Tort:
Cases and Materials

Fourth edition

B. A. HEPPLE, MA, LLB
of Gray's Inn, Barrister;
Professor of English Law
Dean and Head of Dept of Laws,
University College, London

M. H. MATTHEWS, MA, LLB, BCL
of Gray's Inn, Barrister;
Fellow of University College, Oxford

London, Dublin, Edinburgh
Butterworths
1991

United Kingdom	Butterworths, a Division of Reed Elsevier (UK) Ltd, Halsbury House, 35 Chancery Lane, LONDON WC2A 1EL and 4 Hill Street, EDINBURGH EH2 3JZ
Australia	Butterworths, a Division of Reed International Books Australia Pty Ltd, CHATSWOOD, New South Wales
Canada	Butterworths Canada Ltd, MARKHAM, Ontario
Hong Kong	Butterworths Asia (Hong Kong), HONG KONG
India	Butterworths India, NEW DELHI
Ireland	Butterworth (Ireland) Ltd, DUBLIN
Maylasia	Malayan Law Journal Sdn Bhd, KUALA LUMPUR
New Zealand	Butterworths of New Zealand Ltd, WELLINGTON
Singapore	Butterworths Asia, SINGAPORE
South Africa	Butterworths Publishers (Pty) Ltd, DURBAN
USA	Lexis Law Publishing, CHARLOTTESVILLE, Virginia

© B. A. Hepple & M. H. Matthews 1991

Reprinted 1992, 1993, 1994, 1995, 1996, 1998, 1999

A CIP Catalogue record for this book is available from the British Library.

ISBN 0 406 54001 2

Typeset by Colset Singapore
Printed by Redwood Books, Trowbridge, Wiltshire

Visit us at our website: http://www.butterworths.co.uk

Preface

This edition, like its predecessors, is a collection of cases, statutes and other materials on the English law of tort, with connecting notes and questions. It is intended primarily for those studying for a first degree in law. The fairly extensive references to the literature and to other sources are intended as an aid for the teacher and for those students who wish to do research on particular topics.

The book retains the distinctive features of previous editions, namely an emphasis on the interests which the law of tort serves and a contextual approach. So far as context is concerned, there has been an encouraging growth in empirical and theoretical studies in the 25 years since this collection was first produced (1966) as a set of course materials at the University of Nottingham. We have referred to some of this literature, although for reasons of space the length of extracts is limited. Among the particularly important new work from which we have extracts is that of Hazel Genn on the settlement process (chaps. 1 and 19), and Richard Lewis on structured settlements (chap. 8). There are some quotations from new reports by law reforming bodies (e.g. the Calcutt Committee on Privacy, chap. 16), and we have thought it worthwhile to keep some of the extracts from the Pearson Report (especially in chaps. 1, 8 and 19) in view of the renewed debate on the reform of the law relating to compensation for personal injuries. We have also updated the selected bibliography on law reform, including comparative materials, in chap. 19.

The arrangement of the book is in general the same as in the third edition. However, the short chapter on malicious abuse of power, a topic which is now usually taught in the context of administrative law and civil liberties, has been dropped, one reason for this being the publishers' reasonable demands in respect of space. (This edition is 120 pages longer than the third edition.) We also no longer include the text of the statutory immunities in tort for those acting in contemplation or furtherance of trade disputes (chap. 15), because these are studied in courses on labour law. The immunities are, however, explained in notes wherever relevant to an understanding of the development of the economic torts. Liability for animals (chap. 11) has been placed in a separate chapter from liability for things (chap. 10) so as to allow a clearer focus in the latter on products liability.

We are told that teachers have found the first chapter, which attempts to put an action for damages in perspective, a useful way of introducing students to the subject. The asbestosis cases, used for this purpose in previous editions, were looking distinctly weary and so we have substituted materials from the more recent Bradford Football Fire litigation. We are grateful to Roger Suddards, Bill Hudson, Timothy Barnes QC, Edwin

Glasgow QC, M. S. E. Grime QC and Robert Smith QC for their assistance in this respect.

Since the third edition (1985), the House of Lords has retreated from expansive principle to restrictive pragmatism in relation to the duty of care. This is reflected in the partial overruling of *Anns v Merton London Borough Council* by a seven-member House of Lords in *Murphy v Brentwood District Council*, and the reinterpretation of *Hedley Byrne & Co Ltd v Heller & Partners* in *Smith v Eric S. Bush* and in *Caparo Industries plc v Dickman*. Developments such as these have left many areas of doubt and uncertainty, and have created not a few new problems to tease the minds of tort lawyers. They have made our task of selection exceedingly difficult. For example, we have thought it necessary to continue to include extracts from *Anns* in relation to the exercise of statutory powers (chap. 2), and the position of the builder (chap. 9). While dropping *Junior Books* from its former prominence as the harbinger of what we thought in 1985 might be a developing principle of 'detrimental reliance', we have considered it necessary, particularly in view of some cryptic messages in *Murphy* about its continuing relevance, to continue to discuss the case in note form (chap. 4). While there has been a move away from imposing duties in tort in the context of contractual obligations, the interrelationships of contract and tort are sufficiently complex to warrant a new subsection in chapter 4 on this topic in relation to economic loss. Many other new cases have found their way into this edition, including *Smith v Littlewoods* (chap. 2), *Reid v Rush & Tompkins Group plc*, and *The Aliakmon* in the House of Lords (chap. 4), *Hotson v East Berkshire Area Health Authority* and *Wilsher v Essex Area Health Authority* (chap. 6), *Pitts v Hunt* (chap. 7), *F v West Berkshire Health Authority* (chap. 13), *Metall und Rohstoff AG v Donaldson Lufkin and Jenrette Inc.*, *Edwin Hill & Partners v First National Finance Corpn plc*, *Associated British Ports v Transport and General Workers' Union* and *Lonrho plc v Fayed* (chap. 15), *Sutcliffe v Pressdram Ltd* (chap. 16), and *Smith v Stages* (chap. 17). There is also new legislation including extracts from the Latent Damage Act 1986 (chap. 9) and the Consumer Protection Act 1987 (chap. 10).

We have endeavoured to state the law on the basis of materials available to us up to 1 October 1990, but have been able to incorporate some later material.

We are grateful to all those who have made suggestions for improvements, notably our students and colleagues, and to those who have assisted in the preparation of this edition. Butterworths have shown enormous patience, co-operation and good humour in the face of many delays. Special thanks are due to Dr. Gillian Morris for assistance with chaps. 15 and 17, Professor Phillip Capper with chap. 9, Dr. Jane Stapleton with chaps. 9 and 10, and Elliane Moran with chaps. 8 and 16, as well as to Seonaid Cooke, Roger Halson and Michael Davie for help with proofreading. The greatest debt of all is owed to Shirley Hepple and Elizabeth Matthews for their personal support and encouragement through four editions of a book which seems to make ever-increasing demands on our time and energies.

B.A.H.
M.H.M.   11 March 1991

Contents

xii   Contents

Acknowledgments

The publishers and authors wish to thank the following for permission to reprint material from the sources indicated:

Professor P. S. Atiyah: *Vicarious Liability in the Law of Torts*, and with Peter Cane: *Accidents, Compensations and the Law*, 4th edn.

Cambridge University Press and Mr. R. W. M. Dias: *Cambridge Law Journal*, 1962, pp. 179–180; 1967, p. 66.

Canada Law Book Co.: *Dominion Law Reports (3d)*, vol. 145, pp. 21–25.

Criminal Injuries Compensation Board: Text of the 1990 Scheme.

Colston Research Society, Mr. Donald Harris and Dr. Cento Veljanovski: 'Liability for Economic Loss in Tort', in *The Law of Tort* (ed. M. Furmston) 1985.

Estates Gazette: *Estates Gazette*, 1966, vol. 197, pp. 877–879.

Lord Goodman: *New Statesman*, 31 March 1972, p. 426.

Guardian Royal Exchange Assurance Group: Extracts from Liability Policy, Business Interruption Policy and Libel Policy.

The Controller of Her Majesty's Stationery Office: Extracts from official reports Cmnd. 5012, Cmnd. 7054, Cm. 394, Cm. 1102, Law Commission No. 21; Lord Chancellor's Department, Civil Justice Review Consultation Paper; Text of the Agreement dated 21 December 1988 (Motor Insurers' Bureau).

Incorporated Council of Law Reporting for England and Wales: *The Law Reports; The Weekly Law Reports*.

Kenneth Mason Publications Ltd.: *Road Traffic Reports*, 1981, p. 461.

The Law Book Co. Ltd. and Professor John G. Fleming: *The Law of Torts*, 7th edn, pp. 375–377.

Richard Lewis: *Journal of Law and Society*, 1988, vol. 15, pp. 392–395, 403–404, 415.

xiv   Acknowledgments

Lloyd's of London Press Ltd.: *Lloyd's Law Reports*, 1971, vol. 2, pp. 411, 412, 419.

Professor M. A. Millner: *Negligence in Modern Law*.

Modern Law Review Ltd., Mr. A. Evans, Estate O. Kahn-Freund, Dr. P. M. North, Mr. P. J. Pace, Mr. D. M. A. Strachan and Professor Glanville Williams: *Modern Law Review*, 1982, vol. 45, p. 331, 1951, vol. 14, pp. 505-506, 1966, vol. 29, p. 31, 1977, vol. 40, pp. 151-153, 1970, vol. 33, p. 391.

Oxford University Press: *Compensation and Support for Illness and Injury*, by Donald Harris et al. © Social Science Research Council, 1984, pp. 317-23, 327; *Hard Bargaining* by Hazel Genn. © Economic and Social Research Council, 1987, pp. 11-13, 163-169.

Scottish Council of Law Reporting: *Session Cases*.

Society of Public Teachers of Law and Mr. R. Kidner: *Legal Studies*, 1987, vol. 7, pp. 331-332.

Stevens and Sons Ltd., Mr. W. Bishop, Mr. P. P. Craig, Professor B. S. Markesinis, Dr. J. Stapleton and Professor Glanville Williams: *Law Quarterly Review*, 1980, vol. 96, p. 378, 1978, vol. 94, p. 440, 1987, vol. 103, pp. 386-387, 389-390, 1988, vol. 104, pp. 392-393, 404, 405, 1961, vol. 77, p. 196.

Sugden and Spencer, solicitors, Timothy Barnes Esq., QC, Edwin Glasgow, Esq., QC, M. S. E. Grime, Esq., QC, Robert Smith, Esq.: Extracts from pleadings in *Fletcher v Bradford City Association Football Club (1983) Ltd* et al.

Sweet & Maxwell Ltd. and editors: *Clerk & Lindsell on Torts*, 16th edn, paras 10-10, 15-20, *Salmond and Heuston on Torts*, 19th edn, pp. 46, 160, 437, *Winfield and Jolowicz on Tort*, 13th edn, p. 157.

Times Publishing Co. Ltd.: *Times Law Reports*

Professor Glanville Williams: 'Two Cases of False Imprisonment', in *Law, Justice and Equity*, chapter 5, p. 51; and (1951) 4 Current LP, p. 137.

Table of statutes

References in this Table to *Statutes* are to Halsbury's Statutes of England (Fourth Edition) showing the volume and page at which the annotated text of the Act will be found.
Page references printed in **bold** type indicate where the Act is set out in part or in full.

List of cases

Page numbers printed in **bold** type indicate where the facts of a case are set out.

Table of abbreviations

Glanville Williams—Joint Torts and Contributory Negligence, by Glanville L. Williams (London, 1951)

Williams & Hepple—Foundations of the Law of Tort, by Glanville Williams and B. A. Hepple, 2nd edn (London, 1984)

Winfield & Jolowicz—Winfield & Jolowicz on Tort, 13th edn by W. V. H. Rogers (London, 1989)

Introduction

'I have gathered a posie of other men's flowers and
nothing but the thread that binds them is my own.'

MONTAIGNE

The materials in this book are concerned with the protection against *harm*
afforded by the English common law and statutory extensions of the common law to a variety of *interests*. The primary function of the law of tort is
to define the circumstances in which a person whose interests are harmed by
another may seek *compensation*. Scots law, more accurately than English
law, calls this branch of the law reparation. The name given to it by most
civil law systems is delict which, like the old Norman French word 'tort',
simply means a wrong.

Compensation is not the only function of the law of tort. It can sometimes
be used as an alternative to the law of contract where a person has relied on
a promise (e.g. to do work carefully) or to supplement the law of contract
(e.g. where lies induce a person to contract (p. 155)). Torts relating to
wrongful interference with goods are useful appendages to the law of restitution which is concerned with preventing unjust enrichment. An award of
damages for tort may have an admonitory effect (p. 403); an injunction
granted to stop a threatened or continuing tort (e.g. nuisance, p. 623, or
inducing breach of contract, p. 693) may act as a specific deterrent. Tort law
may also be used as a vehicle for determining rights. Disputed possession of
land may be tested through an action for trespass; the misappropriation of
chattels is peculiarly dealt with in English law through the tort of conversion,
which is primarily concerned with questions of title, although the ultimate
remedy is to compensate the owner for his loss. Important questions of civil
liberty may be tested by an action for nominal damages (e.g. the right to
vote; trespass to the person (p. 570); trespass to land (p. 611); or trespass to
goods, such as the seizure of a passport).

These subsidiary functions of the law of tort make it particularly difficult
to present a rational or logical classification of the subject. The lawyer in a
civil law system does not face exactly this problem, largely because questions
of title to property are not dealt with through the law of delict, but by means
of the vindicatory action of the owner, that is, as a part of property law.
Infringements of the citizen's constitutional rights (rather than liberties) are
a part of a relatively distinct body of public law. Even in the uncodified
hybrid systems (like Roman-Dutch law and Scots law) there is a body of
general principle, traceable to the Roman law of Justinian as received in
medieval Europe, which gives the law of delict an inner coherence and unity.
This is a quality which the English law of tort still lacks, although several
attempts have been made by writers and judges to lay down certain general
propositions. Of these attempts, Pollock and Winfield's suggested principle
that the infliction of harm is tortious unless justified and Lord Atkin's
famous principle of a duty of care to one's neighbours (p. 43) stand out as

1

landmarks. In the 1970s there were judicial attempts to make the 'neighbour' principle apply in all situations unless there was a policy justification for excluding it. But these attempts to find a single unifying principle have usually raised more questions than they have resolved, for example, what conduct is 'justified', who is my 'neighbour' to whom a duty of care is owed, and what should judicial 'policy' be in regard to matters such as liability for omissions (p. 65) or for economic loss (p. 149)? More recently, there has been reversion to the older 'incremental' approach in which duties of care are developed by analogy with established categories rather than by reference to a general principle of liability restrained only by indefinable considerations of 'policy' (p. 51).

The really striking and all-important development has been the emergence of negligence into a distinct tort (p. 39) and its subsequent octopus-like spread into the waters once occupied by older torts such as trespass (p. 570). The creation of new duty-situations in the tort of negligence (p. 39) paradoxically reveals both the flexible, open-ended nature of this tort (e.g. in regard to the duty to control the conduct of others, p. 67, and nervous shock, p. 118) and the difficulties in formulating a general principle of liability or non-liability (e.g. in regard to loss to economic interests, p. 149).

The fact is that common lawyers (and this is as true in other common law jurisdictions as it is in England), like the classical Roman lawyers, are far more interested in finding a practical solution to the immediate case than in dogma. Here too, the growth of negligence has had a liberating effect on the judges. Once a 'duty-situation' (i.e. a duty in tort) has been found to exist (e.g. the duty owed by a prison authority to those in the locality in respect of damage done by prisoners negligently allowed to escape, p. 72) that operates as a precedent binding on judges of the lower courts for the decision of future cases. But the question whether there has been a breach of that duty, and the connection between that breach and the resultant damage, are ultimately questions of fact for the court to decide, according to the objective standards of the 'reasonable person'. Here there are no precedents, only analogies. The skilful use of maxims such as res ipsa loquitur (the matter speaks for itself) can enable a judge to require relatively high standards of behaviour (p. 287); alternatively, by an unsympathetic attitude to the plaintiff, he can allow the defendant considerable freedom of action.

The empiricism of the courts, coupled with the piecemeal nature of statutory reform, means that the student of tort is immediately confronted with a confusing and contradictory use of concepts. Here are some examples—

Duty— which may be used to refer to the existence of a tort (created by judicial precedent or statute, pp. 39, 536) or to the standard of behaviour required of the defendant (p. 248) or, in the case of contributory fault, of the plaintiff (p. 354).

Cause— which may refer to the factual chain of events (p. 299) or to a legal policy decision as to the extent of damage for which the wrongdoer should be made to pay (p. 329).

Damage— which may refer to a particular interest (e.g. in property, person etc.) or to the manner in which that interest was harmed (e.g. by fire, by impact etc., p. 346).

Reasonable— an oft-repeated incantation of tort law capable of
foresight including (a) a mere possibility of harm or (b) the pro-
of harm bability of harm or (c) a high degree of probability of
harm ('very likely') or (d) that the marginal cost of
preventing the harm is less than the marginal expected
damages (p. 275). Reasonable foresight of harm to the
plaintiff is said to be the first necessary ingredient of a
duty of care (p. 39), and reasonable foresight of harm is
also part of the test for the breach of a duty of care
(p. 250). Reasonable foresight of a kind or type of harm
is used as part of the test for determining the extent of
the consequences for which the defendant should pay
(p. 329). It may involve different degrees of probability,
at least in these last two cases.

Proximity— used in determining the existence of a duty of care
(p. 51), this suggests that different degrees of 'closeness'
will apply to different kinds of claim (e.g. physical harm,
p. 40, or economic loss, p. 56), but it is by no means clear
that this can be done without reference to one of the tests
of 'reasonable foresight' or to broad considerations of
what is 'just and reasonable' (see p. 52).

Policy— at one time used to limit the prima facie duty of care
based on the 'neighbour' principle, but now said to be
relevant in more restricted circumstances (p. 52) in the
context of deciding whether to impose a duty of care. In
the broad sense 'policy' indicates a social or economic
goal and is sometimes seen to be based on the intuitive
'reason' or 'good sense' of the judge (p. 62).

Risk— sometimes used as a shorthand description of the
foreseeability test in relation to the standard of care
(p. 268), and sometimes as the basis for the imposition of
strict liability (e.g. the person who collects explosives on
his premises *risks* an explosion, p. 650).

These examples could be multiplied. The student should be careful to ask
what purpose a word is being made to serve, instead of simply mouthing the
judicial formula. An analysis of language in this way is an essential part of
the study of law, but it is not sufficient in itself to convey an understanding
of what the law is trying to achieve and, more important, what it in fact
achieves.

It has been in an attempt to find this deeper understanding that the study
of tort law has recently been moving away from the purely conceptual
approach, that is, from the law's internal logic as expressed in the specialised
language of lawyers, towards a study of the law as it actually operates in
society. This means that the questions are no longer simply, is there a duty,
or is the defendant in breach of duty, or what formula is to be applied to the
assessment of damages? Further questions have to be asked by those wishing
to understand the aims and future of tort law, such as, what is the effect of
granting or denying the plaintiff compensation, as the case may be, what
other sources of compensation are available to her, how is this loss
absorbed, either by the group to which the plaintiff (e.g. houseowners) or
the defendant (e.g. motorists or employers or manufacturers) belongs, or by

taxpayers, and how is the spreading of that loss administered (e.g. through private insurance or a form of social security)? It means taking into account the reality of insurance and the various other methods of compensation which exist. This approach has certain consequences for the classification of the law of tort, and this is reflected in the arrangement of this book.

If, as was suggested earlier, the primary function of tort law is compensation for harm, then, following this functional approach, we are bound to ask what are the main interests which may be harmed? A textbook which aims to set out these interests in detail might contain a number of divisions such as (i) interests in personal security; (ii) interests in one's own property (here distinguishing land and chattels); (iii) interests in another's life (e.g. a breadwinner or employee); (iv) interests in another's property (e.g. a car hirer's interest in the car she has hired); (v) interests of a purely economic nature (e.g. loss of production through a strike, competition by a rival trader); (vi) interests in reputation (protected by the torts of libel and slander); (vii) interests in privacy (a nascent interest only partially protected by some existing torts, p. 795). A sourcebook, in the existing state of English law, cannot make these detailed classifications for the simple reason that several of these interests are discussed interchangeably in many of the cases. This is particularly true of interests in persons and property (Lord Atkin's 'duty' test clearly applies to both). The limited acceptance by the judiciary of duty-situations in the case of negligent interference with pure economic interests (p. 149) cannot be realistically explained in terms of the absence of foresight (p. 230). The question is sometimes confused by calling this 'pecuniary' loss and saying that there is no obvious or intrinsic reason why this should be differently treated from other kinds of loss. Of course, all compensation is 'pecuniary' in the sense that the harm to the interest affected must be translated into money terms. The real distinction is between the different *interests* which the law seeks to protect, and not between the money terms in which those interests are compensated for harm.

The interests which the law protects are neither static nor rigidly defined. In the feudal period it was interests in land, the predominant economic asset, which were regarded as meriting the greatest degree of protection. They were vindicated through the writ of trespass. So important were the interests in land that very little attention was paid to the quality of the defendant's behaviour. Unless he was not the master of his own volition (p. 620), he was liable for the act of trespass irrespective of his mental state or the consequences. The need to restore law and order after the ruinous Barons' Wars meant that trespass to the person (particularly assault and battery) and trespass to goods were used as devices to suppress feuding. These wrongs also did not rest on any notion of fault, although, as Winfield showed, liability was never absolute. Reputation was another interest which received early protection, on the basis of strict liability; here the social need was to provide a legal alternative to duelling.

The rise of industrial capitalism, with the consequent proliferation of dangerous machinery, railways, road traffic and polluting activities, brought other interests to the fore. Interests in personal security became important. The interests of entrepreneurs ran counter to those of the people whom their activities hurt: their workers, the consumers of their products, travellers on their railways and so on. A balance was struck by the judges. This worked as follows. First, there was to be no liability without fault. This principle was not established overnight or without exceptions; indeed it was only in 1959 that it was finally established that the plaintiff in a personal injuries case must prove fault (p. 570) and there are still exceptional situations in which liability for personal injuries is strict, such as where a lamp overhanging a highway falls on a passerby (public nuisance, p. 636), dangerous escapes from land (p. 650) and damage by certain classes of animal (p. 521). Secondly, an important class of plaintiffs, that is employees, were denied compensation from their employers when they were injured by the fault of fellow-employees. This doctrine of common employment, invented in 1837 (p. 565), was qualified by statute in 1880 and by-passed by the Workmen's Compensation Acts after 1897, but it remained a part of the law until scrapped by Parliament in 1948. In the changed economic and social climate at the end of the 19th century, the judiciary found ways around the doctrine, for example by creating torts out of industrial safety legislation to which the doctrine did not apply (p. 536) and by expanding the concept of 'personal' duties owed by an employer to his employees (p. 566). But the fault principle has risen to its zenith in this century as a limitation on the protection of physical interests, in particular interests in personal security. In the words of Professor Friedmann, 'as emphasis shifted from definition by the kind of *interest* injured (as in the older torts) to the kind of *conduct* which engenders liability, negligence was obviously better fitted to become the modern tort action *par excellence*' (*Law in a Changing Society*, 2nd edn, p. 162).

This emphasis on negligence is reflected in Part I of this sourcebook (Principles and policy of negligence). Part II of the sourcebook deals with a number of specific duties and interests, relating to defective premises (p. 441), defective products (p. 491), personal security (p. 569) and land (p. 609), all of which have been greatly influenced by the fault principle, as have statutory torts (p. 531). A distinctive feature of several of the torts relating to interference with trade or business (p. 673) and with interests in reputation (p. 739) and to the abuse of power is that three parties are usually involved. There is a plaintiff (P) who has suffered damage, a middleman (X) who has been the vehicle through which that loss has been inflicted on P, and a defendant (D) who is alleged to be responsible. The loss arises not from an infringement of personal security or tangible property, but from an interference with P's relations with X. That is why these are sometimes called *relational* interests. Examples are D's inducement of X to break his contract with P (p. 693) or intentionally causing loss to P by the use of some 'unlawful means' involving X (e.g. threatening X with violence or some other wrong if he does not break off relations with P, p. 718). Relational interests are also considered in Part I in cases where D interferes with P's interest in the life of X, by tortiously killing X (p. 239), and where D harms P's economic interests by negligently damaging X's property (p. 230).

The protection of relational interests conjures up a spectre which haunts the law of tort, but one which is not confined to relational interests. This is the prospect of limitless liability to an unlimited range of plaintiffs. When harm is done to physical interests there are natural safeguards — bodies and tangible property are finite — and the fault principle operates to limit the extent of liability and the range of plaintiffs still further. But when harm is done to relational interests the prospects of loss appear to be infinite. Not surprisingly therefore the law has generally preferred a principle of non-liability for interference with non-physical interests to a general principle of liability. The presumption which favours freedom of action in the economic sphere is compatible with an economic and political system which is committed to the notion of workable competition.

Reputation might, if one preferred, be classed as an aspect of personal security, but it is a relational interest in English law because liability depends on publication to a third party: the plaintiff's esteem in the eyes of others and not his own injured feelings are at stake. The tort of defamation (p. 739) might be considered from another angle as an aspect of English civil liberty, since the essential task of the court (within an over-complex set of technical rules) is to balance reputation against free speech. Liberty, in its constitutional sense, is also underpinned by the protection given by the law of tort to the right to vote, freedom from abuse of legal procedure, and abuse of governmental or monopoly power.

The rules and concepts through which tort law seeks to balance the plaintiff's interest against the defendant's claim for freedom of action are essentially judge-made in the area of torts to physical interests. Where statutes have intervened it has principally been to reform areas where the case by case development of principles has led to anomalous or socially undesirable results. Examples are the continuation of claims by and against the estates of deceased persons (1934) (p. 237), the establishment of a general right of contribution between tortfeasors (1935, revised in 1978) (p. 871), the replacement of the 'all or nothing rule' with a rule of comparative fault where the plaintiff has contributed to his damage (1945) (p. 357), the reform of the complex rules about an occupier's duty to those who enter his land with permission (1957) (p. 442), and to trespassers (1984) (p. 462), the reform of the law relating to liability for damage caused by animals (1971) (p. 521) and for defective premises (1972) (p. 480), and defective products (1987) (p. 504), the provision of a remedy to children born with a disability attributable to a prenatal injury (1976) (p. 142) and minor reforms of the assessment of damages for personal injury (1982) (p. 419).

But legislative intervention has been of overwhelming importance for the so-called 'economic torts' (chap. 15). The relatively short heyday of economic liberalism, which economic historians date from abolition of the Corn Laws in 1846 to the ending of free trade in 1931, was reflected in deliberate Parliamentary abstention from economic regulation. Where the judges appeared to be following a different policy, as in the development of torts of conspiracy and inducing breach of contract in the context of trade disputes, Parliament intervened to protect economic liberties. In the new era of state regulation particularly since World War II, however, the common law of torts to economic interests was replaced by a statutory law of tort in some fields. Monopolies and restrictive practices in the business market are controlled by complex legislation justiciable before a special body, the Restrictive Practices Court, and by the rules of the European Communities. Misappropriation of ideas and other intellectual property is regulated by a specialised body of patents, trade marks and copyright legislation. The judges have an important function in interpreting these and other statutes, but their unique role as creators of tort law in some spheres continues and has even been expanded by Parliament in the field of labour relations since 1980. The new specialised bodies of law, while in theory a part of the law of tort, are in practice best studied in the context of subjects such as labour law, monopolies and restrictive practices, and industrial and intellectual property.

Judge-made law in the sphere of torts to physical interests — in particular personal injuries — has reached a crisis point. The theoretical underpinning of the law of tort as it has been developed since the 19th century is that losses are being shifted from plaintiffs to defendants on the basis of fault. The economic and sociological reality is that losses are typically not simply shifted, but are absorbed by being *spread* or *distributed*. Part III of this sourcebook is concerned with some of the legal devices for loss distribution. The oldest method for ensuring that the person best able to absorb the loss is made to bear it, is itself judge-made. Vicarious liability, while not exempting the person actually inflicting the loss from personal liability, means that his employer or principal is made a joint tortfeasor (p. 803). The statutory rules for contribution between tortfeasors (p. 871) mean that the defendant who pays may be able to recover from other tortfeasors on the basis of comparative fault. But the most significant modern influence towards loss distribution is the practice of liability insurance. When victims of industrial accidents became entitled, under the Workmen's Compensation Act 1897, to claim compensation from employers regardless of fault, employers looked to liability insurance to cover themselves; the cost of premiums was widely spread by employers, being reflected (at least in theory) in the price of products and the wages paid to workers. The risks of tort liability created by the driving of motor vehicles gave another major impetus to liability insurance. When it became clear that this insurance was beneficial not only to potential tortfeasors, but also to their victims, Parliament intervened, first in 1930, to make it compulsory. Employers' liability insurance has been compulsory since 1972. This kind of loss distribution has been described by Professor John Fleming as 'vertical' in contrast to the 'horizontal' spreading of losses, by making collateral sources of compensation available to the plaintiff. In the United Kingdom, social security benefits (and also criminal injuries compensation) are the most important of these collateral sources (p. 917). Social security, which has broken away entirely from the theory of tort law, is already a more significant source of compensation for personal injuries than tort law (p. 35).

In the two-dimensional world of loss-shifting, writers and judges tended to emphasise the admonitory or deterrent functions of the law of tort. In the three-dimensional reality of loss distribution, the emphasis has come to rest upon the compensatory aims of the law. The conflict between this aim and the working of the fault principle has led to a widespread attack on the whole edifice of the law and practice of personal injury compensation. This phenomenon is not confined to England, nor to countries of the common law tradition, and is prevalent even in those which impose some measure of strict liability in the field of road accidents.

The practical objections to the present systems are manifold. For example, it is argued that courts are congested (despite some recent procedural improvements); that litigation is a 'lottery' because of the uncertainty produced by the vagaries of the fault rules and the difficulties of reconstructing, usually years after the event, the minute details of 'negligent' conduct upon which liability is made to turn; that the assessment of damages, and in particular the calculation of lump-sums, means that some plaintiffs get too much and many get too little or nothing at all; that the insurers and lawyers engaged in the 'injury industry' cream off as administrative costs (estimates put these at about 85 per cent of the value of tort compensation payments, or about 45 per cent of the combined total of compensation and operating costs, p. 33) money which could be more efficiently distributed among accident victims; that there are legal gaps in insurance protection although nearly all of these are now covered by an arrangement between the Motor Insurers' Bureau and the government (p. 898), so far as motor insurance is concerned; and that the excessive concentration on compensation results in little time being devoted to the problems of accident prevention and rehabilitation of accident victims.

The theoretical arguments against the present system of personal injuries compensation proceed on the assumption that these and other practical defects merely reflect fundamental weaknesses. The debate raises legal, economic and political issues. From the legal vantage point, writers such as Professor André Tunc, point out that the tort rules, historically designed to deal with damage caused by fault, that is either intentional or through a lack of the standard of care of the 'reasonable' man, are now indiscriminately applied to human errors – such as a momentary lack of attention or an unfortunate reaction to danger – which are the main causes of traffic and industrial 'accidents'. The very word 'accident' – usually applied to occurrences whether or not fault, in the legal sense, can be established – reveals the fortuitous nature of the facts to which the legal principles have to be applied. According to this view, the historic task now facing law reformers is to separate the moral, or deterrent, function of tort law, based on the fault principle, from the compensatory function, which arises in the case of human errors. Another legal aspect of the debate is the argument about co-ordination of the rules of insurance with those of tort law: to avoid the duplication of compensation; and to rationalise the distribution of losses, for example by replacing the tort-and-liability insurance system with a system of compulsory first party insurance, as has already occurred, to a limited extent, in regard to road accidents, in several American states. A more far-reaching reform has been initiated in New Zealand with abolition of tort liability for personal injuries and its replacement by a state accident compensation scheme (p. 929). The Royal Commission on Civil Liability and Compensation for Personal Injury (under the Chairmanship of Lord Pearson), which spent five years considering these questions, recommended the retention of a 'mixed system' of tort liability complementing social security (p. 931). They contented themselves with recommending either no-fault or strict liability for specific types of accidents like road, airline and vaccination, with proposals for avoiding duplication between tort damages and other forms of compensation, and numerous minor reforms. This pleased those who wished to see state intervention kept to a minimum and who saw the Report as a triumph of political compromise and pragmatism, but the result has been damned by others who regarded it as a shabby surrender to the vested interests of the legal profession and the insurance industry (see the reading list, p. 938). However one views the Report's conclusions, one has to note that all the sound and fury which it generated came to virtually nothing, with only a handful of its 188 recommendations being implemented. This is a fate suffered by other law reforming bodies, such as the Faulks Committee on defamation (p. 739).

The apparent complacency about the present state of the law among our legislators has, in recent years, revived academic controversy about the aims and effect of tort law. Is the goal the maintenance of a balance between injurer and victim for moral reasons, or is it to reduce the cost of accidents and so increase overall social welfare? Does the negligence standard promote incentives to avoid accidents in the cheapest possible way? And what of the ideas of community responsibility and social justice which have motivated reforms such as those in New Zealand? These debates are highly relevant to contemporary campaigns for the introduction of no-fault compensation for medical misfortunes and for road accidents.

The student who works her way through the pages which follow is likely to be left with a sense of unease. This is a period of legislative inaction for tort law; but, the very right of an important part of the subject to continue to exist is in question. This, then, is one of those times in legal and social history when the student has to live through the process of profound controversy which may lead to future change. A most important lesson of tort law is the one that Shelley wrote of Man: 'Naught may endure but mutability.'

Principles and policy of negligence

1 An action for damages in perspective

The purpose of this chapter is to give the student a bird's-eye view of an action for damages before beginning a detailed study of the technical rules. The consolidated actions which have been used for this purpose suggest a number of fundamental questions about the aims and functions of the law of tort. These questions are raised at the end of the chapter where they might serve as the basis for a preliminary discussion of issues which will recur throughout this sourcebook. Some reading has been suggested. The student will want to return to these writings at the end of the course and may by then also be equipped to read some of the materials, and the proposals to reform tort law which are collected in the select bibliography, p. 938, post.

1 The Bradford football fire

(a) The background

On 11th May 1985 Bradford City Football Club, having gained promotion to the Second Division of the Football League, was playing a match at the Bradford City ground, Valley Parade, Bradford which should have been a celebratory occasion. However, during the match a fire of 'horrifying proportions and severity' occurred, spreading through the main stand within a period of not more than five minutes.[1] The stand, which had a seating capacity of 2,119 was full of spectators. Fifty-six persons who had been occupying seats in the stand lost their lives and many others were seriously injured.

The grandstand had been built around 1909 by the Bradford City Association Football Club (1908) Ltd. (the 'old club'). In 1983 that company had become insolvent and was wound up. The ground, including the stand, was taken over by a new club, the Bradford City Association Football Club (1983) Ltd. The stand was built on a hillside which sloped upwards from the level of the pitch at an angle of about 15 degrees. The seating consisted of a staggered timber framework bearing footboards and square wooden seats nailed onto continuous planking. The footboards consisted of two parallel close boarded planks. Shrinkage and usage over time had caused gaps to

---

1. This account is taken from the judgment in the action by *Susan Fletcher and Martin Lee Fletcher v Bradford City AFC (1983) Ltd.*, Leeds, 23rd February 1987, and information provided by the plaintiffs' solicitors; see too A. MacDonald (1987) 137 NLJ 481.

open between these planks. Each row of seats was raised above the row in front. There was a gap under each seat which was closed off by a sloping board called a kick board, but some of the kick boards had become dislodged or damaged and where this happened there was an open gap into a continuous void nine inches or more deep which extended under the whole of the floor of that part of the stand.

An investigation by a senior forensic scientist immediately after the fire revealed that large quantities of inflammable rubbish had accumulated in the void. That the debris had accumulated over a long period was shown by the discovery in the void of a pre-decimal price tag (placing the sale before February 1971) and a copy of a local newspaper dated 1968. The scientist concluded that the fire must have been caused by a lighted match or a burning cigarette or some burning tobacco falling through a gap or hole in the floor. The combination of an upward sloping bed of inflammable debris overlaid by the staggered wooden structure was an 'ideal situation for flames to spread rapidly up the slope as they did'.

(b) The actions

In August 1985, Mrs Susan Fletcher, the widow of John Fletcher, who died in the fire, commenced an action claiming damages, as administratrix, on behalf of his estate and under the Fatal Accidents Acts for the benefit of his dependants. She also sued as mother and next friend of her minor son, Martin Fletcher, who claimed damages in respect of his injuries sustained in the fire. Their action was against the Bradford City Association Football Club (1983) Ltd. (the first defendants). These plaintiffs alleged that the fire, the death of John Fletcher and the injuries to Martin were caused by the negligence of the Club.

The Club denied negligence, and alleged that the death and injuries were caused by the negligence and/or breach of statutory duty of the Health and Safety Executive and/or the West Yorkshire Metropolitan County Council. The Executive is a statutory body, whose duty, as defined by s. 18 of the Health and Safety at Work etc. Act 1974, is to make adequate arrangements for the enforcement of the safety provisions of that Act. The County Council was the fire authority on whom certain duties were imposed by the Fire Precautions Act 1971 in respect of premises within its area. The County Council was also the local authority which had powers and duties under the Safety of Sports Grounds Act 1975 to ensure safety at sports grounds and which was alleged by the Club to have been negligent and/or in breach of duty in respect of two quite distinct functions. The Club issued 'third party' notices against the Executive and County Council claiming an indemnity against the plaintiffs' claim and costs or a contribution. Third party notices enable a defendant to claim that a person who is not a party to the proceedings should be responsible in whole or in part for any damages the defendant may have to pay to the plaintiff. This has the effect that the issues between the defendant and the third party can be determined in the proceedings between the plaintiff and the defendant. The Executive and County Council were then joined by the plaintiffs as second and third defendants respectively in the action, thus enabling the plaintiffs to obtain judgment in the same action against whichever parties were held liable.

In accordance with pre-trial directions, the action was consolidated with that of a serving police officer, David Britton, who was injured in the course of rescuing spectators in the blazing stand. The actions were tried, on the issue whether or not the defendants were liable, by Sir Joseph Cantley, sitting as a deputy High Court Judge, in Leeds over 11 working days in November 1986 and he gave judgment on 23rd February 1987. Extracts from the pleadings and his judgment are set out post. These are preceded by an outline of the stages of procedure in an action for damages for personal injuries.

(c)   The stages of procedure

Lord Chancellor's Department. Civil Justice Review. Consultation Paper. Personal Injuries Litigation. February 1986.

40.   The formal rules of procedure governing the conduct of cases are contained in the Rules of the Supreme Court 1965 and the County Court Rules 1981. Despite some differences of administrative organisation and terminology, the procedures of the two courts, at least in personal injuries cases, are effectively the same. For the purposes of this paper they will for the most part be treated as one. The principal purposes of the procedure may be summarised as follows:

   (i)   To ensure that the defendant has notice of the plaintiff's claim and is able to respond if he so wished.
  (ii)   To give each party a clear statement of the other's case.
 (iii)   To ensure that both parties are fully prepared if the case goes to trial.
  (iv)   To eliminate before trial all matters that are not in dispute.
   (v)   To avoid surprise at trial by ensuring that all relevant documentary and other material (with the important exception of witness statements) is disclosed in advance.
  (vi)   To bring cases to trial, in accordance with a timetable, within a reasonable period.

41.   There follows an outline of the main procedural steps that would be taken in the most straightforward kind of High Court case. The time limits mentioned are those laid down by Rules of Court. [Recent amendments since the Consultation Paper are indicated in square brackets — Ed.]

(1)   *Issue of writ.*   Proceedings are initiated by the issue of a *writ*, which is sealed in the court office. The writ formally notifies the defendant of the claim against him and requires him to indicate whether or not he proposes to defend it. It must be issued within 3 years of the accident giving rise to the claim.
(2)   *Service of writ.*   The writ must be served upon the defendant within [4][1] months of issue. The commonest methods of service are by post, upon the defendant in person or (by agreement) upon the defendant's solicitor.
(3)   *Exchange of pleadings.*   This process starts with service of the writ. The purpose of the pleadings is to define and narrow the issues between the parties. The plaintiff's *statement of claim*, which may appear on the writ or which may be served afterwards, will state the facts of the accident, the respects in which

---

1. Since 4th June 1990, the writ is valid for service for 4 months, instead of the former period of 12 months: Rules of the Supreme Court (Amendment No. 4) 1989 S.I. 1989 No. 2427.

the defendant is said to be negligent, and the damage suffered. It will not contain the evidence by which the facts are to be proved. Neither will it indicate the total amount of damages sought, i.e. it is not itself an offer of settlement. [Since 4th June 1990, the plaintiff in an action for personal injuries must serve with the statement of claim (a) a medical report and (b) a statement of the special damages claimed.] In his *defence*, the defendant is required to make clear whether or not he admits the particular allegations. [Since 4th June 1990, the defendant must plead any facts on which he relies in relation to the amount of damages.] In addition, parties may require, and if necessary obtain an order for, 'further and better particulars' of each others' pleadings.

(4) *Close of pleadings.*   The pleadings are said to be closed 14 days after the service of the last pleading (which is usually the defence).

(5) *Directions for trial.*   In actions other than for personal injuries the plaintiff takes out a summons for a court appointment, at which procedural directions are given. In personal injury cases, certain directions for the preparation of the case take effect automatically as from the close of pleadings, unless the court otherwise orders. The main automatic directions are as follows:—

(a) Within 14 days each party must give *'discovery'* of documents, which means exchanging a list of all relevant documents which are or have been in that party's possession. Within a further 7 days, each must allow the other an opportunity to inspect and copy the documents.

(b) If a party intends to rely on an expert's report as evidence at trial, he must (within 10 weeks) disclose its substance to the other party. [In the case of a medical report this is no longer usually necessary if the report was served with the statement of claim.]

(c) Assuming the reports are not agreed, each side is limited, by way of expert witnesses, to two medical experts and one other.

(d) Photographs, a sketch plan and the contents of any police report are receivable in evidence at the trial.

(e) The action is to be tried by a judge alone, i.e. without jury.

(f) The case is to be set down for trial (see (6) below) within 6 months.

[(g) As a result of the Rules of the Supreme Court (Amendment) 1988, S.I. 1988 No. 1340, the court may now order the disclosure of non-expert evidence and such disclosure may be a precondition to a witness's statement being received at trial.]

(6) *Setting down.*   By setting down the case in the court office the plaintiff indicates to the other party and to the court that he is ready for it to be listed for trial. The case will be set down in the place where it is to be tried—the Royal Courts of Justice or one of the provincial trial centres. The plaintiff files in the court office copies of the writ and pleadings, which serve as the court's file at the hearing of the action.

(7) *Trial.*   Personal injury actions are heard by a judge without a jury. The trial is intended to be a continuous session at which all arguments and evidence are submitted and evaluated orally, judgment being given immediately afterwards if possible. The Court may order a split trial in which the issue of liability is tried separately and in advance of the issue of damages. [Since 5th February 1990, the Court has had power to order this without application by the parties.]

42.   The time-limits, the rules about pleadings and the basic order of events are the same in County Court actions. The main difference in the County Court is that once a defence is filed, the court fixes a hearing called a *pre-trial review*. The purpose of this is to give directions for the preparation of the case on the same lines as the automatic High Court directions mentioned at paragraph 41(5) above. In practice, it is not uncommon for the parties' solicitors to agree the necessary directions without attending Court. In principle, the County Court Registrar has power at the pre-trial review to enter judgment for the plaintiff or strike out the plaintiff's action as the case may be. He may also, if the evidence seems sufficient, treat the pre-trial review as though it were the hearing of the action itself. In personal injury actions, however, it is rare for the pre-trial review to be concerned with anything other than directions.

43.   The County Court Rules contain no formal procedure for setting down actions for trial and it had been the practice in many County Courts to fix a date for the trial of the action at the end of the pre-trial review. However, the practice increasingly is to wait as in the High Court until one of the parties signifies readiness for a hearing and the case will not be listed for trial until that happens.

44.   It should be said that all the steps just described are formal ones related to the requirements of the courts. The very important informal process of seeking a negotiated settlement will usually continue alongside the formal process and may bring the latter to an end at any time.

Costs
45.   The courts have a discretion as to who should bear the legal costs of an action but the basic rule is that 'costs follow the event', that is, the winner is normally entitled to recover the costs which he has incurred from the loser. His own costs ('solicitor and client costs') will often be greater than those which he is entitled to recover from the loser ('party and party costs'), which means in practice that the winning party may have to pay his solicitor an additional sum out of his own pocket. (Amendments to Rules of Court are in hand which will simplify the basis on which costs are awarded.)

46.   The risk of having to bear all the costs, which can be very substantial, at the end of the case is a major inducement to settlements short of trial. This risk bears more heavily on the economically weaker party which, in personal injury cases, is usually the plaintiff. A defendant can seek to protect himself against the risk of costs by means of the system of payment into court. Without admitting liability he may choose to pay a sum of money into court in satisfaction of the plaintiff's claim. If the plaintiff accepts that sum the proceedings are terminated and the plaintiff is entitled to his costs up to the date of payment into court. If he does not accept the payment and the action proceeds to trial, he will only be entitled to his full costs if the amount awarded at trial exceeds the amount paid into court by the defendant. Otherwise, the plaintiff will have to pay the costs incurred by the defendant from the date of the payment into court up to the date of judgment. Since these will include the cost of the trial itself, they are likely to be substantial.

Note

Since this Paper, the Report of the Review Body on Civil Justice (Cm. 394, 1988) has made recommendations for speeding up and improving the handling of cases in both the High Court and the county courts. In the light of these recommendations, the Courts and Legal Services Act 1990 will enable the courts to take a more active role in the management of case progress in order to reduce delay before trial. This will take some years to develop and in the meantime the recent amendments, indicated in square brackets in the text ante, are designed to reduce pre-trial delay in personal injury cases. The Courts and Legal Services Act 1990 removes the upper financial limit of county court jurisdiction and regulates eligibility for High Court trial.

(d) The pleadings

Note

The following are extracts from the pleadings and it has not been possible to set out the pleadings in full. Consequently there are some references in these pleadings to certain documents which are not included in this book.

IN THE HIGH COURT OF JUSTICE   1985. – F   . – No. 10605

QUEENS BENCH   **Division**

[Group   ]

[LEEDS   **District Registry**]

Between

SUSAN FLETCHER   First **Plaintiff**
(Widow and Administratrix of the Estate of John Fletcher deceased)

AND

MARTIN LEE FLETCHER   Second Plaintiff
(An infant, suing by his mother and next friend Susan Fletcher)

AND

BRADFORD CITY ASSOCIATION FOOTBALL CLUB (1983) LIMITED
                                                                        Defendants

To the Defendant BRADFORD CITY ASSOCIATION FOOTBALL CLUB (1983) LIMITED
whose Registered Office is situate at Valley Parade Ground, Valley Parade, Bradford West Yorkshire.

This Writ of Summons has been issued against you by the above-named Plaintiff in respect of the claim set out overleaf.

Within 14 days after the service of the Writ on you, counting the day of service, you must either satisfy the claim or return to the Court Office mentioned below the accompanying **Acknowledgment of Service** stating therein whether you intend to contest these proceedings.

If you fail to satisfy the claim or to return the Acknowledgment within the time stated, or if you return the Acknowledgment without stating therein an intention to contest the proceedings the Plaintiff may proceed with the action and judgment may be entered against you forthwith without further notice.

Issued from the [Central Office]   [LEEDS   District Registry]
of the High Court this   14th   day of   August   1985.

Statement of Claim

1.   The First Plaintiff is the widow and administratrix of the Estate of John Fletcher (hereinafter called 'the deceased') who died on the 11th May 1985. Letters of Administration were granted to the First Plaintiff out of the District Probate Registry at Manchester on the 7th August 1985. She brings this action for the benefit of the estate of the deceased under the Law Reform (Miscellaneous Provisions) Act 1934[1] and for the benefit of the dependants of the deceased under the provisions of the Fatal Accidents Act 1976 (as amended).[2]

2.   The Second Plaintiff is an infant having been born on the 12th December 1972. He is the son of the deceased and brings this action by his mother and next friend, Susan Fletcher.

3.   On the 11th May 1985, the deceased, together with the Second Plaintiff, the deceased's son Andrew and other members of their family, attended a 3rd Division football league match at the Defendants Valley Parade ground in Bradford. Each of them paid to gain admittance to the ground and were the Defendants lawful visitors within the meaning of the Occupiers' Liability Act 1957.[3] Each of them was seated in Block G of the main stand.

4.   At about 3.40 p.m. a fire started in Block G of the main stand. In about 5 minutes the whole stand was in total flames. The deceased and the Second Plaintiff's brother, uncle and grandfather were among the 56 people who lost their lives. The Second Plaintiff escaped with burns.

5.   The said fire, the death of the deceased and the injuries to the Second Plaintiff were caused by the negligence of the Defendants, their servants or agents.

PARTICULARS OF NEGLIGENCE

(a) Causing or permitting the main stand to become a fire hazard and a danger to spectators.
   (i)   The stand was constructed of wooden planking which was close boarded. The roof was made of timber covered with bitumen or asphalt. The whole stand was therefore composed of combustible materials.
   (ii) There was a void beneath the floor of the stand.
   (iii) The age of the structure and shrinkage of timber had caused gaps to develop between the close boarding. Kick boards were missing and further gaps thereby created. These gaps were sufficient to permit combustible rubbish to fall into the void.
   (iv) Combustible debris to a depth of between 6 and 12 inches had accumulated in the void. This debris consisted of empty cigarette packets, matchboxes, matchsticks, polystyrene drinking cups, sweet wrappers and newspapers. The debris had accumulated over many years, was dry and was capable of being ignited by a burning match or cigarette end.
(b) Failing to take any or any adequate steps to prevent or reduce the risk of accidental outbreak of fire in this stand. In particular:
   (i)   Failing to seal off the gaps, cracks and holes in the stand so as to prevent combustible rubbish from falling into and accumulating in the void.
   (ii) Failing to clear the void of rubbish by frequent sweeping operations.

---

1. [See p. 237, post.]
2. [See p. 240, post.]
3. [See p. 442, post.]

      (iii) Failing to carry out frequent and detailed inspection of the void.

(c) Failing to take the steps set out in Paragraph (b) herein or any or any adequate steps to prevent or reduce the risk of accidental outbreak of fire in this stand when they knew or ought to have known of the fire risk which had been created. The Plaintiffs will rely upon the following matters for the purposes of establishing that the Defendants either knew or ought to have known of the risk [A number of matters were set out].

(d) Failing to take any or any sufficient note of the recommendations made in the Green Guide.[1] Reference will be made below to specific recommendations within the Guide which were not observed by the Defendants. The following will in any event be relied upon as particulars of negligence independently of the recommendations contained within the Green Guide.

[A number of matters relating to stand construction, fire fighting and evacuation were set out.]

(e) By reason of the foregoing, failing to exercise reasonable care for the safety of spectators at the ground and exposing them to the risk of serious injury in circumstances such as those which in fact occurred.

6.   Further, the matters set out in paragraph 5 herein constituted a failure by the Defendants, their servants or agents to discharge the statutory common duty of care which they owed to the deceased and to the Second Plaintiff by virtue of the provisions of the Occupiers' Liability Act 1957.

7.   By reason of the matters aforesaid the dependants of the deceased have suffered damage and loss.

PARTICULARS PURSUANT TO STATUTE

A.   The particulars of the persons for whose benefit the action under the Fatal Accidents Act 1976 is brought are as follows: —

Susan Fletcher, the First Plaintiff and widow of the deceased, who was born on the 15th March 1951.

Martin Lee Fletcher, the Second Plaintiff and son of the deceased, whose date of birth is set out above.

The nature of the claim in respect of which damages are sought is as follows: —

The deceased was born on the 8th October 1950 and was 34 years of age at the time of his death, was a man in good health, who was Managing Director of Aalco Limited a subsidiary of Amari PLC whose work involved the supply of structural aluminium and other building materials. His net salary for the tax year ending 5th April 1985 averaged £340.00 per week, the substantial part of which was spent for the benefit of the said dependants and this would have continued and increased had he remained alive. In addition the deceased had the benefit of a Company car, and membership of the Amari pension plan, and BUPA scheme. No dependants were in employment themselves.

8.   The deceased's estate has suffered damage and loss.

---

1. See p. 26, post.

PARTICULARS OF SPECIAL DAMAGE

Funeral expenses.   £ 425.32

Jewellery and personal effects
including 9 carat gold ring, Accurist wrist watch
and clothing.   £ 435.00

9.   The Second Plaintiff has sustained personal injuries damage and loss.

PARTICULARS OF PERSONAL INJURIES

Burns to the back and face necessitating his detention in hospital overnight and leaving him with some permanent scarring. Nervous shock[1] consequent upon the terrifying circumstances of the incident and the death of his father, brother, uncle and grandfather. The prognosis is guarded.

AND the First Plaintiff claims:

(1) Damages for bereavement.
(2) Damages for the benefit of the dependants of the deceased.
(3) Damages for the benefit of the deceased's estate.
(4) Interest pursuant to Section 35A of the Supreme Court Act 1981.

AND the Second Plaintiff claims:

(1) Damages.
(2) Interest pursuant to Section 35A of the Supreme Court Act 1981.

[Counsel]

Amended pursuant to the Order of Sir Joseph
Cantley sitting as a Deputy High Court Judge
Dated November 1986

IN THE HIGH COURT OF JUSTICE   1985. – F   . – No. 10605
QUEEN'S BENCH Division
LEEDS District Registry

Between

SUSAN FLETCHER   First **Plaintiff**
(Widow and Administratrix of the Estate of John Fletcher deceased)

AND

MARTIN LEE FLETCHER   Second Plaintiff
(An infant suing by his mother and next friend Susan Fletcher)

---

1. See p. 118, post.

AND

**BRADFORD CITY ASSOCIATION FOOTBALL
CLUB (1983) LIMITED**   First **Defendants**

AND

HEALTH AND SAFETY EXECUTIVE   Second Defendants

AND

**WEST YORKSHIRE METROPOLITAN
COUNTY COUNCIL**   Third Defendants

AMENDED DEFENCE OF FIRST DEFENDANTS

1.   Subject to the provision of the material documents, Paragraphs 1 and 2 of the Re-amended Statement of Claim are admitted.

2.   Paragraphs 3 and 4 of the Re-amended Statement of Claim are admitted.

3.   It is denied that the **First** Defendants their servants or agents acted negligently or in breach of duty as alleged or at all.

4.   Further and in the alternative it is denied that any negligence or breach of duty on the part of the **First** Defendants their servants or agents caused or contributed to the loss of life, or the alleged or any injuries loss or damage the nature and extent of which is not admitted.

5.   Without prejudice to the generality of their denials pleaded above, the First Defendants make the following admissions or averments: —

   (i)   The loss of life and injuries which occurred were caused by the extreme rapidity with which the fire took hold and spread, and which the **First** Defendants, as non-expert occupiers, could not reasonably have been expected to foresee;
   (ii) The stand was constructed of combustible material but there were no reasonably practicable steps, short of total rebuilding, which the **First** Defendants could or should have taken so as effectively to render the same fireproof or to reduce its inflammable properties;
   (iii) Some litter had inevitably found its way into the voids underneath the floor. The only method by which that litter could have been removed would have involved the substantial demolition of the stand, and it would not at any material time have been reasonable for the First Defendants to do that;
   (iv) Because the risks of football hooliganism were at all material times manifest, no firefighting equipment could sensibly be placed within the stand and, in the events which occurred, no such equipment could have been brought effectively into use.

6.   At all material times, the West Yorkshire Metropolitan County Council were the Local Authority, the Fire Authority and the Police Authority responsible for the premises, and the Health and Safety Executive were responsible for the enforcement of the provisions of the Health and Safety at Work Act 1974, which applied to those premises, and they carried out inspections of the same.

7.A   The death of the deceased and such injuries as the Second Plaintiff sustained were caused by the negligence and/or breach of statutory duty of the Health and

Safety Executive and/or the West Yorkshire Metropolitan County Council, their servants or agents:

PARTICULARS OF NEGLIGENCE AND BREACH OF DUTY
BY THE HEALTH AND SAFETY EXECUTIVE

(i) Failing to give any advice or warning to the **First** Defendants of the extreme rapidity with which the fire would be likely to spread in the conditions existing in the stand;

(ii) Having concluded, both in 1981 and 1984, that conditions in the stand created a substantial risk of injury to the public through fire, failing adequately or at all to warn or to communicate that fact to the **First** Defendants or to anybody else;

(iii) Failing to take any adequate steps to ensure that the said risk of injury through fire was understood by the **First** Defendants and others, and was prevented or even minimised;

(iv) Failing, in breach of the duty imposed by Section 18 of the Health and Safety at Work Act 1974, to make adequate arrangements for the enforcement of the provisions of that Act.

PARTICULARS OF NEGLIGENCE AND BREACH OF DUTY
BY WEST YORKSHIRE METROPOLITAN COUNTY COUNCIL

(a) Failing to give any advice or warning to the **First** Defendants, or to their predecessors, as to the extreme rapidity with which fire was likely to spread in the conditions existing in the stand;

(b) Having, in 1976, authorised Bradford City Football Club to admit to the stand more than 5,000 members of the public as spectators, failing to give any or adequate consideration or regard to the questions: —
   (i) of whether it was a fire hazard
       and
   (ii) of suitable evacuation procedures in the case of any emergency and/or to advise the **First** Defendants in regard to the said matters;

(c) Failing to make any inspection of the stand between 1976 and 1984 — when they were invited to do so;

(d) By their letter dated 18th July 1984, indicating to the **First** Defendants that the fire hazard which the stand presented was one of a number of matters which should receive consideration at some time in the future, when they ought to have clearly advised the **First** Defendants that immediate emergency action should be taken, and ensured that this was done;

(e) Failing, in breach of the duty imposed on them by Section 18 of the Fire Precautions Act 1971 to give any or adequate consideration to the enforcement of the provisions of the said Act, if necessary by the exercise of their powers, as the relevant Fire Authority, pursuant to Section 10 (ii) of the Act.

7.B   The First Defendants will additionally rely upon the matters pleaded against the Second and Third Defendants by paragraph 7(b) of the Re-amended Statement of Claim.

8. No admissions are made as to any of the matters alleged under Paragraphs 8, 9 or 10 of the *Re-amended* Statement of Claim.

[Counsel]

DEFENCE OF THE SECOND DEFENDANTS

1. Subject to the provision of the material documents paragraphs 1 and 2 of the Statement of Claim are admitted.

2. Paragraphs 3 and 4 of the Statement of Claim are admitted.

3. It is denied that the Second Defendants, their servants or agents were negligent and/or in breach of statutory duty as alleged in paragraph 7 of the Amended Statement of Claim or at all.

4. Without prejudice to the generality of the foregoing the Second Defendants answer the particulars of negligence alleged by the First Defendants in their Defence and adopted by the Plaintiff in the Amended Statement of Claim as follows:

(a) It is denied that the Second Defendants were under a duty at any material time to give advice or warning to the First Defendants as to the rapidity with which fire could spread in the main stand. The Third Defendants were at all material times the enforcing authority under the Fire Precautions Act 1971 charged with responsibility for fire precautions at the premises. In so far as any authority was under a duty to advise the First Defendants as to fire risk, and the existence of such a duty is denied, it was the Third Defendants.

(b) It is admitted that inspectors employed by the Second Defendants visited the premises in 1981 and 1984. It is denied that they examined the stand on the occasion of such visits or concluded that there was a substantial risk of injury to the public through fire in relation to such stand.

(c) If, which is denied, there was any duty on the Second Defendants to warn the First Defendants of the risk of injury through fire in relation to the stand, the Second Defendants duty discharged that duty. Reliance will be placed on letters dated 10th September 1980 and 22nd July 1981 from Mr Laird and Mr Bennett respectively inspectors employed by the Second Defendants to the First Defendants. Reference will be made to the said letters at the trial hereof for their full terms and effects. The First Defendants failed to reply to and/or to take action upon those letters.

(d) It is denied that the Second Defendants were in breach of duty under Section 18 of the Health and Safety at Work Act. It is further denied that any such breach as may be established provides the Plaintiff with a cause of action against the Second Defendants.

(e) It is further denied that matters complained of were caused by any negligence or breach of duty on the part of the Second Defendants.

5. The injuries sustained by the deceased and by the Second Plaintiff were caused by the negligence and/or breach of statutory duty of the First and/or Third Defendants their servants or agents.

PARTICULARS OF NEGLIGENCE AND/OR BREACH OF STATUTORY DUTY OF THE FIRST DEFENDANTS

The Second Defendants repeat and adopt paragraph 5 of the Amended Statement of Claim.

PARTICULARS OF NEGLIGENCE AND/OR BREACH OF STATUTORY DUTY OF THE THIRD DEFENDANTS

The Second Defendants repeat and adopt the Particulars of Negligence and Breach of Duty in paragraph 7 of the Defence of the First Defendants.

6.   No admissions are made as to any of the matters alleged in paragraphs 8, 9 and 10 of the Amended Statement of Claim.

[Counsel]

DEFENCE OF THIRD DEFENDANTS

1.   Subject to formal proof of marriage and production of the relevant Letters of Administration the first two sentences of paragraph 1 of the Amended Statement of Claim are admitted.

2.   Subject to formal proof the facts alleged in paragraph 2 of the Amended Statement of Claim are admitted.

3.   These Defendants admit that the deceased and the Second Plaintiff attended the football match at the First Defendants' football ground referred to in paragraph 3 of the Amended Statement of Claim.

4.   These Defendants admit that during the said football match a fire started in the main stand of the said ground and further admit that the deceased lost his life in consequence of injuries sustained in the said fire as did other members of the First Plaintiff's family and further admit that the Second Plaintiff sustained personal injury as a result of the said fire.

5.   Save that the Bradford City Council also bore certain responsibilities in respect of the area in which the First Defendants' premises were situated these Defendants admit so much of paragraph 6 of the Defence of the First Defendants as refers to them.

6.   These Defendants deny that they their servants or agents were negligent or in breach of any statutory duty which they bore to the deceased or to the Second Plaintiff or that the said fire, the death of the deceased or such injuries (as to which no admissions are made) as may have been sustained by the Second Plaintiff were sustained as a result thereof.

7.   The said fire and its consequences were caused by the negligence and/or breach of statutory duty of the First Defendants their servants or agents against whom these Defendants will repeat and adopt the allegations contained in the Amended Statement of Claim herein.

[Counsel]

(e) Judgment

SIR JOSEPH CANTLEY: ... There is no dispute as to the cause of the fire. It was caused accidentally by a lighted match or a burning cigarette or some burning tobacco falling through a gap or hole in the floor. ... There it ignited inflammable debris which lay in large quantities under the wooden floor. ... This accumulation of inflammable rubbish was not recent. It had built up over the years. ... This was a fire hazard of long standing.

[His Lordship found that build-up of combustible materials was visible even on a casual inspection and that the Club had notice of the existence of the hazard of fire following a visit in September 1980 by an inspector of the Health and Safety Executive and in July 1984 by an engineer employed by the County Council.]. ...

In his final submission to me [counsel for the first defendants] conceded that the club was at fault in not finding a way to clear the void of inflammable material. They could ... have done so with assistance from the City Council. It was a proper and I think inevitable concession. However the duty of the club at common law and under the Occupiers Liability Act 1957 goes beyond finding a way to make the stand safe. If an occupier has a stand which he uses for the accommodation of 2,000 spectators of all ages and conditions and he knows or ought to know that the state of affairs in the stand is such that there is a real and constant risk of a fire starting and developing under them he cannot be absolved from his duty towards them by establishing that he is not able to find or not able to afford a way of removing that danger from the stand. He must not expose spectators to the danger even if it means that he must take the stand entirely out of use. ...

The omission of the club to take any action to deal with this dangerous situation of which it had notice and knowledge and of which it should have been aware without notice from outside parties is enough in itself to establish the claim of the plaintiffs against the first defendant. It is only right that I should say that I think it would be unfair to conclude that [the Chairman, the vice-Chairman], the board of directors or any of them were intentionally and callously indifferent to the safety of spectators using the stand. They were at fault, but the fault was that no one in authority seems ever to have properly appreciated the real gravity of this fire hazard and consequently no one gave it the attention it certainly ought to have received. The board had many other problems to contend with. The new club had taken over a distinctly ramshackle set of premises. The main stand needed a new roof. The terraces were in disrepair to an extent which could be regarded as dangerous. Almost everything needed attention. [The Chairman] told me that it was obvious in 1983 that no repairs had been done in the previous 10 years. In addition the new club was immediately and chronically short of money. ... They had to avoid all expenditure which did not seem to them to be immediately necessary. ...

[His Lordship went on to find that there were precautions which if they had been taken would have prevented all or at least most of the deaths and injuries which occurred. These included the provision of accessible and sufficient exits and an evacuation system for operation in emergencies. In these and other respects his Lordship referred to the 'Guide to Safety at Sports Grounds', an official publication of 1976 popularly called the 'Green Guide'.] In case I am misunderstood I should make it clear that I am not using the Green Guide as if it were law. It has no legal force. It is expressed to be a voluntary code devised for improving spectators' safety at football grounds to provide a reasonable degree of safety. It is recognised in the code itself that the problem of crowd safety in football grounds is complex and further complicated by the rampant pestilence of hooliganism. ...

I respectfully agree with the conclusion in Popplewell J.'s interim report [Committee of Inquiry into Crowd Safety and Control at Sports Grounds, Home Office] that this tragedy with its appalling number of injuries was caused by the devastating effects of a rapidly developing fire and by the available exits being insufficient to enable the spectators to escape. For both these causes the first defendant must be held responsible.

The Health and Safety Executive

I turn now to the case alleged against the Health and Safety Executive. It is a statutory public body exercising its relevant functions under the Health and Safety at Work etc. Act 1974 and I have to apply the principles laid down by the House of Lords in *Anns v Merton London Borough* [1978] AC 728; [1977] 2 All ER 492 [p. 99, post], and *Home Office v Dorset Yacht Co Ltd* [1970] AC 1004; [1970] 2 All ER 294 [p. 72, post].[1]

Like most statutes relating to public authorities the Health and Safety at Work etc. Act 1974 contains areas of discretion where the decision as to what to do and what not to do is for the authority or its officers to make. A judge is not entitled to substitute his discretion for that conferred by the statute on the authority. If a discretionary decision is made responsibly it cannot involve the authority in liability to a plaintiff in a civil action merely because the judge considers that the wrong decision was made. To succeed in an action for damages for negligence the plaintiff must prove not only that what was done or omitted was negligent but that it was also outside the limits of discretion responsibly and bona fide exercised. [His Lordship then considered the relevant provisions of the Act of 1974. He noted that in relation to fire risks there was an overlap between the powers of the Executive and the powers of the fire authority under the Fire Precautions Act 1971 and the powers of the local authority under the Safety of Sports Grounds Act 1975. The Executive had recognised this was so and had, in 1978, issued a memorandum of advice to their inspectors stating that the Executive would only be responsible for the manner in which undertakings were conducted. It also indicated the primary responsibility for fire risks should reside with the fire authority. In September 1980 an inspector had visited the ground and noted the litter in the void, advising that it should be removed and the void blanked off. He went on to advise the club of the Green Guide.] . . .
In evidence [the inspector] told me that he thought that the presence of this rubbish was a hazard which came within s. 3 of the 1974 Act because it was reasonably practicable for the club to deal with it. . . . [He] told me that he did not regard this rubbish as a matter of serious concern to be reported to the fire authority. Had he so regarded it he would have reported it. He told me that at the time he thought it inconceivable that the fire brigade did not inspect the club and he was anxious not to tread on the toes of the authority which was primarily concerned with fire matters. With hindsight of course it seems obvious that [the inspector's] assessment of the gravity of this risk was wrong and that it ought to have been reported to the fire authority. . . . Although he might at the time have made further investigation and inquiry which would have altered the opinion he formed I certainly do not feel justified in holding that he made his decision irresponsibly or otherwise than in good faith. [His Lordship found that there had been a number of other visits by the same inspector and others, but the question of the litter was never raised again. The risks of an emergency in the stand were raised in 1981 and the club was advised to consider their evacuation procedures. His Lordship considered some of the pleaded allegations against the Executive and rejected them all.] . . . Having seen and heard [the inspector] I do not consider myself justified in holding that he acted so carelessly and unreasonably that he acted in abuse or excess of his power . . . I have come to the conclusion that the action against the second defendant must fail. . . .

---

1. On these principles, see p. 105, post.

West Yorkshire Metropolitan County Council

The third defendant was the fire authority for the purposes of the Fire Precautions Act 1971. It was also the local authority for the purposes of the Safety of Sports Grounds Act 1975. [His Lordship found that as the club was in the Third Division and had not been 'designated' by the Secretary of State no safety certificate was required under the Act of 1975. The fire authority had the power, but were under no statutory duty to inspect the premises of the club. However, His Lordship found that in July 1984 an engineering member of a safety team set up by the local authority had noticed that litter lay in the voids. A letter was subsequently sent to the club on 19th July 1984 pointing out the fire hazard. A copy of the letter was sent to the deputy fire prevention officer but there was no evidence whether that letter was received or considered by him. The club was not again visited or mentioned at meetings of the fire and public protection committee of the authority. No one thought to follow up the letter.] . . . My conclusion is that either the letter was not considered at all, or that an irresponsible decision was made without proper consideration. In either case it was not a valid exercise of discretion and was negligent. If it was an exercise of discretion at all it was to quote Lord Reid [in *Home Office v Dorset Yacht Co Ltd* [1970] AC at p. 1031] 'exercised so carelessly or unreasonably that it was no exercise of the discretion which Parliament conferred.'

[Counsel] on behalf of the County Council conceded very properly in my opinion, that on common law principles there was a sufficient relationship between the County Council and members of the public to establish a prima facie duty of care by the Council towards members of the public. The declared object of the Fire Precautions Act 1971 is the protection of persons from fire risks and under section 18 it was the duty of the Council, as fire authority, to enforce its provisions. . . . The Safety of Sports Grounds Act 1975 is . . . specifically directed to the safety of spectators at sports grounds. . . .

[Counsel] submitted that the death of Mr Fletcher and the injuries of Martin Fletcher and Sergeant Britton were too remote a consequence of any negligence attributable to the Council because the continuing negligence of the Football Club is what is called a 'novus actus interveniens' breaking the chain of causation. . . . The primary duty was, of course, that of the club and the County Council's function was only a supervisory one; but one which was a supervisory one in the interests of the public. They embarked on it but left it unfinished. It was at all times foreseeable to a competent fire officer, or I would have thought, to any intelligent person, that if the club did not take proper action before the season started a fire might start at any time during the season, as in fact it did. If the proper, and in my view obvious, action had been taken by the fire prevention department, as it should have been, they would have exercised their powers of inspection and discovered the nature of the void and a sufficient indication of the extent of the inflammable deposit to realise that [the letter of 19 July] . . . referred to a quite alarming danger. They could, of course, have threatened or even taken action under section 10 of either of the statutes, but that would probably have been unnecessary. It might even have been sufficient, in the case of this club, to have told the club firmly, without making an inspection at once, that this danger must not be allowed to continue into the next season and that compulsory powers would have to be used if it was not dealt with before the season began. . . .

In my view the continuing negligence of the club and their continued inaction or indifference of the County Council through its various departments and officers after it had been alerted to the existence of the danger, were concurrent causes of this disaster, and I hold both of them to be liable in damages to the plaintiffs.

There only remains the apportionment of responsibility between the first and third defendants. As I have already stated, the primary duty was on the club and the functions of the County Council were supervisory and its liability is for negligent breach of a common law duty arising out of the way in which they dealt with or ignored their statutory powers. That duty was not a duty to the club but a duty to the spectators and other persons in the stand. However, the responsibility of the club is, in my view, very much greater and I apportion responsibility between the two defendants as to two-thirds on the first defendant and one-third on the third defendant.

(f)   The compensation

The plaintiffs, together with a group of about 200 other claimants represented by the same solicitors, subsequently received lump sums by way of damages. The amounts were negotiated by their solicitors with the insurers of the Club and the Council. The solicitors took the opinion of leading counsel on a specimen cross-section of cases reflecting the types of injury sustained. By far the greatest number of cases were burn injuries and these were sub-divided into categories. Based on counsel's figures and the solicitors' assessments, settlements were negotiated with the defendants' insurers. The amounts have not been disclosed.

No account was taken of payments made to them by the Bradford Disaster Appeal Fund which was set up as a discretionary trust soon after the tragedy. The Trust distributed about £4 million, raised by public donations, to the dependants of the 56 who died and to the 300 who suffered injuries. Ninety-five per cent of these payments were made within 10 months of the tragedy, that is, nearly a year before the judgment in the negligence actions. The amounts paid to individuals and the criteria used for the distribution of the Fund have not been disclosed. Assessment was undertaken by a team comprising a burns specialist, a psychiatric specialist and a claims assessor. The administration of the Fund has been regarded as a model in later disasters. See R. W. Suddards, *Bradford Disaster Appeal: the administration of an appeal fund* (London, 1986).

2   Points for discussion

(a)   The plaintiffs

Questions

Discuss the following views, in the context of the above case:

'[T]he tort system reveals its inefficiencies in starkest colour in dealing with mass tort claims' (J. G. Fleming, *The American Tort Process* (Oxford, 1988), p. 264).

'In operation, tort law serves as a grotesquely expensive and terribly slow compensation scheme providing unpredictable benefits. Moreover, its beneficiaries are people who, although typically innocent, are no more deserving than other victims who are not fortuitous enough to have access to the [tort] mechanism' (S. D. Sugarman, *Doing Away with Personal Injury Law* (New York and London, 1989), p. 41).

Notes

1. Mrs Fletcher and her son were victims of a disaster or 'mass tort' in which a large number of persons claimed to have been hurt in essentially the same way by the defendants' conduct. There is no formal court-supervised

procedure ('class action') in the English legal system (unlike several other common law jurisdictions) for a group of individuals to pursue claims for damages for negligence collectively. This meant that the plaintiffs' claims were 'lead' actions chosen to settle the common issue of liability for all members of the group. In the absence of agreement with the defendants, it is doubtful whether the judgment would have been binding in respect of all the plaintiffs. In the Bradford cases the defendants co-operated, but the absence of a formal procedure means that defendants can cause protracted delays by refusing to agree, or they can 'buy off' the lead claims by out-of-court settlements thus depriving the other claimants of a decision on the common issue.

2. There is also no proper means of financing such collective claims. An individual plaintiff, chosen for a 'lead' action, is clearly unable to find the resources necessary to conduct complex litigation. In the Bradford cases, the plaintiffs could not obtain legal aid because it was a group action. Initial funding was, therefore, by way of contribution by members of the group, a complex exercise. Even if a legally aided plaintiff were found for the lead action, the legal aid fund would have first call for costs on the amount recovered in the event of his winning. This would be likely to wipe out his damages. In the subsequent litigation arising from use of the drug Opren, the Court of Appeal upheld an order by Hirst J. that the costs incurred by the plaintiffs in the lead actions should be borne by all the parties equally: *Davies v Eli Lilly & Co* [1987] 3 All ER 94.

This is of little comfort even to those fortunate enough to be on legal aid. Sir John Donaldson MR pointed out (at p. 97):

'Unfortunately for the temporarily happy plaintiff, Parliament has required the defendant to pay the damages not to him but to the legal aid fund. That fund is required to use his damages to pay itself back every penny of costs which it has incurred in assisting him to fight his case. It is only if, after this has been done, that anything which is left will be paid to him. It may be nothing will be left or it may be relatively small change.'

Victims who are not eligible for legal aid may not be able to afford to litigate at all. For example, it has been claimed that half the 1,200 haemophiliacs suing the Department of Health on grounds that they were negligently infected by the Aids virus HIV are not eligible for legal aid and will face legal bills of £10,000 or more before the case even goes to trial: H. Witcomb (1990) 140 NLJ 1179. Changes have been made in the legal aid eligibility rules from April 1990, and the Government predicts that this will increase the proportion of the population eligible for legal aid in personal injury cases from 56 per cent to 74 per cent, but without some limit on the amount which the Legal Aid Fund can claw back (ante) many claimants will still not find it worthwhile to sue. In May 1989 the Legal Aid Board recommended that legal aid should be extended to all cases in a group irrespective of income, but this has not been accepted by the Government.

3. The extract, post, from the report of a survey carried out during 1976 and 1977 for the Oxford Centre for Socio-Legal Studies, shows that only about 12 per cent of accidental injuries attract tort compensation. This report, and other studies, identify a number of factors which inhibit use of the law of tort. Among these are:

(a)   ignorance of the law, and lack of knowledge as to where to find an expert in personal injury litigation;

(b)   lack of precision in the concept of negligence leading to uncertainty;

(c)   problems about providing evidence of fault;

(d)   delays in the legal process;

(e)   lack of resources to cover the costs of litigation.

These and other pressures deter accident victims from going to law and result in premature and inadequate settlements (see further H. Genn, *Hard Bargaining: Out of Court Settlement in Personal Injury Actions* (Oxford, 1987)). The problems are even more acute for the victims of 'man-made' diseases who face special difficulties in proving that the defendant's fault caused their illness, and, because of the gradual onset and latency of many diseases, in bringing their claims within the usual three-year period allowed by the Limitation Acts (see generally J. Stapleton, *Disease and the Compensation Debate* (Oxford, 1986)).

Compensation and Support for Illness and Injury Donald Harris et al. Oxford Socio-Legal Studies (Clarendon Press: Oxford, 1984), pp. 317–321

The survey showed that only a small minority of all accident victims initiate legal claims and obtain damages for the losses they have suffered. . . . For all types of accident taken together, the figure is 12 per cent of cases, but there are important differences in the success rates between different categories of accident. While fewer than one in three of road accident victims, and one in five of work accident victims obtained damages, fewer than one in fifty of all other types of accident victims obtained damages, despite the fact that this represented the largest category of accidents suffered by victims in the sample. Although the chances of obtaining damages were very high once there had been contact with a solicitor about the possibility of making a claim, the vast majority of victims either never considered the question of claiming compensation, or if they did so, failed to take any positive steps to make a definite claim.

Elderly victims and young victims appeared on the whole to be reluctant to claim damages, irrespective of the type of accident suffered, and, for elderly victims at least, irrespective of the degree of residual disability suffered as a result of the accident. Women suffering work accidents claimed less often than men suffering work accidents, although for road and other accidents the proportions were similar. In general, accident victims in full- or part-time employment were considerably more likely to claim damages than those not in employment. Contrary to our expectations, accident victims in lower status socio-economic groups were proportionately *more* likely to obtain damages than victims in professional or managerial groups. The seriousness of injury in both physical terms and the amount of time taken off work was not consistently associated with the likelihood that damages would be obtained, underlining the fact that the tort system is based on the cause of accidents rather than on the consequences.

Detailed analysis of the steps involved in actually perceiving an accident as a problem for which legal advice should be sought indicated that women and the elderly were both less likely to consider the question of compensation, and having done so, were less likely than other groups actually to seek legal advice. For those accident victims who did succeed in obtaining damages it was clear that advice obtained *before* getting in touch with a solicitor was very important in providing or reinforcing the incentive to claim damages. More than two-thirds of those people in contact with a solicitor claimed that the idea of obtaining legal advice *first* came from another person. For victims who have accidents on the road or at work there are normally certain procedures for reporting the accident which have to be followed and during which advice about claiming may spontaneously be offered. For victims who have accidents elsewhere there are no such procedures and the people who disproportionately suffer these types of accidents — women, the elderly, children — are more isolated than those at work from networks of information and advice. Trade union activity in pressing claims for damages provides an important example of both the value of immediate advice and easy access to the legal system.

The reasons given for not proceeding with a claim by those people who had at some time considered the possibility indicate that lack of claims-consciousness, problems about providing evidence, and fear of the legal costs involved in making a claim represent important constraints.

The actual operation of the damages system . . . produced relatively low amounts for our sample: a mean of £1,135, but a median of only £500. Many pressures on claimants led them to accept amounts which heavily discounted the full award which a court would make. There may be a discount for each risk or uncertainty facing the claimant: the risks that his evidence might not prove fault on the part of the defendant, that he himself might be found partly at fault (contributory negligence), or that the medical reports on his prognosis might be wrong; the uncertainties about whether he could bear the further delay and expense of waiting for a court hearing, and about how much a judge would award for his injuries. The cumulative effect of all these uncertainties was that nearly all claimants agreed to compromise their cases in out-of-court settlements for sums much lower than 'full' legal liability would justify. Every uncertainty and risk is a negotiating weapon in the hands of the insurance company; a particularly powerful weapon is an allegation of contributory negligence, as was shown by solicitors' reports that it was taken into account in nearly half the settlements. The pressures to settle meant that very few cases (five out of 1,177, or 0.4 per cent) actually reached the stage of a contested hearing in court, although formal court proceedings were commenced in about 40 per cent of the claims ultimately settled. . . .

Delay is an inescapable part of the present tort system. In the survey, the average delay between the date of the accident and the actual receipt of damages was a little over nineteen months; nearly all successful claimants had returned to work before receiving damages. Solicitors had advised delay in 40 per cent of the claims, in order to wait until medical treatment was complete or until the medical condition of the claimant had stabilised. Several trends are clear from the data — the delay is likely to be longer, the longer the victim is off work, and the greater the degree of his residual disability. The data also indicated that the longer the delay before a lawyer is consulted, the worse the chance of obtaining damages: the difficulties of collecting evidence increase with the delay. Two thirds of the solicitors reported difficulties in negotiating with insurance companies, but their clients seemed unaware of many of the difficulties, and reported far fewer. The two main problems for solicitors were to establish liability, and to negotiate the amount of damages. The difficulties led 29 per cent of those who had formally made a claim, or who had consulted a solicitor or trade union about claiming, to decide to abandon it: they reported that they had done so because of problems of obtaining evidence (45 per cent); their own fault (18 per cent); fear of legal expenses (16 per cent); firm denials of liability by the defendants (15 per cent); and problems over trade unions' handling of the claims (15 per cent). . . .

Our data showed that it was not victims' attributions of fault which motivated them to make a damages claim. . . . Fault was not always seen as appropriate grounds for compensation, nor was it necessarily seen as a precondition if a claim was to be made. In only half those cases where the victim took steps to initiate a claim for damages had he also attributed fault to the person against whom the claim would be made. Only about half of those who said their accident was someone else's fault said they had at any time thought that that person should compensate them. Moreover, the pattern of responses for different types of accidents suggested that even in those cases where attributions of fault did coincide with the initiation of a claim, the attribution of fault was a justification rather than a reason for the claim, and that, without the prospect of a possible damages award, fault might have been attributed quite differently, if at all. The question of fault was certainly not unimportant to the victims. In particular, holding someone to blame was clearly seen as threatening to a relationship. However, the factors determining whether or not fault was attributed to someone else, and if so how, were extremely complex, and included many factors beside the causes and circumstances of the accident. Rather than the law reflecting the ordinary man's view of fault and liability, the victims' attributions of fault and liability reflected legal norms and the likelihood of a successful damages claim. The findings also confirmed that the attribution of fault in the context of a particular damages claim is very much a function of that context. It cannot be assumed that the type of attribution of fault generated by the tort system will be appropriate also for purposes of deterrence or accident prevention, where it may be far more effective to focus on quite different causal factors.

Notes

1. An earlier, but less comprehensive survey carried out in 1974 for the Pearson Commission (vol. 2, chap. 18) found that only about 6.5 per cent of all injuries attracted tort compensation, and gave broadly similar reasons to those above. The Pearson Commission (vol. 1, para. 83) estimated that the operating costs of the tort system amounted to about 87 per cent of tort compensation payments, while the costs of the social security system were only 11 per cent of social security benefits (para. 261). The Oxford study (ante) found that the average cost of settling claims ranged from 15 per cent of damages obtained in larger claims, to 29 per cent of damages in smaller claims. The Report of the Review Body on Civil Justice (Cm. 394, 1988), para. 427 found that county court personal injury cases were particularly expensive for successful plaintiffs: plaintiffs' costs alone amounted to more than 50 per cent of compensation in 85 per cent of cases, compared with nearly 50 per cent of cases in the High Court.

2. The Report of the Review Body on Civil Justice, para. 432 reported the following findings of a factual study carried out by Inbucon Management Consultants between June and November 1985 on the basis of court records, solicitors' records and bills of costs:

Delay
   (i) High Court cases frequently took 4,5,6 or more years from incident to conclusion.
  (ii) County Court cases, where the amount in dispute was usually no more than £3,000, could take 3 years or more from incident to conclusion.
 (iii) Cases which were settled by agreement sometimes took as long as those which went to trial.
 (iv) It sometimes took 3 years after the incident to get a case started.
  (v) After the commencement of a case it took nearly 2 years in the High Court in London before the defendant was given details of the plaintiff's case.
 (vi) When the two sides were ready for trial it took the best part of a year in the High Court before a judge could be made available.

Costs

(vii) In the High Court, for every £100 of damages awarded the costs added up to £50, or £70, depending on the basis of calculation. The lower figure is obtained from the solicitors' questionnaires, and the higher one from the taxed bills sample.

(viii) In the County Court both the damages and the costs were less than in the High Court, but for every £100 awarded legal costs added up to £125, or £175, depending on the basis of calculation. Again, the lower figure is obtained from the solicitors' questionnaires, and the higher one from the taxed bills sample.

(b)   The defendants

Question

The directors of the Club, and the officers of the County Council were found to have been negligent. Why was it that the plaintiffs sued the corporations which they served, rather than the individuals?

Notes

1. The Bradford City Association Football Club (1983) Ltd. and the Council are corporate bodies which were insured. These features are relevant to financial responsibility: if an aim of tort law is to compensate the victim, how does it ensure that the defendant can pay?

It was the insurers of the Club and the Council which defended the proceedings in their insureds' names and dealt with the settlement negotiations. The right to do so arose under the terms of insurance contracts. (A specimen policy – not the ones in this case or with the same insurers – will be found in chap. 19, p. 903, post.) Such insurance is not compulsory in the case of football clubs, but it is in respect of employers' liability (p. 894, post), and road traffic accidents (p. 885, post). As to the plaintiff's rights if the defendant becomes insolvent, see p. 896, post, or if the defendant fails to insure where this is compulsory, see p. 892, post. See generally, *Atiyah*, chaps. 9 and 10.

2. In the Bradford case about 200 claimants were able to pool resources and to instruct two firms of solicitors who coordinated the actions and were able to bargain on an equal footing with the insurers. The position may be different where there is a single plaintiff: See the extract from Genn, op cit, set out at p. 913, post.

(c)   The cause of action

Question

What did the plaintiffs have to prove in order to succeed against (1) the Club; (2) the Health and Safety Executive; (3) the County Council?

Note

The elements of negligence and causation, which featured in this case, are the subject of chaps. 2 to 6 of this book. Of special interest in Sir Joseph Cantley's judgment are his findings that (1) the Club was liable for 'fault' even though the directors had not been 'intentionally or callously indifferent', and the Club was impecunious; (2) the Health and Safety Executive were not liable even though 'with hindsight . . . the [inspector's] assessment of the gravity of the risk was wrong and . . . it ought to have been reported to the fire authority'; and (3) the County Council were held liable for 'continued inaction or indifference' which amounted to a concurrent 'cause' of the fire and injuries.

(d) Sources of compensation

Questions

1. What are the main sources of compensation for victims of accident and 'man-made' disease? Consider in particular (a) social security benefits (p. 917, post); (b) criminal injuries compensation (p. 920, post); (c) 'personal' (sometimes called loss or 'first party') insurance (specimens, p. 903, post); (d) occupational and statutory sick pay (p. 917, post); (e) disaster funds and other donations.

2. To what extent is 'double compensation' or 'overcompensation' possible? (For the deductions which may be made from common law damages, see p. 429, post.)

Notes

1. In the settlements in the Bradford case private insurance was disregarded as were the substantial payments received before the trial from the highly successful disaster appeal (see ante). In the larger claims social security benefits were taken into account (see p. 429, post).

2. According to the Report of the Review Body on Civil Justice, para. 391 some 1.8 m new claimants obtain social security payments each year, 1 m obtain occupational sick pay and 250,000 benefit from personal insurance, while only 340,000 victims make claims in tort on the basis of negligence or breach of statutory duty. Ninety-nine per cent of all tort claims are settled without going to trial.

Compensation and Support for Illness and Injury Donald Harris et al. Oxford Socio-Legal Studies (Clarendon Press: Oxford, 1984), pp. 321–323, 327

The main financial support for victims in the survey came from social security . . . ; but only four out of ten actually received some benefit (averaging £731 up to the time of the interview, but with some future entitlement to benefits which could be worth thousands of pounds. . . . About a third of the social security beneficiaries in the survey had to rely on means-tested supplementary benefits, which fact indicates that, for many victims of illness and injury, minimum income levels are not being maintained by the social security benefits specifically designed for illness and injury. A third of the beneficiaries received the long-term invalidity benefits, and a fifth the short-term sickness benefit. In practice entitlement to social security benefit depends largely on previous work status. Nearly three-quarters of those in full-time work before the illness or injury received some benefit but fewer than one in five of other victims received any benefit. This goes some way to explain the fact that many more men than women received support from the social security system.

Data from the survey suggest that difficulties in the administration of social security arise from two factors — the complexity of the criteria for entitlement to some benefits (e.g. means-tested supplementary benefit) and the need for special medical examinations for some benefits (e.g. attendance allowance).

Only seven of the twenty-one victims of criminal injury in our sample obtained an award from the Criminal Injuries Compensation Board. . . . One person applied for an award but was refused for reasons which were not clear in the account given by the victim. Those people who did not apply were either confused about the regulations regarding awards (for example, they might have thought that it was only possible to apply if the identity of the offender was known) or did not think that they would have been entitled to compensation because the injury was caused in a domestic dispute or in a fight between acquaintances. The criminal injuries reported were generally of a serious nature and in some cases caused long periods off work. The amounts awarded were quite small (mean £245, median £207) and most claims were made direct by the victim to the Board rather than through a solicitor.

Although occupational sick pay is obviously confined to employees, it is an important form of support for those who have lost earnings as the result of illness or injury. . . . Our data showed that official statistics on membership of sick pay schemes (to the effect that about 80 per cent of full-time workers are covered) are not a reliable guide to actual receipts of sick pay. In the survey, of those who had held their employment for less than six months, only 25 per cent obtained some sick pay; for those with six months but less than two years' service, 49 per cent obtained some; and for those with more than five years' service, 62 per cent obtained some. The mean total amount of sick pay received was £248; a typical recipient was someone absent for up to twenty-six weeks being paid £20 to £30 per week. When added to social security benefits, these amounts can provide total compensation equal to full pay for the whole or part of the period of absence, but the longer the absence, the less likely that sick pay will continue to be received: only a relatively small amount of sick pay was received for absences beyond six months.

Our data indicated that private, first-party insurance is an insignificant proportion of present support for illness and injury. . . . Only 14 per cent of people in the survey held a policy of this type, and they were mainly work and road accident victims (who were also those most likely to obtain some damages). Fewer than half those with policies received a payment, and the mean amount was only £81.

The survey data on social care . . . showed that, on average, illness has more serious medical consequences than accidents: those who are ill are more likely to be in hospital for more than a week, and to use the services of general practitioners; they are also more likely to suffer residual disabilities. . . . The same holds for local authority and community health services: illness victims (particularly the elderly) make nearly three times as much use of these services as do accident victims. . . . On the basis of service use, therefore, the 'needs' of illness victims would appear to be greater than those of accident victims, yet the tort system in practice benefits only the latter group.

More than half the victims in the survey received informal care and support from family, relatives or neighbours. . . . This assistance often continued on a daily basis for more than six months and came largely from family members: it was not dependent on the age of the victim, nor the cause of his incapacity. Informal support is given without payment, and often in addition to, rather than instead of, local authority support.

A comparison of the different combinations of support received by the various categories of victims showed that those who obtain damages (almost exclusively work and road accident victims) are more likely than other victims to receive in addition some social security support, and slightly more likely to receive some private insurance payment. . . .

In practice, compensation under the damages system is virtually confined to accident cases. Illness caused by the fault of another person can rarely be proved: out of the 182 cases where damages were paid in the survey, only two were for illness — both were claims against employers, one for pneumoconiosis suffered by a miner, and one for poisoning from asbestos dust suffered by a factory worker. In a similar way, benefits under the industrial injuries scheme are concentrated almost entirely on accident cases: only one in fifty of the injury benefits commencing in 1976–7 (the year nearest to our survey period) were for diseases prescribed under the scheme (*Social Security Statistics 1977*, Table 20.50). It should be noted, however, that the preference shown by existing compensation systems is not for accident cases in general, but rather for restricted categories of accidents — injuries suffered at work, on the roads, by criminal violence, or through service with the Armed Forces. . . . Our survey data indicate that although those injured in other categories of accident form the vast majority of accident victims . . . only one in fifty of them obtains any payment of damages. . . .

(e)   The aims of the law of tort

Questions

To what extent does the judgment in the Bradford case:

   (a) deter clubs and supervisory authorities from allowing or continuing similar dangerous hazards in future?
   (b) relieve the suffering of individual victims by spreading their losses through liability insurance or the price mechanism?
   (c) satisfy the principle of justice that one who has been damaged by the fault of another ought to be compensated by that other?

Notes

1. The argument for tort law as a deterrent assumes that, without tort liability, people would put their selfish interests ahead of the safety of others. Compare this with Sir Joseph Cantley's observation that it might have been sufficient simply to have told the Club that 'this danger must not be allowed to continue.' It is often argued that other social mechanisms, such as regulatory agencies, are more effective means than tort law for making people act reasonably, despite the failures of agencies like the fire authority in the Bradford case. Since the Bradford tragedy, regulation to prevent similar occurrences has been strengthened by the Fire Safety and Safety of Places of Sport Act 1987.

Generally on deterrence theories see *Williams & Hepple*, pp. 138–142; Gl. Williams (1951) 4 CLP 137; *Atiyah*, pp. 489–542; S. D. Sugarman, *Doing Away with Personal Injury Law* (New York and London, 1989), pp. 3–34; G. Calabresi, *The Costs of Accidents* (New Haven, 1970); *Harris et al*, pp. 139–163.

2. Compensation is usually seen as the principal goal of tort law. This springs from a natural compassion for victims of accident and disease but rests on the dubious assumptions that tort defendants are the best loss-spreaders, that the forensic and out-of-court mechanisms for determining fault and assessing damages are capable of delivering compensation to most victims, and that other means of compensation (such as social security) are inadequate.

For the arguments for and against compensation theories, see *Williams & Hepple*, pp. 24–30, 78–86, 206–208; *Atiyah*, pp. 467–483; Sugarman, op cit, pp. 35–54; A. I. Ogus (1984) 37 CLP 29.

3. The corrective justice theory of tort law, looked at from the point of view of the victim, is sometimes called the principle of 'ethical compensation', and from the offender's viewpoint, 'ethical retribution': see Gl. Williams (1951) 4 CLP at p. 140ff. Whatever the attractions of doing justice between two individuals, in practice the amount that claimants recover is likely to be far less than they 'deserve' and the amount an uninsured defendant might have to pay is far greater that he or she 'deserves' to pay for momentary inattention or 'negligence'.

See *Williams & Hepple*, pp. 136–137; *Atiyah*, pp. 484–488; Sugarman, op cit, pp. 55–72.

2 The duty of care

The tort of negligence has been the subject of varying classifications. It is sometimes said that it involves a duty, a breach of that duty, and damage caused to the plaintiff by that breach. One can delve deeper, as R. W. M. Dias (particularly in [1967] CLJ 62 at 66) has done, in putting forward the following questions as determining liability:

'(1) Is the careless infliction, by act or omission, of this kind of harm on this type of plaintiff by this type of defendant recognised by law as remediable? (2) Was the defendant's conduct in the given situation careless, i.e. did it fall short of the standard, and come within the scope, set by law? (3) Was it reasonably foreseeable that the defendant's carelessness would have inflicted on this plaintiff the kind of harm of which he complains? (4) Was it the defendant's conduct that caused the plaintiff's damage? If the answers are in the affirmative, the defendant is liable in negligence.'

All these questions are covered at one point or another in this sourcebook. Question 1 and that part of question 3 which is concerned with the foreseeability of the plaintiff are traditionally dealt with under the 'duty of care' heading and are covered by the materials in chaps. 2–4. Question 2 relates to breach of duty and is covered in chap. 5; the remaining part of question 3 and question 4 relate to causation and remoteness of damage and are covered by materials in chap. 6.

The traditional point at which to commence a consideration of the duty of care is the broad 'neighbour principle' enunciated by Lord Atkin in *M'Alister* (or *Donoghue*) *v Stevenson* [1932] AC 562 (p. 43, post) in which he attempted to rationalise and develop the earlier case law. The principle works fairly well when applied to negligent interference with physical interests. Indeed, in *Home Office v Dorset Yacht Co Ltd* [1970] AC 1004; [1970] 2 All ER 294 (p. 72, post) Lord Reid went so far as to say 'the time has come when we can and should say that it ought to apply unless there is some justification or valid explanation for its exclusion' and there was a similar approach in *Anns v Merton London Borough Council* [1978] AC 728; [1977] 2 All ER 492. However, recent years have witnessed a shift away from any general principle and a retreat to a more individual and compartmentalised approach: see e.g. *Caparo Industries plc v Dickman* [1990] 1 All ER 568; [1990] 2 WLR 358 (p. 56, post).

Over the years a significant distinction has been drawn between what is variously called 'financial' or 'pecuniary' or 'economic' loss, on the one hand, and physical damage, on the other hand. At times the validity of this distinction has been questioned and the complexity of the issues involved merits a separate chapter for discussion of the scope of the protection of a person's economic interests. Pragmatic objections, which have been raised to the extension of the 'neighbour principle' to the question of recovery of damages for economic loss, have not been raised to the same extent in regard to the kinds of conduct – such as omissions and control of the conduct of others (p. 65, post) – which may give rise to a duty of care.

The use of the concept of 'duty-situations' has become so deeply entrenched in judicial thinking that the academic controversies about whether it is a necessary element in the tort of negligence now seem somewhat strange (but W. W. Buckland (1935) 51 LQR 637 still repays reading; see also the views expressed more recently in *Atiyah*, chap. 3). It has been generally recognised that concepts such as 'duty', 'remoteness', 'causation' and 'negligence' (in the sense of breach of duty) are interchangeably used as mechanisms to control liability; at times the ambiguity inherent in the notion of 'foreseeability' has been stretched to provide a sole determinant of liability, but its very ambiguity and the realisation that defendants are not always made responsible for foreseeable harm have revitalised other verbal mechanisms. It is not a new suggestion that instead of putting the decisions into pigeon-holes such as 'no duty' or 'too remote' or 'unforeseeable' it would be better, as Lord Denning MR has expressed it (p. 232, post) 'to consider the particular relationship in hand' and decide whether, 'as a matter of policy', the loss should be recoverable. This approach would confront the judiciary with an uncontrolled choice of policy, sometimes in matters which may be more rationally dealt with through the informed processes of the Law Commission and Parliament. But the rapid growth of technology and new situations of danger mean that the judiciary will always have to deal with the unexpected. It is this which gives to the duty of care cases a special importance for understanding the judicial process.

1   The activity duty

Donoghue (or M'Alister) *v* Stevenson House of Lords [1932] All ER Rep 1

Appeal from an interlocutor of the Second Division of the Court of Session in Scotland.

On 26 August 1928, the appellant, a shop assistant, drank a bottle of ginger-beer manufactured by the respondent, which a friend had ordered on her behalf from a retailer in a shop at Paisley and given to her. She stated that the shopkeeper, who supplied the ginger-beer, opened the bottle, which she said was sealed with a metal cap and was made of dark opaque glass, and poured some of its contents into a tumbler which contained some ice cream, and that she drank some of the contents of the tumbler, that her friend then lifted the bottle and was pouring the remainder of the contents into the tumbler, when a snail which had been in the bottle floated out in a state of decomposition. As a result, the appellant alleged, she had contracted a serious illness, and she claimed from the respondent damages for negligence. She alleged that the respondent, as the manufacturer of an article intended for consumption and contained in a receptacle which prevented inspection, owed a duty to her as consumer of the article to take care that there was no noxious element in the article, that he neglected such duty, and that he was, consequently, liable for any damage caused by such neglect. The case then came before the Lord Ordinary, who rejected the plea in law of the respondent and allowed the parties a proof of their averments, but on a reclaiming note the Second Division (the Lord Justice Clerk, Lord Ormidale and Lord Anderson; Lord Hunter dissenting) recalled the interlocutor of the Lord Ordinary and dismissed the action. The plaintiff (pursuer) appealed.

LORD BUCKMASTER (dissenting): . . . The general principle of [*Langridge v Levy*[1], *Longmeid v Holliday*[2] and *Winterbottom v Wright*[3]] is stated by Lord Sumner (then Hamilton, J.) in *Blacker v Lake and Elliot Ltd*[4] (in these terms 106 LT at p. 536):

'The breach of the defendant's contract with A. to use care and skill in and about the manufacture or repair of an article does not of itself give any cause of action to B. when he is injured by reason of the article proving to be defective.'

From this general rule there are two well-known exceptions:
(i) in the case of an article dangerous in itself, and (ii) where the article, not in itself dangerous, is in fact dangerous on account of some defect or for any other reason, and this is known to the manufacturer. Until *George v Skivington*[5] I know of no further modification of the general rule.
As to (i), in the case of things dangerous in themselves, there is, in the words of Lord Dunedin,

'a peculiar duty to take precaution imposed upon those who send forth or install such articles when it is necessarily the case that other parties will come within their proximity':

Dominion Natural Gas Co Ltd v Collins[6] ([1909] AC at p. 646). And as to (ii), this depends on the fact that the knowledge of the danger creates the obligation to warn, and its concealment is in the nature of fraud.
In the present case no one can suggest that the ginger-beer was an article dangerous in itself, and the words of Lord Dunedin show that the duty attaches only to such articles, for I read the words 'a peculiar duty' as meaning a duty peculiar to the special class of subject mentioned. . . .

[LORD BUCKMASTER went on to survey other authorities and continued:] . . . In my view, therefore, the authorities are against the appellant's contention and apart from authority it is difficult to see how any common law proposition can be formulated to support her claim.
The principle contended for must be this — that the manufacturer, or, indeed, the repairer, of any article, apart entirely from contract, owes a duty to any person by whom the article is lawfully used to see that it has been carefully constructed. All rights in contract must be excluded from consideration of this principle, for such rights undoubtedly exist in successive steps from the original manufacturer down to the ultimate purchaser, embraced in the general rule that an article is warranted as reasonably fit for the purpose for which it is sold. Nor can the doctrine be confined to cases where inspection is difficult or impossible to introduce. This conception is simply to misapply to tort doctrines applicable to sale and purchase.
The principle of tort lies completely outside the region where such considerations apply, and the duty, if it exists, must extend to every person who, in lawful

---

1. (1837) 2 M&W 519; affd (1838) 4 M&W 337.
2. (1851) 6 Exch 761.
3. (1842) 10 M&W 109.
4. (1912) 106 LT 533.
5. (1869) LR 5 Exch 1.
6. [1909] AC 640.

circumstances, uses the article made. There can be no special duty attaching to the manufacture of food, apart from those implied by contract or imposed by statute. If such a duty exists it seems to me it must cover the construction of every article, and I cannot see any reason why it should not apply to the construction of a house. If one step, why not fifty? Yet if a house be, as it sometimes is, negligently built, and in consequence of that negligence the ceiling falls and injures the occupier or anyone else, no action against the builder exists according to the English law, although I believe such a right did exist according to the laws of Babylon. Were such a principle known and recognised, it seems to me impossible, having regard to the numerous cases that must have arisen to persons injured by its disregard, that with the exception of *George v Skivington*[1] no case directly involving the principle has ever succeeded in the courts, and were it well known and accepted much of the discussion of the earlier cases would have been waste of time. . . .

LORD ATKIN: The sole question for determination in this case is legal: Do the averments made by the pursuer in her pleading, if true, disclose a cause of action? I need not re-state the particular facts. The question is whether the manufacturer of an article of drink sold by him to a distributor in circumstances which prevent the distributor or the ultimate purchaser or consumer from discovering by inspection any defect is under any legal duty to the ultimate purchaser or consumer to take reasonable care that the article is free from defect likely to cause injury to health. I do not think a more important problem has occupied your Lordships in your judicial capacity, important both because of its bearing on public health and because of the practical test which it applies to the system of law under which it arises. The case has to be determined in accordance with Scots law, but it has been a matter of agreement between the experienced counsel who argued this case, and it appears to be the basis of the judgments of the learned judges of the Court of Session, that for the purposes of determining this problem the law of Scotland and the law of England are the same. I speak with little authority on this point, but my own research, such as it is, satisfies me that the principles of the law of Scotland on such a question as the present are identical with those of English law, and I discuss the issue on that footing. The law of both countries appears to be that in order to support an action for damages for negligence the complainant has to show that he has been injured by the breach of a duty owed to him in the circumstances by the defendant to take reasonable care to avoid such injury. In the present case we are not concerned with the breach of the duty; if a duty exists, that would be a question of fact which is sufficiently averred and for the present purposes must be assumed. We are solely concerned with the question whether as a matter of law in the circumstances alleged the defender owed any duty to the pursuer to take care.

It is remarkable how difficult it is to find in the English authorities statements of general application defining the relations between parties that give rise to the duty. The courts are concerned with the particular relations which come before them in actual litigation, and it is sufficient to say whether the duty exists in those circumstances. The result is that the courts have been engaged upon an elaborate classification of duties as they exist in respect of property, whether real or personal, with further divisions as to ownership, occupation or control, and distinctions based on the particular relations of the one side or the other, whether manufacturer, salesman or landlord, customer, tenant, stranger, and so on. In this way it can be ascertained at any time whether the law recognises a duty, but only where the case can be referred to some particular species which has been examined and classified. And yet the duty which is common to all the cases where liability is established must logically be based upon some element common to the cases where it is found to exist. To exist[2] a complete logical definition of the general principle is probably to go

---

1. (1869) LR 5 Exch 1.
2. [This word does not appear in the Law Reports, [1932] AC 562 at 580, but is replaced by the word 'seek'.]

beyond the function of the judge, for, the more general the definition, the more likely it is to omit essentials or introduce non-essentials. The attempt was made by Lord Esher in *Heaven v Pender*[1] . . . As framed it was demonstrably too wide, though it appears to me, if properly limited, to be capable of affording a valuable practical guide.

At present I content myself with pointing out that in English law there must be and is some general conception of relations giving rise to a duty of care, of which the particular cases found in the books are but instances. The liability for negligence, whether you style it such or treat it as in other systems as a species of 'culpa', is no doubt based upon a general public sentiment of moral wrongdoing for which the offender must pay. But acts or omissions which any moral code would censure cannot in a practical world be treated so as to give a right to every person injured by them to demand relief. In this way rules of law arise which limit the range of complainants and the extent of their remedy. The rule that you are to love your neighbour becomes in law: You must not injure your neighbour, and the lawyers' question: Who is my neighbour? receives a restricted reply. You must take reasonable care to avoid acts or omissions which you can reasonably foresee would be likely to injure your neighbour. Who then, in law, is my neighbour? The answer seems to be persons who are so closely and directly affected by my act that I ought reasonably to have them in contemplation as being so affected when I am directing my mind to the acts or omissions which are called in question. This appears to me to be the doctrine of *Heaven v Pender*[1] as laid down by Lord Esher when it is limited by the notion of proximity introduced by Lord Esher himself and A. L. Smith LJ in *Le Lievre v Gould*[2]. Lord Esher MR says ([1893] 1 QB at p. 497):

'That case established that, under certain circumstances, one man may owe a duty to another, even though there is no contract between them. If one man is near to another, or is near to the property of another, a duty lies upon him not to do that which may cause a personal injury to that other, or may injure his property.'

So A. L. Smith LJ says ([1893] 1 QB at p. 504):

'The decision of *Heaven v Pender*[1] was founded upon the principle that a duty to take due care did arise when the person or property of one was in such proximity to the person or property of another that, if due care was not taken damage might be done by the one to the other.'

I think that this sufficiently states the truth if proximity be not confined to mere physical proximity, but be used, as I think it was intended, to extend to such close and direct relations that the act complained of directly affects a person whom the person alleged to be bound to take care would know would be directly affected by his careless act. That this is the sense in which nearness or 'proximity' was intended by Lord Esher is obvious from his own illustration in *Heaven v Pender*[1] (11 QBD at p. 510) of the application of his doctrine to the sale of goods.

'This [i.e., the rule he has just formulated] includes the case of goods, &c., supplied to be used immediately by a particular person or persons, or one of a class of persons, where it would be obvious to the person supplying, if he thought, that the goods would in all probability be used at once by such persons before a reasonable opportunity for discovering any defect which might exist, and where the thing supplied

---

1. (1883) 11 QBD 503.
2. [1893] 1 QB 491.

would be of such a nature that a neglect of ordinary care or skill as to its condition or the manner of supplying it would probably cause danger to the person or property of the person for whose use it was supplied, and who was about to use it. It would exclude a case in which the goods are supplied under circumstances in which it would be a chance by whom they would be used, or whether they would be used or not, or whether they would be used before there would probably be means of observing any defect, or where the goods would be of such a nature that a want of care or skill as to their condition or the manner of supplying them would not probably produce danger of injury to person or property.'

I draw particular attention to the fact that Lord Esher emphasises the necessity of goods having to be 'used immediately' and 'used at once before a reasonable opportunity of inspection'. This is obviously to exclude the possibility of goods having their condition altered by lapse of time, and to call attention to the proximate relationship, which may be too remote where inspection even by the person using, certainly by an intermediate person, may reasonably be interposed. With this necessary qualification of proximate relationship, as explained in *Le Lievre v Gould*,[1] I think the judgment of Lord Esher expresses the law of England. Without the qualification, I think that the majority of the court in *Heaven v Pender*[2] was justified in thinking that the principle was expressed in too general terms. There will, no doubt, arise cases where it will be difficult to determine whether the contemplated relationship is so close that the duty arises. But in the class of case now before the court I cannot conceive any difficulty to arise. A manufacturer puts up an article of food in a container which he knows will be opened by the actual consumer. There can be no inspection by any purchaser and no reasonable preliminary inspection by the consumer. Negligently in the course of preparation he allows the contents to be mixed with poison. It is said that the law of England and Scotland is that the poisoned consumer has no remedy against the negligent manufacturer. If this were the result of the authorities, I should consider the result a grave defect in the law and so contrary to principle that I should hesitate long before following any decision to that effect which had not the authority of this House. . . . There are other instances than of articles of food and drink where goods are sold intended to be used immediately by the consumer, such as many forms of goods sold for cleaning purposes, when the same liability must exist. The doctrine supported by the decision below would not only deny a remedy to the consumer who was injured by consuming bottled beer or chocolates poisoned by the negligence of the manufacturer, but also to the user of what should be a harmless proprietary medicine, an ointment, a soap, a cleaning fluid or cleaning powder. I confine myself to articles of common household use, where everyone, including the manufacturer, knows that the articles will be used by persons other than the actual ultimate purchaser—namely, by members of his family and his servants, and, in some cases, his guests. I do not think so ill of our jurisprudence as to suppose that its principles are so remote from the ordinary needs of civilised society and the ordinary claims which it makes upon its members as to deny a legal remedy where there is so obviously a social wrong.

It will be found, I think, on examination, that there is no case in which the circumstances have been such as I have just suggested where the liability has been negatived. There are numerous cases where the relations were much more remote where the duty has been held not to exist. There are also dicta in such cases which go further than was necessary for the determination of the particular issues, which have caused the difficulty experienced by the courts below. I venture to say that in the branch of the law which deals with civil wrongs, dependent in England, at any rate, entirely upon

---

1. [1893] 1 QB 491.
2. (1883) 11 QBD 503.

the application by judges of general principles also formulated by judges, it is of particular importance to guard against the danger of stating propositions of law in wider terms than is necessary, lest essential factors be omitted in the wider survey and the inherent adaptability of English law be unduly restricted. For this reason it is very necessary, in considering reported cases in the law of torts, that the actual decision alone should carry authority, proper weight, of course, being given to the dicta of the judges. . . .

I do not find it necessary to discuss at length the cases dealing with duties where a thing is dangerous, or, in the narrower category, belongs to a class of things which are dangerous in themselves. I regard the distinction as an unnatural one so far as it is used to serve as a logical differentiation by which to distinguish the existence or non-existence of a legal right. In this respect I agree with what was said by Scrutton LJ in *Hodge & Sons v Anglo-American Oil Co*[1] (12 Ll L Rep at p. 187), a case which was ultimately decided on a question of fact:

'Personally, I do not understand the difference between a thing dangerous in itself as poison and a thing not dangerous as a class, but by negligent construction dangerous as a particular thing. The latter, if anything, seems the more dangerous of the two; it is a wolf in sheep's clothing instead of an obvious wolf.'

The nature of the thing may very well call for different degrees of care, and the person dealing with it may well contemplate persons as being within the sphere of his duty to take care who would not be sufficiently proximate with less dangerous goods, so that not only the degree of care but the range of persons to whom a duty is owed may be extended. But they all illustrate the general principle. . . .

If your Lordships accept the view that the appellant's pleading discloses a relevant cause of action, you will be affirming the proposition that by Scots and English law alike a manufacturer of products which he sells in such a form as to show that he intends them to reach the ultimate consumer in the form in which they left him, with no reasonable possibility of intermediate examination, and with the knowledge that the absence of reasonable care in the preparation or putting up of the products will result in injury to the consumer's life or property, owes a duty to the consumer to take that reasonable care.

It is a proposition that I venture to say no one in Scotland or England who was not a lawyer would for one moment doubt. It will be an advantage to make it clear that the law in this matter, as in most others, is in accordance with sound common sense. I think that this appeal should be allowed.

LORD THANKERTON: . . . The duties which the appellant accuses the respondent of having neglected may be summarised as follows: (a) that the ginger-beer was manufactured by the respondent or his servants to be sold as an article of drink to members of the public (including the appellant), and that, accordingly, it was his duty to exercise the greatest care in order that snails should not get into the bottles, render the ginger-beer dangerous and harmful, and be sold with the ginger-beer; (b) a duty to provide a system of working his business which would not allow snails to get into the sealed bottles, and, in particular, would not allow the bottles when washed to stand in places to which snails had access; (c) a duty to provide an efficient system of inspection, which would prevent snails from getting into the sealed bottles; and (d) a duty to provide clear bottles, so as to facilitate the said system of inspection.

There can be no doubt, in my opinion, that equally in the law of Scotland and of England it lies upon the party claiming redress in such a case to show that there was some relation of duty between her and the defender which required the defender to exercise due and reasonable care for her safety. It is not at all necessary that there

---

1. (1922) 12 Ll L Rep 183.

should be any direct contract between them, because the action is not based upon contract but upon negligence; but it is necessary for the pursuer in such an action to show there was a duty owed to her by the defender, because a man cannot be charged with negligence if he has no obligation to exercise diligence; *Kemp and Dougall v Darngavil Coal Co*[1] per Lord Kinnear (1909 SC at p. 1319); see also *Clelland v Robb*[2] per Lord President Dunedin and Lord Kinnear (1911 SC at p. 256). The question in each case is whether the pursuer has established, or, in the stage of the present appeal, has relevantly averred, such facts as involve the existence of such a relation of duty.

We are not dealing here with a case of what is called an article per se dangerous or one which was known by the defender to be dangerous, in which cases a special duty of protection or adequate warning is placed upon the person who uses or distributes it. The present case is that of a manufacturer and a consumer, with whom he has no contractual relation, of an article which the manufacturer did not know to be dangerous, and, unless the consumer can establish a special relationship with the manufacturer, it is clear, in my opinion, that neither the law of Scotland nor the law of England will hold that the manufacturer has any duty towards the consumer to exercise diligence. In such a case the remedy of the consumer, if any, will lie against the intervening party from whom he has procured the article. . . .

The special circumstances, from which the appellant claims that such a relationship of duty should be inferred, may, I think, be stated thus, namely, that the respondent, in placing his manufactured article of drink upon the market, has intentionally so excluded interference with, or examination of, the article by any intermediate handler of the goods between himself and the consumer that he has, of his own accord, brought himself into direct relationship with the consumer, with the result that the consumer is entitled to rely upon the exercise of diligence by the manufacturer to secure that the article shall not be harmful to the consumer. If that contention be sound, the consumer, on her showing that the article has reached her intact, and that she has been injured by the harmful nature of the article owing to the failure of the manufacturer to take reasonable care in its preparation before its enclosure in the sealed vessel, will be entitled to reparation from the manufacturer.

In my opinion, the existence of a legal duty in such circumstances is in conformity with the principles of both the law of Scotland and the law of England. The English cases demonstrate how impossible it is finally to catalogue, amid the ever-varying types of human relationships, those relationships in which a duty to exercise care arises apart from contract, and each of these cases relates to its own set of circumstances, out of which it was claimed that the duty had arisen. In none of these cases were the circumstances identical with the present case as regards that which I regard as the essential element in this case, namely, the manufacturer's own action in bringing himself into direct relationship with the party injured. . . .

I am of opinion that the contention of the appellant is sound and that she has relevantly averred a relationship of duty as between the respondent and herself, as also that her averments of the respondent's neglect of that duty are relevant. . . .

LORD MACMILLAN: . . . At your Lordships' Bar counsel for both parties to the present appeal, accepting, as I do also, the view that there is no distinction between the law of Scotland and the law of England in the legal principles applicable to the case, confined their arguments to the English authorities. The appellant endeavoured to establish that according to the law of England the pleadings disclose a good cause of action; the respondent endeavoured to show that on the English decisions the appellant had stated no admissible case. I propose, therefore, to address myself at once to an examination of the relevant English precedents.

---

1. 1909 SC 1314.
2. 1911 SC 253.

I observe in the first place that there is no decision of this House upon the point at issue, for I agree with Lord Hunter that such cases as *Cavalier v Pope*[1] and *Cameron v Young*[2] which decided that

'a stranger to a lease cannot found upon a landlord's failure to fulfil obligations undertaken by him under contract with his lessee,'

are in a different chapter of the law. Nor can it by any means be said that the cases present 'an unbroken and consistent current' of authority, for some flow one way and some the other.

It humbly appears to me that the diversity of view which is exhibited in such cases as *George v Skivington*[3] on the one hand, and *Blacker v Lake and Elliot*[4] on the other hand—to take two extreme instances—is explained by the fact that in the discussion of the topic which now engages your Lordships' attention two rival principles of the law find a meeting place where each has contended for supremacy. On the one hand, there is the well-established principle that no one other than a party to a contract can complain of a breach of that contract. On the other hand, there is the equally well-established doctrine that negligence, apart from contract, gives a right of action to the party injured by that negligence—and here I use the term negligence, of course, in its technical legal sense, implying a duty owed and neglected. The fact that there is a contractual relationship between the parties which may give rise to an action for breach of contract does not exclude the co-existence of a right of action founded on negligence as between the same parties independently of the contract though arising out of the relationship in fact brought about by the contract. Of this the best illustration is the right of the injured railway passenger to sue the railway company either for breach of the contract of safe carriage or for negligence in carrying him. And there is no reason why the same set of facts should not give one person a right of action in contract and another person a right of action in tort. . . .

Where, as in cases like the present, so much depends upon the avenue of approach to the question it is very easy to take the wrong turning. If you begin with the sale by the manufacturer to the retail dealer, then the consumer who purchases from the retailer is at once seen to be a stranger to the contract between the retailer and the manufacturer and so disentitled to sue upon it. There is no contractual relation between the manufacturer and the consumer, and thus the plaintiff if he is to succeed is driven to try to bring himself within one or other of the exceptional cases where the strictness of the rule that none but a party to a contract can found on a breach of that contract has been mitigated in the public interest, as it has been in the case of a person who issues a chattel which is inherently dangerous or which he knows to be in a dangerous condition. If, on the other hand, you disregard the fact that the circumstances of the case at one stage include the existence of a contract of sale between the manufacturer and the retailer and approach the question by asking whether there is evidence of carelessness on the part of the manufacturer and whether he owed a duty to be careful in a question with the party who has been injured in consequence of his want of care, the circumstance that the injured party was not a party to the incidental contract of sale becomes irrelevant and his title to sue the manufacturer is unaffected by that circumstance. The appellant in the present instance asks that her case be approached as a case of delict, not as a case of breach of contract. She does not require to invoke the exceptional cases in which a person not a party to a contract has been held to be entitled to complain of some defect in the subject-matter

---

1. [1906] AC 428.
2. [1908] AC 176.
3. (1869) LR 5 Exch 1.
4. (1912) 106 LT 533.

of the contract which has caused him harm. The exceptional case of things dangerous in themselves or known to be in a dangerous condition has been regarded as constituting a peculiar category outside the ordinary law both of contract and of tort. I may observe that it seems to me inaccurate to describe the case of dangerous things as an exception to the principle that no one but a party to a contract can sue on that contract. I rather regard this type of case as a special instance of negligence where the law exacts a degree of diligence so stringent as to amount practically to a guarantee of safety. . . .

. . . Having regard to the inconclusive state of the authorities in the courts below, and to the fact that the important question involved is now before your Lordships for the first time, I think it desirable to consider the matter from the point of view of the principles applicable to this branch of law which are admittedly common to both English and Scottish jurisprudence.

The law takes no cognizance of carelessness in the abstract. It concerns itself with carelessness only where there is a duty to take care and where failure in that duty has caused damage. In such circumstances carelessness assumes the legal quality of negligence and entails the consequences in law of negligence. What then are the circumstances which give rise to this duty to take care? In the daily contacts of social and business life human beings are thrown into or place themselves in an infinite variety of relationships with their fellows, and the law can refer only to the standards of the reasonable man in order to determine whether any particular relationship gives rise to a duty to take care as between those who stand in that relationship to each other. The grounds of action may be as various and manifold as human errancy, and the conception of legal responsibility may develop in adaptation to altering social conditions and standards. The criterion of judgment must adjust and adapt itself to the changing circumstances of life. The categories of negligence are never closed. The cardinal principle of liability is that the party complained of should owe to the party complaining a duty to take care and that the party complaining should be able to prove that he has suffered damage in consequence of a breach of that duty. Where there is room for diversity of view is in determining what circumstances will establish such a relationship between the parties as to give rise on the one side to a duty to take care and on the other side to a right to have care taken.

To descend from these generalities to the circumstances of the present case I do not think that any reasonable man or any twelve reasonable men would hesitate to hold that if the appellant establishes her allegations the respondent has exhibited carelessness in the conduct of his business. For a manufacturer of aerated water to store his empty bottles in a place where snails can get access to them and to fill his bottles without taking any adequate precautions by inspection or otherwise to ensure that they contain no deleterious foreign matter may reasonably be characterised as carelessness without applying too exacting a standard. But, as I have pointed out, it is not enough to prove the respondent to be careless in his process of manufacture. The question is: Does he owe a duty to take care, and to whom does he owe that duty? I have no hesitation in affirming that a person who for gain engages in the business of manufacturing articles of food and drink intended for consumption by members of the public in the form in which he issues them is under a duty to take care in the manufacture of these articles. That duty, in my opinion, he owes to those whom he intends to consume his products. He manufactures his commodities for human consumption; he intends and contemplates that they shall be consumed. By reason of that very fact he places himself in a relationship with all the potential consumers of his commodities, and that relationship, which he assumes and desires for his own ends, imposes upon him a duty to take care to avoid injuring them. He owes them a duty not to convert by his own carelessness an article which he issues to them as wholesome and innocent into an article which is dangerous to life and health.

It is sometimes said that liability can arise only where a reasonable man would have foreseen and could have avoided the consequences of his act or omission. In the present case the respondent, when he manufactured his ginger-beer, had directly in contemplation that it would be consumed by members of the public. Can it be said that he could not be expected as a reasonable man to foresee that if he conducted his process of manufacture carelessly he might injure those whom he expected and desired to consume his ginger-beer? The possibility of injury so arising seems to me in no sense so remote as to excuse him from foreseeing it. Suppose that a baker through carelessness allows a large quantity of arsenic to be mixed with a batch of his bread, with the result that those who subsequently eat it are poisoned, could he be heard to say that he owed no duty to the consumers of his bread to take care that it was free from poison, and that, as he did not know that any poison had got into it, his only liability was for breach of warranty under his contract of sale to those who actually bought the poisoned bread from him? Observe that I have said 'through carelessness' and thus excluded the cases of a pure accident such as may happen where every care is taken. I cannot believe, and I do not believe, that neither in the law of England nor in the law of Scotland is there redress for such a case. The state of facts I have figured might well give rise to a criminal charge, and the civil consequences of such carelessness can scarcely be less wide than its criminal consequences. Yet the principle of the decision appealed from is that the manufacturer of food products intended by him for human consumption does not owe to the consumers whom he has in view any duty of care, not even the duty to take care that he does not poison them. . . .

I am anxious to emphasise that the principle of judgment which commends itself to me does not give rise to the sort of objection stated by Parke B in *Longmeid v Holliday*,[1] where he said (6 Exch at p. 768):

'But it would be going much too far to say that so much care is required in the ordinary intercourse of life between one individual and another, that if a machine not in its nature dangerous — a carriage for instance — but which might become so by a latent defect entirely unknown, although discoverable by the exercise of ordinary care, should be lent or given by one person, even by the person who manufactured it, to another, the former should be answerable to the latter for a subsequent damage accruing by the use of it.'

I read this passage rather as a note of warning that the standard of care exacted in the dealings of human beings with one another must not be pitched too high than as giving any countenance to the view that negligence may be exhibited with impunity. It must always be a question of circumstances whether the carelessness amounts to negligence and whether the injury is not too remote from the carelessness. I can readily conceive that where a manufacturer has parted with his product and it has passed into other hands it may well be exposed to vicissitudes which may render it defective or noxious and for which the manufacturer could not in any view be held to be to blame. It may be a good general rule to regard responsibility as ceasing when control ceases. So also where between the manufacturer and the user there is interposed a party who has the means and opportunity of examining the manufacturer's product before he reissues it to the actual user. But where, as in the present case, the article of consumption is so prepared as to be intended to reach the consumer in the condition in which it leaves the manufacturer and the manufacturer takes steps to ensure this by sealing or otherwise closing the container, so that the contents cannot be tampered with, I regard his control as remaining effective until the article reaches the consumer and the container is opened by him. The intervention of any exterior agency is intended to be excluded, and was in fact in the present case excluded. It is doubtful whether in such a case there is any redress against the retailer: *Gordon v M'Hardy*.[2]

---

1. (1851) 6 Exch 761.
2. (1903) 6 F 210.

The burden of proof must always be upon the injured party to establish that the defect which caused the injury was present in the article when it left the hands of the party whom he sues, that the defect was occasioned by the carelessness of that party, and that the circumstances are such as to cast upon the defender a duty to take care not to injure the pursuer. There is no presumption of negligence in such a case as the present, nor is there any justification for applying the maxim res ipsa loquitur. Negligence must be both averred and proved. The appellant accepts this burden of proof and, in my opinion, she is entitled to have an opportunity of discharging it if she can. I am, accordingly, of opinion that this appeal should be allowed, the judgment of the Second Division of the Court of Session reversed, and the judgment of the Lord Ordinary restored.

[LORD TOMLIN delivered a speech in favour of dismissing the appeal.]

Appeal allowed

Questions

1. It has been said that this case exploded the 'privity of contract fallacy'. What does this mean?

2. What policy reasons might there have been for the existence of this 'fallacy'?

3. What is the ratio decidendi of the case? (See R. F. V. Heuston (1957) 20 MLR 1 at 5–9.)

Notes

1. Whether a snail was present in the ginger-beer bottle was never judicially determined. (See e.g. (1955) 71 LQR 472; G. Lewis, *Lord Atkin* (London, 1983), pp. 52–53. For more background to the case see Lewis, op cit, p. 51 et seq; M. R. Taylor (1983) 17 UBCL Rev 59; A. M. Linden ibid. 67; A. Rodger (1988) 41 Current LP 1; W. W. McBryde in *Obligations in Context: Essays in Honour of Professor D. M. Walker*, edited by A. J. Gamble, (Edinburgh, 1990), p. 13.

2. This case has been important in the general development of the tort of negligence as well as the more specific area of liability for products. This latter point is dealt with in chap. 10, p. 491, post, where it will be seen that there is now a statutory strict liability regime for defective products (although the tort of negligence co-exists with it).

3. In *Deyong v Shenburn* [1946] KB 227; [1946] 1 All ER 226 Du Parcq LJ stated (at p. 229):

'It is not true to say that wherever a man finds himself in such a position that unless he does a certain act another person may suffer, or that if he does something another person will suffer, then it is his duty in the one case to be careful to do the act and in the other case to be careful not to do the act. Any such proposition is much too wide. One has to find that there has been a breach of a duty which the law recognises, and to see what the law recognises one can only look at the decisions of the courts.'

For example, in *Stephens v Anglian Water Authority* [1987] 3 All ER 379; [1987] 1 WLR 1381, noted by J. G. Fleming (1988) 104 LQR 183, the Court of Appeal regarded itself as bound by the authorities to conclude that no duty of care is owed by a landowner in abstracting percolating water under his land where such abstraction causes subsidence to another's land.

The result of the inquiry into the precedents, which Du Parcq LJ required in *Deyong v Shenburn*, ante, may, of course, be that there is no answer, or at least no clear, binding answer. The judges will then have a choice whether to accept that the foreseeable harm in question should be compensated or not (i.e. to say that there is or is not a duty of care). This is the question to which we must now turn.

Governors of the Peabody Donation Fund *v* Sir Lindsay Parkinson & Co Ltd House of Lords [1984] 3 All ER 529

LORD KEITH OF KINKEL: . . . Lord Atkin's famous enunciation of the general principles on which the law of negligence is founded, in *Donoghue v Stevenson* [1932] AC 562 at 580, [1932] All ER Rep 1 at 11, has long been recognised as not intended to afford a comprehensive definition, to the effect that every situation which is capable of falling within the terms of the utterance and which results in loss automatically affords a remedy in damages. Lord Reid said in *Home Office v Dorset Yacht Co Ltd* [1970] 2 All ER 294 at 297–298, [1970] AC 1004 at 1027:

'It is not to be treated as if it were a statutory definition. It will require qualification in new circumstances. But I think that the time has come when we can and should say that it ought to apply unless there is some justification or valid explanation for its exclusion. For example, causing economic loss is a different matter; for one thing it is often caused by deliberate action. Competition involves traders being entitled to damage their rivals' interests by promoting their own, and there is a long chapter of the law determining in what circumstances owners of land can, and in what circumstances they may not, use their proprietary rights so as to injure their neighbours. But where negligence is involved the tendency has been to apply principles analogous to those stated by Lord Atkin (cf *Hedley Byrne & Co Ltd v Heller & Partners Ltd* [1963] 2 All ER 575, [1964] AC 465). And when a person has done nothing to put himself in any relationship with another person in distress or with his property mere accidental propinquity does not require him to go to that person's assistance. There may be a moral duty to do so, but it is not practicable to make it a legal duty.'

Lord Wilberforce spoke on similar lines in *Anns v Merton London Borough* [1977] 2 All ER 492 at 498, [1978] AC 728 at 751–752:

'Through the trilogy of cases in this House, *Donoghue v Stevenson* [1932] AC 562, [1932] All ER Rep 1; *Hedley Byrne & Co Ltd v Heller & Partners Ltd* [1963] 2 All ER 575, [1964] AC 465, and *Home Office v Dorset Yacht Co Ltd* [1970] 2 All ER 294, [1970] AC 1004, the position has now been reached that in order to establish that a duty of care arises in a particular situation, it is not necessary to bring the facts of that situation within those of previous situations in which a duty of care has been held to exist. Rather the question has to be approached in two stages. First one has to ask whether, as between the alleged wrongdoer and the person who has suffered damage there is a sufficient relationship of proximity or neighbourhood such that, in the reasonable contemplation of the former, carelessness on his part may be likely to cause damage to the latter, in which case a prima facie duty of care arises. Secondly, if the first question is answered affirmatively, it is necessary to consider whether there are any considerations which ought to negative, or to reduce or limit the scope of the duty or the class of person to whom it is owed or the damages to which a breach of it may give rise (see the *Dorset Yacht* case [1970] 2 All ER 294 at 297–298, [1970] AC 1004 at 1027 per Lord Reid).'

There has been a tendency in some recent cases to treat these passages as being themselves of a definitive character. This is a temptation which should be resisted. The true question in each case is whether the particular defendant owed to the particular plaintiff a duty of care having the scope which is contended for, and whether he was in breach of that duty with consequent loss to the plaintiff. A relationship of proximity in Lord Atkin's sense must exist before any duty of care can arise, but the scope of the duty must depend on all the circumstances of the case. In *Home Office v Dorset Yacht Co Ltd* [1970] 2 All ER 294 at 307–308, [1970] AC 1004 at 1038–1039 Lord Morris, after observing that at the conclusion of his speech in *Donoghue v Stevenson* [1932] AC 562 at 599, [1932] All ER Rep 1 at 20 Lord Atkin said that it was advantageous if the law 'is in accordance with sound common sense' and expressing the view that a special relation existed between the prison officers and the yacht company which gave rise to a duty on the former to control their charges so as to prevent them doing damage, continued:

'Apart from this I would conclude that in the situation stipulated in the present case it would not only be fair and reasonable that a duty of care should exist but that it would be contrary to the fitness of things were it not so. I doubt whether it is necessary to say, in cases where the court is asked whether in a particular situation a duty existed, that the court is called on to make a decision as to policy. Policy need not be invoked where reasons and good sense will at once point the way. If the test whether in some particular situation a duty of care arises may in some cases have to be whether it is fair and reasonable that it should so arise the court must not shrink from being the arbiter. As Lord Radcliffe said in his speech in *Davis Contractors Ltd v Fareham Urban District Council* [1956] 2 All ER 145 at 160, [1956] AC 696 at 728, the court is "the spokesman of the fair and reasonable man".'

So in determining whether or not a duty of care of particular scope was incumbent on a defendant it is material to take into consideration whether it is just and reasonable that it should be so. . . .

[LORD SCARMAN, LORD BRIDGE OF HARWICH, LORD BRANDON OF OAKBROOK and LORD TEMPLEMAN agreed with LORD KEITH OF KINKEL's speech.]

Question

Consider the extract (set out in *Peabody*) from Lord Morris' speech in the *Dorset Yacht* case. How do 'policy' and 'reasons and good sense' differ?

Note

Lord Wilberforce's two-stage test in *Anns*, which is set out in *Peabody* ante, was for some time cited with approval in the subsequent case law. Writing in 1984, *Williams & Hepple*, p. 102, saw its significance as lying in the shift of the 'neighbour principle' 'from being an argument to support new areas of liability, if there were policy considerations in favour of doing so, into a principle that would apply unless there was a policy justification for excluding it. The onus of argument shifted, with "policy" operating only as a long-stop where the logical application of the factual test of reasonable foreseeability would lead to obviously undesirable social or financial consequences'. *Peabody*, however, marked something of a turning-point, and the downgrading of the importance of the *Anns* two-stage test has continued, as the next two extracts will show.

Yuen Kun-yeu v A-G of Hong Kong Judicial Committee of the Privy Council [1987] 2 All ER 705

LORD KEITH OF KINKEL (delivering the judgment of the Board): . . . The foremost question of principle is whether in the present case the commissioner owed to members of the public who might be minded to deposit their money with deposit-taking companies in Hong Kong a duty, in the discharge of his supervisory powers under the ordinance, to exercise reasonable care to see that such members of the public did not suffer loss through the affairs of such companies being carried on by their managers in a fraudulent or improvident fashion. That question is one of law, which is capable of being answered on the averments, assumed to be true, contained in the appellants' pleadings. If it is answered in the negative, the appellants have no reasonable cause of action, and their statement of claim was rightly struck out.

The argument for the appellants in favour of an affirmative answer to the question started from the familiar passage in the speech of Lord Wilberforce in *Anns v Merton London Borough* [1977] 2 All ER 492 at 498, [1978] AC 728 at 751 [see p. 51, ante].

. . . This passage has been treated with some reservation in subsequent cases in the House of Lords, in particular by Lord Keith in *Governors of the Peabody Donation Fund v Sir Lindsay Parkinson & Co Ltd* [1984] 3 All ER 529 at 534, [1985] AC 210 at 240, by Lord Brandon in *Leigh & Sillivan Ltd v Aliakmon Shipping Co Ltd* [1986] 2 All ER 145 at 153, [1986] AC 785 at 815 and by Lord Bridge in *Curran v Northern Ireland Co-ownership Housing Association Ltd* [1987] 2 All ER 13 at 17, [1987] 2 WLR 1043 at 1047–1048. The speeches containing these reservations were concurred in by all the other members of the House who were party to the decisions. In *Sutherland Shire Council v Heyman* (1985) 60 ALR 1 Brennan J in the High Court of Australia indicated his disagreement with the nature of the approach indicated by Lord Wilberforce, saying (at 43–44):

'Of course, if foreseeability of injury to another were the exhaustive criterion of a prima facie duty to act to prevent the occurrence of that injury, it would be essential to introduce some kind of restrictive qualification—perhaps a qualification of the kind stated in the second stage of the general proposition in *Anns*. I am unable to accept that approach. It is preferable, in my view, that the law should develop novel categories of negligence incrementally and by analogy with established categories, rather than by a massive extension of a prima facie duty of care restrained only by indefinable "considerations which ought to negative, or to reduce or limit the scope of the duty or the class of person to whom it is owed". The proper role of the "second stage", as I attempted to explain in *Jaensch v Coffey* ((1984) 54 ALR 417 at 437), embraces no more than "those further elements [in addition to the neighbour principle] which are appropriate to the particular category of negligence and *which confine the duty of care within narrower limits* than those which would be defined by an unqualified application of the neighbour principle".' (My emphasis.)

Their Lordships venture to think that the two-stage test formulated by Lord Wilberforce for determining the existence of a duty of care in negligence has been elevated to a degree of importance greater than it merits, and greater perhaps than its author intended. Further, the expression of the first stage of the test carries with it a risk of misinterpretation. As Gibbs CJ pointed out in *Sutherland Shire Council v Heyman* (at 13) there are two possible views of what Lord Wilberforce meant. The first view, favoured in a number of cases mentioned by Gibbs CJ, is that he meant to test the sufficiency of proximity simply by the reasonable contemplation of likely harm. The second view, favoured by Gibbs CJ himself, is that Lord Wilberforce meant the expression 'proximity or neighbourhood' to be a composite one, importing the whole concept of necessary relationship between plaintiff and defendant described by Lord Atkin in *Donoghue v Stevenson* [1932] AC 562 at 580, [1932] All

ER Rep 1 at 11. In their Lordships' opinion the second view is the correct one. As Lord Wilberforce himself observed in *McLoughlin v O'Brian* [1982] 2 All ER 298 at 303, [1983] 1 AC 410 at 420, it is clear that foreseeability does not of itself, and automatically, lead to a duty of care. There are many other statements to the same effect. The truth is that the trilogy of cases referred to by Lord Wilberforce each demonstrate particular sets of circumstances, differing in character, which were adjudged to have the effect of bringing into being a relationship apt to give rise to a duty of care. Foreseeability of harm is a necessary ingredient of such a relationship, but it is not the only one. Otherwise there would be liability in negligence on the part of one who sees another about to walk over a cliff with his head in the air, and forbears to shout a warning.

Donoghue v Stevenson established that the manufacturer of a consumable product who carried on business in such a way that the product reached the consumer in the shape in which it left the manufacturer, without any prospect of intermediate examination, owed the consumer a duty to take reasonable care that the product was free from defect likely to cause injury to health. The speech of Lord Atkin stressed not only the requirement of foreseeability of harm but also that of a close and direct relationship of proximity. The relevant passages are:

'Who, then, in law is my neighbour? The answer seems to be — persons who are so closely and directly affected by my act that I ought reasonably to have them in contemplation as being so affected when I am directing my mind to the acts or omissions which are called in question.'

(See [1932] AC 562 at 580, [1932] All ER Rep 1 at 11.)

'I think that this sufficiently states the truth if proximity be not confined to mere physical proximity, but be used, as I think it was intended, to extend to such close and direct relations that the act complained of directly affects a person whom the person alleged to be bound to take care would know would be directly affected by his careless act.'

(See [1932] AC 562 at 581, [1932] All ER Rep 1 at 12.)

'There will no doubt arise cases where it will be difficult to determine whether the contemplated relationship is so close that the duty arises.'

(See [1932] AC 562 at 582, [1932] All ER Rep 1 at 12.)

Lord Atkin clearly had in contemplation that all the circumstances of the case, not only the foreseeability of harm, were appropriate to be taken into account in determining whether a duty of care arose.

[His Lordship then cited *Hedley Byrne & Co Ltd v Heller & Partners Ltd* [1964] AC 465, [1963] 2 All ER 575 (p. 161, post) and *Home Office v Dorset Yacht Co Ltd* [1970] AC 1004, [1970] 2 All ER 294 (p. 72, post), in further discussing the issue concerning the close and direct relationship, and continued:] . . . The second stage of Lord Wilberforce's test is one which will rarely have to be applied. It can arise only in a limited category of cases where, notwithstanding that a case of negligence is made out on the proximity basis, public policy requires that there should be no liability. One of the rare cases where that has been held to be so is *Rondel v Worsley* [1967] 3 All ER 993, [1969] 1 AC 191, dealing with the liability of a barrister for negligence in the conduct of proceedings in court . . .

[His Lordship also referred to the discussion of policy by Glidewell LJ in *Hill v Chief Constable of West Yorkshire* [1988] QB 60, [1987] 1 All ER 1173. This case has since gone on appeal to the House of Lords, [1989] AC 53, [1988] 2 All ER 238 (p. 62, post). He continued:] . . . In view of the direction in which the law has since been developing, their Lordships consider that for the future it should be recognised that the two-stage test in *Anns* is not to be regarded as in all circumstances a suitable guide to the existence of a duty of care.

The primary and all-important matter for consideration, then, is whether in all the circumstances of this case there existed between the commissioner and would-be depositors with the company such close and direct relations as to place the commissioner, in the exercise of his functions under the ordinance, under a duty of care towards would-be depositors . . .

[LORD KEITH went on to decide that no duty of care existed: see p. 229, post.]

Questions

1. Do you think that Lord Wilberforce intended anything more than a test of reasonable foresight to operate at the first stage of his *Anns* test?

2. In what circumstances do you think Lord Keith intended the two-stage test in *Anns* to be 'a suitable guide to the existence of a duty of care'?

3. Why do you think there has been this retreat from the *Anns* two-stage test? (Consider *Rowling v Takaro Properties Ltd* [1988] AC 473 at 501 (p. 108, post); R. Kidner (1987) 7 LS 319 at 326–327.)

Note

In *Yuen Kun-yeu* Lord Keith mentioned two House of Lords cases (in addition to *Peabody*) in relation to the treatment of *Anns*. In one of these (*Leigh and Sillivan Ltd v Aliakmon Shipping Co Ltd* [1986] AC 785; [1986] 2 All ER 145, p. 203, post) Lord Brandon (with the agreement of his brethren) expressed the view that the test neither is, nor was intended to be, universally applicable in deciding on the existence and scope of a duty of care and he quoted the passage from the *Peabody* case (pp. 51–52, ante) warning against it being treated as of a definitive character. Lord Brandon then continued ([1986] 2 All ER at p. 153):

'The second observation which I would make is that Lord Wilberforce was dealing, as is clear from what he said, with the approach to the questions of the existence and scope of a duty of care in a novel type of factual situation which was not analogous to any factual situation in which the existence of such a duty had already been held to exist. He was not, as I understand the passage, suggesting that the same approach should be adopted to the existence of a duty of care in a factual situation in which the existence of such a duty had repeatedly been held not to exist.'

For examples of the application of Lord Brandon's view, see *Banque Keyser Ullman SA v Skandia (UK) Insurance Co Ltd* [1990] 1 QB 665; [1989] 2 All ER 952, noted p. 174, post (not specifically discussed when that case went to the House of Lords, [1990] 2 All ER 947; [1990] 3 WLR 364; *Reid v Rush & Tompkins Group plc* [1989] 3 All ER 228; [1990] 1 WLR 212 (p. 196, post) (per Ralph Gibson LJ).

Lord Keith also mentioned *Curran v Northern Ireland Co-ownership Housing Association Ltd* [1987] AC 718; [1987] 2 All ER 13. Here Lord Bridge (in a speech concurred in by the other members of the House of Lords) commented (at p. 17):

'. . . *Anns v Merton London Borough* may be said to represent the high-water mark of a trend in the development of the law of negligence by your Lordships' House towards the elevation of the "neighbourhood" principle derived from the speech of Lord Atkin in *Donoghue v Stevenson* [1932] AC 562; [1932] All ER Rep 1 into one of general application from which a duty of care may always be derived unless there are clear countervailing considerations to exclude it. In an article by Professor J. C Smith and Professor Peter Burns, 'Donoghue v Stevenson—The Not So Golden Anniversary' (1983) 46 MLR 147, the trend to which I have referred was cogently criticised, particularly in its tendency to obscure the important distinction between misfeasance and non-feasance.'

(On liability for omissions, see further p. 65, post.)

Caparo Industries plc *v* Dickman House of Lords [1990] 1 All ER 568

For the facts and further extracts from this case, see p. 181, post.

LORD BRIDGE OF HARWICH: . . . In determining the existence and scope of the duty of care which one person may owe to another in the infinitely varied circumstances of human relationships there has for long been a tension between two different approaches. Traditionally the law finds the existence of the duty in different specific situations each exhibiting its own particular characteristics. In this way the law has identified a wide variety of duty situations, all falling within the ambit of the tort of negligence, but sufficiently distinct to require separate definition of the essential ingredients by which the existence of the duty is to be recognised. Commenting on the outcome of this traditional approach, Lord Atkin, in his seminal speech in *Donoghue v Stevenson* [1932] AC 562 at 579–580, [1932] All ER Rep 1 at 11, observed:

'The result is that the Courts have been engaged upon an elaborate classification of duties as they exist in respect of property, whether real or personal, with further divisions as to ownership, occupation or control, and distinctions based on the particular relations of the one side or the other, whether manufacturer, salesman or landlord, customer, tenant, stranger, and so on. In this way it can be ascertained at any time whether the law recognizes a duty, but only where the case can be referred to some particular species which has been examined and classified. And yet the duty which is common to all the cases where liability is established must logically be based upon some element common to the cases where it is found to exist.'

It is this last sentence which signifies the introduction of the more modern approach of seeking a single general principle which may be applied in all circumstances to determine the existence of a duty of care. Yet Lord Atkin himself sounds the appropriate note of caution by adding:

'To seek a complete logical definition of the general principle is probably to go beyond the function of the judge, for the more general the definition the more likely it is to omit essentials or to introduce non-essentials.'

Lord Reid gave a large impetus to the modern approach in *Home Office v Dorset Yacht Co Ltd* [1970] 2 All ER 294 at 297, [1970] AC 1004 at 1026–1027, where he said:

'In later years there has been a steady trend towards regarding the law of negligence as depending on principle so that, when a new point emerges, one should ask not whether it is covered by authority but whether recognised principles apply to it. *Donoghue v Stevenson* may be regarded as a milestone, and the well-known passage in Lord Atkin's speech should I think be regarded as a statement of principle. It is not to be treated as if it were a statutory definition. It will require qualification in new circumstances. But I think that the time has come when we can and should say that it ought to apply unless there is some justification or valid explanation for its exclusion.'

The most comprehensive attempt to articulate a single general principle is reached in the well-known passage from the speech of Lord Wilberforce in *Anns v Merton London Borough* [1977] 2 All ER 492 at 498, [1978] AC 728 at 751-752 [see p. 51, ante] . . .

But since *Anns*'s case a series of decisions of the Privy Council and of your Lordships' House, notably in judgments and speeches delivered by Lord Keith, have emphasised the inability of any single general principle to provide a practical test which can be applied to every situation to determine whether a duty of care is owed and, if so, what is its scope: see *Peabody Donation Fund v Sir Lindsay Parkinson & Co Ltd* [1984] 3 All ER 529 at 533-534, [1985] AC 210 at 239-241, *Yuen Kun-yeu v A-G of Hong Kong* [1987] 2 All ER 705 at 709-712, [1988] AC 175 at 190-194, *Rowling v Takaro Properties Ltd* [1988] 1 All ER 163 at 172, [1988] AC 473 at 501 and *Hill v Chief Constable of West Yorkshire* [1988] 2 All ER 238 at 241, [1989] AC 53 at 60. What emerges is that, in addition to the foreseeability of damage, necessary ingredients in any situation giving rise to a duty of care are that there should exist between the party owing the duty and the party to whom it is owed a relationship characterised by the law as one of 'proximity' or 'neighbourhood' and that the situation should be one in which the court considers it fair, just and reasonable that the law should impose a duty of a given scope on the one party for the benefit of the other. But it is implicit in the passages referred to that the concepts of proximity and fairness embodied in these additional ingredients are not susceptible of any such precise definition as would be necessary to give them utility as practical tests, but amount in effect to little more than convenient labels to attach to the features of different specific situations which, on a detailed examination of all the circumstances, the law recognises pragmatically as giving rise to a duty of care of a given scope. Whilst recognising, of course, the importance of the underlying general principles common to the whole field of negligence, I think the law has now moved in the direction of attaching greater significance to the more traditional categorisation of distinct and recognisable situations as guides to the existence, the scope and the limits of the varied duties of care which the law imposes. We must now, I think, recognise the wisdom of the words of Brennan J in the High Court of Australia in *Sutherland Shire Council v Heyman* (1985) 60 ALR 1 at 43-44, where he said:

'It is preferable in my view, that the law should develop novel categories of negligence incrementally and by analogy with established categories, rather than by a massive extension of a prima facie duty of care restrained only by indefinable "considerations which ought to negative, or to reduce or limit the scope of the duty or the class of person to whom it is owed".'

One of the most important distinctions always to be observed lies in the law's essentially different approach to the different kinds of damage which one party may have suffered in consequence of the acts or omissions of another. It is one thing to owe a duty of care to avoid causing injury to the person or property of others. It is quite another to avoid causing others to suffer purely economic loss. . . .

. . . It is never sufficient to ask simply whether A owes B a duty of care. It is always necessary to determine the scope of the duty by reference to the kind of damage from which A must take care to save B harmless:

'The question is always whether the defendant was under a duty to avoid or prevent that damage, but the actual nature of the damage suffered is relevant to the existence and extent of any duty to avoid or prevent it.'

(See *Sutherland Shire Council v Heyman* (1985) 60 ALR 1 at 48 per Brennan J.) . . .

LORD ROSKILL: . . . I agree with your Lordships that it has now to be accepted that there is no simple formula or touchstone to which recourse can be had in order to provide in every case a ready answer to the questions whether, given certain facts, the law will or will not impose liability for negligence or, in cases where such liability can be shown to exist, determine the extent of that liability. Phrases such as 'fore-seeability', 'proximity', 'neighbourhood', 'just and reasonable', 'fairness', 'voluntary acceptance of risk' or 'voluntary assumption of responsibility' will be found used from time to time in the different cases. But, as your Lordships have said, such phrases are not precise definitions. At best they are but labels or phrases descriptive of the very different factual situations which can exist in particular cases and which must be carefully examined in each case before it can be pragmatically determined whether a duty of care exists and, if so, what is the scope and extent of that duty. If this conclusion involves a return to the traditional categorisation of cases as point-ing to the existence and scope of any duty of care, as my noble and learned friend Lord Bridge, suggests, I think this is infinitely preferable to recourse to somewhat wide generalisations which leave their practical application matters of difficulty and uncertainty. This conclusion finds strong support from the judgment of Brennan J in the High Court of Australia in the passage cited by my noble and learned friends (see *Sutherland Shire Council v Heyman* (1985) 60 ALR 1 at 43–44). . . .

LORD OLIVER OF AYLMERTON: . . . [I]t is now clear from a series of decisions in this House that, at least so far as concerns the law of the United Kingdom, the duty of care in tort depends not solely on the existence of the essential ingredient of the foreseeability of damage to the plaintiff but on its coincidence with a further ingre-dient to which has been attached the label 'proximity' and which was described by Lord Atkin in the course of his speech in *Donoghue v Stevenson* [1932] AC 562 at 581, [1932] All ER Rep 1 at 12 as —

'such close and direct relations that the act complained of directly affects a person whom the person alleged to be bound to take care would know would be directly affected by his careless act.'

It must be remembered, however, that Lord Atkin was using these words in the con-text of loss caused by physical damage where the existence of the nexus between the careless defendant and the injured plaintiff can rarely give rise to any difficulty. To adopt the words of Bingham LJ in the instant case ([1989] 1 All ER 789 at 808, [1989] QB 653 at 686):

'It is enough that the plaintiff chances to be (out of the whole world) the person with whom the defendant collided or who purchased the offending ginger beer.'

The extension of the concept of negligence since the decision of this House in *Hedley Byrne & Co Ltd v Heller & Partners Ltd* [1963] 2 All ER 575, [1964] AC 465 to cover cases of pure economic loss not resulting from physical damage has given rise to a considerable and as yet unsolved difficulty of definition. The opportunities for the infliction of pecuniary loss from the imperfect performance of everyday tasks on the proper performance of which people rely for regulating their affairs are illimitable and the effects are far reaching. A defective bottle of ginger beer may injure a single consumer but the damage stops there. A single statement may be repeated endlessly with or without the permission of its author and may be relied on in a different way by many different people. Thus the postulate of a simple duty to avoid any harm that is, with hindsight, reasonably capable of being foreseen becomes untenable without the imposition of some intelligible limits to keep the law of negligence within the bounds of common sense and practicality. Those limits have been found by the requirement of what has been called a 'relationship of proximity' between plaintiff and defendant and by the imposition of a further requirement that the attachment of liability for harm which has occurred be 'just and reasonable'. But, although the cases in which the courts have imposed or withheld liability are capable of an approximate categorisation, one looks in vain for some common denominator by which the existence of the essential relationship can be tested. Indeed, it is difficult to resist a conclusion that what have been treated as three separate requirements are, at least in most cases, in fact merely facets of the same thing, for in some cases the degree of foreseeability is such that it is from that alone that the requisite proximity can be deduced, whilst in others the absence of that essential relationship can most rationally be attributed simply to the court's view that it would not be fair and reasonable to hold the defendant responsible. 'Proximity' is, no doubt, a convenient expression so long as it is realised that it is no more than a label which embraces not a definable concept but merely a description of circumstances from which, pragmatically, the courts conclude that a duty of care exists.

There are, of course, cases where, in any ordinary meaning of the words, a relationship of proximity (in the literal sense of 'closeness') exists but where the law, whilst recognising the fact of the relationship, nevertheless denies a remedy to the injured party on the ground of public policy. *Rondel v Worsley* [1967] 3 All ER 993, [1969] 1 AC 191 was such a case, as was *Hill v Chief Constable of West Yorkshire* [1988] 2 All ER 238, [1989] AC 53, so far as concerns the alternative ground of that decision. But such cases do nothing to assist in the identification of those features from which the law will deduce the essential relationship on which liability depends and, for my part, I think that it has to be recognised that to search for any single formula which will serve as a general test of liability is to pursue a will-o'-the wisp. The fact is that once one discards, as it is now clear that one must, the concept of foreseeability of harm as the single exclusive test, even a prima facie test, of the existence of the duty of care, the attempt to state some general principle which will determine liability in an infinite variety of circumstances serves not to clarify the law but merely to bedevil its development in a way which corresponds with practicality and common sense . . .

Perhaps . . . the most that can be attempted is a broad categorisation of the decided cases according to the type of situation in which liability has been established in the past in order to found an argument by analogy. Thus, for instance, cases can be classified according to whether what is complained of is the failure to prevent the infliction of damage by the act of the third party (such as *Home Office v Dorset Yacht Co Ltd* [1970] 2 All ER 294, [1970] AC 1004, *P Perl (Exporters) Ltd v Camden London BC* [1983] 3 All ER 161, [1984] QB 342, *Smith v Littlewoods Organisation Ltd (Chief Constable, Fife Constabulary, third party)* [1987] 1 All ER 710, [1987] AC 241 and, indeed, *Anns v Merton London Borough* [1977] 2 All ER 492, [1978] AC 728 itself), in failure to perform properly a statutory duty claimed to have been imposed for the protection of the plaintiff either as a member of a class or as a member of the public (such as *Anns*'s case, *Ministry of Housing and Local Government v Sharp* [1970] 1 All ER 1009, [1970] 2 QB 223, *Yuen Kun-yeu v A-G of Hong Kong* [1987] 2 All ER 705, [1988] AC 175) or in the making by the defendant of some statement or advice which has been communicated, directly or indirectly, to the plaintiff and on which he has relied. Such categories are not, of course, exhaustive. Sometimes they overlap as in the *Anns* case, and there are cases which do not readily fit into easily definable categories (such as *Ross v Caunters (a firm)* [1979] 3 All ER 580, [1980] Ch 297). Nevertheless, it is, I think, permissible to regard negligent statements or advice as a separate category displaying common features from which it is possible to find at least guidelines by which a test for the existence of the relationship which is essential to ground liability can be deduced.

The damage which may be occasioned by the spoken or written word is not inherent. It lies always in the reliance by somebody on the accuracy of that which the word communicates and the loss or damage consequential on that person having adopted a course of action on the faith of it. In general, it may be said that when any serious statement, whether it takes the form of a statement of fact or of advice, is published or communicated, it is foreseeable that the person who reads or receives it is likely to accept it as accurate and to act accordingly. It is equally foreseeable that if it is inaccurate in a material particular the recipient who acts on it may suffer a detriment which, if the statement had been accurate, he would not have undergone. But it is now clear that mere foreseeability is not of itself sufficient to ground liability unless by reason of the circumstances it itself constitutes also the element of proximity (as in the case of direct physical damage) or unless it is accompanied by other circumstances from which that element may be deduced. One must, however, be careful about seeking to find any general principle which will serve as a touchstone for all cases, for even within the limited category of what, for the sake of convenience, I may refer to as 'the negligent statement cases', circumstances may differ infinitely and, in a swiftly developing field of law, there can be no necessary assumption that those features which have served in one case to create the relationship between the plaintiff and the defendant on which liability depends will necessarily be determinative of liability in the different circumstances of another case. There are, for instance, at least four and possibly more situations in which damage or loss may arise from reliance on the spoken or written word and it must not be assumed that because they display common features of reliance and foreseeability they are necessarily in all respects analogous. To begin with, reliance on a careless statement may give rise to direct physical injury which may be caused either to the person who acts on the faith of the statement or to a third person. One has only to consider, for instance, the chemist's assistant who mislabels a dangerous medicine, a medical man who gives negligent telephonic advice to a parent with regard the treatment of a sick child or an architect who negligently instructs a bricklayer to remove the keystone of an archway (as in *Clayton v Woodman & Son (Builders) Ltd* [1962] 2 All ER 33, [1962] 2 QB 533). In such cases it is not easy to divorce foreseeability simpliciter and the proximity which flows from the virtual inevitability of damage if the advice is followed. Again, economic loss may be inflicted on a third party as a result of the act of the recipient of the advice or information carried out in reliance on it (as, for instance, the testator in *Ross v Caunters (a firm)* [1979] 3 All ER 580, [1980] Ch 297 or the purchaser in *Ministry of Housing and Local Government v Sharp* [1970] 1 All ER 1009, [1970] 2 QB 223, both cases which give rise to certain difficulties of analysis) . . .

Notes

1. On the approach to the duty of care in *Anns* and the later case law, see further *Murphy v Brentwood District Council* [1990] 2 All ER 908; [1990] 3 WLR 414 (p. 212, post).

2. It will already have been seen that four factors can be considered on the question of the existence of a duty of care: foresight, proximity, whether the imposition of a duty would be just and reasonable and policy. They will not necessarily all be referred to in any particular case. For example *Yuen Kun Yeu v A-G of Hong Kong* [1988] AC 175; [1987] 2 All ER 705 (p. 229, ante) does not specifically refer to the third, and *Norwich City Council v Harvey* [1989] 1 All ER 1180; [1989] 1 WLR 828 mentions the first three, but not the fourth.

The relationship between some of these factors, which is referred to by

Lord Oliver in *Caparo* (p. 59, ante), might be considered at this stage. What is the connection between foresight and proximity? As was mentioned by Lord Oliver in *Caparo* (pp. 59 and 60, ante) (and see in addition his view in *Murphy v Brentwood District Council* [1990] 2 All ER 908 at 934), mere foresight can constitute the element of proximity in cases of direct physical damage. Note further *Al Saudi Banque v Clark Pixley (a firm)* [1989] 3 All ER 361 at 366 where Millett J expressed the opinion that in 'cases of negligence which causes physical damage, it is seldom necessary to consider the concept of proximity in order to impose a reasonable limit on the ambit of the duty of care. The physical damage itself usually provides a sufficient limiting factor'. Consider, however, the following passage from the speech of Lord Keith (with whom three other members of the House of Lords agreed) in *Hill v Chief Constable of West Yorkshire* [1988] 2 All ER 238 at 241:

'It has been said almost too frequently to require repetition that foreseeability of likely harm is not in itself a sufficient test of liability in negligence. Some further ingredient is invariably needed to establish the requisite proximity of relationship between the plaintiff and defendant, and all the circumstances of the case must be carefully considered and analysed in order to ascertain whether such an ingredient is present. The nature of the ingredient will be found to vary in a number of different categories of decided cases.'

This was said in the context of a case which concerned the question of liability for the acts of a third party — see p. 62, post — and the word 'invariably' should be considered in the light of the view mentioned at the beginning of this paragraph. In *Caparo* [1989] 1 All ER 798 at 803 (when that case was in the Court of Appeal) Bingham LJ said that when considering proximity, where the court is looking at the closeness and directness of the parties' relationship, foresight is of importance because 'the more obvious it is that A's act or omission will cause harm to B, the less likely a court will be to hold that the relationship of A and B is insufficiently proximate to give rise to a duty of care' (and see Lord Oliver's view in *Caparo*, p. 59, ante concerning the degree of foreseeability).

What about any overlap between the 'just and reasonable' category and that of 'proximity'? Lord Oliver in *Caparo* (p. 59, ante) suggests that failure to satisfy the former category may lead to a failure to satisfy the latter category as well. Note also that in *Davis v Radcliffe* [1990] 2 All ER 536 at 540 Lord Goff, delivering the Privy Council's opinion, stated that proximity was an 'expression which refers to such a relation between the parties as renders it just and reasonable that liability in negligence may be imposed on the defendant for loss or damage suffered by the plaintiff by reason of the act or omission of the defendant of which complaint is made'. See further *James McNaughton Papers Group Ltd v Hicks Anderson & Co (a firm)* [1991] 1 All ER 134 at 142 (fairness 'is elusive and may indeed be no more than one of the criteria by which proximity is to be judged'). If a court decides there was insufficient proximity, could it ever be just and reasonable that there should be a duty of care? Are there any cases in which it might be said not to be just and reasonable that there should be a duty even though proximity exists? Consider, for example, *Norwich City Council v Harvey* [1989] 1 All ER 1180; [1989] 1 WLR 828, on which see C.A. Hopkins [1990] CLJ 21. Lord Oliver's speech in *Caparo* serves to emphasise that the three categories considered so far are not watertight compartments. For consideration of the relationship of public policy and duty, see p. 64, post.

3. For further discussion of proximity and the retreat from *Anns* (written before *Caparo* and *Murphy v Brentwood District Council* [1990] 2 All ER 908; [1990] 3 WLR 414, p. 212, post), see Kidner, op cit. At pp. 331–332 he states:

The law of negligence is being required to deal with very difficult problems such as economic loss, nervous shock. . . . It has to become more sophisticated in order to respond to such demands and a blanket notion of a *prima facie* duty based on foreseeability alone is inadequate to deal with these tasks. The law needs to be able to respond to each new area of claims in a more specific way, better adapted to the issues involved and thus must accept the variable nature of the duty of care. This is easily achieved by adopting existing concepts and requiring different levels of 'proximity' in different areas of claims. This notion of proximity has existed since the foundation of negligence but has too often been used as a synonym for foreseeability, when what it has really expressed is the degree of relationship between plaintiff and defendant for the duty of care to arise.

Bringing out the true nature of proximity and adopting different levels of relationship will cause problems of categorisation and definition but such cases can be resolved, not by references to the dictionary definition of the area involved, such as nervous shock, but rather by asking whether the instant case is within the mischief which led to a more restricted level of proximity being applied. Thus the policy behind the principles will always be in issue and this view of the law in no way resiles from the understanding that policy is at the heart of the duty issue.

Nor should it be suggested that this view will stultify the law, but rather it should remove some of the fears of the floodgates argument which is always raised in relation to new areas of duty, by permitting the courts to set up barriers to the flood by means of a restricted area of duty. Recent cases in the House of Lords and in the High Court of Australia resiling from the *Anns* principle should not necessarily be seen as blocking progress, but while a period of consolidation is likely the concepts are there to allow the law to move forward, perhaps in the future by shorter steps.

Hill *v* Chief Constable of West Yorkshire House of Lords [1988] 2 All ER 238

This was an action on behalf of the estate of a murder victim. The allegations in the statement of claim were that murders and attempted murders had previously been committed by the murderer (and they were set out), that it was reasonable to infer that the same person had committed these offences, that it was foreseeable he would commit further offences of the same nature if not caught and that the police owed a duty of care to catch him so as to protect potential future victims. The House of Lords held that there was insufficient proximity for a duty to exist (see p. 86, post), but also considered the question of public policy.

LORD KEITH OF KINKEL . . . [T]here is another reason why an action for damages in negligence should not lie against the police in circumstances such as those of the present case, and that is public policy. In *Yuen Kun-yeu v A-G of Hong Kong* [1987] 2 All ER 705 at 712, [1988] AC 175 at 193, I expressed the view that the category of cases where the second stage of Lord Wilberforce's two-stage test in *Anns v Merton London Borough* [1977] 2 All ER 492 at 498, [1978] AC 728 at 752 might fall to be applied was a limited one, one example of that category being *Rondel v Worsley* [1967] 3 All ER 993, [1969] 1 AC 191. Application of that second stage is, however, capable of constituting a separate and independent ground for holding that the existence of liability in negligence should not be entertained. Potential existence of such liability may in many instances be in the general public interest, as tending towards the observance of a higher standard of care in the carrying on of various different types of activity. I do not, however, consider that this can be said of police activities. The general sense of public duty which motivates police forces is unlikely to be appreciably reinforced by the imposition of such liability so far as concerns their function in the investigation and suppression of crime. From time to time they make mistakes in the exercise of that function, but it is not to be doubted that they apply their best endeavours to the performance of it. In some instances the imposition of liability may lead to the exercise of a function being carried on in a detrimentally defensive frame of mind. The possibility of this happening in relation to the investigative operations of the police cannot be excluded. Further, it would be reasonable to expect that if potential liability were to be imposed it would be not uncommon for actions to be raised against police forces on the ground that they had failed to catch some criminal as soon as they might have done, with the result that he went on to commit further crimes. While some such actions might involve allegations of a simple and straightforward types of failure, for example that a police officer negligently tripped and fell while pursuing a burglar, others would be likely to enter deeply into the general nature of a police investigation, as indeed the present action would seek to do. The manner of conduct of such an investigation must necessarily involve a variety of decisions to be made on matters of policy and discretion, for example as to which particular line of inquiry is most advantageously to be pursued and what is the most advantageous way to deploy the available resources. Many such decisions would not be regarded by the courts as appropriate to be called in question, yet elaborate investigation of the facts might be necessary to ascertain whether or not this was so. A great deal of police time, trouble and expense might be expected to have to be put into the preparation of the defence to the action and the attendance of witnesses at the trial. The result would be a significant diversion of police manpower and attention from their most important function, that of the suppression of crime. Closed investigations would require to be reopened and retraversed, not with the object of bringing any criminal to justice but to ascertain whether or not they had been competently conducted. I therefore consider that Glidewell LJ, in his judgment in the Court of Appeal in the present case, was right to take the view that the police were immune from an action of this kind on grounds similar to those which in *Rondel v Worsley* were held to render a barrister immune from actions for negligence in his conduct of proceedings in court (see [1987] 1 All ER 1173 at 1183–1184, [1988] QB 60 at 76). . . .

[LORD BRANDON OF OAKBROOK, LORD OLIVER OF AYLMERTON and LORD GOFF OF CHIEVELEY agreed with LORD KEITH's speech. LORD TEMPLEMAN delivered a speech in which he was also against allowing the action.]

Question

To what extent might, for example, the medical profession make similar policy arguments against the duty of care which they undoubtedly owe to their patients?

Notes

1. On the immunity of advocates from actions for negligence on policy grounds see p. 173, post.

2. Consider further *Calveley v Chief Constable of the Merseyside Police*

[1989] AC 1228; [1989] 1 All ER 1025 where the House of Lords denied that the police investigating a possible crime owed a duty of care to a suspect. One point made was that 'all other considerations apart, it would plainly be contrary to public policy . . . to prejudice the fearless and efficient discharge by police officers of their vitally important public duty of investigating crime by requiring them to act under the shadow of a potential action for damages for negligence by the suspect' ([1989] 1 All ER at p. 1030). On public policy militating against police liability, see further *Clough v Bussan (West Yorkshire Police Authority, third party)* [1990] 1 All ER 431; *Alexandrou v Oxford* (1990) Times, 19th February.

3. The interrelationship between various of the constituent elements of the duty of care was considered p. 61, ante. What about the interrelationship of public policy and the 'just and reasonable' criterion? Could the former be accommodated within the latter? In *Minories Finance Ltd v Arthur Young (a firm) (Bank of England, third party)* [1989] 2 All ER 105 at 110, for example, the two categories seem to be treated as separate, and consider Lord Oliver's speech in *Caparo Industries plc v Dickman* [1990] 1 All ER 568 at 585 (p. 59, ante). What about the relationship between the 'just and reasonable' criterion and the older, broader sense of policy which was used before the movement away from *Anns v Merton London Borough Council* [1978] AC 728; [1977] 2 All ER 492 in the 1980s that we have seen in this chapter (see the quotation from *Williams & Hepple* set out p. 52, ante)? When *Caparo* was in the Court of Appeal, Bingham LJ stated ([1989] 1 All ER 798 at 803) that this former category (i.e. 'just and reasonable') 'covers very much the same ground as Lord Wilberforce's second stage test in *Anns's* case . . . and what in cases such as *Spartan Steel and Alloys Ltd v Martin & Co (Contractors) Ltd* [1973] QB 27; [1972] 3 All ER 557 [p. 230, post] and *McLoughlin v O'Brian* [1983] 1 AC 410; [1982] 2 All ER 298 [p. 119, post] was called policy'. *Winfield & Jolowicz*, p. 78, note 39a think that this 'may well accord with what Lord Wilberforce intended but it is hard to reconcile with *Yuen Kun Yeu*' [see p. 53, ante]. How does this stand in the light of the House of Lords' views in *Caparo*?

4. For argument as to the unsuitability of a court restricting liability on the ground of policy rather than following principle (i.e. the 'neighbour' principle, seen as a reasonable foresight of harm test), see Lord Scarman's speech in *McLoughlin v O'Brian* [1983] 1 AC 410; [1982] 2 All ER 298 (p. 124, post). However, the majority in *McLoughlin v O'Brian* took the view that policy considerations could restrict liability even where the harm to the plaintiff was reasonably foreseeable, although note that policy is being used here in the older, broader sense mentioned ante.

Contrast with Lord Scarman's speech the following opinion of Robert Goff LJ in *Paterson Zochonis & Co Ltd v Merfarken Packaging Ltd* [1986] 3 All ER 522 at 540 (although again the more restricted scope attached to the label 'policy' in recent times must be borne in mind):

'It is plain that, in considering whether the duty of care should be negatived or limited in any new situation, the courts are making what is usually called a decision of policy. . . . Presented with such a case, the courts have to do their limited best. They have no secretariat, or apparatus for inquiry. They have to derive all the guidance they can from the authorities, and from the writings of scholars; and they have the inestimable benefit of the assistance of counsel. But they are also fully entitled to, and do, draw on their own professional and practical experience. In the end, the choice must be one of judgment, in the balancing of conflicting interests; and in the exercise of that judgment the courts must strive neither unjustifiably to deprive potential plaintiffs of remedies for their injuries, nor unjustifiably to impose too heavy a legal responsibility on potential defendants.'

5. As has been mentioned ante, the label 'policy' used to have a broader scope in this context than it has received of late. Various policy arguments (in the broader sense) that have been raised will be found in the materials in this and the following two chapters although not all of them would fall under the term 'policy' today. For example, how would the 'floodgates argument', on which see p. 130, post, be classified under the duty concept? For general discussion of policy in relation to the duty of care prior to the recent developments in that concept and the more restricted use of the word 'policy', see C. R. Symmons (1971) 34 MLR 394 and 528; J. Bell, *Policy Arguments in Judicial Decisions* (Oxford, 1983), chap. 3. One factor that has received little attention over the years has been the insurance position (Bell, op cit, p. 76), though for an example of it being considered, see *Spartan Steel & Alloys Ltd v Martin & Co (Contractors) Ltd* [1973] QB 27; [1972] 3 All ER 557 (p. 230, post). It would, of course, seem unfair to insurance companies (or their premium payers) to make a defendant liable in a particular case just because he was insured when a non-insured defendant would not be so liable; nevertheless, do you think considerations as to the general availability of different types of insurance, whether the potential plaintiffs or defendants could more easily insure etc. should be irrelevant, relevant, cogent or conclusive when a court is deciding on the existence of a duty of care? If relevant, under which aspect of duty should it come? Consider further *Morgans v Launchbury* [1973] AC 127; [1972] 2 All ER 606 (p. 819, post) although note that it did not concern the duty of care. For argument that the recent problems over the duty of care concept are related to the inability to obtain unlimited insurance, see M. Davies (1989) 9 LS 67. (On the effect which insurance has had on the law of tort, and the different types of insurance, see pp. 883–885, post.)

2 The duty of positive action

Anns *v* London Borough of Merton, p. 99, post

Notes

1. As will be stated p. 99, post, it is important to realise that — without at this stage going into detail, as to which see p. 475, post — in *Murphy v Brentwood District Council* [1990] 2 All ER 908; [1990] 3 WLR 414 (pp. 212 and 466, post) the House of Lords basically overturned the ruling in *Anns* concerning the duty of care which it was held in that case that a local authority owed; however, they left open whether there might be a duty of care on the part of a local authority in respect of injury to a person or other property. Because this point was left open, *Anns* remains of relevance, albeit of diminished practical relevance, in the sphere of omissions; furthermore, it is submitted that the treatment of *East Suffolk Rivers Catchment Board v Kent* [1941] AC 74; [1941] 4 All ER 527 in *Anns* is still of importance after *Murphy*. For the relevance of *Anns* to the exercise of statutory powers, see

p. 99, post. When the House of Lords in *Anns* was discussing the case on the assumption that there had been an inspection, was it considering liability for misfeasance or nonfeasance? (See *Atiyah* 3rd edn, p. 104.)

2. It has been argued that Lord Atkin did not intend his 'neighbour principle' to cover any omissions other than those occurring in the course of some activity (e.g. failing to give a hand-signal while driving a car, when clearly there can be liability): see J. C. Smith and P. Burns (1983) 46 MLR 147 at 155–156. Whatever position one takes on this question of interpretation, it is clear that there are many cases of omission in which the law imposes no liability on people who fail to act. Referring to the parable of the Good Samaritan, Deane J in *Jaensch v Coffey* (1984) 54 ALR 417 at 439–440 has said that 'both priest and Levite ensured performance of any common law duty of care to the stricken traveller when, by crossing to the other side of the road, they avoided any risk of throwing up dust in his wounds'. The 'fundamental distinction' that tort law draws between acts and omissions was acknowledged in *Banque Keyser Ullman SA v Skandia (UK) Insurance Co Ltd* [1990] 1 QB 665; [1989] 2 All ER 952, noted p. 174, post, when that case was in the Court of Appeal, where reference was made to the view of Lord Goff in *Smith v Littlewoods Organisation Ltd* [1987] AC 241 at 271 (p. 92, post), to that of Lord Keith in *Yuen Kun Yeu v A-G of Hong Kong* [1988] AC 175 at 192 (p. 54, ante) and to that of Lord Bridge in *Curran v Northern Ireland Co-Ownership Housing Association Ltd* [1987] AC 718 at 724, set out at p. 56, ante. Cf. *Clough v Bussan* (*West Yorkshire Police Authority, third party*) [1990] 1 All ER 431 at 433. In the Court of Appeal in *Banque Keyser* it was further stated (at p. 798) that the reluctance of the courts to render pure omissions actionable in tort 'applies, perhaps even more so, when the omission is a failure to prevent economic harm'.

On occasions, however, the law will impose a duty to act and failure to act can involve liability. See generally *Fleming*, pp. 133–144. One example which will be found in this section is that the law may impose liability on those who fail to control others when there is a sufficient relationship between them. Other instances of liability for omissions can be found in *Barnett v Chelsea and Kensington Hospital Management Committee* [1969] 1 QB 428; [1968] 1 All ER 1068, noted p. 311, post and in the law relating to occupiers' liability (though see *Winfield & Jolowicz*, p. 93, note 24). See further *Kirkham v Chief Constable of the Greater Manchester Police* [1990] 3 All ER 246; [1990] 2 WLR 987 where liability was established when the police, who were aware of the suicidal tendencies of the plaintiff's husband, had not passed this information on to the prison authorities when he was remanded in custody by a magistrates' court. Lloyd LJ accepted that there could be liability for an omission where a plaintiff had relied on an assumption of responsibility to him by the defendant. In *Kirkham* Lloyd LJ found an assumption of responsibility by the police to relay to the prison authorities, upon the transfer of the plaintiff's husband from police custody to them, information potentially relevant to his well-being and he inferred that there had been reliance by him on that assumption of responsibility. Note the point in *Fleming*, p. 137, that even where there is no close personal relationship, 'a duty may be found in justifiable reliance on a more general assumption of protective care'. He cites cases on the liability of railways for accidents on level crossings such as *Smith v South Eastern Railway Co* [1896]

1 QB 178 (reliance by person crossing railway track on practice of defendant's servant signalling to approaching trains). (See, however, *Fleming*, p. 138, note 78 for an argument that misfeasance may be involved here.)

3. Why should the law be chary of imposing liability for omissions? Possible reasons can be found in *Atiyah*, pp. 80-85. The factors put forward by *Atiyah* are the more burdensome nature of affirmative obligations, the idea that the defendant has not identified himself in the way in which affirmative conduct leading to damage identifies a person and causal arguments, in that the defendant may merely have failed to prevent harm occurring. For criticism of these views, however, see *Atiyah*, pp. 85-86. For further discussion of policy factors, see J. G. Logie [1989] CLJ 115 at 117-120. More generally, Logie argues that liability for failure to warn only exists in limited circumstances at present, but that a common basis for such liability 'could be provided if cases dealing with a negligent failure to warn were dealt with by the principles applied in ordinary negligence actions rather than by special rules which depend on whether the failure was considered to be an act or an omission' (op cit, p. 133).

Carmarthenshire County Council *v* Lewis House of Lords [1955] 1 All ER 565

A lorry driver was killed when, in swerving to avoid a child (approaching his fourth birthday) who ran on to the road, the lorry struck a lamp post. It was admitted that the lorry driver himself had not been at fault. The child (David Morgan) attended a nursery school which was maintained by the appellants, the local education authority, and which was near to this road. A teacher, Miss Morgan, was about to take this child and a girl (Shinoa Evans) out for a walk, but found that a third child had cut himself, and spent ten minutes looking after that child. During this period, the child who was to be involved in the accident left the classroom. He went across the playground, through the gate, down a lane and one hundred yards along the road in question to the point where the accident occurred. The widow of the driver (the respondent) brought an action alleging that her husband's death was due to the appellants' or their servant's negligence. The Court of Appeal, [1953] 2 All ER 1403, dismissed an appeal from the judgment of Devlin J, [1953] 1 All ER 1025, who held that the teacher had been negligent, and there was a further appeal to the House of Lords:

LORD GODDARD: . . . The question of general importance that is raised is whether there is a duty on the occupiers of premises adjoining a highway to prevent young children from escaping on to the highway so as to endanger other persons lawfully passing on it. By young children I mean those of such tender years that they may be presumed to be unable to take any care for their own safety, and whom a prudent parent would not allow to go into a street unaccompanied. . . .

The position, then, is that the appellants maintain a nursery and infant school in premises adjoining a highway in a town and are, in my opinion, under a duty to take care that the children neither themselves [become] involved in or cause a traffic accident. . . .

[Having decided that the teacher had not been negligent, he continued:] But this does not conclude the matter as far as the appellants are concerned. They maintain a nursery school and an infant school on these premises. In the former they accept the care of children from three to five years and in the latter those of five to seven. During the time when this child was in their care, he is found outside the school premises wandering in the street. That, in my opinion, clearly calls for an explanation from the appellants. They have only shown that the child left the room in the temporary absence of the teacher and so got into the playground. In the playground he would have been safe at least from traffic risks. All we know is that the gates must have been open, or so easy to open that a child of three or four could open them. True, the nursery children are put, when out of school, into the play-pen, but infants from five to seven play in the playground. If it is possible for children of that age, when a teacher's back may be turned for a moment, to get out into a busy street, this does seem to indicate some lack of care or of precautions which might reasonably be required. There is no analogy between a school playground and the home in this respect. At any rate, no satisfactory explanation has been given for this child being found in the street at a time when he was in the care of the appellants, and for this reason I would dismiss the appeal.

LORD REID: . . . [T]wo questions arise for decision. In the first place, was the escape of the child David into the street attributable to negligence of the appellants or of those for whom they are responsible? It it was, then it appears to me to be obvious that his being there alone might easily lead to an accident, and, if the child had been killed or injured, the appellants would have been liable in damages, for they certainly owed a duty to the child to protect him from injury. But then a second question is raised by the appellants. They say that, although they owed a duty to the child they owed no duty to other users of the highway, and that, even if they were negligent in letting the child escape on to the street, they cannot be held responsible for damage to others caused by the action of the child when there.

On the first question, I am of opinion that the appellants were negligent. However careful the mistresses might be, minor emergencies and distractions were almost certain to occur from time to time so that some child or children would be left alone without supervision for an appreciable time. The actions of a child of this age are unpredictable and I think that it ought to have been anticipated by the appellants, or their responsible officers, that, in such a case, a child might well try to get out on to the street and that, if it did, a traffic accident was far from improbable. It would have been very easy to prevent this, and either to lock the gates or, if that was thought undesirable, to make them sufficiently difficult to open to ensure that they could not be opened by a child so young that it could not be trusted alone on the street. The classroom door was not an obstacle and, no doubt, it was convenient that the children should be able to open this door themselves, but that meant that the way to the street was open unless the outer gate was so fastened or constructed as to be an obstacle to them.

There was much argument whether Miss Morgan was negligent in leaving these children for ten minutes. I do not think that she was negligent in the first instance because she intended to come back very soon: the real question is whether, when she found that she had to be absent to attend to the injured child, she ought to have paid some attention to the two who were waiting for her. She was next door to the classroom while attending to the injured child, and, without delaying her attention to the injured child, she could have called to David and Shinoa to come into the play-pen where they would have been under supervision or, at least, she could have opened the door of the classroom to see that all was well. But, no doubt, her whole attention was concentrated on the injured child, and the question whether her omission to give any attention to the other children amounted to negligence is, I think, a very narrow one. I prefer to base my judgment on the fact that such a situation ought to have been anticipated by the appellants and provided for.

The appellants argued that, even if they were negligent and even if they owed some duty to the deceased lorry driver, the accident which caused his death was not reasonably foreseeable; his death, if it was a consequence of their negligence, was too remote to involve them in liability for it. I would deal with that argument in this way. Was it foreseeable by an ordinary reasonable and careful person that a child might sometimes be left alone in the nursery school for a short period? I think it was. I see nothing very extraordinary in the circumstances which caused these children to be left alone. Was it, then, foreseeable that such a child might not sit still but might move out of the classroom? If I am right in my view that it is not safe to make assumptions about the behaviour of such young children, again I think it was. Was it then foreseeable that such a child might go into the street, there being no obstacle in its way? I see no ground for assuming that such a child would stay in an empty playground when the gate was not more than twenty yards or so from the classroom. And once the child was in the street anything might happen. It was argued that it might be reasonable to foresee injury to the child but not reasonable to foresee that the child's action would cause injury to others. I can see no force in that. One knows that every day people take risks in order to save others from being run over, and if a child runs into the street the danger to others is almost as great as the danger to the child. . . .

I turn now to the second question which is one of novelty and general importance. If the appellants are right, it means that, no matter how careless the person in charge of a young child may be and no matter how obvious it may be that the child may stray into a busy street and cause an accident, yet that person is under no liability for damage to others caused solely by the action of the child, because his only duty is towards the child under his care. There appears to be no reported case of an action of this kind, and the appellants say that this indicates that no one has hitherto supposed that such an action would lie, for there must have been many instances of the driver of a vehicle suffering damage caused by a young child running in front of it. But in most cases of that kind it would not be worth while to sue the person who was in charge of the child, and, in any event, 'the categories of negligence are never closed'.

The case most relied on by the appellants was *Hay* (or *Bourhill*) *v Young*,[1] where it was held that a motor cyclist was under no duty to a woman who was not in any physical danger from his driving and who did not even see the accident in which he was involved, but who suffered shock from hearing the noise of it. Those facts have not the faintest resemblance to the facts of this case, but the appellants say that the reasoning with regard to remoteness assists them. I do not think that it does. Lord Thankerton ([1942] 2 All ER at 399) said that the cyclist's duty was to drive 'with such reasonable care as will avoid the risk of injury to such persons as he can reasonably foresee might be injured by failure to exercise such reasonable care' and he referred to 'the area of potential danger'. Lord Russell of Killowen (ibid, at p. 401) cited the well-known passage in the speech of Lord Atkin in *M'Alister* (or *Donoghue*) *v Stevenson*[2] ([1932] AC at p. 580), beginning 'Who, then, in law is my neighbour?', as did Lord Porter ([1942] 2 All ER at p. 409). Lord Macmillan said (ibid, at p. 403) that a

'duty is owed to those to whom injury may reasonably and probably be anticipated if the duty is not observed,'

and Lord Wright (ibid, at p. 404) referred to the

'general concept of reasonable foresight as the criterion of negligence or breach of duty.'

If I am right in the view which I have already expressed that injury to other road users was reasonably foreseeable if this child was allowed to escape on to the street, then the reasoning in *Hay* (or *Bourhill*) *v Young*,[1] is very much against the appellants, and they could only succeed on this argument if there were, in connection with the care of young children, some special feature which would prevent the application of the general principle.

The appellants say that it would be unreasonable to apply that principle here

---

1. [1943] AC 92; [1942] 2 All ER 396.
2. [1932] AC 562.

because, if such a duty is held to exist, it will put an impossible burden on harassed mothers who will have to keep a constant watch on their young children. I do not think so. There is no absolute duty, there is only a duty not to be negligent, and a mother is not negligent unless she fails to do something which a prudent or reasonable mother in her position would have been able to do, and would have done. Even a housewife who has young children cannot be in two places at once, and no one would suggest that she must neglect her other duties, or that a young child must always be kept cooped up. But I think that all but the most careless mothers do take many precautions for their children's safety, and the same precautions serve to protect others. I cannot see how any person in charge of a child could be held to have been negligent in a question with a third party injured in a road accident unless he or she had failed to take reasonable and practicable precautions for the safety of the child.

What precautions would have been practicable and what precautions would have been reasonable in any particular case must depend on a great variety of circumstances. But, in this case, it was not impracticable for the appellants to have their gate so made or fastened that a young child could not open it and, in my opinion, that was a proper and reasonable precaution for them to take. . . .

I am, therefore, of opinion that the appeal should be dismissed.

LORD TUCKER: . . . I think that, in principle, there can be no doubt that both courts below were right in holding that persons in charge of tiny children (the child in question was just under four years of age) in premises adjoining a busy highway owe a duty to persons using the highway to take reasonable care to see that such children — being of an age when they cannot have acquired sufficient 'road sense' to permit of their being allowed to travel unattended to and from school — shall not, during school hours, escape unattended on to such a highway, it being reasonably foreseeable that an accident involving injury to other road users as well as to the children may well result therefrom.

In the present case, a child named David Morgan, a week or so before his fourth birthday, had been taken to the nursery school managed by the appellants at Ammanford and left there in charge of the school authorities. Between 12.15 and 12.30 pm during school hours the child had somehow got out into College Street — a busy thoroughfare — and caused an accident which resulted in the death of the respondent's husband. My Lords, such an occurrence, I think, calls for an explanation from the appellants. Not because the facts and circumstances are exclusively within their knowledge — a theory to which I do not subscribe — but because it was an event which should not have happened and which prima facie indicates negligence on the part of those in charge of the child, just as much as the presence of a motor car on the foot pavement prima facie points to negligence on the part of the driver. . . .

My Lords, on this issue I agree with my noble and learned friends Lords Oaksey and Goddard, that the evidence disclosed no negligence on the part of Miss Morgan. It is easy after the event to think of several things she might have done which would have avoided the accident which resulted from her absence, but the question is whether her failure to take such action in the circumstances which existed amounted to negligence. For myself, I have no hesitation in holding that Miss Morgan was not shown to have been guilty of any negligence, and that no responsibility for the death of the deceased man attaches to her.

This does not, however, dispose of the case. The explanation put forward by the appellants entirely fails to explain how or why it was possible for this tiny child to escape from the school premises on to the street. The trial judge drew the inference that the child got out through the unlocked side gate opening on to a lane leading into the street. This was the way the child was brought to, and taken from, school, and I think the judge's inference was the most probable one. No explanation was given why the gate was kept unlocked, or in such a condition that it was possible for a child of four to push it open or unlatch it. Nor was any other means of exit suggested as likely, except by going through other portions of the school premises not forming part of the nursery school and out of a gate leading directly on to the street.

My Lords, I think the appellants failed altogether to show that the child's presence in the street was not due to any negligence on their part, or of those for whom they are responsible. . . .

While entirely absolving Miss Morgan from the finding of negligence against her, I am none the less of opinion that the appellants do not thereby escape responsibility, and for these reasons I would dismiss the appeal.

LORD KEITH OF AVONHOLM [agreeing that the appeal should be dismissed]: . . . I wish to make it clear that I am dealing with the case of a child so young that it cannot safely be allowed on a busy street by itself. With a child of an age to be allowed to find its own way to school, or to traverse the streets alone, different considerations arise. There can normally be no duty to prevent such a child from getting on to a street and, in the case of a traffic accident in which it is involved, the question of responsibility for the accident will be considered in general with reference to the conduct of the child itself and of the other person involved in the accident. There may also be special cases of country children from wayside cottages using a road in full sight of approaching traffic, or tiny tots on some side street obviously used as a children's playground. Such cases will have to be considered on their special circumstances. . . .

[LORD OAKSEY delivered a speech in favour of allowing the appeal.]

Appeal dismissed

Notes

1. The relationship between parents and their children is such that if negligence on the part of a parent is established, that parent can be liable to someone injured by his or her child: see e.g. *Gorely v Codd* [1966] 3 All ER 891; [1967] 1 WLR 19 (though here the defendant parent was found not to have been negligent). Cf. s. 26 of the Criminal Justice Act 1982, as amended and note *Leeds City Council v West Yorkshire Metropolitan Police* [1983] 1 AC 29; [1982] 1 All ER 274. Why should not parents be automatically liable for the torts of their children?

2. In the sort of situation involved in the extract above, the appellants could have found themselves facing not just a claim by a road user, but also a claim from the child himself if he had been injured. Indeed Lord Reid in *Carmarthenshire County Council v Lewis* thought that the appellants would have been liable if the child had suffered damage. By way of example, mention might also be made of *Barnes v Hampshire County Council* [1969] 3 All ER 746; [1969] 1 WLR 1563 where a schoolgirl, aged five, was seriously injured when she ran into a lorry on a busy road which was a short distance from her school. The official time for release from the school she attended was 3.30 pm, but the trial judge found that on this occasion she was let out of the school at or very shortly after 3.25 pm, and that, if she had been let out at the official time, her mother would probably have met the child before the latter reached the busy road. The House of Lords held that the respondents, the education authority, were liable to the child. (Cf. *Van Oppen v Clerk to the Bedford Charity Trustees* [1989] 3 All ER 389; [1990] 1 WLR 235, noted p. 200, post.) Could the driver of a stationary ice-cream van be liable to a child knocked down by a car whilst he or she was crossing a road in the course of going to or leaving the van? (Consider *Arnold v Teno* (1978) 83 DLR (3d) 609.) Might a licensee of a public house be liable to a customer

who, as a result of the consumption of drink on the premises, was knocked over by a car on a busy road or fell over a nearby cliff? Consider *Jordan House Ltd v Menow and Honsberger* (1973) 38 DLR (3d) 105; *Munro v Porthkerry Park Holiday Estates Ltd* [1984] LS Gaz R 1368.

3. *Barnes v Hampshire County Council* concerned the liability of an education authority, but the question of parental liability to children has also been discussed: see e.g. the Australian case of *Hahn v Conley* [1972] ALR 247. Here, having examined the case law, Barwick CJ thought that one proposition — and in his view it was correct — clearly emerged. At p. 251 he stated this proposition as follows:

'. . . if there be a cause of action available to the child, the blood relationship of the defendant to the child will not constitute a bar to the maintenance by the child of the appropriate proceeding to enforce the cause of action. Whilst perhaps there is no clear decision of an appellate court in the United Kingdom, New Zealand or Australia to that effect, I think that the view for which there is most judicial support, and the view which commends itself to me, is that the moral duties of conscientious parenthood do not, as such, provide the child with any cause of action when they are not, or badly, performed or neglected. Further, I think that the predominant judicial view [to be][1] extracted from those cases, and again a view which commends itself to me as correct is that, whilst in particular situations and because of their nature or elements, there will be a duty on the person into whose care the child has been placed and accepted to take reasonable care to protect the child against foreseeable danger, there is no general duty of care in that respect imposed by the law upon a parent simply because of the blood relationship. Also parents like strangers may become liable to the child if the child is led into danger by their actions. . . . In the case of the parent, as in the case of a stranger it seems to me that the duty of care springs out of the particular situation: the extent and nature of the steps which it may be necessary to take to discharge the duty may well be influenced by the fact of parenthood, though parenthood is not itself the source of the duty.'

On the question of parental liability, see also *McCallion v Dodd* [1966] NZLR 710; *Rogers v Rawlings* [1969] Qd R 262; *Arnold v Teno; J Eastham v B Eastham and I Eastham* [1982] CLY 2141; *Posthuma and Posthuma v Campbell* (1984) 37 SASR 321; P. M. Bromley and N. V. Lowe, *Bromley's Family Law* 7th edn (London, 1987), pp. 282–283. Might there be any justification for not allowing a child to sue its parents? Although this would be out of line with the approach of the courts, is there a case for restricting recovery to those situations where the parent is actually insured, or, so as not to discriminate against a child with less prudent parents, those cases where there is compulsory insurance (e.g. road traffic)? Consider also s. 1 and s. 2 of the Congenital Disabilities (Civil Liability) Act 1976 (p. 142, post).

Home Office *v* Dorset Yacht Co Ltd House of Lords [1970] 2 All ER 294

This was an appeal by the Home Office from the order of the Court of Appeal (Lord Denning MR and Edmund Davies and Phillimore LJJ) dated 10 March 1969 and

---

1. [These words do not appear in the report of the case at [1972] ALR at p. 251, but are to be found in the report of the case at (1971) 45 ALJR at p. 635.]

reported, [1969] 2 All ER 564, dismissing the appeal of the Home Office from a judgment of Thesiger J dated 19 December 1968 who decided a preliminary issue on a point of law in favour of the respondents, the Dorset Yacht Co Ltd. The facts are set out in the opinion of Lord Reid.

LORD REID: My Lords, on 21 September 1962, a party of borstal trainees were working on Brownsea Island in Poole Harbour under the supervision and control of three borstal officers. During that night seven of them escaped and went aboard a yacht which they found nearby. They set this yacht in motion and collided with the respondents' yacht which was moored in the vicinity. Then they boarded the respondents' yacht. Much damage was done to this yacht by the collision and some by the subsequent conduct of these trainees. The respondents sue the appellant, the Home Office, for the amount of this damage.

The case comes before your Lordships on a preliminary issue whether the Home Office or these borstal officers owed any duty of care to the respondents capable of giving rise to a liability in damages. So it must be assumed that the respondents can prove all that they could prove on the pleadings if the case goes to trial. The question then is whether on that assumption the Home Office would be liable in damages. It is admitted that the Home Office would be vicariously liable if an action would lie against any of these borstal officers.

The facts which I think we must assume are that this party of trainees was in the lawful custody of the governor of the Portland Borstal Institution and was sent by him to Brownsea Island on a training exercise in the custody and under the control of the three officers with instructions to keep them in custody and under control. But in breach of their instructions these officers simply went to bed leaving the trainees to their own devices. If they had obeyed their instructions they could and would have prevented these trainees from escaping. They would therefore be guilty of the disciplinary offences of contributing by carelessness or neglect to the escape of a prisoner and to the occurrence of loss, damage or injury to any person or property. All the escaping trainees had criminal records and five of them had a record of previous escapes from borstal institutions. The three officers knew or ought to have known that these trainees would probably try to escape during the night, would take some vessel to make good their escape and would probably cause damage to it or some other vessel. There were numerous vessels moored in the harbour, and the trainees could readily board one of them. So it was a likely consequence of their neglect of duty that the respondents' yacht would suffer damage.

The case for the Home Office is that under no circumstances can borstal officers owe any duty to any member of the public to take care to prevent trainees under their control or supervision from injuring him or his property. If that is the law then enquiry into the facts of this case would be a waste of time and money because whatever the facts may be the respondents must lose. That case is based on three main arguments. First, it is said that there is virtually no authority for imposing a duty of this kind. Secondly, it is said that no person can be liable for a wrong done by another who is of full age and capacity and who is not the servant or acting on behalf of that person. And thirdly, it is said that public policy (or the policy of the relevant legislation) requires that these officers should be immune from any such liability.

[In rejecting the first argument for denying a duty of care (in a passage of which part has been set out at p. 51, ante), LORD REID concluded that there was 'nothing to prevent our approaching the present case with Lord Atkin's principles [in M'Alister (or Donoghue) v Stevenson [1932] AC 562 at 580] in mind': on the role of Lord Atkin's approach today, see pp. 40–65, ante. LORD REID continued:] Even so it is said that the respondents must fail because there is a general principle that no person can be responsible for the acts of another who is not his servant or acting on his behalf. But here the ground of liability is not responsibility for the acts of the escaping trainees; it is liability for damage caused by the carelessness of these officers in the knowledge that their carelessness would probably result in the trainees causing damage of this kind. So the question is really one of remoteness of damage. . . .

[Having quoted passages from the judgments in *The Oropesa*,[1] *Haynes v Harwood*[2] and *Scott's Trustees v Moss*,[3] he continued:] These cases show that, where human action forms one of the links between the original wrongdoing of the defendant and the loss suffered by the plaintiff, that action must at least have been something very likely to happen if it is not to be regarded as novus actus interveniens breaking the chain of causation. I do not think that a mere foreseeable possibility is or should be sufficient, for then the intervening human action can more properly be regarded as a new cause than as a consequence of the original wrongdoing. But if the intervening action was likely to happen I do not think it can matter whether that action was innocent or tortious or criminal. Unfortunately tortious or criminal action by a third party is often the 'very kind of thing' which is likely to happen as a result of the wrongful or careless act of the defendant. And in the present case, on the facts which we must assume at this stage, I think that the taking of a boat by the escaping trainees and their unskilful navigation leading to damage to another vessel were the very kind of thing that these borstal officers ought to have seen to be likely.

There was an attempt to draw a distinction between loss caused to the plaintiff by failure to control an adult of full capacity and loss caused by failure to control a child or mental defective. As regards causation, no doubt it is easier to infer novus actus interveniens in the case of an adult but that seems to me to be the only distinction. In the present case on the assumed facts there would in my view be no novus actus when the trainees damaged the respondents' property and I would therefore hold that damage to have been caused by the borstal officers' negligence.

If the carelessness of the borstal officers was the cause of the respondents' loss what justification is there for holding that they had no duty to take care? The first argument was that their right and power to control the trainees was purely statutory and that any duty to exercise that right and power was only a statutory duty owed to the Crown. I would agree but there is very good authority for the proposition that, if a person performs a statutory duty carelessly so that he causes damage to a member of the public which would not have happened if he had performed his duty properly, he may be liable. In *Geddis v Proprietors of Bann Reservoir*[4] Lord Blackburn said:

'For I take it, without citing cases, that it is now thoroughly well established that no action will lie for doing that which the legislature has authorised, if it be done without negligence, although it does occasion damage to anyone; but an action does lie for doing that which the legislature has authorised, if it be done negligently.'

The reason for that is, I think, that Parliament deems it to be in the public interest that things otherwise unjustifiable should be done, and that those who do such things with due care should be immune from liability to persons who may suffer thereby. But Parliament cannot reasonably be supposed to have licensed those who do such things to act negligently in disregard of the interests of others so as to cause them needless damage.

Where Parliament confers a discretion the position is not the same. Then there may, and almost certainly will, be errors of judgment in exercising such a discretion and Parliament cannot have intended that members of the public should be entitled to sue in respect of such errors. But there must come a stage when the discretion is exercised so carelessly or unreasonably that there has been no real exercise of the discretion which Parliament has conferred. The person purporting to exercise his

---

1. [1943] P 32 at 37; [1943] 1 All ER 211 at 214.
2. [1935] 1 KB 146 at 156; [1934] All ER Rep 103 at 107.
3. (1889) 17 R 32 at 36 and 37.
4. (1878) 3 App Cas 430 at 455, 456.

discretion has acted in abuse or excess of his power. Parliament cannot be supposed to have granted immunity to persons who do that. The present case does not raise that issue because no discretion was given to these borstal officers. They were given orders which they negligently failed to carry out. But the county court case of *Greenwell v Prison Comrs.*[1] was relied on and I must deal with it. Some 290 trainees were held in custody in an open borstal institution. During the previous year there had been no less than 172 escapes. Two trainees escaped and took and damaged the plaintiff's motor truck; one of these trainees had escaped on three previous occasions from this institution. For three months since his last escape the question of his removal to a more secure institution had been under consideration but no decision had been reached. The learned judge held that the authorities there had been negligent. In my view, this decision could only be upheld if it could be said that the failure of those authorities to deal with the situation was so unreasonable as to show that they had been guilty of a breach of their statutory duty and that this had caused the loss suffered by the plaintiff.

. . . [T]he responsible authorities must weigh on the one hand the public interest of protecting neighbours and their property from the depredations of escaping trainees and on the other hand the public interest of promoting rehabilitation. Obviously there is much room here for differences of opinion and errors of judgment. In my view there can be no liability if the discretion is exercised with due care. There could only be liability if the person entrusted with discretion either unreasonably failed to carry out his duty to consider the matter or reached a conclusion so unreasonable as again to show failure to do his duty. . . .

We were also referred to *Holgate v Lancashire Mental Hospitals Board, Gill and Robertson*[2] where the alleged fault was in releasing a mental patient. For similar reasons I think this decision could only be supported if it could be said that the release was authorised so carelessly that there had been no real exercise of discretion. . . .

It was suggested that a decision against the Home Office would have very far reaching effects; it was indeed suggested in the Court of Appeal[3] that it would make the Home Office liable for the loss occasioned by a burglary committed by a trainee on parole or a prisoner permitted to go out to attend a funeral. But there are two reasons why in the vast majority of cases that would not be so. In the first place it would have to be shown that the decision to allow any such release was so unreasonable that it could not be regarded as a real exercise of discretion by the responsible officer who authorised the release. And secondly it would have to be shown that the commission of the offence was the natural and probable, as distinct from merely a foreseeable, result of the release—that there was no novus actus interveniens. *Greenwell's* case[4] received a good deal of publicity at the time; it was commented on in the Law Quarterly Review.[5] But it has not been followed by a series of claims. I think the fears of the Home Office are unfounded; I cannot believe that negligence or dereliction of duty is widespread among prison or borstal officers.

Finally, I must deal with public policy. It is argued that it would be contrary to public policy to hold the Home Office or its officers liable to a member of the public for this carelessness—or indeed any failure of duty on their part. The basic question is who shall bear the loss caused by that carelessness—the innocent respondents or the Home Office who are vicariously liable for the conduct of their careless officers? I do not think that the argument for the Home Office can be put better than it was put by the Court of Appeals of New York in *Williams v New York State*:[6]

---

1. (1951) 101 L Jo 486.
2. [1937] 4 All ER 19.
3. [1969] 2 QB 412; [1969] 2 All ER 564.
4. (1951) 101 L Jo 486.
5. Vol. 68, p. 18.
6. 127 NE (2d) 545 (1955) at 550.

'... public policy also requires that the State be not held liable. To hold otherwise would impose a heavy responsibility upon the State, or dissuade the wardens and principal keepers of our prison system from continued experimentation with "minimum security" work details—which provide a means for encouraging better-risk prisoners to exercise their senses of responsibility and honor and so prepare themselves for their eventual return to society. Since 1917, the Legislature has expressly provided for out-of-prison work, Correction Law, §182, and its intention should be respected without fostering the reluctance of prison officials to assign eligible men to minimum security work, lest they thereby give rise to costly claims against the State, or indeed inducing the State itself to terminate this "salutary procedure" looking towards rehabilitation.'

It may be that public servants of the State of New York are so apprehensive, easily dissuaded from doing their duty, and intent on preserving public funds from costly claims, that they could be influenced in this way. But my experience leads me to believe that Her Majesty's servants are made of sterner stuff. So I have no hesitation in rejecting this argument. I can see no good ground in public policy for giving this immunity to a government department. I would dismiss this appeal.

LORD PEARSON: ... It may be artificial and unhelpful to consider the question as to the existence of a duty of care in isolation from the elements of breach of duty and damage. The actual damage alleged to have been suffered by the respondents may be an example of a kind or range of potential damage which was foreseeable, and if the act or omission by which the damage was caused is identifiable, it may put one on the trail of a possible duty of care of which the act or omission would be a breach. In short, it may be illuminating to start with the damage and work back through the cause of it to the possible duty which may have been broken. ...

What would be the nature of the duty of care owed by the Home Office to the respondents if it existed? In my opinion, the Home Office did not owe to the respondents any general duty to keep the borstal boys in detention. If the Home Office had, in the exercise of its discretion, released some of these boys, taking them on shore and putting them on trains or buses with tickets to their homes, there would have been no prospect of damage to the respondents as boatowners and the respondents would not have been concerned and would have had nothing to complain of. Again the boys might have escaped in such a way that no damage could be caused to the respondents as boatowners; for instance, they might have escaped by swimming ashore or by going ashore in a boat belonging to or hired by the borstal authorities or by having their friends bring a rescue boat from outside and carry them off to a refuge in the Isle of Wight or Portsmouth or elsewhere. On the other hand the boys might interfere with the boats from motives of curiosity and desire for amusement without having any intention to escape from borstal detention. The essential feature of this case is not the 'escape' (whatever that may have amounted to) but the interference with the boats. The duty of care would be simply a duty to take reasonable care to prevent such interference. The duty would not be broken merely by the Home Office's failure to prevent an escape from borstal detention or from borstal training. Performance of the duty might incidentally involve an element of physical detention, if interference with the boats by some particular boy could not be prevented by any other means. But if some other means—such as supervision, keeping watch, dissuasion or deterrence—would suffice, physical detention would not be required for performance of the duty.

Can such a duty be held to exist on the facts alleged here? On this question there is no judicial authority except the one decision in the Ipswich county court in *Greenwell v Prison Comrs.*[1] In this situation it seems permissible, indeed almost

---

1. (1951) 101 L Jo 486.

inevitable, that one should revert to the statement of basic principle by Lord Atkin in *M'Alister* (or *Donoghue*) *v Stevenson*[1]. . . . It seems to me that prima facie, in the situation which arose in this case according to the allegations, the respondents as boatowners were in law 'neighbours' of the Home Office and so there was a duty of care owing by the Home Office to the respondents. It is true that the *M'Alister* (or *Donoghue*) *v Stevenson*[1] principle as stated in the passage which has been cited is a basic and general but not universal principle and does not in law apply to all the situations which are covered by the wide words of the passage. To some extent the decision in this case must be a matter of impression and instinctive judgment as to what is fair and just. It seems to me that this case ought to, and does, come within the *M'Alister* (or *Donoghue*) *v Stevenson*[1] principle unless there is some sufficient reason for not applying the principle to this case. Therefore, one has to consider the suggested reasons for not applying the principle here.[2]

Proximity or remoteness. As there is no evidence, one can only judge from the allegations in the statement of claim. It seems clear that there was sufficient proximity; there was geographical proximity and it was foreseeable that the damage was likely to occur unless some care was taken to prevent it. In other cases a difficult problem may arise as to how widely the 'neighbourhood' extends, but no such problem faces the respondents in this case.

Act of third party. In *Weld-Blundell v Stephens*[3] Lord Sumner said:

'In general (apart from special contracts and relations and the maxim Respondeat superior), even though A is in fault, he is not responsible for injury to C which B, a stranger to him, deliberately chooses to do.'

In *Smith v Leurs*[4] Dixon J said:

'. . . apart from vicarious responsibility, one man may be responsible to another for the harm done to the latter by a third person; he may be responsible on the ground that the act of the third person could not have taken place but for his own fault or breach of duty. There is more than one description of duty the breach of which may produce this consequence. For instance, it may be a duty of care in reference to things involving special danger. It may even be a duty of care with reference to the control of actions or conduct of the third person. It is, however, exceptional to find in the law a duty to control another's actions to prevent harm to strangers. The general rule is that one man is under no duty of controlling another to prevent his doing damage to a third. There are, however, special relations which are the source of a duty of this nature. It appears now to be recognised that it is incumbent upon a parent who maintains control over a young child to take reasonable care so to exercise that control as to avoid conduct on his part exposing the person or property of others to unreasonable danger. Parental control, where it exists, must be exercised with due care to prevent the child inflicting intentional damage on others or causing damage by conduct involving unreasonable risk of injury to others.'

In my opinion, this case falls under the exception and not the rule, because there was a special relation. The borstal boys were under the control of the Home Office's officers, and control imports responsibility. The boys' interference with the boats appears to have been a direct result of the Home Office's officers' failure to exercise proper control and supervision. Problems may arise in other cases as to the

---

1. [1932] AC 562 at 580; [1932] All ER Rep 1 at 11.
2. [But on the approach to the duty of care today, see pp. 40–65, ante.]
3. [1920] AC 956 at 986; [1920] All ER Rep 32 at 47.
4. (1945) 70 CLR 256 at 261, 262.

responsibility of the Home Office's officers for acts done by borstal boys when they have completed their escape from control and are fully at large and acting independently. No such problem faces the respondents in this case.

Statutory duty. Not only with respect to the detention of borstal boys but also with respect to the discipline, supervision and control of them the Home Office's officers were acting in pursuance of statutory duties. These statutory duties were owed to the Crown and not to private individuals such as the respondents. The respondents, however, do not base their claim on breach of statutory duty. The existence of statutory duties does not exclude liability at common law for negligence in the performance of the statutory duties. . . . Be it assumed that the Home Office's officers were acting in pursuance of statutory powers (or statutory duties which must include powers) in bringing the borstal boys to Brownsea Island to work there under the supervision and control of the Home Office's officers. No complaint could be made of the Home Office's officers doing that. But in doing that they had a duty to the respondents as 'neighbours' to make proper exercise of the powers of supervision and control for the purpose of preventing damage to the respondents as 'neighbours'.

Public policy. It is said, and in the absence of evidence I assume (and perhaps it is common knowledge and can be judicially noticed) that one method of borstal training, which is employed in relation to boys who may be able to respond to it, is to give them a considerable measure of freedom, initiative and independence in order that they may develop their self-reliance and sense of responsibility. This method, at any rate when it is intensively applied, must diminish the amount of supervision and control which can be exercised over the borstal boys by the Home Office's officers, and there is then a risk, which is not wholly avoidable, that some of the boys will escape and may in the course of escaping or after escaping do injury to persons or damage to property. There is no evidence to show whether or not this method was being employed, intensively or at all, in the present case. But supposing that it was, I am of opinion that it would affect only the content or standard and not the existence of the duty of care. It may be that when the method is being intensively employed there is not very much that the Home Office's officers can do for the protection of the neighbours and their property. But it does not follow that they have no duty to do anything at all for this purpose. They should exercise such care for the protection of the neighbours and their property as is consistent with the due carrying out of the borstal system of training. The needs of the borstal system, important as they no doubt are, should not be treated as so paramount and all-important as to require or justify complete absence of care for the safety of the neighbours and their property and complete immunity from any liability for anything that the neighbours may suffer.

. . . I would say that the Home Office owed no duty to the respondents with regard to the detention of the borstal boys (except perhaps incidentally as an element in supervision and control) nor with regard to the treatment or employment of them, but the Home Office did owe to the respondents a duty of care, capable of giving rise to a liability in damages, with respect to the manner in which the borstal boys were disciplined, controlled and supervised.

I would dismiss the appeal.

LORD DIPLOCK: . . . The only cause of action relied on is the 'negligence' of the officers in failing to prevent the youths from escaping from their custody and control. It is implicit in this averment of 'negligence' and must be treated as admitted not only that the officers by taking reasonable care could have prevented the youths from escaping, but also that it was reasonably foreseeable by them that if the youths did escape they would be likely to commit damage of the kind which they did commit, to some craft moored in the vicinity of Brownsea Island.

The specific question of law raised in this appeal may therefore be stated as: is any duty of care to prevent the escape of a borstal trainee from custody owed by the Home Office to persons whose property would be likely to be damaged by the tortious acts of the borstal trainee if he escaped? This is the first time that this specific question has been posed at a higher judicial level than that of a county court. Your Lordships in answering it will be performing a judicial function similar to that performed in *M'Alister* (or *Donoghue*) *v Stevenson*[1] and more recently in *Hedley Byrne & Co Ltd v Heller & Partners Ltd*[2] of deciding whether the English law of civil wrongs should be extended to impose legal liability to make reparation for the loss caused to another by conduct of a kind which has not hitherto been recognised by the courts as entailing any such liability.

This function, which judges hesitate to acknowledge as law-making, plays at most a minor role in the decision of the great majority of cases, and little conscious thought has been given to analysing its methodology. Outstanding exceptions are to be found in the speeches of Lord Atkin in *M'Alister* (or *Donoghue*) *v Stevenson*[1] and of Lord Devlin in *Hedley Byrne & Co Ltd v Heller & Partners Ltd*.[2] It was because the former was the first authoritative attempt at such an analysis that it has had so seminal an effect on the modern development of the law of negligence.

It will be apparent that I agree with Lord Denning MR[3] that what we are concerned with in this appeal 'is . . . at bottom a matter of public policy which we, as judges, must resolve'. He cited in support Lord Pearce's dictum in *Hedley Byrne & Co Ltd v Heller & Partners Ltd*:[4]

'How wide the sphere of the duty of care in negligence is to be laid depends ultimately on the courts' assessment of the demands of society for protection from the carelessness of others.'

The reference in this passage to 'the courts' in the plural is significant for —

'As always in English law the first step in such an inquiry is to see how far the authorities have gone, for new categories in the law do not spring into existence overnight;'

per Lord Devlin.[5]

The justification of the courts' role in giving the effect of law to the judges' conception of the public interest in the field of negligence is based on the cumulative experience of the judiciary of the actual consequences of lack of care in particular instances. And the judicial development of the law of negligence rightly proceeds by seeking first to identify the relevant characteristics that are common to the kinds of conduct and relationship between the parties which are involved in the case for decision and the kinds of conduct and relationships which have been held in previous decisions of the courts to give rise to a duty of care.

The method adopted at this stage of the process is analytical and inductive. It starts with an analysis of the characteristics of the conduct and relationship involved in each of the decided cases. But the analyst must know what he is looking for; and this involves his approaching his analysis with some general conception of conduct and relationships which *ought* to give rise to a duty of care. This analysis leads to a proposition which can be stated in the form: 'In all the decisions that have been analysed a duty of care has been held to exist wherever the conduct and the relationship possessed each of the characteristics A, B, C, D etc., and has not so far been found to exist when any of these characteristics were absent.'

---

1. [1932] AC 562; [1932] All ER Rep 1.
2. [1964] AC 465; [1963] 2 All ER 575.
3. [1969] 2 QB at p. 426; [1969] 2 All ER at p. 567.
4. [1964] AC at p. 536; [1963] 2 All ER at p. 615.
5. [1964] AC at p. 525; [1963] 2 All ER at p. 608.

For the second stage, which is deductive and analytical, that proposition is converted to: 'In all cases where the conduct and relationship possess each of the characteristics A, B, C, D etc., a duty of care arises.' The conduct and relationship involved in the case for decision is then analysed to ascertain whether they possess each of these characteristics. If they do the conclusion follows that a duty of care does arise in the case for decision.

But since ex hypothesi the kind of case which we are now considering offers a choice whether or not to extend the kinds of conduct or relationships which give rise to a duty of care, the conduct or relationship which is involved in it will lack at least one of the characteristics A, B, C, or D etc. And the choice is exercised by making a policy decision whether or not a duty of care ought to exist if the characteristic which is lacking were absent or redefined in terms broad enough to include the case under consideration. The policy decision will be influenced by the same general conception of what ought to give rise to a duty of care as was used in approaching the analysis. The choice to extend is given effect to by redefining the characteristics in more general terms so as to exclude the necessity to conform to limitations imposed by the former definition which are considered to be inessential. The cases which are landmarks in the common law, such as *Lickbarrow v Mason*;[1] *Rylands v Fletcher*;[2] *Indermaur v Dames*;[3] *M'Alister* (or *Donoghue*) *v Stevenson*,[4] to mention but a few, are instances of cases where the cumulative experience of judges has led to a restatement in wide general terms of characteristics of conduct and relationships which give rise to legal liability.

Inherent in this methodology, however, is a practical limitation which is imposed by the sheer volume of reported cases. The initial selection of previous cases to be analysed will itself eliminate from the analysis those in which the conduct or relationship involved possessed characteristics which are obviously absent in the case for decision. The proposition used in the deductive stage is not a true universal. It needs to be qualified so as to read: 'In all cases where the conduct and relationship possess each of the characteristics A, B, C and D etc., *but do not possess any of the characteristics Z, Y or X etc., which were present in the cases eliminated from the analysis*, a duty of care arises.' But this qualification, being irrelevant to the decision of the particular case, is generally left unexpressed.

[LORD DIPLOCK went on to express the opinion that the case could not be decided by treating Lord Atkin's 'neighbour principle' in *M'Alister* (or *Donoghue*) *v Stevenson* [1932] AC 562 at 580 (p. 43, ante) 'as a universal' (and on the treatment of the 'neighbour principle' today, see pp. 40–65, ante). LORD DIPLOCK continued:] In the present appeal . . . the conduct of the Home Office which is called in question differs from the kind of conduct discussed in *M'Alister* (or *Donoghue*) *v Stevenson*[4] in at least two special characteristics. First, the actual damage sustained by the respondents was the direct consequence of a tortious act done with conscious volition by a third party responsible in law for his own acts and this act was interposed between the act of the Home Office complained of and the sustension of damage by the respondents. Secondly, there are two separate 'neighbour relationships' of the Home Office involved, a relationship with the respondents and a relationship with the third party. These are capable of giving rise to conflicting duties of care. This appeal, therefore, also[5] raises the lawyer's question 'Am I my brother's keeper'? A question which may also[5] receive a restricted reply.

---

1. (1787) 2 Term Rep 63; [1775–1802] All ER Rep 1.
2. (1868) LR 3 HL 330; [1861–73] All ER Rep 1.
3. [1866] LR 1 CP 274; [1861–73] All ER Rep 15.
4. [1932] AC 562; [1932] All ER Rep 1.
5. [The word 'also' would appear to be a reference to Lord Atkin's speech in *M' Alister* (or *Donoghue*) *v Stevenson* [1932] AC 562 at 580 (p. 43, ante) where Lord Atkin mentions the lawyer's question as to who is my neighbour which, he says, receives a restricted reply.]

I start, therefore, with an examination [of] the previous cases in which both or one of these special characteristics are present. . . .

[Having discussed the county court case of *Greenwell v Prison Comrs*[1] where both characteristics were present, he continued:] In two cases, *Ellis v Home Office*[2] and *D'Arcy v Prison Comrs*,[3] it was assumed, in the absence of argument to the contrary, that the legal custodian of a prisoner detained in a prison owed to the plaintiff, another prisoner confined in the same prison, a duty of care to prevent the first prisoner from assaulting the plaintiff and causing him physical injuries. Unlike the present case, at the time of the tortious act of the prisoner for the consequences of which it was assumed that the custodian was liable the prisoner was in the actual custody of the defendant and the relationship between them gave to the defendant a continuing power of physical control over the acts of the prisoner. The relationship between the defendants and the plaintiffs in these two cases too bore no obvious analogy to that between the respondents and the Home Office in the present case. In each of the cases the defendant in the exercise of a legal right and physical power of custody and control of the plaintiff had required him to be in a position in which the defendant ought reasonably and probably to have foreseen that he was likely to be injured by his fellow prisoner.

In my view, it is the combination of these two characteristics, one of the relationship between the defendant custodian and the person actually committing the wrong to the plaintiff and the other of the relationship between the defendant and the plaintiff which supply the reason for the existence of the duty of care in these two cases — which I conceded as counsel in *Ellis v Home Office*.[2] The latter characteristic would be present also in the relationship between the defendant and any other person admitted to the prison who sustained similar damage from the tortious act of a prisoner, since the Home Office as occupier and manager of the prison has the legal right to control the admission and the movements of a visitor while he is on the prison premises. A similar duty of care would thus be owed to him. But I do not think that, save as a deliberate policy decision, any proposition of law based on the decisions in these two cases would be wide enough to extend to a duty to take reasonable care to prevent the escape of a prisoner from actual physical custody and control owed to a person whose property is situated outside the prison premises and is damaged by the tortious act of the prisoner *after his escape*. . . .

[His Lordship discussed *Holgate v Lancashire Mental Hospitals Board, Gill and Robertson*[4] and *Carmarthenshire County Council v Lewis*,[5] and continued:] I do not find it useful to refer to the many other cases cited in which the damage to the plaintiff was not caused by an act of conscious volition of a responsible third person whose conduct the defendant had a legal right to control. The result of the survey of previous authorities can be summarised in the words of Dixon J in *Smith v Leurs*:[6]

'The general rule is that one man is under no duty of controlling another man to prevent his doing damage to a third. There are, however, special relations which are the source of a duty of this nature.'

From the previous decisions of the English courts, in particular those in *Ellis v Home Office*[2] and *D'Arcy v Prison Comrs*[3] which I accept as correct, it is possible to

---

1. (1951) 101 L Jo 486.
2. [1953] 2 QB 135; [1953] 2 All ER 149.
3. [1956] Crim LR 56.
4. [1937] 4 All ER 19.
5. [1955] AC 549; [1955] 1 All ER 565.
6. (1945) 70 CLR at p. 262.

arrive by induction at an established proposition of law as respects one of those special-relations: viz. A is responsible for damage caused to the person or property of B by the tortious act of C (a person responsible in law for his own acts) where the relationship between A and C has the characteristics: (1) that A has the legal right to detain C in penal custody and to control his act while in custody; (2) that A is actually exercising his legal right of custody of C at the time of C's tortious act; and (3) that A if he had taken reasonable care in the exercise of his right of custody could have prevented C from doing the tortious act which caused damage to the person or property of B; and where also the relationship between A and B has the characteristics; (4) that at the time of C's tortious act A has the legal right to control the situation of B or his property as respects physical proximity to C; and (5) that A can reasonably foresee that B is likely to sustain damage to his person or property if A does not take reasonable care to prevent C from doing tortious acts of the kind which he did.

On the facts which your Lordships are required to assume for the purposes of the present appeal the relationship between the Home Office, A, and the borstal trainees, C, did possess characteristics (1) and (3) but did not possess characteristic (2); while the relationship between the Home Office, A, and the respondents, B, did possess characteristic (5) but did not possess characteristic (4). What your Lordships have to decide as respects each of the relationships is whether the missing characteristic is essential to the existence of the duty or whether the facts assumed for the purposes of this appeal disclose some other characteristic which if substituted for that which is missing would produce a new proposition of law which *ought* to be true.

As any proposition which relates to the duty of controlling another man to prevent his doing damage to a third deals with a category of civil wrongs of which the English courts have hitherto had little experience it would not be consistent with the methodology of the development of the law by judicial decision that any new proposition should be stated in wider terms than are necessary for the determination of the present appeal. Public policy may call for the immediate recognition of a new sub-category of relations which are the source of a duty of this nature additional to the sub-category described in the established proposition; but further experience of actual cases would be needed before the time became ripe for the coalescence of sub-categories into a broader category of relations giving rise to the duty, such as was effected with respect to the duty of care of a manufacturer of products in *M'Alister* (or *Donoghue*) *v Stevenson*.[1] Nevertheless, any new sub-category will form part of the English law of civil wrongs and must be consistent with its general principles.

[LORD DIPLOCK went on to distinguish *Geddis v Proprietors of Bann Reservoir*,[2] and to state that the 'public law concept of ultra vires has replaced the civil law concept of negligence as the test of the legality, and consequently of the actionability, of acts or omissions of government departments or public authorities done in the exercise of a discretion conferred on them by Parliament as to the means by which they are to achieve a particular public purpose.' Having discussed the application of the ultra vires concept to the Borstal system, he continued:] In a civil action which calls in question an act or omission of a subordinate officer of the Home Office on the ground that he has been 'negligent' in his custody and control of a borstal trainee who has caused damage to another person the initial inquiry should be whether or not the act or omission was ultra vires for one or other of these reasons. Where the act or omission is done in pursuance of the officer's instructions, the court may have to form its own view as to what is in the interests of borstal trainees, but only to the limited extent of determining whether or not any reasonable person could bona fide come to the conclusion that the trainee causing the damage or other trainees in the same custody could be benefited in any way by the act or omission. This does not involve the court in attempting to substitute, for that of the Home Office, its own

---

1. [1932] AC 562; [1932] All ER Rep 1.
2. (1878) 3 App Cas 430.

assessment of the comparative weight to be given to the benefit to the trainees and the detriment to persons likely to sustain damage. If on the other hand the officer's act or omission is done contrary to his instructions it is not protected by the public law doctrine of intra vires. Its actionability falls to be determined by the civil law principles of negligence, like the acts of the statutory undertakers in *Geddis v Proprietors of Bann Reservoir*.[1]

This, as it seems to me, is the way in which the courts should set about the task of reconciling the public interest in maintaining the freedom of the Home Office to decide on the system of custody and control of borstal trainees which is most likely to conduce to their reformation and the prevention of crime, and the public interest that borstal officers should not be allowed to be completely disregardful of the interests both of the trainees in their charge and of persons likely to be injured by their carelessness, without the law providing redress to those who in fact sustain injury.

Ellis v Home Office[2] and *D'Arcy v Prison Comrs*[3] are decisions which are consistent with this principle as respects the initial inquiry. In neither of them was it sought to justify the alleged acts or omissions of the prison officers concerned as being done in compliance with instructions given to them by the appropriate authority (at that date the prison commissioners) or as being in the interests of the prisoner whose tortious act caused the damage or of any other immates of the prison. If the test suggested were applied to acts and omissions alleged in those two cases they would in public law be ultra vires.

If this analogy to the principle of ultra vires in public law is applied as the relevant condition precedent to the liability of a custodian for damage caused by the tortious act of a person (the detainee) over whom he has a statutory right of custody, the characteristic of the relationship between the custodian and the detainee which was present in those two cases, viz. that the custodian was actually exercising his right of custody at the time of the tortious act of the detainee, would not be essential. A cause of action is capable of arising from failure by the custodian to take reasonable care to prevent the detainee from escaping, if his escape was the consequence of an act or omission of the custodian falling outside the limits of the discretion delegated to him under the statute.

The practical effect of this would be that no liability in the Home Office for 'negligence' could arise out of the escape from an 'open' borstal of a trainee who had been classified for training at a borstal of this type by the appropriate officer to whom the function of classification had been delegated, on the ground that the officer had been negligent in so classifying him or in failing to reclassify him for removal to a 'closed' borstal. The decision as to classification would be one which lay within the officer's discretion. The court could not inquire into its propriety as it did in *Greenwell v Prison Comrs*[4] in order to determine whether he had given what the court considered to be sufficient weight to the interests of persons whose property the trainee would be likely to damage if he should escape. For this reason I think that *Greenwell v Prison Comrs*[4] was wrongly decided by the county court judge. But to say this does not dispose of the present appeal for the allegations of negligence against the borstal officers are consistent with their having acted outside any discretion delegated to them and having disregarded their instructions as to the precautions they should take to prevent members of the working party of trainees from escaping from Brownsea Island. Whether they had or not could only be determined at the trial of the action. But this is only a condition precedent to the existence of any liability. Even if the acts and omissions of the borstal officer[s] alleged in the particulars of

---

1. (1878) 3 App Cas 430.
2. [1953] 2 QB 135; [1953] 2 All ER 149.
3. [1956] Crim LR 56.
4. (1951) 101 L Jo 486.

negligence were done in breach of their instructions and so were ultra vires in public law it does not follow that they were also done in breach of any duty of care owed by the officers to the respondents in civil law.

... To give rise to a duty on the part of the custodian owed to a member of the public to take reasonable care to prevent a borstal trainee from escaping from his custody before completion of the trainee's sentence there should be some relationship between the custodian and the person to whom the duty is owed which exposes that person to a particular risk of damage in consequence of that escape which is different in its incidence from the general risk of damage from criminal acts of others which he shares with all members of the public.

What distinguishes a borstal trainee who has escaped from one who has been duly released from custody, is his liability to recapture, and the distinctive added risk which is a reasonably foreseeable consequence of a failure to exercise due care in preventing him from escaping is the likelihood that in order to elude pursuit immediately on the discovery of his absence the escaping trainee may steal or appropriate and damage property which is situated in the vicinity of the place of detention from which he has escaped.

So long as Parliament is content to leave the general risk of damage from criminal acts to lie where it falls without any remedy except against the criminal himself, the courts would be exceeding their limited function in developing the common law to meet changing conditions if they were to recognise a duty of care to prevent criminals escaping from penal custody owed to a wider category of members of the public than those whose property was exposed to an exceptional added risk by the adoption of a custodial system for young offenders which increased the likelihood of their escape unless due care was taken by those responsible for their custody.

I should therefore hold that any duty of a borstal officer to use reasonable care to prevent a borstal trainee from escaping from his custody was owed only to persons whom he could reasonably foresee had property situate in the vicinity of the place of detention of the detainee which the detainee was likely to steal or to appropriate and damage in the course of eluding immediate pursuit and recapture. Whether or not any person fell within this category would depend on the facts of the particular case including the previous criminal and escaping record of the individual trainee concerned and the nature of the place from which he escaped.

So to hold would be a rational extension of the relationship between the custodian and the person sustaining the damage which was accepted in *Ellis v Home Office*[1] and *D'Arcy v Prison Comrs*[2] as giving rise to a duty of care on the part of the custodian to exercise reasonable care in controlling his detainee. In those two cases the custodian had a legal right to control the physical proximity of the person or property sustaining the damage to the detainee who caused it. The extended relationship substitutes for the right to control the knowledge which the custodian possessed or ought to have possessed that physical proximity in fact existed.

In the present appeal the place from which the trainees escaped was an island from which the only means of escape would presumably be a boat accessible from the shore of the island. There is thus material, fit for consideration at the trial, for holding that the respondents, as the owners of a boat moored off the island, fell within the category of persons to whom a duty of care to prevent the escape of the trainees was owed by the officers responsible for their custody.

If therefore it can be established at the trial of this action: (1) that the borstal officers in failing to take precautions to prevent the trainees from escaping were acting in breach of their instructions and not in bona fide exercise of a discretion delegated to them by the Home Office as to the degree of control to be adopted; and (2) that it was reasonably foreseeable by the officers that if these particular trainees

---

1. [1953] 2 QB 135; [1953] 2 All ER 149.
2. [1956] Crim LR 56.

did escape they would be likely to appropriate a boat moored in the vicinity of Brownsea Island for the purpose of eluding immediate pursuit and to cause damage to it, the borstal officers would be in breach of a duty of care owed to the respondents and the respondents would, in my view, have a cause of action against the Home Office as vicariously liable for the 'negligence' of the borstal officers.

I would accordingly dismiss the appeal on the preliminary issue of law and allow the case to go for trial on those issues of fact.

[LORD MORRIS OF BORTH-Y-GEST delivered a speech in favour of dismissing the appeal. VISCOUNT DILHORNE delivered a speech in favour of allowing the appeal.]

Appeal dismissed

Question

Would the Home Office have been liable on the facts of this case (see Lord Reid's speech) if an escaping Borstal boy had reached the mainland and (a) immediately burgled a house, (b) attacked and robbed a man in that house, or (c) robbed a bank in Poole a week later? Consider *Marti v Smith and Home Office* (1981) 131 NLJ 1028, and see *Lamb v Camden London Borough Council* [1981] QB 625; [1981] 2 All ER 408, part of which is set out p. 323, post.

Notes

1. Lord Reid's treatment of novus actus interveniens has been criticised in recent times and must be considered in the light of later cases: see pp. 89 and 323–328, post.

2. On the question of actions in negligence against public authorities, see p. 99, post.

3. For discussion of how French law approaches 'Borstal boys' cases, see C. J. Hamson [1969] CLJ 273 (but note that the *Dorset Yacht* case, which is discussed in the article, had only been before the Court of Appeal at that stage).

4. Even if not legally liable, the Home Office may make an ex gratia payment of compensation where damage has been caused by an absconding prisoner or borstal boy: see C. Harlow and R. Rawlings, *Law and Administration* (London, 1984), pp. 409–411. Note that in general no compensation will be paid if the loss in question is covered by insurance.

5. Compare the *Dorset Yacht* case with *Smith v Scott* [1973] Ch 314; [1972] 3 All ER 645. In this case the Scott family had been placed in a house by the London Borough of Lewisham. The Scotts' behaviour was found by Pennycuick V-C to have been 'altogether intolerable both in respect of physical damage and of noise', and the Smiths, who lived in an adjoining house, moved out. Several points were argued for the plaintiff (Mr Smith) in this unsuccessful action against the Borough, but it might be noted at this stage that the court held that the Borough owed no duty of care to the neighbours in this situation, i.e. in the selection of a tenant. Particular reference was made to Lord Reid's speech in *Home Office v Dorset Yacht Co Ltd* [1970] AC 1004 at 1027 where he mentioned the 'long chapter of the law' governing

the use by a landowner of his proprietary rights. Pennycuick V-C declined to alter the law by the introduction of a duty of care, although he acknowledged that the position could well have been different if this had been an area of the law which was being brought to the court's attention for the first time. See further *O'Leary v London Borough of Islington* (1983) 9 HLR 83.

6. *Dorset Yacht* was distinguished in *Hill v Chief Constable of West Yorkshire* [1989] AC 53; [1988] 2 All ER 238 which raised the question whether the police owed a duty of care to individual members of the public who might be injured by criminals. (For more details of the case see p. 62, ante where the question of public policy in relation to such a claim was considered.) Distinguishing features were (a) the criminal was never in the police's custody and (b) the victim was one of a very large number of females potentially at risk; on this latter point a contrast was drawn with the special risk to those whose yachts were moored off Brownsea Island in the *Dorset Yacht* case – and see Lord Diplock's speech in that case (p. 84, ante) which was cited in *Hill*. The requisite proximity was therefore lacking in *Hill*. On the question of a duty of care being owed by the police, compare *Clough v Bussan* (*West Yorkshire Police Authority, third party*) [1990] 1 All ER 431 and see *Alexandrou v Oxford* (1990) Times, 19th February.

7. On the problem under discussion here see further the cases discussed pp. 187–188, post in the context of economic loss. Note that in one of these cases (*Davis v Radcliffe* [1990] 2 All ER 536; [1990] 1 WLR 821) the Privy Council's opinion indicates that it will be even harder to establish liability for the acts of third parties when economic rather than physical loss is involved.

8. The degree of control over the third party is obviously important. On this point see further p. 106, post.

Smith *v* Littlewoods Organisation Ltd (Chief Constable, Fife Constabulary, third party) House of Lords [1987] 1 All ER 710

Littlewoods bought a cinema in Dunfermline. Their intention was to demolish the cinema and build a supermarket on the site. During a period when the cinema was empty and when none of Littlewoods' employees or contractors were in attendance, a fire was deliberately started by children (or teenagers) and the fire spread to and damaged the appellants' buildings. The appellants' actions succeeded before the Lord Ordinary, but this was reversed by the First Division of the Inner House of the Court of Session, 1986 SLT 272. There were then appeals to the House of Lords.

LORD GRIFFITHS. My Lords, I regard these appeals as turning on the evaluation and application of the particular facts of this case to a well-established duty and standard of care. . . .

The duty of care owed by Littlewoods was to take reasonable care that the condition of the premises they occupied was not a source of danger to neighbouring property.

The standard of care required of them was that stated in general terms by Lord Radcliffe in *Bolton v Stone* [1951] 1 All ER 1078 at 1087, [1951] AC 850 at 868–869 and expanded in more particularity by Lord Wilberforce in *Goldman v Hargrave* [1966] 2 All ER 989 at 995–996, [1967] 1 AC 645 at 662–663 when dealing with a fire on premises caused by an outside agency. . . .

The fire in this case was caused by the criminal activity of third parties on Littlewoods' premises. I do not say that there will never be circumstances in which the law will require an occupier of premises to take special precautions against such a contingency but they would surely have to be extreme indeed. It is common ground that only a 24-hour guard on these premises would have been likely to prevent this fire, and even that cannot be certain, such is the determination and ingenuity of young vandals.

There was nothing of an inherently dangerous nature stored in the premises, nor can I regard an empty cinema stripped of its equipment as likely to be any more alluring to vandals than any other recently vacated premises in the centre of a town. No message was received by Littlewoods from the local police, fire brigade or any neighbour that vandals were creating any danger on the premises. In short, so far as Littlewoods knew, there was nothing significantly different about these empty premises from the tens of thousands of such premises up and down the country. People do not mount 24-hour guards on empty properties and the law would impose an intolerable burden if it required them to do so save in the most exceptional circumstances. I find no such exceptional circumstances in this case and I would accordingly dismiss the appeals.

I doubt myself if any search will reveal a touchstone that can be applied as a universal test to decide when an occupier is to be held liable for a danger created on his property by the act of a trespasser for whom he is not responsible. I agree that mere foreseeability of damage is certainly not a sufficient basis to found liability. But with this warning I doubt that more can be done than to leave it to the good sense of the judges to apply realistic standards in conformity with generally accepted patterns of behaviour to determine whether in the particular circumstances of a given case there has been a breach of duty sounding in negligence.

LORD MACKAY OF CLASHFERN: . . . The claims are based on the allegation that Littlewoods, as owners and occupiers of the Regal Cinema, had a duty to take reasonable care for the safety of premises adjoining, that they knew or ought to have known that a disused cinema would be a ready target for vandals, and that they knew or ought to have known that their cinema was, in fact, the subject of extensive vandalism and that if they did not take steps to prevent the entry of vandals they would cause damage not only to their own property, whether by fire or otherwise, but further such fire might spread and cause damage to adjoining properties. In the circumstances, it was claimed that Littlewoods had a duty to take reasonable care to keep and maintain the premises lockfast, to cause frequent and regular inspection to be made and to lock and board up any doors and windows found to be open or smashed and to employ a caretaker to watch over the premises and to prevent the entry of vandals. In the course of the hearing before your Lordships counsel for the appellants accepted that, in the light of the evidence, the only precaution that was likely to be effective in preventing the entry of vandals was to arrange for a 24-hour watch to be maintained on the premises. Littlewoods, while accepting that as owners and occupiers of the premises they had a duty to take reasonable care for the safety of premises adjoining, strenuously denied that they owed the duties on which these claims are founded.

. . . The judges of the First Division unanimously concluded that . . . in the circumstances it had not been shown that it was reasonably to be foreseen by Littlewoods that if they took no steps to discourage widespread use of the cinema by youngsters, including vandals, one or more of them, or some other intruder, would be likely deliberately to set fire to the building or deliberately to set such a fire in such a place as would be likely to engulf the building.

. . . [I]t has to be borne in mind that the damage to the neighbouring properties, on which the claims against Littlewoods are founded, is damage by fire or otherwise resulting from vandalism in Littlewoods' premises. A duty of care to prevent this damage is the only duty alleged to be incumbent on Littlewoods relevant to this case. From this it follows that, unless Littlewoods were bound reasonably to anticipate and guard against this danger, they had no duty of care, relevant to this case, requiring them to inspect their premises. Unless, therefore, Littlewoods, on taking control of these premises without any knowledge of the subsequent history of the property after they assumed control, ought reasonably to have anticipated that they would be set on fire and thus or otherwise create a substantial risk of damage to neighbouring properties if they did not take precautions, the claims must fail. . . . In my opinion, their Lordships of the First Division applied their minds to the correct question. In my opinion, the question whether, in all the circumstances described in evidence, a reasonable person in the position of Littlewoods was bound to anticipate as probable, if he took no action to keep these premises lockfast, that, in a comparatively short time before the premises were demolished, they would be set on fire with consequent risk to the neighbouring properties is a matter for the judges of fact to determine. Once it has been determined on the correct basis, an appeal court should be slow to interfere with the determination: see, for example, Lord Thankerton in *Glasgow Corp v Muir* [1943] 2 All ER 44 at 47, [1943] AC 448 at 454 and Lord Porter in *Bolton v Stone* [1951] 1 All ER 1078 at 1082, [1951] AC 850 at 860.

The cases to which counsel for the appellants drew attention in his argument, and s 78 of the [Criminal Justice (Scotland) Act 1980], illustrate that a consequence of this kind, if premises are left unoccupied, is a possibility, but the extent to which such an occurrence is probable must depend on the circumstances of the particular case. While no doubt in this case, as the judges in the courts below have found, it was probable that children and young persons might attempt to break into the vacated cinema, this by no means establishes that it was a probable consequence of its being vacated with no steps being taken to maintain it lockfast that it would be set on fire with consequent risk of damage to neighbouring properties. A telling point in favour of Littlewoods is that, although Littlewoods' particulars were shown on a board prominently displayed at the front of the premises, no one made any protest to them about the state of the premises, or indicated to them any concern that, unless they took some action, neighbouring premises were at risk. If, in the light of the common knowledge in the neighbourhood, it had been anticipated that the cinema might be set on fire, with consequent risk to adjoining properties, I should have thought the persons concerned with the safety of adjoining properties, who were certainly among those acquainted with the situation, would have communicated their anxieties to Littlewoods. Neither is there evidence that the police were ever informed of the situation with regard to the cinema, and this I would take as further confirmation that, in the circumstances, no one anticipated any adverse consequences arising from it. It is true that Mr Scott, the beadle[1], spoke of anxiety for the safety of children, and also made some reference, in that connection, to the possibility of fire, but any concern he had was not apparently sufficiently substantial to prompt him to take any action whatever in the way of seeking to have the situation remedied by the owners or the police.

This is sufficient for the disposal of this appeal but in view of the general importance of some of the matters raised in the parties' submissions it is right that I should add some observations on these.

First, counsel for the appellants urged us to say that the ordinary principle to be deduced from Lord Atkin's speech in *Donoghue v Stevenson* should apply to cases where the damage in question was caused by human agency. It is plain from the authorities that the fact that the damage, on which a claim is founded, was caused by a human agent quite independent of the person against whom a claim in negligence is made does not, of itself, preclude success of the claim, since breach of duty on the part of the person against whom the claim is made may also have played a part in causing the damage.

[Having quoted the passage concerning human action and novus actus interveniens from Lord Reid's speech in the *Dorset Yacht* case [1970] AC 1004 at 1030 (p. 74,

---

1. [Of St Paul's Church (which was damaged by the fire).]

ante), LORD MACKAY continued:] . . . It has to be borne in mind that Lord Reid was demonstrating only that the submission with which he was dealing was incorrect. If a person can be responsible for damage caused by acts of another who is not his servant or acting on his behalf that sufficed to answer the question that Lord Reid had before him in the respondent's favour. It was accordingly not critical whether the test was foreseeability of that damage as likely or very likely. At the stage at which Lord Reid used the phrase 'very likely' he was giving his view on what the two cases he had cited showed. In the first of these, the phrase used is 'the very kind of thing which is likely to happen' (see [1935] 1 KB 146 at 156, [1934] All ER Rep 103 at 107 per Greer LJ) and, in the second, the consequence that was being considered was described in the passage quoted from the Lord President (Inglis) as 'the natural and almost inevitable consequence' of the defender's action which was the foundation of the claim (see 17 R (Ct of Sess) 32 at 36). When Lord Reid turns to state his own position, he does so on the basis that the intervening action was likely to happen. In *Glasgow Corp v Muir* [1943] 2 All ER 44, [1943] AC 448 the issue was whether the defender's manageress was negligent in allowing two members of a picnic party to bring a tea urn along a passage in her tea room without taking certain precautions. The damage in question, in that case, might therefore have arisen from the conduct of the two persons carrying the tea urn, who were not employees of the defenders or in any way accountable to them. The test of liability set out by Lord Macmillan in *Hay* (or *Bourhill*) *v Young* [1942] 2 All ER 396 at 403, [1943] AC 92 at 104, namely:

'The duty to take care is the duty to avoid doing or omitting to do anything the doing or omitting to do which may have as its reasonable and *probable* consequence injury to others and the duty is owed to those to whom injury may reasonably and *probably* be anticipated if the duty is not observed' (my emphasis),

was expressly used by Lord Thankerton and Lord Macmillan.

[Having also quoted from the speeches of Lords Wright, Romer and Clauson in *Glasgow Corp v Muir* [1943] AC at 465, 467–468 and 468, his Lordship continued:] . . . There is no hint that any special qualification fell to be introduced into the test in consequence of the urn being carried by two persons not in the employment of the defenders and for whom they would have no vicarious responsibility.

It is true, as has been pointed out by Oliver LJ in *Lamb v Camden London Borough* [1981] 2 All ER 408 at 418, [1981] QB 625 at 642, that human conduct is particularly unpredictable and that every society will have a sprinkling of people who behave most abnormally. The result of this consideration, in my opinion, is that, where the only possible source of the type of damage or injury which is in question is agency of a human being for whom the person against whom the claim is made has no responsibility, it may not be easy to find that as a reasonable person he was bound to anticipate that type of damage as a consequence of his act or omission. The more unpredictable the conduct in question, the less easy to affirm that any particular result from it is probable and in many circumstances the only way in which a judge could properly be persuaded to come to the conclusion that the result was not only possible but reasonably foreseeable as probable would be to convince him that, in the circumstances, it was highly likely. In this type of case a finding that the reasonable man should have anticipated the consequence of human action as just probable may not be a very frequent option. Unless the judge can be satisfied that the result of the human action is highly probable or very likely he may have to conclude that all that the reasonable man could say was that it was a mere possibility. Unless the needle that measures the probability of a particular result flowing from the conduct of a human agent is near the top of the scale it may be hard to conclude that it has risen sufficiently from the bottom to create the duty reasonably to foresee it.

In summary I conclude, in agreement with both counsel, that what the reasonable man is bound to foresee in a case involving injury or damage by independent human agency, just as in cases where such agency plays no part, is the probable consequences of his own act or omission, but that, in such a case, a clear basis will be required on which to assert that the injury or damage is more than a mere possibility. To illustrate, it is not necessary to go further than the decision of this House in *Home Office v Dorset Yacht Co Ltd*, where I consider that all the members of the majority found such a possible basis in the facts that the respondents' yacht was situated very close to the island on which the borstal boys escaped from their custodians, that the only effective means of avoiding recapture was to escape by the use of some nearby vessel and that the only means of providing themselves with the means to continue their journey was likely to be theft from such nearby vessels. These considerations so limited the options open to the escaping boys that it became highly probable that the boys would use, damage or steal from one or more of the vessels moored near the island. . . .

Cases of theft where the thief uses a neighbour's premises to gain access to the premises of the owner of the stolen goods are, in my opinion, in an important respect different from cases of fire such as that with which your Lordships are concerned in the present appeal. In the case of fire, a hazard is created on the first occupier's premises and it is that hazard which operating from the first occupier's premises creates danger to the neighbouring properties. . . . [E]ven though that hazard is created by the act of a trespasser on the first premises the occupier of these premises, once he knows of the physical facts giving rise to the hazard, has a duty to take reasonable care to prevent the hazard causing damage to neighbouring properties. In the ordinary case of theft where the thief uses the first proprietor's property only as an access to the property of the person from whom the stolen property is taken there is no similar hazard on the first proprietor's land which causes the damage to the neighbouring property. Success of the theft depends very much on its mode and occasion being unexpected. The only danger consists in the thief or thieves who, having passed from trespassing on the first proprietor's property, go on to trespass on his neighbour's. There is also a sense in which neighbouring proprietors can, independently, take action to protect themselves against theft in a way that is not possible with fire. Once the fire had taken hold on Littlewoods' building, St Paul's proprietors[1] could not be expected to take effective steps to prevent sparks being showered over on their property. . . .

Where the question is whether or not the duty to take a particular precaution is incumbent on a defendant, the probability of the risk emerging is not the only consideration, as was pointed out by Lord Reid giving the opinion of the Board in *The Wagon Mound (No 2)*, *Overseas Tankship (UK) Ltd v Miller Steamship Co Pty Ltd* [1966] 2 All ER 709 at 718, [1967] 1 AC 617 at 642–643 in reference to *Bolton v Stone* [1951] 1 All ER 1078, [1951] AC 850. Lord Reid said:

'The House of Lords held that the risk was so small that in the circumstances a reasonable man would have been justified in disregarding it and taking no steps to eliminate it. It does not follow that, no matter what the circumstances may be, it is justifiable to neglect a risk of such a small magnitude. A reasonable man would only neglect such a risk if he had some valid reason for doing so: e.g., that it would involve considerable expense to eliminate the risk. He would weigh the risk against the difficulty of eliminating it. If the activity which caused the injury to Miss Stone had been an unlawful activity there can be little doubt but that *Bolton v Stone* would have been decided differently. In their lordships' judgment *Bolton v Stone* did not alter the general principle that a person must be regarded as negligent if he does not take steps to eliminate a risk which he knows or ought to know is a real risk and not a mere possibility which would never influence the mind of a reasonable man. What that decision did was to recognise and give effect to the qualification that it is justifiable

---

1. [St Paul's Church was damaged by the fire and had to be demolished.]

not to take steps to eliminate a real risk if it is small and if the circumstances are such that a reasonable man, careful of the safety of his neighbour, would think it right to neglect it.'

In my opinion this observation demonstrates that, when the word 'probable' is used in this context in the authorities, it is used as indicating a real risk as distinct from a mere possibility of danger. It is not used in the sense that the consequence must be more probable than not to happen, before it can be reasonably foreseeable. And again, in *Goldman v Hargrave* [1966] 2 All ER 989 at 995–996, [1967] 1 AC 645 at 662–663, Lord Wilberforce giving the opinion of the Board, referring to a number of textbooks as well as an article by Dr A L Goodhart, says:

'All of these endorse the development, which their lordships find in the decisions, towards a measured duty of care by occupiers to remove or reduce hazards to their neighbours. So far it has been possible to consider the existence of a duty, in general terms; but the matter cannot be left there without some definition of the scope of his duty. How far does it go? What is the standard of the effort required? What is the position as regards expenditure? It is not enough to say merely that these must be "reasonable" since what is reasonable to one man may be very unreasonable, and indeed ruinous, to another: the law must take account of the fact that the occupier on whom the duty is cast, has, ex hypothesi, had this hazard thrust on him through no seeking or fault of his own. His interest, and his resources whether physical or material, may be of a very modest character either in relation to the magnitude of the hazard, or as compared with those of his threatened neighbour. A rule which required of him in such unsought circumstances in his neighbour's interest a physical effort of which he is not capable, or an excessive expenditure of money, would be unenforceable or unjust. One may say in general terms that the existence of a duty must be based on knowledge of the hazard, ability to foresee the consequences of not checking or removing it, and the ability to abate it. Moreover in many cases, as for example in Scrutton, LJ's hypothetical case of stamping out a fire [see *Job Edwards Ltd v Birmingham Navigations* [1924] 1 KB 341 at 357] or the present case, where the hazard could have been removed with little effort and no expenditure, no problem arises; but other cases may not be so simple. In such situations the standard ought to be to require of the occupier what it is reasonable to expect of him in his individual circumstances. Thus, less must be expected of the infirm than of the able bodied: the owner of a small property where a hazard arises which threatens a neighbour with substantial interests should not have to do so much as one with larger interests of his own at stake and greater resources to protect them: if the small owner does what he can and promptly calls on his neighbour to provide additional resources, he may be held to have done his duty: he should not be liable unless it is clearly proved that he could, and reasonably in his individual circumstances should, have done more.'

My Lords, I think it is well to remember as Lord Radcliffe pointed out in *Bolton v Stone* [1951] 1 All ER 1078 at 1087, [1951] AC 850 at 868–869:

'. . . a breach of duty has taken place if [the facts] show the appellants guilty of a failure to take reasonable care to prevent the accident. One may phrase it [as] "reasonable care" or "ordinary care" or "proper care" — all these phrases are to be found in decisions of authority — but the fact remains that, unless there has been something which a reasonable man would blame as falling beneath the standard of conduct that he would set for himself and require of his neighbour, there has been no breach of legal duty . . .'

This is the fundamental principle and in my opinion various factors will be taken into account by the reasonable man in considering cases involving fire on the one hand and theft on the other, but since this is the principle the precise weight to be given to these factors in any particular case will depend on the circumstances and rigid distinctions cannot be made between one type of hazard and another. I consider that much must depend on what the evidence shows is done by ordinary people in like circumstances to those in which the claim of breach of duty arises.

In my view, if the test of the standard of the reasonable man is applied to the steps an occupier of property must take to protect neighbouring properties from the hazard of fire arising on his property no further consideration of policy arises that should lessen the responsibility of the occupier in a case such as this. . . .

In my opinion, these appeals should be refused. . . .

LORD GOFF OF CHIEVELEY. My Lords, the Lord President (Lord Emslie)[1] founded his judgment on the proposition that the defenders, who were both owners and occupiers of the cinema, were under a general duty to take reasonable care for the safety of premises in the neighbourhood.

Now if this proposition is understood as relating to a general duty to take reasonable care *not to cause damage* to premises in the neighbourhood (as I believe that the Lord President intended it to be understood) then it is unexceptionable. But it must not be overlooked that a problem arises when the pursuer is seeking to hold the defender responsible for having failed to *prevent* a third party from causing damage to the pursuer or his property by the third party's own deliberate wrongdoing. In such a case, it is not possible to invoke a general duty of care; for it is well recognised that there is no *general* duty of care to prevent third parties from causing such damage. The point is expressed very clearly in Hart and Honoré *Causation in the Law* (2nd edn, 1985) p. 196, where the authors state:

'The law might acknowledge a general principle that, whenever the harmful conduct of another is reasonably foreseeable, it is our duty to take precautions against it . . . But, up to now, no legal system has gone so far as this . . .'

The same point is made in Fleming *The Law of Torts* (6th edn, 1983) p. 200, where it is said: '. . . there is certainly no *general* duty to protect others against theft or loss.' (Fleming's emphasis.)

I wish to add that no such general duty exists even between those who are neighbours in the sense of being occupiers of adjoining premises. There is no general duty on a householder that he should act as a watchdog, or that his house should act as a bastion, to protect his neighbour's house.

Why does the law not recognise a general duty of care to prevent others from suffering loss or damage caused by the deliberate wrongdoing of third parties? The fundamental reason is that the common law does not impose liability for what are called pure omissions. If authority is needed for this proposition, it is to be found in the speech of Lord Diplock in *Home Office v Dorset Yacht Co Ltd* [1970] 2 All ER 294 at 326, [1970] AC 1004 at 1060, where he said:

'The very parable of the Good Samaritan (Luke 10:30) which was evoked by Lord Atkin in *Donoghue v Stevenson* [1932] AC 562, [1932] All ER Rep 1 illustrates, in the conduct of the priest and of the Levite who passed by on the other side, an omission which was likely to have as its reasonable and probable consequence damage to the health of the victim of the thieves, but for which the priest and Levite would have incurred no civil liability in English law.'

Lord Diplock then proceeded to give examples which show that, carried to extremes, this proposition may be repugnant to modern thinking. It may therefore require one day to be reconsidered especially as it is said to provoke an 'invidious comparison with affirmative duties of good-neighbourliness in most countries outside the

---

1. [In the First Division of the Inner House of the Court of Session.]

Common Law orbit' (see Fleming *The Law of Torts* (6th edn, 1983) p. 138). But it is of interest to observe that, even if we do follow the example of those countries, in all probability we will, like them, impose strict limits on any such affirmative duty as may be recognised. In one recent French decision, the condition was imposed that the danger to the claimant must be 'grave, imminent, constant . . . nécessitant une intervention immédiate', and that such an intervention must not involve any 'risque pour le prévenu ou pour un tiers': see Lawson and Markesinis *Tortious Liability for Unintentional Harm in the Common Law and the Civil Law* (1982) vol 1, pp 74–75. The latter requirement is consistent with our own law, which likewise imposes limits on steps required to be taken by a person who is under an *affirmative* duty to prevent harm being caused by a source of danger which has arisen without his fault (see *Goldman v Hargrave* [1966] 2 All ER 989, [1967] 1 AC 645), a point to which I shall return later. But the former requirement indicates that any affirmative duty to prevent deliberate wrongdoing by third parties, if recognised in English law, is likely to be strictly limited. I mention this because I think it important that we should realise that problems like that in the present case are unlikely to be solved by a simple abandonment of the commom law's present strict approach to liability for pure omissions.

Another statement of principle, which has been much quoted, is the observation of Lord Sumner in *Weld-Blundell v Stephens* [1920] AC 956 at 986, [1920] All ER Rep 32 at 47:

'In general . . . even though A. is in fault, he is not responsible for injury to C. which B., a stranger to him, deliberately chooses to do.'

This dictum may be read as expressing the general idea that the voluntary act of another, independent of the defender's fault, is regarded as a novus actus interveniens which, to use the old metaphor, 'breaks the chain of causation'. But it also expresses a general perception that we ought not to be held responsible in law for the deliberate wrongdoing of others. Of course, if a duty of care is imposed to guard against deliberate wrongdoing by others, it can hardly be said that the harmful effects of such wrongdoing are not caused by such breach of duty. We are therefore thrown back to the duty of care. But one thing is clear, and that is that liability in negligence for harm caused by the deliberate wrongdoing of others cannot be founded simply on foreseeability that the pursuer will suffer loss or damage by reason of such wrongdoing. There is no such general principle. We have therefore to identify the circumstances in which such liability may be imposed.

That there are special circumstances in which a defender may be held responsible in law for injuries suffered by the pursuer through a third party's deliberate wrongdoing is not in doubt. For example, a duty of care may arise from a relationship between the parties which gives rise to an imposition or assumption of responsibility on or by the defenders, as in *Stansbie v Troman* [1948] 1 All ER 599, [1948] 2 KB 48, where such responsibility was held to arise from a contract. In that case a decorator, left alone on the premises by the householder's wife, was held liable when he went out leaving the door on the latch and a thief entered the house and stole property. Such responsibility might well be held to exist in other cases where there is no contract, as for example where a person left alone in a house has entered as a licensee of the occupier. Again, the defender may be vicariously liable for the third party's act; or he may be held liable as an occupier to a visitor on his land. Again, as appears from the dictum of Dixon J in *Smith v Leurs* (1945) 70 CLR 256 at 262, a duty may arise from a special relationship between the defender and the third party, by virtue of which the defender is responsible for controlling the third party: see, for example, *Home Office v Dorset Yacht Co Ltd*. More pertinently, in a case between adjoining occupiers of land, there may be liability in nuisance if one occupier causes or permits persons to g[a]ther on his land, and they impair his neighbour's enjoyment of his land. Indeed, even if such persons come onto his land as trespassers, the occupier may, if they constitute a nuisance, be under an affirmative duty to abate the nuisance.

As I pointed out in *P Perl (Exporters) Ltd v Camden London BC* [1983] 3 All ER 161 at 172, [1984] QB 342 at 359, there may well be other cases.

These are all special cases. But there is a more general circumstance in which a defender may be held liable in negligence to the pursuer, although the immediate cause of the damage suffered by the pursuer is the deliberate wrongdoing of another. This may occur where the defender negligently causes or permits to be created a source of danger, and it is reasonably foreseeable that third parties may interfere with it and, sparking off the danger, thereby cause damage to persons in the position of the pursuer. The classic example of such a case is, perhaps, *Haynes v Harwood* [1935] 1 KB 146, [1934] All ER Rep 103[1] . . .

Haynes v Harwood was a case concerned with the creation of a source of danger in a public place. We are concerned in the present case with an allegation that the defenders should be held liable for the consequences of deliberate wrongdoing by others who were trespassers on the defenders' property. In such a case it may be said that the defenders are entitled to use their property as their own and so should not be held liable if, for example, trespassers interfere with dangerous things on their land. But this is, I consider, too sweeping a proposition. It is well established that an occupier of land may be liable to a trespasser who has suffered injury on his land; though in *British Rlys Board v Herrington* [1972] 1 All ER 749, [1972] AC 877[2], in which the nature and scope of such liability was reconsidered by your Lordships' House, the standard of care so imposed on occupiers was drawn narrowly so as to take proper account of the rights of occupiers to enjoy the use of their land. It is, in my opinion, consistent with the existence of such liability that an occupier who negligently causes or permits a source of danger to be created on his land, and can reasonably foresee that third parties may trespass on his land and, interfering with the source of danger, may spark it off, thereby causing damage to the person or property of those in the vicinity, should be held liable to such a person for damage so caused to him. . . .

There is another basis on which a defender may be held liable for damage to neighbouring property caused by a fire started on his (the defender's) property by the deliberate wrongdoing of a third party. This arises where he has knowledge or means of knowledge that a third party has created or is creating a risk of fire, or indeed has started a fire, on his premises, and then fails to take such steps as are reasonably open to him (in the limited sense explained by Lord Wilberforce in *Goldman v Hargrave* [1966] 2 All ER 989 at 995–996, [1967] 1 AC 645 at 663–664)[3] to prevent any such fire from damaging neighbouring property . . .

Turning to the facts of the present case, I cannot see that the defenders should be held liable under either of these two possible heads of liability. First, I do not consider that the empty cinema could properly be described as an unusual danger in the nature of a fire hazard. As the Lord President pointed out (*Squires v Perth and Kinross DC* 1986 SLT 272 at 276):

'There was nothing about the building, so far as we know from the evidence, to suggest that it could easily be set alight.'

This conclusion was, in my judgment, entirely justified on the evidence in the case; and it is, I consider, fatal to any allegation that the defenders should be held liable on the ground that they negligently caused or permitted the creation of an unusual source of danger in the nature of a fire hazard.

Nor can I see that the defenders should be held liable for having failed to take reasonable steps to abate a fire risk created by third parties on their property without

---

1. [See p. 140, post.]
2. [See now the Occupiers' Liability Act 1984, p. 462, post.]
3. [See p. 91, ante.]

their fault. If there was any such fire risk, they had no means of knowing that it existed. . . .

In the course of his argument before your Lordships, counsel for the appellants placed reliance on the decision of the Inner House of the Court of Session in *Squires v Perth and Kinross DC* 1986 SLT 30. That was a case concerned not with liability in respect of a fire hazard, but with liability in respect of a theft by a burglar who had gained access to the pursuers' jeweller's shop through a flat above, which was empty because it was being renovated by building contractors who were held to be in occupation of the flat. It was held that the contractors, as occupiers, were liable in negligence to the pursuers for the loss of the jewellery stolen from the shop, on the ground that any person in occupancy and control of the flat above would have readily foreseen the likelihood of what in fact occurred. It appears that the fact that the flat above was empty was plainly apparent from, in particular, the presence of scaffolding at the front of the building; and complaints had been made on a number of occasions that the contractors did not keep the flat secure, for example, because windows were left open and unglazed to accommodate scaffolding. It was a remarkable feature of the case that the burglar himself, one Sneddon, gave evidence at the trial; and it transpired from his evidence that, although his attention was drawn to the possibility of breaking into the jeweller's shop through the empty flat by seeing the scaffolding and open windows of the flat facing the High Street, he in fact approached the flat from behind, climbing over a building of about 12 to 15 feet high overall. He found the door into the yard behind the shop and flat unsecured, but nevertheless climbed over a wall into the yard and then climbed a drainpipe to a balcony, from which he entered the flat through a door which was open. Having entered the flat, he broke into the jeweller's shop through the floor of the flat and the ceiling of the shop. In these circumstances, assuming that the defenders were in breach of duty in leaving the flat insecure, I feel, with all respect, serious doubts about the decision on the issue of causation, since it is difficult to imagine that an experienced and practised housebreaker, as Sneddon was held to be, would have been deterred from entering the flat even if the door on the balcony had been secured. I am not surprised therefore to find that Lord Dunpark shared the same doubts (at 40). Furthermore, I find it difficult to understand why the question of contributory negligence on the part of the pursuers was not considered. The pursuers were just as aware of the risk as the defenders were; yet, although (as was found) an alarm system is often fitted to the roof of premises such as those of the pursuers, and is relatively inexpensive, they did not take this precaution. They seem to have assumed that, although it was their shop which was likely to attract thieves, they were entitled to rely on the contractors working above, rather than on themselves, to prevent thieves entering through the ceiling of the shop. Indeed, if it had been thought appropriate, in the circumstances, to employ a watchman to guard the jeweller's shop, the pursuers would apparently have considered that that expense should fall not on themselves but on the contractors working above. I do not think that that can be right.

In truth the case raises a more fundamental question, which is whether an occupier is under a general duty of care to occupiers of adjacent premises to keep his premises lockfast in order to prevent thieves entering his premises and thereby gaining access to the adjacent premises. Let us suppose that in *Squires v Perth and Kinross DC*, the defenders had expressly warned the pursuers, by notice, that extensive work was going to be done to the flat above, and that this would mean that for a period of time scaffolding would be erected and all the windows of the flat would be removed. Would it then be objectionable that the pursuers should have to look to their own defences against thieves, in the light of these circumstances? I do not think so. Then, should it make any difference that no such notice was given, but it was obvious what the contractors were doing? Again, I do not think so. Then, suppose that the occupiers of the flat above the shop were an ordinary family and, when they went away on holiday, in all the hustle and bustle of getting their children and animals and possessions into their car, they forgot to lock their front door. While they were away a passing thief, seeing that the flat was unoccupied because the curtains were drawn, went up and tried the front door and, finding it unlocked, gained access to the flat and thence entered the jeweller's shop below and robbed it. Should the occupiers of the flat be held liable to the jewellers in negligence? Again, I do not think so; and I add that I do not think that it would make any difference that it was well known that burglars were operating in the neighbourhood. It is not difficult to multiply these homely examples of cases where a thief may gain access to a house or flat which is not lockfast: for example, where an old lady goes out to spend the day with her married daughter and leaves a ground floor window open for her cat; or where a stone deaf asthmatic habitually sleeps with his bedroom window wide open at night; or where an elderly gentleman leaves his french windows open when he is weeding at the bottom of his garden, so that he can hear the telephone. For my part, I do not think that liability can be imposed on an occupier of property in negligence simply because it can be said that it is reasonably foreseeable, or even (having regard, for example, to some particular temptation to thieves in adjacent premises) that it is highly likely, that if he fails to keep his property lockfast a thief may gain access to his property and thence to the adjacent premises. So to hold must presuppose that the occupier of property is under a general duty to *prevent* thieves from entering his property to gain access to neighbouring property, where there is a sufficient degree of foresight that this may occur. But there is no general duty to *prevent* third parties from causing damage to others, even though there is a high degree of foresight that they may do so. The practical effect is that everybody has to take such steps as he thinks fit to protect his own property, whether house or flat or shop, against thieves. He is able to take his own precautions; and, in deciding what precautions to take, he can and should take into account the fact that, in the ordinary course of life, adjacent property is likely to be from time to time unoccupied (often obviously so, and sometimes for a considerable period of time) and is also likely from time to time not to be lockfast. He has to form his own judgment as to the precautions which he should take, having regard to all the circumstances of the case, including (if it be the case) the fact that his premises are a jeweller's shop which offers a special temptation to thieves. I must confess that I do not find this practical result objectionable. For these reasons I consider, with all respect, that *Squires v Perth and Kinross DC* was wrongly decided.

The present case is, of course, concerned with entry not by thieves but by vandals. Here the point can be made that, whereas an occupier of property can take precautions against thieves, he cannot (apart from insuring his property and its contents) take effective precautions against physical damage caused to his property by a vandal who has gained access to adjacent property and has there created a source of danger which has resulted in damage to his property by, for example, fire or escaping water. Even so, the same difficulty arises. Suppose, taking the example I have given of the family going away on holiday and leaving their front door unlocked, it was not a thief but a vandal who took advantage of that fact; and that the vandal, in wrecking the flat, caused damaged to the plumbing which resulted in a water leak and consequent damage to the shop below. Are the occupiers of the flat to be held liable in negligence for such damage? I do not think so, even though it may be well known that vandalism is prevalent in the neighbourhood. The reason is the same, that there is no general duty to *prevent* third parties from causing damage to others, even though there is a high degree of foresight that this may occur. In the example I have given, it cannot be said that the occupiers of the flat have caused or permitted the creation of a source of danger (as in *Haynes v Harwood* [1935] 1 KB 146, [1934] All ER Rep 103 . . .) which they ought to have guarded against; nor of course were there any special circumstances giving rise to a duty of care. The practical effect is that it is the owner of the damaged premises (or, in the vast majority of cases, his insurers) who is left with a worthless claim against the vandal, rather than the occupier of the property which the vandal entered (or his insurers), a conclusion which I find less objectionable than one which may throw an unreasonable burden on ordinary householders.

For these reasons, I consider that both *Lamb v Camden London Borough* [1981] 2 All ER 408, [1981] QB 625 and *King v Liverpool City Council* [1986] 3 All ER 544, [1986] 1 WLR 890 were rightly decided; but I feel bound to say, with all respect, that the principle propounded by Lord Wylie in *Evans v Glasgow DC* 1978 SLT 17 at 19, viz that there is —

'a general duty on owners or occupiers of property . . . to take reasonable care to see that it [is] proof against the kind of vandalism which was calculated to affect adjoining property,'

is, in my opinion, too wide.

I wish to emphasise that I do not think that the problem in these cases can be solved simply through the mechanism of foreseeability. When a duty *is* cast on a person to take precautions against the wrongdoing of third parties, the ordinary standard of foreseeability applies; and so the possibility of such wrongdoing does not have to be very great before liability is imposed. I do not myself subscribe to the opinion that liability for the wrongdoing of others is limited because of the unpredictability of human conduct. So, for example, in *Haynes v Harwood* [1935] 1 KB 146, [1934] All ER Rep 103, liability was imposed although it cannot have been at all likely that a small boy would throw a stone at the horses left unattended in the public road, and in *Stansbie v Troman* [1948] 1 All ER 599, [1948] 2 KB 48 liability was imposed although it cannot have been at all likely that a thief would take advantage of the fact that the defendant left the door on the latch while he was out. Per contra, there is at present no general duty at common law to prevent persons from harming others by their deliberate wrongdoing, however foreseeable such harm may be if the defender does not take steps to prevent it.

Of course, if persons trespass on the defender's property and the defender either knows or has the means of knowing that they are doing so and that in doing so they constitute a danger to neighbouring property, then the defender may be under an affirmative duty to take reasonable steps to exclude them, in the limited sense explained by Lord Wilberforce in *Goldman v Hargrave* [1966] 2 All ER 989 at 995-996, [1967] 1 AC 645 at 663-664, but that is another matter. I incline to the opinion that this duty arises from the fact that the defender, as occupier, is in exclusive control of the premises on which the danger has arisen.

In preparing this opinion, I have given careful consideration to the question whether *P Perl (Exporters) Ltd v Camden London BC* [1983] 3 All ER 161, [1984] QB 342, in which I myself was a member of the Court of Appeal, was correctly decided. I have come to the conclusion that it was, though on rereading it I do not think that my own judgment was very well expressed. But I remain of the opinion that to impose a general duty on occupiers to take reasonable care to prevent others from entering their property would impose an unreasonable burden on ordinary householders and an unreasonable curb on the ordinary enjoyment of their property; and I am also of the opinion that to do so would be contrary to principle. It is very tempting to try to solve all problems of negligence by reference to an all-embracing criterion of foreseeability, thereby effectively reducing all decisions in this field to questions of fact. But this comfortable solution is, alas, not open to us. The law has to accommodate all the untidy complexity of life; and there are circumstances where considerations of practical justice impel us to reject a general imposition of liability for foreseeable damage. An example of this phenomenon is to be found in cases of pure economic loss . . . As the present case shows, another example of this phenomenon is to be found in cases where the plaintiff has suffered damage through the deliberate wrongdoing of a third party; and it is not surprising that once again we should find the courts seeking to identify specific situations in which liability can properly be imposed. Problems such as these are solved in Scotland, as in England, by means of the mechanism of the duty of care . . .

For these reasons I would dismiss these appeals.

[LORD KEITH OF KINKEL agreed with LORD MACKAY OF CLASHFERN and LORD GOFF OF CHIEVELEY. LORD BRANDON OF OAKBROOK delivered a speech in favour of dismissing the appeals.]

Appeals dismissed

Questions

1. Is Lord Griffiths' approach more similar to that of Lord Mackay or that of Lord Goff?

2. Can Lord Mackay's speech be squared with the approach in *Yuen Kun Yeu v A-G of Hong Kong* [1988] AC 175; [1987] 2 All ER 705 (p. 53, ante)?

Notes

1. Lord Brandon decided that Littlewoods owed the appellants a general duty of care to see that its property was not and did not become a source of danger to the neighbouring buildings. However, this did not in his view include a specific duty to take reasonable care to stop young people gaining unlawful access to the property and unlawfully setting fire to it because this was not reasonably foreseeable. For discussion of *Smith v Littlewoods* see B. S. Markesinis (1989) 105 LQR 104. Arguing that Lords Brandon, Griffiths and Mackay did not rule out liability on the basis of any general rule of no duty in this situation but decided it on its facts, he goes on to speculate as to the potential impact of these speeches in opening up liability in the situation where one person fails to stop another harming himself: see op cit, pp. 119–124.

2. The question of the liability for the acts of third parties can arise in discussion of causation and remoteness of damage as well as duty, and will be further considered at that stage. The two issues are of course interrelated. As Oliver LJ pointed out in *P Perl (Exporters) Ltd v Camden London Borough Council* [1984] QB 342 at 353 if there is a duty of care to to stop a third party causing damage, then it is difficult to see how damage caused in breach of that duty can be too remote. See further *King v Liverpool City Council* [1986] 3 All ER 544 at 552–553, and for Lord Mackay's comments on that case, see [1987] AC 241 at 266–267.

3. When considering cases such as *Smith v Littlewoods*, bear in mind that property owners can normally be expected to insure against damage to their property, but note Markesinis' point (op cit, p. 111) that it may be difficult to obtain insurance against fire (or theft) in some inner city areas.

4. *Smith v Littlewoods* on its facts was concerned with damage to the appellants' property caused by fire but the situation where thieves gain access to a plaintiff's property from the defendant's premises was also discussed. In the earlier case of *P Perl (Exporters) Ltd v Camden London Borough Council* [1984] QB 342; [1983] 3 All ER 161 the defendant council owned adjoining premises, one (no. 144) being divided into flats and the other (no. 142) being let to the plaintiff which used its basement to store clothing. The evidence showed that, for example, there was no lock on the front door of no. 144 at the relevant time. Thieves entered an unoccupied basement

flat in no. 144, knocked a hole in the common wall between the basement
flat in no. 144 and the basement in no. 142 and more than 700 garments were
stolen from the latter basement. The Court of Appeal decided that the defendant council were not liable. Mere foreseeability of harm was regarded as
insufficient to establish a duty of care. In *Smith v Littlewoods* [1987] AC at
pp. 263–266 Lord Mackay justified the decision on the basis that the mode
of entry onto the plaintiffs' premises was only a foreseeable possibility: cf.
Lord Goff's speech. Lord Mackay did also state that if a proprietor came
upon a thief on his premises boring a hole into a neighbour's property, then
the proprietor would have to take reasonable steps to stop him endeavouring
to effect entry in this way.

For further discussion of liability for harm caused by third parties see
Paterson Zochonis & Co Ltd v Merfarken Packaging Ltd [1986] 3 All ER
522 and especially Robert Goff LJ's judgment in that case. He expresses the
view, which he repeated in *Perl*, that a person who entrusts a car to someone
who is obviously drunk or incompetent can be liable. On the other hand,
Robert Goff LJ also thought that a dealer selling a car to someone he knows
is an alcoholic would surely not be liable when an accident occurs some time
later due to the alcoholic driving while drunk. Might a licensee of a public
house be liable to a person in a car injured in a road accident brought about
by a customer's drunkenness? (Cf. pp. 71–72, ante.) Note further the discussion by J. Horder (1988) 51 MLR 735 which also deals with the position of
a 'social host'.

3   The exercise of statutory powers

Home Office v Dorset Yacht Club Ltd, p. 72, ante

Anns v London Borough of Merton House of Lords [1977] 2 All ER 492

The plaintiffs were lessees of flats in a block which had been built under plans passed
by the Mitcham Borough Council, to the duties and liabilities of which the defendant
Council had succeeded. The plaintiffs claimed that there had been structural
movements in the block of flats because it had been erected on inadequate foundations which did not comply with the plans. The negligence alleged in the claim against
the Council related to approving the foundations and/or failing to inspect them.
When *Anns* reached the House of Lords, leave was given for the Council to argue
that it owed no duty of care to the plaintiffs. (The Court of Appeal in *Dutton v
Bognor Regis UDC* [1972] 1 QB 373; [1972] 1 All ER 462 had previously decided that
a council could be liable if there had been negligent approval of foundations.) It is
important to realise that – without at this stage going into detail, as to which see
p. 475, post – in *Murphy v Brentwood District Council* [1990] 2 All ER 908; [1990]
3 WLR 414 (pp. 212 and 466, post) the House of Lords basically overturned the ruling in *Anns* concerning the duty of care which it was held in that case that a local
authority owed in respect of defects in and damage to the building itself; however,
they left open whether there might be a duty of care on the part of a local authority
in respect of physical injury to a person or other property. *Anns* was referred to in
the context of omissions p. 65, ante. This extract also covers the related question of
liability in the tort of negligence when the defendant is exercising a statutory power
or duty, something that does not as a general matter appear to have been affected
by *Murphy*.

LORD WILBERFORCE [having earlier stated that the factual relationship between the Council and owners and occupiers of new dwellings constructed in their area must be considered in the relevant statutory setting under which the Council acts]: ...
To summarise the statutory position. The Public Health Act 1936, in particular Part II[1], was enacted in order to provide for the health and safety of owners and occupiers of buildings, including dwelling-houses, by, inter alia, setting standards to be complied with in construction, and by enabling local authorities, through building byelaws[2], to supervise and control the operations of builders. One of the particular matters within the area of local authority supervision is the foundations of buildings, clearly a matter of vital importance, particularly because this part of the building comes to be covered up as building proceeds. Thus any weakness or inadequacy will create a hidden defect which whoever acquires the building has no means of discovering: in legal parlance there is no opportunity for intermediate inspection. So, by the byelaws, a definite standard is set for foundation work ... ; the builder is under a statutory (sc byelaw) duty to notify the local authority before covering up the foundations; the local authority has at this stage the right to inspect and to insist on any correction necessary to bring the work into conformity with the byelaws. It must be in the reasonable contemplation not only of the builder but also of the local authority that failure to comply with the byelaws' requirement as to foundations may give rise to a hidden defect which in the future may cause damage to the building affecting the safety and health of owners and occupiers. And as the building is intended to last, the class of owners and occupiers likely to be affected cannot be limited to those who go in immediately after construction.

What then is the extent of the local authority's duty towards these persons? ... I do not think that a description of the council's duty can be based on the 'neighbourhood' principle alone or on merely any such factual relationship as 'control' as suggested by the Court of Appeal[3]. So to base it would be to neglect an essential factor which is that the local authority is a public body, discharging functions under statute: its powers and duties are definable in terms of public not private law. The problem which this type of action creates, is to define the circumstances in which the law should impose, over and above, or perhaps alongside, these public law powers and duties, a duty in private law towards individuals such that they may sue for damages in a civil court. It is in this context that the distinction sought to be drawn between duties and mere powers has to be examined.

Most, indeed probably all, statutes relating to public authorities or public bodies, contain in them a large area of policy. The courts call this 'discretion', meaning that the decision is one for the authority or body to make, and not for the courts. Many statutes, also, prescribe or at least presuppose the practical execution of policy decisions: a convenient description of this is to say that in addition to the area of policy or discretion, there is an operational area. Although this distinction between the policy area and the operational area is convenient, and illuminating, it is probably a distinction of degree; many 'operational' powers or duties have in them some element of 'discretion'. It can safely be said that the more 'operational' a power or duty may be, the easier it is to superimpose on it a common law duty of care.

I do not think that it is right to limit this to a duty to avoid causing extra or additional damage beyond what must be expected to arise from the exercise of the power or duty. That may be correct when the act done under the statute *inherently* must

---

1. [See now the Building Act 1984, noted p. 478, post.]
2. Since 1965 building work has been subject to building regulations made by the Minister ... and local authorities no longer have the power to make building byelaws. [See now the Building Act 1984. Byelaw 18(1)(b) required foundations to be of such a depth or design and construction as to safeguard against damage by the subsoil shrinking or swelling.]
3. [In *Dutton v Bognor Regis UDC* [1972] 1 QB 373; [1972] 1 All ER 462.]

adversely *affect* the interest of individuals. But many other acts can be done without causing any harm to anyone — indeed may be directed to preventing harm from occurring. In these cases the duty is the normal one of taking care to avoid harm to those likely to be affected.

Let us examine the Public Health Act 1936 in the light of this. Undoubtedly it lays out a wide area of policy. It is for the local authority, a public and elected body, to decide on the scale of resources which it can make available in order to carry out its functions under Part II of the Act — how many inspectors, with what expert qualifications, it should recruit, how often inspections are to be made, what tests are to be carried out, must be for its decision. It is no accident that the Act is drafted in terms of functions and powers rather than in terms of positive duty. As was well said, public authorities have to strike a balance between the claims of efficiency and thrift (du Parcq LJ in *Kent and Porter v East Suffolk Rivers Catchment Board*[1]): whether they get the balance right can only be decided through the ballot box, not in the courts. It is said, there are reflections of this in the judgments in *Dutton's* case[2], that the local authority is under no duty to inspect, and this is used as the foundation for an argument, also found in some of the cases, that if it need not inspect at all, it cannot be liable for negligent inspection: if it were to be held so liable, so it is said, councils would simply decide against inspections. I think that this is too crude an argument. It overlooks the fact that local authorities are public bodies operating under statute with a clear responsibility for public health in their area. They must, and in fact do, make their discretionary decisions responsibly and for reasons which accord with the statutory purpose; cf *Ayr Harbour Trustees v Oswald*[3], per Lord Watson:

'. . . the powers which [s. 10] confers are discretionary . . . But it is the plain import of the clause that the harbour trustees . . . shall be vested with, and shall avail themselves of, these discretionary powers, whenever and as often as they may be of opinion that the public interest will be promoted by their exercise.'

If they do not exercise their discretion in this way they can be challenged in the courts. Thus, to say that councils are under no duty to inspect, is not a sufficient statement of the position. They are under a duty to give proper consideration to the question whether they should inspect or not. Their immunity from attack, in the event of failure to inspect, in other words, though great is not absolute. And because it is not absolute, the necessary premise for the proposition 'if no duty to inspect, then no duty to take care in inspection' vanishes.

Passing then to the duty as regards inspection, if made. On principle there must surely be a duty to exercise reasonable care. The standard of care must be related to the duty to be performed, namely to ensure compliance with the byelaws. It must be related to the fact that the person responsible for construction in accordance with the byelaws is the builder, and that the inspector's function is supervisory. It must be related to the fact that once the inspector has passed the foundations they will be covered up, with no subsequent opportunity for inspection. But this duty, heavily operational though it may be, is still a duty arising under the statute. There may be a discretionary element in its exercise, discretionary as to the time and manner of inspection, and the techniques to be used. A plaintiff complaining of negligence must prove, the burden being on him, that action taken was not within the limits of a discretion bona fide exercised, before he can begin to rely on a common law duty of care. But if he can do this, he should, in principle, be able to sue.

Is there, then, authority against the existence of any such duty or any reason to restrict it? It is said that there is an absolute distinction in the law between statutory

---

1. [1940] 1 KB 319 at 338; [1939] 4 All ER 174 at 184.
2. [1972] 1 QB 373; [1972] 1 All ER 462.
3. (1883) 8 App Cas 623 at 639.

duty and statutory power – the former giving rise to possible liability, the latter not; or at least not doing so unless the exercise of the power involves some positive act creating some fresh or additional damage.

My Lords, I do not believe that any such absolute rule exists: or perhaps, more accurately, that such rules as exist in relation to powers and duties existing under particular statutes, provide sufficient definition of the rights of individuals affected by their exercise, or indeed their non-exercise, unless they take account of the possibility that, parallel with public law duties there may coexist those duties which persons, private or public, are under at common law to avoid causing damage to others in sufficient proximity to them. This is, I think, the key to understanding of the main authority relied on by the council, *East Suffolk Rivers Catchment Board v Kent*[1].

The statutory provisions in that case were contained in the Land Drainage Act 1930 and were in the form of a power to repair drainage works including walls or banks. The facts are well known. There was a very high tide which burst the banks protecting the respondent's land. The catchment board, requested to take action, did so with an allocation of manpower and resources (graphically described by MacKinnon LJ) which was hopelessly inadequate and which resulted in the respondent's land being flooded for much longer than it need have been. There was a considerable difference of judicial opinion. Hilbery J[2] who tried the case held the board liable for the damage caused by the extended flooding and his decision was upheld by a majority of the Court of Appeal[3]. This House, by majority of four to one reached the opposite conclusion. The speeches of their Lordships contain discussion of earlier authorities, which well illustrate the different types of statutory enactment under which these cases may arise. There are private Acts conferring powers, necessarily, to interfere with the rights of individuals: in such cases, an action in respect of damage caused by the exercise of the powers generally does not lie, but it may do so 'for doing that which the legislature has authorised, if it be done negligently' (*Geddis v Bann Reservoir Proprietors*[4], per Lord Blackburn). Then there are cases where a statutory power is conferred, but the scale on which it is exercised is left to a local authority, *Sheppard v Glossop Corpn*[5]. That concerned a power to light streets and the corporation decided, for economy reasons, to extinguish the lighting on Christmas night. Clearly this was within the discretion of the authority but Scrutton LJ[6] in the Court of Appeal contrasted this situation with one where 'an option is given by statute to an authority to do or not to do a thing and it elects to do the thing and does it negligently'. (Compare *Indian Towing Co v United States*[7], which makes just this distinction between a discretion to provide a lighthouse, and at operational level, a duty, if one is provided, to use due care to keep the light in working order.) Other illustrations are given.

My Lords, a number of reasons were suggested for distinguishing the *East Suffolk* case[1], apart from the relevant fact that it was concerned with a different Act, indeed type of Act. It was said to be a division on causation: I think that this is true of at least two of their Lordships (Viscount Simon LC and Lord Thankerton). It was said that the damage was already there before the board came on the scene. So it was, but the board's action or inaction undoubtedly prolonged it, and the action was in respect of the prolongation. I should not think it right to put the case aside on such arguments. To me the two significant points about the case are, first, that it is an

---

1. [1941] AC 74; [1940] 4 All ER 527.
2. [1939] 2 All ER 207.
3. [1940] 1 KB 319; [1939] 4 All ER 174.
4. (1878) 3 App Cas 430 at 455, 456.
5. [1921] 3 KB 132; [1921] All ER Rep 61.
6. [1921] 3 KB 132 at 145, 146; [1921] All ER Rep 61 at 68.
7. 350 US 61 (1955).

example, and a good one, where operational activity, at the breach in the wall, was still well within a discretionary area, so that the plaintiff's task in contending for a duty of care was a difficult one. This is clearly the basis on which Lord Romer, whose speech is often quoted as a proposition of law, proceeded. Secondly, although the case was decided in 1940, only one of their Lordships considered it in relation to a duty of care at common law. It need cause no surprise that this was Lord Atkin. His speech starts with this passage[1]:

'On the first point [sc whether there was a duty owed to the plaintiffs and what was its nature], I cannot help thinking that the argument did not sufficiently distinguish between two kinds of duties — (i) a statutory duty to do or abstain from doing something, and (ii) a common law duty to conduct yourself with reasonable care so as not to injure persons liable to be affected by your conduct.'

And later he refers to *Donoghue v Stevenson*[2], the only one of their Lordships to do so, though I think it fair to say that Lord Thankerton (who decided the case on causation) in his formulation of the duty must have been thinking in terms of that case. My Lords, I believe that the conception of a general duty of care, not limited to particular accepted situations, but extending generally over all relations of suffient proximity, and even pervading the sphere of statutory functions of public bodies, had not at that time become fully recognised. Indeed it may well be that full recognition of the impact of *Donoghue v Stevenson*[2] in the latter sphere only came with the decision of this House in *Home Office v Dorset Yacht Co Ltd*[3].

In that case the borstal officers, for whose actions the Home Office was vicariously responsible, were acting, in their control of the boys, under statutory powers. But it was held that, nevertheless they were under a duty of care as regards persons who might suffer damage as the result of their carelessness: see per Lord Reid[4], Lord Morris of Borth-y-Gest[5], Lord Pearson[6] ('The existence of the statutory duties does not exclude liability at common law for negligence in the performance of the statutory duties'.) Lord Diplock[7] in his speech gives this topic extended consideration with a view to relating the officers' responsibility under public law to their liability in damages to members of the public under private, civil law. My noble and learned friend points out that the accepted principles which are applicable to powers conferred by a private Act of Parliament, as laid down in *Geddis v Bann Reservoir Proprietors*[8], cannot automatically be applied to public statutes which confer a large measure of discretion on public authorities. As regards the latter, for a civil action based on negligence at common law to succeed, there must be acts or omissions taken outside the limits of the delegated discretion; in such a case 'its actionability falls to be determined by the civil law principles of negligence[9]'.

It is for this reason that the law, as stated in some of the speeches in the *East Suffolk* case[10], but not in those of Lord Atkin or Lord Thankerton, requires at the present time to be understood and applied with the recognition that, quite apart from such consequences as may flow from an examination of the duties laid down by the particular statute, there may be room, once one is outside the area of legitimate

---

1. [1941] AC 74 at 88; [1940] 4 All ER 527 at 533.
2. [1932] AC 562; [1932] All ER Rep 1.
3. [1970] AC 1004; [1970] 2 All ER 294 [though see now pp. 40–65, ante].
4. [1970] AC 1004 at 1030; [1970] 2 All ER 294 at 300.
5. [1970] AC 1004 at 1036; [1970] 2 All ER 294 at 305.
6. [1970] AC 1004 at 1055; [1970] 2 All ER 294 at 322.
7. [1970] AC 1004 at 1064 et seq; [1970] 2 All ER 294 at 329 et seq.
8. (1878) 3 App Cas 430.
9. [1970] AC 1004 at 1068; [1970] 2 All ER 294 at 332.
10. [1941] AC 74; [1940] 4 All ER 527.

discretion or policy, for a duty of care at common law. It is irrelevant to the existence of this duty of care whether what is created by the statute is a duty or a power: the duty of care may exist in either case. The difference between the two lies in this, that, in the case of a power, liability cannot exist unless the act complained of lies outside the ambit of the power. In *Home Office v Dorset Yacht Co Ltd*[1] the officers may (on the assumed facts) have acted outside any discretion delegated to them and having disregarded their instructions as to the precautions which they should take to prevent the trainees from escaping (see per Lord Diplock[2]). So in the present case, the allegations made are consistent with the council or its inspector having acted outside any delegated discretion either as to the making of an inspection, or as to the manner in which an inspection was made. Whether they did so must be determined at the trial. In the event of a positive determination, and only so, can a duty of care arise. . . .

To whom the duty is owed. There is, in my opinion, no difficulty about this. A reasonable man in the position of the inspector must realise that if the foundations are covered in without adequate depth or strength as required by the byelaws, injury to safety or health may be suffered by owners or occupiers of the house. The duty is owed to them, not of course to a negligent building owner, the source of his own loss. I would leave open the case of users, who might themselves have a remedy against the occupier under the Occupiers' Liability Act 1957. A right of action can only be conferred on an owner or occupier, who is such when the damage occurs . . . This disposes of the possible objection that an endless, indeterminate class of potential plaintiffs may be called into existence.

The nature of the duty. This must be related closely to the purpose for which powers of inspection are granted, namely to secure compliance with the byelaws. The duty is to take reasonable care, no more, no less, to secure that the builder does not cover in foundations which do not comply with byelaw requirements. . . .

Nature of the damages recoverable and arising out of the cause of action. There are many questions here which do not directly arise at this stage and which may never arise if the actions are tried. . . . The damages recoverable include all those which foreseeably arise from [any] breach of the duty of care which, as regards the council, I have held to be a duty to take reasonable care to secure compliance with the byelaws. Subject always to adequate proof of causation, these damages may include damages for personal injury and damage to property. . . .

[LORD DIPLOCK, LORD SIMON OF GLAISDALE and LORD RUSSELL OF KILLOWEN agreed with LORD WILBERFORCE's speech. LORD SALMON delivered a speech in favour of dismissing the appeal.]

Questions

1. In what sense or senses did Lord Wilberforce use the term 'discretion' in *Anns*? (See M. Aronson and H. Whitmore, *Public Torts and Contracts* (Sydney, 1982), pp. 69–73; S. H. Bailey and M. J. Bowman [1986] CLJ 430 at 437–439.)

2. Why are public authorities put in a special position as regards a negligence action?

3. Should public authorities be in this special position? (Consider C. Harlow (1980) 43 MLR 241 but see P.P. Craig, *Administrative Law* 2nd edn

---

1. [1970] AC 1004; [1970] 2 All ER 294.
2. [1970] AC 1004 at 1069; [1970] 2 All ER 294 at 333.

(London, 1989), pp. 450–452; R. A. Buckley, *The Modern Law of Negligence* (London, 1988), para. 12–09. See further *The Economic Approach to Law*, edited by P. Burrows and C. G. Veljanovski (London, 1981), pp. 183–184.)

Notes

1. These cases are obviously of great importance in relation to the problems posed by actions for damages against public bodies and detailed treatment of this subject and of the concept of ultra vires must be left to administrative law courses. In addition to the standard textbooks on administrative law, see Aronson and Whitmore, op cit, chap. 2. For further discussion of *Anns*, and especially the relationship between negligence and ultra vires activity or inactivity, see P. P. Craig (1978) 94 LQR 428 (a more extended but less up-to-date treatment than can be found in Craig, *Administrative Law* 2nd edn, pp. 448–458). For further appraisal of *Anns*, see e.g. M. J. Bowman and S. H. Bailey [1984] PL 277; Bailey and Bowman, op cit.

2. *Anns* suggests that there can be liability in the tort of negligence when the defendant performs a statutory duty as well as when he exercises a statutory power. See also *Home Office v Dorset Yacht Co Ltd* [1970] AC 1004 at 1055 where Lord Pearson stated that the existence of statutory duties, which in that case were owed to the Crown, 'does not exclude liability at common law for negligence in the performance of the statutory duties'. Cf. *Haydon v Kent County Council* [1978] QB 343; [1978] 2 All ER 97, on which see Beatson and Matthews, op cit, p. 579.

3. Craig (1978) 94 LQR at p. 440, note 60 is critical of the way in which Lord Wilberforce distinguished the rather difficult case of *East Suffolk Rivers Catchment Board v Kent* [1941] AC 74; [1940] 4 All ER 527. In particular he defines the second distinguishing feature as being that 'the House of Lords in the *East Suffolk* case were not accustomed to the idea that a duty of care extended to all relations involving proximity, including public bodies performing under statutory powers,' and continues:

'This is, with respect open to criticism. Du Parcq LJ in the Court of Appeal and Lord Porter and Lord Romer in the House of Lords were aware of the nineteenth-century cases concerning the imposition of a common law duty of care. In fact their judgments proceed on the hypothesis that such a duty did exist; it is the scope of that duty that concerned them. Liability was restricted to the creation of new damage because of the fear that the courts would otherwise be forced to adjudicate on policy decisions whether a policy determination was involved or not. If the dichotomy between policy and operation had been utilised by the House of Lords in 1940 they would have avoided the problem.'

(For the background to the *East Suffolk* case, see Bowman and Bailey, op cit, pp. 296–299.) It was confirmed in *Fellowes v Rother District Council* [1983] 1 All ER 513 that fresh damage need not be proved in a case based on an alleged negligent exercise of a statutory power, and, despite what was said in *Murphy v Brentwood District Council* [1990] 2 All ER 908; [1990] 3 WLR 414 (pp. 212 and 466, post) about *Anns*, it is submitted that this point is unaffected.

4. In *Curran v Northern Ireland Co-ownership Housing Association Ltd* [1987] AC 718; [1987] 2 All ER 13 the plaintiffs alleged that an extension to a house they had bought was so defective that it needed complete rebuilding. The extension had been built by their predecessor in title with an improvement grant from the Northern Ireland Housing Executive paid under the Housing (Northern Ireland) Order 1976, and the question for the House of Lords on the preliminary issue of law raised in the appeal was whether the Housing Executive could be liable. Lord Bridge, delivering their Lordships' judgment, took a cautious approach to *Anns* and, on the basis of considerations partly set out at p. 56, ante, was 'wary' of any extension of *Anns* to create a duty of care in exercising statutory power to supervise third parties so as to protect people who might otherwise be adversely affected by their activities. In relation to the decision in *Anns*, attention must now, of course, be paid to *Murphy v Brentwood District Council* [1990] 2 All ER 908; [1990] 3 WLR 414 (p. 212, post) in which *Anns* was overruled. However, some attention might still be paid to *Curran*, in which three aspects of the ratio in *Anns* were identified:(i) the statutory power must be directed to protecting the public (or the part to which the plaintiff belongs) from the danger which has manifested itself; (ii) the danger must have been potentially remediable by the proper exercise of the power; and (iii) the fact that the power is not exercised or is exercised negligently must have created a hidden defect not discoverable or remediable before the onset of the damage. In *Curran* a duty of care was rejected. There was no power of control once an application was granted other than the power to withhold the grant (or an instalment of it) if work was not done to the Executive's satisfaction. Any duty imposed by the Order concerning the proper execution of the work was for the purpose of protecting the public purse not the recipients of the grant or their successors.

Consider further *Yuen Kun Yeu v A-G of Hong Kong* [1988] AC 175; [1987] 2 All ER 705, noted p. 187, post and see the reference there to the legislative change that has taken place in Hong Kong. (As *Yuen Kun Yeu* shows, the fact that one of the purposes of a statutory power is the protection of the group to which the plaintiff belongs does not necessarily mean that there will be a duty of care.) Note also *Minories Finance Ltd v Arthur Young (a firm) (Bank of England, third party)* [1989] 2 All ER 105, noted p. 188, post, and see *Davis v Radcliffe* [1990] 2 All ER 536; [1990] 1 WLR 821, noted p. 188, post. In this last-mentioned case it was pointed out (at p. 541) that the emphasis on the broader public interest which is involved in the characteristic task of modern regulatory agencies 'militates strongly against the imposition of a duty of care being imposed on such an agency in favour of any particular section of the public'. For discussion of the liability of regulatory bodies, see H. McLean (1988) 8 Oxf JLS 442.

5. The fact that a statutory power is involved in a case may influence the scope of the duty of care. It might lead to its restriction or militate against its existence altogether (see the *Minories Finance* case), but it might, on the other hand, increase the liability to which a defendant would otherwise be subject: see P. Cane (1988) 52 MLR 200 at 208, note 28 (although his example would need to be changed today in the light of *Murphy v Brentwood District Council* [1990] 2 All ER 908; [1990] 3 WLR 414, p. 212, post).

Rowling v Takaro Properties Ltd Judicial Committee of the Privy Council [1988] 1 All ER 163

The Minister of Finance in New Zealand refused consent to the issue of shares in Takaro to an overseas company. Such consent was required by a statutory regulation but, when challenged in the courts, the refusal was held to have been ultra vires on the ground that an irrelevant factor had been taken into account ([1975] 2 NZLR 62). The issue of the shares was part of a financial rescue scheme for Takaro and the delay caused by the legal proceedings to challenge the refusal of consent contributed in part to the main sponsors of the scheme pulling out of it.

When an action claiming damages for negligence was brought against the Minister, Quilliam J, [1986] 1 NZLR 22 decided there was a duty of care in relation to the exercise of power under the relevant statutory provision, but that there had been no breach. The New Zealand Court of Appeal found both duty and breach, but on appeal the Judicial Committee of the Privy Council decided that there had been no negligence. This extract from the Privy Council's opinion concerns the question of the duty of care.

LORD KEITH OF KINKEL (delivering the judgment of the Board): . . . For reasons which will appear, their Lordships do not find it necessary to reach any final conclusion on the question of the existence, or (if it exists) the scope, of the duty of care resting on a minister in a case such as the present; and they have come to the conclusion that it would not be right for them to do so, because the matter was not fully exposed before them in argument. In particular, no reference was made in argument to the extensive academic literature on the subject of the liability of public authorities in negligence, study of which can be of such great assistance to the courts in considering areas of the law which, as in the case of negligence, are in a continuing state of development. Even so, such is the importance of the present case, especially in New Zealand, that their Lordships feel that it would be inappropriate, and perhaps be felt to be discourteous, if they were to make no reference to the relevant considerations affecting the decision whether a duty of care should arise in a case such as the present.

Quilliam J considered the question with particular reference to the distinction between policy (or planning) decisions and operational decisions. His conclusion was expressed as follows ([1986] 1 NZLR 22 at 35):

'The distinction between the policy and the operational areas can be both fine and confusing. Various expressions have been used instead of operational, e.g, "administrative" or "business powers". It may not be easy to attach any of these labels to the decision of the Minister in this case, but what appears to me to emerge clearly enough is that for the reasons I have indicated his decision was the antithesis of policy or discretion. I therefore equate it with having been operational. The result of that conclusion is that I consider the prima facie existence of a duty of care has been established.'

Their Lordships feel considerable sympathy with Quilliam J's difficulty in solving the problem by simple reference to this distinction. They are well aware of the references in the literature to this distinction (which appears to have originated in the United States of America) and of the critical analysis to which it has been subjected. They incline to the opinion, expressed in the literature, that this distinction does not provide a touchstone of liability, but rather is expressive of the need to exclude altogether those cases in which the decision under attack is of such a kind that a question whether it has been made negligently is unsuitable for judicial resolution, of which notable examples are discretionary decisions on the allocation of scarce resources or the distribution of risks (see especially the discussion in Craig *Administrative Law*

(1983) pp. 534–538). If this is right, classification of the relevant decision as a policy or planning decision in this sense may exclude liability; but a conclusion that it does not fall within that category does not, in their Lordships' opinion, mean that a duty of care will necessarily exist.

It is at this stage that it is necessary, before concluding that a duty of care should be imposed, to consider all the relevant circumstances. One of the considerations underlying certain recent decisions of the House of Lords (*Governors of the Peabody Donation Fund v Sir Lindsay Parkinson & Co Ltd* [1984] 3 All ER 529, [1985] AC 210) and of the Privy Council (*Yuen Kun-yeu v A-G of Hong Kong* [1987] 2 All ER 705, [1987] 3 WLR 776) is the fear that a too literal application of the well-known observation of Lord Wilberforce in *Anns v Merton London Borough* [1977] 2 All ER 492 at 498, [1978] AC 728 at 751–752 may be productive of a failure to have regard to, and to analyse and weigh, all the relevant considerations in considering whether it is appropriate that a duty of care should be imposed. Their Lordships consider that question to be of an intensely pragmatic character, well suited for gradual development but requiring most careful analysis. It is one on which all common law jurisdictions can learn much from each other, because, apart from exceptional cases, no sensible distinction can be drawn in this respect between the various countries and the social conditions existing in them. It is incumbent on the courts in different jurisdictions to be sensitive to each other's reactions; but what they are all searching for in others, and each of them is striving to achieve, is a careful analysis and weighing of the relevant competing considerations.

It is in this spirit that a case such as the present has, in their Lordships' opinion, to be approached. They recognise that the decision of the minister is capable of being described as having been of a policy rather than an operational character; but, if the function of the policy/operational dichotomy is as they have already described it, the allegation of negligence in the present case is not, they consider, of itself of such a character as to render the case unsuitable for judicial decision. Be that as it may, there are certain considerations which militate against imposition of liability in a case such as the present.

Their Lordships wish to refer in particular to certain matters which they consider to be of importance. The first is that the only effect of a negligent decision, such as is here alleged to have been made, is delay. This is because the processes of judicial review are available to the aggrieved party; and, assuming that the alleged error of law is so serious that it can properly be described as negligent, the decision will assuredly be quashed by a process which, in New Zealand as in the United Kingdom, will normally be carried out with promptitude.

The second is that, in the nature of things, it is likely to be very rare indeed that an error of law of this kind by a minister or other public authority can properly be categorised as negligent. As is well known, anybody, even a judge, can be capable of misconstruing a statute; and such misconstruction, when it occurs, can be severely criticised without attracting the epithet 'negligent'. Obviously, this simple fact points rather to the extreme unlikelihood of a breach of duty being established in these cases . . .; but it is nevertheless a relevant factor to be taken into account when considering whether liability in negligence should properly be imposed.

The third is the danger of overkill. It is to be hoped that, as a general rule, imposition of liability in negligence will lead to a higher standard of care in the performance of the relevant type of act; but sometimes not only may this not be so, but the imposition of liability may even lead to harmful consequences. In other words, the cure may be worse than the disease. There are reasons for believing that this may be so in cases where liability is imposed on local authorities whose building inspectors have been negligent in relation to the inspection of foundations, as in the *Anns* case itself, because there is a danger that the building inspectors of some local authorities may react to that decision by simply increasing, unnecessarily, the requisite depth of foundations, thereby imposing a very substantial and unnecessary financial burden on members of the community.[1] A comparable danger may exist in cases such as the present, because, once it became known that liability in negligence may be imposed on the ground that a minister has misconstrued a statute and so acted ultra vires, the cautious civil servant may go to extreme lengths in ensuring that legal advice, or even the opinion of the court, is obtained before decisions are taken, thereby leading to unnecessary delay in a considerable number of cases.

Fourth, it is very difficult to identify any particular case in which it can properly be said that a minister is under a duty to seek legal advice. It cannot, their Lordships consider, reasonably be said that a minister is under a duty to seek legal advice in every case in which he is called on to exercise a discretionary power conferred on him by legislation; and their Lordships find it difficult to see how cases in which a duty to seek legal advice should be imposed should be segregated from those in which it should not. In any event, the officers of the relevant department will be involved; the matter will be processed and presented to the minister for decision in the usual way, and by this means his mind will be focused on the relevant issue. Again, it is not to be forgotten that the minister, in exercising his statutory discretion, is acting essentially as a guardian of the public interest; in the present case, for example, he was acting under legislation enacted not for the benefit of applicants for consent to share issues but for the protection of the community as a whole. Furthermore, he is, so far as their Lordships are aware, normally under no duty to exercise his discretion within any particular time; and if, through a mistaken construction of the statute, he acts ultra vires and delay thereby occurs before he makes an intra vires decision, he will have in any event to exercise his discretion anew and, if his discretion is then exercised in the plaintiff's favour, the effect of the delay will only be to postpone the receipt by the plaintiff of a benefit which he had no absolute right to receive.

No doubt there may be possible answers to some of these points, taken individually. But, if the matter is looked at as a whole, it cannot be said to be free from difficulty. Indeed their Lordships share the opinion expressed by Richmond P in *Takaro Properties Ltd v Rowling* [1978] 2 NZLR 314 at 318 that the whole subject is of the greatest importance and difficulty, as is well demonstrated by the valuable, though understandably inconclusive, discussions of the problem by Woodhouse and Richardson JJ in the same case. Doubtless it was considerations such as those to which their Lordships have already referred that led Lord Diplock in *Dunlop v Woollahra Municipal Council* [1981] I All ER 1202 at 1209, [1982] AC 158 at 171 to express doubts whether a duty of care can exist in such circumstances. In particular, it is being suggested that liability in negligence should be imposed in cases such as the present, when the effect of any such imposition of liability will on the one hand lead to recovery only in very rare cases and then only for the consequences of delay, which should not be long, and may, on the other hand, lead to considerable delay occurring in a greater number of cases, for which there can be no redress. In all the circumstances, it must be a serious question for consideration whether it would be appropriate to impose liability in negligence in these cases, or whether it would not rather be in the public interest that citizens should be confined to their remedy, as at present, in those cases where the minister or public authority has acted in bad faith.

Their Lordships do not think it would be right for them to answer that question in the present case; indeed they must not be thought to be expressing any opinion on the point. This is partly because, as they have said, the matter was not fully exposed in argument. But in any event they are very conscious of the fact, already referred to, that, in the great majority of cases where it is alleged that there has been negligence in the construction of a statute, it is likely to prove that the error cannot

---

1. [See now *Murphy v Brentwood District Council* [1990] 2 All ER 908; [1990] 3 WLR 414 (pp. 212 and 466, post).]

be described as negligent; and they have come to the conclusion that, on the findings of fact of Quilliam J, the present is quite simply a typical example of such a case. They will therefore leave the question of the duty of care. . . .

Question

It was argued by B. A. Hepple All ER Rev 1987 p. 287 that the reinterpretation of *Anns* in *Curran v Northern Ireland Co-Ownership Housing Association Ltd* [1987] AC 718; [1987] 2 All ER 13, noted p. 106, ante (where the overruling of *Anns* was referred to), 'all but abandons Lord Wilberforce's much-criticised and "difficult dichotomy" between an exercise of statutory powers which is a matter of policy or discretion and an exercise of powers which is "operational" in favour of the critical test whether the exercise of the powers enables the authority to control the acts of third parties.' Does the dichotomy find more favour in *Takaro*? Do you agree with Woolf, *Protection of the Public–A New Challenge* (London, 1990), p. 60 that Lord Keith's opinion in *Takaro* 'strongly suggests that the distinction that Lord Wilberforce drew in *Anns v Merton*, between policy or planning decisions and operational decisions is likely to be consigned to the same fate as the test Lord Wilberforce laid down in the same case for ascertaining whether a duty of care exists'?

Notes

1. The distinction drawn in *Anns*, and referred to in *Takaro*, between operational and policy or discretionary areas had previously been found in cases in the United States, on which see Craig (1978) 94 LQR at pp. 442–447. It has, not surprisingly, also arisen in the English case law since *Anns* and a few examples of classification might usefully be set out.

In *Bird v Pearce* [1978] RTR 290 a highway authority had, in the course of road re-surfacing, obliterated some double dotted white lines on the minor road at a crossing; the white lines were not replaced until some days after an accident had occurred at the crossing and no temporary warning sign had been in position in the meantime. Wood J classified the re-surfacing work as something done at the operational level. He also referred to the highway authority's traffic system and to its decision to maintain that system (which involved warning users of the minor roads to give way) in that the system was reinstated once the re-surfacing was completed; the authority had 'exercised a discretion as to the siting, type and existence of the necessary road signs at this particular road junction' ([1978] RTR at p. 298). Wood J then applied normal negligence principles in relation to the authority. It had been argued by counsel for the authority that the decision not to put up a warning sign was a policy decision, but this seems to have been overridden by Wood J by virtue of the classification he adopted. On appeal ([1979] RTR 369) the Court of Appeal did not specifically mention the policy/operational distinction; for discussion of the appeal proceedings, in relation to which commentators have expressed different views, see J. Beatson and M. H. Matthews, *Administrative Law: Cases and Materials* 2nd edn (Oxford, 1989), pp. 581–582.

On the question of the discretionary area, see *Haydon v Kent County Council* [1978] QB 343; [1978] 2 All ER 97 where Goff LJ, for example, regarded the giving of priority to the gritting of roads rather than footpaths in wintry conditions as within that area. Note also *Rigby v Chief Constable of Northamptonshire* [1985] 2 All ER 985; [1985] 1 WLR 1242 — police decision (under a statutory power) not to obtain, or to defer acquisition of, a particular CS gas device to replace the use of CS gas canisters was said to be at the policy level: the decision to use the gas canister would seem to have been at the operational level. For critical comment on the policy/operational distinction, see Bailey and Bowman, op cit (writing before *Takaro*).

2. There has been uncertainty as to whether the need to show ultra vires activity by a public body before it can be liable in the tort of negligence covers the operational as well as the policy or discretionary area. See Beatson and Matthews, op cit, pp. 579–580. If it can cover the former, any unjustified immunity which it might be thought to give to a public body can be met by regarding negligence as constituting excess or abuse of power at this stage (see Craig (1978) 94 LQR 428 at 453–454). Does the passage from *Takaro* ante concerning this distinction suggest that it does not in any event cover this operational area?

3. For the difficulty that might arise where a case falls into the policy area but where the ultra vires hurdle can be surmounted, see Beatson and Matthews, op cit, pp. 580–581.

4. For further consideration of the question of the duty of care owed by public bodies, see, in addition to p. 106, ante, *Jones v Department of Employment* [1989] QB 1; [1988] 1 All ER 725 where an allegation of negligence related to the disallowance by an adjudication officer of the plaintiff's unemployment benefit. Glidewell LJ denied that the officer owed any duty of care, relying on the non-judicial nature of the officer's responsibilities and the statutory framework of appeals. This was discussed by his Lordship under the 'just and reasonable' aspect of duty. The appeal procedure was also important for Slade LJ who thought that it would be contrary to the relevant legislative intent for a common law duty of care to be imposed. If it was appropriate to consider the 'just and reasonable' requirement, then any duty would also be negated in his opinion on this ground, the importance of the right of appeal in this context lying in the remedy it provided for recovery of the unemployment benefit. Glidewell LJ in fact stated (at p. 736), with the approval of the other members of the Court of Appeal, that 'it is a general principle that if a government department or officer, charged with the making of decisions whether certain payments should be made, is subject to a statutory right of appeal against his decisions, he owes no duty of care in private law'. For comment on *Jones*, see W. J. Swadling [1989] PL 328.

Consider also *Mills v Winchester Diocesan Board of Finance* [1989] Ch 428; [1989] 2 All ER 317, noted p. 188, post, where an effective right of appeal was influential in rejecting the alleged duty. It should be noted, however, that the existence of alternative remedies can also militate against the imposition of a duty of care where the defendant is not a public body: see *Pacific Associates Inc v Baxter* [1990] 1 QB 993; [1989] 2 All ER 159, noted p. 210, post.

3 Protected persons

In this chapter attention will be paid to the particular categories of plaintiffs who come within the ambit of the duty of care. The first section confirms the general requirement, already seen in Lord Atkin's 'neighbour principle' in *M'Alister* (or *Donoghue*) *v Stevenson* [1932] AC 562 (p. 43, ante), that the plaintiff be someone to whom injury is reasonably foreseeable, either as an individual or as one of a class.

Plaintiffs who claim to have suffered nervous shock have been treated somewhat warily by the courts; particular concerns in the past have been over the danger of fraudulent claims and of too widespread a liability. The courts may find themselves concerned with difficult questions of medical causation, and the legal and medical professions have not always seen eye to eye on the problems involved in nervous shock cases. (See J. Harvard (1956) 19 MLR 478 and on liability for nervous shock from a medical viewpoint, see further H. Teff (1983) 99 LQR 100.) Doubts have been cast, for example, from the point of view of the medical profession on the number of miscarriages *really* caused by emotional shock — see (1956) 19 MLR at p. 481, note 16. On the other hand, note Lord Bridge's reference in *McLoughlin v O'Brian* [1983] 1 AC 410 at 433 (p. 125, post) to the suspicious attitude on the part of earlier generations of judges towards psychiatry; but, as the rest of that passage shows, attitudes have changed.

The cases this century have revealed a general expansion of the area of liability for nervous shock and one question that arises in this chapter is whether, in *McLoughlin v O'Brian* [1983] 1 AC 410; [1982] 2 All ER 298 (p. 119, post), the law has now reached the position that reasonable foreseeability is both a necessary and a sufficient condition of liability for nervous shock. The damage that is compensated can be some psychiatric illness (and see further p. 127, post) or some physical consequence brought on by the shock (e.g. a heart condition — see *Galt v British Railways Board* (1983) 133 NLJ 870). It is important to note that mere mental distress *on its own* is not compensated in the tort of negligence. See, however, p. 409, post in the context of damages; and if grief as a result of what has happened to a third party means that the plaintiff's injuries have a worse effect, then this is compensatable: *Kralj v McGrath* [1986] 1 All ER 54 at 62. Note further that, by virtue of statute, damages for bereavement can now be obtained by a limited category of people (see p. 241, post). See more generally J. Murdoch (1989) 5 PN 52.

Rescuers are a category of plaintiff who have in general received a sympathetic reception from the courts. Policy might be thought to be at work here in the sense of a desire to encourage the Good Samaritan who is unlikely to encounter much difficulty overcoming the foreseeability hurdle. Problems of medical causation, which have been mentioned in relation to nervous shock cases, do not pose a particular difficulty in relation to rescuers; however, such problems can arise in respect of the final category of plaintiff discussed in this chapter. This is the category of the 'unborn child', the child which is injured before birth and which is later born with a physical or mental defect. As will be seen (p. 144, post), English law had not clearly decided that such a plaintiff could sue in the tort of negligence by the time that legislation came on the scene. The thalidomide tragedy in particular had focused public attention on the plight of those born disabled, and the question of liability for antenatal injuries was referred to the Law Commission in 1972. That body produced a report in 1974 (*Report on Injuries to Unborn Children*, Law Com. No. 60, Cmnd. 5709), and the legislation which was later enacted (the Congenital Disabilities (Civil Liability) Act 1976, p. 142, post) is based on the draft Bill contained in that Report.

1   The foreseeable plaintiff

Hay or Bourhill *v* Young House of Lords [1942] 2 All ER 396

The appellant had just alighted from a tramcar when a motor cyclist, who had ridden past the tramcar, was killed as a result of a collision with a motor car forty-five or fifty feet from where the appellant was standing. The appellant had not seen the motor cyclist and did not see the collision, although she did hear the sound of it. She later saw the blood on the road. The appellant, who was almost eight months pregnant at the time of the accident, claimed damages for nervous shock from the estate of the motor cyclist (John Young) who was found to have been travelling excessively fast. Her action failed before the Lord Ordinary and the Second Division of the Court of Session, and there was an appeal to the House of Lords. The appeal was dealt with on the basis of an amendment to the appellant's pleading which stated that she did not reasonably fear immediate bodily injury to herself.

LORD MACMILLAN: . . . It is no longer necessary to consider whether the infliction of what is called mental shock may constitute an actionable wrong. The crude view that the law should take cognizance only of physical injury resulting from actual impact has been discarded, and it is now well recognised that an action will lie for injury by shock sustained through the medium of the eye or the ear without direct contact. The distinction between mental shock and bodily injury was never a scientific one, for mental shock is presumably in all cases the result of, or at least accompanied by, some physical disturbance in the sufferer's system, and a mental shock may have consequences more serious than those resulting from physical impact. In the case of mental shock, however, there are elements of greater subtlety than in the case of an ordinary physical injury and these elements may give rise to debate as to the precise scope of legal liability.

Your Lordships have here to deal with a common law action founded on negligence. The pursuer's plea is that she has 'sustained loss, injury and damage through the fault of the said John Young,' and that she is 'entitled to reparation therefor out of his estate.' She can recover damages only if she can show that in relation to her the late John Young acted negligently. To establish this she must show that he owed her a duty of care which he failed to observe and that, as a result of this failure in duty on his part, she suffered as she did. . . . The duty to take care is the duty to avoid doing or omitting to do anything the doing or omitting to do which may have as its reasonable and probable consequence injury to others and the duty is owed to those to whom injury may reasonably and probably be anticipated if the duty is not observed.

There is no absolute standard of what is reasonable and probable. It must depend on circumstances and must always be a question of degree. In the present instance the late John Young was clearly negligent in a question with the occupants of the motor car with which his cycle collided. He was driving at an excessive speed in a public thoroughfare and he ought to have foreseen that he might consequently collide with any vehicle which he might meet in his course, for such an occurrence may reasonably and probably be expected to ensue from driving at a high speed in a street. But can it be said that he ought further to have foreseen that his excessive speed, involving the possibility of collision with another vehicle, might cause injury by shock to the pursuer? The pursuer was not within his line of vision, for she was on the other side of a tramway car which was standing between him and her when he passed and it was not until he had proceeded some distance beyond her that he collided with the motor car. The pursuer did not see the accident and she expressly admits that her 'terror did not involve any element of reasonable fear of immediate bodily injury to herself.' She was not so placed that there was any reasonable likelihood of her being affected by the deceased's careless driving.

In these circumstances I am of opinion with the majority of the judges of the second division that the late John Young was under no duty to the pursuer to foresee that his negligence in driving at an excessive speed and consequently colliding with a motor car might result in injury to the pursuer, for such a result could not reasonably and probably be anticipated. He was, therefore, not guilty of negligence in a question with the pursuer. . . .

LORD WRIGHT: My Lords, that damage by mental shock may give a cause of action is now well-established and is not disputed in this case, but as Phillimore J pointed out in his admirable judgment in *Dulieu v White & Sons*,[1] the real difficulty in questions of this kind is to decide whether there has been a wrongful act or breach of duty on the part of the defendant vis-à-vis the plaintiff. That being the prior question, if it is answered against the plaintiff, the matter is concluded. I shall, therefore, consider that issue in the first place. . . .

This general concept of reasonable foresight as the criterion of negligence or breach of duty (strict or otherwise) may be criticised as too vague; but negligence is a fluid principle, which has to be applied to the most diverse conditions and problems of human life. It is a concrete not an abstract idea. It has to be fitted to the facts of the particular case. Willes J defined it as absence of care according to the circumstances (*Vaughan v Taff Vale Rail Co*[2] at 688). It is also always relative to the individual affected. This raises a serious additional difficulty in the cases where it has to be determined not merely whether the act itself is negligent against someone but whether it is negligent vis-à-vis the plaintiff. This is a crucial point in cases of nervous shock. Thus in the present case John Young was certainly negligent in an issue between himself and the owner of the car which he ran into, but it is another question whether he was negligent vis-à-vis the appellant.

In such cases terms like 'derivative' and 'original' and 'primary' and 'secondary' have been applied to define and distinguish the type of the negligence. If, however, the appellant has a cause of action, it is because of a wrong to herself. She cannot build on a wrong to someone else. Her interest, which was in her own bodily security, was of a different order from the interest of the owner of the car. . . .

The present case, like many others of this type, may, however, raise the . . . question whether the appellant's illness was not due to her peculiar susceptibility. She was 8 months gone in pregnancy. Can it be said, apart from everything else, that it was

---

1. [1901] 2 KB 669.
2. (1860) 5 H & N 679.

likely that a person of normal nervous strength would have been affected in the circumstances by illness as the appellant was? Does the criterion or[1] reasonable foresight extend beyond people of ordinary health or susceptibility, or does it take into account the peculiar susceptibilities or infirmities of those affected which the defendant neither knew of nor could reasonably be taken to have foreseen? Must the manner of conduct adapt itself to such special individual peculiarities? If extreme cases are taken, the answer appears to be fairly clear, unless, indeed, there is knowledge of the extraordinary risk. One who suffers from the terrible tendency to bleed on slight contact, which is denoted by the term 'a bleeder,' cannot complain if he mixes with the crowd and suffers severely, perhaps fatally, from being merely brushed against. There is no actionable wrong done there. A blind or deaf man who crosses the traffic on a busy street cannot complain if he is run over by a careful driver who does not know of and could not be expected to observe and guard against the man's infirmity. These questions go to 'culpability, not compensation', as Bankes LJ said in the *Polemis* case,[2] at 571. No doubt it has long ago been stated and often restated that, if the wrong is established, the wrongdoer must take the victim as he finds him. That, however, is only true, as the *Polemis* case[2] shows, on the condition that the wrong has been established or admitted. The question of liability is anterior to the question of the measure of the consequences which go with the liability. . . .

What is now being considered is the question of liability, and this, I think, in a question whether there is a duty owing to members of the public who come within the ambit of the act, must generally depend on a normal standard of susceptibility.

This, it may be said, is somewhat vague. That is true; but definition involves limitation, which it is desirable to avoid further than is necessary in a principle of law like negligence, which is widely ranging and is still in the stage of development. It is here, as elsewhere, a question of what the hypothetical reasonable man, viewing the position, I suppose ex post facto, would say it was proper to foresee. What danger of particular infirmity that would include must depend on all the circumstances; but generally, I think, a reasonably normal condition, if medical evidence is capable of defining it, would be the standard. The test of the plaintiff's extraordinary susceptibility, if unknown to the defendant, would in effect make the defendant an insurer. The lawyer likes to draw fixed and definite lines and is apt to ask where the thing is to stop. I should reply it should stop where in the particular case the good sense of the jury, or of the judge, decides. . . .

However, when I apply the considerations which I have been discussing to the present appeal, I come to the conclusion that the judgment should be affirmed. . . . I cannot accept that John Young could reasonably have foreseen, or, more correctly, the reasonable hypothetical observer could reasonably have foreseen, the likelihood that anyone placed as the appellant was, could be affected in the manner in which she was. In my opinion John Young was guilty of no breach of duty to the appellant and was not in law responsible for the hurt she sustained. I may add that the issue of duty or no duty is indeed a question for the court, but it depends on the view taken of the facts. In the present case both courts below have taken the view that the appellant has, on the facts of the case, no redress and I agree with their view. . . .

LORD PORTER [referring to *Hambrook v Stokes Bros*[3]] . . . It will be observed that . . . all the Lords Justices were careful to point out that the vital problem was the extent of the duty and not the remoteness of damages — a view in which they were supported by the opinions of Kennedy and Phillimore JJ in *Dulieu v White*.[4] With this

---

1. [This word should be 'of' not 'or' — see [1943] AC 92 at 109.]
2. [1921] 3 KB 560.
3. [1925] 1 KB 141.
4. [1901] 2 KB 669.

view I agree, and ask myself whether the defenders in the present case owed any duty to the pursuer.

In the case of a civil action there is no such thing as negligence in the abstract: there must be neglect of the use of care towards a person towards whom the defendant owes the duty of observing care. And I am content to take the statement of Lord Atkin in *M'Alister* (or *Donoghue*) *v Stevenson*[1] at 580, as indicating the extent of the duty:

'You must take reasonable care to avoid acts and omissions which you can reasonably foresee would be likely to injure your neighbour. Who, then, in law is my neighbour? The answer seems to be — persons who are so closely and directly affected by my act that I ought reasonably to have them in contemplation as being so affected when I am directing my mind to the acts or omissions which are called in question.'

Is the result of this view that all persons in or near the street down which the negligent driver is progressing are potential victims of his negligence? Though from their position it is quite impossible that any injury should happen to them and though they have no relatives or even friends who might be endangered, is a duty of care to them owed and broken because they might have been but were not in a spot exposed to the errant driving of the peccant car? I cannot think so. The duty is not to the world at large. It must be tested by asking with reference to each several complainant was a duty owed to him or her. If no one of them was in such a position that direct physical injury could reasonably be anticipated to them or their relations or friends, normally I think no duty would be owed: and, if in addition no shock was reasonably to be anticipated to them as a result of the defender's negligence, the defender might, indeed, be guilty of actionable negligence to others but not of negligence towards them.

In the present case the defender was never herself in any bodily danger nor reasonably in fear of danger either for herself or others. She was merely a person who as a result of the action was emotionally disturbed and rendered physically ill by that emotional disturbance. The question whether emotional disturbance or shock, which a defender ought reasonably to have anticipated as likely to follow from his reckless driving, can ever form the basis of a claim is not in issue. It is not every emotional disturbance or every shock which should have been foreseen. The driver of a car or vehicle even though careless is entitled to assume that the ordinary frequenter of the streets has sufficient fortitude to endure such incidents as may from time to time be expected to occur in them, including the noise of a collision and the sight of injury to others, and is not to be considered negligent towards one who does not possess the customary phlegm. . . .

In order . . . to establish a duty towards herself, the pursuer must show that the cyclist should reasonably have foreseen emotional injury to her as a result of his negligent driving, and . . . I do not think she has done so. . . .

[LORD THANKERTON and LORD RUSSELL OF KILLOWEN delivered speeches in favour of dismissing the appeal.]

Appeal dismissed

Question

Suppose a man attacks and injures his wife as a result of mental disturbance which in turn is a result of a negligent act for which the defendant is responsible. Should the wife's claim for damages in negligence against the defendant

---

1. [1932] AC 562.

be rejected on the ground that she is building on a wrong to another? (Consider *Marx v A-G* [1974] 1 NZLR 164, but note the criticism by W. Binchy (1975) 38 MLR 468.)

Notes

1. The question of liability for nervous shock will be considered in the next section and, as an authority on nervous shock, *Bourhill v Young* must be viewed in the light of the materials there (esp. p. 119, post).

2. The requirement that the plaintiff be reasonably foreseeable, which was enshrined in Lord Atkin's 'neighbour principle' (p. 43, ante), should not be taken to mean that foreseeability of the plaintiff as an individual is required. It is sufficient that he is foreseeable as one of a class (*Farrugia v Great Western Rly Co* [1947] 2 All ER 565). *Awad v Pillai* [1982] RTR 266 also merits attention in this context. In this case the first defendant (D1), who had possession of the plaintiff's car so as to respray it, lent that car to the second defendant (D2) because he had not finished respraying D2's car. D1 led D2 to believe that this car belonged to D1 and that D2's use of the car was covered by insurance. The car was damaged whilst D2 was driving it and in the ensuing court proceedings the question arose whether in this situation the true owner fell within the category of those to whom a duty of care was owed. Applying the 'neighbour principle', it was decided that it was the true owner who was most 'closely affected' and hence to whom a duty was owed. It did not matter that D2 was mistaken as to that person's identity. For critical comment on the case concerning the issue of D2's position as a sub-bailee, see N. E. Palmer and J. R. Murdoch (1983) 46 MLR 73.

3. On the interpretation of the 'neighbour principle' generally, see chap. 2 ante. Lord Atkin's 'neighbour principle' requires the reasonable foresight of injury to the plaintiff to be a 'likely' result of the defendant's act or omission. In *Cunningham v O'Brien* [1982] NI 75 the argument that 'likely' here means 'probable' was rejected: 'likely' covered 'not unlikely' and it was enough that 'a real risk of danger to the plaintiff' was reasonably foreseeable. Consider further Lord Mackay's speech in *Smith v Littlewoods Organisation Ltd* [1987] AC 241; [1987] 1 All ER 710 (p. 87, ante).

2   Nervous shock

Hay or Bourhill *v* Young, p. 114, ante

Notes

1. There has been support in the authorities for two theories of recovery—the 'area of impact' theory and the 'area of shock' theory. *Clerk & Lindsell* propound these two theories in the following passage (at para. 10–10):

'. . . [A]ccording to the [impact theory], as long as it was reasonably foreseeable that the defendant's conduct would have inflicted injury on the plaintiff by actual impact of some sort, he can recover for illness resulting from shock even though he sustained no injury from impact. . . . [A]ccording to the [shock theory], as long as it was reasonably foreseeable that the defendant's conduct would have caused even only shock to an ordinarily strong-nerved person, situated in the position of the plaintiff, then the plaintiff can recover in respect of the shock to him.'

Both these theories had some support in *Bourhill v Young*; see A. L. Goodhart (1944) 8 CLJ 265; cf. *Street*, p. 179. The matter need not be pursued further here, since, as will become apparent, the 'shock theory' is preferred today.

2. It is apparent from *Bourhill v Young* that foresight of nervous shock is to be gauged by the reaction to the events in question of a reasonably strong-nerved person (unless the defendant knew or ought to have known of the plaintiff's special sensitivity). This does not mean that a plaintiff who is more susceptible to shock than the average person will be debarred from recovering compensation: *if* a reasonably strong-nerved person would foreseeably have suffered shock, then a more sensitive person may also be able to claim. Of course, this person may suffer more serious consequences or an unforeseeable type of psychiatric illness, and this problem is considered pp. 342–343, post.

McLoughlin *v* O'Brian House of Lords [1982] 2 All ER 298

LORD WILBERFORCE: My Lords, this appeal arises from a very serious and tragic road accident which occurred on 19 October 1973 near Withersfield, Suffolk. The appellant's husband, Thomas McLoughlin, and three of her children, George, aged 17, Kathleen, aged 7, and Gillian, nearly 3, were in a Ford motor car; George was driving. A fourth child, Michael, then aged 11, was a passenger in a following motor car driven by Mr Pilgrim; this car did not become involved in the accident. The Ford car was in collision with a lorry driven by the first respondent and owned by the second respondent. That lorry had been in collision with another lorry driven by the third respondent and owned by the fourth respondent. It is admitted that the accident to the Ford car was caused by the respondents' negligence. It is necessary to state what followed in full detail.

As a result of the accident, the appellant's husband suffered bruising and shock; George suffered injuries to his head and face, cerebral concussion, fractures of both scapulae and bruising and abrasions; Kathleen suffered concussion, fracture of the right clavicle, bruising, abrasions and shock; Gillian was so seriously injured that she died almost immediately.

At the time, the appellant was at her home about two miles away; an hour or so afterwards the accident was reported to her by Mr Pilgrim, who told her that he thought George was dying, and that he did not know the whereabouts of her husband or the condition of her daughter. He then drove her to Addenbrooke's hospital, Cambridge. There she saw Michael, who told her that Gillian was dead. She was taken down a corridor and through a window she saw Kathleen, crying, with her face cut and begrimed with dirt and oil. She could hear George shouting and screaming. She was taken to her husband who was sitting with his head in his hands. His shirt was hanging off him and he was covered in mud and oil. He saw the appellant and started sobbing. The appellant was then taken to see George. The whole of his left face and left side was covered. He appeared to recognise the appellant and then lapsed into unconsciousness. Finally, the appellant was taken to Kathleen who by now had been cleaned up. The child was too upset to speak and simply clung to her mother. There can be no doubt that these circumstances, witnessed by the appellant, were distressing in the extreme and were capable of producing an effect going well beyond that of grief and sorrow.

The appellant subsequently brought proceedings against the respondents. At the trial, the judge assumed, for the purpose of enabling him to decide the issue of legal liability, that the appellant subsequently suffered the condition of which she complained. This was described as severe shock, organic depression and a change of personality. Numerous symptoms of a physiological character are said to have been manifested. The details were not investigated at the trial, the court being asked to assume that the appellant's condition had been caused or contributed to by shock, as distinct from grief or sorrow, and that the appellant was a person of reasonable fortitude.

On these facts, or assumed facts, the trial judge, Boreham J, gave judgment for the respondents holding, in a most careful judgment reviewing the authorities, that the respondents owed no duty of care to the appellant because the possibility of her suffering injury by nervous shock, in the circumstances, was not reasonably foreseeable.

On appeal by the appellant, the judgment of Boreham J was upheld, but not on the same ground (see [1981] 1 All ER 809; [1981] QB 599). Stephenson LJ took the view that the possibility of injury to the appellant by nervous shock *was* reasonably foreseeable and that the respondents owed the appellant a duty of care. However, he held that considerations of policy prevented the appellant from recovering. Griffiths LJ held that injury by nervous shock to the appellant was 'readily foreseeable' but that the respondents owed no duty of care to the appellant. The duty was limited to those on the road nearby. Cumming-Bruce LJ agreed with both judgments. The appellant now appeals to this House. The critical question to be decided is whether a person in the position of the appellant, i.e. one who was not present at the scene of grievous injuries to her family but who comes on those injuries at an interval of time and space, can recover damages for nervous shock.

Although we continue to use the hallowed expression 'nervous shock', English law, and common understanding, have moved some distance since recognition was given to this symptom as a basis for liability. Whatever is unknown about the mind-body relationship (and the area of ignorance seems to expand with that of knowledge), it is now accepted by medical science that recognisable and severe physical damage to the human body and system may be caused by the impact, through the senses, of external events on the mind. There may thus be produced what is as identifiable an illness as any that may be caused by direct physical impact. It is safe to say that this, in general terms, is understood by the ordinary man or woman who is hypothesised by the courts in situations where claims for negligence are made. Although in the only case which has reached this House (*Hay* (or *Bourhill*) *v Young* [1942] 2 All ER 396; [1943] AC 92) a claim for damages in respect of 'nervous shock' was rejected on its facts, the House gave clear recognition to the legitimacy, in principle, of claims of that character. As the result of that and other cases, assuming that they are accepted as correct, the following position has been reached:

1. While damages cannot, at common law, be awarded for grief and sorrow, a claim for damages for 'nervous shock' caused by negligence can be made without the necessity of showing direct impact or fear of immediate personal injuries for oneself. The reservation made by Kennedy J in *Dulieu v White & Sons* [1901] 2 KB 669; [1900-3] All ER Rep 353, though taken up by Sargant LJ in *Hambrook v Stokes Bros* [1925] 1 KB 141; [1924] All ER Rep 110, has not gained acceptance, and although the respondents, in the courts below, reserved their right to revive it, they did not do so in argument. I think that it is now too late to do so. The arguments on this issue were fully and admirably stated by the Supreme Court of California in *Dillon v Legg* (1968) 29 ALR 3d 1316.

2. A plaintiff may recover damages for 'nervous shock' brought on by injury caused not to him or herself but to a near relative, or by the fear of such injury. So far (subject to 5 below), the cases do not extend beyond the spouses or children of the plaintiff (*Hambrook v Stokes Bros* [1925] 1 KB 141; [1924] All ER Rep 110, *Boardman v Sanderson* [1964] 1 WLR 1317, *Hinz v Berry* [1970] 1 All ER 1074; [1970] 2 QB 40, including foster children (where liability was assumed), and see *King v Phillips* [1953] 1 All ER 617; [1953] 1 QB 429).

3. Subject to the next paragraph, there is no English case in which a plaintiff has been able to recover nervous shock damages where the injury to the near relative

occurred out of sight and earshot of the plaintiff. In *Hambrook v Stokes Bros* an express distinction was made between shock caused by what the mother saw with her own eyes and what she might have been told by bystanders, liability being excluded in the latter case.

4. An exception from, or I would prefer to call it an extension of, the latter case has been made where the plaintiff does not see or hear the incident but comes on its immediate aftermath. In *Boardman v Sanderson* the father was within earshot of the accident to his child and likely to come on the scene; he did so and suffered damage from what he then saw. In *Marshall v Lionel Enterprises* (1971) 25 DLR (3d) 141 the wife came immediately on the badly injured body of her husband. And in *Benson v Lee* [1972] VR 879 a situation existed with some similarity to the present case. The mother was in her home 100 yards away, and, on communication by a third party, ran out to the scene of the accident and there suffered shock. Your Lordships have to decide whether or not to validate these extensions.

5. A remedy on account of nervous shock has been given to a man who came on a serious accident involving people immediately thereafter and acted as a rescuer of those involved (*Chadwick v British Transport Commission* [1967] 2 All ER 945: [1967] 1 WLR 912). 'Shock' was caused neither by fear for himself nor by fear or horror on account of a near relative. The principle of 'rescuer' cases was not challenged by the respondents and ought, in my opinion, to be accepted. But we have to consider whether, and how far, it can be applied to such cases as the present.

Throughout these developments, as can be seen, the courts have proceeded in the traditional manner of the common law from case to case, on a basis of logical necessity. If a mother, with or without accompanying children, could recover on account of fear for herself, how can she be denied recovery on account of fear for her accompanying children? If a father could recover had he seen his child run over by a backing car, how can he be denied recovery if he is in the immediate vicinity and runs to the child's assistance? If a wife and mother could recover if she had witnessed a serious accident to her husband and children, does she fail because she was a short distance away and immediately rushes to the scene? (cf *Benson v Lee*). I think that, unless the law is to draw an arbitrary line at the point of direct sight and sound, these arguments require acceptance of the extension mentioned above under principle 4 in the interests of justice.

If one continues to follow the process of logical progression, it is hard to see why the present plaintiff also should not succeed. She was not present at the accident, but she came very soon after on its aftermath. If, from a distance of some 100 yards (cf *Benson v Lee*), she had found her family by the roadside, she would have come within principle 4 above. Can it make any difference that she comes on them in an ambulance, or, as here, in a nearby hospital, when, as the evidence shows, they were in the same condition, covered with oil and mud, and distraught with pain? If Mr Chadwick can recover when, acting in accordance with normal and irresistible human instinct, and indeed moral compulsion, he goes to the scene of an accident, may not a mother recover if, acting under the same motives, she goes to where her family can be found?

I could agree that a line can be drawn above her case with less hardship than would have been apparent in *Boardman's* and *Hinz's* cases, but so to draw it would not appeal to most people's sense of justice. To allow her claim may be, I think it is, on the margin of what the process of logical progression would allow. But where the facts are strong and exceptional, and, as I think, fairly analogous, her case ought, prima facie, to be assimilated to those which have passed the test.

To argue from one factual situation to another and to decide by analogy is a natural tendency of the human and legal mind. But the lawyer still has to inquire whether, in so doing, he has crossed some critical line behind which he ought to stop. That is said to be the present case. . . .

[Having dealt with the views of the Court of Appeal on this matter and having referred to Lord Atkin's 'neighbour principle' in *M'Alister* (or *Donoghue*) *v Stevenson*

[1932] AC 562 at 580 (p. 43, ante), LORD WILBERFORCE continued:] This is saying that foreseeability must be accompanied and limited by the law's judgment as to persons who ought, according to its standards of value or justice, to have been in contemplation. Foreseeability, which involves a hypothetical person, looking with hindsight at an event which has occurred, is a formula adopted by English law, not merely for defining, but also for limiting the persons to whom duty may be owed, and the consequences for which an actor may be held responsible. It is not merely an issue of fact to be left to be found as such. When it is said to result in a duty of care being owed to a person or a class, the statement that there is a 'duty of care' denotes a conclusion into the forming of which considerations of policy have entered. That foreseeability does not of itself, and automatically, lead to a duty of care is, I think, clear. . . . I may add what Lord Reid said in *McKew v Holland & Hannen & Cubitts (Scotland) Ltd* [1969] 3 All ER 1621 at 1623: 'A defender is not liable for a consequence of a kind which is not foreseeable. But it does not follow that he is liable for every consequence which a reasonable man could foresee.'

We must then consider the policy arguments. In doing so we must bear in mind that cases of 'nervous shock' and the possibility of claiming damages for it are not necessarily confined to those arising out of accidents in public roads. . . .

The policy arguments against a wider extension can be stated under four heads. First, it may be said that such extension may lead to a proliferation of claims, and possibly fraudulent claims, to the establishment of an industry of lawyers and psychiatrists who will formulate a claim for nervous shock damages, including what in America is called the customary miscarriage, for all, or many, road accidents and industrial accidents. Second, it may be claimed that an extension of liability would be unfair to defendants, as imposing damages out of proportion to the negligent conduct complained of. In so far as such defendants are insured, a large additional burden will be placed on insurers, and ultimately on the class of persons insured: road users or employers. Third, to extend liability beyond the most direct and plain cases would greatly increase evidentiary difficulties and tend to lengthen litigation. Fourth, it may be said (and the Court of Appeal agreed with this) that an extension of the scope of liability ought only to be made by the legislature, after careful research. This is the course which has been taken in New South Wales and the Australian Capital Territory.

The whole argument has been well summed up by Dean Prosser in *The Law of Torts* (4th edn, 1971) p. 256:

'The reluctance of courts to enter this zone even where the mental injury is clearly foreseeable, and the frequent mention of the difficulties of proof, the facility of fraud and the problem of finding a place to stop and draw the line, suggest that here it is the nature of the interest invaded and the type of damages which is the real obstacle.'

Since he wrote, the type of damage has, in this country at least, become more familiar and less deterrent to recovery. And some of the arguments are susceptible of answer. Fraudulent claims can be contained by the courts, which, also, can cope with evidentiary difficulties. The scarcity of cases which have occurred in the past, and the modest sums recovered, give some indication that fears of a flood of litigation may be exaggerated: experience in other fields suggests that such fears usually are. If some increase does occur, that may only reveal the existence of a genuine social need; that legislation has been found necessary in Australia may indicate the same thing.

But, these discounts accepted, there remains, in my opinion, just because 'shock' in its nature is capable of affecting so wide a range of people, a real need for the law to place some limitation on the extent of admissible claims. It is necessary to consider three elements inherent in any claim: the class of persons whose claims should be recognised; the proximity of such persons to the accident; and the means by which the shock is caused. As regards the class of persons, the possible range is between the closest of family ties, of parent and child, or husband and wife, and the ordinary bystander. Existing law recognises the claims of the first; it denies that of the second,

either on the basis that such persons must be assumed to be possessed of fortitude sufficient to enable them to endure the calamities of modern life or that defendants cannot
be expected to compensate the world at large. In my opinion, these positions are
justifiable, and since the present case falls within the first class it is strictly unnecessary
to say more. I think, however, that it should follow that other cases involving less close
relationships must be very carefully scrutinised. I cannot say that they should never be
admitted. The closer the tie (not merely in relationship, but in care) the greater the
claim for consideration. The claim, in any case, has to be judged in the light of the
other factors, such as proximity to the scene in time and place, and the nature of
the accident.

As regards proximity to the accident, it is obvious that this must be close in both
time and space. It is after all, the fact and consequence of the defendant's negligence
that must be proved to have caused the 'nervous shock'. Experience has shown that to
insist on direct and immediate sight or hearing would be impractical and unjust and
that under what may be called the 'aftermath' doctrine, one who, from close proximity
comes very soon on the scene, should not be excluded. In my opinion, the result in
Benson v Lee [1972] VR 879 was correct and indeed inescapable. It was based, soundly,
on 'direct perception of some of the events which go to make up the accident as an
entire event, and this includes . . . the immediate aftermath'. The High Court of
Autralia's majority decision in *Chester v Waverley Municipal Council* (1939) 62 CLR
1, where a child's body was found floating in a trench after a prolonged search, may
perhaps be placed on the other side of a recognisable line (Evatt J in a powerful dissent
placed it on the same side), but in addition, I find the conclusion of Lush J in *Benson
v Lee* to reflect developments in the law.

Finally, and by way of reinforcement of 'aftermath' cases, I would accept, by
analogy with 'rescue' situations, that a person of whom it could be said that one could
expect nothing else than that he or she would come immediately to the scene (normally
a parent or a spouse) could be regarded as being within the scope of foresight and duty.
Where there is not immediate presence, account must be taken of the possibility of
alterations in the circumstances, for which the defendant should not be responsible.

Subject only to these qualifications, I think that a strict test of proximity by sight
or hearing should be applied by the courts.

Lastly, as regards communication, there is no case in which the law has compensated
shock brought about by communication by a third party. In *Hambrook v Stokes Bros*
[1925] 1 KB 141; [1924] All ER Rep 110, indeed, it was said that liability would not
arise in such a case, and this is surely right. It was so decided in *Abramzik v Brenner*
(1967) 65 DLR (2d) 651. The shock must come through sight or hearing of the event
or of its immediate aftermath. Whether some equivalent of sight or hearing, e.g.
through simultaneous television, would suffice may have to be considered.

My Lords, I believe that these indications, imperfectly sketched, and certainly to be
applied with common sense to individual situations in their entirety, represent either
the existing law, or the existing law with only such circumstantial extension as the common law process may legitimately make. They do not introduce a new principle. Nor
do I see any reason why the law should retreat behind the lines already drawn. I find
on this appeal that the appellant's case falls within the boundaries of the law so drawn.
I would allow her appeal.

LORD RUSSELL OF KILLOWEN: . . . [I]f the effect on this wife and mother of the results
of the negligence is considered to have been reasonably foreseeable, I do not see the
justification for not finding the defendants liable in damages therefor. I would not
shrink from regarding in an appropriate case policy as something which may feature
in a judicial decision. But in this case what policy should inhibit a decision in favour
of liability to the plaintiff? Negligent driving on the highway is only one form of
negligence which may cause wounding or death and thus induce a relevant mental
trauma in a person such as the plaintiff. There seems to be no policy requirement that
the damage to the plaintiff should be on or adjacent to the highway. In the last analysis

any policy consideration seems to be rooted in a fear of floodgates opening, the tacit question: what next? I am not impressed by that fear, certainly not sufficiently to deprive this plaintiff of just compensation for the reasonably foreseeable damage done to her. I do not consider that such deprivation is justified by trying to answer in advance the question posed, What next? by a consideration of relationships of plaintiff to the sufferers or deceased, or other circumstances; to attempt in advance solutions, or even guidelines, in hypothetical cases may well, it seems to me, in this field, do more harm than good.

I also would allow this appeal.

LORD SCARMAN [having earlier agreed with LORD BRIDGE's approach to the law (post)]:
. . . The importance to be attached to certainty and the size of the 'floodgates' risk vary from one branch of the law to another. What is required of the law in its approach to a commercial transaction will be very different from the approach appropriate to problems of tortious liability for personal injuries. In some branches of the law, notably that now under consideration, the search for certainty can obstruct the law's pursuit of justice, and can become the enemy of the good.

. . . [C]ommon law principle requires the judges to follow the logic of the 'reasonably foreseeable test' so as, in circumstances where it is appropriate, to apply it untrammelled by spatial, physical or temporal limits. Space, time, distance, the nature of the injuries sustained and the relationship of the plaintiff to the immediate victim of the accident are factors to be weighed, but not legal limitations, when the test of reasonable foreseeability is to be applied.

But I am by no means sure that the result is socially desirable. The 'floodgates' argument may be exaggerated. Time alone will tell; but I foresee social and financial problems if damages for 'nervous shock' should be made available to persons other than parents and children who without seeing or hearing the accident, or being present in the immediate aftermath, suffer nervous shock in consequence of it. There is, I think, a powerful case for legislation such as has been enacted in New South Wales and the Australian Capital Territory.

Why then should not the courts draw the line, as the Court of Appeal manfully tried to do in this case? Simply, because the policy issue where to draw the line is not justiciable. The problem is one of social, economic, and financial policy. The considerations relevant to a decision are not such as to be capable of being handled within the limits of the forensic process. . . .

LORD BRIDGE OF HARWICH: . . . The basic difficulty of the subject arises from the fact that the crucial answers to the questions which it raises lie in the difficult field of psychiatric medicine. The common law gives no damages for the emotional distress which any normal person experiences when someone he loves is killed or injured. Anxiety and depression are normal human emotions. Yet an anxiety neurosis or a reactive depression may be recognisable psychiatric illnesses, with or without psychosomatic symptoms. So, the first hurdle which a plaintiff claiming damages of the kind in question must surmount is to establish that he is suffering, not merely grief, distress or any other normal emotion, but a positive psychiatric illness. That is here not in issue. A plaintiff must then establish the necessary chain of causation in fact between his psychiatric illness and the death or injury of one or more third parties negligently caused by the defendant. Here again, this is not in dispute in the instant case. But, when causation in fact is in issue, it must no doubt be determined by the judge on the basis of the evidence of psychiatrists. Then, here comes the all important question. Given the fact of the plaintiff's psychiatric illness [caused] by the defendant's negligence in killing or physically injuring another, was the chain of causation from the one event to the other, considered ex post facto in the light of all that has happened, 'reasonably foreseeable' by the 'reasonable man'? A moment's thought will show that the answer to that question depends on what knowledge is to be attributed to the hypothetical reasonable man of the operation of cause and effect in medicine. . . . It would seem that the consensus of informed judicial opinion is probably the best yardstick available to determine whether, in any given circumstances, the emotional trauma resulting from the death or injury of third parties, or indeed the threat of such death or injury, ex hypothesi attributable to the defendant's negligence, was a foreseeable cause in law, as well as the actual cause in fact, of the plaintiff's psychiatric or psychosomatic illness. But the word I would emphasise in the foregoing sentence is 'informed'. For too long earlier generations of judges have regarded psychiatry and psychiatrists with suspicion, if not hostility. Now, I venture to hope, that attitude has quite disappeared. No judge who has spent any length of time trying personal injury claims in recent years would doubt that physical injuries can give rise not only to organic but also to psychiatric disorders. The sufferings of the patient from the latter are no less real and frequently no less painful and disabling than from the former. Likewise, I would suppose that the legal profession well understands that an acute emotional trauma, like a physical trauma, can well cause a psychiatric illness in a wide range of circumstances and in a wide range of individuals whom it would be wrong to regard as having any abnormal psychological make-up. It is in comparatively recent times that these insights have come to be generally accepted by the judiciary. It is only by giving effect to these insights in the developing law of negligence that we can do justice to an important, though no doubt small, class of plaintiffs whose genuine psychiatric illnesses are caused by negligent defendants. . . .

In approaching the question whether the law should, as a matter of policy, define the criterion of liability in negligence for causing psychiatric illness by reference to some test other than that of reasonable foreseeability it is well to remember that we are concerned only with the question of liability of a defendant who is, ex hypothesi, guilty of fault in causing the death, injury or danger which has in turn triggered the psychiatric illness. A policy which is to be relied on to narrow the scope of the negligent tortfeasor's duty must be justified by cogent and readily intelligible considerations, and must be capable of defining the appropriate limits of liability by reference to factors which are not purely arbitrary. A number of policy considerations which have been suggested as satisfying these requirements appear to me, with respect, to be wholly insufficient. I can see no ground whatever for suggesting that to make the defendant liable for reasonably foreseeable psychiatric illness caused by his negligence would be to impose a crushing burden on him out of proportion to his moral responsibility. However liberally the criterion of reasonable foreseeability is interpreted, both the number of successful claims in this field and the quantum of damages they will attract are likely to be moderate. I cannot accept as relevant the well-known phenomenon that litigation may delay recovery from a psychiatric illness. If this were a valid policy consideration, it would lead to the conclusion that psychiatric illness should be excluded altogether from the heads of damage which the law will recognise. It cannot justify limiting the cases in which damages will be awarded for psychiatric illness by reference to the circumstances of its causation. To attempt to draw a line at the furthest point which any of the decided cases happen to have reached, and to say that it is for the legislature, not the courts, to extend the limits of liability any further, would be, to my mind, an unwarranted abdication of the court's function of developing and adapting principles of the common law to changing conditions, in a particular corner of the common law which exemplifies, par excellence, the important and indeed necessary part which that function has to play. In the end I believe that the policy question depends on weighing against each other two conflicting considerations. On the one hand, if the criterion of liability is to be reasonable foreseeability simpliciter, this must, precisely because questions of causation in psychiatric medicine give rise to difficulty and uncertainty, introduce an element of uncertainty into the law and open the way to a number of arguable claims which a more precisely fixed criterion of liability would exclude. I accept that the element of uncertainty is an important factor. I believe that the 'floodgates' argument, however, is, as it always has been, greatly exaggerated. On the other hand, it seems to me inescapable that any attempt to define the limit of liability by requiring, in addition to reasonable foreseeability, that the plaintiff claiming damages for psychiatric illness should have witnessed the relevant accident, should have been present at or near the place where it happened, should have come on its aftermath and thus have some direct perception of it, as opposed to merely learning of it after the event, should be related in some particular degree to the accident victim – to draw a line by reference to any of these criteria must impose a largely arbitrary limit of liability. I accept, of course, the importance of [such] factors . . . as bearing on the *degree* of foreseeability of the plaintiff's psychiatric illness. But let me give two examples to illustrate what injustice would be wrought by any such hard and fast lines of policy as have been suggested. First, consider the plaintiff who learned after the event of the relevant accident. Take the case of a mother who knows that her husband and children are staying in a certain hotel. She reads in her morning newspaper that it has been the scene of a disastrous fire. She sees in the paper a photograph of unidentifiable victims trapped on the top floor waving for help from the windows. She learns shortly afterwards that all her family have perished. She suffers an acute psychiatric illness. That her illness in these circumstances was a reasonably foreseeable consequence of the events resulting from the fire is undeniable. Yet, is the law to deny her damages as against a defendant whose negligence was responsible for the fire simply on the ground that an important link in the chain of causation of her psychiatric illness was supplied by her imagination of the agonies of mind and body in which her family died, rather than by direct perception of the event? Second, consider the plaintiff who is unrelated to the victims of the relevant accident. If rigidly applied, an exclusion of liability to him would have defeated the plaintiff's claim in *Chadwick v British Transport Commission*. The Court of Appeal treated that case as in a special category because Mr Chadwick was a rescuer. Now, the special duty owed to a rescuer who voluntarily places himself in physical danger to save others is well understood, and is illustrated by *Haynes v Harwood* [1935] 1 KB 146; [1934] All ER Rep 103, the case of the constable injured in stopping a runaway horse in a crowded street. But, in relation to the psychiatric consequences of witnessing such terrible carnage as must have resulted from the Lewisham train disaster, I would find it difficult to distinguish in principle the position of a rescuer, like Mr Chadwick, from a mere spectator, as, for example, an uninjured or only slightly injured passenger in the train, who took no part in the rescue operations but was present at the scene after the accident for some time, perforce observing the rescue operations while he waited for transport to take him home.

My Lords, I have no doubt that this is an area of the law of negligence where we should resist the temptation to try yet once more to freeze the law in a rigid posture which would deny justice to some who, in the application of the classic principles of negligence derived from *Donoghue v Stevenson* [1932] AC 562; [1932] All ER Rep 1, ought to succeed, in the interests of certainty, where the very subject matter is uncertain and continuously developing in the interests of saving defendants and their insurers from the burden of having sometimes to resist doubtful claims. I find myself in complete agreement with Tobriner J[1] that the defendant's duty must depend on reasonable foreseeability and –

'must necessarily be adjudicated only upon a case-by-case basis. We cannot now predetermine defendant's obligation in every situation by a fixed category; no immutable rule can establish the extent of that obligation for every circumstance of the future.'

To put the matter in another way, if asked where the thing is to stop, I should answer, in an adaptation of the language of Lord Wright[2] and Stephenson LJ[3],

1. [In *Dillon v Legg* (1968) 29 ALR 3d 1316].
2. [In *Bourhill v Young* [1943] AC 92 at 110.]
3. [In the Court of Appeal in this case.]

'Where in the particular case the good sense of the judge, enlightened by progressive awareness of mental illness, decides'. . . .

My Lords, I would accordingly allow the appeal.

[LORD EDMUND-DAVIES delivered a speech in favour of allowing the appeal.]

Appeal allowed

Questions

1. Would Lord Wilberforce reject a claim for damages for nervous shock by a bystander witnessing an accident on the ground that shock is unforeseeable or is he saying that it is irrecoverable even if foreseeable? How would Lord Bridge approach the matter?

2. Would a mother in a situation similar to that in *McLoughlin v O'Brian* have recovered for nervous shock if she had been abroad at the time of the accident and had only suffered shock on visiting her family in hospital three days later?

3. Can a claim be made for nervous shock where the shock occurs by witnessing events over a lengthy period rather than by a sudden event? (See N. Grace (1986) 2 PN 46 at 48–49, discussing *Kralj v McGrath* [1986] 1 All ER 54.)

4. Would a defendant be liable if he placed *himself* in danger and the plaintiff suffered nervous shock in consequence? See p. 137, post in the context of rescuers and see the comment in *R v Criminal Injuries Compensation Board, ex p Webb* [1986] QB 184 at 196 when that case was in the Divisional Court; cf. *Jaensch v Coffey* (1984) 54 ALR 417. Note also the indication from Oliver LJ in *Leigh and Sillivan Ltd v Aliakmon Shipping Co Ltd* [1985] QB 350 at 376, when that case was in the Court of Appeal, that a person does not 'owe a legal duty to those who have affection for [him] not, either carelessly or deliberately, to injure [himself]'.

Notes

1. On Lord Scarman's approach in general, see pp. 64–65, ante. It should also be noted that *McLoughlin v O'Brian* was decided when the approach to the duty of care to be found in *Anns v Merton London Borough Council* [1978] AC 728; [1977] 2 All ER 492, set out p. 51, ante, was in favour, but see now pp. 51–65, ante.

2. Lord Wilberforce in *McLoughlin v O'Brian* confirmed the view, mentioned p. 113, ante, that damages will not be awarded for mere mental distress on its own. This was followed in *Whitmore v Euroways Express Coaches Ltd* (1984) Times, 4th May, in which a wife witnessed an accident as a result of which her husband sustained serious injuries; nevertheless, Comyn J regarded it as 'harsh' that her distress, brought about by the injuries to her husband, could not be the subject of compensation. This distress was, however, distinguished from shock 'in its ordinary everyday meaning' which the plaintiff had suffered and which, as a result of the nature of her husband's injuries, had lasted for nearly two months. The plaintiff received £2,000 under this head even though it was not a 'psychiatric shock': for the latter type of shock to be recoverable,

medical evidence would have to be introduced. Although the shock in this case was said not to be 'psychiatric in character', it was presumably something that psychiatrists would recognise, but, as a judge was just as capable as a psychiatrist to decide whether it had been sustained, there was no need for medical evidence to support such a claim for damages. On *Whitmore* see further *Street*, p. 178, note 21 who refers to the requirement, restated in *McLoughlin*, p. 124, ante, by Lord Bridge, that the plaintiff suffer a psychiatric illness; on such a requirement see also *Attia v British Gas plc* [1988] QB 304; [1987] 3 All ER 455, noted p. 130, post. See further N. Grace, op cit and note her point that in awarding damages for nervous shock in *Kralj v McGrath* [1986] 1 All ER 54 Woolf J did not appear to decide whether a psychiatric illness had been suffered.

3. On the issue of liability for nervous shock Lord Edmund-Davies in *McLoughlin v O'Brian* saw no policy reason for limiting the application of the reasonable foreseeability test in that particular case, although he accepted that policy could so limit it. (See *Street*, p. 180.)

Some similarity in approach between his speech and that of Lord Wilberforce can be found. The former suggested ([1982] 2 All ER at p. 306) that the appellant's position 'in visiting her family in hospital immediately she heard of the accident [was] basically indistinguishable from that of a "rescuer", being intent on comforting the injured'. Note also, in addressing the 'floodgates argument', on which see post, he thought that, for the reasons set out in Lord Wilberforce's speech, to allow the appellant to recover for nervous shock in this case would not substantially increase the number and area of claims.

Do you think that liability for nervous shock is now totally governed by the reasonable foresight test? To what extent does Lord Russell in *McLoughlin v O'Brian* agree with Lord Scarman and Lord Bridge? What does Lord Scarman indicate by the phrase 'where it is appropriate' near the beginning of the extract from his speech (and see *Jaensch v Coffey* (1984) 54 ALR at p. 459)? See further Bingham LJ in *Attia v British Gas plc* [1988] QB 304 at 319–320; cf. *Wigg v British Railways Board* (1986) Times, 4 February and note the relationship in this latter case (train driver/ passenger). A particular problem to consider is whether a person (e.g. the mother of a victim) can recover if nervous shock is suffered as a result of merely hearing of the accident. Lord Wilberforce would reject such a claim even if the shock was foreseeable in the circumstances, and this has been the traditional view (see *Hambrook v Stokes Bros* [1925] 1 KB 141; cf. *Schneider v Eisovitch* [1960] 2 QB 430; [1960] 1 All ER 169 on which see J. A. Jolowicz [1960] CLJ 156). What would Lord Scarman and Lord Bridge say? Do we know Lord Russell's opinion on this matter?

Lord Wilberforce (p. 123, ante) did leave open the position where the shock was caused by 'some equivalent of sight or hearing' such as simultaneous television. This was one issue recently addressed by Hidden J in *Jones v Wright* [1991] 1 All ER 353 which concerned the disaster at the Hillsborough football ground: see L. M. Lomax (1990) 140 NLJ 1155. His Lordship ruled that shock caused by watching live television pictures could give rise to claims for damages (so long as they met the appropriate family relationship test, on which see post), but that claims based on hearing radio reports were barred. However, in the case of live radio reports, should any distinction be made between seeing and hearing? In relation to the question of radio reports, and indeed the contents of this note more generally, consider the point made by H.Teff (1983) 99 LQR 100 at 107 that 'there is medical support for the view that, in some circumstances, hearing of the loss of a loved one in an accident could prompt an even stronger reaction than seeing it, given the human mind's propensity for constructing an image of an event even more gruesome than the reality'. See further *Hevican v Ruane* [1991] NLJR 235 acting upon Lord Bridge's speech in *McLoughlin v O'Brian*.

Related to the question of the role of reasonable foresight is the issue whether some sort of family relationship with a victim is required, in addition to reasonable foreseeability of nervous shock, before a claim for damages for nervous shock can succeed. Lord Wilberforce's speech in *McLoughlin v O'Brian* (pp. 122–123, ante) suggests that it is (though note his comment on 'rescuer cases' (p. 121, ante)), but he leaves open whose claims are permitted outside the parent/child or spousal relationships. What was the position of the other members of the House of Lords in *McLoughlin v O'Brian*? On the case law before *McLoughlin v O'Brian* note that in *Hinz v Berry* [1970] 2 QB 40; [1970] 1 All ER 1074 Lord Denning MR had said (at p. 1075) that 'for these last 25 years, it has been settled that damages can be given for nervous shock caused by the sight of an accident, at any rate to a close relative'; cf. Atkin LJ's judgment in *Hambrook v Stokes Bros* [1925] 1 KB 141 where his Lordship had suggested (obiter) that a mere bystander could recover.

In *Jones v Wright* Hidden J, on the basis of reasonable foresight, restricted claims to those who were parents, children, spouses, brothers or sisters of a victim. The claims of those people who were in one of the stands at Hillsborough and had watched the disaster but who did not fall within one of these relationships, were not allowed. Is shock to brothers or sisters more foreseeable than shock to a fiancée? What about foresight of shock to a cohabitee? Another category of case (although it is not one mentioned by Lord Wilberforce in his outline of the development of the law) is that of fear for the safety of a fellow workman. In *Dooley v Cammell Laird & Co Ltd and Mersey Insulation Co Ltd* [1951] 1 Lloyd's Rep 271 materials in a sling hoisted by a crane fell into the hold of a ship when an unsound piece of rope broke. The plaintiff, whose fellow workmen were in the hold, was the crane operator and he recovered damages for shock which he suffered as a result of fear for their safety. (See also *Carlin v Helical Bar Ltd* (1970) 9 KIR 154; *Mount Isa Mines Ltd v Pusey* [1971] ALR 253.) *Dooley*'s case was not in fact mentioned by any of their Lordships in *McLoughlin v O'Brian*. Would it be decided the same way today by all of them? In *Jones v Wright* Hidden J did not exclude such a case, nor a rescuer's claim, but explained them as turning on the plaintiff's particular activity, e.g. the act of operating equipment or of rescue: see [1991] 1 All ER at pp. 382–383.

4. In relation to the 'reasonable foreseeability' test, note also that in *Brice v Brown* [1984] 1 All ER 997, noted p. 342, post, Stuart-Smith J required nervous shock to be reasonably foreseeable as a natural and probable consequence of the tortfeasor's breach of duty. For criticism of this use of 'natural and probable' see C. Gearty [1984] CLJ 238 at 240, who points out that it is omitted in a later part of the judgment.

5. The question whether someone can recover damages for nervous shock suffered as a result of witnessing damage to their property was raised in *Attia*

v British Gas plc [1988] QB 304; [1987] 3 All ER 455 where the defendants admitted that their employees had negligently caused a fire at the plaintiff's house. The plaintiff alleged that she had suffered nervous shock by virtue of seeing her home and its contents on fire, but did not allege that she feared for her own or anyone else's safety. The preliminary issue raised was whether such a claim could, as a matter of law, successfully be made. The Court of Appeal thought it could. Dillon LJ's judgment laid stress on the fact that in relation to the damage to the house and its contents a duty was already owed to the plaintiff not to start a fire; problems of proximity were thereby avoided. Woolf LJ also placed emphasis on a duty of care already being owed to the plaintiff. In addition to the position concerning property damage, he pointed out the plaintiff would have been owed a duty of care in relation to physical injuries if she had been injured when she had entered her house (as she had in fact done) to telephone the fire brigade; in his view, if policy was relevant in nervous shock cases (and see p. 128, ante), there was no policy reason for treating the two types of injury differently. Bingham LJ agreed that the claim should not be struck out as a matter of law, but seemed less influenced by the consideration of a duty of care already being owed to the plaintiff. Is there any reason to deny liability where property damage leads to foreseeable nervous shock to a person to whom a duty is not otherwise owed (e.g. a worshipper who is not physically endangered but who witnesses the destruction of an article of extreme religious importance)?

The *Attia* case shows that the question of liability for nervous shock can be treated as an issue of remoteness of damage (see chap. 6, post) rather than at the level of duty (as in e.g. *McLoughlin v O'Brian*). In *Attia* the existence of a duty to the plaintiff (referred to ante) led Dillon and Woolf LJJ to treat the nervous shock issue as one of remoteness: Bingham LJ acknowledged that the matter could be decided at the level of duty, but preferred to treat it as one of remoteness. For criticism of Bingham LJ's approach, see R. Kidner (1989) 9 LS 1 at 5-6.

6. The 'floodgates argument' was much in issue in *McLoughlin v O'Brian*; indeed all of Lord Wilberforce's four heads of policy arguments are so classified by J. Bell, *Policy Arguments in Judicial Decisions*, pp. 71-72. In *McLoughlin v O'Brian* the 'floodgates argument' was unsuccessful in preventing recovery by the appellant; nevertheless, it seems to have influenced Lord Wilberforce's approach to the general question of recovery for nervous shock. Furthermore, Lord Edmund-Davies stated that the 'floodgates argument' cannot 'invariably be dismissed as lacking cogency' and needed to be 'weighed carefully' although admitting that he had 'often seen it disproved by later events' ([1982] 2 All ER at p. 307). Would Lord Scarman regard it as (a) cogent or (b) relevant? What of Lord Bridge? On the 'floodgates argument' note further the view of Bingham LJ in *Attia v British Gas plc* [1988] QB 304 at 320—'not an argument to be automatically discarded [b]ut nor is it, I think, an argument which can claim a very impressive record of success'; and, in a different context, see the opinion of Lord Roskill in *Junior Books Ltd v Veitchi Co Ltd* [1983] 1 AC 520 at 539 and that of Robert Goff LJ in *Leigh and Sillivan Ltd v Aliakmon Shipping Co Ltd* [1985] QB 350 at 393, when that case was in the Court of Appeal.

7. In *McLoughlin v O'Brian* Lord Scarman thought there was a 'powerful case for legislation such as has been enacted in New South Wales and the

Australian Capital Territory'; and note that a similar provision exists in the Australian Northern Territory. (For discussion of this legislation, see P. G. Heffey (1978) 48 ALJ 240 at 248–254.) The relevant provision in New South Wales is the Law Reform (Miscellaneous Provisions) Act 1944 (NSW), s. 4(1) of which states:

'The liability of any person in respect of injury caused after the commencement of this Act by an act, neglect or default by which any other person is killed, injured or put in peril, shall extend to include liability for injury arising wholly or in part from mental or nevous shock sustained by—
  (a) a parent or the husband or wife of the person so killed, injured or put in peril; or
  (b) any other member of the family of the person so killed, injured or put in peril where such person was killed, injured or put in peril within the sight or hearing of such member of the family.'

'Member of the family' 'husband', 'wife' and 'parent' are defined in s. 4(5), as amended, and s. 4, it seems, provides a statutory cause of action in addition to the common law. Presumably Lord Scarman, in seeing a need for legislation, did not think that its provisions should necessarily follow the New South Wales enactment.

8. For further discussion of *McLoughlin v O'Brian* in an Australian context, see *Jaensch v Coffey* (1984) 54 ALR 417 where the High Court of Australia did not speak with one voice. For general discussion of liability for negligently inflicted nervous shock before *McLoughlin v O'Brian*, see P. G. Heffey (1974) 48 ALJ 196 and 240, and for more recent discussion incorporating that case, see F. A. Trindade [1986] CLJ 476. See also Teff, op cit. He argues (at p. 104) that from a medical viewpoint the critical factor in determining whether a person suffers a recognisable psychiatric illness 'is almost invariably the nature of his relationship with the victim'; and see his point in note 3, ante. On the causes of psychiatric illness, see further *Jaensch v Coffey* (1984) 54 ALR at pp. 456–457.

3   Rescuers

Baker *v* T. E. Hopkins & Son Ltd Court of Appeal [1959] 3 All ER 225

The defendant company was employed to clean out a contaminated well at a farm, and it was decided to use a pump powered by a petrol engine inside the well. This method would lead to a build-up of carbon monoxide in the well, and was very dangerous. Mr Hopkins, the defendant company's managing director, who had decided on this method, was not aware of its grave dangers, but, some time later on the day when the pumping started, he said to Ward, one of the company's employees engaged on the job: 'Don't go down the well tomorrow until the fumes have cleared.' Mr Hopkins paid another visit to the well that evening, and the next morning the two men involved in the job (Ward and Wileman) were forcefully told by him not to go down the well until he arrived. However, Ward did go down, and he was later followed by Wileman who feared that Ward was ill. In response to a call he had received, Dr Baker arrived at the farm, and was informed of the position. He was also told about the petrol engine, and that the fire brigade had been sent for. Attempts were made to discourage him from going down the well, but, 'prompted by the finest instincts of humanity' (per Morris LJ), Dr Baker, having attached a rope to himself, went down the well, but was overcome by the fumes. Unfortunately, the rope became caught, and he could not be pulled out of the well. All three men in the well died, and actions relating to the deaths of Ward and Dr Baker were brought against the defendant company. These succeeded before Barry J, although Ward was found to have been contributorily negligent, and his responsibility for the accident was assessed at 10%. The defendant company appealed. Only the claim in respect of Dr Baker's death is considered in these extracts, although the Court of Appeal dismissed the appeal in relation to each action.

MORRIS LJ: . . . It will be convenient to deal first with Dr Baker's case. The claim which was put forward was that there was negligence, for which the defendant company were responsible and that such negligence resulted in the death of Dr Baker.

The first stage in the proof of the claim involves proof that the defendant company were negligent towards their employees, the second that such negligence caused such employees to be in peril, the third that this could reasonably have been foreseen, and the fourth that it could also have been reasonably foreseen that someone would be likely to seek to rescue them from their peril and might either suffer injury or lose his life. . . .

[Having discussed the evidence and taken the view that the workmen ought to have been warned of the perils that existed, he continued:] It was . . . as a result of the company's negligence (or at least was in part a result of it) that the time came when Ward was in dire peril in the well. The company could and should in my judgment have anticipated that, if as a result of their negligence their men were exposed to great danger in the well, it would be a natural and probable consequence that someone would attempt a rescue. Subject to a consideration of certain further submissions made by the defendant company, it seems to me, therefore, that it is shown that Dr Baker's death was a result of the company's negligence.

It is submitted, however, that the action of Dr Baker in descending the well was a novus actus interveniens, and it is further submitted that the defendant company could not reasonably have foreseen the possibility of such a disaster as that which occurred. In my judgment these submissions are wholly unsustainable once it is held that the company were negligent in creating a situation of great danger and further in failing to warn their servants of it or in failing to ensure that their servants would not be exposed to it. There is happily in all men of good will an urge to save those who are in peril. Those who put men in peril can hardly be heard to say that they never thought that rescue might be attempted or be heard to say that the rescue attempt was not caused by the creation of the peril. As Greer LJ said in *Haynes v Harwood*:[1]

'If what is relied upon as novus actus interveniens is the very kind of thing which is likely to happen if the want of care which is alleged takes place, the principle embodied in the maxim is no defence.'

Equally unavailing in my judgment is the plea which is expressed in the words volenti non fit injuria. In *Letang v Ottawa Electric Rly Co*[2] it was said:

'It is quite a mistake to treat volenti non fit injuria as if it were the legal equipollent of scienti non fit injuria.'

Approval was given of the proposition in the judgment of Wills J in *Osborne v London and North Western Rly Co*[3] that:

---

1. [1935] 1 KB 146 at 156; [1934] All ER Rep 103 at 107.
2. [1926] AC 725 at 730.
3. (1888) 21 QBD 220 at 223, 224.

'If the defendants desire to succeed on the ground that the maxim volenti non fit injuria is applicable, they must obtain a finding of fact that the plaintiff freely and voluntarily, with full knowledge of the nature and extent of the risk he ran, impliedly agreed to incur it.'

In *Dann v Hamilton*[1] Asquith J said:

'Where a dangerous physical condition has been brought about by the negligence of the defendant, and, after it has arisen, the plaintiff, fully appreciating its dangerous character, elects to assume the risk thereof, the maxim has often been held to apply, and to protect the defendant.'

If, however, A by negligence places B in peril in such circumstances that it is a foreseeable result that someone will try to rescue B and if C does so try—ought C in any appropriate sense to be described as a 'volunteer'? In my judgment the answer is No. I confess that it seems to me to be indeed ungracious of A even to suggest it. C would not have agreed to run the risk that A might be negligent, for C would only play his part after A had been negligent. C's intervention comes at the moment when there is some situation of peril and the cause of or the responsibility for the creation of the peril may be quite unknown to C. If C, actuated by an impulsive desire to save life, acts bravely and promptly and subjugates any timorous over-concern for his own well-being or comfort, I cannot think that it would be either rational or seemly to say that he freely and voluntarily agreed to incur the risks of the situation which had been created by A's negligence.

When Dr Baker arrived at the well, he proceeded to act as the promptings of humanity directed. He tried to save life. He tried to save the defendant company's servants. He was doubtless trying to do the very thing that the company hoped could be done. But in any event what he did was brought about by and was caused by the negligence of the company. In these circumstances, the company cannot say that he was a volunteer.

It was further said that Dr Baker himself acted with negligence and that his death was caused or was partly caused thereby. This contention was not advanced harshly or in the language of any carping criticism: it was said that Dr Baker had been 'unreasonably' brave. If a rescuer acts with a wanton disregard of his own safety it might be that in some circumstances it might be held that any injury to him was not the result of the negligence that caused the situation of danger. Such a contention cannot be here asserted. Dr Baker tied a strong rope round his body and arranged for the rope to be held by those on the surface and arranged to maintain oral communication with them. It must be remembered also that the chances of success of his attempt would diminish moment by moment if he tarried. He in no way acted recklessly or negligently. In my judgment, the learned judge came to a correct conclusion in regard to the claim made by his widow. . . .

WILLMER LJ: . . . Dr Baker's case falls to be determined on the basis that Mr Hopkins' own negligence was at least a substantial cause of the peril in which the two men, Ward and Wileman, found themselves, and which led to their death. The case, therefore, raises once more the not unfamiliar problems, much discussed in the so-called 'Rescue cases', which arise where A's wrongful act puts B in a situation of peril, and C, a stranger, suffers injury in the course of attempting to rescue B.

It seems to me that in this case, as in any case where a plaintiff is injured in going to the rescue of a third party put in peril by the defendants' wrongdoing, the questions which have to be answered are fourfold. (1) Did the wrongdoer owe any duty to the rescuer in the circumstances of the particular case? (2) If so, did the rescuer's injury

---

1. [1939] 1 KB 509 at 517; [1939] 1 All ER 59 at 63.

result from a breach of that duty, or did his act in going to the rescue amount to a novus actus? (3) Did the rescuer, knowing the danger, voluntarily accept the risk of injury, so as to be defeated by the maxim volenti non fit injuria? (4) Was the rescuer's injury caused or contributed to by his own failure to take reasonable care for his own safety? All these questions are raised by the circumstances of this case, and have much been canvassed in argument before us. I will endeavour to deal with each in turn.

(1) The question whether the wrongdoer owed any duty to the rescuer must be determined, in my judgment, by reference to Lord Atkin's familiar statement of the law in *M'Alister* (or *Donoghue*) *v Stevenson*[1] when he said:

'You must take reasonable care to avoid acts or omissions which you can reasonably foresee would be likely to injure your neighbour.'

In the circumstances of the particular case, is the rescuer in law the 'neighbour' of the wrongdoer, in the sense that he is so closely and directly affected by the wrongdoer's act that the latter ought reasonably to have him in contemplation as being so affected? Where the act of the wrongdoer has been such as to be likely to put someone in peril, reasonable foresight will normally contemplate the probability of an attempted rescue, in the course of which the rescuer may receive injury. In the American case of *Wagner v International Rly Co*[2] Cardozo J, as it seems to me, foreshadowed in a remarkable way Lord Atkin's statement of principle, and applied it to a typical rescue case. He said:[3]

'Danger invites rescue. The cry of distress is the summons to relief. The law does not ignore these reactions of the mind in tracing conduct to its consequences. It recognises them as normal. It places their effects within the range of the natural and probable. The wrong that imperils life is a wrong to the imperilled victim; it is a wrong also to his rescuer.'

Then a little later he went on:[4]

'The risk of rescue, if only it be not wanton, is born of the occasion. The emergency begets the man. The wrongdoer may not have foreseen the coming of a deliverer. He is accountable as if he had.'

The judgment of Cardozo J was referred to with approval by Lord Wright in *Hay* (or *Bourhill*) *v Young*[5] and Lord Wright went on to say:

'This again shows how the ambit of the persons affected by negligence or misconduct may extend beyond persons who are actually subject to physical impact. There, indeed, may be no one injured in a particular case by actual impact; but still a wrong may be committed to anyone who suffers nervous shock or is injured in an act of rescue.'

I should also refer to *Lord v Pacific Steam Navigation Co Ltd, The Oropesa*[6] where Lord Wright said, quoting from the speech of Lord Haldane in *Canadian Pacific Rly Co v Kelvin Shipping Co Ltd, The Melagama*:[7]

---

1. [1932] AC 562 at 580; [1932] All ER Rep 1 at 11.
2. 232 NY Rep 176 (1921).
3. 232 NY Rep (1921) at p. 180.
4. 232 NY Rep (1921) at p. 180.
5. [1943] AC 92 at 108, 109; [1942] 2 All ER 396 at 405.
6. [1943] P 32 at 39; [1943] 1 All ER 211 at 216.
7. (1927) 138 LT 369 at 370.

'Reasonable human conduct is part of the ordinary course of things . . .'

Assuming the rescuer not to have acted unreasonably, therefore, it seems to me that he must normally belong to the class of persons who ought to be within the contemplation of the wrongdoer as being closely and directly affected by the latter's act. In the present case the fact that Dr Baker was a doctor is of itself significant. Having regard to the nature of the peril created by the wrongful act of Mr Hopkins, it was only too likely that a doctor would be summoned – as Dr Baker in fact was – and, if summoned, would attempt to do all he could for the victim, even at the risk of his own safety. In such circumstances I am satisfied that Dr Baker was one of the class who ought to have been within the contemplation of Mr Hopkins when he brought about the dangerous situation in this well. I do not think, therefore, that it is open to the defendant company to contend that no duty was owed by Mr Hopkins to Dr Baker.

(2) The question whether the act of the rescuer amounts to a novus actus answers itself, in my judgment, as soon as it is determined that it is the kind of act which ought to have been within the contemplation of the wrongdoer, so as to bring the rescuer within the class of persons to whom a duty was owed. . . . In my judgment, it was a natural and probable result of the wrongdoing of Mr Hopkins that, in the likely event of someone being overcome by the carbon monoxide poisoning, a doctor would be called in, and that such doctor, having regard to the traditions of his profession, would, even at the risk of his own safety, descend the well for the purpose of attempting a rescue. Unless it can be shown, therefore, that Dr Baker displayed such an unreasonable disregard for his own safety as to amount to negligence on his own part – with which suggestion I will presently deal – I do not think that it can be said that his act constituted a novus actus interveniens.

(3) The next question is whether the plaintiffs in Dr Baker's case are defeated by the maxim volenti non fit injuria. . . . It seems to me that, when once it is determined that the act of the rescuer was the natural and probable consequence of the defendant's wrongdoing, there is no longer any room for the application of the maxim volenti non fit injuria. It would certainly be a strange result if the law were held to penalise the courage of the rescuer by depriving him of any remedy. Greer LJ in *Haynes v Harwood*[1] was clearly of the view that the maxim cannot be applied to defeat the plaintiff's claim in a rescue case. He quotes from an article by Professor Goodhart in the *Cambridge Law Journal* (vol. V, at p. 196) as follows:[2]

'The American rule is that the doctrine of the assumption of risk does not apply where the plaintiff has, under an exigency caused by the defendants' wrongful misconduct, consciously and deliberately faced a risk, even of death, to rescue another from imminent danger of personal injury or death, whether the person endangered is one to whom he owes a duty of protection, as a member of his family, or is a mere stranger to whom he owes no such special duty.'

Greer LJ goes on:[2]

'In my judgment, that passage not only represents the law of the United States but also the law of this country.'

It is by no means clear that the other two members of the court were prepared to go so far as Greer LJ in stating the principle, and they appear to have based their

---

1. [1935] 1 KB at p. 159; [1934] All ER Rep at p. 109.
2. [1935] 1 KB at p. 157; [1934] All ER Rep at p. 108.

judgments to a great extent on the fact that in the particular case the plaintiff was a police officer. But for my part I am content to accept Greer LJ's statement of the law, and to hold that the maxim volenti non fit injuria cannot be invoked in this case to defeat the second plaintiff's claim. In my judgment, the real question to be determined in a case such as the present is, not whether the rescuer voluntarily accepted the risk of injury, but whether his injury was caused or contributed to by any failure on his part to take reasonable care for his own safety. This was the view expressed by Swift J in *Brandon v Osborne, Garrett & Co*[1] and I think that it is the right view.

(4) I pass, therefore, to the fourth and last question, which is raised by the defendant company's plea that the death of Dr Baker was caused or contributed to by his own negligence. The burden of proof with regard to this allegation is on the defendant company, and in order to succeed I think they would have to show that the conduct of Dr Baker was so foolhardy as to amount to a wholly unreasonable disregard for his own safety. Bearing in mind that danger invites rescue, the court should not be astute to accept criticism of the rescuer's conduct from the wrongdoer who created the danger. Moreover, I think it should be remembered that it is fatally easy to be wise after the event. It is not enough that, when all the evidence has been sifted and all the facts ascertained in the calm and deliberate atmosphere of a court of law, the rescuer's conduct can be shown ex post facto to have been misguided or foolhardy. He is entitled to be judged in the light of the situation as it appeared to him at the time, i.e., in a context of immediate and pressing emergency. Here Dr Baker was faced with a situation in which two men were in danger of speedy death in the well, unless something were done very quickly. He was a doctor, and he had been specially summoned to help. Any man of courage in his position would have felt impelled to act, even at the risk of his own safety. Time was pressing; immediate action was necessary if the men in danger were to be helped; there was virtually no opportunity for reflection, or for estimating the risks involved in an act of rescue. If Dr Baker in such circumstances had instinctively gone straight down the well, without stopping to take any precautions at all, it would, I think, have been difficult enough to criticise him; but in point of fact he did take the very wise precaution of securing himself with a rope, whereby those on the surface could pull him up if he himself were overcome. The immediate cause of his death was the sheer mischance of the rope becoming caught on some obstruction, so as to make it impossible for those on the surface to pull him to safety. I do not think that, having regard to the emergency in which he was acting, he is to be blamed for not foreseeing and guarding against the possibility of such a mischance. On the contrary, I entirely agree with the view expressed by the learned judge that the defendant company, whose negligence brought about the danger, must accept the risk of mischances of this kind. In all the circumstances, I find it impossible to accept the contention that Dr Baker was guilty of any negligence either causing or contributing to his death. . . .

[ORMEROD LJ delivered a judgment in favour of dismissing both appeals.]

Appeals dismissed

Questions

1. Would the defendant company have been liable if the rope had snapped without fault on anyone's part before Dr Baker died, and he had fallen and drowned in the well?

2. Could an action have been brought in respect of Dr Baker's death against the estates of Ward or Wileman?

---

1. [1924] 1 KB 548 at 554, 555.

3. Would a kidney donor be able to recover damages from a person who is liable in tort to the donee for the loss of the donee's kidney? (Consider *Urbanski v Patel* (1978) 84 DLR (3d) 650, noted by J. R. Spencer [1979] CLJ 45; G. Robertson (1980) 96 LQR 19; cf. *Sirianni v Anna* 285 NYS (2d) 709 (1967).)

Notes

1. In relation to the second question above see the judgment of Barry J at first instance — [1958] 3 All ER 147 — in *Baker v Hopkins* where he stated (at p. 153):

'Although no one owes a duty to anyone else to preserve his own safety, yet if, by his own carelessness a man puts himself into a position of peril of a kind that invites rescue, he would in law be liable for any injury caused to someone whom he ought to have foreseen would attempt to come to his aid.'

This view has recently been confirmed by the decision of Boreham J in *Harrison v British Railways Board* [1981] 3 All ER 679, relying on *Videan v British Transport Commission* post. See further *Chapman v Hearse* (1961) 106 CLR 112.

2. On contributory negligence which is discussed in *Baker v Hopkins*, see chap. 7, p. 354, post. For the reasons given in *Baker v Hopkins* there are unlikely to be many occasions on which a rescuer is found to be contributorily negligent, but for an example see *Harrison v British Railways Board* (20% reduction in damages).

Question

If X goes potholing, and, through his own carelessness, gets stuck, and Y is injured in trying to rescue him, would X be liable if he had left a note saying that no rescue attempts were to be made if he got into any trouble?

Videan *v* British Transport Commission Court of Appeal [1963] 2 All ER 860

The two year old child of a stationmaster, who lived in the station house, had strayed on to the railway line. His father and a porter saw him there but they also saw a trolley, driven by a petrol engine, fast approaching him. The trolley driver was signalled to stop by the stationmaster and the porter. He slowed down a little, but only saw the child at the last moment when he applied the brake as hard as he could. In an endeavour to save his son, the stationmaster jumped on to the line in the path of the trolley. His son was saved, though injured, but the stationmaster was killed. The trolley driver, Souness, was found by the trial judge to have been at fault in not keeping a proper look-out, in travelling too fast and in not applying his brakes hard enough, soon enough. An action was brought by the stationmaster's widow who also sued as the next friend for her infant son who claimed damages for the injuries he had sustained. The Court of Appeal held the child to be a trespasser and, although his claim was dismissed, the discussion in this case of the duty owed to trespassers was controversial (see p. 461, post). However, the law on this topic has now been set out in statutory form (p. 462, post), and the extracts here only deal with the claim relating to the stationmaster's death, which had been dismissed by the trial judge.

LORD DENNING MR: . . . I turn now to the widow's claim in respect of the death of her husband. In order to establish it, the widow must prove that Souness owed a duty of care to the stationmaster, that he broke that duty, and that, in consequence of the breach, the stationmaster was killed. Counsel for the defendants says that the widow can prove none of these things. All depends, he says, on the test of foreseeability; and, applying that test, he puts the following dilemma: If Souness could not reasonably be expected to foresee the presence of the child, he could not reasonably be expected to foresee the presence of the father. He could not foresee that a trespasser would be on the line. So how could he be expected to foresee that anyone would be attempting to rescue him? Counsel for the defendants points out that, in all the rescue cases that have hitherto come before the courts, such as *Haynes v G Harwood & Son*[1] and *Baker v T E Hopkins & Sons Ltd*,[2] the conduct of the defendant was a wrong to the victim or the potential victim. How can he be liable to the rescuer when he is not liable to the rescued?

I cannot accept this view. The right of the rescuer is an independent right, and is not derived from that of the victim. The victim may have been guilty of contributory negligence — or his right may be excluded by contractual stipulation — but still the rescuer can sue. So, also, the victim may, as here, be a trespasser and excluded on that ground, but still the rescuer can sue. Foreseeability is necessary, but not foreseeability of the particular emergency that arose. Suffice it that he ought reasonably to foresee that, if he did not take care, some emergency or other might arise, and that someone or other might be impelled to expose himself to danger in order to effect a rescue. Such is the case here. Souness ought to have anticipated that some emergency or other might arise. His trolley was not like an express train which is heralded by signals and whistles and shouts of 'Keep clear'. His trolley came silently and swiftly on the unsuspecting quietude of a country station. He should have realised that someone or other might be put in peril if he came too fast or did not keep a proper look-out; and that, if anyone was put in peril, then someone would come to the rescue. As it happened, it was the stationmaster trying to rescue his child; but it would be the same if it had been a passer-by. Whoever comes to the rescue, the law should see that he does not suffer for it. It seems to me that, if a person by his fault creates a situation of peril, he must answer for it to any person who attempts to rescue the person who is in danger. He owes a duty to such a person above all others. The rescuer may act instinctively out of humanity or deliberately out of courage. But whichever it is, so long as it is not wanton interference, if the rescuer is killed or injured in the attempt, he can recover damages from the one whose fault has been the cause of it. . . .

HARMAN LJ: . . . The father's case seems to have attracted much less attention than the son's. The judge, I think, decided against the father on the ground that he could not be in a better position than his son was, and the burden of counsel for the defendants' argument was similar, namely, that, if the trolley driver had no reason to expect the presence of the infant on the line, still less reason had he to expect to find the father there. I do not think that the two cases stand or fall together like this. These trolleys are not a part of the regular train service which runs (or ought to run) at stated hours and with the arrival of which the employees of the defendants must be taken to be familiar. The trolleys are occasional visitors, with no stated times and no warning of their approach. It is, to my mind, most significant that it is an instruction to trolley drivers that they must approach stations with care. The inference from this is that they must take care that there are no persons on the line, more especially railway servants engaged in maintenance and like duties. One of these servants was the dead station-master. He was a person whose presence on the track was well within the contemplation

---

1. [1935] 1 KB 146; [1934] All ER Rep 103.
2. [1959] 3 All ER 225.

of the driver. He could not be said to be a trespasser. If the infant had suffered nothing and action had been brought on behalf of the father alone, I do not see what answer the defendants could have to a claim for vicarious liability for the negligent act of their servant, the trolley driver. The fact that the father acted rather as a father than as stationmaster seems to me to obscure the issue. The infant might not have been his son but a child of a passenger. It would clearly be within the scope of the stationmaster's employment to take all steps to rescue such a child. It is not necessary that the exact event should be foreseeable. The presence of the stationmaster, one of the defendants' employees, on the track was within the sphere of contemplation. Whether, if the rescuer had been a member of the public, there would have been liability, I leave out of account.

It is, perhaps, rather a different point of view to hold that the emergency justified the father's presence on the line. In the policeman's case, *Haynes v Harwood*,[1] the policeman dashed into the highway to stop the horse which was a menace to children on the highway. It may be said to be different in that such children were lawfully on the highway and were not trespassers, but the emergency is the like and the rescuer has an independent right. . . .

PEARSON LJ: . . . I now come to the appeal of the plaintiff widow, who claims damages for the death of her husband caused, as she contends, by the negligence of Souness acting as the servant of the defendants. It is clear from the evidence and the learned judge's findings that Souness, in his approach to the station, was acting negligently in relation to anyone to whom he owed a duty of care, and that the conduct of Souness in this respect caused the accident. The only disputable question is whether Souness owed any relevant duty of care to the deceased. The [defendants'] argument, evidently accepted by the learned judge, has been that the position of the rescuer could not be any better than the position of the person rescued, and that, as the infant plaintiff's trespass was unforeseeable, so the act of his father in trying to rescue him was unforeseeable, and that, therefore, both the infant plaintiff and his father were outside the zone of reasonable contemplation and the scope of duty. That would no doubt have been a formidable argument if the deceased had been only a father rescuing his son. But the deceased was the stationmaster, having a general responsibility for dealing with any emergency that might arise at the station. It was foreseeable by Souness that, if he drove his trolley carelessly into the station, he might imperil the stationmaster, as the stationmaster might well have some proper occasion for going on to the track in the performance of his duties. For this purpose, it is not necessary that the particular accident which happened should have been foreseeable. It is enough that it was foreseeable that some situation requiring the stationmaster to go on the line might arise, and, if any such situation did arise, a careless approach to the station by Souness with his vehicle would be dangerous to the stationmaster. On that ground, I hold that Souness's careless approach to the station was a breach of a duty owing by him to the deceased as stationmaster, and it caused the accident, and that, consequently, the defendants are liable to the widow and her appeal should be allowed. I agree that this court has no ground for interfering with the learned judge's assessment of the widow's damages at £6,348.

Appeal in relation to the stationmaster's death allowed

Notes

1. Two earlier cases on rescuers may usefully be contrasted. In *Cutler v United Dairies (London) Ltd* [1933] 2 KB 297 the plaintiff saw a horse and

1. [1935] 1 KB 146; [1934] All ER Rep 103.

cart, used by the defendants to deliver milk, going quickly past his house without a driver. He was worried about the safety of his children, but found them playing safely in the garden at the rear of the house. He also saw the driver of the cart trying to calm the horse down in an adjoining field, and the driver called out 'Help, help'. The plaintiff went over the hedge and into the field and endeavoured to hold the horse's head. However, the horse reared, the plaintiff was knocked down and he suffered injury. The jury at the trial of the action found the defendants to have been negligent in employing the horse on this job. The horse had, in fact, bolted once, if not twice, before. The Court of Appeal assumed that the jury's finding was correct, but the defendants' appeal was allowed on the grounds that, on the evidence, the jury was not entitled to find that the defendants' negligence was the cause of the plaintiff's damage, and the defence of volenti non fit injuria was applicable (on which see p. 373, post).

The *Cutler* case was distinguished in the later decision of *Haynes v Harwood* [1935] 1 KB 146 where an appeal from a judgment in the plaintiff's favour was dismissed. In that case, Bird, the defendants' servant, had left his two-horse van in the street, but the horses ran away when a boy threw a stone at them. When the horses had reached a spot opposite a police station, the plaintiff, a policeman, saw that a woman was in great danger and that some children would also be in serious danger if the horses were not stopped. He got hold of one of the horses, but, although he stopped them both within fifteen yards, he was injured when one of the horses fell on him. It was held that there was negligence in leaving the horses unattended in the circumstances of this case (this was a crowded street and children were likely to be present). It was further held that the claim did not fail on causation grounds and that the maxim volenti non fit injuria did not provide a defence.

2. In *Chadwick v British Transport Commission* [1967] 2 All ER 945; [1967] 1 WLR 912 a rescuer suffered nervous shock. His illness was caused by the horror of his experiences in helping at the scene of a serious railway accident at Lewisham, in which ninety people lost their lives. The test of whether a duty was owed to Mr Chadwick (the rescuer) was stated to be – 'What ought the defendants to have foreseen?' – and it was held that a duty was owed to him. The defendants had been negligent towards their passengers, and, in the court's view, injury and danger to the passengers could have been foreseen, as could injury to someone who was trying to rescue them. It was argued by the defendants' counsel that the risk which the rescuer underwent was not quite the same as that undergone by the passengers. In fact, the court did not accept that the risk was different, but, in any event, Waller J took the view than 'once the possibility of rescue occurs, the precise manner of rescue is immaterial'.

3. For confirmation of the view in *Videan* that the *particular* accident befalling the rescuer need not be foreseen, see *Knightley v Johns* [1982] 1 All ER 851; [1982] 1 WLR 349, noted p. 329, post. The Court of Appeal's conclusion from its review of various rescuer cases was that a defendant who has, through his negligence, created a danger which invites rescue is liable for 'accidents of a kind or class which might normally be foreseen or contemplated, though the particular accidents could not be expected' ([1982] 1 All ER at p. 860).

Consider, however, *Crossley v Rawlinson* [1981] 3 All ER 674 which should be compared with *Videan*. In *Crossley v Rawlinson* a tarpaulin covering on a lorry caught fire due to the defendant's negligence and the plaintiff, an AA patrolman, was injured whilst running towards it with a fire extinguisher. He was running along a trodden path on the grass verge of the road when, while still some distance from the lorry, his foot went into a hole which was on the path and hidden from his view by grass. The plaintiff's ensuing fall led to a back injury. It was conceded that it was reasonably foreseeable that the plaintiff would run along the path with a fire extinguisher, but the trial judge stated (at p. 678) that it was not reasonably foreseeable that 'the plaintiff would suffer this or any other injury while running along the path', and he gave judgment for the defendant. Do you think the plaintiff would have recovered if he had been injured because the lorry had exploded when he reached it? If so, would he have been able to recover if he had been injured while still some distance away on the path running towards the lorry, but by an explosion on the lorry rather than by the fall (see M. A. Jones (1982) 45 MLR 342 at 344)? And for comment on this decision see generally the note by Jones, which deals with the issue of remoteness of damage that is raised by the case. See further D. Fleming [1982] CLJ 33.

4. It should also be noted that there may be liability to a plaintiff who intervenes where property rather than life or limb is threatened—see *Hyett v Great Western Rly Co* [1948] 1 KB 345; [1947] 2 All ER 264 and p. 142, post.

5. Interesting problems were raised in *Horsley v Maclaren, The Ogopogo* [1971] 2 Lloyd's Rep 410. Matthews fell by accident from Maclaren's boat (on which he was a guest) into a lake. Maclaren manoeuvred the boat whilst rescue attempts were unsuccessfully made, and, after some minutes, Horsley, another guest, dived into the water in an attempt to rescue Matthews. Matthews' body, in fact, was never found, and Horsley also died. Ritchie J, delivering the majority judgment of the Supreme Court of Canada, held that there was a duty on Maclaren 'in his capacity as a host and as the owner and operator of the *Ogopogo*, to do the best he could to effect the rescue of one of his guests who had accidentally fallen overboard'. (Laskin J (with Hall J concurring) delivered a dissenting judgment, but on this point was prepared to find that Maclaren had a duty to take reasonable care for his guests' safety, and his obligation extended to 'rescue from perils of the sea where this is consistent with his duty to see to the safety of his other passengers and with concern for his own safety'.) Ritchie J went on to say (at p. 412):

'In the present case a situation of peril was created when Matthews fell overboard, but it was not created by any fault on the part of Maclaren, and before Maclaren can be found to have been in any way responsible for Horsley's death, it must be found that there was such negligence in his method of rescue as to place Matthews in an apparent position of increased danger subsequent to and distinct from the danger to which he had been initially exposed by his accidental fall. In other words, any duty owing to Horsley must stem from the fact that a new situation of peril was created by Maclaren's negligence which induced Horsley to act as he did.'

Ritchie J, however, held that Maclaren had, in fact, not been negligent. In this situation, should there be a requirement of increased danger 'distinct from' the initial danger? Should a first rescuer, who was not under an existing duty to rescue, be liable to a second rescuer who only attempts a rescue because of the first rescuer's careless efforts? For discussion of these and other issues, see E. R. Alexander (1972) XXII Univ Tor LJ 98. *The Ogopogo* is also discussed by W. Binchy (1974) 25 NILQ 147.

6. A fireman is a professional rescuer. Should this alter the position in any way? In certain states in the USA, under what is known as the 'fireman's rule', firemen injured while attending a fire cannot sue. No such rule operates in English law, however: see *Ogwo v Taylor* [1988] AC 431; [1987] 3 All ER 961. In this case the plaintiff fireman, who had entered the roof space of the defendant's house so as to control a fire with a hose, sustained serious burns from scalding steam, despite wearing protective clothing. The fire in question had been started by the defendant's negligent use of a blowlamp. The defendant argued that there could only be liability to a fireman where the injury was suffered as a result of an exceptional risk foreseeable by the defendant and which he could avoid in some way, for example by a warning: no liability, it was contended, arose for an injury caused by the 'ordinary risks' involved in fire-fighting. This contention was rejected by the House of Lords, who went on to approve the views expressed in *Salmon v Seafarer Restaurants Ltd* [1983] 3 All ER 729; [1983] 1 WLR 1264 and in particular the following statement in Woolf J's judgment in *Salmon* (at p. 736):

'Where it can be foreseen that the fire which is negligently started is of the type which could, first of all, require firemen to attend to extinguish that fire, and where, because of the very nature of the fire, when they attend they will be at risk even though they exercise all the skill of their calling, there seems no reason why a fireman should be at any disadvantage when the question of compensation for his injuries arises.'

The position is, therefore, governed by a straightforward foresight test, and, of course, as the House of Lords acknowledged, even though the fire brigade have been called out, there may be no foreseeable risk to them in the circumstances. It was expressly pointed out in *Salmon* that the special skills of the fireman will affect the question whether injury is foreseeable or not. On the position of firemen, see further p. 454, post.

4 The unborn child

The Congenital Disabilities (Civil Liability) Act 1976[1]

1. **Civil liability to child born disabled.** — (1) If a child is born disabled as the result of such an occurrence before its birth as is mentioned in subsection (2) below, and a person (other than the child's own mother) is under this section answerable to the child in respect of the occurrence, the child's disabilities are to be regarded as damage resulting from the wrongful act of that person and actionable accordingly at the suit of the child.
   (2) An occurrence to which this section applies is one which—
   (*a*) affected either parent of the child in his or her ability to have a normal, healthy child; or

---

1. [For amendments to this Act dealing with infertility treatments, see s. 43 of the Human Fertilisation and Embryology Act 1990 and see also s. 35 of that Act. (Neither was in force at the time of writing.)]

(b)   affected the mother during her pregnancy, or affected her or the child in the course of its birth, so that the child is born with disabilities which would not otherwise have been present.

(3) Subject to the following subsections, a person (here referred to as 'the defendant') is answerable to the child if he was liable in tort to the parent or would, if sued in due time, have been so; and it is no answer that there could not have been such liability because the parent suffered no actionable injury, if there was a breach of legal duty which, accompanied by injury, would have given rise to the liability.

(4) In the case of an occurrence preceding the time of conception, the defendant is not answerable to the child if at that time either or both of the parents knew the risk of their child being born disabled (that is to say, the particular risk created by the occurrence); but should it be the child's father who is the defendant, this subsection does not apply if he knew of the risk and the mother did not.

(5) The defendant is not answerable to the child, for anything he did or omitted to do when responsible in a professional capacity for treating or advising the parent, if he took reasonable care having due regard to then received professional opinion applicable to the particular class of case; but this does not mean that he is answerable only because he departed from received opinion.

(6) Liability to the child under this section may be treated as having been excluded or limited by contract made with the parent affected, to the same extent and subject to the same restrictions as liability in the parent's own case; and a contract term which could have been set up by the defendant in an action by the parent, so as to exclude or limit his liability to him or her, operates in the defendant's favour to the same, but no greater, extent in an action under this section by the child.

(7) If in the child's action under this section it is shown that the parent affected shared the responsibility for the child being born disabled, the damages are to be reduced to such extent as the court thinks just and equitable having regard to the extent of the parent's responsibility.

2. Liability of woman driving when pregnant. – A woman driving a motor vehicle when she knows (or ought reasonably to know) herself to be pregnant is to be regarded as being under the same duty to take care for the safety of her unborn child as the law imposes on her with respect to the safety of other people; and if in consequence of her breach of that duty her child is born with disabilities which would not otherwise have been present, those disabilities are to be regarded as damage resulting from her wrongful act and actionable accordingly at the suit of the child.

4. Interpretation and other supplementary provisions. – (1) References in this Act to a child being born disabled or with disabilities are to its being born with any deformity, disease or abnormality, including predisposition (whether or not susceptible of immediate prognosis) to physical or mental defect in the future.

(2) In this Act –
(a)   'born' means born alive (the moment of a child's birth being when it first has a life separate from its mother), and 'birth' has a corresponding meaning; and
(b)   'motor vehicle' means a mechanically propelled vehicle intended or adapted for use on roads.

(3) Liability to a child under section 1 or 2 of this Act is to be regarded –
(a)   as respects all its incidents and any matters arising or to arise out of it; and
(b)   subject to any contrary context or intention, for the purpose of construing references in enactments and documents to personal or bodily injuries and cognate matters,
as liability for personal injuries sustained by the child immediately after its birth.

(5) This Act applies in respect of births after (but not before) its passing, and in respect of any such birth it replaces any law in force before its passing, whereby a

person could be liable to a child in respect of disabilities with which it might be born; but in section 1(3) of this Act the expression 'liable in tort' does not include any reference to liability by virtue of this Act, or to liability by virtue of any such law.

. . .

5. Crown application. – This Act binds the Crown.

Questions

1. Why should the mother have an immunity from liability which is not possessed by the father?

2. Why should a mother be liable in the circumstances set out in s. 2 of the Act, but not otherwise?

Notes

1. Before this Act was passed, no English court had decided whether at common law the child injured whilst en ventre sa mere could successfully maintain an action for damages after birth if he or she could establish negligence; nevertheless, it was thought that such an action would have been allowed, as it had been in other jurisdictions, if the issue had arisen squarely for decision. This view was supported by inter alia an obiter dictum of Lord Denning MR in *Re Taylor's Application* [1972] 2 QB 369 at 377 and by the Law Commission (para. 8 of the *Report on Injuries to Unborn Children*, Law Com. No. 60, Cmnd. 5709, 1974). See further the decision at first instance of Lawson J and the concession of counsel in the Court of Appeal in *McKay v Essex Area Health Authority* [1982] QB 1166; [1982] 2 All ER 771, a case which was decided after the 1976 Act but which, because of the date of the birth in question, was governed by the common law. Recently in *B v Islington Health Authority* [1991] 1 All ER 825; [1991] 1 WLR 501, where for a similar reason the common law applied, it was decided that such a claim was permissible. For discussion of the position prior to the 1976 Act, see e.g. P. A. Lovell and R. H. Griffith-Jones (1974) 90 LQR 531.

As will have been seen, in the case of births occurring after 22 July 1976 (the date of the passing of the Congenital Disabilities (Civil Liability) Act 1976), the Act replaces any action that existed at common law (s. 4(5)). This is important; for example, it may have been that at common law English courts would have allowed an action against the mother in circumstances going beyond those set out in s. 2. See further J. M. Eekelaar and R. W. M. Dingwall [1984] JSWL 258 who are critical of the effect of the Act on the position of the child.

2. In relation to s. 1(6) of the Act, note the restriction imposed by the Unfair Contract Terms Act 1977 (p. 389, post). It has been pointed out – see *Current Law Statutes Annotated* 1976, vol. 1 – that, when it does operate, s. 1(6) provides an exception to the doctrine of privity of contract.

3. As has been mentioned (p. 114, ante) the question of liability for ante-natal injuries was referred to the Law Commission in 1972. In 1973, however, the Pearson Commission was established and the topic of compensation for ante-natal injuries was also within that body's terms of reference; see the discussion in vol. 1, chap. 26 of the Report. The Report contains the recommendations (by a majority) that 'a child born alive suffering from the effects of ante-natal injury caused by the fault of another person should con-

tinue to have a right of action for damages against that person', but that 'a child should not have a right of action for damages against either parent for ante-natal injury', unless the ante-natal injury arose 'from any activity for which insurance is compulsory'. It was also recommended that 's. 1(7) of the Congenital Disabilities (Civil Liability) Act 1976 should be repealed', and that 'there should be no change in the provisions of the Congenital Disabilities (Civil Liability) Act 1976 relating to pre-conception injury, beyond the removal of the father as a potential defendant'.

It is interesting to note that whereas the Law Commission suggested that one of the obvious difficulties in this field — causation — would become less of a problem in the future, the Pearson Commission concluded that increases in knowledge brought with them increases in uncertainty in the sphere of causation, and that 'only a minute proportion of those who are born with congenital defects may be able to establish causation and prove that it was due to negligence, and that there is little prospect that this proportion will increase' (para. 1452).

The Pearson Commission concluded that children suffering from injuries inflicted ante-natally should be regarded as part of the more general problem concerning the provision of compensation for all injured children, on which see vol. 1, chap. 27 of the Report.

4. Note that a posthumous child may claim under the Fatal Accidents Act 1976, p. 240, post, (*The George and Richard* (1871) LR 3 A&E 466); thus a child born financially disabled may be compensated. For a statutory provision dealing with compensation for the child who is severely disabled as a result of a vaccination against particular diseases given in certain circumstances to that child's mother before the child's birth, see s. 1(3) of the Vaccine Damage Payments Act 1979; note, however, the conditions of entitlement set out in s. 2 of that Act, and in particular the age requirement in s. 2(1)(c).

5. Section 3 of the Congenital Disabilities (Civil Liability) Act 1976, which is concerned with the operation of the Nuclear Installations Act 1965, is summarised at p. 534, post.

6. For the effect of s. 1 of the 1976 Act in relation to the Consumer Protection Act 1987 (strict liability for defective products), see s. 6(3) of the latter Act (p. 508, post).

Civil Liability for Pre-Natal Injuries P. J. Pace (1977) 40 MLR 141 at 151–153

The Act requires that the child should be born alive disabled or with disabilities. According to section 4(1) this means that the child must be born with 'any deformity, disease or abnormality, including predisposition (whether or not susceptible of immediate prognosis) to physical or mental defect in the future.' This obviously limits the operation of the Act to damage which is capable of being assessed in pecuniary terms, so that the courts will not be faced with the novel situation in the American case of *Williams v State of New York*[1]. There an illegitimate child was born to her

---

1. 18 NY 2d 481 (1966). The Act would presumably cover injuries causing traumatic nymphomania, see *Gloria Sykes v San Francisco Municipal Rly* 11 Med Sci & Law 51 (1971).

mentally deficient mother as a result of a sexual assault upon her mother, then a mental patient in a State institution. The plaintiff alleged that the State had been negligent in failing to provide proper supervision and protection for her mother, and that this alleged negligence had caused her (the plaintiff) to bear the stigma of illegitimacy and to be prejudiced in her property rights. The court dismissed the claim because it found it impossible to decide whether non-existence was preferable to existence as an illegitimate child. Such a disability would not fall within the definition of 'disability' proposed by the Act. The Law Commission disapproved of the approach in *Williams* and differentiated between the situation in which, e.g. the child's disability was caused by syphilitic intercourse when an action would lie, and the situation where, e.g. negligent treatment of a pregnant woman prevented spontaneous abortion[1], when no action would lie. This difference is attributable, according to the Law Commission, to the fact that, in the latter case only, logic dictates that the child's claim must be based on the contention that he would have been better off had the spontaneous abortion succeeded and he had never been born. To guard against the possibility of so-called 'wrongful life' actions, section 1(2)(b) states that an action lies only where, but for the conduct giving rise to the disabled birth, the child would have been born normal – not that it would not have been born at all. There is, however, a difficulty in not treating the former case as a 'wrongful life' claim. As Tedeschi has pointed put[2]:

'How could the Manhattan hospital have prevented the unlawful birth and the mental heredity of Christine Williams without preventing her conception as well? And even assuming, for the sake of argument, that it could have been possible to create that life without those adverse circumstances – the fact remains that a single act had been committed, an act on which the plaintiff relied as her cause of action without it being open artificially to a split so as to advance the plaintiff's case.'

Pre-conception fault

Although it is a considerable extension of the existing Commonwealth and American authorities, the Act provides that pre-conception occurrences may found a cause of action. This situation could arise where negligent X-ray treatment or defective birth-control substances affected a parent's reproductive system to such an extent that the child subsequently conceived was born disabled.[3] The child has no right of action if at the time of the occurrence either parent knew of the risk of the child being born disabled, though this does not apply if the father is the defendant or where the occurrence is coincident with or *post* conception. This poses problems since 'new embryological data . . . purport to indicate that conception is a "process" overtime, rather than an event.'[4] Apart from this difficulty, the point has been made[5] that to allow recovery for pre-conception negligence would be to recognise a legal interest in *not* being conceived. If this analysis is correct then English law will recognise the validity of 'wrongful life' actions and, indeed, Tedeschi would argue that pre-conception negligence does give rise to a 'wrongful life' action:

---

1. See *Gleitman v Cosgrove* 49 NJ 22 (1967).
2. I. Tedeschi, 'On tort liability for "wrongful life"' [1966] Israel LR 513, 531.
3. Edwards, 'The Problem of Compensation for Antenatal Injuries' (1973) 246 *Nature* 54, 55, draws attention to the lack of clear evidence of a causal link between pre-conception damage to gametic cells and post-natal injury.
4. *Roe v Wade* 35 L Ed 2d 147, 93 S Ct (1973) per Blackmun J at p. 181.
5. 'The Impact of Medical Knowledge on the Law Relating to Pre-Natal Injuries' (1962) 110 University of Pennsylvania Law Review 554, 584, n.

'When a person fathers a child and infects it with a disease by one and the same act, then either the semen was already infected when it came into contact with the ovum, so that the new entity created is diseased from its conception (and this is the true meaning of congenital disease), or the single act results in paternity and in the infection of the mother, which will be transmitted from her to the infant. In the first case it is obvious that there was only one alternative to the new being, either not to exist or to exist with the disease. But in the second case as well no separation can be made between the act of the parent causing paternity and that causing the infection, as we are faced with a single act.'[1]

The Law Commission, favouring an action in such circumstances, approached the situation on the basis that, if a child has a legal right to begin life with a sound mind and body, and this is the effect of the proposed legislation, there is a correlative duty on its parents and others to avoid producing conception where the circumstances are likely to result in birth of a disabled child. In other words, the remedy is sought not for being born but 'for compensation for the disability resulting from the sexual intercourse.'[2] It should also be noted that in pre-conception cases compensation would not, without the help of the fiction provided by the Act, fulfil the function, as in other areas of tort, of restoring, as far as money can, the status quo. The fiction is contained in section 4(3) which states that 'Liability under this Act is to be regarded . . . as liability for personal injuries sustained by the child immediately after its birth.'

Notes

1. This article discusses other aspects of the Congenital Disabilities (Civil Liability) Act 1976, on which see also K. M. Stanton (1976) 6 Fam Law 206; P. F. Cane (1977) 51 ALJ 704; Eekelaar and Dingwall, op cit.

2. The Pearson Commission agreed with the Law Commission that there should be no cause of action for damages for 'wrongful life' (para. 1486), and in *McKay v Essex Area Health Authority* [1982] QB 1166; [1982] 2 All ER 771 the Court of Appeal accepted (obiter) that s. 1(2)(b) of the 1976 Act did indeed achieve that goal (though note the points in Pace's article (ante)). In the *McKay* case the birth in question occurred before 22 July 1976 and so the matter was governed by the common law which the Court of Appeal decided did not allow such an action. *McKay* is noted by G. Robertson (1982) 45 MLR 697 and T. Weir [1982] CLJ 225. See further H. Teff (1985) 34 ICLQ 423; J.E.S. Fortin [1981] JSWL 306; R. Lee in *Birthrights*, edited by R. Lee and D. Morgan, (London, 1989), chap. 10.

As Robertson points out, the position of a child denied an action for 'wrongful life' can be ameliorated if the parents have an action for 'wrongful birth'; and for the implications of the *McKay* case on this point, see Robertson, op cit, pp. 700–701. The question of an action for 'wrongful birth' was discussed by Jupp J in *Udale v Bloomsbury Area Health Authority* [1983] 2 All ER 522; [1983] 1 WLR 1098 in which a child had been born after a sterilisation operation had been negligently carried out on the mother. He regarded some of the policy considerations which were discussed in the *McKay* case in relation to the denial of the child's action, as also relevant to the claim by the mother in this case for the cost of extending the family home

---

1. Op cit, p. 531.
2. Op cit, [note 1, p. 144, ante] para. 88.

and of the child's upbringing until he was sixteen. For example, he argued that there would be subconcious pressure on doctors to advise an abortion so as to avoid a negligence action but cf. Griffiths LJ's view in *McKay* [1982] 2 All ER at p. 790. See [1983] 2 All ER at p. 531 for the other policy arguments which led Jupp J to the conclusion that the claim for such costs should be denied (though he did manage to award some compensation for 'disturbance to the family finances' from the unexpected pregnancy without detracting from this public policy — see [1983] 2 All ER at pp. 531–532). However, Peter Pain J in *Thake v Maurice* [1986] QB 644; [1984] 2 All ER 513 dealing with a contract claim (cf. [1986] 1 All ER 497 at 503–506) took a different view. The decision was reversed in part on appeal but not on this point, [1986] QB 644; [1986] 1 All ER 497, and Peter Pain J's view on the issue met with approval in the Court of Appeal's decision in *Emeh v Kensington and Chelsea and Westminster Area Health Authority* [1985] QB 1012; [1984] 3 All ER 1044. In this case the court refused to accept that public policy barred recovery of damages by a parent for the costs of a child which would not have been born in the absence of negligence; indeed Waller LJ, with whose judgment Slade LJ agreed, argued that if damages could not be awarded in this sort of case, then there might be an incentive for a woman to have a late abortion. (More generally, Waller LJ referred to Lord Scarman's speech in *McLoughlin v O'Brian* [1983] 1 AC 410; [1982] 2 All ER 298, noted p. 64, ante and stated that the court 'should not be too ready to lay down lines of public policy', on which see pp. 64–65, ante.) *Emeh* has resolved the matter at the level of the Court of Appeal: see *Thake v Maurice* and *Gold v Haringey Health Authority* [1988] QB 481; [1987] 3 All ER 888, though the tenor of Lloyd LJ's judgment in the latter case suggests that he might otherwise have decided the issue differently. For discussion of policy factors in this area, see C. R. Symmons (1989) 50 MLR 269, and for more general discussion of the action see W. V. H. Rogers (1985) 5 LS 296 (though note that it was written before the Court of Appeal's decision in *Thake v Maurice*); A. Grubb in *Medicine, Ethics and the Law*, edited by M. D. A. Freeman, (London, 1988), p. 121.

4 Protected economic interests

The law of tort serves to protect wealth. Wealth is made up of all those things which can be used or exchanged. The 'things' may be tangible such as land and goods or they may be intangible such as debts, patents and copyrights. Wealth may include rights under a contract as well as the expectation of pecuniary advantage from a business transaction or employment relationship, or the capital of a company or the investments in a fund managed by trustees. In a broad sense, all of these are 'economic interests'.

The *kind* of damage recoverable in the tort of negligence is usually said to be limited to those 'economic' losses which are consequent upon some *physical* harm to the plaintiff's person or to his tangible property. In the case of personal injury this includes loss of earning capacity and expenses, such as the value of services provided by others to the injured plaintiff (p. 418, post). Where property is destroyed by the defendant's tort the normal measure of damages is the value of the property at the time of destruction or, where it is damaged, the cost of repair. There may also be other recoverable ('foreseeable') losses (chap. 6, p. 329, post) such as the loss of profits on property used in the course of a business (p. 331, post).

There has been reluctance to protect other kinds of economic interest through the mechanism of tort. This reluctance has sometimes been expressed in doctrinal terms (e.g. the view that some professional persons could be sued only in contract, p. 201, post), or on policy grounds, in particular the familiar 'floodgates' argument, the fear of 'liability for an indeterminate amount to an indeterminate class' (p. 233, post). In part, limitations on liability are rooted in the market economy and the idea that harm caused by free trade and competition should not be actionable. It is usually thought to be 'legitimate' for the businessman or worker to bear the risk of economic losses, unless these are *deliberately* inflicted in violation of existing contractual rights or, in the absence of such rights, if 'unlawful' means are used (chap. 15, p. 673, post).

With the rise of financial interests, it is scarcely surprising that the rule excluding claims for *negligently* causing 'pure' economic loss came under increasing pressure. The first breakthrough was in the case of false information and advice. In order to understand the developments one must begin with the tort of deceit (p. 155, post), of which there have been traces since the 13th century as part of the legal control of trickery. This usually arises in the context of business dealings. The famous case of *Pasley v Freeman* (1789) 3 Term Rep 51 is the basis of the modern rule that A is liable to B if he knowingly or recklessly, not caring whether it is true or false, makes a false statement to B with intent that it shall be acted upon by B, who does act upon it and thereby suffers damage. *Fleming*, p. 598, observes that 'the close association of deceit with bargaining transactions has inevitably coloured the elements of the action which largely reflect the ethical and moral standards of the market place as they relate to permissible methods of obtaining contractual or other benefits and of inflicting pecuniary loss through reliance on false statements'. In *Derry v Peek* (1889) 14 App Cas 337 (p. 155, post) the House of Lords set itself firmly against any liability for negligent, as distinct from dishonest, statements of fact. Those who wanted protection could buy it, by means of a contract with the representor, but could not utilise the law of tort. This separation of tort and contract had emerged in the 18th century. Before then actions for breach of a warranty made by the seller at the time of sale as to the quality and fitness of goods sold were treated as a deceit. But by the end of that century a warranty was treated as a promise or contract that the facts stated were true, enabling the buyer to claim back what he had paid on grounds of a total failure of consideration. The result was that damages were recoverable for a false statement only if either (a) it was made dishonestly (tort), or (b) there was a breach of warranty (contract). Where a fraudulent false statement had induced the representee to make a contract with the representor, rescission of the contract could be obtained in addition to damages. But where the representation was innocent, only rescission and not damages was available. This unsatisfactory state of affairs in respect of pre-contractual dealings was remedied by the Misrepresentation Act 1967 (p. 159, post) which (a) extended the right to rescission; (b) allowed damages in lieu of rescission in respect of a representation made otherwise than fraudulently where to grant rescission would be inequitable to the representor; and (c) extended the right to claim damages, quite apart from any right to rescission, to certain forms of negligent misrepresentation.

Meanwhile, in *Hedley Byrne & Co Ltd v Heller & Partners Ltd* [1964] AC 465; [1963] 2 All ER 575 (p. 161, post) the House of Lords removed the earlier restrictions on liability for careless information and advice causing economic loss. But their Lordships were cautious, being unwilling to apply Lord Atkin's 'neighbour' principle (p. 43, ante) literally. It was said that negligent *words* were different from negligent *acts* (p. 161, post). They limited the boundaries of the new duty of care not to cause loss by negligent information or advice by saying that there had to be an implied undertaking to exercise care. Although this need not be supported by consideration, some 'special relationship' between the parties would be necessary, the common factor in their Lordships' various descriptions of such relationships being reasonable *reliance* on the skill and judgment of the person making the statement.

It was uncertain for some time whether *Hedley Byrne* had simply established a special category of case by way of exception to the general exclusionary rule against recovery of 'pure' economic loss, or had laid the foundation for a general duty of care not to cause economic loss by undertaking a responsibility upon which another relies to his or her detriment. The first section in this chapter (*voluntary undertakings*) is dominated by the attempts of the courts to work out the relationship between the neighbour principle in *M'Alister* (or *Donoghue*) *v Stevenson* [1932] AC 562 (p. 40, ante) which was limited by Lord Atkin to cases of physical damage, and the detrimental reliance principle in *Hedley Byrne*. In the 1970s and early 1980s, a series of House of Lords decisions presaged an expansion of the scope of

Donoghue v Stevenson liability. For example in *Anns v Merton London Borough Council* [1978] AC 728; [1977] 2 All ER 492 (p. 99, ante) and cases which purported to follow it, an expanded meaning was given to 'physical harm'. In *Junior Books Ltd v Veitchi Co Ltd* [1983] 1 AC 520; [1982] 3 All ER 201, noted p. 226, post, a majority in the House of Lords broke down the barrier between physical harm and economic loss and treated detrimental reliance as the touchstone of liability in 'most cases', so linking (in very uncertain fashion) *Donoghue v Stevenson* and *Hedley Byrne* principles. At the same time there was a rejection of the traditional notion that if the defendant owed a duty of care under a contract with the plaintiff there could be no concurrent liability in tort (see *Midland Bank Trust Co Ltd v Hett, Stubbs and Kemp (a firm)* [1979] Ch 384; [1978] 3 All ER 571, noted p. 201, post). Third parties who suffered loss as a result of A's breach of undertaking to B were allowed to recover their lost benefits (*Ministry of Housing and Local Government v Sharp* [1970] 2 QB 223; [1970] 1 All ER 1009, p. 189, post; *Ross v Caunters* [1980] Ch 297; [1979] 3 All ER 580, p. 192, post). Under the guise of an expansion of the tort of negligence, a single law of obligations seemed to be emerging. The pressure for this arose because of the inadequate and rigid traditional conceptions of the scope of contractual liability, circumscribed by doctrines such as those of consideration and privity of contract.

During the 1980s, however, there has been a reversion to the traditional view that economic benefits can be conferred only by contract, and a striking reassertion of the general principle of non-liability in tort for pure economic loss. It is, perhaps, not surprising that the instincts of the judiciary have matched the growth of an 'enterprise' culture in Britain in this period. The risks of a failed investment in some circumstances (p. 181, post), or of a failure to take out insurance (p. 196, post), or of not taking adequate precautions to protect one's interests when renegotiating a contract (p. 203, post), or the risks of leasing premises or buying products which are worth less than one reasonably expected (p. 212, post), or of having one's business interrupted by a cut in the electricity supply (p. 230, post), are seen as risks inherent in business, 'and the essence of a capitalist society is that businessmen pit their wits against each other in assessing these risks' (*Atiyah*, pp. 74–75). Unfortunately, these risks have been adjudged to fall not only on businessmen but also on employees (p. 196, post), rugby-playing schoolboys (p. 200, post) and ordinary tenants and consumers (p. 212, post). To this extent there has been a retreat of the common law from the philosophy of welfarism, leaving the protection of vulnerable sections of society to Parliament, which itself has in recent years shown a preference for self-regulation of financial and other markets.

Whatever the social basis for the restriction of tort liability, the conceptual framework in which these results have been achieved is bewildering and unsatisfactory. This area of law has lacked an Atkin (see Wedderburn (1983) 46 MLR 223 at 226 referring to the economic torts), and the courts confess that their decisions are of an 'intensely pragmatic' character (per Lord Keith in *Yuen Kun Yeu v A-G of Hong Kong* [1988] AC 175 at 194). The problem is to know which of a number of sometimes inconsistent concepts are being used to control the possibility of crushing liability, and to ensure that the person in the best position to avoid the costs of accidents bears the risk. Judicial preferences change. For example, the notion of 'voluntary assumption of responsibility', in vogue since the *Hedley Byrne* case, was said in *Smith v Eric S Bush (a firm)* [1989] 2 All ER 514 at 534 (p. 177 post) by Lord Griffiths not to be 'a helpful or realistic test of liability'. The test of detrimental 'reliance' on the defendant's undertaking, also central to the *Hedley Byrne* approach, was shown in *Muirhead v Industrial Tank Specialities Ltd* [1985] 3 All ER 705 at 714, noted p. 501, post, by Robert Goff LJ to be of limited value in relation to promises that goods are of sound quality. However, in *Murphy v Brentwood District Council* [1990] 2 All ER 908; [1990] 3 WLR 414, (p. 212, post) both Lord Keith and Lord Oliver recognised that a narrowly drawn notion of 'reliance' may still be used in near-contractual situations, at least against the builder of defective premises.

In the *Murphy* case, a seven-member Judicial Committee of the House of Lords had an opportunity to clear away the doctrinal rubble which surrounds economic loss. They used the freedom given to them by the Practice Statement of 26 July 1966 (see *Practice Note* [1966] 3 All ER 77; [1966] 1 WLR 1234) to overrule *Anns v Merton London Borough Council* [1978] AC 728; [1977] 2 All ER 492 (p. 99, ante), which had been undermined by several decisions before *Murphy*. The House has now put beyond doubt the proposition that no duty of care is owed in respect of economic loss caused by defects in the quality of buildings or products which render them less valuable. Beyond this, however, it is difficult to extract any general principles from the judgments in this and other recent House of Lords decisions. As P. Cane (1989) 52 MLR 200 at 214 remarks, 'it seems unlikely that the law of tort liability for economic loss is yet in its final form'. Indeed, the complex and dynamic nature of economic relationships renders illusory the goal of a single all-embracing principle. The growing interdependence of markets, particularly within the EEC, suggests that the courts and legislature in Britain will have to pay increasing attention to solutions to these problems in other countries. One example is the solution in some European countries to the question of transferred loss (p. 209, post).

For the present, the following guidelines may help the student through the conceptual morass.

(1) There is a duty of care in respect of words or advice given in the course of business or a professional relationship upon which the plaintiff reasonably relies to his detriment (p. 161, post).

(2) There has been a tendency to return to the concept of 'proximity' (as distinct from the broader notion of reasonable foreseeability) so as to limit liability to an identified individual or a member of an identifiable class in respect of a particular transaction (e.g. *Yuen Kun Yeu v A-G of Hong Kong* [1988] AC 175; [1987] 2 All ER 705, noted p. 187, post; *Caparo Industries plc v Dickman* [1990] 1 All ER 568; [1990] 2 WLR 358, p. 181 post). In general, it is only where B directly relies on a statement or advice by A that liability in negligence will arise. However, in a limited and anomalous category of three-party situations (consider *Ministry of Housing and Local Government v Sharp* [1970] 2 QB 223; [1970] 1 All ER 1009, p. 189, post and *Ross v Caunters* [1980] Ch 297; [1979] 3 All ER 580, p. 192, post) there may be liability where B relies on a statement made by A and in so doing causes loss to a third party, C.

(3) The principle, established in the late 19th century in the context of

involuntary relationships, that only a person with a possessory or proprietary interest in a chattel is entitled to be compensated for economic loss by a party who negligently damaged the chattel, has been reasserted, after a period of uncertainty (*Candlewood Navigation Corpn Ltd v Mitsui OSK Lines Ltd* [1986] AC 1; [1985] 2 All ER 935, noted p. 236, post), and has been indiscriminately applied in the context of bilateral or trilateral exchange relationships (*Leigh and Sillivan Ltd v Aliakmon Shipping Co Ltd* [1986] AC 785; [1986] 2 All ER 145, p. 203, post).

(4) Beyond the established exceptions, the negligent causing of economic loss does not need to be justified. In the words of Lord Oliver (in *Murphy v Brentwood District Council* [1990] 2 All ER at 934, p. 225, post) 'if it is to be categorised as wrongful it is necessary to find some factor beyond the mere occurrence of the loss and the fact that its occurrence could be foreseen'. The solution to borderline cases (such as *Spartan Steel and Alloys Ltd v Martin & Co (Contractors) Ltd* [1973] QB 27; [1972] 3 All ER 557, p. 230, post) has so far been achieved pragmatically 'not by the application of logic but by the perceived necessity as a matter of policy to place some limits, perhaps arbitrary limits, to what would otherwise be an endless, cumulative causation chain bounded only by theoretical foreseeability' per Lord Oliver, ibid.

In this fertile field of legal policy-making, it is helpful to start with an extract from an article which draws a distinction, on economic as well as legal grounds, between voluntary undertakings and involuntary relationships, and explains the different considerations which should apply to each (p. 154, post). This distinction is followed in the arrangement of the chapter. In the first section, *voluntary undertakings*, we begin with liability for false information and advice, now clearly established as an important exception to the general principle of non-liability for economic loss. After considering deceit and the Misrepresentation Act 1967, s. 2(1), we look at the common law of negligence (p. 159, post). The *Hedley Byrne* case is the basis for an examination of situations where the communication is made by A, or his agent, to B, or his agent. This must be distinguished from the next group of cases (such as *Smith v Eric S Bush*) where A, or his agent, makes a statement to B, or his agent, and it is passed on to C, who suffers loss by relying upon it (p. 175, post). Both of these situations are distinct from three-party situations (consider *Ministry of Housing and Local Government v Sharp* and *Ross v Caunters*), where B relies on a statement made by A and in so doing causes loss to C (p. 189, post). We then turn to the more general question of the relationship between tort and contract in two-party situations (p. 196, post), and finally to attempts which have been made to use the law of tort to avoid the rigid doctrines of contract law, by rendering a promise made by A to B enforceable in tort by C who suffers loss, or fails to obtain a benefit, as a result of the breach of undertaking (p. 203, post). This includes cases where A is alleged to have failed to exercise supervision over B, causing loss to C (p. 212, post).

The second section deals with involuntary relationships. Here the interests sought to be protected are characterised as *relational interests*. The plaintiff (C) suffers economic loss as a result of his or her relationship to the primary victim (B) of the defendant (A)'s negligence. The first category of relational interest is where C suffers loss as a result of physical harm to B's property by A. The *Spartan Steel* case (p. 230, post) is the best illustration of the hard line between this case (no liability) and the one in which C's losses result from harm to his own property (liability). The use of this line in the context of involuntary relationships serves the purpose of avoiding crushing liability, but it is by no means clear that such an arbitrary distinction in fact allocates the risk to the party best able to take preventive action to reduce the cost of accidents (p. 234, post).

The second relational interest is that in another's life or services. If the interference results in B's death then the common law rule is that C cannot complain in a civil court (p. 239, post). Like the Romans, the medieval English lawyers took the view that it was impossible to place a value on the life of a free man. In the emerging industrial society of the 19th century, the rule had the socially inconvenient result of imposing the main burden of supporting the widows and children of victims of machines upon the rate-payers instead of upon the entrepreneurs whose activities had created the new risks. Lord Campbell was able to persuade Parliament, despite the opposition of the railway companies, that there should be a statutory exception for the benefit of certain members of the family, where the death of the breadwinner could be attributed to the fault of the defendant (p. 240, post). The family circle has been expanded by recent legislation (p. 241, post) but non-family dependants must still bear their own losses. Apart from the statutory exception, C has no cause of action against A for negligent interference with C's relations with B. (The ancient actions, resting upon feudal conceptions, which allowed an employer of a menial servant to claim for loss of his services, a husband to claim for loss of the society and services of his wife and parents to claim for depriving them of a child's services, were abolished by s. 5 of the Law Reform (Miscellaneous Provisions) Act 1970 and s. 2 of the Administration of Justice Act 1982.)

Liability for Economic Loss in Tort Donald Harris and Cento Veljanovski in *The Law of Tort: Policies and Trends in Liability for Damage to Property and Economic Loss*, edited by M. Furmston, (Duckworth for Colston Research Society, 1986) pp. 45–46

The first issue is whether the loss takes place in a situation which involves some form of agreed exchange between the parties. If it does, then the goal of the law should be to give effect to the parties' wishes, provided that there were no defects in the bargaining process (e.g. duress, fraud, misrepresentation, monopoly) which would suggest that the bargain did not genuinely benefit both parties. Most exchange relationships, even when there is a formal contract, are incompletely specified because of the costs and computational burden of negotiating. This is particularly so for those events with low probabilities which can impede or frustrate performance. One of the functions of the law of contract (and that part of tort law affecting consensual relationships) is to fill in the gaps which have been left in the voluntary agreement of the parties because they did not choose to incur the costs of bargaining over them.

An exchange relationship is a voluntary transaction, which we wish to distinguish from an involuntary relationship. A voluntary transaction is one where the parties wish and intend to enter into a relationship with each other because they have agreed upon a set of goals which they regard as mutually advantageous. By combining together to achieve that set of goals, each of them intends to *improve* his position in some respects (or at least to minimise an expected worsening of his situation). The main function of the law in regard to voluntary transaction is to facilitate their making, and to implement their provisions in those cases where the parties do not voluntarily perform them. The law does not need to provide any incentive to the parties to enter the transaction because their own self-interest provides the incentive. The law's concern is only to provide the appropriate incentives to perform what each party previously promised to do: even here, the law is merely implementing the common intention (at the time of contracting) that neither should be permitted to withdraw from the transaction without the other's consent. In a voluntary transaction the parties' autonomy is almost complete: virtually all aspects of the transaction may be regulated by the parties themselves, should they wish to do so.

In an involuntary relationship (one typically covered by tort) the parties neither wish nor intend to enter into a relationship with the other. Their coming into the relationship is an 'accident' which both parties would have wished to avoid, if it were possible. Before the accident there is in practice no real possibility of bargaining between the parties. There is no agreed set of goals which they wish to achieve by combining together; it is only the facts of the accident situation which bring them together normally because one (the victim) claims that his interests have been adversely affected by some act, omission (or, more generally, some activity) of the other (the actor). Once the harm has occurred, there is, in the absence of a peremptory legal rule governing their enforced relationship, no incentive for the actor to enter into any agreement with the victim to deal with the loss. Unless the law imposes a rule of liability upon the actor in favour of the victim, the latter must bear his own loss. The concern of the victim is, as far as possible, to be restored to the *status quo ante*: he does not seek an improvement in his position, but restoration to his previous position.

In our view, many of the economic loss cases involve exchange relationships, which should be clearly distinguished from those which do not. . . . We have deliberately avoided the use of the word 'contract'. Our concept of exchange relationships is much broader than the legal concept of contract and is arranged along a continuum. At one extreme lies the spot contract where there is simultaneous exchange of money for goods or services; at the other, the vertically integrated firm where exchange relations or contracts are replaced by the administrative direction of decision-making bodies within the firm. . . . The important insight derived from viewing contract as part of a continuum of exchange relationships is that we should not be blinded by legal categorisations and forms as to the true nature of the underlying problem and its economic basis. . . .

1   Voluntary undertakings

(a)   False information and advice

(i)   Deceit

Derry v Peek House of Lords [1886–90] All ER Rep 1

The Plymouth, Devonport and District Tramways Co Ltd was authorised by statute to make certain tramways. The enabling Act provided that the tramways might be moved by animal power and, with the Board of Trade's consent, by steam or mechanical power. The defendants, as directors of the company, issued a prospectus containing the following paragraph:

'One great feature of this undertaking, to which considerable importance should be attached, is, that by the special Act of Parliament obtained, the company has the right to use steam or mechanical motive power, instead of horses, and it is fully expected that by the means of this a considerable saving will result in the working expenses of the line as compared with other tramways worked by horses.'

Sir Henry Peek, the plaintiff, relying upon the representations in this paragraph, applied for and obtained shares in the company. The Board of Trade subsequently refused its consent to the use of steam or mechanical power except on certain portions of the tramways. In the result, the company was wound up, and the plaintiff brought an action against the appellants claiming damages for fraudulent misrepresentations by the defendants whereby he was induced to take shares in the company.

Stirling J dismissed the action. This decision was reversed by the Court of Appeal, which held that negligence was sufficient to support liability. The House of Lords reversed the decision of the Court of Appeal.

LORD HERSCHELL: . . . 'This action is one which is commonly called an action of deceit, a mere common law action.' This is the description of it given by Cotton LJ in delivering judgment. I think it important that it should be borne in mind that such an action differs essentially from one brought to obtain rescission of the contract on the ground of misrepresentation of a material fact. The principles which govern the two actions differ widely. Where rescission is claimed it is only necessary to prove that there was misrepresentation. Then, however honestly it may have been made, however free from blame the person who made it, the contract, having been obtained by misrepresentation, cannot stand. In an action of deceit, on the contrary, it is not enough to establish misrepresentation alone; it is conceded on all hands that something more must be proved to cast liability upon the defendant, though it has been a matter of controversy what additional elements are requisite. . . .

To make a statement careless whether it be true or false, and, therefore, without any real belief in its truth, appears to me to be an essentially different thing from making, through want of care, a false statement which is nevertheless honestly believed to be true. And it is surely conceivable that a man may believe that what he states is the fact, though he has been so wanting in care that the court may think that there were no sufficient grounds to warrant his belief.

I shall have to consider hereafter whether the want of reasonable ground for believing the statement made is sufficient to support an action of deceit. I am only concerned for the moment to point out that it does not follow that it is so because there is authority for saying that a statement made recklessly, without caring whether it be true or false, affords sufficient foundation for such an action. . . .

I think there is here some confusion between that which is evidence of fraud, and that which constitutes it. A consideration of the grounds of belief is no doubt an important aid in ascertaining whether the belief was really entertained. A man's mere assertion that he believed the statement he made to be true is not accepted as conclusive proof that he did so. There may be such an absence of reasonable ground for his belief as, in spite of his assertion, to carry conviction to the mind that he had not really the belief which he alleges. If the learned Lord[1] intended to go further, as apparently he did, and to say that, though the belief was really entertained, yet, if there were no reasonable ground for it, the person making the statement was guilty of fraud in the same way as if he had known what he stated to be false, I say, with all respect, that the previous authorities afford no warrant for the view that an action of deceit would lie under such circumstances. A man who forms his belief carelessly, or is unreasonably credulous, may be blameworthy when he makes a representation

1. [I.e. Lord Chelmsford in *Western Bank of Scotland v Addie* (1862) LR 1 Sc & Div 145 at 162.]

on which another is to act, but he is not, in my opinion, fraudulent in the sense in which that word was used in all the cases from *Pasley v Freeman*[1] down to that with which I am now dealing. Even when the expression 'fraud in law' has been employed, there has always been present, and regarded as an essential element, that the deception was wilful either because the untrue statement was known to be untrue, or because belief in it was asserted without such belief existing. . . .

I think the authorities establish the following propositions: First, in order to sustain an action of deceit, there must be proof of fraud, and nothing short of that will suffice. Secondly, fraud is proved when it is shown that a false representation has been made (i) knowingly, or (ii) without belief in its truth, or (iii) recklessly, careless whether it be true or false. Although I have treated the second and third as distinct cases, I think the third is but an instance of the second, for one who makes a statement under such circumstances can have no real belief in the truth of what he states. To prevent a false statement being fraudulent, there must, I think, always be an honest belief in its truth. And this probably covers the whole ground, for one who knowingly alleges that which is false has obviously no such belief. Thirdly, if fraud be proved, the motive of the person guilty of it is immaterial. It matters not that there was no intention to cheat or injure the person to whom the statement was made.

I think these propositions embrace all that can be supported by decided cases from the time of *Pasley v Freeman*[1] down to *Addie's Case*[2] in 1867, when the first suggestion is to be found that belief in the truth of what he has stated will not suffice to absolve the defendant if his belief be based on no reasonable grounds.

[His Lordship considered the evidence of the defendants and continued:] I think they were mistaken in supposing that the consent of the Board of Trade would follow as a matter of course because they had obtained their Act. It was absolutely in the discretion of the Board whether such consent should be given. The prospectus was, therefore, inaccurate. But that is not the question. If they believed that the consent of the Board of Trade was practically concluded by the passing of the Act, has the plaintiff made out, which it was for him to do, that they have been guilty of a fraudulent misrepresentation? I think not. I cannot hold it proved as to any one of them that he knowingly made a false statement, or one which he did not believe to be true, or was careless whether what he stated was true or false. In short, I think they honestly believed that what they asserted was true, and I am of opinion that the charge of fraud made against them has not been established. . . . Whenever it is necessary to arrive at a conclusion as to the state of mind of another person, and to determine whether his belief under given circumstances was such as he alleges, we can only do so by applying the standard of conduct which our own experience of the ways of men has enabled us to form, and by asking ourselves whether a reasonable man would be likely under the circumstances so to believe. I have applied this test, with the result that I have a strong conviction that a reasonable man situated as the defendants were, with their knowledge and means of knowledge, might well believe what they state they did believe and consider that the representation made was substantially true. . . .

[LORD HALSBURY LC, LORD WATSON, LORD BRAMWELL and LORD FITZGERALD delivered speeches in favour of allowing the appeal.]

Notes

1. As a result of this decision the Directors' Liability Act 1890 imposed certain statutory obligations on persons issuing a prospectus. These are now

---

1. (1789) 3 Term Rep 51.
2. (1862) LR 1 Sc & Div 145.

contained in the Companies Act 1985, s. 67. (See L. C. B. Gower, *Principles of Modern Company Law*, 4th edn (London, 1979), pp. 384 et seq.)

2. A person may obtain compensation, without satisfying the requirements of the tort of deceit, where a court convicting the representor of a criminal offence makes a compensation order under s. 35 of the Powers of Criminal Courts Act 1973 as amended. Among the relevant offences are obtaining property by deception (Theft Act 1968, s. 15) and applying a false description to goods in the course of business or deliberately or recklessly making a false statement about the provision or nature of services, facilities or accommodation (Trade Descriptions Act 1968). On compensation orders, where a criminal offence is committed, see further note 3, p. 582, post.

3. In order to establish liability for deceit 'there must . . . be some active misstatement of fact, or, at all events, such a partial and fragmentary statement of fact as that the withholding of that which is not stated makes that which is stated absolutely false': per Lord Cairns in *Peek v Gurney* (1873) LR 6 HL 377 at 403. The reference to 'statements of fact' should not be read too literally. Statements of opinion may be actionable in the tort of deceit where they import some information not equally available to the representee, such as an expert's opinion based on his background knowledge. Cf. *Bisset v Wilkinson* [1927] AC 177 (statement that land would support 2,000 sheep held to be opinion and not actionable since both parties had no knowledge of facts and no special expertise). Statements of present intention may also be a representation of an existing fact. 'The state of a man's mind is as much a fact as the state of his digestion': per Bowen LJ in *Edgington v Fitzmaurice* (1885) 29 Ch D 459 at 483. 'Where a . . . customer orders a meal in a restaurant, he must be held to make an implied representation that he can and will pay for it before he leaves': *DPP v Ray* [1974] AC 370 at 379.

   If an airline states on a ticket that the reservation is 'OK', and does not mention its deliberate policy of overbooking, is there an implied representation of fact that the seat is guaranteed? If the airline subsequently becomes aware that the seats are overbooked, must it inform the passenger immediately? In either of these circumstances would liability, if it existed, be based on (a) deceit, or (b) breach of contract? On statements which prove to be false, see *Winfield & Jolowicz*, pp. 266–267, and p. 174, post.

4. The damages for deceit cover all the losses flowing *directly* from the tort. Unlike damages for negligence (p. 329, post) they need not be foreseeable. In *Doyle v Olby (Ironmongers) Ltd* [1969] 2 QB 158; [1969] 2 All ER 119, where the plaintiff was induced by fraud to buy a business property, he could claim not only the difference between the price and the market value (the foreseeable loss) but also his expenses in reasonably trying to run the business profitably. But the measure of damages for this tort, unlike damages for breach of a contractual undertaking, does not include damages for loss of bargain (*Saunders v Edwards* [1987] 2 All ER 651 at 655 per Kerr LJ, approving *McGregor on Damages*, now 15th edn., para. 1718). So in contract the plaintiff may recover the difference between the actual value of the propery and the value it would have had if the statement had been true. In tort, the plaintiff is simply restored to the position he would have been in had the statement not been made. However, aggravated damages for injured feelings and inconvenience may also be awarded in this tort: see *Archer v Brown*

[1985] QB 401; [1984] 2 All ER 267, where a 'moderate' award of £500 was made to a plaintiff who had been induced by deceit to buy shares from a defendant who did not own them. In this case it was left open whether exemplary damages are recoverable (cf. Purchas LJ in *Metall und Rohstoff AG v ACLI Metals (London) Ltd* [1984] 1 Lloyds Rep 598 at 612, who said obiter that they are not); see generally p. 407, post.

5. Where the deceit has permanently deprived the plaintiff of the goods, the correct measure of damages is the market value of the goods. For example, assume that drugs are obtained from a manufacturer by deceit, and the manufacturer can produce them at less than the market value (because most of his costs are attributable to research and development), he is entitled to the market value: *Smith Kline & French Laboratories Ltd v Long* [1988] 3 All ER 887; [1989] 1 WLR 1.

6. Although deceit is mainly relevant to the protection of economic interests, it may also be utilised where there has been physical harm: *Langridge v Levy* (1837) 2 M & W 519 (liability for fraudulent misrepresentation as to condition of a gun which burst and injured plaintiff). (Compare *Wilkinson v Downton* [1897] 2 QB 57 p. 591, post.)

The Statute of Frauds Amendment Act 1828

6. Action not maintainable on representations of character, etc., unless they be in writing signed by the party chargeable. – No action shall be brought whereby to charge any person upon or by reason of any representation or assurance made or given concerning or relating to the character, conduct, credit, ability, trade, or dealings of any other person, to the intent or purpose that such other person may obtain credit, money, or goods upon, unless such representation or assurance be made in writing signed by the party to be charged therewith.

Note

The purpose of this section (relating to representations as to credit or credit worthiness) was to prevent evasion of the requirement in the Statute of Frauds, that guarantees be in writing, by suing in tort instead of contract. For this reason the courts have held that the section does not apply to actions for breach of contract. Moreover it is limited to fraudulent representations, or those which are alleged to give rise to liability under s. 2(1) of the Misrepresentation Act 1967 (post) (*UBAF Ltd v European American Banking Corpn* [1984] QB 713; [1984] 2 All ER 226) and does not extend to representations giving rise to a common law duty of care (*W B Anderson & Sons v Rhodes (Liverpool) Ltd* [1967] 2 All ER 850). This appears to be the only situation in which there is liability for a negligent act where there would not be liability if it were done intentionally.

(ii)   Negligence

The Misrepresentation Act 1967

2. Damages for misrepresentation. – (1) Where a person has entered into a contract after a misrepresentation has been made to him by another party thereto and as a result thereof he has suffered loss, then, if the person making the misrepresentation would be liable to damages in respect thereof had the misrepresentation been made fraudulently, that person shall be so liable notwithstanding that the misrepresentation was not made fraudulently, unless he proves that he had reasonable ground to believe and did believe up to the time the contract was made that the facts represented were true.

(2) Where a person has entered into a contract after a misrepresentation has been made to him otherwise than fraudulently, and he would be entitled, by reason of the misrepresentation, to rescind the contract, if it is claimed, in any proceedings arising out of the contract, that the contract ought to be or has been rescinded the court or arbitrator may declare the contract subsisting and award damages in lieu of rescission, if of opinion that it would be equitable to do so, having regard to the nature of the misrepresentation and the loss that would be caused by it if the contract were upheld, as well as to the loss that rescission would cause to the other party.

(3) Damages may be awarded against a person under subsection (2) of this section whether or not he is liable to damages under subsection (1) thereof, but where he is so liable any award under the said subsection (2) shall be taken into account in assessing his liability under the said subsection (1).

Notes

1. Section 2(1) of the Misrepresentation Act 1967 creates a statutory tort which extends the tort of deceit. It enables a party who was induced by the defendant to enter into a contract with him by means of a false representation to recover damages for resulting loss without proving fraud. It is more favourable to the representee than the common law action for careless statements (post) because (a) there is no need to prove a 'special relationship' such as to justify the imposition of a duty of care; and (b) the burden of proof on the representor to show that he had reasonable grounds to believe the facts represented to be true is not easily discharged: *Howard Marine and Dredging Co Ltd v A Ogden & Sons (Excavations) Ltd* [1978] QB 574 at 592–593, 596 and 601 (during negotiations for hire of barges owner's representative honestly misstated their deadweight capacity in reliance on wrong information in Lloyd's register; the correct figure was available in shipping documents in the owner's possession: held burden not discharged). However, where the representation was made by someone not a party to the subsequent contract, the representee will have to rely on the tort of negligence (post). On the sort of misrepresentation which is within s. 2(1) of the 1967 Act, see *Banque Keyser Ullmann SA v Slzandia (UK) Insurance Co Ltd* [1990] 1 QB 665 at 790, when that case was in the Court of Appeal.

2. The wording of s. 2(1) does not make it clear whether damages may include loss of bargain. In *Watts v Spence* [1976] Ch 165; [1975] 2 All ER 528 (criticised by *McGregor on Damages*, paras. 1746–1749) Graham J awarded damages for loss of bargain where the defendant had misrepresented that he was sole owner of a house but in fact he owned it jointly with his wife who had refused to consent to the sale. These damages were the market value of the house at the date when completion should have taken place less the contract price. In later cases it has been said that the *tortious* measure of damages applies: *André & Cie SA v Ets Michel Blanc et Fils* [1977] 2 Lloyds Rep 166 at 181; affd [1979] 2 Lloyd's Rep 427, CA; and that in tort loss of bargain damages may not, in every case, be recoverable: per Mervyn Davies J in *Sharneyford Supplies Ltd v Edge* [1985] 1 All ER 976 at 990; this point was

not argued in the Court of Appeal, but Balcombe LJ [1987] Ch 305 at 323 found the criticisms of *Watts v Spence* 'entirely convincing'.

3. Section 2(2) gives the court a discretion to award damages in lieu of rescission of the contract to the victim of a misrepresentation which is not fraudulent. The remedy of rescission and the circumstances where damages may be obtained in lieu are dealt with in books on contract. See, in particular, J. C. Smith and J. A. C. Thomas, *A Casebook on Contract*, 8th edn (London, 1987), chap. 9.

Hedley Byrne & Co Ltd *v* Heller & Partners Ltd House of Lords [1963] 2 All ER 575

The plaintiffs, a firm of advertising agents, booked advertising time on television channels and space in newspapers, on behalf of a customer, Easipower Ltd, on terms that they became personally liable. Becoming doubtful of the financial position of Easipower Ltd they asked their bankers, the National Provincial Bank Ltd, to obtain a report from the defendants, merchant bankers with whom Easipower Ltd had an account. This was done, in the first place, by telephone conversation in the course of which the defendants said that they believed Easipower 'to be respectably constituted and considered good for its normal business engagements' and that 'we believe that the company would not undertake any commitments they were unable to fulfil'. Three months later, a further inquiry was made by letter as to whether Easipower were 'trustworthy . . . to the extent of £100,000 per annum advertising contract'. The defendants replied in a letter headed: 'Confidential. For your private use and without responsibility on the part of this bank or its officials.' The letter continued: '. . . Respectably constituted company, considered good for its ordinary business engagements. Your figures are larger than we are accustomed to see.' The plaintiffs relied on these statements and as a result they lost sums, calculated as £17,661 18s 6d, when Easipower went into liquidation. In their statement of claim an allegation of fraud was originally made, but this was abandoned. McNair J held that the defendants were negligent but that they owed no duty of care to the plaintiffs. The Court of Appeal likewise held that there was no duty of care and it was therefore unnecessary to consider whether the finding of negligence was correct. The House of Lords affirmed the judgment on different grounds.

LORD REID: . . . Apart altogether from authority I would think that the law must treat negligent words differently from negligent acts. The law ought so far as possible to reflect the standards of the reasonable man, and that is what *M'Alister* (or *Donoghue*) *v Stevenson*[1] sets out to do. The most obvious difference between negligent words and negligent acts is this. Quite careful people often express definite opinions on social or informal occasions, even when they see that others are likely to be influenced by them; and they often do that without taking that care which they would take if asked for their opinion professionally, or in a business connexion. The appellants agreed that there can be no duty of care on such occasions, and we were referred to American and South African authorities where that is recognised, although their law appears to have gone much further than ours has yet done. But it is at least unusual casually to put into circulation negligently-made articles which are dangerous. A man might give a friend a negligently-prepared bottle of home-made wine and his friend's guests might drink it with dire results; but it is by

---

1. [1932] AC 562; [1932] All ER Rep 1.

no means clear that those guests would have no action against the negligent manufacturer. Another obvious difference is that a negligently-made article will only cause
one accident, and so it is not very difficult to find the necessary degree of proximity
or neighbourhood between the negligent manufacturer and the person injured. But
words can be broadcast with or without the consent or the foresight of the speaker
or writer. It would be one thing to say that the speaker owes a duty to a limited class,
but it would be going very far to say that he owes a duty to every ultimate 'consumer'
who acts on those words to his detriment. It would be no use to say that a speaker
or writer owes a duty, but can disclaim responsibility if he wants to. He, like the
manufacturer,[1] could make it part of a contract that he is not to be liable for his
negligence: but that contract would not protect him in a question with a third party
at least if the third party was unaware of it.

So it seems to me that there is good sense behind our present law that in general
an innocent but negligent misrepresentation gives no cause of action. There must
be something more than the mere misstatement.... [After considering earlier
authorities including a statement by Lord Haldane in *Robinson v Bank of Scotland*[1]]:
... He speaks of other special relationships and I can see no logical stopping
place short of all those relationships where it is plain that the party seeking information or advice was trusting the other to exercise such a degree of care as the
circumstances required, where it was reasonable for him to do that, and where
the other gave the information or advice when he knew or ought to have known
that the inquirer was relying on him. I say 'ought to have known' because in questions
of negligence we now apply the objective standard of what the reasonable man would
have done.

A reasonable man, knowing that he was being trusted or that his skill and judgment
were being relied on, would, I think have three courses open to him. He could keep
silent or decline to give the information or advice sought: or he could give an answer
with a clear qualification that he accepted no responsibility for it or that it was given
without that reflection or inquiry which a careful answer would require: or he could
simply answer without any such qualification. If he chooses to adopt the last course
he must, I think, be held to have accepted some responsibility for his answer being
given carefully, or to have accepted a relationship with the inquirer which requires
him to exercise such care as the circumstances require....

What the appellants complain of is not negligence in the ordinary sense of carelessness, but rather misjudgment in that Mr Heller, while honestly seeking to give a
fair assessment, in fact made a statement which gave a false and misleading impression of his customer's credit. It appears that bankers now commonly give references
with regard to their customers as part of their business. I do not know how far their
customers generally permit them to disclose their affairs, but even with permission
it cannot always be easy for a banker to reconcile his duty to his customer with his
desire to give a fairly balanced reply to an inquiry; and inquirers can hardly expect
a full and objective statement of opinion or accurate factual information such as
skilled men would be expected to give in reply to other kinds of inquiry. So it seems
to me to be unusually difficult to determine just what duty, beyond a duty to be
honest, a banker would be held to have undertaken if he gave a reply without an adequate disclaimer of responsibility or other warning....

Here, however, the appellants' bank, who were their agents in making the enquiry,
began by saying that 'they wanted to know in confidence and without responsibility
on our part', i.e. on the part of the respondents. So I cannot see how the appellants
can now be entitled to disregard that and maintain that the respondents did incur a
responsibility to them.

The appellants founded on a number of cases in contract where very clear words
were required to exclude the duty of care which would otherwise have flowed from

---

1. 1916 SC (HL) 154 at 157.

the contract. To that argument there are, I think, two answers. In the case of a contract it is necessary to exclude liability for negligence, but in this case the question is whether an undertaking to assume a duty to take care can be inferred; and that is a very different matter. Secondly, even in cases of contract general words may be sufficient if there was no other kind of liability to be excluded except liability for negligence: the general rule is that a party is not exempted from liability for negligence 'unless adequate words are used' — per Scrutton LJ in *Rutter v Palmer*.[1] It being admitted that there was here a duty to give an honest reply, I do not see what further liability there could be to exclude except liability for negligence: there being no contract there was no question of warranty.

I am therefore of opinion that it is clear that the respondents never undertook any duty to exercise care in giving their replies. The appellants cannot succeed unless there was such a duty and therefore in my judgment this appeal must be dismissed.

LORD MORRIS OF BORTH-Y-GEST: . . . My lords, it seems to me that if A assumes a responsibility to B to tender him deliberate advice there could be a liability if the advice is negligently given. I say 'could be' because the ordinary courtesies and exchanges of life would become impossible if it were sought to attach legal obligation to every kindly and friendly act. But the principle of the matter would not appear to be in doubt. . . .

My lords, I consider that . . . it should now be regarded as settled that if someone possessed of a special skill undertakes, quite irrespective of contract, to apply that skill for the assistance of another person who relies on such skill, a duty of care will arise. The fact that the service is to be given by means of, or by the instrumentality of, words can make no difference. Furthermore, if, in a sphere in which a person is so placed that others could reasonably rely on his judgment or his skill or on his ability to make careful inquiry, a person takes it on himself to give information or advice to, or allows his information or advice to be passed on to, another person who, as he knows or should know, will place reliance on it, then a duty of care will arise.

I do not propose to examine the facts of particular situations or the facts of recent decided cases in the light of this analysis, but I proceed to apply it to the facts of the case now under review. As I have stated, I approach the case on the footing that the bank knew that what they said would in fact be passed on to some unnamed person who was a customer of National Provincial Bank Ltd. The fact that it was said that 'they', i.e. National Provincial Bank Ltd, 'wanted to know' does not prevent this conclusion. In these circumstances I think that some duty towards the unnamed person, whoever it was, was owed by the bank. There was a duty of honesty. The great question, however, is whether there was a duty of care. The bank need not have answered the inquiry from National Provincial Bank Ltd. It appears, however, that it is a matter of banking convenience or courtesy and presumably of mutual business advantage that inquiries as between banks will be answered. The fact that it is most unlikely that the bank would have answered a direct inquiry from Hedleys does not affect the question as to what the bank must have known as to the use that would be made of any answer that they gave but it cannot be left out of account in considering what it was that the bank undertook to do. It does not seem to me that they undertook before answering an inquiry to expend time or trouble 'in searching records, studying documents, weighing and comparing the favourable and unfavourable features and producing a well-balanced and well-worded report.' (I quote the words of Pearson LJ)[2] Nor does it seem to me that the inquiring bank (nor therefore their customer) would expect such a process. . . . There was in the present case no contemplation of receiving anything like a formal and detailed report such as might be

---

1. [1922] 2 KB 87 at 92; cf. [1922] All ER Rep 367 at 370.
2. [1962] 1 QB at p. 414; [1961] All ER at p. 902, letter E.

given by some concern charged with the duty (probably for reward) of making all proper and relevant inquiries concerning the nature, scope and extent of a company's activities and of obtaining and marshalling all available evidence as to its credit, efficiency, standing and business reputation. There is much to be said, therefore, for the view that if a banker gives a reference in the form of a brief expression of opinion in regard to credit-worthiness he does not accept, and there is not expected from him, any higher duty than that of giving an honest answer. I need not, however, seek to deal with this aspect of the matter which perhaps cannot be covered by any statement of general application, because in my judgment the bank in the present case, by the words which they employed, effectively disclaimed any assumption of a duty of care. They stated that they only responded to the inquiry on the basis that their reply was without responsibility. If the inquirers chose to receive and act upon the reply they cannot disregard the definite terms upon which it was given. They cannot accept a reply given with a stipulation and then reject the stipulation. Furthermore, within accepted principles (as illustrated in *Rutter v Palmer*[1]) the words employed were apt to exclude any liability for negligence.

LORD DEVLIN: . . . A simple distinction between negligence in word and negligence in deed might leave the law defective but at least it would be intelligible. This is not, however, the distinction that is drawn in counsel for the respondents' argument and it is one which would be unworkable. A defendant who is given a car to overhaul and repair if necessary is liable to the injured driver (a) if he overhauls it and repairs it negligently and tells the driver that it is safe when it is not; (b) if he overhauls it and negligently finds it not to be in need of repair and tells the driver that it is safe when it is not; and (c) if he negligently omits to overhaul it at all and tells the driver that it is safe when it is not. It would be absurd in any of these cases to argue that the proximate cause of the driver's injury was not what the defendant did or failed to do but his negligent statement on the faith of which the driver drove the car and for which he could not recover. In this type of case where if there were a contract there would undoubtedly be a duty of service, it is not practicable to distinguish between the inspection or examination, the acts done or omitted to be done, and the advice or information given. . . .

In my opinion the appellants in their argument tried to press *M'Alister* (or *Donoghue*) *v Stevenson*[2] too hard. They asked whether the principle of proximity should not apply as well to words as to deeds. I think that it should, but as it is only a general conception it does not yet get them very far. Then they take the specific proposition laid down by *Donoghue v Stevenson*[2] and try to apply it literally to a certificate or a banker's reference. That will not do, for a general conception cannot be applied to pieces of paper in the same way as to articles of commerce, or to writers in the same way as to manufacturers. An inquiry into the possibilities of intermediate examination of a certificate will not be fruitful. The real value of *M'Alister* (or *Donoghue*) *v Stevenson*[2] to the argument in this case is that it shows how the law can be developed to solve particular problems. Is the relationship between the parties in this case such that it can be brought within a category giving rise to a special duty? As always in English law the first step in such an inquiry is to see how far the authorities have gone, for new categories in the law do not spring into existence overnight.

It would be surprising if the sort of problem that is created by the facts of this case had never until recently arisen in English law. As a problem it is a by-product of the doctrine of consideration. If the respondents had made a nominal charge for the reference, the problem would not exist. If it were possible in English law to construct

---

1. [1922] 2 KB 87; [1922] All ER Rep 367.
2. [1932] AC 562; [1932] All ER Rep 1.

a contract without consideration, the problem would move at once out of the first and general phase into the particular; and the question would be, not whether on the facts of the case there was a special relationship, but whether on the facts of the case there was a contract.

The respondents in this case cannot deny that they were performing a service. Their sheet anchor is that they were performing gratuitously and therefore no liability for its performance can arise. My lords, in my opinion this is not the law. A promise given without consideration to perform a service cannot be enforced as a contract by the promisee; but if the service is in fact performed and done negligently, the promisee can recover in an action in tort. This is the foundation of the liability of a gratuitous bailee. In the famous case of *Coggs v Bernard*,[1] where the defendant had charge of brandy belonging to the plaintiff and had spilt a quantity of it, there was a motion in arrest of judgment 'for that it was not alleged in the declaration that the defendant was a common porter, nor averred that he had anything for his pains'. The declaration was held to be good notwithstanding that there was not any consideration laid. Gould J said:[1]

'The reason of the action is, the particular trust reposed in the defendant, to which he has concurred by his assumption, and in the executing which he has miscarried by his neglect.'

This proposition is not limited to the law of bailment. In *Skelton v London and North Western Rly Co.*[2] Willes J applied it generally to the law of negligence. He said:[3]

'Actionable negligence must consist in the breach of some duty . . . if a person undertakes to perform a voluntary act, he is liable if he performs it improperly, but not if he neglects to perform it. Such is the result of the decision in the case of *Coggs v Bernard.*'[4]

Likewise in *Banbury v Bank of Montreal*[5] where the bank had advised a customer on his investments, Lord Finlay LC said[6]: 'He is under no obligation to advise, but if he takes upon himself to do so, he will incur liability if he does so negligently.'

The principle has been applied to cases where as a result of the negligence no damage was done to person or to property and the consequential loss was purely financial. In *Wilkinson v Coverdale*[7] the defendant undertook gratuitously to get a fire policy renewed for the plaintiff but, in doing so, neglected formalities, the omission of which rendered the policy inoperative. It was held that an action would lie. In two similar cases, the defendants succeeded on the ground that negligence was not proved in fact. Both cases were thus decided on the basis that in law an action would lie. In the first of them, *Shiells v Blackburne*,[8] the defendant had, acting voluntarily and without reward, made an entry of the plaintiff's leather as wrought leather instead of dressed leather, with the result that the leather was seized. In *Dartnall v Howard*[9] the defendants purchased an annuity for the plaintiff but on the personal security of two insolvent persons. The court, after verdict, arrested the judgment on the ground that the defendants appeared to be gratuitous agents and that it was not

---

1. (1703) 2 Ld Raym 909.
2. (1867) LR 2 CP 631.
3. (1867) LR 2 CP at p. 636.
4. (1703) 2 Ld Raym 909.
5. [1918] AC 626; [1918–19] All ER Rep 1.
6. [1918] AC at p. 654.
7. (1793) 1 Esp 74.
8. (1789) 1 Hy Bl 159.
9. (1825) 4 B & C 345.

averred that they had acted either with negligence or dishonesty. . . .

De la Bere v Pearson Ltd[1] is an example of a case . . . decided on the ground that there was a sufficiency of consideration. The defendants advertised in their newspaper that their city editor would answer inquiries from readers of the paper desiring financial advice. The plaintiff asked for the name of a good stockbroker. The editor recommended the name of a person whom he knew to be an outside broker and whom he ought to have known, if he had made proper inquiries, to be an undischarged bankrupt. The plaintiff dealt with him and lost his money. The case being brought in contract, Vaughan Williams LJ thought[2] that there was sufficient consideration in the fact that the plaintiff consented to the publication of his question in the defendants' paper if the defendants so chose. For Barnes P the consideration appears to have lain in the plaintiff addressing an inquiry as invited.[3] In the same way when in *Everett v Griffiths*[4] the Court of Appeal was considering the liability of a doctor towards the person he was certifying, Scrutton LJ[5] said that the submission to treatment would be a good consideration.

My lords, I have cited these instances so as to show that in one way or another the law has ensured that in this type of case a just result has been reached. But I think that today the result can and should be achieved by the application of the law of negligence and that it is unnecessary and undesirable to construct an artificial consideration. I agree with Sir Frederick Pollock's note on the case of *De la Bere v Pearson Ltd*[1] where he wrote in *Pollock on Contract* (13th edn) 140 (note 31) that 'the cause of action is better regarded as arising from default in the performance of a voluntary undertaking independent of contract'.

My lords, it is true that this principle of law has not yet been clearly applied to a case where the service which the defendant undertakes to perform is or includes the obtaining and imparting of information. But I cannot see why it should not be: and if it had not been thought erroneously that *Derry v Peek*[6] negatived any liability for negligent statements, I think that by now it probably would have been. It cannot matter whether the information consists of fact or of opinion or is a mixture of both, nor whether it was obtained as a result of special inquiries or comes direct from facts already in the defendant's possession or from his general store of professional knowledge. One cannot, as I have already endeavoured to show, distinguish in this respect between a duty to inquire and a duty to state.

I think, therefore, that there is ample authority to justify your lordships in saying now that the categories of special relationships, which may give rise to a duty to take care in word as well as deed, are not limited to contractual relationships or to relationships of fiduciary duty, but include also relationships which in the words of Lord Shaw in *Nocton v Lord Ashburton*[7] are 'equivalent to contract' that is, where there is an assumption of responsibility in circumstances in which, but for the absence of consideration, there would be a contract. Where there is an express undertaking, an express warranty as distinct from mere representation, there can be little difficulty. The difficulty arises in discerning those cases in which the undertaking is to be implied. In this respect the absence of consideration is not irrelevant. Payment for information or advice is very good evidence that it is being relied on and that the informer or adviser knows that it is. Where there is no consideration, it will be necessary to exercise greater care in distinguishing between social and professional relationships and between those which are of a contractual character and those

---

1. [1908] 1 KB 280; [1904–7] All ER Rep 755.
2. [1908] 1 KB at p. 287; [1904–7] All ER Rep at p. 756.
3. [1908] 1 KB at p. 289; [1904–7] All ER Rep at p. 757.
4. [1920] 3 KB 163; *affd* [1921] 1 AC 631.
5. [1920] 3 KB at p. 191.
6. (1889) 14 App Cas 337.
7. [1914] AC at p. 972; [1914–15] All ER Rep at p. 62.

which are not. It may often be material to consider whether the adviser is acting purely out of good nature or whether he is getting his reward in some indirect form. The service that a bank performs in giving a reference is not done simply out of a desire to assist commerce. It would discourage the customers of the bank if their deals fell through because the bank had refused to testify to their credit when it was good.

I have had the advantage of reading all the opinions prepared by your lordships and of studying the terms which your lordships have framed by way of definition of the sort of relation which gives rise to a responsibility towards those who act on information or advice and so creates a duty of care towards them. I do not understand any of your lordships to hold that it is a responsibility imposed by law on certain types of persons or in certain sorts of situations. It is a responsibility that is voluntarily accepted or undertaken either generally where a general relationship, such as that of solicitor and client or banker and customer, is created, or specifically in relation to a particular transaction. In the present case the appellants were not, as in *Woods v Martins Bank, Ltd*[1] the customers or potential customers of the bank. Responsibility can attach only to the single act, i.e., the giving of the reference, and only if the doing of that act implied a voluntary undertaking to assume responsibility. This is a point of great importance because it is, as I understand it, the foundation for the ground on which in the end the House dismisses the appeal. I do not think it possible to formulate with exactitude all the conditions under which the law will in a specific case imply a voluntary undertaking, any more than it is possible to formulate those in which the law will imply a contract. But in so far as your lordships describe the circumstances in which an implication will ordinarily be drawn, I am prepared to adopt any one of your lordships' statements as showing the general rule; and I pay the same respect to the statement by Denning LJ in his dissenting judgment in *Candler v Crane, Christmas & Co*[2] about the circumstances in which he says a duty to use care in making a statement exists. . . .

I shall therefore content myself with the proposition that wherever there is a relationship equivalent to contract there is a duty of care. Such a relationship may be either general or particular. . . .

I regard this proposition as an application of the general conception of proximity. Cases may arise in the future in which a new and wider proposition, quite independent of any notion of contract, will be needed.

On the facts of the present case counsel for the respondents . . . submits, first, that it ought not to be inferred that the respondents knew that National Provincial Bank Ltd were asking for the reference for the use of a customer. If the respondents did know that, then counsel submits that they did not intend that the reference itself should be communicated to the customer; it was intended only as material upon which the customer's bank could advise the customer on its own responsibility. I should consider it necessary to examine these contentions were it not for the general disclaimer of responsibility which appears to me in any event to be conclusive. I agree entirely with the reasoning and conclusion on this point of my noble and learned friend Lord Reid. A man cannot be said voluntarily to be undertaking a responsibility if at the very moment when he is said to be accepting it he declares that in fact he is not. The problem of reconciling words of exemption with the existence of a duty arises only when a party is claiming exemption from a responsibility which he has already undertaken or which he is contracting to undertake. For this reason alone, I would dismiss the appeal.

[LORD HODSON and LORD PEARCE delivered speeches in favour of dismissing the appeal.]

Appeal dismissed

---

1. [1959] 1 QB 55; [1958] 3 All ER 166.
2. [1951] 2 KB 164 at 179; [1951] 1 All ER 426 at 433.

Notes

1. The basis of the decision in this case is that as a result of the disclaimer of responsibility there had been no assumption of a duty of care. The only duty was to act honestly. Would the result have been the same had s. 2(2) of the Unfair Contract Terms Act 1977 (p. 389, post) been in force at the time? Consider *Smith v Eric S Bush* [1990] 1 AC 831; [1989] 2 All ER 514 (p. 175, post).

2. Before the decision in this case there could be liability in damages for careless misstatements causing economic loss only if there was a contractual duty to take care (which might be artificially devised as in *De la Bere v Pearson Ltd* [1908] 1 KB 280, referred to by Lord Devlin p. 166, ante) or if there was a fiduciary relationship between the parties (e.g. solicitor and client: *Nocton v Lord Ashburton* [1914] AC 932; banker and customer, see p. 172, post). In *Hedley Byrne*, the House of Lords confined the requirements set out in *Derry v Peek* (p. 155, ante) exclusively to the tort of deceit. But, as the speeches show, their Lordships were not willing to apply Lord Atkin's neighbour principle (p. 43, ante) literally. Despite the criticisms which may be made of the distinctions drawn in the speeches between words and acts and between physical damage and economic loss (the clearest discussion is by A. M. Honoré (1965) 8 JSPTL (NS) 284, and R. Stevens (1964) 27 MLR 121), Hedley Byrne must be taken as direct authority in two-party situations. These are cases where A makes an oral or written communication to B upon which B places reasonable reliance. This includes situations, like that in *Hedley Byrne* itself, where the communication is made to an agent of B or by an agent of A. However, in three-party situations, where the statement is made by A or his agent to B or his agent and is passed on to C, who suffers loss by relying on it, it may be more appropriate to consider liability within the terms of reference of a general principle of reasonable proximity (p. 175, post). Even more so where B relies on a statement made by A which leads B to act in a manner which causes loss to C (even though C himself placed no reliance on the statement), the courts are unlikely to extend the *Hedley Byrne* decision to this 'three-party' situation, but instead will apply general notions of reasonable proximity (p. 189, post).

3. What then are the requirements of the *Hedley Byrne* tort? *First, there must be a communication from the defendant or his agent to the plaintiff or his agent.*

(a) The courts, since *Hedley Byrne*, have not been willing to draw any distinction between representations, statements of fact, opinions and advice: see *Midland Bank Trust Co Ltd v Hett, Stubbs and Kemp (a firm)* [1979] Ch 384; [1978] 3 All ER 571, noted p. 201, post; *Ross v Caunters* [1980] Ch 297; [1979] 3 All ER 580 (p. 192, post). However, as Shaw LJ pointed out in *Howard Marine and Dredging Co Ltd v A Ogden and Sons (Excavations) Ltd* [1978] QB 574 at 600, where the plaintiff *asks* the defendant for a specific *fact*, which the plaintiff has no direct means of ascertaining, this may go to show 'the gravity of the inquiry or the importance and influence attached to the answer'. On the other hand, 'cases of liability for statements volunteered negligently must be rare': per Stephenson LJ in *Lexmead (Basingstoke) Ltd v*

Lewis [1982] AC 225 at 264, a point not considered by the House of Lords [1982] AC at p. 271 (see further on this point, p. 502, post).

(b) There can be liability for advice only where the plaintiff made it clear that he was seeking *considered* advice, and intended to act upon it in a specific way (per Lord Reid and Lord Morris in their dissenting opinion in the Privy Council in *Mutual Life and Citizens' Assurance Co Ltd v Evatt* [1971] AC 793 at 812, which has been adopted in England). This excludes from the ambit of liability 'representations made during a casual conversation in the street; or in a railway carriage; or an impromptu opinion given offhand; or "off the cuff" on the telephone' (in the words of Lord Denning MR in the *Howard Marine* case, although it is to be noted that he did not draw the distinction between facts and advice made by Shaw LJ). In *Chaudhry v Prabhakar* [1988] 3 All ER 718; [1989] 1 WLR 29 a young woman asked a close family friend, who claimed to know something about motor cars, to look out for a suitable second-hand car for her to buy. She specifically asked him to find out if the car had been involved in an accident. Without any direct inquiry despite some fairly obvious signs that it had been damaged, he highly recommended a car being sold by a panel beater. A few months later it became apparent that it had been involved in a very bad accident, had been poorly repaired and was unroadworthy. Counsel for the friend conceded that, as a gratuitous agent, a duty of care was owed to the woman, but argued that the standard of care required of such a person is a subjective one, to take such care towards his principal as he would towards his own affairs. This was rejected by all three members of the Court of Appeal, on the grounds that the appropriate standard is an objective one, to take such care as is reasonable in all the circumstances. May LJ, however, doubted whether counsel's concession of the existence of a duty of care had been rightly made in law. To impose a duty on a family friend in these circumstances would he thought 'make social regulations [sic] and responsibilities between friends unnecessarily hazardous' (at 725). Stuart-Smith LJ, on the other hand, said that 'the fact that principal and agent are friends does not in my judgment affect the existence of a duty of care, although conceivably it might be a relevant circumstance in considering the degree or standard of care' (at 721; cf. Stocker LJ at 723.). How would an economic analyst view this case? See Note 5, p. 171, post.

(c) If the defendant bankers in *Hedley Byrne* had simply said, 'We have not had time to check our files, but we believe that Easipower is good for its ordinary business engagements', would they have been held liable? Their duty would presumably have been one of honesty and no more (see A. M. Honoré, op cit, pp. 290–291, and R. Stevens, op cit, p. 146).

4. A second requirement is that a *'special relationship' must exist between the plaintiff and the defendant*. The common factor in the various descriptions of 'special relationships' given in *Hedley Byrne* is whether the circumstances were such that the reasonable person would appreciate that his words were likely to be acted upon. But the different judicial characterisations of the circumstances should be noted:

(a) According to one view a 'special relationship' is one 'equivalent to contract' (Lord Devlin, p. 167, ante), or 'very much nearer to contract than tort' (per Hewson J in *The World Harmony* [1967] P 341 at 362 (For some of the perplexing implications of applying the law of tort to 'near-contractual' situations, see p. 196, post.)

(b) According to the majority opinion of the Privy Council in *Mutual Life and Citizens' Assurance Co Ltd v Evatt* [1971] AC 793; [1971] 1 All ER 150, the duty is limited to professional advisers (such as accountants, investment advice businesses, valuers, analysts, surveyors, architects and solicitors). In the *Mutual Life* case, the plaintiff alleged that he was a policy holder in the defendant company and had asked them for advice on the financial stability of an associated company. He said that the defendants knew that if the advice given was favourable he would invest in the company, but they carelessly gave him false information upon which he relied and consequently lost money on his investment. He did not allege that the defendants carried on the business of supplying information or advice on investments or that they claimed any qualification, skill or competence to do so greater than that of the ordinary reasonable man. A majority of the Judicial Committee of the Privy Council, reversing a majority of the High Court of Australia who had upheld a majority of the Supreme Court of New South Wales, held that the absence of any such allegation was fatal to the pleading.

(c) According to the minority opinion of Lord Reid and Lord Morris in the *Mutual Life* case ([1971] 1 All ER at p. 163) 'when an enquirer consults a businessman in the course of his business and makes it plain to him that he is seeking considered advice and intends to act upon it in a particular way, any reasonable businessman would realise that, if he chooses to give advice without any warning or qualification, he is putting himself under a moral obligation to take some care ... [and that it is] within the principles established by the *Hedley Byrne* case to regard his action in giving such advice as creating a special relationship between him and the enquirer and to translate his moral obligation into a legal obligation to take such care as is reasonable in the whole circumstances'.

The English Court of Appeal has preferred (c), the minority opinion in *Mutual Life*, to (b): see *Esso Petroleum Co Ltd v Mardon* [1976] QB 801; [1976] 2 All ER 5, in which Ormrod LJ said (at p. 827) that 'if the majority view were to be accepted the effect of *Hedley Byrne* would be so radically curtailed as to be virtually eliminated' (but this is questionable); and *Howard Marine and Dredging Co Ltd v A Ogden & Sons (Excavations) Ltd* [1978] QB 574; [1978] 2 All ER 1134.

(d) It has sometimes been argued that it is essential to found liability for negligent misstatements to show that there has been a 'voluntary assumption of responsibility' on the part of the person giving the advice. This was emphatically rejected by Lord Griffiths in *Smith v Eric S Bush* [1990] 1 AC 831 at 862 (p. 175, post). In *Caparo Industries plc v Dickman* [1990] 1 All ER 568 at 587 (p. 181, post) Lord Oliver warned against the danger of seeking to find any general principle, 'for even within the limited category of ... the "negligent statement cases", circumstances may differ infinitely and, in a swiftly developing field of law, there can be no necessary assumption that those features which have served in one case to create the relationship between the plaintiff and the defendant on which liability depends will necessarily be determinative of liability in another case.' He added (at p. 589) that the phrase 'voluntary assumption of responsibility' 'was not intended to be the test for the existence of the duty for, on analysis, it means no more than that the act of the defendant in making the statement was voluntary and that the law attributes to it an assumption of responsibility if the statement or advice is inaccurate and is acted upon. It tells us nothing about the circumstances from which such attribution arises.' These statements were made in the context of 'three-party' situations, considered p. 175, post. In 'two-party' situations, the 'course of business' or 'professional relationship' tests appear still to be the touchstone of liability.

5. Could the suggested requirement of professional skill be justified on economic grounds? *Fleming*, p. 609, points out that an 'unexpressed premise [of the majority opinion in *Mutual Life*] may well have been that professional advisers alone would be insured against this risk and capable of internalising the cost of liability among their professional customers'. A more sophisticated economic analysis by W. Bishop (1980) 96 LQR 360 at 378 (also in *The Economic Approach to Law*, edited by P. Burrows and C. G. Veljanovski (London, 1981), pp. 167–186) suggests the following approach to cases of negligent misrepresentation:

'Courts should in general apply ordinary rules of negligence. However where the misrepresentation in question results in the production of valuable information there is a prima facie case for more restricted liability. Liability should be restricted when (a) the information is of a type that is valuable to many potential users, (b) the producer of the information cannot capture in his prices the benefits flowing to all users of the information, and (c) the imposition of liability to all persons harmed would raise potential costs significantly enough to discourage information production altogether. When these three conditions are met the court should impose liability in relation to a limited class only. This class should include all information users with whom the producer has a trading relationship whether direct or indirect. The class can be extended beyond this, but such extension should be limited by the principle expressed in (c), that is it should not be extended so widely that potential defendants would be discouraged from engaging in the activity that generates the information.'

(See further for economic perspectives on professional negligence and the quality of legal services, C. G. Veljanovski and C. J. Whelan (1983) 46 MLR 700 and R. Bowles and P. Jones, *Professional Liability: an Economic Analysis* (Aberdeen, 1989), pp. 34–50.)

This type of economic analysis may be applied to the question of liability for statements made in *pre-contractual negotiations*. In *Esso Petroleum Co Ltd v Mardon* [1976] QB 801; [1976] 2 All ER 5, Esso's representative induced the plaintiff to enter into a contract of tenancy of an Esso petrol filling station by an honest but negligent misrepresentation that the consumption of petrol would reach 200,000 gallons in the third year of operations. The consumption never got anywhere near this figure and as a result the plaintiff (Mardon) lost all the capital he had put into the station and incurred a substantial overdraft. The facts took place before s. 2(1) of the Misrepresentation Act 1967 (p. 159, ante), came into force. The Court of Appeal held that *Hedley Byrne* could be used to impose liability for pre-contractual statements. Bishop, op cit, pp. 371–372 comments:

'Almost certainly the cost of care to Esso was less than the cost of error to Mardon so that a rule making Esso liable is likely to minimise transaction costs. Furthermore, parties probably expect care in cases of this kind. Where parties normally trade under standard expectations the assignment of liability to the party who is expected to perform up to the normal level of care will serve an additional economic purpose. It induces a party who is not performing at that standard to *signal this fact to the other party*, through disclaimer. The information about the other party's standard of performance is valuable information. This is a cheap way of providing it in the market place and its cost of production to Esso (i.e. the transactional costs of disclaiming) is almost certainly lower than its value to Mardon. . . .'

(On the question of disclaimer, see p. 389, post.)

6. Apart from pre-contractual misrepresentations, the *Hedley Byrne* tort has been applied to a number of other commercial relationships, for example:

(a) A dealer who informs sellers of goods that a company, for whom he is purchasing the goods, can safely be given credit: *WB Anderson Ltd v Rhodes (Liverpool) Ltd* [1967] 2 All ER 850 (a decision apparently approved by the majority in *Mutual Life* [1971] AC 793 at 809 on the ground that the representor, a commission agent, had a financial interest in the advice).

(b) A banker who advises a third party on the creditworthiness of one of the banker's customers: *Woods v Martins Bank* [1959] 1 QB 55; [1958] 3 All ER 166 (a 'fiduciary' relationship classified as a 'special' relationship by Lord Hodson in *Hedley Byrne*). But the extent of the duty of care may be limited by contract, as in *Williams and Glyn's Bank Ltd v Barnes* [1981] Com LR 205 where the bank had agreed to provide a loan to a business customer and it was held that the bank's duty was simply to provide the facilities without being under a duty to advise with care on the commercial advisability of the loan. However, the bank may have to give an adequate explanation of the nature and effect of the transaction: *Cornish v Midland Bank plc* [1985] 3 All ER 513.

(c) An estate agent acting for the vendor of a property who provides information about the property to a potential purchaser: *Dodds v Millman* (1964) 45 DLR (2d) 472; *Richardson v Norris Smith Real Estate Ltd* [1977] 1 NZLR 152; cf. *Presser v Caldwell Estates Pty Ltd* [1971] 2 NSWLR 471.

(d) Public authorities may be liable in negligence for supplying inaccurate information or advice. For example in *L Shaddock and Associates Pty Ltd v Parramatta City Council* (1981) 36 ALR 385, the High Court of Australia held that the defendant council was liable for failing to take care in responding to a request from a solicitor acting for a prospective purchaser of land for information as to road widening proposals, although the council was under no statutory duty to provide the information. Mason J (with whom Aickin J agreed) said it was enough to impose a duty of care that the speaker knew or ought to have known that the inquirer was requesting information for a serious purpose, that he proposed to act on it, and might suffer loss if it proved to be inaccurate. In 'distinguishing' the *Mutual Life* case, noted p. 170, ante, the other judges came close to rejecting it. A similar result would be reached in England. For example, negligent advice by a local planning authority regarding rights under an enforcement notice may give rise to liability in tort: see *Davy v Spelthorne Borough Council* [1984] AC 262; [1983] 3 All ER 278. Consider also *Ministry of Housing and Local Government v Sharp* [1970] 2 QB 223; [1970] 1 All ER 1009 (p. 189, post) (a three-party situation). Generally, as regards the negligent exercise of statutory powers, see p. 99, ante.

(e) What about a negligent misrepresentation made *after* the formation of contract? Say that A has contracted to provide B with a burglar alarm system. After a burglary at another customer's premises, A negligently assures B that the system performs properly, but in fact it does not, so causing loss to B. In *J Nunes Diamonds Ltd v Dominion Electric Protection Co* (1972) 26 DLR (3d) 699, the Supreme Court of Canada held (by a narrow majority) on these facts that there was no duty of care on the ground, among others, that liability in tort could be based only on a tort unconnected with performance of the contract. Would an English court reach the same conclusion? The answer depends upon which of two rival views are adopted: either (a) a *Hedley Byrne* 'special relationship' can arise where the relationship is contractual and is not limited to the situation where the duty is owed by one exercising a common calling or exercising a professional skill (e.g. *Batty v Metropolitan Property Realisations Ltd* [1978] QB 554; [1978] 2 All ER 445); or (b) tort has no role to play where the parties' relationship is governed by contract (e.g. *Tai Hing Cotton Mill Ltd v Liu Chong Hing Bank Ltd* [1986] AC 80; [1985] 2 All ER 947, in which it was held that a customer owes no duty in contract to his bank to take reasonable care in drawing cheques beyond the duty not to facilitate fraud or forgery and the duty to inform the bank of unauthorised cheques of which he becomes aware, and so no such duty of care should be imposed in tort. (Cf. *Blackpool and Fylde Aero Club Ltd v Blackpool Borough Council* [1990] 3 All ER 25; [1990] 1 WLR 1195.) The current trend of authorities in England favours the latter view: see generally the cases at p. 200, post.

7. Occasionally a duty of care in respect of information or advice may be denied on explicit policy grounds. Judges have a wide immunity from suit (*Sirros v Moore* [1975] QB 118; [1974] 3 All ER 776), 'otherwise no man but a beggar, or a fool, would be a judge' (Stair, *Institutions*, Bk 4, tit. 1, s. 5, quoted by Lord Fraser in *Arenson v Casson, Beckman, Rutley & Co* [1977] AC 405 at 440). And see further p. 778, post. For much the same reason, arbitrators are said to be immune from actions for negligence, although in *Arenson*'s case Lord Kilbrandon and Lord Fraser expressed some doubt about this exception, and Lord Salmon suggested that arbitrators ought not in all cases to be accorded immunity. In order to fall within the supposed exception, the defendant must show that a formulated dispute between at least two parties has been remitted to him to resolve in such a manner that he is called upon to exercise a judicial function and the parties have agreed to accept his decision (per Lord Simon, Lord Wheatley and Lord Salmon in *Arenson*'s case). A surveyor appointed to determine rent under a rent review clause in a lease has been held not to enjoy immunity as an arbitrator or quasi-arbitrator: *Palacath Ltd v Flanagan* [1985] 2 All ER 161. A sequestrator appointed under a writ of sequestration is an officer of the court but is not immune from liability for negligence: *IRC v Hoogstraten* [1985] QB 107; [1984] 3 All ER 25.

Barristers and solicitor-advocates are neither beggars nor fools, yet they have been accorded the special privilege of immunity from actions for negligence in the conduct and management of litigation (*Rondel v Worsley* [1969] 1 AC 191; [1967] 3 All ER 993), including those matters of pre-trial work which are so intimately connected with the conduct of the case in court that they can be fairly said to be preliminary decisions affecting the way that the case is conducted when it comes to hearing (*Saif Ali v Sydney Mitchell*

Co (a firm) [1980] AC 198; [1978] 3 All ER 1033). This immunity extends to advice as to a plea in criminal proceedings (*Somasundaram v M Julius Melchior & Co (a firm)* [1989] 1 All ER 129; [1988] 1 WLR 1394). The main grounds of public policy advanced for immunity are that the advocate owes a duty to the court that transcends the duty to his client, that an advocate cannot fulfil his public duty if he stands in fear of action by a disgruntled client, that a barrister cannot choose his client (the 'cab rank' rule) and that a suit against an advocate would inevitably involve undesirable relitigation of the matters in dispute between the client and the other party. These arguments have also convinced the High Court of Australia (*Giannarelli v Wraith* (1988) 81 ALR 417; see K. Nicholson (1989) 5 PN 126) but not courts in Canada (*Demarco v Ungaro* (1979) 95 DLR (3d) 385). The immunity may have no application where loss is suffered by a third party as a result of the negligence of a legal representative or adviser: see p. 180, post. For the traditional arguments against the immunity see M. Zander, *Legal Services for the Community* (London, 1978), chap. 4, and for a critical economic analysis see C. G. Veljanovski and C. J. Whelan (1983) 46 MLR at pp. 711–718. The Courts and Legal Services Bill 1990 proposes to put the immunity into statutory form.

8. Even if a duty-situation exists, the plaintiff may have difficulty in proving that an adviser acted negligently, a mere 'error of judgment' not necessarily being sufficient (see p. 278, post).

9. Does the duty extend to correcting information when a chance of circumstances has made it unsafe to rely on information which was accurate when first given? In *Argy Trading Development Co Ltd v Lapid Developments Ltd* [1977] 3 All ER 785; [1977] 1 WLR 444 (criticised by N. P. Gravells (1978) 94 LQR 334) Croom-Johnson J held that although a landlord may be under a duty to give a tenant correct information about the insurance of the premises at the commencement of the lease, there was no duty to inform the tenant when subsequently the insurance cover lapsed. But this may be compared with the greater willingness to find a duty to speak up in *J & JC Abrams Ltd v Ancliffe* [1978] 2 NZLR 420, affd. [1981] 1 NZLR 244 (builder liable for failure to correct estimate before client legally bound), and *Cherry v Allied Insurance Brokers* [1978] 1 Lloyd's Rep 274. Deliberate failure to disclose that the information has been falsified would qualify as deceit (p. 158, ante).

10. More generally, can a mere failure to speak ever give rise to liability in negligence under *Hedley Byrne* principles? This issue arose in *Banque Financière de la Cité SA v Westgate Insurance Co Ltd* [1990] 2 All ER 947; [1990] 3 WLR 364 (known as the *Keyser Ullman* case). The plaintiff banks had made loans to B, who had perpetrated a massive fraud on them by pledging as security gemstones which turned out to be worthless. The hapless banks were also the victims of dishonest conduct by L, the manager of the firm which had arranged insurance policies (containing fraud exclusion clauses) to protect the lending banks in the event of the borrowing companies being unable to repay the loans. His misconduct, unconnected with that of B, consisted of representing to the banks that they had full cover when that was not the case. D, an employee of the insurers, had become aware of L's dishonesty but had failed to disclose it to the banks. The banks claimed that had L's

dishonesty been disclosed to them, they would have lent no further sums to B and so would have incurred no further losses. The Court of Appeal held that there was no duty of care on *Hedley Byrne* principles because on the facts there had been no assumption of responsibility by D and no reliance by the banks. An alternative submission for the banks was that even without an assumption and reliance, there could be a duty of care not to cause economic loss. The Court of Appeal [1990] 1 QB 665; [1989] 2 All ER 952 held that such a duty could arise only in rare cases and that even if it was possible in respect of positive statements, it could not arise from a mere failure to disclose L's dishonesty. The House of Lords affirmed the decision of the Court of Appeal, taking the view that *Hedley Byrne* principles were not relevant because in this case there was no negligent misstatement and the silence of D did not amount to an assertion that L was trustworthy and the banks did not rely on the silence of D. The House also found that the losses suffered by the banks were not the consequence of any breach of duty to disclose the misconduct of L. In relation to the duty to disclose, the House was plainly influenced by the fact that to impose a duty in tort to make disclosure in these circumstances would be to contradict the basic principle of the law of contract that there is no obligation to disclose a material fact during pre-contractual negotiations before entering into an ordinary commercial contract. The existence of an established business relationship between the parties was not enough to turn the insurers' omission into a misrepresentation in tort any more than it could do so in contract. According to Lord Templeman (at p. 959), an insurer's breach of obligation to deal with the proposer of insurance with the utmost good faith does not give rise to a remedy in damages but only to a right of rescission and recovery of the premium. The decision offers yet another warning that, as the Court of Appeal had stated, 'it should be no part of the general function of the law of tort to fill in contractual gaps' ([1990] 1 QB at p. 800), even if 'the legal obligation falls short of the moral imperatives' (at p. 802). See further p. 196, post, on the relationship with contract, and p. 179, post, on the 'assumption of responsibility' test.

11. Does the *Hedley Byrne* principle cover the situation where A makes a statement to B, and it is passed on to C, who suffers loss by relying on it? This three-party situation is considered in the next case.

Smith *v* Eric S. Bush; Harris v Wyre Forest District Council
House of Lords [1989] 2 All ER 514

In the first of these two cases (in which the appeals were heard together), Mrs Smith (the respondent) applied to the Abbey National Building Society for a mortgage to enable her to purchase a house. The Society instructed Eric S Bush (the appellants), an independent firm of surveyors and valuers, to prepare a written valuation report so as to ensure that there would be adequate security for the loan to Mrs Smith. Mrs Smith paid the Society the standard inspection fee, and signed an application form which stated that she would be provided with a copy of the report and also contained a disclaimer to the effect that neither the Society nor the surveyor warranted that the report and the valuation would be accurate and that the report would be supplied without any assumption of responsibility. The copy of the report which she received contained a similar disclaimer. In sole reliance on the report, which said that no essential repairs were necessary, she purchased the house. The surveyors, who knew that the report would be shown to the purchaser, were found to be negligent in failing to discover and report upon a structural defect in one of the chimneys. As a result of this defect one of the chimney flues had collapsed, eighteen months after the purchase, crashing through the bedroom ceiling and causing considerable damage. The trial judge held the surveyors liable and awarded £4,379 damages. The Court of Appeal [1987] 3 All ER 179, affirmed this decision. The surveyors appealed to the House of Lords which affirmed the decision of the Court of Appeal.

In the second case, Mr and Mrs Harris (the appellants) applied to a local council for their mortgage. The council instructed one of their own employees, Mr Lee, to carry out the survey. The mortgage application form stated that the valuation was confidential and was intended solely for the information of the council and that no responsibility whatsoever was implied or accepted for the value or condition of the property. The council's employee valued the house at the asking price of £9,450, and the council offered to advance Mr and Mrs Harris 90 per cent of that sum subject to some minor repairs being done to the house. The report was not made available to Mr and Mrs Harris, but they assumed that the house was worth at least the amount of the valuation and that the surveyor had found no serious defects. They purchased the house for £9,000. When they tried to re-sell it, three years later, a new survey revealed that the house was subject to settlement, was virtually unsaleable, and could be repaired, if at all, at a cost more than the purchase price. The trial judge, [1987] 1 EGLR 231, awarded damages for negligence against the council, who were vicariously responsible for their employee, but the Court of Appeal, [1988] 1 All ER 691, reversed this decision on the ground that the disclaimer notice had excluded liability. The House of Lords reversed the Court of Appeal's decision.

LORD TEMPLEMAN: My Lords, these appeals involve consideration of three questions. The first question is whether a valuer instructed by a building society or other mortgagee to value a house, knowing that his valuation will probably be relied on by the prospective purchaser and mortgagor of the house, owes to the purchaser in tort a duty to exercise reasonable skill and care in carrying out the valuation unless the valuer disclaims liability. If so, the second question is whether a disclaimer of liability by or on behalf of the valuer is a notice which purports to exclude liability for negligence within the Unfair Contract Terms Act 1977[1] and is, therefore, ineffective unless it satisfies the requirement of reasonableness. If so, the third question is whether, in the absence of special circumstances, it is fair and reasonable for the valuer to rely on the notice excluding liability. . . .

[In relation to the first question his Lordship referred to the speech of Lord Devlin in the *Hedley Byrne* case (p. 164, ante), and said:] In the present appeals the relationship between the valuer and the purchaser is 'akin to contract'. The valuer knows that the consideration which he receives derives from the purchaser and is passed on by the mortgagee, and the valuer also knows that the valuation will determine whether or not the purchaser buys the house. . . .

In general, I am of the opinion that in the absence of a disclaimer of liability the valuer who values a house for the purpose of a mortgage, knowing that the mortgagee will rely and the mortgagor will probably rely on the valuation, knowing that the purchaser mortgagor has in effect paid for the valuation, is under a duty to exercise reasonable skill and care and that duty is owed to both parties to the mortgage for which the valuation is made. Indeed, in both the appeals now under consideration the existence of such a dual duty is tacitly accepted and acknowledged because notices excluding liability for breach of the duty owed to the purchaser were drafted by the mortgagee and imposed on the purchaser. In these circumstances it is necessary to consider the second question which arises in these appeals, namely whether the

---

1. [See p. 389, post.]

disclaimers of liability are notices which fall within the Unfair Contract Terms Act 1977.

In *Harris v Wyre Forest DC* the Court of Appeal (Kerr, Nourse LJJ and Caufield J) accepted an argument that the 1977 Act did not apply because the council by their express disclaimer refused to obtain a valuation save on terms that the valuer would not be under any obligation to Mr and Mrs Harris to take reasonable care or exercise reasonable skill. The council did not exclude liability for negligence but excluded negligence so that the valuer and the council never came under a duty of care to Mr and Mrs Harris and could not be guilty of negligence. This construction would not give effect to the manifest intention of the 1977 Act but would emasculate the Act. The construction would provide no control over standard form exclusion clauses which individual members of the public are obliged to accept. A party to a contract or a tortfeasor could opt out of the 1977 Act by declining, in the words of Nourse LJ, to recognise 'their own answerability to the plaintiff' (see [1988] 1 All ER 691 at 697, [1988] QB 835 at 845). Caulfield J said that the Act 'can only be relevant where there is on the facts a potential liability' (see [1988] 1 All ER 691 at 704, [1988] QB 835 at 850). But no one intends to commit a tort and therefore any notice which excludes liability is a notice which excludes a potential liability. Kerr LJ sought to confine the Act to 'situations where the existence of a duty of care is not open to doubt' or where there is 'an inescapable duty of care' (see [1988] 1 All ER 691 at 702, [1988] QB 835 at 853). I can find nothing in the 1977 Act or in the general law to identify or support this distinction. In the result the Court of Appeal held that the Act does not apply to 'negligent misstatements where a disclaimer has prevented a duty of care from coming into existence' (see [1988] 1 All ER 691 at 699–700, [1988] QB 835 at 848 per Nourse LJ). My Lords, this confuses the valuer's report with the work which the valuer carries out in order to make his report. The valuer owed a duty to exercise reasonable skill and care in his inspection and valuation. If he had been careful in his work, he would not have made a 'negligent misstatement' in his report.

Section 11(3) of the 1977 Act provides that, in considering whether it is fair and reasonable to allow reliance on a notice which excludes liability in tort, account must be taken of 'all the circumstances obtaining when the liability arose or (but for the notice) would have arisen'. Section 13(1) of the Act prevents the exclusion of any right or remedy and (to that extent) s 2 also prevents the exclusion of liability 'by reference to . . . notices which exclude . . . the relevant obligation or duty'. Nourse LJ dismissed s 11(3) as 'peripheral' and made no comment on s 13(1). In my opinion both these provisions support the view that the 1977 Act requires that all exclusion notices which would in common law provide a defence to an action for negligence must satisfy the requirement of reasonableness.

The answer to the second question involved in these appeals is that the disclaimer of liability made by the council on its own behalf in *Harris's* case and by the Abbey National on behalf of the appellant surveyors in *Smith's* case constitute notices which fall within the 1977 Act and must satisfy the requirement of reasonableness.

[His Lordship went on to decide the third question in relation to each exclusion clause and held that it was not 'fair and reasonable' to allow reliance on each clause.]

LORD GRIFFITHS: . . . Counsel for the council and Mr Lee drew attention to the doubts expressed about the correctness of this decision by Kerr LJ in the course of his judgment in the Court of Appeal, and submitted, on the authority of *Hedley Byrne & Co Ltd v Heller & Partners Ltd* [1963] 2 All ER 575, [1964] AC 465, that it was essential to found liability for a negligent misstatement that there had been 'a voluntary assumption of responsibility' on the part of the person giving the advice. I do not accept this submission and I do not think that voluntary assumption of responsibility is a helpful or realistic test for liability. It is true that reference is made in a number of the speeches in the *Hedley Byrne* case to the assumption of responsibility as a test of liability but it must be remembered that those speeches were made in the context of a case in which the central issue was whether a duty of care could arise when there had been an express disclaimer of responsibility for the accuracy of the advice. Obviously, if an adviser expressly assumes responsibility for his advice, a duty of care will arise, but such is extremely unlikely in the ordinary course of events. The House of Lords approved a duty of care being imposed on the facts in *Cann v Willson* (1888) 39 Ch D 39 and in *Candler v Crane Christmas & Co* [1951] 1 All ER 426, [1951] 2 KB 164. But, if the surveyor in *Cann v Willson* or the accountant in *Candler v Crane Christmas & Co* had actually been asked if he was voluntarily assuming responsibility for his advice to the mortgagee or the purchaser of the shares, I have little doubt he would have replied: 'Certainly not. My responsibility is limited to the person who employs me.' The phrase 'assumption of responsibility' can only have any real meaning if it is understood as referring to the circumstances in which the law will deem the maker of the statement to have assumed responsibility to the person who acts on the advice.

In *Ministry of Housing and Local Government v Sharp* [1970] 1 All ER 1009, [1970] 2 QB 223 both Lord Denning MR and Salmon LJ rejected the argument that a voluntary assumption of responsibility was the sole criterion for imposing a duty of care for the negligent preparation of a search certificate in the local land charges register.

The essential distinction between the present case and the situation being considered in the *Hedley Byrne* case and in the two earlier cases is that in those cases the advice was being given with the intention of persuading the recipient to act on it. In the present case the purpose of providing the report is to advise the mortgagee but it is given in circumstances in which it is highly probable that the purchaser will in fact act on its contents, although that was not the primary purpose of the report. I have had considerable doubts whether it is wise to increase the scope of the duty for negligent advice beyond the person directly intended by the giver of the advice to act on it to those whom he knows may do so. Certainly in the field of the law of mortgagor and mortgagee there is authority that points in the other direction. . . .

[His Lordship considered these cases. He then concluded that *Yianni v Edwin Evans & Sons* [1982] QB 438; [1981] 3 All ER 592, in which Park J held that in the circumstances of the case a valuer and surveyor employed by a building society to inspect and value a house owed a duty of care to the purchaser who had applied to the building society for a loan, was correctly decided. He continued:] I have already given my view that the voluntary assumption of responsibility is unlikely to be a helpful or realistic test in most cases. I therefore return to the question in what circumstances should the law deem those who give advice to have assumed responsibility to the person who acts on the advice or, in other words, in what circumstances should a duty of care be owed by the adviser to those who act on his advice? I would answer: only if it is foreseeable that if the advice is negligent the recipient is likely to suffer damage, that there is a sufficiently proximate relationship between the parties and that it is just and reasonable to impose the liability. In the case of a surveyor valuing a small house for a building society or local authority, the application of these three criteria leads to the conclusion that he owes a duty of care to the purchaser. If the valuation is negligent and is relied on damage in the form of economic loss to the purchaser is obviously foreseeable. The necessary proximity arises from the surveyor's knowledge that the overwhelming probability is that the purchaser will rely on his valuation, the evidence was that surveyors knew that approximately 90% of purchasers did so, and the fact that the surveyor only obtains the work because the purchaser is willing to pay his fee. It is just and reasonable that the duty should be imposed for the advice is given in a professional as opposed to a social context and liability for breach of the duty will be limited both as to its extent and amount. The extent of the liability is limited to the purchaser of the house: I would not extend it to subsequent purchasers. The amount of the liability cannot be very great because it relates to a modest house. There is no question here of creating a liability of indeterminate amount to an indeterminate class. I would certainly wish to stress, that in cases where the advice has not been given for the specific purpose of the recipient acting on it, it should only be in cases when the adviser knows that there is a high degree of probability that some other identifiable person will act on the advice that a duty of care should be imposed. It would impose an intolerable burden on those who give advice in a professional or commercial context if they were to owe a duty not only to those to whom they give the advice but to any other person who might choose to act on it.

I accept that the mere fact of a contract between mortgagor and mortgagee will not of itself in all cases be sufficient to found a duty of care. But I do not accept the view of the Court of Appeal in *Curran v Northern Ireland Co-ownership Housing Association Ltd* (1986) 8 NIJB 1 that a mortgagee who accepts a fee to obtain a valuation of a small house owes no duty of care to the mortgagor in the selection of the valuer to whom he entrusts the work. In my opinion, the mortgagee in such a case, knowing that the mortgagor will rely on the valuation, owes a duty to the mortgagor to take reasonable care to employ a reasonably competent valuer. Provided he does this the mortgagee will not be held liable for the negligence of the independent valuer who acts as an independent contractor. . . .

[LORD JAUNCEY OF TULLICHETTLE delivered a speech in favour of dismissing the appeal in the first case and allowing the appeal in the second case. LORD KEITH OF KINKEL and LORD BRANDON OF OAKBROOK agreed with all the speeches.]

Notes

1. It is difficult to fit this type of case into the *Hedley Byrne* principle of 'voluntary assumption of responsibility'. A contract existed between the Building Society and the surveyors in *Smith v Bush*, and there was no contract between the purchasers and the surveyor. Although Lord Templeman (p. 176, ante) regarded the situation as one 'equivalent to contract', Lord Jauncey ([1989] 2 All ER at p. 541) said that when Lord Devlin used this concept in *Hedley Byrne* (p. 167, ante) he did not have in mind the sort of tripartite situation which obtained here, but rather he was considering a situation where the provider and receiver of information were in contact with one another either directly or through their agents, and where, but for the lack of payment, a contract would have existed between them. Moreover, although Lord Templeman stated that the 'valuer assumes responsibility to both mortgagee and purchaser', both Lord Griffiths (p. 177, ante) and Lord Jauncey ([1989] 2 All ER at p. 541) based the duty on a 'deemed' rather than an actual assumption of responsibility by the valuers to the purchasers because of the close degree of proximity between them. It was emphasised that the mere fact that the valuation will be shown to the purchaser is not enough: knowledge, actual or implied, of the purchaser's 'highly probable' (per Lord Griffiths, p. 178, ante) or 'likely' (per Lord Jauncey [1989] 2 All ER at p. 541) reliance must be brought home to the surveyor. While such an implication can readily be made in relation to a potential mortgagor at the lower end of the housing market, it is far less likely in the case of an expensive residential or commercial property where the purchaser may be expected to rely on her own survey. Moreover, like Lord Griffiths (p. 178, ante) Lord Jauncey ([1989] 2 All ER at p. 542) would not extend the duty to 'strangers' who might subsequently derive an interest in the house from her.

2. If the surveyor, employed by the purchaser's building society, negligently reported a fault which did not exist, as a result of which the sale fell through and the vendor lost the chance to buy another property for which she had

already made an offer subject to contract, would the vendor have a cause of action against the surveyor? See T. Kaye (1989) 52 MLR 841 at 851.

3. Will the effect of this decision be to cause mortgagees to make prospective mortgagors pay more for inspections, and to deter valuers from undertaking such surveys? Note the comments of Lord Griffiths (p. 178, ante) concerning the advantages of loss-spreading by insurance, and compare the views of P. A Chandler (1988) 51 MLR 377 at 379, commenting on the Court of Appeal's decision in *Smith v Bush*, who thought this might happen, with those of Kaye, op cit, pp. 848–851, who points out that surveyors have acted for some years under the impression that they owe a duty of care to purchasers, and are unlikely to refuse simple valuations since they are heavily dependent upon the goodwill of the building societies which employ them. He suggests that a more probable result of these cases is a change in the format of the valuation so as to limit its scope and make the purchaser much more aware of what has actually been inspected by the surveyor. Another possible development is a change in conveyancing practice under which the vendor would obtain a survey (as tentatively proposed by the Law Commission's Conveyancing Standing Committee, *Caveat Emptor in Sales of Land*, London, 1988). The purchaser could rely on the contents because the valuer would owe both vendor and purchaser a duty to exercise reasonable care and skill in preparing the report.

4. Is the failure of a building society borrower to have his own structural survey done capable of amounting to contributory negligence? See generally M. Harwood (1987) 50 MLR 588.

5. Another example of a tripartite situation is where a claim is brought by a party to legal proceedings against the solicitor or barrister who represented the other party. In *Business Computers International Ltd v Registrar of Companies* [1988] Ch 229; [1987] 3 All ER 465, Scott J held that a person who institutes legal process does not owe a duty of care to the respondent in regard to the service of proceedings or any other step in the proceedings. The judge held that it would not be 'just and reasonable' to impose such a duty, on the ground that the safeguard against impropriety lies in the rules and procedures governing litigation and not in superimposed tortious duties of care. In *Al-Kandari v J R Brown & Co* [1988] QB 665; [1988] 1 All ER 833; Lord Donaldson MR (at pp. 835–836) and Bingham LJ (at p. 839) went even further than this, stating that in the ordinary course of adversarial litigation a solicitor does not owe a duty of care to his or her client's adversary. The reason for this is said to be one of public policy, namely to avoid endless re-litigation of disputes (see p. 174, ante). On the wholly exceptional facts of the case itself (which did not concern pure economic loss), however, there was found to be a duty of care. The solicitor had stepped outside his role as his client's representative and had given an undertaking (embodied in a consent order in matrimonial proceedings) as to the custody of his client's passport. By so doing he had assumed a duty to the other party to litigation (his client's wife) to take reasonable care not to allow the passport to come into his own client's hands. Somehow the passport did get into his hands, he had his wife kidnapped and he then abducted their children to Kuwait, using the passport to do so. The children were never recovered. There was held to be a breach of the assumed duty of care. The Court of Appeal (reversing the

trial judge on this point) found that the damages for physical illness and psychiatric illness suffered by the wife were a natural and probable consequence of the breach of duty and not too remote.

6. Can there be a 'special relationship' where the communication is not to an identified person, like the purchaser in *Smith v Bush*, but to a larger *class* of persons? This is considered in the next case.

Caparo Industries plc *v* Dickman House of Lords [1990] 1 All ER 568

Caparo (the respondents) owned shares in Fidelity, a public company. Fidelity's accounts were audited by Touche Ross & Co (the appellants). After receipt of the audited accounts for the year ended 31 March 1984, Caparo purchased more shares in Fidelity and later that year made a successful take-over bid for the company. Following the take-over, Caparo brought an action for damages against Touche Ross & Co, alleging that the purchases of shares and the subsequent bid were made in reliance on the accounts of Fidelity, and that those accounts were inaccurate and misleading in that they showed a pre-tax profit of some £1.3 m for the year ended 31 March 1984 when in fact there had been a loss of over £400,000. It was alleged that Touche Ross & Co were negligent in certifying that the accounts showed a true and fair view of Fidelity's position at the date to which they related.

On the trial of a preliminary issue, the judge, [1988] BCLC 387, held that (1) the auditors owed no duty at common law to Caparo as investors and (2) whilst auditors might owe statutory duties to shareholders as a class, there was no common law duty to individual shareholders such as would enable an individual shareholder to recover damages for loss sustained by him in acting in reliance on the audited accounts. Caparo appealed to the Court of Appeal, [1989] 1 All ER 798, which, by a majority (O'Connor LJ dissenting) allowed the appeal holding that, whilst there was no relationship between an auditor and a potential investor sufficiently proximate to give rise to a duty of care at common law, there was such a relationship with individual shareholders, so that an individual shareholder who suffered loss by acting in reliance on negligently prepared accounts, was entitled to recover in tort. From that decision, the auditors appealed, and Caparo cross-appealed against the rejection by the Court of Appeal of their claim that the auditors owed them a duty of care as potential investors.

LORD BRIDGE OF HARWICH: [After considering the general approach to the duty of care, set out p. 56, ante, his Lordship continued:] The damage which may be caused by the negligently spoken or written word will normally be confined to economic loss sustained by those who rely on the accuracy of the information or advice they receive as a basis for action. The question what, if any, duty is owed by the maker of a statement to exercise due care to ensure its accuracy arises typically in relation to statements made by a person in the exercise of his calling or profession. In advising the client who employs him the professional man owes a duty to exercise that standard of skill and care appropriate to his professional status and will be liable both in contract and in tort for all losses which his client may suffer by reason of any breach of that duty. But the possibility of any duty of care being owed to third parties with whom the professional man was in no contractual relationship was for long denied because of the wrong turning taken by the law in *Le Lievre v Gould* [1893] 1 QB 491 in overruling *Cann v Willson* (1888) 39 Ch D 39. In *Candler v Crane Christmas & Co* [1951] 1 All ER 426, [1951] 2 KB 164 Denning LJ, in his dissenting judgment, made a valiant attempt to correct the error. But it was not until the decision of this House in *Hedley Byrne & Co Ltd v Heller & Partners Ltd* [1963] 2 All ER 575, [1964] AC 465 that the law was once more set on the right path.

Consistently with the traditional approach it is to these authorities and to subsequent decisions directly relevant to this relatively narrow corner of the field that we should look to determine the essential characteristics of a situation giving rise, independently of any contractual or fiduciary relationship, to a duty of care owed by one party to another to ensure that the accuracy of any statement which the one party makes and on which the other party may foreseeably rely to his economic detriment. . . .

[His Lordship reviewed the authorities and continued:] The salient feature of all these cases is that the defendant giving advice or information was fully aware of the nature of the transaction which the plaintiff had in contemplation, knew that the advice or information would be communicated to him directly or indirectly and knew that it was very likely that the plaintiff would rely on that advice or information in deciding whether or not to engage in the transaction in contemplation. In these circumstances the defendant could clearly be expected, subject always to the effect of any disclaimer of responsibility, specifically to anticipate that the plaintiff would rely on the advice or information given by the defendant for the very purpose for which he did in the event rely on it. So also the plaintiff, subject again to the effect of any disclaimer, would in that situation reasonably suppose that he was entitled to rely on the advice or information communicated to him for the very purpose for which he required it. The situation is entirely different where a statement is put into more or less general circulation and may foreseeably be relied on by strangers to the maker of the statement for any one of a variety of different purposes which the maker of the statement has no specific reason to anticipate. To hold the maker of the statement to be under a duty of care in respect of the accuracy of the statement to all and sundry for any purpose for which they may choose to rely on it is not only to subject him, in the classic words of Cardozo CJ, to 'liability in an indeterminate amount for an indeterminate time to an indeterminate class' (see *Ultramares Corp v Touche* (1931) 255 NY 170 at 179), it is also to confer on the world at large a quite unwarranted entitlement to appropriate for their own purposes the benefit of the expert knowledge or professional expertise attributed to the maker of the statement. Hence, looking only at the circumstances of these decided cases where a duty of care in respect of negligent statements has been held to exist, I should expect to find that the 'limit or control mechanism . . . imposed on the liability of a wrongdoer towards those who have suffered economic damage in consequence of his negligence' (see the *Candlewood* case [1985] 2 All ER 935 at 9455, [1986] AC 1 at 25) rested on the necessity to prove in this category of the tort of negligence, as an essential ingredient of the 'proximity' between the plaintiff and the defendant, that the defendant knew that his statement would be communicated to the plaintiff, either as an individual or as a member of an identifiable class, specifically in connection with a particular transaction or transactions of a particular kind (eg in a prospectus inviting investment) and that the plaintiff would be very likely to rely on it for the purpose of deciding whether or not to enter on that transaction or on a transaction of that kind. . . .

[His Lordship reviewed other authorities, and then considered the position of auditors in relation to the shareholders of a public limited company arising from the provisions of the Companies Act 1985]

No doubt these provisions establish a relationship between the auditors and the shareholders of a company on which the shareholder is entitled to rely for the protection of his interest. But the crucial question concerns the extent of the shareholder's interest which the auditor has a duty to protect. The shareholders of a company have a collective interest in the company's proper management and in so far as a negligent failure of the auditor to report accurately on the state of the company's finances deprives the shareholders of the opportunity to exercise their powers in general meeting to call the directors to book and to ensure that errors in management are corrected, the shareholders ought to be entitled to a remedy. But in practice no problem arises in this regard since the interest of the shareholders in the proper management of the company's affairs is indistinguishable from the interest of the company itself and any loss suffered by the shareholders, eg by the negligent failure of the auditor to discover and expose a misappropriation of funds by a director of the company, will be recouped by a claim against the auditor in the name of the company, not by individual shareholders.

I find it difficult to visualise a situation arising in the real world in which the individual shareholder could claim to have sustained a loss in respect of his existing shareholding referable to the negligence of the auditor which could not be recouped by the company. But on this part of the case your Lordships were much pressed with the argument that such a loss might occur by a negligent undervaluation of the company's assets in the auditor's report relied on by the individual shareholder in deciding to sell his shares at an undervalue. The argument then runs thus. The shareholder, qua shareholder, is entitled to rely on the auditor's report as the basis of his investment decision to sell his existing shareholding. If he sells at an undervalue he is entitled to recover the loss from the auditor. There can be no distinction in law between the shareholder's investment decision to sell the shares he has or to buy additional shares. It follows, therefore, that the scope of the duty of care owed to him by the auditor extends to cover any loss sustained consequent on the purchase of additional shares in reliance on the auditor's negligent report.

I believe this argument to be fallacious. Assuming without deciding that a claim by a shareholder to recover a loss suffered by selling his shares at an undervalue attributable to an undervaluation of the company's assets in the auditor's report could be sustained at all, it would not be by reason of any reliance by the shareholder on the auditor's report in deciding to sell: the loss would be referable to the depreciatory effect of the report on the market value of the shares before ever the decision of the shareholder to sell was taken. A claim to recoup a loss alleged to flow from the purchase of overvalued shares, on the other hand, can only be sustained on the basis of the purchaser's reliance on the report. The specious equation of 'investment decisions' to sell or to buy as giving rise to parallel claims thus appears to me to be untenable. Moreover, the loss in the case of the sale would be of a loss of part of the value of the shareholder's existing holding, which, assuming a duty of care owed to individual shareholders, it might sensibly lie within the scope of the auditor's duty to protect. A loss, on the other hand, resulting from the purchase of additional shares would result from a wholly independent transaction having no connection with the existing shareholding.

I believe it is this last distinction which is of critical importance and which demonstrates the unsoundness of the conclusion reached by the majority of the Court of Appeal. It is never sufficient to ask simply whether A owes B a duty of care. It is always necessary to determine the scope of the duty by reference to the kind of damage from which A must take care to save B harmless:

'The question is always whether the defendant was under a duty to avoid or prevent that damage, but the actual nature of the damage suffered is relevant to the existence and extent of any duty to avoid or prevent it.'

(See *Sutherland Shire Council v Heyman* (1985) 60 ALR 1 at 48 per Brennan J.)

Assuming for the purpose of the argument that the relationship between the auditor of a company and individual shareholders is of sufficient proximity to give rise to a duty of care, I do not understand how the scope of that duty can possibly extend beyond the protection of any individual shareholder from losses in the value of the shares which he holds. As a purchaser of additional shares in reliance on the auditor's report, he stands in no different position from any other investing member of the public to whom the auditor owes no duty.

I would allow the appeal and dismiss the cross-appeal.

LORD OLIVER OF AYLMERTON: [After considering the general approach to the duty of care, set out p. 58, ante, his Lordship said:] What can be deduced from the *Hedley Byrne* case . . . is that the necessary relationship between the maker of a statement or giver of advice (the adviser) and the recipient who acts in reliance on it (the advisee) may typically be held to exist where (1) the advice is required for a purpose, whether particularly specified or generally described, which is made known, either actually or inferentially, to the adviser at the time when the advice is given, (2) the adviser knows, either actually or inferentially, that his advice will be communicated to the advisee, either specifically or as a member of an ascertainable class, in order that it should be used by the advisee for that purpose, (3) it is known, either actually or inferentially, that the advice so communicated is likely to be acted on by the advisee for that purpose without independent inquiry and (4) it is so acted on by the advisee to his detriment. That is not, of course, to suggest that these conditions are either conclusive or exclusive, but merely that the actual decision in the case does not warrant any broader propositions. . . .

My Lords, no decision of this House has gone further than *Smith v Eric S Bush*, but your Lordships are asked by Caparo to widen the area of responsibility even beyond the limits to which it was extended by the Court of Appeal in this case and to find a relationship of proximity between the adviser and third parties to whose attention the advice may come in circumstances in which the reliance said to have given rise to the loss is strictly unrelated either to the intended recipient or to the purpose for which the advice was required. My Lords, I discern no pressing reason of policy which would require such an extension and there seems to me to be powerful reasons against it. As Lord Reid observed in the course of his speech in the *Hedley Byrne* case [1963] 2 All ER 575 at 581, [1964] AC 465 at 483, words can be broadcast with or without the consent or foresight of the speaker or writer; and in his speech in the same case Lord Pearce drew attention to the necessity for the imposition of some discernible limits to liability in such cases. . . .

In seeking to ascertain whether there should be imposed on the adviser a duty to avoid the occurrence of the kind of damage which the advisee claims to have suffered it is not, I think, sufficient to ask simply whether there existed a 'closeness' between them in the sense that the advisee had a legal entitlement to receive the information on the basis of which he has acted or in the sense that the information was intended to serve his interest or to protect him. One must, I think, go further and ask, in what capacity was his interest to be served and from what was he intended to be protected? A company's annual accounts are capable of being utilised for a number of purposes and if one thinks about it it is entirely foreseeable that they may be so employed. But many of such purposes have absolutely no connection with the recipient's status or capacity, whether as a shareholder, voting or non-voting, or as a debenture-holder. Before it can be concluded that the duty is imposed to protect the recipient against harm which he suffers by reason of the particular use that he chooses to make of the information which he receives, one must, I think, first ascertain the purpose for which the information is required to be given. Indeed, the paradigmatic *Donoghue v Stevenson* case of a manufactured article requires, as an essential ingredient of liability, that the article has been used by the consumer in the manner in which it was intended to be used (see *Grant v Australian Knitting Mills Ltd* [1936] AC 85 at 104, [1935] All ER Rep 209 at 217 and *Junior Books Ltd v Veitchi Co Ltd* [1982] 3 All ER 201 at 216, 218, [1983] 1 AC 520 at 549, 552). I entirely follow that if the conclusion is reached that the very purpose of providing the information is to serve as the basis for making investment decisions or giving investment advice, it is not difficult then to conclude also that the duty imposed on the adviser extends to protecting the recipient against loss occasioned by an unfortunate investment decision which is based on carelessly inaccurate information. . . .

. . . I do not believe and I see no grounds for believing that, in enacting the statutory provisions, Parliament had in mind the provision of information for the assistance of purchasers of shares or debentures in the market, whether they be already the holders of shares or other securities or persons having no previous proprietary interest in the company. It is unnecessary to decide the point on this appeal, but I can see more force in the contention that one purpose of providing the statutory information might be to enable the recipient to exercise whatever rights he has in relation to his proprietary interest by virtue of which he receives it, by way, for instance of disposing of that interest. I can, however, see no ground for supposing that the legislature was intending to foster a market for the existing holders of shares or debentures by providing information for the purpose of enabling them to acquire such securities from other holders who might be minded to sell.

For my part, I think that the position as regards the auditor's statutory duty was correctly summarised by O'Connor LJ in his dissenting judgment when he said ([1989] 1 All ER 798 at 830, [1989] QB 653 at 714):

'The statutory duty owed by auditors to shareholders is, I think, a duty owed to them as a body. I appreciate that it is difficult to see how the overstatement of the accounts can cause damage to the shareholders as a body: it will be the underlying reasons for the overstatement which cause damage, for example fraudulent abstraction of assets by directors or servants, but such loss is recoverable by the company. I am anxious to limit the present case to deciding whether the statutory duty operates to protect the individual shareholder as a potential buyer of further shares. If I am wrong in thinking that under the [Companies Act 1985] no duty is owed to shareholders as individuals, then I think that the duty must be confined to transactions in which the shareholder can only participate because he is a shareholder. The statute imposes a duty to shareholders as a class and the duty should not extend to an individual save as a member of the class in respect of some class activity. Buying shares in a company is not such an activity.'

In my judgment, accordingly, the purpose for which the auditors' certificate is made and published is that of providing those entitled to receive the report with information to enable them to exercise in conjunction those powers which their respective proprietary interests confer on them and not for the purposes of individual speculation with a view to profit. The same considerations as limit the existence of a duty of care also, in my judgment, limit the scope of the duty and I agree with O'Connor LJ that the duty of care is one owed to the shareholders as a body and not to individual shareholders.

To widen the scope of the duty to include loss caused to an individual by reliance on the accounts for a purpose for which they were not supplied and were not intended would be to extend it beyond the limits which are so far deducible from the decisions of this House. It is not, as I think, an extension which either logic requires or policy dictates and I, for my part, am not prepared to follow the majority of the Court of Appeal in making it. In relation to the purchase of shares of other shareholders in a company, whether in the open market or as a result of an offer made to all or a majority of the existing shareholders, I can see no sensible distinction, so far as a duty of care is concerned, between a potential purchaser who is, vis-à-vis the company, a total outsider and one who is already the holder of one or more shares. I accordingly agree with what has already fallen from my noble and learned friend Lord Bridge, and I, too, would allow the appeal and dismiss the cross-appeal.

[LORD ROSKILL and LORD JAUNCEY OF TULLICHETTLE delivered speeches in favour of allowing the appeal and dismissing the cross-appeal. LORD ACKNER agreed with all the speeches.]

Appeal allowed; cross-appeal dismissed

Notes

1. In *Candler v Crane Christmas & Co* [1951] 2 KB 164; [1951] 1 All ER 426, Denning LJ delivered a dissenting judgment on the liability of accountants.

This was later approved by Lord Hodson, Lord Devlin and Lord Pearce in *Hedley Byrne & Co Ltd v Heller & Partners Ltd*, and was described by Lord Bridge ([1990] 1 All ER at p. 577) in the *Caparo* case as a 'masterly analysis' requiring 'little, if any amplification or modification in the light of later authority'. Denning LJ suggested (at p. 435) that the duty of care extended only to those transactions

'for which the accountants knew their accounts were required. . . . Thus a doctor, who negligently certifies a man to be a lunatic when he is not, is liable to him, although there is no contract in the matter, because the doctor knows that his certificate is required for the very purpose of deciding whether the man should be detained or not, but an insurance company's doctor owes no duty to the insured person, because he makes his examination only for the purpose of the insurance company . . . .Again a scientist or expert (including a marine hydrographer) is not liable to his readers for careless statements in his published works. He publishes his work simply to give information, and not with any particular transaction in mind. When, however, a scientist or an expert makes an investigation and report for the very purpose of a particular transaction, then, in my opinion, he is under a duty of care in respect of that transaction.'

2. Would it have made a difference in the *Caparo* case if the auditors had actual knowledge of the specific purpose for which the investors intended to use the accounts? Lord Bridge (at·p. 579) and Lord Oliver (at p. 596) approved the dictum of Richmond P in *Scott Group Ltd v McFarlane* [1978] 1 NZLR 553 at 566, that

'[I]t does not seem reasonable to attribute an assumption of responsibility unless the maker of the statement ought in all the circumstances, both in preparing himself for what he said and in saying it, to have directed his mind, and to have been able to direct his mind, to some particular and specific purpose for which he was aware that his information or advice would be relied on. In many situations that purpose will be obvious. But the annual accounts of a company can be relied on in all sorts of ways and for many purposes.'

3. Since *Caparo*, courts have closely scrutinised the purposes for which company accounts have been prepared. So, in *Al Nakib Investments (Jersey) Ltd v Longcroft* [1990] 3 All ER 321; [1990] 1 WLR 1390 Mervyn Davies J held that directors of a company who issued a prospectus for the particular purpose of encouraging shareholders to take up a rights issue did not owe a duty of care to those shareholders who relied upon the prospectus for the purpose of buying the shares in the market. In *James McNaughton Paper Group Ltd v Hicks Anderson & Co* [1991] 1 All ER 134, the Court of Appeal held that accountants who had prepared, at short notice, draft accounts of their client company for the company's chairman, owed no duty of care to a bidder who took over the company after having inspected those accounts. Neill LJ identified a number of (overlapping) matters which are likely to be of importance in determining whether or not a duty exists: (a) the purpose for which the statement was made; (b) the purpose for which the statement was communicated; (c) the relationship between the adviser, the advisee and any relevant third party; (d) the size of any class to which the advisee belonged; (e) the state of knowledge of the adviser; (f) reliance by the advisee. (The test of 'reliance' suggested by Stephenson LJ in *JEB Fasteners Ltd v Marks, Bloom & Co (a firm)* [1983] 1 All ER 583 at 589 is whether the statement plays a 'real and substantial part, though not by itself a decisive part, in inducing the plaintiff to act'.) These criteria were approved by a dif-

ferently constituted Court of Appeal in *Morgan Crucible Co plc v Hill Samuel Bank Ltd* [1991] 1 All ER 148, but with a different result. In that case the assumed facts were that during the course of a takeover bid the directors and financial advisers of the target company had made express representations regarding the accuracy of profit forecasts and financial statements after an identified bidder had emerged and they intended that the bidder should rely on those representations. The bidder did rely on them. It was held that it was arguable, on these pleadings, that there was sufficient proximity between the directors, their advisers, and the bidder to give rise to a duty of care not to mislead the bidder. The Court accepted that it would be right for the court at the trial not to close its eyes to the possible economic consequences of its decision as to a duty of care. In this regard, although Hoffman J's decision that there was no duty of care was overruled, it was worth noting his view that the reason why the House of Lords was willing in *Smith v Eric S Bush* (p. 175, ante) but not in *Caparo* (ante) to extend the duty of care to a statement of which the statutory and declared purpose was different from that for which it was used by the plaintiff, lay in the different economic relationships between the parties and the nature of the markets in which they were operating:

'First, Mr Smith had paid for the survey; although he had no contract with the surveyor, the relationship was, as Lord Templeman said "akin to contract". Economically there was no distinction. Caparo Industries plc, on the other hand, had not paid for the audit. Secondly, the typical plaintiff in a *Smith*-type case is a person of modest means and making the most expensive purchase of his or her life. He is very unlikely to be insured against the manifestation of inherent defects. The surveyor can protect himself relatively easily by insurance. The take-over bidder, on the other hand, is an entrepreneur taking high risks for high rewards and while some accountants may be able to take out sufficient insurance, others may not. Furthermore, the take-over bidder is a limited liability company and the accountants are individuals for whom, save so far as they are covered by insurance, liability would mean personal ruin. Thirdly, the imposition of liability upon surveyors would probably not greatly increase their insurance costs and push up the cost of surveys because the typical buyer who relies upon a building society survey is buying a relatively modest house. Take-overs on the Stock Exchange involve huge amounts and the effects on accountants' insurance and fees are unpredictable.' ([1990] NLJR at p. 1272).

However, the Court of Appeal was not willing, by reference to economic considerations, 'to dismiss as unarguable an otherwise arguable case.'

4. The *Caparo* case, which is noted by T. Weir [1990] CLJ 212, is yet another illustration of judicial reluctance to add common law liabilities on to a statutory framework of control. Section 384 of the Companies Act 1985 regulates the duty of statutory auditors, and ss. 228 et seq. of the Act lay down in considerable detail what statutory accounts must contain (see generally M. J. Sterling (1987) 50 MLR 468 on the duty to shareholders and Bowles and Jones, op cit, pp. 51–61 for an economic perspective). Although not strictly concerned with false information and advice, the Privy Council's decision in *Yuen Kun yeu v A-G of Hong Kong* [1988] AC 175; [1987] 2 All ER 705 showed the limits of the common law in providing investor protection. It was decided that the Commissioner of Deposit-taking Companies in Hong Kong did not owe a duty to members of the public who might be minded to deposit their money in companies registered by the Commissioner to exercise reasonable care to see that they did not suffer loss through the

companies being carried on by their managers in a fraudulent or improvident fashion. The Judicial Board decided the case on a 'no proximity' basis (see p. 53, ante). The decisive factors in this connection appear to have been that (a) the Commissioner had no power to control the day-to-day activities of those who allegedly caused the loss; and (b) the Commissioner had not voluntarily assumed any responsibility to investors, and reliance by them on the fact of registration as a guarantee of the soundness of a particular company would be neither reasonable nor justifiable, nor should the Commissioner reasonably be expected to know of such reliance if it existed. As to (a), on the appellants' averments (which were assumed to be true for the purposes of the question of law before the court) the Commissioner of Deposit-taking Companies had available to him information concerning a company's affairs, information to which the public did not have access and which raised serious doubts about the company's stability. Could this bring the case within the principle in *Home Office v Dorset Yacht Co Ltd* [1970] AC 1004; [1970] 2 All ER 294 (p. 72, ante)? Lord Keith thought not. As stated ante, the Commissioner lacked powers of day-to-day control and was confined under his discretionary powers in the relevant ordinance to stopping the company carrying on business. The Privy Council accordingly denied that there was any special relationship between either the Commissioner and the company or between the Commissioner and those members of the public who were potential depositors with the company. (The Hong Kong legislation has subsequently been amended to give the Commissioner immunity from civil suit. There are comparable provisions in England in the Financial Services Act 1986, s. 186 (1) and the Banking Act 1987, s. 1(4).) In *Minories Finance Ltd v Arthur Young (a firm) (Bank of England, third party)* [1989] 2 All ER 105, Saville J pointed out that the *Yuen Kun Yeu* case concerned a different supervisory authority and could not be considered conclusive so far as the liability of the Bank of England to a depositor in a commercial bank which failed was concerned (although on the facts of the case there was a statutory bar to recovery). Compare *Davis v Radcliffe* [1990] 2 All ER 536; [1990] 1 WLR 821 in which the Privy Council applied *Yuen Kun-yeu* in order to hold that the Isle of Man Finance Board and Treasurer owed no duty of care, in the exercise of their statutory functions of licensing and supervising banks, to depositors in a bank which collapsed. Where the loss is economic, the plaintiff is an unascertained member of a large class of investors or depositors, and the immediate cause of the loss is the wrongful act of a third party, the dicta in *Caparo* point against any common law duty of care. The existence of a statutory right of appeal in respect of an erroneous opinion or advice is another pointer against a common law duty of care: see *Mills v Winchester Diocesan Board of Finance* [1989] Ch 428; [1989] 2 All ER 317 (negligence action against Charity Commissioners proceeding concurrently with charity proceedings under s. 28 of Charities Act 1960 struck out, and doubts expressed whether there was sufficient proximity between the objects of a charity and the Commissioner).

5. There is another three-party situation to be considered. What if B relies on a statement made by A, and in so doing causes loss to C? This was the main issue in the next two cases.

Ministry of Housing and Local Government *v* Sharp Court of Appeal [1970] 1 All ER 1009

The Ministry had registered a planning charge in the local land charges registry after the payment of compensation to a Mr Neale who had been refused permission to develop his land. Any later developer of the land would have to repay this sum to the Ministry before development of the land could take place. Two years later planning permission was granted, and a prospective purchaser of the land requested an official search in the register of local land charges. The certificate omitted to mention the Ministry's charge, as a result of the carelessness of a clerk employed by the local authority. The Ministry conceded that the purchaser was not liable to repay the sum because the clear certificate was conclusive in his favour. Compensation for the loss was sought from the local registrar of land charges for breach of statutory duty and from the local authority who, it was alleged, were vicariously liable for the clerk's mistake.

Fisher J dismissed the Ministry's action for damages. The Court of Appeal, by a majority (Salmon and Cross LJJ, Lord Denning MR dissenting) held that the registrar was not under an absolute statutory obligation to issue an accurate certificate and since no negligence on the part of the registrar was alleged, the claim against the registrar failed. However, the Court of Appeal, reversing the judgment of Fisher J in this respect, held that the clerk was liable to the Ministry and the local authority was vicariously liable for his fault.

LORD DENNING MR: . . . I have no doubt that the clerk is liable. He was under a duty at common law to use due care. That was a duty which he owed to any person—incumbrancer or purchaser—who, he knew or ought to have known, might be injured if he made a mistake. The case comes four square within the principles which are stated in *Candler v Crane Christmas & Co*,[1] and which were approved by the House of Lords in *Hedley Byrne & Co Ltd v Heller & Partners Ltd*.[2]

Counsel for the defendants submitted to us, however, that the correct principle did not go that length. He said that a duty to use due care (where there was no contract) only arose when there was a voluntary assumption of responsibility. I do not agree. He relied particularly on the words of Lord Reid in *Hedley Byrne & Co Ltd v Heller & Partners Ltd*[3] and of Lord Devlin.[4] I think that they used those words because of the special circumstances of that case (where the bank disclaimed responsibility). But they did not in any way mean to limit the general principle.

In my opinion the duty to use due care in a statement arises, not from any voluntary assumption of responsibility, but from the fact that the person making it knows, or ought to know, that others, being his neighbours in this regard, would act on the faith of the statement being accurate. That is enough to bring the duty into being. It is owed, of course, to the person to whom the certificate is issued and who he knows is going to act on it, see the judgment of Cardozo J in *Glanzer v Sheppard*.[5] But it also is owed to any person who he knows or ought to know, will be injuriously affected by a mistake, such as the incumbrancer here. . . .

SALMON LJ: . . . The present case does not precisely fit into any category of negligence yet considered by the courts. The Ministry has not been misled by any

---

1. [1951] 2 KB 164 at 179–185; [1951] 1 All ER 426 at 433–436.
2. [1964] AC 465; [1963] 2 All ER 575.
3. [1964] AC at p. 487; [1963] 2 All ER at p. 583.
4. [1964] AC at p. 529; [1963] 2 All ER at pp. 610, 611.
5. 23 NY 236 (1922).

careless statement made to it by the defendants to someone else who the defendants knew would be likely to pass it on to a third party such as the Ministry, in circumstances in which the third party might reasonably be expected to rely on it, see for example, Denning LJ's dissenting judgment in *Candler v Crane Christmas & Co*[1] which was adopted and approved by the House of Lords in *Hedley Byrne & Co Ltd v Heller & Partners Ltd.*[2] I am not, however, troubled by the fact that the present case is, in many respects, unique. I rely on the celebrated dictum of Lord MacMillan that 'The categories of negligence are never closed', *M'Alister* (or *Donoghue*) *v Stevenson*,[3] and the words of Lord Devlin in *Hedley Byrne & Co Ltd v Heller & Partners Ltd.*[2] . . .

It has been argued, in the present case, that since the council did not voluntarily make the search or prepare the certificate for their clerk's signature they did not voluntarily assume responsibility for the accuracy of the certificate and, accordingly, owed no duty of care to the Minister. I do not accept that, in all cases, the obligation to take reasonable care necessarily depends on a voluntary assumption of responsibility. Even if it did, I am far from satisfied that the council did not voluntarily assume responsibility in the present case. On the contrary, it seems to me that they certainly chose to undertake the duty of searching the register and preparing the certificate. There was nothing to compel them to discharge this duty through their servant. It obviously suited them better than this somewhat pedestrian task should be performed by one of their comparatively minor servants than by their clerk so that he might be left free to carry out other far more difficult and important functions on their behalf.

I do not think that it matters that the search was made at the request of the purchasers and that the certificate issued to him. It would be absurd if a duty of care were owed to a purchaser but not to an incumbrancer. The rules made under many of the statutes creating local land charges do not apply s. 17(3); they do, however, apply s. 17(1) and (2) of the Land Charges Act 1925. If, in such cases, a clear certificate is carelessly given, it will be the purchasers and not the incumbrancer who will suffer. Clearly land may be worth much more unincumbered than if it is subject to a charge. The purchaser who buys on the faith of a clear certificate might suffer very heavy financial loss if the certificate turns out to be incorrect. Such a loss is reasonably to be foreseen as a result of any carelessness in the search of the register or the preparation of the certificate. The proximity between the council and the purchaser is even closer than that between the plaintiff and the defendants in *Candler v Crane Christmas & Co.*[4] The council even receive a fee, although a small one, for the certificate. Clearly a duty to take care must exist in such a case. Our law would be grievously defective if the council did owe a duty of care to the purchaser in the one case but no duty to the incumbrancer in the other. The damage in each case is equally foreseeable. It is in my view irrelevant that in the one case the certificate is issued to the person it injures and in the other case it is not. The purchaser is deceived by the certificate about his legal rights when s. 17(3) of the Land Charges Act 1925 does not apply whilst the incumbrancer's legal rights are taken away by the certificate when s. 17(3) does apply. In my view the proximity is as close in one case as in the other and certainly sufficient to impose on the council through their servant a duty to take reasonable care. . . .

[CROSS LJ delivered a judgment in favour of allowing the appeal.]

Appeal allowed

---

1. [1951] 2 KB 164 at 179–185; [1951] 1 All ER 426 at 433–436.
2. [1964] AC 465; [1963] 2 All ER 575.
3. [1932] AC at p. 619; [1932] All ER Rep at p. 30.
4. [1951] 2 KB 164; [1951] 1 All ER 426.

Notes

1. If the facts of the above case occurred today, the purchaser would be bound by a local land charge not revealed by an official search, by virtue of s. 10 of the Local Land Charges Act 1975, but would have a statutory claim for compensation against the registering authority. Cf. the Land Charges Act 1972, which has no such provision for compensation against the Central Land Charges Registry.

2. *Winfield & Jolowicz*, p. 292 suggest that it was the issue of the certificate and not the purchase of the land which caused the Ministry's loss in the *Sharp* case. But, against this view, it can be argued that if the proposed purchase had fallen through, despite the favourable certificate, no loss would have been suffered by the Ministry. In other words, it was not only the issue of the certificate but also the completion of the purchase which caused the loss.

3. Can *Ministry of Housing and Local Government v Sharp* survive as an authority in the light of the restricted definition of 'proximity' in *Caparo Industries plc v Dickman* [1990] 1 All ER 568; [1990] 2 WLR 358 (p. 181 ante)? Lord Oliver (at p. 588) said that *Sharp* (and *Ross v Caunters* [1980] Ch 297; [1979] 3 All ER 580, p. 192 post) 'give rise to certain difficulties of analysis' but it was not necessary for the purposes of the decision in *Caparo* to consider the situation where economic loss is inflicted on C as the result of the reliance by B on information or advice given by A. Will it in future make a difference whether C is simply a member of a relatively large class, or is an identified person? In this regard, it may be noted that *Sharp* was referred to, with apparent approval, in the speeches in the House of Lords in *Smith v Eric S Bush* [1990] 1 AC 831; [1989] 2 All ER 514 (p. 175, ante), a case where the third party was an identified person.

4. D is requested to provide a character reference for P, a former employee, by X, P's new employer, before X will make P's new job a permanent one. D provides an unfavourable reference, as a result of which X dismisses P, who remains unemployed for some years. Can P sue D for damages if he is able to prove that D negligently provided an inaccurate or unfair reference? In *Lawton v BOC Transhield Ltd* [1987] 2 All ER 608; [1987] ICR 7, Tudor Evans J decided that *Ministry of Housing and Local Government v Sharp* was 'conclusively' in favour of a duty of care to ensure that the opinions in the reference were based on accurate facts. However, P lost because there was ample evidence to support D's opinions expressed in the reference and it was found that it was honest, accurate and not negligently written. There are several difficulties with the application of *Sharp* to this type of situation. The first is the status of the case in the light of later House of Lords decisions: see Note 3 ante. (It is to be noted that Tudor Evans J relied, in the alternative, on *Junior Books Ltd v Veitchi Co Ltd* [1983] 1 AC 520; [1982] 3 All ER 201 to find that there was sufficient proximity, and the reasoning in that case has subsequently been confined by the House of Lords: see p. 218, post.). Secondly, the judge was willing to overcome the need for reliance, if that was necessary in all cases, by finding that P was 'relying' on D to give an accurate reference to X. What is missing in this formulation is that the statement was not requested by P nor passed on to him. The 'reliance' found by Tudor Evans J was no more specific than that of

Mrs Donoghue on the quality of the ginger beer, and that is not sufficient to give rise to liability for pure economic loss (see p. 212, post). Thirdly, it was suggested by Tudor Evans J that an employer could protect himself with a disclaimer of responsibility as the respondents did in *Hedley Byrne*. However, the decision in *Smith v Bush* (p. 175, ante) now makes it clear that such a disclaimer would be subject to the test of reasonableness in the Unfair Contract Terms Act 1977. Presumably the employer could discharge his duty by an adequate warning that, although the statement was honestly made, the facts on which it was based had not been checked. Unlike a claim in defamation (p. 778, post), there is no defence of qualified privilege to a claim based on negligence. But those asked for references can make it clear that the information or advice they are giving is 'off the cuff'. For further comment see B. W. Napier (1987) NLJ 824; R. Townshend-Smith (1987) 3 PN 73; A. M. Tettenborn [1987] CLJ 391; P. S. C. Lewis (1988) 17 ILJ 108; and cf. *Bell-Booth Group Ltd v AG* [1989] 3 NZLR 148.

5. Jack opens a grocer's shop across the road from Jill's shop and falsely states that all the eggs he stocks are guaranteed free from salmonella. As a result many of Jill's customers transfer their custom to Jack. Advise Jill, giving consideration to the torts of (a) negligence; (b) interference with a legal right by unlawful means (p. 724, post); and (c) malicious falsehood (p. 760, post).

6. A government minister states that 'most of the eggs produced in this country are infected by salmonella'. Egg sales plummet. The egg producers want to sue the minister for damages. Why would their action be 'riddled with difficulties' (*Financial Times,* 17th November 1988, reporting Professor Basil Markesinis)?

Ross *v* Caunters (a firm) Chancery Division [1979] 3 All ER 580

By virtue of s. 15 of the Wills Act 1837, if the spouse of a beneficiary under a will witnesses that will, then any gift to the beneficiary is void. The plaintiff's husband had in 1974 witnessed the will of William Philp and as a result the plaintiff could not receive what had been left to her under the will (certain chattels and a share in the residue of the estate). She brought an action claiming damages for negligence against the firm of solicitors employed by William Philp in drawing up the will.

SIR ROBERT MEGARRY V-C read the following judgment: In this case, the facts are simple and undisputed, and the point of law that it raises is short; yet it has taken five days to argue, and over 30 authorities, from both sides of the Atlantic, have very properly been cited, some at considerable length. In broad terms, the question is whether solicitors who prepare a will are liable to a beneficiary under it if, through their negligence, the gift to the beneficiary is void. The solicitors are liable, of course, to the testator or his estate for a breach of the duty that they owed to him, though as he has suffered no financial loss it seems that his estate could recover no more than nominal damages. Yet it is said that however careless the solicitors were, they owed no duty to the beneficiary, and so they cannot be liable to her.

If this is right, the result is striking. The only person who has a valid claim has suffered no loss, and the only person who has suffered a loss has no valid claim. However grave the negligence, and however great the loss, the solicitors would be under no liability to pay substantial damages to anyone. No doubt they would be liable to the testator if the mistake was discovered in his lifetime, though in that case the damages would, I think, be merely for the cost of making a new and valid will, or otherwise putting matters right. But the real question is whether the solicitors are under any liability to the disappointed beneficiary. On behalf of the plaintiff in this case counsel says Yes, and on behalf of the defendant solicitors counsel says No. . . .

The negligence alleged against the solicitors may be put under four heads, which to some extent overlap. These are, first, the failure to inform or warn the testator properly about s. 15; second, the failure, on the return of the will,[1] to check whether it had been duly executed in conformity with the Act; third, the failure to observe that an attesting witness was the plaintiff's husband, so that the gifts to her would be void; and fourth, the failure to draw this to the testator's attention. It is alleged that if his atention had been drawn to it, he would have re-executed the will before different attesting witnesses, or would have made a new and valid will in the same terms. The solicitors have not attempted to quibble or make fine distinctions, but with commendable frankness have by their defence admitted all these allegations, subject to the overriding contention that their obligation to take reasonable care in and about the making of the 1974 will was owed to the testator, and to him alone, and that they owed no duty of care to the plaintiff. . . .

. . . The question is whether a solicitor owes a duty of care to a beneficiary under a will that he makes for a client, and, if so, on what basis that duty rests. This is, of course, the central core of the case.

In considering this, three features of the case before me seem to stand out. First, there is the close degree of proximity of the plaintiff to the defendants. There is no question of whether the defendants could fairly have been expected to contemplate the plaintiff as a person likely to be affected by any lack of care on their part, or whether they ought to have done so: there is no 'ought' about the case. This is not a case where the only nexus between the plaintiff and the defendants is that the plaintiff was the ultimate recipient of a dangerous chattel or negligent mis-statement which the defendants had put into circulation. The plaintiff was named and identified in the will that the defendants drafted for the testator. Their contemplation of the plaintiff was actual, nominate and direct. It was contemplation by contract, though of course the contract was with a third party, the testator.

Second, this proximity of the plaintiff to the defendants was a product of the duty of care owed by the defendants to the testator: it was in no way casual or accidental or unforeseen. The defendants accepted a duty towards the testator to take reasonable care that the will would, inter alia, carry a share of residue from the testator's estate to the plaintiff. In all that they did (or failed to do) in relation to the will, the solicitors were bound by the duty of care towards the testator that they had accepted; and that duty included a duty to confer a benefit on the plaintiff. When a solicitor undertakes to a client to carry through a transaction which will confer a benefit on a third party, it seems to me that the duty to act with due care which binds the solicitor to his client is one which may readily be extended to the third party who is intended to benefit.

Third, to hold that the defendants were under a duty of care towards the plaintiff would raise no spectre of imposing on the defendants an uncertain and unlimited liability. The liability would be to one person alone, the plaintiff. The amount would be limited to the value of the share of residue intended for the plaintiff. There would be no question of widespread or repeated liability, as might arise from some published mis-statement on which large numbers might rely, to their detriment. There would be no possibility of the defendants being exposed, in the well-known expression of Cardozo CJ, 'to a liability in a indeterminate amount for an indeterminate time to an indeterminate class': see *Ultramares Corpn v Touche*.[2] Instead, there would be a

---

1. [By the testator to the firm of solicitors.]
2. 174 NE 441 (1931) at 444.

finite obligation to a finite number of persons, in this case one. . . .

. . . On the facts of the present case, I do not think that it matters much whether that result is reached by extending the *Hedley Byrne*[1] principle to such cases, as Lord Denning MR did[2], or whether it is reached by determining liability on *Donoghue v Stevenson*[3] principles, and then using *Hedley Byrne*[1] to extend those principles to cases of pure financial loss, as I think was done by Salmon LJ[2]. In view of what Denning LJ said in *Candler v Crane, Christmas & Co*[4] about the persons to whom the duty of care is owed, I find some difficulty in seeing how the principles stated in the judgment apply to someone to whom no statement will be made or shown but who will be injured by a negligent statement being acted on by some third party. With great respect and considerable hesitation, I would prefer the approach of Salmon LJ, though I am happy not [to] be required to decide anything on the point.

It seems to me that the *Sharp* case[5] is conclusive of the point before me. Indeed, it seems to me that despite the factual differences between that case and the case before me, they are closely similar in principle. Let me take P as the plaintiff in each case, D as the defendant (ignoring any distinction between the clerk and the local authority in the *Sharp* case[5]) and X as the third party, the purchaser in the *Sharp* case[5] and the testator in the case before me. I will take five points. First, D was guilty of negligent omissions in his dealings with X: he failed to discover the land charge or failed to include it in the certificate that he gave to the purchaser, or he failed to warn the testator about attestation by a beneficiary's spouse, warning him only about attestation by a beneficiary . . . Second, X acted on the negligent omission but suffered no loss. Third, by acting in this way X caused financial loss to P: P's charge became void against the purchaser, and P's legacy was invalidated. Fourth, D contemplated, or ought to have contemplated that his negligent omissions would injure P, an identified or identifiable person. Fifth, there was no possible liability for an indeterminate amount to an indeterminate number of persons. The *Sharp* case[5] accordingly seems to me, particularly when read in the context of the other cases that I have cited, to provide ample authority . . . for holding that the defendants are liable to the plaintiff in negligence, and for holding that the fact that the claim is for purely financial loss is no bar to that liability. . . .

It may be of assistance if I summarise my main conclusions:

(1) . . . [T]here is no longer any rule that a solicitor who is negligent in his professional work can be liable only to his client in contract; he may be liable both to his client and to others for the tort of negligence.

(2) The basis of the solicitor's liability to others is either an extension of the *Hedley Byrne*[1] principle or, more probably, a direct application of the principle of *Donoghue v Stevenson*[3].

(3) A solicitor who is instructed by his client to carry out a transaction that will confer a benefit on an identified third party owes a duty of care towards that third party in carrying out that transaction, in that the third party is a person within his direct contemplation as someone who is likely to be so closely and directly affected by his acts or omissions that he can reasonably foresee that the third party is likely to be injured by those acts or omissions.

(4) The mere fact that the loss to such a third party caused by the negligence is purely financial, and is in no way a physical injury to person or property, is no bar to the claim against the solicitor.

---

1. [1964] AC 465; [1963] 2 All ER 575.
2. [In *Ministry of Housing and Local Government v Sharp* [1970] 2 QB 223; [1970] 1 All ER 1009.]
3. [1932] AC 562; [1932] All ER Rep 1.
4. [1951] 2 KB 164 at 180–181; [1951] 1 All ER 426 at 434.
5. [1970] 2 QB 223; [1970] 1 All ER 1009.

(5) In such circumstances there are no considerations which suffice to negative or limit the scope of the solicitor's duty to the beneficiary.

From what I have said, it follows that the plaintiff's claim succeeds, and she is entitled to damages against the defendants for the loss of the benefits that the 1974 will would have carried to her but for the negligence of the defendants. . . .

Judgment for the plaintiff

Notes

1. The limits of the duty of care established in this case are illustrated by *Clarke v Bruce Lance & Co (a firm)* [1988] 1 All ER 364; [1988] 1 WLR 881. A solicitor was instructed to draw up a will which included a devise of a service station owned by the testator. The will was duly prepared and executed. Subsequently the solicitor acted for the testator in drawing up a variation of the lease of the service station under which the lessee was given a fixed price option to purchase the service station after the death of the testator or his wife, whichever was the later. At the testator's death the value of the service station had increased substantially. The testator's widow was still alive but the potential beneficiary brought an action for damages against the solicitor alleging that he had suffered or would suffer damage if, as seemed inevitable, the option to purchase were in due course exercised. The negligence alleged was the failure of the solicitor to advise the testator that the granting of the fixed-price option was an uncommercial and misconceived transaction, likely to harm the interests of the potential beneficiary under the will. The Court of Appeal held that there was no duty of care and struck out the claim, giving four main reasons: (a) there was no close degree of proximity between the potential devisee and the solicitors; (b) the transaction in which the option was granted did not have as its object the benefit of the potential beneficiary under the will; (c) if the solicitors were liable to the potential beneficiary, this would open up the prospect of indeterminate liability to an indeterminate class of potential beneficiaries; and (d) if the solicitors had been negligent they could be sued by the testator in his lifetime, or by his personal representatives after his death. These factors were said to distinguish the case from *Ross v Caunters.*

2. *Ross v Caunters* is sometimes distinguished from *Ministry of Housing and Local Government v Sharp* (p. 189, ante) on the ground that the disappointed legatee did not suffer a 'loss' but only the disappointment of an expected advantage, and a mere hope (*spes successionis*) at that, because the testator could have changed his will at any time before death. In *Seale v Perry* [1982] VR 193, the Supreme Court of Victoria, fearful of undermining privity of contract, did not follow *Ross v Caunters*, mainly on the grounds that the beneficiaries had lost only a 'windfall' and that they had placed no reliance on the validity of the will (see H. Luntz (1983) 3 Oxf JLS 284). The New Zealand Court of Appeal, on the other hand, has followed *Ross v Caunters*: *Gartside v Sheffield, Young and Ellis* [1983] NZLR 37.

(b) Duties in Tort and Contract

Reid v Rush & Tompkins Group plc Court of Appeal [1989] 3 All ER 228

The plaintiff, Frederick Reid, was employed by the defendants as a quarry foreman on a project in Ethiopia. In the course of his employment, while driving the defendants' Land Rover on a bush road, he was severely injured in a collision solely due to the negligence of a hit and run driver. There was no system of compulsory third party motor insurance and no scheme to cover uninsured third parties in Ethiopia (unlike England: see p. 894, post). The plaintiff brought an action in England claiming damages against the defendants alleging that (a) they were in breach of an implied term of his contract of employment to take out appropriate insurance cover or to advise him to obtain such cover, and (b) they were in breach of a duty in tort to take all reasonable steps to protect his economic welfare, arising out of a risk of personal injury whilst he was acting in the course of his employment.

This claim was struck out as disclosing no cause of action. The plaintiff appealed to the Court of Appeal. In his submissions for the plaintiff, counsel did not seek to argue separately for the existence of an implied contractual term but argued that the duty was based on an implied assumption of responsibility under the *Hedley Byrne* principle, and that this would be sufficient also to support an implied contractual term.

RALPH GIBSON LJ: . . .

The defendants' submissions
Counsel for the defendants submitted that there are rules of law which render the plaintiff's claim unarguable. Firstly, he contended that the economic loss suffered by the plaintiff is not recoverable under *Donoghue v Stevenson* [1932] AC 562, [1932] ER Rep 1 because it was not caused by any injury or apprehended injury, whether to him or his property, for which the defendants were responsible: see *D & F Estates Ltd v Church Comrs for England* [1988] 2 All ER 992 at 1003, [1989] AC 177 at 202, where the reasoning in Lord Brandon's dissenting speech in *Junior Books Ltd v Veitchi Co Ltd* [1982] 3 All ER 201, [1983] 1 AC 520, was said to contain 'principles of fundamental importance'. The economic losses claimed by the plaintiff, it was submitted, involve the assertion and creation of obligations suitable only to contract. Economic loss, divorced from actual or apprehended physical injury or damage for which the defendants are responsible, is recoverable, in the absence of contract, only when there is an assumption of responsibility, and corresponding reliance by the plaintiff, under the principles stated in *Hedley Byrne & Co Ltd v Heller & Partners Ltd* [1963] 2 All ER 575, [1964] AC 465.

Next, the plaintiff was in a contractual relationship with the defendants under the contract of employment. No term in the contract provides for the defendants to incur the obligations alleged, therefore the plaintiff is precluded from suing for economic loss in tort: See *Tai Hing Cotton Mill Ltd v Liu Chong Hing Bank Ltd* [1985] 2 All ER 947, [1986] AC 80 and *Greater Nottingham Co-op Society Ltd v Cementation Piling and Foundations Ltd* [1988] 2 All ER 971, [1989] QB 71. . . .

The ordinary duty of care of master to servant
It is first necessary to examine the plaintiff's claim, which counsel for the plaintiff has acknowledged to be a claim for pure economic loss as against the defendants, with reference to the ordinary duty of care owed by a master to his servant. The duty has for very many years always been referred to in terms of the physical safety and well-being of the servant: see *Smith v Baker & Sons* [1891] AC 325, [1891–4] All ER Rep 69 and *Wilsons & Clyde Coal Co Ltd v English* [1937] 3 All ER 628, [1938] AC 57. No case has been cited in which it has been held to extend to protect the servant from economic loss. In *Deyong v Shenburn* [1946] 1 All ER 226, [1946] KB 227, where the plaintiff's clothing was stolen from the dressing-room provided for his use at a theatre, the county court judge held that the defendant had been negligent in failing to provide

a lock on the dressing-room door, but he held also that the defendant was not under a duty to protect the plaintiff's clothing from theft. His decision was upheld by this court (Lord Greene MR, du Parcq and Tucker LJJ) on the ground that there was no relevant implied term of the contract and no duty at law to provide such a system of work as would protect his servant's clothing from theft. . . .

The position is, accordingly, that although the duty of a master to his servant may extend to warning him of unavoidable risks of physical injury, it has hitherto not been extended to the taking of reasonable care to protect the servant from economic loss. . . .

The plaintiff's claim in tort: damages for financial loss without assumption of responsibility

I turn now to the question whether the plaintiff's claim reveals any reasonable cause of action in tort. As to the claim based on Lord Wilberforce's two-stage test stated in *Anns v Merton London Borough* [1977] 2 All ER 492 at 498, [1978] AC 728 at 751-752 and the comments thereon of Lord Keith in *Governors of the Peabody Donation Fund v Sir Lindsay Parkinson & Co Ltd* [1984] 3 All ER 529 at 536, [1985] AC 210 at 240-241, it was not disputed that on the facts alleged it was reasonably foreseeable by the defendants that the plaintiff might suffer economic loss as a result of the special risk to which he was exposed in this work in Ethiopia. The questions remain whether the relationship of master and servant was, in the circumstances, arguably of such proximity as to cause any of the alleged duties to arise, and whether it could be held to be just and reasonable for the court to hold that any such duty was owed by the defendants to the plaintiff. . . .

[His Lordship then considered the submission that, without proof of voluntary assumption of risk and reliance, there could be no liability by reason of the fact that the plaintiff's claim was for economic loss not caused by any physical injury or damage for which the defendants were responsible. He concluded:] I would therefore hold in this case, as this court was prepared to accept for the purposes of the judgment in *Banque Financière de la Cité SA v Westgate Insurance Co Ltd* [1989] 2 All ER 952 at 1009, [1989] 3 WLR 25 at 103-104, that—

'in some cases (if rare) of pure economic loss the court may be willing to find the existence of a duty of care owed by a defendant to a plaintiff even in the absence of evidence of any actual voluntary assumption by the defendant of such duty and/or of any reliance on such assumption.'

That conclusion means that one of the grounds on which the defendants have asserted that the plaintiff can have no reasonable cause of action has not been made out. It does not establish that this is arguably one of those rare cases in which a duty of care can be found.

The plaintiff's case on implied term

The next submission, based on the two cases of *Tai Hing Cotton Mill Ltd v Liu Chong Hing Bank Ltd* [1985] 2 All ER 947, [1986] AC 80 and *Greater Nottingham Co-op Society Ltd v Cementation Piling and Foundations Ltd* [1988] 2 All ER 971, [1989] QB 71, was that, since there was between the parties the contract of employment, the plaintiff can only recover damages for economic loss if a term in that contract so provides and not in tort. It is necessary first to determine whether there was any implied term in the contract of employment to the effect that the defendants would give to the plaintiff all necessary advice relating to the special risk and would advise the plaintiff that he should himself obtain appropriate insurance cover. The alleged implied assumption of responsibility gave rise, it is alleged, to a similar duty.

In my judgment, it is impossible to hold on the facts pleaded that an implied term arose on the particular relationship of this plaintiff to these defendants as his employers.

[His Lordship gave reasons based on the nature of the contract between the parties.]

Voluntary assumption of responsibility

The next question is whether, in the absence of a special term implied on the facts between these parties, or of a term implied by law, the alleged specific duty to inform and advise can be held arguably to have arisen by reason of an 'assumption of responsibility' by the defendants.

[His Lordship cited Lord Devlin's speech in the *Hedley Byrne* case (p. 166 ante) and continued:] The concept of 'voluntary assumption of responsibility' as used in the *Hedley Byrne* case seems to me to refer to an act by a defendant whereby he voluntarily does something, which affects the plaintiff, and it is such an act that a reasonable man would recognise that in the circumstances he is required to perform it with due care. The defendant's knowledge, actual or implied, that the plaintiff is relying on him to act with such care is a vital, and in many circumstances indispensable, factor. Where there is a contract between the parties, and any 'voluntary assumption of responsibility' occurred, if at all, at the time of making and by reason of the contract, it seems unreal to me to try to separate a duty of care arising from the relationship created by the contract from one 'voluntarily assumed' but not specifically assumed by a term of the contract itself. There was at no time any reference by either side to the special risk or to what might be done with reference to it. For these reasons, I conclude that this plaintiff has no reasonable cause of action based on voluntary assumption of responsibility.

The general duty of the defendants as employers

It remains then to consider whether any of the duties asserted by the plaintiff could be held in the circumstances to fall within the scope of the duty owed by a master to his servant.

As to the duty to provide personal accident insurance at the expense of the defendants for the plaintiff, it is in my judgment impossible to hold that the scope of the duty in tort could extend so far. The legislation has not in general extended even the duty of compulsory employer's liability insurance in respect of employment out of this country. It has not been suggested that the master is required to provide personal accident insurance in those cases where in this country his servant is exposed to the risk of suffering injury in the course of his employment through the fault of a third party who cannot pay. The common law cannot in my judgment devise such a duty which the legislature has not thought fit to impose and it could not be just or reasonable for the court to impose it.

As to the alleged duty to inform and advise, however, the answer seems to me to be less clear. . . .

[After referring to the arguments in favour of extending the scope of the employer's duty, his Lordship mentioned earlier decisions limiting the duty to protection against physical harm or disease, and continued:] I have had much difficulty in concluding that the general duty at common law on a master to take care for the protection of his servant's physical well-being cannot be extended by decision of the courts to include protection for the financial well-being of his servant in special circumstances where the foreseeable financial loss arises from foreseeable physical injury suffered in the course of the employment and the duty claimed would extend only to a warning of a special risk. If this view be right the only way in which an employer's general duty of care, and I emphasise that I am referring only to the general duty of care which arises out of the relationship, will be capable of extension to cover financial loss will be by legislation, or by a contractual term, express or implied on the particular facts, or by a term which the court is able to say must be implied by law. At this point consideration must be given to the submission of counsel for the defendants based on *Tai Hing Cotton Mill Ltd v Liu Chong Hing Bank Ltd* [1985] 2 All ER 947, [1986] AC 80 to the effect that a duty in tort cannot be imposed to enlarge the duties assumed, whether expressly or impliedly or by rule of law, under the contract of employment. That case was concerned with the mutual responsibilities of banker and customer and might be thought to be remote from the responsibilities between master and servant. The judgment of their Lordships in the Privy Council was delivered by Lord Scarman, who said ([1985] 2 All ER 947 at 957, [1986] AC 80 at 107):

'Their Lordships do not believe that there is anything to the advantage of the law's development in searching for a liability in tort where the parties are in a contractual relationship. This is particularly so in a commercial relationship. Though it is possible as a matter of legal semantics to conduct an analysis of the rights and duties inherent in some contractual relationships including that of banker and customer either as a matter of contract law when the question will be what, if any, terms are to be implied or as a matter of tort law when the task will be to identify a duty arising from the proximity and character of the relationship between the parties, their Lordships believe it to be correct in principle and necessary for the avoidance of confusion in the law to adhere to the contractual analysis: on principle because it is a relationship in which the parties have, subject to a few exceptions, the right to determine their obligations to each other and for the avoidance of confusion because different consequences do follow according to whether liability arises from contract or tort, eg in the limitation of action.'

Lord Scarman was referring to the 'right' to determine obligations and was not dealing with the probable capacity of a party to procure changes in the contract. Their Lordships, however, clearly thought that the principle could be applicable to master and servant. Lord Scarman continued to cite a passage from the speech of Lord Radcliffe in *Lister v Romford Ice and Cold Storage Co Ltd* [1957] 1 All ER 125 at 139, [1957] AC 555 at 587, . . . in support of the proposition that new implied terms are capable of being implied by law into the contract between master and servant. Lord Scarman said:

'Their Lordships respectfully agree with some wise words of Lord Radcliffe . . . After indicating that there are cases in which a duty arising out of the relationship between employer and employee could be analysed as contractual or tortious Lord Radcliffe said: "Since, in any event, the duty in question is one which exists by imputation or implication of law and not by virtue of any express negotiation between the parties, I should be inclined to say that there is not real distinction between the two possible sources of obligation. But it is certainly, I think, as much contractual as tortious. Since, in modern times, the relationship between master and servant, between employer and employed, is inherently one of contract, it seems to me entirely correct to attribute the duties which arise from that relationship to implied contract."'

It therefore seems to me that, on the facts alleged, it is not open to this court to extend the duty of care owed by these defendants to the plaintiff by imposing a duty in tort which, if I am right, is not contained in any express or implied term of contract. . . .

[NEILL and MAY LJJ delivered judgments agreeing with RALPH GIBSON LJ that the appeal should be dismissed, but reserving their opinions as to the circumstances in which damages may be recovered in tort for pure economic loss.]

Appeal dismissed

Notes

1. The procedure followed in this case, a successful application to strike out the plaintiff's statement of claim on the grounds that it disclosed no reasonable cause of action, meant that the plaintiff was deprived of the opportunity to lead evidence of the common practice throughout British companies employing large numbers of staff overseas of arranging insurance against

accidental injury in the course of employment: see R. G. Billins (1989) 139 NLJ 1639. Had such a custom and practice been proved, it would have been incorporated as a term of the contract of employment (see *Sagar v Ridehalgh & Son Ltd* [1931] 1 Ch 310). In order to succeed in contract, in the absence of such a custom, the plaintiff had to prove either a term implied in fact or, failing this, a term implied by law in all contracts where the employer engages the employee to work abroad. The decision in *Lister v Romford Ice and Cold Storage Co Ltd* [1957] AC 555; [1957] 1 All ER 125 (p. 875, post) was a strong pointer against any such implied term. In that case the House of Lords, by a majority, refused to imply a term that employers would indemnify a lorry driver against liability to third parties if as reasonable and prudent employers they ought to have been insured. The plaintiff sought to fill the gap in contract law by relying on the tort theories of implied assumption of responsibility or proximity. The failure to do so left Mr Reid 'crippled, unemployed, with his engagement broken off, and his house lost' and no compensation (Billins, op cit). Had the accident happened in England, there would have been compulsory third party and employer's liability insurance (see p. 885, post). The underlying policy of the Employer's Liability (Compulsory Insurance) Act 1969 (p. 894, post) is that the employer is the best cost avoider of industrial accidents because he is in a better position than the employee to estimate the risks, to prevent accidents and to absorb or pass on the costs to employees and customers. Why did the Court of Appeal brush aside such policy arguments?

2. *Reid*'s case was followed by another division of the Court of Appeal in *Van Oppen v Clerk to the Bedford Charity Trustees* [1989] 3 All ER 389; [1990] 1 WLR 235, where it was held that a school was under no duty of care in tort to take out personal accident insurance for pupils playing rugby or to advise parents to do so. The result was that Simon van Oppen was left uncompensated for severe spinal injuries sustained during an inter-house school rugby match. (The trial judge, [1989] 1 All ER 273, had found that the injuries were the result of an accident rather than negligence on anyone's part, and there was no appeal against this finding.) The Court of Appeal was unwilling to find any assumption of responsibility in relation to insurance, or reasonable reliance on it, in the particular circumstances of the case. The court also held that there was no general duty to have regard to the economic welfare of pupils arising from the relationship of school and pupil.

3. Lord Scarman's statement in *Tai Hing Cotton Mill Ltd v Liu Chong Hing Bank Ltd* [1986] AC 80 at 107 (quoted p. 199 ante) to the effect that tort duties should not be superimposed on a contractual relationship, was made in the context of a banker–customer relationship, without any review of the earlier cases which have permitted concurrent liability in contract and tort for professional negligence. The dictum has been relied upon in a number of subsequent cases involving commercial relationships. For example, in *National Bank of Greece SA v Pinlos Shipping Co No 1, The Maira* [1990] 1 AC 637; [1989] 1 All ER 213 (revsd on other grounds [1990] 1 AC 637; [1990] 1 All ER 78) the Court of Appeal held that there was no duty of care on a bank, which had entered into a tripartite management agreement with owners of a vessel mortgaged to the bank and a management agent, to see that the management agent did not under-insure the vessel. Having held that there was no

contractual duty of care, the Court of Appeal decided that 'if the plaintiff fails in contract he must necessarily fail in tort' (Lloyd LJ at p. 223; see too, Nicholls LJ at p. 232). Lloyd LJ pointed out that the position would be different if the contract and tort lay in different fields: 'If, to take a simple example, I give my employee a lift home and injure him by my careless driving, then obviously he will not be prevented from recovering from me in tort because of the existence between us of a contract of employment' (at pp. 223–224). This refusal to fill contractual gaps by duties in tort was approved and followed in *Bank of Nova Scotia v Hellenic Mutual War Risks Association (Bermuda) Ltd* [1990] 1 QB 818 at 900–914; see A. McGee (1990) 6 PN 28; see too the *Banque Keyser Ullman* case [1990] 1 QB 665 at 799–802, noted p. 174, ante. (Both of these cases subsequently went to the House of Lords.)

4. These recent cases which hold that tort has no role to play where the relationship between the parties is governed by a contract between them rest, ultimately, on the view that 'it would be unfair to impose on the promisor any harsher consequences of tort liability. In the opposing view, the plaintiff should be free to choose from among concurrent causes of action, for why should he forfeit his tort rights merely by entering into a formal contract unless he actually agreed to limit or exclude them?' (*Fleming*, p. 169). At one time it was thought that concurrent liability was restricted to certain common callings such as innkeepers and carriers. Later there was a tendency to find concurrent liability in tort only for misfeasance (doing something badly) which made the plaintiff's position worse, for example the longstanding recognition of concurrent liability for negligent medical care. Economic losses (caused e.g. by stockbrokers, architects and solicitors), particularly if arising from failure to confer a benefit, were generally recoverable only in contract. This rested upon the doctrine that a person who promises or undertakes to confer a benefit on another will not normally be liable for failing to confer it if the promisee gave no consideration for the promise. Moreover, a third party for whom the benefit was intended but who did not give consideration cannot sue for the enforcement of the promise. As *Dias and Markesinis*, p. 12 point out, sometimes contract law was expanded to give damages for economic loss where 'it was by no means certain that the doctrine of consideration was satisfied' (e.g. *De la Bere v Pearson* [1908] 1 KB 280 and see p. 166, ante). More recently, tort law has expanded 'provoked by a rigid law of contract' (*Dias and Markesinis*, p. 13). This was stimulated by the rediscovery of voluntary assumption of responsibility as a source of obligation in the *Hedley Byrne* case (p. 161, ante). Once it was established that a professional person who gratuitously assumed responsibility could be liable in tort to a client who relied on his undertaking, it seemed absurd to deny such liability to the client who *paid* for the service. The result was to enable the plaintiff to use a more favourable tort rule, unless a specific provision of the contract excluded this. So in *Midland Bank Trust Co Ltd v Hett, Stubbs and Kemp (a firm)* [1979] Ch 384; [1978] 3 All ER 571, a solicitor carelessly failed to register as an estate contract an option which had been given to the plaintiff, their client, to purchase a farm. The owner of the farm conveyed it to his wife, so the plaintiff lost the chance of exercising the option. Oliver J held that the plaintiff's executors (he having died) could sue the solicitor for damages concurrently in tort and contract. The result was that the more favourable tort limitation rule could be applied. (See Note 5, post.) Consider the view of Lloyd LJ in *Lee v Thompson* [1989]

2 EGLR 151 at 153, but see *Bell v Peter Browne & Co* [1990] 3 All ER 124; [1990] 3 WLR 510 although note the comments on the *Midland Bank* case.

The significance of the *Midland Bank* decision is that the solicitor was made liable in tort not for making the plaintiff's position worse than it would have been if he had not engaged the solicitor, but rather for failing to confer the benefit on the plaintiff of having his option registered. Moreover, Oliver J ([1979] Ch at 416) said that 'once the duty is established it cannot, in my judgment, matter whether the breach takes the form of malfeasance or non-feasance'. So, too, in *McPherson v Prunty* [1983] VR 573, the Supreme Court of Victoria held a solicitor liable in tort and contract for mere inactivity for failing to commence an 'unassailable' action for damages on behalf of a client. This does not mean, however, that there is a general positive duty to act in tort (p. 65, ante), but these and other decisions show that a professional person who undertakes to perform a service can be liable in tort if the quality of the service provided is below that expected of a reasonably skilled person, even if the damages claimed are not simply for making the plaintiff's position worse but are for the failure to confer a benefit. See generally A. J. E. Jaffey (1985) 5 LS 77 at 79–87.

The same reasoning was applied in *Batty v Metropolitan Property Realisations Ltd* [1978] QB 554; [1978] 2 All ER 445, where land developers as vendors of a house were held liable to the purchasers not only in contract for breach of an express warranty that the dwelling had been built in a workmanlike manner of proper materials so as to be fit for habitation, but also in tort for (at least) dangerous defects in quality rendering the house worthless. This aspect of the decision in *Batty* was not considered by the House of Lords in *D & F Estates Ltd v Church Comrs for England* [1989] AC 177; [1988] 2 All ER 992, although the result against the builder in *Batty* (with whom there was no direct contractual relationship) was questioned; see p. 477, post. In *Ketteman v Hansel Properties Ltd* [1987] AC 189; [1988] 1 All ER 38 (decided before the *D & F Estates* case) the House of Lords assumed that an architect could be liable in tort for economic loss suffered by his client. The implications of the speeches in the *D & F Estates* case and *Murphy v Brentwood District Council* [1990] 2 All ER 908; [1990] 3 WLR 414 (p. 212, post) for these professional relationships remain to be worked out. *Clerk & Lindsell*, para. 11–03 state that 'the fundamental principle on which the judgment in *D & F Estates Ltd* rests is that a person involved in the construction of a chattel or a building does not warrant the *quality* of the work done save by virtue of his contract with his customer.' Does it follow that an architect or surveyor can be liable to his client for negligence only in contract?

5. The post-*Hedley Byrne* cases which recognise concurrent liability in tort and contract for failure of a professional person to confer an economic benefit on his client, are difficult to reconcile with the more recent trend in employment cases like *Reid v Rush & Tompkins* (ante) and those involving commercial relationships. One ground of distinction may be that in the commercial cases, the terms under which services are provided are detailed in a contract with the client and so a contract-only rule may seem more appropriate (cf. *Clerk & Lindsell*, para. 11–05). But this results in the

anomaly that a third person may be in a more favourable position than the client because he can rely on tort. One area where the distinction between tort and contract is crucial relates to the time limit for bringing an action. In personal injury cases there is a three-year limitation period, and time begins to run either from when the cause of action accrues or from the date of the plaintiff's knowledge (Limitation Act 1980, ss. 2, 5 and 11(1)). A cause of action accrues from the moment of breach in the case of contract, but only from the time when the damage is suffered in tort. In actions for latent damage (other than personal injury) in the tort of negligence the period is six years either from when the cause of action accrues or (subject to a long-stop of 15 years) three years from the date of the plaintiff's knowledge whichever is longer (Limitation Act 1980, s. 14A inserted by Latent Damage Act 1986, s. 1, p. 484, post). If an architect's client is limited to a contractual claim when a negligently designed chimney collapses, he will find that his claim is statute-barred six years from the time of breach, while his neighbour on whose property the chimney fell retains a claim in tort for a longer period.

6. Another way in which attempts have been made to use the law of tort to avoid the doctrines of contract law, has been by rendering a promise made by A to B enforceable in tort by C. These are cases in which C complains that he has failed to receive a benefit or has been provided with a product or premises or services of poor quality arising from something done or made by A under a contract with B. One such case was *Ross v Caunters* [1980] Ch 297; [1979] 3 All ER 580 (p. 192 ante). Strong encouragement for such claims by third parties was given by a majority of the House of Lords in *Junior Books Ltd v Veitchi Co Ltd* [1983] 1 AC 520; [1982] 3 All ER 201, noted p. 226, post. But that decision was progressively eroded in all the subsequent cases, with a return in general to the principle that foreseeable economic loss is recoverable in tort by a third party only if it arises immediately out of physical damage to property of the third party. This principle is elaborated in the cases and notes which follow.

(c) Duties to third parties

Leigh and Sillivan Ltd *v* Aliakmon Shipping Co Ltd, The Aliakmon House of Lords [1986] 2 All ER 145

LORD BRANDON OF OAKBROOK: My Lords, this appeal arises in an action in the Commercial Court in which the appellants, who were the c & f buyers of goods carried in the respondents' ship, the Aliakmon, claim damages against the latter for damage done to such goods at a time when the risk, but not yet the legal property in them, had passed to the appellants. The main question to be determined is whether, in the circumstances just stated, the respondents (the shipowners) owed a duty of care in tort to the appellants (the buyers) in respect of the carriage of such goods; and, if so, whether and to what extent such duty was qualified by the terms of the bill of lading under which the goods were carried.

The buyers' claim was put forward originally in both contract and tort. Staughton J at first instance gave judgment for the buyers on their claim in contract, so making it unnecessary for him to reach a decision on their further claim in tort (see [1983] 1 Lloyd's Rep 203). However, on appeal by the shipowners to the Court of Appeal (Sir John Donaldson MR, Oliver and Robert Goff LJJ), that court set aside the judgment of Staughton J and dismissed the buyers' claims in both contract and tort (see [1985] 2 All ER 44, [1985] QB 350). Sir John Donaldson MR and Oliver LJ rejected the claim in tort on the ground that the shipowners did not at the material time owe any duty of care to the buyers. Robert Goff LJ rejected the claim in tort on the ground that, although the shipowners owed a duty of care to the buyers, they had not, on the facts, committed any breach of that duty.

My Lords, the facts relating to what I have called the main question to be determined are unusual and need to be set out with some particularity. By a contract of sale made in July 1976 the buyers agreed to buy from Kinsho-Mataichi Corp (the sellers) a quantity of steel coils (the goods) to be shipped from Korea to Immingham on c & f terms, free out Immingham. The price of the goods was to be paid by a 180-day bill of exchange to be indorsed by the buyers' bank in return for a bill of lading relating to the goods. The buyers, who were traders in steel rather than users of it, intended to finance the transaction by making a contract for the resale of the goods to sub-buyers before the bill of lading was tendered by the sellers.

The goods were loaded on board the Aliakmon (the ship) at Inchon in South Korea and a bill of lading dated 14 September 1976 was issued in respect of them. The bill of lading showed the carrying ship as the Aliakmon, the shippers as Illsen Steel Co Ltd, the port of shipment as Inchon, the port of discharge as Immingham and the consignees as the buyers. It is to be inferred that Illsen Steel Co Ltd, in shipping the goods, were acting as agents for the sellers. The bill of lading further expressly incorporated the Hague Rules.

The buyers later found themselves unable to make the contract for the resale of the goods which they had intended to make with the result that their bank declined to back the bill of exchange by which payment for the goods was to be made. In this situation representatives of the buyers and the sellers met on 7 October 1976 in an effort to find a solution to the problem. Following that meeting the sellers sent the bill of lading to the buyers under cover of a letter dated 11 October 1976, and receipt of these was acknowledged by the buyers by a letter dated 18 October 1976. The Court of Appeal has held, and the buyers now accept, that the effect of the letters so exchanged was to vary the original contract of sale in the following respects. First, the sellers, despite delivery of the bill of lading to the buyers, were to reserve the right of disposal of the goods represented by it. Second, while the buyers were to present the bill of lading to the ship at Immingham and take delivery of the goods there, they were to do so, not as principals on their own account, but solely as agents for the sellers. Third, after the goods had been discharged, they were to be stored in a covered warehouse to the sole order of the sellers.

On arrival of the ship at Immingham the buyers duly carried out the terms of the contract of sale as varied in the manner described above. On discharge of the goods they proved to be in a damaged condition. Staughton J found, and his finding has not been challenged, that a substantial part of this damage, but not all, has been caused by improper stowage of the goods in two respects: first, the stowage of steel and timber in the same compartment, resulting in condensation from the timber causing rusting of the steel; and, second, overstowage of the goods in such a way as to cause crushing of them. He further assessed the amount of damage at £83,006.07, a figure which is likewise not in dispute.

The buyers subsequently paid the price of the goods to the sellers, after certain claims for alleged defects in them had been settled. The result of this was that the legal ownership of the goods, which had until then remained in the sellers by reason of their reservation of the right of disposal of them, finally passed to the buyers.

My Lords, under the usual kind of cif or c & f contract of sale, the risk in the goods passes from the seller to the buyer on shipment, as is exemplified by the obligation of the buyer to take up and pay for the shipping documents even though the goods may already have suffered damage or loss during their carriage by sea. The property in the goods, however, does not pass until the buyer takes up and pays for the shipping documents. Those include a bill of lading relating to the goods which has been indorsed by the seller in favour of the buyer. By acquiring the bill of lading so indorsed the buyer becomes a person to whom the property in the goods has passed on or by reason of such indorsement, and so, by virtue of s 1 of the Bills of Lading Act 1855, has vested in him all the rights of suit, and is subject to the same liabilities in respect of the goods, as if the contract contained in the bill of lading had been made with him.

In terms of the present case this means that, if the buyers had completed the c & f contract in the manner intended, they would have been entitled to sue the shipowners for the damage to the goods in contract under the bill of lading, and no question of any separate duty of care in tort would have arisen. In the events which occurred, however, what had originally been a usual kind of c & f contract of sale had been varied so as to become, in effect, a contract of sale ex warehouse at Immingham. The contract as so varied was, however, unusual in an important respect. Under an ordinary contract of sale ex warehouse both the risk and the property in the goods would pass from the seller to the buyer at the same time, that time being determined by the intention of the parties. Under this varied contract, however, the risk had already passed to the buyers on shipment because of the original c & f terms, and there was nothing in the new terms which caused it to revert to the sellers. The buyers, however, did not acquire any rights of suit under the bill of lading by virtue of s 1 of the Bills of Lading Act 1855. This was because, owing to the sellers' reservation of the right of disposal of the goods, the property in the goods did not pass to the buyers on or by reason of the indorsement of the bill of lading, but only on payment of the purchase price by the buyers to the sellers after the goods had been discharged and warehoused at Immingham. Hence the attempt of the buyers to establish a separate claim against the shipowners founded in the tort of negligence.

My Lords, there is a long line of authority for a principle of law that, in order to enable a person to claim in negligence for loss caused to him by reason of loss of or damage to property, he must have had either the legal ownership of or a possessory title to the property concerned at the time when the loss or damage occurred, and it is not enough for him to have only had contractual rights in relation to such property which have been adversely affected by the loss of or damage to it. The line of authority to which I have referred includes the following cases: *Cattle v Stockton Waterworks Co* (1875) LR 10 QB 453, [1874–80] All ER Rep 220 (contractor doing work on another's land unable to recover from a waterworks company loss suffered by him by reason of the company's want of care in causing or permitting water to leak from a water pipe laid and owned by it on the land concerned); *Simpson & Co v Thomson* (1877) 3 App Cas 279 (insurers of two ships A and B, both owned by C, unable to recover from C loss caused to them by want of care in the navigation of ship A in consequence of which she collided with and damaged ship B); *SA de Remorquage à Hélice v Bennetts* [1911] 1 KB 243 (tug owners engaged to tow ship A unable to recover from owners of ship B loss of towage remuneration caused to them by want of care in the navigation of ship B in consequence of which she collided with and sank ship A); *Chargeurs Rèunis Cie Française de Navigation à Vapeur v English and American Steamship Co, The Ceylan, The Merida* (1921) 9 Ll LR 464 (time charterer of ship A unable to recover from owners of ship B loss caused to them by want of care in the navigation of ship B in consequence of which she collided with and damaged ship A); *Konstantinidis v World Tanker Corp Inc, The World Harmony* [1965] 2 All ER 139, [1967] P 341 (same as preceding case). The principle of law referred to is further supported by the observations of Scrutton LJ in *Elliott Steam Tug Co Ltd v Shipping Controller* [1922] 1 KB 127 at 139–140.

None of these cases concerns a claim by cif or c & f buyers of goods to recover from the owners of the ship in which the goods are carried loss suffered by reason of want of care in the carriage of the goods resulting in their being lost or damaged at a time when the risk in the goods, but not yet the legal property in them, has passed to such buyers. The question whether such a claim would lie, however, came up for decision in *Margarine Union GmbH v Cambay Prince Steamship Co Ltd, The Wear Breeze*

[1967] 3 All ER 775, [1969] 1 QB 219. In that case cif buyers had accepted four delivery orders in respect of as yet undivided portions of a cargo of copra in bulk shipped under two bills of lading. It was common ground that, by doing so, they did not acquire either the legal property in, or a possessory title to, the portions of copra concerned; they only acquired the legal property later when four portions each of 500 tons were separated from the bulk on or shortly after discharge in Hamburg. The copra having been damaged by want of care by the shipowners' servants or agents in not properly fumigating the holds of the carrying ship before loading, the question arose whether the buyers were entitled to recover from the shipowners in tort for negligence the loss which they had suffered by reason of the copra having been so damaged. Roskill J held that they were not, founding his decision largely on the principle of law established by the line of authority to which I have referred. . . .

My Lords, counsel for the buyers did not question any of the cases in the long line of authority to which I have referred except *The Wear Breeze*. . . . He contended, however, that *The Wear Breeze* was either wrongly decided at the time, or at any rate should be regarded as wrongly decided today, and should accordingly be over-ruled. . . .

[His Lordship then considered each of the five grounds on which counsel for the buyers relied. First he held that the fact that a buyer under a cif or c & f contract was the prospective legal owner of the goods was not a material distinction from the other non-recovery cases in which the plaintiffs were not persons who had contracted to buy the property. Secondly, he held that even if an equitable property in the goods could be created or passed under the contract of sale (of which he was 'extremely doubtful'), an equitable owner not in possession has no right to sue without joining the legal owner as a party to the action. Thirdly, he decided that there was nothing in what Lord Wilberforce said in *Anns v Merton London Borough Council* [1978] AC 728 at 751–752, set out at p. 51, ante, about the role of policy in negativing a prima facie duty of care, which would compel a departure from the line of authorities against recovery, and went on to say:] Counsel for the buyers said, rightly in my view, that the policy reason for excluding a duty of care in cases like [*Candlewood Navigation Corpn Ltd v Mitsui OSK Lines Ltd*], *The Mineral Transporter* [1986] AC 1; [1985] 2 All ER 935 and what I earlier called the other non-recovery cases was to avoid the opening of the floodgates so as to expose a person guilty of want of care to unlimited liability to an indefinite number of other persons whose contractual rights have been adversely affected by such want of care. Counsel for the buyers went on to argue that recognition by the law of a duty of care owed by shipowners to a cif or c & f buyer, to whom the risk, but not yet the property in the goods carried in such shipowners' ship has passed, would not of itself open any floodgates of the kind described. It would, he said, only create a strictly limited exception to the general rule, based on the circumstance that the considerations of policy on which that general rule was founded did not apply to that particular case. I do not accept that argument. If an exception to the general rule were to be made in the field of carriage by sea, it would no doubt have to be extended to the field of carriage by land, and I do not think that it is possible to say that no undue increase in the scope of a person's liability for want of care would follow. In any event, where a general rule, which is simple to understand and easy to apply, has been established by a long line of authority over many years, I do not think that the law should allow special pleading in a particular case within the general rule to detract from its application. If such detraction were to be permitted in one particular case, it would lead to attempts to have it permitted in a variety of other particular cases, and the result would be that the certainty, which the application of the general rule presently provides, would be seriously undermined. Yet certainty of the law is of the utmost importance, especially but by no means only, in commercial matters. I therefore think that the general rule, reaffirmed as it has been so recently by the Privy Council in *The Mineral Transporter*, ought to apply to a case like the present one, and that there is nothing in what Lord Wilberforce said in the *Anns* case which would compel a different conclusion.

. . . [C]ounsel for the buyers submitted that your Lordships should hold that a duty of care did exist in the present case, but that it was subject to the terms of the bill of lading. With regard to this suggestion Sir John Donaldson MR said in the present case ([1985] 2 All ER 44 at 54, [1985] QB 350 at 368):

'I have, of course, considered whether any duty of care in tort to the buyer could in some way be equated to the contractual duty of care owed to the shipper, but I do not see how this could be done. The commonest form of carriage by sea is one on the terms of the Hague Rules. But this is an intricate blend of responsibilities and liabilities (art III), rights and immunities (art IV), limitations in the amount of damages recoverable (art IV, r 5), time bars (art III, r 6), evidential provisions (art III, rr 4 and 6), indemnities (art III, r 5 and art IV, r 6) and liberties (art IV, rr 4 and 6). I am quite unable to see how these can be synthesised into a standard of care.'

I find myself suffering from the same inability to understand how the necessary synthesis could be made as the Master of the Rolls. . . .

Ground 4: the requirements of a rational system of law
My Lords, under this head counsel for the buyers submitted that any rational system of law ought to provide a remedy for persons who suffered the kind of loss which the buyers suffered in the present case, with the clear implication that, if your Lordships' House were to hold that the remedy for which he contended was not available, it would be lending its authority to an irrational feature of English law. I do not agree with this submission for, as I shall endeavour to show, English law does, in all normal cases, provide a fair and adequate remedy for loss of or damage to goods the subject matter of a cif or c & f contract, and the buyers in this case could easily, if properly advised at the time when they agreed to the variation of the original c & f contract, have secured to themselves the benefit of such a remedy.

As I indicated earlier, under the usual cif or c & f contract the bill of lading issued in respect of the goods is indorsed and delivered by the seller to the buyer against payment by the buyer of the price. When that happens, the property in the goods passes from the sellers to the buyers on or by reason of such indorsement, and the buyer is entitled, by virtue of s 1 of the Bills of Lading Act 1855, to sue the shipowner for loss of or damage to the goods on the contract contained in the bill of lading. The remedy so available to the buyer is adequate and fair to both parties, and there is no need for any parallel or alternative remedy in tort for negligence. In the present case, as I also indicated earlier, the variation of the original c & f contract agreed between the sellers and the buyers produced a hybrid contract of an extremely unusual character. It was extremely unusual in that what had originally been an ordinary c & f contract became, in effect, a sale ex warehouse at Immingham, but the risk in the goods during their carriage by sea remained with the buyers as if the sale had still been on a c & f basis. In this situation the persons who had a right to sue the shipowners for loss of or damage to the goods on the contract contained in the bill of lading were the sellers, and the buyers, if properly advised, should have made it a further term of the variation that the sellers should either exercise this right for their account (see *The Albazero* [1976] 3 All ER 129, [1977] AC 774) or assign such right to them to exercise for themselves. If either of these two precautions had been taken, the law would have provided the buyers with a fair and adequate remedy for their loss.

These considerations show, in my opinion, not that there is some lacuna in English law relating to these matters, but only that the buyers, when they agreed to the variation of the original contract of sale, did not take the steps to protect themselves which, if properly advised, they should have done. To put the matter quite simply the buyers, by the variation to which they agreed, were depriving themselves of the right of suit under s 1 of the Bills of Lading Act 1855 which they would otherwise have had, and commercial good sense required that they should obtain the benefit of an equivalent right in one or other of the two different ways which I have suggested.

Ground 5: the judgment of Robert Goff LJ
My Lords, after a full examination of numerous authorities relating to the law of negligence Goff LJ said[1] ([1985] 2 All ER 44 at 77, [1985] QB 350 at 399):

'In my judgment, there is no good reason in principle or in policy, why the c & f buyer should not have . . . a direct cause of action. The factors which I have already listed point strongly towards liability. I am particularly influenced by the fact that the loss in question is of a character which will ordinarily fall on the goods' owner, who will have a good claim against the shipowner, but in a case such as the present the loss may, in practical terms, fall on the buyer. It seems to me that the policy reasons pointing towards a direct right of action by the buyer against the shipowner in a case of this kind outweigh the policy reasons which generally preclude recovery for purely economic loss. There is here no question of any wide or indeterminate liability being imposed on wrongdoers; on the contrary, the shipowner is simply held liable to the buyer in damages for loss for which he would ordinarily be liable to the goods' owner. There is a recognised principle underlying the imposition of liability, which can be called "the principle of transferred loss". Furthermore, that principle can be formulated. For the purposes of the present case, I would formulate it in the following deliberately narrow terms, while recognising that it may require modification in the light of experience. Where A owes a duty of care in tort not to cause physical damage to B's property, and commits a breach of that duty in circumstances in which the loss of or physical damage to the property will ordinarily fall on B but (as is reasonably foreseeable by A) such loss or damage, by reason of a contractual relationship between B and C, falls on C, then C will be entitled, subject to the terms of any contract restricting A's liability to B, to bring an action in tort against A in respect of such loss or damage to the extent that it falls on him, C. To that proposition there must be exceptions. In particular, there must, for the reasons I have given, be an exception in the case of contracts of insurance. I have also attempted so to draw the principle as to exclude the case of the time charterer who remains liable for hire for the chartered ship while under repair following collision damage, though this could if necessary be treated as another exception having regard to the present state of the authorities.'

With the greatest possible respect to Robert Goff LJ, the principle of transferred loss which he there enunciated, however useful in dealing with special factual situations it may be in theory, is not only not supported by authority, but is on the contrary inconsistent with it. Even if it were necessary to introduce such a principle in order to fill a genuine lacuna in the law, I should myself, perhaps because I am more faint hearted than Robert Goff LJ, be reluctant to do so. As I have tried to show earlier, however, there is in truth no such lacuna in the law which requires to be filled. Neither Sir John Donaldson MR nor Oliver LJ was prepared to accept the introduction of such a principle and I find myself entirely in agreement with their unwillingness to do so.

My Lords, I have now examined and rejected all the five grounds on which counsel for the buyers relied in support of his contention that *The Wear Breeze* [1967] 3 All ER 775, [1969] 1 QB 219 was either wrongly decided at the time, or at any rate should be regarded as wrongly decided today, and should accordingly be overruled. The conclusion which I have reached is that *The Wear Breeze* was good law at the time when it was decided and remains good law today. . . .

[LORD KEITH OF KINKEL, LORD BRIGHTMAN, LORD GRIFFITHS and LORD ACKNER all agreed that the appeal should be dismissed for the reasons given by LORD BRANDON OF OAKBROOK.]

Appeal dismissed

---

1. [In the Court of Appeal in this case.]

An Expanding Tort Law – the Price of a Rigid Contract Law
B. S. Markesinis (1987) 103 LQR 354 at 386 and 389–390

. . . Lord Brandon failed to consider adequately the full implications of his negative ruling. But was this ruling fair at least in the specific factual situation of *The Aliakmon*? Lord Brandon obviously considered that it was, since he clearly thought that the particular buyer's misfortune was the result of his own failure to stipulate that the seller exercise his contractual rights against the carrier or for failing to have the seller transfer such rights to him by means of assignment. With great respect, even this solution, in addition to being commercially inconvenient, does not always adequately protect the buyer. For a buyer who follows Lord Brandon's advice will only obtain such rights as the seller himself had under the contract of carriage. This means that he (like the seller who is the original shipper) would not be able to claim that the goods (or part of them) were already damaged at the time of shipment where a clean bill of lading had been issued. (This was, in fact, the case in *The Aliakmon*). If, on the other hand, the buyer is allowed to sue in contract under the Bills of Lading Act 1855 he would then have the benefit of any estoppels arising from the false statements in the bill of lading. The question, therefore, is not whether the plaintiffs in all these cases should be allowed to recover from the tortfeasor. Rather the real issue is to make sure that their defendants are not placed in a worse position than they would have been in had they been sued by their co-contractors. Finding the proper doctrinal explanation seems infinitely more important than trying to re-establish the shaken authority of the non-liability rule. As the Supreme Court of New Jersey put it in its most recent decision [*People Express Airlines v Consolidated Rail* 100 NJ 246, 495 A 2d 107 at [p. 111] (1985)]: 'In the end, the challenge is to fashion a rule that limits liability but permits adjudication of meritorious claims.'. . .

The Aliakmon judgment, however, is just as remarkable for what it failed to do as for the way in which it tried to achieve its aims. The main omission lies in its failure to consider adequately the imaginative judgment delivered by Robert Goff LJ in the Court of Appeal. But the Court, in its own words, was too 'faint-hearted' to attempt the task of elaboration. It thus took the view that it was impossible to shape a duty of care in tort that would reflect the contractual duties owed by the carrier to the shipper.

The task was seen as near impossible given the intricate blend of rights, immunities and responsibilities contained in the Hague Rules. The German theory of *Drittschadensliquidation* ['transferred loss'] would provide an answer here, and . . . its similarity with the reasoning of the judgment of Robert Goff LJ must be obvious. The third party who had suffered the loss is given the *contractual* action of the creditor against the debtor. The difficulties that Sir John Donaldson MR and Lord Brandon experienced in this respect have, apparently, been resolved by Scandinavian and Dutch lawyers, and they would also vanish into thin air if one were prepared to adopt the German reasoning. But traditional English lawyers would object, however, that such a contractually flavoured action, even though it does not amount to a fully-fledged contract in favour of third parties, remains impossible while English law adheres to its own notion of privity of contract. The main contribution of Robert Goff LJ in *The Aliakmon* was his attempt at the end of his judgment to circumvent this difficulty by showing how the *permissibie tort action could be fashioned by the underlying contractual relationship*. In this he identified the real problem in *The Aliakmon*. For surely what matters is that the carrier's liability in tort is no greater than his liability in contract under the Hague/Visby Rules rather than whether he can be sued by the buyer. Why could not the standard and ambit of the tort duty be determined by the contract? Why could not the exclusion clauses in the Rules apply in the tort action? In fact Article IV bis of the Hague/Visby Rules expressly states that the carrier's defences shall apply 'whether the action be found in contract or in tort'. The wording and the history of this Rule could be taken to envisage tort actions, *whether or not the claimant had a contract with the defendant/carrier*. Courts have limited a tort action in terms of a contract between the *same* parties. Why should this not be also possible when the terms are found in a contract between different parties but are clearly known to all the world?

Notes

1. The principle that a person who has not got a possessory or proprietary interest in a chattel is not entitled to be compensated for economic loss by a party who negligently damaged the chattel is well established, and was reasserted by the Privy Council in *Candlewood Navigation Corpn Ltd v Mitsui OSK Lines Ltd, The Mineral Transporter* [1986] AC 1; [1985] 2 All ER 935, noted p. 236, post. It provides a clear rule, preventing 'indeterminate liability to an indeterminate class' of plaintiffs in the context of involuntary relationships (see 'relational interests', p. 230, post). The question is whether this simple principle is equally appropriate where the tripartite relationships are regulated by contracts, as in *The Aliakmon* where there was a contract between B (the sellers) and C (the buyers), and a contract between B (the sellers) and A (the shippers), but no contract between A and C.

2. Since *The Aliakmon*, it seems that Parliament may inadvertently have given the consignee of goods a non-contractual cause of action against a carrier in respect of damage negligently caused to the goods by the carrier and occurring before the consignee obtains ownership. This appears to be the result of s. 3 of the Latent Damage Act 1986, which in effect allows a person who had no proprietary interest at the time that damage (other than personal injury) was suffered to sue provided that the material facts were not known to the previous owner: see p. 486, post; and E. Griew (1986) 136 NLJ 1201.

3. The reluctance of the courts to superimpose duties in tort upon carefully structured tripartite relationships may also be seen in recent cases in construction law. In *Pacific Associates Inc v Baxter* [1990] 1 QB 993; [1989] 2 All ER 159 a contractor successfully tendered for dredging and reclamation work for the employer, the Ruler of Dubai. The contractor knew that the work would be supervised by a consultant engineer retained by the employer and that the contractor would only be paid sums on account when they were certified by the engineer. There was no direct contractual relationship between the contractor and the engineer. The contract with the employer provided that the contractor was entitled to additional payment if it encountered hard material in the course of dredging which could not reasonably have been foreseen. The contractor's repeated claims for such payments were rejected by the engineer on the ground that the hard materials should have been foreseen. The contractor brought an action for £45 m damages against the engineer alleging negligence or breach of a duty to act fairly and impartially in administering the contract by failing to certify and rejecting the claims for payment for hard materials. The duty was said to arise either from a voluntary assumption of responsibility under *Hedley Byrne* principles or from the close and direct proximity between the contractor and engineer. Both these arguments were rejected by the Court of Appeal which held that the engineer did not owe a duty in tort to act with due care to avoid economic loss to the contractor under the contract with the employer. As regards the

alleged assumption of responsibility, there was no request to the engineer by or on behalf of the contractor for the engineer to render any service to the contractor. The relationship between the engineer and contractor was the result of a contract between the contractor and the employer, and of the engineer having agreed with the employer to perform the functions of engineer under the contract. The engineer was not employed to exercise due care in the interest of the contractor, and so could not be regarded as having assumed responsibility to do so. This kind of tripartite relationship was seen as different from the direct assumption in *Hedley Byrne*. Various reasons were given for rejecting the second basis of argument. Either economic loss to the contractor was not reasonably contemplated, in part because the contract provided for the correction of mistakes by the engineer by process of arbitration (Ralph Gibson LJ at p. 1031, but Russell LJ at p. 1036 had reservations); or there was insufficient proximity (Ralph Gibson LJ at p. 1031; but Russell LJ considered that the proximity test was satisfied; and Purchas LJ thought there was a degree of proximity in the sense that the engineer relied on the contractor, but regarded this as not the same quality of proximity as required to establish a duty of care in the *Hedley Byrne* sense); or it was not 'just and reasonable' to impose a duty given that the parties had chosen to structure their relationships so that there was no contract between contractor and engineer (Russell LJ at pp. 1035–1039 regarded this as the 'heart of the matter'; see, to like effect, Ralph Gibson LJ at pp. 1031–1032; Purchas LJ at pp. 1009–1010). See too *Greater Nottingham Co-operative Society Ltd v Cementation Piling and Foundations Ltd* [1989] QB 71; [1988] 2 All ER 971.

4. *The Aliakmon* was a case in which loss that would have been suffered by B (the sellers), as a result of A's breach of duty of care, was in fact suffered by C (the buyers), because of an intervening transfer of risk, i.e. the goods were damaged at a time when title was still with B but the risk had passed to C. The House of Lords denied C a tort-based claim on the grounds that precedent barred recovery by a non-owner of chattels. This rule was seen as a well-established control mechanism for avoiding crushing liability. Lord Brandon (p. 207, ante) was particularly concerned that allowing a claim in tort would deprive A of the contractual limitations set out in the Hague/Visby rules. Markesinis (ante) criticises both the consequences of the decision, and the use of a single rigid rule which bars recovery by a non-owner of chattels. He supports Robert Goff LJ's suggested principle of 'transferred loss', which was rejected by the House of Lords, by reference to the analogous contractual solution in German law, and the tort action under the Dutch Commercial Code. For further details of the German theory, see B. S. Markesinis, *A Comparative Introduction to the German Law of Torts* 2nd edn (Oxford, 1990), pp. 73–74 and 233–234; and see too W. Lorenz in *Essays in Memory of Professor F. H. Lawson*, edited by P. Wallington and R. M. Merkin (London, 1986), chap. 8. What would the effect be of Robert Goff LJ's suggested principle on the doctrine of privity of contract? (Here consider the difference between a third party beneficiary who has no right to sue the promisor for performance of a primary contractual obligation, and a third party who suffers loss as a result of a breach of one of the secondary contractual obligations: see Markesinis, op cit, p. 358; and cf. *Ross v Caunters* [1980] Ch 297; [1979] 3 All ER 580, p. 192, ante.)

5. Robert Goff LJ remarked in *The Aliakmon* in the Court of Appeal [1985] 2 All ER 44 at 73 that 'the philosophy of the market place presumes that it is lawful to gain profit by causing others economic loss'. The economic justification for this is greater efficiency and consumer welfare. Can a single rigid rule which bars recovery by non-owners achieve the economic objectives of (a) deterrence, i.e. making potential defendants (in this case the shipowners) act more carefully and thereby reduce the cost of accidents to consumers; (b) optimal risk allocation, i.e. imposing liability on the party best able to avoid or minimise the loss and to insure against the risk, in return for a premium on the price; and (c) control of default by the potentially negligent party, i.e. imposing liability on the party with the greatest incentive to monitor conduct? The arrangements in *The Aliakmon* were negotiated. Sir John Donaldson MR (at p. 53) made the following analysis:

'The relationship between buyer and seller on the one hand and cargo owner and shipowner on the other are quite distinct. In each case the parties seek to establish an economic balance, but there is no reason why it should be the same balance. The buyer may well be able to obtain the goods more cheaply if he undertakes not to hold the seller liable if the goods are lost or damaged after shipment and before they are delivered to him and to pay the price in any event. The shipowner may well charge a lower freight if, in return, he is to enjoy the protection of exceptions and limitations on his liability. Indeed he may be unwilling to accept the goods for carriage at all, if to do so will involve him in assuming any more extended duty of care or more extended liability for breach of that duty.'

This reflects the view that where the parties have voluntarily negotiated the terms of their 'exchange relationships', on the basis of a clear legal rule which bars the non-owner from recovery, it must be presumed that as far as they are concerned this represents what is in their mutual interests: see generally, Harris and Veljanowski, op cit, pp. 45–57.

6. Do these reasons for the non-liability principle apply with equal force where C is outside the 'exchange relationship' or chain of contracts and suffers economic loss due to negligence in the performance of a contract between B and A? Specifically, if A builds premises or manufactures a product under a contract with B, and C, the ultimate user, suffers loss because the premises or product are defective, should C be allowed to recover damages for that loss from A? In other words, could Mrs Donoghue (p. 40, ante) have claimed damages from the manufacturer because she received a worthless bottle of ginger-beer (even assuming she had not been injured)? This is considered in the case and notes which follow.

Murphy v Brentwood District Council House of Lords [1990] 2 All ER 908

In 1970 the plaintiff purchased one of a pair of newly-built semi-detached houses from a construction company. The houses were built over filled ground on concrete raft foundations. The design had been submitted to the defendant council for approval under building regulations. The council had sought the advice of independent consulting engineers who recommended the approval of the plans. In 1981 serious cracks appeared and it was discovered that as a result of defective design the concrete raft had cracked and become distorted so causing differential settlement and cracks in some walls and the fracturing of a gas pipe and soil pipe. The plaintiff sold the house subject to defects for £35,000 less than its value in sound condition. He brought an action against the council claiming damages on the grounds that they were liable for the consultant engineer's negligence.

The trial judge (1988) 13 Con LR 96, found that the council's consultant engineers had been negligent in approving the design, and that there was an imminent danger to the health and safety of the occupants of the house. He awarded damages of £38,777 being the loss on the sale of the house and expenses.

The Court of Appeal, [1990] 2 All ER 269, upheld this judgment on the basis of the decision of the House of Lords in *Anns v Merton London Borough Council* [1978] AC 728; [1977] 2 All ER 492 and held that the council owed a duty of care to the plaintiff to see that the house was properly built so as to avoid injury to the safety and health of those who lived in it. The Court of Appeal decided that the council were in breach of this duty in approving the plans for a defective raft foundation.

The council appealed to the House of Lords.

LORD KEITH OF KINKEL: . . . Before your Lordships' House it was argued on behalf of the council that *Anns* was wrongly decided and should be departed from under the practice statement of 26 July 1966 (see *Note* [1966] 3 All ER 77, [1966] 1 WLR 1234). The speeches of Lord Bridge and Lord Oliver in *D & F Estates Ltd v Church Comrs for England* [1988] 2 All ER 992, [1989] AC 177 contain some passages expressing doubts as to the extent to which the decision in *Anns* is capable of being reconciled with pre-existing principle. It is therefore appropriate to subject the decision to careful reconsideration.

As is well known, it was held in *Anns* that a local authority might be liable in negligence to long lessees occupying maisonettes built on inadequate foundations not complying with relevant building regulations, on the ground of failure by the authority to discover by inspection the inadequacy of the foundations before they were covered over. The proceedings arose out of the trial of a preliminary issue whether or not the plaintiffs had any cause of action against the local authority, and the damages claimed by them were not specified in the pleadings. It appeared, however, that such damages would include the cost of repairing cracks in the structure and of underpinning the foundations of the block of maisonettes.

The leading speech was that of Lord Wilberforce. His examination of law started with the formulation of the two-stage test of liability in negligence . . .

[His Lordship quoted the passage from Lord Wilberforce's speech set out p. 51, ante, and continued:] I observe at this point that the two-stage test has not been accepted as stating a universally applicable principle. Reservations about it were expressed by myself in *Governors of the Peabody Donation Fund v Sir Lindsay Parkinson & Co Ltd* [1984] 3 All ER 529 at 534, [1985] AC 210 at 240, by Lord Brandon in *Leigh & Sillavan Ltd v Aliakmon Shipping Co Ltd, The Aliakmon* [1986] 2 All ER 145 at 153, [1986] AC 785 at 815 and by Lord Bridge in *Curran v Northern Ireland Co-ownership Housing Association Ltd (Stewart, third party)* [1987] 2 All ER 13, [1987] AC 718. In *Sutherland Shire Council v Heyman* (1985) 60 ALR 1 at 43–44, where the High Court of Australia declined to follow *Anns*, Brennan J expressed his disagreement with Lord Wilberforce's approach, saying:

'It is preferable, in my view, that the law should develop novel categories of negligence incrementally and by analogy with established categories, rather than by a massive extension of a prima facie duty of care restrained only by indefinable "considerations which ought to negative, or to reduce or limit the scope of the duty or the class of person to whom it is owed".'

In the Privy Council case of *Yuen Kun-yeu v A-G of Hong Kong* [1987] 2 All ER 705 at 710, [1988] AC 175 at 191 that passage was quoted with approval and it was said ([1987]) 2 All ER 705 at 712, [1988] AC 175 at 194):

'In view of the direction in which the law has since been developing, their Lordships consider that for the future it should be recognised that the two-stage test . . . is not to be regarded as in all circumstances a suitable guide to the existence of a duty of care.'

Finally, in *Yuen Kun-yeu's* case [1987] 2 All ER 705 at 712, [1988] AC 175 at 193 and in *Hill v Chief Constable of West Yorkshire* [1988] 2 All ER 238 at 243, [1989] AC 53 at 63 I expressed the opinion, concurred in by the other members of the House who participated in the decisions, that the second stage of the test only came into play where some particular consideration of public policy excluded any duty of care. As regards the ingredients necessary to establish such a duty in novel situations, I consider that an incremental approach on the lines indicated by Brennan J in the *Sutherland Shire Council* case is to be preferred to the two-stage test.

Lord Wilberforce thereafter went on to consider the purposes of the 1936 Act, to hold that the local authority were under a duty to give proper consideration to the question whether they should inspect or not and to hold further that in relation to an inspection which it was decided to make there was a duty to exercise reasonable care in making it. Having considered *East Suffolk Rivers Catchment Board v Kent* [1940] 4 All ER 527, [1941] AC 74 and *Home Office v Dorset Yacht Co Ltd* [1970] 2 All ER 294, [1970] AC 1004, he continued ([1977] 2 All ER 492 at 504, [1978] AC 728 at 758):

'*To whom the duty is owed.* There is, in my opinion, no difficulty about this. A reasonable man in the position of the inspector must realise that if the foundations are covered in without adequate depth or strength as required by the byelaws, injury to safety or health may be suffered by owners or occupiers of the house. The duty is owed to them, not of course to a negligent building owner, the source of his own loss. I would leave open the case of users, who might themselves have a remedy against the occupier under the Occupiers' Liability Act 1957. A right of action can only be conferred on an owner or occupier, who is such when the damage occurs (see below). This disposes of the possible objection that an endless, indeterminate class of potential plaintiffs may be called into existence.

The nature of the duty. This must be related closely to the purpose for which powers of inspection are granted, namely to secure compliance with the byelaws. The duty is to take reasonable care, no more, no less, to secure that the builder does not cover in foundations which do not comply with byelaw requirements. The allegations in the statements of claim, insofar as they are based on non-compliance with the plans, are misconceived.'

Lord Wilberforce went on to consider the position of the builder, on the view that it would be unreasonable to impose liability in respect of defective foundations on the council if the builder, whose primary fault it was, should be immune from liability (see [1977] 2 All ER 492 at 504–505, [1978] AC 728 at 758–759). This consideration was, I think, a necessary part of the reasoning which led to his conclusion about the liability of the local authority. The *Dorset Yacht* case, on which Lord Wilberforce was proceeding, was concerned with the liability of prison officers for failing to take reasonable care to prevent the borstal boys in their charge from acting tortiously towards the owners of yachts moored in the vicinity of their encampment. If the conduct of the boys had not been tortious there would have been no liability on the prison officers. So, likewise, if the builder of defective foundations had been under no liability in tort, the local authority could have been under no liability for not taking reasonable care to see that he did not construct defective foundations. Lord Wilberforce took the view that the principle of *Donoghue v Stevenson* [1932] AC 562, [1932] All ER Rep 1 applied to the builder of defective premises, there being no sound reason why that principle should be limited to defective chattels.

I see no reason to doubt that the principle of *Donoghue v Stevenson* does indeed apply so as to place the builder of premises under a duty to take reasonable care to avoid injury through defects in the premises to the person or property of those whom he should have in contemplation as likely to suffer such injury if care is not taken. But it is against injury through latent defects that the duty exists to guard. I shall consider this aspect more fully later.

Lord Wilberforce went on ([1977]) 2 All ER 492 at 505, [1978] AC 728 at 759–760):

'*Nature of the damages recoverable and arising out of the cause of action.* There are many questions here which do not directly arise at this stage and which may never arise if the actions are tried. But some conclusions are necessary if we are to deal with the issue as to limitation. The damages recoverable include all those which foreseeably arise from the breach of the duty of care which, as regards the council, I have held to be a duty to take reasonable care to secure compliance with the byelaws. Subject always to adequate proof of causation, these damages may include damages for personal injury and damage to property. In my opinion they may also include damage to the dwelling-house itself; for the whole purpose of the byelaws in requiring foundations to be of certain standard is to prevent damage arising from weakness of the foundations which is certain to endanger the health or safety of occupants. To allow recovery for such damage to the house follows, in my opinion, from normal principle. If classification is required, the relevant damage is in my opinion material, physical damage, and what is recoverable is the amount of expenditure necessary to restore the dwelling to a condition in which it is no longer a danger to the health or safety of persons occupying and possibly (depending on the circumstances) expenses arising from necessary displacement. On the question of damages generally I have derived much assistance from the judgment (dissenting on this point, but of strong persuasive force) of Laskin CJ in the Canadian Supreme Court case of *Rivtow Marine Ltd v Washington Iron Works* [1974] SCR 1189 at 1220–1221 and from the judgments of the New Zealand Court of Appeal . . . in *Bowen v Paramount Buildings (Hamilton) Ltd* [1977] 1 NZLR 394.

When does the cause of action arise? We can leave aside cases of personal injury or damage to other property as presenting no difficulty. It is only the damage for the house which required consideration. In my respectful opinion the Court of Appeal was right when, in *Sparham-Souter v Town and Country Developments (Essex) Ltd* [1976] 2 All ER 65, [1976] QB 858, it abjured the view that the cause of action arose immediately on delivery, ie conveyance of the defective house. It can only arise when the state of the building is such that there is present or imminent danger to the health or safety of persons occupying it. We are not concerned at this stage with any issue relating to remedial action nor are we called on to decide on what the measure of the damages should be; such questions, possibly very difficult in some cases, will be for the court to decide. It is sufficient to say that a cause of action arises at the point I have indicated.'

Counsel for the council did not seek to argue that a local authority owes no duty at all to persons who might suffer injury through a failure to take reasonable care to secure compliance with building byelaws. He was content to accept that such a duty existed but maintained that its scope did not extend beyond injury to person or health and (possibly) damage to property other than the defective building itself. Not having heard argument on the matter, I prefer to reserve my opinion on the question whether any duty at all exists. So far as I am aware, there has not yet been any case of claims against a local authority based on injury to person or health through a failure to secure compliance with building byelaws. If and when such a case arises, that question may require further consideration. The present problem is concerned with the scope of the duty. The question is whether the defendant council owed the plaintiff a duty to take reasonable care to safeguard him against the particular kind of damage which he has in fact suffered, which was not injury to person or health nor damage to anything other than the defective house itself (see *Overseas Tankship*

(UK) Ltd v Morts Dock and Engineering Co Ltd, The Wagon Mound (No 1) [1961] 1 All ER 404 at 414–415 [1961] AC 388 at 425 per Viscount Simonds, *Caparo Industries plc v Dickman* [1990] 1 All ER 568 at 580–581, 599–600, [1990] 2 WLR 358 at 373, 396 per Lord Bridge and Lord Oliver, quoting the judgment of Brennan J in the *Sutherland Shire Council* case (1985) 60 ALR 1 at 48.

Lord Wilberforce, in the passage last quoted from his speech in *Anns*, does not devote precise consideration to the scope of the duty owed by a local authority as regards securing compliance with building byelaws. The question whether recovery could be allowed for damage to the house and for the cost of putting it in such a state as to be no longer a danger to health or safety was treated in the context of the measure of damages and the answer was said to follow from normal principle. It appears that the normal principle concerned was that which emerged from *Donoghue v Stevenson*, as extended to the sphere of stautory functions of public bodies in *Home Office v Dorset Yacht Co Ltd*. However, an essential feature of the species of liability in negligence established by *Donoghue v Stevenson* was that the carelessly manufac-tured product should be intended to reach the injured consumer in the same state as that in which it was put up with no reasonable prospect of intermediate examination (see [1932] AC 562 at 599, [1932] All ER Rep 1 at 20 per Lord Atkin; see also *Grant v Australian Knitting Mills Ltd* [1936] AC 85 at 103–105, [1935] All ER Rep 209 at 217–218 per Lord Wright). It is the latency of the defect which constitutes the mischief. There may be room for disputation whether the likelihood of inter-mediate examination and consequent actual discovery of the defect has the effect of negativing a duty of care or of breaking the chain of causation (compare *Farr v Butters Bros & Co* [1932] 2 KB 606, [1932] All ER Rep 339 with *Denny v Supplies and Transport Co Ltd* [1950] 2 KB 374). But there can be no doubt that, whatever the rationale, a person who is injured through consuming or using a product of the defective nature of which he is well aware has no remedy against the manufacturer. In the case of a building, it is right to accept that a careless builder is liable, on the principle of *Donoghue v Stevenson*, where a latent defect results in physical injury to anyone, whether owner, occupier, visitor or passer-by, or to the property of any such person. But that principle is not apt to bring home liability towards an occupier who knows the full extent of the defect yet continues to occupy the building. The *Dorset Yacht* case was concerned with the circumstances under which one person might come under a duty to another to take reasonable care to prevent a third party from committing a tort against that other. So the case had affinities with *Anns*, where a local authority was held to be under a duty to take reasonable care to prevent a builder from causing damage through carelessness to subsequent occupiers of houses built by him. In the *Dorset Yacht* case, however, the damage caused was physical damage to property, and, as I explained in *Hill v Chief Constable of West Yorkshire* [1988] 2 All ER 238 at 242, [1989] AC 53 at 61, the prison officers in charge of the borstal boys had created a potential situation of danger for the owners of yachts moored in the vicinity of the encampment by bringing the boys into that locality. No such feature was present in *Anns*.

In *Anns* the House of Lords approved, subject to explanation, the decision of the Court of Appeal in *Dutton v Bognor Regis United Building Co Ltd* [1972] 1 All ER 462, [1972] 1 QB 373. In that case Lord Denning MR said ([1972] 1 All ER 462 at 474, [1972] 1 QB 373 at 396):

'Counsel for the Council submitted that the liability of the council would, in any case, be limited to those who suffered bodily harm; and did not extend to those who only suffered economic loss. He suggested, therefore, that although the council might be liable if the ceiling fell down and injured a visitor, they would not be liable simply because the house was diminished in value . . . I cannot accept this submission. The damage done here was not solely economic loss. It was physical damage to the house. If counsel's submission were right, it would mean that, if the inspector negligently passes the house as properly built and it collapses and injures a person, the council are liable; but, if the owner discovers the defect in time to repair it — and he does repair it — the council are not liable. That is an impossible distinction. They are liable in either case. I would say the same about the manufacturer of an article. If he makes it negligently, with a latent defect (so that it breaks to pieces and injures someone), he is undoubtedly liable. Suppose that the defect is discovered in time to prevent the injury. Surely he is liable for the cost of repair.'

The jump which is here made from liability under the *Donoghue v Stevenson* principle for damage to person or property caused by a latent defect in a carelessly manufactured article to liability for the cost of rectifying a defect in such an article which is ex hypothesi no longer latent is difficult to accept. As Stamp LJ recognised in the same case, there is no liability in tort on a manufacturer towards the purchaser from a retailer of an article which turns out to be useless or valueless through defects due to careless manufacture (see [1972] 1 All ER 426 at 489–490 [1972] 1 QB 373 at 414–415). The loss is economic. It is difficult to draw a distinction in principle between an article which is useless or valueless and one which suffers from a defect which would render it dangerous in use but which is discovered by the purchaser in time to avert any possibility of injury. The purchaser may incur expense in putting right the defect, or, more probably, discard the article. In either case the loss is purely economic. Stamp LJ appears to have taken the view that in the case of a house the builder would not be liable to a purchaser where the defect was discovered in time to prevent injury but that a local authority which had failed to discover the defect by careful inspection during the course of construction was so liable.

Batty v Metropolitan Property Realizations Ltd [1978] 2 All ER 445, [1978] QB 554 was a case where a house which suffered no defects of construction had been built on land subject to the danger of slippage. A landslip carried away part of the garden but there was no damage to the house itself. Due to the prospect, however, that at some future time the house might be completely carried away, it was rendered valueless. There was no possibility of remedial works such as might save the house from being carried away. The Court of Appeal allowed recovery in tort against the builder of damages based on loss of the value of the house. That again was purely economic loss.

Consideration of the nature of the loss suffered in this category of cases is closely tied up with the question of when the cause of action arises. Lord Wilberforce in *Anns v Merton London Borough* [1977] 2 All ER 492 at 505, [1978] AC 728 at 760 regarded it as arising when the state of the building is such that there is present an imminent danger to the health or safety of persons occupying it. That state of affairs may exist when there is no actual physical damage to the building itself, though Lord Wilberforce had earlier referred to the relevant damage being material physical damage. So his meaning may have been that there must be a concurrence of material physical damage and also present or imminent danger to the health or safety of occupants. On that view there would be no cause of action where the building had suffered no damage (or possibly, having regard to the word 'material', only very slight damage) but a structural survey had revealed an underlying defect, presenting imminent danger. Such a discovery would inevitably cause a fall in the value of the building, resulting in economic loss to the owner. That such is the nature of the loss is made clear in cases where the owner abandons the building as incapable of being put in a safe condition (as in *Batty's* case) or where he chooses to sell it at the lower value rather than undertake remedial works. In *Pirelli General Cable Works Ltd v Oscar Faber & Partners (a firm)* [1983] 1 All ER 65, [1983] 2 AC 1 it was held that the cause of action in tort against consulting engineers who had negligently approved a defective design for a chimney arose when damage to the chimney caused by the defective design first occurred, not when the damage was discovered or with reasonable diligence might have been discovered. The defendants there had in relation to the design been in contractual relations with the plaintiffs, but it was common ground that a claim in contract was time-barred. If the plaintiffs had happened to discover the defect before any damage had occurred there would seem to be no good reason for holding that they would not have had a cause of action in tort at that stage, without having to wait until some damage had occurred. They would have suffered economic loss through having a defective chimney on which they required to expend money for the purpose of removing the defect. It would seem that in a case such as the *Pirelli General Cable Works* case, where the tortious liability arose out of a contractual relationship with professional people, the duty extended to take reasonable care not to cause economic loss to the client by the advice given. The plaintiffs built the chimney as they did in reliance on that advice. The case would accordingly fall within the principle of *Hedley Byrne & Co Ltd v Heller & Partners Ltd* [1963] 2 All ER 575, [1964] AC 465. I regard *Junior Books Ltd v Veitchi Co Ltd* [1982] 3 All ER 201, [1983] 1 AC 520 as being an application of that principle.

In my opinion it must now be recognised that, although the damage in *Anns* was characterised as physical damage by Lord Wilberforce, it was purely economic loss. In *Sutherland Shire Council v Heyman* (1985) 60 ALR 1 at 60–61 where, as observed above, the High Court of Australia declined to follow *Anns* when dealing with a claim against a local authority in respect of a defectively constructed house, Deane J said:

'Nor is the respondents' claim in the present case for ordinary physical damage to themselves or their property. Their claim, as now crystallized, is not in respect of damage to the fabric of the house or to other property caused by collapse or subsidence of the house as a result of the inadequate foundations. It is for the loss or damage represented by the actual inadequacy of the foundations, that is to say, it is for the cost of remedying a structural defect in their property which already existed at the time when they acquired it. In *Anns v Merton London Borough Council*, it was held by the House of Lords that a local government authority owed a relevant duty of care, in respect of inspection of the foundations of a building, to persons who subsequently became long term lessees (either as original lessees or as assignees) of parts of the building. Lord Wilberforce, in a speech with which three of the other four members of the House of Lords agreed, expressed the conclusion that the appropriate classification of damage sustained by the lessees by reason of the inadequacy of the foundations of the completed building was 'material, physical damage, and what is recoverable is the amount of expenditure necessary to restore the dwelling to a condition in which it is no longer a danger to the health or safety of persons occupying and possibly (depending on the circumstances) expenses arising from necessary displacement' (see [1977] 2 All ER 492 at 505, [1978] AC 728 at 759). While, in a case where a subsequent purchaser or long term tenant reasonably elects to retain the premises and to reinforce the foundations, one possible measure of the damages involved in the actual inadequacy would (if such damages were recoverable) be that suggested by his Lordship, I respectfully disagree with the classification of the loss sustained in such circumstances as 'material, physical damage'. Whatever may be the position with respect to consequential damage to the fabric of the building or to other property caused by subsequent collapse or subsidence, the loss or injury involved in the actual inadequacy of the foundations cannot, in the case of a person who purchased or leased the property after the inadequacy existed but before it was known or manifest, properly be seen as ordinary physical or material damage. The only property which could be said to have been damaged in such a case is the building. The building itself could not be said to have been subjected to 'material, physical damage' by reason merely of the inadequacy of its foundations since the building never existed otherwise than with its foundations in that state. Moreover, even if the inadequacy of the foundations could be seen as material, physical damage to the building, it would be damage to property in which a future purchaser or tenant had no interest at all at the time when it occurred. Loss or injury could only be sustained by such a purchaser or tenant on or after the acquisition of the freehold or leasehold estate without knowledge of the faulty foundations. It is arguable that any such loss or injury should be seen as being sustained at the time of acquisition when, because of ignorance of the inadequacy of the foundations, a higher price is paid (or a higher rent is agreed to be paid) than is warranted by the intrinsic worth of the freehold or leasehold estate that is being acquired. Militating against that approach is the consideration that, for so long as the inadequacy of the foundations is neither known nor manifest, no identifiable loss has come home: if the purchaser or tenant sells the freehold or leasehold estate within that time, he or she will sustain no loss by reason of the inadequacy of the foundations. The alternative, and in my view preferable, approach is that any loss or injury involved in the actual inadequacy of the foundations is sustained only at the time when that inadequacy is first known or manifest. It is only then that the actual diminution in the market value of the premises occurs. On either approach, however, any loss involved in the actual inadequacy of the foundations by a person who acquires an interest in the premises after the building has been completed is merely economic in its nature.'

I find myself in respectful agreement with the reasoning contained in this passage, which seem to me to be incontrovertible.

It being recognised that the nature of the loss held to be recoverable in *Anns* was pure economic loss, the next point for examination is whether the avoidance of loss of that nature fell within the scope of any duty of care owed to the plaintiffs by the local authority. On the basis of the law as it stood at the time of the decision the answer to that question must be in the negative. The right to recover for pure economic loss, not flowing from physical injury, did not then extend beyond the situation where the loss had been sustained through reliance on negligent misstatements, as in *Hedley Byrne*. There is room for the view that an exception is to be found in *Morrison Steamship Co v Greystoke Castle (cargo owners)* [1946] 2 All ER 696, [1947] AC 265. That case, which was decided by a narrow majority, may, however, be regarded as turning on specialties of maritime law concerned in the relationship of joint adventurers at sea. Further, though the purposes of the 1936 Act as regards securing compliance with building byelaws covered the avoidance of injury to the safety or health of inhabitants of houses and of members of the public generally, these purposes did not cover the avoidance of pure economic loss to owners of buildings (see *Governors of the Peabody Donation Fund v Sir Lindsay Parkinson & Co Ltd* [1984] 3 All ER 529 at 534–535, [1985] AC 210 at 241). On analysis, the nature of the duty held by *Anns* to be incumbent on the local authority went very much further than a duty to take reasonable care to prevent injury to safety or health. The duty held to exist may be formulated as one to take reasonable care to avoid putting a future inhabitant owner of a house in a position in which he is threatened, by reason of a defect in the house, with avoidable physical injury to person or health and is obliged, in order to continue to occupy the house without suffering such injury, to expend money for the purpose of rectifying the defect.

The existence of a duty of that nature should not, in my opinion, be affirmed without a careful examination of the implications of such affirmation. To start with, if such a duty is incumbent on the local authority, a similar duty must necessarily be incumbent also on the builder of the house. If the builder of the house is to be so subject, there can be no grounds in logic or in principle for not extending liability on like grounds to the manufacturer of a chattel. That would open on an exceedingly wide field of claims, involving the introduction of something in the nature of a transmissible warranty of quality. The purchaser of an article who discovered that it suffered from a dangerous defect before that defect had caused any damage would be entitled to recover from the manufacturer the cost of rectifying the defect, and, presumably, if the article was not capable of economic repair, the amount of loss sustained through discarding it. Then it would be open to question whether there should not also be a right to recovery where the defect renders the article not dangerous but merely useless. The economic loss in either case would be the same. There would also be a problem where the defect causes the destruction of the article itself, without causing any personal injury or damage to other property. A similar problem could arise, if the *Anns* principle is to be treated as confined to real property, where a building collapses when unoccupied.

In America the courts have developed the view that in the case of chattels damage to the chattel itself resulting from careless manufacture does not give a cause of action in negligence or in product liability. Thus in *East River Steamship Corp v Transamerica Delaval Inc* (1986) 476 US 858 charterers of a supertanker were denied recovery on either of these grounds, against the manufacturers of turbines which had suffered damage through design or manufacturing defect and which had had to be replaced. Blackmun J, delivering the judgment of the Supreme Court, expressed the opinion (at 870–873) that a claim of this character fell properly into the sphere of warranty under contract law. This judgment was followed by the United States Court of Appeals, Third Circuit, in *Aloe Coal Co v Clark Equipment Co* (1987) 816 F 2d 110, where recovery in negligence was refused in respect of damage to a tractor shovel which caught fire and was destroyed, allegedly due to careless manufacture. The view of these courts is in line with the dissenting judgment of Lord Brandon in *Junior Books Ltd v Veitchi Co Ltd* [1982] 3 All ER 201, [1983] 1 AC 520.

These American cases would appear to destroy the authority of the earlier decision in *Quackenbush v Ford Motor Co* (1915) 167 AD 433, founded on by the New Zealand Court of Appeal in *Bowen v Paramount Builders (Hamilton) Ltd* [1977] 1 NZLR 394, from which Lord Wilberforce in *Anns v Merton London Borough* [1977] 2 All ER 492 at 505, [1978] AC 728 at 759–760 said that he had derived assistance. He referred similarly to the dissenting judgment of Laskin J in the Canadian Supreme Court case of *Rivtow Marine Ltd v Washington Iron Works* [1974] SCR 1189 at 1220–1221. That was a case where a crane installed on the plaintiffs' barge was revealed as being dangerously defective as a result of a similar crane having collapsed and killed a man while being operated elsewhere. The manufacturers and the suppliers were aware of this occurrence but delayed considerably in warning the plaintiffs, so that they were placed under the necessity of taking the crane out of service for rectification at the height of the logging season instead of in the slack season. The majority of the Supreme Court held the manufacturers and suppliers liable for the loss of profit sustained by the plaintiffs through not having been given earlier warning of the defect. This was on the *Hedley Byrne* principle. They did not allow recovery for the cost of putting right the defect. The minority, Laskin and Hall JJ, were in favour of allowing recovery of that cost. For my part, I consider that the decision of the majority was correct. The defect in the crane was discovered before it had done any damage, so that there could be no question of application of the *Donoghue v Stevenson* principle. The cost of rectifying the defect was incurred for the purpose of enabling the crane to be profitably operated. The danger of injury from the defect, once it was known, could have been averted simply by laying up the crane. The loss was purely economic.

In *D & F Estates Ltd v Church Comrs for England* [1988] 2 All ER 992, [1989] AC 177 both Lord Bridge and Lord Oliver expressed themselves as having difficulty in reconciling the decision in *Anns* with pre-existing principle and as being uncertain as to the nature and scope of such new principle as it introduced. Lord Bridge suggested that in the case of a complex structure such as a building one element of the structure might be regarded for *Donoghue v Stevenson* purposes as distinct from another element, so that damage to one part of the structure caused by a hidden defect in another part might qualify to be treated as damage to 'other property' (see [1988] 2 All ER 992 at 1006, [1989] AC 177 at 206). I think that it would be unrealistic to take this view as regards a building the whole of which had been erected and equipped by the same contractor. In that situation the whole package provided by the contractor would, in my opinion, fall to be regarded as one unit rendered unsound as such by a defect in the particular part. On the other hand, where, for example, the electric wiring had been installed by a sub-contractor and due to a defect caused by lack of care a fire occurred which destroyed the building, it might not be stretching ordinary principles too far to hold the electrical sub-contractor liable for the damage. If in the

East River case the defective turbine had caused the loss of the ship the manufacturer of it could consistently with normal principles, I would think, properly have been held liable for that loss. But, even if Lord Bridge's theory were to be held acceptable, it would not seem to extend to the founding of liability on a local authority, considering that the purposes of the 1936 Act are concerned with averting danger to health and safety, not danger or damage to property. Further, it would not cover the situation which might arise through discovery, before any damage had occurred, of a defect likely to give rise to damage in the future.

Liability under the *Anns* decision is postulated on the existence of a present or imminent danger to health or safety. But, considering that the loss involved in incurring expenditure to avert the danger is pure economic loss, there would seem to be no logic in confining the remedy to cases where such danger exists. There is likewise no logic in confining it to cases where some damage (perhaps comparatively slight) has been caused to the building, but refusing it where the existence of the danger has come to light in some other way, for example through a structural survey which happens to have been carried out, or where the danger inherent in some particular component or material has been revealed through failure in some other building. Then there is the question whether the remedy is available where the defect is rectified, not in order to avert danger to an inhabitant occupier himself, but in order to enable an occupier, who may be a corporation, to continue to occupy the building through its employees without putting those employees at risk.

In my opinion it is clear that *Anns* did not proceed on any basis of established principle, but introduced a new species of liability governed by a principle indeterminate in character but having the potentiality of covering a wide range of situations, involving chattels as well as real property, in which it had never hitherto been thought that the law of negligence had any proper place.

The practice statement of 26 July 1966 (see *Note* [1966] 3 All ER 77, [1966] 1 WLR 1234) leaves it open to this House to depart from a previous decision of its own if it so chooses. In *Jones v Secretary of State for Social Services* [1972] 1 All ER 145 at 149, [1972] AC 944 at 966 Lord Reid said:

'The old view was that any departure from rigid adherences to precedent would weaken [the certainty in the law]. I did not and do not accept that view. It is notorious that where an existing decision is disapproved but cannot be overruled courts tend to distinguish it on inadequate grounds. I do not think that they act wrongly in so doing; they are adopting the less bad of the only alternatives open to them. But this is bound to lead to uncertainty for no one can say in advance whether in a particular case the court will or will not feel bound to follow the old unsatisfactory decision. On balance it seems to me that overruling such a decision will promote and not impair the certainty of the law.'

In my opinion there can be no doubt that *Anns* has for long been widely regarded as an unsatisfactory decision. In relation to the scope of the duty owed by a local authority it proceeded on what must, with due respect to its source, be regarded as a somewhat superficial examination of principle and there has been extreme difficulty, highlighted most recently by the speeches in the *D & F Estates* case, in ascertaining on exactly what basis of principle it did proceed. I think it must now be recognised that it did not proceed on any basis of principle at all, but constituted a remarkable example of judicial legislation. It has engendered a vast spate of litigation, and each of the cases in the field which have reached this House has been distinguished. Others have been distinguished in the Court of Appeal. The result has been to keep the effect of the decision within reasonable bounds, but that has been achieved only by applying strictly the words of Lord Wilberforce and by refusing to accept the logical implications of the decision itself. These logical implications show that the case properly considered has potentiality for collision with long-established principles regarding liability in the tort of negligence for economic loss. There can be no doubt that to depart from the decision would re- establish a degree of certainty in this field of law which it has done a remarkable amount to upset.

So far as policy considerations are concerned, it is no doubt the case that extending the scope of the tort of negligence may tend to inhibit carelessness and improve standards of manufacture and construction. On the other hand, overkill may present its own disadvantages, as was remarked in *Rowling v Takaro Properties Ltd* [1988] 1 All ER 163 at 173, [1988] AC 473 at 502. There may be room for the view that *Anns*-type liability will tend to encourage owners of buildings found to be dangerous to repair rather than run the risk of injury. The owner may, however, and perhaps quite often does, prefer to sell the building at its diminished value, as happened in the present case.

It must, of course, be kept in mind that the decision has stood for some 13 years. On the other hand, it is not a decision of the type that is to a significant extent taken into account by citizens or indeed local authorities in ordering their affairs. No doubt its existence results in local authorities having to pay increased insurance premiums, but to be relieved of that necessity would be to their advantage, not to their detriment. To overrule it is unlikely to result in significantly increased insurance premiums for householders. It is perhaps of some significance that most litigation involving the decision consists in contests between insurance companies, as is largely the position in the present case. The decision is capable of being regarded as affording a measure of justice, but as against that the impossibility of finding any coherent and logically based doctrine behind it is calculated to put the law of negligence into a state of confusion defying rational analysis. It is also material that *Anns* has the effect of imposing on builders generally a liability going far beyond that which Parliament thought fit to impose on house builders alone by the Defective Premises Act 1972, a statute very material to the policy of the decision but not adverted to in it. There is much to be said for the view that in what is essentially a consumer protection field, as was observed by Lord Bridge in *D & F Estates Ltd v Church Comrs for England* [1988] 2 All ER 992 at 1007, [1989] AC 177 at 207, the precise extent and limits of the liabilities which in the public interest should be imposed on builders and local authorities are best left to the legislature.

My Lords, I would hold that *Anns* was wrongly decided as regards the scope of any private law duty of care resting on local authorities in relation to their function of taking steps to secure compliance with building byelaws or regulations and should be departed from. It follows that *Dutton v Bognor Regis United Building Co Ltd* [1972] 1 All ER 462, [1972] 1 QB 373 should be overruled, as should all cases subsequent to *Anns* which were decided in reliance on it.

In the circumstances I do not consider it necessary to deal with the question whether, assuming that the council was under a duty of the scope contended for by the plaintiff, it discharged that duty by acting on the advice of competent consulting engineers.

My Lords, for these reasons I would allow the appeal.

LORD BRIDGE OF HARWICH: My Lords, the speech of my noble and learned friend Lord Keith addresses comprehensively all the issues on which the outcome of this appeal depends. I find myself in full agreement with it . . .

Dangerous defects and defects of quality
If a manufacturer negligently puts into circulation a chattel containing a latent defect which renders it dangerous to persons or property, the manufacturer, on the well-known principles established by *Donoghue v Stevenson* [1932] AC 562, [1932] All ER Rep 1, will be liable in tort for injury to persons or damage to property which the chattel causes. But if a manufacturer produces and sells a chattel which is merely defective in quality, even to the extent that it is valueless for the purpose for which it is intended, the manufacturer's liability at common law arises only under and by reference to the terms of any contract to which he is a party in relation to the chattel;

the common law does not impose on him any liability in tort to persons to whom he owes no duty in contract but who, having acquired the chattel, suffer economic loss because the chattel is defective in quality. If a dangerous defect in a chattel is discovered before it causes any personal injury or damage to property, because the danger is now known and the chattel cannot be safely used unless the defect is repaired, the defect becomes merely a defect in quality. The chattel is either capable of repair at economic cost or it is worthless and must be scrapped. In either case the loss sustained by the owner or hirer of the chattel is purely economic. It is recoverable against any party who owes the loser a relevant contractual duty. But it is not recoverable in tort in the absence of a special relationship of proximity imposing on the tortfeasor a duty of care to safeguard the plaintiff from economic loss. There is no such special relationship between the manufacturer of a chattel and a remote owner or hirer.

I believe that these principles are equally applicable to buildings. If a builder erects a structure containing a latent defect which renders it dangerous to persons or property, he will be liable in tort for injury to persons or damage to property resulting from that dangerous defect. But, if the defect becomes apparent before any injury or damage has been caused, the loss sustained by the building owner is purely economic. If the defect can be repaired at economic cost, that is the measure of the loss. If the building cannot be repaired, it may have to be abandoned as unfit for occupation and therefore valueless. These economic losses are recoverable if they flow from breach of a relevant contractual duty, but, here again, in the absence of a special relationship of proximity they are not recoverable in tort. The only qualification I would make to this is that, if a building stands so close to the boundary of the building owner's land that after discovery of the dangerous defect it remains a potential source of injury to persons or property on neighbouring land or on the highway, the building owner ought, in principle, to be entitled to recover in tort from the negligent builder the cost of obviating the danger, whether by repair or by demolition, so far as that cost is necessarily incurred in order to protect himself from potential liability to third parties. . . .

LORD OLIVER OF AYLMERTON: My Lords, I have had the advantage of reading in draft the speeches prepared by my noble and learned friends Lord Keith and Lord Bridge. For the reasons which they have given I too would allow this appeal. . . .

It does not, of course, at all follow as a matter of necessity from the mere fact that the only damage suffered by a plaintiff in an action for the tort of negligence is pecuniary or 'economic' that his claim is bound to fail. It is true that, in an uninterrupted line of cases since 1875, it has consistently been held that a third party cannot successfully sue in tort for the interference with his economic expectations or advantage resulting from injury to the person or property of another person with whom he has or is likely to have a contractual relationship (see *Cattle v Stockton Waterworks Co* (1875) LR 10 QB 453, [1874–80] All ER Rep 220, *Simpson & Co v Thomson* (1877) 3 App Cas 279, *SA de Remorquage à Hélice v Bennetts* [1911] 1 KB 243). That principle was applied more recently by Widgery J in *Weller & Co v Foot and Mouth Disease Research Institute* [1965] 3 All ER 560, [1966] 1 QB 569 and received its most recent reiteration in the decision of this House in *Leigh Sillavan Ltd v Aliakmon Shipping Co Ltd, The Aliakmon* [1986] 2 All ER 145, [1986] AC 785. But it is far from clear from these decisions that the reason for the plaintiff's failure was simply that the only loss sustained was 'economic'. Rather they seem to have been based either on the remoteness of the damage as a matter of direct causation or, more probably, on the 'floodgates' argument of the impossibility of containing liability within any acceptable bounds if the law were to permit such claims to succeed. The decision of this House in *Morrison Steamship Co Ltd v Greystoke Castle (cargo owners)* [1946] 2 All ER 696, [1947] AC 265 demonstrates that the mere fact that the primary damage suffered by a plaintiff is pecuniary is no necessary bar to an action in negligence given the proper circumstances (in that case, what was said to be the 'joint venture' interest of shipowners and the owners of cargo carried on board) and if the matter remained in doubt that doubt was conclusively resolved by the decision of this House in *Hedley Byrne & Co Ltd v Heller & Partners Ltd* [1963] 2 All ER 575 at 606–603, [1964] AC 465 at 517, where Lord Devlin convincingly demonstrated the illogicality of a distinction between financial loss caused directly and financial loss resulting from physical injury to personal property.

The critical question, as was pointed out in the analysis of Brennan J in his judgment in *Sutherland Shire Council v Heyman* (1985) 60 ALR 1, is not the nature of the damage in itself, whether physical or pecuniary, but whether the scope of the duty of care in the circumstances of the case is such as to embrace damage of the kind which the plaintiff claims to have sustained (see *Caparo Industries plc v Dickman* [1990] 1 All ER 568, [1990] 2 WLR 358). The essential question which has to be asked in every case, given that damage which is the essential ingredient of the action has occurred, is whether the relationship between the plaintiff and the defendant is such, or, to use the favoured expression, whether it is of sufficient 'proximity', that it imposes on the latter a duty to take care to avoid or prevent that loss which has in fact been sustained. That the requisite degree of proximity may be established in circumstances in which the plaintiff's injury results from his reliance on a statement or advice on which he was entitled to rely and on which it was contemplated that he would be likely to rely is clear from *Hedley Byrne* and subsequent cases, but *Anns* was not such a case and neither is the instant case. It is not, however, necessarily to be assumed that the reliance cases form the only possible category of cases in which a duty to take reasonable care to avoid or prevent pecuniary loss can arise. *Morrison Steamship Co Ltd v Greystoke Castle (cargo owners)*, for instance, clearly was not a reliance case. Nor indeed was *Ross v Caunters (a firm)* [1979] 3 All ER 580, [1980] Ch 297 so far as the disappointed beneficiary was concerned. Another example may be *Ministry of Housing and Local Government v Sharp* [1970] 1 All ER 1009, [1970] 2 QB 223, although this may, on analysis, properly be categorised as a reliance case.

Nor is it self-evident logically where the line is to be drawn. Where, for instance, the defendant's careless conduct results in the interruption of the electricity supply to business premises adjoining the highway, it is not easy to discern the logic in holding that a sufficient relationship of proximity exists between him and a factory owner who has suffered loss because material in the course of manufacture is rendered useless but that none exists between him and the owner of, for instance, an adjoining restaurant who suffers the loss of profit on the meals which he is unable to prepare and sell. In both cases the real loss is pecuniary. The solution to such borderline cases has so far been achieved pragmatically (see *Spartan Steel and Alloys Ltd v Martin & Co (Contractors) Ltd* [1972] 3 All ER 557, [1973] QB 27) not by the application of logic but by the perceived necessity as a matter of policy to place some limits, perhaps arbitrary limits, to what would otherwise be an endless, cumulative causative chain bounded only by theoretical foreseeability.

I frankly doubt whether, in searching for such limits, the categorisation of the damage as 'material', 'physical', 'pecuniary' or 'economic' provides a particularly useful contribution. Where it does, I think, serve a useful purpose is in identifying those cases in which it is necessary to search for and find something more than the mere reasonable foreseeability of damage which has occurred as providing the degree of 'proximity' necessary to support the action. In his classical exposition in *Donoghue v Stevenson* [1932] AC 562 at 580–581, [1932] All ER Rep 1 at 11 Lord Atkin was expressing himself in the context of the infliction of direct physical injury resulting from a carelessly created latent defect in a manufactured product. In his analysis of the duty in those circumstances he clearly equated 'proximity' with the reasonable foresight of damage. In the straightforward case of the direct infliction of physical injury by the act of the plaintiff there is, indeed, no need to look beyond the foreseeability by the defendant of the result in order to establish that he is in a 'proximate' relationship with the plaintiff. But, as was pointed out by Lord Diplock in *Home Office v Dorset Yacht Co Ltd* [1970] 2 All ER 294 at 326, [1970] AC 1004 at 1060, Lord Atkin's test, though a useful guide to characteristics which will be found to exist in conduct and relationships giving rise to a legal duty of care, is manifestly false if misused as a universal; and Lord Reid, in the course of his speech in the same case, recognised that the statement of principle enshrined in that test necessarily required qualification in cases where the only loss caused by the defendant's conduct was economic. The infliction of physical injury to the person or property of another universally requires to be justified. The causing of economic loss does not. If it is to be categorised as wrongful it is necessary to find some factor beyond the mere occurrence of the loss and the fact that its occurrence could be foreseen. Thus the categorisation of damage as economic serves at least the useful purpose of indicating that something more is required and it is one of the unfortunate features of *Anns* that it resulted initially in this essential distinction being lost sight of.

   ... Whether, as suggested in the speech of my noble and learned friend Lord Bridge, [the builder] could be held responsible for the cost necessarily incurred by a building owner in protecting himself from potential liability to third parties is a question on which I prefer to reserve my opinion until the case arises, although I am not at the moment convinced of the basis for making such a distinction. ...

[LORD MACKAY OF CLASHFERN LC and LORD JAUNCEY OF TULLICHETTLE delivered speeches in favour of allowing the appeal. LORD BRANDON OF OAKBROOK agreed that the appeal should be allowed for the reasons given by LORD KEITH OF KINKEL. LORD ACKNER agreed that the appeal should be allowed for the reasons given by LORD KEITH OF KINKEL, LORD BRIDGE OF HARRWICH, LORD OLIVER OF AYLMERTON and LORD JAUNCEY.]

Appeal allowed

Notes

1. The practical importance of this decision is that it establishes that a local authority is not liable in negligence to a building owner or occupier for the cost of remedying a dangerous latent defect in the building which resulted from negligent failure by the local authority to ensure that the building was designed or erected in accordance with building regulations. The decision was applied by the House of Lords, in a case considered at the same time, *Department of the Environment v Thomas Bates & Son Ltd* [1990] 2 All ER 943; [1990] 3 WLR 457, to hold that a builder was not liable in tort for the cost of remedying defects in a building in order to make it safe and suitable for its intended purpose where there was no damage to the building and no imminent danger to personal safety and health. The implications for the law relating to defective premises are considered p. 466, post, and defective products, p. 500, post.

2. The case is of general interest because it marks a significant contraction in the scope of the duty of care, at least so far as liability for economic loss is concerned. The major developments are outlined in the Introduction to this chapter. Here it is worth noting that a seven-member House of Lords found it necessary to overrule their own earlier decision in *Anns v Merton London Borough Council* [1978] AC 728; [1977] 2 All ER 492. The assumed facts in that case were that there was a threat to health or safety due to defective foundations, the defective foundations having caused cracks in the walls of the building. The damages which the occupiers were allowed to recover

consisted in such sums as each of them had to expend in order to put his dwelling in a state that it was no longer a danger to health or safety. P. Cane (1979) 95 LQR 117 described these as 'preventive' damages. The case was regarded as one of 'physical damage', although all that seemed to be needed was a 'present and imminent threat' of physical damage (see L. N. Duncan-Wallace (1978) 94 LQR 60; P. Cane (1984) 10 Monash Univ LR 17, 45). J. Stapleton, (1988) 104 LQR 213 at 222, suggests that 'the practical advantage of this view was that it would allow a plaintiff who for some reason knew that the condition of the property posed such a threat (e.g. because all other box girder bridges of that design had collapsed within 5 years of construction) to sue before physical changes occurred in the structure'. The effect of *Murphy* and *Bates* is to rule out the possibility of preventive damages, subject to Lord Bridge's view (p. 223, ante) concerning the building close to the boundary of land, though see Lord Oliver's speech (p. 224, ante). P. Cane (1989) 52 MLR 200 at 207 (commenting on the earlier case of *D & F Estates Ltd v Church Comrs for England* [1989] AC 177; [1988] 2 All ER 992) argues that this may be 'economically unjustified in that prevention is often cheaper than cure' (see generally on the earlier law, J. Stapleton (1988) 104 LQR 213, 389).

3. In *Junior Books Ltd v Veitchi Co Ltd* [1983] 1 AC 520; [1982] 3 All ER 201, the assumed facts were that the pursuers contracted with a firm of builders to construct a factory for them. The pursuer's architects nominated the defenders as specialist sub-contractors to lay the flooring. The defenders entered into a contract with the builders but not with the pursuers to carry out this work. Owing to the negligence of the defenders the floor became defective and developed cracks. It was not suggested that there was a threat to health and safety or threatened damage to any other property of the pursuers. The entire floor surface needed replacement. The House of Lords held (by a majority of 4–1) that the pursuers could recover from the flooring sub-contractors (a) the cost of replacement of the floor surface; and (b) the consequential economic loss arising from storing their books elsewhere, moving machinery, loss of profits, payment of wages to employees and overheads during the period of treatment. Lord Roskill (with whom Lords Fraser and Russell agreed, Lord Keith agreeing with the result on a narrower ground) rejected any distinction in principle between 'pure' economic loss and economic loss caused by physical damage, and he said that the requirement of 'proximity' 'must always involve, at least in most cases, some degree of reliance'. Both he and Lord Fraser emphasised that the relationship between the pursuers and the sub-contractors fell only just short of contract, and there was reliance on the skill and judgment of the sub-contractors. Although this decision was hailed as 'a milestone in the development of the law of negligence' (M. Jones (1982) 132 NLJ 1091) and as 'throwing doubt upon the traditional division between contract and tort' (N. E. Palmer and J. R. Murdoch (1983) 46 MLR 213 at 241), it was also strongly criticised for leaving 'a host of problems unresolved' without adequate consideration of precedent or policy (Hepple, All ER Rev 1982, pp. 301–305; see further F. Reynolds (1985) 11 NZULR 215; M. McGrath (1985) 3 Oxf JLS 350.) In all the subsequent cases, reasons were found for distinguishing and not following it. The very first time the House of Lords considered *Junior Books*, they treated it (surprisingly) as a case of physical damage (*Tate and*

Lyle Industries Ltd v Greater London Council [1983] 2 AC 509; [1983] 1 All ER 1159). When Walton J had to consider whether a sub-agent could be liable in tort to his principal, he distinguished *Junior Books* on the ground that the decision could not be used to sidestep the doctrine of privity of contract (*Balsamo v Medici* [1984] 2 All ER 304; [1984] 1 WLR 951). Despite the apparently wide view of the majority in *Junior Books* that there could be a duty of care to prevent damage to the defective property itself, the Court of Appeal held there was insufficient proximity between an ordinary purchaser and the manufacturer of defective products to impose a duty of care in respect of pure economic loss (*Muirhead v Industrial Tank Specialities Ltd* [1986] QB 507; [1985] 3 All ER 705), and, notwithstanding the impositiion of liability on the builder in the absence of a contractual relationship in *Junior Books*, the Court of Appeal held that liability for qualitative defects in products falls within the exclusive scope of contract law (*Simaan General Contracting Co v Pilkington Glass Ltd (No 2)* [1988] QB 758; [1988] 1 All ER 791). Rather rashly perhaps, Dillon LJ remarked in the latter case (at p. 805): 'I find it difficult to see that future citation from *Junior Books* can ever serve any useful purpose.' In *D & F Estates Ltd v Church Comrs for England* [1988] 2 All ER at p. 1003 Lord Bridge said:

'The consensus of judicial opinion, with which I concur, seems to be that the decision of the majority is so far dependent on the unique, non-contractual, relationship between the pursuer and the defender in that case and the unique scope of the duty of care owed by the defender to the pursuer arising from that relationship that the decision cannot be regarded as laying down any principle of general application in the law of tort or delict.'

Lord Oliver ([1988] 2 All ER at p. 1013) said that *Junior Books* 'rests, in any event, on the *Hedley Byrne* doctrine of reliance' (see Note 5, post). In view of the fact that both Lord Bridge and Lord Oliver adopted what was said by Lord Brandon in his dissenting speech in *Junior Books* (see Note 4, post), it is surprising that the House of Lords did not expressly overrule the majority decision. However, in *Murphy v Brentwood District Council* both Lord Keith and Lord Oliver referred to *Junior Books* as falling within 'reliance' principles. It does seem likely that if the facts of *Junior Books* had arisen in England an *implied contract* between the defendant sub-contractors and the plaintiffs to exercise reasonable care and skill in laying the floor would have been alleged (as in *Charnock v Liverpool Corpn* [1968] 3 All ER 473; [1968] 1 WLR 1498).

4. Why has there been reluctance to impose a duty on A not to cause economic loss to C by his negligent performance of his contract with B? Among the reasons put forward by Lord Brandon in his dissenting speech in *Junior Books* [1983] 1 AC 520 at pp. 549–551 (approved in the *D & F Estates* case, ante), in the context of defective premises (or products), were the following:

(a) The duty of care in *M'Alister* (or *Donoghue*) *v Stevenson* [1932] AC 562 (p. 40 ante) was based on a danger of physical injury to persons and property, and the relevant property for this purpose was 'property other than the very property which gave rise to the danger of physical damage concerned'. 'To dispense with that essential ingredient ... would ... involve a radical departure from long-established authority.'

The student may wonder whether *Donoghue v Stevenson* or *Hedley Byrne* would have been decided in the way they were if the House of Lords in those cases had shown the same deference to precedent.

(b) The effect of a wider duty would be to create contractual-type obligations in the absence of a contractual relationship (e.g. in the case of a manufacturer a warranty to the ultimate consumer that the goods were as well designed, and free from defects as reasonable care could make them). In *D & F Estates* ([1988] 2 All ER at p. 1005) Lord Bridge cited with approval the opinion of Blackmun J in the decision of the Supreme Court of the United States of America in *East River Steamship Corpn v Transamerica Delaval Inc* 106 S Ct 2295 (1986) at 2300–2302 that the 'loss due to repair costs, descreased value, and lost profits is essentially the failure of the purchaser to receive the benefit of its bargain—traditionally the core concern of contract law', and that there is 'the need to keep products liability [i.e. tort law] and contract law in separate spheres and to maintain a realistic limitation on damages'. P. Cane (1989) 52 MLR 200 at 208–209 comments:

'None of these reasons seems very compelling. A rule allowing recovery for damage to the defective property is not indeterminate, nor would it impose unlimited liability if recovery were limited to the owner of the property (or, perhaps, in appropriate cases the occupier) at some relevant time. Furthermore repair costs, decreased value (in the sense of difference between price and actual value) and lost profits do not, as such, fall outside the province of the law of torts—they are recoverable as damages for negligent damage to property; they are only outside the province of the law of torts if awarded in circumstances which are themselves defined as falling outside the province of the law of torts. Finally, the simple assertion of a need to keep the spheres of tort and contract separate tells us nothing about where the border should be drawn.'

(c) It would be difficult to ascertain the standard of care by which the question of defectiveness was to be decided. Would this be the standard of care prescribed by the contract between the sub-contractors and the main contractor? Would the defendant be excused if the contract with the third party had been terminated (e.g. by frustration or on grounds of fundamental breach), or he had been relieved of his obligation to the contracting party to perform? Would any exclusion clauses in the contract apply? It is to be noted, however, that Lord Roskill in *Junior Books* saw no difficulty in applying the contractual standard to the tort action, nor did Robert Goff LJ in *The Aliakmon* [1985] QB 350 at 397–398. The latter also suggested, in the context of transferred loss (p. 208, ante), that the defendant could pose against the tort plaintiff all defences which are available to him against the other contracting party (see B. S. Markesinis (1987) 103 LQR 354 at 392–395). On the other hand, when *The Aliakmon* went to the House of Lords, Lord Brandon ([1986] AC 785 at 817), with whose speech the other members of the House agreed, did not find in Lord Roskill's comments in *Junior Books* concerning exclusion clauses 'any convincing legal basis for qualifying a duty of care owed by A to B by reference to a contract to which A is, but B is not, a party'. Compare the comments of Purchas LJ in *Pacific Associates Inc v Baxter* [1990] 1 QB 993 at 1022–1023 and consider also *Norwich City Council v Harvey* [1989] 1 All ER 1180; [1989] 1 WLR 828, on which see C. A. Hopkins [1990] CLJ 21.

5. The major question prompted by the cases in this section is why there is a duty of care in respect of false information or advice causing pure economic loss, at least to a limited class of plaintiffs, but no such duty in relation to the construction of buildings or the manufacture and supply of products? Why has the *Hedley Byrne* principle of detrimental reliance not been generalised into a general principle in 'breach of voluntary undertaking' situations? One of the reasons may be that the concept of reliance is very difficult to apply. As Robert Goff LJ remarked in *Muirhead v Industrial Tank Specialities Ltd* [1986] QB 507 at 527: 'There is, of course, a sense in which it can be said that every successful plaintiff in an action of negligence has relied on the defendant not to be negligent, as every motorist relies on every other motorist in the vicinity to drive carefully.' 'Reliance' was not used in *Hedley Byrne* in this wide sense, but rather in the narrower sense that the words or conduct of the defendant imply an undertaking to an identifiable plaintiff to act in a certain way. It is this narrow sense of 'reliance' which Lord Oliver appears to have had in mind when explaining the *Junior Books* case (Note 3, ante); see P. Cane (1989) 52 MLR 200 at 202 and 213. One function of the 'detrimental reliance' concept is to limit the class of potential plaintiffs, but it seems that this can be achieved just as well by a narrow definition of 'proximity': see e.g. the discussion of the floodgates argument by the High Court of Australia in *Caltex Oil (Australia) Pty Ltd v Dredge Willemstad* (1976) 136 CLR 529, where the majority of the court held that there was sufficient proximity to justify a claim for economic loss because the defendant knew (in the words of the headnote) 'that a particular person not merely a member of an unascertained class [would] be likely to suffer economic loss as a consequence of his negligence'.

This test of proximity has been widely applied in later cases in Commonwealth jurisdictions. The approach taken by the Privy Council in *Yuen Kun Yeu v A-G of Hong Kong* [1988] AC 175; [1987] 2 All ER 705 was to use the *absence* of reasonable reliance as one of the indications that there was insufficient proximity. It was decided that the Commissioner of Deposit-Taking Companies in Hong Kong did not owe a duty of care to members of the public who might be minded to invest in companies registered by the Commissioner to see that they did not suffer financial loss through the companies being carried on by their managers in a fraudulent fashion. Not only had the Commissioner not voluntarily assumed responsibility to them but it was neither reasonable nor justifiable for them to place reliance on the fact of registration as a guarantee of the soundness of a particular company, and so the relationship was not sufficiently close to found a duty of care: see further on this case, pp. 53 and 187, ante.

Another objection to the 'reliance' test is that it is not capable of explaining those 'breach of voluntary undertaking' situations where the plaintiff is owed a duty of care in respect of economic loss even though he has not relied on the undertaking (e.g. *Ross v Caunters* [1980] Ch 297; [1979] 3 All ER 580, p. 192, ante). We must, therefore, conclude that the 'breach of undertaking' situations in which damages for economic loss may be claimed are too varied and complex to be brought within a single, all-embracing principle such as detrimental reliance. A simple rule has, however, existed for over 100 years in respect of 'relational interests', that is, situations where the relationships between the parties are involuntary: see the next case.

2   Relational interests

(a)   Another's property

Spartan Steel and Alloys Ltd v Martin & Co (Contractors) Ltd
Court of Appeal [1972] 3 All ER 557

LORD DENNING MR: The plaintiffs, Spartan Steel & Alloys Ltd, have a factory in Birmingham where they manufacture stainless steel. The factory obtains its electricity by a direct cable from a power station of the Midlands Electricity Board.

In June 1969 contractors called Martin & Co (Contractors) Ltd, the defendants, were doing work on a road about a quarter of a mile away. They were going to dig up the road with a big power-driven excavating shovel. They made enquiries about the place of the cables, mains and so forth, under the road. They were given plans showing them. But unfortunately their men did not take reasonable care. The shovel damaged the cable which supplied electricity to the plaintiffs' works. The electricity board shut down the power whilst they mended the cable.

The factory was at that time working continuously for 24 hours all round the clock. The electric power was shut off at 7.40 pm on 12 June 1969, and was off for 14½ hours until it was restored at 10.00 am on 13 June 1969. This was all through the night and a couple of hours more. But, as this factory was doing night work, it suffered loss. At the time when the power was shut off, there was an arc furnace in which metal was being melted in order to be converted into ingots. Electric power was needed throughout in order to maintain the temperature and melt the metal. When the power failed, there was a danger that the metal might solidify in the furnace and do damage to the lining of the furnace. So the plaintiffs used oxygen to melt the material and poured it from a tap out of the furnace. But this meant that the melted material was of much less value. The physical damage was assessed at £368. In addition, if that particular melt had been properly completed, the plaintiffs would have made a profit on it of £400. Furthermore, during those 14½ hours, when the power was cut off, the plaintiffs would have been able to put four more melts through the furnace; and, by being unable to do so, they lost a profit of £1,767.

The plaintiffs claim all those sums as damages against the defendants for negligence. No evidence was given at the trial, because the defendants admitted that they had been negligent. The contest was solely on the amount of damages. The defendants take their stand on the recent decision in this court of *SCM (United Kingdom) Ltd v W. J. Whittall & Son Ltd.*[1] They admit that they are liable for the £368 physical damages. They did not greatly dispute that they are also liable for the £400 loss of profit on the first melt, because that was truly consequential on the physical damages and thus covered by *SCM v Whittall.*[1] But they deny that they are liable for the £1,767 for the other four melts. They say that was economic loss for which they are

---

1. [1971] 1 QB 337; [1970] 3 All ER 245.

not liable. The judge rejected their contention and held them liable for all the loss. The defendants appeal to this court. . . .

At bottom I think the question of recovering economic loss is one of policy. Whenever the courts draw a line to mark out the bounds of *duty*, they do it as a matter of policy so as to limit the responsibility of the defendant. Whenever the courts set bounds to the *damages* recoverable – saying that they are, or are not, too remote – they do it as matter of policy so as to limit the liability of the defendant.

In many of the cases where economic loss has been held not to be recoverable, it has been put on the ground that the defendant was under no *duty to the plain-tiff*. Thus where a person is injured in a road accident by the negligence of another, the negligent driver owes a duty to the injured man himself, but he owes no duty to the servant of the injured man: see *Best v Samuel Fox & Co Ltd*;[1] nor to the master of the injured man: *IRC v Hambrook*;[2] nor to anyone else who suffers loss because he had a contract with the injured man: see *Simpson & Co v Thomson*;[3] nor indeed to anyone who only suffers economic loss on account of the accident: see *Kirkham v Boughey*.[4] Likewise, when property is damaged by the negligence of another, the negligent tortfeasor owes a duty to the owner or possessor of the chattel, but not to one who suffers loss only because he had a contract entitling him to use the chattel or giving him a right to receive it at some later date: see *Elliot Steam Tug Co v Shipping Controller*[5] and *Margarine Union GmbH v Cambay Prince SS Co Ltd*.[6]

In other cases, however, the defendant seems clearly to have been under a duty to the plaintiff, but the economic loss has not been recovered because it is too remote. Take the illustration given by Blackburn J in *Cattle v Stockton Waterworks Co*[7] when water escapes from a reservoir and floods a coalmine where many men are working; those who had their tools or clothes destroyed could recover, but those who only lost their wages could not. Similarly, when the defendants' ship negligently sank a ship which was being towed by a tug, the owner of the tug lost his remuneration, but he could not recover it from the negligent ship although the same duty (of navigation with reasonable care) was owed to both tug and tow: see *Société Remorquage à Hélice v Bennetts*.[8] In such cases if the plaintiff or his property had been physically injured, he would have recovered; but, as he only suffered economic loss, he is held not entitled to recover. This is, I should think, because the loss is regarded by the law as too remote: see *King v Phillips*.[9]

On the other hand, in the cases where economic loss by itself has been held to be recoverable, it is plain that there was a duty to the plaintiff and the loss was not too remote. Such as when one ship negligently runs down another ship, and damages it, with the result that the cargo has to be discharged and reloaded. The negligent ship was already under a duty to the cargo-owners; and they can recover the cost of discharging and reloading it, as it is not too remote: see *Morrison SS Co Ltd v Greystoke Castle*.[10] Likewise, when a banker negligently gives a reference to one who acts on it, the duty is plain and the damage is not too remote: see *Hedley Byrne & Co Ltd v Heller & Partners Ltd*.[11]

---

1. [1952] AC 716 at 731; [1952] 2 All ER 394 at 398.
2. [1956] 2 QB 641 at 660; [1956] 3 All ER 338 at 339, 340.
3. (1877) 3 App Cas 279 at 289.
4. [1958] 2 QB 338 at 341; [1957] 3 All ER 153 at 155.
5. [1922] 1 KB 127 at 139.
6. [1969] 1 QB 219 at 251, 252; [1967] 3 All ER 775 at 794.
7. (1875) LR 10 QB 453 at 457; [1874–80] All ER Rep 220 at 223.
8. [1911] 1 KB 243 at 248.
9. [1953] 1 QB 429 at 439, 440; [1953] 1 All ER 617 at 622.
10. [1947] AC 265; [1946] 2 All ER 696.
11. [1964] AC 465; [1963] 2 All ER 575.

The more I think about these cases, the more difficult I find it to put each into its proper pigeon-hole. Sometimes I say: 'There was no duty.' In others I say: 'The damage was too remote.' So much so that I think the time has come to discard those tests which have proved so elusive. It seems to me better to consider the particular relationship in hand, and see whether or not, as a matter of policy, economic loss should be recoverable. Thus in *Weller & Co v Foot and Mouth Disease Research Institute*[1] it was plain that the loss suffered by the auctioneers was not recoverable, no matter whether it is put on the ground that there was no duty or that the damage was too remote. Again, in *Electrochrome Ltd v Welsh Plastics Ltd*[2] it is plain that the economic loss suffered by the plaintiffs' factory (due to the damage to the fire hydrant) was not recoverable, whether because there was no duty or that it was too remote.

So I turn to the relationship in the present case. It is of common occurrence. The parties concerned are the electricity board who are under a statutory duty to maintain supplies of electricity in their district; the inhabitants of the district, including this factory, who are entitled by statute to a continuous supply of electricity for their use; and the contractors who dig up the road. Similar relationships occur with other statutory bodies, such as gas and water undertakings. The cable may be damaged by the negligence of the statutory undertaker, or by the negligence of the contractor, or by accident without any negligence by anyone; and the power may have to be cut off whilst the cable is repaired. Or the power may be cut off owing to a short-circuit in the power house; and so forth. If the cutting off of the supply causes economic loss to the consumers, should it as matter of policy be recoverable? And against whom?

The first consideration is the position of the statutory undertakers. If the board do not keep up the voltage or pressure of electricity, gas or water—or, likewise, if they shut it off for repairs—and thereby cause economic loss to their consumers, they are not liable in damages, not even if the cause of it is due to their own negligence. The only remedy (which is hardly ever pursued) is to prosecute the board before the justices. Such is the result of many cases, starting with a water board: *Atkinson v Newcastle and Gateshead Waterworks Co*;[3] going on to a gas board: *Clegg, Parkinson & Co v Earby Gas Co*;[4] and then to an electricity company: *Stevens v Aldershot Gas, Water and District Lighting Co*.[5] In those cases the courts, looking at the legislative enactments, held that Parliament did not intend to expose the board to liability for damages to the inhabitants en masse: see what Lord Cairns LC said[6] and Wills J.[7] No distinction was made between economic loss and physical damage; and taken at their face value the reasoning would mean that the board was not liable for physical damage either. But there is another group of cases which go to show that, if the board, by their negligence in the conduct of their supply, cause direct physical damage to person or property, the cases seem to show that they are liable: see *Milnes v Huddersfield Corpn*[8] per Lord Blackburn; *Midwood & Co Ltd v Manchester Corpn*;[9] *Heard v Brymbo Steel Co Ltd*[10] and *Hartley v Mayoh & Co*.[11] But one thing is clear, the board have never been held liable for economic loss only.

1. [1966] 1 QB 569; [1965] 3 All ER 560.
2. [1968] 2 All ER 205.
3. (1877) 2 Ex D 441; [1874–80] All ER Rep 757.
4. [1896] 1 QB 592.
5. (1932) 102 LJKB 12.
6. In *Atkinson v Newcastle and Gateshead Waterworks Co* (1877) 2 Ex D at p. 445.
7. In *Clegg, Parkinson & Co v Earby Gas Co* [1896] 1 QB at p. 595.
8. (1886) 11 App Cas 511 at 530.
9. [1905] 2 KB 597.
10. [1947] KB 692.
11. [1954] 1 QB 383; [1954] 1 All ER 375.

If such be the policy of the legislature in regard to electricity boards, it would seem right for the common law to adopt a similar policy in regard to contractors. If the electricity boards are not liable for economic loss due to negligence which results in the cutting off of the supply, nor should a contractor be liable.

The second consideration is the nature of the hazard, namely, the cutting of the supply of electricity. This is a hazard which we all run. It may be due to a short circuit, to a flash of lightning, to a tree falling on the wires, to an accidental cutting of the cable, or even to the negligence of someone or other. And when it does happen, it affects a multitude of persons; not as a rule by way of physical damage to them or their property, but by putting them to inconvenience, and sometimes to economic loss. The supply is usually restored in a few hours, so the economic loss is not very large. Such a hazard is regarded by most people as a thing they must put up with – without seeking compensation from anyone. Some there are who install a stand-by system. Others seek refuge by taking out an insurance policy against breakdown in the supply. But most people are content to take the risk on themselves. When the supply is cut off, they do not go running round to their solicitor. They do not try to find out whether it was anyone's fault. They just put up with it. They try to make up the economic loss by doing more work next day. This is a healthy attitude which the law should encourage.

The third consideration is this. If claims for economic loss were permitted for this particular hazard, there would be no end of claims. Some might be genuine, but many might be inflated, or even false. A machine might not have been in use anyway, but it would be easy to put it down to the cut in supply. It would be well-nigh impossible to check the claims. If there was economic loss on one day, did the applicant do his best to mitigate it by working harder next day? And so forth. Rather than expose claimants to such temptation and defendants to such hard labour – on comparatively small claims – it is better to disallow economic loss altogether, at any rate when it stands alone, independent of any physical damage.

The fourth consideration is that, in such a hazard as this, the risk of economic loss should be suffered by the whole community who suffer the losses – usually many but comparatively small losses – rather than on the one pair of shoulders, that is, on the contractor on whom the total of them, all added together, might be very heavy.

The fifth consideration is that the law provides for deserving cases. If the defendant is guilty of negligence which cuts off the electricity supply and causes actual physical damage to person or property, that physical damage can be recovered; see *Baker v Crow Carrying Co Ltd*[1] referred to by Buckley LJ in *SCM v Whittall*[2] and also any economic loss truly consequential on the material damage: see *British Celanese Ltd v A H Hunt (Capacitors) Ltd*[3] and *SCM v Whittall*.[4] Such cases will be comparatively few. They will be readily capable of proof and will be easily checked. They should be and are admitted.

These considerations lead me to the conclusion that the plaintiffs should recover for the physical damage to the one melt (£368), and the loss of profit on that melt consequent thereon (£400); but not for the loss of profit on the four melts (£1,767), because that was economic loss independent of the physical damage. I would, therefore, allow the appeal and reduce the damages to £768.

EDMUND-DAVIES LJ (dissenting on the question of the pure economic loss): . . . For my part, I cannot see why the £400 loss of profit here sustained should be recoverable and not the £1,767. It is common ground that both types of loss were equally

---

1. (1 February 1960, unreported).
2. [1971] 1 QB at p. 356; [1970] 3 All ER at p. 261.
3. [1969] 2 All ER 1252; [1969] 1 WLR 959.
4. [1971] 1 QB 337; [1970] 3 All ER 245.

foreseeable and equally direct consequences of the defendants' admitted negligence, and the only distinction drawn is that the former figure represents the profit loss as a result of the physical damage done to the material in the furnace at the time when the power was cut off. But what has that purely fortuitous fact to do with legal principle? In my judgment, nothing. . . .

Having considered the intrinsic nature of the problem presented in this appeal, and having consulted the relevant authorities, my conclusion . . . is that an action lies in negligence for damages in respect of purely economic loss, provided that it was a reasonably foreseeable and direct consequence of failure in a duty of care. The application of such a rule can undoubtedly give rise to difficulties in certain sets of circumstances, but so can the suggested rule that economic loss may be recovered *provided* it is directly consequential on physical damage. Many alarming situations were conjured up in the course of counsel's arguments before us. In their way, they were reminiscent of those formerly advanced against awarding damages for nervous shock; for example, the risk of fictitious claims and expensive litigation, the difficulty of disproving the alleged cause and effect, and the impossibility of expressing such a claim in financial terms. But I suspect that they . . . would for the most part be resolved either on the ground that no duty of care was owed to the injured party or that the damages sued for were irrecoverable *not* because they were simply financial but because they were too remote. . . .

[LAWTON LJ delivered a judgment in favour of allowing the appeal and reducing the damages to £768.]

Appeal allowed.

Notes

1. This case affords the best illustration of the line drawn by the courts between (a) liability for negligently causing reasonably foreseeable physical harm to the plaintiff or his property which leads to economic loss to the plaintiff consequent upon that physical harm (the value of the melt actually in the furnace and the loss of profit on that melt, the first loss), and (b) no liability for reasonably foreseeable economic loss suffered by the plaintiff as the result of the defendant causing physical harm to a third person or his property (loss of profit on the four melts which they normally would have completed in the time that the electricity supply was cut-off, the second loss). The test used by the majority of the court is the (fortuitous) presence of physical damage to the property of the plaintiff. Edmund-Davies LJ (dissenting) regarded the second loss as recoverable because it was a 'direct consequence' of the breach of duty. This brings the issue within the sphere of remoteness of damage (p. 329, post) rather than the existence of a duty of care. In other words, since the plaintiff had suffered some recoverable foreseeable damage (the first loss) the plaintiff could also recover more remote kinds of damage provided these were reasonably foreseeable as a result of the defendant's negligence. Harris and Veljanovski, op cit, pp. 62–64 argue that these legal criteria have no economic relevance, and that the critical factors are (a) the nature of the precautions which both parties could have taken; and (b) the need to avoid crushing liability. In regard to both these factors it should be noted that in *Spartan Steel* the defendants knew there was a cable under the road which was a direct feeder from the electricity board to the plaintiffs' works, and the power line provided electricity only to the plaintiffs' works. 'Is there a defensible line to be drawn

between cases where only one (or a small number) is at risk, and cases where a large number of potential victims is at risk?' (ibid.). Compare the *Spartan Steel* case with *Ross v Caunters* [1980] Ch 297; [1979] 3 All ER 580, p. 192 ante (identifiable plaintiff allowed to recover loss of benefit under will); and also with *Caltex Oil (Australia) Pty Ltd v Dredge Willemstad* (1976) 136 CLR 529 (A negligently damaged oil pipeline belonging to B, causing loss to C who supplied oil *only* to B through it: held C were entitled to recover from A the cost of alternative means of transport until the pipeline could be used again).

2. In *Weller & Co v Foot & Mouth Disease Research Institute* [1966] 1 QB 569; [1965] 3 All ER 560 (referred to by Lord Denning p. 239, ante) the assumed facts were that there was an escape from the defendant's premises of foot and mouth disease virus which infected cattle on neighbouring land, that the plaintiffs were not in occupation of this land, that an order was made closing Guildford and Farnham markets as a result of the outbreak of the disease and that the plaintiffs who were cattle auctioneers suffered a loss of business because of this closure. It was further assumed that this loss was foreseeable and that the escape of the virus was caused by the defendant's negligence. Widgery J held that a duty of care was owed to the owners of the cattle in the neighbourhood but not to the plaintiffs who had no proprietary interest in anything which might conceivably be damaged by the virus if it escaped. In *The Irene's Success* [1982] QB 481; [1982] 1 All ER 218, Lloyd J explained the decision as being that 'the loss suffered by the plaintiffs, though foreseeable, was, as it were, at one remove from the physical damage to the cattle. If the defendants were to be liable to the plaintiffs as auctioneers why not, for example, to the transport contractors who would also foreseeably suffer economic loss as a result of the cattle being affected? And if the transport contractors could sue why not others as well? The number of potential plaintiffs would be almost unlimited.' Harris and Veljanovski, op cit, pp. 64–67, point out that 'the negligent act of the defendant did not directly affect the [auctioneers'] production activities, but only led to a change in the market for their services — a fall in demand which was similar to other falls caused by other fluctuations in the market resulting from non-negligent or political factors'. They argue that it was sufficient in this case for the defendant Institute to compensate the farmers; this would give them an incentive to take care in future. The auctioneers (whose fees could reflect the risks they took) would not suffer any permanent loss in the demand for their services; on the other hand, if the Institute had to compensate the auctioneers (and logically others whose markets were affected) they would be exposed to crushing liability which would halt or limit their research activities.

3. It was made clear by the House of Lords in *Esso Petroleum Co Ltd v Hall Russell & Co Ltd* [1989] AC 643; [1989] 1 All ER 37 that the mere fact that the plaintiff who has suffered economic loss has also sustained damage to his own property is not sufficient to entitle him to claim for the economic loss unless it is consequent upon, and not merely additional to, the damage to his property. The *Esso Bernicia* had collided with the jetty at Sullon Voe terminal in the Shetlands and bunker oil escaped polluting the foreshore. This had happened when a coupling blew out of a hydraulic pipe above the starboard engine of the *Stanechakker*, one of three tugs helping to berth the

Bernicia. A fire started and the towing line was cast off causing the *Bernicia* to go out of control. This action was raised by Esso, the shipowners, against Hall, Russell, the designers and builders of the *Stanechakker*, averring negligence. The claims were for (a) £170,000-odd for the value of bunker oil lost, cost of repair to the *Bernicia* etc; (b) £527,000 for sums paid by Esso to local crofters in respect of damage to sheep due to pollution of the foreshore; and (c) £3.7 m paid by Esso to BP, the terminal operators, to clean up the foreshore. These two last-mentioned sums had been paid in terms of an agreement, called TOVALOP, under which tanker operators have agreed *inter se* to assume liability to victims for pollution damage caused by oil escaping or discharged from their tankers. The House of Lords held that the physical damage to the *Bernicia*, loss of use and loss of bunker oil were reasonably foreseeable consequences of the negligence. However, they held that the payments to the crofters and to BP under TOVALOP were irrecoverable economic loss because they were not consequent upon the physical damage to the tanker, but a result of the damage to property of third parties (the sheep and terminal) which Esso had agreed under TOVALOP to indemnify. This is an application of the same principle which prevents C, an insurer of B's property from suing in its own name A, the tortfeasor who destroyed it, but C may be subrogated to B's rights and so entitled to sue in B's name having satisfied the claim: *Simpson v Thomson* (1877) 3 App Cas 279. In the *Esso Bernicia* case, Esso had not taken an assignation (known as an assignment in English law) of the crofters' and BP's claims against Hall Russell, and were not allowed to sue in their own name. For critical comment see Weir [1989] LMCLQ 1, and Hepple, All ER Rev 1989, p. 329.

4. The principle, accepted by the majority in *Spartan Steel*, that a person must have a proprietary interest (i.e. ownership or possession) in the damaged property at the time the damage was inflicted in order to recover economic loss which results from not being able to use the property was reaffirmed by the Privy Council, after a period of uncertainty, in *Candlewood Navigation Corpn Ltd v Mitsui OSK Lines Ltd, The Mineral Transporter* [1986] AC 1; [1985] 2 All ER 935, noted by M.A. Jones (1986) 102 LQR 13; A. Tettenborn [1986] CLJ 13. The first plaintiffs were the owners of the *Ibaraki Maru* which was damaged by the negligence of the defendant's vessel, *The Mineral Transporter*. At the time of the collision the *Ibaraki Maru* had been let on a bareboat charter to the second plaintiffs, who were liable under the terms of this charter to bear the cost of repairs. The effect of the bareboat charter was to put the second plaintiffs in possession of the vessel. The second plaintiffs had, in turn, re-let the vessel to the first plaintiffs under a time sub-charter, which did not confer possession on the first plaintiffs. The Privy Council held that the second plaintiffs, being in possession, were entitled to recover the cost of repairs from the defendants. But the first plaintiffs were not entitled to recover either (a) the hire charges they had to pay while the vessel was being repaired, or (b) their loss of profits during the same period. It was argued that the first plaintiffs, as owners, were entitled to sue but this was rejected on the ground that they had suffered the loss as time sub-charterers, not owners. The example may be put in non-marine terms. If B, the owner of a van, lets it to C on a self-drive basis and then engages C under a separate contract to do some removals for him using the van, B would not be able to recover from A, who negligently damaged

the van, the hire charges for another van and his loss of pofits while the van was being repaired. This assumes that C was obliged to repair the van. If C was under no such obligation and had returned it to B in a damaged condition B, as owner, could sue. What would the position be if C failed to repair in breach of his contract with B (a point left open by the Privy Council)? More generally, does it make sense 'that the tortfeasor was able to escape from paying for part of the loss for which he was responsible merely because that loss was divided between two victims' (see Hepple All ER Rev 1985, p. 295)? *The Mineral Transporter* was approved and followed by the House of Lords in *Leigh and Sillivan Ltd v Aliakmon Shipping Co Ltd* [1986] AC 785; [1986] 2 All ER 145 (p. 203 ante).

(b) Another's life

(i) Transmission of causes of action on death

The Law Reform (Miscellaneous Provisions) Act 1934

1. Effect of death on certain causes of action. — (1) Subject to the provisions of this section, on the death of any person after the commencement of this Act all causes of action subsisting against or vested in him shall survive against, or, as the case may be, for the benefit of, his estate. Provided that this subsection shall not apply to causes of action for defamation. . . .

(1A) The right of a person to claim under section 1A of the Fatal Accidents Act 1976 (bereavement) shall not survive for the benefit of his estate on his death.[1]

(2) Where a cause of action survives as aforesaid for the benefit of the estate of a deceased person, the damages recoverable for the benefit of the estate of that person: —

(a) shall not include —
 (i) any exemplary damages;
 (ii) any damages for loss of income in respect of any period after that person's death;[2]
 . . .
(c) where the death of that person has been caused by the act or omission which gives rise to the cause of action, shall be calculated without reference to any loss or gain to his estate consequent on his death, except that a sum in respect of funeral expenses may be included.

(4) Where damage has been suffered by reason of any act or omission in respect of which a cause of action would have subsisted against any person if that person had not died before or at the same time as the damage was suffered, there shall be deemed, for the purposes of this Act, to have been subsisting against him before his death such cause of action in respect of that act or omission as would have subsisted if he had died after the damage was suffered.

(5) The rights conferred by this Act for the benefit of the estates of deceased persons shall be in addition to and not in derogation of any rights conferred on the dependants of deceased persons by the Fatal Accidents Acts 1846–1908,[3] . . . and so much of this Act as relates to causes of action against the estates of deceased

---

1. [Inserted by the Administration of Justice Act 1982, s. 4.]
2. [Ibid.]
3. [This now includes a reference to the Fatal Accidents Act 1976.]

persons shall apply in relation to causes of action under the said Acts as it applies in relation to other causes of action not expressly excepted from the operation of subsection (1) of this section.

Notes

1. *Section 1 (1)*. This Act comes into play if either the plaintiff or the defendant is killed instantaneously or otherwise dies before the commencement of proceedings. The Act enables the personal representatives of the deceased victim to recover such damages as he might have received had he lived, subject to certain exceptions. Likewise, if the tortfeasor dies there can be recovery against the estate. (As regards the exclusion of actions for defamation, see p. 620, post.) Quite independently of the survival of the plaintiff's cause of action under this Act, the surviving dependants have their own cause of action for economic loss which they have suffered as a result of the death of their breadwinner (p. 240, post) (s. 1(5)).

2. *Section 1(1A)*. The action for damages for bereavement is discussed p. 243, post.

3. *Section 1(2)(a)*. (i) Exemplary damages are discussed in chap 8, p. 407, post. (ii) 'Loss of income in respect of any period after that person's death': This was excluded from survival by s. 4(2) of the Administration of Justice Act 1982, which gives effect to the substance of recommendations by the Law Commission (Law Com. No. 56, Draft Bill, cl. 16(3)), and the Pearson Commission vol. 1, paras. 433–437. The intention is to exclude the possibility of double recovery against the defendant. This possibility arose because in *Pickett v British Rail Engineering Ltd* [1980] AC 136; [1979] 1 All ER 774 (p. 421, post), the House of Lords decided that a *living* plaintiff could claim damages in respect of the income which he would have earned during the years of his life which he expects to 'lose' as a result of the tort, and in *Gammell v Wilson* [1982] AC 27; [1981] 1 All ER 578, the House of Lords held that this applied as well to a person who had died when the action was commenced. 'Double' recovery could arise if either (a) the dependants were not the beneficiaries of the estate, so that the defendants would have to pay damages both to the estate for the 'lost' years, and to the dependants for their loss of dependency in those years, or (b) the damages awarded to the estate for the 'lost' years were substantially larger than the damages for loss of dependency; in this case, if the dependants were the beneficiaries of the estate they would be entitled to the larger amount. P. Cane and D. Harris (1983) 46 MLR 478 criticise the new s. 1(2)(*a*)(ii) as a 'lesson in how not to reform the law' on a number of grounds. One of these is that the abolition of damages for the 'lost' years in *all* claims by estates, even where the dependants have no claim for loss of dependency (e.g. where the injury to the plaintiff caused a loss in his earnings but he died from some other nontortious cause), leaves the dependants in some cases without provision. On the other hand, the beneficiaries of the estate may still receive the windfall of damages for loss of amenity suffered by (even) an unconscious victim before he died (p. 413, post). It is also worth nothing that s. 1(2)(*a*)(ii) refers only to loss of 'income'. This leaves open the possibility that the estate may claim for the loss of opportunity to inherit capital, which falls within the *Pickett* rule: see *Adsett v West* [1983] QB 826; [1983] 2 All ER 985.

4. *Section 1(2)(c)*. The damages recoverable are the same as would have been recovered by the victim subject to the exceptions mentioned. Apart from funeral expenses, this is true also where the death has been caused by the act or omission which gives rise to the cause of action, for example the loss of an annuity ceasing on death or the gain arising from a life insurance policy payable upon death are disregarded.

5. *Section 1(4)*. This deals with the situation where the tortfeasor dies.

(ii) Death as a cause of action

Admiralty Commissioners *v* Steamship Amerika (Owners). *The Amerika* House of Lords [1916–17] All ER Rep 177

A submarine sank due to the negligent navigation of the respondents' steamship. All but one of the crew were drowned. The Commissioners of Admiralty brought this action to recover the damage they had sustained. This included the capitalised amount of pensions payable by them to relatives of the deceased.

The House of Lords dismissed an appeal from a decision of the Court of Appeal which had disallowed this as an item of damages. Their Lordships held that (1) the payments had been made on compassionate grounds; since a person may not increase his claim for damages by a voluntary act, the payments were not recoverable from the tortfeasor; (2) the rule in *Baker v Bolton* (set out in Lord Sumner's speech, post) applied.

LORD SUMNER: This appeal has been brought principally to test the rule in *Baker v Bolton*,[1] that 'in a civil court the death of a human being cannot be complained of as an injury', a rule which has long been treated as universally applicable at common law. Some attempt was made to contest it only in its application to the case of master and servant. I will discuss both the narrower and the wider proposition, but it is clear that the action was not brought for the loss to a master of the services of his employee, but for the respondents' bad navigation, which sank the Crown's submarine, and the item of damage now in dispute, namely, pensions and allowances to dependants of seamen who were drowned, was claimed merely as one of the natural consequences of the tort, which consisted in sinking the ship. . . .

Never during the many centuries that have passed since reports of the decisions of English courts first began has the recovery of damages for the death of a human being as a civil injury been recorded. Since Lord Ellenborough's time the contrary has been uniformly decided by the Court of Exchequer and by the Court of Appeal. In addition to the weight of Lord Ellenborough's name (no mean authority even when sitting at nisi prius in spite of Lord Campbell's sneer), the rule has been definitely asserted by Lord Selborne (*Clarke v Carfin Coal Co* [1891] AC 412 at 414), Lord Bowen (*The Vera Cruz (No 2)* (1884) 9 PD 96 at 101), and Lord Alverstone and Lord Gorell (*Clark v London General Omnibus Co Ltd*[2]). It has been accepted as the rule of the common law by the Supreme Court of the Dominion of Canada (*Re The Garland, Monaghan v Horn*[3]), and the Supreme Court of the United States of America (*The Corsair*[4]). That the rule has also received statutory recognition appears to me

---

1. (1808) 1 Camp 493 per Lord Ellenborough.
2. [1906] 2 KB 648.
3. (1881) 7 SCR 409.
4. 145 US 335 (1892).

to be abundantly plain. I agree that the preamble to s. 1 of the Fatal Accidents Act 1846, should be read as applying to the particular defect in the existing law, which it was passed to remedy, namely, the disadvantageous position of widows and children, and not to the limited rights of masters and employers though only Bramwell B's intrepid individualism could dismiss it as a 'loose recital in an incorrectly drawn section of a statute, on which the courts had to put a meaning from what it did not rather than what it did say' (*Osborn v Gillett* (1873) LR 8 Exch 88 at 95). Still I think that the view taken by the legislature in 1846 is clear. . . . It provided a new cause of action and did not merely regulate or enlarge an old one. It excluded Scotland from its operation because a sufficient remedy already existed there, when in England none existed at all. So much seems to me to be indubitable. It did not deal with the case of master and servant as such, presumably because the legislature found nothing in the common law rule in this regard which called for reconsideration. . . .

[EARL LOREBURN LC and LORD PARKER OF WADDINGTON delivered speeches to the same effect.]

Hansard's Parliamentary Debates, Third Series, House of Lords, 24 April 1846, cols. 967–968

LORD CAMPBELL (moving the second reading of the Death By Accident Compensation Bill [which, when enacted, became popularly known as Lord Campbell's Act, and was given the title the Fatal Accidents Act by the Short Titles Act 1896]) . . . said that he had a great respect for the common law; but still he felt that there could be no doubt that some of its doctrines were not applicable to the present state of society. One of these doctrines was that the life of a man was so valuable that they could not put any estimate upon it in case of a death by accident; and, therefore, if a man had his leg broken, on account of negligence on the part of coach-proprietors or of a railway company, he had his remedy in a court of justice; but if the negligence were still grosser, and if a life were destroyed, there was no remedy whatever. In Scotland, and in foreign countries, the general rule was that where there was a wrong which worked injuriously to another, the law gave compensation . . . He was sorry to perceive that some disposition appeared to exist among hon. and learned gentlemen elsewhere to oppose this measure; but this he could say that his noble and learned Friend the Lord Chief Justice of England has expressed his unqualified approbation of its merits. Some of his learned Friends thought, however, that the law of England was absolute perfection, and that any attempt to infringe it should be resisted. He was told that resistance to this measure, in the other House of Parliament, would be also increased by the influence of the railway companies there, and that the influence was so great that one railway company alone could muster not less than eighty votes. . . .

Note

For a critique of the historical reasoning in *The Amerika* see W. S. Holdsworth, *History of English Law*, vol. iii, pp. 231–236 and Appendix viii, pp. 676–677.

The Fatal Accidents Act 1976

1. Right of action for wrongful act causing death. (1) If death is caused by any wrongful act, neglect or default which is such as would (if death had not ensued) have entitled the person injured to maintain an action and recover damages in respect thereof, the person who would have been liable if death had not ensued shall be liable to an action for damages, notwithstanding the death of the person injured.

(2) Subject to section 1A(2) below, every such action shall be for the benefit of the

dependants of the person ('the deceased') whose death has been so caused.

(3) In this Act 'dependant' means –

(a) the wife or husband or former wife or husband of the deceased;

(b) any person who –

(i) was living with the deceased in the same household immediately before the date of the death; and

(ii) had been living with the deceased in the same household for at least two years before that date; and

(iii) was living during the whole of that period as the husband or wife of the deceased;

(c) any parent or other ascendant of the deceased;

(d) any person who was treated by the deceased as his parent;

(e) any child or other descendant of the deceased;

(f) any person (not being a child of the deceased) who, in the case of any marriage to which the deceased was at any time a party, was treated by the deceased as a child of the family in relation to that marriage;

(g) any person who is, or is the issue of, a brother, sister, uncle or aunt of the deceased.

(4) The reference to the former wife or husband of the deceased in subsection (3)(a) above includes a reference to a person whose marriage to the deceased has been annulled or declared void as well as a person whose marriage to the deceased has been dissolved.

(5) In deducing any relationship for the purposes of subsection (3) above –

(a) any relationship by affinity shall be treated as a relationship by consanguinity, any relationship of the half blood as a relationship of the whole blood, and the stepchild of any person as his child, and

(b) an illegitimate person shall be treated as the legitimate child of his mother and reputed father.

(6) Any reference in this Act to injury includes any disease and any impairment of a person's physical or mental condition.

1A. Bereavement. – (1) An action under this Act may consist of or include a claim for damages for bereavement.

(2) A claim for damages for bereavement shall only be for the benefit –

(a) of the wife or husband of the deceased; and

(b) where the deceased was a minor who was never married –

(i) of his parents, if he was legitimate; and

(ii) of his mother, if he was illegitimate.

(3) Subject to subsection (5) below, the sum to be awarded as damages under this section shall be £3,500 [£7,500 from 1st April 1991].

(4) Where there is a claim for damages under this section for the benefit of both the parents of the deceased, the sum awarded shall be divided equally between them (subject to any deduction falling to be made in respect of costs not recovered from the defendant).

(5) The Lord Chancellor may by order made by statutory instrument, subject to annulment in pursuance of a resolution of either House of Parliament, amend this section by varying the sum for the time being specified in subsection (3) above.

2. Persons entitled to bring the action. – (1) The action shall be brought by and in the name of the executor or administrator of the deceased.

(2) If –

(a) there is no executor or administrator of the deceased, or

(b) no action is brought within six months after the death by and in the name of an executor or administrator of the deceased,

the action may be brought by and in the name of all or any of the persons for whose benefit an executor or administrator could have brought it.

(3) Not more than one action shall lie for and in respect of the same subject matter of complaint.

(4) The plaintiff in the action shall be required to deliver to the defendant or his solicitor full particulars of the persons for whom and on whose behalf the action is brought and of the nature of the claim in respect of which damages are sought to be recovered.

3. Assessment of damages. — (1) In the action such damages, other than damages for bereavement, may be awarded as are proportioned to the injury resulting from the death to the dependants respectively.

(2) After deducting the costs not recovered from the defendant any amount recovered otherwise than as damages for bereavement shall be divided among the dependants in such shares as may be directed.

(3) In an action under this Act where there fall to be assessed damages payable to a widow in respect of the death of her husband there shall not be taken into account the re-marriage of the widow or her propects of re-marriage.

(4) In an action under this Act where there fall to be assessed damages payable to a person who is a dependant by virtue of section 1(3)(*b*) above in respect of the death of the person with whom the dependant was living as husband or wife there shall be taken into account (together with any other matter that appears to the court to be relevant to the action) the fact that the dependant had no enforceable right to financial support by the deceased as a result of their living together.

(5) If the dependants have incurred funeral expenses in respect of the deceased, damages may be awarded in respect of those expenses.

(6) Money paid into court in satisfaction of a cause of action under this Act may be in one sum without specifying any person's share.

4. Assessment of damages: disregard of benefits. — In assessing damages in respect of a person's death in an action under this Act, benefits which have accrued or will or may accrue to any person from his estate or otherwise as a result of his death shall be disregarded.[1]

5. Contributory negligence. — Where any person dies as the result partly of his own fault and partly of the fault of any other person or persons, and accordingly if an action were brought for the benefit of the estate under the Law Reform (Miscellaneous Provisions) Act 1934 the damages recoverable would be reduced under section 1(1) of the Law Reform (Contributory Negligence) Act 1945, any damages recoverable in an action . . . [2] under this Act shall be reduced to a proportionate extent.

Notes

1. The Fatal Accidents Act (Lord Campbell's Act) was first passed in 1846. The present Act, consolidating earlier legislation, was itself amended in important respects by the Administration of Justice Act 1982 in the light of recommendations by the Law Commission (Law Com. No. 56) and the Pearson Commission (vol. 1, paras. 399–477 and 537–539). It is to be noted that one of the changes made is that benefits derived from the deceased's estate are now disregarded in the assessment of damages for lost dependency (s. 4, and see p. 238, ante). Has the Act outlived its usefulness? See S. M. Waddams (1984) 47 MLR 437.

---

1. [Sections 1–4 were substituted by s. 3 of the Administration of Justice Act 1982.]
2. [Words deleted by s. 4(2) of the Administration of Justice Act 1982.]

2. *Section 1(1) '... would (if death had not ensued) have entitled the person injured to maintain an action'.* The dependants have no right of action if the deceased himself could not have sued during his lifetime. The defences of volenti non fit injuria and illegality might avail a defendant who killed the deceased during a criminal affray instigated by the deceased for the purpose of harming the defendant: *Murphy v Culhane* [1977] QB 94; [1976] 3 All ER 533 (p. 594, post). The dependants may also be barred if the support they were afforded before the death of the deceased emanated from the proceeds of crime: *Burns v Edman* [1970] 2 QB 541; [1970] 1 All ER 886, noted p. 401, post, and see the questions p. 400, post concerning the views expressed in *Kirkham v Chief Constable of the Greater Manchester Police* [1990] 3 All ER 246; [1990] 2 WLR 927.

3. *Section 1(2)-(5): classes of dependants.* Although the action must be brought by and in the name of the executor or administrator of the deceased (s. 2), it exists for the benefit of those classes of dependants set out in the Act. In respect of the claim for loss of dependency, among the most important additions by the Administration of Justice Act 1982 were the former wife or husband of the deceased (s. 1(3)(*a*)) and the so-called 'common law spouse' (s. 1(3)(*b*)), but in assessing damages payable to the latter account must be taken of the fact that the dependant has no enforceable right to financial support (s. 3(4)). The claim in respect of bereavement (s. 1A) may be brought only by a far narrower class of mourners, namely the (lawful) wife or husband of the deceased, the parents of a legitimate child or the mother of an illegitimate child. The Act creates an exception to the common law rule (p. 239, ante) so no classes other than those named may sue for economic loss.

4. *Section 1A: bereavement.* Section 1(1) of the Administration of Justice Act 1982 abolished the former head of damages in respect of loss of expectation of life caused to the injured person by his injuries. The conventional sum awarded (not exceeding £1,250 in respect of a child) under this head could survive for the benefit of the estate. The new claim is analogous to that in Scotland under s. 1(4) of the Damages (Scotland) Act 1976 in respect of 'such non-patrimonial benefit as the relative might have been expected to derive from the deceased's society and guidance if he had not died'.

5. *Section 3: assessment of damages.* The method of assessing damages under the Fatal Accidents Act was enunciated by Lord Wright in *Davies v Powell Duffryn Associated Collieries Ltd* [1942] AC 601; [1942] 1 All ER 657:

'The starting point is the amount of wages which the deceased was earning, the ascertainment of which to some extent may depend upon the regularity of his employment. Then there is an estimate of how much was required or expected for his own personal and living expenses. The balance will give a datum or base figure which will generally be turned into a lump sum by taking a certain number of years' purchase. That sum, however, has to be taxed down by having due regard to uncertainties.'

In other words, the annual value of the dependency is estimated (this is called the multiplicand) and is multiplied by a figure related to how long the dependency would have lasted (the multiplier). For various reasons (see p. 430, post) this will usually not be greater than 16, however many years the dependency would have lasted. In *Graham v Dodds* [1983] 2 All ER 953; [1983] 1 WLR 808, the House of Lords held that this multiplier is to be calculated from the date of death rather than the date of the trial of the action, otherwise 'the longer the trial of the dependants' claims could be delayed the more they would eventually recover' (per Lord Bridge at p. 958). As regards the effect of inflation, see the speech of Lord Scarman in *Lim Poh Choo v Camden and Islington Area Health Authority* [1980] AC 174; [1979] 2 All ER 910 (p. 410, post).

6. *Section 3(2)* contains provisions formerly in s. 4(1) of the Law Reform (Miscellaneous Provisions) Act 1971 because Parliament agreed with Phillimore J in *Buckley v John Allen and Ford (Oxford) Ltd* [1967] 2 QB 637 at 644, that it was distasteful for a judge to have to put a money value upon a widow's chances of remarriage. The resulting legislation contains what the Pearson Commission (vol. I, para. 411) described as 'the manifest absurdity of awarding damages for a loss which is known to have ceased', and accordingly it recommended (para. 412) that the remarriage of a widow or widower before trial should be taken into account. The Law Commission (Law Com. No. 56, draft Bill cl. 9(b)) also proposed removing two further anomalies, by making the provision apply to claims made by children of the deceased, and to a claim by a widower. If the Pearson Commission's proposals for periodic payments (p. 430, post) were adopted, the problem would take on a new aspect. The Commission was divided as to whether or not such benefits should cease on remarriage, with the possibility of a dowry in the form of a lump sum equivalent to five years' compensation.

7. *Section 5* has the effect of allowing a reduction of damages if the deceased was contributorily negligent. What if the *dependant* was partly responsible for the breadwinner's death? In *Mulholland v McCrea* [1961] NI 135 the deceased was a passenger in a car driven by her husband. The husband was partly responsible for the accident. He claimed as personal representative under the Fatal Accidents Acts and under the Northern Irish Law Reform (Miscellaneous Provisions) Act 1937 (which corresponds to the English Act of 1934). The Northern Irish Court of Appeal held by a majority that the amount awarded to the husband as dependant should be reduced having regard to his share in the responsibility for his wife's death. However, the negligence of one dependant cannot affect the claim of another dependant. In *Dodds v Dodds* [1978] QB 543; [1978] 2 All ER 539, the deceased was killed wholly as a result of his wife's negligence. It was conceded that she had no claim as a dependant, but this did not affect her son's claim as dependant against her (in effect against the insurers standing behind her).

Davies *v* Taylor House of Lords [1972] 3 All ER 836

LORD REID: . . . The appellant is the widow of a man who was killed in a road accident owing to the negligence of the respondent. She claims under s. 2 of the Fatal Accidents Act 1846. To succeed she must show that she has suffered 'injury' resulting from her husband's death. Admittedly the injury must be of a financial character. In the ordinary case where the spouses were living together on the husband's earnings what the widow loses is the prospect of future financial support. There can be no question of proving as a fact that she would have received a certain amount of benefit. No one can know what might have happened had he not been killed. But the value of the prospect chance or probability of support can be estimated by taking all significant factors into account. But, perhaps on an application of the de minimis principle, speculative possibilities would be ignored. I think that must apply equally whether the contention is that for some reason or reasons the support might have increased, decreased, or ceased altogether. The court or jury must do its best to evaluate all the chances, large or small, favourable or unfavourable.

The peculiarity in the present case is that the appellant had left her husband some five weeks before his death and there was no immediate prospect of her returning to him. He wanted her to come back but she was unwilling to come. But she says that there was a prospect or chance or probability that she might have returned to him later and it is only in that event that she would have benefited from his survival. To my mind the issue and the sole issue is whether that chance or probability was substantial. If it was it must be evaluated. If it was a mere possibility it must be ignored. Many different words could be and have been used to indicate the dividing line. I can think of none better than 'substantial' on the one hand, or 'speculative' on the other. It must be left to the good sense of the tribunal to decide on broad lines, without regard to legal niceties, but on a consideration of all the facts in proper perspective.

I am well aware of the fact that in real life chances rarely are or can be estimated on mathematical terms. But for simplicity or argument let me suppose two cases of a widow who had separated from her husband before he was killed. In one case it is estimated that the chance that she would have returned to him is a 60 per cent probability (more likely than not) but in the other the estimate of that chance is a 40 per cent probability (quite likely but less than an even chance). In each case the tribunal would determine what its award would have been if the spouses had been living together when the husband was killed, and then discount it or scale it down to take account of the probability of her not returning to him.

But in the present case the trial judge applied a different test. He held that there was an onus on the appellant to prove that on a balance of probabilities she had an expectation of continued dependency — that it was more probable than not that there would have been a reconciliation. In fairness to him I must note that he understood that this had been agreed by counsel. But we were informed that that was not so and counsel for the respondent very properly did not seek to found on this. I think that the learned judge was misled.

When the question is whether a certain thing is or is not true — whether a certain event did or did not happen — then the court must decide one way or the other. There is no question of chance or probability. Either it did or it did not happen. But the standard of civil proof is a balance of probabilities. If the evidence shows a balance in favour of it having happened then it is proved that it did in fact happen. But here we are not and could not be seeking a decision either that the wife would or that she would not have returned to her husband. You can prove that a past event happened, but you cannot prove that a future event will happen and I do not think that the law is so foolish as to suppose that you can. All that you can do is to evaluate the chance. Sometimes it is virtually 100 per cent, sometimes virtually nil. But often it is somewhere in between. And if it is somewhere in between I do not see much difference between a probability of 51 per cent and a probability of 49 per cent.

'Injury' in the Fatal Accidents Act 1846 does not and could not possibly mean loss of a certainty. It must and can only mean loss of a chance. The chance may be a probability of over 99 per cent but it is still only a chance. So I can see no merit in adopting here the test used for proving whether a fact did or did not happen. There it must be all or nothing.

If the balance of probability were the proper test what is to happen in the two cases which I have supposed of a 60 per cent and a 40 per cent probability? The 40 per cent case will get nothing but what about the 60 per cent case? Is it to get a full award on the basis that it has been proved that the wife would have returned to her husband? That would be the logical result. I can see no ground at all for saying that the 40 per cent case fails altogether but the 60 per cent case gets 100 per cent. But it would be almost absurd to say that the 40 per cent case gets nothing while the 60 per cent case award is scaled down to that proportion of what the award would have been if the spouses had been living together. That would be applying two different rules to the two cases. So I reject the balance of probability test in this case.

But I agree with your Lordships that even on the test which I think ought to be applied the appellant has not shewn any significant chance or probability that she suffered any injury financially by her husband's death. So I am of opinion that this appeal must be dismissed.

[LORD MORRIS OF BORTH-Y-GEST, VISCOUNT DILHORNE, LORD SIMON OF GLAISDALE and LORD CROSS OF CHELSEA delivered speeches in favour of dismissing the appeal.]

5 Breach of duty

The tort of negligence, as its very name implies, requires fault to be proved against the defendant. If there is a duty of care imposed upon the defendant, the plaintiff must prove inter alia that the defendant acted, or omitted to act, negligently. This is sometimes called the 'negligence issue' and it is with this issue that the materials in this chapter are concerned. The courts are not consistent in their terminology however, and not infrequently the word 'duty' is used in relation to this issue (e.g. *Haley v London Electricity Board* [1965] AC 778; [1964] 3 All ER 185, p. 268, post). The student must therefore question the sense in which the judges use this concept. The standard of care which is formulated is that of the 'reasonable man', but it is important to realise that he is a fictional character, the reference to whom is a thin disguise for the value judgment which is made by the judge; nevertheless, as has been pointed out (M. A. Millner (1976) 92 LQR 131 at 133), 'by and large there is a substantial measure of objectivity in the assessment of prudent and sensible behaviour, reflecting the behavioural norms of the time and place, even though it be filtered . . . through the judge's personal experience'. Although in general the courts will hold negligent anyone who has fallen below the standard of the reasonable man (but see the heading 'Infants', p. 264, post), the amount of care and skill required of the defendant may be greater than that which could be expected of the ordinary man in the street (e.g. where he is a member of a trade or profession or holds himself out as possessing a particular skill, p. 258, post). The cases reveal the factors which the courts take into account in deciding whether a person has been negligent. This is essentially a balancing process, but for the plaintiff it is vital that, at the end of the day, the scales are tipped in his favour. Yet this may be a difficult task for the plaintiff. His case may founder for lack of witnesses – the victim of a 'hit-and-run' driver is the most obvious but not the only example. Thus the practical problem of proving negligence, even though the plaintiff may be assisted in certain cases by the maxim res ipsa loquitur or by statute (pp. 286–297, post), should not be underestimated.

It has been pointed out that one merit of the present system is that the courts may exercise some influence in raising standards in businesses or professions by deciding that a defendant has still been negligent, although he has adhered to a common practice (p. 276, post). In many cases it will be the reaction, not of the defendant, but of his insurers which will be more important (see *Clerk & Lindsell*, para. 10–75; cf. *Atiyah*, pp. 499–506).

For an appraisal of the fault principle generally in the law of tort, see *Atiyah*, chap. 19; *Williams & Hepple*, pp. 135–142. See further T. Honoré (1988) 104 LQR 530; *Harris et al*, chap. 4. Recent judicial dissatisfaction with the requirement of fault can be found in *Ashcroft v Mersey Regional Health*

Authority [1983] 2 All ER 245 (medical treatment) and *Snelling v Whitehead* (1975) Times, 31st July (road accident). In the latter case, for example, in which a seriously injured child failed to recover damages because the defendant driver was not proved to have been negligent, Lord Wilberforce felt that the case was one 'which should attract automatic compensation regardless of any question of fault'. The Pearson Commission considered both these areas. For its views on road accidents, see vol. 1, chap. 18 of the Report. In relation to medical injuries (discussed in vol. 1, chap. 24), the Commission concluded that a no-fault scheme should not be introduced for medical accidents (para. 1370) (though it favoured strict liability to volunteers for medical research or clinical trials who suffer severe damage (para. 1341)).

1   The reasonable person

(a)   The average standard

Glasgow Corporation *v* Muir House of Lords [1943] 2 All ER 44

A church party, desiring accommodation where they could eat their tea, obtained permission for 12s 6d to use the tea room in a mansion house belonging to the appellants. They had to carry their tea urn to the mansion house, and the route to the tea room then lay along a passage-way, the width of which narrowed from five feet to three feet three inches. There were some children from another party buying sweets and ices at a counter at the beginning of this passage and, just after McDonald (a church officer) and Taylor, who were carrying the urn, had turned down the passage, the church officer let go of one handle of the urn, and the scalding tea which escaped injured six children. The action brought on their behalf was grounded on the alleged negligence of Mrs Alexander (the manageress) who had given the permission to use the tea room. The First Division of the Court of Session reversed the dismissal of the action by the Lord Ordinary. On appeal to the House of Lords:

LORD MACMILLAN: My Lords, the degree of care for the safety of others which the law requires human beings to observe in the conduct of their affairs varies according to the circumstances. There is no absolute standard, but it may be said generally that the degree of care required varies directly with the risk involved. Those who engage in operations inherently dangerous must take precautions which are not required of persons engaged in the ordinary routine of daily life. It is no doubt true that in every act which an individual performs there is present a potentiality of injury to others. All things are possible and, indeed, it has become proverbial that the unexpected always happens. But while the precept *alterum non laedere* requires us to abstain from intentionally injuring others, it does not impose liability for every injury which our conduct may occasion. In Scotland, at any rate, it has never been a maxim of the law that a man acts at his peril. Legal liability is limited to those consequences of our acts which a reasonable man of ordinary intelligence and experience so acting would have in contemplation. . . .

The standard of foresight of the reasonable man is in one sense an impersonal test. It eliminates the personal equation and is independent of the idiosyncrasies of the particular person whose conduct is in question. Some persons are by nature unduly timorous and imagine every path beset with lions; others, of more robust temperament, fail to foresee or nonchalantly disregard even the most obvious dangers. The reasonable man is presumed to be free both from over-apprehension and from over-confidence. But there is a sense in which the standard of care of the reasonable man involves in its application a subjective element. It is still left to the judge to decide what in the circumstances of the particular case the reasonable man would have had in contemplation and what accordingly the party sought to be made liable ought to have foreseen. Here there is room for diversity of view, as, indeed, is well illustrated in the present case. What to one judge may seem far-fetched may seem to another both natural and probable.

... The question, as I see it, is whether Mrs Alexander, when she was asked to allow a tea urn to be brought into the premises under her charge, ought to have had in mind that it would require to be carried through a narrow passage in which there were a number of children and that there would be a risk of the contents of the urn being spilt and scalding some of the children. If as a reasonable person she ought to have had these considerations in mind, was it her duty to require that she should be informed of the arrival of the urn and, before allowing it to be carried through the narrow passage, to clear all the children out of it, in case they might be splashed with scalding water?

The urn was an ordinary medium-sized cylindrical vessel of about 15 ins. diameter and about 16 ins. in height, made of light sheet metal with a fitting lid, which was closed. It had a handle at each side. Its capacity was about 9 gallons, but it was only a third or a half full.[1] It was not in itself an inherently dangerous thing and could be carried quite safely and easily by two persons exercising ordinary care. A caterer, called as a witness on behalf of the pursuers, who had large experience of the use of such urns, said that he had never had a mishap with an urn while it was being carried. The urn was in charge of two responsible persons, McDonald, the church officer, and the lad Taylor, who carried it between them. When they entered the passage-way they called out to the children there congregated to keep out of the way and the children drew back to let them pass. Taylor who held the front handle had safely passed the children when, for some unexplained reason, McDonald loosened hold of the other handle, the urn tilted over and some of its contents were spilt, scalding several of the children who were standing by. The urn was not upset but came to the ground on its base.

In my opinion, Mrs Alexander had no reason to anticipate that such an event would happen as a consequence of granting permission for a tea urn to be carried through the passage-way where the children were congregated, and consequently there was no duty incumbent on her to take precautions against the occurrence of such an event. I think that she was entitled to assume that the urn would be in charge of responsible persons (as it was) who would have regard for the safety of the children in the passage (as they did have regard) and that the urn would be carried with ordinary care, in which case its transit would occasion no danger to bystanders. The pursuers have left quite unexplained the actual cause of the accident. The immediate cause was not the carrying of the urn through the passage, but McDonald's losing grip of his handle. How he came to do so is entirely a matter of speculation. He may have stumbled or he may have suffered a temporary muscular failure. We do not know and the pursuers have not chosen to enlighten us by calling McDonald as a witness. Yet is is argued that Mrs Alexander ought to have foreseen the possibility, nay, the reasonable probability of an occurrence the nature of which is unascertained. Suppose that McDonald let go his handle through carelessness. Was Mrs Alexander bound to foresee this as reasonably probable and to take precautions against the possible consequences? I do not think so. The only ground on which the view of the majority of the judges of the first division can be justified is that Mrs Alexander ought to have foreseen that some accidental injury might happen to the children in the passage if she allowed an urn containing hot tea to be carried through the passage and ought, therefore, to have cleared out the children entirely during its

---

1. [Lord Thankerton thought it was no more than two-thirds full.]

transit, which Lord Moncrieff describes as 'the only effective step'. With all respect I think that this would impose upon Mrs Alexander a degree of care higher than the law exacts. . . . As, in my opinion, no negligence has been established I agree with what I understand to be the view of all your Lordships that the appeal should be allowed and the judgment of the Lord Ordinary restored.

[LORD WRIGHT, LORD CLAUSON, LORD THANKERTON and LORD ROMER delivered speeches in favour of allowing the appeal.]

Appeal allowed

Question

To what extent should it be relevant when a public body is sued that 'resources available for the public service are limited and that the allocation of resources is a matter for Parliament' (*Knight v Home Office* [1990] 3 All ER 237 at 243)?

Note

In *Hall v Brooklands Auto-Racing Club* [1932] All ER Rep 208 at 217, Greer LJ said that the reasonable member of the public 'is sometimes described as "the man in the street", or "the man in the Clapham omnibus", or, as I recently read in an American author, "the man who takes the magazines at home, and in the evening pushes the lawn mower in his shirt sleeves".'

(b) Foreseeability and the standard of care

Bolton v Stone House of Lords [1951] 1 All ER 1078

A cricket club had played cricket on their ground since about 1864. The respondent, Miss Stone, who was standing on the road outside her house, was hit by a cricket ball which had been straight-driven by a batsman playing for a visiting team. She was nearly one hundred yards from where the ball was struck. The ball cleared a fence which was approximately seventy-eight yards from the striker of the ball, the fence being seven feet high and, in fact, the slope of the ground meant that the top of the fence was seventeen feet above the level of the pitch. A witness with a house nearer the ground than that of Miss Stone, said that cricket balls had hit his house or gone into his yard five or six times in the preceding few years. There was other evidence that the hit was an exceptional one, and that—as was accepted by the trial judge (Oliver J)—it was a rare occurrence for the ball to go over the fence during a match. The respondent sued the committee and members of the club, the appellants here, for damages for negligence and nuisance. Oliver J, [1949] 1 All ER 237, dismissed both claims, but the Court of Appeal, [1949] 2 All ER 851, held the appellants liable in negligence. On appeal to the House of Lords:

LORD OAKSEY: . . . Cricket has been played for about ninety years on the ground in question and no ball has been proved to have struck anyone on the highways near the ground until the respondent was struck, nor has there been any complaint to the appellants. In such circumstances was it the duty of the appellants, who are the committee of the club, to take some special precautions other than those they did take to prevent such an accident as happened? The standard of care in the law of negligence is the standard of an ordinarily careful man, but, in my opinion, an ordinarily careful man does not take precautions against every foreseeable risk. He can, of course, foresee the possibility of many risks, but life would be almost impossible if he were to attempt to take precautions against every risk which he can foresee. He takes precautions against risks which are reasonably likely to happen. Many foreseeable risks are extremely unlikely to happen and cannot be guarded against except by almost complete isolation. The ordinarily prudent owner of a dog does not keep his dog always on a lead on a country highway for fear it may cause injury to a passing motor cyclist, nor does the ordinarily prudent pedestrian avoid the use of the highway for fear of skidding motor cars. It may very well be that after this accident the ordinarily prudent committee man of a similar cricket ground would take some further precaution, but that is not to say that he would have taken a similar precaution before the accident. . . .

LORD REID: My Lords, it was readily foreseeable that an accident such as befell the respondent might possibly occur during one of the appellants' cricket matches. Balls had been driven into the public road from time to time, and it was obvious that if a person happened to be where a ball fell that person would receive injuries which might or might not be serious. On the other hand, it was plain that the chance of that happening was small. The exact number of times a ball has been driven into the road is not known, but it is not proved that this has happened more than about six times in about thirty years. If I assume that it has happened on the average once in three seasons I shall be doing no injustice to the respondent's case. Then there has to be considered the chance of a person being hit by a ball falling in the road. The road appears to be an ordinary side road giving access to a number of private houses, and there is no evidence to suggest that the traffic on this road is other than what one might expect on such a road. On the whole of that part of the road where a ball could fall there would often be nobody and seldom any great number of people. It follows that the chance of a person ever being struck even in a long period of years was very small.

This case, therefore, raises sharply the question what is the nature and extent of the duty of a person who promotes on his land operations which may cause damage to persons on an adjoining highway. Is it that he must not carry out or permit an operation which he knows or ought to know clearly can cause such damage, however improbable that result may be, or is it that he is only bound to take into account the possibility of such damage if such damage is a likely or probable consequence of what he does or permits, or if the risk of damage is such that a reasonable man, careful of the safety of his neighbour, would regard that risk as material? I do not know of any case where this question has had to be decided or even where it has been fully discussed. Of course there are many cases in which somewhat similar questions have arisen, but, generally speaking, if injury to another person from the defendants' acts is reasonably foreseeable the chance that injury will result is substantial and it does not matter in which way the duty is stated. In such cases I do not think that much assistance is to be got from analysing the language which a judge has used. More assistance is to be got from cases where judges have clearly chosen their language with care in setting out a principle, but even so, statements of the law must be read in light of the facts of the particular case. Nevertheless, making all allowances for this, I do find at least a tendency to base duty rather on the likelihood of damage to others than on its foreseeability alone. . . . I think that reasonable men do, in fact, take into account the degree of risk and do not act on a bare possibility as they would if the risk were more substantial. . . .

Counsel for the respondent in the present case had to put his case so high as to say that, at least as soon as one ball had been driven into the road in the ordinary course of a match, the appellants could and should have realised that that might happen again, and that, if it did, someone might be injured, and that that was enough to put on the appellants a duty to take steps to prevent such an occurrence. If the true test is foreseeability alone I think that must be so. Once a ball has been driven on to a road without there being anything extraordinary to account for the fact, there is clearly a risk that another will follow and if it does there is clearly a chance, small though it may be, that somebody may be injured. On the theory that it is foreseeability alone that matters it would be irrelevant to consider how often a ball might be expected to land in the road and it would not matter whether the road was the busiest street or the quietest country lane. The only difference between these cases is in the degree of risk. It would take a good deal to make me believe that the law has departed so far from the standards which guide ordinary careful people in ordinary life. In the crowded conditions of modern life even the most careful person cannot avoid creating some risks and accepting others. What a man must not do, and what I think a careful man tries not to do, is to create a risk which is substantial. Of course, there are numerous cases where special circumstances require that a higher standard shall be observed and where that is recognised by the law, but I do not think that this case comes within any such special category. . . . In my judgment, the test to be applied here is whether the risk of damage to a person on the road was so small that a reasonable man in the position of the appellants, considering the matter from the point of view of safety, would have thought it right to refrain from taking steps to prevent the danger. In considering that matter I think that it would be right to take into account, not only how remote is the chance that a person might be struck, but also how serious the consequences are likely to be if a person is struck, but I do not think that it would be right to take into account the difficulty of remedial measures. If cricket cannot be played on a ground without creating a substantial risk, then it should not be played there at all. I think that this is in substance the test which Oliver J applied in this case. He considered whether the appellants' ground was large enough to be safe for all practical purposes and held that it was. This is a question, not of law, but of fact and degree. It is not an easy question, and it is one on which opinions may well differ. I can only say that, having given the whole matter repeated and anxious consideration, I find myself unable to decide this question in favour of the respondent. I think, however, that this case is not far from the borderline. If this appeal is allowed, that does not, in my judgment, mean that in every case where cricket has been played on a ground for a number of years without accident or complaint those who organise matches there are safe to go on in reliance on past immunity. I would have reached a different conclusion if I had thought that the risk here had been other than extremely small because I do not think that a reasonable man, considering the matter from the point of view of safety, would or should disregard any risk unless it is extremely small.

This case was also argued as a case of nuisance, but counsel for the respondent admitted that he could not succeed on that ground if the case on negligence failed. I, therefore, find it unnecessary to deal with the question of nuisance and I reserve my opinion as to what constitutes nuisance in cases of this character. In my judgment, the appeal should be allowed.

LORD RADCLIFFE: . . . It seems to me that a reasonable man, taking account of the chances against an accident happening, would not have felt himself called on either to abandon the use of the ground for cricket or to increase the height of his surrounding fences. He would have done what the appellants did. In other words, he would have done nothing. . . .

I agree with the others of your Lordships that, if the respondent cannot succeed in negligence, she cannot succeed on any other head of claim.

[LORD PORTER and LORD NORMAND delivered speeches in favour of allowing the appeal.]

Appeal allowed

Question

Would the appellants have been liable if Miss Stone had been one of a large procession which, to their knowledge, was assembling in the road outside?

Note

Compare with *Bolton v Stone* the decision relating to liability in negligence in *Miller v Jackson* [1977] QB 966; [1977] 3 All ER 338. (As in *Bolton v Stone* the question of nuisance was also raised in this case, and on this point see p. 648, post.) In *Miller v Jackson* a housing estate had been built next to a cricket ground and the plaintiffs, Mr and Mrs Miller who owned one of the houses on the estate, sued the chairman and secretary of the club on their own behalf and on behalf of the other members of the club. Between 1972 and 1974 cricket balls had on a number of occasions gone on to the plaintiffs' property, causing some property damage, though no personal injury. In 1975 the height of the fence between the ground and the estate was increased so it stood nearly fifteen feet high, the maximum height possible because of the wind. Nevertheless, cricket balls were still hit over the fence. According to the club's count, balls had gone over the fence six times in the 1975 season and on eight or nine occasions in the 1976 season, and according to the plaintiffs some of these balls had come on to their property. In the opinion of the majority of the Court of Appeal the 'risk of injury to persons and property is so great that on each occasion when a ball comes over the fence and causes damage to the plaintiffs, the defendants are guilty of negligence' ([1977] 3 All ER at p. 348). See further *Hilder v Associated Portland Cement Manufacturers Ltd* [1961] 3 All ER 709; [1961] 1 WLR 1434.

The Wagon Mound (No 2), Overseas Tankship (UK) Ltd *v* The Miller Steamship Co Pty Ltd Judicial Committee of the Privy Council [1966] 2 All ER 709

LORD REID: This is an appeal from a judgment of Walsh J,[1] dated 10 October 1963, in the Supreme Court of New South Wales (Commercial Causes) by which he awarded to the respondents sums of £80,000 and £1,000 in respect of damage from fire sustained by their vessels, Corrimal and Audrey D, on 1 November 1951. These vessels were then at Sheerlegs Wharf, Morts Bay, in Sydney Harbour undergoing repairs. The appellant was charterer by demise of a vessel, the Wagon Mound, which in the early hours of 30 October 1951, had been taking in bunkering oil from Caltex Wharf not far from Sheerlegs Wharf. By reason of carelessness of the Wagon Mound engineers a large quantity of this oil overflowed from the Wagon Mound on to the surface of the water. Some hours later much of the oil had drifted to and accumulated round Sheerlegs Wharf and the respondents' vessels. About 2 p.m. on 1 November this oil was set alight: the fire spread rapidly and caused extensive damage to the wharf and to the respondents' vessels.

An action was raised against the present appellant by the owners of Sheerlegs Wharf on the ground of negligence. On appeal to the Board it was held that the plaintiffs were not entitled to recover on the ground that it was not foreseeable that such

1. [1963] 1 Lloyd's Rep 402.

oil on the surface of the water could be set alight (*Overseas Tankship (UK) Ltd v Morts Dock and Engineering Co Ltd*).[1] Their lordships will refer to this case as the *Wagon Mound (No. 1)*. The issue of nuisance was also raised but their lordships did not deal with it: they remitted this issue to the Supreme Court and their lordships now understand that the matter was not pursued there in that case.

In the present case the respondents sue alternatively in nuisance and in negligence. Walsh J[2] had found in their favour in nuisance but against them in negligence. Before their lordships the appellant appeals against his decision on nuisance and the respondents appeal against his decision on negligence. Their lordships are indebted to that learned judge for the full and careful survey of the evidence which is set out in his judgment.[3] Few of his findings of fact have been attacked, and their lordships do not find it necessary to set out or deal with the evidence at any length; but it is desirable to give some explanation of how the fire started before setting out the learned judge's findings.

In the course of repairing the respondents' vessels the Morts Dock Co, the owners of Sheerlegs Wharf, were carrying out oxy-acetylene welding and cutting. This work was apt to cause pieces or drops of hot metal to fly off and fall in the sea. So when their manager arrived on the morning of 30 October and saw the thick scum of oil round the Wharf, he was apprehensive of fire danger and he stopped the work while he took advice. He consulted the manager of Caltex Wharf and, after some further consultation, he was assured that he was safe to proceed: so he did so, and the repair work was carried on normally until the fire broke out on 1 November. Oil of this character with a flash point of 170°F is extremely difficult to ignite in the open; but we now know that that is not impossible. There is no certainty about how this oil was set alight, but the most probable explanation, accepted by Walsh J, is that there was floating in the oil-covered water some object supporting a piece of inflammable material, and that a hot piece of metal fell on it when it burned for a sufficient time to ignite the surrounding oil.

The findings of the learned trial judge are as follows:[4]

'(i) Reasonable people in the position of the officers of the Wagon Mound would regard furnace oil as very difficult to ignite on water.

'(ii) Their personal experience would probably have been that this had very rarely happened.

'(iii) If they had given attention to the risk of fire from the spillage, they would have regarded it as a possibility, but one which could become an actuality only in very exceptional circumstances.

'(iv) They would have considered the chances of the required exceptional circumstances happening whilst the oil remained spread on the harbour waters, as being remote.

'(v) I find that the occurrence of damage to [the respondents'] property as a result of the spillage, was not reasonably foreseeable by those for whose acts [the appellant] would be responsible.

'(vi) I find that the spillage of oil was brought about by the careless conduct of persons for whose acts [the appellant] would be responsible.

'(vii) I find that the spillage of oil was a cause of damage to the property of each of [the respondents].

'(viii) Having regard to those findings, and because of finding (v), I hold that the claim of each of [the respondents] framed in negligence fails.' . . .

---

1. [1961] AC 388; [1961] 1 All ER 404.
2. [1963] 1 Lloyd's Rep 402.
3. [1963] 1 Lloyd's Rep at pp. 406–408.
4. [1963] 1 Lloyd's Rep at p. 426.

It is now necessary to turn to the respondents' submission that the trial judge was wrong in holding that damage from fire was not reasonably foreseeable. In *Wagon Mound (No. 1)*[1] the finding on which the Board proceeded was that of the trial judge:

'... [the appellants] did not know and could not reasonably be expected to have known that [the oil] was capable of being set afire when spread on water.'

In the present case the evidence led was substantially different from the evidence led in *Wagon Mound (No. 1)*[2] and the findings of Walsh J[3] are significantly different. That is not due to there having been any failure by the plaintiffs in *Wagon Mound (No. 1)*[2] in preparing and presenting their case. The plaintiffs there were no doubt embarrassed by a difficulty which does not affect the present plaintiffs. The outbreak of the fire was consequent on the act of the manager of the plaintiffs in *Wagon Mound (No. 1)*[2] in resuming oxy-acetylene welding and cutting while the wharf was surrounded by this oil. So if the plaintiffs in the former case had set out to prove that it was foreseeable by the engineers of the Wagon Mound that this oil could be set alight, they might have had difficulty in parrying the reply that then this must also have been foreseeable by their manager. Then there would have been contributory negligence and at that time contributory negligence was a complete defence in New South Wales.

The crucial finding of Walsh J[4] in this case is in finding (v): that the damage was 'not reasonably foreseeable by those for whose acts the defendant would be responsible.' That is not a primary finding of fact but an inference from the other findings, and it is clear from the learned judge's judgment that in drawing this inference he was to a large extent influenced by his view of the law. The vital parts of the findings of fact which have already been set out in full are (i) that the officers of the Wagon Mound 'would regard furnace oil as very difficult to ignite on water'—not that they would regard this as impossible: (ii) that their experience would probably have been 'that this had very rarely happened'—not that they would never have heard of a case where it had happened, and (iii) that they would have regarded it as a 'possibility, but one which could become an actuality only in very exceptional circumstances'—not, as in *Wagon Mound (No. 1)*,[2] that they could not reasonably be expected to have known that this oil was capable of being set afire when spread on water. The question which must now be determined is whether these differences between the findings in the two cases do or do not lead to different results in law.

In *Wagon Mound (No. 1)*[2] the Board were not concerned with degrees of foreseeability because the finding was that the fire was not foreseeable at all. So Viscount Simonds[5] had no cause to amplify the statement that the 'essential factor in determining liability is whether the damage is of such a kind as the reasonable man should have foreseen'. Here the findings show, however, that some risk of fire would have been present to the mind of a reasonable man in the shoes of the ship's chief engineer. So the first question must be what is the precise meaning to be attached in this context to the words 'foreseeable' and 'reasonably foreseeable'.

Before *Bolton v Stone*[6] the cases had fallen into two classes: (i) those where, before the event, the risk of its happening would have been regarded as unreal either because the event would have been thought to be physically impossible or because the

---

1. [1961] AC at p. 413; [1961] 1 All ER at p. 407.
2. [1961] AC 388; [1961] 1 All ER 404.
3. [1963] 1 Lloyd's Rep 402.
4. [1963] 1 Lloyd's Rep at p. 426.
5. [1961] AC at p. 426; [1961] 1 All ER at p. 415.
6. [1951] AC 850; [1951] 1 All ER 1078.

possibility of its happening would have been regarded as so fantastic or far-fetched that no reasonable man would have paid any attention to it—'a mere possibility which would never occur to the mind of a reasonable man' (per Lord Dunedin in *Fardon v Harcourt-Rivington*[1])—or (ii) those where there was a real and substantial risk or chance that something like the event which happens might occur and then the reasonable man would have taken the steps necessary to eliminate the risk.

Bolton v Stone[2] posed a new problem. There a member of a visiting team drove a cricket ball out of the ground on to an unfrequented adjacent public road and it struck and severely injured a lady who happened to be standing in the road. That it might happen that a ball would be driven on to this road could not have been said to be a fantastic or far-fetched possibility: according to the evidence it had happened about six times in twenty-eight years. Moreover it could not have been said to be a far-fetched or fantastic possibility that such a ball would strike someone in the road: people did pass along the road from time to time. So it could not have been said that, on any ordinary meaning of the words, the fact that a ball might strike a person in the road was not foreseeable or reasonably foreseeable. It was plainly foreseeable; but the chance of its happening in the foreseeable future was infinitesimal. A mathematician given the data could have worked out that it was only likely to happen once in so many thousand years. The House of Lords held that the risk was so small that in the circumstances a reasonable man would have been justified in disregarding it and taking no steps to eliminate it.

It does not follow that, no matter what the circumstances may be, it is justifiable to neglect a risk of such a small magnitude. A reasonable man would only neglect such a risk if he had some valid reason for doing so: e.g. that it would involve considerable expense to eliminate the risk. He would weigh the risk against the difficulty of eliminating it. If the activity which caused the injury to Miss Stone had been an unlawful activity there can be little doubt but that *Bolton v Stone*[2] would have been decided differently. In their lordships' judgment *Bolton v Stone*[2] did not alter the general principle that a person must be regarded as negligent if he does not take steps to eliminate a risk which he knows or ought to know is a real risk and not a mere possibility which would never influence the mind of a reasonable man. What that decision did was to recognise and give effect to the qualification that it is justifiable not to take steps to eliminate a real risk if it is small and if the circumstances are such that a reasonable man, careful of the safety of his neighbour, would think it right to neglect it.

In the present case there was no justification whatever for discharging the oil into Sydney Harbour. Not only was it an offence to do so, but also it involved considerable loss financially. If the ship's engineer had thought about the matter there could have been no question of balancing the advantages and disadvantages. From every point of view it was both his duty and his interest to stop the discharge immediately.

It follows that in their lordships' view the only question is whether a reasonable man having the knowledge and experience to be expected of the chief engineer of the Wagon Mound would have known that there was a real risk of the oil on the water catching fire in some way: if it did, serious damage to ships or other property was not only foreseeable but very likely. Their lordships do not dissent from the view of the trial judge that the possibilities of damage[3] 'must be significant enough in a practical sense to require a reasonable man to guard against them', but they think that he may have misdirected himself in saying[4]

'there does seem to be a real practical difficulty, assuming that some risk of fire

---

1. [1932] All ER Rep 81 at 83.
2. [1951] AC 850; [1951] 1 All ER 1078
3. [1963] 1 Lloyd's Rep at p. 411.
4. [1963] 1 Lloyd's Rep at p. 413.

damage was foreseeable, but not a high one, in making a factual judgment as to whether this risk was sufficient to attract liability if damage should occur.'

In this difficult chapter of the law decisions are not infrequently taken to apply to circumstances far removed from the facts which give rise to them, and it would seem that here too much reliance has been placed on some observations in *Bolton v Stone*[1] and similar observations in other cases.

In their lordships' view a properly qualified and alert chief engineer would have realised there was a real risk here, and they do not understand Walsh J to deny that; but he appears to have held that, if a real risk can properly be described as remote, it must then be held to be not reasonably foreseeable. That is a possible interpretation of some of the authorities; but this is still an open question and on principle their lordships cannot accept this view. If a real risk is one which would occur to the mind of a reasonable man in the position of the defendant's servant and which he would not brush aside as far-fetched, and if the criterion is to be what that reasonable man would have done in the circumstances, then surely he would not neglect such a risk if action to eliminate it presented no difficulty, involved no disadvantage and required no expense.

In the present case the evidence shows that the discharge of so much oil on to the water must have taken a considerable time, and a vigilant ship's engineer would have noticed the discharge at an early stage. The findings show that he ought to have known that it is possible to ignite this kind of oil on water, and that the ship's engineer probably ought to have known that this had in fact happened before. The most that can be said to justify inaction is that he would have known that this could only happen in very exceptional circumstances; but that does not mean that a reasonable man would dismiss such risk from his mind and do nothing when it was so easy to prevent it. If it is clear that the reasonable man would have realised or foreseen and prevented the risk, then it must follow that the appellants are liable in damages. The learned judge found this a difficult case: he said that this matter is[2] 'one on which different minds would come to different conclusions'. Taking a rather different view of the law from that of the learned judge, their lordships must hold that the respondents are entitled to succeed on this issue. . . .

Appeal and cross-appeal allowed. [The appeal which related to the question of nuisance is dealt with p. 632, post.]

Notes

1. On the relevance of the difficulty and cost of remedial measures, compare Lord Reid's views in this case with those in *Bolton v Stone* (p. 252, ante) and see also *Latimer v AEC Ltd* [1953] AC 643; [1953] 2 All ER 449 (p. 273, post).

2. *The Wagon Mound (No. 1)* [1961] AC 388; [1961] 1 All ER 404 (p. 333, post) is the leading authority on remoteness of damage in negligence. A given set of facts may give rise to claims in the torts of nuisance and negligence, and nuisance itself can be subdivided into public and private nuisance. (See chap. 14, p. 623, post). There are important differences between these torts, but, in the sphere of remoteness of damage, *The Wagon Mound*

---

1. [1951] AC 850; [1951] 1 All ER 1078.
2. [1963] 1 Lloyd's Rep at p. 424.

(*No. 2*) (in a part of the judgment which has been omitted at this stage) establishes that in nuisance, as in the tort of negligence, there must be foreseeability of the kind of damage suffered before the defendant will be held liable for that particular item of damage. (See p. 632, post where the Privy Council's judgment on this aspect of the case is set out.) Foreseeability plays a large and varied role in the tort of negligence. Not only is it relevant to breach of duty (which is under consideration at this point) and remoteness of damage (as has just been mentioned), but it is also relevant to the question whether a duty is owed to this particular plaintiff (p. 114, ante). It is important that the different uses of the foreseeability doctrine should be appreciated, and discussion of this point can be found in an article by R. W. M. Dias [1967] CLJ 62.

(c) Special skill

Philips *v* William Whiteley Ltd King's Bench Division [1938] 1 All ER 566

The plaintiff went to the defendants' jewellery department to arrange for her ears to be pierced to enable her to wear earrings. The defendants did not have any member of their own staff who did this job, but arranged for Mr Couzens, an employee of another firm, to pierce the ears. Approximately twelve or thirteen days after the piercing she felt pain in her neck. An abscess developed which had to be operated on and the operation left a small scar. It appeared that Mr Couzens had performed over one thousand ear piercings and nothing of this nature had happened on any other occasion. The plaintiff claimed damages, alleging negligence against Mr Couzens, the defendants' agent.

GODDARD J: . . . In this case, the first thing that I have to consider is the standard of care demanded from Mr Couzens—or, I should say, from Whiteleys, because Whiteleys were the people who undertook to do this piercing. It is not easy in any case to lay down a particular canon or standard by which the care can be judged, but, while it is admitted here, and admitted on all hands, that Mr Couzens did not use the same precautions of procuring an aseptic condition of his instruments as a doctor or a surgeon would use, I do not think that he could be called upon to use that degree of care. Whiteleys have to see that whoever they employ for the operation uses the standard of care and skill that may be expected from a jeweller, and, of course, if the operation is negligently performed—if, for instance, a wholly unsuitable instrument were used, so that the ear was badly torn, or something of that sort happened— undoubtedly they would be liable. So, too, if they did not take that degree of care to see that the instruments were clean which one would expect a person of the training and the standing of a jeweller to use. To say, however, that a jeweller warrants or undertakes that he will use instruments which have the degree of surgical cleanliness that a surgeon brings about when he is going to perform a serious operation, or indeed any operation, is, I think, putting the matter too high. The doctors all seem to agree in this case that, if a lady went to a surgeon for the piercing of her ears, he would render his instruments sterile. After all, however, aseptic surgery is a thing of very modern growth. As anybody who has read the life of Lord Lister or the history of medicine in the last fifty or sixty years knows, it is not so many years ago that the best surgeon in the land knew nothing about even antiseptic surgery. Then antiseptic surgery was introduced, and that was followed by aseptic surgery. I do not think that a jeweller holds himself out as a surgeon or professes that he is going to conduct the operation of piercing a lady's ears by means of aseptic surgery, about which it is not to be supposed that he knows anything.

If a person wants to ensure that the operation of piercing her ears is going to be carried out with that proportion of skill and so forth that a Fellow of the Royal College of Surgeons would use, she must go to a surgeon. If she goes to a jeweller, she must expect that he will carry it out in the way that one would expect a jeweller to carry it out. One would expect that he would wash his instruments. One would expect that he would take some means of disinfecting his instrument, just in the same way as one knows that the ordinary layman, when he is going to use a needle to prick a blister or prick a little gathering on a finger, generally takes the precaution to put the needle in a flame, as I think Mr Couzens did. I accept the evidence of Mr Couzens as to what he says he did on this occasion – how he put his instrument in a flame before he left his shop, and how he washed his hands, and so forth. I think that he did. I see no reason to suppose that he is not telling me the absolute truth when he says what he did, and, as Dr Pritchard, who holds the very high qualification of a Fellow of the Royal College of Physicians, said, for all practical purposes that is enough. That is to say, for the ordinary every-day matters that would be regarded as enough. It is not a degree of surgical cleanliness, which is a very different thing from ordinary cleanliness. It is not the cleanliness which a doctor would insist upon, because, as I say, Mr Couzens is not a doctor. He was known not to be a doctor. One does not go to a jeweller to get one's ears attended to if one requires to have a doctor in attendance to do it. If one wants a doctor in attendance, one goes to his consulting room or one has him come to see one. I do not see any ground here for holding that Mr Couzens was negligent in the way in which he performed this operation. It might be better, and I think that it probably would, if he boiled his instrument beforehand at his place, or if he took a spirit lamp with him and boiled his instrument at the time, but in view of the medical evidence, the evidence of Dr Pritchard, which I accept, I see no ground for holding that Mr Couzens departed from the standard of care which you would expect that a man of his position and his training, being what he held himself out to be, was required to possess. Therefore, the charge of negligence fails.

Even if I am wrong in that, and even if another court were to take the view that a person who undertakes to pierce an ear is bound, although he holds himself out to be more than a jeweller, to take all the precautions that a trained surgeon would take, I am quite unable, on the evidence, to find that the abscess from which Mrs Philips suffered was due to any action of Mr Couzens. . . .

Judgment for the defendants

Questions

1. What is the standard of care of a first aid volunteer? (See G. Ll. H. Griffiths (1990) 53 MLR 255.)

2. Should the standard of care in a prison hospital match that of a psychiatric hospital outside prison? (See *Knight v Home Office* [1990] 3 All ER 237.)

Notes

1. In relation to the position of skilled defendants, see the oft-quoted test in *Bolam v Friern Hospital Management Committee* [1957] 2 All ER 118; [1957] 1 WLR 582, noted p. 277, post, that 'the test is the standard of the ordinary skilled man exercising and professing to have that special skill'.

2. The following warning delivered by Denning LJ in *Roe v Minister of Health* [1954] 2 QB 66; [1954] 2 All ER 131 should be borne in mind. He said (at p. 137):

'It is so easy to be wise after the event and to condemn as negligence that which was only a misadventure. We ought always to be on our guard against it, especially in cases against hospitals and doctors. Medical science has conferred great benefits on mankind, but these benefits are attended by considerable risks. Every surgical operation is attended by risks. We cannot take the benefits without taking the risks. Every advance in technique is also attended by risks. Doctors, like the rest of us, have to learn by experience; and experience often teaches in a hard way. Something goes wrong and shows up a weakness, and then it is put right.... We must not look at the 1947 accident with 1954 spectacles.'

On the position of medical practitioners, see further *Whitehouse v Jordan* [1981] 1 All ER 267; [1981] 1 WLR 246; *Maynard v West Midlands Regional Area Health Authority* [1985] 1 All ER 635; [1984] 1 WLR 634; *Sidaway v Board of Governors of the Bethlem Royal Hospital and the Maudsley Hospital* [1985] AC 871; [1985] 1 All ER 643 (p. 278, post). Note further the analogy drawn with general medical practitioners in *Luxmoore-May v Messenger May Baverstock (a firm)* [1990] 1 All ER 1067 at 1075–1076, which concerned a firm of provincial auctioneers and valuers.

3. There may of course be specialities within a particular profession. In *Maynard* it was stated (at p. 638) that 'a doctor who professes to exercise a special skill must exercise the ordinary skill of his speciality', and see *Sidaway* (at pp. 892 and 897 – the latter can be found p. 279, post; *Wilsher v Essex Area Health Authority* [1987] QB 730; [1986] 3 All ER 801, noted p. 264, post.) See further A. M. Dugdale and K. M. Stanton, *Professional Negligence* 2nd edn (London, 1988), para. 15–20; R. M. Jackson and J. L. Powell, *Professional Negligence* 2nd edn (London, 1987), paras. 1.27–1.29; J. Holyoak (1985) 1 PN 32. Is the position of someone who is more knowledgeable than other professionals within his field affected by this greater knowledge? (Consider *Wimpey Construction UK Ltd v D V Poole* [1984] 2 Lloyd's Rep 499.) Note also A. H. Hudson's comments, (1986) 102 LQR 11 at 12 on Sir John Donaldson MR's dicta in *Condon v Basi* [1985] 2 All ER 453 at 454 that 'there will of course be a higher degree of care required of a player in a First Division football match than of a player in a local league football match'.

Nettleship *v* Weston Court of Appeal [1971] 3 All ER 581

The plaintiff agreed to teach the defendant to drive in the defendant's husband's car after he had been correctly told, in response to a remark of his about the insurance position, that he was covered as a passenger by the fully comprehensive insurance if there was an accident. During the third lesson he in fact assisted her by moving the gear lever, applying the hand brake and occasionally helping with the steering. In the course of that lesson, they made a slow left turn after having stopped at a halt sign. However, the defendant did not straighten out the wheel and panicked. Although the plaintiff got hold of the hand brake with one hand and tried to get hold of the steering wheel with the other hand so as to correct it, the car hit a lamp standard. The plaintiff's left knee-cap was broken and he appealed against the dismissal of his claim for damages from the defendant who had been convicted of driving without due care and attention.

MEGAW LJ: . . . The important question of principle which arises is whether, because of Mr Nettleship's knowledge that Mrs Weston was not an experienced driver, the standard of care which was owed to him by her was lower than would otherwise have been the case.

In *Insurance Comr v Joyce*,[1] Dixon J stated persuasively the view that there is, or may be, a 'particular relation' between the driver of a vehicle and his passenger resulting in a variation of the standard of duty owed by the driver. . . . He summarised the same principle in these words[2]:

'It appears to me that the circumstances in which the defendant accepts the plaintiff as a passenger and in which the plaintiff accepts the accommodation in the conveyance should determine the measure of duty . . .'

Theoretically, the principle as thus expounded is attractive. But, with very great respect, I venture to think that the theoretical attraction should yield to practical considerations.

As I see it, if this doctrine of varying standards were to be accepted as part of the law on these facts, it could not logically be confined to the duty of care owed by learner-drivers. There is no reason, in logic, why it should not operate in a much wider sphere. The disadvantages of the resulting unpredictability, uncertainty and, indeed, impossibility of arriving at fair and consistent decisions outweigh the advantages. The certainty of a general standard is preferable to the vagaries of a fluctuating standard.

As a first example of what is involved, consider the converse case: the standard of care (including skill) owed not by the driver to the passenger, but by the passenger-instructor to the learner-driver. Surely the same principle of varying standards, if it is a good principle, must be available also to the passenger, if he is sued by the driver for alleged breach of the duty of care in supervising the learner-driver. On this doctrine, the standard of care, or skill, owed by the instructor, vis-à-vis the driver, may vary according to the knowledge which the learner-driver had, at some moment of time, as to the skill and experience of the particular instructor. Indeed, if logic is to prevail, it would not necessarily be the knowledge of the driver which would be the criterion. It would be the expectation which the driver reasonably entertained of the instructor's skill and experience, if that reasonable expectation were greater than the actuality. Thus, if the learner-driver knew that the instructor had never tried his hand previously even at amateur instructing, or if, as may be the present case, the driver knew that the instructor's experience was confined to two cases of amateur instructing some years previously, there would, under this doctrine, surely be a lower standard than if the driver knew or reasonably supposed that the instructor was a professional or that he had had substantial experience in the recent past. But what that standard would be, and how it would or should be assessed, I know not. For one has thus cut oneself adrift from the standard of the competent and experienced instructor, which up to now the law has required without regard to the particular personal skill, experience, physical characteristics or temperament of the individual instructor, and without regard to a third party's knowledge or assessment of those qualities or characteristics.

Again, when one considers the requisite standard of care of the learner-driver, if this doctrine were to apply, would not logic irresistibly demand that there should be something more than a mere, single, conventional, standard applicable to anyone who falls into the category of learner-driver, i.e. of anyone who has not yet qualified for (or perhaps obtained) a full licence? That standard itself would necessarily vary

---

1. (1948) 77 CLR 39 at 56, 60.
2. (1948) 77 CLR at p. 59.

over a wide range, not merely with the actual progress of the learner, but also with the passenger's knowledge of that progress; or, rather, if the passenger has in fact over-estimated the driver's progress, it would vary with the passenger's reasonable assessment of that progress at the relevant time. The relevant time would not necessarily be the moment of the accident.

The question, what is the relevant time? would itself have to be resolved by reference to some principle. The instructor's reasonable assessment of the skill and competence of the driver (and also the driver's assessment of the instructor's skill and competence) might alter drastically between the start of the first lesson and the start of a later lesson, or even in the course of one particular spell of driving. I suppose the principle would have to be that the relevant time is the last moment when the plaintiff (whether instructor or driver) could reasonably have refused to continue as passenger or driver in the light of his then knowledge. That factor in itself would introduce yet another element of difficulty, uncertainty and, I believe, serious anomaly. I for my part, with all respect, do not think that our legal process could successfully or satisfactorily cope with the task of fairly assessing, or applying to the facts of a particular case, such varying standards, depending on such complex and elusive factors, including the assessment by the court, not merely of a particular person's actual skill or experience, but also of another person's knowledge or assessment of that skill or experience at a particular moment of time.

Again, if the principle of varying standards is to be accepted, why should it operate, in the field of driving motor vehicles, only up to the stage of the driver qualifying for a full licence? And why should it be limited to the quality of inexperience? If the passenger knows that his driver suffers from some relevant defect, physical or temperamental, which could reasonably be expected to affect the quality of his driving, why should not the same doctrine of varying standards apply? Dixon J thought it should apply. Logically there can be no distinction. If the passenger knows that his driver, though holding a full driving licence, is blind in one eye or has the habit of taking corners too fast, and if an accident happens which is attributable wholly or partly to that physical or that temperamental defect, why should not some lower standard apply vis-à-vis the fully informed passenger, if standards are to vary? Why should the doctrine, if it be part of the law, be limited to cases involving the driving of motor cars? Suppose that to the knowledge of the patient a young surgeon, whom the patient has chosen to operate on him, has only just qualified. If the operation goes wrong because of the surgeon's inexperience, is there a defence on the basis that the standard of skill and care was lower than the standard of a competent and experienced surgeon? Does the young, newly-qualified, solicitor owe a lower standard of skill and care, when the client chooses to instruct him with knowledge of his inexperience?

True, these last two examples may fall within the sphere of contract; and a contract may have express terms which deal with the question, or it may have implied terms. But in relationships such as are involved in this case, I see no good reason why a different term should be implied where there is a contract from the term which the law should attach where there is, or may be, no contract. Of course, there may be a difference — not because of any technical distinction between cases which fall within the law of tort and those which fall within the law of contract — but because the very factor or factors which create the contractual relationship may be relevant on the question of the implication of terms. . . .

In my judgment, in cases such as the present it is preferable that there should be a reasonably certain and reasonably ascertainable standard of care, even if on occasion that may appear to work hardly against an inexperienced driver, or his insurers. The standard of care required by the law is the standard of the competent and experienced driver; and this is so, as defining the driver's duty towards a passenger who knows of his experience, as much as towards a member of the public outside the car; and as much in civil as in criminal proceedings.

It is not a valid argument against such a principle that it attributes tortious liability to one who may not be morally blameworthy. For tortious liability has in many cases ceased to be based on moral blameworthiness. For example, there is no doubt whatever that if Mrs Weston had knocked down a pedestrian on the pavement when the accident occurred, she would have been liable to the pedestrian. Yet so far as any moral blame is concerned, no different considerations would apply in respect of the pedestrian from those which apply in respect of Mr Nettleship. . . .

[LORD DENNING MR adopted the view that the standard of care did not vary—it was that of the skilled, experienced and careful driver. SALMON LJ thought that the standard of care could vary, but that on the facts of this case the standard of the ordinary driver should be applied. LORD DENNING MR and SALMON LJ (MEGAW LJ dissenting on this point) accepted the apportionment of responsibility which had been made by the trial judge and damages were reduced by one-half because of the plaintiff's contributory negligence.]

Appeal allowed

Question

Does the learner driver hold himself out as possessing the skill and experience required by this case in the light of the fact that 'L' plates must be displayed on the car? Why do the courts require him to attain the standard of 'the competent and experienced driver'?

Notes

1. The judgments in *Nettleship v Weston* also discuss the defence of volenti non fit injuria. (See p. 377, post.)

2. In *Cook v Cook* (1986) 68 ALR 353, noted by S. Todd (1989) 105 LQR 24, the High Court of Australia was unconvinced by Megaw LJ's arguments in *Nettleship v Weston* concerning the practical disadvantages which he saw as arising from the adoption of Dixon J's approach in *Insurance Comr v Joyce* (1948) 77 CLR 39: see (1987) 68 ALR at pp. 359–360. Whilst accepting that normally the standard applicable to a driver would be that of the experienced and competent driver, in their view (at pp. 360–361) 'when special and exceptional circumstances clearly transform the relationship between a particular driver and a particular passenger into a special or different class or category of relationship . . . the case will be one in which the duty of care owed by the particular driver to the particular passenger will be either expanded or confined by reference to the objective standard of skill or care which is reasonably to be expected of a driver to a passenger in the category of a case where that special or different relationship exists'. An example given of a lower standard of care was that owed by a pupil receiving his first driving lesson to a professional driving instructor.

3. It is perhaps worth underlining at this point that the relevant standard is one of reasonable care in all the circumstances. Thus when a police officer is driving a car in pursuit of another car the 'stressful circumstances' are to be taken into account: see *Marshall v Osmond* [1983] QB 1034; [1983] 2 All ER 225 in which the Court of Appeal held that there had been an error of judgment by the officer but that he had not been negligent.

4. If a driver was in a state of automatism at the relevant time so that his actions were totally beyond his control, then he will not be liable to an injured person. However, if there was merely some impairment of consciousness, the driver will be liable if his driving did not match the standard laid down in *Nettleship v Weston*; *Roberts v Ramsbottom* [1980] 1 All ER 7; [1980] 1 WLR 823.

5. Should the fact that a junior hospital doctor is involved in the process of learning and acquiring experience in particular areas while actually performing his duties in those areas affect the standard of care? This point was raised in *Wilsher v Essex Area Health Authority* [1987] QB 730; [1986] 3 All ER 801 where Sir Nicolas Browne-Wilkinson V-C was of the opinion that, as liability was based on personal fault, then the standard should be that of a doctor with the qualifications and experience of the particular defendant. However, the majority view in the Court of Appeal was more objective. In particular, Mustill LJ saw the test as being the degree of care that could reasonably be required not from someone of the defendant's rank but from a holder of the defendant's post. (This matter was not discussed when the case went to the House of Lords, [1988] AC 1074; [1988] 1 All ER 871, p. 305, post.) See further I. Kennedy and A. Grubb, *Medical Law: Text and Materials* (London, 1989), pp. 399–404.

6. Even where odd jobs are done around the house, the courts are prepared to demand a certain level of skill from a defendant householder. In *Wells v Cooper* [1958] 2 QB 265; [1958] 2 All ER 527 where the defendant had fixed a handle to a door, it was held that he must keep to the standard of a reasonably competent carpenter.

(d) Infants

McHale *v* Watson Full Court of the High Court of Australia [1966] ALR 513

This was an appeal from a judgment of Windeyer J, [1965] ALR 788, dismissing the appellant's action.

KITTO J: The appellant, a girl of nine, was hit in the eye by a piece of steel welding rod, about six inches in length and a quarter of an inch in diameter, which had been sharpened at the end that struck her. According to findings which are not challenged, the spike, as it has been called, was thrown by the respondent, a boy of 12, with the intention of endeavouring to make it stick into a hardwood post at a point at which he aimed, but it glanced off the post and struck the appellant. The respondent, it has been found, had no intention of either hitting the appellant or frightening her. The question whether he is liable in damages for the injury which the appellant sustained depends upon whether by throwing the spike as he did he committed a breach of a duty of care which he owed her.

The respondent was standing a foot or two from the post, and the appellant was at most four or five feet from him and to his left. He knew that the spike was sharp, and, therefore, that it might injure anyone whom its sharpened end should strike. If he had been an adult the question to be decided would have been whether an ordinary person in his situation, exercising reasonable foresight, would have realised that if he should throw the spike at the point on the post at which in fact he aimed there was such a likelihood of its glancing off the post and hitting the appellant that in ordinary prudence he ought not to throw it as he did. The learned trial judge did not express a concluded opinion as to the answer he would have given to this question. Saying that he did not think he was required to disregard altogether the fact that the respondent was at the time only 12 years old, his Honour reached the conclusion that the injury to the appellant 'was not the result of a lack of foresight and appreciation of the risk that might reasonably have been expected, or of a want of reasonable care in aiming the dart'. I take this to mean that the test to be applied in determining whether the appellant's injury resulted from a breach of duty owed to her by the respondent should be stated not in terms of the reasonable foresight and prudence of an ordinary person, but in terms of the reasonable foresight and prudence of an ordinary boy of 12; and that the respondent should succeed because an ordinary boy of 12 would not have appreciated that any risk to the appellant was involved in what he did. . . .

[Having mentioned the strict liability existing some centuries ago, he continued:] Partly, no doubt, as a development of the idea always recognized that this strict liability should extend only to immediate and not to remote consequences of the act, the law came in time to limit it to acts involving a shortcoming on the part of the defendant: *Holdsworth*, op cit,[1] vol. 3, at p. 379. Act of God and inevitable necessity thus came to be admitted as excuses; and, those steps having been taken, liability not unnaturally became further restricted so as not to attach to acts which, though causes of harm, were inherently proper and were for that reason to be considered not so proximate as to entail liability: *Holdsworth*, op cit,[1] vol. 8, at pp. 455 et seq. But propriety, in the relevant sense, has never been a matter of a morally blameless state of mind: see Pollock's excursus on negligence in *The Law of Torts*, 15th edn (1951) at p. 336, and the observations of Lord Denning as to unsoundness of mind in *White v White* [1950] P 39 at 58; [1949] 2 All ER 339. In so far as 'proper' is an apt word to use in this connexion it connotes nothing but conformity with an objective standard of care, namely, the care reasonably to be expected in the like circumstances from the normal person exercising reasonable foresight and consideration for the safety of others. Thus a defendant does not escape liability by proving that he is abnormal in some respect which reduces his capacity for foresight or prudence.

The principle is of course applicable to a child. The standard of care being objective, it is no answer for him, any more than it is for an adult, to say that the harm he caused was due to his being abnormally slow-witted, quick-tempered, absentminded or inexperienced. But it does not follow that he cannot rely in his defence upon a limitation upon the capacity for foresight or prudence, not as being personal to himself, but as being characteristic of humanity at his stage of development and in that sense normal. By doing so he appeals to a standard of ordinariness, to an objective and not a subjective standard. In regard to the things which pertain to foresight and prudence — experience, understanding of causes and effects, balance of judgment, thoughtfulness — it is absurd, indeed it is a misuse of language, to speak of normality in relation to persons of all ages taken together. In those things normality is, for children, something different from what normality is for adults; the very concept of normality is a concept of rising levels until 'years of discretion' are attained. The law does not arbitrarily fix upon any particular age for this purpose, and tribunals of fact may well give effect to different views as to the age at which normal adult foresight and prudence are reasonably to be expected in relation to particular sets of circumstances. But up to that stage the normal capacity to exercise those two qualities necessarily means the capacity which is normal for a child of the relevant age; and it seems to me that it would be contrary to the fundamental principle that a person is liable for harm that he causes by falling short of an objective

---

1. [*History of English Law.*]

criterion of 'propriety' in his conduct — propriety, that is to say, as determined by a comparison with the standard of care reasonably to be expected in the circumstances from the normal person — to hold that where a child's liability is in question the normal person to be considered is someone other than a child of corresponding age.

Assistance on the subject is not to be found in the shape of specific decision in England or in this country, and judicial opinions in the United States and Canada have varied both in result and in reasoning. It seems to me, however, that strong support for the view I have indicated is provided by decisions on the cognate subject of contributory negligence. It is true that contributory negligence is not a breach of legal duty; it is only a failure to take reasonable care for one's own safety. But I must respectfully disagree with those who think that the deficiencies of foresight and prudence that are normal during childhood are irrelevant in determining what care it is reasonable for a child to take for the safety of others though relevant in determining what care it is reasonable for a child to take for himself. The standard is objective in contributory negligence no less than in negligence, in the sense that an ordinary capacity for care is postulated and is notionally applied to the circumstances of the case in order to determine what a reasonable person would have done or refrained from doing, regardless of the actual capacity for foresight or prudence possessed by the individual plaintiff or defendant. . . .

I am, therefore, of opinion that the learned trial judge did not misdirect himself on the question of law. There remains the question of fact: did the respondent, in throwing the spike as he did, though aware of the proximity of the appellant, do anything which a reasonable boy of his age would not have done in the circumstances — a boy, that is to say, who possessed and exercised such degree of foresight and prudence as is ordinarily to be expected of a boy of 12, holding in his hand a sharpened spike and seeing the post of a tree-guard before him? On the findings which must be accepted, what the respondent did was the unpremeditated, impulsive act of a boy not yet of an age to have an adult's realization of the danger of edged tools or an adult's wariness in the handling of them. It is, I think, a matter for judicial notice that the ordinary boy of 12 suffers from a feeling that a piece of wood and a sharp instrument have a special affinity. To expect a boy of that age to consider before throwing the spike whether the timber was hard or soft, to weigh the chances of being able to make the spike stick in the post, and to foresee that it might glance off and hit the girl, would be, I think, to expect a degree of sense and circumspection which nature ordinarily withholds till life has become less rosy. . . .

In my opinion the appeal should be dismissed.

OWEN J: . . . There is, then, a considerable body of opinion amongst the textbook writers, supported by decisions in Canada and the United States, that where an infant defendant is charged with negligence, his age is a circumstance to be taken into account and the standard by which his conduct is to be measured is not that to be expected of a reasonable adult but that reasonably to be expected of a child of the same age, intelligence and experience. In none of the other textbooks which I have examined does the question appear to have been considered.

. . . I am of opinion that Windeyer J rightly took into consideration the fact that Barry Watson was only 12 years old and that he did not misdirect himself as to the degree of care reasonably to be expected of a boy of that age.

I would dismiss the appeal.

[McTIERNAN ACJ delivered a judgment in favour of dismissing the appeal. MENZIES J delivered a judgment in favour of allowing the appeal.]

Appeal dismissed

Questions

1. If it is accepted that the child's age is relevant when considering whether he has been negligent, should the child's own intelligence and experience also be taken into account? (See the extract from Owen J's judgment, ante.)

2. In the light of *Nettleship v Weston* [1971] 2 QB 691; [1971] 3 All ER 581 (p. 260, ante), what standard of skill and care would be required of a person aged seventeen who is driving a car? Would his age be taken into account?

3. Did the standard expected of a nineteen-year-old person change after the coming into force of s. 1 of the Family Law Reform Act 1969 which reduced the age of majority to eighteen?

4. Is there also a separate category of old age pensioners? (Compare *Daly v Liverpool Corpn* [1939] 2 All ER 142.)

5. Are there any other categories of people to whom special consideration should be given? What standard should be expected of those suffering from mental disorders?

Notes

There has been a surprising dearth of direct English authority on the standard of care expected of infants. It may be, as McTiernan ACJ pointed out in *McHale v Watson*, that a child is not in general worth suing (but see *Salmond & Heuston*, p. 486). Thus, in fact, the plaintiff who has been injured by a child's act will on occasion sue not the child but one of its parents (or the appropriate school authority) alleging negligence in some respect, e.g. in not properly supervising the child's use of a firearm — see *Donaldson v McNiven* [1952] 2 All ER 691 (father found not negligent).

Where English courts have dealt with the contributory negligence of infants (p. 370, post) they have taken age into consideration, and it has seemed likely that they would adopt the same approach when the issue arose directly for decision in a case where an infant was the defendant. See further P. J. Rowe (1976) 126 NLJ 354. In *Watkins v Birmingham City Council* (1976) 126 NLJ 442, noted p. 844, post, the Court of Appeal supported the view (obiter) that the age of a child should be taken into account, but that the standard of care was otherwise objective Furthermore, in *Staley v Suffolk County Council and Dean Mason*, an unreported decision in 1985 set out in *Clerk & Lindsell*, para 10-60, where there was a defendant who was aged twelve, the standard required of him by Staughton J was the degree of care to be expected of a boy of that age. Compare *Williams v Humphrey* (1975) Times, 20th February, noted p. 577, post (injury suffered at a swimming pool: defendant who was nearly sixteen years old to be judged by the standard of an adult), but in *Foskett v Mistry* [1984] RTR 1 in the context of contributory negligence where the plaintiff had run out into the road, it was thought 'to be putting it a little too high' to equate a sixteen and a half year old with a fully grown adult in respect of road safety.

2 Application of the standard of care

(a) The likelihood of the occurrence of injury

Bolton v Stone, p. 250, ante
The Wagon Mound (No. 2), p. 253, ante

Haley v London Electricity Board House of Lords [1964] 3 All ER 185

The respondents had, under statutory power, made an excavation in the pavement. One of the precautions which they took was to leave, at one end of this excavation, a punner (a heavy weight attached to a long handle). The weighted end was on the pavement and the other end of the handle was lodged two feet high in some railings so the handle was sloping between these two points. The appellant, who often walked along this stretch of the pavement to reach a bus stop, was blind but could avoid ordinary obstacles by the use of his white stick. He used the stick correctly, but missed the punner handle and tripped over it. When he fell, he banged his head on the pavement and as a result became deaf. The Court of Appeal, [1963] 3 All ER 1003, dismissed an appeal from the judgment of Marshall J who had dismissed the appellant's action for damages. On appeal to the House of Lords:

LORD REID: . . . The trial judge held that what the respondents' men did gave adequate warning to ordinary people with good sight, and I am not disposed to disagree with that. . . .

On the other hand, if it was the duty of the respondents to have in mind the needs of blind or infirm pedestrians, I think that what they did was quite insufficient. Indeed the evidence shows that an obstacle attached to a heavy weight and only nine inches above the ground may well escape detection by a blind man's stick and is for him a trap rather than a warning. So the question for your lordships' decision is the nature and extent of the duty owed to pedestrians by persons who carry out operations on a city pavement. The respondents argue that they were only bound to have in mind or to safeguard ordinary able-bodied people and were under no obligation to give particular consideration to the blind or infirm. If that is right, it means that a blind or infirm person, who goes out alone goes at his peril. He may meet obstacles which are a danger to him, but not to those with good sight, because no one is under any obligation to remove or protect them; and if such an obstacle causes him injury he must suffer the damage in silence.

I could understand the respondents' contention if it was based on an argument that it was not reasonably foreseeable that a blind person might pass along that pavement on that day; or that, although foreseeable, the chance of a blind man coming there was so small and the difficulty of affording protection to him so great that it would have been in the circumstances unreasonable to afford that protection. Those are well recognised grounds of defence; but in my judgment neither is open to the respondents in this case.

In deciding what is reasonably foreseeable one must have regard to common knowledge. We are all accustomed to meeting blind people walking alone with their white sticks on city pavements. No doubt there are many places open to the public where for one reason or another one would be surprised to see a blind person walking alone, but a city pavement is not one of them; and a residential street cannot be different from any other. The blind people whom we meet must live somewhere, and most of them probably left their homes unaccompanied. It may seem surprising that blind people can avoid ordinary obstacles so well as they do, but we must take account of the facts. There is evidence in this case about the number of blind people in London and it appears from government publications that the proportion in the whole country is near one in five hundred. By no means all are sufficiently skilled or confident to venture out alone, but the number who habitually do so must be very large. I find it quite impossible to say that it is not reasonably foreseeable that a blind person may pass along a particular pavement on a particular day.

No question can arise in this case of any great difficulty in affording adequate protection for the blind. In considering what is adequate protection again one must have regard to common knowledge. One is entitled to expect of a blind person a high degree of skill and care because none but the most foolhardy would venture to go out alone without having that skill and exercising that care. We know that in fact blind people do safely avoid all ordinary obstacles on pavements; there can be no question of padding lamp posts as was suggested in one case.[1] A moment's reflection, however, shows that a low obstacle in an unusual place is a grave danger: on the other hand it is clear from the evidence in this case and also I think from common knowledge that quite a light fence some two feet high is an adequate warning. There would have been no difficulty in providing such a fence here. The evidence is that the Post Office always provide one, and that the respondents have similar fences which are often used. Indeed the evidence suggests that the only reason why there was no fence here was that the accident occurred before the necessary fences had arrived. So, if the respondents are to succeed, it can only be on the ground that there was no duty to do more than safeguard ordinary able-bodied people.

The respondents rely on the case of *Pritchard v Post Office*[2] a decision of the Court of Appeal not reported in either of the more commonly cited series of reports. The facts are not fully stated, but it would appear that servants of the Post Office had protected a hole where they were working by surrounding it with their usual light fence, but a blind woman stumbled through the fence and was injured. I would think that the decision was clearly right, the sole cause of the accident being the plaintiff's contributory negligence; but the county court judge based his decision on there being no special duty to protect the blind or infirm and that was repeated by the Court of Appeal in dismissing an appeal. I am aware that the current practice is to regard the ratio of a decision as equally authoritative whether the judgment was given ex tempore after inadequate argument or given after full argument and mature consideration. I think that this places a wholly unreasonable burden on the Court of Appeal. The argument before your lordships in this case occupied three days, which was not at all too long in view of the novelty and difficulty of the points involved. *Pritchard*'s case[2] was argued and disposed of in one day, and it would be quite unreasonable to prolong the hearing of a small county court appeal which must obviously fail in order to have a full legal argument even assuming that counsel were prepared to deal fully with the general question of law. . . .

I can see no justification for laying down any hard and fast rule limiting the classes of persons for whom those interfering with a pavement must make provision. It is said that it is impossible to tell what precautions will be adequate to protect all kinds of infirm pedestrians or that taking such precautions would be unreasonably difficult or expensive. I think that such fears are exaggerated, and it is worth recollecting that when the courts sought to lay down specific rules as to the duties of occupiers the law became so unsatisfactory that Parliament had to step in and pass the Occupiers Liability Act 1957. It appears to me that the ordinary principles of the common law must apply in streets as well as elsewhere, and that fundamentally they depend on what a reasonable man, careful of his neighbour's safety, would do having the knowledge which a reasonable man in the position of the defendant must be deemed

---

1. See *M'Kibbin v Glasgow City Corpn* 1920 SC 590 at 598.
2. (1950) 114 JP 370.

to have. I agree with the statement of law at the end of the speech of Lord Sumner in *Glasgow Corpn v Taylor*[1] —

'a measure of care appropriate to the inability or disability of those who are immature or feeble in mind or body is due from others who know of, or ought to anticipate, the presence of such persons within the scope and hazard of their own operations.'

I would therefore allow this appeal. The assessment of damages has been deferred and the case must be remitted for such assessment.

LORD MORTON OF HENRYTON: . . . There is no dispute as to the facts, and only two questions arise for decision—first, what is the duty owed by those who engage on operations on the pavement of a highway and, secondly, was that duty discharged in the present case.

My lords, I would answer the first question as follows. It is their duty to take reasonable care not to act in a way likely to endanger other persons who may reasonably be expected to walk along the pavement. That duty is owed to blind persons if the operators foresee or ought to have foreseen that blind persons may walk along the pavement and is in no way different from the duty owed to persons with sight, though the carrying out of the duty may involve extra precautions in the case of blind pedestrians. I think that everyone living in greater London must have seen blind persons walking slowly along on the pavement and waving a white stick in front of them, so as to touch any obstruction which may be in their way, and I think that the respondents' workmen ought to have foreseen that a blind person might well come along the pavement in question.

I have not found it easy to answer the second question, but I have come to the conclusion that the workmen failed adequately to discharge the duty which I have stated, though I would accept the finding of the learned trial judge that 'what the [respondents] did was adequate to give reasonable and proper warning to normal pedestrians'. . . .

I would allow the appeal. Counsel for the respondents submitted that a decision against them would have very far-reaching consequences and would make it necessary for persons working in any public place to take elaborate and extreme precautions to prevent blind persons from suffering injury. My lords, I do not think that the consequences would be so serious as counsel suggests, bearing in mind, first, that there are many places to which one would not reasonably expect a blind person to go unaccompanied and, secondly, that workmen are entitled to assume that such a person will take reasonable care to protect himself, for example by using a stick in order to ascertain if there is anything in his way and by stopping if his stick touches any object.

[LORD EVERSHED, LORD HODSON and LORD GUEST delivered speeches in favour of allowing the appeal.]

Appeal allowed

Note

In addition to the protection that the decision in *Haley* affords to blind persons, s. 1 of the Disabled Persons Act 1981 requires a highway authority, local authority or anyone exercising statutory power to carry out work on

---

1. [1922] 1 AC 44 at 67; [1921] All ER Rep 1 at 13.

a highway to have regard to the needs of disabled or blind persons where the work may impede their mobility. In particular, the needs of blind persons to have openings in the street properly protected must be taken into account.

(b)   The gravity of the injury which may be suffered

Paris v Stepney Borough Council House of Lords [1951] 1 All ER 42

LORD SIMONDS: My Lords, this is an appeal from an order of the Court of Appeal[1] setting aside a judgment of Lynskey J, in favour of the appellant for £5,250 damages and costs. On 13 May 1942, the appellant entered the service of the respondents as a garage hand in their cleansing department. He was then for all practical purposes blind in his left eye, having suffered serious injury in May 1941, as the result of enemy action, but this fact was not known to the respondents at that time. On or about 19 July 1946, he was medically examined with a view to his becoming a member of the permanent staff and joining the superannuation scheme, and on 22 July 1946, the medical officer reported to a Mr Boden, the respondents' public cleansing officer, that the appellant was not fit on account of his disablement to join the super-annuation scheme. On 16 May 1947, he was given two weeks' notice expiring on 30 May 1947, to terminate his employment. I will assume that at this date the respondents had notice of his physical disability, including the blindness of his left eye. On 28 May 1947, the accident occurred which gave rise to the present action. The appellant was engaged in dismantling the chassis of a gulley cleaner, a type of vehicle generally used by local authorities for the cleansing and flushing of street gulleys. The vehicle had been raised about four and a half feet from the garage floor by means of a ramp. The appellant had to remove a U-bolt holding the springs of an axle, and, to release it, he hit the U-bolt with a steel hammer. As the result of his doing so a piece of metal flew off and entered his right eye with the disastrous consequences that he lost the sight of it altogether. On 8 August 1947, he commenced his action against the respondents claiming damages for their negligence and breach of statutory duty. The respondents put in a defence denying negligence and raising an alternative plea of contributory negligence which has not been pursued. Nor has the appellant pursued his claim for breach of statutory duty. The single question is whether the appellant proved the negligence of the respondents, a question answered in the affirmative by Lynskey J, in the negative by the Court of Appeal.

What, then, was the negligence alleged by the appellant and denied by the respondents? It was that it was the duty of the respondents to supply the appellant with suitable goggles for the protection of his eyes while he was engaged in such work and to require him to use them. . . . I will say at once that I do not dissent from the view that an employer owes a particular duty to each of his employees. His liability in tort arises from his failure to take reasonable care in regard to the particular employee and it is clear that, if so, all the circumstances relevant to that employee must be taken into consideration. I see no valid reason for excluding as irrelevant the gravity of the damage which the employee will suffer if an accident occurs, and with great respect to the judgments of the Court of Appeal I cannot accept the view, neatly summarised by Asquith LJ ([1949] 2 All ER 845), that the greater risk of injury is, but the risk of greater injury is not, a relevant circumstance. I find no authority for such a proposition nor does it appear to me to be founded on any logical principle. . . .

---

1. [1950] 1 KB 320; [1949] 2 All ER 843.

LORD MORTON OF HENRYTON: My Lords, it cannot be doubted that there are occupations in which the possibility of an accident occurring to any workman is extremely remote, while there are other occupations in which there is constant risk of accident to the workmen. Similarly, there are occupations in which, if an accident occurs, it is likely to be of a trivial nature, while there are other occupations in which, if an accident occurs, the result to the workman may well be fatal. Whether one is considering the likelihood of an accident occurring, or the gravity of the consequences if an accident happens, there is in each case a gradually ascending scale between the two extremes which I have already mentioned. In considering generally the precautions which an employer ought to take for the protection of his workmen it must, in my view, be right to take into account both elements, the likelihood of an accident happening and the gravity of the consequences. I take as an example two occupations in which the risk of an accident taking place is exactly equal. If an accident does occur in the one occupation, the consequences to the workman will be comparatively trivial; if an accident occurs in the other occupation the consequences to the workman will be death or mutilation. Can it be said that the precautions which it is the duty of an employer to take for the safety of his workmen are exactly the same in each of these occupations? My Lords, that is not my view. I think that the more serious the damage which will happen if an accident occurs, the more thorough are the precautions which an employer must take. If I am right as to this general principle, I think it follows logically that if A and B, who are engaged on the same work, run precisely the same risk of an accident happening, but if the results of an accident will be more serious to A than to B, precautions which are adequate in the case of B may not be adequate in the case of A, and it is a duty of the employer to take such additional precautions for the safety of A as may be reasonable. The duty to take reasonable precautions against injury is one which is owed by the employer to every individual workman.

In the present case it is submitted by counsel for the appellant that, although the appellant ran no greater risk of injury than the other workmen engaged in the maintenance work, he ran a risk of greater injury. Counsel points out that an accident to one eye might transform the appellant into a blind man, and this event in fact happened. A similar accident to one of his comrades would transform that comrade into a one-eyed man, a serious consequence indeed, but not so serious as the results have been to the appellant. My Lords, the Court of Appeal thought that the one-eyed condition of the appellant, known to his employers, was wholly irrelevant in determining the question whether the employer did or did not take reasonable precautions to avoid an accident of this kind. I do not agree. Applying the general principle which I have endeavoured to state, I agree with your Lordships and with Lynskey J, that the condition of the appellant was a relevant fact to be taken into account. . . .

[LORD OAKSEY, LORD MACDERMOTT and LORD NORMAND delivered speeches to a similar effect on this point. However, on the facts of the case, it was only by a majority (LORD SIMONDS and LORD MORTON OF HENRYTON dissenting) that the judgment of LYNSKEY J on liability was restored.]

Appeal allowed

Note

In *Withers v Perry Chain Co Ltd* [1961] 3 All ER 676; [1961] 1 WLR 1314 the plaintiff had had an attack of dermatitis from a reaction to grease used in her job. When she returned to work, the defendants put her on work which in their opinion was the best available for her in the circumstances, but she suffered further attacks and sued her employers alleging negligence in employing her on work which they ought to have known could cause (or exacerbate) dermatitis. Sellers LJ stated (at p. 680) that the duty of the defendants 'was to take all reasonable care for the plaintiff in the employment in which she was engaged, including, of course, a duty to have regard to the fact that she had had dermatitis previously', but it was held that no breach of duty had been established in the case. Devlin LJ said (also at p. 680):

'It may be also (on the principle of *Paris v Stepney Borough Council*) that when the susceptibility of an employee to dermatitis is known there is a duty on the employer to take extra or special precautions to protect such an employee. But it is not suggested that there were any extra or special precautions here which could have been taken.'

(c) The cost and practicability of measures necessary to overcome the risk

Latimer v AEC Ltd House of Lords [1953] 2 All ER 449

The respondents' large factory was flooded by an unusually heavy rainstorm and the water mixed with an oily liquid usually collected in channels in the floor. This mixture when it drained away left a film making the surface very slippery. Sawdust was then spread on the floor but there was insufficient to cover all the area, even though the respondents had had enough there to meet any situation they could have been expected to foresee. The appellant, who was working in the factory on the night shift, slipped on a part of the floor which had not had sawdust applied to it, and a barrel, which he was putting on to a trolley, rolled on to and injured his ankle. Pilcher J, [1952] 1 All ER 443, gave judgment for the appellant against the respondents in negligence, but the Court of Appeal, [1952] 1 All ER 1302, reversed this decision. On appeal to the House of Lords:

LORD TUCKER: . . . In the present case, the respondents were faced with an unprecedented situation following a phenomenal rain storm. They set forty men to work on cleaning up the factory when the flood subsided and used all the available supply of sawdust, which was approximately three tons. The judge has found that they took every step which could reasonably have been taken to deal with the conditions which prevailed before the night shift came on duty, and he has negatived every specific allegation of negligence as pleaded, but he has held the respondents liable because they did not close down the factory, or the part of the factory where the accident occurred, before the commencement of the night shift. I do not question that such a drastic step may be required on the part of a reasonably prudent employer if the peril to his employees is sufficiently grave, and to this extent it must always be a question of degree, but, in my view, there was no evidence in the present case which could justify a finding of negligence for failure on the part of the respondents to take this step. This question was never canvassed in evidence, nor was sufficient evidence given as to the condition of the factory as a whole to enable a satisfactory conclusion to be reached. The learned judge seems to have accepted the reasoning of counsel for the appellant to the effect that the floor was slippery, that slipperiness is a potential danger, that the respondents must be taken to have been aware of this, that in the circumstances nothing could have been done to remedy the slipperiness, that the respondents allowed work to proceed, that an accident due to slipperiness occurred, and that the respondents are, therefore, liable.

This is not the correct approach. The problem is perfectly simple. The only question was: Has it been proved that the floor was so slippery that, remedial steps not being possible, a reasonably prudent employer would have closed down the factory rather than allow his employees to run the risks involved in continuing work? The learned judge does not seem to me to have posed this question to himself, nor was there sufficient evidence before him to have justified an affirmative answer. The absence of any evidence that anyone in the factory during the afternoon or night shift, other than the appellant, slipped, or experienced any difficulty, or that any complaint was made by or on behalf of the workers, all points to the conclusion that the danger was, in fact, not such as to impose on a reasonable employer the obligation placed on the respondents by the trial judge. I agree that the appeal be dismissed.

[On the question of common law negligence, LORD REID agreed with LORD TUCKER and LORD PORTER, LORD OAKSEY and LORD ASQUITH OF BISHOPSTONE delivered speeches in favour of dismissing the appeal. A claim for breach of statutory duty was rejected.]

Appeal dismissed

(d)   The purpose of the defendant's acts

Daborn *v* Bath Tramways Motor Co Ltd and T. Smithey Court of Appeal [1946] 2 All ER 333

The plaintiff was driving an ambulance with a left-hand drive. A notice on the back of the vehicle stated 'Caution – Left hand drive – No signals'. The ambulance was shut in at the back, but, by using a mirror on the left hand side, the plaintiff could see vehicles some yards behind her. She gave evidence that she signalled with her left hand that she was going to make a right turn. However, as the ambulance was turning right, it was hit by a bus, and the plaintiff suffered grave injuries when she was thrown out of the ambulance as a result of the collision. In an unsuccessful appeal by the defendants from a decision of Croom-Johnson J awarding the plaintiff damages, it was argued that the plaintiff had been negligent.

ASQUITH LJ: . . . In determining whether a party is negligent, the standard of reasonable care is that which is reasonably to be demanded in the circumstances. A relevant circumstance to take into account may be the importance of the end to be served by behaving in this way or in that. As has often been pointed out, if all the trains in this country were restricted to a speed of 5 miles an hour, there would be fewer accidents, but our national life would be intolerably slowed down. The purpose to be served, if sufficiently important, justifies the assumption of abnormal risk. The relevance of this applied to the present case is this: during the war which was, at the material time, in progress, it was necessary for many highly important operations to be carried out by means of motor vehicles with left-hand drives, no others being available. So far as this was the case, it was impossible for the drivers of such cars to give the warning signals which could otherwise be properly demanded of them. Meanwhile, it was essential that the ambulance service should be maintained. It seems to me, in those circumstances, it would be demanding too high and an unreasonable standard of care from the drivers of such cars to say to them: 'Either you must give signals which the structure of your vehicle renders impossible or you must not drive at all.' It was urged by counsel for the defendants that these alternatives were not exhaustive, since the driver of such a car should, before executing a turn, stop his car, move to the right-hand seat and look backwards to see if another car was attempting to overtake him and then start up again. Counsel for the plaintiff has satisfied me that such a procedure, besides involving possible delay, might be wholly ineffective. I think the plaintiff did all that in the circumstances she could reasonably be required to do if you include in those circumstances, as I think you should: (i) the necessity in time of national emergency of employing all transport resources which were available, and (ii) the inherent limitations and incapacities of this particular form of transport. In considering whether reasonable care has been observed, one must balance the risk against the consequences of not assuming that risk, and in the present instance this calculation seems to me to work out in favour of the plaintiff. I agree . . . that this appeal should be dismissed.

[MORTON and TUCKER LJJ delivered judgments in favour of dismissing the appeal.]

Notes

1. Attention might also be paid to *Watt v Hertfordshire County Council* [1954] 2 All ER 368; [1954] 1 WLR 835; where the plaintiff, a fireman, was in a team called out to an emergency. A jack was to be taken out as the call said that a woman was trapped under a heavy vehicle a few hundred yards away. There was a vehicle specially fitted to carry this jack, which weighed two or three hundredweight, but it was out on other service, and so the jack was lifted on to a lorry. Unfortunately the driver had to brake suddenly, and the plaintiff was injured when the jack, which stood on four small wheels, moved and caught his leg. It was held that the defendants, his employers, had not been negligent. Saving life and limb, Denning LJ said, justified a considerable risk being taken. He went on to state (at p. 371) that 'I quite agree that fire engines, ambulances and doctors' cars should not shoot past the traffic lights when they show a red light. That is because the risk is too great to warrant the incurring of the danger.' Would this view still prevail if the driver of a fire engine, seeing a man ahead of him in dire peril from a fire, had looked both ways before crossing the red light, but had collided with a car which had just come round a bend?

2. In *United States v Carroll Towing Co Inc* 159 F 2d 169 (1947) Learned Hand J set out a formula for deciding on negligence that encapsulates factors which have just been covered in (*a*)–(*d*) ante. He stated (at p. 173) that 'if the probability be called P; the injury, L; and the burden, B; liability depends upon whether B is less than L multiplied by P: i.e., whether $B < PL$'. For discussion of this formula as part of the economic analysis of law see e.g. R. A. Posner (1972) 1 J Leg Stud 29 esp. at 32–33; *Tort Law: Cases and Economic Analysis* (Boston, 1982), esp. chap. 1; C. Veljanovski, *The Economics of Law: An Introductory Text* (London, 1990), pp. 64–72.

(e) Competitions

Wooldridge *v* Sumner, p. 383, post

Note

See also note 1, p. 387, post, following the extract from *Wooldridge v Sumner*.

(f) Common practice

Morton v William Dixon Ltd Court of Session 1909 SC 807

LORD DUNEDIN: . . . Where the negligence of the employer consists of what I may call a fault of omission, I think it is absolutely necessary that the proof of that fault of omission should be one of two kinds, either—to shew that the thing which he did not do was a thing which was commonly done by other persons in like circumstances, or—to shew that it was a thing which was so obviously wanted that it would be folly in anyone to neglect to provide it. . . .

Notes

1. This passage from Lord Dunedin's judgment has been cited and interpreted in several cases, on which see *Salmond & Heuston*, pp. 263–264, who state that the word 'folly' 'really means no more than "imprudent" or "unreasonable"'.

2. It should be noted, however, that a defendant can be held to have been negligent, even though there is evidence that he acted in accordance with common practice. (See e.g. *Cavanagh v Ulster Weaving Co Ltd* [1960] AC 145; [1959] 2 All ER 745; Dugdale and Stanton, op cit, paras. 15.22–15.23; Jackson and Powell, op cit, paras. 1-25–1-26; J. Holyoak (1990) 10 LS 201; and see further p. 278, post.) On the other hand, a defendant is not necessarily negligent if he does not adopt a common practice. In *Brown v Rolls Royce Ltd* [1960] 1 All ER 577; [1960] 1 WLR 210, among the facts found by the court below (the Court of Session) were that the appellant contracted industrial dermatitis from contact with oil in his work, that, although there were ample washing facilities, barrier cream was not supplied by his employers (on the advice of their medical officer who was not at fault) and that its value in relation to dermatitis was the subject of strong differences of opinion amongst the medical profession. In addition, it had been found that barrier cream was commonly supplied by employers to men doing the sort of work in which the appellant was involved, but that it was not proved that it would stop them, or would probably have stopped him, contracting dermatitis. The House of Lords held that the employers were not at fault in failing to supply barrier cream. Lord Keith of Avonholm said (at p. 581):

'A common practice in like circumstances not followed by an employer may no doubt be a weighty circumstance to be considered by judge or jury in deciding whether failure to comply with this practice, taken along with all the other material circumstances in the case, yields an inference of negligence on the part of the employers.'

However, he added that the 'ultimate test is lack of reasonable care for the safety of the workman in all the circumstances of the case'. Note also Lord Denning's speech in which he stated (at p. 582):

'If defenders do not follow the usual precautions, it raises a prima facie case against them in this sense, that it is evidence from which negligence *may* be inferred, but not in the sense that it *must* be inferred unless the contrary is proved. At the end of the day, the court has to ask itself whether the defenders were negligent or not.'

3. Further consideration was given to the effect of a general practice in the context of employers' liability by Swanwick J in *Stokes v Guest, Keen and Nettlefold (Bolts and Nuts) Ltd* [1968] 1 WLR 1776. After referring to several authorities relating to employers' duty to workmen, he deduced the following principles (at p. 1783):

'. . . that the overall test is still the conduct of the reasonable and prudent employer, taking positive thought for the safety of his workers in the light of what he knows or ought to know; where there is a recognised and general practice which has been followed for a substantial period in similar circumstances without mishap, he is entitled to follow it, unless in the light of common sense or newer knowledge it is clearly bad; but, where there is developing knowledge, he must keep reasonably abreast of it and not be too slow to apply it; and where he has in fact greater than average knowledge of the risks, he may be thereby obliged to take more than the average or standard precautions.'

Is the last part of the quotation an encouragement to ignorance?

Swanwick J's principles were adopted (though added to) by Mustill J in *Thompson v Smiths Shiprepairers (North Shields) Ltd* [1984] QB 405; [1984] 1 All ER 881. He pointed out that there may be a situation where a particular practice is regularly followed in an industry but *not* 'without mishap': the risk may have been 'an inescapable feature of the industry' and, if so, the employer is not liable (though in certain circumstances there will be a duty to warn (see *White v Holbrook Precision Castings Ltd* [1985] IRLR 215 at 218)). Mustill J went on to point out (at p. 889) that common practice in an industry is relevant (though not conclusive) on the issue of negligence, not only when the negligence is said to be constituted by a failure to take known precautions, 'but also where the omission involves an absence of initiative in seeking out knowledge of facts which are not in themselves obvious.' Although the employer 'must keep up to date . . . the court must be slow to blame him for not ploughing a lone furrow'.

4. What is the position when there are conflicting views as to the proper practice to adopt? In *Bolam v Friern Hospital Management Committee* [1957] 2 All ER 118; [1957] 1 WLR 582 McNair J, directing the jury, told them that a doctor was not negligent if he adopted a practice which a responsible body of skilled medical men accepted as proper, and that this was unaffected by the mere fact that there was a contrary body of opinion. This view has been approved in later cases (see e.g. *Maynard v West Midlands Regional Health Authority* [1985] 1 All ER 635; [1984] 1 WLR 634 referring to a practice accepted as proper by a responsible body of medical opinion), and it was acknowledged in *Gold v Haringey Health Authority* [1988] QB 481; [1987] 2 All ER 888 that it is not confined to the medical profession but applies to 'any other profession or calling which requires special skill, knowledge or experience'. Nevertheless, as has been mentioned earlier (p. 276, ante), courts can (exceptionally) find adherence to an accepted practice to be negligent. There has been debate whether this is indeed the case with the medical profession (see e.g. Jackson and Powell, op cit, paras. 6–26 – 6–30; Kennedy and Grubb, op cit, pp. 406–420; A. Grubb in *Medicine, Ethics and the Law*, edited by M. D. A. Freeman, (London, 1988), pp. 136–137); and on the interpretation of the *Bolam* case itself, see J. L. Montrose (1958) 21 MLR 529 (set out in Kennedy and Grubb, op cit, pp. 417–419); Kennedy and Grubb, op cit, pp. 407–408; P. D. G. Skegg, *Law, Ethics and Medicine*

(Oxford, 1988 reprint), p. 83, note 39. In relation to the test in *Bolam* note the following statement by Hirst J in *Hills v Potter* [1983] 3 All ER 716 at 728:

'In every case the court must be satisfied that the standard contended for on [doctors'] behalf accords with that upheld by a substantial body of medical opinion, and that this body of medical opinion is both respectable and responsible and experienced in [the] particular field of medicine.'

If a court thought that a practice was negligent, would it qualify as a practice accepted as proper by a *responsible* body of medical opinion on this matter? Furthermore, the treatment of *Bolam* in *Gold* as a test applicable beyond the medical profession suggests that medical opinion is not conclusive. How conclusive is medical opinion under s. 1(5) of the Congenital Disabilities (Civil Liability) Act 1976 (p. 143, ante)?

The next case is concerned with the issue whether the 'responsible body of medical opinion' test should be applied, not only to diagnosis and treatment, but also to the amount of information a medical practitioner must give to a patient as to the risks involved in a course of treatment. This test can be refered to as the *Bolam* test (see p. 283, post), but so can the 'skilled man' test mentioned p. 259, ante (see p. 279, post) and indeed the phrase 'the *Bolam* test' may be used so as to encompass both: for an example see the *Gold* case.

Sidaway *v* Bethlem Royal Hospital Governors House of Lords [1985] 1 All ER 643

This was an appeal from the Court of Appeal, [1984] 1 All ER 1018, which had dismissed an appeal from a decision of Skinner J who had dismissed the appellant's action.

LORD BRIDGE OF HARWICH: . . . The appellant underwent at the hospital for which the first respondents are the responsible authority an operation on her cervical vertebrae performed by a neuro-surgeon, since deceased, whose executors are the second respondents. The nature of the operation was such that, however skilfully performed, it involved a risk of damage to the nerve root at the site of the operation or to the spinal cord. The trial judge described that risk as 'best expressed to a layman as a 1% or 2% risk of ill-effects ranging from the mild to the catastrophic'. The appellant in fact suffered, without negligence on the surgeon's part in the performance of the operation, a degree of damage to the spinal cord of which the effects, if not catastrophic, were certainly severe. Damages have been agreed, subject to liability, in the sum of £67,500.

The appellant denied that she had seen the surgeon at all before the operation was performed. This evidence the judge rejected. He found that, before the appellant consented to undergo the operation, the surgeon explained the nature of the operation to her in simple terms and warned her of the possibility and likely consequences of damage to the nerve root, but did not refer to the risk of damage to the spinal cord. Most unfortunately, the surgeon who performed the operation died before these proceedings were instituted. Accordingly, the trial judge, the Court of Appeal and your Lordships' House have all been denied the advantage of what would clearly have been vital evidence on the issue of liability, not only the surgeon's own account of precisely what he had told this appellant, but also his explanation of the reasons for his clinical judgment that, in her case, the information he gave her about the operation and its attendant risk was appropriate and sufficient. The judge was thus driven to base the finding, to which I have earlier referred, in part on inference from documents, but mainly on the evidence of other doctors as to what they knew of the deceased surgeon's customary practice when discussing with patients an operation of the kind the appellant was to undergo. The result is that liability falls to be considered, in effect, in relation to that customary practice, independently of the vitally important individual doctor/patient relationship which must play so large a part in any discussion of a proposed operation with a patient. That introduces an element of artificiality into the case which we may deplore but cannot avoid.

There was a difference of opinion between the neuro-surgeons called as expert witnesses whether they themselves would, in the circumstances, have warned the appellant specifically of the risk of damage to the spinal cord. But the one expert witness called for the appellant agreed readily and without reservation that the deceased surgeon, in omitting any such warning, would have been following a practice accepted as proper by a responsible body of competent neuro-surgeons.

Broadly, a doctor's professional functions may be divided into three phases: diagnosis, advice and treatment. In performing his functions of diagnosis and treatment, the standard by which English law measures the doctor's duty of care to his patient is not open to doubt. 'The test is the standard of the ordinary skilled man exercising and professing to have that special skill.' These are the words of McNair J in *Bolam v Friern Hospital Management Committee* [1957] 2 All ER 118 at 121, [1957] 1 WLR 582 at 586, approved by this House in *Whitehouse v Jordan* [1981] 1 All ER 267 at 277, [1981] 1 WLR 246 at 258 per Lord Edmund-Davies and in *Maynard v West Midlands Regional Health Authority* [1985] 1 All ER 635 per Lord Scarman. The test is conveniently referred to as the *Bolam* test. In *Maynard*'s case Lord Scarman, with whose speech the other four members of the Appellate Committee agreed, further cited with approval the words of the Lord President (Clyde) in *Hunter v Hanley* 1955 SLT 213 at 217:

'In the realm of diagnosis and treatment there is ample scope for genuine difference of opinion and one man clearly is not negligent merely because his conclusion differs from that of other professional men . . . The true test for establishing negligence in diagnosis or treatment on the part of a doctor is whether he has been proved to be guilty of such failure as no doctor of ordinary skill would be guilty of if acting with ordinary care. . . .'

The language of the *Bolam* test clearly requires a different degree of skill from a specialist in his own special field than from a general practitioner. In the field of neuro-surgery it would be necessary to substitute for the Lord President's phrase 'no doctor of ordinary skill', the phrase 'no neuro-surgeon of ordinary skill'. All this is elementary and, in the light of the two recent decisions of this House referred to, firmly established law.

The important question which this appeal raises is whether the law imposes any, and if so what, different criterion as the measure of the medical man's duty of care to his patient when giving advice with respect to a proposed course of treatment. It is clearly right to recognise that a conscious adult patient of sound mind is entitled to decide for himself whether or not he will submit to a particular course of treatment proposed by the doctor, most significantly surgical treatment under general anaesthesia. This entitlement is the foundation of the doctrine of 'informed consent' which has led in certain American jurisdictions to decisions and, in the Supreme Court of Canada, to dicta on which the appellant relies, which would oust the *Bolam* test and substitute an 'objective' test of a doctor's duty to advise the patient of the advantages and disadvantages of undergoing the treatment proposed and more particularly to advise the patient of the risks involved.

There are, it appears to me, at least theoretically, two extreme positions which could be taken. It could be argued that, if the patient's consent is to be fully informed, the doctor must specifically warn him of *all* risks involved in the treatment offered, unless he has some sound clinical reason not to do so. Logically, this would seem to be the extreme to which a truly objective criterion of the doctor's duty would lead. Yet this position finds no support from any authority to which we have been referred in any jurisdiction. It seems to be generally accepted that there is no need to warn of the risks inherent in all surgery under general anaesthesia. This is variously explained on the ground that the patient may be expected to be aware of such risks or that they are relatively remote. If the law is to impose on the medical profession a duty to warn of risks to secure 'informed consent' independently of accepted medical opinion of what is appropriate, neither of these explanations for confining the duty to special as opposed to general surgical risks seems to me wholly convincing.

At the other extreme it could be argued that, once the doctor has decided what treatment is, on balance of advantages and disadvantages, in the patient's best interest, he should not alarm the patient by volunteering a warning of any risk involved, however grave and substantial, unless specifically asked by the patient. I cannot believe that contemporary medical opinion would support this view, which would effectively exclude the patient's right to decide in the very type of case where it is most important that he should be in a position to exercise that right and, perhaps even more significantly, to seek a second opinion whether he should submit himself to the significant risk which has been drawn to his attention. I should perhaps add at this point, although the issue does not strictly arise in this appeal, that, when questioned specifically by a patient of apparently sound mind about risks involved in a particular treatment proposed, the doctor's duty must, in my opinion, be to answer both truthfully and as fully as the questioner requires.

The decision mainly relied on to establish a criterion of the doctor's duty to disclose the risks inherent in a proposed treatment which is prescribed by the law and can be applied independently of any medical opinion or practice is that of the District of Columbia Circuit Court of Appeals in *Canterbury v Spence* 464 F 2d 772 (1972). The judgment of the court (Wright, Leventhal and Robinson JJ), delivered by Robinson J, expounds the view that an objective criterion of what is a sufficient disclosure of risk is necessary to ensure that the patient is enabled to make an intelligent decision and cannot be left to be determined by the doctors. He said (at 784):

'Respect for the patient's right of self-determination on particular therapy demands a standard set by law for physicians rather than one which physicians may or may not impose upon themselves.'

In an attempt to define the objective criterion it is said (at 787) that —

'the issue on non-disclosure must be approached from the viewpoint of the reasonableness of the physician's divulgence in terms of what he knows or should know to be the patient's informational needs.'

A risk is required to be disclosed —

'when a reasonable person, in what the physician knows or should know to be the patient's position, would be likely to attach significance to the risk or cluster of risks in deciding whether or not to forego the proposed therapy.'

The judgment adds (at 788): 'Whenever non-disclosure of particular risk information is open to debate by reasonable-minded men, the issue is for the finder of facts.'

The court naturally recognises exceptions from the duty laid down in the case of an unconscious patient, an immediate emergency or a case where the doctor can establish that disclosure would be harmful to the patient.

Expert medical evidence will be needed to indicate the nature and extent of the risks and benefits involved in the treatment (and presumably of any alternative course). But the court affirms (at 792): 'Experts are unnecessary to a showing of the materiality of a risk to a patient's decision on treatment, or to the reasonably, expectable effect of risk disclosure on the decision.' In English law, if this doctrine were adopted, expert medical opinion whether a particular risk should or should not have been disclosed would presumably be inadmissible in evidence.

I recognise the logical force of the *Canterbury* doctrine, proceeding from the premise that the patient's right to make his own decision must at all costs be safeguarded against the kind of medical paternalism which assumes that 'doctor knows best'. But, with all respect, I regard the doctrine as quite impractical in application for three principal reasons. First, it gives insufficient weight to the realities of the doctor/patient relationship. A very wide variety of factors must enter into a doctor's clinical judgment not only as to what treatment is appropriate for a particular patient, but also as to how best to communicate to the patient the significant factors necessary to enable the patient to make an informed decision whether to undergo the treatment. The doctor cannot set out to educate the patient to his own standard of medical knowledge of all the relevant factors involved. He may take the view, certainly with some patients, that the very fact of his volunteering, without being asked, information of some remote risk involved in the treatment proposed, even though he describes it as remote, may lead to that risk assuming an undue significance in the patient's calculations. Second, it would seem to me quite unrealistic in any medical negligence action to confine the expert medical evidence to an explanation of the primary medical factors involved and to deny the court the benefit of evidence of medical opinion and practice on the particular issue of disclosure which is under consideration. Third, the objective test which *Canterbury* propounds seems to me to be so imprecise as to be almost meaningless. If it is to be left to individual judges to decide for themselves what 'a reasonable person in the patient's position' would consider a risk of sufficient significance that he should be told about it, the outcome of litigation in this field is likely to be quite unpredictable.

I note with interest from a learned article entitled 'Informed Consent to Medical Treatment' (1981) 97 LQR 102 at 108 by Mr Gerald Robertson ... that only a minority of states in the United States of America have chosen to follow *Canterbury* and that since 1975 'there has been a growing tendency for individual states to enact legislation which severely curtails the operation of the doctrine of informed consent.' I should also add that I find particularly cogent and convincing the reasons given for declining to follow *Canterbury* by the Supreme Court of Virginia in *Bly v Rhoads* 222 SE 2d 783 (1976).

Having rejected the *Canterbury* doctrine as a solution to the problem of safeguarding the patient's right to decide whether he will undergo a particular treatment advised by his doctor, the question remains whether that right is sufficiently safeguarded by the application of the *Bolam* test without qualification to the determination of the question what risks inherent in a proposed treatment should be disclosed. The case against a simple application of the *Bolam* test is cogently stated by Laskin CJC, giving the judgment of the Supreme Court of Canada in *Reibl v Hughes* (1980) 114 DLR (3d) 1 at 13:

'To allow expert medical evidence to determine what risks are material and, hence, should be disclosed and, correlatively, what risks are not material is to hand over to the medical profession the entire question of the scope of the duty of disclosure, including the question whether there has been a breach of that duty. Expert medical evidence is, of course, relevant to findings as to the risks that reside in or are a result of recommended surgery or other treatment. It will also have a bearing on their materiality but this is not a question that is to be concluded on the basis of the expert medical evidence alone. The issue under consideration is a different issue from that involved where the question is whether the doctor carried out his professional activities by applicable professional standards. What is under consideration here is the patient's right to know what risks are involved in undergoing or foregoing certain surgery or other treatment.'

I fully appreciate the force of this reasoning, but can only accept it subject to the important qualification that a decision what degree of disclosure of risks is best calculated to assist a particular patient to make a rational choice whether or not to undergo a particular treatment must primarily be a matter of clinical judgment. It would follow from this that the issue whether non-disclosure in a particular case should be condemned as a breach of the doctor's duty of care is an issue to be decided primarily on the basis of expert medical evidence, applying the *Bolam* test. But I do not see that this approach involves the necessity 'to hand over to the medical profession the entire question of the scope of the duty of disclosure, including the question whether there has been a breach of that duty'. Of course, if there is a conflict of evidence whether a responsible body of medical opinion approves of non-disclosure in a particular case, the judge will have to resolve that conflict. But, even in a case where, as here, no expert witness in the relevant medical field condemns the non-disclosure as being in conflict with accepted and responsible medical practice, I am of opinion that the judge might in certain circumstances come to the conclusion that disclosure of a particular risk was so obviously necessary to an informed choice on the part of the patient that no reasonably prudent medical man would fail to make it. The kind of case I have in mind would be an operation involving a substantial risk of grave adverse consequences, as for example the 10% risk of a stroke from the operation which was the subject of the Canadian case of *Reibl v Hughes* (1980) 114 DLR (3d) 1. In such a case, in the absence of some cogent clinical reason why the patient should not be informed, a doctor, recognising and respecting his patient's right of decision, could hardly fail to appreciate the necessity for an appropriate warning.

In the instant case I can see no reasonable ground on which the judge could properly reject the conclusion to which the unchallenged medical evidence led in the application of the *Bolam* test. The trial judge's assessment of the risk at 1% or 2% covered both nerve root and spinal cord damage and covered a spectrum of possible ill-effects 'ranging from the mild to the catastrophic'. In so far as it is possible and appropriate to measure such risks in percentage terms (some of the expert medical witnesses called expressed a marked and understandable reluctance to do so), the risk of damage to the spinal cord of such severity as the appellant in fact suffered was, it would appear, certainly less than 1%. But there is no yardstick either in the judge's findings or in the evidence to measure what fraction of 1% that risk represented. In these circumstances, the appellant's expert witness's agreement that the non-disclosure complained of accorded with a practice accepted as proper by a responsible body of neuro-surgical opinion afforded the respondents a complete defence to the appellant's claim.

I would dismiss the appeal.

LORD SCARMAN: . . . The issue is whether Mr Falconer failed to exercise due care (his skill was not challenged) in the advice which he gave his patient when recommending an operation; I use the word 'advice' to cover information as to risk and the options of alternative treatment. Whatever be the correct formulation of the applicable law, the issue cannot be settled positively for or against the doctor without knowing what advice, including any warning of inherent risk in the operation, he gave his patient before she decided to undergo it and what was his assessment of the mental, emotional and physical state of his patient. The trial judge derived no help on these two vital matters from the evidence of the appellant. Mr Falconer was not an available witness, having died before trial, and the medical records afforded no sure guide on either matter. Regrettable though a 'non-proven' verdict is, it is not, therefore, surprising. Where the court lacks direct evidence as to the nature and extent of the advice and warning (if any) given by the doctor and as to his assessment of his patient the court may well have to conclude that the patient has failed to prove her case.

This lack of evidence is unsatisfactory also from a purely legal point of view. I am satisfied, for reasons which I shall develop, that the trial judge and the Court of

Appeal erred in law in holding that, in a case where the alleged negligence is a failure to warn the patient of a risk inherent in the treatment proposed, the *Bolam* test, (see *Bolam v Friern Hospital Management Committee* [1957] 2 All ER 118, [1957] 1 WLR 582) . . . is to be applied. In my view the question whether or not the omission to warn constitutes a breach of the doctor's duty of care towards his patient is to be determined not exclusively by reference to the current state of responsible and competent professional opinion and practice at the time, though both are, of course, relevant consideration[s], but by the court's view whether the doctor in advising his patient gave the consideration which the law requires him to give to the right of the patient to make up her own mind in the light of the relevant information whether or not she will accept the treatment which he proposes. This being my view of the law, I have tested the facts found by the trial judge by what I believe to be the correct legal criterion. In my view the appellant has failed to prove that Mr Falconer was in breach of the duty of care which he owed to her in omitting to disclose the risk which the trial judge found as a fact he did not disclose to her.

. . . [W]as [the judge in *Bolam*] correct in treating the 'standard of competent professional opinion' as the criterion in determining whether a doctor is under a duty to warn his patient of the risk, or risks, inherent in the treatment which he recommends? Skinner J and the Court of Appeal have in the instant case held that [he] was correct. Bristow J adopted the same criterion in *Chatterton v Gerson* [1981] 1 All ER 257; [1981] QB 432. The implications of this view of the law are disturbing. It leaves the determination of a legal duty to the judgment of doctors. Responsible medical judgment may, indeed, provide the law with an acceptable standard in determining whether a doctor in diagnosis or treatment has complied with his duty. But is it right that medical judgment should determine whether there exists a duty to warn of risk and its scope? It would be a strange conclusion if the courts should be led to conclude that our law, which undoubtedly recognises a right in the patient to decide whether he will accept or reject the treatment proposed, should permit the doctors to determine whether and in what circumstances a duty arises requiring the doctor to warn his patient of the risks inherent in the treatment which he proposes.

The right of 'self-determination', the description applied by some to what is no more and no less than the right of a patient to determine for himself whether he will or will not accept the doctor's advice, is vividly illustrated where the treatment recommended is surgery. A doctor who operates without the consent of his patient is, save in cases of emergency or mental disability, guilty of the civil wrong of trespass to the person; he is also guilty of the criminal offence of assault. The existence of the patient's right to make his own decision, which may be seen as a basic human right protected by the common law, is the reason why a doctrine embodying a right of the patient to be informed of the risks of surgical treatment has been developed in some jurisdictions in the United States of America and has found favour with the Supreme Court of Canada. Known as the 'doctrine of informed consent', it amounts to this: where there is a 'real' or a 'material' risk inherent in the proposed operation (however competently and skilfully performed) the question whether and to what extent a patient should be warned before he gives his consent is to be answered not by reference to medical practice but by accepting as a matter of law that, subject to all proper exceptions (of which the court, not the profession, is the judge), a patient has a right to be informed of the risks inherent in the treatment which is proposed. The profession, it is said, should not be judge in its own cause; or, less emotively but more correctly, the courts should not allow medical opinion as to what is best for the patient to override the patient's right to decide for himself whether he will submit to the treatment offered him. . . .

. . . The proliferation of medical malpractice suits in the United States of America has led some courts and some legislatures to curtail or even to reject the operation of the doctrine in an endeavour to restrict the liability of the doctor and so discourage the practice of 'defensive medicine', by which is meant the practice of doctors advising and undertaking the treatment which they think is legally safe even though they may believe that it is not the best for their patient.

The danger of defensive medicine developing in this country clearly exists, though the absence of the lawyer's 'contingency fee' (a percentage of the damages for him as his fee if he wins the case but nothing if he loses) may make it more remote. However that may be, in matters of civil wrong or tort courts are concerned with legal principle; if policy problems emerge, they are best left to the legislature: see *McLoughlin v O'Brian* [1982] 2 All ER 298, [1983] 1 AC 410.

. . . In a medical negligence case where the issue is as to the advice and information given to the patient as to the treatment proposed, the available options and the risk, the court is concerned primarily with a patient's right. The doctor's duty arises from his patient's rights. If one considers the scope of the doctor's duty by beginning with the right of the patient to make his own decision whether he will or will not undergo the treatment proposed, the right to be informed of significant risk and the doctor's corresponding duty are easy to understand, for the proper implementation of the right requires that the doctor be under a duty to inform his patient of the material risks inherent in the treatment. And it is plainly right that a doctor may avoid liability for failure to warn of a material risk if he can show that he reasonably believed that communication to the patient of the existence of the risk would be detrimental to the health (including, of course, the mental health) of his patient. . . .

My conclusion as to the law is therefore this. To the extent that I have indicated, I think that English law must recognise a duty of the doctor to warn his patient of risk inherent in the treatment which he is proposing; and especially so if the treatment be surgery. The critical limitation is that the duty is confined to material risk. The test of materiality is whether in the circumstances of the particular case, the court is satisfied that a reasonable person in the patient's position would be likely to attach significance to the risk. Even if the risk be material, the doctor will not be liable if on a reasonable assessment of his patient's condition he takes the view that a warning would be detrimental to his patient's health. . . .

[Having applied the principles in his speech, LORD SCARMAN was in favour of dismissing the appeal.]

[LORD KEITH OF KINKEL agreed with LORD BRIDGE OF HARWICH. LORD DIPLOCK and LORD TEMPLEMAN delivered speeches in favour of dismissing the appeal.]

Appeal dismissed

Notes

1. On the relationship of policy and principle to which Lord Scarman refers (ante), see p. 64 ante; S. Lee (1985) 101 LQR 93.

2. Lord Diplock in *Sidaway* did not think any distinction should be made between cases concerning the amount of information a medical practitioner should reveal and other aspects of a practitioner's duty. He mentioned (at p. 657) that 'the criterion of the duty of care owed by a doctor to his patient is whether he has acted in accordance with a practice accepted as proper by a body of responsible and skilled medical opinion' and acknowledged that there might be several such practices in relation to a particular matter. However, he underlined at a later stage that the court must be satisfied by expert evidence that the body of medical opinion is a responsible one. (See further p. 278, ante.)

3. Consider again the comments on the *Bolam* case at p. 278, ante. In this note we are primarily concerned with the 'responsible body of medical opinion' test to be found in that case. I. Kennedy, *Treat Me Right* (Oxford,

1988), pp. 193-212 (and see Skegg, op cit, p. 263) views Lord Diplock alone as applying it, and is unhappy with the reliance solely on his speech from *Sidaway* in *Gold v Haringey Health Authority* [1988] QB 481; [1987] 2 All ER 888 which stated that the House of Lords in *Sidaway* applied the *Bolam* test: see Kennedy, op cit, pp. 210-212. See further A. Grubb [1988] CLJ 12 and in *Medicine, Ethics and the Law*, edited by M. D. A. Freeman, (London, 1988), pp. 133-139 and note his reference (at p. 139) to the unreported case in 1987 of *Palmer v Eadie*. But is Lord Bridge's opinion (with which Lord Keith agreed) really any different from that of Lord Diplock? Is Lord Diplock leaving the decision to the medical profession in all cases? If confronted with Lord Bridge's example (p. 282, ante) where it was said that compliance with a common practice would not avoid a finding of negligence, might not Lord Diplock decide, having heard the evidence from the medical witnesses, that this was not a responsible body of medical opinion? On the interpretation of Lord Templeman's speech, consider Kennedy, op cit, pp. 205-209; Skegg, op cit, p. 262. Note, however, that in *Blyth v Bloomsbury Health Authority* (1989) 5 PN 167 Kerr LJ thought that Lord Templeman was saying that the *Bolam* test was 'all-pervasive' although as Kennedy and Skegg point out, the case is not expressly cited in Lord Templeman's speech.

It should also be mentioned that *Gold* rejected the idea that the *Bolam* test would not apply to advice on non-therapeutic matters. Such a distinction was thought to go against the 'thrust' of the majority view in *Sidaway*, particular attention being paid to Lord Diplock's speech in that case for the point that the *Bolam* test applied to all cases where a person performed a professional skill. One area where it was thought that the *Bolam* test did not apply was where a patient asked for advice: see e.g. Lord Bridge's speech, p. 280, ante. However, in *Blyth v Bloomsbury Health Authority* Kerr LJ was of the opinion that the *Bolam* test applied to the same extent to the provision of information in response to a general inquiry as in the case where no inquiry was made and (obiter) was unconvinced that it was irrelevant even if a specific inquiry was made. Consider also Neill LJ's opinion that the *Bolam* test applied 'as a general proposition' in relation to the amount of information to be provided when the patient had asked questions.

4. For more general discussion of the question of the provision of information by medical practitioners, see Kennedy, op cit, chap. 9; Kennedy and Grubb, op cit, pp. 215-277 and 581-587; Skegg, op cit, pp. 75-95 and 260-263; H. Teff (1985) 101 LQR 432; M. Brazier (1987) 7 LS 169; S. Lee, *Law and Morals* (Oxford, 1986), chap. 10; and *Oxford Essays in Jurisprudence* 3rd series, edited by J. Eekelaar and J. Bell, (Oxford, 1987), pp. 199-202 and 212-220. For an empirical study of the effect in Canada of the adoption by that country's Supreme Court of the 'informed consent' doctrine (*Reibl v Hughes* (1980) 114 DLR (3d) 1), see G. B. Robertson (1984) 22 Osgoode Hall LJ 139; for comment on the post-*Reibl v Hughes* case law in Canada, see Kennedy, op cit, p. 212, citing A. N. Dugdale (1986) 2 PN 108 at 108-111. In Dugdale's opinion the fear expressed in *Sidaway*, that defensive medicine would be brought about by a concern that breach of a duty to warn would open up widespread liability, is unlikely to be realised because of the requirement of showing causation, which in Canada has been approached on an objective basis: see further Grubb, op cit, pp. 139-142 and see p. 146, note 23.

3 Aids in discharging the burden of proof

(a) Statute

The Civil Evidence Act 1968

11. Convictions as evidence in civil proceedings. — (1) In any civil proceedings the fact that a person has been convicted of an offence by or before any court in the United Kingdom or by a court-martial there or elsewhere shall (subject to subsection (3) below) be admissible in evidence for the purpose of proving, where to do so is relevant to any issue in those proceedings, that he committed that offence, whether he was so convicted upon a plea of guilty or otherwise and whether or not he is a party to the civil proceedings; but no conviction other than a subsisting one shall be admissible in evidence by virtue of this section.

(2) In any civil proceedings in which by virtue of this section a person is proved to have been convicted of an offence by or before any court in the United Kingdom or by a court-martial there or elsewhere —

    (a) he shall be taken to have committed that offence unless the contrary is proved; and

    (b) without prejudice to the reception of any other admissible evidence for the purpose of identifying the facts on which the conviction was based, the contents of any document which is admissible as evidence of the conviction, and the contents of the information, complaint, indictment or charge-sheet on which the person in question was convicted, shall be admissible in evidence for that purpose.

(3) Nothing in this section shall prejudice the operation of section 13[1] of this Act or any other enactment whereby a conviction or a finding of fact in any criminal proceedings is for the purposes of any other proceedings made conclusive evidence of any fact.

Notes

1. For discussion of this provision, see Sir R. Cross, *Evidence*, 7th edn (London, 1990), pp. 102–103.

2. Another way in which statute might help a plaintiff discharge the burden of proof should be noted. Although a breach of statutory duty can constitute a tort in its own right (see chap.12, p. 531, post), nevertheless a breach of statutory duty can be evidence of negligence; and for a more radical suggestion from the Supreme Court of Canada, see p. 551, post. On the other hand, it might be noted here that compliance with a legislative standard can be evidence that the defendant has not been negligent, although it does not necessarily rule out a contrary finding (*Bux v Slough Metals Ltd* [1974] 1 All ER 262; [1973] 1 WLR 1358, noted p. 551, post; cf. *Budden v BP Oil Ltd and Shell Oil Ltd* [1980] JPL 586 on which see R. B. Macrory [1981] JPL 258).

---

1. [See p. 768, post.]

(b)   Common law — res ipsa loquitur

Scott v London and St Katherine Docks Co Court of Exchequer Chamber [1861-73] All ER Rep 246

The plaintiff by his declaration alleged that the defendants were possessed of certain docks, and warehouses therein, that the plaintiff was lawfully therein, that the defendants by their servants were lowering bags of sugar by means of a crane or hoist, and that by the negligence of the defendants' servants a bag of sugar fell upon the plaintiff and injured him. The defendants denied liability. At the trial before Martin B and a special jury, the plaintiff, who was the only witness called, gave evidence relative to the accident, and stated that he was a Custom House officer of twenty six years' standing; that on 19 January 1864, the occasion in question, he was at the defendants' docks, and had performed his duty at the East Quay there as superintendent of the weighing of goods; that he was directed by Mr Lilley, his superior officer, to go from the East Quay to the Spirit Quay, which he proceeded to do, having to pass the warehouses in his way. Not being able to find Lilley, he inquired of a workman where he was, and was told he was in a warehouse, which was pointed out to him, and, in passing from the doorway of one warehouse to the other, he was felled to the ground by the falling upon him of six bags of sugar which were being lowered to the ground from the upper part of the warehouse by means of a crane or jigger hoist. The plaintiff said that he had no warning, and there was no fence or barrier to show persons that the place was dangerous, and nobody called out to him to stop him from going through the door or under the hoist. He also said that instantly before the bags fell he 'heard the rattling of a chain overhead.' No other evidence being given, the learned judge proposed to nonsuit the plaintiff for want of evidence showing negligence in defendants, but on the plaintiff's resisting that course, with a view to a bill of exceptions, his Lordship directed the jury to find a verdict for the defendants. A rule was subsequently obtained to set that verdict aside, and for a new trial, on the ground that there was evidence of negligence by the defendants' servants, which rule after argument was made absolute by the Court of Exchequer, on the authority of Byrne v Boadle[1] (dubitante Pollock CB, and dissentiente Martin B, on the authority of Hammack v White[2]), and against that decision the defendants now appealed.

ERLE CJ: The majority of the court have come to the following conclusion. There must be reasonable evidence of negligence, but, where the thing is shown to be under the management of the defendant, or his servants, and the accident is such as, in the ordinary course of things, does not happen if those who have the management of the machinery use proper care, it affords reasonable evidence, in the absence of explanation by the defendant, that the accident arose from want of care. We all assent to the principle laid down in the cases cited for the defendants; but the judgment turns upon the construction to be put on the judge's notes. As my brother Mellor and myself read those notes, we cannot find that reasonable evidence in the present case of the want of care which seems apparent to the rest of the court. The judgment of the court below is, therefore, affirmed, and the case must go down to a new trial, when the real effect of the evidence will, in all probability, be more correctly ascertained.

Appeal dismissed

---

1. (1863) 2 H & C 722.
2. (1862) 11 CBNS 588.

Notes

1. It is reported at (1865-6) 13 LT (NS) 148 at 149 that at the second trial there was a verdict for the defendants.

2. In *Barkway v South Wales Transport Co Ltd* [1950] AC 185n; [1950] 1 All ER 392, Lord Porter referred to Erle CJ's exposition of the doctrine (ante) and stated (at pp. 394-395):

'The doctrine is dependant on the absence of explanation, and, although it is the duty of the defendants, if they desire to protect themselves, to give an adequate explanation of the cause of the accident, yet, if the facts are sufficiently known, the question ceases to be one where the facts speak for themselves, and the solution is to be found by determining whether, on the facts as established, negligence is to be inferred or not.'

3. The maxim res ipsa loquitur has been raised in the sphere of the protection of economic interests. In *Stafford v Conti Commodity Services Ltd* [1981] 1 All ER 691 where the defendants were a company of brokers dealing on the commodities futures market, the case for its application was that only ten out of forty six transactions in an eight month period had been profitable. Reference was made to Erle CJ's classic statement of the doctrine (ante), and the defendants contended that the maxim was inapplicable. One argument concerned the requirement that the loss be such as would not in the ordinary course of things happen if due care was taken. This, it was argued, was not satisfied in the case of transactions on the commodities market, a point seemingly accepted by Mocatta J since he thought that in such a volatile area negligence could not be established by res ipsa loquitur, but would require 'exceedingly strong evidence from expert brokers in relation to individual transactions'. See further *Merrill Lynch Futures Inc v York House Trading Ltd* (1984) Times, 24th May in which Griffiths LJ stopped short of saying there could never be circumstances from which an inference of negligence could be drawn, but agreed with Mocatta J's view which has been quoted in the latter part of the previous sentence.

4. For discussion of res ipsa loquitur in the context of products liability, see p. 503, post.

5. There are conflicting authorities on the effect of res ipsa loquitur. The following extracts represent recent expressions of opinion by appellate courts. (For discussion of some of the recent cases, see P. S. Atiyah (1972) 35 MLR 337.)

Henderson *v* Henry E. Jenkins & Sons House of Lords [1969] 3 All ER 756

The hydraulic brakes of a lorry suddenly failed whilst it was descending a hill and it collided with two vehicles and killed the appellant's husband. The reason for the failure was a hole in a corroded part of the brake pipe. Although part of the pipe could be seen whilst it remained on the lorry, the part which in fact was badly corroded could not have been inspected without the pipe being removed. The evidence showed that it was unusual for there to be complete and sudden failure of brakes from corrosion. The respondents pleaded that the brake failure resulted 'from a latent defect . . . which occurred without any fault on the part of the [respondents and the driver] and the existence of which was not discoverable by the exercise of reasonable care by them.' They argued that ordinary practice only required that the visible parts of the pipe be regularly inspected (which they had done), and it was established that neither the Ministry of Transport nor the manufacturers advised that the pipes be removed for inspection. The appellant's action for damages against the respondents and the driver was dismissed by Nield J. She appealed to the Court of Appeal, [1969] 1 All ER 401, against the dismissal of the action against the respondents and, after that appeal had been dismissed, she appealed to the House of Lords.

LORD REID [having earlier referred to the evidence of the respondents' 'leading expert' who, in response to a question, had agreed that the pipe 'was subjected to some unusual treatment from outside', continued:]

If there were nothing in the evidence to indicate a probability that something unusual must have happened to this lorry to cause the very unusual type of brake failure which the learned trial judge has held in fact occurred here, then undoubtedly the respondents would have proved that they had exercised all proper care in this case. But if the evidence indicates a likelihood that something unusual has occurred to cause a break-down, then I do not see how the owner can say that he has exercised all proper care unless he can prove that he neither knew nor ought to have known of any such occurrence. For if he did know of it he would have been bound to take adequate steps to prevent any resulting break-down. It may well be that it would be sufficient for him to prove that he had a proper system for drivers reporting all unusual occurrences and that none had been reported to him.

. . . It may be that they [the respondents] could have proved that, so far as they knew or could have discovered by reasonable enquiry, nothing unusual ever happened to it which could have led to this corrosion. Or it may be that they did know of something but did not realise the possible danger resulting from it although they ought to have done so. We do not know. They had to prove that in all the circumstances which they knew or ought to have known that they took all proper steps to avoid danger. In my opinion they have failed to do that, and I am therefore of opinion that this appeal should be allowed. Damages have been agreed to be £5,700.

LORD DONOVAN: . . . The plea of 'latent defect' made by the respondents had to be made good by them. It was for them to show that they [had] taken all reasonable care, and that despite this, the defect remained hidden.

They proved that the pipe in question was visually inspected in situ once a week; that the brake pedal was on these occasions depressed to check for leaks from the pipe and none seen; that nothing more than such visual inspection of the pipe was required by the Ministry of Transport rules or the maker's advice. On the question of the likelihood of corrosion of the pipe they produced two expert witnesses, the first of whom said there was nothing unusual about it, and the second of whom said it was extremely unusual. The appellant's expert witness had testified without challenge that corrosion occurred quite often. The trial judge did not resolve this discord by any finding of his own. The respondents' second expert witness considered that the pipe had been subjected to some unusual treatment from outside by some chemical agent.

It is obvious that visual inspection of the pipe in situ, however frequent, could not disclose corrosion on the hidden part of it. The question, therefore, suggests itself at once: did not reasonable care require the removal of the pipe at suitable intervals so that the whole of it could be inspected? It is equally obvious that the answer to this question must depend partly on the age of the vehicle, partly on the mileage it had done, and partly on the load it had been carrying. All these things affected the measure of reasonable care which the respondents had to exercise.

The lorry was an Albion lorry, five years old. The speedometer showed that it had done 52,000 miles, but since speedometers begin again at nought once they have registered 100,000 miles, nobody has suggested that reliance could be placed on the reading of 52,000. But no evidence was tendered as to mileage. So that the lorry might have done either 150,000 or 250,000 miles in its five years of life. As to the loads it carried, we know no more than that on the day of the accident it was carrying 9½ tons of concrete pipes.

Yet the kind of load this lorry had been carrying in the past was something which had to be known in order to assess the measure of the duty of reasonable care resting on the respondents. For the corrosion of the pipe was caused by some chemical agent. Had the lorry, therefore, been carrying chemicals of any kind? Or had it operated under conditions where salt (also a corrosive agent) might come in contact with the pipe? Or had it at some time been adapted for carrying cattle and done so? If any of these things were the case then clearly visual inspection of the pipe in situ would not have been enough. It should have been removed at intervals so that the whole of it, and not merely part of it, could be examined.

It was for the respondents to deal with these matters by evidence. They were asserting, and had to prove, that they exercised all reasonable care; but whether they had or not depended on what the facts were in the foregoing respects. Yet on these matters they chose to give no evidence at all. The result was that they failed to establish their defence and should have lost the case.

Nield J, however, decided in their favour. His final conclusion was thus expressed:

'In these circumstances there is no negligence proved against the driver or against the [respondents].'

The real question, however, was whether the respondents had proved that they had exercised all reasonable care; and, I repeat, facts essential to a conclusion on this point had not been put before the court. Furthermore the learned judge said, after stating that the issue was whether the defect would have been discovered by reasonable care according to standards current at the time—

'In considering that part of the case, the first matter to notice is that it is agreed that visual inspection was all that could reasonably be required of the owners of such a vehicle and I am much impressed by the evidence that to remove these pipes involves considerable danger in the sense that they may kink or fracture, and thus it is plainly the custom in the ordinary course of things not to remove these fluid pipes.'

I am unable to discover how and where it was agreed by the appellant that visual inspection in situ was all that could reasonably be required. Neither she nor her advisers could possibly so agree unless they knew among other things what loads the lorry had been in the habit of carrying. And while the pipes might not be removed 'in the ordinary course of things' it was for the respondents to prove that this lorry's life had conformed to 'the ordinary course of things'. But they chose to leave the case in the state where, for all one knew, the lorry might have been carrying carboys of acid about regularly, or had been coming into contact with sea water or salt frequently, or had been engaged in carrying cattle. One of the respondents' expert witnesses, a Mr Tyndall, who was a vehicle examiner employed by the Ministry of Transport, said:

'Unless you had some suspicion of anything, I would never suggest that they [i.e. brakes pipes] are removed; unless, of course, they had been making trips to a seaside place where they had been near salt water and then, of course, one would definitely request them to be removed.'

It was, therefore, incumbent on the respondents, if they were to sustain their plea of latent defect undiscoverable by the exercise of ordinary care, to prove where the vehicle had been and what it had been carrying whilst in their service and in what conditions it had operated. Only then could the standard of reasonable care be ascertained, and their conduct measured against it. . . .

I differ from Nield J with regret. But the tenor of his judgment suggests that he dealt with this case as though it were the more usual type where the onus of proof lay on the appellant; whereas in fact the burden of proof that they had taken all reasonable care rested on the respondents. For these reasons, which are substantially those given by Sachs LJ in his dissenting judgment below,[1] I am of the opinion that the appeal should be allowed and the appellant should recover from the respondents the agreed damages of £5,700. . . .

LORD PEARSON: My Lords, in my opinion, the decision in this appeal turns on what is sometimes called 'the evidential burden of proof', which is to be distinguished from the formal (or legal or technical) burden of proof. . . . For the purposes of the present case the distinction can be simply stated in this way. In an action for negligence the plaintiff must allege, and has the burden of proving, that the accident was caused by negligence on the part of the defendants. That is the issue throughout the trial, and in giving judgment at the end of the trial the judge has to decide whether he is satisfied on a balance of probabilities that the accident was caused by negligence on the part of the defendants, and if he is not so satisfied the plaintiff's action fails. The formal burden of proof does not shift. But if in the course of the trial there is proved a set of facts which raises a prima facie inference that the accident was caused by negligence on the part of the defendants, the issue will be decided in the plaintiff's favour unless the defendants by their evidence provide some answer which is adequate to displace the prima facie inference. In this situation there is said to be an evidential burden of proof resting on the defendants. I have some doubts whether it is strictly correct to use the expression 'burden of proof' with this meaning, as there is a risk of it being confused with the formal burden of proof, but it is a familiar and convenient usage. . . .

. . . The respondents and the driver were, by this plea [of latent defect], alleging and, therefore, admitting that the accident was caused by a sudden brake failure resulting from corrosion of the brake fluid pipe, and were assuming an evidential burden of proving that the corrosion occurred without any fault on their part and that its existence was not discoverable by the exercise of reasonable care by them.

That was the effect of the pleading of the respondents and the driver, but in any case the physical facts of the case raise a strong prima facie inference that the respondents and the driver[2] were at fault and that their fault was a cause of the accident. . . .

[Having referred to the facts of the case, he continued:] From these facts it seems to me clear, as a prima facie inference, that the accident must have been due to default of the respondents in respect of inspection or maintenance or both. Unless they had a satisfactory answer, sufficient to displace the inference, they should have been held liable.

The respondents' answer was that they had followed a practice of relying solely on visual inspection of the pipes, and that this was a general and proper practice. The learned judge's finding was that 'it is plainly the custom in the ordinary course of things not to remove these fluid pipes.' This may be a general and proper practice for an ordinary case in which there are no special circumstances increasing the risk. But I think the respondents' answer should not have been accepted without evidence from the respondents sufficiently showing that this was an ordinary case without special circumstances increasing the risk.

---

1. [1969] 1 All ER at p. 403; [1969] 2 WLR at p. 149.
2. [But note that there was no appeal from the dismissal of the action against the driver.]

. . . The respondents might perhaps have been able to show by evidence that the lorry had not been used in any way, or involved in any incident, that would cause abnormal corrosion or require special inspection or treatment, or at any rate that they neither knew nor ought to have known of any such use or incident. But they did not call any such evidence. Their answer was incomplete. They did not displace the inference, arising from the physical facts of the case, that the accident must have been due to their default in respect of inspection or maintenance or both.

While fully accepting the learned judge's findings of primary fact, I am of opinion that he drew a wrong conclusion in holding that the accident was not caused by negligence of the respondents. I would allow the appeal.

[LORD GUEST and VISCOUNT DILHORNE delivered speeches in favour of dismissing the appeal.]

Appeal allowed

Question

There is no express mention of res ipsa loquitur in the speeches in this case. Is it, nevertheless, correctly classified under this heading?

Notes

1. See the discussion of this case by Atiyah, op cit. At p. 341, he points out that, in their dissenting speeches, both Lord Guest and Viscount Dilhorne 'seem to have accepted that the defendants had the burden of disproving negligence but both held that the defendants had in fact discharged the burden'. See further the note, p. 293, post.

2. In *Colvilles Ltd v Devine* [1969] 2 All ER 53; [1969] 1 WLR 475, Lord Guest stated (at p. 57) that if res ipsa loquitur applied, the appellants in that case were 'absolved if they can give a reasonable explanation of the accident and show this explanation was consistent with no lack of care on their part.' See also Lord Upjohn at p. 58; cf. Lord Donovan also at p. 58, and see generally Atiyah, op cit, pp. 342–344, especially in relation to Lord Donovan's speech.

3. *Rees v Saville* [1983] RTR 332 also concerned a latent defect in a motor vehicle. The plaintiff's parked car was damaged in a collision with the defendant's car, the accident occurring as a result of the defendant losing control of his car because of a failure of part of the suspension. On the facts the defendant was absolved from any negligence but the test proposed by Cumming-Bruce LJ (at p. 340) was 'whether, in the light of [the] facts, the defendant had discharged the evidential burden that lay upon him to prove on the balance of probability that he had exercised all reasonable care when he decided to act as he did'. Is this consistent with Lord Pearson's speech in *Henderson v Jenkins* (and see further Sir R. Cross, op cit, pp. 113–114)? Sir David Cairns' approach was different. Having distinguished *Henderson v Jenkins* on the basis that the cause of the defect in this case was known, he referred for assistance to Lord Porter's speech in *Barkway v South Wales Transport Co Ltd* [1950] 1 All ER 392 at 394–395 (most of which can be found p. 288, ante), and went on to decide that the question of the onus of proof was not in issue.

Lloyde *v* West Midlands Gas Board Court of Appeal [1971] 2 All ER 1240

MEGAW LJ: . . . I doubt whether it is right to describe res ipsa loquitur as a 'doctrine'. I think it is no more than an exotic, though convenient, phrase to describe what is in essence no more than a common sense approach, not limited by technical rules, to the assessment of the effect of evidence in certain circumstances. It means that a plaintiff prima facie establishes negligence where: (i) it is not possible for him to prove precisely what was the relevant act or omission which set in train the events leading to the accident; but (ii) on the evidence as it stands at the relevant time it is more likely than not that the effective cause of the accident was *some* act or omission of the defendant or of someone for whom the defendant is responsible, which act or omission constitutes a failure to take proper care for the plaintiff's safety.

I have used the words 'evidence as it stands at the relevant time'. I think this can most conveniently be taken as being at the close of the plaintiff's case. On the assumption that a submission of no case is then made, would the evidence, as it then stands, enable the plaintiff to succeed because, although the precise cause of the accident cannot be established, the proper inference on balance of probability is that that cause, whatever it may have been, involved a failure by the defendant to take due care for the plaintiff's safety? If so, res ipsa loquitur. If not, the plaintiff fails. Of course, if the defendant does not make a submission of no case, the question still falls to be tested by the same criterion, but evidence for the defendant, given thereafter, may rebut the inference. The res, which previously spoke for itself, may be silenced, or its voice may, on the whole of the evidence, become too weak or muted. . . .

Note

Megaw LJ's approach in this case met with approval in *Turner v Mansfield Corpn* (1975) 119 Sol Jo 629. See also the Privy Council's view in *Ng Chun Pui v Lee Chuen Tat* [1988] RTR 298 where this passage from Megaw LJ's judgment and the bulk of the first paragraph in the extract from Lord Pearson's speech in *Henderson v Henry E Jenkins & Sons* (p. 291, ante) were adopted 'as most clearly expressing the true meaning and effect of the so-called doctrine of res ipsa loquitur'.

Ward *v* Tesco Stores Ltd Court of Appeal [1976] 1 All ER 219

LAWTON LJ delivered the first judgment at the invitation of Megaw LJ: This is an appeal by the defendants from a judgment of his Honour Judge Nance given in the Liverpool County Court on 21 February 1975, whereby he adjudged that the plaintiff should recover against the defendants £178.50 damages and her costs on scale 2, for personal injuries said to have been caused by the negligence of the defendants in the maintenance of the floor in their supermarket at Smithdown Road, Liverpool. By consent the sum awarded has been reduced to £137.10. The higher figure was due to an arithmetical error.

On 29 June 1974, at about midday, the plaintiff went to the defendants' supermarket. It is a large one and is carried on in premises which used to be a cinema. Inside, the premises were laid out in the way which is usual nowadays in super-markets. On duty there was a total of about 30 to 35 staff; but in the middle of the day that number was reduced because staff had to be relieved in order to enable them to get their midday meals.

The plaintiff went round the store, carrying a wire basket, as shoppers are expected to do in supermarkets. She was doing her shopping at the back of the store when she felt herself slipping. She appreciated that she was slipping on something which was sticky. She fell to the ground, and sustained minor injuries. She had not seen what had caused her to slip. It was not suggested, either at the trial or in this court, that she had in any way been negligent in failing to notice what was on the floor as she walked along doing her shopping. When she was picking herself up she appreciated that she had slipped on some pink substance which looked to her like yoghourt. Later, somebody on the defendants' staff found a carton of yoghourt in the vicinity which was two-thirds empty.

A member of the staff helped to pick the plaintiff up. The manager was called. The plaintiff was taken to his office. She was dealt with there in a kindly and considerate way. The defendants offered to, and did, arrange for such of her clothes as had been soiled by the fall to be cleaned.

That is all the plaintiff was able to prove, save for one additional fact. About three weeks later when she was shopping in the same store she noticed that some orange squash had been spilt on the floor. She kept an eye on the spillage for about a quarter of an hour. During that time nobody came to clear it up.

The trial judge was of the opinion that the facts which I have related constituted a prima facie case against the defendants. . . .

. . . [T]hose in charge of the store knew that during the course of a working week there was a likelihood of spillages occurring from time to time. It was accepted at the trial that shoppers, intent on looking to see what is on offer, cannot be expected to look where they are putting their feet. The management should have appreciated that if there are patches of slippery substances on the floor people are liable to step into them and that, if they do, they may slip. It follows too that if those are the conditions to be expected in the store there must be some reasonably effective system for getting rid of the dangers which may from time to time exist. The only precautions which were taken were, first, the system of having the floor brushed five or six times during the working day and, secondly, giving instructions to the staff that if they saw any spillage on the floor they were to stay where the spill had taken place and call somebody to clean it up.

The main complaint of the defendants in this case has been that the trial judge should never have taken the view that the plaintiff had proved a prima facie case. . . .

. . . This case . . . has to be decided on its own facts, to which established principles must be applied. The relevant principles were enunciated in the classical judgment of Erle CJ in *Scott v London and St Katherine Docks Co*[1]:

'But where the thing is shewn to be under the management of the defendant or his servants, and the accident is such as in the ordinary course of things does not happen if those who have the management use proper care, it affords reasonable evidence, in the absence of explanation by the defendants that the accident arose from want of care.'

In this case the floor of this supermarket was under the management of the defendants and their servants. The accident was such as in the ordinary course of things does not happen if floors are kept clean and spillages are dealt with as soon as they occur. If an accident does happen because the floors are covered with spillage, then in my judgment some explanation should be forthcoming from the defendants to show that the accident did not arise from any want of care on their part; and in the absence of any explanation the judge may give judgment for the plaintiff. Such burden of proof as there is on defendants in such circumstances is evidential, not probative. The trial judge thought that prima facie this accident would not have happened had the defendants taken reasonable care. In my judgment he was justified in taking that view because the probabilities were that the spillage had been on the floor

---

1. (1865) 3 H & C 596 at 601.

long enough for it to have been cleaned up by a member of the staff.

The next question is whether the defendants by their evidence gave any explanation to show that they had taken all reasonable care. . . . The judge weighed the evidence and decided as a matter of fact from which in this case there can be no appeal that the precautions taken were not enough, and that the plaintiff in consequence had proved her case. In coming to that conclusion he followed the judgment of Lord Goddard CJ in *Turner v Arding and Hobbs Ltd*[1]:

'The duty of the shopkeeper in this class of case is well established. It may be said to be a duty to use reasonable care to see that the shop floor, on which people are invited, is kept reasonably safe, and if an unusual danger is present of which the injured person is unaware, and the danger is one which would not be expected and ought not to be present, the onus of proof is on the defendants to explain how it was that the accident happened.'

It is clear from a later passage in his judgment that Lord Goddard CJ, in referring to the burden of proof, was not saying that the defendant had to disprove negligence. What he had intended to say is apparent from what he said later[1]:

'Here, however, I think that there is a burden thrown on the defendants either of explaining how this thing got on the floor or giving me far more evidence than they have as to the state of the floor and the watch that was kept on it immediately before the accident.'

The learned judge had that passage in mind when he decided as he did. In my judgment he was right; and accordingly I would dismiss this appeal.

ORMROD LJ: I have the misfortune to disagree with the judgment of Lawton LJ. Starting from the beginning, I do not think that it was established that this accident was caused by any want of care on the part of the defendants. The accident described by the plaintiff—and she did no more than describe the accident, namely that she slipped in some yoghourt which was on the floor of the supermarket—could clearly have happened no matter what degree of care these defendants had taken. The crucial question is how long before the accident the yoghourt had been on the floor. Had some customer knocked it off the shelf a few moments before, then no reasonable system which the defendants could be expected to operate would have prevented this accident. So I think that the plaintiff fails at the outset.

So far as the proposition which Lawton LJ has cited from Erle CJ[2] is concerned, all I would say is that, since this accident could quite easily have happened without any want of care on the part of the defendants, I do not think that that broad proposition is applicable. . . .

MEGAW LJ: I agree with the conclusion expressed by Lawton LJ, and with the reasons given by him for that conclusion. But as unfortunately the court is not unanimous I feel that it is desirable that I should add a few words of my own, not, I believe, in any way departing from the reasons given by Lawton LJ.

. . . It is for the plaintiff to show that there has occurred an event which is unusual and which, in the absence of explanation, is more consistent with fault on the part of the defendants than the absence of fault; and to my mind the learned judge was wholly right in taking that view of the presence of this slippery liquid on the floor of the supermarket in the circumstances of this case: that is that the defendants knew

---

1. [1949] 2 All ER 911 at 912.
2. *Scott v London and St Katherine Docks Co* (1865) 3 H & C 596 at 601.

or should have known that it was a not uncommon occurrence; and that if it should happen, and should not be promptly attended to, it created a serious risk that customers would fall and injure themselves. When the plaintiff has established that, the defendants can still escape from liability. They could escape from liability if they could show that the accident must have happened, or even on balance of probability would have been likely to have happened, irrespective of the existence of a proper and adequate system, in relation to the circumstances, to provide for the safety of customers. But, if the defendants wish to put forward such a case, it is for them to show that, on balance of probability, either by evidence or by inference from the evidence that is given or is not given, this accident would have been at least equally likely to have happened despite a proper system designed to give reasonable protection to customers. That, in this case, they wholly failed to do. . . .

Appeal dismissed

Question

Are the judgments of Lawton and Megaw LJJ in this case and the judgment of Megaw LJ in *Lloyde*'s case (p. 293, ante) consistent with *Henderson v Henry E Jenkins & Sons* (p. 288, ante)?

Notes

1. In applying Erle CJ's well-known proposition in *Scott v London and St Katherine Docks Co* (1865) 3 H & C 596 at 601 (p. 287, ante) to the facts of the case, Lawton LJ appears to be equating 'proper care' with keeping the floors clean and dealing with spillages immediately. This, in the view of one commentator on the case (C. Manchester (1979) 93 LQR 13 at 14), 'seems to be imposing an extremely high duty of care on the defendants, one which, in effect, is almost tantamount to strict liability'.

2. The High Court of Australia took a different line in a somewhat similar case (*Dulhunty v J B Young Ltd* (1975) 7 ALR 409) decided shortly before *Ward v Tesco Stores Ltd*; the approach, as pointed out in a note on the Australian case, (1977) 93 LQR 486, is reminiscent of that of Ormrod LJ in *Ward*'s case. In *Dulhunty v J B Young Ltd* the appellant sustained injury as a result of slipping on a grape that was lying on the floor of a passageway in the respondent's store. The store did not sell food, though a store eighty yards away did. There was evidence that occasionally people had been seen by one of the respondent's employees eating their lunches in the passageway. The appellant's accident happened at approximately 3.45 pm. The High Court of Australia approved the view of the trial judge that it was an essential part of the appellant's case to show when the grape had been dropped and hence how long it had been on the floor, and the appeal from the judgment in the respondent's favour was dismissed.

3. The case of a spillage in a supermarket has been treated as different from that of a spillage in an office block: see *Bell v Department of Health and Social Security* (1989) Times, 13th June, rejecting the application of res ipsa loquitur on the facts and distinguishing *Ward v Tesco Stores Ltd*.

4. M. A. Millner in his book *Negligence in Modern Law* (London, 1967) expresses the following opinion (at pp. 92–93, footnotes omitted):

'Res ipsa loquitur is an immensely important vehicle for importing strict liability into negligence cases. In practice, there are many cases where res ipsa loquitur is properly invoked in which the defendant is unable to show affirmatively either that he took all reasonable precautions to avoid injury or that the particular cause of the injury was not associated with negligence on his part. Industrial and traffic accidents, and injuries caused by defective merchandise [though see now p. 504, post], are so frequently of this type that the theoretical limitations of the maxim are quite overshadowed by its practical significance. The result is a certain disparity between the theory of fault liability underlying negligence and the actual functioning of the remedy, which could best be resolved by the open recognition of certain spheres of conduct as carrying an "insurance" against risk. Injuries sustained in the sphere of such guaranteed safety would then cease to be governed by negligence considerations, and the incipient tendency of res ipsa loquitur towards strict liability would, in a defined class of case, be consummated by appropriate legislation.'

6 Causation and remoteness of damage

This topic is relevant to all torts, although most of the decided cases are on the tort of negligence. A connection must be shown between the defendant's breach of duty and the damage suffered by the plaintiff. The language used by writers and judges to describe this problem is perplexing. For example, it is said that a defendant is not liable unless he 'caused' the damage; on the other hand, it is said that he is not liable for all the damage he has 'caused'. Adjectives such as 'legal', 'proximate' or 'remote' do little to unravel the mysteries of this topic.

The courts are involved in various inquiries. One is the question of 'cause-and-effect'. This is sometimes called 'factual causation', and is said to depend upon notions of the physical sequence of events. The 'but for' test — the defendant's breach of duty is a cause of the damage if that damage would not have occurred *but for* it — is widely applied, but does not solve all problems particularly where there are multiple causes (p. 311, post). Furthermore, at the next stage when the courts have to select among the operative factual causes, they do not view causation in the same way as a scientist or metaphysician, but in the manner of the 'man in the street' (per Lord Wright in *Yorkshire Dale SS Co Ltd v Minister of War Transport, The Coxwold* [1942] AC 691 at 706).

The courts must decide how far the defendant should be held liable for the consequences of his breach of duty. A single act of negligence, for example, may lead to disastrous consequences, bearing heavily on the defendant. Some practical and reasonable limitation has to be placed on loss-shifting. In the tort of negligence, the courts have moved towards the formulation that the kind of harm to this plaintiff must be foreseeable (*The Wagon Mound* [1961] AC 388; [1961] 1 All ER 404, p. 333, post). The earlier 'direct consequences' test (*Re Polemis* [1921] 3 KB 560, p. 329, post) still provides an interesting contrast, and, indeed, may not be wholly irreconcilable with the 'foreseeability' approach.

1 Factual causation

Hotson v East Berkshire Area Health Authority House of Lords [1987] 2 All ER 909

LORD BRIDGE OF HARWICH: My Lords, the respondent plaintiff is now 23 years of age. On 26 April 1977, as a schoolboy of 13, whilst playing in the school lunch hour he climbed a tree to which a rope was attached, lost his hold on the rope and fell some 12 feet to the ground. He sustained an acute traumatic fracture of the left femoral epiphysis. Within hours he was taken to St Luke's Hospital, Maidenhead, for which the appellant health authority (the authority) was responsible. Members of the hospital staff examined him, but failed to diagnose the injury and he was sent home. For five days he was in severe pain. On 1 May 1977 he was taken to the hospital once more and this time X-rays of his hip yielded the correct diagnosis. He was put on immediate traction, treated as an emergency case and transferred to the Heatherwood Hospital where, on the following day, he was operated on by manipulation and reduction of the fracture and pinning of the joint. In the event the plaintiff suffered an avascular necrosis of the epiphysis. The femoral epiphysis is a layer of cartilage separating the bony head from the bony neck of the femur in a growing body. Avascular necrosis results from a failure of the blood supply to the epiphysis and causes deformity in the maturing head of the femur. This in turn involves a greater or lesser degree of disability of the hip joint with a virtual certainty that it will in due course be aggravated by osteoarthritis developing within the joint.

The plaintiff sued the authority, who admitted negligence in failing to diagnose the injury on 26 April 1977. Simon Brown J, in a judgment delivered on 15 March 1985, sub nom *Hotson v Fitzgerald* [1985] 3 All ER 167, [1985] 1 WLR 1036, awarded £150 damages for the pain suffered by the plaintiff from 26 April to 1 May 1977 which he would have been spared by prompt diagnosis and treatment. This element of the damages is not in dispute. The authority denied liability for any other element of damages. The judge expressed his findings of fact as follows ([1985] 3 All ER 167 at 171, [1985] 1 WLR 1036 at 1040–1041):

'1. Even had the defendants correctly diagnosed and treated the plaintiff on 26 April there is a high probability, which I assess as a 75% risk, that the plaintiff's injury would have followed the same course as it in fact has, ie he would have developed avascular necrosis of the whole femoral head with all the same adverse consequences as have already ensued and with all the same adverse future prospects. 2. That 75% risk was translated by the defendants' admitted breach of duty into inevitability. Putting it the other way, the defendants' delay in diagnosis denied the plaintiff the 25% chance that, given immediate treatment, avascular necrosis would not have developed. 3. Had avascular necrosis not developed, the plaintiff would have made a very nearly full recovery. 4. The reason why the delay sealed the plaintiff's fate was because it followed the pressure caused by haemarthrosis (the bleeding of ruptured blood vessels into the joint) to compress and thus block the intact but distorted remaining vessels with the result that even had the fall left intact sufficient vessels to keep the epiphysis alive (which, as finding no 1 makes plain, I think possible but improbable) such vessels would have become occluded and ineffective for this purpose.'

On the basis of these findings he held, as a matter of law, that the plaintiff was entitled to damages for the loss of the 25% chance that, if the injury had been promptly diagnosed and treated, it would not have resulted in avascular necrosis of the epiphysis and the plaintiff would have made a very nearly full recovery. He proceeded to assess the damages attributable to the consequences of the avascular necrosis at £46,000. Discounting this by 75%, he awarded the plaintiff £11,500 for the lost chance of recovery. The authority's appeal against this element in the award of damages was dismissed by the Court of Appeal (Sir John Donaldson MR, Dillon and Croom-Johnson LJJ) ([1987] 1 All ER 210, [1987] 2 WLR 287). The authority now appeal by leave of your Lordship's House. . . .

In analysing the issue of law arising from his findings the judge said ([1985] 3 All ER 167 at 175, [1985] 1036 at 1034–1044):

'In the end the problem comes down to one of classification. Is this on true analysis a case where the plaintiff is concerned to establish causative negligence or is it rather a case where the real question is the proper quantum of damage? Clearly the case hovers near the border. Its proper solution in my judgment depends on categorising it correctly between the two. If the issue is one of causation then the defendants succeed since the plaintiff will have failed to prove his claim on the balance of probabilities. He will be lacking an essential ingredient of his cause of action. If, however, the issue is one of quantification then the plaintiff succeeds because it is trite law that the quantum of a recognised head of damage must be evaluated according to the chances of the loss occurring.'

He reached the conclusion that the question was one of quantification and thus arrived at his award to the plaintiff of one quarter of the damages appropriate to compensate him for the consequences of the avascular necrosis.

It is here, with respect, that I part company with the judge. The plaintiff's claim was for damages for physical injury and consequential loss alleged to have been caused by the authority's breach of their duty of care. In some cases, perhaps particularly medical negligence cases, causation may be so shrouded in mystery that the court can only measure statistical chances. But that was not so here. On the evidence there was a clear conflict as to what had caused the avascular necrosis. The authority's evidence was that the sole cause was the original traumatic injury to the hip. The plaintiff's evidence, [at] its highest, was that the delay in treatment was a material contributory cause. This was a conflict, like any other about some relevant past event, which the judge could not avoid resolving on a balance of probabilities. Unless the plaintiff proved on a balance of probabilities that the delayed treatment was at least a material contributory cause of the avascular necrosis he failed on the issue of causation and no question of quantification could arise. But the judge's findings of fact, as stated in the numbered paragraphs (1) and (4) which I have set out earlier in this opinion, are unmistakably to the effect that on a balance of probabilities the injury caused by the plaintiff's fall left insufficient blood vessels intact to keep the epiphysis alive. This amounts to a finding of fact that the fall was the sole cause of the avascular necrosis.

The upshot is that the appeal must be allowed on the narrow ground that the plaintiff failed to establish a cause of action in respect of the avascular necrosis and its consequences. Your Lordships were invited to approach the appeal more broadly and to decide whether, in a claim for damages for personal injury, it can ever be appropriate, where the cause of the injury is unascertainable and all the plaintiff can show is a statistical chance which is less than even that, but for the defendant's breach of duty, he would not have suffered the injury, to award him a proportionate fraction of the full damages appropriate to compensate for the injury as the measure of damages for the lost chance.

There is a superficially attractive analogy between the principle applied in such cases as *Chaplin v Hicks* [1911] 2 KB 786, [1911–13] All ER Rep 224 (award of damages for breach of contract assessed by reference to the lost chance of securing valuable employment if the contract had been performed) and *Kitchen v Royal Air Forces Association* [1958] 2 All ER 241, [1958] 1 WLR 563 (damages for solicitors' negligence assessed by reference to the lost chance of prosecuting a successful civil action) and the principle of awarding damages for the lost chance of avoiding personal injury or, in medical negligence cases, for the lost chance of a better medical result which might have been achieved by prompt diagnosis and correct treatment. I think there are formidable difficulties in the way of accepting the analogy. But I do not see this appeal as a suitable occasion for reaching a settled conclusion as to whether the analogy can ever be applied.

As I have said, there was in this case an inescapable issue of causation first to be resolved. But if the plaintiff had proved on a balance of probabilities that the authority's negligent failure to diagnose and treat his injury promptly had materially contributed to the development of avascular necrosis, I know of no principle of English law which would have entitled the authority to a discount from the full measure of damage to reflect the chance that, even given prompt treatment, avascular necrosis might well still have developed. The decisions of this House in *Bonnington Castings Ltd v Wardlaw* [1956] 1 All ER 615, [1956] AC 613 and *McGhee v National Coal Board* [1972] 3 All ER 1008, [1973] 1 WLR 1 give no support to such a view.

I would allow the appeal to the extent of reducing the damages awarded to the plaintiff by £11,500 and the amount of any interest on that sum which is included in the award.

LORD MACKAY OF CLASHFERN: My Lords, I have had the advantage of reading in draft the speeches prepared by my noble and learned friends Lord Bridge and Lord Ackner. I agree with them that this appeal should be allowed for the reasons which they have given. . . .

When counsel for the plaintiff was invited to say what he meant by a chance he said that in relation to the facts of this case as found by the judge what was meant by a chance was that if 100 people had suffered the same injury as the plaintiff 75 of them would have developed avascular necrosis of the whole femoral head and 25 would not. This, he said, was an asset possessed by the plaintiff when he arrived at the authority's hospital on 26 April 1977. It was this asset which counsel submits the plaintiff lost in consequence of the negligent failure of the authority to diagnose his injury properly until 1 May 1977.

. . . [W]hat was the plaintiff's condition on being first presented at the hospital? Did he have intact sufficient blood vessels to keep the affected epiphysis alive? The judge had evidence from the authority's expert which amounted to an assertion that the probability was 100% that the fall had not left intact sufficient vessels to keep the epiphysis alive while he had evidence from Mr Bucknill, for the plaintiff, which although not entirely consistently suggested that the probability was perhaps between 40% and 60%, say 50%, that sufficient vessels were left intact to keep the epiphysis alive. The concluding sentence in the judge's fourth finding in fact makes it plain, in my opinion, that he took the view, weighing that testimony along with all the other matters before him, that it was more probable than not that insufficient vessels had been left intact by the fall to maintain an adequate blood supply to the epiphysis and he expressed this balance by saying that it was 75% to 25%, a result reached perhaps as counsel for the plaintiff suggested by going for a figure midway between the competing estimates given by the parties' experts in evidence. Although various statistics were given in evidence, I do not read any of them as dealing with the particular probability which the judge assessed at 75% to 25%. In the circumstances of this case the probable effect of delay in treatment was determined by the state of facts existing when the plaintiff was first presented to the hospital. It is not, in my opinion, correct to say that on arrival at the hospital he had a 25% chance of recovery. If insufficient blood vessels were left intact by the fall he had no prospect of avoiding complete avascular necrosis whereas if sufficient blood vessels were left intact on the judge's findings no further damage to the blood supply would have resulted if he had been given immediate treatment, and he would not have suffered the avascular necrosis.

As I have said, the fundamental question of fact to be answered in this case related to a point in time before the negligent failure to treat began. It must, therefore, be a matter of past fact. It did not raise any question of what might have been the situation in a hypothetical state of facts. To this problem the words of Lord Diplock in *Mallett v McMonagle* [1969] 2 All ER 178 at 191, [1970] AC 166 at 176 apply:

'In determining what did happen in the past a court decides on the balance of probabilities. Anything that is more probable than not it treats as certain.'
. . .

On the other hand, I consider that it would be unwise in the present case to lay it down as a rule that a plaintiff could never succeed by proving loss of a chance in a medical negligence case.[1] . . .

---

1. [See note 1, p. 304 post.]

LORD ACKNER: My Lords, this appeal, as counsel for the plaintiff submitted, raises a short point of classification. Adopting, although somewhat adapting, the words of Dillon LJ in his short judgment, the fundamental question is: what does the law regard as the damage which the plaintiff has suffered? Was it the onset of avascular necrosis or was it the loss of the chance of avoiding that condition? (See [1987] 1 All ER 210 at 219, [1987] 2 WLR 287 at 298.) . . .

In the result the judge had by his clear findings decided that the negligence of the authority in failing to diagnose and treat for a period of five days, had not caused the deformed left hip. The judge, in agreement with the submission made to your Lordships by counsel for the authority, said in terms that in the end the problem came down to one of classification ([1985] 3 All ER 167 at 175, [1985] 1 WLR 1036 at 1043–1044):

'Is this on true analysis a case where the plaintiff is concerned to establish causative negligence or is it rather a case where the real question is the proper quantum of damage?'

The learned judge thought, that the case 'hovers near the border'. To my mind, the first issue which the judge had to determine was an issue of causation: did the breach of duty cause the damage alleged? If it did not, as the judge so held, then no question of quantifying damage arises. The debate on the loss of a chance cannot arise where there has been a positive finding that before the duty arose the damage complained of had already been sustained or had become inevitable.

Kitchen v Royal Air Forces Association [1958] 2 All ER 241, [1958] 1 WLR 563 has no relevance to this appeal. In that case there was an undoubted breach of contract which caused the plaintiff to suffer more than nominal damages. By reason of the solicitor's negligence, she had lost a worthwhile action. What the court there had to do was to value that action. It is, of course, obvious that it is not only actions that are bound to succeed that have a value. Every action with a prospect of success has a value and it is a familiar task for the court to assess that value where negligence has prevented such an action being brought. Again, *Chaplin v Hicks* [1911] 2 KB 786, [1911–13] All ER Rep 224 strongly relied on by the plaintiff, provides no assistance. In that case a young lady actress-to-be had made a contract with the defendant under which she had an opportunity of appearing in a competition in which, if successful, she would have obtained a remunerative engagement as an actress. In the words of Fletcher Moulton LJ ([1911] 2 KB 786 at 797, [1911–13] All ER Rep 224 at 231):

'The contract gave the plaintiff a right of considerable value, one for which many people would give money; therefore to hold that the plaintiff was entitled to no damages for being deprived of such a right because the final result depended on a contingency or chance would have been a misdirection.'

In a sentence, the plaintiff was not entitled to any damages in respect of the deformed hip because the judge had decided that this was not caused by the admitted breach by the authority of their duty of care but was caused by the separation of the left femoral epiphysis when he fell some 12 feet from a rope on which he had been swinging.

On this simple basis I would allow this appeal. I have sought to stress that this case was a relatively simple case concerned with the proof of causation, on which the plaintiff failed, because he was unable to prove, on the balance of probabilities, that his deformed hip was caused by the authority's breach of duty in delaying over a period of five days a proper diagnosis and treatment. Where *causation* is in issue, the judge decides that issue on the balance of the probabilities. Unless there is some special situation, eg joint defendants where the apportionment of liability between them is required, there is no point or purpose in expressing in percentage terms the certainty or near certainty which the plaintiff has achieved in establishing his cause of action.

Once liability is established, on the balance of probabilities, the loss which the plaintiff has sustained is payable in full. . . .

Of course, where the cause of action has been established, the assessment of that part of the plaintiff's loss where the future is uncertain, involves the evaluation of that uncertainty. . . .

[LORD BRANDON OF OAKBOOK and LORD GOFF OF CHIEVELEY agreed with the speeches of LORD BRIDGE OF HARWICH, LORD MACKAY OF CLASHFERN and LORD ACKNER.]

Appeal allowed

Question

Do you agree with Lord Mackay's view (p. 302, ante, and consider Lord Ackner's speech, p. 303, ante) that it is not 'correct to say that on arrival at the hospital [the plaintiff] had a 25% chance of recovery'? (See J. Stapleton (1988) 104 LQR 389 at 393–394.)

Notes

1. Lord Mackay left open the position of recovery for loss of a chance because of the decision in *McGhee v National Coal Board* [1972] 3 All ER 1008; [1973] 1 WLR 1 and felt that 'unless and until this House departs from the decision in *McGhee* your Lordships cannot affirm the proposition that in no circumstances can evidence of loss of a chance resulting from the breach of a duty of care found a successful claim of damages . . . ([1987] 2 All ER at p. 916, though cf. ibid. p. 919). Consider now the treatment of *McGhee* in *Wilsher v Essex Area Health Authority* [1988] AC 1074; [1988] 1 All ER 871 (p. 305, post).

2. Compare with *Hotson* the decision in *Davies v Taylor* [1974] AC 207; [1972] 3 All ER 836 (p. 244, ante). If the allegation in a case is that the defendant failed to provide a safety device, then it is established that the plaintiff must show on the balance of probabilities that he would have used it. As this is an eventuality that did not happen, is this consistent with *Hotson* and *Davies v Taylor*? Consider Dugdale and Stanton, *Professional Negligence* 2nd edn, paras. 18–06 – 18–09.

3. Commenting on *Hotson*, Stapleton, op cit, pp. 392–393 writes:

'Once the plaintiff had identified his loss as loss of a chance and the Court of Appeal had held it was compensatable as such, the plaintiff was entitled to damages for the value of that lost chance because he could establish *on the balance of probabilities* that the defendants' fault had caused *that* damage. The balance of probability test on the issue of causation of past events is retained but its effects are transformed by the reformulation of the damage which forms the gist of the action.

Unhappily the House of Lords did not resolve the difficult question raised by the plaintiff's argument—namely whether reformulation of the gist in terms of loss of a chance should now be acceptable. Their Lordships focused on the traditional (but in this context, irrelevant) question of whether the plaintiff had shown a causal connection on the balance of probabilities to the *necrosis*, which of course he had and could not. The defendants, therefore, succeeded in their appeal because the plaintiff had failed on the issue of causation as it related to damage formulated in terms of necrosis. Their Lordships regarded this finding as releasing them from having to determine whether loss of a chance could form the gist of a complaint in negligence. The loss of a chance issue was classified as one of valuation/quantification and it was held that unless the plaintiff first succeeded on causation no question of quantification of the loss could arise. This reasoning unfortunately fails to address the essence of the plaintiff's argument, which was whether a claim formulated in a different way (i.e. in terms of loss of a chance) was acceptable. In other words, the loss of a chance issue here is not about the quantification/valuation of the interest destroyed (all judges accepted the trial judge's valuation of the lost chance as 25%) but whether loss of a chance could constitute the gist to which the causation enquiry would be directed. Consideration of the plaintiff's argument was, therefore, essential before any issue of causation could be addressed. It cannot be over-emphasised that the formulation of the "damage" forming the gist of the action *defines* the causation question. Logically one can only deal with causation after one knows what the damage forming the gist of the action is.'

Cf. D. P. T. Price (1989) 38 ICLQ 735 at 746–748. See further Stapleton, op cit, pp. 390–400 and 406–407 on *Hotson* where, inter alia, the wider implications of accepting the loss of a chance argument are explored (e.g. the chance it presents for a closer relationship between the defendant's responsibility and the risk he has created which assists the idea of deterrence). On *Hotson* (and the next case extracted) see Price, op cit; J. G. Fleming (1989) 68 Can Bar Rev 661. On loss of a chance see further F. C. Cownie (1989) 5 PN 194 where (at p. 198) there is an exploration of whether a cost benefit analysis justifies distinguishing the position for recovery of loss of a chance in contract and tort; B. Coote (1988) 62 ALJ 761. Inter alia, Coote refers (at p. 772) to the argument which appealed to the Court of Appeal in *Hotson* (i.e. that the breach of duty had lost the plaintiff the benefit of a chance of recovery, which loss was a sufficient injury to establish the cause of action) and continues that this argument:

'would seek to substitute the loss of a valuable benefit for the requirement of physical injury or damage. So long as the existence of a tort depends on the presence of such injury or damage, the loss of a mere valuable benefit could not be a sufficient compliance with that requirement. The tort itself would first have to be changed.'

Where economic loss is recoverable, should the chance of economic gain, which, because of the defendant's negligence, the plaintiff has now lost, have to be proved to have been more than 50 per cent or not? (See Coote, op cit, pp. 769–770.)

Wilsher v Essex Area Health Authority House of Lords [1988] 1 All ER 871

The plaintiff, who was born almost three months prematurely, sustained retrolental fibroplasia (RLF) which caused him to be totally blind in one eye and to suffer from seriously impaired vision in the other. His claim was that the RLF was caused by an excess of oxygen tension in his blood in the early weeks after birth and that this was due to negligence in the management of his oxygen supply. In the Court of Appeal, [1986] 3 All ER 801, a finding of negligence was upheld against a registrar for failure to notice from an X-ray that a catheter, used to measure the partial pressure of oxygen (Po_2), had been misplaced (i.e. put in a vein rather than an artery). In this situation it would give a misleading reading and this led to the administration of too much oxygen. This finding of negligence was not challenged in the House of Lords, where the question of causation was in issue.

LORD BRIDGE OF HARWICH: . . . There was in the voluminous expert evidence given at the trial an irreconcilable conflict of opinion as to the cause of Martin's [i.e. the plaintiff's] RLF. It was common ground that a sufficiently high level of Po_2 in the arterial blood of a very premature baby, if maintained for a sufficiently long period of time, can have a toxic effect on the immature blood vessels in the retina leading to a condition which may either regress or develop into RLF. It was equally common ground, however, that RLF may occur in premature babies who have survived without any artificial administration of oxygen and that there is evidence to indicate a correlation between RLF and a number of other conditions from which premature babies commonly suffer (eg apnoea, hypercarbia, intraventricular haemorrhage, patent ductus arteriosus, all conditions which afflicted Martin) although no causal mechanisms linking these conditions with the development of RLF have been positively identified. However, what, if any, part artificial administration of oxygen causing an unduly high level of Po_2 in Martin's arterial blood played in the causation of Martin's RLF was radically in dispute between the experts. There was certainly evidence led in support of the plaintiff's case that high levels of Po_2 in general and, more particularly, the level of Po_2 maintained when the misplaced catheter was giving misleadingly low readings of the level in the arterial blood were probably at least a contributory cause of Martin's RLF. If the judge had directed himself that it was for the plaintiff to discharge the onus of proving causation on a balance of probabilities and had indicated his acceptance of this evidence in preference to the contrary evidence led for the authority, a finding in favour of the plaintiff would have been unassailable. That is why it is conceded by counsel for the authority that the most he can ask for, if his appeal succeeds, is an order for retrial of the causation issue. However, the burden of the relevant expert evidence led for the authority, to summarise it in very general terms, was to the effect that any excessive administration of oxygen which resulted from the misplacement of the catheter did not result in the Po_2 in the arterial blood being raised to a sufficiently high level for a sufficient length of time to have been capable of playing any part in the causation of Martin's RLF. . . .

The Court of Appeal, although it felt unable to resolve the primary conflict in the expert evidence as to the causation of Martin's RLF, did make a finding that the levels of Po_2 which Martin experienced in consequence of the misplacement of the catheter were of a kind capable of causing RLF. Mustill LJ expressed his anxiety whether 'by making a further finding on an issue where there was a sharp conflict between the expert witnesses, we are not going too far in the effort to avoid a retrial' (see [1986] 3 All ER 801 at 825, [1987] QB 730 at 766). But he concluded that it was 'legitimate, after reading and rereading the evidence,' to make this finding based on 'the weight of the expert evidence'. This finding by the Court of Appeal is challenged by counsel for the authority as one which it was not open to it to make. I must return to this later. But assuming, as I do for the present, that the finding was properly made, it carried the plaintiff's case no further than to establish that oxygen administered to Martin as a consequence of the negligent failure to detect the misplacement of the catheter was one of a number of possible causes of Martin's RLF.

Mustill LJ subjected the speeches in *McGhee v National Coal Board* [1972] 3 All ER 1008, [1973] 1 WLR 1 to a careful scrunity and analysis and concluded that they established a principle of law which he expressed in the following terms ([1986] 3 All ER 801 at 829, [1987] QB 730 at 771–772):

'If it is an established fact that conduct of a particular kind creates a risk that injury will be caused to another or increases an existing risk that injury will ensue, and if the two parties stand in such a relationship that the one party owes a duty not to conduct himself in that way, and if the first party does conduct himself in that way, and if the other party does suffer injury of the kind to which the risk related, then the first party is taken to have caused the injury by his breach of duty, even though the existence and extent of the contribution made by the breach cannot be ascertained.'

Applying this principle to the finding that the authority's negligence was one of the possible causes of Martin's RLF, he held that this was sufficient to enable the court to conclude that the negligence was 'taken to have caused the injury'. Glidewell LJ reached the same conclusion by substantially the same process of reasoning. Sir Nicolas Browne-Wilkinson V-C took the opposite view.

The starting point for any consideration of the relevant law of causation is the decision of this House in *Bonnington Castings Ltd v Wardlaw* [1956] 1 All ER 615, [1956] AC 613. This was the case of a pursuer who, in the course of his employment by the defenders, contracted pneumoconiosis over a period of years by the inhalation of invisible particles of silica dust from two sources. One of these (pneumatic hammers) was an 'innocent' source, in the sense that the pursuer could not complain that his exposure to it involved any breach of duty on the part of his employers. The other source (swing grinders), however, arose from a breach of statutory duty by the employer.

[His Lordship then set out certain passages from the speeches of Lords Reid, Tucker and Keith in that case [1956] AC at pp. 619–620, 624–625 and 625 to the effect that the pursuer had the burden of proof that the defenders' breach of duty caused or materially contributed to his damage. He continued:] Their Lordships concluded, however, from the evidence that the inhalation of dust to which the pursuer was exposed by the defender's breach of statutory duty had made a material contribution to his pneumoconiosis which was sufficient to discharge the onus on the pursuer of proving that his damage was caused by the defenders' tort. . . .

In *McGhee v National Coal Board* [1972] 3 All ER 1008, [1973] 1 WLR 1 the pursuer worked in a brick kiln in hot and dusty conditions in which brick dust adhered to his sweaty skin. No breach of duty by his employers, the defenders, was established in respect of his working conditions. However, the employers were held to be at fault in failing to provide adequate washing facilities which resulted in the pursuer having to bicycle home after work with his body still caked in brick dust. The pursuer contracted dermatitis and the evidence that this was caused by the brick dust was accepted. Brick dust adhering to the skin was a recognised cause of industrial dermatitis and the provision of showers to remove it after work was a usual precaution to minimise the risk of the disease. The precise mechanism of causation of the disease however, was not known and the furthest the doctors called for the pursuer were able to go was to say that the provsion of showers would have materially reduced the risk of dermatitis. They were unable to say that it would probably have prevented the disease.

The pursuer failed before the Lord Ordinary and the First Division of the Court of Session on the ground that he had not discharged the burden of proof of causation. He succeeded on appeal to the House of Lords. Much of the academic discussion to which this decision has given rise has focused on the speech of Lord Wilberforce, particularly on two paragraph[s]. He said ([1972] 3 All ER 1008 at 1012, [1973] 1 WLR 1 at 6):

'But the question remains whether a pursuer must necessarily fail if, after he has shown a breach of duty, involving an increase of risk of disease, he cannot positively prove that this increase of risk caused or materially contributed to the disease while his employers cannot positively prove the contrary. In this intermediate case there is an appearance of logic in the view that the pursuer, on whom the onus lies, should fail – a logic which dictated the judgments below. The question is whether we should be satisfied in factual situations like the present, with this logical approach. In my opinion, there are further considerations of importance. First, it is a sound principle that where a person has, by breach of duty of care, created a risk, and injury occurs within the area of that risk, the loss should be borne by him *unless he shows that it had some other cause*. Secondly, from the evidential point of view, one may ask, why should a man who is able to show that his employer should have taken certain precautions, because without them there is a risk, or an added risk, of injury or disease, and who in fact sustains exactly that injury or disease, have to assume the burden of proving more: namely, that it was the addition to the risk, caused by the breach of duty, which caused or materially contributed to the injury? In many cases of which the present is typical, this is impossible to prove, just because honest medical opinion cannot segregate the causes of an illness between compound causes. And if one asks which of the parties, the workman or the employers should suffer from this inherent evidential difficulty, the answer as a matter in policy or justice should be that it is the creator of the risk who, ex hypothesi, must be taken to have foreseen the possibility of damage, who should bear its consequences.' (My emphasis.)

He then referred to *Bonnington Castings Ltd v Wardlaw* and *Nicholson v Atlas Steel Foundry and Engineering Co Ltd* [1957] 1 All ER 776, [1957] 1 WLR 613 and added ([1972] 3 All ER 1008 at 1013, [1973] 1 WLR 1 at 7):

'The present factual situation has its differences: the default here consisted not in adding a material quantity to the accumulation of injurious particles but by failure to take a step which materially increased the risk that the dust already present would cause injury. And I must say that, at least in the present case, to bridge the evidential gap by inference seems to me something of a fiction, since it was precisely this inference which the medical expert declined to make. But I find in the cases quoted an analogy which suggests the conclusion that, *in the absence of proof that the culpable condition had, in the result, no effect*, the employers should be liable for an injury, squarely within the risk which they created and that they, not the pursuer, should suffer the consequence of the impossibility, foreseeably inherent in the nature of his injury, of segregating the precise consequence of their default.' (My emphasis).

My Lords, it seems to me that both these paragraphs, particularly in the words I have emphasised, amount to saying that, in the circumstances, the burden of proof of causation is reversed and thereby to run counter to the unanimous and emphatic opinions expressed in *Bonnington Castings Ltd v Wardlaw* [1956] 1 All ER 615, [1956] AC 613 to the contrary effect. I find no support in any of the other speeches for the view that the burden of proof is reversed and, in this respect, I think Lord Wilberforce's reasoning must be regarded as expressing a minority opinion.

A distinction is, of course, apparent between the facts of *Bonnington Castings Ltd v Wardlaw*, where the 'innocent' and 'guilty' silica dust particles which together caused the pursuer's lung disease were inhaled concurrently and the facts of *McGhee v National Coal Board* where the 'innocent' and 'guilty' brick dust was present on the pursuer's body for consecutive periods. In the one case the concurrent inhalation of 'innocent' and 'guilty' dust must both have contributed to the cause of the disease. In the other case the consecutive periods when 'innocent' and 'guilty' brick dust was present on the pursuer's body may both have contributed to the cause of the disease or, theoretically at least, one or other may have been the sole cause. But where the layman is told by the doctors that the longer the brick dust remains on the body, the greater the risk of dermatitis, although the doctors cannot identify the process of causation scientifically, there seems to be nothing irrational in drawing the inference, as a matter of common sense, that the consecutive periods when brick dust remained on the body probably contributed cumulatively to the causation of the dermatitis.

I believe that a process of inferential reasoning on these general lines underlies the decision of the majority in *McGhee*'s case.

[LORD BRIDGE then quoted certain passages from the speeches of Lords Reid, Simon, Kilbrandon and Salmon in *McGhee* [1972] 3 All ER at pp. 1010, 1011, 1014, 1016, 1017 and 1018 in support of his view and continued:] The conclusion I draw from these passages is that *McGhee v National Coal Board* laid down no new principle of law whatever. On the contrary, it affirmed the principle that the onus of proving causation lies on the pursuer or plaintiff. Adopting a robust and pragmatic approach to the undisputed primary facts of the case, the majority concluded that it was a legitimate inference of fact that the defenders' negligence had materially contributed to the pursuer's injury. The decision, in my opinion, is of no greater significance than that and the attempt to extract from it some esoteric principle which in some way modifies, as a matter of law, the nature of the burden of proof of causation which a plaintiff or pursuer must discharge once he has established a relevant breach of duty is a fruitless one.

In the Court of Appeal in the instant case Sir Nicolas Browne-Wilkinson V-C, being in a minority, expressed his view on causation with understandable caution. But I am quite unable to find any fault with the following passage in his dissenting judgment ([1986] 3 All ER 801 at 834–835, [1987] QB 730 at 779):

'To apply the principle in *McGhee v National Coal Board* [1972] 3 All ER 1008, [1973] 1 WLR 1 to the present case would constitute an extension of that principle. In *McGhee* there was no doubt that the pursuer's dermatitis was physically caused by brick dust; the only question was whether the continued presence of such brick dust on the pursuer's skin after the time when he should have been provided with a shower caused or materially contributed to the dermatitis which he contracted. There was only one possible agent which could have caused the dermatitis, viz brick dust, and there was no doubt that the dermatitis from which he suffered was caused by that brick dust. In the present case the question is different. There are a number of different agents which could have caused the RLF. Excess oxygen was one of them. The defendants failed to take reasonable precautions to prevent one of the possible causative agents (eg excess oxygen) from causing RLF. But no one can tell in this case whether excess oxygen did or did not cause or contribute to the RLF suffered by the plaintiff. The plaintiff's RLF may have been caused by some completely different agent or agents, eg hypercarbia, intraventricular haemorrhage, apnoea or patent ductus arteriosus. In addition to oxygen, each of those conditions has been implicated as a possible cause of RLF. This baby suffered from each of those conditions at various times in the first two months of his life. There is no satisfactory evidence that excess oxygen is more likely than any of those other four candidates to have caused RLF in this baby. To my mind, the occurrence of RLF following a failure to take a necessary precaution to prevent excess oxygen causing RLF provides no evidence and raises no presumption that it was excess oxygen rather than one or more of the four other possible agents which caused or contributed to RLF in this case. The position, to my mind, is wholly different from that in *McGhee*, where there was only one candidate (brick dust) which could have caused the dermatitis, and the failure to take a precaution against brick dust causing dermatitis was followed by dermatitis caused by brick dust. In such a case, I can see the common sense, if not the logic, of holding that, in the absence of any other evidence, the failure to take the precaution caused or contributed to the dermatitis. To the extent that certain members of the House of Lords decided the question on inferences from evidence or presumptions, I do not consider that the present case falls within their reasoning. A failure to take preventive measures against one out of five possible causes is no evidence as to which of those five caused the injury.'

Since, on this view, the appeal must, in any event, be allowed, it is not strictly necessary to decide whether it was open to the Court of Appeal to resolve one of the conflicts between the experts which the judge left unresolved and to find that the oxygen administered to Martin in consequence of the misleading Po_2 levels derived from the misplaced catheter was capable of having caused or materially contributed to his RLF. I very well understand the anxiety of the majority to avoid the necessity for ordering a retrial if that was at all possible. But, having accepted, as your Lordships and counsel have had to accept, that the primary conflict of opinion between the experts whether excessive oxygen in the first two days of life probably did cause or materially contribute to Martin's RLF cannot be resolved by reading the transcript, I doubt, with all respect, if the Court of Appeal was entitled to try to resolve the secondary conflict whether it could have done so. Where expert witnesses are radically at issue about complex technical questions within their own field and are examined and cross-examined at length about their conflicting theories, I believe that the judge's advantage in seeing them and hearing them is scarcely less important than when he has to resolve some conflict of primary fact between lay witnesses in purely mundane matters. So here, in the absence of relevant findings of fact by the judge, there was really no alternative to a retrial. At all events, the judge who retries the issue of causation should approach it with an entirely open mind uninfluenced by any view of the facts bearing on causation expressed in the Court of Appeal.

To have to order a retrial is a highly unsatisfactory result and one cannot help feeling the profoundest sympathy for Martin and his family that the outcome is once again in doubt and that this litigation may have to drag on. Many may feel that such a result serves only to highlight the shortcomings of a system in which the victim of some grievous misfortune will recover substantial compensation or none at all according to the unpredictable hazards of the forensic process. But, whether we like it or not, the law, which only Parliament can change, requires proof of fault causing damage as the basis of liability in tort. We should do society nothing but disservice if we made the forensic process still more unpredictable and hazardous by distorting the law to accommodate the exigencies of what may seem hard cases.

Leave to appeal was given by the Court of Appeal on terms that the authority should not seek an order for costs in this House or for variation of the orders for costs in the courts below. For the reasons I have indicated I would allow the appeal, set aside the order of the Court of Appeal save as to costs and order retrial of the issue whether the negligence of the authority, as found by the Court of Appeal, caused or materially contributed to the plaintiff's RLF.

[LORD FRASER OF TULLYBELTON, LORD LOWRY, LORD GRIFFITHS and LORD ACKNER agreed with LORD BRIDGE OF HARWICH's speech.]

Appeal allowed

Notes

1. In *Fitzgerald v Lane* [1987] QB 781; [1987] 2 All ER 455 the plaintiff was badly injured in a road accident. While walking briskly across a pelican crossing which had the red light showing against him, he was struck by D1's car, propelled onto its bonnet, into its windscreen and then onto the road where he was struck by D2's car. Both D1 and D2 were found to have been negligent and the plaintiff was found to have been contributorily negligent. The trial judge took the view that there were three equally possible causes for the partial tetraplegia which the plaintiff had sustained: the impact with the windscreen, the impact with the ground and D2's car striking the plaintiff. The case was decided by the Court of Appeal before *Wilsher* had reached the House of Lords, and, relying on the principle formulated by

Mustill LJ in *Wilsher* (see p. 307, ante), a causal link was found to have been established between D2's negligence and the tetraplegia. Would this case survive the rejection of Mustill LJ's principle by the House of Lords in *Wilsher*? See the notes on *Wilsher* by A. Boon (1988) 51 MLR 508 at 514–516.; A. Grubb [1988] CLJ at 352. (*Fitzgerald v Lane* did in fact later go to the House of Lords, [1989] AC 328; [1988] 2 All ER 961, noted pp. 373 and 874, post, but this causation issue was not discussed.)

2. For discussion of *McGhee v National Coal Board* [1972] 3 All ER 1008; [1973] 1 WLR 1 prior to the treatment of it in the recent case law, see E. J. Weinrib (1975) 38 MLR 518. The case is also discussed by Stapleton, op cit pp. 401–407. An objection raised by Stapleton to *Bonnington Castings Ltd v Wardlaw* [1956] AC 613; [1956] 1 All ER 615 and to *McGhee*, even as interpreted by the House of Lords in *Wilsher*, is that the defendant is paying for some damage that has not been shown on the balance of probabilities to have been caused by him. Stapleton's point is unaffected by *Wilsher*. She continues (at pp. 404–405):

'[Allowing the pursuer in *McGhee* (and in *Bonnington Castings*)] to recover for the *entire* injury, not just for the portion of that injury which he had proved to have been caused by the defender's fault . . . is tantamount to allowing the gist of the claim to be formulated in terms of the entire outcome while the causation requirement which the plaintiff is asked to satisfy is limited to only a portion of that gist damage. This non-coincidence of gist damage and the damage in respect of which the causal issue is formulated means that a plaintiff is also able to recover for that part of the overall injury to which he has been unable on the balance of probabilities to show any causal connection. Thus, even though the form of the causal issue in these cases may now be seen as the orthodox one, the outcome still represents an abandonment of the traditional rule that the defendant should only pay for past injuries which he has been shown on the balance of probabilities to have caused. It over-internalises costs to the defendant and over-deters his conduct. This radical, pro-plaintiff result seems to be unaffected by Lord Bridge's analysis in *Wilsher*.'

Stapleton goes on to argue that this is more pro-plaintiff than the Court of Appeal's view in *Hotson v East Berkshire Area Health Authority* [1987] AC 750; [1987] 1 All ER 210, on which see pp. 304 and 305, ante. which would not help a plaintiff where there is an evidentiary gap: see op cit, p. 407.

3. The 'but for' test has already been referred to p. 299, ante. *Barnett v Chelsea and Kensington Hospital Management Committee* [1969] 1 QB 428; [1968] 1 All ER 1068 is often mentioned by writers in this context. Nield J found that there had been negligence in the failure on the part of the defendants' casualty officer to see and examine the plaintiff's husband who arrived at the casualty department. He was in fact suffering from, and died of, arsenic poisoning. However, the casual link was not established since the plaintiff's husband would have died even if all care had been taken. See further *Robinson v Post Office* [1974] 2 All ER 737; [1974] 1 WLR 1176.

It should be noted that the 'but-for' test does not provide a complete answer to all the difficulties provided by factual causation, as the following passage by D. M. A. Strachan (1970) 33 MLR 386 at 391 reveals (footnotes omitted):

'The "but-for" test, though attractive and serviceable because of its basic simplicity, is incapable of dealing with all questions of factual causation. In certain situations common sense demands that a person be held responsible for a certain injury although that injury would have occurred without his participation. It is in situations where there are two independent factors, each being sufficient to produce the injury, that the test proves unsatisfactory. Such factors may operate either concurrently or successively. They operate concurrently if two independent fires, both negligently started, converge on a house and demolish it. Short shrift should be given to the contention that the damage is not caused by one, since another set of circumstances existed which would have caused the damage independently. The logical conclusion, if such a contention were to succeed, would be that the house-owner would be left with no redress since neither fire could be said to have caused the loss. . . .

The problem becomes more convoluted when the independent factors, each of which is sufficient to produce the injury, are successive rather than concurrent.'

Baker *v* Willoughby House of Lords [1969] 3 All ER 1528

The appellant, when crossing a road, had been knocked down by the respondent's car and his left leg and ankle were injured, the ankle becoming stiff. Apart from suffering pain, he lost those 'amenities of life' which are dependent on the ability to move freely and his earning capacity was reduced. The House of Lords restored the trial judge's apportionment of 75% responsibility on the respondent motorist for the accident. After the accident but before the trial of the action the appellant was involved in several different sorts of employment. One day he was sorting scrap metal when he was shot by one of two men who had unsuccessfully demanded money from him. His left leg was so badly affected by the shot that its amputation was necessary and the substitution of an artificial limb for what had been a stiff leg increased his disability. On the question of the effect on the respondent's liability of the second injury:

LORD REID: . . . The appellant argues that the loss which he suffered from the car accident has not been diminished by his second injury. He still still suffers from reduced capacity to earn although these[1] may have been to some extent increased. And he will suffer these losses for as long as he would have done because it is not said that the second injury curtailed his expectation of life.[2] The respondent on the other hand argues that the second injury removed the very limb from which the earlier disability had stemmed, and that therefore no loss suffered thereafter can be attributed to the respondent's negligence. He says that the second injury submerged or obliterated the effect of the first and that all loss thereafter must be attributed to the second injury. The trial judge[3] rejected this argument which he said was more ingenious than attractive. But it was accepted by the Court of Appeal.[4]

The respondent's argument was succinctly put to your Lordships by his counsel. He could not run before the second injury; he cannot run now. But the cause is now quite different. The former cause was an injured leg but now he has no leg and the former cause can no longer operate. His counsel was inclined to agree that if the first injury had caused some neurosis or other mental disability, that disability might be regarded as still flowing from the first accident; even if it had been increased by the second accident the respondent might still have to pay for that part which he caused. I agree with that and I think that any distinction between a neurosis and a physical injury depends on a wrong view of what is the proper subject for compensation.

---

1. [I.e. these losses.]
2. [Compare *Pickett v British Rail Engineering Ltd* [1980] AC 136; [1979] 1 All ER 774 (p. 421, post).]
3. [1969] 1 QB 38; [1968] 2 All ER 236.
4. [1969] 2 All ER 549; [1969] 2 WLR 489.

A man is not compensated for the physical injury; he is compensated for the loss which he suffers as a result of that injury. His loss is not in having a stiff leg; it is in his inability to lead a full life, his inability to enjoy those amenities which depend on freedom of movement and his inability to earn as much as he used to earn or could have earned if there had been no accident. In this case the second injury did not diminish any of these. So why should it be regarded as having obliterated or superseded them?

If it were the case that in the eye of the law an effect could only have one cause then the respondent might be right. It is always necessary to prove that any loss for which damages can be given was caused by the defendant's negligent act. But it is commonplace that the law regards many events as having two causes; that happens whenever there is contributory negligence, for then the law says that the injury was caused both by the negligence of the defendant and by the negligence of the plaintiff. And generally it does not matter which negligence occurred first in point of time.

I see no reason why the appellant's present disability cannot be regarded as having two causes, and if authority be needed for this I find it in *Harwood v Wyken Colliery Co*[1]. . . .

[Having discussed various other cases, LORD REID continued:] These cases exemplify the general rule that a wrongdoer must take the plaintiff (or his property) as he finds him: that may be to his advantage or disadvantage. In the present case the robber is not responsible or liable for the damage caused by the respondent; he would only have to pay for additional loss to the appellant by reason of his now having an artificial limb instead of a stiff leg. . . .

If . . . later injury suffered before the date of the trial either reduces the disabilities from the injury for which the defendant is liable, or shortens the period during which they will be suffered by the plaintiff then the defendant will have to pay less damages. But if the later injuries merely become a concurrent cause of the disabilities caused by the injury inflicted by the defendant, then in my view they cannot diminish the damages. . . .

Finally, I must advert to the pain suffered and to be suffered by the appellant as a result of the car accident. If the result of the amputation was that the appellant suffered no more pain thereafter, then he could not claim for pain after the amputation which he would never suffer. But the facts with regard to this are not clear, the amount awarded for pain subsequent to the date of the amputation was probably only a small part of the £1,600 damages and counsel for the respondent did not make a point of this. So in these circumstances we can neglect this matter. . . .

LORD PEARSON: . . . There is a plausible argument for the respondent on the following lines. The original accident, for which the respondent is liable, inflicted on the appellant a permanently injured left ankle, which caused pain from time to time, diminished his mobility and so reduced his earning capacity, and was likely to lead to severe arthritis. The proper figure of damages for those consequences of the accident, as assessed by the judge before making his apportionment, was £1,600. That was the proper figure for those consequences if they were likely to endure for a normal period and run a normal course. But the supervening event, when the robbers shot the appellant in his left leg, necessitated an amputation of the left leg above the knee. The consequences of the original accident therefore have ceased. He no longer suffers pain in his left ankle, because there no longer is a left ankle. He will never have the arthritis. There is no longer any loss of mobility through stiffness or weakness of the left ankle, because it is no longer there. The injury to the left ankle, resulting from the original accident, is not still operating as one of two concurrent causes both producing discomfort and disability. It is not operating at all nor causing anything. The present state of disablement, with the stump and the artificial leg on the left side, was caused wholly by the supervening event and not at all by the

1. [1913] 2 KB 158.

the original accident. Thus the consequences of the original accident have been submerged and obliterated by the greater consequences of the supervening event.

That is the argument, and it is formidable. But it must not be allowed to succeed, because it produces manifest injustice. The supervening event has not made the appellant less lame nor less disabled nor less deprived of amenities. It has not shortened the period over which he will be suffering. It has made him more lame, more disabled, more deprived of amenities. He should not have less damages through being worse off than might have been expected.

The nature of the injustice becomes apparent if the supervening event is treated as a tort (as indeed it was) and if one envisages the appellant suing the robbers who shot him. They would be entitled, as the saying is, to 'take the plaintiff as they find him'. (*Performance Cars Ltd v Abraham*.[1]) They have not injured and disabled a previously fit and able-bodied man. They have only made an already lame and disabled man more lame and more disabled. Take, for example, the reduction of earnings. The original accident reduced his earnings from £x per week to £y per week, and the supervening event further reduced them from £y per week to £z per week. If the respondent's argument is correct, there is, as counsel for the appellant has pointed out, a gap. The appellant recovers from the respondent the £x − y not for the whole period of the remainder of his working life, but only for the short period up to the date of the supervening event. The robbers are liable only for the £y − z from the date of the supervening event onwards. In the Court of Appeal[2] an ingenious attempt was made to fill the gap by holding that the damages recoverable from the later tortfeasors (the robbers) would include a novel head of damage, viz., the diminution of the appellant's damages recoverable from the original tortfeasor (the respondent). I doubt whether that would be an admissible head of damage; it looks too remote. In any case it would not help the appellant, if the later tortfeasors could not be found or were indigent and uninsured. These later tortfeasors cannot have been insured in respect of the robbery which they committed.

I think a solution of the theoretical problem can be found in cases such as this by taking a comprehensive and unitary view of the damage caused by the original accident. Itemisation of the damages by dividing them into heads and sub-heads is often convenient, but is not essential. In the end judgment is given for a single lump sum of damages and not for a total of items set out under heads and sub-heads. The original accident caused what may be called a 'devaluation' of the plaintiff, in the sense that it produced a general reduction of his capacity to do things, to earn money and to enjoy life. For that devaluation the original tortfeasor should be and remain responsible to the full extent, unless before the assessment of the damages something has happened which either diminishes the devaluation (e.g. if there is an unexpected recovery from some of the adverse effects of the accident) or by shortening the expectation of life diminishes the period over which the plaintiff will suffer from the devaluation. If the supervening event is a tort, the second tortfeasor should be responsible for the additional devaluation caused by him. . . .

[LORD GUEST, VISCOUNT DILHORNE and LORD DONOVAN concurred with LORD REID.]

Appeal allowed

Note

In *Performance Cars Ltd v Abraham* [1962] 1 QB 33; [1961] 3 All ER 413, which is referred to in *Baker v Willoughby*, the defendant, whose car had

---

1. [1962] 1 QB 33; [1961] 3 All ER 413.
2. [1969] 2 All ER 549; [1969] 2 WLR 489.

collided with the plaintiffs' Rolls-Royce causing damage to its wing and bumper, accepted responsibility for the accident. The damage to the wing necessitated a respray of the lower part of the car. A fortnight before, this same Rolls-Royce had been in a collision caused by the fault of another person and the damages in that case included the cost of a respray which had not yet been carried out. Nothing had been recovered under that judgment and the claim against the defendant in the present case included the cost of a respray. This was held by the Court of Appeal to be irrecoverable from this defendant. The second collision had not caused the need for a respray: such a need already existed.

Jobling v Associated Dairies Ltd House of Lords [1981] 2 All ER 752

In 1973 the appellant injured his back at work, an injury for which the respondents were held liable, and this injury led to his earning capacity being reduced by 50%. However, in 1976 (before the trial of the action) the appellant was rendered totally unfit for work by the onset of a condition known as spondylotic myelopathy, a disease of the spine. This condition had developed after the original accident and was in no way connected with it. Reeve J decided, on the basis of *Baker v Willoughby*, that he had to ignore the later condition in assessing damages, but the Court of Appeal disagreed, [1980] 3 All ER 769. On appeal to the House of Lords:

LORD WILBERFORCE: . . . In an attempt to solve the present case, and similar cases of successive causes of incapacity according to some legal principle, a number of arguments have been invoked.

1. Causation arguments. The unsatisfactory character of these is demonstrated by the case of *Baker v Willoughby* [1970] AC 467; [1969] 3 All ER 1528. I think that it can now be seen that Lord Reid's theory of concurrent causes even if workable on the particular facts of *Baker v Willoughby* (where successive injuries were sustained by the same limb) is as a general solution not supported by the authority he invokes (*Harwood v Wyken Colliery Co* [1913] 2 KB 158) or workable in other cases. . . .

2. The 'vicissitudes' argument. This is that since, according to accepted doctrine, allowance, and if necessary some discount, has to be made in assessing loss of future earnings for the normal contingencies of life, amongst which 'illness' is normally enumerated, so, if one of these contingencies becomes actual before the date of trial, this actuality must be taken into account. Reliance is here placed on the apophthegm 'the court should not speculate when it knows'. This argument has a good deal of attraction. But it has its difficulties: it raises at once the question whether a discount is to be made on account of all possible 'vicissitudes' or only on account of 'non-culpable' vicissitudes (ie such that if they occur there will be no cause of action against anyone, the theory being that the prospect of being injured by a tort is not a normally foreseeable vicissitude) or only on account of 'culpable' vicissitudes (such as per contra). And if this distinction is to be made how is the court to act when a discounted vicissitude happens before trial? Must it attempt to decide whether there was culpability or not? And how is it to do this if, as is likely, the alleged culprit is not before it?

This actual distinction between 'culpable' and 'non-culpable' events was made, with supporting argument, in the Alberta case of *Penner v Mitchell* [1978] 5 WWR 328. One may add to it the rider that, as pointed out by Dickson J in the Supreme Court of Canada in *Andrews v Grand & Toy Alberta Ltd* (1978) 83 DLR (3d) 452 at 470, there are in modern society many public and private schemes which cushion the individual against adverse circumstances. One then has to ask whether a discount should be made in respect of (a) such cases or (b) cases where there is no such cushion.

There is indeed in the 'vicissitude' argument some degree of circularity, since a discount in respect of possible events would only be fair if the actual event, discounted as possible, were to be taken into account when happening. But the whole question is whether it should be. One might just as well argue from what happens in 'actual' cases to what should happen in discountable cases.

In spite of these difficulties, the 'vicissitude' argument is capable in some, perhaps many, cases of providing a workable and reasonably just rule, and I would certainly not discountenance its use, either in the present case or in others.

The fact, however, is that to attempt a solution of these and similar problems, where there are successive causes of incapacity in some degree, on classical lines ('the object of damages for tort is to place the plaintiff in as good a position as if etc'; 'the defendant must compensate for the loss caused by his wrongful act, no more'; 'the defendant must take the plaintiff as he finds him etc') is, in many cases, no longer possible. We do not live in a world governed by the pure common law and its logical rules. We live in a mixed world where a man is protected against injury and misfortune by a whole web of rules and dispositions, with a number of timid legislative interventions. To attempt to compensate him on the basis of selected rules without regard to the whole must lead either to logical inconsistencies or to over- or under-compensation. As my noble and learned friend Lord Edmund-Davies has pointed out, no account was taken in *Baker v Willoughby* of the very real possibility that the plaintiff might obtain compensation from the Criminal Injuries Compensation Board. If he did in fact obtain this compensation he would, on the ultimate decision, be over-compensated.

In the present case, and in other industrial injury cases, there seems to me no justification for disregarding the fact that the injured man's employer is insured (indeed since 1972 compulsorily insured) against liability to his employees. The state has decided, in other words, on a spreading of risk. There seems to me no more justification for disregarding the fact that the plaintiff (presumably; we have not been told otherwise), is entitled to sickness and invalidity benefit in respect of his myelopathy, the amount of which may depend on his contribution record, which in turn may have been affected by his accident. So we have no means of knowing whether the plaintiff would be over-compensated if he were, in addition, to receive the assessed damages from his employer, or whether he would be under-compensated if left to his benefit. It is not easy to accept a solution by which a partially incapacitated man becomes worse off in terms of damages and benefit through a greater degree of incapacity. Many other ingredients, of weight in either direction, may enter into individual cases. Without any satisfaction I draw from this the conclusion that no general, logical or universally fair rules can be stated which will cover, in a manner consistent with justice, cases of supervening events, whether due to tortious, partially tortious, non-culpable or wholly accidental events. The courts can only deal with each case as best they can in a manner so as to provide just and sufficient but not excessive compensation, taking all factors into account. I think that this is what *Baker v Willoughby* did, and indeed that Lord Pearson reached his decision in this way; the rationalisation of the decision, as to which I at least have doubts, need and should not be applied to other cases. In the present case the Court of Appeal reached the unanswerable conclusion that to apply *Baker v Willoughby* to the facts of the present case would produce an unjust result, and I am willing to accept the corollary that justice, so far as it can be perceived, lies the other way and that the supervening myelopathy should not be disregarded. If rationalisation is needed, I am willing to accept the 'vicissitudes' argument as the best available. I should be more firmly convinced of the merits of the conclusion if the whole pattern of benefits had been considered, in however general a way. The result of the present case may be lacking in precision and rational justification, but so long as we are content to live in a mansion of so many different architectures this is inevitable.

I would dismiss the appeal.

LORD KEITH OF KINKEL: . . . Counsel for the appellant sought to draw a distinction between the case where the plaintiff, at the time of the tortious injury, is already suffering from a latent undetected condition which later develops into a disabling illness and the case where the inception of the illness occurs wholly at a later date. In the former case, so it was maintained, the illness would properly fall to be taken into account in diminution of damages, on the principle that the tortfeasor takes his victim as he finds him, but in the latter case it would not. There is no trace of the suggested distinction in any of the authorities, and in my opinion it is unsound and apt to lead to great practical difficulties, providing ample scope for disputation among medical men. What would be the position, it might be asked, of an individual having a constitutional weakness making him specially prone to illness generally, or an hereditary tendency to some specific disease?

I am . . . of opinion that the majority in *Baker v Willoughby* were mistaken in approaching the problems common to the case of a supervening tortious act and to that of supervening illness wholly from the point of view of causation. While it is logically correct to say that in both cases the original tort and the supervening event may be concurrent causes of incapacity, that does not necessarily, in my view, provide the correct solution. In the case of supervening illness, it is appropriate to keep in view that this is one of the ordinary vicissitudes of life, and when one is comparing the situation resulting from the accident with the situation, had there been no accident, to recognise that the illness would have overtaken the plaintiff in any event, so that it cannot be disregarded in arriving at proper compensation, and no more than proper compensation.

Additional considerations come into play when dealing with the problems arising where the plaintiff has suffered injuries from two or more successive and independent tortious acts. In that situation it is necessary to secure that the plaintiff is fully compensated for the aggregate effects of all his injuries. As Lord Pearson noted in *Baker v Willoughby* [1970] AC 467 at 495; [1969] 3 All ER 1528 at 1535 it would clearly be unjust to reduce the damages awarded for the first tort because of the occurrence of the second tort, damages for which are to be assessed on the basis that the plaintiff is already partially incapacitated. I do not consider it necessary to formulate any precise juristic basis for dealing with this situation differently from the case of supervening illness. It might be said that a supervening tort is not one of the ordinary vicissitudes of life, or that it is too remote a possibility to be taken into account, or that it can properly be disregarded because it carries its own remedy. None of these formulations, however, is entirely satisfactory. The fact remains that the principle of full compensation requires that a just and practical solution should be found. In the event that damages against two successive tortfeasors fall to be assessed at the same time, it would be highly unreasonable if the aggregate of both awards were less than the total loss suffered by the plaintiff. The computation should start from an assessment of that total loss. The award against the second tortfeasor cannot in fairness to him fail to recognise that the plaintiff whom he injured was already to some extent incapacitated. In order that the plaintiff may be fully compensated, it becomes necessary to deduct the award so calculated from the assessment of the plaintiff's total loss and award the balance against the first tortfeasor. If that be a correct approach, it follows that, in proceedings against the first tortfeasor alone, the occurrence of the second tort cannot be successfully relied on by the defendant as reducing the damages which he must pay. That, in substance, was the result of the decision in *Baker v Willoughby*, where the supervening event was a tortious act, and to that extent the decision was, in my view, correct.

Before leaving the case, it is right to face up to the fact that, if a non-tortious supervening event is to have the effect of reducing damages but a subsequent tortious act is not, there may in some cases be difficulty in ascertaining whether the event in question is or is not of a tortious character, particularly in the absence of the alleged tortfeasor. Possible questions of contributory negligence may cause additional complications. Such difficulties are real, but are not sufficient, in my view, to warrant the conclusion that the distinction between tortious and non-tortious supervening events should not be accepted. The court must simply do its best to arrive at a just assessment of damages in a pragmatical way in the light of the whole circumstances of the case.

My Lords, for these reasons I would dismiss the appeal.

LORD BRIDGE OF HARWICH: . . . The vicissitudes principle itself, it seems to me, stems from the fundamental proposition of law that the object of every award of damages for monetary loss is to put the party wronged so far as possible in the same position, no better and no worse, as he would be in if he had not suffered the wrong in respect of which he claims. To assume that an injured plaintiff, if not injured, would have continued to earn his full wages for a full working life, is very probably to over-compensate him. To apply a discount in respect of possible future loss of earnings arising from independent ca[u]ses may be to under-compensate him. When confronted by future uncertainty, the court assesses the prospects and strikes a balance between these opposite dangers as best it can. But, when the supervening illness or injury which is the independent cause of loss of earning capacity has manifested itself before trial, the event has demonstrated that, even if the plaintiff had never sustained the tortious injury, his earnings would now be reduced or extinguished. To hold the tortfeasor, in this situation, liable to pay damages for a notional continuing loss of earnings attributable to the tortious injury is to put the plaintiff in a better position than he would be in if he had never suffered the tortious injury. Put more shortly, applying well-established principles for the assessment of damages at common law, when a plaintiff injured by the defendant's tort is wholly incapacitated from earning by supervening illness or accidental injury, the law will no longer treat the tort as a continuing cause of any loss of earning capacity. . . .

[LORD EDMUND-DAVIES and LORD RUSSELL OF KILLOWEN delivered speeches in favour of dismissing the appeal.]

Appeal dismissed

Notes

1. All their Lordships in *Jobling* criticised Lord Reid's reliance in *Baker v Willoughby* (p. 313, ante) on *Harwood v Wyken Colliery Co* [1913] 2 KB 158 which concerned the old Workmen's Compensation Scheme. However, note A. Evans' argument — (1982) 45 MLR 329 at 331 — that this criticism was 'not so much in his use of that decision to found a causation argument but in his failure to recognise the inadequacies of causation arguments on their own and, in particular, to take account of the "vicissitudes" argument which Hamilton LJ in *Harwood* had clearly recognised as pertaining in a tortious context.' (Cf. *Bushby v Morris* (1979–80) 28 ALR 611 at 616.) The actual decision in *Baker v Willoughby* was not challenged by counsel for the respondents in *Jobling* and it was not reversed by the House of Lords. In addition to the views of Lord Wilberforce and Lord Keith set out ante, Lord Edmund-Davies thought it possible for the decision in *Baker v Willoughby* to be accepted 'on its own facts', although he was worried by a couple of features of the decision (see [1981] 2 All ER at p. 759). Lord Russell 'was not prepared to state disagreement' with the decision in *Baker v Willoughby*, but Lord Bridge was not willing to go even this far. Given the approach of the respondents' counsel mentioned ante, Lord Bridge was content to leave open the current status of the decision.

2. Lord Wilberforce said that although no account was taken in *Baker v Willoughby* of the chance that the plaintiff might be awarded compensation by the Criminal Injuries Compensation Board, he thought there was a 'very real possibility' that he would be. Lord Wilberforce concluded that, if this happened, the plaintiff would be over-compensated. The scheme under which the Board now operates can be found at p. 920, post, and it would seem that the Board would only pay for the additional losses brought about by the shooting (i.e. the increased disability); this would reflect the position in the law of tort (see e.g. *Baker v Willoughby*, pp. 313 and 314, ante) and will remain the position even when the new statutory scheme (see p. 927, post) comes into operation. Consider also para. 21 of the Scheme (p. 924, post). On the other hand, the first tortfeasor in *Baker v Willoughby* did not have to pay for the additional disability resulting from the shooting. How, therefore, could the plaintiff have been over-compensated?

3. One of Lord Keith's suggestions for reconciling *Baker v Willoughby* with *Jobling* – that a supervening tort is not one of the ordinary vicissitudes of life – met with some support from Lord Russell who was 'prepared to suggest' that physical damage from such an event would not be a 'relevant vicissitude'. Compare the approach of Lord Wilberforce and Lord Bridge set out ante.

To distinguish the situation in *Baker v Willoughby* is one thing, but the question of the justification for such a distinction must also be considered. It does seem unfair to allow a person such as the plaintiff in *Baker v Willoughby* to be worse off because he has been the victim of two torts rather than of one; and of course the decision obviates that result. However, it should be borne in mind that, as Lord Wilberforce made clear in *Jobling*, tort is not the only system of compensation. See T. Hervey (1981) 97 LQR 210 at 211 – 212 who, in commenting on the Court of Appeal's decision in *Jobling*, points out that an injured person can suffer, not just from 'falling between' two tortfeasors (which *Baker v Willoughby* does manage to avoid), but also from 'falling between' tort and another compensation system. See e.g. reg. 11(3) of the Social Security (General Benefit) Regulations S.I. 1982, No. 1408. In the light of this should a distinction be drawn between tortious and non-tortious supervening events?

4. For further discussion of the issues in this section, see J. D. Fraser and D. R. Howarth (1984) 4 LS 131.

2 Selection among operative factual causes

Stapley *v* Gypsum Mines Ltd House of Lords [1953]
2 All ER 478

LORD ASQUITH OF BISHOPSTONE: . . . Courts of law must accept the fact that the philosophic doctrine of causation and the juridical doctrine of responsibility for the consequences of a negligent act are not congruent. To a philosopher – a term which I use in no disparaging sense, for what is a philosopher but one who, inter alia, reasons severely and with precision? – to a philosopher, the whole legal doctrine of responsibility must seem anomalous. To him, if event C could not occur unless each of two previous events — A and B — had preceded it, it would be unmeaning to say that A was more responsible for the occurrence of C than was B, or that B was more responsible for its occurrence than was A. The whole modern doctrine of contributory negligence,[1] however, proceeds on the contrary assumption. If not, there would be no question of apportionment. But the fission between law and strict logic goes deeper than that. For I am persuaded that it is still part of the law of this country that two causes may both be necessary preconditions of a particular result — damage to X — yet the one may, if the facts justify that conclusion, be treated as the real, substantial, direct or effective cause, and the other dismissed as at best a causa sine qua non and ignored for purposes of legal liability. . . .

McKew v Holland and Hannen and Cubitts (Scotland) Ltd
Second Division of the Court of Session, and the House of Lords [1969] 3 All ER 1621

The appellant was slightly injured as a result of the fault of the respondents and one consequence was that for a short time thereafter he occasionally lost control of his left leg. Shortly after sustaining these injuries, the appellant, along with his wife, child and brother-in-law, went to inspect a flat to which access was provided by a steep flight of stairs with no handrail. Having inspected the flat, he was about to go down the stairs with his child, ahead of his wife and brother-in-law. According to his evidence, his left leg gave way, he thrust the child back and, to avoid going down head first, he threw himself and landed mainly on his right leg. His ankle was broken, and the question was whether the appellant could recover for the damage caused by this accident. The claim failed before the Lord Ordinary and the Court of Session. The following passage from the opinion of the Lord Justice-Clerk in the Court of Session received approval in the House of Lords:

THE LORD JUSTICE-CLERK: . . . It may well be that, in the situation in which he [the appellant] thought he was placed and with, apparently, an immediate choice to be made between two evils, the [appellant] was not unreasonable in jumping as he did. In my opinion, however, the chain of causation had already been broken. On his own evidence, his left leg had 'gone away' from him on several occasions before the second accident, both in the street and in his house. Yet, with this knowledge and experience, he set out to descend a flight of stairs without a stick or other support and without the assistance, which was available, of his wife or brother-in-law. I cannot regard this as a reasonable act and it was, in my opinion, an intervening act which broke the chain of causation. But for the first accident and the resulting weakness of the left leg the second accident would, no doubt, not have happened. The latter was indirectly connected with the former, but it was not the result of it, except possibly in some remote and indirect way, and a fortiori it was not the natural and direct or probable result of it, in whatever sense these words be used. . . .

[On appeal to the House of Lords:]

LORD REID: . . . In my view the law is clear. If a man is injured in such a way that his leg may give way at any moment he must act reasonably and carefully. It is quite possible that in spite of all reasonable care his leg may give way in circumstances such that as a result he sustains further injury. Then that second injury was caused by his disability which in turn was caused by the defender's fault. But if the injured man acts unreasonably he cannot hold the defender liable for injury caused by his own

---

1. [See chap. 7 (p. 357, post).]

unreasonable conduct. His unreasonable conduct is novus actus interveniens. The chain of causation has been broken and what follows must be regarded as caused by his own conduct and not by the defender's fault or the disability caused by it. Or one may say that unreasonable conduct of the pursuer and what follows from it is not the natural and probable result of the original fault of the defender or of the ensuing disability. I do not think that foreseeability comes into this. A defender is not liable for a consequence of a kind which is not foreseeable. But it does not follow that he is liable for every consequence which a reasonable man could foresee. What can be foreseen depends almost entirely on the facts of the case, and it is often easy to foresee unreasonable conduct or some other novus actus interveniens as being quite likely. But that does not mean that the defender must pay for damage caused by the novus actus. It only leads to trouble . . . if one tries to graft on to the concept of foreseeability some rule of law to the effect that a wrongdoer is not bound to foresee something which in fact he could readily foresee as quite likely to happen. For it is not at all unlikely or unforeseeable that an active man who has suffered such a disability will take some quite unreasonable risk. But if he does he cannot hold the defender liable for the consequences.

So in my view the question here is whether the second accident was caused by the appellant doing something unreasonable. It was argued that the wrongdoer must take his victim as he finds him and that that applies not only to a thin skull[1] but also to his intelligence. But I shall not deal with that argument because there is nothing in the evidence to suggest that the appellant is abnormally stupid. This case can be dealt with equally well by asking whether the appellant did something which a moment's reflection would have shown him was an unreasonable thing to do.

He knew that his left leg was liable to give way suddenly and without warning. He knew that this stair was steep and that there was no handrail. He must have realised, if he had given the matter a moment's thought, that he could only safely descend the stair if he either went extremely slowly and carefully so that he could sit down if his leg gave way, or waited for the assistance of his wife and brother-in-law. But he chose to descend in such a way that when his leg gave way he could not stop himself. I agree with what the Lord Justice-Clerk[2] says at the end of his opinion and I think that this is sufficient to require this appeal to be dismissed.

But I think it right to say a word about the argument that the fact that the appellant made to jump when he felt himself falling is conclusive against him. When his leg gave way the appellant was in a very difficult situation. He had to decide what to do in a fraction of a second. He may have come to a wrong decision; he probably did. But if the chain of causation had not been broken before this by his putting himself in a position where he might be confronted with an emergency, I do not think that he would put himself out of court by acting wrongly in the emergency unless his action was so utterly unreasonable that even on the spur of the moment no ordinary man would have been so foolish as to do what he did. In an emergency it is natural to try to do something to save oneself and I do not think that his trying to jump in this emergency was so wrong that it could be said to be . . . more than an error of judgment. But for the reasons already given I would dismiss this appeal.

[LORD HODSON and VISCOUNT DILHORNE concurred with LORD REID. LORD GUEST delivered a speech in favour of dismissing the appeal, and LORD UPJOHN concurred generally.]

Appeal dismissed

---

1. [See p. 338, post.]
2. [Ante.]

Notes

1. In considering causation reference should also be made to the section on rescuers in chap. 3 (p. 131, ante).

2. *Wieland v Cyril Lord Carpets Ltd* [1969] 3 All ER 1006 is a case dealing with a similar problem, but one in which the court came to a different decision. The first accident was caused by the defendants' negligence. Two days after the accident, the plaintiff, who wore bi-focal spectacles, returned to the hospital where she had originally been taken, and her neck was fitted with a special collar. The position of her neck in the collar 'deprived her of her usual ability to adjust herself automatically to the bi-focals'. After leaving the hospital, the plaintiff was in a nervous state as a result of her visit to the doctor and her involvement in the accident, and this fact, coupled with the problem which the bi-focal spectacles now presented, meant that the plaintiff was somewhat unsteady. She went to her son's office to ask him to take her home. He accompanied her down the stairs in the office building, but, on nearing the foot of the stairs, the plaintiff fell and injured her ankles. Eveleigh J held that the fall and consequent injury were caused by the defendants' negligence in the first accident. The plaintiff's skill in descending stairs whilst wearing the bi-focal spectacles had been impaired, resulting in the fall.

3. It has even been held that the chain of causation was not broken by a suicide: see *Pigney v Pointers Transport Services Ltd* [1957] 2 All ER 807; [1957] 1 WLR 1121, noted p. 342, post. Note also *Kirkham v Chief Constable of the Greater Manchester Police* [1989] 3 All ER 882. Here it was decided that a suicide was not too remote a consequence of the negligence in a case where the police in the circumstances were held to owe a duty to take reasonable care to stop the deceased's suicide. See also the opinion of O'Connor LJ in *Hyde v Thameside Area Health Authority* (1986) 2 PN 26 at 32 to which reference is made in *Kirkham*: cf. the view of Lord Denning MR at p. 29 in the *Hyde* case. When *Kirkham* went on appeal, [1990] 3 All ER 246; [1990] 2 WLR 987, noted p. 400, post, this remoteness point was not expressly discussed in the Court of Appeal's judgments, but the award of damages was upheld. See further p. 342, post.

4. On the question whether failure to have an abortion could constitute a novus actus interveniens in a 'wrongful birth' action (p. 147, ante), see *Emeh v Kensington and Chelsea and Westminster Area Health Authority* [1985] QB 1012; [1984] 3 All ER 1044. Although none of the members of the Court of Appeal ruled out the *possibility* of such failure constituting a novus actus (A. Grubb [1985] CLJ 30), Slade LJ did say (at p. 1053):

'Save in the most exceptional circumstances, I cannot think it right that the court should ever declare it unreasonable for a woman to decline to have an abortion, in a case where there is no evidence that there were any medical or psychiatric grounds for terminating the particular pregnancy.'

Home Office *v* Dorset Yacht Co Ltd, p. 74, ante

Note

The speech of Lord Reid is the one that is particularly important in this context. However, Sir R. Cooke [1978] CLJ 288 at 294–295 argues that the other members of the House of Lords in the *Dorset Yacht* case did not take 'the same line as a matter of principle', and he points out that Lord Reid did not regard the resumption of welding as 'of any particular significance' in *The Wagon Mound (No 2)* [1967] 1 AC 617; [1966] 2 All ER 709 (p. 253, ante and p. 632, post). The author of this article, sitting as a member of the New Zealand Court of Appeal, expressed similar views in *Taupo Borough Council v Birnie* [1978] 2 NZLR 397 at 410–411. Lord Reid's comments have also been subject to interpretation in English courts as the next extract will show.

Lamb *v* London Borough of Camden Court of Appeal [1981] 2 All ER 408

Contractors employed by the defendant local authority broke into a water main whilst replacing a sewer near to the plaintiff's house. The owner (Mrs Lamb) was in the USA at the time and had let her house to a tenant. The water that came out of the broken main affected the foundations of the house, rendering it unsafe for habitation, and thus the tenant moved out of the premises. Having arrived back in England Mrs Lamb put her furniture in store because of the extent of the repairs necessary to the house and then returned to the USA. Thereafter squatters moved into the house but they left after proceedings to evict them had been started. Boards were then put up in an effort to secure the house but squatters got in again and after the gas and electricity services were cut off, they burnt panelling which they had pulled off the walls. They also took other things in the house. There was a claim for compensation (including the cost of damage done by the squatters) and the defendant council admitted liability for nuisance (on which see chap. 14, p. 623, post). The damages were assessed by an official referee, who thought that squatting was a reasonably foreseeable risk but that it was not likely. Applying Lord Reid's speech in the *Dorset Yacht* case, he held that the damage caused by the squatters was too remote, and an appeal was taken from this decision to the Court of Appeal. The judgments in the Court of Appeal refer to *The Wagon Mound* [1961] AC 388; [1961] 1 All ER 404 (p. 333, post) and *The Wagon Mound (No 2)* [1967] 1 AC 617; [1966] 2 All ER 709 (p. 253, ante and p. 632, post). These cases will be considered later, but basically establish that in both negligence and nuisance the kind of damage must be reasonably foreseeable.

LORD DENNING MR [having criticised Lord Reid's test in the *Dorset Yacht* case (p. 74, ante) as including too much and as difficult to reconcile with *Stansbie v Troman* [1948] 2 KB 48; [1948] 1 All ER 599 and *The Wagon Mound* and *The Wagon Mound (No 2)*:] If Lord Reid's test is wrong, what is the alternative test? Logically, I suppose that liability and compensation should go hand in hand. If reasonable foresight is the criterion in negligence, so also it should be in remoteness of damage. That was the test for which counsel for Mrs Lamb contended. . . .

To my mind that alternative test is also not acceptable. It would extend the range of compensation far too widely. . . . Take . . . the illustration I took from the *Dorset Yacht* case of the criminal who escapes (owing to the negligence of the prison staff) and breaks into people's houses. Although it could reasonably be foreseen, the Home Office are not liable for his depredations. . . .

The truth
The truth is that all these three, duty, remoteness and causation, are all devices by which the courts limit the range of liability for negligence or nuisance. As I said recently in *Compania Financiera Soleada SA v Hamoor Tanker Corpn Inc, The Borag*

[1981] 1 All ER 856 at 861, [1981] 1 WLR 274 at 281: '. . . it is not every consequence of a wrongful act which is the subject of compensation. The law has to draw a line somewhere.'

Sometimes it is done by limiting the range of the persons to whom duty is owed. Sometimes it is done by saying that there is a break in the chain of causation. At other times it is done by saying that the consequence is too remote to be a head of damage. All these devices are useful in their way. But ultimately it is a question of policy for the judges to decide. . . .

Looking at the question as one of policy, I ask myself: whose job was it to do something to keep out the squatters? And, if they got in, to evict them? To my mind the answer is clear. It was the job of the owner of the house, Mrs Lamb, through her agents. That is how everyone in the case regarded it. It has never been suggested in the pleadings or elsewhere that it was the job of the council. No one ever wrote to the council asking them to do it. The council were not in occupation of the house. They had no right to enter it. All they had done was to break the water main outside and cause the subsidence. After they had left the site, it was Mrs Lamb *herself* who paved the way for the squatters by moving out all her furniture and leaving the house unoccupied and unfurnished. There was then, if not before, on the judge's findings, a reasonably foreseeable risk that squatters might enter. She ought to have taken steps to guard against it. She says that she locked the doors and pulled the shutters. That turned out to be insufficient, but it was her responsibility to do more. At any rate, when the squatters did get in on the first occasion in 1974, it was then her agents who acted on her behalf. They got the squatters out. Then, at any rate, Mrs Lamb or her agents ought to have done something effective. But they only put up a few boards at a cost of £10. Then there was the second invasion in 1975. Then her agents did recognise her responsibility. They did what they could to get the squatters out. They eventually succeeded. But no one ever suggested throughout that it was the responsibility of the council.

In her evidence Mrs Lamb suggested that she had not the money to do more. I do not think the judge accepted the suggestion. Her agents could well have made the house secure for a modest sum which was well within her capabilities.

On broader grounds of policy, I would add this: the criminal acts here, malicious damage and theft, are usually covered by insurance. By this means the risk of loss is spread throughout the community. It does not fall too heavily on one pair of shoulders alone. The insurers take the premium to cover just this sort of risk and should not be allowed, by subrogation, to pass it on to others. . . . It is commonplace nowadays for the courts, when considering policy, to take insurance into account. . . .

So here, it seems to me, that, if Mrs Lamb was insured against damage to the house and theft, the insurers should pay the loss. If she was not insured, that is her misfortune.

Taking all these policy matters into account, I think the council are not liable for the acts of these squatters.

I would dismiss this appeal.

OLIVER LJ [having quoted from Lord Reid's speech in the *Dorset Yacht* case concerning intervening human action:] The views which Lord Reid there expressed are not reflected in the speeches of the others of their Lordships in the case, and were, I think, obiter, since there was no scope for argument on the assumed facts that the damage which occurred was not the very thing that was likely to happen. But, obiter or no, Lord Reid's opinion must be at least of the very highest persuasive authority. For my part, however, I very much doubt whether he was, in what he said regarding the likelihood of the act of a third party, intending to bring back into the test of remoteness some further philosophical consideration of nexus or direct or indirect causation. As it seems to me, all that Lord Reid was saying was this, that, where as a matter of fact the consequence which the court is considering is one which results from, or would not have occurred but for, the intervention of some independent human agency over which the tortfeasor has no control it has to approach the problem of what could be reasonably foreseen by the tortfeasor, and thus of the damage for which he is responsible, with particular care. The immediate cause is known: it is the independent human agency; and one has therefore to ask: on what basis can the act of that person be attributed back to the tortfeasor? It may be because the tortfeasor is responsible for his actions or because the third party act which has precipitated the damage is the very thing that the tortfeasor is employed to prevent. But what is the position in the absence of some such consideration? Few things are less certainly predictable than human behaviour, and if one is asked whether in any given situation a human being may behave idiotically, irrationally or even criminally the answer must always be that that is a possibility, for every society has its proportion of idiots and criminals. It cannot be said that you cannot foresee the possibility that people will do stupid or criminal acts, because people are constantly doing stupid or criminal acts. But the question is not what is foreseeable merely as a possibility but what would the reasonable man actually foresee if he thought about it, and all that Lord Reid seems to me to be saying is that the hypothetical reasonable man in the position of the tortfeasor cannot be said to foresee the behaviour of another person unless that behaviour is such as would, viewed objectively, be very likely to occur. Thus, for instance, if by my negligent driving I damage another motorist's car, I suppose that theoretically I *could* foresee that, whilst he leaves it by the roadside to go and telephone his garage, some ill-intentioned passer-by may jack it up and remove the wheels. But I cannot think that it could be said that, merely because I have created the circumstances in which such a theft might become possible, I ought reasonably to foresee that it would happen.

Now if this is right, it does raise a difficulty over the official referee's finding. If the likelihood of human behaviour is an element in reasonable foreseeability the official referee's disposition to say that the invasion of squatters was reasonably foreseeable is inconsistent with his actual finding of fact that squatting was unlikely, and that is the only actual finding. What I think, with respect, he was doing in this passage of his judgment was confusing 'foreseeable' with 'reasonably foreseeable'. That indeed would be consistent with the passage from Lord Reid's speech on which he was relying as stating the principle. Lord Reid said in terms that foreseeability 'as a possibility' was not sufficient and I think that what the official referee has done is to treat that as meaning, in the context, '*reasonable* foreseeability as a possibility'. In the context in which, as I think, Lord Reid was using the expression 'as a possibility' (that is to say, as meaning '*only* a bare possibility and no more') that seems to me to be a contradiction in terms, and for the reasons which I have endeavoured to explain it was not what Lord Reid intended and it was not what he said. The critical finding here is, to my mind, that the incursion of squatters was in fact unlikely.

Given this finding, it seems to me that, accepting Lord Reid's test as correct (which counsel for the plaintiff challenges), it must be fatal to the plaintiff's contentions on this appeal, because it constitutes in effect a finding that the damage claimed is not such as could be reasonably foreseen. And that, indeed, seems to me to accord with the common sense of the matter. . . .

I should perhaps add that I do not dissent from the view of Lord Denning MR that the test expressed by Lord Reid (with, as I think, the intention of restricting the ambit of the duty in tort) was incorrect, in that it was not exhaustive and did not go far enough in that direction. To apply a straight test of foreseeability or likelihood to hypothetical circumstances which could arise in relation to the acts of independent third parties in the case of, for instance, carelessness on the part of servants of the Home Office does, as Lord Denning MR points out, produce some astonishing results. Suppose that as a result of the carelessness of a prison officer a prisoner escapes and commits a crime of the same type as that for which he is in custody a fortnight later and 400 miles away from the place at which he escaped. Is it any less foreseeable that he will do so than that he will steal his rail fare from a house adjoining the prison? And is the Home Office to be liable without limit until the prisoner is apprehended? Does it make any difference if he is, at the date of his escape, on remand or due for parole? Happily, such hypothetical questions do not, on the view that I take, have to be answered in the instant case, but whether or not it is right to regard questions of remoteness according to some flexible test of the policy of the law from time to time (on which I prefer at the moment to express no view) I concur with Lord Denning MR in regarding the straight test of foreseeability, at least in cases where the acts of independent third parties are concerned, as one which can, unless subjected to some further limitation, produce results which extend the ambit of liability beyond all reason. Speaking for myself, I would respectfully regard Lord Reid's test as a work-able and sensible one, subject only to this, that I think that he may perhaps have understated the *degree* of likelihood required before the law can or should attribute the free act of a responsible third person to the tortfeasor. Such attribution cannot, as I think, rationally be made simply on the basis of some geographical or temporal proximity, and even 'likelihood' is a somewhat uncertain touchstone. It may be that some more stringent standard is required. There may, for instance, be circumstances in which the court would require a degree of likelihood amounting almost to inevita-bility before it fixes a defendant with responsibility for the act of a third party over whom he has and can have no control. On the official referee's finding, however, that does not arise here, and the problem can be left for a case in which it directly arises.

WATKINS LJ: ... I feel bound to say with respect that what Lord Reid said in the *Dorset Yacht* case does nothing to simplify the task of deciding for or against remote-ness, especially where the fresh damage complained of has been caused by the interven-ing act of a third party. It may be that in respect of such an act he is to be understood as saying, without using his remarkable and usual clarity of expression, that damage is inevitably too remote unless it can reasonably be foreseen as likely to occur. If that be so, it could be said that he was not intending to depart from the *Wagon Mound*[1] test save in cases involving intervening human action to which he would apply a rather stricter than usual test by placing acts which are *not likely to occur* within the realm of remoteness.

    ... [The decision in *McKew v Holland & Hannen & Cubitts (Scotland) Ltd* [1969] 3 All ER 1621 (p. 320, ante)] has in some quarters been criticised on the basis that it would have been more in accordance with principle to have treated the plaintiff's unreasonable conduct as contributory negligence. I do not agree. I prefer to regard the decision in *McKew* as a good example of a determination to bring realistic con-sideration to bear on the question of fresh damage arising from an event or act occurring subsequently to the initial negligent act in the context of remoteness of damage.

    It seems to me that if the sole and exclusive test of remoteness is whether the fresh damage has arisen from an event or act which is reasonably foreseeable, or reasonably foreseeable as a possibility, or likely or quite likely to occur, absurd, even bizarre, results might ensue in actions for damages for negligence. Why, if this test were to be rigidly applied to the facts in the *Dorset Yacht* case, one can envisage the Home Office being found liable for the damage caused by an escaped borstal boy committing a burglary in John o'Groats. This would plainly be a ludicrous conclusion.

    I do not think that words such as, among others, 'possibility', 'likely' or 'quite likely' assist in the application of the test of reasonable foreseeability. If the crisply stated test which emanates from *The Wagon Mound (No. 2)*[1] is to be festooned with additional words supposedly there for the purpose of amplification or qualification, an understandable application of it will become impossible.

    In my view the *Wagon Mound* test should always be applied without any of the gloss which is from time to time being applied to it.

    But when so applied it cannot in all circumstances in which it arises conclude consideration of the question of remoteness, although in the vast majority of cases it

---

1. [See p. 323, ante.]

will be adequate for this purpose. In other cases, the present one being an example of these in my opinion, further consideration is necessary, always providing, of course, a plaintiff survives the test of reasonable foreseeability.

This is because the very features of an event or act for which damages are claimed themselves suggest that the event or act is not on any practical view of it remotely in any way connected with the original act of negligence. These features will include such matters as the nature of the event or act, the time it occurred, the place where it occurred, the identity of the perpetrator and his intentions, and responsibility, if any, for taking measures to avoid the occurrence and matters of public policy.

A robust and sensible approach to this very important area of the study of remoteness will more often than not produce, I think, an instinctive feeling that the event or act being weighed in the balance is too remote to sound in damages for the plaintiff. I do not pretend that in all cases the answer will come easily to the inquirer. But that the question must be asked and answered in all these cases I have no doubt.

To return to the present case, I have the instinctive feeling that the squatters' damage is too remote. I could not possibly come to any other conclusion, although on the primary facts I, too, would regard that damage or something like it as reasonably foreseeable in these times.

We are here dealing with unreasonable conduct of an outrageous kind. It is notorious that squatters will take the opportunity of entering and occupying any house, whether it be damaged or not, which is found to be unoccupied for more than a very temporary duration. In my opinion this kind of antisocial and criminal behaviour provides a glaring example of an act which inevitably, or almost so, is too remote to cause a defendant to pay damages for the consequences of it.

Accordingly, I would hold that the damage caused by the squatters in the present case is too remote to be recovered from these defendants. . . .

Appeal dismissed

Notes

1. In relation to Lord Denning's views in *Lamb* as to the insurance position, consider the comments of R. G. Lee and R. M. Merkin (1981) 131 NLJ 965. They point out that both household contents and building insurance policies are unlikely to cover damage to a property which has been unoccupied for thirty consecutive days, whereas the contractors were likely to have carried all risks insurance. *Lamb* is also noted by J. Murdoch (1982) 98 LQR 22. On policy see further p. 352, post.

2. The fact that the reasoning of the judges in *Lamb* was not uniform was acknowledged in *P Perl* (*Exporters*) *Ltd v Camden London Borough Council* [1984] QB 342; [1983] 3 All ER 161, noted p. 98, ante, by Waller LJ who expressed a preference for Oliver LJ's opinion. See further *Crossley v Rawlinson* [1981] 3 All ER 674 at 678 where in particular part of Watkins LJ's judgment was cited, and see also *Meah v McCreamer* (*No 2*) [1986] 1 All ER 943 at 950. For further discussion of the speeches in *Lamb*, see *Ward v Cannock Chase District Council* [1986] Ch 546; [1985] 3 All ER 537 where Scott J stated (at p. 552):

'Although the three judgments in *Lamb v Camden London Borough* give different reasons for coming to the same conclusion, a common ratio is, to my mind, identifiable at least in the judgments of Oliver and Watkins LJJ. Both start with the reasonable foreseeability test as expressed in *The Wagon Mound* (*No 2*). Both, where damage caused by independent third parties is concerned, require something more than merely the foreseeable possibility of the occurrence of the damage. Oliver LJ would ask what the reasonable man, if he thought about the consequences of the negligent act or omission, would actually foresee. Unless a reasonable man would actually foresee the intervening acts in question, Oliver LJ would hold the damage too remote. Watkins LJ would exclude the damage if, on a practical view, it did not seem sufficiently connected with the negligent act or omission. Lord Reid [in *Dorset Yacht*] would ask whether the intervening acts were the very kind of thing likely to happen.

I do not think there is any real difference between Lord Reid's and Oliver LJ's formulations. Each, in my view, expresses in different language the same essential requirements. There is, however, a difference between their approach and that of Watkins LJ. Both Lord Reid and Oliver LJ would examine the nature of the damage in question from the anterior moment when the negligent act or omission took place. From that standpoint they would ask whether the damage would be actually foreseen by a reasonable man, or would be regarded as the very kind of thing likely to happen. Watkins LJ's approach, however, would start with the damage under review and look back to the negligent act or omission in order to find some sufficient connection. In most cases, this difference of approach would I think make no difference to the result.'

Scott J went on to decide that on either approach certain vandal damage to buildings that had occurred in that case as a result of the buildings being unoccupied, which in turn resulted from the defendant's breach of duty, was not too remote; on the other hand, certain vandal damage to, and theft of, chattels kept on the premises was found to be too remote.

Consider further Lord Mackay's comments on *Lamb* in *Smith v Littlewoods Organisation Ltd* [1987] AC 241; [1987] 1 All ER 710 (p. 86, ante). He stated that his view of Lord Reid's speech in *Dorset Yacht* (see p. 89, ante) was somewhat different from that of Lord Denning MR and Oliver LJ in *Lamb* and continued (at p. 723):

'While I do not consider that it is correct to base the decision in *Lamb v Camden London Borough* on a proposition as a matter of policy that no wrongdoer could ever be liable for outrageous or anti social conduct that had followed his wrongdoing and had contributed to the damage resulting therefrom, I respectfully and entirely agree with the result to which the Court of Appeal came in that case, and particularly with the reason expressed for it by Oliver LJ where he said ([1981] 2 All ER 408 at 419, [1981] QB 625 at 643).

"I confess that I find it inconceivable that the reasonable man, wielding his pick in the road in 1973, could be said reasonably to foresee that his puncturing of a water main would fill the plaintiff's house with uninvited guests in 1974."'

For Lord Goff's view in *Smith v Littlewoods* on *Lamb*, see p. 97, ante.

3. Despite the views expressed in *Lamb*, Lord Reid's comments in the *Dorset Yacht* case were quoted without any qualification in *Paterson Zochonis & Co Ltd v Merfarken Packaging Ltd* [1986] 3 All ER 522 at 534 and 541–542. The Court of Appeal was more cautious in *Knightley v Johns* [1982] 1 All ER 851 at 863 saying that Lord Reid's 'insistence on human actions being less easily foreseeable or less likely effects of carelessness than a sequence of natural "inanimate" reactions' may need reconsideration in the light of *Lamb*, and consider now Lord Mackay's speech in *Smith v Littlewoods* (p. 89, ante – mentioned in the previous note). In addition to the question of its relationship with *Lamb*, is Lord Mackay's general approach consistent with *McKew v Holland and Hannen and Cubitts (Scotland) Ltd* [1969] 3 All ER 1621 (p. 320, ante)? Does it leave any room for a court to reject as too remote damage that results from a foreseeable intervening event?

4. In *Knightley v Johns* [1982] 1 All ER 851; [1982] 1 WLR 349, J negligently overturned his car near the exit of a tunnel carrying one-way traffic. S, the police inspector in charge, who had forgotten to close the tunnel, ordered K to ride on his motorcycle the wrong way along the tunnel to close the entrance. In doing so K collided with a car being driven by C who was not negligent. K was not negligent. The Court of Appeal held that S had been negligent in not closing the tunnel and in ordering or allowing K to do so by a dangerous manoeuvre, and that there had been a new cause interrupting the sequence of events between J's negligence and K's accident. Accordingly S (and his chief constable) were liable to K, and J was not.

Knightley v Johns should be compared with *McKew v Holland and Hannen and Cubitts (Scotland) Ltd* [1969] 3 All ER 1621 (p. 320, ante) and with *Lamb*, since it suggests that the only test for a novus actus interveniens is whether it is reasonably foreseeable (and see note 3, ante). It also appears to equate the test, which can be found in the older authorities, that a natural and probable consequence of the defendant's act will not be a novus actus interveniens with the test of reasonable foreseeability. Cf. *The Wagon Mound* [1961] AC 388 at 422–423 (pp. 334–335, post) which suggests that they may not always be the same and this passage was quoted by the court: consider further *Slipper v BBC* [1991] 1 All ER 165; [1990] 3 WLR 967. The reasonable foreseeability test was defined in *Knightley v Johns* (at p. 865) as 'foreseeability of something of the same sort being likely to happen, as against its being a mere possibility which would never occur to the mind of a reasonable man or, if it did, would be neglected as too remote to require precautions or to impose responsibility'. Stephenson LJ went on to say:

'The question to be asked is accordingly whether that whole sequence of events is a natural and probable consequence of Mr Johns's negligence and a reasonably foreseeable result of it. In answering the question it is helpful but not decisive to consider which of these events were deliberate choices to do positive acts and which were mere omissions [or] failures to act; which acts and omissions were innocent mistakes or miscalculations and which were negligent having regard to the pressures and the gravity of the emergency and the need to act quickly. Negligent conduct is more likely to break the chain of causation than conduct which is not; positive acts will more easily constitute new causes than inaction. Mistakes and mischances are to be expected when human beings, however well trained, have to cope with a crisis; what exactly they will be cannot be predicted, but if those which occur are natural the wrongdoer cannot, I think, escape responsibility for them and their consequences simply by calling them improbable or unforeseeable. He must accept the risk of some unexpected mischances . . .'

3   Foreseeability of the kind of damage

Re Polemis and Furness, Withy & Co Ltd   Court of Appeal [1921] All ER Rep 40

The charterers of a ship carried in it a cargo which included benzine or petrol in cases. Whilst the vessel was being unloaded at Casablanca, a plank fell into the hold, and there was an explosion leading to a fire which destroyed the ship. The owners alleged that negligence on the part of the charterers' servants caused the loss of the ship, and one of the charterers' arguments was that the damage was too remote. The following findings of fact were made by the arbitrators:

'(a) That the ship was lost by fire. (b) That the fire arose from a spark igniting petrol vapour in the hold. (c) That the spark was caused by the falling board coming into contact with some substance in the hold. (d) That the fall of the board was caused by the negligence of the Arabs (other than the winchman) engaged in the work of discharging. (e) That the said Arabs were employed by the charterers or their agents the Cie Transatlantique on behalf of the charterers, and that the said Arabs were the servants of the charterers. (f) That the causing of the spark could not reasonably have been anticipated from the falling of the board, though some damage to the ship might reasonably have been anticipated. (g) There was no evidence before us that the Arabs chosen were known or likely to be negligent. (h) That the damages sustained by the owners through the said accident amount to the sum of £196,165 1s 11d. . . .'

Sankey J affirmed the award. The charterers appealed.

BANKES LJ: . . . In the present case the arbitrators have found as a fact that the falling of the plank was due to the negligence of the defendants' servants. The fire appears to me to have been directly caused by the falling of the plank. In these circumstances I consider that it is immaterial that the causing of the spark by the falling of the plank could not have been reasonably anticipated. The charterers' junior counsel sought to draw a distinction between the anticipation of the extent of damage resulting from a negligent act, and the anticipation of the type of damage resulting from such an act. He admitted that it could not lie in the mouth of a person whose negligent act had caused damage to say that he could not reasonably have foreseen the extent of the damage, but he contended that the negligent person was entitled to rely upon the fact that he could not reasonably have anticipated the type of damage which resulted from his negligent act. I do not think that the distinction can be admitted. Given the breach of duty which constitutes the negligence, and given the damage as a direct result of that negligence, the anticipations of the person whose negligent act has produced the damage appear to me to be irrelevant. I consider that the damages claimed are not too remote. . . .

WARRINGTON LJ: . . . The presence or absence of reasonable anticipation of damage determines the legal quality of the act as negligent or innocent. If it be thus determined to be negligent, then the question whether particular damages are recoverable depends only on the answer to the question whether they are the direct consequence of the act. . . . In the present case it is clear that the act causing the plank to fall was in law a negligent act, because some damage to the ship might reasonably be anticipated. If this is so then the charterers are liable for the actual loss, that being on the findings of the arbitrators the direct result of the falling board: see per Lord Sumner in *Weld-Blundell v Stephens*[1] ([1920] AC at p. 983). On the whole, in my opinion, the appeal must be dismissed with costs.

SCRUTTON LJ: . . . To determine whether an act is negligent, it is relevant to determine whether any reasonable person would foresee that the act would cause damage; if he would not, the act is not negligent. But if the act would or might probably cause damage, the fact that the damage it in fact causes is not the exact kind of damage one would expect is immaterial, so long as the damage is in fact caused sufficiently directly by the negligent act, and not by the operation of independent causes having no connection with the negligent act, except that they could not avoid its results. Once the act is negligent, the fact that its exact operation was not foreseen is immaterial. . . . In the present case it was negligent in discharging cargo to knock down the planks of the temporary staging, for they might easily cause some damage either to workmen, or cargo, or the ship. The fact that they did directly produce an

1. [1920] AC 956.

unexpected result, a spark in an atmosphere of petrol vapour which caused a fire, does not relieve the person who was negligent from the damage which his negligent act directly caused. For these reasons the experienced arbitrators and the judge appealed from came, in my opinion, to a correct decision, and the appeal must be dismissed with costs.

Appeal dismissed

Note

In [1962] CLJ 178 R. W. M. Dias writes (at pp. 179–180, footnotes omitted):

'A convenient point of departure would be to ask, for what is *Polemis* supposed to be an authority? The decision is open to two possible interpretations, a dichotomy which has considerably obscured the discussions centred upon it. One of these, to be called the "wide" principle, is that the defendant is liable for all the damage directly resulting from his careless behaviour, however caused, and even to a plaintiff who was not foreseeably endangered by it. The other, to be called the "narrow" principle, is that so long as the plaintiff was in foreseeable danger, the defendant is liable to him to the full extent of the damage that directly results, though neither the manner of its incidence nor its extent may have been foreseeable. The second of these versions will be accepted here. This is because, in the *first* place, the point of distinction between the two statements, namely, the foresight of damage to the plaintiff, accords with an abundance of authority which would appear to have submerged the alternative view, although occasional support for the latter does bubble forth from beneath the tide. *Secondly*, the "narrow" proposition is warranted by the facts in *Polemis* where some damage to the plaintiff's ship was found to have been reasonably foreseeable as the result of dropping a plank into its hold, but not the fire which unexpectedly developed. *Thirdly*, only on this footing is the case reconcilable with certain subsequent decisions of the House of Lords, in each of which the defendant was held not liable on the ground that no damage to the plaintiff was initially foreseeable. . . .'

Cf. M. Davies (1982) 45 MLR 534 at 548–549.

The Edison House of Lords [1933] All ER Rep 144

The *Edison*, in leaving the port of Patras, came into contact with the *Liesbosch*'s moorings and pulled that vessel, which had no crew on board, out to sea. In the heavy sea, the *Liesbosch* sank, and the respondents admitted liability. The *Liesbosch* was being used by the appellants for dredging operations as part of certain works they had contracted to carry out. There were penalties for delay. The appellants at that time were unable to buy a substitute dredger as their liquid resources were tied up in the contract, and so they hired a dredger, the *Adria*, at a high rate and the work was restarted. In the light of this high rate of hire, the Harbour Board bought the dredger shortly after its arrival, and resold it to the appellants, payment being on an instalment basis. In assessing the damages, the Registrar of the Admiralty Division took the view that in their circumstances the appellants had acted reasonably in hiring the dredger, and that their acts were the natural and direct results of the defendants' (respondents) wrongful act. He allowed the appellants (1) the actual value to them of the *Liesbosch* (2) reasonable expenses while the work was stopped (3) hiring expenses of the *Adria* until bought by the Harbour Board (4) the extra cost of working the *Adria* (5) loss of interest during the period of delay. He awarded the appellants £19,820. Langton J, [1931] P 230, basically affirmed the Registrar's report, but an appeal was allowed by the Court of Appeal, [1932] P 52, and the damages were reduced. On further appeal to the House of Lords:

LORD WRIGHT: . . . The substantial issue is what in such a case as the present is the true measure of damage. It is not questioned that when a vessel is lost by collision due to the sole negligence of the wrong-doing vessel the owners of the former vessel are entitled to what is called restitutio in integrum, which means that they should recover such a sum as will replace them so far as can be done by compensation in money, in the same position as if the loss had not been inflicted on them, subject to the rules of law as to remoteness of damage. The respondents contend that all that is recoverable as damages is the true value to the owners of the lost vessel, as at the time and place of loss. Before considering what is involved in this contention, I think it desirable to examine the claim made by the appellants, which found favour with the registrar and Langton J, and which in effect is that all their circumstances, in particular their want of means, must be taken into account, and hence the damages must be based on their actual loss, provided only that, as the registrar and the judge have found, they acted reasonably in the unfortunate predicament in which they were placed, even though but for their financial embarrassment they could have replaced the *Liesbosch* at a moderate price and with comparatively short delay.

In my judgment, the appellants are not entitled to recover damages on this basis. The respondents' tortious act involved the physical loss of the dredger; that loss must somehow be reduced to terms of money. But the appellants' actual loss in so far as it was due to their impecuniosity arose from that impecuniosity as a separate and concurrent cause, extraneous to and distinct in character from the tort; the impecuniosity was not traceable to the respondents' acts, and, in my opinion, was outside the legal purview of the consequences of these acts. The law cannot take account of everything that follows a wrongful act; it regards some subsequent matters as outside the scope of its selection, because 'it were infinite to trace the cause of causes,' or consequences of consequences. Thus, the loss of a ship by collision due to the other vessel's sole fault may force the shipowner into bankruptcy, and, that again, may involve his family in suffering, loss of education, or opportunities, in life, but no such loss could be recovered from the wrongdoer. In the varied web of affairs the law must abstract some consequences as relevant, not, perhaps, on grounds of pure logic but simply for practical reasons. In the present case, if the appellants' financial embarrassment is to be regarded as a consequence of the respondents' tort, I think it is too remote, but I prefer to regard it as an independent cause, though its operative effect was conditioned by the loss of the dredger. . . .

Polemis and Furness, Withy & Co,[1] a case in tort of negligence, was cited as illustrating the wide scope possible in damages for tort. That case, however, was concerned with the immediate physical consequences of the negligent act, and not with the co-operation of an extraneous matter such as the plaintiffs' want of means. I think, therefore, that it is not material further to consider that case here. Nor is the appellants' financial disability to be compared with that physical delicacy or weakness which may aggravate the damage in the case of personal injuries, or with the possibility that the injured man in such a case may be either a poor labourer or a highly paid professional man. The former class of circumstances goes to the extent of actual physical damage, and the latter consideration goes to interference with profit-earning capacity; whereas the appellants' want of means was, as already stated, extrinsic.

I agree with the conclusion of the Court of Appeal that the registrar and Langton J proceeded on a wrong basis, and that the damages must be assessed as if the appellants had been able to go into the market and buy a dredger to replace the *Liesbosch*. . . .

. . . [T]he value of the *Liesbosch* to the appellants, capitalized as at the date of the loss, must be assessed by taking into account: (i) the market price of a comparable dredger in substitution; (ii) costs of adaptation, transport, insurance, &c., to Patras;

---

1. [1921] 3 KB 560.

(iii) compensation for disturbance and loss in carrying out their contract over the period of delay between the loss of the *Liesbosch* and the time at which the substituted dredger could reasonably have been available for use in Patras, including in that loss such items as overhead charges, expenses of staff and equipment, and so forth, thrown away, but neglecting any special loss due to the appellants' financial position. . . .

[LORD BUCKMASTER, LORD WARRINGTON, LORD TOMLIN and LORD RUSSELL OF KILLOWEN concurred. The matter was referred back to the Registrar to assess the measure of damages on the principles which had been laid down by the House of Lords.]

Questions

1. How far does this case limit the decision in *Re Polemis*?

2. The tortfeasor takes his victim as he finds him. If he injures a man earning a large salary, this may cost him more in damages than a similar injury to a low wage earner. Thus the varying earning capacity is taken into account by the law. Is there any logical justification for excluding from this doctrine of taking the victim as you find him his want of means, as in *The Edison*? (Consider Harris, *Remedies*, p. 220.)

Note

The Edison has been subject to a certain amount of reinterpretation in recent years: see e.g. *Dodd Properties (Kent) Ltd v Canterbury City Council* [1980] 1 All ER 928; [1980] 1 WLR 433. Extracts from the *Dodd Properties* case will appear at a later stage in the chapter (p. 343, post) when the doctrine that a tortfeasor must take the plaintiff as he finds him is considered, and the current status and importance of *The Edison* must be viewed in the light of the extracts and notes found at that point.

Overseas Tankship (UK) Ltd *v* Morts Dock and Engineering Co Ltd, The Wagon Mound Judicial Committee of the Privy Council [1961] 1 All ER 404

The appellants were charterers of the SS *Wagon Mound* which was taking on bunkering oil at the Caltex wharf in Sydney harbour. As a result of the appellants' servants' carelessness, some of the oil spilt into the bay, spreading over a large part of it, and, in particular, there was a thick concentration of the oil near to the respondents' wharf (the Sheerlegs Wharf). The respondents' workmen had been using electric and oxy-acetylene welding equipment, and, on becoming aware of the situation, their works manager prohibited any welding or burning until further orders. After making further enquiry, he took the view that their operations could be continued with safety, and he gave the appropriate instructions, but in addition ordered all safety precautions to be taken to prevent inflammable material getting into the oil from the wharf. About two days later the oil caught fire because, the trial judge found, molten metal had fallen from the wharf and set fire to some cotton waste or rag floating in the oil on a piece of débris. The wharf also caught fire and was damaged, as was some equipment on the wharf, and the respondents claimed damages. The trial judge found that the appellants 'did not know, and could not reasonably be expected to have known, that [the oil] was capable of being set afire when spread on water', [1958] 1 Lloyd's Rep at p. 582, and also that some damage was caused to the respondents as a direct result of the spilling of the oil, namely the oil congealing on the slipways of their wharf, although no compensation was claimed for this damage. The Full Court of the Supreme Court of New South Wales dismissed an appeal from Kinsella J, who held the appellants liable, and there was a further appeal to the Judicial Committee of the Privy Council.

VISCOUNT SIMONDS: . . . It is inevitable that first consideration should be given to *Re Polemis and Furness, Withy & Co Ltd*,[1] which will henceforward be referred to as *Polemis*. For it was avowedly in deference to that decision and to decisions of the Court of Appeal that followed it that the full court was constrained to decide the present case in favour of the respondents. . . .

There can be no doubt that the decision of the Court of Appeal in *Polemis*[1] plainly asserts that, if the defendant is guilty of negligence, he is responsible for all the consequences, whether reasonably foreseeable or not. The generality of the proposition is, perhaps, qualified by the fact that each of the lords justices refers to the outbreak of fire as the direct result of the negligent act. There is thus introduced the conception that the negligent actor is not responsible for consequences which are not 'direct', whatever that may mean. . . .

If the line of relevant authority had stopped with *Polemis*,[1] their Lordships might, whatever their own views as to its unreason, have felt some hesitation about overruling it. But it is far otherwise. It is true that, both in England and in many parts of the Commonwealth, that decision has from time to time been followed; but in Scotland it has been rejected with determination. It has never been subject to the express scrutiny of either the House of Lords or the Privy Council, though there have been comments on it in those supreme tribunals. Even in the inferior courts, judges have, sometimes perhaps unwittingly, declared themselves in a sense adverse to its principle. . . .

[Having referred to several authorities decided after *Re Polemis*,[1] he continued:] Enough has been said to show that the authority of *Polemis*[1] has been severely shaken, though lip-service has from time to time been paid to it. In their Lordships' opinion, it should no longer be regarded as good law. It is not probable that many cases will for that reason have a different result, though it is hoped that the law will be thereby simplified, and that, in some cases at least, palpable injustice will be avoided. For it does not seem consonant with current ideas of justice or morality that, for an act of negligence, however slight or venial, which results in some trivial foreseeable damage, the actor should be liable for all consequences, however unforeseeable and however grave, so long as they can be said to be 'direct'. It is a principle of civil liability, subject only to qualifications which have no present relevance, that a man must be considered to be responsible for the probable consequences of his act. To demand more of him is too harsh a rule, to demand less is to ignore that civilised order requires the observance of a minimum standard of behaviour. This concept, applied to the slowly developing law of negligence, has led to a great variety of expressions which can, as it appears to their Lordships, be harmonised with little difficulty with the single exception of the so-called rule in *Polemis*.[1] For, if it is asked why a man should be responsible for the natural or necessary or probable consequences of his act (or any other similar description of them), the answer is that it is not because they are natural or necessary or probable, but because, since they have this quality, it is judged, by the standard of the reasonable man, that he ought to have foreseen them. Thus it is that, over and over again, it has happened that, in different judgments in the same case and sometimes in a single judgment, liability for a consequence has been imposed on the ground that it was reasonably foreseeable, or alternatively on the ground that it was natural or necessary or probable. The two

---

1. [1921] 3 KB 560; [1921] All ER Rep 40.

grounds have been treated as coterminous, and so they largely are. But, where they are not, the question arises to which the wrong answer was given in *Polemis*.[1] For, if some limitation must be imposed on the consequences for which the negligent actor is to be held responsible — and all are agreed that some limitation there must be — why should that test (reasonable foreseeability) be rejected which, since he is judged by what the reasonable man ought to foresee, corresponds with the common conscience of mankind, and a test (the 'direct' consequence) be substituted which leads to nowhere but the never ending and insoluble problems of causation. 'The lawyer' said Sir Frederick Pollock 'cannot afford to adventure himself with philosophers in the logical and metaphysical controversies that beset the idea of cause.' Yet this is just what he has most unfortunately done and must continue to do if the rule in *Polemis*[1] is to prevail. A conspicuous example occurs when the actor seeks to escape liability on the ground that the 'chain of causation' is broken by a 'nova causa' or 'novus actus interveniens'.

The validity of a rule or principle can sometimes be tested by observing it in operation. Let the rule in *Polemis*[1] be tested in this way. In *The Edison*,[2] the appellants, whose vessel had been fouled by the respondents, claimed damages under various heads. The respondents were admittedly at fault; therefore, said the appellants, invoking the rule in *Polemis*,[1] they were responsible for all damage whether reasonably foreseeable or not. Here was the opportunity to deny the rule or to place it secure on its pedestal. But the House of Lords took neither course; on the contrary, it distinguished *Polemis*[1] on the ground that, in that case, the injuries suffered were the 'immediate physical consequences' of the negligent act. It is not easy to understand why a distinction should be drawn between 'immediate physical' and other consequences, nor where the line is to be drawn. It was, perhaps, this difficulty which led Denning LJ in *Roe v Ministry of Health*[3] to say that foreseeability is only disregarded when the negligence is the immediate or *precipitating* cause of the damage. This new word may well have been thought as good a word as another for revealing or disguising the fact that he sought loyally to enforce an unworkable rule. In the same connexion may be mentioned the conclusion to which the full court finally came in the present case. Applying the rule in *Polemis*[1] and holding, therefore, that the unforeseeability of the damage by fire afforded no defence, they went on to consider the remaining question. Was it a 'direct' consequence? On this, Manning J said:

'Notwithstanding that, if regard is had separately to each individual occurrence in the chain of events that led to this fire, each occurrence was improbable and, in one sense, improbability was heaped upon improbability, I cannot escape from the conclusion that if the ordinary man in the street had been asked, as a matter of common sense, without any detailed analysis of the circumstances, to state the cause of the fire at Morts Dock, he would unhesitatingly have assigned such cause to spillage of oil by the appellants' employees.'

Perhaps he would, and probably he would have added 'I never should have thought it possible.' But, with great respect to the full court, this is surely irrelevant, or, if it is relevant, only serves to show that the *Polemis* rule[1] works in a very strange way. After the event even a fool is wise. Yet it is not the hindsight of a fool, but it is the foresight of the reasonable man which alone can determine responsibility. The *Polemis* rule,[1] by substituting 'direct' for 'reasonably foreseeable' consequence, leads to a conclusion equally illogical and unjust.

---

1. [1921] 3 KB 560; [1921] All ER Rep 40.
2. [1933] AC 449; [1933] All ER Rep 144.
3. [1954] 2 QB 66 at 85; [1954] 2 All ER 131 at 138.

At an early stage in this judgment, their Lordships intimated that they would deal with the proposition which can best be stated by reference to the well-known dictum of Lord Sumner:[1] 'This, however, goes to culpability, not to compensation.' It is with the greatest respect to that very learned judge and to those who have echoed his words that their Lordships find themselves bound to state their view that this proposition is fundamentally false.

It is, no doubt, proper when considering tortious liability for negligence to analyse its elements and to say that the plaintiff must prove a duty owed to him by the defendant, a breach of that duty by the defendant, and consequent damage. But there can be no liability until the damage has been done. It is not the act but the consequences on which tortious liability is founded. Just as (as it has been said) there is no such thing as negligence in the air, so there is no such thing as liability in the air. Suppose an action brought by A for damage caused by the carelessness (a neutral word) of B, for example a fire caused by the careless spillage of oil. It may, of course, become relevant to know what duty B owed to A, but the only liability that is in question is the liability for damage by fire. It is vain to isolate the liability from its context and to say that B is or is not liable, and then to ask for what damage he is liable. For his liability is in respect of that damage and no other. If, as admittedly it is, B's liability (culpability) depends on the reasonable foreseeability of the consequent damage, how is that to be determined except by the foreseeability of the damage which in fact happened – the damage in suit? And, if that damage is unforeseeable so as to displace liability at large, how can the liability be restored so as to make compensation payable? But, it is said, a different position arises if B's careless act has been shown to be negligent and has caused some foreseeable damage to A. Their Lordships have already observed that to hold B liable for consequences, however unforeseeable, of a careless act, if, but only if, he is at the same time liable for some other damage, however trivial, appears to be neither logical nor just. This becomes more clear if it is supposed that similar unforeseeable damage is suffered by A and C, but other foreseeable damage, for which B is liable, by A only. A system of law which would hold B liable to A but not to C for the similar damage suffered by each of them could not easily be defended. Fortunately, the attempt is not necessary. For the same fallacy is at the root of the proposition. It is irrelevant to the question whether B is liable for unforeseeable damage that he is liable for foreseeable damage, as irrelevant as would the fact that he had trespassed on Whiteacre be to the question whether he had trespassed on Blackacre. Again, suppose a claim by A for damage by fire by the careless act of B. Of what relevance is it to that claim that he has another claim arising out of the same careless act? It would surely not prejudice his claim if that other claim failed; it cannot assist it if it succeeds. Each of them rests on its own bottom and will fail if it can be established that the damage could not reasonably be foreseen. We have come back to the plain common sense stated by Lord Russell of Killowen in *Hay (or Bourhill) v Young*.[2] As Denning LJ said in *King v Phillips*[3] '. . . there can be no doubt since *Hay (or Bourhill) v Young*[2] that the test of *liability for shock* is foreseeability of *injury by shock*.' Their Lordships substitute the word 'fire' for 'shock' and indorse this statement of the law.

Their Lordships conclude this part of the case with some general observations. They have been concerned primarily to displace the proposition that unforeseeability is irrelevant if damage is 'direct'. In doing so, they have inevitably insisted that the essential factor in determining liability is whether the damage is of such a kind as

---

1. [1920] AC 956 at 984. [The preceding words are 'What a defendant ought to have anticipated as a reasonable man is material when the question is whether or not he was guilty of negligence, that is, of want of due care according to the circumstances.']
2. [1943] AC 92; [1942] 2 All ER 396.
3. [1953] 1 QB 429 at 441; [1953] 1 All ER 617 at 623.

the reasonable man should have foreseen. This accords with the general view thus stated by Lord Atkin in *M'Alister* (or *Donoghue*) *v Stevenson*:[1]

'The liability for negligence, whether you style it such or treat it as in other systems as a species of "culpa," is no doubt based upon a general public sentiment of moral wrongdoing for which the offender must pay.'

It is a departure from this sovereign principle if liability is made to depend solely on the damage being the 'direct' or 'natural' consequence of the precedent act. Who knows or can be assumed to know all the processes of nature? But if it would be wrong that a man should be held liable for damage unpredictable by a reasonable man because it was 'direct' or 'natural', equally it would be wrong that he should escape liability, however 'indirect' the damage, if he foresaw or could reasonably foresee the intervening events which led to its being done; cf. *Woods v Duncan*.[2] Thus foreseeability becomes the effective test. In reasserting this principle, their Lordships conceive that they do not depart from, but follow and develop, the law of negligence as laid down by Alderson B, in *Blyth v Birmingham Waterworks Co*.[3]

It is proper to add that their Lordships have not found it necessary to consider the so-called rule of 'strict liability' exemplified in *Rylands v Fletcher*[4] and the cases that have followed or distinguished it. Nothing that they have said is intended to reflect on that rule. . . .

[An alternative claim in nuisance was remitted to the Full Court to be dealt with as may be thought proper.]

Appeal allowed

Questions

1. Is this a 'plaintiffs' decision' or a 'defendants' decision'?

2. Is *The Edison* affected by this decision?

3. Does the rule that one takes one's victim as one finds him still remain? (See *Smith v Leech Brain & Co Ltd*, post.)

4. Should the doctrine of novus actus interveniens still be relevant after this case? If so, what is its relationship with the test of remoteness in this case? (See M. A. Millner (1971) 22 NILQ 168.)

Notes

1. For further litigation arising out of this incident, but with a different plaintiff, see *The Wagon Mound* (*No 2*) [1967] 1 AC 617; [1966] 2 All ER 709 (p. 253, ante, and p. 632, post).

2. In terms of precedent, the Judicial Committee of the Privy Council does not bind other English courts. Therefore it is arguable that *Re Polemis* in strict theory should still survive and be a binding precedent for certain courts. However, it is clear that the decision has been treated as effectively

---

1. [1932] AC 562 at 580; [1932] 1 All ER 617 at 623.
2. [1946] AC at p. 442.
3. (1856) 11 Exch 781; [1843–60] All ER Rep 478.
4. (1868) LR 3 HL 330; [1861–73] All ER Rep 1.

overruled by *The Wagon Mound*, whatever the theoretical precedent position: see *Smith v Leech Brain & Co Ltd* (post).

3. For further discussion of *Re Polemis* and *The Wagon Mound*, see M. Davies, op cit, who, inter alia, describes the difficult financial situation facing the shipping industry at the time of the decision in *Re Polemis*. The decision would have been particularly welcomed by shipowners because of the protection it provided if their ships were damaged. Davies also points out that at the time *Re Polemis* was decided the effect of any wide-ranging remoteness rule was limited by a narrower conception of duty than has prevailed in more recent times; before *M'Alister* (or *Donoghue*) *v Stevenson* [1932] AC 562 (p. 40, ante) a duty of care only existed in certain relationships (e.g. bailment). It was the advent of a more general duty of care based on Lord Atkin's 'neighbour principle' which led to criticism of the results of the application of *Re Polemis*. Therefore, in assessing the merits of *Re Polemis at the time* this point should be borne in mind.

4 Development of *The Wagon Mound* doctrine

(a)   The degree of foreseeability

The Wagon Mound (No. 2), p. 253, ante

(b)   The thin skull rule

Smith *v* Leech Brain & Co Ltd Queen's Bench Division [1961] 3 All ER 1159

The plaintiff's husband was a labourer and galvaniser employed by the defendants at the Glaucus Iron Works, Poplar. The articles to be galvanised were lowered into a tank containing molten metallic zinc and flux. The method used depended on the size of the article. All articles were first dipped in hydrochloric acid and the larger articles were then lowered into the tank by means of an overhead crane, from a position behind a sheet of corrugated iron. On 15 August 1950, the plaintiff's husband was operating the overhead crane, using the corrugated iron sheet supplied, when a piece of molten metal or flux struck and burned his lower lip. The burn was treated at the time but he thought nothing of it. Ultimately the place where the burn had been began to ulcerate and get larger. He consulted his general practitioner who sent him to hospital where cancer was diagnosed. Treatment by radium needles enabled the lip to heal and destroy the primary growth. Subsequently, however, secondary growths were observed. Thereafter he had some six or seven operations, and he died of cancer on 14 October 1953.

Lord Parker CJ found that the defendants were negligent, that there had been no contributory negligence on the part of the plaintiff's husband, and that the burn was the promoting agency, promoting cancer in tissues which already had a premalignant condition as a result of his having worked at gas works, where he would have been in contact with tar or tar vapours from 1926 to 1935.

The case is reported only on the question of remoteness of damage.

LORD PARKER CJ: I am confronted with the recent decision of the Privy Council in *Overseas Tankship (UK) Ltd v Morts Dock and Engineering Co Ltd.*[1] For convenience, that case is always referred to as *The Wagon Mound*. But for *The Wagon Mound*,[1] it seems to me perfectly clear that, assuming negligence proved, assuming that the burn caused in whole or in part the cancer and the death, this plaintiff would be entitled to recover. It is said on the one side by counsel for the defendants, that, although I am not strictly bound by *The Wagon Mound*[1] since it is a Privy Council case, I should treat myself as free, using the arguments to be derived from that case, to say that other cases in the Court of Appeal have been wrongly decided, and, particularly, that *Re Polemis and Furness, Withy & Co Ltd*[2] was wrongly decided, and that a further ground for taking that course is to be found in the various criticisms that have from time to time in the past been made by members of the House of Lords in regard to *Re Polemis*.[2] On the other hand, it is said by counsel for the plaintiff that I should hold that *Re Polemis*[2] was rightly decided and, secondly, that, even if that is not so, I must treat myself as completely bound by it. Thirdly, he said that in any event, whatever the true view is in regard to *Re Polemis*,[2] *The Wagon Mound*[1] has no relevance at all to this case.

For my part, I am quite satisfied that the Judicial Committee in *The Wagon Mound*[1] did not have what I may call, loosely, the 'thin skull' cases in mind. It has always been the law of this country that a tortfeasor takes his victim as he finds him. It is unnecessary to do more than refer to the short passage in the decision of Kennedy J in *Dulieu v White & Sons*,[3] where he said:

'If a man is negligently run over or otherwise negligently injured in his body, it is no answer to the sufferer's claim for damages that he would have suffered less injury, or no injury at all, if he had not had an unusually thin skull or an unusually weak heart.'

To the same effect is a passage in *The Arpad*.[4] But quite apart from those two references, as is well-known, the work of the courts for years and years has gone on on that basis. There is not a day that goes by where some trial judge does not adopt that principle, that the tortfeasor takes his victim as he finds him. If the Judicial Committee had any intention of making an inroad into that doctrine, I am quite satisfied that they would have said so.

It is true that, if one takes the wording in the advice given by Viscount Simonds in *The Wagon Mound*[1] and applies it strictly to such a case as this, it could be said that they were dealing with this point. But, as I have said, it is, to my mind, quite impossible to conceive that they were, and, indeed, it has been pointed out that they disclose the distinction between such a case as this and the one which they were considering, when they comment on *Smith v London & South Western Rly Co*[5]. Lord Simonds, in dealing with that case in *The Wagon Mound*[1] said this:

'Three things may be noted about this case: the first, that, for the sweeping proposition laid down, no authority was cited; the second, that the point to which the court directed its mind was not unforeseeable damage of a different kind from that which was foreseen, but more extensive damage of the same kind . . .'

In other words, Lord Simonds is clearly there drawing a distinction between the question whether a man could reasonably anticipate a type of injury, and the question

---

1. [1961] AC 388; [1961] 1 All ER 404.
2. [1921] 3 KB 560; [1921] All ER Rep 40.
3. [1901] 2 KB 669 at 679.
4. [1934] P 189 at 202, 203; [1934] All ER Rep 326 at 331.
5. (1870) LR 6 CP 14.

whether a man could reasonably anticipate the extent of injury of the type which could be foreseen. The Judicial Committee were, I think, disagreeing with the decision in *Re Polemis*[1] that a man is no longer liable for the type of damage which he could not reasonably anticipate. The Judicial Committee were not, I think, saying that a man is only liable for the extent of damage which he could anticipate, always assuming the type of injury could have been anticipated. That view is really supported by the way in which cases of this sort have been dealt with in Scotland. Scotland has never, as far as I know, adopted the principle laid down in *Re Polemis*,[1] and yet I am quite satisfied that they have throughout proceeded on the basis that the tortfeasor takes the victim as he finds him.

In those circumstances, it seems to me that this is plainly a case which comes within the old principle. The test is not whether these defendants could reasonably have foreseen that a burn would cause cancer and that Mr Smith would die. The question is whether these defendants could reasonably foresee the type of injury which he suffered, namely, the burn. What, in the particular case, is the amount of damage which he suffers as a result of that burn, depends on the characteristics and constitution of the victim. Accordingly, I find that the damages which the plaintiff claims are damages for which these defendants are liable. Before leaving that part of the case, I should say, in case the matter goes further, that I would follow, sitting as a trial judge, the decision in *The Wagon Mound*;[2] or rather, more accurately, I would treat myself, in the light of the arguments in that case, able to follow other decisions of the Court of Appeal, prior to *Re Polemis*,[1] rather than *Re Polemis*[1] itself. As I have said, *Re Polemis*[1] has been criticised by individual members of the House of Lords, although followed by the Court of Appeal in *Thurogood v Van Den Berghs and Jurgens Ltd*.[3] I should treat myself as at liberty to do that, and, for my part, I would do so the more readily, because I think that it is important that the common law, and the development of the common law, should be homogeneous in the various sections of the Commonwealth. It would be lamentable if a court sitting here had to say that, while the common law in the Commonwealth and Scotland has been developed in a particular way, yet we in this country, and sitting in these courts, are going to proceed in a different way. However, as I have said, that does not strictly arise in this case.

Judgment for the plaintiff

Question

Could Lord Parker CJ have classified the type of damage here as cancer? If so, what would have been the result of the case?

Notes

1. The relationship of the 'thin skull' rule to *The Wagon Mound* doctrine is no easy one. This consideration was in evidence in the South African case of *Alston v Marine and Trade Insurance Co Ltd* 1964 (4) SA 112, noted by C. C. Turpin [1965] CLJ 34, where *The Wagon Mound* doctrine was not accepted; Hiemstra J spoke in the following terms (at p. 115):

'This question, whether there can be a different criterion for determining culpability and compensation, so *The Wagon Mound* rightly says, "goes to the root of the

---

1. [1921] 3 KB 560; [1921] All ER Rep 40.
2. [1961] AC 388; [1961] 1 All ER 404.
3. [1951] 2 KB 537; [1951] 1 All ER 682.

matter". *The Wagon Mound* sweeps away all difference, and here it immediately becomes unconvincing. An accident and some injury can be foreseeable but the form and extent of the damage hardly ever. The escape from this truism is to say that the *type* of damage can be foreseen, namely, fire or bodily injury, and that the extent thereof was not meant to be included in the foreseeability test. . . .

The Wagon Mound has laid down a rule of thumb which will in most cases be easy to apply but is neither intellectually satisfying nor always just. It already breaks down upon the "eggshell skull" cases. Or, differently put, it has to be lovingly accommodated before it will harmonise with the well-established rule "You must take your victim as you find him". It is probably unforeseeable that you will run down a millionaire in a slum, but he is nevertheless entitled to his much higher compensation than the pauper. These considerations convince me that the dichotomy between culpability and compensation is not as fundamentally false as *The Wagon Mound* would make out.'

2. As *Smith v Leech Brain & Co Ltd* shows, the thin skull rule has been accommodated by English courts, however uneasily, with *The Wagon Mound* doctrine. See further *Wieland v Cyril Lord Carpets Ltd* [1969] 3 All ER 1006 and for discussion of the thin skull rule, see P. J. Rowe (1977) 40 MLR 377. Particular reference should also be made to *Robinson v Post Office* [1974] 2 All ER 737; [1974] 1 WLR 1176. The relevant facts for present purposes were that, as the result of an allergy, the plaintiff contracted encephalitis after he had been injected with an anti-tetanus serum. The injection had been given because the plaintiff had sustained an injury at work. The Court of Appeal was concerned with the liability of the Post Office (the plaintiff's employer) for the encephalitis, the Post Office's liability for the injury itself not being in dispute. In meeting the argument that the Post Office was not liable for the encephalitis as it was not reasonably foreseeable that the plaintiff would contract this illness, Orr LJ (delivering the judgment of the Court of Appeal) stated (at p. 750):

'In our judgment the principle that a defendant must take the plaintiff as he finds him involves that if a wrongdoer ought reasonably to foresee that as a result of his wrongful act the victim may require medical treatment he is, subject to the principle of novus actus interveniens, liable for the consequences of the treatment applied although he could not reasonably foresee those consequences or that they could be serious.'

Does this test require a kind of damage to be foreseen? (See further the note on this case by R. W. M. Dias [1975] CLJ 15.)

Robinson's case was one where there was a pre-existing susceptibility. Unforeseeable damage following on from a foreseeable kind of damage may, of course, occur without any pre-existing susceptibility; the first injury may have *created* a new risk or susceptibility—e.g. where the foreseeable injury becomes infected and leads to more serious injury. In a New Zealand case, *Stephenson v Waite, Tileman Ltd* [1973] 1 NZLR 152, Richmond J (with Turner P concurring) discussed this last point (as well as the relationship of the thin skull cases with *The Wagon Mound*). At p. 168 he summarised his conclusions as follows:

'1 In cases of damage by physical injury to the person the principles imposing liability for consequences flowing from the pre-existing special susceptibility of the victim and/or from new risk or susceptibility created by the initial injury remain part of our law.

2 In such cases the question of foreseeability should be limited to the initial injury. The tribunal of fact must decide whether that injury is of a kind, type or character which the defendant ought reasonably to have foreseen as a real risk.

3 If the plaintiff establishes that the initial injury was within a reasonably foreseeable kind, type or character of injury, then the necessary link between the ultimate consequences of the initial injury and the negligence of the defendant can be forged simply as one of cause and effect — in other words by establishing an adequate relationship of cause and effect between the initial injury and the ultimate consequence.

If I am correct in the foregoing conclusions then juries will be left to deal with the question of foreseeability in an area which is readily comprehensible and in which the test of the ordinary reasonable man can be applied in an atmosphere of reality. They will not have to decide the ability of the ordinary man to foresee the risks of "kinds" of harm resulting from a "sub-compartmentalisation" of secondary consequences of an initial injury. Nor will it be necessary to decide whether a doctor driving a motor car is to be made liable for a greater field of injury than would the ordinary layman in similar circumstances.'

3. The case of *Pigney v Pointers Transport Services Ltd* [1957] 2 All ER 807; [1957] 1 WLR 1121 was mentioned at an earlier stage (see p. 322, ante). In that case the plaintiff's husband, an employee of the defendants, had been injured in an accident in July 1955, which occurred whilst he was working at the defendants' premises. He suffered an injury to his head due to the defendants' negligence, and, as a result of the accident, experienced an 'acute anxiety neurosis with depressive features'. He underwent treatment in a mental hospital as a voluntary patient, but some months later in January 1957, whilst suffering from depression caused by the anxiety neurosis, he hanged himself. Pilcher J held that the injury was the cause of the husband's death. He had earlier quoted part of the judgment of Scrutton LJ in *Re Polemis* [1921] 3 KB 560 and stated (at p. 810) that 'Whilst the death of the deceased was not the kind of damage that one would expect to result from the injury he received, I am satisfied that his death was, to use Scrutton LJ's words, "directly traceable" to the physical injury which he sustained due to the lack of care of the defendants for his safety.' In the light of *The Wagon Mound*, it might be thought that the case would be decided differently today. However, in an article — (1961) 77 LQR 179 — G. Williams, in referring to this decision, writes (at p. 196):

'The learned judge based his decision on *Re Polemis*, but it can be supported independently of that case. Either the victim's suicide was a normal reaction to his injuries, or it was abnormal. If it was normal, it should be taken as reasonably foreseeable; if it was abnormal, it comes within the thin skull rule as applied to psychic states.'

See further *Cotic v Gray* (1981) 124 DLR (3d) 641 which deals with various Commonwealth authorities, and see p. 322, ante.

4. The application of the 'thin skull' rule to 'nervous shock cases' was raised in *Brice v Brown* [1984] 1 All ER 997. It will be remembered that foresight of nervous shock is tested by the reaction of the reasonably strong-nerved person to the events in question (*Bourhill v Young* [1943] AC 92; [1942] 2 All ER 396, p. 114, ante and see p. 119, ante). Once that test is satisfied — though see p. 129, ante for a complication here arising from *Brice v Brown* — and once causation and breach of duty are also proved, then, according to

Brice v Brown (at pp. 1006–1007), 'the plaintiff is entitled to compensation for nervous shock and such of its direct consequences as were not dissimilar in type or kind, whether or no the same were initially reasonably to be foreseen.' Thus in *Brice v Brown* it was decided that, as nervous shock was reasonably foreseeable, it did not matter that the precise mental process leading to the plaintiff's condition and the precise name given by the psychiatrists to the condition were unforeseeable; nor did it matter that the reasonably strong-nerved person would not have suffered the same consequences as the plaintiff. See also *Meah v McCreamer (No 2)* [1986] 1 All ER 943 at 946 referring to the egg-shell personality issue in *Meah v McCreamer* [1985] 1 All ER 367.

One issue here is what constitutes a type of damage. Nervous shock was defined in *Brice v Brown* so as to cover mental injury or psychiatric illness, and it would seem that this was the type of damage. See also *The Wagon Mound* [1961] AC 388 at 426 (p. 336, ante); *Mount Isa Mines Ltd v Pusey* [1971] ALR 253 at 264; cf. the terminology which was favoured by Bingham LJ in *Attia v British Gas plc* [1987] 3 All ER 455 at 462. What do you think Stuart-Smith J meant by the phrase 'not dissimilar in type or kind'? Does it suggest that nervous shock can be subdivided? See C. Gearty [1984] CLJ 238 at 240. Is Stuart-Smith J's general approach consistent with the 'thin skull' rule? On the 'thin skull' rule and nervous shock, see further *Galt v British Railways Board* (1983) 133 NLJ 870; *Hevican v Ruane* [1991] NLJR 235.

5. On foreseeability and the extent of damage to property, see *Clerk & Lindsell*, para. 10–154, and see *Vacwell Engineering Co Ltd v BDH Chemicals Ltd* [1971] 1 QB 88 at 110.

The Edison, p. 331, ante

Dodd Properties (Kent) Ltd *v* Canterbury City Council Court of Appeal [1980] 1 All ER 928

The first plaintiffs owned a garage which they leased to the second plaintiffs. In 1968 the three defendants in this case were involved in the erection of a multi-storey car park near to this garage and were liable in the tort of nuisance (on which see chap. 15, p. 623, post) for damage caused to the garage by pile driving carried out in the course of building the car park. The main issue for the Court of Appeal concerned the date when the cost of repairs was to be assessed. The plaintiffs argued that it should be the date of the judgment (1978) but the trial judge (Cantley J), [1979] 2 All ER 118, fixed it at 1970, the date to which he decided it was reasonable to postpone carrying out the repairs. The importance of the issue lay in the fact that inflation had vastly increased the cost of repairs between 1970 and 1978. Cantley J found that *one* of the reasons for the fact that the repairs had not been carried out by the time of the trial of the action was that the plaintiffs, although not impecunious, had been 'very short of ready cash'. However, he held, following *The Edison*, that in deciding on what was a reasonable time at which to do the repairs any impecuniosity or financial stringency had to be disregarded and he opted for the 1970 date. The Court of Appeal thought that it was reasonable to postpone repairs until 1978 and it is the approach to *The Edison* (referred to in this case under its alternative name *The Liesbosch*) which is of particular interest here. For further discussion of the question of the date for assessment of damages, see pp. 436–438, post.

MEGAW LJ: . . . I agree with the analysis of the *Liesbosch* case[1] and the comments thereon in the judgment which Donaldson LJ will deliver hereafter. I do not think that, on any fair view of the ratio decidendi of the *Liesbosch* case[1], it applies to the issue with which we are concerned. Amongst other reasons, there are these two. First, it was not 'financial stringency', let alone 'impecuniousness' as in the *Liesbosch* case[1], which on any fair view, on the judge's findings, was *the* cause, or even, I think, an effective cause, of the decision to postpone repairs. The 'financial stringency' which would have been created by carrying out the repairs was merely one factor among a number of factors which together produced the result that commercial good sense pointed towards deferment of the repairs. The second reason which I would mention is that, once it is accepted that the plaintiffs were not in any breach of any duty owed by them to the defendants in failing to carry out repairs earlier than the time when it was reasonable for the repairs to be put in hand, this becomes, for all practical purposes, if not in theory, equated with a plaintiff's ordinary duty to mitigate his damages. Lord Wright in his speech in the *Liesbosch* case[2] accepted Lord Collins's dictum in *Clippens Oil Co Ltd v Edinburgh and District Water Trustees*[3]: '. . . in my opinion the wrong-doer must take his victim talem qualem, and if the position of the latter is aggravated because he is without the means of mitigating it, so much the worse for the wrong-doer . . .' I agree with the observations of Oliver J in *Radford v De Froberville*[4] as to the relationship between the duty to mitigate and the measure, or amount, of damages in relation to a question such as the question with which we are here concerned. A plaintiff who is under a duty to mitigate is not obliged, in order to reduce the damages, to do that which he cannot afford to do, particularly where, as here, the plaintiff's 'financial stringency', so far as it was relevant at all, arose, as a matter of common sense, if not as a matter of law, solely as a consequence of the defendant's wrongdoing. . . .

DONALDSON LJ: . . . Whatever the difficulties inherent in the *Liesbosch*[1] decision, and it is not at once apparent why a tortfeasor must take his victim as he finds him in terms of exceptionally high or low profit earning capacity, but not in terms of pecuniosity or impecuniosity which may be their manifestations, it binds this court as much as it bound Cantley J unless and until it is reviewed by the House of Lords. However, it is important to see precisely what it did decide. . . .

As I understand Lord Wright's speech, he took the view that in so far as the plaintiffs in fact suffered more than the loss assessed on a market basis, the excess loss flowed directly from their lack of means and not from the tortious act, or alternatively it was too remote in law. In modern terms, I think that he would have said that it was not foreseeable.

The position of the plaintiffs in the present case seems to me to be quite different. They were not impecunious in the *Liesbosch*[1] sense of one who could not go out into the market. On the contrary, they were financially able to carry out the work of reinstatement in 1970. However, on the judge's findings, they were commercially prudent in not incurring the cash flow deficiency which would have resulted from their undertaking the work in the autumn of 1970 and waiting for reimbursement until after the hearing, particularly when the defendants were denying liability and there was a dispute as to what works could and should be done by way of reinstatement. In my judgment, the decision in the *Liesbosch* case[1] has no application to such a situation, which is distinguishable.

If the decision whether to adopt 1970 or 1978 costs turns on whether, bearing in

---

1. [1933] AC 449, [1933] All ER Rep 144.
2. [1933] AC 449 at 461, [1933] All ER Rep 144 at 158–159.
3. [1907] AC 291 at 303.
4. [1978] 1 All ER 33 at 44, [1977] 1 WLR 1262 at 1272.

mind the likelihood that prices would rise, the plaintiffs should have undertaken the work in 1970 in pursuance of their duty to mitigate their damage, there is another ground for distinguishing the *Liesbosch* case[1] and for taking full account of the plaintiffs' financial position. This is that Lord Wright's explanation of the decision in *Clippens Oil Co Ltd v Edinburgh and District Water Trustees*[2], where Lord Collins said that the tortfeasor must take his victim as he found him, including any lack of means, was that that decision represented the rule in relation to the duty to minimise damage. . . .

Notes

1. Browne LJ agreed with the reasons given by Megaw and Donaldson LJJ for not regarding *The Edison* as requiring the choice of the 1970 date. He also expressly agreed with Oliver J's views in *Radford v De Froberville* [1978] 1 All ER 33; [1977] 1 WLR 1262 concerning mitigation and the measure of damages. Oliver J stated (at p. 44):

'No doubt the measure of damages and the plaintiff's duty and ability to mitigate are logically distinct concepts: see, for instance, the speech of Lord Wright in *Owners of Dredger Liesbosch v Owners of Steamship Edison*. But to some extent, at least, they are mirror images, particularly in cases of damages for breach of contract; for the measure of damages can be, very frequently, arrived at only by postulating and answering the question, what can this particular plaintiff reasonably do to alleviate his loss and what would be the cost to him of doing so at the time when he could reasonably be expected to do it? What this is may vary with individual circumstances.'

2. Donaldson LJ's treatment of *The Edison* has been cited with apparent approval by Kerr LJ in *Perry v Sydney Phillips & Son (a firm)* [1982] 3 All ER 705; [1982] 1 WLR 1297 and was found helpful by Peter Pain J in *Archer v Brown* [1985] QB 401; [1984] 2 All ER 267 where he applied a reasonable foreseeability test. *The Edison* is also mentioned in the other judgments in *Perry v Phillips*, and Lord Denning MR was prepared (at p. 709) to go so far as to dismiss Lord Wright's view concerning the non-recovery of loss due to impecuniosity as 'not of general application' and 'restricted to the facts of the *Liesbosch* case'; cf. the judgment of Oliver LJ. Consider also the earlier decision of the Court of Appeal (with Lord Denning sitting as a member of the court) in *Compania Financeria Soleada SA v Hamoor Tanker Corpn Inc, The Borag* [1981] 1 All ER 856; [1981] 1 WLR 274 (although this was not a tort case). Here unforeseeable interest charges that were incurred because a business was run on an overdraft were held to be irrecoverable. Do you think that under Donaldson LJ's approach in *Dodd Properties* foreseeability (exceptionally) plays a role in relation to the extent of damage (consider *Clerk & Lindsell*, para. 10–162)?

As *Winfield & Jolowicz*, p. 150 point out, *The Edison* was applied more recently 'without qualification' in *Ramwade Ltd v W. J. Emson & Co* [1987] RTR 72. Compare its treatment by M. A. Jones, *Textbook on Torts* 2nd edn (London, 1989), p. 141 'foreseeable financial loss . . . held irrecoverable' with Dugdale and Stanton, *Professional Negligence* 2nd edn, para. 18.34,

---

1. [1933] AC 449, [1933] All ER Rep 144.
2. [1907] AC 291 at 303.

note 8 'loss resulting from impecuniosity was unforeseeable, and hence, irrecoverable'.

3. For an example where impecuniosity was found to be the 'direct and foreseeable' result of a defendant's tort and was not held against the plaintiff, see *Jarvis v T Richards & Co* (1980) 124 Sol Jo 793, discussed by P. J. Davies [1982] JBL 21. What does 'direct' signify here? Cf. *Archer v Brown* (ante). More generally on *The Edison*, see G. Phillips (1982) 20 Osgoode Hall LJ 18; S. M. Wexler (1987) 66 Can Bar Rev 129.

4. In *Malcolm v Broadhurst* [1970] 3 All ER 508 a woman and her husband had been involved in a road accident caused by the defendant's negligent driving. She recovered damages for her injuries and for certain loss of wages in respect of her full-time job. However, she had also worked as a part-time secretary for her husband who had been injured in the accident. For about a year (until February 1968) her own injuries stopped her from working, but from that time onwards she lost this part-time employment purely because, as a result of his injuries, her husband had ceased to be self-employed, rendering the wife's secretarial services unnecessary. Although any other part-time employment was impractical in her circumstances, she was denied damages for her loss of wages after February 1968. Geoffrey Lane J refused to extend the rule that one takes one's victim as one finds him so as to cover a person's 'infirmities of employment', and this unforeseeable loss was irrecoverable.

(c)   The type or kind of damage

Hughes *v* Lord Advocate House of Lords [1963] 1 All ER 705

Some men employed by the Post Office were working on cables under a road and they reached the cables by means of a ladder in a manhole. There was a tent over the manhole and at the material time there were red warning paraffin lights around the site. Before going for their teabreak, the men took the ladder from the manhole and put it on the ground outside the tent and they pulled some tarpaulin over the entrance to the tent, leaving a gap of about two feet six inches between it and the ground. In their absence, the appellant and another ten year old boy (his uncle) took one of the lamps and the ladder into the tent and went down the manhole. After they had come out of the manhole, the appellant stumbled over the lamp which was knocked into the hole. There was a violent explosion and flames reached a height of thirty feet. The appellant fell into the hole and was badly burnt. On appeal to the House of Lords from the First Division of the Court of Session, 1961 SC 310, who, affirming the Lord Ordinary's decision, had held the respondent not liable:

LORD REID: My Lords, I have had an opportunity of reading the speech which my noble and learned friend Lord Guest is about to deliver. I agree with him that this appeal should be allowed and I shall only add some general observations. I am satisfied that the Post Office workmen were in fault in leaving this open manhole unattended and it is clear that if they had done as they ought to have done this accident would not have happened. It cannot be said that they owed no duty to the appellant. But it has been held that the appellant cannot recover damages.

It was argued that the appellant cannot recover because the damage which he suffered was of a kind which was not foreseeable. That was not the ground of judgment of the First Division or of the Lord Ordinary and the facts proved do not, in my judgment, support that argument. The appellant's injuries were mainly caused by burns, and it cannot be said that injuries from burns were unforeseeable. As a warning to traffic the workmen had set lighted red lamps around the tent which covered the manhole, and if boys did enter the dark tent it was very likely that they would take one of these lamps with them. If the lamp fell and broke it was not at all unlikely that the boy would be burned and the burns might well be serious. No doubt it was not to be expected that the injuries would be as serious as those which the appellant in fact sustained. But a defender is liable, although the damage may be a good deal greater in extent than was foreseeable. He can only escape liability if the damage can be regarded as differing in kind from what was foreseeable.

So we have (first) a duty owed by the workmen, (secondly) the fact that if they had done as they ought to have done there would have been no accident, and (thirdly) the fact that the injuries suffered by the appellant, though perhaps different in degree, did not differ in kind from injuries which might have resulted from an accident of a foreseeable nature. The ground on which this case has been decided against the appellant is that the accident was of an unforeseeable type. Of course the pursuer has to prove that the defender's fault caused the accident and there could be a case where the intrusion of a new and unexpected factor could be regarded as the cause of the accident rather than the fault of the defender. But that is not this case. The cause of this accident was a known source of danger, the lamp, but it behaved in an unpredictable way. The explanation of the accident which has been accepted, and which I would not seek to question, is that, when the lamp fell down the manhole and was broken, some paraffin escaped, and enough was vaporized to create an explosive mixture which was detonated by the naked light of the lamp. The experts agree that no one would have expected that to happen: it was so unlikely as to be unforeseeable. The explosion caused the boy to fall into the manhole: whether his injuries were directly caused by the explosion or aggravated by fire which started in the manhole is not at all clear. . . .

. . . This accident was caused by a known source of danger, but caused in a way which could not have been foreseen, and in my judgment that affords no defence. I would therefore allow the appeal.

LORD JENKINS: . . . It is true that the duty of care expected in cases of this sort is confined to reasonably foreseeable dangers, but it does not necessarily follow that liability is escaped because the danger actually materialising is not identical with the danger reasonably foreseen and guarded against. Each case must depend on its own particular facts. For example . . . in the present case the paraffin did the mischief by exploding, not burning, and it is said that, while a paraffin fire (caused, e.g. by the upsetting of the lighted lamp or otherwise allowing its contents to leak out) was a reasonably foreseeable risk so soon as the pursuer got access to the lamp, an explosion was not. To my mind the distinction drawn between burning and explosion is too fine to warrant acceptance. . . .

LORD GUEST: . . . In dismissing the appellant's claim the Lord Ordinary and the majority of the judges of the First Division reached the conclusion that the accident which happened was not reasonably foreseeable. In order to establish a coherent chain of causation it is not necessary that the precise details leading up to the accident should have been reasonably foreseeable: it is sufficient if the accident which occurred is of a type which should have been foreseeable by a reasonably careful person (*Miller v South of Scotland Electricity Board* per Lord Keith of Avonholm;[1]

---

1. 1958 SC (HL) 20 at 34.

Harvey v Singer Manufacturing Co Ltd per Lord Patrick[1]); or as Lord Mackintosh,[2] expressed it in *Harvey*'s case[3] the precise concatenation of circumstances need not be envisaged. Concentration has been placed in the courts below on the explosion which it was said could not have been foreseen because it was caused in a unique fashion by the paraffin forming into vapour and being ignited by the naked flame of the wick. But this, in my opinion, is to concentrate on what is really a non-essential element in the dangerous situation created by the allurement. The test might better be put thus: — Was the igniting of paraffin outside the lamp by the flame a foreseeable consequence of the breach of duty? In the circumstances there was a combination of potentially dangerous circumstances against which the Post Office had to protect the appellant. If these formed an allurement to children it might have been foreseen that they would play with the lamp, that it might tip over, that it might be broken, and that when broken the paraffin might spill and be ignited by the flame. All these steps in the chain of causation seem to have been accepted by all the judges in the courts below as foreseeable. But because the explosion was the agent which caused the burning and was unforeseeable, therefore the accident, according to them, was not reasonably foreseeable. In my opinion this reasoning is fallacious. An explosion is only one way in which burning can be caused. Burning can also be caused by the contact between liquid paraffin and a naked flame. In the one case paraffin vapour and in the other case liquid paraffin is ignited by fire. I cannot see that these are two different types of accident. They are both burning accidents and in both cases the injuries would be burning injuries. On this view the explosion was an immaterial event in the chain of causation. It was simply one way in which burning might be caused by the potentially dangerous paraffin lamp. . . .

I have therefore reached the conclusion that the accident which occurred and which caused burning injuries to the appellant was one which ought reasonably to have been foreseen by the Post Office employees and that they were at fault in failing to provide a protection against the appellant entering the shelter and going down the manhole.

I would allow the appeal.

LORD PEARCE: . . . Did the explosion create an accident and damage of a different type from the misadventure and damage that could be foreseen? In my judgment it did not. The accident was but a variant of the foreseeable. It was, to quote the words of Denning LJ in *Roe v Ministry of Health*[4] 'within the risk created by the negligence.' No unforeseeable extraneous, initial occurrence fired the train. . . .

[LORD MORRIS OF BORTH-Y-GEST delivered a speech in favour of allowing the appeal.]

Appeal allowed

Question

Is *Crossley v Rawlinson* [1981] 3 All ER 674, noted p. 141, ante, consistent with *Hughes v Lord Advocate*? (Consider M. A. Jones (1982) 45 MLR 342 at 343; *Street*, p. 229, note 12.)

---

1. 1960 SC 155 at 168.
2. 1960 SC at p. 172.
3. 1960 SC 155.
4. [1954] 2 QB 66 at 85; [1954] 2 All ER 131 at 138.

Notes

1. *Doughty v Turner Manufacturing Co Ltd* [1964] 1 QB 518; [1964] 1 All ER 98 has caused problems. Two cauldrons containing molten liquid at 800° centigrade had loose covers made of an asbestos/cement compound. One of the covers, which were between four and six inches above the liquid, was inadvertently knocked, and slid into the cauldron, becoming submerged in the liquid. This was not regarded as dangerous. Less than two minutes later the liquid erupted, and the plaintiff, who had taken a message to a foreman who was near the cauldrons, suffered burns. The eruption was a consequence, it was later discovered, of a chemical change in the cover because of the heat, but, in the light of the knowledge at the time when the plaintiff was injured, the accident was unforeseeable. Counsel for the plaintiff argued that the accident 'was merely a variant of foreseeable accidents by splashing'. More than one ground can be put forward as to why the plaintiff should fail on the facts of this case – see *Clerk & Lindsell*, para. 10-157 – but Harman LJ did state (at p. 529) that the damage in the case 'was of an entirely different kind from the foreseeable splash' (and see also Lord Pearce at p. 527). Can Harman LJ's view be reconciled with *Hughes v Lord Advocate*?

2. For an application of the *Hughes* approach in the sphere of economic loss, see *Banque Keyser Ullman SA v Skandia (UK) Insurance Co Ltd* [1990] 1 QB 665 at 767–769, but see the view of the House of Lords when the case went on appeal, [1990] 2 All ER 947 at 957–958. On this case generally, see p. 174, ante.

Tremain *v* Pike Exeter Assizes [1969] 3 All ER 1303

PAYNE J: The plaintiff in this case, William Tremain, is claiming damages for a disease which he contracted, and which he alleges to be due to the negligence of the defendants. The case is conveniently summarised in the plaintiff's statement of claim in which it is said that, at the material time, he was employed as a herdsman by the defendants, who are farmers, at Bovey Barton Farm at Beer, Seaton, in Devonshire, and that in the course of his employment he used a water trough and a milking parlour, and also washed his hands in the water trough; further, that at times he handled hay on the farm; that in or about March 1967, and before that date, the premises were infested and over-run with rats; that in or about March 1967, or previously, the water in the trough, or alternatively hay handled by the plaintiff, became infected by rats with the germs and organisms of a disease commonly known as Weil's disease; that in or about March 1967, in the course of his employment, through carrying out the operations described, he contracted Weil's disease and suffered injury. The particulars of negligence, which I need not read in full, concentrate on these complaints; that the defendants permitted the farm to become infested and over-run with rats and that they failed to take adequate steps to keep the farm free from rats or to reduce their number. There are further particulars: they say that the defendants failed to keep the buildings on the farm, and in particular the milking parlour, in good repair so as to prevent rats from entering and breeding in the buildings, they failed to take adequate steps to prevent the water trough or the hay from being infected, and in consequence of all those matters the plaintiff contracted this disease. . . .

[Having referred to the fact that he had heard evidence from Dr Alston, an authority on the disease, he continued:] . . . The defendants do not dispute that in March 1967 the plaintiff became infected with Weil's disease, and they accept that it would be proper for me to find on the balance of probabilities that he contracted the disease in consequence of his employment on the farm.

Dr Alston has made a special study of Weil's disease or leptospirosis for the last 35 years. It is now known that the leptospires are present in about 40 to 50 per cent of the rats in this country, and that the leptospires are passed from the kidney to the urine of the rat, and remain active in the urine for two or three days if they remain in wet or damp conditions. Rats infect each other and so perpetuate the disease. Human beings contract the disease through contact with the rodent urine and contamination of the skin, especially if the skin is cut, eroded or sodden with water. The incidence of the disease in human beings is rare in spite of the prevalence of the leptospires in rats because of the very slight susceptibility of human beings to the disease. The risk is very low indeed. . . .

[His Lordship considered the evidence as to infestation of rats in and around the farm buildings, and continued:] On that evidence I am satisfied that, in March 1967, there was a growing population of rats in and around the farm buildings, the farmyard and their precincts, and that the time had arrived when a prudent and experienced farmer, once the facts had come to his knowledge, would call in the rodent officer or a contractor, and arrange for an intensive attack on the rats. He would, however, take that course with a view to protecting his milk supply, preventing the contamination of foodstuffs, preserving his animal feed and generally improving cleanliness. He would not have in mind the safety of his farm staff in the performance of their work as his servants as there was no reason for him to suppose that they were in any danger in their daily work. Moreover, I am not satisfied that in March 1967 the defendants knew, or ought reasonably to have known: (i) that the rat population had reached the proportions which the evidence before me establishes; or (ii) that any more precautions were required than those which they applied as a matter of routine. . . .

. . . I feel able on the evidence to find that, on the balance of probabilities, the plaintiff became infected on the farm, but any greater precision would not be justified. The employer's duty to his servants is to take reasonable care for their safety, and this safety extends to the safety of the premises and the plant, and to the method and conduct of the work, but is not restricted to those matters. Put in slightly different words, his duty is to take reasonable steps to avoid exposing his servants to a reasonably foreseeable risk of injury.

It follows from the contents of this judgment that, in my opinion, the defendants were not in breach of any duty of care to the plaintiff, nor was his disease attributable to any such breach. If, contrary to my view, it should be held that the defendants were in breach of duty in that they ought to have known of the extent of the infestation in March 1967, and ought to have foreseen that the plaintiff was, or might be, exposed to some general hazard involving personal injury, illness or disease in consequence of the infestation, the defendants, as I think, are still immune from liability on the grounds that Weil's disease was at best a remote possibility which they could not reasonably foresee, and that the damage suffered by the plaintiff was, therefore, unforeseeable and too remote to be recoverable.

I do not accept the contention of counsel for the plaintiff that it is sufficient to show that the plaintiff was exposed generally to the risk of disease because of the possible contamination of animal feed or of milk at the farm, or the possibility of the plaintiff being bitten, itself, in my view, an unlikely event. Weil's disease is not comparable to the other human disabilities which may flow from an infestation of rats. One must not overlook the fact that, if the defendants had to take effective precautions against Weil's disease, it would not be sufficient merely to keep the rat population in check by poisoning, trapping, hunting and so forth. A rat population of varying size would still remain on the farm as it does on all farms. It would be necessary to introduce protective clothing for the hands and arms, some check on cuts and abrasions and a system of washing facilities and hygiene which, in my view, would be out of all proportion in cost and effort to the risk which had to be countered. . . .

The kind of damage suffered here was a disease contracted by contact with rats' urine. This, in my view, was entirely different in kind from the effect of a rat-bite, or food poisoning by the consumption of food or drink contaminated by rats. I do not accept that all illness or infection arising from an infestation of rats should be regarded as of the same kind. One cannot say in this case, as was said by Lord Reid in *Hughes*, case:[1] '. . . if they [the defenders] had done as they ought to have done there would have been no accident . . .'

It may be that it is less satisfactory in this case to ask the question whether the infection is different in kind from other sequelae of rat infestation which might be foreseeable, as that leads to disputation about what is meant by difference in kind, than to ask the direct question whether, on the facts of this case, the leptospirosis was reasonably foreseeable by the defendants. In my opinion, one has only to ask that question and the answer is inescapably 'No'. . . .

Judgment for the defendants

Notes

1. In *Bradford v Robinson Rentals Ltd* [1967] 1 All ER 267; [1967] 1 WLR 337 the plaintiff, a 57-year-old man, was employed by the defendants in Exeter as a radio service engineer, and he travelled to and from his jobs in a van. One day, when there was snow and ice on the roads, he was told to drive a colleague's van to Bedford to change it for a new one, and to drive the new one back. The chance to change vehicles might have been lost if it were not taken up quickly. Both the AA and a BBC broadcast advised that only essential journeys should be made. The plaintiff, who was reluctant to make the journey, protested in vain, and he set off the next day. The van's heater at that time was disconnected, and the radiator had to be topped up frequently during the journey. The plaintiff took all reasonable precautions against the cold, but the lack of a heater meant that his breath formed ice on the windscreen so he had to keep a window open. The new van had no heater either, so a window had to be kept open on the return journey as well. The plaintiff suffered permanent injury to his hands and feet through frostbite. Had the plaintiff established that this was a reasonably foreseeable type of injury? Rees J apparently thought so. He held that the risk of injury from exposure to extreme cold and tiredness was reasonably foreseeable, and that the defendants were liable to the plaintiff. This was so even if the latter was peculiarly susceptible to frostbite, since a tortfeasor takes his victim as he finds him, although there was no evidence of such susceptibility in fact in the case. In *Tremain v Pike* Payne J thought the distinction between *Smith v Leech Brain & Co Ltd* [1962] 2 QB 405; [1961] 3 All ER 1159 (p. 338, ante) and the *Bradford* case on the one hand, and the case he was considering on the other hand, to be 'crystal clear'. He said — [1969] 3 All ER at p. 1309 — that 'the risk of injury from a burn in the first case and from extreme cold in the second was foreseeable, and it was only the degree of injury or the development of the sequelae which was not foreseeable. In this case, the risk of the initial infection of the plaintiff was, in my view, not reasonably foreseeable.' For a note discussing *Tremain v Pike* and *Bradford v Robinson Rentals Ltd* see R. W. M. Dias [1970] CLJ 28. Contrast also with

---

1. [1963] AC at p. 845; [1963] 1 All ER at p. 706.

Tremain v Pike the approach of Edmund Davies LJ in *Draper v Hodder* [1972] 2 QB 556; [1972] 2 All ER 210.

2. On the question of types of damage and nervous shock, see p. 343, ante.

3. As Harris, *Remedies* p. 218 points out, citing *Pritchard v J. H. Cobden Ltd* [1988] Fam 22 at pp. 39–40 and 48–49 and *Meah v McCreamer (No 2)* [1986] 1 All ER 943 at 947–950, policy can be brought into play at the causation and remoteness stage to deny liability even if a foreseeable kind of damage is involved. (Policy has already been referred to in this chapter when consideration was given to *Lamb v Camden London Borough Council* [1981] QB 625; [1981] 2 All ER 408 (p. 323, ante)). In *Pritchard v Cobden*, where the plaintiff's divorce was causally connected with the personal injuries he had received due to negligence for which the defendants were responsible, any financial losses consequent on the divorce were not regarded as a loss caused by a third party, but rather were a redistribution of assets (though see S. Juss [1987] CLJ 210 at 212). However, even if this were not the case, it was decided by the Court of Appeal, going against *Jones v Jones* [1985] QB 704; [1984] 3 All ER 1003, that on grounds of policy such a head of damage was not recoverable. For example, the trial of the personal injuries action and the matrimonial proceedings might not be heard together, and the introduction of matters relevant to the matrimonial position in the former hearing would raise difficult questions for the judge to decide – and in the later proceedings the evidence might prove to have been wrong – and it would lengthen litigation. Consider also *Meah v McCreamer (No 2)* [1986] 1 All ER 943 where it was decided that the plaintiff could not recover damages he had to pay to two victims of attacks which he had carried out: the attacks were a result of a personality change in the plaintiff consequent upon injuries he had suffered in a road accident caused by the defendant's negligence. For comment see B. A. Hepple All ER Rev 1985, pp. 309–310.

For general discussion of causation and remoteness of damage raising policy considerations see *Atiyah*, chap. 4; J. G. Merrills [1973] Ottawa LR 18; Harris, *Remedies*, pp. 217–223. For economists' arguments see Harris, *Remedies*, pp. 206–209.

7 Defences: contributory negligence, volenti non fit injuria, exclusion of liability and illegality and public policy

Although the question of causation has been considered in an earlier chapter, it also plays an important role in the defence of contributory negligence, which, if successful, serves to reduce the plaintiff's damages. (See e.g. *Stapley v Gypsum Mines Ltd* [1953] AC 663; [1953] 2 All ER 478, p. 361, post.) As the phrase contributory negligence would imply, the plaintiff must not only have been negligent, but his negligence must have contributed to the damage which he has suffered, and in the absence of this causal connection, the plaintiff's damages will not be reduced. On the other hand, in certain situations, the plaintiff's negligence, occurring after the defendant's negligent act, may not only have contributed to some item of damage for which he is claiming compensation, but may be held to have gone so far as to sever the chain of causation between the defendant's act and this damage, with the result that the plaintiff recovers nothing for this particular item. The result here is achieved not by virtue of the defence of contributory negligence, but because there is no sufficient causal connection between the defendant's act and the damage — see *McKew v Holland & Hannen & Cubitts (Scotland) Ltd* [1969] 3 All ER 1621 (p. 320, ante); *Winfield & Jolowicz*, pp. 155–156; M. A. Millner (1971) 22 NILQ 168 at 176–179.

Whereas the phrase contributory negligence gives some idea of the nature of that defence, the maxim volenti non fit injuria needs a greater amount of explanation. In the sphere of intentional interference this defence will be found under the heading 'Consent', p. 594, post, and see further *Street*, p. 75. (For the position with regard to the defence of contributory negligence in this context, consider *Murphy v Culhane* [1977] QB 94; [1976] 3 All ER 533, p. 594, post and p. 596, post.) In this chapter the volenti maxim is considered as a defence to the unintentional infliction of injuries and, in this context, writers (e.g. *Fleming*) use the term 'voluntary assumption of risk'. One difficulty concerns the way in which the volenti maxim operates. *Salmond & Heuston* (at pp. 557–558) mention one view — that there has been a breach of duty, which the plaintiff waives — but then state that 'the better view is that consent here means the agreement of the plaintiff, express or implied, to exempt the defendant from the duty of care which he would otherwise have owed'. This view was quoted by John Stephenson J in *Buckpitt v Oates* [1968] All ER 1145 at 1148 and seemingly adopted obiter in the House of Lords in *Titchener v British Railways Board* [1983] 3 All ER 770 at 776 (although on the position in Scotland, cf. *Winnik v Dick* 1984 SLT 185). Compare the view in *Freeman v Home Office (No 2)* [1984] QB 524; [1984] 1 All ER 1036, noted p. 598, post. (See also R. W. M. Dias [1966] CLJ 75 esp. at 79.)

Contributory negligence and volenti non fit injuria are separate defences, but they can both be pleaded as defences in the same action. If the volenti defence fails, damages may still be reduced for contributory negligence, and there are important differences between the two defences. These should become apparent from a consideration of the nature of the defences through a study of the materials in this chapter. The most obvious is that the volenti maxim, if successful, provides a complete defence, but a successful plea of contributory negligence leads to a reduction of the damages by the court in accordance with the Law Reform (Contributory Negligence) Act 1945. There is a limit to the percentage reduction that is permissible: it has been held that there cannot be a 100 per cent reduction under the 1945 Act (*Pitts v Hunt* [1990] 3 All ER 344 at 357 and 359).

The contributory negligence defence must today be considered in the light of the Law Reform (Contributory Negligence) Act 1945. Statute plays a less important role in the volenti or assumption of risk doctrine, but it can, of course, intervene so as to negate the defence where it might otherwise apply, e.g. s. 149 of the Road Traffic Act 1988 (p. 888, post), and consider s. 2(3) of the Unfair Contract Terms Act 1977 (p. 390, post). In certain contexts, however, the doctrine seems to have been enshrined in statutory form. Examples are provided by s. 2(5) of the Occupiers' Liability Act 1957 (p. 443, post) and by s. 5(2) of the Animals Act 1971 (p. 522, post) but see s. 6(5) of that Act (p. 523, post) and see also the view of Ormrod LJ in *Cummings v Granger* [1977] QB 397 at 408 (p. 528, post).

Statute, in particular the Unfair Contract Terms Act 1977 (p. 389, post), has severely restricted the defendant's freedom to exclude liability in tort. The obvious method of attempting to exclude liability is by contract, but see also *White v Blackmore* [1972] 2 QB 651; [1972] 3 All ER 158 (p. 456, post). The student should consider the relationship between the volenti defence and exclusion of liability, a subject which will be mentioned later in the context of occupiers' liability (p. 460, post) but which is referred to initially in the third section of this chapter.

The final defence considered in this chapter has been variously termed illegality, public policy or ex turpi causa non oritur actio. For the history of this Latin maxim and criticism of its use, see Windeyer J's judgment in *Smith v Jenkins* [1970] ALR 519 at 527–530. The essence of this defence is that, by virtue of his involvement in some illegal or other conduct, the plaintiff cannot recover damages for his loss. In a given situation the defences of contributory negligence, volenti and illegality or public policy can all be raised. The statutory restrictions on volenti do not rule out the 'illegality' defence which may therefore prove attractive to defendants: see C. R. Symmons (1973) 123 NLJ 373 at 375; *Pitts v Hunt* (p. 392, post).

1   Contributory negligence

(a)   Before 1945

Note

At common law the rule was that a plaintiff who was contributorily negligent failed in his action (see e.g. *Butterfield v Forrester* (1809) 11 East 60, but see the doctrine of 'last opportunity', p. 361, post). In contrast to the position at common law the rule which developed in Admiralty was one of equal apportionment of a loss if a collision was caused by the negligence of both vessels, but this was altered by the Maritime Conventions Act 1911. For the history of the Admiralty rule, see Marsden, *The Law of Collisions at Sea*, 11th edn (London, 1961), esp. chap. 4; *Glanville Williams*, pp. 341–342.

The Maritime Conventions Act 1911

1. Rule as to division of loss. — (1) Where, by the fault of two or more vessels; damage or loss is caused to one or more of those vessels, to their cargoes or freight, or to any property on board, the liability to make good the damage or loss shall be in proportion to the degree in which each vessel was in fault:
Provided that —
(a) if, having regard to all the circumstances of the case, it is not possible to establish different degrees of fault, the liability shall be apportioned equally; and
(b) nothing in this section shall operate so as to render any vessel liable for any loss or damage to which her fault has not contributed; and
(c) nothing in this section shall affect the liability of any person under a contract of carriage or any contract, or shall be construed as imposing any liability upon any person from which he is exempted by any contract or by any provision of law, or as affecting the right of any person to limit his liability in the manner provided by law.

Admiralty Commissioners *v Volute* (Owners), The *Volute*
House of Lords [1921] All ER Rep 193

There was a collision between the *Volute* (an oil tank ship) and the *Radstock*, one of two destroyers in charge of a convoy of which the *Volute* was a member. The Court of Appeal had held the *Radstock* to be alone to blame. However, there was an appeal, and the House of Lords held on the evidence that the *Volute* had been negligent in not giving a short blast on her whistle on altering her course. They also held the *Radstock* to blame for increasing her speed shortly before the collision.

VISCOUNT BIRKENHEAD LC: . . . The matter, therefore, rests in this way. On the one hand, if the *Volute* had signalled or had postponed her porting unless and until she signalled there would have been no collision. On the other hand, if the *Radstock* had not gone full speed ahead after the position of danger brought about by the action of the *Volute*, there would have been no collision. In all cases of damage by collision on land or sea, there are three ways in which the question of contributory negligence may arise. A is suing for damage thereby received. He was negligent, but his negligence had brought about a state of things in which there would have been no damage if B had not been subsequently and severably negligent. A recovers in full: see, among other cases, *Spaight v Tedcastle*[1] and *The Margaret* (*Cayzer v Carron Co*).[2] At the other end of the chain, A's negligence makes collision so threatening that, though by the appropriate measure B could avoid it, B has not really time to think and by mistake takes the wrong measure. B is not held to be guilty of any negligence and A wholly fails: *The Bywell Castle*;[3] *Stoomvart Maatschappy*

---

1. (1881) 6 App Cas 217.
2. (1884) 9 App Cas 873.
3. (1879) 4 PD 219.

Nederland v Peninsula and Oriental Co.[1] In between these two termini come the cases where the negligence is deemed contributory, and the plaintiff in common law recovers nothing [but now see Law Reform (Contributory Negligence) Act 1945, s. 1(1)], while in Admiralty damages are divided in some proportion or other. Lord Blackburn, in *The Margaret*,[2] was of opinion that the area of this middle space was the same for Admiralty as for common law, and his opinion may be accepted subject to a possible qualification arising out of the subsequent passing of the Maritime Conventions Act 1911. How, then, are its limits to be ascertained? Contributory negligence certainly arises when the negligence is contemporaneous, but are the only cases of contributory negligence cases where the negligence is contemporaneous? Is it to be the rule in all cases if the tribunal can find a period at which A's negligence has ceased and after which B's negligence has begun that then the negligence of A is to be disregarded? If such should be the rule it will be found that the cases of contributory negligence would be few. If two roads intersect each other at right angles and there is a large building at the point of intersection, and two people are running or riding or driving at a reckless pace, one down each street, and meet at the corner, it would be easy to say that both were in fault and equally so. If the courses of two motor-cars cross and there is no rule of the road such as that at sea requiring one to give way and the other to keep her course and both hold on both are equally to blame. In *The Margaret*[2] a badly navigated barge came into collision with a schooner which was improperly carrying her anchor over her bows in a dangerous way contrary to the rule. An impact ensued which would have done no damage but for the fact that the fluke of the anchor knocked a hole in the barge. Sir Robert Phillimore put the whole blame on the badly navigated barge, but the Court of Appeal thought that, though the collision was solely due to her, the damage was due to both, and divided it. But even this class of case was varied by the subsequent decision of Gorell Barnes J in *The Monte Rosa*,[3] where he distinguished *The Margaret*,[2] saying that the collision there occurred at night and the anchor could not be seen and held the badly navigated vessel alone to blame for the collision because those on board of her might have seen the dangerous position of the anchor.

It is very difficult, except in the cases just mentioned, to think of any cases where there is strictly synchronous negligence. And if that be the rule the application of the doctrine of contributory negligence to collisions, whether on land or sea, would be rare. Still rarer would be cases where the more minute calculations required by the Maritime Conventions Act could find place. . . .

Upon the whole I think that this question of contributory negligence must be dealt with somewhat broadly and upon commonsense principles as a jury would probably deal with it. While, no doubt, where a clear line can be drawn, the subsequent negligence is the only one to look to, there are cases in which the two acts come so closely together, and the second act of negligence is so much mixed up with the state of things brought about by the first act that the party secondly negligent, while not held free from blame under *The Bywell Castle*[4] rule, might, on the other hand, invoke the prior negligence as being part of the cause of the collision so as to make it a case of contribution. The Maritime Conventions Act with its provisions for nice qualifications as to the quantum of blame and the proportions in which contribution is to be made may be taken as to some extent declaratory of the Admiralty rule in this respect.

Your Lordships have now to apply these considerations of law to the facts of the present case. As already stated, if the *Volute* had not neglected to give the appropriate whistle signal when she ported there would have been no collision. On the other hand, if the *Radstock*, in the position of danger brought about by the action of the *Volute*

---

1. (1880) 5 App Cas 876.
2. (1881) 6 PD 76.
3. [1893] P 23.
4. (1879) 4 PD 219.

had not gone full speed ahead, there would have been no collision. The case seems to me to resemble somewhat closely that of *The Hero*.[1] In that case, as in this, notwithstanding the negligent navigation of the first ship, the collision could have been avoided if proper action had been taken by the second ship. Indeed, that case is remarkable because the proper order was actually given, but unfortunately countermanded. In that case this House held both vessels to blame, apparently considering the acts of navigation on the two ships as forming parts of one transaction, and the second act of negligence as closely following upon and involved with the first. In the present case there does not seem to be a sufficient separation of time, place or circumstance between the negligent navigation of the *Radstock* and that of the *Volute* to make it right to treat the negligence on board the *Radstock* as the sole cause of the collision. The *Volute*, in the ordinary plain common sense of this business, having contributed to the accident, it would be right for your Lordships to hold both vessels to blame for the collision. Accordingly, I move your Lordships to reverse the order appealed from, and to pronounce the *Volute* partly to blame for the said collision, with the usual consequential directions. . . .

[VISCOUNT CAVE, VISCOUNT FINLAY, LORD SHAW and LORD PHILLIMORE concurred.]

Appeal allowed

Note

In *Marvin Sigurdson v British Columbia Electric Rly Co Ltd* [1953] AC 291, (a post-1945 case) Lord Tucker, delivering judgment in the Privy Council, referred to certain of the passages quoted above in Viscount Birkenhead's judgment in *The Volute* and expressed the following opinion (at p. 299):

'This was an Admiralty case, but now that common law courts have to apply the same principles to cases of collisions on land it seems to their Lordships that this language will be found particularly suited to the exposition to a jury of the principles which they have to apply in these cases, and is much to be preferred to attempts to classify acts in relation to one another with reference to time or with regard to the knowledge of one party at a particular moment of the negligence of the other party and his appreciation of the resulting danger, and by such tests to create categories in some of which one party is solely liable and others in which both parties are liable. Time and knowledge may often be decisive factors, but it is for the jury or other tribunal of fact to decide whether in any particular case the existence of one of these factors results or does not result in the ascertainment of that clear line to which Viscount Birkenhead referred—moreover, their Lordships do not read him as intending to lay down that the existence of "subsequent" negligence will alone enable that clear line to be found.'

(b) The defence since 1945

The Law Reform (Contributory Negligence) Act 1945

1. Apportionment of liability in case of contributory negligence.—(1) Where any person suffers damage as the result partly of his own fault and partly of the fault of any other person or persons, a claim in respect of that damage shall not be defeated by reason of the fault of the person suffering the damage, but the damages recoverable

---

1. [1912] AC 300.

in respect thereof shall be reduced to such extent as the court thinks just and equitable having regard to the claimant's share in the responsibility for the damage:

Provided that —

(a) this subsection shall not operate to defeat any defence arising under a contract;

(b) where any contract or enactment providing for the limitation of liability is applicable to the claim, the amount of damages recoverable by the claimant by virtue of this subsection shall not exceed the maximum limit so applicable.

(2) Where damages are recoverable by any person by virtue of the foregoing subsection subject to such reduction as is therein mentioned, the court shall find and record the total damages which would have been recoverable if the claimant had not been at fault.

(5) Where, in any case to which subsection (1) of this section applies, one of the persons at fault avoids liability to any other such person or his personal representative by pleading the Limitation Act 1939[1], or any other enactment limiting the time within which proceedings may be taken, he shall not be entitled to recover any damages . . . from that other person or representative by virtue of the said subsection.

(6) Where any case to which subsection (1) of this section applies is tried with a jury, the jury shall determine the total damages which would have been recoverable if the claimant had not been at fault and the extent to which those damages are to be reduced.

3. Saving for Maritime Conventions Act 1911, and past cases. – (1) This Act shall not apply to any claim to which section one of the Maritime Conventions Act 1911 applies and that Act shall have effect as if this Act had not been passed. . . .

4. Interpretation. — The following expressions have the meanings hereby respectively assigned to them, that is to say —

'court' means, in relation to any claim, the court or arbitrator by or before whom the claim falls to be determined;
'damage' includes loss of life and personal injury;
'fault' means negligence, breach of statutory duty or other act or omission which gives rise to a liability in tort or would, apart from this Act, give rise to the defence of contributory negligence;

Note

On the question of the Act's applicability in a contractual action, see the Court of Appeal's decision in *Forsikringsaktieselskapet Vesta v Butcher* [1989] AC 852; [1988] 2 All ER 43 (Act only applies where liability in contract matches a liability in negligence imposed independently of any contract). This point did not arise on the appeal to the House of Lords, [1989] AC 852; [1989] 1 All ER 402. Cf. *Tennant Radiant Heat Ltd v Warrington Development Corp* [1988] 1 EGLR 41 (apportionment on the basis of causation in a case where the 1945 Act was held not applicable), but note the comments on this case in the Court of Appeal in *Bank of Nova Scotia v Hellenic Mutual War Risks Association (Bermuda) Ltd, The Good Luck* [1989] 3 All ER 628 at 672. See further The *'Superhulls Cover' Case* [1990] 2 Lloyd's Rep 431; P. L. Newman (1990) 53 MLR 201; the Law Commission's Working Paper No. 114 (*Contributory Negligence as a Defence in Contract*).

---

1. [This Act was repealed by the Limitation Act 1980 which was a consolidating measure.]

Nance v British Columbia Electric Railway Co Ltd Judicial Committee of the Privy Council [1951] 2 All ER 448

VISCOUNT SIMON: . . . The statement that, when negligence is alleged as the basis of an actionable wrong, a necessary ingredient in the conception is the existence of a duty owed by the defendants to the plaintiff to take due care, is, of course, indubitably correct. But when contributory negligence is set up as a defence, its existence does not depend on any duty owed by the injured party to the party sued and all that is necessary to establish such a defence is to prove to the satisfaction of the jury that the injured party did not in his own interest take reasonable care of himself and contributed, by this want of care, to his own injury. For when contributory negligence is set up as a shield against the obligation to satisfy the whole of the plaintiff's claim, the principle involved is that, where a man is part author of his own injury, he cannot call on the other party to compensate him in full. . . .

Jones v Livox Quarries Ltd Court of Appeal [1952] 2 QB 608

The plaintiff, an employee of the defendants, stood contrary to his instructions on the back of a traxcavator, a vehicle which travelled at about two and a half mph. The lunchtime whistle had gone, and the traxcavator was travelling along the route to the canteen. The driver gave evidence that he was not aware of the plaintiff's presence on the vehicle. Having driven the traxcavator round a stationary excavator and made a sharp left turn, the traxcavator was stopped (or nearly stopped) by the driver so that he could change gear. A dumper, travelling behind the traxcavator, collided with the back of that vehicle, injuring the plaintiff. Hallett J found that the dumper driver had been negligent, but that the plaintiff had been contributorily negligent, and reduced his damages by one-fifth. There was an appeal by the plaintiff, and a cross-appeal by the defendants (the employers of the dumper driver) to the Court of Appeal.

DENNING LJ: . . . The case of *Davies v Swan Motor Co (Swansea) Ltd*[1] has been much discussed before us. It has been said that the three judgments in that case do not proceed on precisely the same lines. That is true, but it is, I suggest, quite understandable, because the court was there feeling its way in difficult country. Since that time, however, the ground has been cleared considerably. It can now be safely asserted that the doctrine of last opportunity[2] is obsolete; and also that contributory negligence does not depend on the existence of a duty. But the troublesome problem of causation still remains to be solved.

Although contributory negligence does not depend on a duty of care, it does depend on foreseeability. Just as actionable negligence requires the foreseeability of harm to others, so contributory negligence requires the foreseeability of harm to oneself. A person is guilty of contributory negligence if he ought reasonably to have foreseen that, if he did not act as a reasonable, prudent man, he might be hurt himself; and in his reckonings he must take into account the possibility of others being careless.

Once negligence is proved, then no matter whether it is actionable negligence or contributory negligence, the person who is guilty of it must bear his proper share of responsibility for the consequences. The consequences do not depend on foreseeability, but on causation. The question in every case is: What faults were there which caused the damage? Was his fault one of them? The necessity of causation is shown by the word 'result' in s. 1(1) of the Act of 1945, and it was accepted by this court in *Davies v Swan Motor Co (Swansea) Ltd.*[1]

---

1. [1949] 2 KB 291; [1949] 1 All ER 620.
2. [See p. 360, post.]

There is no clear guidance to be found in the books about causation. All that can be said is that causes are different from the circumstances in which, or on which, they operate. The line between the two depends on the facts of each case. It is a matter of common sense more than anything else. In the present case, as the argument of Mr Arthian Davies proceeded, it seemed to me that he sought to make foreseeability the decisive test of causation. He relied on the trial judge's statement that a man who rode on the towbar of the traxcavator 'ran the risk of being thrown off and no other risk'. That is, I think, equivalent to saying that such a man could reasonably foresee that he might be thrown off the traxcavator, but not that he might be crushed between it and another vehicle.

In my opinion, however, foreseeability is not the decisive test of causation. It is often a relevant factor, but it is not decisive. Even though the plaintiff did not foresee the possibility of being crushed, nevertheless in the ordinary plain common sense of this business the injury suffered by the plaintiff was due in part to the fact that he chose to ride on the towbar to lunch instead of walking down on his feet. If he had been thrown off in the collision, Mr Arthian Davies admits that his injury would be partly due to his own negligence in riding on the towbar; but he says that, because he was crushed, and not thrown off, his injury is in no way due to it. That is too fine a distinction for me. I cannot believe that that purely fortuitous circumstance can make all the difference to the case. . . .

In order to illustrate this question of causation, I may say that if the plaintiff, whilst he was riding on the towbar, had been hit in the eye by a shot from a negligent sportsman, I should have thought that the plaintiff's negligence would in no way be a cause of his injury. It would only be the circumstance in which the cause operated. It would only be part of the history. But I cannot say that in the present case. The man's negligence here was so much mixed up with his injury that it cannot be dismissed as mere history. His dangerous position on the vehicle was one of the causes of his damage. . . .

The present case is a good illustration of the practical effect of the Act of 1945. In the course of the argument my Lord suggested that before the Act of 1945 he would have regarded this case as one where the plaintiff should recover in full. That would be because the negligence of the dumper driver would then have been regarded as the predominant cause. Now, since the Act, we have regard to all the causes, and one of them undoubtedly was the plaintiff's negligence in riding on the towbar of the traxcavator. His share in the responsibility was not great—the trial judge assessed it at one-fifth—but, nevertheless, it was his share, and he must bear it himself. . . .

It all comes to this: If a man carelessly rides on a vehicle in a dangerous position, and subsequently there is a collision in which his injuries are made worse by reason of his position than they otherwise would have been, then his damage is partly the result of his own fault, and the damages recoverable by him fall to be reduced accordingly.

[SINGLETON and HODSON LJJ delivered judgments in favour of dismissing the appeal and cross-appeal.]

Appeal and cross-appeal dismissed

Notes

1. For comment on Denning LJ's treatment of causation in *Jones v Livox Quarries Ltd*, see I. Fagelson (1979) 42 MLR 646 at 655–656.

2. The effect of the complicated 'last opportunity' doctrine (which in Denning LJ's opinion is obsolete) is explained by the following passage from *Winfield & Jolowicz* (p. 157 – footnotes omitted):

'The common law rule produced hardship where one of the two negligent parties suffered the greater loss although his negligence was not the major cause of the accident. Accordingly, the courts modified the defence of contributory negligence by the so-called rule of last opportunity. This enabled the plaintiff to recover notwithstanding his own negligence, if upon the occasion of the accident the defendant could have avoided the accident while the plaintiff could not. The authorities were confused, and confusion was made worse confounded by the extension of the rule, in *British Columbia Electric Ry. Co v Loach* [1916] 1 AC 719, to cases of "constructive last opportunity." This meant that if the defendant would have had the last opportunity but for his own negligence, he was in the same position as if he had actually had it, and the plaintiff again recovered in full.'

For further reading on this topic, see *Glanville Williams*, chap. 9 and §66; *Salmond & Heuston*, pp. 573–576 and 589–590; A. L. Goodhart (1949) 65 LQR 237; *Rouse v Squires* [1973] QB 889; [1973] 2 All ER 903. In *Lloyds Bank Ltd v Budd* [1982] RTR 80 Lord Denning MR re-iterated his opinion about the 'last opportunity' rule, saying that it had 'gone forever'.

Stapley *v* Gypsum Mines Ltd House of Lords [1953] 2 All ER 478

Appeal from an order of the Court of Appeal (Singleton, Birkett and Morris LJJ), dated 7 April 1952, and reported, [1952] 1 All ER 1092, reversing an order of Sellers J, dated 20 December 1951.

The appellant, the widow of a miner employed in the respondents' gypsum mine, claimed damages against the respondents . . . in respect of the death of her husband which was caused by the fall of the roof of a stope in which he was working. The deceased and a fellow workman had been charged by the respondents with the duty of bringing down the roof so as to make the stope safe to work in, but they had failed to do so, and the deceased had gone to work in the stope. The learned judge found in favour of the appellant on the ground that the respondents were liable for the negligence or breach of statutory duty of the workman who was working with the deceased, but he deducted one half of the award which he would otherwise have made, as he held that the deceased was partly to blame for the accident. On an appeal by the respondents and cross-appeal by the appellant, the Court of Appeal held that the deceased's own negligence and breach of statutory duty, and not that of the respondents, was the substantial cause of the deceased's death, and, accordingly, they allowed the appeal and dismissed the cross-appeal.

LORD REID: My Lords, in the respondents' mines the workings are driven at right angles away from the main haulage way. The actual working place is the stope and the part between it and the haulage way is the twitten. The miners all work in pairs, one being the borer and the other the breaker. There is no sharp demarcation between their work and neither can give orders to the other, though the borer appears to be the senior man. Before the accident Stapley and Dale were working together, Stapley being the breaker. He was a steady workman with long experience, but rather slow. He had for a time been a borer but had reverted to being a breaker. A well recognised danger in the mine is a fall of part of the roof. The roof is not generally shored up as any weakness in it can be detected by tapping it. If it is 'drummy', giving a hollow sound, it is unsafe and must be taken down. There are three ways of doing this — with a pick, or with a pinch bar or crow bar, or by firing a shot. Whichever way is adopted, of course, men doing the necessary work must not stand immediately below the dangerous part of the roof. One morning when Stapley and Dale arrived at their stope they tested the roof and found it to be drummy. They saw the foreman, Church, about it and he ordered them to fetch it down. They all knew that that meant that no one was to work under the roof before it had come down. Church did not say which method was to be adopted. Both men were accustomed to this work and the method was properly left to their discretion. They used picks, but after half an hour had made no impression. The work was awkwardly placed as a fault ran across the mouth of the stope, the floor and roof inside being about eighteen inches higher than outside it. Probably they could not use a pinch bar, but they could easily have prepared the place for firing a shot and sent for the shot-firer. Instead, according to Dale whose evidence was accepted, they agreed that the roof was safe enough for them to resume their ordinary work, and did so. There was a quantity of gypsum lying in the stope and if the roof had been safe their first task would have been to get this to the haulage way. To do that, Stapley had to enter the stope and break the gypsum into smaller pieces and Dale had to make preparations in the twitten. So they separated, and when Dale came back half an hour later he found Stapley lying dead in the stope under a large piece of the roof which had fallen on him.

There is no doubt that if these men had obeyed their orders the accident would not have happened. Both acted in breach of orders and in breach of safety regulations, and both ought to have known quite well that it was dangerous for Stapley to enter the stope. The present action against the respondents is chiefly based on Dale's fault having contributed to the accident, and on the respondents being responsible for it, the defence of common employment being no longer available. So it is necessary to consider what would have happened if Dale had done his duty. It was his duty either to try a pinch bar or to start boring holes for the shot-firer, and on the evidence I think that it is highly probable that, if he had insisted on doing that instead of agreeing with Stapley to neglect their orders and the regulations, Stapley would not have stood out against him or tried to resume his ordinary work. Stapley had nothing to gain from his disobedience, and, if he had not found Dale in agreement with him, it appears to me unlikely that he would have persisted. But if he had persisted and thereby prevented Dale from carrying out his orders – because Dale could not have worked at the roof if Stapley had persisted in going below it – then it was Dale's duty to go for the foreman, as he, Dale, could not give orders to Stapley. We do not know how soon the roof fell or how long it would have taken Dale to find and bring the foreman, but it is, at least, quite likely that the foreman would have arrived in time to prevent the accident. If Dale's failure did contribute to the accident, then I do not see on what ground the respondents can escape liability in respect of that failure.

In these circumstances it is necessary to determine what caused the death of Stapley. If it was caused solely by his own fault, then the appellant cannot succeed. But if it was caused partly by his own fault and partly by the fault of Dale, then the appellant can rely on the Law Reform (Contributory Negligence) Act 1945. To determine what caused an accident from the point of view of legal liability is a most difficult task. If there is any valid logical or scientific theory of causation, it is quite irrelevant in this connection. In a court of law, this question must be decided as a properly instructed and reasonable jury would decide it. . . . The question must be determined by applying common sense to the facts of each particular case. One may find that, as a matter of history, several people have been at fault and that if any one of them had acted properly the accident would not have happened, but that does not mean that the accident must be regarded as having been caused by the faults of all of them. One must discriminate between those faults which must be discarded as being too remote and those which must not. Sometimes it is proper to discard all but one and to regard that one as the sole cause, but in other cases it is proper to regard two or more as having jointly caused the accident. I doubt whether any test can be applied generally. It may often be dangerous to apply to this kind of case tests which have been used in traffic accidents by land or sea, but in this case I think it useful to adopt phrases from the speech of Viscount Birkenhead LC ([1922] 1 AC 129, pp. 144, 145) in *Admiralty Comrs v SS Volute*, and to ask: Was Dale's fault 'so much mixed up with the state of things brought about' by Stapley that 'in the ordinary plain common sense of this business' it must be regarded as having contributed to the accident? I can only say that I think it was and that there was no 'sufficient separation of time, place or circumstance' between them to justify its being excluded. Dale's fault was one of omission rather than commission and it may often be impossible to say that, if a man had done what he omitted to do, the accident would certainly have been prevented. It is enough, in my judgment, if there is a sufficiently high degree of probability that the accident would have been prevented. I have already stated my view of the probabilities in this case and I think that it must lead to the conclusion that Dale's fault ought to be regarded as having contributed to the accident.

Finally, it is necessary to apply the Law Reform (Contributory Negligence) Act 1945. Sellers J reduced the damages by one half holding both parties equally to blame. Normally one would not disturb such an award, but Sellers J does not appear to have taken into account the fact that Stapley deliberately and culpably entered the stope. By doing so, it appears to me that he contributed to the accident much more directly than Dale. Section 1(1) of the Act directs that the damages

'. . . shall be reduced to such extent as the court thinks just and equitable having regard to the claimant's share in the responsibility for the damage.'

A court must deal broadly with the problem of apportionment, and, in considering what is just and equitable, must have regard to the blameworthiness of each party, but 'the claimant's share in the responsibility for the damage' cannot, I think, be assessed without considering the relative importance of his acts in causing the damage apart from his blameworthiness. It may be that in this case Dale was not much less to blame than Stapley, but Stapley's conduct in entering the stope contributed more immediately to the accident than anything that Dale did or failed to do. I agree with your Lordships that in all the circumstances it is proper in this case to reduce the damages by eighty per cent and to award twenty per cent of the damages to the appellant. I have not dealt with the question whether, at the time of the accident, the respondents were in breach of reg. 7(3) of the Metalliferous Mines General Regulations 1938, because, whichever way that question was decided, it would not in this case affect my view as to the amount by which the damages should be reduced.

[LORD TUCKER and LORD OAKSEY delivered speeches in favour of allowing the appeal. LORD PORTER and LORD ASQUITH OF BISHOPSTONE delivered speeches in favour of dismissing the appeal.]

Appeal allowed

Froom *v* Butcher Court of Appeal [1975] 3 All ER 520

Mr Froom was driving his car carefully along a road at a speed of between 30–35 mph with his wife sitting beside him in the front and his daughter in the back seat. The front seats of the car were fitted with seat belts but neither Mr nor Mrs Froom was wearing them. Unfortunately Mr Froom's car was struck head on by a car travelling quickly in the opposite direction and on its wrong side of the road as it had pulled out to overtake a line of traffic. Nield J, [1974] 3 All ER 517, held that failure to wear a seat belt was not contributory negligence. There was an appeal to the Court of Appeal. It should be noted that at the time this case was decided it was not compulsory to wear seat belts: see p. 368, post.

LORD DENNING MR: . . . Mr Froom and his wife and daughter were all injured. Mr Froom was forced up against the steering column. He had a broken rib and bruises on his chest. He had abrasions on his head. He would probably have been saved from these injuries if he had worn a seat belt. He also had a broken finger, but the seat belt would not have saved that. These injuries were not at all severe. He was back at work next day. The judge assessed his general damages at £450. Mrs Froom was also injured but the seat belt would not have saved her from them. The question that arises is whether Mr Froom's damages are to be reduced because he was not wearing a seat belt. The judge held they were not. The defendant appeals to this court.

This is the first case to reach this court about seat belts. But there have been a dozen or more cases in the lower courts; and they have disclosed a remarkable conflict of opinion. Half the judges think that, if a person does not wear a seat belt, he is guilty of contributory negligence and his damages ought to be reduced. The other half think that it is not contributory negligence and they ought not to be reduced. . . .

The cause of the damage

In these seat belt cases, the injured plaintiff is in no way to blame for the accident itself. Sometimes he is an innocent passenger sitting beside a negligent driver who goes off the road. At other times he is an innocent driver of one car which is run into by the bad driving of another car which pulls out on to its wrong side of the road. It may well be asked: Why should the injured plaintiff have his damages reduced? The accident was solely caused by the negligent driving by the defendant. Sometimes outrageously bad driving. It should not lie in his mouth to say: 'You ought to have been wearing a seat belt.' . . .

I do not think that is the correct approach. The question is not what was the cause of the accident. It is rather what was the cause of the damage. In most accidents on the road the bad driving, which causes the accident, also causes the ensuing damage. But in seat belt cases the cause of the accident is one thing. The cause of the damage is another. The *accident* is caused by the bad driving. The *damage* is caused in part by the bad driving of the defendant, and in part by the failure of the plaintiff to wear a seat belt. If the plaintiff was to blame in not wearing a seat belt, the damage is in part the result of his own fault. He must bear some share in the responsibility for the damage and his damages fall to be reduced to such extent as the court thinks just and equitable. . . .

The sensible practice

It is compulsory for every motor car to be fitted with seat belts for the front seats. The regulations[1] so provide. They apply to every motor car registered since [1 Jan] 1965. In the regulations seat belts are called, in cumbrous language, 'body-restraining seat belts.' A 'seat belt' is defined[2] as 'a belt intended to be worn by a person in a vehicle and designed to prevent or lessen injury to its wearer in the event of an accident to the vehicle . . .'

Seeing that it is compulsory to fit seat belts, Parliament must have thought it sensible to wear them. But it did not make it compulsory for anyone to wear a seat belt. Everyone is free to wear it or not, as he pleases.[3] Free in this sense, that if he does not wear it, he is free from any penalty by the magistrates. Free in the sense that everyone is free to run his head against a brick wall, if he pleases. He can do it if he likes without being punished by the law. But it is not a sensible thing to do. If he does it, it is his own fault; and he has only himself to thank for the consequences.

Much material has been put before us about the value of wearing a seat belt. It shows quite plainly that everyone in the front seats of a car should wear a seat belt. Not only on long trips, but also on short ones. Not only in the town, but also in the country. Not only when there is fog, but also when it is clear. Not only by fast drivers, but also by slow ones. Not only on motorways, but also on side roads. . . . This material confirms the provision of the Highway Code which contains this advice: 'Fit seat belts in your car and make sure they are always used.' This advice has been in

---

1. Motor Vehicles (Construction and Use) Regulations 1973 (S.I. 1973 No. 24).
2. Regulation 17(9).
3. [But see now p. 368, post.]

the Highway Code since 1968, and should have been known to Mr Froom at the time of his accident in November 1972.

The Road Traffic [Act] 1972 says that a failure to observe that provision does not render a person liable to criminal proceedings of any kind, but it can be relied on in civil proceedings as tending to establish or negative liability: see s. 37(5)[1]. . . .

The effect of failure to wear a seat belt

(i) *Majority versus minority*
Quite a lot of people, however, think differently about seat belts. Some are like Mr Froom here. They think that they would be less likely to be injured if they were thrown clear than if they were strapped in. They would be wrong. The chances of injury are four times as great. Yet they believe it honestly and firmly. On this account Nield J thought they should not bear any responsibility. He recognised that such persons are in a minority, but he thought that proper respect should be paid to the minority view. He said[2]:

'. . . I do not feel that the courts are justified in invading the freedom of choice of the motorist by holding it to be negligence, lack of care or fault to act on an opinion firmly and honestly held and shared by many other sensible people.'

I am afraid I do not agree. In determining responsibility, the law eliminates the personal equation. It takes no notice of the views of the particular individual; or of others like him. It requires everyone to exercise all such precautions as a man of ordinary prudence would observe: see *Vaughan v Menlove*[3]; *Glasgow Corpn v Muir*[4] by Lord Macmillan. Nowadays, when we have no juries to help us, it is the duty of the judge to say what a man of ordinary prudence would do. He should make up his own mind, leaving it to the Court of Appeal to correct him if he is wrong.

(ii) *The high risk argument*
Other people take the view that the risk of an accident is so remote that it is not necessary to wear a seat belt on all occasions; but only when there are circumstances which carry a high risk, for example, driving on a motorway in conditions of fog, ice or snow; or engaging in road racing activities. . . . I cannot accept this view either. You never know when a risk may arise. It often happens suddenly and when least anticipated, when there is no time to fasten the seat belt. Besides, it is easy to forget when only done occasionally. But, done regularly, it becomes automatic. Every time that a car goes out on the road there is the risk of an accident. Not that you yourself will be negligent. But that someone else will be. That is a possibility which a prudent man should, and will, guard against. He should always, if he is wise, wear a seat belt.

(iii) *Mere forgetfulness*
Lastly, there are many people who do not wear their seat belts, simply through forgetfulness or inadvertence or thoughtlessness. Their fault is far less serious than that of the negligent driver who causes an accident. Some judges have expressed themselves strongly about this . . . I am afraid I cannot share this view. The case for wearing seat belts is so strong that I do not think the law can admit forgetfulness as an excuse. If it were, everyone would say: 'Oh, I forgot.' In order to bring home the importance of wearing seat belts, the law should say that a person who fails to wear it must share some responsibility for the damages.

---

1. [See now s. 38(7) of the Road Traffic Act 1988.]
2. [1974] 3 All ER at p. 520; [1974] 1 WLR at p. 1302.
3. (1837) 3 Bing NC 468; [1835–42] All ER Rep 156.
4. [1943] AC 448 at 457; [1943] 2 All ER 44 at 48.

Thus far I have spoken only of the ordinary run of cases. There are, of course, exceptions. A man who is unduly fat or a woman who is pregnant may rightly be excused because, if there is an accident, the strap across the abdomen may do more harm than good. But, apart from such cases, in the ordinary way a person who fails to wear a seat belt should accept some share of responsibility for the damage—if it could have been prevented or lessened by wearing it.

The share of responsibility
Whenever there is an accident, the negligent driver must bear by far the greater share of responsibility. It was his negligence which caused the accident. It also was a prime cause of the whole of the damage. But insofar as the damage might have been avoided or lessened by wearing a seat belt, the injured person must bear some share. But how much should this be? Is it proper to enquire whether the driver was grossly negligent or only slightly negligent? or whether the failure to wear a seat belt was entirely inexcusable or almost forgivable? If such an enquiry could easily be undertaken, it might be as well to do it. In *Davies v Swan Motor Co*[1] we said that consideration should be given not only to the causative potency of a particular factor, but also its blameworthiness. But we live in a practical world. In most of these cases the liability of the driver is admitted; the failure to wear a seat belt is admitted; the only question is: what damages should be payable? This question should not be prolonged by an expensive enquiry into the degree of blame-worthiness on either side, which would be hotly disputed. Suffice it to assess a share of responsibility which will be just and equitable in the great majority of cases.

Sometimes the evidence will show that the failure made no difference. The damage would have been the same, even if a seat belt had been worn. In such cases the damages should not be reduced at all. At other times the evidence will show that the failure made all the difference. The damage would have been prevented altogether if a seat belt had been worn. In such cases I would suggest that the damages should be reduced by 25 per cent. But often enough the evidence will only show that the failure made a considerable difference. Some injuries to the head, for instance, would have been a good deal less severe if a seat belt had been worn, but there would still have been some injury to the head. In such case I would suggest that the damages attributable to the failure to wear a seat belt should be reduced by 15 per cent.

Conclusion
Everyone knows, or ought to know, that when he goes out in a car he should fasten the seat belt. It is so well-known that it goes without saying, not only for the driver, but also the passenger. If either the driver or the passenger fails to wear it and an accident happens—and the injuries would have been prevented or lessened if he had worn it—then his damages should be reduced. Under the Highway Code a driver may have a duty to invite his passenger to fasten his seat belt, but adult passengers possessed of their faculties should not need telling what to do. If such passengers do not fasten their seat belts, their own lack of care for their own safety may be the cause of their injuries. In the present case the injuries to the head and chest would have been prevented by the wearing of a seat belt and the damages on that account might be reduced by 25 per cent. The finger would have been broken anyway and the damages for it not reduced at all. Overall the judge suggested 20 per cent and Mr Froom has made no objection to it. So I would not interfere.

I would allow the appeal and reduce the damages by £100.

[LAWTON and SCARMAN LJJ agreed.]

Appeal allowed

---

1. [1949] 2 KB at p. 326; [1949] 1 All ER at p. 632.

Questions

1. Is it consistent with s. 1(1) of the Law Reform (Contributory Negligence) Act 1945 for Lord Denning to suggest fixed percentage reductions in certain types of cases? (See further J. R. Spencer [1976] CLJ 44 at 45.)

2. Do Lord Denning's suggested percentage reductions apply in the case of a driver who fails to wear a seat belt and who is also partly to blame for the occurrence of the accident?

3. Suppose a person injured in a car accident did not wear a seat belt because he or she found it unbearable to wear one as a result of the fear of being trapped in the car if an accident should occur. Is the position of a person with such a phobia analogous to that of fat men or pregnant women who, according to *Froom v Butcher*, are not contributorily negligent if they do not wear a seat belt? (Consider *Condon v Condon* [1978] RTR 483 (*sed quaere*).)

4. In a case where the injuries that did occur would have been avoided or lessened by the use of a seat belt, should the court take account of any different injuries that *might* have occurred if the plaintiff had been wearing a seat belt (e.g. by being crushed or burnt if he had been restrained in his seat, rather than being projected through the windscreen)? Compare the approach in *Patience v Andrews* [1983] RTR 447 with that in *Mackay v Borthwick* 1982 SLT 265.

5. Do you think this decision in fact encouraged people to wear seat belts? (See further p. 368, post.)

Notes

1. Compare with *Froom v Butcher* the discussion of the policy issues in an article written before the Court of Appeal's decision by J. C. Hicks (1974) 37 MLR 308 at 314–316. As Hicks makes clear, one point to appreciate is that a contributorily negligent plaintiff will have to bear part of the loss himself in this sort of case, whereas a negligent defendant will nearly always be insured. See *Atiyah*, pp. 119–120, for a similar point in a more general context.

2. It may not be contributory negligence for a passenger in the back of an ambulance not to use a seat belt: see *Eastman v South West Thames Health Authority* [1990] RTR 315 which discusses the question of warning passengers about seat belts (cf. *Froom v Butcher*, p. 366, ante).

3. A few years before *Froom v Butcher* the Court of Appeal decided that it could be contributory negligence to ride a motor bike without wearing a crash helmet: *O'Connell v Jackson* [1972] 1 QB 270; [1971] 3 All ER 129. In 1973, as a result of subordinate legislation made under s. 32 of the Road Traffic Act 1972, it became compulsory to wear protective headgear whilst riding a motor bike: see now s. 16 of the Road Traffic Act 1988. Section 16(2), re-enacting the prior position under the Motor-Cycle Crash-Helmets (Religious Exemption) Act 1976, provides that any requirement imposed under the law-making powers granted by s. 16 'shall not apply to any follower of the Sikh religion while he is wearing a turban.' Does this mean that a follower of the Sikh religion who wears a turban whilst riding a motor

bike and who suffers injury which a crash helmet would have avoided would not have his damages reduced for contributory negligence? Cf. s. 11 of the Employment Act 1989 dealing with the position of Sikhs wearing turbans on building sites.

After more than one attempt to introduce it, the wearing of seat belts in the front seats of cars was made compulsory by s. 33A of the Road Traffic Act 1972 (enacted by s. 27 of the Transport Act 1981) and subordinate legislation made under that provision (The Motor Vehicles (Wearing of Seat Belts) Regulations 1982, S.I. 1982 No. 1203). See now s. 14 of the Road Traffic Act 1988. (For the position of children under the age of fourteen, see now s. 15 of the Road Traffic Act 1988 (replacing earlier legislation) and The Motor Vehicles (Wearing of Seat Belts by Children) Regulations 1982, S.I. 1982 No. 1342 and The Motor Vehicle (Wearing of Seat Belts by Children in Rear Seats Regulations 1989, S.I. 1989 No. 1219.) Reg. 5 of S.I. 1982 No. 1203 sets out exceptions to the requirement that a seat belt be worn (e.g. drivers reversing, taxi drivers): in particular reg. 5 provides an exception for a person in respect of whom a doctor has signed a certificate 'to the effect that it is inadvisable on medical grounds for him to wear a seat belt'.

Breach of or compliance with the regulations could be introduced as evidence either for or against an allegation of contributory negligence. It would seem unlikely that a plaintiff possessing a certificate of exemption would be held to be contributorily negligent if a seat belt were not worn. What do you think the courts' attitude would be to (a) a pregnant woman who has not got a medical certificate; (b) a pregnant woman who had sought but been refused a medical certificate by a doctor?

In the first eleven months since the wearing of seat belts was made compulsory, there were over 7,000 fewer fatal and serious casualties in the front seats of cars than in the previous year (65 H. C. Debs (6th Series) col. 11). To what extent does this suggest that the criminal law is a more effective deterrent than the tort 'fine' involved in the application of contributory negligence?

4. In *Capps v Miller* [1989] 2 All ER 333; [1989] 1 WLR 839 it was accepted that Lord Denning MR's guidelines in *Froom v Butcher* should normally also be applied in cases where a crash helmet was not worn. However, Glidewell and May LJJ distinguished the case where the straps were not fastened or not properly fastened (albeit this is also a breach of statutory duty). In Glidewell LJ's opinion, the blame was less in such a case and this would be reflected in the percentage deduction that was made. May LJ, who agreed with Glidewell LJ's 10% reduction in this case (cf. the approach of Croom-Johnson LJ), pointed out that he reached this conclusion on his 'best consideration' of the facts and circumstances of the case without embarking on what Lord Denning MR referred to in *Froom v Butcher* as an 'expensive enquiry into the degree of blameworthiness on either side which would be hotly disputed'.

5. In *Capps v Miller* Croom-Johnson LJ thought it was of great importance that Lord Denning MR's guidelines should be adhered to 'for the sake of the swift conduct, and it may be settlement, of litigation'. (As has been seen ante, he would have applied them more widely than his brethren in that case, but see May LJ's comment also referred to ante.) On the increase in uncertainty produced by the mere raising of contributory negligence in the settlement

process and its effect in making plaintiffs more likely to accept an offer (as well as justifying a lower offer), see H. Genn, *Hard Bargaining: Out of Court Settlement in Personal Injury Actions*, pp. 112–113. Adoption of Lord Denning MR's guidelines increases certainty. Do you think that this means that less cases are settled?

6. The percentage reductions suggested in *Froom v Butcher* may be increased in suitable circumstances. For example, in *Gregory v Kelly* [1978] RTR 426 the plaintiff, who was suing the driver of the car in which he had been a passenger, would have suffered no injury if he had been wearing a seat belt. He also knew that the car had no operative footbrake and Kenneth Jones J reduced the damages by 40 per cent. Consider further *Ashton v Turner* [1981] QB 137; [1980] 3 All ER 870; *Salmon v Newland* (1983) Times, 16th May.

Even if a seat belt is worn, it is surely normally still contributory negligence to ride in a car knowing that it has no operative footbrake. Similarly, knowledge on the plaintiff's part that the driver has been drinking may also mean that it is contributory negligence to ride in the car with him. In *Owens v Brimmell* [1977] QB 859; [1976] 3 All ER 765 Tasker Watkins J stated (at p. 771):

'. . . [I]t appears to me that there is widespread and weighty authority abroad for the proposition that a passenger may be guilty of contributory negligence if he rides with the driver of a car whom he knows has consumed alcohol in such quantity as is likely to impair to a dangerous degree that driver's capacity to drive properly and safely. So, also, may a passenger be guilty of contributory negligence if he, knowing that he is going to be driven in a car by his companion later, accompanies him on a bout of drinking which has the effect, eventually of robbing the passenger of clear thought and perception and diminishes the driver's capacity to drive properly and carefully. Whether this principle can be relied on successfully is a question of fact and degree to be determined in the circumstances out of which the issue is said to arise.'

See further *Meah v McCreamer* [1985] 1 All ER 367; cf. *Malone v Rowan* [1984] 3 All ER 402; and see further *Ashton v Turner*. For comment on *Owens v Brimmell*, see C. R. Symmons (1977) 40 MLR 350 who points in particular to the difficulties of assessing the passenger's share in the responsibility in such a case. *Owens v Brimmell* is also discussed by N. P. Gravells (1977) 93 LQR 581, although the article ranges more widely. See further p. 376, post.

(c) Emergencies

Jones v Boyce Nisi Prius (1816) 1 Stark 493

This was an action on the case against the defendant, a coach proprietor, for so negligently conducting the coach, that the plaintiff, an outside passenger, was obliged to jump off the coach, in consequence of which his leg was broken.

It appeared that soon after the coach had set off from an inn, the coupling rein broke, and one of the leaders being ungovernable, whilst the coach was on a descent, the coachman drew the coach to one side of the road, where it came in contact with some piles, one of which it broke, and afterwards the wheel was stopped by a post. Evidence was adduced to shew that the coupling rein was defective, and that the breaking of the rein had rendered it necessary for the coachman to drive to the side of the road in order to stop the career of the horses. Some of the witnesses stated that the wheel was forced against the post with great violence; and one of the witnesses stated, that at that time the plaintiff, who had before been seated on the back part of the coach, was jerked forwards in consequence of the concussion, and that one of the wheels was elevated to the height of eighteen or twenty inches; but whether the plaintiff jumped off, or was jerked off, he could not say. A witness also said, I should have jumped down had I been in his (the plaintiff's) place, as the best means of avoiding the danger. The coach was not overturned, but the plaintiff was immediately afterwards seen lying on the road with his leg broken, the bone having been protruded through the boot.

Upon this evidence, Lord Ellenborough was of opinion, that there was a case to go to the jury, and a considerable mass of evidence was then adduced, tending to shew that there was no necessity for the plaintiff to jump off.

LORD ELLENBOROUGH, in his address to the jury, said, — This case presents two questions for your consideration; first, whether the proprietor of the coach was guilty of any default in omitting to provide the safe and proper means of conveyance, and if you should be of that opinion, the second question for your consideration will be, whether that default was conducive to the injury which the plaintiff has sustained; for if it was not so far conducive as to create such a reasonable degree of alarm and apprehension in the mind of the plaintiff, as rendered it necessary for him to jump down from the coach in order to avoid immediate danger, the action is not maintainable. To enable the plaintiff to sustain the action, it is not necessary that he should have been thrown off the coach; it is sufficient if he was placed by the misconduct of the defendant in such a situation as obliged him to adopt the alternative of a dangerous leap, or to remain at certain peril; if that position was occasioned by the default of the defendant, the action may be supported. On the other hand, if the plaintiff's act resulted from a rash apprehension of danger, which did not exist, and the injury which he sustained is to be attributed to rashness and imprudence, he is not entitled to recover. The question is, whether he was placed in such a situation as to render what he did a prudent precaution, for the purpose of self-preservation. — His Lordship, after recapitulating the facts, and commenting upon them, and particularly on the circumstance of the rein being defective, added: — If the defect in the rein was not the constituent cause of the injury, the plaintiff will not be entitled to your verdict. Therefore it is for your consideration, whether the plaintiff's act was the measure of an unreasonably alarmed mind, or such as a reasonable and prudent mind would have adopted. If I place a man in such a situation that he must adopt a perilous alternative, I am responsible for the consequences; if, therefore, you should be of opinion, that the reins were defective, did this circumstance create a necessity for what he did, and did he use proper caution and prudence in extricating himself from the apparently impending peril. If you are of that opinion, then, since the original fault was in the proprietor, he is liable to the plaintiff for the injury which his misconduct has occasioned. This is the first case of the kind which I recollect to have occurred. A coach proprietor certainly is not to be responsible for the rashness and imprudence of a passenger; it must appear that there existed a reasonable cause for alarm.

The jury found a verdict for the plaintiff. Damages £300.

(d) Infants

Gough v Thorne Court of Appeal [1966] 3 All ER 398

LORD DENNING MR: On 13 June 1962, a group of children were crossing the New Kings Road, Chelsea, London. They were Malcolm Gough, who was seventeen; his brother John, who was ten; and his sister Elizabeth, the plaintiff, who was 13½. They were coming from the Wandsworth Bridge Road, crossing the New Kings Road, and going to a swimming pool on the other side. They waited on the pavement for some little time to see if it was safe to cross. Then a lorry came up, coming up the Wandsworth Bridge Road and turning left into the New Kings Road. The lorry driver had got pretty well half-way across the road, towards the bollards, and he stopped at about five feet from the bollards. He put his right hand out to warn the traffic which was coming up the road. He saw the children waiting; he beckoned to them to cross; and they did. They had got across just beyond the lorry when a 'bubble' car, driven by the defendant, came through the gap between the front of the lorry and the bollard, about five feet, just missed the eldest boy, and struck the young boy of ten, but ran into and seriously injured the plaintiff, Elizabeth, aged 13½. Now, on the plaintiff's behalf, there is a claim against the driver of the 'bubble' car for negligence.

The judge has found that the defendant driver was negligent. He said that the 'bubble' car was going too fast in the circumstances, and that the driver did not keep a proper look-out because he ought to have seen the lorry driver's signal and he did not see it. He found, therefore, that the defendant, the driver of the 'bubble' car, was to blame and negligent. Then there came the question whether the little girl, the plaintiff, was herself guilty of contributory negligence. As to that, the judge found that she was one-third to blame for this accident. I will read what the judge said about it. 'Was there contributory negligence?', he asked. He answered:

'I think that there was. I think that the plaintiff was careless in advancing past the lorry into the open road without pausing to see whether there was any traffic coming from her right. I do not think that her responsibility was very great. After all, the lorry driver had beckoned her on. She might have thought it unlikely that any traffic would try to come through the gap. She might have thought that if there were any traffic coming from that direction, it would wait until the lorry started to move or gave the all clear. She was, after all, only thirteen years old. I assess her degree of responsibility at one-third.'

I am afraid that I cannot agree with the judge. A very young child cannot be guilty of contributory negligence. An older child may be; but it depends on the circumstances. A judge should only find a child guilty of contributory negligence if he or she is of such an age as reasonably to be expected to take precautions for his or her own safety: and then he or she is only to be found guilty if blame should be attached to him or her. A child has not the road sense or the experience of his or her elders. He or she is not to be found guilty unless he or she is blameworthy.

In this particular case I have no doubt that there was no blameworthiness to be attributed to the plaintiff at all. Here she was with her elder brother crossing a road. They had been beckoned on by the lorry driver. What more could you expect the child to do than to cross in pursuance of the beckoning? It is said by the judge that she ought to have leant forward and looked to see whether anything was coming. That indeed might be reasonably expected of a grown-up person with a fully developed road sense, but not of a child of 13½.

I am clearly of opinion that the judge was wrong in attributing any contributory negligence to the plaintiff, aged 13½; and I would allow the appeal accordingly.

SALMON LJ: . . . The question as to whether the plaintiff can be said to have been guilty of contributory negligence depends on whether any ordinary child of 13½ could be expected to have done any more than this child did. I say, 'any ordinary child'. I do not mean a paragon of prudence; nor do I mean a scatter-brained child; but the ordinary girl of 13½. . . .

[DANCKWERTS LJ delivered a brief judgment in favour of allowing the appeal, and agreed in particular with LORD DENNING's observations on contributory negligence.]

Appeal allowed

Questions

1. If a young child, who wandered on to the road but who was found not to have been contributorily negligent because of his age, is injured by a negligent motorist, how might the motorist cut down the amount of damages he (or his insurance company) has to pay? (See D. J. Gibson-Watt (1972) 122 NLJ 280.)

2. If a twelve-year-old plaintiff was found to have a mental age of fifteen years, by what standard should the child be judged in deciding whether he has been contributorily negligent?

Notes

1. Compare the position where an infant is the defendant, p. 264, ante.

2. The position in tort should not be confused with that in criminal law, where a child below the age of ten cannot be liable for a crime, whatever mental element that crime might require. (See J. C. Smith and B. Hogan, *Criminal Law* 6th edn (London, 1988), pp. 178–179.)

3. Lord Denning MR states in *Gough v Thorne* that a very young child cannot be contributorily negligent. Of course, in the case of extremely young children, it may seem obvious that this is so, but several of the leading textbooks take the view that there is no age below which it can be said, as a matter of law, that a finding of contributory negligence cannot be made against a child — *Charlesworth & Percy on Negligence* 8th edn (London, 1990), para. 3–38; *Clerk & Lindsell*, para. 1–149; *Winfield & Jolowicz*, p. 163. This view (as stated in *Charlesworth & Percy*) was accepted in *Speirs v Gorman* [1966] NZLR 897. Note also *Barnes v Flucker* 1985 SLT 142 where counsel conceded that as a matter of law the two five year olds hit by a car in that case could be contributorily negligent. The Pearson Commission, however, recommended that in cases of motor vehicle injury contributory negligence should not be a defence if the plaintiff was less than twelve years old (vol. 1, para. 1077).

(e) Workers

Caswell v Powell Duffryn Associated Collieries Ltd, p. 559, post

Note

The comments in the *Caswell* case on the position of workers in relation to contributory negligence were spoken in the context of the tort of breach of statutory duty and it is not certain whether they apply to a negligence action: see *Winfield & Jolowicz*, p. 164. See further I. Fagelson (1979) 42 MLR 646 at 651–652 who submits that they do so apply.

(f) Apportionment of damages

Stapley v Gypsum Mines Ltd, p. 361, ante

Froom v Butcher, p. 363, ante

Notes

1. See generally A. I. Ogus, *The Law of Damages* (London, 1973), pp. 103–107; D. Payne (1955) 18 MLR 344; Gravells op cit, pp. 594–609; Fagelson op cit, pp. 656–663.

2. For 'sub-apportionment', see *The Calliope* [1970] P 172; [1970] 1 All ER 624.

3. Apportionment of damages under the 1945 Act (contributory negligence) must be distinguished from apportionment of damages under the Civil Liability (Contribution) Act 1978 (p. 871, post) (contribution between joint tortfeasors). The former task needs to be kept distinct from the latter: see *Fitzgerald v Lane* [1989] AC 328; [1988] 2 All ER 961, noted by H. McLean [1989] CLJ 14 and see further p. 874, post. According to this decision, in apportionment under the 1945 Act when there are joint tortfeasors, the plaintiff's actions are contrasted with the 'totality of the tortious conduct of the defendants': the responsibility of each individual tortfeasor is not decided in this exercise, but rather in any contribution proceedings between them (though compare the position under s. 1 of the Maritime Conventions Act 1911, p. 355, ante).

2   Volenti non fit injuria

Dann v Hamilton King's Bench Division [1939] 1 All ER 59

The plaintiff and her mother were driven by Hamilton to see the Coronation decorations, and during the evening Hamilton consumed a certain amount of drink. They met a man named Taunton, and he was given a lift in the car. However, he left the car shortly before it was involved in an accident in which the plaintiff was injured and Hamilton was killed. The action was against his widow who represented his estate. It was found by the learned judge (Asquith J) that as Taunton left the car a conversation took place along the following lines (although Asquith J conceded that it was not clear how seriously the words were spoken): — Taunton said to the plaintiff and her mother 'You two have more pluck than I have', to which the plaintiff answered 'You should be like me. If anything is going to happen, it will happen'. The defence relied upon the maxim volenti non fit injuria, negligence being admitted at the trial.

ASQUITH J: . . . As a matter of strict pleading, it seems that the plea volenti is a denial of any duty at all, and, therefore, of any breach of duty, and an admission of negligence cannot strictly be combined with the plea. The plea volenti differs in this respect from the plea of contributory negligence, which is not raised in this case: see the observations of Bowen LJ in *Thomas v Quartermaine.*[1] This technicality,

---

1. (1887) 18 QBD 685.

however, is of no consequence in the present case. . . .

. . . [I]t is common ground that the deceased, Hamilton, negligently caused the collision, and the evidence further satisfies me that his driving at the time of the collision was that of a man, not only negligent, but negligent through excess of drink. The question is whether, on those facts, the rule or maxim volenti non fit injuria applies so as to defeat the plaintiff's claim. It has often been pointed out that the maxim says volenti, not scienti. A complete knowledge of the danger is in any event necessary, but such knowledge does not necessarily import consent. It is evidence of consent, weak or strong according to circumstances. The question whether the plaintiff was volens is one of fact, to be determined on this amongst other evidence: see *Smith v Baker & Sons*,[1] and other authorities.

As to knowledge, I find as a fact that the plaintiff knew at 11.50 pm, when Taunton was set down, that Hamilton, while far from being dead drunk, was under the influence of drink to such an extent as substantially to increase the chances of a collision arising from his negligence, that with this knowledge she re-entered the car, and that, in so doing, she was not acting under the pressure of any legal or social duty, or through the absence of alternative and practicable forms of transport, since she could have gone home by bus for 2*d*. Is this enough to constitute her volens for the purposes of the maxim? Indeed, is it clear that the maxim applies at all to the present case? . . .

The maxim . . . undoubtedly applies in many cases of pure tort, but case law in this field is very scanty. This is not, perhaps, because its application is rare in this field, but because in a large class of cases its applicability is so obvious as not to be brought to the test of litigation. It is manifest, for instance, that the consent of the patient relieves the dentist who extracts a tooth, or the surgeon who extracts an appendix, of liability for assault, to which their action would otherwise amount. In these cases, the certainty of physical injury is consented to. In another class of cases, perhaps more numerous, a man is not courting injury, but wishes to avoid it, but he nevertheless consents to the risk of its occurrence — for example, when he voluntarily engages in a game of cricket, or a boxing-match (with adequately padded gloves), or a fencing bout (with adequately buttoned foils). In such cases, he impliedly consents to the risks ordinarily incident to those sports, and here again, in the absence of consent, the party who sustains injury would be entitled to sue for assault, or otherwise for trespass to the person. . . .

Those are cases of trespass to the person. How stands the matter with regard to the tort of negligence, as we may now venture to call it? Does the maxim apply to negligence at all? . . .

Some text-book writers of authority, notably *Beven on Negligence*, 4th edn, at p. 790, roundly deny that the maxim applies to cases of negligence at all. This is a hard saying, and must be read, I think, subject to some implied limitation. Where a dangerous physical condition has been brought about by the negligence of the defendant, and, after it has arisen, the plaintiff, fully appreciating its dangerous character, elects to assume the risk thereof, the maxim has often been held to apply, and to protect the defendant. Instances are *Torrance v Ilford UDC*[2] and the more recent *Cutler v United Dairies (London) Ltd*.[3] Where, however, the act of the plaintiff relied on as a consent precedes, and is claimed to license in advance, a possible subsequent act of negligence by the defendant (and this, I think, must be the case Beven had in mind), the case may well be different. Here, *Smith v Baker & Sons*[4] does not help as much as might be expected. In any case, it turned on contract, which is not in question here.

---

1. [1891] AC 325.
2. (1909) 73 JP 225.
3. [1933] 2 KB 297.
4. [1891] AC 325.

With some qualifications, *Pollock on Torts*, 13th edn, supports Beven's dictum, declaring, at p. 172:

'The whole law of negligence assumes the principle of volenti non fit injuria not to be applicable.'

He points out, quoting the observations of Lord Halsbury LC in *Smith v Baker & Sons*,[1] that anyone crossing a London street knows that a substantial percentage of drivers are negligent. If a man crosses deliberately, with this knowledge, and is negligently run down, he is certainly not volens, and is not, therefore, precluded from a remedy. Sir Frederick Pollock adds, at p. 173:

'A man is not bound at his peril to fly from a risk from which it is another's duty to protect him, merely because the risk is known.'

In *Woodley v Metropolitan District Rly Co*,[2] Mellish LJ carries this illustration a step further. He says, at p. 394:

'Suppose this case: a man is employed by a contractor for cleansing the street, to scrape a particular street, and for the space of a fortnight he has the opportunity of observing that a particular hansom cabman drives his cab with extremely little regard for the safety of the men who scrape the streets. At the end of a fortnight the man who scrapes the streets is negligently run over by the cabman. An action is brought in the county court, and the cabman says in his defence: "You know my style of driving, you had seen me drive for a fortnight, I was only driving in my usual style."'

The judgment of Mellish LJ in this particular case was a minority judgment, but seems to have been preferred to that of the majority [by] the House of Lords in the later case of *Membery v Great Western Rly Co*.[3]

Cannot a yet further step be safely taken? I find it difficult to believe, although I know of no authority directly in point, that a person who voluntarily travels as a passenger in a vehicle driven by a driver who is known by the passenger to have driven negligently in the past is volens as to future negligent acts of such driver, even though he could have chosen some other form of transport if he had wished. Then, to take the last step, suppose that such a driver is likely to drive negligently on the material occasion, not because he is known to the plaintiff to have driven negligently in the past, but because he is known to the plaintiff to be under the influence of drink. That is the present case. Ought the result to be any different? After much debate, I have come to the conclusion that it should not, and that the plaintiff, by embarking in the car, or re-entering it, with knowledge that through drink the driver had materially reduced his capacity for driving safely, did not impliedly consent to, or absolve the driver from liability for, any subsequent negligence on his part whereby the plaintiff might suffer harm.

There may be cases in which the drunkenness of the driver at the material time is so extreme and so glaring that to accept a lift from him is like engaging in an intrinsically and obviously dangerous occupation, inter-meddling with an unexploded bomb or walking on the edge of an unfenced cliff. It is not necessary to decide whether in such a case the maxim volenti non fit injuria would apply, for in the present case I find as a fact that the driver's degree of intoxication fell short of this degree. I therefore conclude that the defence fails, and the claim succeeds. . . .

Judgment for the plaintiff

---

1. [1891] AC 325.
2. (1877) 2 Ex D 384.
3. (1889) 14 App Cas 179.

Notes

1. For an example where it was thought that, if it had not been for s. 148(3) of the Road Traffic Act 1972 (see now s. 149 of the Road Traffic Act 1988, p. 888, post), the volenti maxim would have precluded a passenger from recovering damages from a driver who had been drinking, see *Winnik v Dick* 1981 SLT 23 and 101 (Sh Ct); 1984 SLT 185. Reference to several earlier Commonwealth cases can be found in D. M. Gordon's article (1966) 82 LQR 62. As has just been indicated, the effect of s. 149 of the Road Traffic Act 1988 must be borne in mind today, on which see p. 389, post.

2. The lack of any statutory equivalent to the Road Traffic Act in the case of aircraft was noted in *Morris v Murray* [1990] 3 All ER 801; [1991] 2 WLR 195. *Dann v Hamilton* was also distinguished in this case in which the plaintiff knowingly and willingly went on a flight in a light aircraft with a drunken pilot, and was injured when the plane crashed. The Court of Appeal allowed the defence of volenti. Rejecting a mere reduction for contributory negligence, Fox LJ stated that 'the wild irresponsibility of the venture is such that the law should not intervene to award damages and should leave the loss where it falls'. What rationale does this suggest for the defence? Cf. A. J. E. Jaffey [1985] CLJ 87 at 88.

3. In *Slater v Clay Cross Co Ltd* [1956] 2 QB 264; [1956] 2 All ER 625, Denning LJ (at pp. 627–628) referring to *Dann v Hamilton* spoke in the following terms:

'Asquith J held that the maxim volenti non fit injuria had no application to the case; and he gave judgment in favour of the injured passenger. I must say that I agree with him. I know that the decision has in some quarters been criticised, but I would point out that Lord Asquith himself wrote a note in the *Law Quarterly Review* for July 1953, vol. 69 at p. 317, which explains what he decided. He wrote:
  "The criticisms . . . were to the effect that even if the volenti doctrine did not apply, there was here a cast iron defence on the ground of contributory negligence. I have since had the pleadings and my notes exhumed, and they very clearly confirm my recollection that contributory negligence was not pleaded. Not merely so, but my notes show that I encouraged counsel for the defence to ask for leave to amend by adding this plea, but he would not be drawn: why, I have no idea. As the case has been a good deal canvassed on the opposite assumption, I hope you will not grudge the space for this not unimportant corrigendum."
In so far as he decided that the doctrine of volenti did not apply, I think the decision was quite correct. In so far as he suggested that the plea of contributory negligence might have been available, I agree with him.'

See further *Owens v Brimmell* [1977] QB 859; [1976] 3 All ER 765, noted p. 369, ante, and see also *Fookes v Slaytor* [1979] 1 All ER 137; [1978] 1 WLR 1293 where this passage from Denning LJ's judgment was treated as impliedly stating that contributory negligence must be pleaded before it is available as a defence in any case.

4. For an example (obiter) of volenti (encapsulated in s. 2(3) of the Occupiers' Liability (Scotland) Act 1960), see *Titchener v British Railways Board* [1983] 3 All ER 770; [1983] 1 WLR 1427, noted p. 455, post; and for comment on this and other cases see Jaffey, op cit. In addition to the discussion of the authorities by Jaffey, see the recent decision in *Morris v Murray*

and consider how far the judgements in general in that case support Jaffey's desired position. Consider also Lloyd LJ's view in *Kirkham v Chief Constable of the Greater Manchester Police* [1990] 3 All ER 246 at 250; cf. *Pitts v Hunt* [1990] 3 All ER 344 at 359–360 per Dillon LJ.

Nettleship *v* Weston Court of Appeal [1971] 3 All ER 581

The facts and part of the judgment have been set out p. 260, ante.

LORD DENNING MR: . . . This brings me to the defence of volenti non fit injuria. Does it apply to the instructor? In former times this defence was used almost as an alternative defence to contributory negligence. Either defence defeated the action. Now that contributory negligence is not a complete defence, but only a ground for reducing the damages, the defence of volenti non fit injuria has been closely considered, and, in consequence, it has been severely limited. Knowledge of the risk of injury is not enough. Nor is a willingness to take the risk of injury. Nothing will suffice short of an agreement to waive any claim for negligence. The plaintiff must agree, expressly or impliedly, to waive any claim for any injury that may befall him due to the lack of reasonable care by the defendant: or more accurately, due to the failure of the defendant to measure up to the standard of care that the law requires of him. That is shown in England by *Dann v Hamilton*[1] and *Slater v Clay Cross Co Ltd*;[2] and in Canada by *Lehnert v Stein*;[3] and in New Zealand by *Morrison v Union S S Co of New Zealand Ltd*.[4] The doctrine has been so severely curtailed that in the view of Diplock LJ: '. . . the maxim, in the absence of express contract, has no application to negligence simpliciter where the duty of care is based solely on proximity or "neighbourship" in the Atkinian sense': see *Wooldridge v Sumner*.[5]

Applying the doctrine in this case, it is clear that Mr Nettleship did not agree to waive any claim for injury that might befall him. Quite the contrary. He enquired about the insurance policy so as to make sure that he was covered. If and insofar as Mrs Weston fell short of the standard of care which the law required of her, he has a cause of action. But his claim may be reduced insofar as he was at fault himself—as in letting her take control too soon or in not being quick enough to correct her error.

I do not say that the professional instructor—who agrees to teach for reward—can likewise sue. There may well be implied in the contract an agreement by him to waive any claim for injury.[6] He ought to insure himself, and may do so, for aught I know. But the instructor who is just a friend helping to teach never does insure himself. He should, therefore, be allowed to sue. . . .

MEGAW LJ [referring to cases where passengers knew a driver was likely to drive unsafely because of drink or drugs, yet still accepted a lift:] . . . There may in such cases sometimes be an element of aiding and abetting a criminal offence; or, if the facts fall short of aiding and abetting, the passenger's mere assent to benefit from the commission of a criminal offence may involve questions of turpis causa. For myself, with great respect, I doubt the correctness on its facts of the decision in *Dann v Hamilton*.[7] But the present case involves no such problem. . . .

---

1. [1939] 1 KB 509; [1939] 1 All ER 59.
2. [1956] 2 QB 264; [1956] 2 All ER 625.
3. (1963) 36 DLR (2d) 159.
4. [1964] NZLR 468.
5. [1963] 2 QB 43 at 69; [1962] 2 All ER 978 at 990.
6. [See now the Road Traffic Act 1988, s. 149, p. 888 post.]
7. [1939] 1 KB 509; [1939] 1 All ER 59.

[MEGAW LJ was not speaking of the volenti maxim here. However he went on to hold the volenti maxim inapplicable for, in his view, the facts did not show that the plaintiff had accepted the risk of injury through the defendant's inexperience. SALMON LJ rejected 'any possible defence' of volenti non fit injuria because of the assurance given about the position regarding insurance.]

Notes

1. There have been several cases where the volenti defence has been pleaded against passengers in cars in which there were notices stating that passengers travelled at their own risk. (See *Buckpitt v Oates* [1968] 1 All ER 1145; *Bennett v Tugwell* [1971] 2 QB 267; [1971] 2 All ER 248; cf. *Birch v Thomas* [1972] 1 All ER 905; [1972] 1 WLR 294.) Section 149 of the Road Traffic Act 1988 (p. 888, post) will today exclude the defence in this situation. *Nettleship*'s case must be read subject to this section.

2. On 'turpis causa', which was mentioned by Megaw LJ, see p. 392, post.

Bowater v The Mayor, Aldermen and Burgesses of the Borough of Rowley Regis Court of Appeal [1944] 1 All ER 465

The plaintiff was employed by the defendants as a carter, and his job was to take away rubbish swept up by the road sweepers. The foreman told him to take out a horse which had tried to run away on more than one occasion when driven by one of the plaintiff's fellow employees. Both the plaintiff and the defendants' foreman were aware of the incidents. The plaintiff expressed his dislike of the proposed course of action, but was told that the borough surveyor had said that he was to take the horse out, and the plaintiff obeyed. About a month later the horse ran away, and the plaintiff was thrown out of the cart and injured. Singleton J upheld the plea of volenti non fit injuria. An appeal to the Court of Appeal was successful and a new trial was ordered on the question of damages.

GODDARD LJ: . . . The maxim volenti non fit injuria is one which in the case of master and servant is to be applied with extreme caution. Indeed, I would say that it can hardly ever be applicable where the act to which the plaintiff is said to be 'volens' arises out of his ordinary duty, unless the work for which the plaintiff is engaged is one in which danger is necessarily involved. Thus a man in an explosives factory must take the risk of an explosion occurring in spite of the observance and provision of all statutory regulations and safeguards. A horse-breaker must take the risk of being thrown or injured by a restive or unbroken horse; it is an ordinary risk of his employment. But a man whose occupation is not one of a nature inherently dangerous but who is asked or required to undertake a risky operation is in a different position. To rely on this doctrine the master must show that the workman undertook that the risk should be on him. It is not enough that, whether under protest or not, he obeyed an order or complied with a request which he might have declined as one which he was not bound either to obey or to comply with. It must be shown that he agreed that what risk there was should lie on him. I do not mean that it must necessarily be shown that he contracted to take the risk, as that would involve consideration, though a simple case of showing that a workman did take a risk upon himself would be that he was paid extra for so doing, and in some occupations 'danger money' is often paid.

This, in my opinion, is the result of *Yarmouth v France*,[1] *Smith v Baker*,[2] and

---

1. (1887) 19 QBD 647.
2. [1891] AC 325.

Monaghan v Rhodes,[1] and the further citation of authority, in support of what I think is now a well-settled principle, is unnecessary. Though the question in the last resort is one of fact I find myself unable to agree with Singleton J on the evidence in this case. I venture to think he approached the case from a wrong angle. A corporation carter or dustman is not like a horse-breaker because he is also a horse-keeper. It is no part of his duty to break or tame the horse which draws the dust cart. Nor is it right to inquire into the mental processes that may lead him to do what he is told or to consider what degree of appreciation of the risk was apparent to him. As Lord Esher MR said in *Yarmouth v France*,[2] that would be to say that for the same accident an unintelligent man might recover while a more intelligent one would not. For this maxim or doctrine to apply it must be shown that a servant who is asked or required to use dangerous plant is a volunteer in the fullest sense; that, knowing of the danger, he expressly or impliedly said that he would do the job at his own risk and not at that of his master. The evidence in this case fell far short of that and, in my opinion, the plaintiff was entitled to recover.

The appeal is allowed with costs and the case must go down for a new trial on damages only, unless the parties will agree to this court assessing the damages. . . .

[SCOTT and DU PARCQ LJJ delivered judgments in favour of allowing the appeal.]

Notes

1. As this case clearly shows, mere knowledge of the risk by the plaintiff will not per se bring him within the scope of the maxim. Indeed, many years earlier, Bowen LJ had stressed that the maxim was volenti non fit injuria and not scienti non fit injuria (*Thomas v Quartermaine* (1887) 18 QBD 685 at 696).

2. In the employment situation, the workman who has knowledge of a danger is unlikely to have true freedom of choice, for this is an area in which economic pressures operate. See further the comments of *Millner*, pp. 102–108. The volenti maxim has, in fact, been of little importance in master and servant cases since *Smith v Baker & Sons* [1891] AC 325. Compare *Burnett v British Waterways Board* [1973] 2 All ER 631; [1972] 1 WLR 1329. It would however be a mistake to suppose that the volenti defence can never apply in this context, for the next case provides an example of its application, though in a rather restricted sphere.

3. Lack of real freedom of choice also exists in the rescuer cases, p. 131, ante, where the volenti defence has been raised (and see *Winfield & Jolowicz*, pp. 694–695 for other reasons why the defence will fail in that context). See further *Ogwo v Taylor* [1988] AC 431; [1987] 3 All ER 961, noted p. 142, ante, where counsel specifically did not raise volenti; indeed, Lord Bridge stated that the application of volenti in the case of professional firemen 'would be utterly repugnant to our notions of contemporary justice'.

4. Where a person's mind was impaired, volenti could not be raised as a defence to a claim against the police in respect of his suicide: *Kirkham v Chief Constable of the Greater Manchester Police* [1990] 3 All ER 246; [1990] 2 WLR 987 (although note Farquharson LJ's alternative point, post).

---

1. [1920] 1 KB 487.
2. (1887) 19 QBD 647.

Lloyd LJ was inclined to hold that hospital or prison authorities (and presumably other potential defendants like the police) could successfully raise the defence in a claim by the estate of a person of sound mind who had committed suicide. Compare Farquharson LJ's view (at p. 254) where he stated that 'the defence is inappropriate where the act of the deceased relied on is the very act which the duty cast upon the defendant required him to prevent'.

Imperial Chemical Industries Ltd v Shatwell House of Lords [1964] 2 All ER 999

This was an appeal from the Court of Appeal who dismissed an appeal from a judgment of Elwes J. Elwes J had held the appellants vicariously liable to the respondent for his fellow servant's negligence and breach of statutory duty. He had further held that the volenti defence was not open to the appellants in the claim based on breach of statutory duty, but reduced the damages by half because of the respondent's share of the blame for the accident. On the tort of breach of statutory duty which is also raised in the speeches in the House of Lords, see chap. 12, p. 531, post.

LORD REID: My Lords, this case arises out of the accidental explosion of a charge at a quarry belonging to the appellants which caused injuries to the respondent George Shatwell and his brother James, who were both qualified shotfirers. On 8 June 1960, these two men and another shotfirer, Beswick, had bored and filled fifty shot holes and had inserted electric detonators and connected them up in series. Before firing it was necessary to test the circuit for continuity. This should have been done by connecting long wires so that the men could go to a shelter some eighty yards away and test from there. They had not sufficient wire with them and Beswick went off to get more. The testing ought not to have been done until signals had been given, so that other men could take shelter, and these signals were not due to be given for at least another hour. Soon after Beswick had left George said to his brother 'Must we test them', meaning shall we test them, and James said 'yes'. The testing is done by passing a weak current through the circuit in which a small galvanometer is included and if the needle of the instrument moves when a connexion is made the circuit is in order. So George got a galvanometer and James handed two short wires to him. Then George applied the wires to the galvanometer and the needle did not move. This showed that the circuit was defective so the two men went round inspecting the connections. They saw nothing wrong and George said that that meant there was a dud detonator somewhere, and decided to apply the galvanometer to each individual detonator. James handed two other wires to him and George used them to apply the galvanometer to the first detonator. The result was an explosion which injured both men.

This method had been regularly used without mishap until the previous year. Then some research done by the appellants showed that it might be unsafe and in October 1959, the appellants gave orders that testing must in future be done from a shelter and a lecture was given to all the shotfirers, including the Shatwells, explaining the position. Then in December 1959, new statutory regulations[1] were made (S.I. 1959 No. 2259) probably because the Ministry had been informed of the results of the appellants' research. These regulations came into operation in February 1960, and the Shatwells were aware of them. But some of the shotfirers appear to have gone on in the old way. An instance of this came to the notice of the management in May 1960, and the management took immediate action and revoked the shotfiring certificate of the disobedient man, and told the other shotfirers about this. George admitted in evidence that he knew all this. He admitted that they would only have had to wait

---

1. The Quarries (Explosives) Regulations 1959.

ten minutes until Beswick returned with the long wires. When asked why he did not wait, his only excuse was that he could not be bothered to wait.

George now sues the appellants on the ground that he and his brother were equally to blame for this accident, and that the appellants are vicariously liable for his brother's conduct. He has been awarded £1,500, being half the agreed amount of his loss. There is no question of the appellants having been in breach of the regulation because the duty under the regulation is laid on the shotfirer personally. So counsel for George frankly and rightly admitted that if George had sued James personally instead of suing his employer the issue would have been the same. If this decision is right it means that if two men collaborate in doing what they know is dangerous and is forbidden and as a result both are injured, each has a cause of action against the other.

The appellants have two grounds of defence, first that James' conduct had no causal connexion with the accident the sole cause being George's own fault, and secondly volenti non fit injuria. I am of opinion that they are entitled to succeed on the latter ground, but I must deal shortly with the former ground because it involves the decision of this House in *Stapley v Gypsum Mines Ltd*,[1] and I think that there has been some misunderstanding of that case. . . . The only issue before the House was whether the conduct of Dale had contributed to cause the accident, and the House decided by a majority that it had. There was little, if any, difference of opinion as to the principles to be applied; the difference was in their application to the facts of the case. The case gives authoritative guidance on the question of causation, but beyond that it decides nothing. It clearly appears from the argument of counsel[2] that the defence volenti non fit injuria was never taken and nothing about it was said by any of their lordships.

Applying the principles approved in *Stapley*'s case[1] I think that James' conduct did have a causal connexion with this accident. It is far from clear that George would have gone on with the test if James had not agreed with him; but, perhaps more important, James did collaborate with him in making the test in a forbidden and unlawful way. His collaboration may not have amounted to much, but it was not negligible. . . . So I do not think that the appellants could succeed entirely on this defence and I turn to consider their second submission.

The defence volenti non fit injuria has had a chequered history. At one time it was very strictly applied. . . . More recently it appears to have been thought in some quarters that, at least as between master and servant, volenti non fit injuria is a dead or dying defence. That, I think, is because in most cases where the defence would now be available it has become usual to base the decision on contributory negligence. Where the plaintiff's own disobedient act is the sole cause of his injury, it does not matter in the result whether one says 100 per cent contributory negligence[3] or volenti non fit injuria; but it does matter in a case like the present. If we adopt the inaccurate habit of using the word 'negligence' to denote a deliberate act done with full knowledge of the risk, it is not surprising that we sometimes get into difficulties. I think that most people would say, without stopping to think of the reason, that there is a world of difference between two fellow servants collaborating carelessly, so that the acts of both contribute to cause injury to one of them, and two fellow servants combining to disobey an order deliberately, though they know the risk involved. It seems reasonable that the injured man should recover some compensation in the former case, but not in the latter. If the law treats both as merely cases of negligence, it cannot draw a distinction. In my view the law does and should draw a distinction. In the first case only the partial defence of contributory negligence is available. In the second volenti non fit injuria is a complete defence, if the employer is not himself

---

1. [1953] AC 663; [1953] 2 All ER 478.
2. See [1953] AC at p. 665.
3. [But see now *Pitts v Hunt* [1990] 3 All ER 344 at 357 and 359, noted p. 354, ante.]

at fault and is only liable vicariously for the acts of the fellow servant. If the plaintiff invited or freely aided and abetted his fellow servant's disobedience, then he was volens in the fullest sense. He cannot complain of the resulting injury either against the fellow servant or against the master on the ground of his vicarious responsibility for his fellow servant's conduct. I need not here consider the common case where the servant's disobedience puts the master in breach of a statutory obligation, and it would be wrong to decide in advance whether that would make any difference. There remain two other arguments for the respondent which I must deal with.

It was argued that in this case it has not been shown that George had a full appreciation of the risk. In my view it must be held that he had. . . .

Finally the respondent argues that there is a general rule that the defence of volenti non fit injuria is not available where there has been a breach of a statutory obligation. It would be odd if that were so. In the present case the prohibition of testing except from a shelter had been imposed by the appellants before the statutory prohibition was made. So it would mean that, if the respondent had deliberately done what he did in full knowledge of the risk the day before the statutory prohibition was made, this defence would have been open to the appellants, but if he had done the same thing the day after the regulation came into operation it would not. . . .

I entirely agree that an employer who is himself at fault in persistently refusing to comply with a statutory rule could not possibly be allowed to escape liability because the injured workman had agreed to waive the breach. If it is still permissible for a workman to make an express agreement with his employer to work under an unsafe system, perhaps in consideration of a higher wage—a matter on which I need express no opinion—then there would be a difference between breach of a statutory obligation by the employer and breach of his common law obligation to exercise due care: it would be possible to contract out of the latter, but not out of the former type of obligation. But all that is very far removed from the present case. . . .

I can find no reason at all why the fact that these two brothers agreed to commit an offence by contravening a statutory prohibition imposed on them as well as agreeing to defy their employer's orders should affect the application of the principle volenti non fit injuria either to an action by one of them against the other or to an action by one against their employer based on his vicarious responsibility for the conduct of the other. I would therefore allow this appeal.

LORD PEARCE: . . . In *Wheeler v New Merton Board Mills Ltd*[1] the Court of Appeal laid down that the defence of volenti non fit injuria was no answer to a claim by a workman against his employer for injury caused through a breach by the employer of a duty imposed on him by statute. They so held (with some reluctance which I do not share) principally because the case of *Baddeley v Earl Granville*[2] had stood for some fifty years. But in those cases the defendants were themselves in breach of statutory duty (as were the defendants in *Stapley*'s case).[3] In the present case the defendants themselves were in breach of no statutory duty. The questions of public policy and fairness which reinforced those decisions do not help the plaintiff in the present case but rather tell the other way. In my opinion, the rule which the courts have rightly created disallowing the defence where the employer is in breach of statutory duty should not apply to a case such as the present. The defence should be available where the employer was not himself in breach of statutory duty and was not vicariously in breach of any statutory duty through the neglect of some person who was of superior rank to the plaintiff and whose commands the plaintiff was bound to obey (or who had some special and different duty of care, see, e.g. *National*

---

1. [1933] 2 KB 669; [1933] All ER Rep 28.
2. (1887) 19 QBD 423; [1886–90] All ER Rep 374.
3. [1955] AC 663; [1953] 2 All ER 478.

Coal Board v England,[1] where a miner was injured by the shotfirer firing the charge) and where the plaintiff himself assented to and took part in the breaking of the statutory duty in question. If one does not allow some such exception one is plainly shutting out a defence which, when applied in the right circumstances, is fair and sensible.

So far as concerns common law negligence, the defence of volenti non fit injuria is clearly applicable if there was a genuine full agreement, free from any kind of pressure, to assume the risk of loss. . . .

In the present case it seems clear that as between George and James there was a voluntary assumption of risk. George was clearly acting without any constraint or persuasion; he was in fact inaugurating the enterprise. On the facts it was an implied term (to the benefit of which the employers are vicariously entitled) that George would not sue James for any injury that he might suffer, if an accident occurred. Had an officious bystander raised the possibility, can one doubt that George would have ridiculed it? . . .

[VISCOUNT RADCLIFFE, LORD HODSON and LORD DONOVAN delivered speeches in favour of allowing the appeal.]

Appeal allowed

Question

Would the result of this case have been any different if James, although employed as a shotfirer, had been George's supervisor?

Wooldridge v Sumner Court of Appeal [1962] 2 All ER 978

The first defendant owned Work of Art, a horse taking part in a competition for heavyweight hunters at the National Horse Show. The horses were required to walk, trot, canter and gallop, and this was a class of competition in which both the horse and its rider, Mr Holladay, were experienced. There was a line of tubs and benches two feet from the edge of the competition arena, which was surrounded by a cinder running track. The plaintiff, a professional photographer, was standing at the end of one of those benches. The defendant's horse was kept close into the corner of the bandstand end of the arena so as to give the horse the best chance to show off its gallop in the straight. However, having rounded the corner, the horse apparently jumped two of the tubs, knocked over a third, and then moved from the line of tubs on to a course taking it several feet behind the bench at the end of which the plaintiff was standing. The plaintiff, who had become frightened by the horse's approach, tried to pull someone away from the bench, but stepped or fell back and was knocked down by the horse. Barry J who dismissed the claim against the second defendants (the organisers of the show, who were occupiers of the stadium) found that the horse was being ridden too fast into and out of the corner, so that it was inevitable that it would come into contact with the tubs, and that Mr Holladay's conduct and control of the horse amounted to negligence for which the first defendant was liable. He also decided that if Mr Holladay had allowed it, the horse would have gone safely on to the cinder track. However, Barry J found that Mr Holladay tried to get the horse back on to the course and so carried along the line of tubs, and that Mr Holladay knew, or should have known, that the people sitting or standing along the line of benches and tubs were highly likely to be endangered by these efforts. The first defendant appealed:

SELLERS LJ: . . . In all the circumstances, in so far as the judgment found that

---

1. [1954] AC 403; [1954] 1 All ER 546.

Mr Holladay was going 'too fast' I would not hold this to be negligence; and in any case its effect had ceased when the horse was straightened up, as it was, some twenty-five yards before the accident, and with regard to the second finding on which the judgment was based, I am unable to find fault in Mr Holladay amounting to negligence. It was, I think, the horse's course and not his which took them along the line of tubs instead of to the right of that line and for this I do not think that he can be blamed. . . .

In my opinion, a competitor or player cannot, at least, in the normal case of competition or game, rely on the maxim volenti non fit injuria in answer to a spectator's claim, for there is no liability unless there is negligence, and the spectator comes to witness skill and with the expectation that it will be exercised. But, provided the competition or game is being performed within the rules and the requirement of the sport and by a person of adequate skill and competence, the spectator does not expect his safety to be regarded by the participant. If the conduct is deliberately intended to injure someone whose presence is known, or is reckless and in disregard of all safety of others so that it is a departure from the standards which might reasonably be expected in anyone pursuing the competition or game, then the performer might well be held liable for any injury his act caused. There would, I think, be a difference, for instance, in assessing blame which is actionable between an injury caused by a tennis ball hit or a racket accidentally thrown in the course of play into the spectators at Wimbledon and a ball hit or a racket thrown into the stands in temper or annoyance when play was not in progress. The relationship of spectator and competitor or player is a special one, as I see it, as the standard of conduct of the participant, as accepted and expected by the spectator, is that which the sport permits or involves. The different relationship involves its own standard of care. There can be no better evidence that Mr Holladay was riding within the rules than that he won, notwithstanding this unfortunate accident in the course of the event, and I do not think that it can be said that he was riding recklessly and in disregard of all safety or even, on this evidence, without skill. . . .

I would allow the appeal and enter judgment for the first defendant also.

DIPLOCK LJ: . . . Accepting, then, the primary facts as found by the trial judge but not those inferences which he drew from them and which, on analysis of the evidence, I think are unjustified, one is left with two acts or omissions by Mr Holladay which were causative factors in the accident. The first was the speed at which he caused Work of Art to negotiate the bend, the second was his omission at some moment before he reached the line of tubs to let the horse run out on to the cinder track. . . .

The matter has to be looked at from the point of view of the reasonable spectator as well as the reasonable participant; not because of the maxim volenti non fit injuria, but because what a reasonable spectator would expect a participant to do without regarding it as blameworthy is as relevant to what is reasonable care as what a reasonable participant would think was blameworthy conduct in himself. The same idea was expressed by Scrutton LJ in *Hall v Brooklands Auto-Racing Club*:[1]

'What is reasonable care would depend on the perils which might be reasonably expected to occur, *and the extent to which the ordinary spectator might be expected to appreciate and take the risk of such perils.*'

A reasonable spectator attending voluntarily to witness any game or competition knows, and presumably desires, that a reasonable participant will concentrate his attention on winning, and if the game or competition is a fast-moving one will have to exercise his judgment and attempt to exert his skill in what, in the analogous context of contributory negligence, is sometimes called 'the agony of the moment'. If the

---

1. [1933] 1 KB 205 at 214; [1932] All ER Rep 208 at 213.

participant does so concentrate his attention and consequently does exercise his judgment and attempt to exert his skill in circumstances of this kind which are inherent in the game or competition in which he is taking part, the question whether any mistake he makes amounts to a breach of duty to take reasonable care must take account of those circumstances.

The law of negligence has always recognised that the standard of care which a reasonable man will exercise depends on the conditions under which the decision to avoid the act or omission relied on as negligence has to be taken. The case of the workman engaged on repetitive work in the noise and bustle of the factory is a familiar example. More apposite for present purposes are the collision cases where a decision has to be made on the spur of the moment.

'... A's negligence makes collision so threatening that, though by the appropriate measure B could avoid it, B has not really time to think and by mistake takes the wrong measure. B is not held to be guilty of any negligence and A wholly fails.'

(*Admiralty Comrs v SS Volute*).[1] A fails not because of his own negligence; there never has been any contributory negligence rule in Admiralty. He fails because B has exercised such care as is reasonable in circumstances in which he has not really time to think. No doubt, if he has got into those circumstances as a result of a breach of duty of care which he owes to A, A can succeed on this antecedent negligence; but a participant in a game or competition gets into the circumstances in which he has no time or very little time to think by his decision to take part in the game or competition at all. It cannot be suggested that the participant, at any rate if he has some modicum of skill, is by the mere act or participating in breach of his duty of care to a spectator who is present for the very purpose of watching him do so. If, therefore, in the course of the game or competition at a moment when he really has no time to think, a participant by mistake takes a wrong measure, he is not, in my view, to be held guilty of any negligence.

Furthermore, the duty which he owes is a duty of care, not a duty of skill. Save where a consensual relationship exists between a plaintiff and a defendant by which the defendant impliedly warrants his skill, a man owes no duty to his neighbour to exercise any special skill beyond that which an ordinary reasonable man would acquire before indulging in the activity in which he is engaged at the relevant time. It may well be that a participant in a game or competition would be guilty of negligence to a spectator if he took part in it when he knew or ought to have known that his lack of skill was such that, even if he exerted it to the utmost, he was likely to cause injury to a spectator watching him. No question of this arises in the present case. It was common ground that Mr Holladay was an exceptionally skilful and experienced horseman.

The practical result of this analysis of the application of the common law of negligence to participant and spectator would, I think, be expressed by the common man in some such terms as these: 'A person attending a game or competition takes the risk of any damage caused to him by any act of a participant done in the course of and for the purposes of the game or competition, notwithstanding that such act may involve an error of judgment or a lapse of skill, unless the participant's conduct is such as to evince a reckless disregard of the spectator's safety'. The spectator takes the risk because such an act involves no breach of the duty of care owed by the participant to him. He does not take the risk by virtue of the doctrine expressed or obscured by the maxim volenti non fit injuria. The maxim states a principle of estoppel applicable originally to a Roman citizen who consented to being sold as a slave. Although pleaded and argued below, it was only faintly relied on by counsel for the first defendant in this court. In my view, the maxim, in the absence of express

1. [1922] 1 AC 129 at 136; [1921] All ER Rep 193 at 197.

contract, has no application to negligence simpliciter where the duty of care is based solely on proximity or 'neighbourship' in the Atkinian sense. The maxim in English law pre-supposes a tortious act by the defendant. The consent that is relevant is not consent to the risk of injury but consent to the lack of reasonable care that may produce that risk (see *Kelly v Tarrants Ltd*,[1] per Lord MacDermott), and requires on the part of the plaintiff at the time at which he gives his consent full knowledge of the nature and extent of the risk that he ran (*Osborne v London and North Western Rly Co*[2], per Wills J approved in *Letang v Ottawa Electric Rly Co*[3]). In *Dann v Hamilton*[4] Asquith J expressed doubts whether the maxim ever could apply to license in advance a subsequent act of negligence, for, if the consent precedes the act of negligence, the plaintiff cannot at that time have full knowledge of the extent as well as the nature of the risk which he will run. Asquith J, however, suggested that the maxim might, nevertheless, be applicable to cases where a dangerous physical condition had been brought about by the negligence of the defendant, and the plaintiff with full knowledge of the existing danger elected to run the risk thereof. With the development of the law of negligence in the last twenty years, a more consistent explanation of this type of case is that the test of liability on the part of the person creating the dangerous physical condition is whether it was reasonably foreseeable by him that the defendant[5] would so act in relation to it as to endanger himself. This is the principle which has been applied in the rescue cases (see *Cutler v United Dairies (London) Ltd*[6] and contrast *Haynes v Harwood*[7]) and that part of Asquith J's judgment in *Dann v Hamilton*[8] dealing with the possible application of the maxim to the law of negligence was not approved by the Court of Appeal in *Ward v TE Hopkins & Son Ltd, Baker v Same*.[9] In the type of case envisaged by Asquith J if I may adapt the words of Morris LJ in *Ward v Hopkins*,[10] the plaintiff could not have agreed to run the risk that the defendant might be negligent for the plaintiff would only play his part after the defendant had been negligent.

Since the maxim has, in my view, no application to this or any other case of negligence simpliciter, the fact that the plaintiff, owing to his ignorance of horses, did not fully appreciate the nature and extent of the risk he ran did not impose on Mr Holladay any higher duty of care towards him than that which he owed to any ordinary reasonable spectator with such knowledge of horses and vigilance for his own safety as might be reasonably expected to be possessed by a person who chooses to watch a heavyweight hunter class in the actual arena where the class is being judged. . . . Beyond saying that the question is one of degree, the learned judge has not expressly stated in his judgment anything which would indicate the considerations which he had in mind in determining that Mr Holladay was in breach of the duty of care owed by a participant in a competition of this character to a spectator who had chosen to watch the event in the arena in which it was taking place. There is, however, no reference in his judgment to the fact, which is, in my view, of the utmost relevance, that Mr Holladay's decisions what he should do once the signal for the gallop had been given had to be made in circumstances in which he had no time to exercise an unhurried judgment. It is, I think, clear that, if the trial judge gave any weight to this factor, he did not make proper allowance for it. . . .

---

1. [1954] NI 41 at 45.
2. (1888) 21 QBD 220 at 223, 224.
3. [1926] AC 725; [1926] All ER Rep 546.
4. [1939] 1 KB 509; [1939] 1 All ER 59.
5. [It would seem that this should be read as 'the plaintiff'.]
6. [1933] 2 KB 297; [1933] All ER Rep 594.
7. [1935] 1 KB 146; [1934] All ER Rep 103.
8. [1939] 1 KB 509; [1939] 1 All ER 59.
9. [1959] 3 All ER 225.
10. [1959] 3 All ER at p. 233.

[Having stated that, in the circumstances of the case, Mr Holladay's 'conduct in taking the corner too fast could not in my view amount to negligence', he continued:] As regards the second respect in which the learned judge found Mr Holladay to be negligent, namely, in his attempt to bring back the horse into the arena after it had come into contact with the first shrub . . . I am unable to accept the judge's inference of fact that the course taken by the horse along the line of shrubs was due to Mr Holladay's attempt to bring it back into the arena instead of letting it run out on to the cinder track. But, even if the judge's inference of fact be accepted, here was a classic case where Mr Holladay's decision what to do had to be taken in the 'agony of the moment' when he had no time to think, and if he took the wrong decision that could not in law amount to negligence. The most that can be said against Mr Holladay is that, in the course of, and for the purposes of, the competition he was guilty of an error or errors of judgment or a lapse of skill. That is not enough to constitute a breach of the duty of reasonable care which a participant owes to a spectator. In such circumstances, something in the nature of a reckless disregard of the spectator's safety must be proved, and of this there is no suggestion in the evidence.

I, too, would allow this appeal.

[DANCKWERTS LJ delivered a judgment in favour of allowing the appeal.]

Appeal allowed

Questions

1. Do you think the phrase 'reckless disregard of the spectator's safety' implies an objective or a subjective standard, i.e. must the competitor actually have foreseen the danger to the spectator?

2. If a policeman who was on duty at a sporting event was carelessly injured by a competitor, would the 'reckless disregard of safety' test apply?

Notes

1. The criticism to which this decision was subjected by A. L. Goodhart (1962) 78 LQR 490, was referred to in *Wilks v Cheltenham Home Guard Motor Cycle and Light Car Club* [1971] 2 All ER 369; [1971] 1 WLR 668. Edmund-Davies LJ stated (at p. 374) that he 'would with deference adopt the view of Dr Goodhart (1962) 78 LQR at p. 496 that the proper test is whether injury to a spectator has been caused "by an error of judgment that a reasonable competitor, being the reasonable man of the sporting world, would not have made".' Although accepting that spectators expected the competitor to be doing his best to win, his Lordship would still require the competitor to exercise reasonable care *in all the circumstances*. Lord Denning MR, however, was still prepared to apply the 'reckless disregard of safety' test to riders in *races* (cf. pp. 370–371). Phillimore LJ stressed that the test was one of negligence and that the circumstances might not warrant the application of the tests to be found in *Wooldridge v Sumner*. For an example of such circumstances consider *Harrison v Vincent* [1982] RTR 8, although note that the plaintiff here was not a spectator but one of the participants in a race for motor bikes with sidecars. In this case the normal standard of care in negligence was regarded as applicable to the maintenance and inspection of equipment before a race; on the other hand, the 'reckless disregard of safety' test was thought to be applicable to activity 'in the flurry and

excitement of the sport'. It is submitted, however, that the test adopted by Edmund-Davies LJ in the *Wilks* case should be followed. It is sufficiently flexible to cater for the special factors which arise in the context of competitions, and, as Dr Goodhart pointed out, the test 'is more in accord with the general principles on which the law of negligence is based'. Cf. the view of Jaffey, op cit, pp. 108–109 who prefers the 'reckless disregard of safety' test.

Consider also the preferred approach in *Condon v Basi* [1985] 2 All ER 453; [1985] 1 WLR 866 where both plaintiff and defendant were participants in a game of soccer in which, as a result of a tackle by the defendant, the plaintiff sustained a broken leg. Sir John Donaldson MR (with whose judgment Stephen Brown LJ and Glidewell J agreed) referred to the decision in *Rootes v Shelton* [1968] ALR 33 with approval and cited from the judgments in that case of Barwick CJ and Kitto J (at pp. 34 and 37 respectively). He then continued (at p. 454):

'I have cited from those two judgments because they show two different approaches which, as I see it, produce precisely the same result. One is to take a more generalised duty of care and modify it on the basis that the participants in the sport or pastime impliedly consent to taking risks which otherwise would be a breach of the duty of care. That seems to be the approach of Barwick CJ. The other is exemplified by the judgment of Kitto J, where he is saying, in effect, that there is a general standard of care, namely the Lord Atkin approach that you are under a duty to take all reasonable care taking account of the circumstances in which you are placed (see *Donoghue (or M'Alister) v Stevenson* [1932] AC 562 at 580, [1932] All ER Rep 1 at 11); which, in a game of football, are quite different from those which affect you when you are going for a walk in the countryside.

For my part I would prefer the approach of Kitto J, but I do not think it makes the slightest difference in the end if it is found by the tribunal of fact that the defendant failed to exercise that degree of care which was appropriate in all the circumstances, or that he acted in a way to which the plaintiff cannot be expected to have consented. In either event, there is liability.'

Note that *Wooldridge v Sumner* was not cited in *Condon v Basi*, and, as A. H. Hudson has pointed out in a note on *Condon v Basi* (1986) 102 LQR 11, support can be found in the obiter dictum of Sir John Arnold P in *Harrison v Vincent* (mentioned ante) for the application in the case of participants of the 'reckless disregard of safety' test to activity in the 'flurry and excitement of the sport'. For a reconciliation of the tests in *Wooldridge v Sumner* and *Condon v Basi* see Hudson, op cit, pp. 12–13. *Condon v Basi* is also noted by C. Gearty [1985] CLJ 371. On *Wooldridge v Sumner* see further *Morris v Murray* [1990] 3 All ER 801; [1991] 2 WLR 195.

2. If a spectator is injured by a competitor in a sporting event, he is not restricted to an action against that person, but may bring an action against the occupier of the place where the event was staged—see *Murray v Harringay Arena Ltd* [1951] 2 KB 529; [1951] 2 All ER 320; cf. *White v Blackmore* [1972] 2 QB 651; [1972] 3 All ER 158 (p. 456, post).

3. For a case where a participant in a sporting event (and not a spectator) sued the organiser of the event, see *Harrison v Vincent* [1982] RTR 8.

The Road Traffic Act 1988

See section 149, p. 888, post.

Note

It has been argued – see C. R. Symmons (1973) 123 NLJ 373 – that s. 148(3) of the Road Traffic Act 1972, which has been re-enacted as s. 149 of the 1988 Act, did not rule out the volenti defence in cases where implied consent is relied upon by the defendant (i.e. where there are no express terms): this is on the basis that the phrase 'a person so carried' means a person carried under the sort of 'antecedent agreement or understanding' referred to earlier in the subsection, which might not cover the implied consent cases. However, the Court of Appeal in *Pitts v Hunt* [1990] 3 All ER 344; [1990] 3 WLR 542 has now decided that it does catch such cases (although it was also accepted in that case that the defence of 'illegality' (p. 392, post) was unaffected, on which see p. 399, post).

The Unfair Contract Terms Act 1977

See section 2(3), post.

Question

What more do you think is required under the terms of s. 2(3) of this Act for the volenti defence to be successful in a case to which s. 2(3) applies? (For discussion of this point in the context of occupiers' liability, see J. Mesher [1979] Conv 58 at 61–62.)

Note

On the interpretation of s. 2(3), see B. Coote (1978) 41 MLR 312 at 316–317.

3 Exclusion of liability

White *v* Blackmore, p. 456, post

The Unfair Contract Terms Act 1977

PART 1. AMENDMENT OF LAW FOR ENGLAND AND WALES AND NORTHERN IRELAND

Introductory

1. **Scope of Part 1.** – (1) For the purposes of this Part of this Act, 'negligence' means the breach –
   (a) of any obligation, arising from the express or implied terms of a contract, to take reasonable care or exercise reasonable skill in the performance of the contract;
   (b) of any common law duty to take reasonable care or exercise reasonable skill (but not any stricter duty);
   (c) of the common duty of care imposed by the Occupiers' Liability Act 1957 or the Occupiers' Liability Act (Northern Ireland) 1957.
   (3) In the case of both contract and tort, sections 2 to 7 apply . . . only to business liability, that is liability for breach of obligations or duties arising –
   (a) from things done or to be done by a person in the course of a business (whether his own business or another's); or

(b) from the occupation of premises used for business purposes of the occupier; and references to liability are to be read accordingly [but liability of an occupier of premises for breach of an obligation or duty towards a person obtaining access to the premises for recreational or educational purposes, being liability for loss or damage suffered by reason of the dangerous state of the premises, is not a business liability of the occupier unless granting that person such access for the purposes concerned falls within the business purposes of the occupier.][1]

(4) In relation to any breach of duty or obligation, it is immaterial for any purpose of this Part of this Act whether the breach was inadvertent or intentional, or whether liability for it arises directly or vicariously.

Avoidance of liability for negligence, breach of contract, etc.

2. Negligence liability. – (1) A person cannot by reference to any contract term or to a notice given to persons generally or to particular persons exclude or restrict his liability for death or personal injury resulting from negligence.

(2) In the case of other loss or damage, a person cannot so exclude or restrict his liability for negligence except in so far as the term or notice satisfies the requirement of reasonableness.

(3) Where a contract term or notice purports to exclude or restrict liability for negligence a person's agreement to or awareness of it is not of itself to be taken as indicating his voluntary acceptance of any risk.

Liability arising from sale or supply of goods

5. 'Guarantee' of consumer goods. – (1) In the case of goods of a type ordinarily supplied for private use or consumption, where loss or damage –
   (a) arises from the goods proving defective while in consumer use; and
   (b) results from the negligence of a person concerned in the manufacture or distribution of the goods,
liability for the loss or damage cannot be excluded or restricted by reference to any contract term or notice contained in or operating by reference to a guarantee of the goods.

(2) For these purposes –
   (a) goods are to be regarded as 'in consumer use' when a person is using them, or has them in his possession for use, otherwise than exclusively for the purposes of a business; and
   (b) anything in writing is a guarantee if it contains or purports to contain some promise or assurance (however worded or presented) that defects will be made good by complete or partial replacement, or by repair, monetary compensation or otherwise.

(3) This section does not apply as between the parties to a contract under or in pursuance of which possession or ownership of the goods passed.

Explanatory provisions

11. The 'reasonableness' test. – (1) In relation to a contract term, the requirement of reasonableness for the purposes of this Part of this Act . . . is that the term shall have been a fair and reasonable one to be included having regard to the circumstances which were, or ought reasonably to have been, known to or in the contemplation of the parties when the contract was made.

(3) In relation to a notice (not being a notice having contractual effect), the requirement of reasonableness under this Act is that it should be fair and reasonable

---

1. [Inserted by s. 2 of the Occupiers' Liability Act 1984 and art. 4 of the Occupiers Liability (Northern Ireland) Order 1987, S.I. 1987 No. 1280 (N.I. 15).]

to allow reliance on it, having regard to all the circumstances obtaining when the liability arose or (but for the notice) would have arisen.

(4) Where by reference to a contract term or notice a person seeks to restrict liability to a specified sum of money, and the question arises (under this or any other Act) whether the term or notice satisfies the requirement of reasonableness, regard shall be had in particular . . . to—

    (a) the resources which he could expect to be available to him for the purpose of meeting the liability should it arise; and

    (b) how far it was open to him to cover himself by insurance.

(5) It is for those claiming that a contract term or notice satisfies the requirement of reasonableness to show that it does.

13. Varieties of exemption clause. — (1) To the extent that this Part of this Act prevents the exclusion or restriction of any liability it also prevents—

    (a) making the liability or its enforcement subject to restrictive or onerous conditions;

    (b) excluding or restricting any right or remedy in respect of the liability, or subjecting a person to any prejudice in consequence of his pursuing any such right or remedy;

    (c) excluding or restricting rules of evidence or procedure;

and (to that extent) sections 2 and 5 . . . also prevent excluding or restricting liability by reference to terms and notices which exclude or restrict the relevant obligation or duty.

(2) But an agreement in writing to submit present or future differences to arbitration is not to be treated under this Part of this Act as excluding or restricting any liability.

14. Interpretation of Part 1 — In this Part of this Act —

    'business' includes a profession and the activities of any
       government department or local or public authority;
    'goods' has the same meaning as in [the Sale of Goods Act 1979]
    . . .
    'negligence' has the meaning given by section 1(1);
    'notice' includes an announcement, whether or not in writing, and
       any other communication or pretended communication; and
    'personal injury' includes any disease and any impairment of
       physical or mental condition.

Notes

1. Exclusion of liability by contract or notice can be found discussed under the heading of volenti or assumption of risk. See e.g. *Fleming*, pp. 265–269; *Atiyah*, pp. 126–127. However, s. 2 of the Occupiers' Liability Act 1957 (p. 443, post), s. 149 of the Road Traffic Act 1988 (p. 888, post) and s. 2 of the Unfair Contract Terms Act 1977 treat volenti and exclusion separately. In *White v Blackmore* [1972] 2 QB 651; [1972] 3 All ER 158 (p. 456, post) it will be seen that volenti failed as a defence but that exclusion of liability was successful, and that Buckley LJ regarded the two defences as 'somewhat analogous'. See further *Fowler v Tierney* 1974 SLT (Notes) 23; *Burnett v British Waterways Board* [1973] 2 All ER 631; [1973] 1 WLR 700; and p. 460, post. One question to consider is whether the knowledge required on the plaintiff's part for exclusion by contract or notice is the same as that required for the volenti defence. The general topic of exclusion clauses must be left to courses on contract.

2. On exclusion of liability and the Unfair Contract Terms Act in the context of occupiers' liability, see p. 456, post.

3. On the interpretation of the scope of the Act, see *Smith v Eric S. Bush* [1990] 1 AC 831; [1989] 2 All ER 514. Lord Templeman's views were set out at p. 177, ante. The matter was also discussed by Lords Griffiths and Jauncey. In rejecting the view that the Act does not apply if the disclaimer (or exclusion notice) stops a duty of care arising (see p. 177, ante), Lord Griffiths stated that he regarded s. 11(3) and s. 13(1) as establishing a 'but-for' test in relation to an exclusion notice. 'They indicate that the existence of the common law duty to take reasonable care, referred to in section 1(1) (*b*), is to be judged by considering whether it would exist "but-for" the notice excluding liability' ([1990] 1 AC at p. 857). The House of Lords went on to hold that it would not be fair and reasonable to allow reliance on the disclaimers on the facts involved. See generally T. Kaye (1989) 52 MLR 841 at 845–848.

4. It has been held that a clause transferring liability from one person to another is caught by the words 'exclud[ing] or restrict[ing] liability' in s. 2 of the 1977 Act: *Phillips Products Ltd v Hyland* [1987] 2 All ER 620; [1987] 1 WLR 659. However, this case was distinguished in *Thompson v T. Lohan (Plant Hire) Ltd* [1987] 2 All ER 631; [1987] 1 WLR 649. Here the same clause was held to be outside s. 2 where it operated not between defendant and plaintiff as was the situation in the *Phillips* case, but between a defendant and the third party: the clause in this situation was not regarded as excluding or restricting the *liability* which had been established between that defendant and the plaintiff. For comment on these two cases, see L. S. Sealey [1988] CLJ 6.

5. For comment on the Unfair Contract Terms Act 1977 generally, see e.g. R. Lawson, *Exclusion Clauses* 3rd edn (London, 1990); W. V. H. Rogers and M. G. Clarke, *The Unfair Contract Terms Act 1977* (London, 1978); P. K. J. Thompson, *Unfair Contract Terms Act 1977* (London, 1978); D. Yates, *Exclusion Clauses in Contracts* 2nd edn (London, 1982); Coote, op cit. In relation to tort liability, note (in addition to the provisions which have been set out) s. 4 of the Act dealing with indemnity clauses.

6. Other instances of statutory provisions invalidating the exclusion of liability will be found in this book; see s. 1(3) of the Law Reform (Personal Injuries) Act 1948 (p. 566, post); s. 1(2) of the Employer's Liability (Defective Equipment) Act 1969 (p. 859, post); s. 149 of the Road Traffic Act 1988 (p. 888, post); s. 6(3) of the Defective Premises Act 1972 (p. 483, post); s. 7 of the Consumer Protection Act 1987 (p. 508, post). To what extent do any of these provisions overlap with those to be found in the Unfair Contract Terms Act 1977?

4 Illegality and public policy

Pitts *v* Hunt Court of Appeal [1990] 3 All ER 344

The first defendant was killed and the plaintiff injured when the first defendant's motor bike, ridden by the first defendant with the plaintiff as a pillion passenger, collided with the second defendant's car. The plaintiff and the first defendant had been drinking prior to the journey on which the collision occurred. The trial judge (Judge Fallon QC, sitting as a Deputy High Court judge) found that the second defendant had not been negligent. As stated by Beldam LJ in the Court of Appeal, the trial judge further 'found that the deceased had drunk so much that he was obviously unfit to drive and that if the plaintiff had been in a proper state he would have realised that. He found that the deceased, very much aided and abetted by the plaintiff, was deliberately trying to frighten others who were on the road. No doubt because they had drunk so much, they viewed it as a joke or a game but it was certainly reckless driving. He found that the plaintiff had supported or encouraged the deceased whom he knew was under age, drunk and uninsured, and he added ([1990] 1 QB 302 at 312):

"On my findings the deceased was riding this motor cycle recklessly and dangerously and at the very least the plaintiff was aiding and abetting that driving. He was not manipulating the controls of the machine but he was fully in agreement with and was encouraging the way in which the deceased was manipulating the controls. Indeed, the eye-witness accounts which I have accepted demonstrate that both the plaintiff and the deceased were actually enjoying their experience, partly if not largely as a result of the very large amount they had drunk that night."'

The trial judge decided that the plaintiff's claim was barred by the operation of the ex turpi maxim, and there was an appeal to the Court of Appeal.

BALCOMBE LJ: . . . (1) *The joint illegal enterprise*
In a case of this kind I find the ritual incantation of the maxim ex turpi causa non oritur actio more likely to confuse than to illuminate. I prefer to adopt the approach of the majority of the High Court of Australia in the most recent of the several Australian cases to which we were referred, *Jackson v Harrison* (1978) 138 CLR 438. That is to consider what would have been the cause of action had there been no joint illegal enterprise, that is the tort of negligence based on the breach of a duty of care owed by the deceased to the plaintiff, and then to consider whether the circumstances of the particular case are such as to preclude the existence of that cause of action. I find myself in complete agreement with the following passage from the judgment of Mason J in *Jackson v Harrison* (at 455–456):

'If a joint participant in an illegal enterprise is to be denied relief against a co-participant for injury sustained in that enterprise, the denial of relief should be related not to the illegal character of the activity but rather to the character and incidents of the enterprise and to the hazards which are necessarily inherent in its execution. A more secure foundation for denying relief, though more limited in its application — and for that reason fairer in its operation — is to say that the plaintiff must fail when the character of the enterprise in which the parties are engaged is such that it is impossible for the court to determine the standard of care which is appropriate to be observed. The detonation of an explosive device is a case of this kind. But the driving of a motor vehicle by an unlicensed and disqualified driver, so long as it does not entail an agreement to drive the car recklessly on the highway (see *Bondarenko v Sommers* (1968) 69 SR (NSW) 269), stands in a somewhat different position. In this case the evidence indicates that the participants contemplated that the vehicle would be driven carefully — an accident or untoward event might, as in fact it did, lead to discovery of their breach of the law. It is not suggested that either party lacked the experience or ability to drive carefully — that they were unlicensed was due to their having been disqualified as a result of earlier traffic offences . . . A plaintiff will fail when the joint illegal enterprise in which he and the defendant are engaged is such that the court cannot determine the particular standard of care to be observed. It matters not whether this in itself provides a complete answer to the plaintiff's claim or whether it leads in theory to the conclusion that the defendant owes no duty of care to the plaintiff because no standard of care can be determined in the particular case.'

The facts of the earlier case in the High Court of Australia, *Smith v Jenkins* (1970) 119 CLR 397, are set out in the judgment of Dillon LJ[1] and I need not repeat them. Of those facts Jacobs J said in *Jackson v Harrison* (1978) 138 CLR 438 at 460:

'It appears to me that these facts lie at the basis of the conclusion that there was a relevant joint criminal enterprise. It was a jaunt, an escapade, a joy-ride even though of a most serious kind from the beginning to the end. How could a standard of care be determined for such a course of criminal activity? I doubt that the decision would have been the same if the accident had occurred days, weeks or months later when the circumstances of the taking of the vehicle had ceased to have any significant relationship to the manner in which the vehicle was being used.'

This approach seems to me to enable the court to differentiate between those joint enterprises which, although involving a contravention of the criminal law and hence illegal, eg the use of a car by an unlicensed and disqualified driver as in *Jackson v Harrison*, are not such as to disable that court from determining the standard of care to be observed, and those, such as the use of a get-away car as in *Ashton v Turner* [1980] 3 All ER 870, [1981] QB 137, where it is impossible to determine the appropriate standard of care.

Counsel for the plaintiff submitted that, however reprehensible the plaintiff's conduct may have been, his culpability involved neither dishonesty nor violence nor any moral turpitude such as is inherent in crimes of dishonesty or violence. Although an assessment of the degree of moral turpitude becomes unnecessary if one adopts, as I do, the approach of the majority of the High Court of Australia in *Jackson v Harrison*, I would not wish it to be thought that I accept this submission. It was only by good fortune that no innocent third party was injured by this disgraceful piece of motor cycle riding, in which the judge found on the facts that the plaintiff was an active participant. If moral turpitude were relevant, here was moral turpitude of a high degree.

However, I prefer to found my judgment on the simple basis that the circumstances of this particular case were such as to preclude the court from finding that the deceased owed a duty of care to the plaintiff. . . .

DILLON LJ: . . . It so happens that the cases where a passenger has been injured by the 'negligence' of the driver when the vehicle in which the passenger was being carried was being used for an illegal purpose in which the passenger was an accomplice have come before the High Court of Australia more often than before the appellate courts in this country. The factual situations in which the Australian courts have held that a passenger injured by the 'negligence' of the driver in the course of a joint

---

1. [Dillon LJ stated ([1990] 3 All ER at pp. 363–364): 'In *Smith v Jenkins* (1970) 119 CLR 397 a group of four youths all about 16 years of age, who had been drinking, robbed a man, stole his car keys, and then, having found out where his car was, stole the car and drove it off on a joyride. The plaintiff was the first driver, but after a couple of changes of driver he was merely a passenger; a relatively few miles from the scene of the theft the car left the road at 80 or 90 mph and hit a tree. The plaintiff was seriously injured and sued the youth who had been the driver at the time of the accident; it was held that he could not recover anything.']

criminal enterprise cannot recover damages from the driver are clear. But the reasoning by which the Australian courts have reached their conclusions from common law principles is, to me, very much less clear, not least because of the extent to which the judgments in one particular decision of the High Court, *Smith v Jenkins* (1970) 119 CLR 397, have been reinterpreted in later decisions of the High Court. There is also the problem of how the Australian approach, purportedly based on common law principles, is reconcilable with certain recent developments in the English courts, also purportedly based on common law principles, in cases to which the judge below was not referred.

It is clear for a start that the fact that a plaintiff was engaged in an illegal activity which brought about his injury does not automatically bring it about that his claim for damages for personal injury as a result of the negligence of the defendant must be dismissed. (See eg *Baker v Market Harborough Industrial Co-op Society Ltd* [1953] 1 WLR 1472, where, as in many cases, the court apportioned liability for a road accident which had been caused by each driver, independently, driving negligently and without due care and attention . . .) . . .

So much is common ground between the parties, but it raises questions which have been the subject of discussion in English and Australian judgments whether a line can be drawn between different grades of illegality, and whether there is a distinction, and if so, on what ground, between the ordinary case of negligence, albeit involving a criminal act . . . and cases where a passenger sues the driver for injuries sustained by reckless driving at the time of the accident when they were both engaged in a joint criminal enterprise of which the reckless driving was an inherent part.

Counsel for the plaintiff founds on certain recent authorities in this country which he relied on as establishing a 'conscience test' to be applied in cases of illegality.

The starting point is the judgment of Hutchison J in *Thackwell v Barclays Bank plc* [1986] 1 All ER 676. In that case the plaintiff claimed damages from the bank for having paid a cheque drawn in favour of the plaintiff to a third party in reliance on a forgery of the plaintiff's signature on an indorsement of the cheque. The claim was rejected on the ground that the cheque represented the proceeds of a fraud on a fourth party, to which the plaintiff, the drawer of the cheque and the forger of the indorsement were all parties. Hutchison J treated the case as one in which public policy would prevent the plaintiff suing just as it would prevent a burglar from whom the stolen goods were snatched by a third party just as the burglar left the victim's house from maintaining an action in conversion against the third party. The judge in reaching that conclusion seems to have accepted a submission from counsel for the defendants that there were two distinct but related lines of authority running through the cases on illegality, the second of which laid down the 'conscience test'. That test was put as follows (at 678):

'That test, he suggested, involved the court looking at the quality of the illegality relied on by the defendant and all the surrounding circumstances, without fine distinctions and seeking to answer two questions: first, whether there had been illegality of which the court should take notice and, second, whether in all the circumstances it would be an affront to the public conscience if by affording him the relief sought the court was seen to be indirectly assisting or encouraging the plaintiff in his criminal act.'

The context in which that submission was put forward in *Thackwell v Barclays Bank plc* [1986] 1 All ER 676 seems to have been one of the proximity of the illegality to the matters of which complaint was made in the action. There is authority in *Sajan Singh v Sardara Ali* [1960] 1 All ER 269, [1960] AC 167 that a person who has acquired property under an illegal contract and has been using it without a permit can none the less maintain an action for damages for conversion against a person, even the vendor of the property, who subsequently, on the facts some three or four years later, wrongly deprives him of that property. The suggestion seems to have been in *Thackwell v Barclays Bank plc* that it would be an affront to the public conscience to allow one thief to maintain an action because a second of the thieves had stolen the first's share in the course of the division of the swag.

The conscience test was approved by this court in *Saunders v Edwards* [1987] 2 All ER 651, [1987] 1 WLR 1116. That was again a case of the proximity, or relevance, of the illegality to the matters of which the plaintiff was complaining. The plaintiff claimed damages for fraudulent misrepresentation, which had induced him to purchase a flat from the defendant. The defendant sought unsuccessfully to defend himself by asserting that the contract for the sale of the flat, and presumably also the conveyance, were tainted with illegality in that in the apportionment of the purchase price in the contract between chattels and the flat itself the amount attributable to the chattels had been fraudulently inflated, and the amount attributable to the flat had been correspondingly reduced, in order to reduce the stamp duty payable to the Revenue. This court applied Hutchison J's test, to which Nicholls LJ added to the end of the formulation the words 'or encouraging others in similar criminal acts' (see [1987] 2 All ER 651 at 664, [1987] 1 WLR 1116 at 1132).

Saunders v Edwards was, it seems to me, a case where the alleged illegality over the stamp duty apportionment was independent of, or unrelated to, the wrong in the way of fraudulent misrepresentation for which the plaintiff was suing. Kerr LJ decided the case, however, on the basis that the cases 'show that there are no rigid rules for or against the ex turpi causa defence' and that the cases 'show that the conduct and relative moral culpability of the parties may be relevant in determining whether or not the ex turpi causa defence falls to be applied as a matter of public policy (see [1987] 2 All ER 651 at 660, [1987] 1 WLR 1116 at 1127). Bingham LJ used rather different language where he said ([1987] 2 All ER 651 at 666, [1987] 1 WLR 1116 at 1134):

'. . . I think that on the whole the courts have tended to adopt a pragmatic approach to those problems, seeking where possible to see that genuine wrongs are righted so long as the court does not thereby promote or countenance a nefarious object or bargain which it is bound to condemn. Where the plaintiff's action in truth arises directly ex turpi causa, he is likely to fail . . . Where the plaintiff has suffered a genuine wrong, to which allegedly unlawful conduct is incidental, he is likely to succeed . . .'

That passage was adopted by Kerr LJ in giving the leading judgment of this court in *Euro-Diam Ltd v Bathurst* [1988] 2 All ER 23 at 29, [1990] 1 QB 1 at 36. The latter part of it is sufficient to cover the decision in *Saunders v Edwards* [1987] 2 All ER 651, [1987] 1 WLR 1116.

I find a test that depends on what would or would not be an affront to the public conscience very difficult to apply, since the public conscience may well be affected by factors of an emotional nature, eg that these boys by their reckless and criminal behaviour happened to do no harm to anyone but themselves. Moreover, if the public conscience happened to think that the plaintiff should be compensated for his injuries it might equally think that the deceased driver of the motor cycle, had he survived and merely been injured, ought to be compensated, and that leads into the much-debated question whether there ought to be a universal scheme for compensation for the victims of accidents without regard to fault.

Beyond that, appeal to the public conscience would be likely to lead to a graph of illegalities according to moral turpitude, and I am impressed by the comments of Mason J in *Jackson v Harrison* (1978) 138 CLR 438 at 455, where he said:

'. . . there arises the difficulty, which I regard as insoluble, of formulating a criterion which would separate cases of serious illegality from those which are not serious. Past distinctions drawn between felonies and misdemeanours, malum in se and malum prohibitum, offences punishable by imprisonment and those which are not, non-statutory and statutory offences offer no acceptable discrimen.'

Bingham LJ's dichotomy between cases where the plaintiff's action in truth arises directly ex turpi causa and cases where the plaintiff has suffered a genuine wrong to which allegedly unlawful conduct is incidental avoids this difficulty, in that it does not involve grading illegalities according to moral turpitude.

In the Australian courts it was held by the High Court of Australia in *Jackson v Harrison* that the maxim ex turpi causa is a maxim of the law of contract which cannot apply in the law of tort. This however is, as it seems to me, a matter of terminology and in the present case rather a red herring. The most commonly cited anglicisation of the maxim is that of Lord Mansfield CJ in *Holman v Johnson* (1775) 1 Cowp 341 at 343, [1775-1802] All ER Rep 98 at 99 that 'No Court will lend its aid to a man who founds his cause of action upon an immoral or an illegal act'. Whether that is or is not (see per Windeyer J in *Smith v Jenkins* (1970) 119 CLR 397 at 412) a correct translation of the maxim is now beside the point since it has been applied continuously as the law of England for over 200 years. Moreover, it has been so applied not only in cases where the cause of action has been laid in contract, but also in cases, such as *Chettiar v Chettiar* [1962] 1 All ER 494, [1962] AC 294, where it was held that a person who was party to an illegal transaction could not be heard to claim that that transaction had given rise to an enforceable trust in his favour. (See also *Re Emery's Investment's Trusts, Emery v Emery* [1959] 1 All ER 577, [1959] Ch 410.)

That a defence of illegality can be pleaded to a case founded in tort is, in my judgment, clear, whether or not the defence is correctly called ex turpi causa. *Thackwell v Barclays Bank plc* [1986] 1 All ER 676 is one instance. Another is *Murphy v Culhane* [1976] 3 All ER 533, [1977] QB 94 [p. 594, post] . . .

[His Lordship went on to examine various Australian authorities (*Smith v Jenkins* (1970) 119 CLR 397; *Bondarenko v Sommers* (1968) 69 SR (NSW) 269; *Jackson v Harrison* (1978) 138 CLR 438; and *Progress and Properties Ltd v Craft* (1976) 135 CLR 651) and continued:] The distillation of the law by the High Court of Australia rests . . . now on the judgment of Jacobs J, with which the other members of the majority of the court concurred, in *Progress and Properties Ltd v Craft* and in the judgments of Mason and Jacobs JJ with whom Aicken J concurred in *Jackson v Harrison* (1978) 138 CLR 438. For relief to be derived on the ground of the illegality, the circumstances of the joint illegal venture in the course of which the accident which caused the plaintiff's injuries occurred must be such as to negate, as between the two of them, any ordinary standard of care. Thus Mason J said in *Jackson v Harrison* (at 456):

'A plaintiff will fail when the joint illegal enterprise in which he and the defendant are engaged is such that the court cannot determine the particular standard of care to be observed,'

And Jacobs J said in *Progress and Properties Ltd v Craft* (1976) 135 CLR 651 at 668:

'Where there is a joint illegal activity the actual act of which the plaintiff in a civil action may be complaining as done without care may itself be a criminal act of a kind in respect of which a court is not prepared to hear evidence for the purpose of establishing the standard of care which was reasonable in the circumstances.'

This formulation would clearly cover . . . the reckless driving, to escape capture, of the getaway car after a robbery as in the English case of *Ashton v Turner* [1980] 3 All ER 870, [1981] QB 137. It was regarded in *Jackson v Harrison* as also covering the factual situations in *Bondarenko v Sommers* (1968) 69 SR (NSW) 269, where there was, in the words of Mason J in *Jackson v Harrison* 138 CLR 438 at 456, 'an agreement to drive the [stolen] car recklessly' for the purpose of racing on the highway, and the factual situation in *Smith v Jenkins* [see note 1, p. 394, ante]. In reference to *Smith v Jenkins*, Jacobs J said in *Jackson v Harrison* 138 CLR 438 at 460:

'It was a jaunt, an escapade, a joy-ride even though of a most serious kind from the beginning to the end. How could a standard of care be determined for such a course of criminal activity?'

I feel unable to draw any valid distinction between the reckless riding of the motor cycle in the present case by the deceased boy, Hunt, and the plaintiff under the influence of drink, and the reckless driving of the cars, albeit stolen, in *Smith v Jenkins* and *Bondarenko v Sommers*. The words of Barwick CJ in *Smith v Jenkins* (1970) 119 CLR 397 at 399–400:

'The driving of the car by the appellant, the manner of which is the basis of the respondent's complaint, was in the circumstances as much a use of the car by the respondent as it was a use by the appellant. That use was their joint enterprise of the moment.'

apply with equal force to the riding of the motor cycle in the present case. This is a case in which, in Bingham LJ's words, the plaintiff's action in truth arises directly *ex turpi causa*. . . .

[BELDAM LJ delivered a judgment in favour of dismissing the appeal.]

Appeal dismissed

Question

What purpose was served by denying the plaintiff a remedy in *Pitts v Hunt*? Was it deterrence, punishment or some other purpose? (See T. Hervey (1981) 97 LQR 537 at 539 commenting on the earlier decision of *Ashton v Turner* [1981] QB 137; [1980] 3 All ER 870.)

Notes

1. In *Pitts v Hunt* the third member of the court (Beldam LJ) seemed to apply the 'public conscience' test on which see the comments in the extracts from *Pitts v Hunt* and see p. 399, post. His primary source for public policy was legislation relating to the use of motor vehicles, supplemented by the reasoning of those decisions in which courts had refused to enforce rights in this sphere. If, for example, public policy would bar a claim by a driver to indemnity under a policy which he is obliged to take out for a passenger's benefit, then in his opinion a passenger, jointly guilty of the offence, was barred by public policy from recovering damages. Beldam LJ went on to rule that the claim was barred in the circumstances of this case, but he was not prepared to decide what degree of seriousness was required in an offence before recovery would be denied. For Beldam LJ decisions in other jurisdictions were merely secondary guidance for finding public policy.

2. *Pitts v Hunt* has already been mentioned in relation to volenti and the Road Traffic Act 1988: see p. 389, ante. In the present context it should also

be said that the case decided that s. 148(3) of the Road Traffic Act 1972 (now re-enacted as s. 149 of the Road Traffic Act 1988) does not affect the defence of illegality. 'The words "agreement or understanding" in section 148(3) do not contemplate an illegal agreement, express or tacit, to carry out an illegal purpose . . .' [1990] 3 All ER at p. 366 per Dillon LJ with whom Balcombe LJ agreed.

3. For argument as to the precise scope of the difference between the approach in *Smith v Jenkins* (1970) 44 ALJR 78 and *Jackson v Harrison* (1978) 148 CLR 438 (two of the High Court of Australia decisions which were considered in *Pitts v Hunt*), see J. Swanton (1981) 9 Sydney LR 304 at 317–322.

4. What is the conduct which may bar an action? The commission of a tort appears to be insufficient: see *Salmond & Heuston*'s reference, p. 569, to the common law position of trespassers (p. 461, post). On the other hand, it has been stated that the conduct in question does not necessarily have to be illegal: see *Kirkham v Chief Constable of the Greater Manchester Police* [1990] 3 All ER 246; [1990] 2 WLR 987, noted p. 400, post and see the summary of *Euro-Diam Ltd v Bathurst* [1990] 1 QB 1; [1988] 2 All ER 23 post. In *Kirkham* Lloyd LJ (cf. Farquharson LJ — Sir Denys Buckley agreed with both judgments) expressly relied for this view on *Thackwell v Barclays Bank Ltd* [1986] 1 All ER 676, *Saunders v Edwards* [1987] 2 All ER 651; [1987] 1 WLR 1116 and *Euro-Diam Ltd v Bathurst*. These cases support what is termed the 'public conscience test', on which see the comments in the extract from *Pitts v Hunt* ante and see post.

Crimes are an obvious category to which the defence might apply, but not all crimes are sufficient to stop the plaintiff from recovering damages. A breach of statutory duty by the plaintiff may or may not be a crime (see *R v Horseferry Road Justices, ex p. Independent Broadcasting Authority* [1987] QB 54; [1986] 2 All ER 666); but, whether or not it is a crime, a breach of a statutory duty imposed for the plaintiff's safety will not bar his claim (*National Coal Board v England* [1954] AC 403; [1954] 1 All ER 546). Note in particular that s. 4 of the Law Reform (Contributory Negligence) Act 1945 (p. 358, ante) includes breach of statutory duty in its definition of 'fault' and which therefore is merely a ground for reducing damages: this suggests that Parliament did not intend it to be an absolute bar.

5. Whether or to what extent the English courts follows the 'public conscience' test in the light of the judgments of Balcombe and Dillon LJJ in *Pitts v Hunt* remains to be seen. In *Howard v Shirlstar Container Transport Ltd* [1990] 3 All ER 366; [1990] 1 WLR 1292, a contract case, Staughton LJ referred to another contract case (*Euro-Diam Ltd v Bathurst* [1990] 1 QB 1; [1990] 2 All ER 23, mentioned ante) in which the Court of Appeal had seemingly regarded the 'public conscience' test as applicable to *both* contract and tort claims. Staughton LJ commented (at p. 371):

'I turn . . . to . . . the effect of illegality under a contract of English domestic law. This was dealt with in three propositions by Kerr LJ in the *Euro-Diam* case [1988] 2 All ER 23 at 28–29, [1990] 1 QB 1 at 35. I can abbreviate them for present purposes. (1) The ex turpi causa defence rests on a principle of public policy. It applies where the plaintiff has been guilty of illegal (or immoral) conduct if in all the circumstances it would be an affront to the public conscience to grant the plaintiff relief, because the court would thereby appear to assist or encourage the plaintiff in his illegal conduct or to encourage others in similar acts, (2) The main situations where the defence will prima facie succeed are (i) where the plaintiff seeks, or is forced, to found his claim on an illegal contract or to plead illegality in order to support his claim, either in the statement of claim or in a reply; (ii) where the grant of relief to the plaintiff would enable him to benefit from his criminal conduct; (iii) where the situation is residually covered by the general principle in (i) above. (3) However, the ex turpi causa defence must be approached pragmatically and with caution, depending on the circumstances.

We were referred to *Pitts v Hunt* ... decided on 13 April. There Dillon LJ said that he did not find the 'public conscience' test satisfactory. ... However, Beldam LJ in that case recorded that, in *Saunders v Edwards* [1987] 2 All ER 651, [1987] 1 WLR 1116, the 'public conscience' test, first clearly set out by Hutchison J in *Thackwell v Barclays Bank plc* [1986] 1 All ER 676, was approved. We do not have a complete transcript of the judgments in that case, nor do we know whether the *Euro-Diam* case was cited. In the circumstances, it seems right to me for us to follow the judgment of Kerr LJ in the *Euro-Diam* case.'

(We now know, of course, that *Euro-Diam* was referred to in *Pitts v Hunt*: see p. 396, ante.) In the *Howard* case Taylor LJ thought that the correct approach to illegality was that set out in the *Thackwell* case as approved in *Saunders v Edwards* (see p. 396, ante). Lord Donaldson of Lymington MR agreed with both judgments. Although, as mentioned ante, the *Howard* case directly concerned contract, the views in it have implications for the position in tort. On the 'public conscience' test, consider further *Rance v Mid-Downs Health Authority* [1991] 1 All ER 801 at 823.

It should also be noted that, shortly before the decision of the Court of Appeal in *Pitts v Hunt*, another differently composed Court of Appeal had decided *Kirkham v Chief Constable of the Greater Manchester Police* [1990] 3 All ER 246; [1990] 2 WLR 987 which concerned a claim in relation to a suicide. In this case liability was established on the part of the police who were aware of the suicidal tendencies of the plaintiff's husband but who had not passed this information on to the prison authorities when he was handed over from police custody to them after being remanded in custody by a magistrates' court. (See p. 66, ante.) Did the fact of the suicide bar the claim? The Court of Appeal held that in the circumstances it did not. Lloyd LJ used the 'public conscience' test, although he would rather test the matter by asking whether to allow the action would 'shock the ordinary citizen'. Cf. Farquharson LJ's approach: Sir Denys Buckley agreed with both judgments. Previously, in *Hyde v Thameside Area Health Authority* (1986) 2 PN 26, Lord Denning MR had expressed the view that public policy should prevent a claim in relation to a suicide or attempted suicide. This was noted in *Kirkham*, but the Court of Appeal did not regard a claim related to a suicide as barred by public policy or the ex turpi causa maxim, at least (per Lloyd LJ) where the deceased was not in full possession of his mind, or where (per Farquharson LJ) a serious mental instability had been proved. The latter did, however, go so far as to acknowledge that the position might be different if the deceased had been wholly sane (and, as has already been mentioned, Sir Denys Buckley agreed with both judgments).

6. It seems that on the 'standard of care' approach the courts will not fix a standard of care even though it might be possible for them to do so (see Swanton, op cit, pp. 320–321). This raises the question as to how different

the 'standard of care' approach referred to in *Pitts v Hunt*, ante, and the
'public conscience' test really are (cf. Swanton, op cit, p. 322). Is the reason
for not fixing a standard of care anything other than that to fix the standard
of care in these cases would offend the public conscience? Another point to
consider is how far the 'standard of care' approach can apply outside the tort
of negligence. The defence under consideration in this section has been
raised in other torts. For an example of its potential use in a different tort
see *Murphy v Culhane* [1977] QB 94; [1976] 3 All ER 533 (p. 594, post) and
see the discussion of *Thackwell v Barclays Bank plc* [1986] 1 All ER 676 and
Saunders v Edwards [1987] 2 All ER 651; [1987] 1 WLR 1116 in *Pitts v Hunt*
(pp. 395–396, ante). Consider further *Shelley v Paddock* [1980] QB 348;
[1980] 1 All ER 1009 where the plea failed (the notion of the innocent plaintiff not being in pari delicto with the defendants was brought into play). Note
also in *Murphy v Culhane* Lord Denning's suggestion that a burglar who was
shot by a householder might be met by a plea of ex turpi (though compare
the case reported (1983) Times, 30th September) and see further his similar
opinion in *Cummings v Granger* [1977] QB 397; [1977] 1 All ER 104 (p. 527,
post) concerning a burglar bitten by a guard dog. These examples are cited
by *Winfield & Jolowicz*, pp. 699–700, in relation to the situation where there
is no joint participation in the illegality. See also the comment in *Winfield
& Jolowicz*, p. 700, on *Marshall v Osmond* [1983] QB 1034; [1983] 2 All ER
225, noted p. 263, ante, and *Meah v McCreamer (No. 2)* [1986] 1 All ER 943.
Consider further *Thackwell v Barclays Bank plc*.

7. For an example of what might be thought to be the harsh effects the
application of this defence can have, see *Burns v Edman* [1970] 2 QB 541;
[1970] 1 All ER 886. In this case, in which a person had been killed in a motor
accident, Crichton J thought it was a 'fair inference' that the support given
by the deceased to his family had come from the proceeds of crime. In this
situation the judge accepted an argument that in the Fatal Accidents Act
claims the injury (i.e. loss of support) to each defendant, who included the
deceased's children, was 'turpis causa' and hence irrecoverable. Could there
have been an action if the deceased in *Burns v Edman* had stolen a bottle of
ginger beer for consumption by his children and they had been injured by
a decomposed snail in the bottle? (This question is suggested by D. E. C.
Yale [1970] CLJ 17 in his comment on the case).

In *Kirkham v Chief Constable of the Greater Manchester Police* [1990] 3
All ER 246; [1990] 2 WLR 987 Farquharson LJ stated that he did not need
to decide whether a claim by a spouse arising from a suicide would be barred
by the ex turpi causa maxim, and Sir Denys Buckley was not satisfied that
a dependant's claim under the Fatal Accidents Act would be barred by any
'turpitude' by the deceased. Are these views distinguishable from *Burns v
Edman*? Can Sir Denys Buckley's view be squared with the point (see pp. 243
and 422, ante) that the dependants cannot sue if the deceased did not have
an action at his death?

8. For discussion of this area of the law, see N. H. Crago (1963–4) 4 Melb
ULR 534; G. H. L. Fridman (1972) 18 McGill LJ 275; E. J. Weinrib (1976)
26 Univ Tor LJ 28; W. J. Ford (1977) 11 Melb ULR 33; Swanton, op cit; C.
Debattista (1984) 13 Anglo-American LR 15.

8 Assessment of damages

1 The aims of an award of damages

Cassell & Co Ltd *v* **Broome** House of Lords [1972] 1 All ER 801

[For the facts and the assessment of damages in defamation cases see chap. 16, p. 790, post.]

LORD HAILSHAM: . . . Of all the various remedies available at common law, damages are the remedy of most general application at the present day, and they remain the prime remedy in actions for breach of contract and tort. They have been defined as 'the pecuniary compensation, obtainable by success in an action, for a wrong which is either a tort or a breach of contract'. They must normally be expressed in a single sum to take account of all the factors applicable to each cause of action. . . .[1]

In almost all actions for breach of contract, and in many actions for tort, the principle of restitutio in integrum is an adequate and fairly easy guide to the estimation of damage, because the damage suffered can be estimated by relation to some material loss. It is true that where loss includes a pre-estimate of future losses, or an estimate of past losses which cannot in the nature of things be exactly computed, some subjective element must enter in. But the estimate is in things commensurable with one another. . . .

In many torts, however, the subjective element is more difficult. The pain and suffering endured, and the future loss of amenity, in a personal injuries case are not in the nature of things convertible into legal tender. . . . Nor, so far as I can judge, is there any purely rational test by which a judge can calculate what sum, greater or smaller, is appropriate. What is surprising is not that there is difference of opinion about such matters, but that in most cases professional opinion gravitates so closely to a conventional scale. Nevertheless, in all actions in which damages, purely compensatory in character, are awarded for suffering, from the purely pecuniary point of view the plaintiff may be better off. The principle of restitutio in integrum, which compels the use of money as its sole instrument for restoring the status quo, necessarily involves a factor larger than any pecuniary loss. . . .

. . . This brings me to the question of terminology. It has been more than once pointed out the language of damages is more than usually confused. For instance, the term 'special damage' is used in more than one sense to denominate actual past losses precisely calculated (as in a personal injuries action), or 'material damage actually suffered' as in describing the factor necessary to give rise to the cause of action in cases, including cases of slander, actionable only on proof of special damage'. If it is not too deeply embedded in our legal language, I would like to see 'special damage' dropped as a term of art in its latter sense and some phrase like 'material loss' substituted. But a similar ambiguity occurs in actions of defamation, the expressions 'at large', 'punitive', 'aggravated', 'retributory', 'vindictive' and

---

1. *Mayne and McGregor on Damages*, 12th edn, para. 1.

'exemplary' having been used in, as I have pointed out, inextricable confusion.

In my view it is desirable to drop the use of the phrase 'vindictive' damages altogether, despite its use by the county court judge in *Williams v Settle*.[1] Even when a purely punitive element is involved, vindictiveness is not a good motive for awarding punishment. In awarding 'aggravated' damages the natural indignation of the court at the injury inflicted on the plaintiff is a perfectly legitimate motive in making a generous rather than a more moderate award to provide an adequate solatium. But that is because the injury to the plaintiff is actually greater and as the result of the conduct exciting the indignation demands a more generous solatium. Likewise the use of 'retributory' is objectionable because it is ambiguous. It can be used to cover both aggravated damages to compensate the plaintiff and punitive or exemplary damages purely to punish the defendant or hold him up as an example.

As between 'punitive' or 'exemplary', one should, I would suppose, choose one to the exclusion of the other, since it is never wise to use two quite interchangeable terms to denote the same thing. Speaking for myself, I prefer 'exemplary', not because 'punitive' is necessarily inaccurate, but 'exemplary' better expresses the policy of the law as expressed in the cases. It is intended to teach the defendant and others that 'tort does not pay' by demonstrating what consequences the law inflicts rather than simply to make the defendant suffer an extra penalty for what he has done, although that does, of course, precisely describe its effect.

The expression 'at large' should be used in general to cover all cases where awards of damages may include elements for loss of reputation, injured feelings, bad or good conduct by either party, or punishment, and where in consequence no precise limit can be set in extent. It would be convenient if, as the appellants' counsel did at the hearing, it could be extended to include damages for pain and suffering or loss of amenity. Lord Devlin uses the term in this sense in *Rookes v Barnard*,[2] when he defines the phrase as meaning all cases where 'the award is not limited to the pecuniary loss that can be specifically proved'. But I suspect that he was there guilty of a neologism. If I am wrong, it is a convenient use and should be repeated.

Finally, it is worth pointing out, although I doubt if a change of terminology is desirable or necessary, that there is danger in hypostatising 'compensatory', 'punitive', 'exemplary' or 'aggravated' damages at all. The epithets are all elements or considerations which may, but with the exception of the first need not, be taken into account in assessing a single sum. They are not separate heads to be added mathematically to one another. . . .

LORD REID: . . . Damages for any tort are or ought to be fixed at a sum which will compensate the plaintiff, so far as money can do it, for all the injury which he has suffered. Where the injury is material and has been ascertained it is generally possible to assess damages with some precision. But that is not so where he has been caused mental distress or when his reputation has been attacked—where to use the traditional phrase he has been held up to hatred, ridicule or contempt. Not only is it impossible to ascertain how far other people's minds have been affected, it is almost impossible to equate the damage to a sum of money. Any one person trying to fix a sum as compensation will probably find in his mind a wide bracket within which any sum could be regarded by him as not unreasonable—and different people will come to different conclusions. So in the end there will probably be a wide gap between the sum which on an objective view could be regarded as the least and the sum which could be regarded as the most to which the plaintiff is entitled as compensation.

It has long been recognised that in determining what sum within that bracket should be awarded, a jury, or other tribunal, is entitled to have regard to the conduct of the defendant. He may have behaved in a high-handed, malicious, insulting or

---

1. [1960] 2 All ER 806.
2. [1964] AC 1129 at 1221; [1964] 1 All ER 367 at 407.

oppressive manner in committing the tort or he or his counsel may at the trial have aggravated the injury by what they there said. That would justify going to the top of the bracket and awarding as damages the largest sum that could fairly be regarded as compensation.

Frequently in cases before *Rookes v Barnard*[1] when damages were increased in that way but were still within the limit of what could properly be regarded as compensation to the plaintiff, it was said that punitive, vindictive or exemplary damages were being awarded. As a mere matter of language that was true enough. The defendant was being punished or an example was being made of him by making him pay more than he would have had to pay if his conduct had not been outrageous. But the damages although called punitive were still truly compensatory; the plaintiff was not being given more than his due.

On the other hand when we came to examine the old cases we found a number which could not be explained in that way. The sums awarded as damages were more — sometimes much more — than could on any view be justified as compensatory and courts, perhaps without fully realising what they were doing, appeared to have permitted damages to be measured not by what the plaintiff was fairly entitled to receive but by what the defendant ought to be made to pay as punishment for his outrageous conduct. That meant that the plaintiff, by being given more than on any view could be justified as compensation, was being given a pure and undeserved windfall at the expense of the defendant, and that insofar as the defendant was being required to pay more than could possibly be regarded as compensation he was being subjected to pure punishment.

I thought and still think that that is highly anomalous. It is confusing the function of the civil law which is to compensate with the function of the criminal law which is to inflict deterrent and punitive penalties. Some objection has been taken to the use of the word 'fine' to denote the amount by which punitive or exemplary damages exceed anything justly due to the plaintiff. In my view the word 'fine' is an entirely accurate description of that part of any award which goes beyond anything justly due to the plaintiff and is purely punitive.

Those of us who sat in *Rookes v Barnard*[1] thought that the loose and confused use of words like 'punitive' and 'exemplary' and the failure to recognise the difference between damages which are compensatory and damages which go beyond that and are purely punitive had led to serious abuses, so we took what we thought was the best course open to us to limit those abuses. Theoretically we might have held that as purely punitive damages had never been sanctioned by any decision of this House (as to which I shall say more later) there was no right under English law to award them. But that would have been going beyond the proper function of this House. There are many well established doctrines of the law which have not been the subject of any decision by this House. We thought we had to recognise that it had become an established custom in certain classes of case to permit awards of damages which could not be justified as compensatory, and that that must remain the law. But we thought and I still think it well within the province of this House to say that that undesirable anomaly should not be permitted in any class of case where its use was not covered by authority. In order to determine the classes of case in which this anomaly had become established it was of little use to look merely at the words which had been used by the judges because, as I have said, words like 'punitive' and 'exemplary' were often used with regard to damages which were truly compensatory. We had to take a broad view of the whole circumstances.

I must now deal with those parts of Lord Devlin's speech which have given rise to difficulties. He set out two categories of cases which in our opinion comprised all or virtually all the reported cases in which it was clear that the court had approved of an award of a larger sum of damages than could be justified as compensatory. Critics

---

1. [1964] AC 1129; [1964] 1 All ER 367.

appear to have thought that he was inventing something new. That was not my understanding. We were confronted with an undesirable anomaly. We could not abolish it. We had to choose between confining it strictly to classes of cases where it was firmly established, although that produced an illogical result, or permitting it to be extended so as to produce a logical result. In my view it is better in such cases to be content with an illogical result than to allow any extension.

It will be seen that I do not agree with Lord Devlin's view that in certain classes of case exemplary damages serve a useful purpose in vindicating the strength of the law. That view did not form an essential step in his argument. Concurrence with the speech of a colleague does not mean acceptance of every word which he has said. If it did there would be far fewer concurrences than there are. So I did not regard disagreement on this side issue as preventing me from giving my concurrence.

I think that the objections to allowing juries to go beyond compensatory damages are overwhelming. To allow pure punishment in this way contravenes almost every principle which has been evolved for the protection of offenders. There is no definition of the offence except that the conduct punished must be oppressive, high-handed, malicious, wanton or its like — terms far too vague to be admitted to any criminal code worthy of the name. There is no limit to the punishment except that it must not be unreasonable. The punishment is not inflicted by a judge who has experience and at least tries not to be influenced by emotion; it is inflicted by a jury without experience of law or punishment and often swayed by considerations which every judge would put out of his mind. And there is no effective appeal against sentence. All that a reviewing court can do is to quash the jury's decision if it thinks the punishment awarded is more than any 12 reasonable men could award. The court cannot substitute its own award. The punishment must then be decided by another jury and if they too award heavy punishment the court is virtually powerless. It is no excuse to say that we need not waste sympathy on people who behave outrageously. Are we wasting sympathy on vicious criminals when we insist on proper legal safeguards for them? The right to give punitive damages in certain cases is so firmly embedded in our law that only Parliament can remove it. But I must say that I am surprised by the enthusiasm of Lord Devlin's critics in supporting this form of palm tree justice.

Lord Devlin's first category is set out in the passage where he said[1]:

'The first category is oppressive, arbitrary or unconstitutional action by the servants of the government. I should not extend this category — I say this with particular reference to the facts of this case — to oppressive action by private corporations or individuals.'

This distinction has been attacked on two grounds: first, that it only includes Crown servants and excludes others like the police who exercise governmental functions but are not Crown servants and, secondly, that it is illogical since both the harm to the plaintiff and the blameworthiness of the defendant may be at least equally great where the offender is a powerful private individual. With regard to the first I think that the context shows that the category was never intended to be limited to Crown servants. The contrast is between 'the government' and private individuals. Local government is as much government as national government, and the police and many other persons are exercising governmental functions. It was unnecessary in *Rookes v Barnard*[2] to define the exact limits of the category. I should certainly read it as extending to all those who by common law or statute are exercising functions of a governmental character.

The second criticism is I think misconceived. I freely admit that the distinction is illogical. The real reason for the distinction was, in my view, that the cases showed

---

1. [1964] AC at p. 1226; [1964] 1 All ER at p. 410.
2. [1964] AC 1129; [1964] 1 All ER 367.

that it was firmly established with regard to servants of 'the government' that damages could be awarded against them beyond any sum justified as compensation, whereas there was no case except one that was overruled where damages had been awarded against a private bully or oppressor to an amount that could not fairly be regarded as compensatory, giving to that word the meaning which I have already discussed. I thought that this House was therefore free to say that no more than that was to be awarded in future.

We are particularly concerned in the present case with the second category.[1] With the benefit of hindsight I think I can say without disrespect to Lord Devlin that it is not happily phrased. But I think the meaning is clear enough. An ill disposed person could not infrequently deliberately commit a tort in contumelious disregard of another's rights in order to obtain an advantage which would outweigh any compensatory damages likely to be obtained by his victim. Such a case is within this category. But then it is said, suppose he commits the tort not for gain but simply out of malice why should he not also be punished. Again I freely admit there is no logical reason. The reason for excluding such a case from the category is simply that firmly established authority required us to accept this category however little we might like it, but did not require us to go farther. If logic is to be preferred to the desirability of cutting down the scope for punitive damages to the greatest extent that will not conflict with established authority then this category must be widened. But as I have already said I would, logic or no logic, refuse to extend the right to inflict exemplary damages to any class of case which is not already clearly covered by authority. On that basis I support this category. . . .

Notes

1. The categories in which Lord Devlin in *Rookes v Barnard* [1964] 1 All ER at p. 410, thought that exemplary damages could serve a useful purpose 'in vindicating the strength of the law' were as follows:

'The first category is oppressive, arbitrary or unconstitutional action by the servants of the government. I should not extend this category—I say this with particular reference to the facts of this case—to oppressive action by private corporations or individuals. Where one man is more powerful than another, it is inevitable that he will try to use his power to gain his ends; and if his power is much greater than the other's, he might perhaps be said to be using it oppressively. If he uses his power illegally, he must of course pay for his illegality in the ordinary way; but he is not to be punished simply because he is the more powerful. In the case of the government it is different, for the servants of the government are also the servants of the people and the use of their power must always be subordinate to their duty of service. It is true that there is something repugnant about a big man bullying a small man and very likely the bullying will be a source of humiliation that makes the case one for aggravated damages, but it is not in my opinion punishable by damages.

Cases in the second category are those in which the defendant's conduct has been calculated by him to make a profit for himself which may well exceed the compensation payable to the plaintiff. I have quoted the dictum of Erle CJ, in *Bell v Midland Rly Co*,[2] Maule J in *Williams v Currie*[3] suggests the same thing; and so does Martin B in an obiter dictum in *Crouch v Great Northern Rly Co*[4]. It is a factor also that is taken into account in damages for libel; one man should not be allowed to sell another man's reputation for profit. Where a defendant with a cynical disregard for a plaintiff's rights has calculated that the money to be made out of his wrongdoing will probably exceed

---

1. [See Note 1, post.]
2. (1861) 10 CBNS 287 at 304.
3. (1845) 1 CB 841 at 848.
4. (1856) 11 Exch 742 at 759.

the damages at risk, it is necessary for the law to show that it cannot be broken with impunity. This category is not confined to moneymaking in the strict sense. It extends to cases in which the defendant is seeking to gain at the expense of the plaintiff some object – perhaps some property which he covets – which either he could not obtain at all or not obtain except at a price greater than he wants to put down. Exemplary damages can properly be awarded whenever it is necessary to teach a wrongdoer that tort does not pay. To these two categories, which are established as part of the common law, there must of course be added any category in which exemplary damages are expressly authorised by statute.'

Only two (Viscount Dilhorne and Lord Wilberforce) of the seven Law Lords who heard *Cassell & Co Ltd v Broome* did not think that the principles as to when exemplary damages are appropriate laid down in *Rookes v Barnard*, were in general correct.

2. Lord Hailsham, [1972] 1 All ER 801 at 829–830, Lord Diplock (at p. 873) and Lord Kilbrandon (at p. 877) agreed with Lord Reid (ante) that the first category should not be limited to servants of the government in the strict sense, but should be extended to others exercising governmental functions. Awards under this category can be a useful means of defending civil liberties, particularly in cases of wrongful arrest. In *Holden v Chief Constable Lancashire* [1987] QB 380; [1986] 3 All ER 836 (where the plaintiff was unlawfully arrested and detained at a police station for about 20 minutes) the Court of Appeal held that wrongful arrest could fall within Lord Devlin's first category regardless of whether there was oppressive behaviour or aggravating circumstances. This case also decided that exemplary damages can be awarded where the defendant is liable only vicariously for the conduct of another person. Fairly substantial awards have been made against Chief Constables for the actions of police officers. For example in *Taylor v Metropolitan Police Comr* (1989) Times, 6th December, an award of £70,000 exemplary damages was made on top of awards of £10,000 for false imprisonment and £10,000 for malicious prosecution, and in *White v Metropolitan Police Comr* (1982) Times, 24th April, a West Indian couple were each awarded £20,000 exemplary damages on top of awards of £6,500 and £4,500 respectively for false imprisonment, assault and malicious prosecution. In the latter case the judge took account of the fact that the police conduct could 'do immense harm to race relations'. In *Alexander v Home Office* [1988] 2 All ER 118 at 123, May LJ could see no reason why exemplary damages should not be awarded for the statutory tort of unlawful racial discrimination. This has been followed by industrial tribunals, although the President of the Employment Appeal Tribunal has suggested that such awards are 'inappropriate and unnecessary' (*Bradford City Metropolitan Council v Arora* [1989] IRLR 442 at 446).

3. The rationale behind Lord Devlin's second category, according to Lord Diplock in *Rookes v Barnard* [1964] AC at p. 1129, is to prevent unjust enrichment of the defendant at the plaintiff's expense, rather than to punish. Arguably, the law of restitution would be better suited to this purpose than the law of tort: see Harris, *Remedies*, pp. 185-186. This category plainly covers cases where the defendant acted tortiously in order to obtain possession of property which he could not buy, as in *Drane v Evangelou* [1978] 2 All ER 437; [1978] 1 WLR 455. One may compare the Housing Act 1988, ss. 27-28, which measures the tenant's damages for unlawful eviction by the difference in value

between the premises with and without vacant possession. *Williams & Hepple*, pp. 74–75, argue that there is a general principle that exemplary damages may be awarded where, in Lord Devlin's words, 'it is necessary to teach a wrongdoer that tort does not pay'.

4. Awards of exemplary damages are most frequently encountered in cases of defamation (p. 790, post). In *Cassell v Broome* Lord Hailsham ([1972] 1 All ER at p. 828) and Lord Diplock (at p. 874) expressed the view that Lord Devlin's speech was not to be interpreted as extending the power to award exemplary damages in torts such as deceit and negligence where this had not previously been done: cf. *Archer v Brown* [1984] 2 All ER 267 at 277–281.

5. Lord Reid's approach to the aims of an award of damages may be compared with that of Lord Wilberforce who said ([1972] 1 All ER at p. 860):

'It cannot lightly be taken for granted, even as a matter of theory, that the purpose of the law of tort is compensation, still less that it ought to be, an issue of large social import, or that there is something inappropriate or illogical or anomalous (a question-begging word) in including a punitive element in civil damages, or, conversely, that the criminal law, rather than the civil law is in these cases the better instrument for conveying social disapproval, or for redressing a wrong to the social fabric; or that damages in any case can be broken down into two separate elements. As a matter of practice English law has not committed itself to either of these theories; it may have been wiser than it knew.'

6. Lord Hailsham ([1972]) 1 All ER at p. 828) suggested that where damages for loss of reputation are concerned, or where a simple outrage to person or property is concerned, *aggravated* damages are appropriate. These are regarded as compensatory and must bear a reasonable relation to the distress caused by the tort. In *Archer v Brown* [1985] QB 401; [1984] 2 All ER 267, £500 aggravated damages were awarded for deceit to compensate the plaintiff for his injured feelings. In cases of rape or sexual assault aggravated damages will be awarded, although in *W v Meah* [1986] 1 All ER 935, Woolf J emphasised that the award should be compensatory and should be related to awards in personal injury cases. The same judge held, in *Kralj v McGrath* [1986] 1 All ER 54, that aggravated damages were 'wholly inapppropriate' in a case of medical negligence where 'horrific and wholly unacceptable' treatment had caused the plaintiff 'excruciating pain'. Aggravated damages may be appropriate in cases of intentional commission of the statutory tort of racial discrimination: see *Alexander v Home Office* [1988] 2 All ER 118; [1988] 1 WLR 968. The line between exemplary damages and aggravated damages is not easy to draw, e.g. in *Ballard v Metropolitan Police Comr* (1983) 133 NLJ 1133 (Westminister County Court) aggravated damages of £400 were awarded because of the unjustified use of truncheons on women demonstrating against male violence; the judge stated that there were no circumstances in the case which would justify an award of exemplary damages.

Awards for injured feelings have been made for breach of contract (*Jarvis v Swans Tours Ltd* [1973] QB 233; [1973] 1 All ER 71) and for tort, although not as a separate item (*Ichard v Frangoulis* [1977] 2 All ER 461; [1977] 1 WLR 566) in respect of the loss of enjoyment of a holiday. In *Perry v Sidney Phillips & Son (a firm)* [1982] 3 All ER 705; [1982] 1 WLR 1297 damages were awarded in respect of the distress and discomfort caused by the negligent survey of a defective house. See further J. Murdoch (1989) 5 PN 52.

7. For general discussion see *Williams & Hepple*, pp. 73–78; Harris, *Remedies*, pp. 228–233; A. S. Burrows, *Remedies for Torts and Breach of Contract* (London, 1987), pp. 236–250; P. R. Ghandi (1990) 10 LS 182.

2 Personal injuries

Todorovic *v* Waller High Court of Australia (1981) 37 ALR 481

GIBBS CJ and WILSON J [in a joint judgment]: ... In the first place, a plaintiff who has been injured by the negligence of the defendant should be awarded such a sum of money as will, as nearly as possible, put him in the same position as if he had not sustained the injuries. Secondly, damages for one cause of action must be recovered once and forever, and (in the absence of any statutory exception) must be awarded as a lump sum; the court cannot order a defendant to make periodic payments to the plaintiff. Thirdly, the court has no concern with the manner in which the plaintiff uses the sum awarded to him; the plaintiff is free to do what he likes with it. Fourthly, the burden lies on the plaintiff to prove the injury or loss for which he seeks damages.

Although the aim of the court in awarding damages is to make good to the plaintiff, so far as money can do, the loss which he has suffered, it is obvious that it is impossible to assess damages for pain and suffering and loss of amenities of life by any process of arithmetical calculation. It may be less obvious, but is no less certain, that the assessment of damages for future pecuniary loss resulting from personal injuries can never be a mere matter of mathematics. It is true that as the assessment of damages has become more sophisticated, calculations are made in an attempt to achieve greater precision. Such calculations may sometimes give a false appearance of accuracy. Some of the figures on which they are based are the result of estimate or speculation. In the case of loss of earning capacity it is necessary to compare what the plaintiff might have earned if he had not suffered the injury with what he is likely to earn in his injured condition. In many cases this means that the court has to engage in 'a double exercise in the art of prophesying': *Paul v Rendell* (1981) 55 ALJR 371 at 372; 34 ALR 569 at 571. . . .

The difficulty inherent in the assessment of damages provides no reason for the courts to shirk the task of arriving at the estimate most likely to provide fair and reasonable compensation. But it may provide a reason for approaching with some caution a proposal to overturn an established method of assessment, in an attempt to achieve an accuracy which it is not humanly possible to attain. . . .

Lim Poh Choo *v* Camden and Islington Area Health Authority House of Lords [1979] 2 All ER 910

LORD SCARMAN: My Lords, on 28 February 1973 Dr Lim Poh Choo, a senior psychiatric registrar employed in the national health service, was admitted to a national health service hospital for a minor operation, which was carried out the next morning. When, following on the operation, she was in the recovery room, she suffered a cardiac arrest. It was the result of the negligence of some person for whom the area health authority is vicariously responsible. The consequences for Dr Lim have been disastrous. Before 1 March 1973 Dr Lim, who was then 36 years old, had a career ahead of her in her chosen speciality of psychiatric medicine. She was described by one who knew her and her work as a 'remarkably intelligent doctor'. She is now the wreck of a human being, suffering from extensive and irremediable brain damage, which has left her only intermittently, and then barely, sentient and totally dependent on others.

On 19 September 1974 Dr Lim, suing by her mother as next friend, issued her writ against the Camden and Islington Area Health Authority, who in due course delivered a defence denying negligence. However, in November 1977, shortly before trial, the defendants admitted liability. The one issue at trial was, therefore, the question of damages. But its complexities are such that it occupied the trial judge for the best part of five days, the Court of Appeal six days, and your Lordships' House five days.

It cannot be said that any of the time judicially spent on these protracted proceedings has been unnecessary. The question, therefore, arises whether the state of the law which gives rise to such complexities is sound. Lord Denning MR in the Court of Appeal declared that a radical reappraisal of the law is needed. I agree. But I part company with him on ways and means. Lord Denning MR believes it can be done by the judges, whereas I would suggest to your Lordships that such a reappraisal calls for social, financial, economic and administrative decisions which only the legislature can take. The perplexities of the present case, following on the publication of the report of the Royal Commission on Civil Liability and Compensation for Personal Injury (the Pearson report)[1], emphasise the need for reform of the law.

The course of the litigation illustrates, with devastating clarity, the insuperable problems implicit in a system of compensation for personal injuries which (unless the parties agree otherwise) can yield only a lump sum assessed by the court at the time of judgment. Sooner or later, and too often later rather than sooner, if the parties do not settle, a court (once liability is admitted or proved) has to make an award of damages. The award, which covers past, present and future injury and loss, must, under our law, be of a lump sum assessed at the conclusion of the legal process. The award is final; it is not susceptible to review as the future unfolds, substituting fact for estimate. Knowledge of the future being denied to mankind, so much of the award as is to be attributed to future loss and suffering (in many cases the major part of the award) will almost surely be wrong. There is really only one certainty: the future will prove the award to be either too high or too low. . . .

The judge awarded Dr Lim a total sum of £254,765. He apportioned it as follows:

(1) Pain, suffering, loss of amenities	£20,000	
Interest from date of writ	£5,930	£25,930
(2) Out-of-pocket expenses, including £680 for cost of stay at Tang Tock Seng Hospital and Singapore nursing home	£3,596	
(3) Cost of care to date of judgment: 40 months at £200 per month	£8,000	
(4) Interest on (2) and (3) from date of accident (1 March 1973) to judgment	£2,482	£14,078
(5) Loss of earnings to date of judgment	£14,213	
(6) Interest on (5) from date of accident to judgment	£3,044	£17,257
(7) Cost of future care:		
Malaysia, 7 years at £2,600 per annum discounted to:	£17,500	
England, 11 years at £8,000 per annum	£88,000	£105,500
(8) Loss of future earnings:		
14 years at £6,000	£84,000	
Loss of pension	£8,000	£92,000

---

1. March 1978, Cmnd. 7054.

On appeal to the Court of Appeal, the defendants attacked the award in many respects. . . .

(A) *The total of damages (£254,765)*

The submission that the total of the award was excessive was one of the broadest generality. Whether or not he can establish duplication or overlap or any other error in calculating the separate items of the award, counsel for the appellants submitted that an award of damages, being a 'jury question', must be fair to both sides, and that in a case such as the present a judge should bear in mind (a) comparable cases, (b) the effect of high awards on the level of insurance premiums or, if, as here, the taxpayer foots the bill, on the taxpayer, (c) the availability of care for the victim under the national health service and (d) public policy. Such generalities as that damages must be treated as a jury question and kept in line with public policy I do not find helpful. Their very breadth merely contributes to uncertainty and inconsistency in an area of the law, the history if not the present practice of which is notorious for both vices. Invoking the memory of the days when juries assessed damages for personal injuries does no more than remind us that the modern practice of reasoned awards by judges is a substantial advance on the inscrutable awards of juries. Of course, awards must be fair. But this means no more than that they must be a proper compensation for the injury suffered and the loss sustained. Nor in this case do I find helpful a comparison of one total award with another. In so far as an award consists of 'conventional' items, e.g. for pain and suffering, comparability with other awards is certainly of value in keeping the law consistent. But pecuniary loss depends on circumstances; and, where (as in the present case) such loss predominates, comparison with total awards in other cases does not help, and may be misleading.

The two specific matters counsel for the appellants mentioned, the burden on the public (through premiums or taxes) and the availability of national health service care, prove on examination to be for the legislator, not the judge. As to the first, the principle of the law is that compensation should as nearly as possible put the party who has suffered in the same position as he would have been in if he had not sustained the wrong (per Lord Blackburn in *Livingstone v Rawyards Coal Co*[1]). There is no room here for considering the consequences of a high award on the wrongdoer or those who finance him. And, if there were room for any such consideration, on what principle, or by what criterion, is the judge to determine the extent to which he is to diminish on this ground the compensation payable?

The second matter, though introduced by counsel for the appellants as part of his general submissions on the total award, is really one, as he recognised, which falls to be considered in assessing the cost of future care. It is convenient, however, to deal with it at this stage. Section 2(4) of the Law Reform (Personal Injuries) Act 1948 provides that in an action for damages for personal injuries there shall be disregarded, in determining the reasonableness of any expenses, the possibility of avoiding those expenses or part of them by taking advantage of facilities available in the national health service. In *Harris v Brights Asphalt Contractors Ltd*[2] Slade J said of the subsection:

'I think all [it] means is that, when an injured plaintiff in fact incurs expenses which are reasonable, that expenditure is not to be impeached on the ground that, if he had taken advantage of the facilities available under the National Health Service Act 1946, those reasonable expenses might have been avoided. I do not understand section 2(4) to enact that a plaintiff shall be deemed to be entitled to recover expenses which in fact he will never incur.'

---

1. (1880) 5 App Cas 25 at 39.
2. [1953] 1 QB 617 at 635.

In *Cunningham v Harrison*[1] the Court of Appeal expressed the same view, Lawton LJ[2] saying that a defendant can, notwithstanding the statute, submit that the plaintiff will probably not incur such expenses because he will be unable to obtain outside the national health service the domestic and nursing help which he requires.

I agree with Slade J and the Court of Appeal. It has not been suggested that expenses so far incurred in the care and treatment of Dr Lim have been unreasonable. They are, therefore, protected by the subsection. But it is open to serious question whether for the rest of her life it will continue to be possible to obtain for Dr Lim, outside the national health service, the domestic and nursing help she will require. However, Lord Denning MR and Lawton LJ both of whom were parties to the decision in *Cunningham v Harrison*[1], have proceeded in the instant case on the basis, which the trial judge must also have accepted, that it will be possible and that the expense of doing so is reasonable, in the absence of any evidence to the contrary, I am not prepared to take a different view, though I recognise the force of the case developed in the Pearson report[3] for legislation repealing the subsection.

The attack, therefore, on the total of damages awarded as being excessive, merely by reason of its size, fails. If the appellants are to succeed, they must show that one or more of the component items of the award are wrong.

(B) *The award for pain and suffering and loss of amenities*
Counsel for the appellants recognised, at the outset of his argument, that, if *Wise v Kaye*[4] and *H West & Son Ltd v Shephard*[5] were correctly decided, his first submission (that the sum awarded should be comparable with the small conventional awards in fatal cases for loss of expectation of life) must fail.

My Lords, I think it would be wrong now to reverse by judicial decision the two rules which were laid down by the majority of the House in *H West & Son Ltd v Shephard*[5], namely (1) that the fact of unconsciousness does not eliminate the actuality of the deprivation of the ordinary experiences and amenities of life (see the formulation used by Lord Morris of Borth-y-Gest[6]) and (2) that, if damages are awarded on a correct basis, it is of no concern to the court to consider any question as to the use that will thereafter be made of the money awarded. The effect of the two cases (*Wise v Kaye*[4] being specifically approved in *H West & Son Ltd v Shephard*[5]) is twofold. First, they draw a clear distinction between damages for pain and suffering and damages for loss of amenities. The former depend on the plaintiff's personal awareness of pain, her capacity for suffering. But the latter are awarded for the fact of deprivation, a substantial loss, whether the plaintiff is aware of it or not. Secondly, they establish that the award in *Benham v Gambling*[7] (assessment in fatal cases of damages for loss of expectation of life) is not to be compared with, and has no application to, damages to be awarded to a living plaintiff for loss of amenities.

I do not underrate the formidable logic and good sense of the minority opinions expressed in *Wise v Kaye*[4] and *H West & Son Ltd v Shephard*[5]. The quality of the minority opinions was, however, matched by the equally formidable logic and good sense of the majority opinions. The question on which opinions differed was, in truth, as old and as obstinate as the philosopher's stone itself. A decision having been taken by this House in 1963 (the year *H West & Son Ltd v Shephard*[5] was decided), its reversal would cause widespread injustice, unless it were to be part and parcel of a comprehensive reform of the law. For since 1962 settlements have proceeded on the

---

1. [1973] QB 942; [1973] 3 All ER 463.
2. [1973] QB 942 at 957; [1973] 3 All ER 463 at 473.
3. Cmnd. 7054-I, paras. 340–342.
4. [1962] 1 QB 638; [1962] 1 All ER 257.
5. [1964] AC 326; [1963] 2 All ER 625.
6. [1964] AC 326 at 349; [1963] 2 All ER 625 at 633.
7. [1941] AC 157; [1941] 1 All ER 7.

basis that the rule adopted in *Wise v Kaye*[1] was correct: and judges have had to assess damages on the same basis in contested cases. We are in the area of 'conventional' awards for non-pecuniary loss, where comparability matters. Justice requires that such awards continue to be consistent with the general level accepted by the judges. If the law is to be changed by the reversal of *H West & Son Ltd v Shephard*[2], it should be done not judicially but legislatively within the context of a comprehensive enactment dealing with all aspects of damages for personal injury.

I now come to the second submission for counsel for the appellants that, even if *H West & Son Ltd v Shephard*[2] be good law, the sum of £29,000 for Dr Lim's pain, suffering and loss of amenities was excessive. The answer to this submission is to be found in one stark but factually correct observation of Bristow J. He said[3]: 'Dr Lim's loss of the amenities of her good and useful life is total.' Accordingly, I think counsel for the appellants' attack on this head of the award fails.

I turn now to consider the respondent's submission that this award was too low. Counsel for the respondent took two points: first, that the judge underestimated Dr Lim's awareness of her condition and her loss; secondly, that bearing in mind the depreciation in the value of money since *Wise v Kaye*[1] and *H West & Son Ltd v Shephard*[2], an award of £20,000 was out of line with the sums awarded in those, and other, cases. Both Lawton and Browne LJJ were impressed by the first point. There are passages in the evidence which suggest that Dr Lim's awareness of her condition is greater and more sustained than the trial judge found. He relied on the conclusions formed by Dr MacQuaide, a very distinguished doctor, who on six occasions in 1976 examined Dr Lim in Penang. Dr MacQuaide found her emotional state to be blank, and that she was completely lacking in volition and spontaneity. He added that her powers of reasoning were impossible to test. I am not prepared to hold that the judge was wrong in his conclusion that 'she is so intellectually impaired that she does not appreciate what has happened to her'.

The second point also fails, in my judgment. An award for pain, suffering and loss of amenities is conventional in the sense that there is no pecuniary guideline which can point the way to a correct assessment. It is, therefore, dependent only in the most general way on the movement in money value. . . . [T]here will be a tendency in times or inflation for awards to increase, if only to prevent the conventional becoming the contemptible. . . . [A] '*West v Shephard*[2] award' . . . has been held by the House of Lords to be compensation for a substantial loss. As long, therefore as the sum awarded is a substantial sum in the context of current money values, the requirement of the law is met. A sum of £20,000 is, even today, a substantial sum. The judge cannot, therefore, be shown to have erred in principle, and his award must stand.

In making his assessment, the judge assumed his award would bear interest from the date of service of writ. Were it not to bear interest, he would have increased it by the amount of interest it would have carried so that it reflected the situation as it was at trial[3]. Since trial, this House has laid down in *Pickett v British Rail Engineering Ltd*[4] that awards for pain, suffering and loss of amenities should bear interest from date of service of writ. The judge's original figure of £20,000 represents therefore his assessment, in current money values at date of trial, of the plaintiff's loss as at date of service of writ, to which, following *Pickett*'s case[4], one must add the appropriate interest.

For these reasons I think the judge's award of £20,000 and interest for pain, suffering and loss of amenities should be upheld.

(C) *Loss of earnings, and duplication* (*overlap*)

The appellants' submission is brief and simple. In para. 8 of their case it was put in three short sentences:

---

1. [1962] 1 QB 638; [1962] 1 All ER 257.
2. [1964] AC 326; [1963] 2 All ER 625.
3. [1979] 1 QB 196 at 204; [1979] 1 All ER 322 at 338.
4. [1979] 1 All ER 774; [1978] 3 WLR 955.

'The Plaintiff ought not to have been awarded damages for loss of earnings as well as for loss of amenities and cost of care. The sum awarded for cost of care exceeded her estimated loss of earnings and *covered all her needs*. The additional award of damages for loss of earnings was duplicatory.'

As developed in argument, the submission was a twofold one. First, it was submitted that in catastrophic cases 'loss of earnings' does not reflect a real loss. Secondly, if damages are recoverable for loss of earnings, duplication with other heads of damage is to be avoided. The law must, therefore, ensure that no more is recovered for loss of earnings than what the plaintiff, if not injured, would have saved, or reserved for the support of his, or her, dependants. Since there was no evidence to suggest that Dr Lim would have accumulated any surplus income after meeting her working and living expenses, the trial judge's award for loss of earnings was wholly wrong.

The first submission is contrary to an established line of authority which, beginning with *Phillips v London and South Western Rly Co*[1], has recently received the seal of this House's approval in *Pickett v British Rail Engineering Ltd*[2]. It is also contrary to the principle of the common law that a genuine deprivation (be it pecuniary or non-pecuniary in character) is a proper subject of compensation. The principle was recognised both in *Phillip*'s case[3], where the loss was pecuniary, and in *H West & Son Ltd v Shephard*[4], where the loss was non-pecuniary.

The second submission is more formidable. Undoubtedly, the courts must be vigilant to avoid not only duplication of damages but the award of a surplus exceeding a true compensation for the plaintiff's deprivation or loss.

The separate items, which together constitute a total award of damages, are inter-related. They are the parts of a whole, which must be fair and reasonable. 'At the end', as Lord Denning MR said in *Taylor v Bristol Omnibus Co Ltd*[5], 'the judges should look at the total figure in the round, so as to be able to cure any overlapping or other source of error'. In most cases the risk of overlap is not great, nor, where it occurs, is it substantial. Living expenses continue, or progressively increase, for most plaintiffs after injury as they would have done if there had been no injury. But where, as in *Pickett*'s case[2], the plaintiff claims damages for the earnings of his 'lost years', or, as in the present case, the claim is in respect of a lifetime's earnings lost because, though she will live, she cannot earn her living, a real risk arises that the plaintiff may recover, not merely compensation for loss, which is the entitlement given by law, but a surplus greater than could have been achieved if there had been no death or incapacity. Two deductions, therefore, fall to be made from the damages to be awarded. First, as the cases have always recognised, the expenses of earning the income which has been lost. Counsel for the respondent conceded this much. Secondly, the plaintiff's living expenses. This is necessarily a hypothetical figure in the case of a 'lost years' claim, since the plaintiff does not survive to earn the money; and, since there is no cost of care claim (the plaintiff being assumed to be dead), it falls to be deducted from the loss of earnings award. But where, as in the present case, the expectancy of life is not shortened but incapacity exists, there will be a cost of care claim as well as a loss of earnings claim. How should living expenses be assessed and deducted in such a case? One approach, analogous to the method necessarily adopted in 'lost years' cases, would be to attempt an assessment of how much the plaintiff would have spent and on what, always a most speculative exercise. How, for instance, could anyone tell how Dr Lim would have ordered her standard of living, had she been able to pursue her career? Another approach is, however,

---

1. (1879) 5 CPD 280; [1874–80] All ER Rep 1176.
2. [1979] 1 All ER 774; [1978] 3 WLR 955.
3. (1879) 5 CPD 280 at 292; [1874–80] All ER Rep 1176 at 1181, per Brett LJ.
4. [1964] AC 326 at 349; [1963] 2 All ER 625 at 633, per Lord Morris.
5. [1975] 2 All ER 1107 at 1111; [1975] 1 WLR 1054 at 1057.

available in the case of a living plaintiff. In *Shearman v Folland*[1] the Court of Appeal deducted what has been described as the 'domestic element' from the cost of care. Inevitably, a surviving plaintiff has to meet her living expenses. This approach, being on the basis of a future actuality (subject to the uncertainties of life), is far less hypothetical than the former (which, faute de mieux, has to be adopted in 'lost years' cases). It is a simpler, more realistic, calculation and accords more closely with the general principle of the law that the courts in assessing compensation for loss are not concerned either with how the plaintiff would have used the moneys lost or how she (or he) will use the compensation received.

In the present case, my Lords, it is perfectly possible to estimate the domestic element in Dr Lim's cost of care. The estimated figure must, therefore, be deducted in the assessment of her damages for the cost of her care. In the result Dr Lim will recover in respect of her future loss a capital sum which, after all proper discounts, will represent her loss of earnings, net after allowing for working expenses, and her cost of care, net after deducting the domestic element. A capital sum so assessed will compensate for a genuine loss and for a genuine item of additional expenditure, both of which arise from the injury she has sustained. It will not contain any element of duplication or go beyond compensation into surplus.

A further argument was addressed to your Lordships in the context of duplication. It was urged that there was an overlap between the sum awarded for loss of amenities and that for loss of future earnings. The amenities which Dr Lim has lost, it was submitted, would have had to be provided out of her earnings. If, therefore, she is to be compensated for the former, she should suffer a deduction from her loss of earnings claim. Reliance was placed on the judgment of Diplock LJ in *Fletcher v Autocar and Transporters Ltd*[2].

The question whether there can be any overlap between damages for non-pecuniary loss and for pecuniary loss does not arise for decision on the facts of this case. As the majority of the Court of Appeal said, the amount of damages awarded to Dr Lim for loss of amenities was a modest sum. It was not assessed by reference to any expensive pleasures or pursuits such as Diplock LJ postulated in *Fletcher*'s case[3]. There was, indeed, no evidence to suggest that Dr Lim had, or was likely to develop, any such tastes or pursuits. There is, therefore, no duplication of damages between the two items in this case.

On the point of principle whether damages for non-pecuniary loss can properly be reduced to avoid an overlap with damages for pecuniary loss I express no final opinion. I confess, however, that I doubt the possibility of overlap; and I note that the Pearson Commission[4] considers it wrong in principle to reduce the one by reason of the size of the other.

(D) *Cost of future care* Both parties were agreed that damages under this head are recoverable. . . .

(E) *Effect of future inflation*
The trial judge said he made allowance for future inflation in the multiplier for cost of future care and in the multiplier for loss of future earnings. The Court of Appeal, in holding that he had made no mistake in principle, relied on a recent decision of this House, *Cookson v Knowles*[5]. In that case Lord Diplock[6] made the comment that

---

1. [1950] 2 KB 43; [1950] 1 All ER 976.
2. [1968] 2 QB 322 esp at 342; [1968] 1 All ER 726 esp at 737.
3. [1968] 2 QB 322 at 342; [1968] 1 All ER 726 at 737.
4. Report of the Royal Commission on Civil Liability and Compensation for Personal Injury (Cmnd. 7054–I), para. 759.
5. [1979] AC 556; [1978] 2 All ER 604.
6. [1978] 2 All ER 604 at 611; [1978] 2 WLR 978 at 986.

future inflation 'is taken care of in a rough and ready way' because the conventional multipliers applied by the judges assume a rate of interest of 4 per cent or 5 per cent, whereas actual rates of interest are much higher. Lord Fraser of Tullybelton[1] added the comment that in 'exceptional cases, where the [assumed] annuity is large enough to attract income tax at a high rate . . . it might be appropriate to increase the multiplier, or to allow for future inflation in some other way'. My Lords, I do not read these passages in the speeches in that case of my noble and learned friends as modifying the law in any way. The law appears to me to be now settled that only in exceptional cases, where justice can be shown to require it, will the risk of future inflation be brought into account in the assessment of damages for future loss. Of the several cases to this effect I would cite as of particular importance *Taylor v O'Connor*[2] and *Young v Percival*[3]. It is perhaps incorrect to call this rule a rule of law. It is better described as a sensible rule of practice, a matter of common sense. Lump sum compensation cannot be a perfect compensation for the future. An attempt to build into it a protection against future inflation is seeking after a perfection which is beyond the inherent limitations of the system. While there is wisdom in Lord Reid's comment in *Taylor v O'Connor*[4] that it would be unrealistic to refuse to take inflation into account at all, the better course in the great majority of cases is to disregard it. And this for several reasons. First, it is pure speculation whether inflation will continue at present, or higher, rates, or even disappear. The only sure comment one may make on any financial prediction is that it is as likely to be falsified as to be borne out by the event. Secondly, as Lord Pearson said in *Taylor v O'Connor*[5], inflation is best left to be dealt with by investment policy. It is not unrealistic in modern social conditions, nor is it unjust, to assume that the recipient of a large capital sum by way of damages will take advice as to its investment and use. Thirdly, it is inherent in a system of compensation by way of a lump sum immediately payable, and, I would think, just, that the sum be calculated at current money values, leaving the recipient in the same position as others, who have to rely on capital for their support to face the future.

The correct approach should be, therefore, in the first place to assess damages without regard to the risk of future inflation. If it can be demonstrated that, on the particular facts of a case, such an assessment would not result in a fair compensation (bearing in mind the investment opportunity that a lump sum award offers), some increase is permissible. But the victims of tort who receive a lump sum award are entitled to no better protection against inflation than others who have to rely on capital for their future support. To attempt such protection would be to put them into a privileged position at the expense of the tortfeasor, and so to impose on him an excessive burden, which might go far beyond compensation for loss. . . .

Conclusion
On the questions of principle argued before the House I find that the appellants have substantially failed in the appeal, but have succeeded on the cross-appeal. Nevertheless, for the reasons I have given and because of the changed circumstances of Dr Lim and her family, the award is diminished, though to no very great extent. Excluding interest, which should be calculated and, if possible, agreed by the parties

---

1. [1978] 2 All ER 604 at 616; [1978] 2 WLR 978 at 991.
2. [1971] AC 115; [1970] 1 All ER 365.
3. [1974] 3 All ER 677; [1975] 1 WLR 17.
4. [1971] AC 115 at 130; [1970] 1 All ER 365 at 368.
5. [1971] AC 115 at 143; [1970] 1 All ER 365 at 378.

when the House makes its decision, the award should, I propose, be as follows:

Pain, suffering, loss of amenities	£20,000
Out-of-pocket expenses	£3,596
Cost of care to date of judgment in this House	
(a) Malaysia	£16,500
(b) travelling	£1,923
(c) (calculated from 4 September 1978 to an arbitrary date, 4 May 1979, it will require to be revised upwards to the actual date of judgment in the House)	£4,266.64
Loss of earnings to date of judgment at trial	£14,213
Cost of future care	£76,800
Loss of future earnings (including pension rights)	£92,000
Total	£229,298.64

to which the appropriate interest will have to be added.

My Lords, I would propose that, subject to the necessary variations to the amount of the award, the appeal be dismissed with costs and the cross-appeal dismissed with no order as to costs.

[LORD DIPLOCK, VISCOUNT DILHORNE and LORD SIMON OF GLAISDALE agreed with the speech of LORD SCARMAN.]

Appeal and cross-appeal dismissed

Report of the Royal Commission on Civil Liability and Compensation for Personal Injury. Cmnd. 7054. Vol. I

Services rendered and expenses incurred by others for the plaintiff's benefit
343 Services may be rendered by others to help the plaintiff to cope with his injury. Probably the most common example is that of a wife who looks after her injured husband at home. A relative or friend of the plaintiff may incur expenses for his benefit, such as travelling expenses when visiting him in hospital.

344 The problem of compensating for losses of this kind was considered by the Court of Appeal in *Donnelly v Joyce* [1974] QB 454. Lord Justice Megaw, delivering the decision of the court, said:

'We do not agree with the proposition . . . that the plaintiff's claim, in circumstances such as the present, is properly to be regarded as being . . . "in relation to someone else's loss" merely because someone else has provided to, or for the benefit of, the plaintiff – the injured person – the money . . . to provide for needs of the plaintiff directly caused by the defendant's wrongdoing. The loss *is* the plaintiff's loss. The question from what source the plaintiff's needs have been met, the question who has paid the money or given the services, the question whether or not the plaintiff is or is not under a legal or moral liability to repay, are, so far as the defendant and his liability are concerned, all irrelevant. The plaintiff's loss, to take this present case, is not the expenditure of money to buy the special boots or to pay for the nursing attention. His loss is the existence of the need for those special boots or for those nursing services, the value of which for purposes of damages – for the purpose of the ascertainment of the amount of his loss – is the proper and reasonable cost of supplying those needs. That, in our judgment, is the key to the problem. So far as the defendant is concerned, the loss is not someone else's loss. It is the plaintiff's loss.'

345   We were attracted by this reasoning. If the plaintiff needs to have services rendered or expenses incurred for his benefit, and if this need arises from an injury for which a defendant is liable, then we think he should be able to recover damages. The way in which the need is met is indeed irrelevant. If, for example, the plaintiff's need for attendance is met gratuitously by his wife rather than by a suitable paid person, he should not recover less damages. This point of equity assumes considerable practical importance where the gratuitous rendering of a service brings about a fall in family income, for example, if a member of the plaintiff's family gives up work to care for him. In such cases, it is in our view just to consider the value of the services rendered, and the impact of the defendant's action on the family as a whole. . . .

347   The English courts, until the decision in *Donnelly v Joyce*, sometimes insisted that the plaintiff should give an undertaking to repay the damages to the person who actually rendered the services or incurred the expense (see, for example, *Schneider v Eisovitch* [1960] 2 QB 430). We understand that the Scottish Law Commission are to propose that the plaintiff should be under a legal duty to account for such damages as are recovered in respect of the services. [The Administration of Justice Act 1982, s. 8(2), now makes provision for this in Scotland] In *Cunningham v Harrison* [1973] QB 942 Lord Denning, Master of the Rolls, said, referring to services rendered by a wife, that the husband should recover compensation for the value of the services and hold it in trust for his wife.

348   We think it follows from Lord Justice Megaw's reasoning in the later case of *Donnelly v Joyce* that such arrangements are unnecessary. The damages are awarded for the plaintiff's loss, and it is for him to dispose of them as he thinks fit. In practice, the damages will often compensate for a loss suffered by a family income pool. . . .

351   **We recommend** that damages should continue to be recoverable for an injured person's need to have services rendered and expenses incurred by others for his benefit; that such damages should be recoverable by the injured person in his own right; that the injured person should not have a legal obligation to account to, or hold the damages in trust for, those rendering the services or incurring the expenses; and that such damages should continue to be assessed on the basis of what is reasonable.

The Administration of Justice Act 1982

5. Maintenance at public expense to be taken into account in assessment of damages
In an action under the law of England and Wales or the law of Northern Ireland for damages for personal injuries (including any such action arising out of a contract) any saving to the injured person which is attributable to his maintenance wholly or partly at public expense in a hospital, nursing home or other institution shall be set off against any income lost by him as a result of his injuries.

Notes

1. The 'radical reappraisal of the law', which their Lordships in the *Lim Poh Choo* case were agreed is needed, has not taken place, despite the detailed proposals by the Law Commission, *Report on Personal Injury Litigation – Assessment of Damages* (Law Com. No. 56, 1973) and by the Pearson Commission, nearly 100 pages of whose Report (vol. I) is devoted to this subject. Some limited changes were made by the Administration of Justice Act 1982.

Section 5 of the Act (ante) prevents overcompensation of the kind in *Daish v Wauton* [1972] 2 QB 262; [1972] 1 All ER 25, which decided that no account should be taken of the saving of expenses when the plaintiff receives hospital treatment at state expense. This follows a recommendation by the Pearson Commission, vol. I, paras. 510–512. However, another proposal by the Commission, vol. I, para. 342, that s. 2(4) of the Law Reform (Personal Injuries) Act 1948 (referred to by Lord Scarman, p. 412, ante) should be repealed and replaced by a requirement that private medical expenses should be recoverable only if it was reasonable on medical grounds to incur them, has not been accepted. In *Thomas v Wignall* [1987] QB 1098; [1987] 1 All ER 1185, there was an award of £435,000 for the cost of the plaintiff's future medical care in the private sector, although during the nine years since the accident she had been in NHS institutions for seven years and in private care for only 18 months. In cases like this, based on speculation as to the plaintiff's future care, no undertaking has to be given by the plaintiff that she will use the damages for private care.

2. The right to claim damages for loss of expectation of life was abolished by s. 1(1)(a) of the Administration of Justice Act 1982, but in assessing damages in respect of pain and suffering caused by the injuries, account must be taken of any suffering caused, or likely to be caused to the plaintiff by awareness that his expectation of life has been so reduced (s. 1(1)(b)). Parliament has recognised the feelings of mourners in a new head of damages for bereavement (see p. 243, ante), and we have seen (p. 409, ante) that the courts have shown an increasing willingness to award damages in tort and for breach of contract in respect of injured feelings, as well as arguably removing 'recognisable psychiatric illness' (p. 119, ante) from any special categorisation in the tort of negligence. In *The Mediana* [1900] AC 113 at 116–117, the Earl of Halsbury LC asked: 'what manly mind cares about pain and suffering that is past?', and critics have claimed that awards for pain and suffering tend to overcompensate the victim, particularly in less serious cases. The Pearson Commission, vol. I, paras. 382–389 proposed the abolition of damages for non-pecuniary loss during the first three months after the injury. In a typical case of tetraplegia, where the plaintiff, with a life expectancy of 25 years, was not in physical pain, but was fully aware of her disability, had powers of sight, speech and hearing and needed help with bodily functions, an award of £75,000 for pain and suffering and loss of amenity was regarded as appropriate in 1985: *Housecroft v Burnett* [1986] 1 All ER 332. 'Loss of amenity' refers to the inability to continue in the lifestyle the plaintiff had before the accident and is based on the post-accident expectation of life.

3. Lord Scarman (p. 414, ante) said it would be wrong to reverse by judicial decision the rule that an unconscious plaintiff is entitled to damages for loss of amenity. The Pearson Commission, which said that damages for non-pecuniary loss serve the functions of a palliative, a means of purchasing alternative sources of satisfaction for those lost and for meeting hidden expenses caused by the injury (para. 360), recommended the abolition of damages for non-pecuniary loss in the case of permanent unconsciousness (paras. 397–398) but no legislation has followed.

4. Dr Lim was a qualified medical practitioner on the brink of a career as a psychiatrist at the time she suffered her catastrophic injuries; her future loss

of earnings could be calculated on that basis. But what of a plaintiff who has suffered a 'loss of earning capacity' rather than any provable loss of earnings? The courts have so far declined to compensate injured housewives on the basis of what they could have earned had they chosen to become *paid* workers. However, in *Daly v General Steam Navigation Co Ltd* [1980] 3 All ER 696; [1981] 1 WLR 120 an injured housewife was compensated for being deprived of her capacity to look after her family regardless of the fact that other members of the family had absorbed her tasks. This appears to have made it unnecessary to implement the proposal by the Law Commission (Law Com. No. 56, 1973), para. 157, and the Pearson Commission, vol. I, paras. 352–358, that damages should enable the plaintiff to replace the services which she would have provided (see further *Hodges v Frost* (1984) 53 ALR 373, a decision of the Federal Court of Australia).

Pickett *v* British Rail Engineering Ltd House of Lords [1979] 1 All ER 774

The plaintiff developed lung disease as a result of inhaling asbestos dust while working in the defendant's workshops, for which the defendant admitted liability. In 1975, when he was 52 years old, he issued a writ and the action was tried in 1976, when the medical evidence put his expectation of life at one year, whereas if he had not been exposed to asbestos he could have looked forward to employment up to the age of 65. Stephen Brown J awarded damages under various heads, including £7,000 for pain and suffering and loss of amenities, together with interest from the date of service of the writ to the date of trial. He awarded only £1,508.88 in respect of loss of earnings, being the amount the plaintiff could have expected to earn during the survival period of one year. Following *Oliver v Ashman* [1962] 2 QB 210; [1961] 3 All ER 323, he decided that the plaintiff should recover nothing in respect of the years of which he had been deprived (the lost years). The plaintiff died 5 months after the trial and his widow as administratrix was substituted as plaintiff. The Court of Appeal increased the general damages to £10,000 but refused to allow any interest on the increased sum and left undisturbed the award in respect of future loss of earnings.

The House of Lords allowed the plaintiff's appeal against the refusal to award interest on the general damages, and also allowed a cross-appeal by the defendant against the increase in general damages. The plaintiff also appealed against the refusal to award any sum for loss of earnings during the lost years.

LORD WILBERFORCE: . . . *Oliver v Ashman*[1] is part of a complex of law which has developed piecemeal and which is neither logical nor consistent. Judges do their best to make do with it but from time to time cases appear, like the present, which do not appeal to a sense of justice. I shall not review in any detail the state of the authorities for this was admirably done by Holroyd Pearce LJ in *Oliver v Ashman*[1]. The main strands in the law as it then stood were: (1) the Law Reform (Miscellaneous Provisions) Act 1934 abolished the old rule *actio personalis moritur cum persona* and provided for the survival of causes of action in tort for the benefit of the victim's estate; (2) the decision of this House in *Rose v Ford*[2] that a claim for loss of expectation of life survived under the 1934 Act, and was not a claim for damages based on the death of a person

---

1. [1962] 2 QB 210; [1961] 3 All ER 323.
2. [1937] AC 826; [1937] 3 All ER 359.

and so barred at common law (cf. *Admiralty Comrs v SS Amerika (Owners)*[1]); (3) the decision of this House in *Benham v Gambling*[2] that damages for loss of expectation of life could only be given up to a conventional figure, then fixed at £200; (4) the Fatal Accidents Acts under which proceedings may be brought for the benefit of dependants to recover the loss caused to those dependants by the death of the breadwinner; the amount of this loss is related to the probable future earnings which would have been made by the deceased during 'lost years'.

This creates a difficulty. It is assumed in the present case, and the assumption is supported by authority, that if an action for damages is brought by the victim during his lifetime, and either proceeds to judgment or is settled, further proceedings cannot be brought after his death under the Fatal Accidents Acts. If this assumption is correct, it provides a basis, in logic and justice, for allowing the victim to recover for earnings lost during his lost years.

This assumption is based on the wording of s. 1 of the 1846 Act (now s. 1 of the Fatal Accidents Act 1976) and is not supported by any decision of this House. It cannot however be challenged in this appeal, since there is before us no claim under the Fatal Accidents Acts. I think, therefore, that we must for present purposes act on the basis that it is well founded, and that if the present claim, in respect of earnings during the lost years, fails it will not be possible for a fresh action to be brought by the deceased's dependants in relation to them. . . .

[His Lordship considered the authorities and then continued]:

As to principle, the passage which best summarises the underlying reasons for the decision in *Oliver v Ashman*[3] is the following:

'. . . what has been lost by the person assumed to be dead is the opportunity to enjoy what he would have earned, whether by spending it or saving it. Earnings themselves strike me as being of no significance without reference to the way in which they are used. To inquire what would have been the value to a person in the position of this plaintiff of any earnings which he might have made after the date when ex hypothesi he will be dead strikes me as a hopeless task.'

Or as Holroyd Pearce LJ put it[4]: 'What is lost is an expectation, not the thing itself.'

My Lords, I think that these are instinctual sentences, not logical propositions or syllogisms, none the worse for that because we are not in the field of pure logic. It may not be unfair to paraphrase them as saying: 'Nothing is of value except to a man who is there to spend or save it. The plaintiff will not be there when these earnings hypothetically accrue: so they have no value to him.' Perhaps there are additional strands, one which indeed Willmer LJ had earlier made explicit, that the whole process of assessment is too speculative for the courts to undertake; another that the only loss is a subjective one, an emotion of distress. But if so I would disagree with them. Assumptions, chances, hypotheses enter into most assessments, and juries had, we must suppose, no difficulties with them; the judicial approach, however less robust, can manage too. And to say that what calls for compensation is injured feelings does not provide an answer to the vital question which is whether, in addition to this subjective element, there is something objective which has been lost.

But is the main line of reasoning acceptable? Does it not ignore the fact that a particular man, in good health, and sound earning, has in these two things an asset of present value quite separate and distinct from the expectation of life which every man possesses? Compare him with a man in poor health and out of a job. Is he not,

---

1. [1917] AC 38; [1916–17] All ER Rep 177.
2. [1941] AC 157; [1941] 1 All ER 7.
3. [1962] 2 QB 210 at 240; [1961] 3 All ER 323 at 338, per Willmer LJ.
4. [1962] 2 QB 210 at 230; [1961] 3 All ER 323 at 332.

and not only in the immediate present, a richer man? Is he not entitled to say, at one moment I am a man with existing capability to earn well for 14 years, the next moment I can only earn less well for one year? And why should he be compensated only for the immediate reduction in his earnings and not for the loss of the whole period for which he has been deprived of his ability to earn them? To the argument that 'they are of no value because you will not be there to enjoy them' can he not reply, 'Yes they are; what is of value to me is not only my opportunity to spend them enjoyably, but to use such part of them as I do not need for my dependants, or for other persons or causes which I wish to support. If I cannot do this, I have been deprived of something on which a value, a present value, can be placed'?

I do not think that the problem can be solved by describing what has been lost as an 'opportunity' or a 'prospect' or an 'expectation'. Indeed these words are invoked both ways, by the Lords Justices as denying a right to recover (on grounds of remoteness, intangibility or speculation), by those supporting the appellant's argument as demonstrating the loss of some real asset of true value. The fact is that the law sometimes allows damages to be given for the loss of things so described (e.g. *Chaplin v Hicks*[1]), sometimes it does not. It always has to answer a question which in the end can hardly be more accurately framed than as: 'Is the loss of this something for which the claimant should and reasonably can be compensated?'

The defendant, in an impressive argument, urged on us that the real loss in such cases as the present was to the victim's dependants and that the right way in which to compensate them was to change the law (by statute; judicially it would be impossible) so as to enable the dependants to recover their loss independently of any action by the victim. There is much force in this, and no doubt the law could be changed in this way. But I think that the argument fails because it does not take account, as in an action for damages account must be taken, of the interest of the victim. Future earnings are of value to him in order that he may satisfy legitimate desires, but these may not correspond with the allocation which the law makes of money recovered by dependants on account of his loss. He may wish to benefit some dependants more than, or to the exclusion of, others; this (subject to family inheritance legislation) he is entitled to do. He may not have dependants, but he may have others, or causes, whom he would wish to benefit, for whom he might even regard himself as working. One cannot make a distinction, for the purposes of assessing damages, between men in different family situations.

There is another argument, in the opposite sense; that which appealed to Streatfield J in *Pope v D Murphy & Son Ltd*[2]. Why, he asked, should the tortfeasor benefit from the fact that as well as reducing his victim's earning capacity he has shortened his victim's life? Good advocacy but unsound principle, for damages are to compensate the victim not to reflect what the wrongdoer ought to pay.

My Lords, in the case of the adult wage earner with or without dependants who sues for damages during his lifetime, I am convinced that a rule which enables the 'lost years' to be taken account of comes closer to the ordinary man's expectations than one which limits his interest to his shortened span of life. The interest which such a man has in the earnings he might hope to make over a normal life, if not saleable in a market, has a value which can be assessed. A man who receives that assessed value would surely consider himself and be considered compensated; a man denied it would not. And I do not think that to act in this way creates insoluble problems of assessment in other cases. In that of a young child (cf. *Benham v Gambling*[3]) neither present nor future earnings could enter into the matter; in the more difficult case of adolescents just embarking on the process of earning (cf. *Skelton v Collins*[4]) the value of 'lost' earnings might be real but would probably be assessable as small. . . .

---

1. [1911] 2 KB 786; [1911–13] All ER Rep 224.
2. [1961] 1 QB 222; [1960] 2 All ER 873.
3. [1941] AC 157; [1941] 1 All ER 7.
4. (1966) 115 CLR 94.

My Lords, I have reached the conclusion which I would recommend so far without reference to *Skelton v Collins*[1] in which the High Court of Australia, refusing to follow *Oliver v Ashman*[2], achieved the same result. The value of this authority is twofold: first in recommending by reference to authority (per Taylor J) and in principle (per Windeyer J) the preferable solution, and, secondly, in demonstrating that this can properly be reached by judicial process. The judgments, further, bring out an important ingredient, which I would accept, namely that the amount to be recovered in respect of earnings in the 'lost' years should be that amount after deduction of an estimated sum to represent the victim's probable living expenses during those years. I think that this is right because the basis, in principle, for recovery lies in the interest which he has in making provision for dependants and others, and this he would do out of his surplus. There is the additional merit of bringing awards under this head into line with what could be recovered under the Fatal Accidents Acts. *Skelton v Collins*[1] has been followed and applied recently by the High Court of Australia in *Griffiths v Kerkemeyer*[3].

I would allow the appeal on this point and remit the action to the Queen's Bench Division for damages to be assessed accordingly. . . .

[LORD SALMON, LORD EDMUND-DAVIES and LORD SCARMAN delivered speeches in favour of allowing the appeal on this point. LORD RUSSELL OF KILLOWEN delivered a speech dissenting on this point.]

Appeal and cross-appeal allowed

Notes

1. The decision in the above case is along the lines of the rule proposed by the Law Commission (Law Com. No. 56, para. 87) and the Pearson Commission (vol. I, para. 335). As a result of s. 4 of the Administration of Justice Act 1982 the claim in respect of the 'lost' years does not survive for the benefit of the victim's estate (see p. 238, ante). There has been some controversy as to the calculation of the living expenses to be deducted from the prospective earnings. In *Harris v Empress Motors Ltd* [1983] 3 All ER 561; [1984] 1 WLR 212 the Court of Appeal, overruling several first instance decisions, held that the sum to be deducted is what the plaintiff would have spent exclusively on himself to maintain his standard of life, but sums he would have spent to maintain his dependants are not deductible.

2. In *Jamil bin Harun v Yang Kamsiah Bte Meor Rasdi* [1984] AC 529; [1984] 2 WLR 668 the passage from Lord Wilberforce's speech in *Pickett* (p. 423, ante) concerning the position of young children and adolescents was quoted in the Privy Council's judgment; but it was interpreted as 'not directed to a case . . . where the infant plaintiff is expected to live for her normal span or, at the very least, for a substantial number of years.' In the Privy Council's view, the court would just have to do its best in making this difficult calculation in relation to the years the child will live.

In the earlier case of *Croke (a minor) v Wiseman* [1981] 3 All ER 852; [1982] 1 WLR 71, noted by P. J. Davies (1982) 45 MLR 333 — and see further *Joyce v Yeomans* [1981] 2 All ER 21; [1981] 1 WLR 549 — a majority of the

1. (1966) 115 CLR 94.
2. [1962] 2 QB 210; [1961] 3 All ER 323.
3. (1977) 51 ALR 387.

Court of Appeal accepted that damages could be awarded for such a period to the plaintiff who was aged 21 months when he suffered catastrophic injury. The approach of the trial judge in this case had been to take the average national earnings for a young man as the basis of the award and this was regarded by the majority of the Court of Appeal as appropriate in the circumstances of the case (cf. *Mitchell v Liverpool Area Health Authority (Teaching)* (1985) Times, 17th June). In the case of the 'lost' years, however, the court in *Croke v Wiseman* was not prepared to award damages for loss of earnings in a case where there would be no need for any such sum of money since there would be no dependants. It was thought that there were no compelling social reasons to justify carrying out what would be a more speculative exercise, more speculative since living expenses would have to be assessed and deducted (but see Davies, op cit, p. 334). On the other hand, it has been regarded as possible for a child to be awarded damages for lost earnings in the 'lost' years in suitable cases where the lost earnings are less speculative: see Lord Scarman's suggestion in *Gammell v Wilson* [1982] AC 27 at 78 of the five-year-old television star and see further *Connolly v Camden and Islington Area Health Authority* [1981] 3 All ER 250 at 256.

Dews *v* National Coal Board House of Lords [1987] 2 All ER 545

The plaintiff, a miner, was awarded damages against his employers for injuries sustained during the course of his employment. As a condition of his employment he contributed 5¼ per cent of his wages to the Mineworkers' Pension Scheme and his employers made an equal contribution. The pension to which he would ultimately become entitled was not directly dependent upon the amount of the contributions. Moreover, since he was off work for less than 18 months he suffered no loss of pensionable service. For part of the period he was off work neither he nor the employer paid contributions. He claimed these 'lost' contributions, amounting to £110 in all (10½ per cent of his wages), as one of his heads of damages.

LORD GRIFFITHS: . . . The employers resisted the claim on the ground that as the plaintiff had not been required to pay these sums and as he had suffered no loss of pension rights he had therefore suffered no damage, and was not entitled to recover a sum that would be in the nature of a windfall rather than compensation for loss actually suffered. It was this issue that was reserved at the trial for a further hearing and which is now the subject of this appeal.

The further argument was heard by Michael Davies J who held that the plaintiff was entitled to recover the £55 which would have been contributed to the scheme out of his wages but that he was not entitled to recover the £55 that represented the employers' contribution.

The employers appealed and the Court of Appeal unanimously allowed the appeal, albeit their reasoning differed (see [1986] 2 All ER 769, [1987] QB 81). The plaintiff, however, did not cross-appeal against the finding that he was not entitled to include the employers' contribution in the claim for damages. This was perhaps a pity because in my view the resolution of the problem requires consideration of both the plaintiff's and the employers' contributions.

It is a fundamental principle of English law that damages for personal injury are compensatory, and intended so far as money can to put the plaintiff in the same financial position as if the accident had never happened. It was the application of this fundamental principle that led the House of Lords in *British Transport Commission v Gourley* [1955] 3 All ER 796, [1956] AC 185 to hold that damages for loss of earnings were to be assessed at the net sum that would be available to the plaintiff after discharging his liability for tax, rather than his gross earnings before deduction of tax.

If this fundamental principle is applied to the facts of this case the plaintiff is not entitled to recover the £55. If he had not been injured he would never have received this sum as under the terms of his contract of employment it would have been paid directly into the scheme, and therefore would not have been available to him to dispose of as he chose as part of his earnings. Furthermore, because of the 18 months' moratorium provided for by the scheme he suffered no loss of future pension. If therefore the plaintiff was to be paid this sum of £55 he would receive £55 more than if he had been in full employment and to that extent would be enriched at the expense of his employers, rather than compensated.

Counsel for the plaintiff acknowledges this result on the facts of this particular case but submits that it should be accepted as an anomaly for to do otherwise would breach a second fundamental principle that governs the award of damages for personal injury, which is that it is no concern of the tortfeasor how the injured plaintiff chooses to dispose of his earnings. It does not lie in the mouth of the tortfeasor to argue that because he has put the plaintiff in a hospital bed for six months he must be given credit for the money that the plaintiff would have spent on his own amusement during that time if he had been able to do so. Applying this principle, as the plaintiff's wages included the 5 ¼ % that was contributed on his behalf to the scheme, it is said that it is no concern of the employers in their capacity as a tortfeasor to inquire how that part of the plaintiff's wages was spent, and he is entitled to be paid it as a part of his wages. . . .

In my view the key to the solution of the present problem is to be found by recognising that in present-day society people generally work with two principal aims in view: the first is to provide themselves with an income available for current spending and the second is to provide money that will be put into a pension scheme to provide them with an income after their retirement. When a plaintiff is injured and as a result is paid no wages his immediate real loss is that part of his net earnings that were available for current expenditure. In respect of this part of his earnings the object of which is to provide income available for current expenditure the tortfeasor is, subject to sums necessarily spent to earn the income, entitled to no credit for expenditure saved as a result of the injury; the principle that it is no concern of the tortfeasor how the plaintiff chooses to spend his income applies.

Different considerations, however, apply to the contributions to a retirement pension. This money is not intended to provide any immediate benefit and the plaintiff suffers no immediate loss as a result of the loss of his wages. He may, of course, as a result of a failure to pay contributions to the pension scheme suffer a future loss of pension. This loss he is entitled to recover. The measure of the loss will depend on the terms of the particular scheme to which the plaintiff is contributing. In some schemes if the period of disability is relatively short it may be that the loss can be compensated for by paying to the plaintiff a sum equivalent to the contributions that have not been paid during his disability, so that he can top up the contributions. But such a payment would have to include not only his own contributions to the scheme but also those of his employer. No doubt for fiscal reasons it is usual for the contributions to a pension scheme to be expressed as a percentage of the plaintiff's wages and a contribution, often a matching contribution, as in this case, from the employer; but both contributions are made as part of the consideration the employer pays for the plaintiff's work and in the example I have been considering the plaintiff would be entitled to recover a sum equivalent to both his own and the employer's contributions. However, if the plaintiff has been off work for a substantial period of time or is permanently disabled it is almost certain that payment of a sum equivalent to the lost contributions will not be sufficient to compensate for his lost pension rights and a more sophisticated calculation will be required to ascertain the loss.

What is certain, however, is that the plaintiff cannot recover both the contributions and the pension that those contributions would have purchased, for that would be to allow double recovery. . . .

. . . I do not regard it as a critical feature that this was a compulsory pension scheme. If the evidence showed that a plaintiff had been regularly making contributions to a voluntary scheme in order to secure a pension so that, but for the accident, the probability pointed to a continuation of those contributions I would apply the same principle. It will, of course, be easier to apply the principle in a compulsory scheme because it is possible to say with certainty that the plaintiff would not have received that part of his wages for his immediate disposal and that it would have gone to the pension scheme. In this case of voluntary contributions the likelihood of the contributions having been continued will have to be taken into account. It may be that the plaintiff would satisfy the court that he was not going to continue with the contributions in which case he would be able to recover what he had hitherto paid as a contribution as a part of his damages. If, on the other hand, the plaintiff asserts that he was going to continue with the contributions and the probabilities support him then his loss is not the contributions but any diminution in his pension rights as a result of the discontinuance of the contributions.

For these reasons, my Lords, I would dismiss the appeal.

LORD MACKAY OF CLASHFERN: . . . The speciality of this case is that the failure to pay contributions because of the terms of the pension scheme does not produce any consequent diminution in pension rights. Counsel for the plaintiff says that this is analogous to an insurance arrangement. He submits that by the terms of the scheme the plaintiff has in effect made an arrangement under which he is insured against loss of pension rights in the event of his being unable to pay contributions due to absence from work for a limited peiod. He likened the position to that which would have obtained if the plaintiff had, out of his own resources, paid for an insurance to provide the contributions during such an absence from work. In my opinion, the situation is similar to that in which an injured plaintiff on going off work in consequence of an accident does not immediately suffer a loss of wages. In such a case the tortfeasor will not be required to compensate him for a loss of wages which he has not suffered even though the position resulting is similar to one in which the plaintiff himself had purchased an insurance to provide payment equal to his wages over this period. In my opinion the correct analysis is that the arrangement under which the plaintiff suffers no loss of pension rights although no contributions were paid during his period of absence from work is part of the arrangement for remuneration under which he worked at the time of the accident. Since viewing that arrangement as a whole he has suffered no loss in respect of the absence of contributions to the pension scheme during his period off work I agree that his claims fails.

[LORD KEITH OF KINKEL, LORD BRANDON OF OAKBROOK and LORD ACKNER agreed with both these speeches.]

Appeal dismissed

Notes

1. Lord Mackay formulated a general principle to govern the assessment of loss in these terms: 'In my opinion the tortfeasor is concerned with the disposal of any part of the plaintiff's remuneration which is applied to obtain benefits which may be affected by the plaintiff's injury and, if affected, would be a proper subject of claim against the tortfeasor' ([1987] 2 All ER at p. 551). This may not always yield the same results as Lord Griffiths' reasoning (ante): see L. J Anderson (1987) 50 MLR 963 at 966–967.

2. The principle in *British Transport Commission v Gourley* [1956] AC 185; [1955] 3 All ER 796 (referred to by Lord Griffiths, ante), that the plaintiff should be compensated for actual loss, that is, the amount left in his hands

after *compulsory* deductions such as tax, has been applied to national insurance contributions (*Cooper v Firth Brown Ltd* [1963] 2 All ER 31; [1963] 1 WLR 418, a wrongful dismissal case). In *Dews* (ante) the principle was extended to *voluntary* contributions. Harris, *Remedies*, p. 265 comments:

'The deduction of tax and other contributions from [the plaintiff's] damages means that the true social cost of accidents is not being borne by tortfeasors (directly or through their insurers), which seriously diminishes the deterrent effect of imposing tort liability. Since the burden of the loss of the tax which [the plaintiff] would have paid is borne by taxpayers in general, [the defendant's] tort imposes an external cost on the community (Bishop and Kaye, 104 LQR 211 (1987)).'

3. It has been difficult to discern any clear principle in the common law approach to offsets or deductions from damages. In the light of recent cases, Harris, *Remedies*, p. 295, suggests the following distinction:

'If the benefit is financed by a large section of the public in an institutionalised way (e.g. taxpayers and contributors to social security) or by the defendant himself (e.g. an employer), it should be deducted from the damages. On the other hand, if [the plaintiff] has himself chosen to arrange the benefit and has himself contributed to its cost, directly or indirectly (e.g. private insurance), or if the benefit comes from voluntary donations to charity, no deduction should be made from his damages. The judges wish to encourage both first-party insurance and charitable giving; it can also be inferred in these cases that the intention of [the plaintiff] or of the donors was not to relieve a potential tortfeasor, but rather to provide support for himself, or the victims, irrespective of any claim in tort which might be brought.'

This is supported by *Hodgson v Trapp* [1989] AC 807; [1988] 3 All ER 870, where the House of Lords decided that a deduction should be made from the damages of £431,840 awarded to a plaintiff, who had suffered catastrophic injuries in a road accident, in respect of statutory attendance and mobility allowances payable to her. Lord Bridge was not willing to countenance 'double recovery in such a case at the expense of both taxpayers and insurers'. (See now p. 429, post, on subsequent statutory changes regarding deductions.) In *Hussain v New Taplow Paper Mills Ltd* [1988] AC 514; [1988] 1 All ER 541, the plaintiff, who had been seriously injured in the course of his employment, was forced to bring into account and deduct long-term sickness benefits payable under an insurance scheme run by the defendant employers. This was justified by Lord Bridge on the ground that the payments were made to the plaintiff as a partial substitute for earnings and were the 'very antithesis' of a pension which would be payable only after the employment ceased (see post). The fact that the defendants had insured their liability to make sickness payments was treated as irrelevant. In *Colledge v Bass Mitchells & Butlers Ltd* [1988] 1 All ER 536; [1988] ICR 125, the Court of Appeal allowed deduction of a redundancy payment from the damages awarded to a plaintiff who had suffered a severe back injury, as a result of negligence for which his employers were responsible, and had later accepted voluntary redundancy. The plaintiff would have been unlikely to be made redundant and would probably have worked for the employers until retirement but for the injury. On the other hand, benefits received under a contract of insurance are not deductible (*Bradburn v Great Western Rly Co* (1874) LR 10 Exch 1; *McCamley v Cammell Laird Shipbuilders Ltd* [1990] 1 All ER 854; [1990] 1 WLR 963), nor are payments from charitable motives, nor occupational disability pensions, whether or not discretionary and whether or not contributory which are treated as a form of insurance (*Parry v Cleaver* [1970] AC 1; [1969] 1 All ER 555, but compare *Hussain v New Taplow Mills Ltd* and query whether the same result would be reached today in *Parry* if the defendant had been the plaintiff's employer?).

4. The main source of compensation for victims of accidents and disease is social security (see chap. 1, p. 35, ante, and chap. 19, p. 917, post). It has for long been controversial whether social security benefits should be offset against damages. The argument for deduction, voiced in the Beveridge Report, is that an injured person should not have the same need met twice. This was supported, in 1946, by a Departmental Committee on Alternative Remedies (the Monckton Committee) (Cmd. 6860) which recommended that 'the injured person or his dependants should not be permitted to recover by way of damages and benefits more than the maximum which he could recover from either source alone.' The argument against deduction, expressed by a minority of the Monckton Committee, is that the claimant earns many social security benefits by contributions in the same way as private insurance. In the result, a compromise was adopted. Section 2(1) of the Law Reform (Personal Injuries) Act 1948 provided that in assessing damages for loss of income due to personal injury, the court should take into account one half of the value of certain social security benefits for five years. Only awards made by the court, and not out of court settlements, were subject to this deduction and the deduction could be made only from the award for past and future loss of earnings. The Pearson Commission (chap. 13, paras. 487–488, and minority opinion, paras. 543–548) recommended that the full value of social security benefits should be deducted from damages, with the proviso that the set-off should only be against the like head of damages.

The Government has accepted the case against 'double compensation', in a way that is expected to save about £55 million a year in government expenditure, without reducing the liability of tortfeasors. Section 22 and Sch. 4 of the Social Security Act 1989, as amended by Sch. 1 to the Social Security Act 1990, and the Recoupment Regulations 1990, S.I. 1990, No. 322, now provide that virtually all social security benefits may be recouped in full by the Department of Social Security from the 'compensator' before the latter makes a 'compensation payment' to the victim in consequence of an accident, injury or disease. This applies to an accident or injury or a claim for benefit in respect of a disease on or after 1 January 1989 where the payment is made on or after 3 September 1990. It covers all payments of compensation for personal injuries (excluding costs) whether made voluntarily or in pursuance of a court order or an agreement, 'or otherwise'. The clawback is made in respect of benefits paid or likely to be paid up to the date of the compensation payment, or the fifth anniversary of the accident or injury or claim for benefit in consequence of a disease, whichever is the earlier. Special rules apply to structured settlements (see p. 433, post). The recoupment of benefits takes place regardless whether the compensation is reduced on account of contributory negligence. This means that if the court awards damages of £10,000 and reduces these by 50 per cent for contributory negligence, and the social security benefits amount to £5,000, the victim will receive nothing from the 'compensator' (see H. Witcomb (1989) 139 NLJ 1006). The clawback is made not only from the loss of earnings award but also from the general damages, so depriving the victim of 'full' compensation for pain, suffering, loss of amenity etc. Certain payments are exempt from clawback, such as payments made to dependants under the Fatal Accidents Act 1976, payments under the Vaccine Damage Payments Act 1979, and any redundancy payment taken into account in the assessment of damages. The clawback scheme also does not apply to 'small payments' (currently fixed as those not exceeding £2,500). In respect of these small payments, the compensator still has the right, under s. 2(1) of the Law Reform (Personal Injuries) Act 1948, as amended, to offset half of any of the relevant benefits covered by s. 22 of the Social Security Act 1989, for the five years beginning with the time when the cause of action accrued, against the award of damages for personal injuries. This means, in effect, that half of the social security benefits for the five-year period will be offset when calculating the award of damages in the case of 'small payments'. In the case of larger awards or settlements, the compensator does not offset against damages, but is liable to repay the relevant benefits in full to the state before making payment of the award or settlement, reduced by the amount of the relevant benefits, to the victim. For details of the recoupment regulations, see M. Churchouse (1990) 14 LS Gaz 19.

Report of the Royal Commission on Civil Liability and Compensation for Personal Injury. Cmnd. 7054. Vol. I

555   The main component of a claim for future pecuniary loss is, almost invariably, loss of income or, in fatal cases, lost dependency. The plaintiff's loss is therefore in periodic form, whether it is made up of weekly wages, a monthly salary, or regular contributions to a family budget. Any expenses included in a claim for future pecuniary loss also tend to be regular outgoings.

556   It seems to most of us that the lump sum is not the most natural form of compensation for losses of this sort, given the objective of tort of restoring the plaintiff as closely as possible to his position before the injury. Yet it is at present the only form of tort compensation. In assessing damages, the court must translate a periodic future loss into a capital sum.

557   This process is inevitably inexact. The court must compare the plaintiff's expected income with the income which he might have enjoyed if he had not been injured. Allowance must be made for the likely duration of incapacity, and for the chances of promotion or increase in earnings; and, on the other hand, for the chances of loss of earnings, unemployment, unconnected illness or death. The court must also make assumptions about future economic conditions. In particular, it must make some assumptions about future rates of inflation, tax, and return on invested capital.

558   None of these factors is certain. The plaintiff may live for a longer or shorter period than was assumed; his medical condition may improve or deteriorate unexpectedly; he may lose his job or fail to find another; or he may be unable to derive the hoped-for return on his investment. As a result, he may be extensively over compensated or under compensated.

560   The lump sum is said, however, to have a number of advantages. Among those urged upon us was finality in litigation. A lump sum completely disposes of a tort claim. This is said to be in the interest both of the parties and of the community, in that there is an end of legal dispute and an end of expense. The defendant can

discharge his liability fully and then forget the matter. In practice, this means that his insurer can close his file without incurring the expenses (which would ultimately be reflected in higher premiums) of continued administration. The plaintiff, if he is not too badly injured, can concentrate his efforts on recovery and put his injury and his grievance behind him. Because people like to finish with their claims a final lump sum award is said to promote settlements, and thus to help to contain the cost of the tort system.

561 The lump sum is also said to give freedom of choice. Although the compensation is awarded for future pecuniary loss, the plaintiff may, if he wishes, spend all or a large part of it immediately. He may, for example, use it to buy a house or to pay off his existing mortgage; or to buy a business; or simply to purchase some luxury which he could not otherwise afford but which may give him pleasure that to some extent makes up for his loss.

564 In the less serious cases, we think, the arguments in favour of lump sums should normally prevail. There is no doubt that any system of periodic payments would require more elaborate and expensive administration than the present system of lump sum awards; and although, as we point out in paragraph 580, we would not rule out periodic payments otherwise than for serious and long term pecuniary losses, we would not expect such cases to be very common. It is in the interests of the community that most of the smaller tort claims, even for future pecuniary loss, should be finally, and so far as possible quickly, disposed of.

565 Most of us feel, however, that in cases of death or serious and lasting injury the arguments in favour of lump sums are not convincing. The finality of the lump sum may operate to the plaintiff's disadvantage if the forecast on which it is based proves erroneous — for example by overstating his chances of physical recovery or underestimating the effect of inflation on income from his invested damages. Its relative immediacy may not be preferable to the provision of assured long term financial support, either from the point of view of the plaintiff or from the point of view of the community who have to support him if his damages prove inadequate. Indeed, the payment of supplementary benefit to a person whose damages were exhausted would be a form of double compensation paid for by taxpayers. Finally, the freedom of choice offered by the lump sum is something which the plaintiff would not have enjoyed if he had not been injured.

566 By contrast, periodic payments seem to us to offer important advantages in serious cases, although we recognise that it would not be practicable to eliminate all the uncertainties of awards of damages for future pecuniary loss.

Notes

1. The survey for the Oxford Centre for Socio-Legal Studies (*Harris et al*, pp. 122–125) found that many of those awarded lump sums used them to buy tangible, durable items; about half saved some for the future; a fifth put some towards a house or other improvements; but only a quarter used some for living expenses. Claimants explained that they had accepted lower sums in out-of-court settlements than they had expected because of their urgent need for money, or their fear of further trouble or delay. H. Genn, *Hard Bargaining: Out of Court Settlement in Personal Injury Actions*, pp. 75–78 found that insurance claims inspectors, and lawyers, had the greatest difficulty in estimating the quantum of damages, especially in relation to future loss of earnings. This imprecision and uncertainty made it hard for

plaintiffs to argue convincingly against low offers of settlement. The majority of the Pearson Commission, vol. I, paras. 574–614, made detailed proposals for the award of periodical payments in cases of serious injury or death, but these proposals, opposed by a minority (ibid., paras. 615–630), have not been implemented. Some attempt to deal with the problem of medical contingencies is made by s. 6 of the Administration of Justice Act 1982 (inserting a new s. 32A in the Supreme Court Act 1981) and Rules of the Supreme Court, O.37) enable the court to award *provisional* damages in cases where there is a chance that at some time in the future the injured person will, as a result of the tortious act or omission, develop some serious disease or suffer some serious deterioriation in his physical or mental condition. In this case damages will be awarded in two stages: first, damages assessed on the assumption that the development or deterioration will not occur, and then further damages at a later date if this does occur. Another way in which advance payments may be encouraged is through 'split' trials, in which the issue of liability can be dealt with early, leaving assessment of damages to a later hearing, pending which interim payments may be made. Since 1990, the court has had power to order a split trial of its own motion.

2. The traditional method of calculating the lump sum is to estimate the net annual loss (the multiplicand) in the manner described in the Pearson Report, vol. I, paras. 557–559 (p. 430, ante), and to apply to this a multiplier worked out on the basis that the income and part of the capital will be spent each year so that the capital will be exhausted at the age until which the loss is assessed. The Pearson Commission stated (vol. I, para. 648):

'The present range of multipliers used by the courts—which has an effective maximum of 18—approximately corresponds to the assumption that a person who invests a sum of money in the United Kingdom will enjoy a rate of return on his investment of 4½ per cent a year, after the effects of tax and inflation have been taken into account. This assumption is not now realistic. The net real rates of return (that is, the net rates after tax, less the rate of inflation) derived from investments in this country have over a number of years been considerably lower than 4½ per cent.'

D. Kemp QC (1984) 3 CJQ 120 argues that the court should assume that the plaintiff will invest in index-linked (i.e. inflation-proof) bonds so as to protect himself against the fall in the value of money, bearing in mind the refusal of the courts, reaffirmed by Lord Scarman in the *Lim Poh Choo* case (p. 416, ante), to speculate about inflationary trends. According to *Kemp & Kemp on Damages*, p. 7018, the net rate of return upon index-linked securities available to private investors, after deduction of basic rate income tax (in 1989) was about 3 per cent. This net rate of interest is referred to as the 'discount rate' which should be taken into account when assessing the lump sum. If this approach were adopted there would be a substantial increase in the multipliers currently applied. For example, in the *Lim Poh Choo* case (p. 410, ante) the multiplier would have been 22 using a discount rate of 2 per cent per annum. However, in *Auty v National Coal Board* [1985] 1 All ER 930, the Court of Appeal not only rejected evidence as to future inflationary trends but also declined to apply a discount rate below the 5 per cent adopted by the trial judge. In *Hodgson v Trapp* [1989] AC 807; [1988] 3 All ER 870, the House of Lords disapproved of the practice of increasing the multiplier to take account of the incidence of higher rates of taxation. See generally W. Bishop and J. Kaye (1987) 104 LQR 211.

3. The English courts remain strangely reluctant to admit actuarial evidence as to future loss (*Mitchell v Mulholland (No. 2)* [1972] 1 QB 65; [1971] 2 All ER 1205), and have even rejected as inadmissible, without proof as to their correctness, actuarial tables compiled by a working party under the chairmanship of Michael Ogden QC, with the assistance of the Government Actuary and published by HMSO (*Spiers v Halliday* (1984) Times, 30th June). The Law Commission (Law Com. No. 56, paras. 215–224) had strongly recommended the use of such tables. In other common law jurisdictions actuarial evidence is generally accepted; see e.g. *Andrews v Grand & Toy Alberta Ltd* (1978) 83 DLR (3d) 452 and generally J. H. Prevett (1972) 35 MLR 140, 257.

4. The lapse of time between the injury and the payment of damages would leave the plaintiff seriously out of pocket, especially in times of inflation, if interest was not awarded on lump sum damages. Section 35A of the Supreme Court Act 1981 (inserted by the Administration of Justice Act 1982) provides that interest should be awarded unless the court is satisfied that there are special reasons for not doing so. In *Cookson v Knowles* [1979] AC 556; [1978] 2 All ER 604 the House of Lords held that claims for pecuniary loss up to the date of trial should bear interest at half the current short-term interest rates, but no interest should be awarded on future pecuniary loss since that has not yet been sustained. In *Wright v British Railways Board* [1983] 2 AC 773; [1983] 2 All ER 698 the House of Lords held that interest at the moderate rate of 2 per cent from the date of service of the writ to date of judgment should be made in respect of non-pecuniary loss. It is customary to calculate the multiplier at the date of trial. This has been criticised for leading to excessive awards and also for putting a premium on delay. In *Pritchard v J. H. Cobden Ltd* [1988] Fam 22; [1987] 1 All ER 300, the Court of Appeal rejected an attempt to reverse this practice. This case had taken nine years to come to trial; interest was disallowed for two years reflecting the period in which the plaintiff's solicitor had been guilty of unjustified delay.

5. In the absence of legislative reform, it has been left to the insurance industry to introduce 'structured settlements' so as to provide pensions in place of lump sum damages for plaintiffs with serious personal injuries. The nature and radical implications of such settlements are discussed in the extract post. See further I. R. Scott (1988) 7 CJQ 99; D. Allen (1988) 104 LQR 448; *Kelly v Dawes* (1990) Times, 27th September.

Pensions Replace Lump Sum Damages: Are Structured Settlements the Most Important Reform of Tort in Modern Times?
Richard Lewis (1988) 15 *Journal of Law and Society* 392–395, 403–404 and 413

A radical change in the way damages for personal injury may be paid has been made without, as yet, much in the way of comment upon it. 'Structured settlements', extensively used in North America, have been introduced into this country. These substitute pensions for the lump sums traditionally paid to plaintiffs for their future losses. The pension derives from an annuity bought by the insurer covering the liability involved, and held for the benefit of the injured person. In contrast to the once-and-for-all award of lump sum damages, the pension can be varied and its payments 'structured' over a period of time. Lump sums can only be replaced in this way if the parties agree out of court to do so. To encourage these private settlements the parties have been given a considerable financial inducement by the state. The result is that structuring will soon frequently be used for the most important cases in tort – where the injury is so serious as to cause earnings and other financial losses to accrue into the future.

A structured settlement enables an insurer to pay out less money than before, whilst at the same time allowing a plaintiff to draw a higher income from the damages obtained. These gains are made at the taxpayers' expense. From the perspective of the accident victim structured settlements offer at least two new advantages over the lump sum: first, the income generated can be guaranteed against erosion by inflation; and secondly, it is paid free of tax into the plaintiff's hands. This favourable tax treatment, recently conceded by the Inland Revenue, is the key to understanding the attractions of a structured settlement. In effect it increases by at least a quarter the value of the lump sum offered by the insurer. It therefore enables insurers to pay out less to generate the same income for the plaintiff. This fact alone should cause all personal injury lawyers and liability insurers to re-examine their traditional practices; they must change their negotiating tactics whenever a large award is contemplated.

The financial package offered by a structured settlement is composed of two elements: the first – also found in the traditional award of damages – is a lump sum to cover the financial losses incurred to the date of the settlement; the second element of the package offers a pension, which usually lasts for the rest of the plaintiff's life. (In some cases it can last for a set number of years if, for example, the plaintiff wishes to provide for dependents after her or his death.) The pension compensates the plaintiff both for non-pecuniary injury, such as pain and suffering, and for the financial loss accruing as the years pass. It therefore includes payments for any future reduction of income caused by the plaintiff being unable to continue with her or his pre-accident job. It also covers any out-of-pocket expenses, medical costs, and generally the future cost of caring for the plaintiff. The package can be individually tailored with increments to cover, for example, medical appliances, education, married life, and support for dependents. In extreme cases the sums involved can be enormous; lump sum damages of over £1 million were awarded last year. Structuring such a payment could result in a very high level of pension indeed.

However, the scope for structuring a settlement is not without limit. There are two factors which confine such agreements. First, they can only be arranged via a settlement out of court. Judges have no power to order the structuring of any damages they award. However, this hardly detracts from the importance of the reform because only one per cent of cases actually proceed to judgment. The rest are settled by the parties themselves. The second limit to structuring is more significant. Because periodic payments for past losses are obviously inappropriate, structuring can only be employed where the financial loss will continue into the future. In addition, the damages must be large enough to justify using the new technique. Initially it is thought that only cases worth more than £50,000 will be considered, but this may change with experience and, in particular, with wider appreciation of the advantages of structuring. Even then, however, only a minority of tort cases will be affected because only seven and a half per cent involve any future financial loss at all. The present tort system is overwhelmingly concerned with minor injuries which have no lasting ill effects. For these a lump sum, averaging only around £2,000, will continue to be the appropriate method of paying damages. Nevertheless, it is the more serious injuries, where structuring may now occur, which attract the attention of the media and thus the public. It is in these cases that the system is seen at its worst, and is criticised as a slow, expensive, and unjust means of compensating seriously disabled people. The cases in which structuring will prove worthwhile are therefore those which attract an importance disproportionate to their number, although not to the amount of damages they involve. They are seen as being the vanguard of the law of tort. . . .

Structured settlements will make one élite group of accident victims — those who can establish liability in tort — even more élite. Already receiving the highest benefits, this group will now receive even more, and at the taxpayers' expense. The extent that the taxpayer, and thus the state, is already involved in subsidising the tort system calls into question its traditional portrayal as a private, individualistic mechanism for the replacement of income and other losses. The state's involvement in tort can be considered together with the support it gives on a haphazard basis to other victims of accidents. As part of a wider welfare system it awards 'subsidies' in various forms of which the tax break given to structured settlements is but one. Elsewhere, for example, special schemes have compensated vaccine-damaged children whilst discriminating against those who suffer adverse reactions from other medical techniques; workers suffering from pneumoconiosis have been similarly favoured compared to those who have developed other industrial diseases; the multiple victims of disasters have gained in contrast to victims of isolated accidents; and the subsidies have preferred haemophiliacs who have contracted the A.I.D.S. virus as against other sufferers, including a mother who contracted the virus from a blood transfusion given during childbirth. Structured settlements can be considered in the context of a series of such *ad hoc* subsidies where it is impossible to discern any common policy beind the various decisions made. There is a general lack of coherence. Why is one group of victims to be preferred to another and how can the varying levels of support be justified? . . .

. . . Many of the problems caused by the lump sum regime will remain, and structured settlements will go only a little way towards pacifying those critics of tort who demand more fundamental reform.

However, structured settlements will provide an effective answer to several of the complaints. First, they will restore a plaintiff more closely to the pre-accident position. . . .

Secondly, such settlements will also relieve plaintiffs of the burden of managing their damages award. The danger . . . of the plaintiff mortgaging her or his future by being given the freedom to dissipate the damages awarded is thus avoided. Thirdly, the settlement at least can be varied to take account of inflation, thus countering a major criticism of lump sums . . . Finally, the payment may last for the plaintiff's lifetime. This prevents overcompensation if death occurs earlier than expected and undercompensation if death occurs later. Structured settlements remove the uncertainty involved in estimating the plaintiff's life expentancy.

The other criticisms of the method of paying damages will continue to apply to structured settlements. . . . [T]he settlement will continue to be expensive to assess, cause payment to be delayed, and discourage rehabilitation. This is because it will still be necessary to calculate the lump sum in order to arrive at the structure for the settlement. The Association of British Insurers' standard form for the agreement, as approved by the Inland Revenue, makes specific provision for inserting the figure for this capital sum. This also means that the assessment will continue to involve . . . speculation and artificiality . . . The present assumptions as to money rates will continue to apply, and the predictions as to the plaintiff's future will not decrease in difficulty or extent. The settlement is not to be varied to take account of any later changes in the plaintiff's medical or financial conditions. Except where allowance is made for inflation, payments cannot alter by one penny from those originally envisaged at the date of the settlement. Overall, structured settlements do little to satisfy those who see extensive review of periodic payments as the only exact and just method of assessing compensation for those who are seriously injured. . . .

. . . Structured settlements offer the tort system more money in exchange for its acceptance of periodic payments. But these payments are subject to very little review, and the change will do little to satisfy those who seek more fundamental reform. In particular, objection can be made to the fact that structuring takes no account of the case for treating people equally according to the extent of disability rather than its cause; the few disabled people who are to benefit already receive the most money. Structuring is the result of a decision taken within a limited framework and in the absence of any coherent policy as to how to compensate disabled people.

Despite this criticism, it is still possible to answer in the affirmative the question posed in the title to this article: for those concerned only with the tort system, structuring can be considered its most important reform in modern times. For those seriously injured it is hard to think of any changes, in either liability or quantum, which are likely to have had an equal effect upon settlements since, perhaps, statutes of the 1940s. There are several reasons for this. First, structuring makes a great deal more money available to those prepared to settle out of court. By doing so it radically alters the framework within which bargaining in tort takes place, and no lawyer, insurer, or plaintiff can afford to ignore the development. Secondly, although at present only seriously injured plaintiffs can benefit from structuring, this group are the most in need of any further allocation of funds from the tort system because they receive the harshest treatment from it. Finally, structuring may appear to some to avoid the major criticisms previously made of the tort system. The stark difference between tort and social security may appear to be reduced. This may forestall other, more fundamental, reforms. Structuring may therefore not only reduce the pressure for new no-fault schemes, but may also prolong still further the life of the tort system itself.

3 Property damage

Edison, p. 331, ante

Dodd Properties (Kent) Ltd v Canterbury City Council Court of Appeal [1980] 1 All ER 928

For the facts of this case see p. 343, ante.

DONALDSON LJ: The general object underlying the rules for the assessment of damages is, so far as is possible by means of a monetary award, to place the plaintiff in the position which he would have occupied if he had not suffered the wrong complained of, be that wrong a tort or a breach of contract. In the case of a tort causing damage to real property, this object is achieved by the application of one or other of two quite different measures of damage, or, occasionally, a combination of the two. The first is to take the capital value of the property in an undamaged state and to compare it with its value in a damaged state. The second is to take the cost of repair or reinstatement. Which is appropriate will depend on a number of factors, such as the plaintiff's future intentions as to the use of the property and the reasonableness of those intentions. If he reasonably intends to sell the property in its damaged state, clearly the diminution in capital value is the true measure of damage. If he reasonably intends to continue to occupy it and to repair the damage, clearly the cost of repairs is the true measure. And there may be in-between situations.

Happily there is no issue in the present case as to which measure of damage falls to be applied. It is the cost of reinstatement. The primary issue is as to how and, more particularly, on what date those costs are to be assessed. This is a very significant issue in the light of the increase in costs over the period between the occurrence of the damage in 1968 and the trial in 1978.

Counsel for the defendants submits, and I for my part would readily accept, that the general rule is that damages fall to be assessed as at the date when the cause of action arose. The rule is so stated by Lord Wilberforce in *Miliangos v George Frank*

(*Textiles*) *Ltd*[1]. And I am inclined to think that in normal circumstances this would be applicable where the relevant measure of damage was diminution in the capital value of the property. But it is only a general or basic rule and is subject to many exceptions. Thus damages for personal injury, excluding consequential loss to which other principles apply, are assessed in the light of the value of money at the date of the hearing. The issue here is whether the assessment of damages based on the cost of repair or reinstatement is another exception, as counsel for the plaintiffs contends. I think that it is. . . .

In the absence of special and extraneous factors, there is no divergence between the interest of a plaintiff and a defendant on the choice of the most propitious moment at which to effect reinstatement. Both wish to achieve the maximum economy, at least so long as the plaintiff is in doubt whether he will be entitled to a full indemnity from the defendant. It follows that, in a case in which a plaintiff has reinstated his property before the hearing, the costs prevailing at the date of that operation which were reasonably incurred by him are prima facie those which are relevant. Equally in a case in which a plaintiff has *not* effected reinstatement by the time of the hearing, there is a prima facie presumption that the costs then prevailing are those which should be adopted in ascertaining the cost of reinstatement. There may indeed be cases in which the court has to estimate costs at some future time as being the reasonable time at which to reinstate, but that is not this case.

This is, however, only a prima facie approach. It may appear on the evidence that the plaintiff, acting reasonably, should have undertaken the reinstatement at some date earlier than that in fact adopted or, as the case may be, earlier than the hearing. If so, the relevant costs are those ruling at that earlier date. Whether this is regarded as arising out of the primary measure of damage, i.e. that the relevant time is when the property should have been reinstated or whether it is regarded as being a reflection of a plaintiff's duty to mitigate his loss, may not matter. . . .

Notes

1. Megaw and Browne LJJ delivered judgments agreeing that the cost of repairs was to be assessed at the earliest date when, having regard to all the circumstances, they could reasonably be undertaken, rather than the date when the damage occurred. Their Lordships all went on to consider the effect of the plaintiffs' financial position and reached the conclusion that the cost of repairs in the present case was to be assessed at the date of the action. This aspect of the case, with relevant extracts from the judgments, is considered p. 345, ante. For discussion of the date for assessment of damages, see D. Feldman and D. F. Libling (1979) 95 LQR 101; I. N. Duncan Wallace (1980) 96 LQR 101, 341; S. M. Waddams (1981) 97 LQR 445.

2. Three basic rules applicable to the assessment of damages are that (a) the plaintiff cannot recover for any loss which he could reasonably have avoided; (b) he can recover for loss reasonably incurred in trying to avoid the loss; and (c) the defendant is liable for the loss only as reasonably mitigated by the plaintiff (*McGregor on Damages*, para. 209). The standard of conduct required is that of reasonableness; it is a question of fact in each case whether the plaintiff has acted reasonably. One point is whether the plaintiff's financial inability to take steps in mitigation will be held against him. The decision in *Dodd Properties (Kent) Ltd v Canterbury City Council* on this point

---

1. [1975] 3 All ER 801 at 813; [1976] AC 443 at 468.

(p. 345, ante) confirms the view that it will not. In the earlier Court of Appeal decision in *Martindale v Duncan* [1973] 2 All ER 355; [1973] 1 WLR 574 it was held that mitigation principles did not prevent the plaintiff from claiming for the full period in which he had hired another car while waiting, because of his impecuniosity, to have the repairs approved by the defendant and his own insurers before having those repairs done. Another point is whether the proper and reasonable compensation for the plaintiff is diminution of value of the property destroyed by the defendant's tort, or the cost of reinstatement. This will depend upon the circumstances of the case: if the property is a profit-making asset, the proper measure of damages will not be limited to their diminution in value. It will be reasonable for the plaintiff to purchase new property to carry on his business since this will mitigate the damage which would have been caused by the loss of profits during the period of repair or rebuilding: *Dominion Mosaics and Tile Co Ltd v Trafalgar Trucking Co Ltd* [1990] 2 All ER 246. See too *Ward v Cannock Chase District Council* [1986] Ch 546; [1985] 3 All ER 537.

3. When assessing damages for economic loss arising from the negligent performance of some service, whether the action is framed in contract or tort, the damages should normally be the amount necessary to put the plaintiff in the position he would have been had there been no wrong. In *Perry v Sidney Phillips & Son (a firm)* [1982] 3 All ER 705; [1982] 1 WLR 1297, the Court of Appeal held that where the plaintiff bought a defective house on the strength of a negligent survey, the correct measure of the damages to be paid by the surveyor was the difference between the value of the house as it was, and what the plaintiff actually paid for it. According to Lord Denning MR and Oliver LJ the measure was not the present day cost of repairs because the economic loss caused by the negligence of the surveyor was making the plaintiff pay more than the house was worth. See too *Simpson v Grove Tompkins & Co* (1982) 126 Sol Jo 347 where the measure of damages awarded against a solicitor who negligently deprived the plaintiff of the chance to purchase a property was held to be the difference between the market value at the time of the later purchase and the original price. Cf. *Murray v Lloyd* [1990] 2 All ER 92; [1989] 1 WLR 1060.

PART TWO

Specific duties and interests

9 Liability for defective premises

In earlier chapters we have examined the main elements of the tort of negligence, defences and the assessment of damages. We turn now to a consideration of liability for defective premises in which judge-made duties and immunities have been affected by statute. This area can be divided into (1) the occupier's liability and (2) the non-occupier's liability in respect of premises. The materials in this chapter will reveal examples of different levels at which 'duty' may be formulated. The occupier's duty to 'visitors' is described as a 'common duty of care' by statute (p. 443, post). The non-occupier doing work on the premises owes a duty of care at common law, while the statutory duty to build dwellings properly (Defective Premises Act 1972, s 1, p. 480, post) appears to be a high one. The occupier's duty to trespassers certainly used to be said to be lower than the normal duty of care (see the views in *British Railways Board v Herrington* [1972] AC 877; [1972] 1 All ER 749, noted p. 480, post – duty of humanity). Today, however, the trespasser's position must be viewed in the light of s. 1 of the Occupiers' Liability Act 1984 (p. 462, post) and the student should consider whether this might also be regarded as imposing a lower duty.

1 Occupiers' liability

(a) To 'visitors'

Note

A consideration of occupiers' liability at common law had to take into account particular categories of entrant on to the premises. The duty of care required of the occupier varied according to whether the lawful entrant was entering under a contract, or as a non-contractual invitee or licensee. The Occupiers' Liability Act 1957 ('a little gem of a statute' per Lord Hailsham, 443 H. L. Debs. (5th Series) col. 720) followed from the Third Report of the Law Reform Committee (Cmd. 9305) 1954 and it brings the invitee and the licensee together into the category of lawful visitors to whom the occupier owes the common duty of care (s. 1(2)). Trespassers remain outside the scope of this Act, as section 1(b) of this chapter will show, and their position is regulated by more recent legislation.

Some doubt has arisen as to the scope of the Act. At common law, if the plaintiff was injured by the occupier's activities on the premises (e.g. driving a car) as opposed to their static condition, then liability could be based on a duty of care arising from those activities. The relevance of the category of lawful entrant in which the law placed the plaintiff was confined to the 'occupancy duty' rather than the 'activity duty'. (For these terms, see F. H. Newark, (1954) 17 MLR 102 at 109; and see generally P. M. North, *Occupiers' Liability* (London, 1971), pp. 71–80.) Writers have disagreed whether the 1957 Act now governs the 'activity duty' as well as the 'occupancy duty'. Comments in *Jauffir v Akhbar* (1984) Times, 10th February and by Stephen Brown LJ in *Ogwo v Taylor* [1987] 1 All ER 668 at 673 support the view that it does not cover the former, as does the fact that when the latter case went on appeal, [1988] AC 431; [1987] 3 All ER 961, noted p. 142, ante, the House of Lords decided it as a common law negligence case: see *Winfield & Jolowicz*, p. 208. Consider further the views in *Ferguson v Welsh* [1987] 3 All ER 777; [1987] 1 WLR 1553; but, in any event, *Winfield & Jolowicz* state (at p. 209) that 'there can be little if any practical difference between the duty of care in negligence and the common duty of care as applied to current activities'. Following from this, it is interesting to note that the Act provides an example of a statutory duty of care in which Parliament has attempted to lay down certain factors for the courts' consideration (see s. 2(3)–(5)). The student should consider how far these factors would be relevant in the common law tort of negligence. The common law nevertheless is relevant in interpreting the Act: see s. 1(2), post.

Occupiers' liability was examined in vol. 1, chap. 28 of the Pearson Commission's Report. The Commission was against the introduction of either a no-fault scheme or strict liability in this area of the law, though in relation to strict liability see the Commission's recommendations mentioned at p. 664, post.

The Occupiers' Liability Act 1957

LIABILITY IN TORT

1. Preliminary. — (1) The rules enacted by the two next following sections shall have effect, in place of the rules of the common law, to regulate the duty which an occupier of premises owes to his visitors in respect of dangers due to the state of the premises or to things done or omitted to be done on them.

(2) The rules so enacted shall regulate the nature of the duty imposed by law in consequence of a person's occupation or control of premises and of any invitation or permission he gives (or is to be treated as giving) to another to enter or use the premises, but they shall not alter the rules of the common law as to the persons on whom a duty is so imposed or to whom it is owed; and accordingly for the purpose of the rules so enacted the persons who are to be treated as an occupier and as his visitors are the same (subject to subsection (4) of this section) as the persons who would at common law be treated as an occupier and as his invitees or licensees.

(3) The rules so enacted in relation to an occupier of premises and his visitors shall also apply, in like manner and to the like extent as the principles applicable at common law to an occupier of premises and his invitees or licensees would apply, to regulate —

   (*a*) the obligations of a person occupying or having control over any fixed or moveable structure, including any vessel, vehicle or aircraft; and

   (*b*) the obligations of a person occupying or having control over any premises or structure in respect of damage to property, including the property of persons who are not themselves his visitors.

(4) A person entering any premises in exercise of rights conferred by virtue of an access agreement or order under the National Parks and Access to the Countryside

Act 1949, is not, for the purposes of this Act, a visitor of the occupier of those premises.

2. Extent of occupier's ordinary duty. – (1) An occupier of premises owes the same duty, the 'common duty of care', to all his visitors, except in so far as he is free to and does extend, restrict, modify or exclude his duty to any visitor or visitors by agreement or otherwise.

(2) The common duty of care is a duty to take such care as in all the circumstances of the case is reasonable to see that the visitor will be reasonably safe in using the premises for the purposes for which he is invited or permitted by the occupier to be there.

(3) The circumstances relevant for the present purpose include the degree of care, and of want of care, which would ordinarily be looked for in such a visitor, so that (for example) in proper cases –

(a)   an occupier must be prepared for children to be less careful than adults; and

(b)   an occupier may expect that a person, in the exercise of his calling, will appreciate and guard against any special risks ordinarily incident to it, so far as the occupier leaves him free to do so.

(4) In determining whether the occupier of premises has discharged the common duty of care to a visitor, regard is to be had to all the circumstances, so that (for example) –

(a)   where damage is caused to a visitor by a danger of which he had been warned by the occupier, the warning is not to be treated without more as absolving the occupier from liability, unless in all the circumstances it was enough to enable the visitor to be reasonably safe; and

(b)   where damage is caused to a visitor by a danger due to the faulty execution of any work of construction, maintenance or repair by an independent contractor employed by the occupier, the occupier is not to be treated without more as answerable for the danger if in all the circumstances he had acted reasonably in entrusting the work to an independent contractor and had taken such steps (if any) as he reasonably ought in order to satisfy himself that the contractor was competent and that the work had been properly done.

(5) The common duty of care does not impose on an occupier any obligation to a visitor in respect of risks willingly accepted as his by the visitor (the question whether a risk was so accepted to be decided on the same principles as in other cases in which one person owes a duty of care to another).

(6) For the purposes of this section, persons who enter premises for any purpose in the exercise of a right conferred by law are to be treated as permitted by the occupier to be there for that purpose, whether they in fact have his permission or not.

3. Effect of contract on occupier's liability to third party. – (1) Where an occupier of premises is bound by contract to permit persons who are strangers to the contract to enter or use the premises, the duty of care which he owes to them as his visitors cannot be restricted or excluded by that contract, but (subject to any provision of the contract to the contrary) shall include the duty to perform his obligations under the contract, whether undertaken for their protection or not, in so far as those obligations go beyond the obligations otherwise involved in that duty.

(2) A contract shall not by virtue of this section have the effect, unless it expressly so provides, of making an occupier who has taken all reasonable care answerable to strangers to the contract for dangers due to the faulty execution of any work of construction, maintenance or repair or other like operation by persons other than himself, his servants and persons acting under his direction and control.

(3) In this section 'stranger to the contract' means a person not for the time being entitled to the benefit of the contract as a party to it or as the successor by assignment or otherwise of a party to it, and accordingly includes a party to the contract who has ceased to be so entitled.

(4) Where by the terms or conditions governing any tenancy (including a statutory tenancy which does not in law amount to a tenancy) either the landlord or the tenant is bound, though not by contract, to permit persons to enter or use premises of which he is the occupier, this section shall apply as if the tenancy were a contract between the landlord and the tenant.

. . .

LIABILITY IN CONTRACT

5. Implied term in contracts. — (1) Where persons enter or use, or bring or send goods to, any premises in exercise of a right conferred by contract with a person occupying or having control of the premises, the duty he owes them in respect of dangers due to the state of the premises or to things done or omitted to be done on them, in so far as the duty depends on a term to be implied in the contract by reason of its conferring that right, shall be the common duty of care.

(2) The foregoing subsection shall apply to fixed and moveable structures as it applies to premises.

(3) This section does not affect the obligations imposed on a person by or by virtue of any contract for the hire of, or for the carriage for reward of persons or goods in, any vehicle, vessel, aircraft or other means of transport, or by or by virtue of any contract of bailment.

. . .

GENERAL

6. Application to Crown. — This Act shall bind the Crown, but as regards the Crown's liability in tort shall not bind the Crown further than the Crown is made liable in tort by the Crown Proceedings Act 1947, and that Act and in particular section two of it shall apply in relation to duties under sections two to four of this Act as statutory duties.

Notes

1. Section 4 of the above Act was repealed by s. 6(4) of the Defective Premises Act 1972, but see now s. 4 of that Act, p. 482, post.

2. Various provisions of the Unfair Contract Terms Act 1977 which affect the operation of s. 2(1) and s. 2(5) of the 1957 Act are set out p. 389, ante.

3. On the relation of s. 2(1) and s. 5(1) of this Act see *Sole v W J Hallt Ltd* [1973] QB 574; [1973] 1 All ER 1032. Swanwick J held that in general a person who came within the scope of s. 5(1) could also claim in tort as a visitor under s. 2(1). His decision that the plaintiff could sue in contract or in tort at his option was an important one since, having found a breach of the common duty of care, he also held that the plaintiff's contributory negligence broke the chain of causation in the contract action under s. 5 but not in the tort action under s. 2 where it merely led to a reduction in the damages. Are there any additional advantages or disadvantages which might lead a plaintiff to choose one of these actions rather than the other? See p. 496, post.

(i) Occupation

Wheat *v* E Lacon & Co Ltd House of Lords [1966] 1 All ER 582

Winn J had dismissed the appellant's action. The majority of Court of Appeal (Harman and Diplock LJJ), [1965] 2 All ER 700, dismissed her appeal, holding that the respondents had not owed the common duty of care to the appellant's deceased husband. On appeal to the House of Lords:

LORD DENNING: My Lords, the 'Golfer's Arms' at Great Yarmouth is owned by the respondents, the brewery company, E. Lacon & Co Ltd. The ground floor was run as a public house by Mr Richardson as manager for the respondents. The first floor was used by Mr and Mrs Richardson as their private dwelling. In the summer Mrs Richardson took in guests for her private profit. Mr and Mrs Wheat and their family were summer guests of Mrs Richardson. About 9 pm one evening, when it was getting dark, Mr Wheat fell down the back staircase in the private portion and was killed. Winn J held that there were two causes: (i) the handrail was too short because it did not stretch to the foot of the stairs; (ii) someone had taken the bulb out of the light at the top of the stairs.

The case raises this point of law: did the respondents owe any duty to Mr Wheat to see that the handrail was safe to use or to see that the stairs were properly lighted? That depends on whether the respondents were 'an occupier' of the private portion of the 'Golfer's Arms', and Mr Wheat was their 'visitor' within the Occupiers' Liability Act 1957: for, if so, the respondents owed him the 'common duty of care'.

In order to determine this question we must have resort to the law before the Occupiers' Liability Act 1957: for it is expressly enacted by s. 1(2) that the Act of 1957

'shall not alter the rules of the common law as to the persons on whom a duty is so imposed or to whom it is owed; and accordingly . . . the persons who are to be treated as an occupier and as his visitors are the same . . . as the persons who would at common law be treated as an occupier and as his invitees or licensees . . .'

At the outset, I would say that no guidance is to be obtained from the use of the word 'occupier' in other branches of the law: for its meaning varies according to the subject-matter.

In the Occupiers' Liability Act 1957, the word 'occupier' is used in the same sense as it was used in the common law cases on occupiers' liability for dangerous premises. It was simply a convenient word to denote a person who had a sufficient degree of control over premises to put him under a duty of care towards those who came lawfully on to the premises. Those persons were divided into two categories, invitees and licensees: and a higher duty was owed to invitees than to licensees; but by the year 1956 the distinction between invitees and licensees had been reduced to vanishing point. The duty of the occupier had become simply a duty to take . . . reasonable care to see that the premises were reasonably safe for people coming lawfully on to them: and it made no difference whether they were invitees or licensees, see *Slater v Clay Cross Co Ltd*.[1] The Act of 1957 confirmed the process. It did away, once and for all, with invitees and licensees and classed them all as 'visitors'; and it put on the occupier the same duty to all of them, namely, the common duty of care. This duty is simply a particular instance of the general duty of care, which each man owes to his 'neighbour'. When Sir Baliol Brett MR first essayed a definition of this general duty, he used the occupiers' liability as an instance of it (see *Heaven v Pender*):[2] and when Lord Atkin eventually formulated the general duty in acceptable terms, he, too, used occupiers' liability as an illustration (see *Donoghue v Stevenson*,[3] and particularly his reference[4] to *Grote v Chester and Holyhead Rly Co*[5]). Translating this general principle into its particular application to dangerous premises, it becomes

---

1. [1956] 2 QB 264 at 269; [1956] 2 All ER 625 at 627.
2. (1883) 11 QBD 503 at 508, 509; [1881–85] All ER Rep 35 at 39, 40.
3. [1932] AC 562 at 580; [1932] All ER Rep 1 at 11.
4. [1932] AC at pp. 586, 587; [1932] All ER Rep at p. 14.
5. (1848) 2 Exch 251.

simply this: wherever a person has a sufficient degree of control over premises that he ought to realise that any failure on his part to use care may result in injury to a person coming lawfully there, then he is an 'occupier' and the person coming lawfully there is his 'visitor'; and the 'occupier' is under a duty to his 'visitor' to use reasonable care. In order to be an 'occupier' it is not necessary for a person to have entire control over the premises. He need not have exclusive occupation. Suffice it that he has some degree of control. He may share the control with others. Two or more may be 'occupiers'. And whenever this happens, each is under a duty to use care towards persons coming lawfully on to the premises, dependent on his degree of control. If each fails in his duty, each is liable to a visitor who is injured in consequence of his failure, but each may have a claim to contribution from the other.

In *Salmond on Torts* (14th edn, 1965) p. 372, it is said that an 'occupier' is 'he who has the immediate supervision and control and the power of permitting or prohibiting the entry of other persons'. This definition was adopted by Roxburgh J in *Hartwell v Grayson Rollo and Clover Docks Ltd*[1] and by Diplock LJ in the present case.[2] There is no doubt that a person who fulfils that test is an 'occupier'. He is the person who says 'come in'; but I think that that test is too narrow by far. There are other people who are 'occupiers', even though they do not say 'come in'. If a person has any degree of control, over the state of the premises it is enough. The position is best shown by examining the cases in four groups.

First, where a landlord let premises by demise to a tenant, he was regarded as parting with all control over them. He did not retain any degree of control, even though he had undertaken to repair the structure. Accordingly, he was held to be under no duty to any person coming lawfully on to the premises, save only to the tenant under the agreement to repair. In *Cavalier v Pope*[3] it was argued that the premises were under the control of the landlord because of his agreement to repair: but the House of Lords rejected that argument. That case has now been overruled by s. 4 of the Act of 1957[4] to the extent therein mentioned.

Secondly, where an owner let floors or flats in a building to tenants, but did not demise the common staircase or the roof or some other parts, he was regarded as having retained control of all parts not demised by him. Accordingly, he was held to be under a duty in respect of those retained parts to all persons coming lawfully on to the premises. So he was held liable for a defective staircase in *Miller v Hancock*,[5] for the gutters of the roof in *Hargroves, Aronson & Co v Hartopp*[6] and for the private balcony in *Sutcliffe v Clients Investment Co*.[7] The extent of the duty was held to be that owed to a licensee, and not to an invitee, see *Fairman v Perpetual Investment Building Society*;[8] *Jacobs v LCC*.[9] Since the Act of 1957 the distinction between invitees and licensees has been abolished, and the extent of the duty is now simply the common duty of care. But the old cases still apply so as to show that the landlord is responsible for all parts not demised by him, on the ground that he is regarded as being sufficiently in control of them to impose on him a duty of care to all persons coming lawfully on to the premises.

Thirdly, where an owner did not let premises to a tenant but only licensed a person to occupy them on terms which did not amount to a demise, the owner still having the right to do repairs, he was regarded as being sufficiently in control of the structure

---

1. [1947] KB 901 at 917.
2. [1965] 2 All ER at p. 711, letter E.
3. [1906] AC 428.
4. [See p. 444, ante and also p. 482, post.]
5. [1893] 2 QB 177; [1891–94] All ER Rep 736.
6. [1905] 1 KB 472.
7. [1924] 2 KB 746.
8. [1923] AC 74.
9. [1950] AC 361, [1950] 1 All ER 737.

to impose on him a duty towards all persons coming lawfully on to the premises. So he was held liable for a visitor who fell on the defective step to the front door in *Hawkins v Coulsdon and Purley UDC*;[1] and to the occupier's wife for the defective ceiling which fell on her in *Greene v Chelsea Borough Council*.[2] The extent of the duty was that owed to a licensee, but since the Act of 1957 the duty is the common duty of care to see that the structure is reasonably safe.

Fourthly, where an owner employed an independent contractor to do work on premises or a structure, the owner was usually still regarded as sufficiently in control of the place as to be under a duty towards all those who might lawfully come there. In some cases he might fulfil that duty by entrusting the work to the independent contractor: see *Haseldine v Daw & Son Ltd*[3] and s. 2(4) of the Act of 1957. In other cases he might only be able to fulfil it by exercising proper supervision himself over the contractor's work, using due diligence himself to prevent damage from unusual danger (see *Thomson v Cremin*[4] as explained by Lord Reid in *Davie v New Merton Board Mills Ltd*[5]). But in addition to the owner, the courts regarded the independent contractor as himself being sufficiently in control of the place where he worked as to owe a duty of care towards all persons coming lawfully there. He was said to be an 'occupier' also (see *Hartwell v Grayson Rollo and Clover Docks Ltd*[6]), but this is only a particular instance of his general duty of care (see *A C Billings & Sons Ltd v Riden*[7] per Lord Reid).

In the light of these cases, I ask myself whether the respondents had a sufficient degree of control over the premises to put them under a duty to a visitor. Obviously they had complete control over the ground floor and were 'occupiers' of it. But I think that they had also sufficient control over the private portion. They had not let it out to Mr Richardson by a demise. They had only granted him a licence to occupy it, having a right themselves to do repairs. That left them with a residuary degree of control which was equivalent to that retained by the Chelsea Corporation in *Greene's* case.[2] They were in my opinion 'an occupier' within the Act of 1957. Mr Richardson, who had a licence to occupy, had also a considerable degree of control. So had Mrs Richardson, who catered for summer guests. All three of them were, in my opinion, 'occupiers' of the private portion of the 'Golfer's Arms'. There is no difficulty in having more than one occupier at one and the same time, each of whom is under a duty of care to visitors. The Court of Appeal so held in the recent case of *Fisher v CHT Ltd*.[8]

What did the common duty of care demand of each of these occupiers towards their visitors? Each was under a duty to take such care as 'in all the circumstances of the case' was reasonable to see that the visitor would be reasonably safe. So far as the respondents were concerned, the circumstances demanded that on the ground floor they should, by their servants, take care not only of the structure of the building, but also the furniture, the state of the floors and lighting, and so forth, at all hours of day or night when the premises were open. In regard to the private portion, however, the circumstances did not demand so much of the respondents. They ought to have seen that the structure was reasonably safe, including the handrail, and that the system of lighting was efficient; but I doubt whether they were bound to see that the lights were properly switched on or the rugs laid safely on the floor. The respondents were entitled to leave those day-to-day matters to Mr and Mrs Richardson. They, too, were occupiers. The circumstances of the case demanded that Mr and Mrs Richardson

---

1. [1954] 1 QB 319; [1954] 1 All ER 97.
2. [1954] 2 QB 127; [1954] 2 All ER 318.
3. [1941] 2 KB 343; [1941] 3 All ER 156.
4. (1941) [1953] 2 All ER 1185.
5. [1959] AC 604 at 642–645; [1959] 1 All ER 346 at 365–367.
6. [1947] KB 901 at 912, 913.
7. [1958] AC 240 at 250; [1957] 3 All ER 1 at 5.
8. [1966] 1 All ER 88.

should take care of those matters in the private portion of the house. And of other matters, too. If they had realised that the handrail was dangerous, they should have reported it to the respondents.

We are not concerned here with Mr and Mrs Richardson. The judge has absolved them from any negligence and there is no appeal. We are only concerned with the respondents. They were, in my opinion, occupiers and under a duty of care. In this respect I agree with Sellers LJ[1] and Winn J, but I come to a different conclusion on the facts. I can see no evidence of any breach of duty by the respondents. So far as the handrail was concerned, the evidence was overwhelming that no-one had any reason before this accident to suppose that it was in the least dangerous. So far as the light was concerned, the proper inference was that it was removed by some stranger shortly before Mr Wheat went down the staircase. Neither the respondents nor Mr and Mrs Richardson could be blamed for the act of a stranger.

I would, therefore, dismiss this appeal.

LORD MORRIS OF BORTH-Y-GEST: . . . Who, then, for this purpose is an occupier? I say 'for this purpose' because in other circumstances there may be different identification (e.g. in connexion with rating or in connexion with the franchise). Section 1(1) of the Act of 1957 speaks of 'an occupier of premises'. Section 1(2) refers to 'a person's occupation or control of premises': it goes on to refer to 'any invitation or permission he gives (or is to be treated as giving) to another to enter or use the premises'. This, I think, shows that exclusive occupation is not necessary to constitute a person an occupier. In his speech in *Glasgow Corpn v Muir*[2] Lord Wright said[3]:

'Before dealing with the facts, I may observe that in cases of invitation the duty has most commonly reference to the structural condition of the premises, but it may clearly apply to the use which the occupier (or whoever has control so far as material) of the premises permits a third party to make of the premises.'

This illustrates that there may be someone who would ordinarily be regarded as the occupier of premises while at the same time there may be another occupier who has 'control so far as material'. . . . Questions of fact may arise as to the nature and extent of occupation and control. Thus in *Prenton v General Steam Navigation Co Ltd*[4] there was a question whether contractors were sufficiently in occupation of the 'tween decks of a ship for the purposes of their work to owe a duty to an employee of their sub-contractors. It was said by Jenkins LJ, in *Pegler v Craven*,[5] that the conception of 'occupation' is not necessarily and in all circumstances confined to the actual personal occupation of the person termed the occupier himself, and that in certain contexts and for certain purposes it extends to vicarious occupation by a caretaker or other servant or by an agent.

[His Lordship referred to the service agreement between the respondents and Mr Richardson, under which, inter alia, the respondents retained the right of entry for certain purposes, including inspection of the state of repair of the property. He also referred to the arrangements allowing guests and continued:] . . . The general result of the agreement and of the arrangements to which I have referred was that the respondents through their servant were in occupation of the whole premises. Their servant was required to be there. The contemplation, it would appear, was that the respondents would see to the condition of the premises and would effect any necessary repairs. As the residential part would constitute the home of the manager

1 [1965] 2 All ER at p. 705, letter B.
2. [1943] AC 448; [1943] 2 All ER 44.
3. [1943] AC at p. 462; [1943] 2 All ER at p. 51.
4. (1944) 77 Ll L Rep 174.
5. [1952] 2 QB 69 at 74; [1952] 1 All ER 685 at 687.

and his family it was a reasonable inference, and it would be mutually assumed, that his privacy in regard to it would be respected. It would be mutually assumed that the respondents could not as of right enter that part save for the defined purpose of viewing its condition and state of repair. There was freedom for the manager or his wife to make contracts with and to receive and entertain visitors for reward.

The conclusion which I reach is that as regards the premises as a whole both the respondents and the manager were occupiers but that by mutual arrangement the respondents would not (subject to certain over-riding considerations) exercise control over some parts. They gave freedom to their manager to live in his home in privacy. They gave him freedom to furnish it as and how he chose. They gave him freedom to receive personal guests and also to receive guests for reward. I think it follows that both the respondents and the Richardsons were 'occupiers' vis-à-vis Mr Wheat and his party. . . .

LORD PEARSON: . . . It seems to me clear that Mr and Mrs Richardson had at least some occupational control of the upper part of the premises to which the appeal relates. They lived there. They provided the furniture. They for their own benefit took in paying guests and received them and looked after them. The paying guests would have been their invitees at common law, and were their visitors under the Act of 1957. Moreover, Mr and Mrs Richardson were present and able to see the state of the premises and what was being done or omitted therein. If anything was wrong, they could take steps to rectify it or have it rectified. If there were any danger, they could protect the paying guests by erecting a barrier or giving a warning or otherwise. Mr and Mrs Richardson were appropriate persons for bearing and fulfilling the common duty of care. . . . I think that the respondents, however, also had some occupational control of the upper part of the premises. The lower part, the licensed part, was occupied by the respondents through their servant Mr Richardson and their agent Mrs Richardson for the purpose of the liquor-selling business of the respondents. The agreement applied to the whole of the premises without distinguishing between the two parts. Mr Richardson as manager for the respondents was required as well as entitled to occupy the whole of the premises on their behalf. He was required to live in the upper part for the better performance of his duties as manager of the business of the respondents. His right to live there, and the permission to take in paying guests, were perquisites of the employment. The paying guests, though invited by the Richardsons, had the respondents' permission to come and were therefore visitors of the respondents as well as of the Richardsons. The fact that the respondents gave permission for the Richardsons to take in paying guests is important as showing that the respondents had some control over the admission of persons to the upper part of the premises. The respondents did not themselves say 'Come in', but they authorised the Richardsons to say 'Come in'. The respondents had, under cl. 5 of the agreement, an express right to enter the premises for viewing the state of repair, and, as was conceded (correctly in my opinion), an implied right to do the repairs found to be necessary. It is fair to attribute to the respondents some responsibility for the safety of the premises for those who would, in pursuance of the authority given by the respondents, be invited to enter as paying guests the upper part of the premises. In matters relating to the design and condition of the structure they would be in a position to perform the common duty of care.

For these reasons I agree that there was, for the purposes of occupiers' liability, dual occupation of the upper part of the premises; but as there was no proof of negligence on the part of the respondents I would dismiss the appeal.

[VISCOUNT DILHORNE and LORD PEARCE delivered speeches in favour of dismissing the appeal.]

Appeal dismissed

Question

What was the basis for the decision that the respondents were in occupation of the area in question? Cf. *Stone v Taffe* [1974] 3 All ER 1016; [1974] 1 WLR 1575.

Note

The four groups of cases to which Lord Denning referred in *Wheat v Lacon* were cited in *Harris v Birkenhead Corpn* [1976] 1 All ER 341; [1976] 1 WLR 279 in support of the view that a person does not need to have actual physical possession to be an occupier. In the *Harris* case a house owned by one person but let out to a tenant was to be compulsorily purchased by the defendant local authority which served notices of entry on the tenant and the owner. The notices stated that the local authority would enter on and take possession of the property fourteen days after service; however, possession was not taken for several months and in fact did not occur until shortly after the relevant date for the purposes of this case. Before the relevant date, though some months after the service of the notices of entry, the tenant left the house which thereafter remained unoccupied. The local authority argued that before it could be an occupier in this case there had to be an actual or symbolic taking of possession on its behalf. This contention was rejected. Whilst the possibility that someone with an immediate right to enter premises might not be an occupier until he physically took possession was left open, the local authority was held by the Court of Appeal to be an occupier on the facts of this case; the facts which were stressed were (a) that the house was uninhabited and (b) that the previous occupier had left because of the local authority's lawful assertion of an immediate right to enter and control which allowed it at any time to dispossess the owner and the person occupying the house at the time of the assertion of the right.

(ii) The common duty of care — relevant factors

Sawyer *v* H and G Simonds Ltd Queen's Bench Division (1966) 197 Estates Gazette 877

In this case Mr Kenneth George Sawyer, of 65 Donnington Gardens, Reading, Berks, claimed damages for personal injury caused by the negligence and/or breach of statutory duty of the defendants, H & G Simonds Ltd, brewers, of Reading, as owners and occupiers of the Ship Hotel, Duke Street, Reading.

Giving judgment, VEALE J, said that on 18 June 1960, Mr Sawyer received an injury when he fell in a bar in the Ship Hotel and damaged his hand in some way on some glass on the floor. It was a very long time ago, and giving evidence in 1966 was a matter of great difficulty in the recollection of anybody. Mr Sawyer's story was that he had ordered a half of bitter for himself, his first drink of the day, and a half of bitter for an acquaintance. He positioned himself on a bar stool and placed his feet on the bar rail, when the stool slipped on some liquor on the floor and he fell backwards. In putting out his hand to break the fall his hand was cut by broken glass from which the liquor had come.

Even if the accident had occurred in the way the plaintiff described it, he still had to prove that there was negligence under the Occupiers' Liability Act 1957. The duty owed by the defendant to the plaintiff was a 'common duty of care' under s. 2 of the Act. This section read: 'The common duty of care is a duty to take such care as in all the circumstances of the case is reasonable to see that the visitor will be reasonably safe in using the premises for the purposes for which he is invited or permitted by the occupier to be there.' This did not extend to the duty of *insuring* the safety of the visitor. Of course it was dangerous to allow broken glass to lie about anywhere where the public came and went. Of course broken glass should be cleared up as soon as possible. But one could not clear up broken glass unless one knew that broken glass was there to be cleared.

The occupier was therefore under a duty to keep a reasonable look-out for this type of danger. The accident had occurred at a busy time in the lunch hour on a Saturday. It was the duty of the hall porter to come in every 20 minutes to clear empty glasses, and if he had seen broken glass on the floor he would have removed it. 'Reasonable care' involved consideration of the nature of the danger, the length of time that the danger was in existence, the steps necessary to remove the danger and the likelihood or otherwise of an injury being caused. The mere fact that this unfortunate accident happened did not connote negligence. There was an adequate system in the hotel for looking out for this kind of danger. The danger of falling from a stool in this way was remote. The barman had no knowledge that glass was on the floor. He (his Lordship) could not find that the defendants were negligent, and he entered judgment for the defendants with costs limited to £85 from the plaintiff, who was legally aided.

Notes

1. Compare this case with *Martin v Middlesbrough Corpn* (1965) 63 LGR 385, where damages were recovered when a schoolgirl slipped and was injured by broken glass. The injury occurred in a school playground and the broken glass was probably part of a milk bottle. The defendants, the local education authority, were held liable, because, in the court's opinion, there should have been better arrangements for disposing of the empty bottles. The standard of care required of the defendants, who owed the common duty of care under the Occupiers' Liability Act 1957, was stated (at p. 386) to be that of 'a prudent parent in relation to his own children': see *North*, pp. 68–70. Compare also *Ward v Tesco Stores Ltd* [1976] 1 All ER 219; [1976] 1 WLR 810 (p. 293, ante) on which see *Clerk & Lindsell*, para. 13–14, note 21.

2. Even if a breach of duty is established, the question of remoteness of damage may rule out a particular claim: *Morgan v Blunden* (1986) Times, 1st February.

Roles *v* Nathan Court of Appeal [1963] 2 All ER 908

A central heating boiler produced a great deal of smoke when lit, and a boiler engineer advised that the flues should be cleaned. Two chimney sweeps were, therefore, engaged to clean the flues of the boiler, which burnt coke and gave off carbon monoxide gas. The engineer warned the sweeps of the danger presented by the fumes, but his warning was disregarded, and one of the sweeps crawled into one of the flues. The next day, after the fire had gone out, the flues were cleaned by the sweeps. However, when the boiler was relit, the fumes still caused problems. Mr Collingwood, an expert, was brought in, and, although he warned the sweeps of the dangers of the fumes, it was only with great difficulty that he could get them to leave the room. Their attitude, he said, was that they were experts. He also advised them, amongst others, that, before the boiler was relit, the vent holes (an inspection chamber in the horizontal flue and a sweep hole in the vertical flue) should be sealed, and he repeated the warning about the gases. Some time later the boiler was lit by an unknown person (it was thought it might have been the caretaker who later disappeared). Whilst the fire was burning, the sweeps carried on with and nearly completed their work. Only the sweep hole in the vertical flue remained to be sealed when they told Mr Corney (the occupier's son-in-law and the man at that time in charge of the rooms where the boiler was situated) that they would finish the job the next day. In fact they came back that evening, but died when they were overcome by the fumes. The widows of the two sweeps sued the occupier of the rooms.

LORD DENNING MR: . . . It is quite plain that these men died because they were overcome by fumes of carbon monoxide. It would appear to a layman that the fumes must have come from the sweep-hole, but the judge on the evidence thought that they probably came from the boiler. But I do not think that it matters. The fumes came from the boiler or the sweep-hole or both. The question is whether anyone was at fault. The judge found Mr Corney guilty of negligence because he 'failed to take such care as should have ensured that there was no fire until the sweep-hole had been sealed'. He said: '. . . unhappily, he did not tell the caretaker to draw the fire, or at any rate not to stoke it up'. On this account he held that Mr Corney was at fault, and the occupier liable. But he found the two sweeps guilty of contributory negligence, and halved the damages. The judge said:

'That negligence [of the chimney sweeps] consisted in the knowledge that there was gas about, or probably would be, the way they ignored explicit warnings, and showed complete indifference to the danger which was pointed out to them in plain language, and this strange indifference to the fact that the fire was alight, when Mr Collingwood had said it ought not to be, until the sweep-hole had been sealed.'

The occupier now appeals and says that it is not a case of negligence and contributory negligence, but that, on the true application of the Occupiers' Liability Act 1957, the occupier was not liable at all. This is the first time that we have had to consider that Act. It has been very beneficial. It has rid us of those two unpleasant characters, the invitee and the licensee, who haunted the courts for years, and it has replaced them by the attractive figure of a visitor, who has so far given no trouble at all. The Act has now been in force six years, and hardly any case has come before the courts in which its interpretation has had to be considered. The draftsman expressed the hope[1] that the Act would

'replace a principle of the common law with a new principle of *the common law*: instead of having the judgment of Willes J[2] construed as if it were a statute, one is to have a statute which can be construed as if it were a judgment of Willes J.'

It seems that his hopes are being fulfilled. All the fine distinctions about traps have been thrown aside and replaced by the common duty of care. . . .

[Having cited s. 2(3) of the 1957 Act, he continued:] That subsection shows that *Christmas v General Cleaning Contractors Ltd*[3] is still good law under this new Act. There a window cleaner (who was employed by independent contractors) was sent to clean the windows of a club. One of the windows was defective; it had not been inspected and repaired as it should have been. In consequence, when the window cleaner was cleaning it, it ran down quickly and trapped his hand, thus causing him to fall. It was held that he had no cause of action against the club. If it had been a

---

1. See *Salmond on Tort* (13th edn) at pp. 512, 513, note 51.
2. In *Indermaur v Dames* (1866) LR 1 CP 274 at 288.
3. [1952] 1 KB 141, [1952] 1 All ER 39; affd sub nom *General Cleaning Contractor Ltd v Christmas* [1953] AC 180; [1952] 2 All ER 1110.

guest who had his fingers trapped by the defective window, the guest could have recovered damages from the club. But the window cleaner could not do so. The reason is this: The householder is concerned to see that the windows are safe for his guests to open and close, but he is not concerned to see that they are safe for a window cleaner to hold on to. The risk of a defective window is a special risk, but it is ordinarily incident to the calling of a window cleaner, and so he must take care for himself, and not expect the householder to do so. Likewise, in the case of a chimney sweep who comes to sweep the chimneys or to seal up a sweep-hole. The householder can reasonably expect the sweep to take care of himself so far as any dangers from the flues are concerned. These chimney sweeps ought to have known that there might be dangerous fumes about and ought to have taken steps to guard against them. They ought to have known that they should not attempt to seal up the sweep-hole whilst the fire was still alight. They ought to have had the fire withdrawn before they attempted to seal it up, or at any rate they ought not to have stayed in the alcove too long when there might be dangerous fumes about. All this was known to these two sweeps; they were repeatedly warned about it, and it was for them to guard against the danger. It was not for the occupier to do it, even though he was present and heard the warnings. When a householder calls in a specialist to deal with a defective installation on his premises, he can reasonably expect the specialist to appreciate and guard against the dangers arising from the defect. The householder is not bound to watch over him to see that he comes to no harm. I would hold, therefore, that the occupier here was under no duty of care to these sweeps, at any rate in regard to the dangers which caused their deaths. If it had been a different danger, as for instance if the stairs leading to the cellar gave way, the occupier might no doubt be responsible, but not for these dangers which were special risks ordinarily incidental to their calling.

Even if I am wrong about this point, and the occupier was under a duty of care to these chimney sweeps, the question arises whether the duty was discharged by the warning that was given to them. This brings us to s. 2(4). . . . We all know the reason for this subsection. It was inserted so as to clear up the unsatisfactory state of the law as it had been left by the decision of the House of Lords in *London Graving Dock Co Ltd v Horton*.[1] That case was commonly supposed to have decided that, when a person comes on to premises as an invitee, and is injured by the defective or dangerous condition of the premises (due to the default of the occupier), it is, nevertheless, a complete defence for the occupier to prove that the invitee knew of the danger, or had been warned of it. Supposing, for instance, that there was only one way of getting into and out of premises, and it was by a footbridge over a stream which was rotten and dangerous. According to *Horton*'s case,[1] the occupier could escape all liability to any visitor by putting up a notice: 'This bridge is dangerous', even though there was no other way by which the visitor could get in or out, and he had no option but to go over the bridge. In such a case, s. 2(4)(a) makes it clear that the occupier would not [2] be liable. But if there were two footbridges, one of which was rotten, and the other safe a hundred yards away, the occupier could still escape liability, even today, by putting up a notice: 'Do not use this footbridge. It is dangerous. There is a safe one further upstream'. Such a warning is sufficient because it does enable the visitor to be reasonably safe.

I think that the law would probably have developed on these lines in any case; see *Greene v Chelsea Borough Council*,[3] where I ventured to say:

'. . . knowledge or notice of the danger is only a defence when the plaintiff is free to act on that knowledge or notice so as to avoid the danger.'

---

1. [1951] AC 737; [1951] 2 All ER 1.
2. [The word should be 'nowadays' – [1963] 1 WLR 1117 at 1124.]
3. [1954] 2 QB 127 at 139; [1954] 2 All ER 318 at 325.

But the subsection has now made it clear. A warning does not absolve the occupier unless it is enough to enable the visitor to be reasonably safe. Apply s. 2(4) to this case. I am quite clear that the warnings which were given to the sweeps were enough to enable them to be reasonably safe. The sweeps would have been quite safe if they had heeded these warnings. They should not have come back that evening and attempted to seal up the sweep-hole while the fire was still alight. They ought to have waited till next morning, and then they should have seen that the fire was out before they attempted to seal up the sweep-hole. In any case they should not have stayed too long in the sweep-hole. In short, it was entirely their own fault. The judge held that it was contributory negligence. I would go further and say that, under the Act, the occupier has, by the warnings, discharged his duty.

I would, therefore, be in favour of allowing this appeal and entering judgment for the defendants.

[HARMAN LJ delivered a judgment in favour of allowing the appeal. PEARSON LJ delivered a judgment in favour of dismissing the appeal, but differing 'only as to the interpretation of the evidence, and not as to any question of law'.]

Appeal allowed

Question

Suppose a plaintiff was injured by a danger of which the normal occupier of premises would not have been aware. If the occupier was in fact aware of this danger, and put up a warning notice, but in the wrong place, could he be liable? (Cf. *Woollins v British Celanese Ltd* (1966) 1 KIR 438.)

Notes

1. Firemen obviously have special skills in dealing with fires and on the position of firemen entering property, see *Ogwo v Taylor* [1988] AC 431; [1987] 3 All ER 961, noted p. 142, ante where the claim by a fireman against the person who started the fire (who was the occupier) was decided as a common law negligence claim by the House of Lords (and see p. 442 ante). Cf. s. 2(3)(b) of the 1957 Act. Liability under that Act can be based on events after the commencement of the fire. An occupier might be liable to an injured fireman if, for example, he negligently failed to warn him of an unexpected danger. Note, however, the view of the House of Lords in *Bermingham v Sher Bros* 1980 SC 67 (dealing with the Occupiers' Liability (Scotland) Act 1960) that there is no duty to provide a safe way of getting into and out of the premises throughout the duration of a fire.

2. *Roles v Nathan* discussed s. 2(3)(b) of the 1957 Act. The other limb of s. 2(3) (i.e. s. 2(3)(a)) requires an occupier to expect children to be less careful than adults. On the other hand, there is the balancing factor that parents have some responsibility for the safety of their children. An occupier is entitled to rely upon parents acting reasonably in protecting their offspring from danger which is obvious to an adult: see *Simkiss v Rhondda Borough Council* (1983) 81 LGR 460 at 467 referring to the pre-1957 Act case of *Glasgow Corpn v Taylor* [1922] 1 AC 44. Consider also *Phipps v Rochester Corpn* [1955] 1 QB 450; [1955] 1 All ER 129.

3. Section 2(4)(a), which was mentioned in *Roles v Nathan*, should also be considered in relation to the decision of the House of Lords in *Titchener v*

British Railways Board [1983] 3 All ER 770; [1983] 1 WLR 1427 decided under the Occupiers' Liability (Scotland) Act 1960 which does not classify categories of entrant. The fifteen-year-old plaintiff was severely injured, and her sixteen-year-old male companion killed, when struck by a train at 11.00 at night at a place where there was a short-cut across a railway line running through a built-up area of Glasgow. Access could be gained to the railway line from the road by climbing up a slope to an embankment on which the railway ran and passing through a gap in the boundary fence, the condition of which, said Lord Hailsham, 'left much to be desired'. Trains crossed by at intervals of about twenty minutes. The British Railways Board were aware that people passed through the gaps in the fence to walk across the line and there was evidence that at least one child had been killed at approximately the same spot. The plaintiff, who had crossed the line on previous occasions, admitted that she was well aware of the existence of the line and of the danger of walking across it, and she said that, when doing so, she normally kept a look-out for trains. No allegation was made that the train was being driven otherwise than in a perfectly proper manner. The House of Lords rejected her claim for damages.

The first reason put forward by Lord Fraser, with whom all their Lordships agreed, was that the Board had discharged its duty to this plaintiff under s. 2(1) of the 1960 Act, the terms of which can be found p. 464, post. This was based on (in addition to the plaintiff's admissions referred to above) the existence of the embankment which meant she could not have unwittingly strayed onto the line, and of the fence which, notwithstanding that it had gaps, gave her warning that she would be on railway premises which she knew to be dangerous. Furthermore, there was no special risk at this part of the line.

In English law the plaintiff might well have been classed as a trespasser (consider *British Railways Board v Herrington* [1972] AC 877; [1972] 1 All ER 749; and see the Occupiers' Liability Act 1984, p. 462, post). However, the case might be examined on the *assumption* that she could have been classed as a licensee in England and hence a 'visitor'. On this basis the approach in the House of Lords is reminiscent of the decision in *London Graving Dock Co Ltd v Horton* [1951] AC 737; [1951] 2 All ER 1 which was criticised by the Law Reform Committee in its Third Report (Cmd. 9305, 1954, para. 77) (although it should be noted that that case concerned an invitee). The decision in *Horton*'s case was to the effect that an occupier discharged his duty to such a visitor by a warning sufficient to convey full knowledge of the nature and extent of the danger. Section 2(4)(a) of the English Act of 1957 abrogates the rule in *Horton*'s case and knowledge of the danger by the visitor, whether as a result of being warned or not, does not necessarily prevent his recovery of damages (see *Bunker v Charles Brand & Son Ltd* [1969] 2 QB 480; [1969] 2 All ER 59). Would a different conclusion have been reached by the House had *Titchener* fallen to be decided under English law and on the basis that the plaintiff would have been classed as a 'visitor'? Note further that Lord Fraser would, if necessary, have been prepared to decide that in the circumstances of the case, no duty was owed to the plaintiff to fence at all, and also that the claim would have failed on grounds of (a) causation and (b) volenti non fit injuria (encapsulated in s. 2(3) of the Scottish Act).

4. Section 2(4)(b) deals with the occupier's liability for independent contractors. For recent discussion in the House of Lords see *Ferguson v Welsh* [1987] 3 All ER 777; [1987] 1 WLR 1553.

(iii) Exclusion of liability

White v Blackmore Court of Appeal [1972] 3 All ER 158

On a Sunday morning, the plaintiff's husband entered as a competitor for some 'jalopy' races. Later that day, he returned with his wife (the plaintiff), baby and mother-in-law to the course, and paid the entrance fee for his wife and mother-in-law. As he was a competitor, he entered free. Near to the entrance there was one of several notices headed 'Warning to the public, Motor Racing is Dangerous'. It stated that it was 'a condition of admission that all persons having any connection with the promotion and/or organisation and/or conduct of the meeting, including. . . . the drivers. . . . of the vehicles. . . . are absolved from all liabilities arising out of accidents causing damage or personal injury (whether fatal or otherwise) howsoever caused to spectators or ticketholders.' In addition, p. 2 of the programme, of which he received three copies when he entered the course with his family, contained a substantially similar clause, although the cover of the programme made no reference to there being any conditions. At one point after a race, the plaintiff's husband went across to join his family who were behind the spectators' rope some way from the track, although he did not cross the rope. After another race had started, a car's wheel became entangled in the safety ropes about ⅓ of a mile away with the result that it pulled up the stakes holding these ropes, and the master stake, which held several ropes, close to where the husband was standing. He was thrown through the air, badly injured and later died. His widow claimed damages from several defendants, two of whom were the chairman of the jalopy club which was holding the races and the racing organiser. The meeting was being held to aid a charity. The widow's claim was rejected by the trial judge on the ground that the maxim volenti non fit injuria applied. The plaintiff appealed, but her appeal was dismissed.

BUCKLEY LJ: The learned judge found the defendants, who are sued personally and as representing the members of the Severn Valley Jalopy Club, guilty of negligence as organisers of the jalopy race meeting on account of the way in which the ropes were attached to the post near which the deceased was standing when the accident happened. Counsel for the defendants has submitted that the judge applied too high a standard in arriving at this decision. There was, in my judgment, material before the learned judge on which he could properly arrive at this conclusion, which I think should not be disturbed. The judge went on to hold that the defendants were nevertheless entitled to succeed in their defence on the ground of the doctrine enshrined in the maxim volenti non fit injuria. Strictly, I think that that doctrine is not applicable in the present case, but the somewhat analogous law relating to exclusion of liability.

The doctrine of volenti non fit injuria affords a shield of defence to a party who would otherwise be liable in tort to an opponent who has by his conduct voluntarily encountered a risk which was fully known to him at the time. . . . The learned judge expressed the view that it might not have been at all obvious to the deceased that he was standing in a particularly dangerous place when the accident occurred. Accepting this, I do not think it can be said in the present case that the deceased had full knowledge of the risk which he was running.

In my judgment the case must turn on the effect of the various warnings which the deceased saw or had ample opportunity to see. If these warnings were, or any of them was, sufficient to exclude any duty of care on the part of the organisers of the meeting towards the deceased, the defendants were not guilty of negligence and consequently they do not need the shield of the doctrine of volenti. The learned judge in fact based his decision on these warnings.

I need not repeat the history of the relevant events on the day of the accident. Counsel for the plaintiff has submitted that when the deceased signed on in the morning of that day he entered into a contractual arrangement with the organisers that he should be permitted to come on to the field for the purpose of competing in the races, and that that contract could not be affected by any of the subsequent events of the day. That contract, he says, was not subject to any limitation of liability except possibly one to the effect that competitors taking part in races did so at their own risk. Consequently, counsel submits, the organisers' liability to the deceased when he came on to the field in the afternoon was subject to no relevant limitation. In my judgment, the evidence does not support the suggestion that the parties had any intention of entering into contractual relations when the deceased signed on in the morning. He was thereby indicating to the organisers, as the learned judge thought and as I think, that he proposed to take part in the racing in the afternoon as a competitor and no more. Accordingly I do not feel able to accept this submission of counsel for the plaintiff.

When the deceased returned with his family in the afternoon, the notice[1] . . . was prominently displayed near the entrance to the ground. The learned judge found as a fact that the deceased saw that notice and appreciated that it was a notice governing the conditions under which people were to be admitted to watch the racing.

No argument was addressed to us based on the Occupiers' Liability Act 1957, s. 2(4). This, I think, was right. To the extent that the notice at the entrance was a warning of danger, I agree with Lord Denning MR[2] that it did not enable a visitor to be reasonably safe, but the notice was more than a warning of a danger: it was designed to subject visitors to a condition that the classes of persons mentioned in it should be exempt from liability arising out of accidents. Section 2(4) has, it seems to me, no application to this aspect of the notice.

In my opinion, when the deceased came on to the field in the afternoon, he did so as a gratuitous licensee. I have already said that, in my view, no contract was made in the morning. The deceased made no payment for entry in the afternoon. Nothing that occurred in the morning could afford consideration for any contract entered into in the afternoon. In my judgment, no contract between the promoters and the deceased was made in the afternoon. The deceased remained willing to take part in the races and the promoters remained willing to allow him to do so. On the evidence, he was not, in my judgment, either bound or entitled contractually to take part in the races. In this state of affairs he was allowed on to the field free of charge.

I think that when the deceased came on to the field in the afternoon he did so in a dual capacity, as a prospective competitor and as a spectator. He was not intending to take part in all the races run on that afternoon, and I can feel no doubt that part of his object in attending the meeting was to enjoy watching those races in which he was not a competitor as well as to compete in those races in which he proposed to compete. There was considerable discussion in the course of the argument whether this notice was applicable to the deceased. Counsel for the plaintiff contended that, if he was wrong about a contract having been entered into in the morning, at least a licence was then granted to the deceased to enter the field in the afternoon for the purpose of competing in the races and counsel contended that such licence was irrevocable until the deceased had completed the purpose for which it was granted, that is to say, until he had completed those races in which he proposed to take part. For my part I think that no licence was granted to the deceased in the morning beyond an implied licence permitting him to leave his jalopy in the pits coupled with a further implied licence allowing him in due course to remove his jalopy from the field. Whether this be right or not, whatever licence was granted to the deceased by the organisers in the morning was, in my judgment, a gratuitous one. It was not, as was suggested, a licence coupled with an interest. It could consequently be revoked or varied by the organisers at any time subject only to the deceased being given a suitable

---

1. [See the statement of facts, ante.]
2. [His dissenting judgment has been omitted.]

opportunity to remove his property from the field. In the absence of any express term, a revocable licence can be revoked by whatever notice is reasonable in the circumstances (*Winter Garden Theatre (London) Ltd v Millennium Productions Ltd*).[1] Since, in my view, the deceased had no legal right to insist on taking part in the races, there is no reason to regard any licence granted to him in the morning as irrevocable until he had completed those races in which he proposed to take part. In the circumstances of this case I think any licence granted to the deceased in the morning was revocable summarily subject only to his right to recover his jalopy. If it was revocable, it was to a like extent variable.

What then was the effect of the situation which arose when the deceased returned to the field in the afternoon? It is clear that the occupier of land, who permits someone else to enter on that land as his licensee, can by imposing suitable conditions limit his own liability to the licensee in respect of any risks which may arise while the licensee is on the land (*Ashdown v Samuel Williams & Sons Ltd*[2]). The Occupiers' Liability Act 1957, which in s. 2(1) refers to an occupier excluding his duty of care to any visitor 'by agreement or otherwise', has not altered the law in this respect. Counsel for the plaintiff concedes that in the present case the notice displayed at the entrance to the ground was sufficient to exclude liability on the part of the organisers of the meeting to all spectators properly so called, but he contends that a distinction is to be drawn between competitors and spectators for this purpose. It is common ground that the deceased was not a ticket-holder within the meaning of the notice, but, in my judgment, he was a spectator. The learned judge so held, and I think that he was right in doing so. The notice was, in my opinion, sufficiently explicit in its application to the deceased. I feel unable to accept the suggestion that the heading 'Warning to the Public' should be read in a restrictive sense excluding competitors. Reading the document as a whole, I think there can be no doubt that it was addressed to all persons answering the descriptions of spectators or ticket-holders. The deceased was not even a member of the Severn Valley Jalopy Club. He was, in my opinion, a member of the public. The organisers are, I think, shown to have taken all reasonable steps to draw the condition contained in the notice to the attention of the deceased. The learned judge found that warnings of this character were a common feature at jalopy races with which the deceased would have been familiar. He also found, as I have already said, that the deceased saw this particular notice and appreciated its character. He also found that the deceased saw a number of other notices in identical terms posted about the field and that he appreciated what these notices were intended to effect. I think that he came on to the field in the afternoon on the terms contained in the notice displayed at the entrance to the ground.

The liability of the organisers of the meeting to visitors attending it for the purpose of taking part in some races and watching others was in my opinion limited in two respects. Such a visitor, in my judgment, [is] a competitor and when engaged in the role of a competitor, accepted all the risks inherent in the sport of jalopy racing. The organisers owed no duty to him to protect him against those risks. . . . As a spectator, such a visitor was, I think, subject to the condition set out in the warning notice. At the time when the accident occurred the deceased was, in my opinion, a spectator. The limitation on the liability of the organisers in these circumstances is to be found in the notice. The condition set out in the notice was that they were to be absolved from all liabilities arising out of accidents causing damage or personal injury howsoever caused. The use of the words 'howsoever caused' makes clear that the absolution was intended to be of a general character. The effect of the condition must, in my judgment, amount to the exclusion of liability for accidents arising from the organisers' own negligence. For these reasons I consider that the learned judge was right in dismissing the action. This makes it unnecessary for me to consider the effect

---

1. [1948] AC 173; [1947] 2 All ER 331.
2. [1957] 1 QB 409; [1957] 1 All ER 35.

of the warning notice which was printed on the inner face of the programme.
I would dismiss this appeal.

[ROSKILL LJ delivered a judgment in favour of dismissing the appeal. LORD DENNING
MR delivered a judgment in favour of allowing the appeal.]

Question

If the deceased had been killed as a result of being run over by a negligently
driven jalopy, would the notice in this case have protected the driver? (See
generally *North*, pp. 126–130.)

Note

The question of exclusion of liability arose in an important case decided just
before the 1957 Act — *Ashdown v Samuel Williams & Sons Ltd* [1957] 1 QB
409; [1957] 1 All ER 35. The plaintiff's place of work was on property leased
by the first defendants to her employers, the second defendants, and to reach
her place of employment the plaintiff used a short cut which lay across land
retained by the first defendants. The short cut crossed several railway lines,
and the plaintiff, when crossing one of these lines, was injured by a truck,
which was being shunted by the first defendants' employees. They were found
to have been negligent. A notice erected by the first defendants could be
seen by people using the short cut, and it stated that those on the property
were there at their own risk, and that they should not have any claim against
these defendants for any injury they received, however caused. The Court of
Appeal held that the plaintiff entered the land as a licensee, and that the terms
of the notice were effective to exclude the first defendants' liability. The defendants had 'taken all reasonable steps to bring the conditions to her notice' (per
Parker LJ): it did not matter that she had only read part of the notice. It was
mentioned above that *Ashdown v Samuel Williams & Sons Ltd* was a pre-
Occupiers' Liability Act decision. In the light of s. 2(1) of that Act, it was
thought that it was still valid after the Act was passed and this view is supported by *White v Blackmore*. See also the comments on this decision in
Burnett v British Waterways Board [1973] 2 All ER 631; [1973] 1 WLR 700.
For further comment on *Ashdown*'s case, see notes by L. C. B. Gower (1956)
20 MLR 532 (dealing with the decision in the court below) and (1957) 20 MLR
181, and see F. J. Odgers [1957] CLJ 39 at 42–54. However, it should be noted
that the actual decision on exclusion in *Ashdown*'s case would not be the same
today because of the statutory provisions referred to post and set out at p. 389,
ante.

The Unfair Contract Terms Act 1977, p. 389, ante

Notes

1. For discussion of the position of the occupier before this Act was passed,
see C. R. Symmons (1974) 38 Conv (NS) 253. Although the Unfair Contract
Terms Act 1977 has curtailed the scope of the occupier's ability to exclude
his liability, it has only brought about a curtailment and not a total ban in
all circumstances.
   In the first place, by virtue of s. 1(3), the relevant part of the Act only applies

to 'business liability'. Section 1(3) does tell us a little more about this phrase and s. 14 includes certain activities within the meaning of the word 'business'; apart from this, however, and apart from such guidance as can be obtained from judicial decisions interpreting the word 'business' in other contexts, we must await future case law for the precise scope of the word 'business' to be made clearer. For general discussion, see e.g. J. Mesher [1979] Conv 58 at 58–60; W. V. H. Rogers and M. G. Clarke, *The Unfair Contract Terms Act 1977*. The Act has obviously affected *Ashdown v Samuel Williams & Sons Ltd* [1957] 1 QB 409; [1957] 1 All ER 35 noted p. 459, ante, but *White v Blackmore* (p. 456, ante) is an example of a case in which liability was excluded, but which may not be caught by s. 2.

The Occupiers' Liability Act 1957 applies to damage to property (though see *North*, pp. 94–112) and therefore the second point to note about s. 2 is that sub-s. (2) allows the occupier to exclude his liability for damage to property if the contract term or notice 'satisfies the requirement of reasonableness'. Thus, to apply this sub-section the student needs to know about the pre-Act position concerning the exclusion of liability, as well as the requirement of reasonableness under the Unfair Contract Terms Act 1977, on which see Mesher, op cit, p. 61.

2. The recent amendment to s. 1 of the Unfair Contract Terms Act 1977 by s. 2 of the Occupiers' Liability Act 1984, which has been set out at p. 390, ante, came into force on 13th May 1984. Its purpose is to promote greater access to the countryside. It was thought that landowners would be more willing to allow access for the purposes laid down by the amendment if liability to such visitors could be excluded. However, during the debates in Parliament, some concern was expressed that the section needed to be amended so as to clarify the position where a charge is made for access. If too uncertain, of course, the section might fail to achieve its object. What is the position of a landowner who charges for entry to his premises purely to cover expenses and no more? Do you think this would take the case into the category of 'business liability'?

Another point to notice is that the amendment to s. 1(3) of the 1977 Act only covers damage arising from the dangerous state of the premises. This raises the distinction between what has been termed the 'activity duty' and the 'occupancy duty' on which see p. 442, ante. Contrast the wording of s. 1(1) of the 1984 Act (p. 462, post). Do you think that activities associated with occupation (e.g. driving a tractor from one field to another, as opposed to driving a car on one's property while on the way to the shops) are not covered by this amendment to the 1977 Act? What about operating machinery fixed in one place on the land?

In relation to the stated purpose of this amendment are there in any event reasons, other than fear of legal liability, which discourage landowners from permitting access and which are not of course affected by the amendment (e.g. fear of the damage the public might do)? See M. A. Jones (1984) 47 MLR 713 at 726. Generally on the interpretation of s. 2 of the 1984 Act, see R. J. Bragg and M. R. Brazier (1986) 130 SJ 251 and 274.

3. Section 2(3) of the Unfair Contract Terms Act 1977 is concerned with the defence of volenti non fit injuria, which in the Occupiers' Liability Act 1957 is enshrined in s. 2(5). This defence has already been discussed in chap. 7 (p. 391, ante) but note at this stage that in *White v Blackmore* (p. 456, ante) Buckley LJ distinguished this defence from the law relating to exclusion of

liability. Nevertheless, according to *Burnett v British Waterways Board* [1973] 2 All ER 631; [1973] 1 WLR 700, exclusion of liability may, as does volenti, require the plaintiff to have had a choice in the matter. (See the note on the *Burnett* case by J. R. M. Lowe (1974) 37 MLR 218, which discusses the point under consideration here, and see further p. 391, ante.)

(b)   To trespassers

Note

The Occupiers' Liability Act 1957 does not regulate the duty which is owed to trespassers. This used to depend on the common law, which, once a person had been classified as a trespasser, traditionally excluded him from the ambit of any duty of reasonable care. This is shown by *R Addie & Sons (Collieries) Ltd v Dumbreck* [1929] AC 358; [1929] All ER Rep 1, where Lord Hailsham LC put forward (at p. 4) the following celebrated proposition:

'Towards the trespasser the occupier has no duty to take reasonable care for his protection or even to protect him from concealed danger. The trespasser comes on to the premises at his own risk. An occupier is in such a case liable only where the injury is due to some wilful act involving something more than the absence of reasonable care. There must be some act done with the deliberate intention of doing harm to the trespasser, or at least some act done with reckless disregard of the presence of the trespasser.'

Whilst it might be said that a burglar deserves no better treatment, it was much more difficult to apply this remark to the case of an 'innocent' trespassing child. Nevertheless, the traditional approach asserted that this was the only duty owed to the 'innocent' child, once he was classified as a trespasser, and it equated the position of the adult and the child within this category. This was a rigid approach which could operate harshly, and yet if the magic tag 'occupier' was absent, then the contractor, who was carrying on activities on the land but who was not an occupier of that land, could be held liable for negligence to a person whom he injured, even though that person was a trespasser vis-à-vis the occupier.

It was not surprising, therefore, that ways were sought to mitigate the harshness of the law. This could be achieved if it were decided that the plaintiff had an implied licence and, therefore, was not a trespasser, a decision which could more readily be reached in the case of a child. A more drastic step was taken in *Videan v British Transport Commission* [1963] 2 QB 650; [1963] 2 All ER 860, in which the Court of Appeal made some progress towards the imposition of liability for negligence. Lord Denning MR took the view that, where the occupier was conducting activities on his land, a duty of care extended to a trespasser whose presence ought to be foreseen, and Harman LJ also based the occupier's liability to trespassers for activities he carried out on his land on the foreseeability doctrine (cf. Pearson LJ). However, it was not long before these views were criticised by the Privy Council in *Railways Comr v Quinlan* [1964] AC 1054; [1964] 1 All ER 897, which basically reaffirmed the *Addie* rule. Undeterred, the Court of Appeal in *Kingzett v British Railways Board* (1968) 112 Sol Jo 625 followed *Videan*, and this conflict of authority remained until, a few years later, the issue reached the House of Lords in *British Railways Board v Herrington* [1972] AC 877; [1972] 1 All ER 749. The House took the opportunity to restate the duty owed to trespassers, but unfortunately did not speak with one voice. Without purporting to give a comprehensive picture of the decision, three particular approaches in the speeches might perhaps be mentioned. In Lord Reid's opinion (at p. 758):

'. . . [T]he question whether an occupier is liable in respect of an accident to a trespasser on his land would depend on whether a conscientious humane man with his knowledge, skill and resources could reasonably have been expected to have done or refrained from doing before the accident something which would have avoided it. If he knew before the accident that there was a substantial probability that trespassers would come, I think that most people would regard as culpable failure to give any thought to their safety.'

On the other hand Lord Pearson thought that if the occupier knew of or should reasonably have anticipated the presence of a trespasser, then he owed that trespasser a duty of humanity. Somewhere between these two views was that of Lord Diplock. The occupier must actually know of the trespasser's presence or of facts that make it likely; similarly he must actually know of facts concerning his land or activities on it which are likely to cause injury to a trespasser. The reasonable man's perception of the likelihood of the trespasser's presence and the danger was then the yardstick, but it had to be based on facts actually known to the occupier. The duty was confined to 'taking reasonable steps to enable the trespasser to avoid the danger'; and for the duty to arise the degree of likelihood 'of the trespasser's presence at the actual time and place of danger to him [must be] such as would impel a man of ordinary humane feelings to take some steps to mitigate the risk of injury to the trespasser to which the particular danger exposes him' ([1972] 1 All ER at p. 796).

The duty owed to a trespasser (the duty of common humanity) was seen in *Herrington* as a lower duty than the common duty of care under the Occupiers' Liability Act 1957. Particularly noteworthy features of the decision were that a majority of the House of Lords favoured the view that the occupier's actual resources should be taken into account, and, as indicated ante, that there was support for some degree of subjectivity in relation to the occupier's knowledge. More detailed treatment of *Herrington* and discussion of the later case law will not be undertaken, however, because of the legislative activity in this field. The question of liability to trespassers was referred to the Law Commission after the *Herrington* decision and its report was published in 1976 (*Report on Liability for Damage or Injury to Trespassers and Related Questions of Occupiers' Liability*, Law Com. No. 75, Cmnd. 6428). The proposals contained in this report in relation to uninvited entrants were approved by the Pearson Commission (vol. 1, chap. 28) and were the basis for s. 1 of the Occupiers' Liability Act 1984, post, although there are differences.

The Occupiers' Liability Act 1984

1. Duty of occupier to persons other than his visitors. — (1) The rules enacted by this section shall have effect, in place of the rules of the common law, to determine —
  (a) whether any duty is owed by a person as occupier of premises to persons other than his visitors in respect of any risk of their suffering injury on the premises by reason of any danger due to the state of the premises or to things done or omitted to be done on them; and
  (b) if so, what that duty is.

(2) For the purposes of this section, the persons who are to be treated respectively as an occupier of any premises (which, for those purposes, include any fixed or movable structure) and as his visitors are —

(a) any person who owes in relation to the premises the duty referred to in section 2 of the Occupiers' Liability Act 1957 (the common duty of care), and

(b) those who are his visitors for the purposes of that duty.

(3) An occupier of premises owes a duty to another (not being his visitor) in respect of any such risk as is referred to in subsection (1) above if —

(a) he is aware of the danger or has reasonable grounds to believe that it exists;

(b) he knows or has reasonable grounds to believe that the other is in the vicinity of the danger concerned or that he may come into the vicinity of the danger (in either case, whether the other has lawful authority for being in that vicinity or not); and

(c) the risk is one against which, in all the circumstances of the case, he may reasonably be expected to offer the other some protection.

(4) Where, by virtue of this section, an occupier of premises owes a duty to another in respect of such a risk, the duty is to take such care as is reasonable in all the circumstances of the case to see that he does not suffer injury on the premises by reason of the danger concerned.

(5) Any duty owed by virtue of this section in respect of a risk may, in an appropriate case, be discharged by taking such steps as are reasonable in all the circumstances of the case to give warning of the danger concerned or to discourage persons from incurring the risk.

(6) No duty is owed by virtue of this section to any person in respect of risks willingly accepted as his by that person (the question whether a risk was so accepted to be decided on the same principles as in other cases in which one person owes a duty of care to another).

(7) No duty is owed by virtue of this section to persons using the highway, and this section does not affect any duty owed to such persons.

(8) Where a person owes a duty by virtue of this section, he does not, by reason of any breach of the duty, incur any liability in respect of any loss of or damage to property.

(9) [I]n this section —

'highway' means any part of a highway other than a ferry or waterway;

'injury' means anything resulting in death or personal injury, including any disease and any impairment of physical or mental condition; and

'movable structure' includes any vessel, vehicle or aircraft.

3. Application to Crown. — Section 1 of this Act shall bind the Crown, but as regards the Crown's liability in tort shall not bind the Crown further than the Crown is made liable in tort by the Crown Proceedings Act 1947.

Question

When introducing at its Second Reading in the House of Lords the provision which became (with some amendment) s. 1 of the 1984 Act, Lord Hailsham stated that it 'does not aim to destroy the existing law but follows the biblical injunction to fulfil it by combining in a single set of propositions the slightly different lines of argument by which the members of the Appellate Committee, who were concerned in *Herrington*'s case, arrived at the same general conclusion' (443 H. L. Debs. (5th Series) col. 720). Do you think that s. 1 has this effect? In relation to the occupier's knowledge do you regard it as most similar to the approach of Lord Reid, Lord Pearson or Lord Diplock in *Herrington*? Are the occupier's actual resources still a relevant factor?

Notes

1. This legislation came into force on 13th May, 1984.

2. Section 1 of the Occupiers' Liability Act 1984 does not cover damage to property; cf. the Occupiers' Liability (Scotland) Act 1960. Any such liability will, therefore, have to be found at common law. It might be thought that the common law would be unlikely to view such a claim favourably (note e.g. the references to 'humanity' in *Herrington*) and thus that the trespasser whose clothes or car are damaged may well have no redress. On the other hand, consider the Law Commission's view, note 5, post and note also *Tutton v AD Walter Ltd* [1986] QB 61; [1985] 3 All ER 757 where (obiter) *Herrington* was regarded as applicable to property damage (bees).

3. The Occupiers' Liability (Scotland) Act 1960 covers both lawful visitors and trespassers. Section 2(1) states:

'The care which an occupier of premises is required, by reason of his occupation or control of the premises, to show towards a person entering thereon in respect of dangers which are due to the state of the premises or to anything done or omitted to be done on them and for which the occupier is in law responsible shall, except in so far as he is entitled to and does extend, restrict, modify or exclude by agreement his obligations towards that person, be such care as in all the circumstances of the case is reasonable to see that that person will not suffer injury or damage by reason of any such danger.'

The Scottish Act contains no provision equivalent to s. 1(3) of the 1984 Act; yet it does not appear to have caused any problems in practice. What cases are excluded by s. 1(3) that would otherwise have been successful under a straightforward 'reasonable care in all the circumstances' requirement? Compare para. 27 of the Law Commission's Report. See generally M. A. Jones (1984) 3 Lit 283 at 284–285.

4. For litigation on the 1984 Act see *White v St Albans City* (1990) Times, 12th March where it was accepted that the mere fact of a defendant having taken measures to stop entry onto land containing some danger did not necessarily mean that the 'reasonable grounds to believe' element in s. 1(3)(b) had been satisfied.

5. It was mentioned at p. 442, ante that it was uncertain whether the Occupiers' Liability Act 1957 covered what has been termed the 'activity duty' as well as the 'occupancy duty'; but it may also be remembered that the issue was unlikely to be of practical importance. On the difficulties of this distinction in the pre-1957 law, see *North*, pp. 71–82. If the 1957 Act does not cover the 'activity duty', nevertheless it should be noted that the 'occupancy duty' it does cover includes activities which affect the safety of the premises. The Law Commission, which took the view that the 1957 Act does not apply to the 'activity duty', thought the scope of its proposed legislation concerning the duty owed to uninvited entrants (which to an extent became the 1984 Act) should be similar. The trespasser injured by, for example, the negligent driving of a car by the person who was the occupier, would be left to bring a claim at common law for negligence; the fact that the plaintiff was trespassing would merely affect the foreseeability of his presence and thereby be relevant to the question of negligence liability.

When assessing the merits of this approach, it should be borne in mind that the distinction between 'occupancy' and 'activity' has not been without difficulty in the past. Consider further the uncertainty surrounding the scope of the 1957 Act which was mentioned p. 442, ante. If the 1957 Act were interpreted by the courts as encompassing the 'activity duty', then this would negate the argument put forward by the Law Commission for so restricting the 1984 Act. A further point to consider arises from *British Railways Board v Herrington* [1972] AC 877; [1972] 1 All ER 749, noted p. 462, ante. Whereas a distinction between the static condition of the land and the occupier's operations on it had been drawn in relation to trespassers in *Videan v British Transport Commission* [1963] 2 QB 650; [1963] 2 All ER 860 (though see *North*, pp. 76–78), this distinction was not accepted by the House of Lords in *Herrington*. If *Herrington* was interpreted as covering all activities by the occupier, even driving his car, then it would appear that the duty of humanity should prevail in the area unaffected by the 1984 Act: cf. the Law Commission's view, ante.

6. The Law Commission's view of the position of the trespasser in relation to the 'activity duty', as outlined in the previous note, is similar to what was thought to be the position of the trespasser vis-à-vis the contractor who was not an occupier of the land: see *Buckland v Guildford Gas, Light and Coke Co* [1949] 1 KB 410; [1948] 2 All ER 1086. There was an indication in *Herrington* that the position of the occupier and contractor might be equated: see [1972] AC at pp. 914 and 929 per Lords Wilberforce and Pearson, but see [1972] AC at p. 943 per Lord Diplock, and consider *Pannett v P McGuinness & Co Ltd* [1972] 2 QB 599; [1972] 3 All ER 137; M. H. Matthews [1972A] CLJ 214 at 217–218. Is this likely to pose any problems after the 1984 Act? See further R. A. Buckley [1984] Conv 413 at 416–417.

7. Suppose a person (A), having a right under a contract to enter one part of the premises of another (B), in fact goes into a different part of the premises, becoming a trespasser there, and is injured. If the contract contains a term excluding liability for any injury to A occurring anywhere on B's property, howsoever caused, would this term be struck down by the Unfair Contract Terms Act 1977 (assuming that this is a case of 'business liability')? If not, note that there was an argument (before the 1984 Act was passed) that at common law as a matter of public policy the courts would not allow exclusion of the duty owed to a trespasser: see e.g. B. Coote (1975) 125 NLJ 752; Law Commission, op cit, para. 60; Mesher, op cit, pp. 63–64. Can this sort of argument now be applied to the 1984 Act? If the 1984 Act provides the minimum duty which an occupier can owe another (though see the following note), it might be assumed by the courts that Parliament did not intend to allow the duty to be derogated from; however, note that the 1984 Act specifically permits the volenti defence.

One point to bear in mind is that the Law Commission did expressly provide (in cl. 3 of its proposed legislation) for exclusion of the duty owed to uninvited entrants by a contract term or notice to the extent that reliance on such a term or notice would be fair or reasonable. (This clause in fact also dealt with the question of exclusion in relation to lawful entrants and its provisions on this matter are inconsistent with the Unfair Contract Terms Act 1977.) No such clause appears in the 1984 Act; cf. s. 2(1) of the 1957 Act. What inferences, if any, should be drawn from this? Should the Act be so interpreted as to permit exclusion of the duty there laid down, but not intentional or reckless conduct by the occupier (M. A. Jones (1984) 47 MLR 713 at 724) or perhaps not even a breach of the duty of humanity? (For the problems concerning the method of exclusion of liability to trespassers (assuming exclusion is possible), see the Law Commission, op cit, paras. 64–66.)

What of the visitor to whom the common duty of care has been excluded? It was arguable that a duty of humanity to him could not be excluded before the 1984 Act. If the duty in the 1984 Act is a non-excludable minimum duty to trespassers, which equally cannot be excluded in relation to a visitor, then it would meet the criticism that such a visitor may otherwise be in a worse position than a trespasser. On the other hand, as *Winfield & Jolowicz*, p. 222, point out, there is a danger that this would effectively destroy the freedom to exclude that Parliament has conferred. Might the duty of humanity remain as an unexcludable minimum duty owed to such a visitor (see Buckley, op cit, p. 422); or might the minimum duty only be a duty not to injure intentionally or recklessly?

8. The duty imposed by the 1984 Act is not only owed to trespassers but also applies to other entrants who are not 'visitors' for the purpose of the Occupiers' Liability Act 1957. This category includes persons exercising private rights of way vis-à-vis the owner of the servient tenement (*Holden v White* [1982] QB 679; [1982] 2 All ER 328, though see J. R. Spencer [1983] CLJ 48) since they were not his invitees or licensees at common law. For another category of 'non-visitor' see s. 1(4) of the Occupiers' Liability Act 1957 (p. 443, ante). Those exercising public rights of way were also not invitees or licensees at common law and were not 'visitors' for the purpose of the 1957 Act (*Greenhalgh v British Railways Board* [1969] 2 QB 286; [1969] 2 All ER 114), but by virtue of s. 1(7) of the 1984 Act they are not owed the duty set out in that section. In the case of highways maintainable at the public expense the position is now governed by the Highways Act 1980 on which see *Winfield & Jolowicz*, pp. 418–420. With respect to highways not so maintainable the common law operates and the traditional position has been that there can be liability for misfeasance (e.g. repairing badly) but not for nonfeasance (e.g. not repairing). However, it has been argued that users of such a highway are protected by the duty of humanity in *British Railways Board v Herrington* [1972] AC 877; [1972] 1 All ER 749, noted p. 462, ante, and that support for this can be found in *Thomas v British Railways Board* [1976] QB 912; [1976] 3 All ER 15: see Buckley, op cit, pp. 415–416; cf. *Brady v Department of the Environment* [1988] 1 NIJB 1.

9. For comment on the Occupiers' Liability Act 1984 see Jones, op cit; Buckley, op cit.

2 Non-occupiers' liability for premises

Murphy v Brentwood District Council House of Lords [1990] 2 All ER 908

For the facts and other extracts from this case, see p. 212, ante. These extracts should be read again at this point in addition to the extracts post.

LORD BRIDGE OF HARWICH [having set out the passage headed '*Dangerous defects and defects of quality*' which can be found p. 222, ante, continued:]

The complex structure theory
In my speech in the *D & F Estates* case [1988] 2 All ER 992 at 1006–1007, [1989] AC
177 at 206–207 I mooted the possibility that in complex structures or complex chattels
one part of a structure or chattel might, when it caused damage to another part of
the same structure or chattel, be regarded in the law of tort as having caused damage
to 'other property' for the purpose of the application of *Donoghue v Stevenson*
principles. I expressed no opinion as to the validity of this theory, but put it forward
for consideration as a possible ground on which the facts considered in *Anns* might
be distinguishable from the facts which had to be considered in *D & F Estates* itself.
I shall call this for convenience 'the complex structure theory' and it is, so far as I
can see, only if and to the extent that this theory can be affirmed and applied that
there can be any escape from the conclusions I have indicated above under the rubric
'Dangerous defects and defects of quality'.

The complex structure theory has, so far as I know, never been subjected to express
and detailed examination in any English authority. . . .

. . . The reality is that the structural elements in any building form a single indivisi-
ble unit of which the different parts are essentially interdependent. To the extent that
there is any defect in one part of the structure it must to a greater or lesser degree
necessarily affect all other parts of the structure. Therefore any defect in the structure
is a defect in the quality of the whole and it is quite artificial, in order to impose a
legal liability which the law would not otherwise impose, to treat a defect in an integral structure, so far as it weakens the structure, as a dangerous defect liable to
cause damage to 'other property'.

A critical distinction must be drawn here between some part of a complex structure
which is said to be a 'danger' only because it does not perform its proper function in
sustaining the other parts and some distinct item incorporated in the structure which
positively malfunctions so as to inflict positive damage on the structure in which it is
incorporated. Thus, if a defective central heating boiler explodes and damages a house
or a defective electrical installation malfunctions and sets the house on fire, I see no
reason to doubt that the owner of the house, if he can prove that the damage was due
to the negligence of the boiler manufacturer in the one case or the electrical contractor
in the other, can recover damages in tort on *Donoghue v Stevenson* principles. But the
position in law is entirely different where, by reason of the inadequacy of the foundations of the building to support the weight of the superstructure, differential settlement
and consequent cracking occurs. Here, once the first cracks appear, the structure as
a whole is seen to be defective and the nature of the defect is known. Even if, contrary
to my view, the initial damage could be regarded as damage to other property caused
by a latent defect, once the defect is known the situation of the building owner is
analogous to that of the car owner who discovers that the car has faulty brakes.[1] He
may have a house which, until repairs are effected, is unfit for habitation, but, subject
to the reservation I have expressed with respect to ruinous buildings at or near the
boundary of the owner's property, the building no longer represents a source of danger
and as it deteriorates will only damage itself.

For these reasons the complex structure theory offers no escape from the conclusion that damage to a house itself which is attributable to a defect in the structure
of the house is not recoverable in tort on *Donoghue v Stevenson* principles, but
represents purely economic loss which is only recoverable in contract or in tort by
reason of some special relationship of proximity which imposes on the tortfeasor a
duty of care to protect against economic loss.

---

1. [Lord Bridge had earlier stated ([1990] 2 All ER at p. 927):
   'If I buy a secondhand car and find it to be faulty, it can make no difference to
   the manufacturer's liability in tort whether the fault is in the brakes or in the
   engine, ie whether the car will not stop or will not start. In either case the car is
   useless until repaired. The manufacturer is no more liable in tort for the cost of
   the repairs in the one case than in the other.']

The relative positions of the builder and the local authority

I have so far been considering the potential liability of a builder for negligent defects in the structure of a building to persons to whom he owes no contractual duty. Since the relevant statutory function of the local authority is directed to no other purpose than securing compliance with building byelaws or regulations by the builder, I agree with the view expressed in *Anns* and by the majority of the Court of Appeal in *Dutton* that a negligent performance of that function can attract no greater liability than attaches to the negligence of the builder whose fault was the primary tort giving rise to any relevant damage. I am content for present purposes to assume, though I am by no means satisfied that the assumption is correct, that where the local authority, as in this case or in *Dutton*, has in fact approved the defective plans or inspected the defective foundations and negligently failed to discover the defect, its potential liability in tort is coextensive with that of the builder.

Only Stamp LJ in *Dutton* was prepared to hold that the law imposed on the local authority a duty of care going beyond that imposed on the builder and extending to protection of the building owner from purely economic loss. I must return later to consider the question of liability for economic loss more generally, but here I need only say that I cannot find in *Hedley Byrne & Co Ltd v Heller & Partners Ltd* [1963] 2 All ER 575, [1964] AC 465 or *Home Office v Dorset Yacht Co Ltd* [1970] 2 All ER 294, [1970] AC 1004 any principle applicable to the circumstances of *Dutton* or the present case that provides support for the conclusion which Stamp LJ sought to derive from those authorities.

Imminent danger to health or safety

A necessary element in the building owner's cause of action against the negligent local authority, which does not appear to have been contemplated in *Dutton* but which, it is said in *Anns*, must be present before the cause of action accrues, is that the state of the building is such that there is present or imminent danger to the health or safety of persons occupying it. Correspondingly the damages recoverable are said to include the amount of expenditure necessary to restore the building to a condition in which it is no longer such a danger, but presumably not any further expenditure incurred in any merely qualitative restoration. I find these features of the *Anns* doctrine very difficult to understand. The theoretical difficulty of reconciling this aspect of the doctrine with previously accepted legal principle was pointed out by Lord Oliver in *D & F Estates* [1988] 2 All ER 992 at 1011, [1989] AC 177 at 212–213. But apart from this there are, as it appears to me, two insuperable difficulties arising from the requirement of imminent danger to health or safety as an ingredient of the cause of action which lead to quite irrational and capricious consequences in the application of the *Anns* doctrine. The first difficulty will arise where the relevant defect in the building, when it is first discovered, is not a present or imminent danger to health or safety. What is the owner to do if he is advised that the building will gradually deteriorate, if not repaired, and will in due course become a danger to health and safety, but that the longer he waits to effect repairs the greater the cost will be? Must he spend £1,000 now on the necessary repairs with no redress against the local authority? Or is he entitled to wait until the building has so far deteriorated that he has a cause of action and then to recover from the local authority the £5,000 which the necessary repairs are now going to cost? I can find no answer to this conundrum. A second difficulty will arise where the latent defect is not discovered until it causes the sudden and total collapse of the building, which occurs when the building is temporarily unoccupied and causes no damage to property except to the building itself. The building is now no longer capable of occupation and hence cannot be a danger to health and safety. It seems a very strange result that the building owner should be without remedy in this situation if he would have been able to recover from the local authority the full cost of repairing the building if only the defect had been discovered before the building fell down.

Liability for economic loss

All these considerations lead inevitably to the conclusion that a building owner can only recover the cost of repairing a defective building on the ground of the authority's negligence in performing its statutory function of approving plans or inspecting buildings in the course of construction if the scope of the authority's duty of care is wide enough to embrace purely economic loss. The House has already held in *D & F Estates* that a builder, in the absence of any contractual duty or of a special relationship of proximity introducing the *Hedley Byrne* principle of reliance, owes no duty of care in tort in respect of the quality of his work. As I pointed out in *D & F Estates*, to hold that the builder owed such a duty of care to any person acquiring an interest in the product of the builder's work would be to impose on him the obligations of an indefinitely transmissible warranty of quality.

By s. 1 of the Defective Premises Act 1972 Parliament has in fact imposed on builders and others undertaking work in the provision of dwellings the obligations of a transmissible warranty of the quality of their work and of the fitness for habitation of the completed dwelling. But, besides being limited to dwellings, liability under that Act is subject to a limitation period of six years from the completion of the work and to the exclusion provided for by s. 2. It would be remarkable to find that similar obligations in the nature of a transmissible warranty of quality, applicable to buildings of every kind and subject to no such limitations or exclusions as are imposed by the 1972 Act, could be derived from the builder's common law duty of care or from the duty imposed by building byelaws or regulations. In *Anns* Lord Wilberforce expressed the opinion that a builder could be held liable for a breach of statutory duty in respect of buildings which do not comply with the byelaws. But he cannot, I think, have meant that the statutory obligation to build in conformity with the byelaws by itself gives rise to obligations in the nature of transmissible warranties of quality. If he did mean that, I must respectfully disagree. I find it impossible to suppose that anything less than clear express language such as is used in s. 1 of the 1972 Act would suffice to impose such a statutory obligation.

As I have already said, since the function of a local authority in approving plans or inspecting buildings in the course of construction is directed to ensuring that the builder complies with building byelaws or regulations, I cannot see how, in principle, the scope of the liability of the authority for a negligent failure to ensure compliance can exceed that of the liability of the builder for his negligent failure to comply.

There may, of course, be situations where, even in the absence of contract, there is a special relationship of proximity between builder and building owner which is sufficiently akin to contract to introduce the element of reliance so that the scope of the duty of care owed by the builder to the owner is wide enough to embrace purely economic loss. The decision in *Junior Books Ltd v Veitchi Co Ltd* [1982] 3 All ER 201, [1983] 1 AC 520 can, I believe, only be understood on this basis.

In *Sutherland Shire Council v Heyman* (1985) 60 ALR 1 the critical role of the reliance principle as an element in the cause of action which the plaintiff sought to establish is the subject of close examination, particularly in the judgment of Mason J. The central theme of his judgment, and a subordinate theme in the judgments of Brennan and Deane JJ, who together with Mason J formed the majority rejecting the *Anns* doctrine, is that a duty of care of a scope sufficient to make the authority liable for damage of the kind suffered can only be based on the principle of reliance and that there is nothing in the ordinary relationship of a local authority, as statutory supervisor of building operations, and the purchaser of a defective building capable of giving rise to such a duty. I agree with these judgments. It cannot, I think, be suggested, nor do I understand *Anns* or the cases which have followed *Anns* in Canada and New Zealand to be in fact suggesting, that the approval of plans or the inspection of a building in the course of construction by the local authority in performance of their statutory function and a subsequent purchase of the building by the plaintiff are circumstances in themselves sufficient to introduce the principle of reliance which is the foundation of a duty of care of the kind identified in *Hedley Byrne*.

In *Dutton* [1972] 1 All ER 462 at 475, [1972] 1 QB 373 at 397–398 Lord Denning MR said:

'. . . Mrs Dutton has suffered a grievous loss. The house fell down without any fault of hers. She is in no position herself to bear the loss. Who ought in justice to bear it? I should think those who were responsible. Who are they? In the first place, the builder was responsible. It was he who laid the foundations so badly that the house fell down. In the second place, the council's inspector was responsible. It was his job to examine the foundations to see if they would take the load of the house. He failed to do it properly. In the third place, the council should answer for his failure. They were entrusted by Parliament with the task of seeing that houses were properly built. They received public funds for the purpose. The very object was to protect purchasers and occupiers of houses. Yet, they failed to protect them. Their shoulders are broad enough to bear the loss.'

These may be cogent reasons of social policy for imposing liability on the authority. But the shoulders of a public authority are only 'broad enough to bear the loss' because they are financed by the public at large. It is pre-eminently for the legislature to decide whether these policy reasons should be accepted as sufficient for imposing on the public the burden of providing compensation for private financial losses. If they do so decide, it is not difficult for them to say so.

I would allow the appeal.

LORD OLIVER OF AYLMERTON: . . . In the 13 years which have elapsed since the decision of this House in *Anns v Merton London Borough* [1977] 2 All ER 492, [1978] AC 728 the anomalies which arise from its literal application and the logical difficulty in relating it to the previously established principles of the tort of negligence have become more and more apparent. This appeal and the appeal in *Dept of the Environment v Thomas Bates & Son Ltd* [1990] 2 All ER 943 which was heard shortly before it, have highlighted some of the problems which *Anns* has created and underline the urgent need for it now to be re-examined.

In approaching such a re-examination there are number of points to be made at the outset. Firstly, it has to be borne in mind that neither in *Anns* nor in *Dutton v Bognor Regis United Building Co Ltd* [1972] 1 All ER 462, [1972] 1 QB 373, which preceded it, was the liability of the local authority based on the proposition that the Public Health Act 1936 gave rise to an action by a private individual for breach of statutory duty of the type contemplated in *Cutler v Wandsworth Stadium Ltd* [1949] 1 All ER 544, [1949] AC 398, a type of claim quite distinct from a claim in negligence (see *London Passenger Transport Board v Upson* [1949] 1 All ER 60 at 67, [1949] AC 155 at 168 per Lord Wright). The duty of the local authority was, as Lord Wilberforce stressed in the course of his speech in *Anns* [1977] 2 All ER 492 at 504, [1978] AC 728 at 758, the ordinary common law duty to take reasonable care, no more and no less.

Secondly, in neither case was it possible to allege successfully that the plaintiffs had relied on the proper performance by the defendant of its Public Health Act duties so as to invoke the principles expounded in *Hedley Byrne & Co Ltd v Heller & Partners Ltd* [1963] 2 All ER 575, [1964] AC 465. In the course of his speech in *Anns* [1977] 2 All ER 492 at 512–513, [1978] AC 728 at 768–769 Lord Salmon was at pains to emphasise that the claim had nothing to do with reliance.

Thirdly, the injury of which the plaintiffs complained in *Anns* was not 'caused' by the defendant authority in any accepted sense of the word. The complaint was not of what the defendant had done but of what it had not done. It had failed to prevent the builder of the flats from erecting a substandard structure. It is true that in *Dutton* the basis for liability was said, by both Lord Denning MR and Sachs LJ, to rest on the defendant's ability to control the building operation, from which it might be inferred that it was so involved in the operation as to be directly responsible for the defective foundations. This, whilst it goes no way towards resolving many of the difficulties arising from the decision, might be thought perhaps to provide a more acceptable basis for liability, but it was specifically rejected in *Anns* [1977] 2 All ER 492 at 500, [1978] AC 728 at 754 per Lord Wilberforce.

Fourthly, although in neither case was the builder who had actually created the defect represented at the hearing, the fact that the claim was, in essence, one based on the failure of the defendant to prevent the infliction of tortious injury by the builder rendered it necessary to determine also the question of what, if any, liability lay on him. If the builder was under no obligation to the plaintiffs to take reasonable care to provide proper foundations it is difficult to see how the defendant authority could be liable for failing to prevent what was, vis-à-vis the plaintiffs, lawful conduct on his part save on the footing that the 1936 Act imposed an absolute statutory duty to ensure that no substandard building was erected. But, as already mentioned, the action was not one for breach of statutory duty. The liability of the local authority and that of the builder are not, therefore, logically separable.

Finally, despite the categorisation of the damage as 'material, physical damage' (see *Anns* [1977] 2 All ER 492 at 505, [1978] AC 728 at 759 per Lord Wilberforce), it is, I think, incontestable on analysis that what the plaintiffs suffered was pure pecuniary loss and nothing more. If one asks, 'What were the damages to be awarded *for*?' clearly they were not to be awarded for injury to the health or person of the plaintiffs, for they had suffered none. But equally clearly, although the 'damage' was described, both in the Court of Appeal in *Dutton* and in this House in *Anns*, as physical or material damage, this simply does not withstand analysis. To begin with, it makes no sort of sense to accord a remedy where the defective nature of the structure has manifested itself by some physical symptom, such as a crack or a fractured pipe, but to deny it where the defect has been brought to light by, for instance, a structural survey in connection with a proposed sale. Moreover, the imminent danger to health or safety which was said to be the essential ground of the action was not the result of the physical manifestations which had appeared but of the inherently defective nature of the structure which they revealed. They were merely the outward signs of a deterioration resulting from the inherently defective condition with which the building had been brought into being from its inception and cannot properly be described as damage caused to the building in any accepted use of the word 'damage'.

In the speech of Lord Bridge and in my own speech in *D & F Estates Ltd v Church Comrs for England* [1988] 2 All ER 992, [1989] AC 177 there was canvassed what has been called 'the complex structure theory'. This has been rightly criticised by academic writers, although I confess that I thought that both Lord Bridge and I had made it clear that it was a theory which was not embraced with any enthusiasm but was advanced as the only logically possible explanation of the categorisation of the damage in *Anns* as 'material, physical damage'. Lord Bridge has, in the course of his speech in the present case, amply demonstrated the artificiality of the theory and, for the reasons which he has given, it must be rejected as a viable explanation of the underlying basis for the decision in *Anns*. However that decision is analysed, therefore, it is in the end inescapable that the only damage for which compensation was to be awarded and which formed the essential foundation of the action was pecuniary loss and nothing more. The injury which the plaintiff suffers in such a case is that his consciousness of the possible injury to his own health or safety or that of others puts him in a position in which, in order to enable him either to go on living in the property or to exploit its financial potentiality without that risk, whether substantial or insubstantial, he has to expend money in making good the defects which have now become patent. . . .

[Having delivered that part of his speech which can be found pp. 223–225, ante, LORD OLIVER continued:] [Proximity] is an expression which persistently defies definition, but my difficulty in rationalising the basis of *Dutton* and *Anns* is and has always been not so much in defining it as in discerning the circumstances from which it could have been derived. For reasons which I have endeavoured to explain, the starting-point in seeking to rationalise these decisions must, as it seems to me, be to establish the basis of the liability of the person who is the direct and immediate cause of the plaintiff's loss. Anyone, whether he be a professional builder or a do-it-yourself enthusiast, who builds or alters a semi-permanent structure must be taken to contemplate that at some time in the future it will, whether by purchase, gift or inheritance, come to be occupied by another person and that if it is defectively built or altered it may fall down and injure that person or his property or may put him in a position in which, if he wishes to occupy it safely or comfortably, he will have to expend money on rectifying the defect. The case of physical injury to the owner or his licensees or to his or their property presents no difficulty. He who was responsible for the defect (and it will be convenient to refer to him compendiously as 'the builder') is, by the reasonable foreseeability of that injury, in a proximate 'neighbour' relationship with the injured person on ordinary *Donoghue v Stevenson* principles. But, when no such injury has occurred and when the defect has been discovered and is therefore no longer latent, whence arises that relationship of proximity required to fix him with responsibility for putting right the defect? Foresight alone is not enough, but from what else can the relationship be derived? Apart from contract, the manufacturer of a chattel assumes no responsibility to a third party into whose hands it has come for the cost of putting it into a state in which it can safely continue to be used for the purpose for which it was intended. *Anns*, of course, does not go so far as to hold the builder liable for every latent defect which depreciates the value of the property but limits the recovery, and thus the duty, to the cost of putting it into a state in which it is no longer an imminent threat to the health or safety of the occupant. But it is difficult to see any logical basis for such a distinction. If there is no relationship of proximity such as to create a duty to avoid pecuniary loss resulting from the plaintiff's perception of non-dangerous defects, on what principle can such a duty arise at the moment when the defect is perceived to be an imminent danger to health? Take the case of an owner-occupier who has inherited the property from a derivative purchaser. He suffers, in fact, no 'loss' save that the property for which he paid nothing is less valuable to him by the amount which it will cost him to repair it if he wishes to continue to live in it. If one assumes the parallel case of one who has come into possession of a defective chattel, for instance a yacht, which may be a danger if it is used without being repaired, it is impossible to see on what principle such a person, simply because the chattel has become dangerous, could recover the cost of repair from the original manufacturer.

The suggested distinction between mere defect and dangerous defect which underlies the judgment of Laskin J in *Rivtow Marine Ltd v Washington Iron Works* [1974] SCR 1189 is, I believe, fallacious. The argument appears to be that because, if the defect had not been discovered and someone had been injured, the defendant would have been liable to pay damages for the resultant physical injury on the principle of *Donoghue v Stevenson* it is absurd to deny liability for the cost of preventing such injury from ever occurring. But once the danger ceases to be latent there never could be any liability. The plaintiff's expenditure is not expenditure incurred in minimising the damage or in preventing the injury from occurring. The injury will not now ever occur unless the plaintiff causes it to do so by courting a danger of which he is aware and his expenditure is incurred not in preventing an otherwise inevitable injury but in order to enable him to continue to use the property or the chattel.

My Lords, for the reasons which I endeavoured to state in the course of my speech in *D & F Estates Ltd v Church Comrs for England* [1988] 2 All ER 992, [1989] AC 177 and which are expounded in more felicitous terms both in the speeches of my noble and learned friends in the instant case and in that of Lord Keith in *Dept of the Environment v Thomas Bates & Son Ltd* [1990] 2 All ER 943, I have found it impossible to reconcile the liability of the builder propounded in *Anns* with any previously accepted principles of the tort of negligence and I am able to see no circumstances from which there can be deduced a relationship of proximity such as to render the builder liable in tort for pure pecuniary damage sustained by a derivative owner with whom he has no contractual or other relationship. Whether, as suggested in the speech of my noble and learned friend Lord Bridge, he could be held responsible for the cost necessarily incurred by a building owner in protecting himself from potential liability to third parties is a question on which I prefer to reserve my opinion until the case arises, although I am not at the moment convinced of the basis for making such a distinction.

If then, the law imposes on the person primarily responsible for placing on the market a defective building no liability to a remote purchaser for expenditure incurred in making good defects which, ex hypothesi, have injured nobody, on what principle is liability in tort to be imposed on a local authority for failing to exercise its regulatory powers so as to prevent conduct which, on this hypothesis, is not tortious? Or, to put it another way, what is it, apart from the foreseeability that the builder's failure to observe the regulations may create a situation in which expenditure by a remote owner will be required, that creates the relationship of proximity between the authority and the remote purchaser? A possible explanation might, at first sight, seem to be that the relationship arises from the mere existence of the public duty of supervision imposed by the statute. That, I think, must have been the view of Stamp LJ in *Dutton*, for he regarded the liability of the local authority as arising quite independently of that of the builder. His was, however, a minority view which derives no support from the reasoning of this House in *Anns* and cannot stand up to analysis except on the basis (a) that the damage sustained was physical damage and (b) that the local authority, by reason of its ability to oversee the operation, was the direct cause of the defective construction. Neither of these propositions in my judgment is tenable.

The instant case is, to an extent, a stronger case than *Anns*, because there the authority was under no duty to carry out an inspection whereas here there was a clear statutory duty to withhold approval of the defective design. This, however, can make no difference in principle and the reasoning of the majority in *Anns*, which clearly links the liability of the local authority to that of the builder, must equally apply. The local authority's duty to future owners of the building to take reasonable care in exercising its supervisory function was expressed in *Anns* to arise 'on principle', but it is not easy to see what the principle was, unless it was simply the foreseeability of possible injury alone, which it is now clear, is not in itself enough. The only existing principle on which liability could be based was that propounded in the *Dorset Yacht* case [1970] 2 All ER 294, [1970] AC 1004, that it is to say that the relationship which existed between the authority and the plaintiff was such as to give arise to a positive duty to prevent another person, the builder, from inflicting pecuniary injury. But in a series of decisions in subsequent cases, in particular *Curran v Northern Ireland Co-ownership Housing Association Ltd* [1987] 2 All ER 13, [1987] AC 718 and *Hill v Chief Constable of West Yorkshire* [1988] 2 All ER 238, [1989] AC 53, this House has been unable to find in the case of other regulatory agencies with powers as wide as or wider than those under the Public Health Acts such a relationship between the regulatory authority and members of the public for whose protection the statutory powers were conferred (see also *Yuen Kun-yeu v A-G of Hong Kong* [1987] 2 All ER 705, [1988] AC 175).

My Lords, I can see no reason why a local authority, by reason of its statutory powers under the Public Health Acts or its duties under the building regulations, should be in any different case. Ex hypothesi there is nothing in the terms or purpose of the statutory provisions which support the creation of a private law right of action for breach of statutory duty. There is equally nothing in the statutory provisions which even suggest that the purpose of the statute was to protect owners of buildings from economic loss. Nor is there any easily discernible reason why the existence of the statutory duties, in contradistinction to those existing in the case of other regulatory agencies, should be held in the case of a local authority to create a special relationship imposing a private law duty to members of the public to prevent the conduct of another person which is not itself tortious. . . . With the greatest deference to the high authority of the opinions expressed in *Anns* and in *Dutton*, I cannot see, once it is recognised, as I think that it has to be, that the only damage sustained by discovery of the defective condition of the structure is pure pecuniary loss, how those decisions can be sustained as either an application or a permissible extension of existing principle.

The question that I have found most difficult is whether, having regard to the time which has elapsed and the enormous amount of litigation which has been instituted in reliance on *Anns*, it is right that this House should now depart from it. . . .

For the reasons which I have endeavoured to express I do not think that *Anns* can be regarded as consistent with [the] general principles [of the English law of civil wrongs]. Nor do I think that it can properly be left to stand as a peculiar doctrine applicable simply to defective buildings, for I do not think that its logical consequences can be contained within so confined a compass. It may be said that to hold local authorities liable in damages for failure effectively to perform their regulatory functions serves a useful social purpose by providing what is, in effect, an insurance fund from which those who are unfortunate enough to have acquired defective premises can recover part at least of the expense to which they have been put or the loss of value which they have sustained. One cannot but have sympathy with such a view, although I am not sure that I see why the burden should fall on the community at large rather than be left to be covered by private insurance. But, in any event, like my noble and learned friends, I think that the achievement of beneficial social purposes by the creation of entirely new liabilities is a matter which properly falls within the province of the legislature and within that province alone. At the date when *Anns* was decided the Defective Premises Act 1972, enacted after a most careful consideration by the Law Commission, had shown clearly the limits within which Parliament had thought it right to superimpose additional liabilities on those previously existing at common law and it is one of the curious features of the case that no mention even of the existence of this important measure, let alone of its provisions, and in particular the provision regarding the accrual of the cause of action, appears in any of the speeches or in the reported summary in the Law Reports of the argument of counsel.

There may be very sound social and political reasons for imposing on local authorities the burden of acting, in effect, as insurers that buildings erected in their areas have been properly constructed in accordance with the relevant building regulations. Statute may so provide. It has not done so and I do not, for my part, think that it is right for the courts not simply to expand existing principles but to create at large new principles in order to fulfil a social need in an area of consumer protection which has already been perceived by the legislature but for which, presumably advisedly, it has not thought it necessary to provide.

I would accordingly allow the appeal. . . .

LORD JAUNCEY OF TULLICHETTLE: . . . My Lords, I agree with the views of my noble and learned friend Lord Bridge in this appeal that to apply the complex structure theory to a house so that each part of the entire structure is treated as a separate piece of property is quite unrealistic. A builder who builds a house from foundations upwards is creating a single integrated unit of which the individual components are interdependent. To treat the foundations as a piece of property separate from the walls or the floors is a wholly artificial exercise. If the foundations are inadequate the whole house is affected. Furthermore, if the complex structure theory is tenable there is no reason in principle why it should not also be applied to chattels consisting of integrated parts such as a ship or a piece of machinery. The consequences of such an application would be far reaching. It seems to me that the only context for the complex structure theory in the case of a building would be where one integral component of the structure was built by a separate contractor and where a defect in such a component had caused damage to other parts of the structure, eg a steel frame erected by a specialist contractor which failed to give adequate support to floors or walls. Defects in such ancillary equipment as central heating boilers or electrical installations would be subject to the normal *Donoghue v Stevenson* principle if such defects gave rise to damage to other parts of the building. . . .

[LORD MACKAY OF CLASHFERN LC delivered a speech in favour of allowing the appeal.

LORD BRANDON OF OAKBROOK agreed that the appeal should be allowed for the reasons given by LORD KEITH. LORD ACKNER agreed that the appeal should be allowed for the reasons given by LORD KEITH, LORD BRIDGE, LORD OLIVER and LORD JAUNCEY.]

Notes

1. *Murphy* is of great significance because of its overruling of *Anns*. This has rendered a good deal of the previous case law redundant. Note, however, that the House of Lords left open the position of the local authority where personal injury or damage to other property is caused. On the question of damage to property see, however, the view of Lord Keith (p. 221, ante) which indicates that he would not be in favour of allowing recovery for this type of damage from a local authority in this context; cf. Lord Bridge's speech (p. 468, ante). Given that the liability of the local authority may not have disappeared totally, let us note two points from the earlier case law. First, could the local authority, in performing its duties in relation to the approval or non-approval of plans under the Public Health Act 1936 (see now the Building Act 1984), be liable where it has sought advice from an independent contractor and the latter has been negligent? (See generally p. 851, post.) The Court of Appeal in *Murphy* [1990] 2 All ER 269; [1990] 2 WLR 944 decided that the authority would be liable in such a situation, the common law duty not being discharged if the delegate is negligent. This aspect of the Court of Appeal's decision in *Murphy* (i.e. liability for a delegate) was another point that the House of Lords left open and it therefore remains of relevance if the courts decide that a local authority does owe the more limited duty of care referred to earlier in this note. Secondly, in *Anns* Lord Wilberforce denied that the local authority owed any duty to a negligent building owner; and later case law decided that normally no duty was owed to a building owner who was in breach of the building regulations even if it was the act of an independent contractor, such as an architect or a builder, which had put him in breach and he was not personally negligent. For discussion see *Richardson v West Lindsey District Council* [1990] 1 All ER 296; [1990] 1 WLR 552 interpreting in particular *Governors of the Peabody Donation Fund v Sir Lindsay Parkinson & Co Ltd* [1985] AC 210; [1984] 3 All ER 529; *Investors in Industry Commercial Properties Ltd v South Bedfordshire District Council* [1986] QB 1034; [1986] 1 All ER 787 and *Dennis v Charnwood Borough Council* [1983] QB 409; [1982] 3 All ER 486. In special circumstances (see the *Dennis* case) the plaintiff could still sue. This will also need to be borne in mind if it transpires that a local authority can be liable in cases of personal injury or damage to other property.

2. The House of Lords was influenced in its decision as to whether to overrule *Anns* by its view of the relationship of the courts and the legislature in this field and in particular by the existence of the Defective Premises Act 1972 (p. 480, ante). See also the approach in *D & F Estates Ltd v Church Comrs for England* [1989] AC 177 at 207–208 (when considering the position of a builder) and *McNerny v Lambeth London Borough Council* (1988) 21 HLR 188, noted p. 480, post (dealing with the position of a landlord). Generally on this point, however, consider the argument of P. Cane (1989) 52 MLR 200 at 211 (commenting on *D & F Estates Ltd*) which will be found p. 484, post after the Defective Premises Act 1972 has been set out).

3. On the significance of *Murphy* in the sphere of defective products, see chap. 10, post and on its relevance to the question of recovery of economic lost generally, see p. 212, ante. Other aspects of the decision will be considered later in this section; for example, we shall return to its treatment of the position of builders after the next extract.

Anns *v* London Borough of Merton House of Lords [1977] 2 All ER 492

For the facts see p. 98, ante. As has just been seen, *Murphy* overrules *Anns* in relation to the position of the local authority (although perhaps not totally). Lord Wilberforce's speech in *Anns* (with which three of the other members of the House of Lords agreed) also contains some comments on the position of the builder.

LORD WILBERFORCE: . . . *The position of the builder.* I agree with the majority in the Court of Appeal in thinking that it would be unreasonable to impose liability in respect of defective foundations on the council, if the builder, whose primary fault it was, should be immune from liability. So it is necessary to consider this point, although it does not directly arise in the present appeal. If there was at one time a supposed rule that the doctrine of *Donoghue v Stevenson*[1] did not apply to realty, there is no doubt under modern authority that a builder of defective premises may be liable in negligence to persons who thereby suffer injury: see *Gallagher v N McDowell Ltd*[2], per Lord MacDermott CJ, a case of personal injury. Similar decisions have been given in regard to architects (*Clayton v Woodman & Son (Builders) Ltd*[3], *Clay v A J Crump & Sons Ltd*[4]. *Gallagher*'s case[2] expressly leaves open the question whether the immunity against action of builder-owners, established by older authorities (e g *Bottomley v Bannister*[5]) still survives.

That immunity, as I understand it, rests partly on a distinction being made between chattels and real property, partly on the principle of 'caveat emptor' or, in the case where the owner leases the property, on the proposition that (fraud apart) there is no law against letting a 'tumbledown house' (*Robbins v Jones*[6], per Erle CJ). But leaving aside such cases as arise between contracting parties, when the terms of the contract have to be considered (see *Voli v Inglewood Shire Council*[7], per Windeyer J), I am unable to understand why this principle or proposition should prevent recovery in a suitable case by a person, who has subsequently acquired the house, on the principle of *Donoghue v Stevenson*[1]: the same rules should apply to all careless acts of a builder: whether he happens also to own the land or not. I agree generally with the conclusions of Lord Denning MR on this point (*Dutton*'s case[8]). In the alternative, since it is the duty of the builder (owner or not) to comply with the byelaws, I would be of opinion that an action could be brought against him, in effect, for breach of statutory duty by any person for whose benefit or protection the byelaw was made. . . .

---

1. [1932] AC 562; [1932] All ER Rep 1.
2 [1961] NI 26.
3 [1962] 2 All ER 33; [1962] 1 WLR 585.
4 [1963] 3 All ER 687; [1964] 1 QB 533.
5 [1932] 1 KB 458, [1931] All ER Rep 99.
6 (1863) 15 CBNS 221; [1861–73] All ER Rep 544.
7 (1863) 110 CLR 74 at 85.
8 *Dutton v Bognor Regis UDC* [1972] 1 All ER 462 at 471, 472; [1972] 1 QB 373 at 392–394.

Questions

1. Why do you think Lord Bridge in *Murphy* (p. 223, ante; cf. Lord Oliver, p. 472, ante) would allow an action against a builder for preventive damages in the case of a building near to the highway or a neighbour's property?

2. To what extent do the speeches in *Murphy* distinguish the case where the electric wiring system is installed by an independent contractor and causes damage to the building and the case where the main builder installs it with the same effects? (See further note 1, post.) Should such a distinction be made? What if the original builder a few years later negligently installed a new electric wiring system which causes damage to the building?

Notes

1. Apart from apparently confirming that builders have no immunity at common law (pp. 214–215, ante) (a point made in the extract from *Anns*; cf. note 5, post), *Murphy* provides guidance on the situations when they can be sued in negligence. (As will be seen, this has implications for the Latent Damage Act 1986, p. 488, post.) Prior to *Murphy, D & F Estates Ltd v Church Comrs for England* [1989] AC 177; [1988] 2 All ER 992 had indicated that the builder might be liable for damage to the building itself on the 'complex structure' theory (i.e. different parts of the building would count as different property and consequently a defect in one part causing damage to another part would be a case of damage to other property). Generally on the *D & F Estates* case see I. N. D. Wallace (1989) 105 LQR 46; (1990) 106 LQR 11; P. Cane (1989) 52 MLR 200. Consider now the comments on the 'complex structure' theory in *Murphy* and see Question 2, ante. For Lord Keith (p. 220, ante) and Lord Jauncey (p. 474, ante) damage to the building can be damage to other property where it is caused by for example, a sub-contractor negligently installing the electric wiring. Lord Bridge (p. 467, ante) appears to be distinguishing different ways in which the damage to another part of the building is caused. Note, however, the reference in his example to the person he envisaged being liable. Does this indicate a similar approach to that adopted by Lords Keith and Jauncey? Sub-contracting is a common practice in the construction industry. Does this mean that the restriction, emphasised in *Murphy*, on recovery for damage to a building will be more apparent than real?

On the position of the builder see further *Department of the Environment v Thomas Bates & Son Ltd* [1990] 2 All ER 943; [1990] 3 WLR 457 where the plaintiffs brought an action against the defendant builders for the cost of strengthening certain pillars in a building. This was not a case in which the building was unsafe (the strengthening was for the purpose of enabling it to be loaded to its design capacity), but in any event *Murphy* rejects a distinction between safe and unsafe buildings in this respect. The House of Lords held that the claim failed. Having mentioned that, since *Anns*, it had been accepted that similar principles governed the liability of the builder and the local authority, Lord Keith, with whom the other members of the House of Lords agreed, went on to say (at p. 946):

'To hold in favour of the plaintiffs would involve a very significant extension of the doctrine of *Anns* so as to cover the situation where there existed no damage to the building and no imminent danger to personal safety or health. If *Anns* was correctly decided, such an extension could reasonably be regarded as entirely logical. The undesirability of such an extension, for the reasons stated in *Murphy v Brentwood District Council*, formed an important part of the grounds which led to the conclusion that *Anns* was not correctly decided. That conclusion must lead inevitably to the result that the plaintiffs' claim fails.'

On the other hand, *Junior Books Ltd v Veitchi Co Ltd* [1983] 1 AC 520; [1982] 3 All ER 201, noted p. 226, ante should also be borne in mind in this context. In that case economic loss was held to be recoverable from a sub-contractor and the decision was explained in *Murphy* as falling within 'reliance' principles: see note 3, p. 226, ante, which also deals with comments in earlier cases (e.g. *D & F Estates Ltd*) on *Junior Books*.

2. In *Anns* Lord Wilberforce (p. 476, ante) said that a builder could be sued for breach of statutory duty if he causes damage as a result of breaching the building byelaws (and see *Eames London Estates Ltd v North Hertfordshire District Council* (1980) 18 BLR 50) but a different view was taken in *Perry v Tendring District Council* (1984) 30 BLR 118; and see D. Keating (1984–5) 1 Const LJ 87 at 94–96). (On actions for breach of statutory duty more generally, see chap. 12 post.) In relation to the building regulations made by a Minister under the Public Health Act 1961 (which replaced building byelaws outside Inner London), note *Worlock v SAWS* (1981) 20 BLR 94 where Woolf J thought it would be wrong to construe these regulation as imposing an absolute liability. This point was not dealt with on appeal, (1983) 22 BLR 26, but Woolf J's view gains a measure of support from *Taylor Woodrow Construction (Midlands) Ltd v Charcon Structures Ltd* (1982) 266 Estates Gazette 40 esp. at 44. (Section 1 of the Building Act 1984 now contains the power to make building regulations and the power has been exercised: see the Building Regulations 1985, S.I. No. 1066 of 1985, as amended (which do apply to Inner London).) More recently *D & F Estates Ltd v Church Comrs for England* [1989] AC 177; [1988] 2 All ER 992 apparently accepted that a builder could be liable for breach of the byelaws (which presumably includes the building regulations as well). Such liability could be wide-ranging: on this point and more generally see Wallace, op cit, pp. 72–74. However, consider now the view of Lord Bridge in *Murphy* (p. 469, ante). To what extent does this go against the builder's liability in this tort? Note also Lord Oliver's speech (p. 473, ante) and Lord Mackay's speech in the same case ([1990] 2 All ER at p. 912) on the liability of *a local authority* for breach of statutory duty under the Public Health Acts (now partly replaced). Lord Mackay stated that 'it is not suggested, and does not appear to have been suggested in *Anns*, that the Public Health Act 1936, in particular Pt II, manifests any intention to create statutory rights in favour of owners and occupiers of premises against the local authority charged with responsibility under that Act'. Might Lord Oliver's comments, which also refer to the building regulations, apply to a builder as well?

On the question of the civil actionability of the building regulations, it should be further noted that s. 71 of the Health and Safety at Work etc. Act 1974 provided that breach of a duty imposed by building regulations was to be actionable if it caused damage unless the regulations provided to the contrary. However, this section was never brought into force for this purpose. A similar provision is to be found in s. 38 of the Building Act 1984 (although it was not in force at the time of writing). On liability for breach of statutory duty in this area see further A. M. Dugdale and K. M. Stanton, *Professional Negligence* 2nd edn, paras. 11-10 to 11-12 (written before *Murphy*).

3. For the relevance of intermediate examination, see *Sutherland v C R Maton & Son Ltd* (1976) 3 BLR 87; *Yianni v Edwin Evans & Sons* [1982] QB 438; [1981] 3 All ER 592; *Perry v Tendring District Council* (1984) 30 BLR 118.

4. On the liability of a non-occupying contractor carrying out work on premises to those coming lawfully there, see *A C Billings & Sons Ltd v Riden* [1958] AC 240; [1957] 3 All ER 1 (normal negligence principles). For the liability of architects and surveyors, see R. M. Jackson and J. L. Powell, *Professional Negligence* 2nd edn, chaps. 2 and 3, and note later case law such as *Smith v Eric S Bush* [1990] 1 AC 831; [1989] 2 All ER 514 (p. 175, ante).

5. It might well be thought that the vendor or lessor of defective premises would have been liable to someone injured as a result of his negligence, if not before *M'Alister* (or *Donoghue*) *v Stevenson* [1932] AC 562, then certainly after that decision. However, for a long time the authorities indicated that a vendor or lessor was not liable in negligence for his acts (or failure to act) prior to the sale or letting where persons on the premises were injured after such sale or letting as a result of the premises' defective state. It was thought that this was an area of law which was unaffected by *M'Alister* (or *Donoghue*) *v Stevenson*. This was to be distinguished from the case of a builder who was not an owner (*Sharpe v E T Sweeting & Sons Ltd* [1963] 2 All ER 455; [1963] 1 WLR 665). It should be noted that the landlord's immunity was cut down by s. 4 of the Occupiers' Liability Act 1957 (now repealed by the Defective Premises Act 1972, but replaced in wider terms by s. 4 of that Act). In *Dutton v Bognor Regis U D C* [1972] 1 QB 373; [1972] 1 All ER 462 Lord Denning MR and Sachs LJ attacked this common law immunity, at least so far as hidden defects created on the premises were concerned (per Sachs LJ) and, as we have seen, in *Anns* the House of Lords rejected the supposed immunity of the builder/vendor, an aspect of *Anns* which was seemingly accepted in *Murphy*.

What is the position at common law of a landlord or vendor who merely omits to repair the floorboards or who omits to warn of a defect which is not of his own creation (although in the case of landlords see the wide terms of s. 4 of the Defective Premises Act 1972, p. 482, post)? In the light of *Anns* and *Murphy* would he now be liable in tort at common law to an injured person? Note *Bowen v Paramount Builders (Hamilton) Ltd* [1977] 1 NZLR 394 at 415 where Richmond P expressed the hope that in the case of a vendor who is not a builder 'the time has now arrived when the courts can recognise a duty in tort on the part of a vendor who has actual knowledge of a dangerous but latent defect to warn his purchaser of the existence of that defect'. See further *Winfield & Jolowicz*, p. 233; J. H. Holyoak and D. K. Allen, *Civil Liability for Defective Premises* (London, 1982), paras. 6.40-6.60; J. Martin (1984) 37 Current LP 85.

In *Rimmer v Liverpool City Council* [1985] QB 1; [1984] 1 All ER 930 the Court of Appeal was not prepared to impose a duty of care on landlords to see that the premises were reasonably safe at the time of the letting. In the current state of the law the imposition of such a duty was thought to be a matter for the House of Lords, if not the legislature. On the other hand, the landlords in that particular case were held to owe a duty of care as they had designed and built the flat in which injury to the plaintiff had occurred; in that capacity they owed a duty of reasonable care, in relation to its design and construction, to see that the premises were reasonably safe on being let to a tenant (though see Martin, op cit, pp. 101–102 on the question whether in the Court of Appeal's view the duty would cover a case of a failure to act on information received by such a landlord before a particular letting but after a non-negligent design and construction). Consider further *Ryan v London Borough of Camden* (1982) 8 HLR 75, on which see Martin, op cit, pp. 99–101. Note also *McNerny v Lambeth London Borough Council* (1988) 21 HLR 188 where the Court of Appeal, regarding itself as bound by *Cavalier v Pope* [1906] AC 428, rejected the idea of a duty in negligence on a landlord (who was not liable as a builder) to take reasonable steps to ensure the premises are habitable. As was suggested in *Rimmer*, the courts are likely to regard legislation as necessary to overrule *Cavalier v Pope*. In *McNerny* Dillon LJ said that even if *Cavalier v Pope* was not binding, the task of creating the new duty (referred to ante) was for Parliament not the courts, since this was 'an area where Parliament has intervened to prescribe the duties for landlords that Parliament thinks appropriate' (e.g. s. 4 of the Defective Premises Act 1972, p. 482, post). Is this too great a self-denying ordinance? See further the approach of the House of Lords in *Murphy v Brentwood District Council* [1990] 2 All ER 908; [1990] 3 WLR 414 (p. 212 and p. 466, ante) but see note 5, p. 484, post. Taylor LJ also expressed the view in *McNerny* that the question of the reform of *Cavalier v Pope* was a matter for Parliament because of the problems and uncertainty its demise would cause.

6. Before the developments in the Court of Appeal and the House of Lords mentioned in the previous note, the Law Commission had given its attention to this area of the law in 1970 (*Civil Liability of Vendors and Lessors of Defective Premises*, Law Com. No. 40), and two years later the Defective Premises Act was passed. Section 3 of the Act must be read subject to the developments mentioned in the preceding note.

The Defective Premises Act 1972

1. Duty to build dwellings properly. — (1) A person taking on work for or in connection with the provision of a dwelling (whether the dwelling is provided by the erection or by the conversion or enlargement of a building) owes a duty —
   (a) if the dwelling is provided to the order of any person, to that person; and
   (b) without prejudice to paragraph (a) above, to every person who acquires an interest (whether legal or equitable) in the dwelling;
to see that the work which he takes on is done in a workmanlike or, as the case may be, professional manner, with proper materials and so that as regards that work the dwelling will be fit for habitation when completed.
   (2) A person who takes on any such work for another on terms that he is to do it in accordance with instructions given by or on behalf of that other shall, to the extent to which he does it properly in accordance with those instructions, be treated for the purposes of this section as discharging the duty imposed on him by subsection (1) above except where he owes a duty to that other to warn him of any defects in the instructions and fails to discharge that duty.

(3) A person shall not be treated for the purposes of subsection (2) above as having given instructions for the doing of work merely because he has agreed to the work being done in a specified manner, with specified materials or to a specified design.

(4) A person who —

(a) in the course of a business which consists of or includes providing or arranging for the provision of dwellings or installations in dwellings; or

(b) in the exercise of a power of making such provision or arrangements conferred by or by virtue of any enactment;

arranges for another to take on work for or in connection with the provision of a dwelling shall be treated for the purposes of this section as included among the persons who have taken on the work.

(5) Any cause of action in respect of a breach of the duty imposed by this section shall be deemed, for the purposes of the Limitation Act 1939, the Law Reform (Limitation of Actions, &c.) Act 1954 and the Limitation Act 1963[1], to have accrued at the time when the dwelling was completed, but if after that time a person who has done work for or in connection with the provision of the dwelling does further work to rectify the work he has already done, any such cause of action in respect of that further work shall be deemed for those purposes to have accrued at the time when the further work was finished.

2. Cases excluded from the remedy under section 1. — (1) Where —

(a) in connection with the provision of a dwelling or its first sale or letting for habitation any rights in respect of defects in the state of the dwelling are conferred by an approved scheme to which this section applies on a person having or acquiring an interest in the dwelling; and

(b) it is stated in a document of a type approved for the purposes of this section that the requirements as to design or construction imposed by or under the scheme have, or appear to have, been substantially complied with in relation to the dwelling;

no action shall be brought by any person having or acquiring an interest in the dwelling for breach of the duty imposed by section 1 above in relation to the dwelling.

(2) A scheme to which this section applies —

(a) may consist of any number of documents and any number of agreements or other transactions between any number of persons; but

(b) must confer, by virtue of agreements entered into with persons having or acquiring an interest in the dwellings to which the scheme applies, rights on such persons in respect of defects in the state of the dwellings. . . .

(7) Where an interest in a dwelling is compulsorily acquired —

(a) no action shall be brought by the acquiring authority for breach of the duty imposed by section 1 above in respect of the dwelling; and

(b) if any work for or in connection with the provision of the dwelling was done otherwise than in the course of a business by the person in occupation of the dwelling at the time of the compulsory acquisition, the acquiring authority and not that person shall be treated as the person who took on the work and accordingly as owing that duty.

3. Duty of care with respect to work done on premises not abated by disposal of premises. — (1) Where work of construction, repair, maintenance or demolition or any other work is done on or in relation to premises, any duty of care owed, because of the doing of the work, to persons who might reasonably be expected to be affected by defects in the state of the premises created by the doing of the work shall not be abated by the subsequent disposal of the premises by the person who owed the duty.

---

1. [And note the Limitation Act 1980, a consolidating statute.]

(2) This section does not apply—

(a) in the case of premises which are let, where the relevant tenancy of the premises commenced, or the relevant tenancy agreement of the premises was entered into, before the commencement of this Act [1 January, 1974];

(b) in the case of premises disposed of in any other way, when the disposal of the premises was completed, or a contract for their disposal was entered into, before the commencement of this Act; or

(c) in either case, where the relevant transaction disposing of the premises is entered into in pursuance of an enforceable option by which the consideration for the disposal was fixed before the commencement of this Act.

4. Landlord's duty of care in virtue of obligation or right to repair premises demised.—(1) Where premises are let under a tenancy which puts on the landlord an obligation to the tenant for the maintenance or repair of the premises, the landlord owes to all persons who might reasonably be expected to be affected by defects in the state of the premises a duty to take such care as is reasonable in all the circumstances to see that they are reasonably safe from personal injury or from damage to their property caused by a relevant defect.

(2) The said duty is owed if the landlord knows (whether as the result of being notified by the tenant or otherwise) or if he ought in all the circumstances to have known of the relevant defect.

(3) In this section 'relevant defect' means a defect in the state of the premises existing at or after the material time and arising from, or continuing because of, an act or omission by the landlord which constitutes or would if he had had notice of the defect, have constituted a failure by him to carry out his obligation to the tenant for the maintenance or repair of the premises; and for the purposes of the foregoing provision 'the material time' means—

(a) where the tenancy commenced before this Act, the commencement of this Act; and

(b) in all other cases, the earliest of the following times, that is to say—

(i) the time when the tenancy commences;

(ii) the time when the tenancy agreement is entered into;

(iii) the time when possession is taken of the premises in contemplation of the letting.

(4) Where premises are let under a tenancy which expressly or impliedly gives the landlord the right to enter the premises to carry out any description of maintenance or repair of the premises, then, as from the time when he first is, or by notice or otherwise can put himself, in a position to exercise the right and so long as he is or can put himself in that position, he shall be treated for the purposes of subsections (1) to (3) above (but for no other purpose) as if he were under an obligation to the tenant for that description of maintenance or repair of the premises; but the landlord shall not owe the tenant any duty by virtue of this subsection in respect of any defect in the state of the premises arising from, or continuing because of, a failure to carry out an obligation expressly imposed on the tenant by the tenancy.

(5) For the purposes of this section obligations imposed or rights given by any enactment in virtue of a tenancy shall be treated as imposed or given by the tenancy.

(6) This section applies to a right of occupation given by contract or any enactment and not amounting to a tenancy as if the right were a tenancy, and 'tenancy' and cognate expressions shall be construed accordingly.

5. Application to Crown.—This Act shall bind the Crown, but as regards the Crown's liability in tort shall not bind the Crown further than the Crown is made liable in tort by the Crown Proceedings Act 1947.

6. Supplemental.—(1) In this Act—

'disposal', in relation to premises, includes a letting, and an assignment or surrender of a tenancy, of the premises and the creation by contract of any other right to occupy the premises, and 'dispose' shall be construed accordingly;

'personal injury' includes any disease and any impairment of a person's physical or mental condition;

'tenancy' means —

(a) a tenancy created either immediately or derivatively out of the freehold, whether by a lease or underlease, by an agreement for a lease or underlease or by a tenancy agreement, but not including a mortgage term or any interest arising in favour of a mortgagor by his attorning tenant to his mortgagee; or

(b) a tenancy at will or a tenancy on sufferance; or

(c) a tenancy, whether or not constituting a tenancy at common law, created by or in pursuance of any enactment;

and cognate expressions shall be construed accordingly.

(2) Any duty imposed by or enforceable by virtue of any provision of this Act is in addition to any duty a person may owe apart from that provision.

(3) Any term of an agreement which purports to exclude or restrict, or has the effect of excluding or restricting, the operation of any of the provisions of this Act, or any liability arising by virtue of any such provision, shall be void.

(4) Section 4 of the Occupiers' Liability Act 1957 (repairing landlords' duty to visitors to premises) is hereby repealed.

Questions

1. How does s. 1 alter the common law position? What is the level of the duty which is imposed? Could s. 1 cover economic loss? (Consider Lord Bridge's view in *Murphy v Brentwood District Council* [1990] 2 All ER 908 at 930, p. 469, ante.)

2. Could s. 1 of the Act cover the case of a local authority in the sort of situations discussed in *Anns v Merton London Borough Council* [1978] AC 728, [1977] 2 All ER 492 and *Murphy*? (Consider *Sparham-Souter v Town and Country Developments (Essex) Ltd* [1976] QB 858 at 869–870 and 877.) If it could, how important would this be after *Murphy*?

3. Would any of the sections of the Act be of assistance to a trespasser? (See P. M. North (1973) 36 MLR 628 at 636.)

Notes

1. For discussion of s. 1 of the Act, see *Alexander v Mercouris* [1979] 3 All ER 305; [1979] 1 WLR 1270.

2. Under s. 2 of the Act, it is for the Secretary of State to approve schemes which he is to do by order exercisable by statutory instrument. Various schemes established by the National House-Building Council (N.H.B.C) have been approved for the purposes of s. 2. The last approval was given to a scheme in 1977, and more recently it has not been the practice of the N.H.B.C to seek approval for its schemes.

3. Section 4 of the Act replaces in wider terms s. 4 of the Occupiers' Liability Act 1957. A landlord of course could be liable in contract to his tenant, on which see Holyoak & Allen, op cit, paras. 7.4–7.20.

4. For detailed consideration of the 1972 Act, see J. R. Spencer [1974] CLJ

307 and [1975] CLJ 48. In relation to his Addendum [1975] CLJ at p. 48 discussing the Health and Safety at Work etc. Act 1974, see p. 478, ante.

5. Note the use made of the existence of the Defective Premises Act in *Murphy v Brentwood District Council* [1990] 2 All ER 908; [1990] 3 WLR 414 (p. 212, ante and p. 466, ante) and the other cases referred to in note 2, p. 475, ante. Consider, however, the following argument of P. Cane (1989) 52 MLR 200 at 211, commenting on the earlier decision in *D & F Estates Ltd v Church Comrs for England* [1989] AC 177; [1988] 2 All ER 992:

'Lord Bridge [in *D & F Estates Ltd*] . . . expressed the view that since the enactment of the Defective Premises Act 1972, it would not be right for the courts to impose liability for losses recoverable under that Act by means of a rule which might allow recovery in circumstances where the Act would not. In particular, the common law should not be used to impose liability for the cost of repairing premises other than dwellings, and it should not be used to evade the limitation period for claims under the Act. This argument seems to be based on the problematic idea that once the legislature has enacted legislation on a particular subject matter-in this case, defective premises, the courts are precluded from developing the common law in that area. It also seems to be based on the misplaced faith that the legislature always does, and indeed did in the Defective Premises Act, lay down a set of rules which are much more precise and more carefully limited and crafted than the common law can achieve. Finally, Lord Bridge expressed the opinion that consumer protection is better left to the legislature. Does this mean that when it has the chance the House of Lords will also reverse *Hedley Byrne v Heller* [[1964] AC 465; [1963] 2 All ER 575] and all other rules and principles of the law of tort (including those based on *Donoghue v Stevenson* [[1932] AC 562]) which are intended to, or can be, or are used to protect the consumers of goods and services against producers?'

The Latent Damage Act 1986

Time limits for negligence actions in respect of latent damage not involving personal injuries

1 Time limits for negligence actions in respect of latent damage not involving personal injuries. – The following sections shall be inserted in the Limitation Act 1980 (referred to below in this Act as the 1980 Act) immediately after section 14 (date of knowledge for purposes of special time limits for actions in respect of personal injuries or death) –

Actions in respect of latent damage not involving personal injuries

14A Special time limit for negligence actions where facts relevant to cause of action are not known at date of accrual. – (1) This section applies to any action for damages for negligence, other than one to which section 11[1] of this Act applies, where the starting date for reckoning the period of limitation under subsection (4)(*b*) below falls after the date on which the cause of action accrued.

(2) Section 2[2] of this Act shall not apply to an action to which this section applies.

---

1. [Section 11 basically applies to actions for damages for personal injuries for negligence, nuisance or breach of duty for which a three year limitation period is laid down (though it is possible for it to be extended).]
2. [Section 2 bars tort actions more than six years after the date when the cause of action accrued (though this period can also be extended, albeit in more limited circumstances, e.g. disability).]

(3) An action to which this section applies shall not be brought after the expiration of the period applicable in accordance with subsection (4) below.

(4) That period is either—

(a) six years from the date on which the cause of action accrued; or

(b) three years from the starting date as defined by subsection (5) below, if that period expires later than the period mentioned in paragraph (a) above.

(5) For the purposes of this section, the starting date for reckoning the period of limitation under subsection (4)(b) above is the earliest date on which the plaintiff or any person in whom the cause of action was vested before him first had both the knowledge required for bringing an action for damages in respect of the relevant damage and a right to bring such an action.

(6) In subsection (5) above "the knowledge required for bringing an action for damages in respect of the relevant damage" means knowledge both—

(a) of the material facts about the damage in respect of which damages are claimed; and

(b) of the other facts relevant to the current action mentioned in subsection (8) below.

(7) For the purposes of subsection (6)(a) above, the material facts about the damage are such facts about the damage as would lead a reasonable person who had suffered such damage to consider it sufficiently serious to justify his instituting proceedings for damages against a defendant who did not dispute liability and was able to satisfy a judgment.

(8) The other facts referred to in subsection (6)(b) above are—

(a) that the damage was attributable in whole or in part to the act or omission which is alleged to constitute negligence; and

(b) the identity of the defendant; and

(c) if it is alleged that the act or omission was that of a person other than the defendant, the identity of that person and the additional facts supporting the bringing of an action against the defendant.

(9) Knowledge that any acts or omissions did or did not, as a matter of law, involve negligence is irrelevant for the purposes of subsection (5) above.

(10) For the purposes of this section a person's knowledge includes knowledge which he might reasonably have been expected to acquire—

(a) from facts observable or ascertainable by him; or

(b) from facts ascertainable by him with the help of appropriate expert advice which it is reasonable for him to seek;

but a person shall not be taken by virtue of this subsection to have knowledge of a fact ascertainable only with the help of expert advice so long as he has taken all reasonable steps to obtain (and, where appropriate, to act on) that advice.

14B Overriding time limit for negligence actions not involving personal injuries.—
(1) An action for damages for negligence, other than one to which section 11[1] of this Act applies, shall not be brought after the expiration of fifteen years from the date (or, if more than one, from the last of the dates) on which there occurred any act or omission—

(a) which is alleged to constitute negligence; and

(b) to which the damage in respect of which damages are claimed is alleged to be attributable (in whole or in part).

(2) This section bars the right of action in a case to which subsection (1) above applies notwithstanding that—

(a) the cause of action has not yet accrued; or

(b) where section 14A of this Act applies to the action, the date which is for the purposes of that section the starting date for reckoning the period mentioned in subsection (4)(b) of that section has not yet occurred;

before the end of the period of limitation prescribed by this section.

---

1. [See note 1, p. 484, ante.]

Accrual of cause of action to successive owners in respect of latent damage to property

3 Accrual of cause of action to successive owners in respect of latent damage to property. — (1) Subject to the following provisions of this section, where —

(a) a cause of action ("the original cause of action") has accrued to any person in respect of any negligence to which damage to any property in which he has an interest is attributable (in whole or in part); and

(b) another person acquires an interest in that property after the date on which the original cause of action accrued but before the material facts about the damage have become known to any person who, at the time when he first has knowledge of those facts, has any interest in the property;

a fresh cause of action in respect of that negligence shall accrue to that other person on the date on which he acquires his interest in the property.

(2) A cause of action accruing to any person by virtue of subsection (1) above —

(a) shall be treated as if based on breach of a duty of care at common law owed to the person to whom it accrues; and

(b) shall be treated for the purposes of section 14A of the 1980 Act (special time limit for negligence actions where facts relevant to cause of action are not known at date of accrual) as having accrued on the date on which the original cause of action accrued.

(3) Section 28 of the 1980 Act (extension of limitation period in case of disability) shall not apply in relation to any such cause of action.

(4) Subsection (1) above shall not apply in any case where the person acquiring an interest in the damaged property is either —

(a) a person in whom the original cause of action vests by operation of law; or

(b) a person in whom the interest in that property vests by virtue of any order made by a court under section 538 of the Companies Act 1985 (vesting of company property in liquidator).

(5) For the purposes of subsection (1)(b) above, the material facts about the damage are such facts about the damage as would lead a reasonable person who has an interest in the damaged property at the time when those facts become known to him to consider it sufficiently serious to justify his instituting proceedings for damages against a defendant who did not dispute liability and was able to satisfy a judgment.

(6) For the purposes of this section a person's knowledge includes knowledge which he might reasonably have been expected to acquire —

(a) from facts observable or ascertainable by him; or

(b) from facts ascertainable by him with the help of appropriate expert advice which it is reasonable for him to seek;

but a person shall not be taken by virtue of this subsection to have knowledge of a fact ascertainable by him only with the help of expert advice so long as he has taken all reasonable steps to obtain (and, where appropriate, to act on) that advice.

(7) This section shall bind the Crown, but as regards the Crown's liability in tort shall not bind the Crown further than the Crown is made liable in tort by the Crown Proceedings Act 1947.

Supplementary

4 Transitional provisions. — (1) Nothing in section 1 or 2 of this Act shall —

(a) enable any action to be brought which was barred by the 1980 Act or (as the case may be) by the Limitation Act 1939 before this Act comes into force: or

(b) affect any action commenced before this Act comes into force.

(2) Subject to subsection (1) above, sections 1 and 2 of this Act shall have effect in relation to causes of action accruing before, as well as in relation to causes of

action accruing after, this Act comes into force.

(3) Section 3 of this Act shall only apply in cases where an interest in damaged property is acquired after this Act comes into force but shall so apply, subject to subsection (4) below, irrespective of whether the original cause of action accrued before or after this Act comes into force.

(4) Where—

(a) a person acquires an interest in damaged property in circumstances to which section 3 would apart from this subsection apply; but

(b) the original cause of action accrued more than six years before this Act comes into force;

a cause of action shall not accrue to that person by virtue of subsection (1) of that section unless section 32(1)(b) of the 1980 Act (postponement of limitation period in case of deliberate concealment of relevant facts) would apply to any action founded on the original cause of action.

5 Citation, interpretation, commencement and extent. — (1) This Act may be cited as the Latent Damage Act 1986.

(2) In this Act—

'the 1980 Act' has the meaning given by section 1; and

'action' includes any proceeding in a court of law, any arbitration and any new claim within the meaning of section 35 of the 1980 Act (new claims in pending actions).

(3) This Act shall come into force at the end of the period of two months beginning with the date [18 July 1986] on which it is passed.

(4) This Act extends to England and Wales only.

Notes

1. Limitation of actions is not generally dealt with in this book, but the importance of the Latent Damage Act 1986 for the area of the law currently under consideration makes some reference to the Act desirable. On the Act generally, see P. Capper, *Latent Damage Act 1986* (London, 1987).

2. The Latent Damage Act 1986 was based on a report from the Law Reform Committee (*Twenty-Fourth Report (Latent Damage)*, Cmnd. 9390, 1984). The difficulties to which the previous law could give rise were shown by *Pirelli General Cable Works Ltd v Oscar Faber & Partners (A Firm)* [1983] 2 AC 1; [1983] 1 All ER 65. In this case the plaintiffs engaged the defendants, who were consulting engineers, to advise them about a particular building that was to be constructed. The building had a tall chimney made of pre-cast concrete and the chimney had been designed and supplied by a nominated sub-contractor. The defendants were found to have accepted responsibility for the design and to have been negligent in passing it. Some of the concrete proved to be unsuitable, cracks developed and the chimney had to be partly demolished and replaced. The cracks occurred more than eight years before the issue of the writ and by virtue of the then relevant statutory provision (s. 2 of the Limitation Act 1939, as amended) the limitation period was six years from the date when the cause of action accrued. The House of Lords decided that the cause of action accrued at the time when the physical damage occurred (i.e. here the cracks) whether or not it was discovered or even capable of being discovered (although it was also stated (at p. 16) that there 'may perhaps be cases where the defect is so gross that the building is doomed from the start, and where the owner's cause of action will accrue as

soon as it is built'). This comment in *Pirelli* about the 'doomed from the start' category gave rise to difficulty (see e.g. *Ketteman v Hansel Properties Ltd* [1987] AC 189; [1988] 1 All ER 38). After *Murphy v Brentwood District Council* [1990] 2 All ER 908; [1990] 3 WLR 414 (p. 212, ante and p. 466, ante), will it be of any relevance?

On the position as stated in *Pirelli*, a person could lose a cause of action without ever being aware that he had one. Section 1 of the Latent Damage Act 1986 (adding in s. 14A to the Limitation Act 1980) mitigates the potential harshness of this position for plaintiffs, but by adding s. 14B to the Limitation Act 1980 and thereby providing a fifteen-year 'long stop' from the time of *the breach of duty*, s. 1 of the 1986 Act gives something in return to defendants. Note that s. 1 does not say anything about when the cause of action accrues, which is left to the common law. The law concerning limitation periods can therefore raise questions about what damage is actionable. In relation to the 'long stop' provision, it should be appreciated that although the time runs from the breach of duty (whereas in tort it normally runs from the occurrence of the damage), this can involve a longer period than might at first sight appear because, for example, of the notion of a continuing duty (see *Rimmer v Liverpool City Council* [1985] QB 1; [1984] 1 All ER 930); and see generally Capper, op cit, pp. 47–50. It has also been argued that rights to contribution under the Civil Liability (Contribution) Act 1978 (p. 871, post) can in effect extend a defendant's liability: see Capper, op cit, pp. 21–23; cf. M. Ross (1987) 3 Const LJ 71 at pp. 80–81. More generally on the 'long stop' provision, see Capper, op cit.

Has the position set out ante been affected by *Murphy*? On the view taken of *Pirelli* by Lord Keith in *Murphy* (p. 218, ante), the plaintiffs in that case could have sued for their loss before the cracks occurred in the chimney. Furthermore, on the general approach in *Murphy* claims against the builder for damage to a building will not be allowed unless they fit into the *Junior Books* category as interpreted in *Murphy*, in which case it would seem that the action would be available before any physical damage occurred to the building. The Act can apply in relation to these sorts of claims, as it can in the case of other defendants such as architects or surveyors where liability for economic loss may be found. The time starts to run when damage occurs and in negligent advice cases this will often be when action is taken in reliance on the advice (see generally *Forster v Outred & Co (a firm)* [1982] 2 All ER 753; [1982] 1 WLR 86; *D W Moore & Co Ltd v Ferrier* [1988] 1 All ER 400; [1988] 1 WLR 267; *Bell v Peter Browne & Co* [1990] 3 All ER 124; [1990] 3 WLR 510). Such damage may be latent and thus the Act will prove to be useful.

Would the ruling in *Pirelli* be important in Lord Bridge's case in *Murphy* (p. 223, ante) of the building near to the highway or a neighbour's property? What is the position where there is a claim based on physical damage to property? A claim brought against the builder will normally have to be for personal injury or damage to property other than the building itself. The ruling in *Pirelli* and its amelioration by the Act will apply to the latter, but their practical importance in respect of an action against the builder has been reduced in the light of *Murphy*. However, it seems they may apply to claims against sub-contractors whose negligent work damages other parts of the building (see p. 477, ante) and in the light of the common practice of sub-contracting in the construction industry, *Pirelli* and the Act may be of more importance than might initially have appeared.

3. It has been decided that the Latent Damage Act does not apply to claims in contract: *Iron Trade Mutual Insurance Co Ltd v J K Buckenham Ltd* [1990] 1 All ER 808.

4. Section 2 of the Latent Damage Act deals with the relationship of the new s. 14A and s. 14B of the Limitation Act 1980 and s. 28 of the Limitation Act 1980 (which concerns the position of persons under a disability) and s. 32 of that Act (which concerns postponement of the running of the period of limitation due to fraud, concealment or mistake).

5. The decision in *Pirelli* had revealed a problem for the successors in title to the person who was the owner of the property when the physical damage occurred. This was because of the general rule that a plaintiff has to have a possessory or proprietary interest in the article which is physically damaged at the time when the damage occurs. See generally p. 230, ante. For comment on this point from *Pirelli* see G. Robertson (1983) 99 LQR 559; Hepple All ER Rev 1983, p. 332; M. A. Jones (1984) 100 LQR 413 which also discuss the opinion expressed in *Pirelli* by Lord Fraser, with whose speech the other members of the House of Lords agreed, that 'the true view is that the duty of the builder . . . is owed to owners of the property as a class, and that if time runs against one owner, it also runs against all his successors in title'. Section 3 of the Latent Damage Act now provides a legislative solution to the difficulty. Has its practical importance been reduced after *Murphy* in the light of the views in that case about the type of damage that is actionable?

An additional point to note about s. 3 is the argument (see E. Griew (1986) 136 NLJ 1201) that it could have a wider impact than might be anticipated and affect the position laid down in *Leigh and Sillivan Ltd v Aliakmon Shipping Co Ltd* [1986] AC 785; [1986] 2 All ER 145 (p. 203, ante): on this issue see note 2, p. 210, ante.

10 Liability for damage caused by things

Those who keep or put into circulation *things* create special dangers. Not surprisingly, therefore, there have been attempts to create special rules, going beyond the tort of negligence, to place responsibility for resulting damage on those who create the risk, subject to certain defences. One situation where the attempt was successful at common law is provided by the rule in *Rylands v Fletcher* (1868) LR 3 HL 330 (p. 650, post) which imposes strict liability for the escape of dangerous things from land. Liability under this rule will be discussed in chap. 14, post because of its close connection with the factual circumstances which may give rise to an action in nuisance, and it will be seen at that point that there are restrictions upon its operation. The courts, it might be noted here, declined the opportunity to use this rule so as to impose strict liability on the part of those using motor vehicles on the road (see J. R. Spencer [1983] CLJ 65); and they also missed the opportunity (in *Phillips v Britannia Hygienic Laundry Co Ltd* [1923] 2 KB 832; 93 LJKB 5, p. 543, post) to develop, through statutory interpretation, a principle of strict liability for damage caused by motor vehicles. More generally, the courts did not follow the lead given by the courts in the United States in developing a principle of strict liability for defective products (see Prosser and Keeton, *The Law of Torts* 5th edn (St. Paul, Minnesota, 1984), chap. 17); as will be seen (p. 504, post), a regime of strict liability in this area of the law has been introduced by legislative means (the Consumer Protection Act 1987). So far as the tort of negligence is concerned, the 'manufacturer's rule' in *M'Alister* (or *Donoghue*) *v Stevenson* [1932] AC 562 (p. 40, ante) has been extended to a wide range of ultimate consumers and has on occasions almost reached the level of strict liability. However, the theory of the tort rests firmly upon the idea of negligence. At one time the classification of a chattel as dangerous or non-dangerous was considered important, and it is still of importance to the rule in *Rylands v Fletcher*; but today it is clear that this classification in the tort of negligence affects only the degree of care which will be required of a defendant in a particular situation.

A consumer does get some degree of protection from the criminal law and the possibility of an action in contract needs to be borne in mind when the materials in this chapter are studied. Recovery of damages on a strict liability basis may, of course, be available in contract. An action for breach of statutory duty (see chap. 12 post), which is a tort action, may also provide a stricter form of liability than negligence and here the student's attention is directed to s. 41 of the Consumer Protection Act 1987. A more general introduction of strict liability for defective products in tort has come about by the implementation, in the Consumer Protection Act 1987 (p. 504, ante), of a European Community Directive (p. 510, ante). It might also be noted that the Law Commission and the Scottish Law Commission (in their Report entitled *Liability for Defective Products*, Law Com. No. 82, Scot Law Com. No. 45) and the Pearson Commission (in chap. 22 of their Report) had proposed the establishment of such a regime. We have referred to the new scheme that has been introduced as involving strict liability, but one of the interesting questions to which the student will need to address his or her mind — and one which our references in this chapter to strict liability should not be taken as pre-empting — is just how strict this liability is. Another point that might be made at this stage is that liability in negligence and contract co-exists with the Consumer Protection Act 1987 and remains of importance because of, for example, the restricted range of damage that is covered by the 1987 Act.

1 Negligence

(a) In general

M'Alister (or Donoghue) *v* Stevenson, p. 40, ante

(b) Development of the law

Grant *v* Australian Knitting Mills Ltd Judicial Committee of the Privy Council [1935] All ER Rep 209

The plaintiff [appellant], Dr Grant, of Adelaide, South Australia, claimed damages on the ground that he had contracted dermatitis by reason of the improper condition of some underpants bought by him from the defendants, John Martin and Co Ltd, and manufactured by the defendants, Australian Knitting Mills Ltd.

The appellant bought the underwear on 3 June 1931. He put on one suit on the morning of 28 June 1931. By the evening of that date he felt itching, but no objective symptoms appeared until the next day, when a redness appeared in front of each ankle over an area of about 2½ in. by 1½ in. His condition got worse, the rash became generalised and very acute, and he was confined to bed for seventeen weeks. In November he became convalescent and went to New Zealand to recuperate. He returned in the following February, but soon had a relapse, and by March his condition was so serious that in April he went into hospital where he remained until July. In April he began this action.

The Supreme Court of South Australia (Murray CJ) gave judgment against both defendants, against the retailers on the contract of sale, and against the manufacturers in tort, following the decision of the House of Lords in *M'Alister* (or *Donoghue*) *v* Stevenson,[1] but the decision of the Supreme Court was reversed by the High Court of Australia by a majority. The plaintiff appealed.

LORD WRIGHT: . . . The appellant's claim was that the disease was caused by the presence in the cuffs or ankle ends of the underpants which he purchased and wore, of an irritating chemical, namely, free sulphite, the presence of which was due to negligence in manufacture, and also involved on the part of the respondents, John Martin & Co Ltd, a breach of the relevant implied conditions under the Sale of Goods Act.

---

1. [1932] AC 562.

[Having held that the retailers were liable in contract and that there was negligence in the manufacture, he continued:] . . . According to the evidence, the method of manufacture was correct; the danger of excess sulphites being left was recognised and was guarded against; the process was intended to be foolproof. If excess sulphites were left in the garment, that could only be because someone was at fault. The appellant is not required to lay his finger on the exact person in all the chain who was responsible or to specify what he did wrong. Negligence is found as a matter of inference from the existence of the defects taken in connection with all the known circumstances; even if the manufacturers could by apt evidence have rebutted that inference they have not done so.

On this basis, the damage suffered by the appellant was caused in fact (because the interposition of the retailers may for this purpose in the circumstances of the case be disregarded) by the negligent or improper way in which the manufacturers made the garments. But this mere sequence of cause and effect is not enough in law to constitute a cause of action in negligence, which is a complex concept, involving a duty as between the parties to take care, as well as a breach of that duty and resulting damage. . . .

. . . Their Lordships, like the judges in the courts in Australia, will follow [M'Alister (or Donoghue) v Stevenson[1]], and the only question here can be what that authority decides and whether this case comes within its principles. . . .

Their Lordships think that the principle of the decision is summed up in the words of Lord Atkin ([1932] AC at p. 599):

'A manufacturer of products, which he sells in such a form as to show that he intends them to reach the ultimate consumer in the form in which they left him with no reasonable possibility of intermediate examination, and with the knowledge that the absence of reasonable care in the preparation or putting up of the products will result in an injury to the consumer's life or property, owes a duty to the consumer to take that reasonable care.'

This statement is in accord with the opinions expressed by Lord Thankerton and Lord Macmillan, who in principle agreed with Lord Atkin.

In order to ascertain whether the principle applies to the present case, it is necessary to define what the decision involves and consider the points of distinction relied upon before their Lordships.

It is clear that the decision treats negligence, where there is a duty to take care, as a specific tort in itself, and not simply as an element in some more complex relationship or in some specialised breach of duty, and still less as having any dependence on contract. All that is necessary as a step to establish the tort of actionable negligence is to define the precise relationship from which the duty to take care is to be deduced. It is, however, essential in English law that the duty should be established; . . . In Donoghue's case,[1] the duty was deduced simply from the facts relied on, namely, that the injured party was one of a class for whose use, in the contemplation and intention of the makers, the article was issued to the world, and the article was used by that party in the state in which it was prepared and issued without it being changed in any way and without there being any warning of, or means of detecting, the hidden danger; there was, it is true, no personal intercourse between the maker and the user; but though the duty is personal, because it is inter partes, it needs no interchange of words, spoken or written, or signs of offer or assent; it is thus different in character from any contractual relationship; no question of consideration between the parties is relevant; for these reasons the use of the word 'privity' in this connection is apt to mislead because of the suggestion of some overt relationship like that in contract, and the word 'proximity' is open to the same

---

1. [1932] AC 562.

objection; if the term proximity is to be applied at all, it can only be in the sense that the want of care and the injury are in essence directly and intimately connected; though there may be intervening transactions of sale and purchase and intervening handling between these two events, the events are themselves unaffected by what happened between them: proximity can only properly be used to exclude any element of remoteness, or of some interfering complication between the want of care and the injury, and, like 'privity' may mislead by introducing alien ideas. Equally also may the word 'control' embarrass, though it is conveniently used in the opinions in *Donoghue*'s case[1] to emphasise the essential factor that the consumer must use the article exactly as it left the maker, that is in all material features, and use it as it was intended to be used. In that sense the maker may be said to control the thing until it is used. But that again is an artificial use, because, in the natural sense of the word, the makers parted with all control when they sold the article and divested themselves of possession and property. An argument used in the present case based on the word 'control' will be noticed later.

It is obvious that the principles thus laid down involve a duty based on the simple facts detailed above, a duty quite unaffected by any contracts dealing with the thing, for instance, of sale by maker to retailer, and again by retailer to consumer or to the consumer's friend.

It may be said that the duty is difficult to define, because when the act of negligence in manufacture occurs there was no specific person towards whom the duty could be said to exist: the thing might never be used: it might be destroyed by accident or it might be scrapped, or in many ways fail to come into use in the normal way: in other words, the duty cannot at the time of manufacture be other than potential or contingent, and only can become vested by the fact of actual use by a particular person. But the same theoretical difficulty has been disregarded in cases like *Heaven v Pender*,[2] or in the case of things dangerous per se or known to be dangerous, where third parties have been held entitled to recover on the principles explained in *Dominion Natural Gas Co Ltd v Collins and Perkins*.[3] In *Donoghue*'s case[1] the thing was dangerous in fact, though the danger was hidden, and the thing was dangerous only because of want of care in making it; as Lord Atkin points out in *Donoghue*'s case[1] ([1932] AC at p. 595), the distinction between things inherently dangerous and things only dangerous because of negligent manufacture cannot be regarded as significant for the purpose of the questions here involved.

One further point may be noted. The principle of *Donoghue*'s case[1] can only be applied where the defect is hidden and unknown to the consumer, otherwise the directness of cause and effect is absent: the man who consumes or uses a thing which he knows to be noxious cannot complain in respect of whatever mischief follows because it follows from his own conscious volition in choosing to incur the risk or certainty of mischance.

If the foregoing are the essential features of *Donoghue*'s case[1] they are also to be found, in their Lordships' judgment, in the present case. The presence of the deleterious chemical in the pants, due to negligence in manufacture, was a hidden and latent defect, just as much as were the remains of the snail in the opaque bottle: it could not be detected by any examination that could reasonably be made. Nothing happened between the making of the garments and their being worn to change their condition. The garments were made by the manufacturers for the purpose of being worn exactly as they were worn in fact by the appellant: it was not contemplated that they should be first washed. It is immaterial that the appellant has a claim in contract against the retailers, because that is a quite independent cause of action, based on different considerations, even though the damage may be the same. Equally irrelevant

---

1. [1932] AC 562.
2. (1883) 11 QBD 503.
3. [1909] AC 640.

is any question of liability between the retailers and the manufacturers on the contract of sale between them. The tort liability is independent of any question of contract.

It was argued, but not perhaps very strongly, that *Donoghue*'s case[1] was a case of food or drink to be consumed internally, whereas the pants here were to be worn externally. No distinction, however, can be logically drawn for this purpose between a noxious thing taken internally and a noxious thing applied externally: the garments were made to be worn next to the skin: indeed Lord Atkin ([1932] AC at p. 583) specifically puts as examples of what is covered by the principle he is enunciating things operating externally, such as 'an ointment, a soap, a cleaning fluid, or cleaning powder'.

Counsel for the respondents, however, sought to distinguish *Donoghue*'s case[1] from the present on the ground that in the former the makers of the ginger beer had retained 'control' over it in the sense that they had placed it in stoppered and sealed bottles, so that it would not be tampered with until it was opened to be drunk, whereas the garments in question were merely put into paper packets, each containing six sets, which in ordinary course would be taken down by the shopkeeper and opened and the contents handled and disposed of separately so that they would be exposed to the air. He contended that, though there was no reason to think that the garments, when sold to the appellant were in any other condition, least of all as regards sulphur contents, than when sold to the retailers by the manufacturers, still the mere possibility and not the fact of their condition having been changed was sufficient to distinguish *Donoghue*'s case[1]: there was no 'control' because nothing was done by the manufacturers to exclude the possibility of any tampering while the goods were on their way to the user. Their Lordships do not accept that contention. The decision in *Donoghue*'s case[1] did not depend on the bottle being stoppered and sealed; the essential point in this regard was that the article should reach the consumer or user subject to the same defect as it had when it left the manufacturer. That this was true of the garment is in their Lordships' opinion beyond question. At most there might in other cases be a greater difficulty of proof of the fact.

. . . [T]heir Lordships hold the present case to come within the principle of *Donoghue*'s case[1] and they think that the judgment of the Chief Justice was right and should be restored as against both respondents, and that the appeal should be allowed with costs here and in the courts below, and that the appellant's petition for leave to adduce further evidence should be dismissed without costs. They will humbly so advise His Majesty.

Appeal allowed

Note

The claim in contract against the retailers also succeeded in this case, and the possibility of such an action must always be borne in mind in the context of products liability. See generally C. J. Miller, *Product Liability and Safety Encyclopaedia*, Division II. A particular advantage for the plaintiff, compared with the tort of negligence, is that liability can be stricter in contract (see e.g. s. 14(2) of the Sale of Goods Act 1979); although strict liability in tort has now been introduced alongside negligence, the type of damage covered is not as wide-ranging as in negligence or contract. Another advantage for the plaintiff is that he avoids the difficulty over the recovery of economic loss in tort: see p. 500, post and p. 507, post. The student should

---

1. [1932] AC 562.

also consider the position relating to contributory negligence (see p. 358, ante) and remoteness of damage (see *H Parsons (Livestock) Ltd v Uttley Ingham & Co Ltd* [1978] QB 791; [1978] 1 All ER 525). Limitation periods may be more favourable in tort than contract.

If sued, the retailer can of course claim in contract from the person who sold him the product and in theory the cost can be laid at the manufacturer's door through the chain of contracts connecting him with the retailer. However, in practice this may not be so easy; for example, one party in the chain of distribution may have gone bankrupt or, as in *Lexmead (Basingstoke) Ltd v Lewis* [1982] AC 225; [1981] 1 All ER 1185, one party may be unable to identify the party from whom the product was obtained. In this situation the party who has been held liable for breach of contract could try to recover this loss from the manufacturer in tort, on which see p. 502, post, but, since the coming into force of the Civil Liability (Contribution) Act 1978 (p. 871, post), there has been the possibility of a claim for contribution even though the party claiming contribution is liable in contract and the party from whom it is claimed is liable in tort if both are liable for the same damage to a third party. This could, therefore, avoid the difficulty of claiming for economic loss in tort if the damage caused by the product was personal injury or damage to property.

Evans *v* Triplex Safety Glass Co Ltd King's Bench Division [1936] 1 All ER 283

In 1934, Mr Evans bought a Vauxhall car which had been fitted by the Vauxhall Motor Co with a windscreen made of 'Triplex Toughened Safety Glass'. In July 1935, he was driving the car, with his wife and son as passengers, when the windscreen cracked and disintegrated. Part of the windscreen fell on the boy, part on Mr Evans and a considerable portion fell on the wife who suffered severe shock. The plaintiffs (Mr Evans and his wife) brought an action against the manufacturers of the windscreen.

PORTER J: . . . In this case I do not think that I ought to infer negligence on the part of the defendants. . . . I cannot draw the inference that the cause of the disintegration was the faulty manufacture. It is true that the human element may fail and then the manufacturers would be liable for negligence of their employee, but then that was not proved in this case. The disintegration may have been caused by any accident. There was every opportunity for failure on the part of the human element in fastening the windscreen, and I think that the disintegration was due rather to the fitting of the windscreen than to faulty manufacture having regard to its use on the road and the damage done to a windscreen in the course of user.

It is true that, as Mr Macaskie[1] points out, in these cases he has not got to eliminate every possible element, but he has got to eliminate every probable element. He has not displaced sufficiently the balance of probabilities in this case. I think that this glass is reasonably safe and possibly more safe than other glasses. One cannot help seeing that in all these cases one has to look with considerable care. One has to consider the question of time. The plaintiff had had the windscreen for about a year. Then there is the possibility of examination. The suppliers of the car had every opportunity to examine the windscreen. I do not propose to lay down any rule of law; it is a question of degree and these elements must be taken into consideration. This

---

1. [Counsel for the plaintiffs.]

article was put into a frame and screwed; one must consider that. As I have said there is the element of time, the opportunity of examination and the opportunity of damage from other causes. One must consider all these factors.

In *M'Alister* (or *Donoghue*) *v Stevenson*[1] there was a snail in the ginger beer bottle and there was no opportunity of seeing it as you could not see through the glass. In *Grant v Australian Knitting Mills Ltd*[2] the article passed on to the purchaser and it is quite clear that a reasonable examination of the garment would not have revealed the presence of the sulphite. That case is different from this. In that case there was found in some of the garments an excess of sulphites and that clearly was the cause of the injury. Here are a number of causes which might have caused disintegration. I do not find any negligence proved against the defendants and I give the defendants judgment with costs.

Kubach v Hollands King's Bench Division [1937] 3 All ER 907

A science teacher bought from the second defendants a powder labelled manganese dioxide, but which was in fact a mixture of that chemical and a much larger quantity of antimony sulphide. The second defendants had purchased the powder as manganese dioxide from a third party, but the invoice stated, inter alia, that the goods 'must be examined and tested by user before use'. The second defendants did not examine or test the powder, nor did they inform the teacher of the need for such examination or test. The use of manganese dioxide in a particular chemical experiment would have been safe but when this powder was used, there was an explosion and a schoolgirl was injured. The plaintiffs (the schoolgirl and her father) unsuccessfully claimed damages against the first defendant (the proprietress of the school). However, the second defendants, who had notice of the powder's intended use, were held liable for negligence, and they claimed contribution or an indemnity from the third party.

LORD HEWART CJ: . . . After hearing and considering the very careful arguments of counsel on both sides, I have come, reluctantly enough, to the conclusion that the third party is entitled to succeed. . . .

[Having quoted Lord Atkin's 'manufacturer principle',[3] he continued:] The case which is there contemplated is, I think, in essential respects the opposite of the present case. The manganese dioxide which the third party ought to have supplied here to the second defendants might have been resold for a variety of purposes or in innocuous compounds or mixtures. The use of it for school experiments was only one of the many possible uses, and the third party, unlike the second defendants, had no notice of the intended use. More than that, it was common ground that a very simple test, if it had been carried out, as the third party's invoice prescribed, and as the first defendant was not warned, would immediately have exhibited the fact that antimony sulphide had erroneously been made up and delivered as manganese dioxide. The second defendants had ample and repeated opportunity of intermediate examination, and, if they had taken the simple precaution which the invoice warned them to take, no mischief would have followed. . . .

Finally, it was attempted, although faintly, to derive some assistance for the second defendants from the provisions of the Law Reform (Married Women and Tortfeasors) Act 1935[4]. . . . In my opinion, there was no joint tort, nor could the plaintiff have sued the third party. . . .

Judgment for the third party against the second defendants

---

1. [1932] AC 562.
2. [1936] AC 85.
3. [1932] AC 562 at 599.
4. [See now the Civil Liability (Contribution) Act 1978, p. 871, post.]

Questions

1. What is the relevance of a warning to the question of intermediate examination?

2. Do you think that there is a duty to warn or take some action in relation to a defect in a product that the manufacturer discovers after the product has left his hands? (Consider *Rivtow Marine Ltd v Washington Ironworks Ltd* (1973) 40 DLR (3d) 530; *V and M Walton v British Leyland (UK) Ltd* [1980] PLI 156.)

Notes

1. It has been suggested that the words 'reasonable possibility' in Lord Atkin's reference (in *M'Alister* (or *Donoghue*) *v Stevenson*) to the opportunity for intermediate examination should be changed to 'probability' (Goddard LJ in *Haseldine v C A Daw & Son Ltd* [1941] 2 KB 343 at 376); but even in this situation *Fleming*, p. 472 argues that the probability of intermediate examination will only excuse 'if the defendant was justified in regarding the expected test as sufficient to defuse the danger prior to use and thus provide a safeguard to persons who might otherwise be harmed'. Note further *Murphy v Brentwood District Council* [1990] 2 All ER 908 at 917 (p. 216, ante) where Lord Keith referred to a 'reasonable prospect of intermediate examination' and Lord Jauncey (at p. 940—and consider also p. 938) mentioned that the duty laid down by Lord Atkin 'only extended to articles which were likely to be used before a reasonable opportunity of inspection had occurred'.

Lord Atkin's reference to intermediate examination was also considered in *Aswan Engineering Establishment Co v Lupdine Ltd* [1987] 1 All ER 135; [1987] 1 WLR 1. Lloyd LJ, with whose judgment Fox LJ agreed, accepted that this had on occasions been treated as an independent requirement for the plaintiff to meet; but, expressing the opinion that this phrase of Lord Atkin's 'take[s] colour from the preceding words', he preferred to see it as a factor to be considered on the question of reasonable foresight of damage to person or property. This approach in *Aswan* related the issue to the question of the scope of the manufacturer's duty of care (and consider Lord Jauncey's view, ante). Compare the earlier case of *The Diamantis Pateras* [1966] 1 Lloyd's Rep 179 in which Lawrence J stated (at p. 188): 'A consideration of modern authorities leads me to the conclusion that the opportunity of intermediate examination is a matter which goes now rather to the question of causation than to the issue of whether or not a duty of care is imposed on the defendants'.

The plaintiff himself may have had a chance to inspect the article and have gained some knowledge of its dangerous nature. In *Denny v Supplies and Transport Co Ltd* [1950] 2 KB 374 the plaintiff, an employee of certain wharfingers, was injured in the course of unloading timber from a barge. The timber had earlier been loaded from a ship on to the barge by stevedores, who were found by the county court judge to have done the job very badly. The movement of the timber from the ship to the land was 'one continuous process'. At one time, before the accident occurred, the plaintiff had asked the wharf superintendent for danger money, complaining that the barge had been badly loaded, and was thus unsafe. However, in the Court of Appeal, Evershed MR would not assent to the proposition that an experienced man must have realised danger was *imminent*: further, in his Lordship's view, there was 'no practical alternative to the course of conduct adopted'. It was held that the chain of causation between the stevedores' acts and the plaintiff's injury remained intact, and that the plaintiff was still the stevedores' 'neighbour'. The stevedores' appeal from the county court judge's decision awarding the plaintiff £100 was dismissed. *Denny*'s case was cited in *Rimmer v Liverpool City Council* [1985] QB 1; [1984] 1 All ER 930. In the latter case, which concerned liability for premises, *Denny*'s case was used as one of the authorities to support the following view of the Court of Appeal (at p. 938):

'. . . [W]e take the law to be that an opportunity for inspection of a dangerous defect, even if successfully taken by A who is injured by it, will not destroy his proximity to B who created the danger, or exonerate B from liability to A, unless A was free to remove or avoid the danger in the sense that it was reasonable to expect him to do so, and unreasonable for him to run the risk of being injured by the danger.'

See also the view in *Fleming* set out ante. Compare *Farr v Butters Bros & Co* [1932] 2 KB 606 and see a note at (1955) 66 LQR 427. Consider further *Murphy v Brentwood District Council* [1990] 2 All ER 908; [1990] 3 WLR 414 (p. 212, ante and p. 466, ante). Lord Keith (p. 216, ante) emphasised that it is the 'latency of the defect which constitutes the mischief' and would disallow a claim if a plaintiff knew of the defect in the product (and see Lord Jauncey [1990] 2 All ER at p. 938). Should this be read subject to the point made by *Fleming* set out ante and in *Rimmer*?

2. In *Kubach v Hollands* Lord Hewart CJ referred to the invoice which warned the second defendants to take a simple precaution. The question of warning by a vendor arose in *Hurley v Dyke* [1979] RTR 265 where the defendant had sold at an auction a car which was dangerously defective; some days later, the plaintiff, who was a passenger in the car and was not its owner, was injured in an accident due to the car's dangerous condition. According to the House of Lords, the highest at which the defendant's knowledge could be put was that he knew 'of the very real potential danger of driving the car without further examination' and without effecting any repairs which were shown to be necessary by that examination. On this finding it was conceded that the defendant had satisfied the duty of care he owed, as the car had been sold at the auction with the warning that it was sold 'As seen and with all its faults'. Furthermore, three of their Lordships subscribed to the view that even if it had been established that the defendant had known the car was dangerous, it should not be assumed that he would have been liable. If a similar case arose today and there was a claim in tort by the purchaser of the car, would the Unfair Contract Terms Act 1977 (p. 389, ante) be relevant? The provisions of this Act must, of course, be borne in mind when liability for defective products is under consideration. On the duty of a purchaser of a second hand car and in particular on the relevance of an MOT certificate, consider *Rees v Saville* [1983] RTR 332, noted p. 292, ante (which concerned injury to a third party's car).

3. *Stennett v Hancock and Peters* [1939] 2 All ER 578, provides an illustration of an increase in the class of plaintiffs (i.e. liability not being restricted to consumers) and also in the class of defendants. The plaintiff's leg was

badly bruised when it was struck by a flange which had come off one of the wheels of the first defendant's lorry, the plaintiff being on the pavement of the highway along which the lorry was being driven. In fact, the wheel had earlier been in the possession of the second defendant whose servants had mended a puncture, re-assembled the wheel and on the day of the accident put it back on the lorry. The cause of the accident was found to be the careless re-assembly of the wheel by one of the second defendant's servants. Neither the first defendant himself nor his driver inspected the wheel to see that its re-assembly had been carried out correctly, but the learned judge (Branson J), relying on the decision in *Phillips v Britannia Hygienic Laundry Co Ltd* [1923] 1 KB 539, took the view that the first defendant could assume that the wheel had been properly assembled. The claim against the first defendant failed, but the second defendant (the repairer) was held liable on the principle of *M'Alister* (or *Donoghue*) *v Stevenson* [1932] AC 562. Each element which according to that decision had been necessary to impose liability on the manufacturer of a product to its ultimate user was, in Branson J's opinion, present in this case. On repairers see further *Haseldine v C A Daw & Son Ltd* [1941] 2 KB 343; [1941] 3 All ER 156. Note also that in *Kubach v Hollands* the second defendants were the owners of the shop from which the chemical had been bought.

4. On liability for products in the sphere of employment, see the Employer's Liability (Defective Equipment) Act 1969 (p. 858, post).

(c) Economic loss

Murphy *v* Brentwood District Council, p. 212, ante and p. 466, ante

Notes

1. Although *Murphy* directly concerned buildings, it is of relevance to the general area of products liability, and the student should consider its implications in this context. The whole question of recovery of damages for economic loss in the tort of negligence has been considered in detail in chap. 4, p. 149, ante, but some particular points will be mentioned here.

If the damage for which the plaintiff claims compensation constitutes damage to other property, the difficulty of recovering for economic loss is, of course, avoided. Nevertheless, a problem which has arisen in the context of products (and it is a problem which we have earlier encountered in the sphere of buildings) is what constitutes other property to which the physical damage must generally occur if it is to be actionable. This issue was discussed in *Aswan Engineering Establishment Co v Lupdine Ltd* [1987] 1 All ER 135; [1987] 1 WLR 1 in which the plaintiffs had purchased in plastic pails manufactured by one company a waterproofing compound ('Lupguard') manufactured by another company. The pails collapsed in the very high temperatures in Kuwait where they were sent and the Lupguard was lost. Lloyd LJ, with whom Fox LJ agreed, inclined to the view that what happened to the Lupguard was injury to other property (i.e. separate from the pails) even though the plaintiffs had purchased the Lupguard in the pails. He also raised the question whether a tyre on a car would be different property from the car even though the tyre was bought as a component part of it, and whether the contents of a bottle were different property from the cork: his provisional view was that a negligent manufacturer of the tyre or cork could be sued for damage caused to the car or contents of the bottle respectively. Nicholls LJ accepted that in 'strict legal analysis' the Lupguard and the pails were different property. However, he was unhappy with the idea that the manufacturer of a container could be liable under *M'Alister* (or *Donoghue)* *v Stevenson* [1932] AC 562 for loss of the contents due to a defect in the container, but did not need to decide the point. In *D & F Estates Ltd v Church Comrs for England* [1989] AC 177; [1988] 2 All ER 992 Lord Bridge, in the context of discussing the concept of complex structures (on which see p. 477, ante), referred to the possible existence of the concept of complex chattels in which different parts could be treated as different property. Does this idea survive the treatment of the concept of complex structures in *Murphy*? Are the views in *Aswan* concerning the pail and the Lupguard or Lloyd LJ's examples on which he expressed his provisional view as to different property being involved consistent with *Murphy*? What if a garage negligently fitted a special set of tyres to a car at the time it was purchased and they led to an accident in which another part of the car was damaged?

2. After *Dutton v Bognor Regis UDC* [1972] 1 QB 373; [1972] 1 All ER 462 and *Anns v Merton London Borough Council* [1978] AC 728; [1977] 2 All ER 492 it was thought that a person who discovered a dangerous defect in a product before it caused harm could recover the cost of repair from a negligent manufacturer. This position was, however, rejected in *D & F Estates Ltd v Church Comrs for England* [1989] AC 177; [1988] 2 All ER 992 and *Murphy* rejects a distinction between safe and unsafe goods in respect of this loss, such economic loss only being recoverable in negligence in the limited circumstances permitted by that case: see the comments on *Junior Books Ltd v Veitchi Co Ltd* [1983] 1 AC 520; [1982] 3 All ER 201, noted p. 226, ante, in *Murphy*. *Junior Books* had discussed the position of an ordinary consumer vis-à-vis a manufacturer where the consumer suffers pure economic loss as a result of buying the manufacturer's goods from a retailer. Lord Roskill (at p. 547) said that sufficient proximity so as to allow an action against the manufacturer would not often be present in the normal everyday transaction 'when it is obvious that in truth the real reliance was upon the immediate vendor and not upon the manufacturer' and see Lord Fraser's speech (at p. 533 – no 'very close proximity' in such a case). Do you agree with this view about reliance in this situation? See Sir G. Borrie, *The Development of Consumer Law and Policy – Bold Spirits and Timorous Souls* (London, 1984), p. 31 and see further N. E. Palmer and J. R. Murdoch (1983) 46 MLR 213 at 216–217.

An example of a situation in which a court held that the purchaser of an article could not successfully sue its manufacturer in tort for pure economic loss is provided by *Muirhead v Industrial Tank Specialities Ltd* [1986] QB 507; [1985] 3 All ER 705. Here the plaintiff could not recover such loss from a manufacturer of electric motors which were used in pumping water for the tank in which the plaintiff kept lobsters, but which were not suitable for use on the UK voltage range. In the court's view there was not sufficient proximity or reliance between the plaintiff and the manufacturer. The case on its facts fell within the category discussed by Lords Roskill and Fraser in *Junior Books* in which, where there is an ordinary purchase of goods, the buyer must seek redress in contract for pure economic loss caused by a defect in the goods. The decision does not, of course, rule out the possibility of such recovery in negligence if sufficient proximity or reliance can be found, and nor does *Murphy*.

On the question of recovery for pure economic loss in relation to products, see also *Simaan General Contracting Co v Pilkington Glass Ltd (No 2)* [1988] QB 758; [1988] 1 All ER 791, in which *Junior Books* was distinguished.

3. For a case prior to *Murphy* in which the House of Lords had hinted at a situation where economic loss might be recoverable, see *Lexmead (Basingstoke) Ltd v Lewis* [1982] AC 225; [1981] 1 All ER 1185. The Court of Appeal in this case had in fact rejected a claim for economic loss based on *M'Alister* (or *Donoghue*) *v Stevenson* [1932] AC 562 (p. 40, ante). Although the point did not arise for decision in the House of Lords, it was stated (at p. 1192) that the dismissal of the appeal should not be taken as indicating approval of the 'proposition that where the economic loss suffered by a distributor in the chain between the manufacturer and the ultimate consumer consists of a liability to pay damages to the ultimate consumer for physical injuries sustained by him, or consists of a liability to indemnify a distributor lower in the chain of distribution for his liability to the ultimate consumer for damages for physical injuries, such economic loss is not recoverable under the *Donoghue v Stevenson* principle from the manufacturer'. Nevertheless, Oliver LJ stated, when *Leigh and Sillivan Ltd v Aliakmon Shipping Co Ltd* was in the Court of Appeal, [1985] QB 350 at 380, that the Court of Appeal's decision in *Lexmead* remained binding on that court.

Contrast *The Kapetan Georgis* [1988] 1 Lloyd's Rep 352 at 356 where Hirst J, having quoted the passage ante from *Lexmead*, continued:

'This suggests that when the case is hallmarked by a physical damage claim somewhere up the chain, there is a strong ground for not applying the general principle [requiring a proprietary or possessory interest in the thing damaged at the time the damage occurs]; indeed it seems to me that the passing down the chain of a claim for physical damage in a case like [*Lexmead*] . . . may well not be regarded as a purely economic loss claim at all.'

His Lordship went on to express the opinion that the point left open in the House of Lords in *Lexmead* was unaffected either by the decision of the House of Lords in *Leigh and Sillivan Ltd v Aliakmon Shipping Co Ltd* [1986] AC 785; [1986] 2 All ER 145 (p. 203, ante) or by the decision of the Privy Council in *Candlewood Navigation Corpn Ltd v Mitsui OSK Lines Ltd* [1986] AC 1; [1985] 2 All ER 935, noted p. 236, ante. Cf. A. M. Clark, *Product Liability* (London, 1989), p. 110. Is the point in *Lexmead* affected by *Murphy*?

4. Suppose a manufacturer sends out advertising material which contains negligent misrepresentations concerning his product. If a distributor of the product who relied on the material suffers economic loss (e.g. by being liable in contract to the person to whom he sold it) or if a consumer, who also relied on it, suffers economic loss because the product does not perform as well as the advertisement had stated, could there be an action against the

manufacturer under *Hedley Byrne & Co Ltd v Heller & Partners Ltd* [1964] AC 465; [1963] 2 All ER 575 (p. 161, ante)? Consider P. F. Cane (1979) 95 LQR 117 at 139–140. The Court of Appeal in *Lexmead (Basingstoke) Ltd v Lewis* [1982] AC 225; [1980] 1 All ER 978 would give a negative answer to this question, since it was stated (at p. 1003):

'... [W]e cannot regard the manufacturer and supplier of an article as putting himself into a special relationship with every distributor who obtains his product and reads what he says or prints about it and so owing him a duty to take reasonable care to give him true information or good advice.... [L]iability for statements volunteered negligently must be rare and ... statements made in such circumstances as these are not actionable at the suit of those who have not asked for them. To make such statements with the serious intention that others will or may rely on them ... is not, in our opinion, enough to establish a special relationship with those others or a duty to them.'

The House of Lords did not comment on this point when the case went on appeal ([1981] 1 All ER 1185). Is more weight put on this distinction between volunteered and requested statements than it can bear?

(d)   The problem of proof

Grant v Australian Knitting Mills Ltd, p. 492, ante

Mason v Williams and Williams Ltd and Thomas Turton & Sons Ltd Chester Assizes [1955] 1 All ER 808

A piece of metal flew off the head of a cold chisel, which the plaintiff was using, and hit him in the eye: the eye later had to be removed. There was no suggestion that the plaintiff had been at fault in using the chisel, which had been supplied by his employers (the first defendants), and manufactured by the second defendants. The chisel, the head of which was dangerously hard, had only been taken out of the stores a few weeks before the accident. On the claim against the manufacturers:

FINNEMORE J: ... I appreciate that I am faced with another problem, as was indicated in the case of *M'Alister* (or *Donoghue*) *v Stevenson*,[1] that res ipsa loquitur does not apply and that the court has to be satisfied, and therefore the plaintiff has got to prove, that there was negligence on the part of the manufacturers. Of course that cannot be proved normally by saying that on such and such a date such and such a workman did this, that or the other. I think that when you have eliminated anything happening in this case at the employers' factory, whither, as is undisputed, this chisel came direct from the manufacturers – and when it came from the manufacturers the head was too hard, and that undue hardness could have been produced only while it was being manufactured by them, and could have been produced by someone there either carelessly or deliberately to make a harder and more durable head – that is really as far as any plaintiff can be expected to take his case. What the plaintiff says here is: 'This is your chisel, you made it and I used it as you made it, in the condition in which you made it, in the way you intended me to use it, and you never relied on any intermediate examination; therefore I have discharged the onus of proof by saying that this trouble must have happened through some act in the manufacture

---

1. [1932] AC 562.

of this chisel in your factory, and that was either careless or deliberate, and in either event it was a breach of duty towards me, a person whom you contemplated would use this article which you made, in the way you intended it to be used.' He is entitled to succeed against the manufacturers. . . .

Judgment for the plaintiff against the manufacturers

Question

What would the defendants have to do to escape liability in a case of this kind?

Notes

1. This extract should be read along with the statements of Lord Macmillan in *M'Alister* (or *Donoghue*) *v Stevenson* [1932] AC 562 (p. 50, ante), and also the views expressed in *Grant v Australian Knitting Mills Ltd* [1936] AC 85 (p. 493, ante).

2. In *Daniels and Daniels v R White & Sons Ltd and Tarbard* [1938] 4 All ER 258 it was decided that a manufacturer could escape liability in negligence if he established that he had a foolproof method of manufacture and that there was proper supervision. The case is said by some textbook writers to be inconsistent with *Grant v Australian Knitting Mills Ltd* [1936] AC 85 (p. 492, ante) and an earlier Court of Appeal decision (*Chaproniere v Mason* (1905) 21 TLR 633): see e.g. *Charlesworth & Percy on Negligence* 8th edn, para. 14–07, note 4. In *Hill v James Crowe (Cases) Ltd* [1978] 1 All ER 812 MacKenna J approved *Charlesworth*'s criticism of *Daniels v R White & Sons Ltd* and stated that a manufacturer did not necessarily escape liability if he established that he had a good system of work and adequate supervision; there could still be vicarious liability for an employee's negligence in the course of his employment (on which see chap. 17, p. 805, post). See further S. L. Malden (1982) 33 NILQ 229 at 231, note 15.

2 Strict liability

Consumer Protection Act 1987

PART I

PRODUCT LIABILITY

1 Purpose and construction of Part I. — (1) This Part shall have effect for the purpose of making such provision as is necessary in order to comply with the product liability Directive and shall be construed accordingly.

   (2) In this Part, except in so far as the context otherwise requires —
      'agricultural produce' means any produce of the soil, of stockfarming or of fisheries;
      'dependant' and 'relative' have the same meaning as they have in, respectively, the Fatal Accidents Act 1976 and the Damages (Scotland) Act 1976;
      'producer', in relation to a product, means —

(a) the person who manufactured it;

(b) in the case of a substance which has not been manufactured but has been won or abstracted, the person who won or abstracted it;

(c) in the case of a product which has not been manufactured, won or abstracted but essential characteristics of which are attributable to an industrial or other process having been carried out (for example, in relation to agricultural produce), the person who carried out that process;

'product' means any goods or electricity and (subject to subsection (3) below) includes a product which is comprised in another product, whether by virtue of being a component part or raw material or otherwise; and

'the product liability Directive' means the Directive of the Council of the European Communities, dated 25th July 1985, (No 85/374/EEC)[1] on the approximation of the laws, regulations and administrative provisions of the member States concerning liability for defective products.

(3) For the purposes of this Part a person who supplies any product in which products are comprised, whether by virtue of being component parts or raw materials or otherwise, shall not be treated by reason only of his supply of that product as supplying any of the products so comprised.

2 Liability for defective products. — (1) Subject to the following provisions of this Part, where any damage is caused wholly or partly by a defect in a product, every person to whom subsection (2) below applies shall be liable for the damage.

(2) This subsection applies to —

(a) the producer of the product;

(b) any person who, by putting his name on the product or using a trade mark or other distinguishing mark in relation to the product, has held himself out to be the producer of the product;

(c) any person who has imported the product into a member State from a place outside the member States in order, in the course of any business of his, to supply it to another.

(3) Subject as aforesaid, where any damage is caused wholly or partly by a defect in a product, any person who supplied the product (whether to the person who suffered the damage, to the producer of any product in which the product in question is comprised or to any other person) shall be liable for the damage if —

(a) the person who suffered the damage requests the supplier to identify one or more of the persons (whether still in existence or not) to whom subsection (2) above applies in relation to the product;

(b) that request is made within a reasonable period after the damage occurs and at a time when it is not reasonably practicable for the person making the request to identify all those persons; and

(c) the supplier fails, within a reasonable period after receiving the request, either to comply with the request or to identify the person who supplied the product to him.

(4) Neither subsection (2) nor subsection (3) above shall apply to a person in respect of any defect in any game or agricultural produce if the only supply of the game or produce by that person to another was at a time when it had not undergone an industrial process.

(5) Where two or more persons are liable by virtue of this Part for the same damage, their liability shall be joint and several.

(6) This section shall be without prejudice to any liability arising otherwise than by virtue of this Part.

---

1. [See p. 510, post.]

3 Meaning of 'defect'. – (1) Subject to the following provisions of this section, there is a defect in a product for the purposes of this Part if the safety of the product is not such as persons generally are entitled to expect; and for those purposes 'safety', in relation to a product, shall include safety with respect to products comprised in that product and safety in the context of risks of damage to property, as well as in the context of risks of death or personal injury.

(2) In determining for the purposes of subsection (1) above what persons generally are entitled to expect in relation to a product all the circumstances shall be taken into account, including –

(a) the manner in which, and purposes for which, the product has been marketed, its get-up, the use of any mark in relation to the product and any instructions for, or warnings with respect to, doing or refraining from doing anything with or in relation to the product;

(b) what might reasonably be expected to be done with or in relation to the product; and

(c) the time when the product was supplied by its producer to another;

and nothing in this section shall require a defect to be inferred from the fact alone that the safety of a product which is supplied after that time is greater than the safety of the product in question.

4 Defences. – (1) In any civil proceedings by virtue of this Part against any person ('the person proceeded against') in respect of a defect in a product it shall be a defence for him to show –

(a) that the defect is attributable to compliance with any requirement imposed by or under any enactment or with any Community obligation; or

(b) that the person proceeded against did not at any time supply the product to another; or

(c) that the following conditions are satisfied, that is to say –

(i) that the only supply of the product to another by the person proceeded against was otherwise than in the course of a business of that person's; and

(ii) that section 2(2) above does not apply to that person or applies to him by virtue only of things done otherwise than with a view to profit; or

(d) that the defect did not exist in the product at the relevant time; or

(e) that the state of scientific and technical knowledge at the relevant time was not such that a producer of products of the same description as the product in question might be expected to have discovered the defect if it had existed in his products while they were under his control; or

(f) that the defect –

(i) constituted a defect in a product ('the subsequent product') in which the product in question had been comprised; and

(ii) was wholly attributable to the design of the subsequent product or to compliance by the producer of the product in question with instructions given by the producer of the subsequent product.

(2) In this section 'the relevant time', in relation to electricity, means the time at which it was generated, being a time before it was transmitted or distributed, and in relation to any other product, means –

(a) if the person proceeded against is a person to whom subsection (2) of section 2 above applies in relation to the product, the time when he supplied the product to another;

(b) if that subsection does not apply to that person in relation to the product, the time when the product was last supplied by a person to whom that subsection does apply in relation to the product.

5 Damage giving rise to liability. — (1) Subject to the following provisions of this section, in this Part 'damage' means death or personal injury or any loss of or damage to any property (including land).

(2) A person shall not be liable under section 2 above in respect of any defect in a product for the loss of or any damage to the product itself or for the loss of or any damage to the whole or any part of any product which has been supplied with the product in question comprised in it.

(3) A person shall not be liable under section 2 above for any loss of or damage to any property which, at the time it is lost or damaged, is not —

(a) of a description of property ordinarily intended for private use, occupation or consumption; and

(b) intended by the person suffering the loss or damage mainly for his own private use, occupation or consumption.

(4) No damages shall be awarded to any person by virtue of this Part in respect of any loss of or damage to any property if the amount which would fall to be so awarded to that person, apart from this subsection and any liability for interest, does not exceed £275.

(5) In determining for the purposes of this Part who has suffered any loss of or damage to property and when any such loss or damage occurred, the loss or damage shall be regarded as having occurred at the earliest time at which a person with an interest in the property had knowledge of the material facts about the loss or damage.

(6) For the purposes of subsection (5) above the material facts about any loss of or damage to any property are such facts about the loss or damage as would lead a reasonable person with an interest in the property to consider the loss or damage sufficiently serious to justify his instituting proceedings for damages against a defendant who did not dispute liability and was able to satisfy a judgment.

(7) For the purposes of subsection (5) above a person's knowledge includes knowledge which he might reasonably have been expected to acquire —

(a) from facts observable or ascertainable by him; or

(b) from facts ascertainable by him with the help of appropriate expert advice which it is reasonable for him to seek;

but a person shall not be taken by virtue of this subsection to have knowledge of a fact ascertainable by him only with the help of expert advice unless he has failed to take all reasonable steps to obtain (and, where appropriate, to act on) that advice.

(8) Subsections (5) to (7) above shall not extend to Scotland.

6 Application of certain enactments. — (1) Any damage for which a person is liable under section 2 above shall be deemed to have been caused —

(a) for the purposes of the Fatal Accidents Act 1976, by that person's wrongful act, neglect or default;

(2) Where —

(a) a person's death is caused wholly or partly by a defect in a product, or a person dies after suffering damage which has been so caused;

(b) a request such as mentioned in paragraph (a) of subsection (3) of section 2 above is made to a supplier of the product by that person's personal representatives or, in the case of a person whose death is caused wholly or partly by the defect, by any dependant or relative of that person; and

(c) the conditions specified in paragraphs (b) and (c) of that subsection are satisfied in relation to that request,

this Part shall have effect for the purposes of the Law Reform (Miscellaneous Provisions) Act 1934, the Fatal Accidents Act 1976 and the Damages (Scotland) Act 1976 as if liability of the supplier to that person under that subsection did not depend on that person having requested the supplier to identify certain persons or on the said conditions having been satisfied in relation to a request made by that person.

(3) Section 1 of the Congenital Disabilities (Civil Liability) Act 1976 shall have effect for the purposes of this Part as if —

(a) a person were answerable to a child in respect of an occurrence caused wholly or partly by a defect in a product if he is or has been liable under section 2 above in respect of any effect of the occurrence on a parent of the child, or would be so liable if the occurrence caused a parent of the child to suffer damage;

(b) the provisions of this Part relating to liability under section 2 above applied in relation to liability by virtue of paragraph (a) above under the said section 1; and

(c) subsection (6) of the said section 1 (exclusion of liability) were omitted.

(4) Where any damage is caused partly by a defect in a product and partly by the fault of the person suffering the damage, the Law Reform (Contributory Negligence) Act 1945 and section 5 of the Fatal Accidents Act 1976 (contributory negligence) shall have effect as if the defect were the fault of every person liable by virtue of this Part for the damage caused by the defect.

(5) In subsection (4) above 'fault' has the same meaning as in the said Act of 1945.

(6) Schedule 1 to this Act shall have effect for the purpose of amending the Limitation Act 1980 and the Prescription and Limitation (Scotland) Act 1973 in their application in relation to the bringing of actions by virtue of this Part.

(7) It is hereby declared that liability by virtue of this Part is to be treated as liability in tort for the purposes of any enactment conferring jurisdiction on any court with respect to any matter.

(8) Nothing in this Part shall prejudice the operation of section 12 of the Nuclear Installations Act 1965 (rights to compensation for certain breaches of duties confined to rights under that Act).

7 Prohibition on exclusions from liability. — The liability of a person by virtue of this Part to a person who has suffered damage caused wholly or partly by a defect in a product, or to a dependant or relative of such a person, shall not be limited or excluded by any contract term, by any notice or by any other provision.

8 Power to modify Part I. — (1) Her Majesty may by Order in Council make such modifications of this Part and of any other enactment (including an enactment contained in the following Parts of this Act, or in an Act passed after this Act) as appear to Her Majesty in Council to be necessary or expedient in consequence of any modification of the product liability Directive which is made at any time after the passing of this Act.

(2) An Order in Council under subsection (1) above shall not be submitted to Her Majesty in Council unless a draft of the Order has been laid before, and approved by a resolution of, each House of Parliament.

9 Application of Part I to Crown. — (1) Subject to subsection (2) below, this Part shall bind the Crown.

(2) The Crown shall not, as regards the Crown's liability by virtue of this Part, be bound by this Part further than the Crown is made liable in tort or in reparation under the Crown Proceedings Act 1947, as that Act has effect from time to time.

45 Interpretation. — (1) In this Act, except in so far as the context otherwise requires —

'aircraft' includes gliders, balloons and hovercraft;

'business' includes a trade or profession and the activities of a professional or trade association or of a local authority or other public authority;

'conditional sale agreement', 'credit-sale agreement' and 'hire-purchase agreement' have the same meanings as in the Consumer Credit Act 1974 but as if in the definitions in that Act 'goods' had the same meaning as in this Act;

. . .

'gas' has the same meaning as in Part I of the Gas Act 1986;

'goods' includes substances, growing crops and things comprised in land by virtue of being attached to it and any ship, aircraft or vehicle;

. . .

'mark' and 'trade mark' have the same meanings as in the Trade Marks Act 1938;

'modifications' includes additions, alterations and omissions, and cognate expressions shall be construed accordingly;

'motor vehicle' has the same meaning as in [the Road Traffic Act 1988][1];

. . .

'personal injury' includes any disease and any other impairment of a person's physical or mental condition;

. . .

'ship' includes any boat and any other description of vessel used in navigation;

. . .

'substance' means any natural or artificial substance, whether in solid, liquid or gaseous form or in the form of a vapour, and includes substances that are comprised in or mixed with other goods;

'supply' and cognate expressions shall be construed in accordance with section 46 below;

. . .

(4) Section 68(2) of the Trade Marks Act 1938 (construction of references to use of a mark) shall apply for the purposes of this Act as it applies for the purposes of that Act.

. . .

46 Meaning of 'supply'. — (1) Subject to the following provisions of this section, references in this Act to supplying goods shall be construed as references to doing any of the following, whether as principal or agent, that is to say —

(a) selling, hiring out or lending the goods;

(b) entering into a hire-purchase agreement to furnish the goods;

(c) the performance of any contract for work and materials to furnish the goods;

(d) providing the goods in exchange for any consideration (including trading stamps) other than money;

(e) providing the goods in or in connection with the performance of any statutory function; or

(f) giving the goods as a prize or otherwise making a gift of the goods;

and, in relation to gas or water, those references shall be construed as including references to providing the service by which the gas or water is made available for use.

(2) For the purposes of any reference in this Act to supplying goods, where a person ('the ostensible supplier') supplies goods to another person ('the customer') under a hire-purchase agreement, conditional sale agreement or credit-sale agreement or under an agreement for the hiring of goods (other than a hire-purchase agreement) and the ostensible supplier —

(a) carries on the business of financing the provision of goods for others by means of such agreements; and

(b) in the course of that business acquired his interest in the goods supplied to the customer as a means of financing the provision of them for the customer by a further person ('the effective supplier'),

the effective supplier and not the ostensible supplier shall be treated as supplying the goods to the customer.

(3) Subject to subsection (4) below, the performance of any contract by the erection of any building or structure on any land or by the carrying out of any other building works shall be treated for the purposes of this Act as a supply of goods in so far as, but only in so far as, it involves the provision of any goods to any person by means of their incorporation into the building, structure or works.

(4) Except for the purposes of, and in relation to, notices to warn or any provision made by or under Part III of this Act, references in this Act to supplying goods shall

---

1. [Substituted by the Road Traffic (Consequential Provisions) Act 1988, Sch. 4.]

not include references to supplying goods comprised in land where the supply is effected by the creation or disposal of an interest in the land.

(8) Where any goods have at any time been supplied by being hired out or lent to any person, neither a continuation or renewal of the hire or loan (whether on the same or different terms) nor any transaction for the transfer after that time of any interest in the goods to the person to whom they were hired or lent shall be treated for the purposes of this Act as a further supply of the goods to that person.

(9) A ship, aircraft or motor vehicle shall not be treated for the purposes of this Act as supplied to any person by reason only that services consisting in the carriage of goods or passengers in that ship, aircraft or vehicle, or in its use for any other purpose, are provided to that person in pursuance of an agreement relating to the use of the ship, aircraft or vehicle for a particular period or for particular voyages, flights or journeys.

50 . . .

(1) This Act may be cited as the Consumer Protection Act 1987.

(2) Nothing in this Act . . . shall make any person liable by virtue of Part I of this Act for any damage caused wholly or partly by a defect in a product which was supplied to any person by its producer before the coming into force of Part I of this Act.

. . .

Council Directive
of 25 July 1985

on the approximation of the laws, regulations and administrative provisions of the Member States concerning liability for defective products
(85/374/EEC)

THE COUNCIL OF THE EUROPEAN COMMUNITIES,

Having regard to the Treaty establishing the European Economic Community, and in particular Article 100 thereof,

Having regard to the proposal from the Commission,

Having regard to the opinion of the European Parliament,

Having regard to the opinion of the Economic and Social Committee,

Whereas approximation of the laws of the Member States concerning the liability of the producer for damage caused by the defectiveness of his products is necessary because the existing divergences may distort competition and affect the movement of goods within the common market and entail a differing degree of protection of the consumer against damage caused by a defective product to his health or property;

Whereas liability without fault on the part of the producer is the sole means of adequately solving the problem, peculiar to our age of increasing technicality, of a fair apportionment of the risks inherent in modern technological production;

Whereas liability without fault should apply only to movables which have been industrially produced; whereas, as a result, it is appropriate to exclude liability for agricultural products and game, except where they have undergone a processing of an industrial nature which could cause a defect in these products; whereas the liability provided for in this Directive should also apply to movables which are used in the construction of immovables or are installed in immovables;

Whereas protection of the consumer requires that all producers involved in the production process should be made liable, in so far as their finished product, component part or any raw material supplied by them was defective; whereas, for the same reason, liability should extend to importers of products into the Community and to persons who present themselves as producers by affixing their name, trade mark or other distinguishing feature or who supply a product the producer of which cannot be identified;

Whereas, in situations where several persons are liable for the same damage, the protection of the consumer requires that the injured person should be able to claim full compensation for the damage from any one of them;

Whereas, to protect the physical well-being and property of the consumer, the defectiveness of the product should be determined by reference not to its fitness for use but to the lack of the safety which the public at large is entitled to expect; whereas the safety is assessed by excluding any misuse of the product not reasonable under the circumstances;

Whereas a fair apportionment of risk between the injured person and the producer implies that the producer should be able to free himself from liability if he furnishes proof as to the existence of certain exonerating circumstances;

Whereas the protection of the consumer requires that the liability of the producer remains unaffected by acts or omissions of other persons having contributed to cause the damage; whereas, however, the contributory negligence of the injured person may be taken into account to reduce or disallow such liability;

Whereas the protection of the consumer requires compensation for death and personal injury as well as compensation for damage to property; whereas the latter should nevertheless be limited to goods for private use or consumption and be subject to a deduction of a lower threshold of a fixed amount in order to avoid litigation in an excessive number of cases; whereas this Directive should not prejudice compensation for pain and suffering and other non-material damages payable, where appropriate, under the law applicable to the case;

Whereas a uniform period of limitation for the bringing of action for compensation is in the interests both of the injured person and of the producer;

Whereas products age in the course of time, higher safety standards are developed and the state of science and technology progresses; whereas, therefore, it would not be reasonable to make the producer liable for an unlimited period of the defectiveness of his product; whereas, therefore, liability should expire after a reasonable length of time, without prejudice to claims pending at law;

Whereas, to achieve effective protection of consumers, no contractual derogation should be permitted as regards the liability of the producer in relation to the injured person;

Whereas under the legal systems of the Member States an injured party may have a claim for damages based on grounds of contractual liability or on grounds of non-contractual liability other than that provided for in this Directive; in so far as these provisions also serve to attain the objective of effective protection of consumers, they should remain unaffected by this Directive; whereas, in so far as effective protection of consumers in the sector of pharmaceutical products is already also attained in a Member State under a special liability system, claims based on this system should similarly remain possible;

Whereas, to the extent that liability for nuclear injury or damage is already covered in all Member States by adequate special rules, it has been possible to exclude damage of this type from the scope of this Directive;

Whereas, since the exclusion of primary agricultural products and game from the scope of this Directive may be felt, in certain Member States, in view of what is expected for the protection of consumers, to restrict unduly such protection, it should be possible for a Member State to extend liability to such products;

Whereas, for similar reasons, the possibility offered to a producer to free himself from liability if he proves that the state of scientific and technical knowledge at the time when he put the product into circulation was not such as to enable the existence of a defect to be discovered may be felt in certain Member States to restrict unduly the protection of the consumer; whereas it should therefore be possible for a Member State to maintain in its legislation or to provide by new legislation that this exonerating circumstance is not admitted; whereas, in the case of new legislation, making use of this derogation should, however, be subject to a Community stand-still procedure, in order to raise, if possible, the level of protection in a uniform manner throughout the Community;

Whereas, taking into account the legal traditions in most of the Member States, it is inappropriate to set any financial ceiling on the producer's liability without fault; whereas, in so far as there are, however, differing traditions, it seems possible to admit that a Member State may derogate from the principle of unlimited liability by providing a limit for the total liability of the producer for damage resulting from a death or personal injury and caused by identical items with the same defect, provided that this limit is established at a level sufficiently high to guarantee adequate protection of the consumer and the correct functioning of the common market;

Whereas the harmonisation resulting from this cannot be total at the present stage, but opens the way towards greater harmonisation; whereas it is therefore necessary that the Council receive at regular intervals, reports from the Commission on the application of this Directive, accompanied, as the case may be, by appropriate proposals;

Whereas it is particularly important in this respect that a re-examination be carried out of those parts of the Directive relating to the derogations open to the Member States, at the expiry of a period of sufficient length to gather practical experience on the effects of these derogations on the protection of consumers and on the functioning of the common market,

HAS ADOPTED THIS DIRECTIVE:

Article 1

The producer shall be liable for damage caused by a defect in his product.

Article 2

For the purpose of this Directive 'product' means all movables, with the exception of primary agricultural products and game, even though incorporated into another movable or into an immovable. 'Primary agricultural products' means the products of the soil, of stock-farming and of fisheries, excluding products which have undergone initial processing. 'Product' includes electricity.

Article 3

1. 'Producer' means the manufacturer of a finished product, the producer of any raw material or the manufacturer of a component part and any person who, by putting his name, trade mark or other distinguishing feature on the product presents himself as its producer.

2. Without prejudice to the liability of the producer, any person who imports into the Community a product for sale, hire, leasing or any form of distribution in the course of his business shall be deemed to be a producer within the meaning of this Directive and shall be responsible as a producer.

3. Where the producer of the product cannot be identified, each supplier of the product shall be treated as its producer unless he informs the injured person, within a reasonable time, of the identity of the producer or of the person who supplied him with the product. The same shall apply, in the case of an imported product, if this product does not indicate the identity of the importer referred to in paragraph 2, even if the name of the producer is indicated.

Article 4

The injured person shall be required to prove the damage, the defect and the causal relationship between defect and damage.

Article 5

Where, as a result of the provisions of this Directive, two or more persons are liable for the same damage, they shall be liable jointly and severally, without prejudice to the provisions of national law concerning the rights of contribution or recourse.

Article 6

1. A product is defective when it does not provide the safety which a person is entitled to expect, taking all circumstances into account, including:

   (a) the presentation of the product;
   (b) the use to which it could reasonably be expected that the product would be put;
   (c) the time when the product was put into circulation.

2. A product shall not be considered defective for the sole reason that a better product is subsequently put into circulation.

Article 7

The producer shall not be liable as a result of this Directive if he proves:

   (a) that he did not put the product into circulation; or
   (b) that, having regard to the circumstances, it is probable that the defect which caused the damage did not exist at the time when the product was put into circulation by him or that this defect came into being afterwards; or
   (c) that the product was neither manufactured by him for sale or any form of distribution for economic purpose nor manufactured or distributed by him in the course of his business; or
   (d) that the defect is due to compliance of the product with mandatory regulations issued by the public authorities; or
   (e) that the state of scientific and technical knowledge at the time when he put the product into circulation was not such as to enable the existence of the defect to be discovered; or
   (f) in the case of a manufacturer of a component, that the defect is attributable to the design of the product in which the component has been fitted or to the instructions given by the manufacturer of the product.

Article 8

1. Without prejudice to the provisions of national law concerning the right of contribution or recourse, the liability of the producer shall not be reduced when the damage is caused both by a defect in the product and by the act or omission of a third party.

2. The liability of the producer may be reduced or disallowed when, having regard to all the circumstances, the damage is caused both by a defect in the product and by the fault of the injured person or any person for whom the injured person is responsible.

Article 9

For the purpose of Article 1, 'damage' means:

(*a*) damage caused by death or by personal injuries;
(*b*) damage to, or destruction of, any item of property other than the defective product itself, with a lower threshold of 500 ECU, provided that the item of property:
    (i) is of a type ordinarily intended for private use or consumption, and
    (ii) was used by the injured person mainly for his own private use or consumption.

This Article shall be without prejudice to national provisions relating to non-material damage.

Article 10

1. Member States shall provide in their legislation that a limitation period of three years shall apply to proceedings for the recovery of damages as provided for in this Directive. The limitation period shall begin to run from the day on which the plaintiff became aware, or should reasonably have become aware, of the damage, the defect and the identity of the producer.
    2. The laws of Member States regulating suspension or interruption of the limitation period shall not be affected by this Directive.

Article 11

Member States shall provide in their legislation that the rights conferred upon the injured person pursuant to this Directive shall be extinguished upon the [expiry] of a period of 10 years from the date on which the producer put into circulation the actual product which caused the damage, unless the injured person has in the meantime instituted proceedings against the producer.

Article 12

The liability of the producer arising from this Directive may not, in relation to the injured person, be limited or excluded by a provision limiting his liability or exempting him from liability.

Article 13

This Directive shall not affect any rights which an injured person may have according to the rules of the law of contractual or non-contractual liability or a special liability system existing at the moment when this Directive is notified.

Article 14

This Directive shall not apply to injury or damage arising from nuclear accidents and covered by international conventions ratified by the Member States.

Article 15

1. Each Member State may:

(*a*) by way of derogation from Article 2, provide in its legislation that within the meaning of Article 1 of this Directive 'product' also means primary agricultural products and game;
(*b*) by way of derogation from Article 7(*e*), maintain or, subject to the procedure set out in paragraph 2 of this Article, provide in this legislation that the producer shall be liable even if he proves that the state of scientific and

technical knowledge at the time when he put the product into circulation was not such as to enable the existence of a defect to be discovered.

2. A Member State wishing to introduce the measures specified in paragraph 1(*b*) shall communicate the text of the proposed measure to the Commission. The Commission shall inform the other Member States thereof.

The Member State concerned shall hold the proposed measure in abeyance for nine months after the Commission is informed and provided that in the meantime the Commission has not submitted to the Council a proposal amending this Directive on the relevant matter. However, if within three months of receiving the said information, the Commission does not advise the Member State concerned that it intends submitting such a proposal to the Council, the Member State may take the proposed measure immediately.

If the Commission does submit to the Council such a proposal amending this Directive within the aforementioned nine months, the Member State concerned shall hold the proposed measure in abeyance for a further period of 18 months from the date on which the proposal is submitted.

3. Ten years after the date of notification of this Directive, the Commission shall submit to the Council a report on the effect that rulings by the courts as to the application of Article 7(*e*) and of paragraph 1(*b*) of this Article have on consumer protection and the functioning of the common market. In the light of this report the Council, acting on a proposal from the Commission and pursuant to the terms of Article 100 of the Treaty, shall decide whether to repeal Article 7(*e*).

Article 16

1. Any Member State may provide that a producer's total liability for damage resulting from a death or personal injury and caused by identical items with the same defect shall be limited to an amount which may not be less than 70 million ECU.

2. Ten years after the date of notification of this Directive, the Commission shall submit to the Council a report on the effect on consumer protection and the functioning of the common market of the implementation of the financial limit on liability by those Member States which have used the option provided for in paragraph 1. In the light of this report the Council, acting on a proposal from the Commission and pursuant to the terms of Article 100 of the Treaty, shall decide whether to repeal paragraph 1.

Article 17

This Directive shall not apply to products put into circulation before the date on which the provisions referred to in Article 19 enter into force.

Article 18

1. For the purposes of this Directive, the ECU shall be that defined by Regulation (EEC) No 3180/78, as amended by Regulation (EEC) No 2626/84. The equivalent in national currency shall initially be calculated at the rate obtaining on the date of adoption of this Directive.

2. Every five years the Council, acting on a proposal from the Commission, shall examine and, if need be, revise the amounts in this Directive, in the light of economic and monetary trends in the Community.

Article 19

1. Member States shall bring into force, not later than three years from the date of notification of this Directive, the laws, regulations and administrative provisions necessary to comply with this Directive. They shall forthwith inform the Commission thereof.

2. The procedure set out in Article 15(2) shall apply from the date of notification of this Directive.

Article 20

Member States shall communicate to the Commission the texts of the main provisions of national law which they subsequently adopt in the field governed by this Directive.

Article 21

Every five years the Commission shall present a report to the Council on the application of this Directive and, if necessary, shall submit appropriate proposals to it.

Article 22

This Directive is addressed to the Member States.

Questions

1. What test of remoteness of damage do you think will be applied to liability under the Consumer Protection Act 1987? (See C. Newdick (1987) 104 LQR 288 at 297–300; S. Whittaker (1985) 5 YEL 233 at 253–254.)

2. In what ways might a plaintiff's misuse of a product affect a claim under the 1987 Act?

Notes

1. The Consumer Protection Act 1987, Part 1 of which came into force on 1 March 1987, implements the Directive on Product Liability 1985 which has just been set out. As will have been seen, certain parts of the Directive were optional, and, as will also have been seen, this country has exercised the option (a) to exclude primary agricultural products and game (s. 2(4)), (b) to allow the development risks defence (s. 4(1) (e)), but (c) not to have an overall financial limit on liability. Consider the views of the Law Commission and the Scottish Law Commission, *Liability for Defective Products*, Law Com. No. 82, Scot. Law Com. No. 45, Cmnd. 6831 and the Pearson Commission, vol. 1, chap. 22 (when considering a strict liability regime for defective products prior to the amended version of the Directive). None of these bodies wanted an overall limit on financial liability, but none favoured a development risks defence. In relation to primary agricultural products and game the Law Commission and the Pearson Commission favoured their inclusion, whereas the Scottish Law Commission wanted consideration to be given to the question of their exclusion.

2. For policy arguments in favour of strict liability for defective products, see the reports of the Law Commission and Scottish Law Commission, op cit, paras. 21–29 and 38–42 and of the Pearson Commission, vol. 1, paras. 1230–1236. The Government were influenced by the policy factors set out by the Pearson Commission, e.g. encouraging producers to achieve the highest possible safety standards, the producer being in the best position to insure and pass on the cost of so doing: see *Implementation of EC Directive on Product Liability; an Explanatory and Consultative Note*, issued by the Department of Trade and Industry in 1985. The Pearson Commission

thought that the imposition of strict liability for products would only constitute a small part of product costs — and, as *Winfield & Jolowicz*, p. 260, note 60 point out, they were not envisaging a development risks defence, on which see note 6, post. (On the question of high risk industries, insurance and the development risks defence, see A. M. Clark, *Product Liability*, pp. 181–182 and 184.) Note also the Pearson Commission's estimate that defective goods (other than drugs) may only cause 1 per cent of personal injuries.

3. It will have been seen that s. 2(2) of the Act covers not only the producer (as defined by s. 1), but also the importer into a member state of the European Community and the 'own brander'. In addition, s. 2(3) provides a potential liability for a supplier of the product unless certain information is given (in the circumstances there set out) to the person who has suffered damage. The advantage for the plaintiff is fairly obvious here and is particularly necessary in cases of 'anonymous' goods: see the Law Commissions, op cit, paras. 100–101. However, J. R. Bradgate and N. Savage (1987) 137 NLJ 935 at 954 comment that the 'keeping and storage of the records needed to avoid liability under s. 2(3) may prove crippling to many small businesses; insurance against liability may be the easiest solution in such cases, but the insurer may want to inspect stock recording systems before fixing a premium, and in any case it is likely that the very businesses most at risk from s. 2(3) [small businesses supplying a large number of small products] are those least likely to know of its provisions'. More generally, what is the disadvantage of providing several potential defendants? Note also that the producer of a complete product is liable for a defect in a component part of the product. Should he be?

4. Liability for defective buildings was considered in the previous chapter. Does the Consumer Protection Act 1987 have any application to the case where a person suffers damage as a result of a defect in a building? Consider the definition of 'product' in s. 1(2), that of 'goods' in s. 45(1) and what is laid down about 'supply' in s. 4(1)(b) and s. 46(3) and (4) (and see *Winfield & Jolowicz*, p. 252). Who might be liable if, for example, a tile on the roof cracks, due to a defect in its manufacture, and falls, thereby causing personal injury? (Consider C. J. Miller, *Product Liability and Safety Encyclopaedia*, Division III, para. 105.) Another point that has been raised is whether books are covered by the Act. See S. Whittaker (1989) 105 LQR 125 on this question and generally on the coverage of intellectual property.

5. To what extent does the Act introduce a standard of liability that is stricter than negligence? This raises the question of how s. 3 of the Act will be interpreted. What test or tests may evolve? The phrase 'such as persons generally are entitled to expect' in s. 3 appears, by its use of the word 'entitled', to be different from the 'consumer expectation' test which is one of the tests that has been deployed in the United States of America where strict liability for defective products has been in existence for some time. A test in which the risks and benefits of the product are balanced (which has also been used in the United States) would seem to be a more likely outcome. This is reminiscent of the tort of negligence and raises the question as to which risks are to be taken into account. In negligence it is the risks which were or which should have been known to the defendant: in a system of strict

liability it should be the risks that in fact existed, whether discoverable or not, and it is on this issue that the development risks defence becomes significant: see the next note. When considering this point, bear in mind, however, that, as Stapleton points out ((1986) 6 Oxf JLS 392 at 393 and 408-413), the notion of 'benefits' involves a consideration of the relative benefits of the product in the light of feasible alternatives at the time of supply, i.e. developments in this respect since that time will not be taken into account: see the last part of s. 3(2) of the 1987 Act.

Types of defect can be classified as 'manufacturing defects', 'design defects' and 'failures to warn'. (See e.g, Newdick, op cit.) Should the same test apply to all? Generally on the test for what is defective, see Clark, op cit, chaps. 2 and 4.

6. Section 4 sets out various defences to the strict liability introduced by the Act. Section 4(1)(e) has been controversial. Compare its wording with Art. 7(1)(e) of the Directive. Are the two compatible? C. Newdick [1988] CLJ 455 argues that they are and that the wording in the Act reflects the true meaning of the Directive. Do you agree? (Cf. Miller, op cit, III, para. 126.1.) In the light of s. 4(1)(e) how does liability under the Act differ from that in negligence? It seems that the question whether s. 4(1)(e) complies with the Directive may be tested within the European Community: see D. McIntosh [1990] PLI 106. If there is a difference between the Directive and the Act in this respect, note the point that s. 1(1) of the Act requires the Act to be construed so that it makes such provision as is necessary to comply with the Directive (though see Miller, op cit; Clark, op cit, p. 154). As was mentioned ante, the development risks defence was one of the optional facets of the Directive, and of the first seven countries to implement it, only one (Luxembourg) did not avail itself of this option (S. Ashworth [1990] PLI 30). Generally on the development risks defence see the article by Newdick ante; Stapleton, op cit, 408-419; Clark, op cit, chap. 6; Miller, op cit, III, paras. 122-131. What are the arguments for and against allowing this defence?

Contributory negligence can also be applicable to a suit under the 1987 Act (s. 6(4)). Should it be? See J. A. Jolowicz in *Accident Compensation after Pearson*, edited by D. K. Allen, C. J. Bourn and J. Holyoak, (London, 1979), pp. 59-61 and cf. P. J. Sherman at p. 133. Compare with the defence of contributory negligence the provision in s. 3(2)(*b*) of the Act. It has been pointed out (Clark, op cit, p. 195) that the defence of volenti is not expressly mentioned in the Act (although disclaimers of liability are banned (s. 7)). For discussion of this omission, see Clark, op cit. pp. 194-196. However, in relation to his comment on p. 195 — that in a case where the harm is caused partly by the actions of the victim the defence of contributory negligence is capable of partial or full exclusion of liability — note the later decision in *Pitts v Hunt* [1990] 3 All ER 344; [1990] 3 WLR 542. As has been mentioned p. 354, ante, this case decides that a 100 per cent deduction is not possible under the Law Reform (Contributory Negligence) Act 1945.

7. The range of recoverable damage is limited under s. 5, and recovery for damage not covered by the Act (e.g. damage to a factory) will have to be sought under other torts or in contract. (It has also been pointed out that negligence may be of practical importance even in relation to types of damage covered by the Act because of limitation periods: note that Sch. 1

to the 1987 Act contains the limitation period for individual cases but also a ten-year 'long stop' from the 'relevant time' within the meaning of s. 4.) The Act covers death and personal injuries. Damage to certain property is compensatable under the Act (provided the monetary threshold of £275 is met); but should such loss be covered by a strict liability scheme? This question is related to the incidence of first party insurance in respect of such damage and what might be thought to be the desirable goal of encouraging it. (See the Law Commissions, op cit, paras. 117–121; Whittaker (1985) 5 YEL at pp. 274–275.) There has been some debate whether economic loss consequent on recoverable damage to property is within the Act (see J. R. Bradgate and N. Savage (1987) 137 NLJ 1025 at 1026), but it would appear that it is. Damage to the product itself is not covered. What if one part of a car (e.g. the brakes) which is supplied by a component manufacturer is defective and causes an accident in which the rest of the car is damaged? (Cf. the position in negligence, p. 500, ante). Are Art. 9 of the Directive and s. 5(2) of the Act consistent on this point? (See Miller, op cit, III, para. 140.2; *Clerk & Lindsell*, para. 12.25.)

11 Liability for animals

We have seen in chap 10 ante that liability for defective products is a blend of common law and statute. This is also the case when damage is caused by animals. In this sphere, however, strict liability at common law was more prevalent than in the case of products (see p. 491, ante), but legislation has taken over and attention now has to be paid to the Animals Act 1971 (post). This Act was based on a report of the Law Commission in 1967 (*Civil Liability for Animals*, Law Com. No. 13), although it should be noted that it departs in some respects from the provisions of the Draft Bill to be found in that report. Liability for damage caused by animals can still be grounded on torts such as negligence, nuisance or *Rylands v Fletcher*. Nevertheless, it should not be forgotten that liability in negligence is affected by the 1971 Act, for s. 8 alters the common law position concerning liability for negligence where animals stray onto a highway (and see *Davies v Davies* [1975] QB 172; [1974] 3 All ER 817). For discussion of this area of the law, in addition to the standard textbooks, see P. M. North, *The Modern Law of Animals* (London, 1972).

The Animals Act 1971

STRICT LIABILITY FOR DAMAGE DONE BY ANIMALS

1. New provisions as to strict liability for damage done by animals. — (1) The provisions of sections 2 to 5 of this Act replace —
   (*a*) the rules of the common law imposing a strict liability in tort for damage done by an animal on the ground that the animal is regarded as ferae naturae or that its vicious or mischievous propensities are known or presumed to be known;
   (*b*) subsections (1) and (2) of section 1 of the Dogs Act 1906 as amended by the Dogs (Amendment) Act 1928 (injury to cattle or poultry); and
   (*c*) the rules of the common law imposing a liability for cattle trespass.
   (2) Expressions used in those sections shall be interpreted in accordance with the provisions of section 6 (as well as those of section 11) of this Act.

2. Liability for damage done by dangerous animals. — (1) Where any damage is caused by an animal which belongs to a dangerous species, any person who is a keeper of the animal is liable for the damage, except as otherwise provided by this Act.
   (2) Where damage is caused by an animal which does not belong to a dangerous species, a keeper of the animal is liable for the damage, except as otherwise provided by this Act, if —
   (*a*) the damage is of a kind which the animal, unless restrained, was likely to cause or which, if caused by the animal, was likely to be severe; and
   (*b*) the likelihood of the damage or of its being severe was due to characteristics

of the animal which are not normally found in animals of the same species or
are not normally so found except at particular times or in particular circumstances; and

(c) those characteristics were known to that keeper or were at any time known to
a person who at that time had charge of the animal as that keeper's servant or,
where that keeper is the head of a household, were known to another keeper
of the animal who is a member of that household and under the age of sixteen.

3. Liability for injury done by dogs to livestock. — Where a dog causes damage by
killing or injuring livestock, any person who is a keeper of the dog is liable for the
damage, except as otherwise provided by this Act.

4. Liability for damage and expenses due to trespassing livestock. — (1) Where
livestock belonging to any person strays on to land in the ownership or occupation
of another and —

(a) damage is done by the livestock to the land or to any property on it which is
in the ownership or possession of the other person; or

(b) any expenses are reasonably incurred by that other person in keeping the
livestock while it cannot be restored to the person to whom it belongs or while
it is detained in pursuance of section 7 of this Act, or in ascertaining to whom
it belongs;

the person to whom the livestock belongs is liable for the damage or expenses, except
as otherwise provided by this Act.

(2) For the purposes of this section any livestock belongs to the person in whose
possession it is.

5. Exceptions from liability under sections 2 to 4. — (1) A person is not liable under
sections 2 to 4 of this Act for any damage which is due wholly to the fault of the
person suffering it.

(2) A person is not liable under section 2 of this Act for any damage suffered by
a person who has voluntarily accepted the risk thereof.

(3) A person is not liable under section 2 of this Act for any damage caused by
an animal kept on any premises or structure to a person trespassing there, if it is
proved either —

(a) that the animal was not kept there for the protection of persons or property; or

(b) (if the animal was kept there for the protection of persons or property) that
keeping it there for that purpose was not unreasonable.

(4) A person is not liable under section 3 of this Act if the livestock was killed or
injured on land on to which it had strayed and either the dog belonged to the occupier
or its presence on the land was authorised by the occupier.

(5) A person is not liable under section 4 of this Act where the livestock strayed
from a highway and its presence there was a lawful use of the highway.

(6) In determining whether any liability for damage under section 4 of this Act is
excluded by subsection (1) of this section the damage shall not be treated as due to
the fault of the person suffering it by reason only that he could have prevented it by
fencing; but a person is not liable under that section where it is proved that the straying of the livestock on to the land would not have occurred but for a breach by any
other person, being a person having an interest in the land, of a duty to fence.

6. Interpretation of certain expressions used in sections 2 to 5. — (1) The following
provisions apply to the interpretation of sections 2 to 5 of this Act.

(2) A dangerous species is a species —

(a) which is not commonly domesticated in the British Islands; and

(b) whose fully grown animals normally have such characteristics that they are
likely, unless restrained, to cause severe damage or that any damage they may
cause is likely to be severe.

(3) Subject to subsection (4) of this section, a person is a keeper of an animal if —

(*a*) he owns the animal or has it in his possession; or

(*b*) he is the head of a household of which a member under the age of sixteen owns the animal or has it in his possession;

and if at any time an animal ceases to be owned by or to be in the possession of a person, any person who immediately before that time was a keeper thereof by virtue of the preceding provisions of this subsection continues to be a keeper of the animal until another person becomes a keeper thereof by virtue of those provisions.

(4) Where an animal is taken into and kept in possession for the purpose of preventing it from causing damage or of restoring it to its owner, a person is not a keeper of it by virtue only of that possession.

(5) Where a person employed as a servant by a keeper of an animal incurs a risk incidental to his employment he shall not be treated as accepting it voluntarily.

DETENTION AND SALE OF TRESPASSING LIVESTOCK

7. Detention and sale of trespassing livestock. — (1) The right to seize and detain any animal by way of distress damage feasant is hereby abolished.

(2) Where any livestock strays on to any land and is not then under the control of any person the occupier of the land may detain it, subject to subsection (3) of this section, unless ordered to return it by a court.

(3) Where any livestock is detained in pursuance of this section the right to detain it ceases —

(*a*) at the end of a period of forty-eight hours, unless within that period notice of the detention has been given to the officer in charge of a police station and also, if the person detaining the livestock knows to whom it belongs, to that person; or

(*b*) when such amount is tendered to the person detaining the livestock as is sufficient to satisfy any claim he may have under section 4 of this Act in respect of the livestock; or

(*c*) if he has no such claim, when the livestock is claimed by a person entitled to its possession.

(4) Where livestock has been detained in pursuance of this section for a period of not less than fourteen days the person detaining it may sell it at a market or by public auction, unless proceedings are then pending for the return of the livestock or for any claim under section 4 of this Act in respect of it.

(5) Where any livestock is sold in the exercise of the right conferred by this section and the proceeds of the sale, less the costs thereof and any costs incurred in connection with it, exceed the amount of any claim under section 4 of this Act which the vendor had in respect of the livestock, the excess shall be recoverable from him by the person who would be entitled to the possession of the livestock but for the sale.

(6) A person detaining any livestock in pursuance of this section is liable for any damage caused to it by a failure to treat it with reasonable care and supply it with adequate food and water while it is so detained.

(7) References in this section to a claim under section 4 of this Act in respect of any livestock do not include any claim under that section for damage done by or expenses incurred in respect of the livestock before the straying in connection with which it is detained under this section.

ANIMALS STRAYING ON TO HIGHWAY

8. Duty to take care to prevent damage from animals straying on to the highway. — (1) So much of the rules of the common law relating to liability for negligence as excludes or restricts the duty which a person might owe to others to take such care as is reasonable to see that damage is not caused by animals straying on to a highway is hereby abolished.

(2) Where damage is caused by animals straying from unfenced land to a highway a person who placed them on the land shall not be regarded as having committed a breach of the duty to take care by reason only of placing them there if —

(a) the land is common land, or is land situated in an area where fencing is not customary, or is a town or village green; and

(b) he had a right to place the animals on that land.

PROTECTION OF LIVESTOCK AGAINST DOGS

9. Killing of or injury to dogs worrying livestock. — (1) In any civil proceedings against a person (in this section referred to as the defendant) for killing or causing injury to a dog it shall be a defence to prove —

(a) that the defendant acted for the protection of any livestock and was a person entitled to act for the protection of that livestock; and

(b) that within forty-eight hours of the killing or injury notice thereof was given by the defendant to the officer in charge of a police station.

(2) For the purposes of this section a person is entitled to act for the protection of any livestock if, and only if —

(a) the livestock or the land on which it is belongs to him or to any person under whose express or implied authority he is acting; and

(b) the circumstances are not such that liability for killing or causing injury to the livestock would be excluded by section 5(4) of this Act.

(3) Subject to subsection (4) of this section, a person killing or causing injury to a dog shall be deemed for the purposes of this section to act for the protection of any livestock if, and only if, either —

(a) the dog is worrying or is about to worry the livestock and there are no other reasonable means of ending or preventing the worrying; or

(b) the dog has been worrying livestock, has not left the vicinity and is not under the control of any person and there are no practicable means of ascertaining to whom it belongs.

(4) For the purposes of this section the condition stated in either of the paragraphs of the preceding subsection shall be deemed to have been satisfied if the defendant believed that it was satisfied and had reasonable ground for that belief.

(5) For the purposes of this section —

(a) an animal belongs to any person if he owns it or has it in his possession; and

(b) land belongs to any person if he is the occupier thereof.

SUPPLEMENTAL

10. Application of certain enactments to liability under sections 2 to 4. — For the purposes of the Fatal Accidents Acts 1846 to 1959[1], the Law Reform (Contributory Negligence) Act 1945 and [the Limitation Act 1980][2] any damage for which a person is liable under sections 2 to 4 of this Act shall be treated as due to his fault.

11. General interpretation. — In this Act —

'common land', and 'town or village green' have the same meanings as in the Commons Registration Act 1965;

'damage' includes the death of, or injury to, any person (including any disease and any impairment of physical or mental condition);

'fault' has the same meaning as in the Law Reform (Contributory Negligence) Act 1945;

---

1. [This now includes a reference to the Fatal Accidents Act 1976. The Fatal Accidents Acts 1846 and 1959 have been repealed.]
2. [Substituted by the Limitation Act 1980, s. 40(2) and Sch. 3.]

'fencing' includes the construction of any obstacle designed to prevent animals from straying;

'livestock' means cattle, horses, asses, mules, hinnies, sheep, pigs, goats and poultry, and also deer not in the wild state and, in sections 3 and 9, also, while in captivity, pheasants, partridges and grouse;

'poultry' means the domestic varieties of the following, that is to say, fowls, turkeys, geese, ducks, guinea-fowls, pigeons, peacocks and quails; and

'species' includes sub-species and variety.

12. Application to Crown. – (1) This Act binds the Crown, but nothing in this section shall authorise proceedings to be brought against Her Majesty in her private capacity.

(2) Section 38(3) of the Crown Proceedings Act 1947 (interpretation of references to Her Majesty in her private capacity) shall apply as if this section were contained in that Act.

13. Short title, repeal, commencement and extent. – (1) This Act may be cited as the Animals Act 1971.

(2) The following are hereby repealed, that is to say –

(a) in the Dogs Act 1906, subsections (1) to (3) of section 1; and

(b) in section 1(1) of the Dogs (Amendment) Act 1928 the words 'in both places where that word occurs'.

(3) This Act shall come into operation on 1 October 1971.

(4) This Act does not extend to Scotland or to Northern Ireland.

Cummings *v* Granger Court of Appeal [1977] 1 All ER 104

The plaintiff was bitten one night by the defendant's Alsatian which was used as a guard-dog in a scrapyard occupied by the defendant. The dog was allowed to run loose at night in the yard, though it could not escape from the yard. In large letters on the gates of the yard there appeared the warning 'Beware of the Dog'. Next to these gates was a wicket gate which the plaintiff's companion (Mr Hobson) used a key to open. The trial judge (O'Connor J), [1975] 2 All ER 1129, found that the plaintiff had gone into the yard, but that she was a trespasser there. O'Connor J held the defendant liable under s. 2(2) of the Animals Act 1971, but found that the plaintiff had been contributorily negligent and reduced the damages by 50 per cent. There was an appeal to the Court of Appeal.

LORD DENNING MR (who had stated that this Alsatian 'was just a typical guard-dog'): . . . This brings me to the law. At common law when a dog bit a man, the owner or keeper of the dog was *strictly* liable if he knew that it had a propensity to bite or attack human beings. Apart from this, however, he was liable for *negligence* if the circumstances were such as to impose on him a duty of care towards the injured plaintiff, which he had failed to observe: see *Fardon v Harcourt-Rivington*[1] by Lord Atkin and *Draper v Hodder*.[2] Now so far as strict liability is concerned, the common law has been replaced by the Animals Act 1971. . . .

The statutory liability for a tame animal like a dog is defined in s. 2(2) of the 1971 Act, subject to exceptions contained in s. 5. Now it seems to me that this is a case where the keeper of the dog is strictly liable unless he can bring himself within one of the exceptions. I say this because the three requirements for strict liability are satisfied. The section is very cumbrously worded and will give rise to several difficulties

---

1. [1932] All ER Rep 81 at 83.
2. [1972] 2 QB 556; [1972] 2 All ER 210.

in future. But in this case the judge[1] held that the three requirements were satisfied and I agree with him for these reasons. Section 2(2)(*a*): this animal was a dog of the Alsatian breed. If it did bite anyone, the damage was 'likely to be severe'. Section 2(2)(*b*): this animal was a guard-dog kept so as to scare intruders and frighten them off. On the owner's own evidence, it used to bark and run round in circles, especially when coloured people approached. Those characteristics — barking and running around to guard its territory — are not normally found in Alsatian dogs except in the circumstances where used as guard-dogs. Those circumstances are 'particular circumstances' within s. 2(2)(*b*). It was 'due' to those circumstances that the damage was likely to be severe if an intruder did enter on its territory. Section 2(2)(*c*): those characteristics were known to the keeper. It follows that the keeper of the dog is strictly liable unless he can bring himself within one of the exceptions in s. 5. Obviously s. 5(1) does not avail. The bite was not *wholly* due to the fault of the [plaintiff] but only *partly* so. Section 5(3) may, however, avail the keeper. It shows that if someone trespasses on property and is bitten or injured by a guard-dog, the keeper of the guard-dog is exempt from liability if it is proved 'that keeping it there for that purpose was not unreasonable'.

The judge held that the owner of this dog was unreasonable in keeping it in this yard. . . .

I take a different view. This was a yard in the East End of London where persons of the roughest type come and go. It was a scrapyard, true, but scrapyards like building sites often contain much valuable property. It was deserted at night and at weekends. If there was no protection allowed there, thieves would drive up in a lorry and remove the scrap, with no one to see them or to stop them. The only reasonable way of protecting the place was to have a guard-dog. True, it was a fierce dog. But why not? A gentle dog would be no good. The thieves would soon make friends with him. It seems to me that it was very reasonable, or, at any rate, not unreasonable for the owner to keep this dog there. Long ago in 1794 Lord Kenyon CJ said: '. . . every man had a right to keep a dog for the protection of his yard or house': see *Brock v Copeland*[2].

Alternatively, there is another defence provided by s. 5(2). It says that a person is not liable 'for any damage suffered by a person who has voluntarily accepted the risk thereof'. This seems to me to warrant a reference back to the common law. This very defence was considered in 1820 in *Ilott v Wilkes*[3]. It was a case about a spring gun which went off and injured a trespasser. But Bayley J[4] put this very case:

'. . . if a trespasser enters into the yard of another, over the entrance to which notice is given, that there is a furious dog loose, and that it is dangerous for any person to enter in without one of the servants or the owner. If the wrong-doer, having read that notice, and knowing, therefore, that he is likely to be injured, in the absence of the owner enters the yard, and is worried by the dog, (which in such a case would be a mere engine without discretion,) it is clear that the party could not maintain any action for the injury sustained by the dog, because the answer would be, as in this case, that he could not have a remedy for an injury which he had voluntarily incurred.'

That reasoning applies here. This lady certainly knew the animal was there. She worked next door. She knew all about it. She must have seen this huge notice on the door 'Beware of the Dog'. Nevertheless she went in, following her man friend. In the circumstances she must be taken voluntarily to have incurred this risk. So with any burglar or thief who goes on to premises knowing that there is a guard-dog there. If

---

1. [1975] 2 All ER 1129; [1975] 1 WLR 1330.
2. (1794) 1 Esp 203 at 203.
3. (1820) 3 Barn & Ald 304; [1814–23] All ER Rep 277.
4. (1820) 3 Barn & Ald 304 at 313; [1814–23] All ER Rep 277 at 280.

he is bitten or injured he cannot recover. He voluntarily takes the risk of it. Even if he does not know a guard-dog is there, he might be defeated by the plea 'ex turpi causa non oritur actio'.

There is only one further point I would mention. This accident took place in November 1971 very shortly after the Animals Act 1971 was passed. In 1975 the Guard Dogs Act 1975 was passed. It does not apply to this case. But it makes it quite clear that in future a person is not allowed to have a guard-dog to roam about on his premises unless the dog is under the control of a handler. If he has no handler, the dog must be chained up so that it is not at liberty to roam around. If a person contravenes the 1975 Act, he can be brought before a magistrate and fined. . . . But it is only criminal liability. It does not confer a right of action in any civil proceedings. It may, however, have this effect in civil proceedings: it may make it unreasonable for the defendant to let a dog free in the yard at night (as this defendant did) and it may thus deprive the defendant of a defence under s. 5(3)(b). But he might still be able to rely on the defence under s. 5(2) of volenti non fit injuria.

Coming back to the present case, I think the defendant is not under any strict liability to the plaintiff because she was a trespasser and also because she voluntarily took the risk. I would therefore allow the appeal and enter judgment for the defendant.

ORMROD LJ: . . . So far as s. 2 of the [Animals] Act 1971 is concerned, the first thing is to see what the word 'species' means, and it is defined in s. 11 as follows: '"species" includes sub-species and variety'. Those words have very much the ring of biological terms of art, and no doubt they should be given that meaning. In other words, it would be wrong to treat, say, a guard-dog as being a variety of a species or sub-species for the purposes of the section. What we have to deal with here is a sub-species of dog or variety of dog called 'Alsatians'.

Having struggled with s. 2(2)(b) for a considerable time to ascertain its meaning through its remarkably opaque language, I agree that the upshot of it can perhaps be put in this way. The plaintiff must prove that the animal has a propensity to cause damage which is not normally found in the variety of dog concerned or only at particular times or in particular circumstances; and an example of that is a bitch with pups or an Alsatian dog running loose in a yard which it regards as its territory when a stranger enters into it.

The plaintiff in this case set out to prove that this Alsatian had a propensity to cause damage which was not normally found in an Alsatian dog. She failed, in my judgment, wholly to show that this dog had any particular characteristic which was not normally found in Alsatians. . . .

Assuming it is open to her to rely on the second limb [of s. 2(2)(b)], I agree that this dog in the particular conditions of running loose in this yard, which it regarded as part of its territory, had characteristics such that, in those circumstances and at that time, it might cause damage. I think that that is probably true. Whether it was ever proved satisfactorily that the defendant knew about that, I doubt, but for the purposes of this judgment I am prepared to accept that he did know about it.

That brings us straight to s. 5, which is the important section providing for defences. It is important, I think, to remember that this is not a negligence action; this is not a fault liability situation; this is a strict liability situation, which is quite different. Therefore the defences which are made available to him by the 1971 Act are very important and ought not to be whittled away. To be fair to him and to be fair to the plaintiff, each of them must have their full statutory rights.

I entirely agree with all that Lord Denning MR has said on s. 5(3), that is liability to a trespasser, the plaintiff being for this purpose a trespasser. . . .

The other defence which is open to him is under s. 5(2), which is, in the words of the 1971 Act:

'A person is not liable under section 2 of this Act for any damage suffered by a person who has voluntarily accepted the risk thereof.'

I would like to read those words in their ordinary English meaning and not to complicate the question too much with the old, long history of the doctrine of volenti. That doctrine was developed in quite different conditions. It has nothing to do with strict liability; and I would not, for my part, like to see that defence whittled down by too fine distinctions as to what 'voluntarily accepted the risk' means. They are, to my mind, fairly simple English words and should in this context be treated as such. In this case I do not think it is open to any doubt whatever on the plaintiff's evidence that, assuming she did go into this yard, she accepted the risk. No doubt she knew about the dog, she said that she was frightened of the dog. For whatever reason she went in (the learned judge seems to think that she might have been relying on Mr Hobson to protect her), I would myself come to the conclusion that she accepted the risk, and it is no answer to say that she had Mr Hobson with her. In those circumstances I agree that this appeal should be allowed.

[BRIDGE LJ delivered a judgment in favour of allowing the appeal and stated that he agreed with the judgments of LORD DENNING MR and ORMROD LJ.]

Appeal allowed

Questions

1. Do you agree with Ormrod LJ's approach to s. 5(2), or do you think that Parliament intended the history of the doctrine of volenti to be rather more relevant to the interpretation of s. 5(2) than Ormrod LJ was prepared to accept?

2. As Lord Denning MR stated, the Guard Dogs Act 1975 does not confer any civil remedy for contravention of the Act (s. 5). In the light of this, do you think a compensation order could be made in criminal proceedings under the Act? (See p. 582, post.)

Notes

1. For an example of an animal falling within s. 2(1) of the Act, see *Tutin v M Chipperfield Promotions Ltd* (1980) 130 NLJ 807 (camel); cf. the pre-1971 Act law as shown by *McQuaker v Goddard* [1940] 1 KB 687; [1940] 1 All ER 471.

2. For comment on an unreported case (*Losner v Barnett*) concerning liability for dog bites, see the note on *Cummings v Granger* by B. S. Jackson (1977) 40 MLR 590. *Cummings v Granger* is also noted by J. R. Spencer [1977] CLJ 39.

3. The interpretation of s. 2(2) of the 1971 Act, which was under consideration in *Cummings v Granger*, has been further discussed by the Court of Appeal recently.

In *Smith v Ainger* (1990) Times, 5th June the plaintiff was injured when the defendants' dog, in making to attack the plaintiff's dog which was on a lead held by the plaintiff, came into contact with the plaintiff's legs and knocked him over. One issue concerned the meaning of the word 'likely' in the context of s. 2(2)(*a*): this was interpreted as having a wider compass than a phrase such as 'more probable than not' and to cover things that *might* happen. Another question was whether what occurred had been a kind of damage that the defendants' dog was likely to cause unless restrained. (Cf.

the 'kind of damage' concept in the discussion of remoteness of damage in chap. 6 ante.) The kind of damage involved in this case was accepted by Neill LJ in the Court of Appeal as being 'personal injury to a human being caused by the direct application of force', any distinction between a bite and injury as a result of buffeting being rejected as unrealistic. Neill LJ concluded that in the circumstances the answer to the question just posed was in the affirmative and consequently that the case fell within the first limb of s. 2(2)(a). The second limb of s. 2(2)(a) ('likely to be severe') was also thought to have been met on the authority of *Cummings v Granger* (see p. 526, ante) and *Curtis v Betts* [1990] 1 All ER 769; [1990] 1 WLR 459 that injury by a large dog fell into this category (although on the facts in the case concerning this particular dog Neill LJ would otherwise have been inclined to decide the matter differently).

Another Court of Appeal case (*Curtis v Betts*) also involved a successful claim for damages for injury caused by a dog, but here the plaintiff had been bitten by a bull mastiff. When considering the second limb of s. 2(2)(a) the Court of Appeal rejected the idea that the animal in question had to have abnormal characteristics for its species which rendered it likely that, if it caused damage, such damage would be severe. Section 2(2)(a) could apply without such abnormal characteristics being present. In relation to *s. 2(2)(b)*, Stuart-Smith LJ stated (at p. 778):

'To my mind the difficulty in the subsection arises from the first three words, "the likelihood of". Without these words, it would be plain that para (*b*) was concerned with the causation of damage. The plaintiff would have to prove that the damage of one of the types in para (*a*) was caused by either a permanent or temporary characteristic specified in para (*b*). This makes good sense. But the first three words seem to connote a concept of foreseeability and not causation. This would have remarkable consequences. If all that is necessary is that it be likely that a bitch with a litter of pups may have a propensity to be fierce and provided she is large enough to cause severe damage, the owner of such a bitch would be liable (if para (*c*) is satisfied) if the bitch causes severe damage at any time, whether or not she has pups or is with them. I cannot think that this was the intention of Parliament. Although I find difficulty in giving content to the words "the likelihood of", I am satisfied that there must be a causal link between the characteristic in question and the damage suffered. In particular where the case falls under the second limb, the temporary characteristic, the time or circumstances in which the damage is caused must be those during which the particular characteristics are or were prone to be exhibited.'

Nourse LJ agreed with Stuart-Smith LJ's comments concerning the phrase 'the likelihood of' in s. 2(2)(*b*) which, for the reasons put forward by the latter, he also agreed had to be given effect to as though the words 'the damage' were substituted for the phrase 'the likelihood of the damage or of its being severe'. The third member of the Court of Appeal (Slade LJ, with whose views on the construction of s. 2(2) Nourse LJ was in general agreement) would meet the difficulty by construing the phrase 'due to' in s. 2(2)(b) as meaning 'attributable to', rather than 'caused by'.

The characteristic which fell within the second limb of s. 2(2)(b) in *Curtis v Betts* was the tendency of bull mastiffs to react fiercely when defending the boundaries of what they regarded as their territory. An example of a characteristic falling within the first limb of s. 2(2)(b) is provided by *Kite v Napp* (1982) Times, 1st June (dog attacked people carrying bags), and see also *Wallace v Newton* [1982] 2 All ER 106; [1982] 1 WLR 375 (horse unreliable and unpredictable in its behaviour).

4. In relation to Lord Denning MR's comments concerning the Guard Dogs Act 1975, note s. 2(1)(c) and s. 2(2) of the Animals (Scotland) Act 1987 which contain the corresponding, though not identically worded, defence to that to be found in s. 5(3) of the Animals Act 1971. The Scottish Act expressly requires that s. 1 of the Guard Dogs Act 1975 be complied with if the animal is kept on the land for the protection of persons or property and is a guard dog within the meaning of the 1975 Act.

5. Under the Dangerous Wild Animals Act 1976 a person keeping a dangerous wild animal (as specified in the Act, as amended) must in general have a licence from a local authority. One of the conditions which s. 1 of that Act lays down must be attached to the licence is that the licensee should be insured against liability for any damage caused by the animal in question. The Pearson Commission's understanding was that this was regarded as requiring unlimited cover, but the Commission doubted whether this 'can realistically be expected'. Therefore an amendment to the Act was recommended so as 'either to specify practical limits to the third party insurance cover required, or to give the licensing authorities discretion to determine what is a satisfactory amount' (vol. 1, para. 1628). Note further the Riding Establishments Acts 1964 and 1970 in relation to which the same recommendation was made. On the position of zoos see the Zoo Licensing Act 1981 which may require their operation to be licensed by a local authority. A condition relating to insurance against liability for damage caused by the animals is something the local authority *may* impose in granting a licence (s. 5); cf. the Dangerous Wild Animals Act 1976. More generally, the Pearson Commission, having discussed in vol. 1, chap. 30 of its Report the question of liability for injuries caused by animals, did not see any need to change English law in this area (para. 1626).

6. The report of the Scottish Law Commission (*Obligations: Report on Civil Liability in Relation to Animals*, Scot Law Com. No 97) led to the Animals (Scotland) Act in 1987. Note the consideration, in Part V of the report, of the question of compulsory insurance and no fault liability in the context of liability for animals.

7. On the plea of ex turpi causa non oritur actio to which Lord Denning MR referred, see p. 392, ante.

8. As was mentioned in the introduction to this chapter, liability for animals is not only governed by the Animals Act 1971. There can be liability in torts such as negligence, nuisance or the rule in *Rylands v Fletcher* (1868) LR 3 HL 330, on which see North, *Animals*, chap. 6.

12 Statutory torts and employer's liability

We have so far considered two effects of statutes in relation to legal duties: (a) the removal of anomalies (e.g. the Occupiers' Liability Act 1957, p. 442, ante; the Defective Premises Act 1972, p. 480, ante, and the Animals Act 1971, p. 521, ante); and (b) the negligent exercise of statutory powers as giving rise to liability in certain circumstances in the tort of negligence (p. 99, ante).

The cases in this chapter are concerned with a third question. When does a *duty* laid down by statute give rise to civil liability? For this purposes statutes may be classified in three broad categories:

(i) those which *create torts by express words*, either in substitution for common law liability for negligence or other torts (e.g. Nuclear Installations Act 1965, p. 533, post) or alongside existing torts (e.g. Mineral Workings (Offshore Installations) Act 1971, noted p. 534, post);

(ii) those which *expressly exclude* civil liability for breach of their provisions (e.g. Medicines Act 1968, p. 535, post);

(iii) those which provide a criminal sanction or some other remedy, but are *silent* on the question of civil liability.

The first two categories give rise to no particular difficulties of statutory interpretation, although compensation for statutory wrongs may sometimes be dealt with by a different tribunal from that which determines liability for common law torts (e.g. the statutory wrongs of racial and sex discrimination in employment are dealt with by industrial tribunals: Race Relations Act 1976, s. 54; Sex Discrimination Act 1975, s. 63).

In dealing with the third category the courts usually pay lip-service to the theory of whether Parliament intended to create civil liability when it laid down the duty. This is a pure fiction because it is only very recently that Parliament has tended to give any thought to this question at all. Even modern statutes, like the Prevention of Oil Pollution Act 1971 (which makes the discharge of oil into navigable waters a criminal offence), are far from explicit. The Law Commission (see Draft Clauses, p. 549, post) proposed, in 1969, that there should be a general statute creating a presumption that the breach of a statutory duty is intended to be actionable at the suit of any person who suffers or apprehends damage, unless a contrary intention is expressly stated. But this would apply only to Acts passed after the statutory presumption is enacted and not to the vast body of existing statute law nor to future delegated legislation made under existing statutory powers. So the problems of interpretation will be with us indefinitely. Indeed, they are likely

531

to become more acute as the courts are called upon to provide remedies in English law for breach of the provisions of the EC Treaties and regulations and directives made by the Council of Ministers of the EC, and issue which lies beyond the scope of this chapter (for discussion see K. M. Stanton, *Breach of Statutory Duty in Tort* (London, 1986), pp. 67–68 and 84–86; J. Steiner (1987) 12 EL Rev 102–110).

In reading the cases, the student will discern various principles according to which the courts have purported to determine the presumed intention of Parliament: for example, whether the Act was passed for the benefit of a defined class of persons or a designated individual (liability) or for the public at large (no liability); whether the kind of harm which the plaintiff suffered was the 'mischief' which the Act was designed to prevent; and whether the remedy provided by the statute is adequate. None of these is particularly helpful and the results are often contradictory: compare *Groves v Lord Wimborne* [1898] 2 QB 402 (p. 536, post) with *Phillips v Britannia Hygienic Laundry Co* [1923] 2 KB 832 (p. 543, post). In attempting to reconcile these decisions one important historical fact should be kept in mind. In 1837 the courts invented the doctrine of common employment which debarred an employee injured by the negligence of a fellow employee from recovering damages from their common employer (*Priestley v Fowler* (1837) 3 M & W 1, p. 565, post). By the end of the century a number of judges realised that this doctrine (although modified by the Employers' Liability Act 1880) was causing much hardship to injured workers; the stream of new factory and mines legislation was being inadequately enforced; and the first Workmen's Compensation Act, passed in 1897, did not provide for full compensation since it was based on the principle of an equal division of the risk of industrial accidents between employer and employee. *Groves v Lord Wimborne* was a response to this situation and enabled the courts to evade the doctrine of common employment.

In other fields, such as road accidents, the social reasons for judicial invention have been less compelling. The few exceptions to the general rule that non-industrial statutes do not give rise to civil liability, in the absence of an express provision, may be regarded as anomalies. *Monk v Warbey* [1935] 1 KB 75 (p. 892, post) was based on the premise that victims of road accidents should not only be entitled to compensation but should actually get it; in the light of the Road Traffic Act 1988 (p. 885, post) this case is now of little practical importance. Cases such as *Dawson v Bingley UDC* [1911] 2 KB 149, noted p. 540, post, and *Read v Croydon Corpn* [1938] 4 All ER 631, noted p. 540, post, are ones in which, quite apart from the statute, a duty-situation could be said to exist: compare *Atkinson v Newcastle Waterworks Co* (1877) LR 2 Ex D 441 (p. 538, post) where, at common law, no duty of positive action could have been said to arise. The reluctance of the courts to create civil wrongs where an Act, other than one dealing with industrial safety, creates an obligation and is silent on the subject of civil enforcement, is shown by *Lonrho Ltd v Shell Petroleum Ltd* [1982] AC 173; [1981] 2 All ER 456 (p. 545, post).

Dissatisfaction with the current English approach has led to considerable interest, on this side of the Atlantic, in the American approach which treats legislative provisions either as setting the standard of care in the tort of negligence, at least if breach is unexcused (negligence per se) or as evidence of negligence. This approach is reviewed in the important decision of the

Supreme Court of Canada in *The Queen in Right of Canada v Saskatchewan Wheat Pool* (1983) 143 DLR (3d) 9 (p. 551, post). In order to put the arguments in context, it is necessary to understand the nature of the personal 'non-delegable' duties which have developed in relation to the duty of care owed by an employer to his employees. This development, itself a response to the stunting effect of the doctrine of common employment, is considered in section 7 of this chapter.

1   Express creation of new torts

The Nuclear Installations Act 1965

7. Duty of licensee of licensed site. — (1) Where a nuclear site licence has been granted in respect of any site, it shall be the duty of the licensee to secure that —
  (a) no such occurrence involving nuclear matter as is mentioned in subsection (2) of this section causes injury to any person or damage to any property of any person other than the licensee, being injury or damage arising out of or resulting from the radioactive properties, or a combination of those and any toxic, explosive or other hazardous properties, of that nuclear matter; and
  (b) no ionising radiations emitted during the period of the licensee's responsibility —
    (i) from anything caused or suffered by the licensee to be on the site which is not nuclear matter; or
    (ii) from any waste discharged (in whatever form) on or from the site, cause injury to any person or damage to any property of any person other than the licensee.
(2) The occurrences referred to in subsection (1)(a) of this section are —
  (a) any occurrence on the licensed site during the period of the licensee's responsibility, being an occurrence involving nuclear matter;
  (b) any occurrence elsewhere than on the licensed site involving nuclear matter which is not excepted matter and which at the time of the occurrence —
    (i) is in the course of carriage on behalf of the licensee as licensee of that site; or
    (ii) is in the course of carriage to that site with the agreement of the licensee from a place outside the relevant territories; and
    (iii) in either case, is not on any other relevant site in the United Kingdom;
  (c) any occurrence elsewhere than on the licensed site involving nuclear matter which is not excepted matter and which —
    (i) having been on the licensed site at any time during the period of the licensee's reponsibility; or
    (ii) having been in the course of carriage on behalf of the licensee as licensee of that site,
  has not subsequently been on any relevant site, or in the course of any relevant carriage, or (except in the course of relevant carriage) within the territorial limits of a country which is not a relevant territory.

13. Exclusion, extension or reduction of compensation in certain cases. —
(4) The duty imposed by section 7, 8, 9, 10 or 11 of this Act —
  (a) shall not impose any liability on the person subject to that duty with respect to injury or damage caused by an occurrence which constitutes a breach of that duty if the occurrence, or the causing thereby of the injury or damage, is attributable to hostile action in the course of any armed conflict, including any armed conflict within the United Kingdom; but

(*b*) shall impose such a liability where the occurrence, or the causing thereby of the injury or damage, is attributable to a natural disaster, notwithstanding that the disaster is of such an exceptional character that it could not reasonably have been foreseen.

Notes

1. Consider the defences in s. 13(4) of the Act. How do these compare with the defences available in an action for negligence, nuisance or under the *Rylands v Fletcher* rule? (See chap. 14, p. 650, post.)

2. Section 13(6) provides that damages may be reduced by reason of the fault of the plaintiff only if he has intentionally caused harm or had reckless disregard for the consequences of his act.

3. 'Injury' is defined as personal injury including loss of life (s. 26(1)). In *Merlin v British Nuclear Fuels plc* [1990] 3 All ER 711; [1990] 3 WLR 383, the plaintiffs' house was contaminated by radionuclides emanating from the Sellafield nuclear power station. They decided to move so as not to expose their children to the health risk they believed would result from long-term occupation of the house. They claimed compensation for the diminution in the value of their house, which they alleged was due to contamination in contravention of s. 7(1) of the Act. Gatehouse J held that the increased risk to the occupants of developing cancer did not amount to 'injury' and that 'damage to property' did not include economic loss or damage to property rights. Compare the common law approach to economic loss, p. 149, ante.

4. An exposure to nuclear matter or ionising radiations may affect the unborn. Section 3 of the Congenital Disabilities (Civil Liability) Act 1976 clarifies the above Act by stating that anything which affects the ability of parents to have a normal healthy child is an 'injury' for the purposes of the Nuclear Installations Act 1965. Disabilities sustained by the child of those parents as a result of the exposure give rise to a claim for compensation under the 1965 Act any time within thirty years of the exposure.

5. This statute in effect replaces common law liability (e.g. in respect of nuisance, negligence, and the rule in *Rylands v Fletcher*) arising from the escape of ionising radiations with a new statutory liability. This liability is concentrated on the licensee (a licence for the operation of a nuclear plant on a particular site being required). The new tort was created as part of a carefully worked out scheme between the Government and the insurance companies. Section 27 of the Energy Act 1983 increased the operator's liability from £5 million to £20 million per incident; the total amount of compensation to be provided in respect of a nuclear incident by the operator and public funds together was increased from £50 million per incident to the equivalent of about £210 million (ss. 28 and 30).

6. Another example of the express creation of an action is s. 11 of the Mineral Workings (Offshore Installations) Act 1971, which provides that breach of any provision of the Act, or of regulations made thereunder, shall be actionable so far as it causes personal injury. This Act, like most other safety legislation in England, was passed in response to a particular tragedy,

in this case the loss of thirteen lives when the drilling rig *Sea Gem* collapsed, capsized and sank. A committee of inquiry (Cmnd. 3409) found that there had been several important breaches of the Institute of Petroleum's voluntary Code of Safe Practice (although these failures were not the direct cause of the loss of life). Compliance with this Code had been a condition of the grant of a drilling licence to the owners of the rig. The committee said nothing about the creation of civil liability for breach of statutory duty. It should be noted that (a) civil liability under the Act is co-existent with common law duties; and (b) certain defences available in criminal proceedings (i.e. under s. 9(3) or regulations made under s. 7(2)(b)) are not available in civil proceedings. (See too s. 30 of the Petroleum and Submarine Pipe-lines Act 1975 and regulations made thereunder.)

7. Examples of other Acts which expressly create a civil remedy are the Misrepresentation Act 1967, s. 2(1) (p. 159, ante), the Consumer Protection Act 1987, s. 41, the Control of Pollution Act 1974, s. 88, the Data Protection Act 1984, ss. 22 and 23, the Telecommunications Act 1984, s. 18, the Electricity Act 1989, s. 39(3) and the Water Act 1989, ss. 30, 45(7) and 58(7).

2   Express exclusion of civil remedy

The Medicines Act 1968

133. **General provisions as to operation of Act.** – (2) Except in so far as this Act otherwise expressly provides, and subject to the provisions of section [18 of the Interpretation Act 1978] (which relates to offences under two or more laws), the provisions of this Act shall not be construed as—
   (*a*) conferring a right of action in any civil proceedings (other than proceedings for the recovery of a fine) in respect of any contravention of this Act or of any regulations or order made under this Act, or
   (*b*) affecting any restrictions imposed by or under any other enactment, whether contained in a public general Act or in a local or private Act, or
   (*c*) derogating from any right of action or other remedy (whether civil or criminal) in proceedings instituted otherwise than under this Act.

Note

The Medicines Act creates various offences in relation to the adulteration of medicinal products and requires compliance with certain standards. But Parliament apparently thought that enforcement could best be left to the criminal law. Do you agree?

Examples of other statutes which expressly exclude a civil remedy for breach of statutory duty are s. 13 of the Safety of Sports Grounds Act 1975, s. 12 of the Fire Safety and Safety of Places of Sport Act 1987 and s. 5 of the Guard Dogs Act 1975.

3 Creation of new torts by judicial interpretation of statutes

The Effect of Penal Legislation in the Law of Tort Glanville Williams (1960) 23 MLR 233

> I'm the Parliamentary Draftsman,
> I compose the country's laws,
> And of half the litigation
> I'm undoubtedly the cause.

J. P. C., *Poetic Justice* (1947).

It is a favourite charge; and yet (if we may breathe it) others than the draftsman are sometimes accountable for the trouble in interpreting statutes. Good rules of interpretation, consistently applied, could do much to reduce the area of doubt. It is the absence of such rules, or the failure to apply existing rules with sufficient regularity to preserve their character as rules, that has brought about the situation in which it is almost impossible to predict when statutory standards of behaviour will be imported into the law of tort.

The present position of penal legislation in the civil law—and it is only of penal legislation that we are speaking, since a study of other legislation would extend the discussion too much—the position of penal legislation may be oversimplified into two generalisations. When it concerns industrial welfare, such legislation results in absolute liability in tort. In all other cases it is ignored. There are exceptions both ways, but, broadly speaking, that is how the law appears from the current decisions. One may make bold to say that both propositions are the result of a wrong approach to the problem of assimilating statutory rules into the civil law.

Groves v **Lord Wimborne** Court of Appeal [1895–9] All ER Rep 147

A. L. SMITH LJ—This is an action brought against the occupier of the Dowlais ironworks, founded upon a breach of the defendant's statutory duty to fence certain machinery at the works, by reason of which breach of duty the plaintiff, in the course of his employment there, suffered personal injuries. At the trial of the action Grantham J gave judgment for the defendant upon the ground that no action would lie for the breach of the statutory duty alleged by the plaintiff.

By the Factory and Workshop Act 1878, certain duties as to fencing machinery are cast upon the occupiers of factories. In imposing these duties that Act has followed the principles of many previous Acts relating to factories and workshops. It is a public Act passed to compel the occupiers of factories to take certain precautions on behalf of their workmen. It is not, as the learned judge at the trial thought it was, in the nature of a private legislative bargain between masters and men, but a legislative enactment in compulsion of the masters. Let us now consider what are the duties imposed by this Act upon occupiers of factories with regard to fencing machinery. Section 5 makes certain provisions 'with respect to the fencing of machinery in a factory', and by sub-s. (3) as amended by the Factory and Workshop Act, 1891, s. 6(2):

'All dangerous parts of the machinery and every part of the mill-gearing shall either be securely fenced or be in such position or of such construction as to be equally safe to every person employed in the factory as it would be if it were securely fenced.'

By sub-s. (4):

'All fencing shall be constantly maintained in an efficient state while the parts required to be fenced are in motion.'

In the present case it is conceded that the machinery which caused the injury to the plaintiff was not fenced as required by the Act. Proof that there has been a breach of the statutory duty to fence inposed on the defendant, and that the plaintiff had been thereby injured would prima facie establish the plaintiff's cause of action.

Assuming that the matter depended on s. 5 alone, and that ss. 81, 82, and 86 had formed no part of the Act, could it be doubted that a person injured as the plaintiff has been could sue for the damage caused to him by the breach of the statutory duty imposed on the defendant? Clearly not. Therefore, unless it can be found from the whole purview of the Act that the legislature intended that the only remedy for a breach of the duty created by the Act should be the infliction of a fine upon the master, it seems clear to me that upon proof of such a breach of duty and of an injury done to the workman, a cause of action is given to the workman against the master.

That brings me to the question whether the cause of action which would prima facie be given by the Act has been taken away by any of the provisions enacted in the statute. Reliance has been placed upon ss. 81, 82 and 86, and it has been argued that, under these sections, the only remedy provided in a case where a workman has been injured by a breach of a duty imposed upon the master by the Act is an application to a court of summary jurisdiction for the infliction of a fine. In considering this question, I ask myself in whose favour was the Act passed? As was pointed out by Kelly CB in *Gorris v Scott*[1] the purposes which the legislature had in view in passing the Act are very material. I feel no doubt that the Act was passed for the benefit of workmen in factories, by compelling the masters to do certain things for their protection. I do not think that ss. 81, 82 and 86 can be interpreted so as to take away from an injured workman the remedy which otherwise he would have under the statute against his master. Not one penny of a fine imposed under these sections need ever go into the pocket of the person injured. It is only when a Secretary of State so determines that any part of the fine is to be applied for the benefit of the injured workman. I cannot think that such an enactment was intended to deprive the workman of his right of action. Moreover, upon what grounds are the magistrates to whom application has been made under these sections to estimate the amount of the fine to be imposed? Suppose that a workman has been killed in consequence of a breach of the master's statutory duty to fence his machinery, should the fine be of the same amount whether the breach of duty was a flagrant one or not? It is contended that the magistrates ought to take into consideration the nature of the injury which the workman has suffered, but I do not feel at all clear that that is what the legislature intended by these sections. I am inclined to think that the object of these provisions is the infliction of punishment on the master who has neglected his duty, and that the fine should be in proportion to his offence. The consideration of these points leads me to the conclusion that it was not the intention of the legislature to take away by means of these sections the right which the workman would otherwise have to be properly compensated for any injury caused to him by his master's neglect of duty.

There is also another ground which I should have mentioned which supports me in arriving at that conclusion. It is this. There is no necessity that the fine inflicted under these sections should be payable by the master, who would presumably be a man of some means. Under ss. 86 and 87 the fine may be imposed upon the actual offender, and it is provided that the master may then obtain exemption from the penalty. The actual offender may be a workman earning weekly wages, and yet it is said that the infliction of a fine on him is to be the only remedy that the injured person

---

1. (1874) 9 LR Exch 125.

is to have. I cannot read this statute in the way in which the defendant seeks to read it. In my opinion, s. 5 gives to a workman a right of action upon the statute, when he has been injured through a breach of the duties created by the statute, and his rights of compensation are not limited by the provisions of the Act with regard to a fine that may be imposed by a court of a summary jurisdiction. . . .

[His Lordship then held that the defence of common employment, abolished by the Law Reform (Personal Injuries) Act 1948, was not available in an action for a breach of a statutory duty incumbent on the defendant, and concluded:] In my opinion the appeal must be allowed, and the judgment entered for the £150 damages assessed by the jury.

[RIGBY and VAUGHAN WILLIAMS LJJ delivered judgments agreeing that the appeal should be allowed.]

Notes

1. It is not every piece of industrial safety legislation that is so interpreted: e.g. *Biddle v Truvox Engineering Co Ltd* [1952] 1 KB 101; [1951] 2 All ER 835 in which it was held that a person who sells or lets defective factory machinery contrary to the provisions of s. 17(2) of the Factories Act 1961 is not civilly liable to a workman injured by reason of the defect. The worker's only remedy is at common law.

2. The modern equivalent of s. 6(2) of the Factory and Workshop Act 1891, which was under consideration in *Groves v Lord Wimborne*, is s. 14(1) of the Factories Act 1961. There is no provision in the 1961 Act for applying the fine recovered in criminal proceedings for breach of that section to the benefit of the victim.

Atkinson *v* Newcastle Waterworks Co Court of Appeal [1874-80] All ER Rep 757

The plaintiff's premises caught fire and owing to the pressure in the defendants' pipes being insufficient the fire could not be extinguished and the premises were burnt down. The plaintiff brought an action for damages against the defendants alleging that they were in breach of the statutory duty imposed on them by s. 42 of the Waterworks Clauses Act 1847. The section provided:

'The undertakers shall, at all times, keep charged with water under [sufficient] pressure . . . all their pipes to which fire-plugs shall be fixed, unless prevented by frost, unusual drought or other unavoidable cause or accident, or during necessary repairs, and shall allow all persons at all times to take and use such water for extinguishing fire without making compensation for the same.'

The defendants demurred to this count. The Court of Exchequer gave judgment for the plaintiff.

On appeal (six years later) to the Court of Appeal:

LORD CAIRNS LC: . . . The statutory duty referred to arises under s. 42 of the Waterworks Clauses Act 1847. The scheme of these clauses seems to be this: The undertakers apply to Parliament for powers to take land and construct works for the supply of water, and in consideration of the powers which they obtain they come under certain obligations. As to fire-plugs they are under an obligation to fix them at intervals along the streets, and, if requested, to fix them near premises used as manufactories, and to keep them charged up to the prescribed pressure, unless prevented by frost, drought, or other unavoidable cause or accident, and to allow all persons to take and use water for the purpose of extinguishing fire, without making compensation. They are willing to accept the Parliamentary obligation to keep the mains charged. That this creates a statutory duty no one can dispute; but does it give a right of action to any individual who can aver, as the plaintiff does here, that his premises were near the pipes, that a fire broke out, that there was no water to extinguish it, and that his premises were burnt? He does not say that he was not allowed to take the water, but he complains of a failure in the duty to keep the mains charged.

The proposition a priori appears to be somewhat startling that a company supplying a town with water — although they are willing to be put under obligation to keep up the pressure, and to be subject to penalties if they fail to do so — should further be willing to assume, or that Parliament should think it necessary to subject them to liability to individual actions by any householder who could make out a case. In the one case they are merely under liability to penalties if they neglect to perform their duty, in the other case they are practically insurers, so far as water can produce safety from damage by fire. It is necessary to look at the provisions of s. 43. Four cases are there specified, which cover all the duties imposed by the former sections, a.nd for neglect of any one of these duties, there is a penalty of £10. For neglect of two of them, viz. to furnish to the town commissioners a sufficient supply of water for public purposes, and to furnish a supply of water to the owner or occupier, there is a further penalty of 40s a day, payable to every person who has paid or tendered the rate, for as long as such neglect or refusal continues after notice in writing has been given of the want of supply. It is not material to say, but it is possible that it might be held that neglect or refusal to fix fire-plugs would also subject the company to the 40s penalty. If so that penalty would be applicable in three cases out of the four. We have to consider why in some cases the penalty should go into the pocket of the individuals injured, and not in others. In the case of the obligation to keep the pipes charged, and allow all persons to use the water for the purpose of extinguishing fires, the provision is for the benefit of the public, and not of any individual specially, and the guarantee for the performance of the obligation is the liability to the public penalty of £10.

Apart from authority, I should be of opinion that the scheme of the Act and its true construction was not to create a duty which should be the subject of an action by any individual who might be injured, not to give a right to an individual to bring an action, but to lay down a series of duties, and provide a guarantee for their performance by s. 43, which imposes penalties in case of neglect or refusal. Where it is convenient that it should be so, the penalty goes into the pocket of the injured party; otherwise they are public penalties, imposed by way of security that all the public duty will be performed. The contrary intention is that we ought to say that where the penalty goes into the pocket of an individual no action will lie, but that otherwise a right of action exists, that in the other cases an individual would have no right of action, but that any one of the public could bring an action if there was no water in the main, and he suffered damage in consequence. I think it is impossible to adopt this view. The scheme must be judged by ss. 42 and 43, taken as a whole. Where we find that in most cases a penalty is imposed which would stop the right to action, it seems to me that the same result would follow in the other case provided for by s. 43. That is my opinion, unless there is some authority to the contrary.

The authority which is said to lead to a different conclusion is *Couch v Steel*.[1] That was a case of some peculiarity. The plaintiff, who was a seaman, and had served on board the defendant's vessel, sued the defendant for not providing a proper supply of medicines for the voyage, which he was bound to do by 7 & 8 Vict, c. 112, s. 18,

---

1. (1854) 3 E & B 402.

in consequence of which the plaintiff suffered from illness. In the declaration no claim was made on the Act of Parliament, but it was produced on the argument, and relied on in support of the plaintiff's case. With regard to that case and that Act of Parliament, if the decision were before us for review, I should desire further time for consideration; but that is not the case here, for the Act we have to deal with is widely different from the Act on which that case was decided. I must venture, with the greatest respect for the learned judges who took part in the decision, to express a doubt whether the authorities referred to by Lord Campbell in giving judgment justified the broad expressions which were used. It is not necessary to go through all the authorities which are there referred to, and which will be found collected in 3 E & B at 411, but it appears to me to be questionable whether they justify the broad general statement that wherever there is a statutory duty imposed, and any person is injured by the non-performance of that duty, an action can be maintained. It must depend on the particular statute, and where it is like a private legislative bargain, into which the undertakers of the works have entered, it differs from the case where a general public duty is imposed. Therefore, I cannot look on *Couch v Steel*[1] as an authority for the decision of the court below in the present case, and no other authority was cited which could govern it.

I have, therefore, come to the conclusion that on the first count of the declaration there is no cause of action, and the demurrer must be allowed.

[COCKBURN CJ and BRETT LJ agreed that there should be judgment for defendants.]

Appeal allowed

Question

Why was the fact that the penalty of £10 could not be applied to the benefit of the plaintiff regarded as an argument *against* the imposition of a civil remedy? (Cf. *Groves v Lord Wimborne*, p. 536, ante. The Water Act 1989, s. 58(7) now allows sums to be recovered by a person who suffers damage due to the supply of unwholesome water.)

Notes

1. In *Dawson v Bingley UDC* [1911] 2 KB 149 a local authority negligently put up a plate with a misleading direction in that it did not correctly denote the position of a fire-plug, as the authority was required to do under s. 66 of the Public Health Act 1875. The fire-plug became covered in dirt and ashes with the result that a fire-brigade coming to a fire was delayed for fifteen or twenty minutes in finding it. The plaintiff's property consequently suffered additional damage in the fire. The local authority was held liable to compensate him. Kennedy LJ distinguished *Atkinson v Newcastle Waterworks Co* on the ground that (a) the defendants there were not a public body but a private company; and (b) the Act in that case imposed remedies in the form of penalties, while s. 66 of the Public Health Act 1875 contained no specific remedy for infringement. Is there any other ground for distinction? Is this case an early example of liability for negligent statements (p. 161, ante)?

2. In *Read v Croydon Corpn* [1938] 4 All ER 631 the corporation supplied impure drinking water as a result of which the infant plaintiff contracted

---

1. (1854) 3 E & B 402.

typhoid. The corporation had negligently failed to take certain precautions during work at the wells which were the source of the water supply. It was held that (a) they were liable for common law negligence; and (b) they were guilty of breach of statutory duty under the Waterworks Clauses Act 1847, s. 35, but that this conferred a right of action upon ratepayers only (and so not the infant plaintiff, but her father who claimed certain special damages he had suffered as a result of her illness). Stable J said (at p. 654) that 'in *Atkinson*'s case, in the absence of the statute, or of any contractual obligation, there could not have been any common law remedy at the suit of a person whose shop was burnt down because the pressure of water in a particular pipe was insufficient to enable the fire engines to put out the fire.' Why? Is this relevant to the existence of an action for breach of statutory duty? Compare *McCall v Abelesz* [1976] QB 585; [1976] 1 All ER 727 in which it was held that the harassment of a tenant contrary to s. 30(2) of the Rent Act 1965 did not give rise to a right to damages, one point being that the tenant already had a possible action for breach of the covenant of quiet enjoyment.

3. Modern legislation, such as the Water Act 1989 and the Electricity Act 1989, has placed express duties on privatised public utilities to pay compensation or damages to consumers for loss or damage suffered from failure or defects in the supply of their services in certain circumstances. It has been argued that the approach in *Atkinson v Newcastle Waterworks Co* had the underlying purpose of protecting the discretionary decisions of *public* bodies from attack by way of an action for damages (R. A. Buckley (1984) 100 LQR 204). The restrictive approach in *Atkinson* raises the wider question of the availability of damages in this tort as a remedy in administrative law: see generally Stanton, op cit, pp. 73–84 and 148–152.

Gorris *v* Scott Court of Exchequer (1874) 9 LR Exch 125

KELLY CB: This is an action to recover damages for the loss of a number of sheep which the defendant, a shipowner, had contracted to carry, and which were washed overboard and lost by reason (as we must take it to be truly alleged) of the neglect to comply with a certain order made by the Privy Council, in pursuance of the Contagious Diseases (Animals) Act 1869. The Act was passed merely for sanitary purposes, in order to prevent animals in a state of infectious disease from communicating it to other animals with which they might come in contact. Under the authority of that Act, certain orders were made; amongst others, an order by which any ship bringing sheep or cattle from any foreign port to ports in Great Britain is to have the place occupied by such animals divided into pens of certain dimensions, and the floor of such pens furnished with battens or foot-holds. The object of this order is to prevent animals from being overcrowded, and so brought into a condition in which the disease guarded against would be likely to be developed. This regulation has been neglected, and the question is, whether the loss, which we must assume to have been caused by that neglect, entitles the plaintiffs to maintain an action.

The argument of the defendant is, that the Act has imposed penalties to secure the observance of its provisions, and that, according to the general rule, the remedy prescribed by the statute must be pursued; that although, when penalties are imposed for the violation of a statutory duty a person aggrieved by its violation may sometimes maintain an action for the damage so caused, that must be in cases where the object of the statute is to confer a benefit on individuals, and to protect them against the evil consequences which the statute was designed to prevent, and which have in fact ensued; but that if the object is not to protect individuals against the consequences which have in fact ensued, it is otherwise; that if, therefore, by reason of the precautions in question not having been taken, the plaintiffs had sustained that damage against which it was intended to secure them, an action would lie, but that when the damage is of such a nature as was not contemplated at all by the statute, and as to which it was not intended to confer any benefit on the plaintiffs, they cannot maintain an action founded on the neglect. The principle may be well illustrated by the case put in argument of a breach by a railway company of its duty to erect a gate on a level crossing, and to keep the gate closed except when the crossing is being actually and properly used. The object of the precaution is to prevent injury from being sustained through animals or vehicles being upon the line at unseasonable times; and if by reason of such a breach of duty, either in not erecting the gate, or in not keeping it closed, a person attempts to cross with a carriage at an improper time, and injury ensues to a passenger, no doubt an action would lie against the railway company, because the intention of the legislature was that, by the erection of the gates and by their being kept closed individuals should be protected against accidents of this description. And if we could see that it was the object, or among the objects of this Act, that the owners of sheep and cattle coming from a foreign port should be protected by the means described against the danger of their property being washed overboard, or lost by the perils of the sea, the present action would be within the principle.

But, looking at the Act, it is perfectly clear that its provisions were all enacted with a totally different view; there was no purpose, direct or indirect, to protect against such dangers; but, as is recited in the preamble, the Act is directed against the possibility of sheep or cattle being exposed to disease on their way to this country. The preamble recites that 'it is expedient to confer on Her Majesty's most honourable Privy Council power to take such measures as may appear from time to time necessary to prevent the introduction into Great Britain of contagious or infectious diseases among cattle, sheep, or other animals, by prohibiting or regulating the importation of foreign animals,' and also to provide against the 'spreading' of such diseases in Great Britain. Then follow numerous sections directed entirely to this object. Then comes s. 75, which enacts that 'the Privy Council may from time to time make such orders as they think expedient for all or any of the following purposes.' What, then, are these purposes? They are 'for securing for animals brought by sea to ports in Great Britain a proper supply of food and water during the passage and on landing,' 'for protecting such animals from unnecessary suffering during the passage and on landing,' and so forth; all the purposes enumerated being calculated and directed to the prevention of disease, and none of them having any relation whatever to the danger of loss by the perils of the sea. That being so, if by reason of the default in question the plaintiffs' sheep had been overcrowded, or had been caused unnecessary suffering, and so had arrived in this country in a state of disease, I do not say that they might not have maintained this action. But the damage complained of here is something totally apart from the object of the Act of Parliament, and it is in accordance with all the authorities to say that the action is not maintainable.

[PIGGOTT, POLLOCK and AMPHLETT BB agreed that the declaration disclosed no cause of action, and judgment was given for the defendant.]

Questions

1. Would the plaintiffs' action have succeeded had their sheep died from an infectious disease communicated by other animals due to the absence of the required pens?

2. It is sometimes argued that an action upon the statute is an aid to law

enforcement, because it encourages the victim to set the law in motion (C. Morris (1933) 46 Harv LR 453 at 458). Can this rationale be reconciled with the decision in *Gorris v Scott*?

Phillips *v* Britannia Hygienic Laundry Co Ltd Court of Appeal [1923] All ER Rep 127

The Motor Cars (Use and Construction) Order 1904, provided: 'the motor car and all fittings thereof shall be in such a condition as not to cause, or to be likely to cause, danger to any person in the motor car or on the highway.' The defendants' vehicle was in a defective condition not due to any negligence on their part but because of the negligence of repairers to whom they had sent the vehicle for overhaul. As a result of the defendants using the vehicle on the highway, in this defective condition, there was a collision with a van belonging to the plaintiff. The plaintiff claimed damages on the ground of a breach of the statutory duty imposed by the Use and Construction regulations. A criminal penalty was provided for the breach of any one of those regulations. The Divisional Court held that the action must be dismissed. An appeal to the Court of Appeal was unsuccessful.

BANKES LJ: . . . We have not here to consider the case of a person injured on the highway. The injury was done to the plaintiff's van, and the plaintiff, as a member of the public, claims a right of action as being a member of a class for whose benefit cl. 6 was enacted. He contends that the public using the highway is the class so favoured. I do not agree. In my view, the public using the highway is not a class; it is the public itself and not a class of the public. I think this clause does not apply to individual members or sections of the public, but to the public generally, and it is included in a batch of regulations for breach of which it cannot have been intended that a person aggrieved should have a civil remedy by way of action in addition to the more appropriate statutory remedy already provided. In my opinion, the plaintiff has failed to show that this case is an exception to the general rule. The appeal, therefore, fails and must be dismissed.

ATKIN LJ: I am of the same opinion. This is an important and a difficult question. I was much impressed by the argument of counsel for the plaintiff when dealing with these regulations, because there can be little doubt that the scope of the regulations was to promote the safety of the public using the highway. The question is whether they were intended to be enforced only by the special penalty attached to them in the Act. I conceive the rule to be that when a statute imposes a duty of commission or omission upon an individual, the question whether a person aggrieved by a breach of the duty has a right of action depends upon the intention of the statute. Was it intended that a duty should be owed to the individual aggrieved as well as to the State, or is it a public duty only? That depends upon the construction of the statute as a whole, and the circumstances in which it was made and to which it relates. One of the matters to be taken into consideration is this: Does the statute on the face of it contain a reference to a remedy for the breach of it? If so, it would, prima facie, be the only remedy, but that is not conclusive. One must still look to the intention of the legislature to be derived from the words used, and one may come to the conclusion that, although the statute creates a duty and imposes a penalty for the breach of that duty, it may still intend that the duty should be owed to individuals. Instances of this are *Groves v Lord Wimborne*[1] and *Britannic Merthyr Coal Co v David*.[2]

---

1. [1898] 2 QB 402.
2. [1910] AC 74.

To my mind, and on this point I differ from McCardie J, the question is not be determined solely by the test whether or not the person aggrieved can fall within some special class of the community, or whether he is some designated individual. It would, I think, be strange if it were so. The duty imposed may be of such paramount importance that it is owed to every member of the public. It would be strange if a less important duty which is owed to a section of the public may be enforced by an action, while a more important duty which is owed to the public at large cannot be so enforced. The right of action does not depend upon whether a statutory enactment or prohibition is proclaimed for the benefit of the public as a whole or for the benefit of a particular class. It may well be enforced by an individual who cannot be otherwise specified than as a member of the public who passed along the highway. Therefore I think McCardie J is applying too narrow a test when he says ([1923] 1 KB at p. 547):

'In my view, the Motor Car Acts and regulations were not enacted for the benefit of any particular class of folk. They are provisions for the benefit of the whole public, whether pedestrians or vehicle users, whether aliens or British citizens, and whether working or walking or standing upon the highway.'

In stating the argument of the defendant in *Gorris v Scott*,[1] Kelly CB refers to the obligation imposed upon railway companies by s. 47 of the Railways Clauses Consolidation Act 1845, to erect gates across public carriage roads crossed by the railway on the level and to keep the gates closed except when the crossing is being actually and properly used, under the penalty of 40*s* for every default. It has never been doubted that if a member of the public crossing the railway were injured by the railway company's breach of duty, either in not erecting a gate or in not keeping it closed, he would have a right of action. Therefore, the question is whether these regulations, having regard to the circumstances in which they were made and to which they relate, were intended to impose a duty, which is a public duty, or whether they were intended also to impose a duty, enforceable by an individual aggrieved. Upon the whole, I have come to the conclusion that it was not intended to impose a duty enforceable by individuals aggrieved, but only a public duty, the sole remedy for breach of which is the remedy provided by way of a fine. The regulations impose obligations of varying degrees of importance; some of them are more concerned with the maintenance of the highway than with the protection of the public. Yet there is one penalty imposed for the breach of any one of them. Upon the whole, I think the true inference is that the legislature did not permit the Department which had been empowered to make regulations for the use and construction of motor vehicles to impose new duties in favour of individuals and new causes of action for breach of them. That seems to me to be the more reasonable conclusion when it is realised that the obligations of those who bring vehicles upon highways have been already well provided for and regulated by the common law. It is not likely that the legislature intended by these regulations to impose upon the owners of vehicles an absolute obligation to make them roadworthy in all events, even in the absence of negligence. For these reasons I am of opinion that the conclusion arrived at by the Divisional Court was correct, and that the appeal should therefore be dismissed.

[YOUNGER LJ agreed.]

Question

Can Atkin LJ's reasoning be reconciled with that of A. L. Smith LJ in *Groves v Lord Wimborne* (p. 536, ante)?

---

1. (1874) LR 9 Exch 125.

Notes

1. In general the courts have refused to create civil remedies out of road traffic legislation. In *Tan Chye Choo v Chong Kew Moi* [1970] 1 All ER 266; [1970] 1 WLR 147 *Phillips*'s case was followed in relation to the similar Motor Vehicles (Construction and Use) Rules of Malaysia. In *Coote v Stone* [1971] 1 All ER 657; [1971] 1 WLR 279 it was held that there is no civil action for breach of the Various Trunk Roads (Prohibition of Waiting) (Clearways) Order S.I 1963 No. 1172, which prohibited waiting on a clearway. The only important exception to this general approach is that the House of Lords has held that there is a civil action for breach of the Pedestrian Crossing Places (Traffic) Regulations (*London Passenger Transport Board v Upson* [1949] AC 155; [1949] 1 All ER 60, p. 550, post). In *Coote v Stone* Davies LJ explained this on the ground that those regulations were 'designed for the safety of pedestrians'. For whose safety were the Motor Vehicle (Use and Construction) Regulations designed?

2. *Atiyah*, p. 135 comments on the *Phillips* case:

'Perhaps the court was influenced—consciously or unconsciously—by the fact that in 1923 it was still not compulsory to insure against third party liability, and the court may have shrunk from imposing a form of liability without fault on individual motorists who might not have had the resources to meet a judgment for damages. Had this problem arisen after compulsory insurance was introduced in 1930 the result might conceivably have been different.'

Lonrho Ltd *v* Shell Petroleum Co Ltd House of Lords [1981] 2 All ER 456

This appeal arose out of a case stated by the umpire and arbitrators under the Arbitration Act 1950 in an arbitration between the appellants (Lonrho) and the respondents (Shell and BP). Lonrho were the claimants in the arbitration. They were the owners of a crude oil pipeline running from the ocean port of Beira in Mozambique to a refinery near Umtali in what was then called Southern Rhodesia. The refinery was owned and operated by a Rhodesian company controlled by Shell and BP and other oil companies. The pipeline was operated under an agreement made between Lonrho and the oil companies, including Shell and BP. On 11 November 1965 the government of Southern Rhodesia unilaterally declared independence (UDI). Five days later the United Kingdom Parliament passed the Southern Rhodesia Act 1965 and pursuant to that Act the Southern Rhodesia (Petroleum) Order 1965 S.I. 1965 No. 2140 was made (replaced in 1968 by a more comprehensive Order in Council) prohibiting any unauthorised person from supplying or delivering crude oil or petroleum products to Southern Rhodesia on a penalty of a fine or imprisonment. As a result from December 1965 no oil was shipped to the Beira terminal and Lonrho's revenue from operating the pipeline ceased. Lonrho claimed damages in excess of £100 million against Shell and BP, alleging that before the making of the sanctions order Shell and BP assured the illegal regime in Rhodesia that an adequate supply of petroleum products would reach that country after UDI and thereby influenced the regime to declare UDI, and that after the sanctions order was made Shell and BP supplied petroleum products to Rhodesia by other means and thereby prolonged the period during which the sanctions order prevented the pipeline from operating. The arbitrators and the umpire, before deciding the facts in issue, decided that Lonrho's points of claim disclosed no cause of action against Shell and BP. This finding was upheld by both the judge at first instance and the Court of Appeal.

Lonrho appealed to the House of Lords on the grounds, inter alia, that contravention of the sanctions order, if proved, would amount to a breach of statutory duty by Shell and BP severally, giving Lonrho a right of action in tort, or a conspiracy by Shell and BP jointly. Those parts of the speech of Lord Diplock which concern the question of conspiracy are to be found p. 688, post. On the question whether breaches of the sanctions order would give rise to a right of action in the claimants for damage alleged to have been caused by those breaches:

LORD DIPLOCK: . . . My Lords, it is well settled by authority of this House in *Cutler v Wandsworth Stadium Ltd* [1949] AC 398; [1949] 1 All ER 544, that the question whether legislation which makes the doing or omitting to do a particular act a criminal offence renders the person guilty of such offence liable also in a civil action for damages at the suit of any person who thereby suffers loss or damage is a question of construction of the legislation.

[His Lordship set out the legislation and continued:] . . . The sanctions order thus creates a statutory prohibition on the doing of certain classes of acts and provides the means of enforcing the prohibition by prosecution for a criminal offence which is subject to heavy penalties including imprisonment. So one starts with the presumption laid down originally by Lord Tenterden CJ in *Doe d Bishop of Rochester v Bridges* (1831) 1 B & Ad 847 at 859, [1824–34] All ER Rep 167 at 170, where he spoke of the 'general rule' that 'where an Act creates an obligation, and enforces the performance in a specified manner . . . that performance cannot be enforced in any other manner', a statement that has frequently been cited with approval ever since, including on several occasions in speeches in this House. Where the only manner of enforcing performance for which the Act provides is prosecution for the criminal offence of failure to perform the statutory obligation or for contravening the statutory prohibition which the Act creates, there are two classes of exception to this general rule.

The first is where on the true construction of the Act it is apparent that the obligation or prohibition was imposed for the benefit or protection of a particular class of individuals, as in the case of the Factories Acts and similar legislation. As Lord Kinnear put it in *Black v Fife Coal Co Ltd* [1912] AC 149 at 165, in the case of such a statute:

'There is no reasonable ground for maintaining that a proceeding by way of penalty is the only remedy allowed by the statute . . . We are to consider the scope and purpose of the statute and in particular for whose benefit it is intended. Now the object of the present statute is plain. It was intended to compel mine owners to make due provision for the safety of the men working in their mines, and the persons for whose benefit all these rules are to be enforced are the persons exposed to danger. But when a duty of this kind is imposed for the benefit of particular persons there arises at common law a correlative right in those persons who may be injured by its contravention.'

The second exception is where the statute creates a public right (i.e. a right to be enjoyed by all those of Her Majesty's subjects who wish to avail themselves of it) and a particular member of the public suffers what Brett J in *Benjamin v Storr* (1874) LR 9 CP 400 at 407 described as 'particular, direct and substantial' damage 'other and different from that which was common to all the rest of the public'. Most of the authorities about this second exception deal not with public rights created by statute but with public rights existing at common law, particularly in respect of use of highways. *Boyce v Paddington Borough Council* [1903] 1 Ch 109 is one of the comparatively few cases about a right conferred on the general public by statute. It is in relation to that class of statute only that Buckley J's oft-cited statement (at 114) as to the two cases in which a plaintiff, without joining the Attorney General, could himself sue in private law for interference with that public right must be understood. The two cases he said were:

'first, where the interference with the public right is such as that some private right of his is at the same time interfered with . . . and, secondly, where no private right is interfered with, but the plaintiff, in respect of his public right, suffers special damage peculiar to himself from the interference with the public right.'

The first case would not appear to depend on the existence of a public right in addition to the private one: while to come within the second case at all it has first to be shown that the statute, having regard to its scope and language, does fall within that class of statutes which create a legal right to be enjoyed by all of Her Majesty's subjects who wish to avail themselves of it. A mere prohibition on members of the public generally from doing what it would otherwise be lawful for them to do is not enough.

My Lords, it has been the unanimous opinion of the arbitrators with the concurrence of the umpire, of Parker J and of each of the three members of the Court of Appeal that the sanctions orders made pursuant to the Southern Rhodesia Act 1965 fell within neither of these two exceptions. Clearly they were not within the first category of exception. They were not imposed for the *benefit* or *protection* of a particular class of individuals who were engaged in supplying or delivering crude oil or petroleum products to Southern Rhodesia. They were intended to put an end to such transactions. Equally plainly they did not create any public right to be enjoyed by all those of Her Majesty's subjects who wished to avail themselves of it. On the contrary, what they did was to withdraw a previously existing right of citizens of, and companies incorporated in, the United Kingdom to trade with Southern Rhodesia in crude oil and petroleum products. Their purpose was, perhaps, most aptly stated by Fox LJ. He said:

'I cannot think that they were concerned with conferring rights either on individuals or the public at large. Their purpose was the destruction, by economic pressure, of the UDI regime in Southern Rhodesia; they were instruments of state policy in an international matter.'

Until the United Nations called on its members to impose sanctions on the illegal regime in Southern Rhodesia it may not be strictly accurate to speak of it as an international matter, but from the outset it was certainly state policy in affairs external to the United Kingdom.

In agreement with all those present and former members of the judiciary who have considered the matter I can see no ground on which contraventions by Shell and BP of the sanctions orders, though not amounting to any breach of their contract with Lonrho, nevertheless constituted a tort for which Lonrho could recover in a civil suit any loss caused to them by such contraventions.

Briefly parting from this part of the case, however, I should mention briefly two cases, one in the Court of Appeal of England, *Ex p Island Records Ltd* [1978] Ch 122; [1978] 3 All ER 824, and one in the High Court of Australia, *Beaudesert Shire Council v Smith* (1966) 120 CLR 145, which counsel for Lonrho, as a last resort, relied on as showing that some broader principle has of recent years replaced those long-established principles that I have just stated for determining whether a contravention of a particular statutory prohibition by one private individual makes him liable in tort to another private individual who can prove that he has suffered damage as a result of the contravention.

Ex p Island Records Ltd was an unopposed application for an Anton Piller order against a defendant who, without the consent of the performers, had made records of musical performances for the purposes of trade. This was an offence, punishable by a relatively small penalty under the Dramatic and Musical Performers' Protection Act 1958. The application for the Anton Piller order was made by performers whose performances had been 'bootlegged' by the defendant without their consent and also by record companies with whom the performers had entered into exclusive contracts.

So far as the application by performers was concerned, it could have been granted for entirely orthodox reasons. The Act was passed for the protection of a particular class of individuals, dramatic and musical performers; even the short title said so. Whether the record companies would have been entitled to obtain the order in a civil action to which the performers whose performances had been bootlegged were not parties is a matter which for present purposes it is not necessary to decide. Lord Denning MR, however, with whom Waller LJ agreed (Shaw LJ dissenting) appears to enunciate a wider general rule, which does not depend on the scope and language of the statute by which a criminal offence is committed, that whenever a lawful business carried on by one individual in fact suffers damage as the consequence of a contravention by another individual of any statutory prohibition the former has a civil right of action against the latter for such damage.

My Lords, with respect, I am unable to accept that this is the law; and I observe that in his judgment rejecting a similar argument by the appellants in the instant appeal Lord Denning MR accepts that the question whether a breach of sanctions orders gives rise to a civil action depends on the object and intent of those orders, and refers to *Ex p Island Records Ltd* as an example of a statute passed for the protection of private rights and interests, viz those of the performers.

Beaudesert Shire Council v Smith is a decision of the High Court of Australia. It appeared to recognise the existence of a novel innominate tort of the nature of an 'action for damages upon the case' available to 'a person who suffers harm or loss as the inevitable consequence of the unlawful, intentional and positive acts of another'. The decision, although now 15 years old, has never been followed in any Australian or other common law jurisdiction. In subsequent Australian cases it has invariably been distinguished, most recently by the Privy Council in *Dunlop v Woollahra Municipal Council* [1981] 1 All ER 1202; [1981] 2 WLR 693, on appeal from the Supreme Court of New South Wales. It is clear now from a later decision of the Australian High Court in *Kitano v Commonwealth of Australia* (1974) 129 CLR 151 that the adjective 'unlawful' in the definition of acts which give rise to this new action for damages on the case does not include *every* breach of statutory duty which in fact causes damage to the plaintiff. It remains uncertain whether it was intended to include acts done in contravention of a wider range of statutory obligations or prohibitions than those which under the principles that I have discussed above would give rise to a civil action at common law in England if they are contravened. If the tort described in *Beaudesert* was really intended to extend that range, I would invite your Lordships to declare that it forms no part of the law of England.

I would therefore answer [the] question . . . No.

[LORD EDMUND-DAVIES, LORD KEITH OF KINKEL, LORD SCARMAN and LORD BRIDGE OF HARWICH agreed with the speech of LORD DIPLOCK in favour of dismissing the appeal.]

Appeal dismissed

Notes

1. The broad principle, stated by Lord Denning MR in *Ex p Island Records Ltd* [1978] Ch 122; [1978] 3 All ER 824, that wherever the violation of a statute causes interference with a lawful trade or calling there is a civil right of action, was treated as wrong by the Court of Appeal in *Rickless v United Artists Corpn* [1988] QB 40 at 54 in view of the *ratio decidendi* of *Lonrho*. The *Rickless* case was concerned with s. 2 of the Dramatic and Musical Performers' Protection Act 1958 (now repealed by the Copyright, Designs and Patents Act 1988) which made it a criminal offence to make unauthorised

recording of dramatic and musical performances without the performer's consent. The Court of Appeal held that despite strong indications in the wording of the Act and its history that the Act did not create private rights of action, the Act was in its terms expressly made for the protection of performers, in accordance with an international convention to which Parliament was giving effect, and so fell within Lord Diplock's first exceptional case (p. 546, ante). Consequently, Peter Sellers' widow was able to claim damages for the unauthorised use of clips from the 'Pink Panther' films. However, in *RCA Corpn v Pollard* [1983] Ch 135; [1982] 3 All ER 771 it was held that the Act gave no civil right of action in favour of the recording companies against defendants who were marketing 'bootlegged' Elvis Presley records. The protection of the business interests of those companies was not regarded as being within the scope of the Act. Part II of the Copyright, Designs and Patents Act 1988 now protects those with recording rights as well as performers.

2. Can the notion that the obligation or prohibition must be imposed for the benefit or protection of a particular class of persons be reconciled with the view of Atkin LJ in the *Phillips* case: 'It would be strange if a less important duty, which is owed to a section of the public, may be enforced by action, while a more important duty owed to the public at large cannot' ([1923] 2 KB at pp. 841–842)?

Law Commission, 'The Interpretation of Statutes' (Law Com. No. 21, 1969)

Appendix A

DRAFT CLAUSES

Presumption as to enforcement of statutory duty

4. Where any Act passed after this Act imposes or authorises the imposition of a duty, whether positive or negative and whether with or without a special remedy for its enforcement, it shall be presumed, unless express provision to the contrary is made, that a breach of the duty is intended to be actionable (subject to the defences and other incidents applying to actions for breach of statutory duty) at the suit of any person who sustains damage in consequence of the breach.

Notes

1. R. Pound (1908) 21 Harv LR 383 at 406–407 preferred legislation above judicial decision as 'the more truly democratic form of law-making'. He thought it followed from this that judicial analogies from the social policies expressed in statutes should be encouraged. Will this draft clause, if enacted, help or hinder this kind of judicial legislation? (See further the note, p. 554, post.)

2. The Law Commission (Law Com. No. 21, 1969) has also proposed that, in ascertaining the meaning of any provision of an Act, the court should be entitled to consider, inter alia, reports of Royal Commissions and committees, relevant treaties, command papers and other relevant documents, but reports of Parliamentary proceedings. The Law Commission's report contains a useful bibliography of material on the interpretation of statutes (pp. 55–56).

London Passenger Transport Board *v* Upson House of Lords [1949] 1 All ER 60

LORD WRIGHT: . . . I think that the authorities such as *Caswell*'s case,[1] *Lewis v Denye*[2] and *Sparks v Edward Ash Ltd*[3] show clearly that a claim for damages for breach of a statutory duty intended to protect a person in the position of the particular plaintiff is a special common law right which is not to be confused in essence with a claim for negligence. The statutory right has its origin in the statute, but the particular remedy of an action for damages is given by the common law in order to make effective for the benefit of the injured plaintiff his right to the performance by the defendant of the defendant's statutory duty. It is an effective sanction. It is not a claim in negligence in the strict or ordinary sense. As I said ([1939] 3 All ER 739) in *Caswell*'s case:[1]

'I do not think that an action for breach of a statutory duty such as that in question is completely or accurately described as an action in negligence. It is a common law action based on the purpose of the statute to protect the workman, and belongs to the category often described as that of strict or absolute liability. At the same time it resembles actions in negligence in that the claim is based on a breach of a duty to take care for the safety of the workman.'

But, whatever the resemblances, it is essential to keep in mind the fundamental differences of the two classes of claim. Here I shall, perhaps, be guilty of hypercriticism if I were to quarrel with the expression of Asquith LJ in the Court of Appeal ([1947] 2 All ER 516) that the common law duty is enhanced by the duty contained in the regulations. One duty does not, in truth, enhance the other, though the same damage may be caused by action which might equally be characterised as ordinary negligence at common law or as breach of the statutory duty. On the other hand, the damage may be due either to negligence or to breach of the statutory duty. In the present case Asquith LJ decided, as I understand, in favour of the respondent, not on the ground of negligence, which he did not find, but specifically on the ground of breach of statutory duty. There is, I think, a logical distinction which accords with what I regard as the correct view that the causes of action are different. It follows that the correct pleading would be to allege each cause of action separately so as to avoid the confusion which seems to me to have crept in at certain points of these proceedings. I have desired before I deal specifically with the regulations to make it clear how, in my judgment, they should be approached, and also to make it clear that a claim for their breach may stand or fall independently of a claim for negligence. There is always a danger, if the claim is not sufficiently specific, that the due consideration of the claim for breach of statutory duty may be prejudiced if it is confused with the claim in negligence. . . .

Notes

1. In *Morris v National Coal Board* [1963] 3 All ER 644; [1963] 1 WLR 1382 it was held that a plaintiff who presents his case exclusively as one of breach of statutory duty cannot on appeal seek to support the decision on grounds that there was common law negligence, even though there is a considerable amount of evidence of breach of a common law duty. Is the result satisfactory in view of the abolition of the forms of action and the fact that the plaintiff is not supposed to plead matters of law? (See *Lewis v Denye* [1940] AC 921 at 924–925.)

1. [1940] AC 152; [1940] 3 All ER 722.
2. [1940] AC 921; [1939] 3 All ER 299.
3. [1943] 1 KB 223; [1943] 1 All ER 1.

2. The independence of the action for breach of statutory duty from common law negligence is illustrated by *Bux v Slough Metals Ltd* [1974] 1 All ER 262; [1973] 1 WLR 1358, in which the plaintiff failed to establish a breach of statutory duty by his employer, who had provided safety goggles which the plaintiff had not worn. The plaintiff succeeded, however, in an action for damages for negligence because the evidence showed that the plaintiff would have worn the goggles had he been instructed to do so in a reasonable and firm manner followed up by supervision. This was a breach of the employer's duty to provide a safe system of work (see p. 566, post). The plaintiff's damages were reduced by 40 per cent on grounds of his contributory negligence.

The Queen in Right of Canada *v* Saskatchewan Wheat Pool
Supreme Court of Canada (1983) 143 DLR (3d) 9

This was an appeal from a decision of the Federal Court of Appeal, (1981) 117 DLR (3d) 70, allowing an appeal from a judgment of Collier J, (1980) 104 DLR (3d) 392, in favour of the plaintiff in an action for damages for breach of statutory duty. The respondent Pool had delivered grain from a terminal elevator into a ship, but there was an infestation of rusty beetle larvae in the grain which was delivered into two of the ship's holds. This was revealed by a particular test, the results of which were only available after the ship had left port, and the Canadian Wheat Board, an agent of the Crown, was ordered by the Canadian Grain Commission to fumigate the affected grain. The ship was therefore directed by the Board to go to Kingston for this operation to take place and, once the cost of unloading and reloading the grain and detention claims were added to the cost of fumigation, the financial consequence for the Board was the payment of $98,261.55. It was this sum which the Board now claimed from the Pool alleging a breach of s. 86(*c*) of the Canada Grain Act 1970–71–72 (Can) c. 7, which prohibited the discharge of infested grain from an elevator. The Act provided for a criminal penalty for breach, but did not expressly grant a civil remedy.

The judgment of the court was delivered by DIXON J: — This case raises the difficult issue of the relation of a breach of a statutory duty to a civil cause of action. Where 'A' has breached a statutory duty causing injury to 'B', does 'B' have a civil cause of action against 'A'? If so, is 'A's' liability absolute, in the sense that it exists independently of fault, or is 'A' free from liability if the failure to perform the duty is through no fault of his? ...

STATUTORY BREACH GIVING RISE TO A CIVIL CAUSE OF ACTION

(a) *General*
The uncertainty and confusion in relation between breach of statute and a civil cause of action for damages arising from the breach is of long standing. The commentators have little but harsh words for the unhappy state of affairs, but arriving at a solution, from the disarray of cases, is extraordinarily difficult. It is doubtful that any general principle or rationale can be found in the authorities to resolve all of the issues or even those which are transcendent.

There does seem to be general agreement that the breach of a statutory provision which causes damage to an individual should in some way be pertinent to recovery of compensation for the damage. Two very different forces, however, have been acting in opposite directions. In the United States the civil consequences of breach of statute have been subsumed in the law of negligence. On the other hand, we have witnessed in England the painful emergence of a new nominate tort of statutory breach. ...

(b) *The English position*
[In the course of reviewing the English authorities and academic writings, DIXON J stated:] The pretence of seeking what has been called a 'will o' the wisp', a non-existent intention of Parliament to create a civil cause of action, has been harshly criticized. It is capricious and arbitrary, 'judicial legislation' at its very worst. . . . Glanville Williams is now of the opinion that the 'irresolute course' of the judicial decisions 'reflect no credit on our jurisprudence' and with respect, I agree. He writes:

'The failure of the judges to develop a governing attitude means that it is almost impossible to predict, outside the decided authorities, when the courts will regard a civil duty as impliedly created. In effect the judge can do what he likes, and then select one of the conflicting principles stated by his predecessors in order to justify his decision.' [(1960) 23 MLR at p. 246]

(c) *The American position*
. . . [T]he American approach . . . has assimilated civil responsibility for statutory breach into the general law of negligence. . . .
There are, however, differing views of the effect of this assimilation: at one end of the spectrum, breach of a statutory duty may constitute negligence *per se*, or at the other, it may merely be evidence of negligence. This distinction finds its roots in the seminal 1913 article by Professor Thayer, 'Public Wrong and Private Action', 27 Harv LR 317 (1913–14), at p. 323:

'Unless the court were prepared to go to this length it would be bound to say that if the breach of the ordinance did in fact contribute to the injury as a cause the defendant is liable as a matter of law; but this is treating it as 'negligence *per se*, to use the ordinary phraseology, and not merely 'evidence of negligence'.
The doctrine that a breach of the law is 'evidence of negligence' is in truth perplexing and difficult of comprehension. It stands as a sort of compromise midway between two extremer views: (1) that a breach of the law cannot be treated as prudent conduct; (2) that the ordinance was passed *alio intuito* and does not touch civil relations.'

Professor Thayer's thesis was essentially that prudent men do not break the law. He thus applied the criminal standard of care, breach of which would give rise to penal consequences under the statute, to the civil action.
The majority view in the United States has been that statutory breach constitutes negligence *per se* — in certain circumstances . . .
This approach has been adopted by the *Restatement, Torts, Second*, para. 288B:

'(1) The unexcused violation of a legislative enactment or an administrative regulation which is adopted by the court as defining the standard of conduct of a reasonable man, is negligence in itself.
(2) The unexcused violation of an enactment or regulation which is not so adopted may be relevant evidence bearing on the issue of negligent conduct.'

It is important to note two qualifications to the finding of negligence *per se*: (1) the violation must not be an 'excused violation' and (2) the enactment must be one which is adopted by the court as defining the standard of conduct of a reasonable man. . . .
The so-called 'minority view' in the United States considers breach of a statute to be merely evidence of negligence. There are, however, varying degrees of evidence. Statutory breach may be considered totally irrelevant, merely relevant, or *prima facie* evidence of negligence having the effect of reversing the onus of proof. . . .
The major criticism of the negligence *per se* approach has been the inflexible application of the legislature's criminal standard of conduct to a civil case. I agree with this criticism. The defendant in a civil case does not benefit from the technical defences or protection offered by the criminal law; the civil consequences may easily outweigh any

penal consequences attaching to the breach of statute; and finally the purposes served by the imposition of criminal as opposed to civil liability are radically different. The compensatory aspect of tort liability has won out over the deterrent and punitive aspect; the perceptible evolution in the use of civil liability as a mechanism of loss shifting to that of loss distribution has only accentuated this change. And so '[t]he doctrine of negligence *per se* is, therefore, not fitted for relentless use, nor is it so used' (Morris, 'The Relation of Criminal Statutes to Tort Liability', 46 Harv. L.R 453 (1932–33), at p. 460). Thus the guidelines in the *Restatement, Torts, Second*.

(d) The Canadian position

... The use of breach of statute as evidence of negligence as opposed to recognition of a nominate tort of statutory breach is, as Professor Fleming has put it, more intellectually acceptable. It avoids, to a certain extent, the fictitious hunt for legislative intent to create a civil cause of action which has been so criticized in England. It also avoids the inflexible application of the legislature's criminal standard of conduct to a civil case. Glanville Williams is of the opinion, with which I am in agreement, that where there is no duty of care at common law, breach of non-industrial penal legislation should not affect civil liability unless the statute provides for it. As I have indicated above, industrial legislation historically has enjoyed special consideration. Recognition of the doctrine of absolute liability under some industrial statutes does not justify extension of such doctrine to other fields, particularly when one considers the jejune reasoning supporting the juristic invention.

Regarding statutory breach as part of the law of negligence is also more consonant with other developments which have taken place in the law. ...

Tort law itself has undergone a major transformation in this century with nominate torts being eclipsed by negligence, the closest the common law has come to a general theory of civil responsibility. The concept of duty of care, embodied in the neighbour principle has expanded into areas hitherto untouched by tort law.

One of the main reasons for shifting a loss to a defendant is that he has been at fault, that he has done some act which should be discouraged. There is then good reason for taking money from the defendant as well as a reason for giving it to the plaintiff who has suffered from the fault of the defendant. But there seems little in the way of defensible policy for holding a defendant who breached a statutory duty unwittingly to be negligent and obligated to pay even though not at fault. The legislature has imposed a penalty on a strictly admonitory basis and there seems little justification to add civil liability when such liability would tend to produce liability without fault. The legislature has determined the proper penalty for the defendant's wrong but if tort admonition of liability without fault is to be added, the financial consequences will be measured, not by the amount of the penalty, but by the amount of money which is required to compensate the plaintiff. Minimum fault may subject the defendant to heavy liability. Inconsequential violations should not subject the violator to any civil liability at all but should be left to the criminal courts for enforcement of a fine.

In this case the Board contends that the duty imposed by the Act is absolute, that is to say, the Pool is liable, even in absence of fault, and all that is requisite to prove a breach of duty is to show that the requirements of the statute have not, in fact, been complied with; it is not necessary to show how the failure to comply arose or that the Pool was guilty of any failure to take reasonable care to comply. ...

For all of the above reasons I would be adverse to the recognition in Canada of a nominate tort of statutory breach. Breach of statute, where it has an effect upon civil liability, should be considered in the context of the general law of negligence. Negligence and its common law duty of care have become pervasive enough to serve the purpose invoked for the existence of the action for statutory breach.

It must not be forgotten that the other elements of tortious responsibility equally apply to situations involving statutory breach, i.e., principles of causation and damages. To be relevant at all, the statutory breach must have caused the damage of which the plaintiff complains. Should this be so, the violation of the statute should be evidence of negligence on the part of the defendant.

THIS CASE

Assuming that Parliament is competent constitutionally to provide that anyone injured by a breach of the *Canada Grain Act* shall have a remedy by civil action, the fact is that Parliament has not done so. Parliament has said that an offender shall suffer certain specified penalties for his statutory breach. We must refrain from conjecture as to Parliament's unexpressed intent. The most we can do in determining whether the breach shall have any other legal consequences is to examine what is expressed. In professing to construe the Act in order to conclude whether Parliament intended a private right of action, we are likely to engage in a process which Glanville Williams aptly described as 'looking for what is not there' (p. 244). The *Canada Grain Act* does not contain any express provision for damages for the holder of a terminal elevator receipt who receives infested grain out of an elevator.

The obligation of a terminal operator under s. 61(1) of the *Canada Grain Act* is to deliver to the holder of an elevator receipt for grain issued by the operator the identical grain or grain of the same kind, grade and quantity as the grain referred to in the surrendered receipt, as the receipt requires. That obligation was discharged.

Breach of s. 86(c) of the *Canada Grain Act* in discharging infested grain into the 'Frankcliffe Hall' does not give rise, in and of itself, to an independent tortious action. The Board has proceeded as if it does. Statutory breach, and not negligence, is pleaded. The case has been presented exclusively on the basis of breach of statutory duty. The Board has not proved what Lord Atkin referred to as statutory negligence, i.e., an intentional or negligent failure to comply with a statutory duty. There is no evidence at trial of any negligence or failure to take care on the part of the Pool. . . .

In sum I conclude that:

(1) Civil consequences of breach of statute should be subsumed in the law of negligence.

(2) The notion of a nominate tort of statutory breach giving a right to recovery merely on proof of breach and damages should be rejected, as should the view that unexcused breach consitutes negligence *per se* giving rise to absolute liability.

(3) Proof of statutory breach, causative of damages, may be evidence of negligence.

(4) The statutory formulation of the duty may afford a specific, and useful, standard of reasonable conduct.

(5) In the case at bar negligence is neither pleaded nor proven. The action must fail.

I would dismiss the appeal with costs.

Appeal dismissed

Note

In view of the widespread criticism of the English approach, which rests upon the fiction of legislative intention, which of the following reforms would you favour? (a) A statutory presumption along the lines recommended by the Law Commission (p. 549, ante). Stanton, op cit, p. 54 suggests instead a presumption of non-actionability unless the statute in question expressly provides the contrary, on the grounds that this would discourage new forms of liability, based on legislation, in the absence of express authority. (b) The negligence *per se* doctrine, on which note the criticisms of the Canadian Supreme Court (ante), and compare C. Morris (1949) 49 Col LR 21; and, for a natural rights approach, J. R. S. Prichard and A. Brudner in *Justice, Rights and Tort Law*, edited by M. D. Bales and B. Chapman (Dordrecht/Boston, 1983), pp. 149–177. (c) The 'evidence of negligence' approach, on which see G. Williams (1960) 23 MLR 233, and M. H. Matthews (1984) 4 Oxf JLS 429 and compare the objections by R. A. Buckley (1984) 100 LQR at pp. 206–210. Buckley (at p. 224) suggests that, notwithstanding the reasoning in the *Saskatchewan Wheat Pool* case, the decision is consistent with the proposition that only fault liability will be imposed if the statutory duty is merely general in nature. It is to be noted that the *Saskatchewan Wheat Pool* case did not concern industrial safety and whether it was intended to reject a separate tort of breach of statutory duty in that area is a matter of debate. See W. V. H. Rogers [1984] CLJ 23 at 25; cf. Matthews, op cit, p. 431; L. N. Klar (1984) 6 Supreme Court LR 309 at 316–317. As has been pointed out, however, the existence in Canada of workmen's compensation schemes makes strict statutory duties in that sphere less important as a source of industrial compensation. Might there be a sound case for having a tort of breach of statutory duty in the case of industrial safety legislation, in the light especially of s. 47(2) of the Health and Safety at Work etc Act 1974 (on which see p. 561, post), but adopting the 'evidence of negligence' approach for other legislation if the legislature has not made its wishes clear? (Consider Matthews, op cit, p. 433.)

4 Causation and breach of statutory duty

Boyle *v* Kodak Ltd House of Lords [1969] 2 All ER 439

The appellant was injured when he fell off a ladder while engaged in painting the outside of a large oil storage tank which was some 30 feet high. The upper part had to be painted by a man standing on a ladder the top of which rested on a rail round the roof of the tank. For safety it was necessary to lash the top of the ladder to this rail to prevent it from slipping sideways, and the accident occurred while the appellant was going up the ladder in order to lash it. For some reason, never discovered, the ladder slipped when he was about twenty feet up and he fell with the ladder.

LORD DIPLOCK: My Lords, in this action negligence and contributory negligence were pleaded but as I read the judgment of Chapman J he found that the ladder from which the appellant fell was so positioned and footed that the risk of its slipping while he was mounting it in order to lash the top of it to the rail of the tank was so small that a reasonable man would not have thought it necessary to expend the time and effort which would have been involved in ascending the staircase to the top of the tank and lashing the ladder before setting foot on it. The judge expressly found that the respondents were not negligent and it is implicit in his judgment that the appellant's conduct did not amount to contributory negligence at common law. All three members of the Court of Appeal agreed with these findings which have not been seriously contested in your Lordships' House.

All that is left in this appeal is the appellant's claim for damages for breach by the respondents of their statutory duty under reg. 29(4) of the Building (Health, Safety and Welfare) Regulations 1948,[1] which so far as is relevant provides: 'Every ladder shall so far as practicable be securely fixed so that it can move neither from its top nor from its bottom points of rest.'

I agree with all your Lordships, with the Court of Appeal and with the trial judge that this regulation applied to the operation on which the appellant was engaged when he fell. I also agree that it was practicable, by lashing the ladder to the rail of the tank before anyone mounted it, to fix the ladder securely so that it could not move from its top points of rest. So the regulation was not complied with. If it had been the top of the ladder would not have slipped and the appellant would not have sustained his physical injuries. So the non-compliance with the regulation was a cause of the appellant's injuries.

The law relating to civil liability for breach of statutory duties imposed by the Factories Act 1961, and its predecessors and by regulations made thereunder is now well settled. It is the creature not of the statutes themselves but of judicial decision by which over the period of 70 years which have passed since *Groves v Lord Wimborne*,[2] a new branch of the law of civil wrongs has been developed. The statutes say nothing about civil remedies for breaches of their provisions. The judgments of the courts say all.

The duty to comply with the requirements of reg. 29(4) of the Building (Health Safety and Welfare) Regulations 1948, is imposed by reg. 4 on the employer who is undertaking the operation. But it is also imposed on the person, in the instant case the appellant, who performs the act, viz. mounting the ladder, to which the relevant requirement of the regulation relates. We have thus a situation where both appellant and respondents were at fault and the only fault of each was their respective failure to comply with the same requirements of the same regulation.

Although the civil liability of the employer has been engrafted by judicial decision on the criminal liability imposed by Parliament its growth has been separate from the parent stem. It is no good looking to the statute and seeing from it where the criminal liability would lie, for we are concerned only with civil liability. We must look to the cases, and in particular to *Ginty v Belmont Building Supplies Ltd*,[3] and those which followed it, by which this branch of the law of civil wrongs is being developed.

The employer's duty to comply with the requirements of the regulation differs from that of his employee. The employer, at any rate when he is a corporation, must needs perform his duty vicariously through his officers, servants, agents or contractors; but he does not thereby rid himself of his duty. He remains vicariously responsible for any failure by any one of them to do whatever was necessary to ensure that the requirements of the regulation were complied with; and among those for whose failure he is prima facie vicariously liable is any employee who is himself under a con-current duty to comply with those requirements. The employee's duty, on the other hand, is in respect of and is limited to his own acts or omissions. He is not vicariously liable for those of anyone else.

What, then, is the liability of an employer who is sued by an employee plaintiff for damages for personal injuries sustained as a result of a breach of statutory duty by the employer in not complying with the requirements of a regulation when the non-compliance relied on was also a breach of statutory duty by the plaintiff himself?

The plaintiff establishes a prima facie cause of action against his employer by proving the fact of non-compliance with a requirement of the regulation and that he suffered injury as a result. He need prove no more. No burden lies on him to prove what steps should have been taken to avert the non-compliance nor to identify the employees whose acts or defaults contributed to it, for the employer is vicariously

---

1. S.I. 1984 No. 1145.
2. [1898] 2 QB 402; [1895-99] All ER Rep 147.
3. [1959] 1 All ER 414.

responsible for them all. But if the employer can prove that the only act or default of anyone which caused or contributed to the non-compliance was the act or default of the plaintiff himself, he establishes a good defence. For the legal concept of vicarious liability requires three parties: the injured person, a person whose act or default caused the injury and a person vicariously liable for the latter's act or default. To say 'You are liable to me for my own wrongdoing' is neither good morals nor good law. But unless the employer can prove this he cannot escape liability. If he proves that it was partly the fault of the employee plaintiff, as ex hypothesi it will be in the postulated case, for the employee's own breach of statutory duty is 'fault' within the meaning of s. 1 of the Law Reform (Contributory Negligence) Act 1945, this may reduce the damages recoverable but it will not constitute a defence to the action.

Since it is only through other persons that the employer can perform his duty of compliance with the requirements of the regulations it is incumbent on him to ensure that all of those persons understand those requirements and their practical application to the particular work being undertaken and possess the skill and are provided with the plant, equipment and personnel needed to secure compliance. Although in the present case the necessary plant, equipment and personnel was provided for the appellant and he possessed the necessary skill the respondents, who called no evidence, made no attempt to prove that they had taken any steps to ensure that the appellant understood the requirements of reg. 4 of the Building (Health, Safety and Welfare) Regulations 1948, or understood that, in the particular circumstances of the work which he was undertaking, these requirements would not be satisfied unless he lashed the ladder at the top to the rail of the tank before he mounted it.

It has been contended on their behalf that as the appellant was a skilled and experienced craftsman they were entitled to assume that he understood all these things. But however reasonable such assumption might be they would not escape liability unless they proved that the appellant did in fact understand them, although the reasonableness of their assumption if mistaken would be relevant to their share in the responsibility for the damage for the purpose of reducing the damages recoverable under the Law Reform (Contributory Negligence) Act 1945.

On the evidence in the present case, which was that of the appellant himself and of a fellow workman who completed the work after the plaintiff was injured, it appeared that neither was given any instruction about the regulations or was told that the regulations required the top of the ladder to be lashed to the rail of the tank before anyone mounted on it. It also appeared that the appellant, for reasons which are intelligible though unconvincing, believed that the ladder should be lashed while he was mounted on it and not before. So far from establishing that the appellant did know what the requirements of the regulation were and their application to the particular circumstances of the operation on which he was engaged, the evidence discloses that the foreman and the ganger through whom, inter alia, the respondents were purporting to perform their statutory duty and for whose omissions they are vicariously liable, took no steps to give to the appellant instructions on either of these matters which, if carried out, would have prevented the breach of statutory duty. The respondents, in my view, therefore failed to satisfy the onus which lay on them to prove that the only act or default of anyone which caused or contributed to the non-compliance was the act or default of the appellant himself.

In your Lordships' House the respondents relied strongly on a finding of the learned judge that their failure to instruct the appellant to lash the ladder at the top before mounting it did not constitute negligence on their part. For reasons that I have already indicated the fact that a failure to give instructions as to the requirements of the regulations is not negligent does not exonerate an employer from liability for breach of his statutory duty to comply with the requirements of the regulations which he owes to the person whom he has failed to instruct. He is only exonerated if he can show that that person did in fact know the requirements. But in the present case the failure goes further than this. It may well be unnecessary to give a skilled and experienced craftsman instructions how to avoid obvious dangers, and the more obvious the danger the less the need to do so. But in the present case on the findings of the learned judge the risk of the ladder slipping while the appellant was mounting it to lash the top of it was so small that a reasonable man would not have thought it necessary in the interests of his own safety to expend the time and effort and incur the possible loss of bonus which would have been involved in ascending the staircase to the top of the tank and lashing the ladder. The more remote the danger in the particular operation on which the employee is engaged the greater the need to instruct him or to remind him of the application of the regulation to it.

Perhaps because he had already dealt with instruction in connection with the issue of negligence, the cognate question of instructions about the application of the regulations to the task in hand escaped the attention of the judge at the trial when he came to deal with breach of statutory duty. This oversight, in my opinion, led him to err in law in treating it as sufficient to exonerate the respondents from all liability that —

'. . . he [the appellant] was the one to see that that breach was not carried out . . . He had the means of securing the ladder and complying with the Regulations and he did not do so.'

In the Court of Appeal, Salmon LJ in his dissenting judgment was the only one to recognise the vital distinction between the need to instruct a craftsman on how to avoid obvious dangers and the need to instruct him about the application of the regulations in situations where no danger is apparent. On this aspect of the case the majority members of the Court of Appeal, in my view, fell into the same error as the learned trial judge. But they also upheld the judgment on the ground that, even if the appellant had been instructed that he was required by the regulations to lash the ladder at the top before and not after mounting and to ascend to the top of the tank by the staircase to do so, and that he would be committing an offence if he did not, the appellant would nevertheless have disregarded those instructions. Failure to give them, therefore, did not cause or contribute to the breach.

Whether the appellant would or would not have obeyed such instructions is a question of fact. The learned judge made no finding on it. It was never put to the appellant in cross-examination. It was never canvassed in evidence at all. It is, in my view, impermissible for an appellate court to decide this case against the appellant on what is no more than speculation as to a fact which the respondents never sought to prove and with which the appellant was given no opportunity to deal.

I would therefore allow the appeal. Both appellant and respondents were in breach of their statutory duty. This was the only 'fault' of each. I find it difficult to apportion their respective shares of the responsibility for the damage. In view of the remoteness of the danger in neither was it a very heinous fault. But however venial the fault of each of them they must share between them the responsibility for the whole of the damage. I would assess the share of each as one-half and reduce the damages recoverable by the appellant accordingly.

I would allow the appeal, declare that the respondents are liable to the appellant for one-half of the damage sustained by him and remit the case for the damages to be assessed.

[LORD REID, with whom LORD MORRIS OF BORTH-Y-GEST concurred, and LORD HODSON, delivered speeches in favour of allowing the appeal. LORD UPJOHN concurred.]

Notes

1. The law of causation applies as much to breach of statutory duties as it does to breach of common law duties (see chap. 6, p. 299, ante), but it is particularly important where the statute lays down a duty on both the

employer and the injured employee, or where the employee is the only person who could carry out the statutory duty. See too *Cummings* (or *McWilliams*) *v Sir William Arrol & Co* [1962] 1 All ER 623; [1962] 1 WLR 295: steel erector killed when he fell from a steel tower; had he been wearing a safety belt he would not have been killed; held his widow could not recover reparation in respect of the breach of statutory duty to provide belts because even had he been provided with a belt he would not have worn one. Compare *Bux v Slough Metals Ltd* [1974] 1 All ER 262; [1973] 1 WLR 1358, noted p. 551, ante.

2. Would the employers have been liable in *Boyle v Kodak Ltd* had they been able to show that, even properly instructed, the appellant would have disobeyed? What kind of evidence would be admissible to show 'what he would have done in circumstances which never arose'? (per Lord Devlin in *McWilliams*'s case, ante). See too *Ross v Associated Portland Cement Manufacturers Ltd* [1964] 2 All ER 452; [1964] 1 WLR 768.

5   Contributory negligence and breach of statutory duty

Caswell *v* Powell Duffryn Associated Collieries Ltd House of Lords [1939] 3 All ER 722

Arthur Caswell, an employee of the respondents, was killed in their mine, and his mother sued for damages alleging breach of statutory duty (s. 55 of the Coal Mines Act 1911, which related to the fencing of machinery).

LORD ATKIN: . . . Though I have come to the conclusion that in this case the defendants failed to prove negligence on the part of the deceased workman, I feel bound to say something on the topic, which was much discussed in argument, whether contributory negligence is ever a defence to an action based upon a breach of a statutory duty, or, more narrowly, based upon a breach of a statutory duty to protect workmen and others imposed by such Acts as the Factory Acts, Mining Acts, etc. Authority for the proposition that contributory negligence in the ordinary sense is not a defence to such an action is to be found in the judgment of the High Court of Australia in *Bourke v Butterfield and Lewis Ltd*.[1] The argument is that safely[2] obligations are placed upon employers for the purpose of protecting not only workmen who are careful but also those who are careless: and that the object of the legislature is defeated if the right to sue for injuries caused by the breach of the safety regulations is denied to the careless workman for whose benefit amongst others the legislation was specially enacted. I venture to think that this attractive theory does not give sufficient weight to the true cause of action in such cases. The statute does not in terms create a statutory cause of action. It does not, for instance, make the employer an insurer. The person who is injured, as in all cases where damage is the gist of the action, must show not only a breach of duty but that his hurt was due to the breach. If his damage is due entirely to his own wilful act no cause of action arises as, for instance, if out of bravado he puts his hand into moving machinery or

---

1. (1927) 38 CLR 354.
2. [This word should be 'safety'—see [1940] AC at p. 164.]

attempts to leap over an unguarded cavity. The injury has not been caused by the defendants' omission but by the plaintiff's own act. The injury may, however, be the result of two causes operating at the same time, a breach of duty by the defendant and the omission on the part of the plaintiff to use the ordinary care for the protection of himself or his property that is used by the ordinary reasonable man in those circumstances. In that case the plaintiff cannot recover because the injury is partly caused by what is imputed to him as his own default.[1] On the other hand, if the plaintiff were negligent, but his negligence was not a cause operating to produce the damage, there would be no defence. I find it impossible to divorce any theory of contributory negligence from the concept of causation. It is negligence which 'contributes to cause' the injury, a phrase which I take from the opinion of Lord Penzance in *Radley v London and North Western Rly Co*.[2] And whether you ask whose negligence was responsible for the injury, or from whose negligence did the injury result, or adopt any other phrase you please, you must in the ultimate analysis be asking who 'caused' the injury: and you must not be deterred because the word 'cause' has in philosophy given rise to embarrassments which in this connection should not affect the judge. . . .

I cannot . . . accept the view that the action for injuries caused by breach of statutory duty differs from an action for injuries caused by any other wrong. I think that the defendant will succeed if he proves that the injury was caused solely or in part by the omission of the plaintiff to take the ordinary care that would be expected of him in the circumstances.[3]

But having come to that conclusion I am of opinion that the care to be expected of the plaintiff in the circumstances will vary with the circumstances; and that a different degree of care may well be expected from a workman in a factory or a mine from that which might be taken by an ordinary man not exposed continually to the noise, strain and manifold risks of factory or mine. I agree with the statement of Lawrence J in *Flower v Ebbw Vale Steel, Iron and Coal Co Ltd*,[4] at p. 140, cited by my noble and learned friend Lord Wright in [1936] AC at p. 214:

'I think, of course, that in considering whether an ordinary prudent workman would have taken more care than the injured man, the tribunal of fact has to take into account all the circumstances of work in a factory and that it is not for every risky thing which a workman in a factory may do in his familiarity with the machinery that a plaintiff ought to be held guilty of contributory negligence.'

This seems to me a sensible practical saying, and one which will afford all the protection which is necessary to the workman. . . . I have already said that I see no ground for imputing any negligence to the deceased man in the present case judged by any standard: but in any case judging the question of fact by the standard suggested by Lawrence J I think that the defence of contributory negligence inevitably failed. . . .

LORD WRIGHT: . . . What is all important is to adapt the standard of what is negligence to the facts, and to give due regard to the actual conditions under which men work in a factory or mine, to the long hours and the fatigue, to the slackening of attention which naturally comes from constant repetition of the same operation, to the noise and confusion in which the man works, to his pre-occupation in what he is actually doing at the cost perhaps of some inattention to his own safety. . . .

---

1. [This statement must now be read in the light of the Law Reform (Contributory Negligence) Act 1945 (p. 000, ante).]
2. (1876) 1 App Cas 754.
3. [This sentence must also, of course, be read in the light of the 1945 Act.]
4. [1934] 2 KB 132.

LORD PORTER: . . . It is the reasonable man who is to be considered, not the particular individual, and therefore the degree of care will not vary from man to man, but it will, I think, vary from mine to mine and from factory to factory. The skill gained by a worker may enable him to take risks and do acts which in an unskilled man would be negligence, and on the other hand the fatiguing repetition of the same work may make a man incapable of the same care, and therefore not guilty of negligence, in doing or failing to do an act which a man less fatigued would do or leave undone. . . .

[LORD MACMILLAN delivered a speech in which he agreed with LORD ATKIN's exposition of the law. LORD THANKERTON concurred with LORD ATKIN.]

Notes

1. For the defence of contributory negligence in general, see p. 354, ante. In *Westwood v Post Office* [1974] AC 1; [1973] 3 All ER 184 Lord Kilbrandon quoted the view of Denning LJ in *Jones v Livox Quarries Ltd* [1952] 2 QB 608 at 615 (p. 359, ante) that 'in his reckonings [a plaintiff] must take into account the possibility of others being careless'; but his Lordship went on to doubt its application when a court is concerned with a question of statutory liability, as opposed to a common law claim. On apportionment see I. Fagelson (1979) 42 MLR 646 at 661–662.

2. For the defence of volenti non fit injuria, see p. 373, ante and especially *ICI Ltd v Shatwell* [1965] AC 656; [1964] 2 All ER 999 (p. 380, ante).

6 The interpretation of industrial safety legislation: a note

The action for breach of statutory duty, when applied to some industrial legislation, was a neat way around the doctrine of common employment (*Groves v Lord Wimborne*, p. 536, ante). Despite the abolition of that doctrine by s. 1 of the Law Reform (Personal Injuries) Act 1948 (p. 566, post) the action has survived. It is not possible in this sourcebook to enter into this complex, capricious and vague area of statutory interpretation of industrial legislation. (A practitioners' book, which also has the merit of being entertainingly written and of use to the student, is J. Munkman, *Employers' Liability at Common Law* 11th edn (London, Dublin, Edinburgh, 1990); see too N. Selwyn, *Law of Health and Safety at Work* (London, 1982) and C. D. Drake and F. D. Wright, *Law of Health and Safety at Work: the New Approach* (London, 1983).) This chapter would, however, be incomplete if the student had failed to appreciate that 'some of the protection to the workman which at first sight might be thought available turns out on closer scrutiny to be illusory' per Lord Hailsham in *F E Callow (Engineers) Ltd v Johnson* [1971] AC 335 at 342.

Given the existence of a civil right of action, the plaintiff must prove: (a) that he belongs to the class of persons whom the statute is designed to protect; (b) that the defendant was in breach of the duty; and (c) that the breach caused the damage. We have seen (section 4, ante) that this third question, the relationship between the breach and the resultant damage, raises questions of fault. The first two questions, particularly the second, may also do so. It all depends upon the precise wording of the statutory duty or, where the meaning is not clear, upon the judicial interpretation of those words.

Unfortunately, industrial legislation has grown up in a piecemeal fashion. Surveying the legal scene, an official Committee of Inquiry (under the Chairmanship of Lord Robens), Cmnd. 5034, reported in 1972 that there were nine main groups of statutes (controlling respectively factories, commercial premises, mining and quarrying, agriculture, explosives, petroleum, nuclear installations, radioactive substances, and alkali etc. works) supported by nearly 500 subordinate statutory instruments, which were added to each year. The mass of statute law comprised – in the words of the Committee – an 'haphazard mass of ill-assorted and intricate detail'. The various Acts showed neither internal logic nor consistency with one another. The rate of technological change meant that they were often out of date; and they were far from comprehensive because, according to a Department of Employment estimate, something like 5 million of the 23 million workers in Britain were not covered by any occupational health and safety legislation. In relation to those who were covered it was found that some duties were strict (the word 'absolute' is a misnomer) while other duties were based on a requirement of some degree of fault. The random distribution of duties between strict and not-so-strict duties depended upon the 'accident of language' (G. Williams (1960) 23 MLR 233 at 243 – a seminal article; and see too, *Williams & Hepple*, pp. 116–123).

As a result of the recommendations of the Committee, the comprehensive Health and Safety at Work etc. Act 1974 (in force since 1975) has been enacted. This places great emphasis on non-statutory codes and standards in promoting accident prevention partly in supplementation of, and partly in place of, statutory regulations. The existing legislation (such as the Factories Act and subordinate legislation) is gradually being replaced by this new system for accident prevention. The Act is comprehensive, covering all persons at work and others against risks to health and safety arising out of or in connection with work activities.

This has considerable implications for damages actions by injured workers. Although there is a general presumption in s. 47(2) that breach of the new regulations will give rise to civil liability unless the particular regulation provides otherwise, it is by no means clear that the new regulations create strict duties or that they are as specific as some of those in existing legislation. They allow defences – such as 'reasonable practicability' – which are at the very least the first cousins of the standard of care expected of the reasonable man. For example, in *Marshall v Gotham Co Ltd* [1954] AC 360; [1954] 1 All ER 937 regulations required the roof of a mine to be made secure so far as reasonably practicable. The usual practice in a gypsum mine is to test the roof with a hammer and bring down unsafe parts of the roof, instead of the practice in coal mines of having systematic support by props. The roof had been tested in this way but it collapsed due to a rare geological fault which had not been known to occur for twenty years. Systematic support might have minimised the fall but would not have eliminated the risk. The House of Lords held that the known risk had to be balanced against safety measures, and that the defence was established. Lord Reid said, however, that 'as men's lives might be at stake it should not lightly be held that to take a practicable precaution is unreasonable' (at p. 942). Their Lordships referred with approval to the test propounded by Asquith LJ in *Edwards v National Coal Board* [1949] 1 All ER 743 at 747: '"Reasonably practicable" is a narrower term than "physically possible", and seems to me to imply that a computation must be made by the owner in which the quantum of risk is placed on one scale and the sacrifice involved in the measures necessary for averting the risk (whether in money, time or trouble) is placed in the other, and that, if it be shown that there is a gross disproportion between them – the risk being insignificant in relation to the sacrifice – the defendants discharge the onus on them.' If the new regulations uniformly allow the defence of 'reasonable practicability', then strict duties arising from statute may become 'codified negligence' but with the burden of proof of absence of negligence being upon the employer. However, the relatively few health and safety regulations made during the first fifteen years of operation of the new Act show no clear movement in this direction. For example, the Classification Packaging and Labelling of Dangerous Substances Regulations, SI 1984/1244 – implementing EEC directives aimed at standardising the labelling of hazardous substances, lays down strict duties on suppliers to label in graphic form with easily understood symbols various dangerous substances. A person injured in consequence of a breach of these regulations would have a civil action for damages by virtue of reg. 15(1)(b). A defence is provided in respect of *criminal* proceedings that a person took 'all reasonable precautions and exercised all due diligence' to avoid the commission of an offence, by the 1974 Act. This does not provide a defence in civil proceedings (s. 47(3) of the 1974 Act). The Pearson Commission, vol. I, para. 917, recommended that a distinction should be drawn between the defences available for criminal and civil proceedings.

This recommendation was made because of the strictures of the Robens Committee, paras. 130, 435 and Appendix 7, against utilising the same body of law for two quite different purposes, one being accident prevention and the other compensation. The prospect of civil litigation may delay remedial measures because of the reluctance to admit breach of statutory duty or negligence, and industrial relations may become strained. For the most part, legal interpretation of the regulations takes place in the context of civil litigation and there are a number of cases where these interpretations have appeared to conflict with the aim of accident prevention. Some of the judicial interpretations have rested upon a compensation theory. They have approached statutory interpretation from the injured worker's point of view. Examples are cases in which it has been held that an employee who is injured when going to a part of his employer's premises where he has no business to be (and hence is trespassing) may claim compensation for breach of the strict statutory duties under the Factories Act 1961 (*Uddin v Associated Portland Cement Manufacturers* [1965] 2 QB 582; [1965] 2 All ER 213) and the Offices, Shops and Railway Premises Act 1963 (*Westwood v Post Office* [1974] AC 1; [1973] 3 All ER 184). Another example is the literal interpretation (refusing to read in an unexpressed exception) in *John Summers & Sons Ltd v Frost* [1955] AC 740; [1955] 1 All ER 870 of s. 14(1) of the Factories Act 1961 which requires 'every dangerous part of any machinery' to be 'securely fenced'. A grindstone wheel moving at 1,450 revolutions per minute was held to be 'dangerous', although the evidence showed that it would be impossible to provide a guard which would make the machine usable. Williams (op cit, p. 238) comments: 'it is hard to imagine that Parliament really intended when it passed . . . the Factories Act . . . that so common a machine as a grindstone should become unlawful. . . .'

Other judicial interpretations have adopted either explicitly (as in *Haigh v Charles W Ireland Ltd* [1973] 3 All ER 1137; [1974] 1 WLR 43) or implicitly, a strict interpretation which resolves what might be thought to be an ambiguity in favour of the defendant employer. Paradoxically, this rule of strict construction is now more often enunciated in the civil courts in actions for breach of statutory duty, than by the criminal courts. Artificial distinctions have been used to limit the scope of particular statutory duties. For example, in regard to s. 14(1) of the Factories Act 1961 it has been held that (a) since it is only *parts* of machinery which have to be fenced there is no obligation to fence a machine if it is dangerous as a *whole* but does not have dangerous parts (*British Railways Board v Liptrot* [1969] 1 AC 136 at 159); (b) a part of machinery does not include a workpiece moving under power and held in the machinery by a chuck, nor does it include materials in the machinery (*Eaves v Morris Motors Ltd* [1961] 2 QB 385; [1961] 3 All ER 233; cf. *Wearing v Pirelli Ltd* [1977] 1 All ER 339; [1977] 1 WLR 48); (c) the dangers against which fencing is required do not include dangers to be apprehended from the ejection of flying materials from the machine even though this is part of the machine itself (*Close v Steel Co of Wales* [1962] AC 367; [1961] 2 All ER 953); and (d) the worker is not protected if what comes into contact with the dangerous part of a machine is a hand tool operated by the worker as distinct from the worker's body or clothes (*Sparrow v Fairey Aviation Co Ltd* [1964] AC 1019; [1962] 3 All ER 706). (For further examples see *Encyclopedia of Health and Safety at Work*, vol. I, part I, chap. 2.)

In view of interpretations such as these, and the absence of any visible progress in enacting a comprehensive body of regulations embodying a standard of 'codified negligence' applicable to civil actions for damages under the Health and Safety at Work etc. Act 1974, it is disappointing that the Pearson Commission having recommended, with one dissentient, that an injured worker's right of action against his employer should be retained, did not go on to recommend that there should be any change in the basis of liability in tort for work injury (vol. I, paras. 914–917). It concluded that 'the widely used action for breach of statutory duty goes far enough' in the direction of strict liability, and it placed its faith in future regulations which would differentiate between civil and criminal liability. It was also not willing to recommend a formal reversal of the burden of proof, so that the onus would be on the employer to show that he was not at fault or not in breach of statutory duty (paras. 918–922).

7 Employer's liability to employees for negligence

An employee who is injured at work may seek to hold his employer responsible on two possible grounds: (a) the personal breach of a common law or statutory duty by the employer; or (b) the breach of a duty owed by a fellow employee of the plaintiff, the employer being vicariously liable for the torts of his employees. The second situation is the more usual one in practice, but before the passing of the Law Reform (Personal Injuries) Act 1948, s. 1 (p. 566, post), such an action was barred by the doctrine of common employment judicially invented in *Priestley v Fowler* (1837) 3 M & W 1 (post). Although the scope of this defence was partially limited by the Employers' Liability Act 1880, and excluded in the case of breach of *statutory* duties (p. 536, ante), it caused much injustice. In order to circumvent the doctrine, the courts came to give an extended and artificial meaning to the concept of the *personal* duty owed by an employer. The high point was reached in *Wilsons and Clyde Coal Co Ltd v English* [1938] AC 57; [1937] 3 All ER 628 (p. 566, post). Despite the abolition of the doctrine of common employment in 1948, the concept of personal non-delegable duties persists in this field. In this section the general nature of this relatively high duty may be examined. One of its principal implications is in regard to the employer's responsibility for faults of an independent contractor which cause injury to an employee. That aspect is considered p. 858, post. Consider also p. 810, post, where *McDermid v Nash Dredging and Reclamation Co Ltd* [1987] AC 906; [1987] 2 All ER 878 is noted.

Priestley *v* Fowler Court of Exchequer [1835–42] All ER Rep 449

The plaintiff was employed by a butcher. He was injured in the course of his employment when the van in which he was being carried was carelessly overloaded by a fellow-servant. A verdict for £100 in his favour was entered. The Court of Exchequer arrested the judgment.

LORD ABINGER CB [delivering the judgment of the Court]: . . . If the master be liable to the servant in this action, the principle of that liability will be found to carry us to an alarming extent. He who is responsible by his general duty, or by the terms of his contract, for all the consequences of negligence in a matter in which he is the principal, is responsible for the negligence of all his inferior agents. If the owner of the carriage is, therefore, responsible for the sufficiency of his carriage to his servant, he is responsible for the negligence of his coach-builder or his harness-maker or his coach-man. The footman, therefore, who rides behind the carriage, may have an action against his master for a defect in the carriage owing to the negligence of the coach-maker or for a defect in the harness arising from the negligence of the harness-maker or for drunkenness, neglect, or want of skill in the coachman; nor is there any reason why the principle should not, if applicable in this class of cases, extend to many others. The master, for example, would be liable to the servant for the negligence of the chambermaid, for putting him into a damp bed; for that of the upholsterer, for sending in a crazy bed-stead, whereby he was made to fall down while asleep and injure himself; for the negligence of the cook, in not properly cleaning the copper vessels used in the kitchen; of the butcher, in supplying the family with meat of a quality injurious to the health; of the builder, for a defect in the foundation of the house, whereby it fell and injured both the master and the servant by the ruins.

The inconvenience, not to say the absurdity of these consequences, affords a sufficient argument against the application of this principle to the present case. But, in truth, the mere relation of the master and the servant never can imply an obligation on the part of the master to take more care of the servant than he may reasonably be expected to do of himself. He is, no doubt, bound to provide for the safety of his servant in the course of his employment, to the best of his judgment, information, and belief. The servant is not bound to risk his safety in the service of his master, and may, if he thinks fit, decline any service in which he reasonably apprehends injury to himself: and in most of the cases in which danger may be incurred, if not in all, he is just as likely to be acquainted with the probability and extent of it as the master. In that sort of employment, especially, which is described in the declaration in this case, the plaintiff must have known as well as his master, and probably better, whether the van was sufficient, whether it was over-loaded, and whether it was likely to carry him safely. In fact, to allow this sort of action to prevail would be an encouragement to the servant to omit that diligence and caution which he is in duty bound to exercise on the behalf of his master, to protect him against the misconduct or negligence of others who serve him, and which diligence and caution, while they protect the master, are a much better security against any injury the servant may sustain by the negligence of others engaged under the same master, than any recourse against his master for damages could possibly afford.

We are, therefore, of opinion that the judgment ought to be arrested.

Note

The unfortunate Priestley spent some years in the debtors' prison because he could not pay the costs of his unsuccessful action. Munkman, op cit, p. 7, comments that Lord Abinger, who owned Inverlochy Castle near Ben Nevis, may have been thinking of 'his own extensive pre-Victorian household, and the liabilities to which he himself might be subjected', when he delivered this judgment. The philosophy it expresses is the same as that in the then popular 'iron law of wages'. From the point of view of accident prevention, the decision led to the dilemma which Byles J saw in *Clarke v Holmes* (1862) 7 H & N 937 at 949: 'If a master's personal knowledge of defects in his machinery be necessary to his liability, the more a master neglects his business and abandons it to others the less will he be liable.' An interesting, but little used scheme to aid factory employees was the machinery of penal compensation originating in the Factories Act 1844 and of importance until 1880: see R. L. Howells (1963) 26 MLR 367.

The Law Reform (Personal Injuries) Act 1948

1. Common employment. – (1) It shall not be a defence to an employer who is sued in respect of personal injuries caused by the negligence of a person employed by him, that that person was at the time the injuries were caused in common employment with the person injured.

(2) Accordingly the Employers' Liability Act, 1880, shall cease to have effect, and is hereby repealed.

(3) Any provision contained in a contract of service or apprenticeship, or in an agreement collateral thereto (including a contract or agreement entered into before the commencement of this Act), shall be void in so far as it would have the effect of excluding or limiting any liability of the employer in respect of personal injuries caused to the person employed or apprenticed by the negligence of persons in common employment with him.

Wilsons and Clyde Coal Co Ltd *v* English House of Lords [1937] 3 All ER 628

The pursuer claimed damages in respect of personal injuries sustained while employed at the defendant company's Glencraig Colliery, Fife. At the end of a day-shift, as he was proceeding to the pit-bottom, he was crushed when the haulage plant was set in motion. His case was that it was a necessary part of a safe system of working, and recognised mining practice, that during the time when day-shift men were being raised to the surface the haulage plant should be stopped. The defendants claimed that they had effectively discharged their duty of providing a safe system of work by appointing a qualified manager, and they relied upon s. 2(4) of the Coal Mines Act 1911 which provided that only a qualified manager could control the technical management of the mine. In an appeal against an interlocutor pronounced by a court of seven judges of the Court of Session the House of Lords unanimously rejected this defence, and dismissed the appeal.

LORD WRIGHT: . . . I do not mean that employers warrant the adequacy of plant, or the competence of fellow-employees, or the propriety of the system of work. The obligation is fulfilled by the exercise of due care and skill. But it is not fulfilled by entrusting its fulfilment to employees, even though selected with due care and skill. The obligation is threefold, 'the provision of a competent staff of men, adequate material, and a proper system and effective supervision'. . . .

The well established, but illogical, doctrine of common employment is certainly one not to be extended, and indeed has never in its long career been pushed so far as the Court of Appeal[1] sought to push it. . . .

I think the whole course of authority consistently recognises a duty which rests on the employer, and which is personal to the employer, to take reasonable care for the safety of his workmen, whether the employer be an individual, a firm, or a company, and whether or not the employer takes any share in the conduct of the operations. The obligation is threefold, as I have explained. The obligation to provide and maintain proper plant and appliances is a continuing obligation. It is not, however, broken by a mere misuse of, or failure to use, proper plant and appliances, due to the negligence of a fellow-servant, or a merely temporary failure to keep in order or adjust plant and appliances, or a casual departure from the system of working, if these matters can be regarded as the casual negligence of the managers, foremen, or other employees. It may be difficult, in some cases, to distinguish, on the facts, between the employer's failure to provide and maintain and the fellow-servants' negligence in the respects indicated. . . .

[LORD THANKERTON, LORD MACMILLAN and LORD MAUGHAM delivered speeches in favour of dismissing the appeal. LORD ATKIN agreed with all the speeches.]

Question

In view of the fact that the defendant company was required by statute to delegate the duty to provide a safe system of work, why did the House of Lords describe it as a duty 'personal' to the company?

Notes

1. For examples of the employer's threefold duty see Munkman, op cit, chap. 4. It should be noted that the duty to provide proper plant, equipment and premises, overlaps with the occupier's duty to visitors, and is stringently interpreted: see e.g. *General Cleaning Contractors Ltd v Christmas* [1953] AC 180; [1952] 2 All ER 1110 (safe system includes an adequate system of instruction and supply of necessary protective equipment); cf. *Wilson v Tyneside Window Cleaning Co* [1958] 2 QB 110; [1958] 2 All ER 265 (duty extends to premises not in employer's occupation, but less will be required of an employer when the employee is on someone else's premises).

---

1. [Inter alia, in *Fanton v Denville* [1932] 2 KB 309.]

2. It is compulsory for employers to insure against their liability to employees: Employers' Liability (Compulsory Insurance) Act 1969, p. 894, post. Reference should also be made to the Employers' Liability (Defective Equipment) Act 1969 (p. 858, post).

3. For the relevance of 'common practice', see p. 276, ante.

4. The provisions of s. 1(3) of the Law Reform (Personal Injuries) Act 1948 (p. 566, ante) prevent contracting-out only of the employer's vicarious liability to an employee who suffers damage as a result of the fault of a fellow-employee. Section 2(1) of the Unfair Contract Terms Act 1977 (p. 389, ante) supplements this by rendering void any term of a contract or notice which excludes or restricts liability for death or personal injury resulting from negligence. Section 2(2) prohibits exclusions or restrictions for negligence in the case of other 'loss or damage' (e.g. to the employee's property) unless the terms or the notice are 'reasonable'. These provisions cover both personal and vicarious liability.

5. As was mentioned p. 564, ante, the Pearson Commission recommended, with one dissentient, that the tort action for work injuries should remain on the present basis of liability (vol. 1, para. 913). For the Pearson Commission's views on work injuries more generally, see vol. 1, chap. 17 of the Report.

13 Intentional interference with the person

This chapter includes not only the torts traditionally known as assault, battery and false imprisonment, which can be grouped under the heading trespass to the person, but also liability for wrongful interference with the person in situations where an action under any of the first three torts may be inappropriate. *Winfield & Jolowicz*, p. 54, define an assault as 'an act of the defendant which causes to the plaintiff reasonable apprehension of the infliction of a battery on him by the defendant', and a battery as 'the intentional and direct application of force to another person'. Whether trespass to the person is still actionable where the defendant has acted negligently rather than intentionally is a disputed question. Compare, for example, *Winfield & Jolowicz*, p. 53 and pp. 70–71 with *Street*, pp. 15–19, 21 and 25 and *Salmond & Heuston*, p. 135 and see pp. 570–578, ante. In relation to this last point, the first section of this chapter (admittedly 'trespassing' to some extent from its title) deals with the interrelationship of the trespass action and an action in the tort of negligence, although the history of these two actions cannot really be explored here.

Whereas an action in the tort of negligence requires proof of damage, trespass to the person is actionable per se and, although this difference is not often of great importance, in *John Lewis & Co Ltd v Tims* [1952] 1 All ER 1203 at 1204, Lord Porter stated (in the context of false imprisonment) that when 'the liberty of the subject is at stake questions as to the damage sustained become of little importance': see also *Murray v Ministry of Defence* [1988] 2 All ER 521 at 529 (p. 585, post). Indeed, the trespass action can be a particularly important weapon in safeguarding the freedom of the individual. Nevertheless, substantial sums of money can be awarded (e.g. *Reynolds v Metropolitan Police Comr* [1982] Crim LR 600 – £12,000 jury award for false imprisonment), and exemplary damages can be awarded against the police (see p. 408, ante).

Assault, battery and false imprisonment are torts, but they are also crimes (see *Smith & Hogan*, chap. 12), and acts giving rise to tortious liability may, therefore, involve criminal liability as well. Criminal cases are used as precedents in determining the scope of these torts, but, since the policy of the law in the two spheres may differ, some caution must be exercised when this is done. Apart from the possibility of the same act giving rise to both civil and criminal liability, a particular factual situation may well involve liability under more than one of the various torts which come within the category of trespass to the person. A battery will usually, but not always, be preceded by an assault, although each can exist independently of the other, and acts amounting to false imprisonment could in addition involve liability for assault or battery. The student should be warned, however, that the word assault is often used loosely to cover both the technical assault and the battery.

The wrongful interference principle has the potential to develop a wide area of liability which has not yet been fully explored by the courts. Very few cases have been brought to their attention (though in addition to the cases set out in this chapter, note the unreported case of *Burnett v George* in 1986, cited by R. Clayton and H. Tomlinson, *Civil Actions against the Police* (London, 1987), p. 119 and the comments of Lord Denning MR in *D v National Society for the Prevention of Cruelty to Children* [1978] AC 171 at 188-189 when that case was in the Court of Appeal). The wrongful interference principle is distinct from the trespass action, and consequently does not suffer from the disadvantages of the latter. For example, there does not appear to be any requirement that the harm be a direct consequence of the defendant's act, a limitation which could still cause problems with the trespass action. (See *Street*, p. 27, for certain cases which, he suggests, are not trespasses, but which may be actionable under this principle: see also ibid, p. 24, note 3.)

1 Trespass, intention and negligence

Fowler *v* Lanning Queen's Bench Division [1959] 1 All ER 290

DIPLOCK J: . . . The writ in this case claims damages for trespass to the person committed by the defendant at Corfe Castle, in the county of Dorset, on 19 November 1957. The statement of claim alleges laconically that at that place and on that date 'the defendant shot the plaintiff', and that by reason thereof the plaintiff sustained personal injuries and has suffered loss and damage. By his defence the defendant, in addition to traversing the allegations of fact, raises the objection

'that the statement of claim is bad in law and discloses no cause of action against him on the ground that the plaintiff does not allege that the said shooting was intentional or negligent.'

An order has been made that this point of law be disposed of before the trial of the issues of fact in the action. That order is binding on me, and, in disposing of it, I can look no further than the pleadings. I must confess that at first glance at the pleadings I felt some anxiety lest I was being invited to decide a point which has long puzzled the professors (see the article by Professors Goodhart and Winfield (1933) 49 Law Quarterly Review 359; *Pollock on Torts* (15th edn) p. 129; *Salmond on Torts* (12th edn) p. 311; *Winfield on Tort* (5th edn) p. 213), only to learn ultimately that, just as in *M'Alister* (or *Donoghue*) *v Stevenson* ([1932] AC 562), there was in fact no snail in the ginger beer bottle, so in this case there was in fact no pellet in the defendant's gun.

The point of law is not, however, a mere academic one even at the present stage of the action. The alleged injuries were, I am told, sustained at a shooting party; it is not suggested that the shooting was intentional. The practical issue is whether, if the plaintiff was in fact injured by a shot from a gun fired by the defendant, the onus lies on the plaintiff to prove that the defendant was negligent, in which case, under the modern system of pleading, he must so plead and give particulars of negligence (see RSC, Ord. 19, r. 4)[1] or whether it lies on the defendant to prove

---

1. [See now RSC, Ord. 18, r. 7(1).]

that the plaintiff's injuries were not caused by the defendant's negligence, in which case the plaintiff's statement of claim is sufficient and discloses a cause of action (see RSC, Ord. 19, r. 25).[1] The issue is thus a neat one of onus of proof.

[Having surveyed the history of this area of the law, DIPLOCK J continued:] I can summarise the law as I understand it from my examination of the cases as follows:

(1) Trespass to the person does not lie if the injury to the plaintiff, although the direct consequence of the act of the defendant, was caused unintentionally and without negligence on the defendant's part.

(2) Trespass to the person on the highway does not differ in this respect from trespass to the person committed in any other place.

(3) If it were right to say with Blackburn J in 1865[2] that negligence is a necessary ingredient of unintentional trespass only where the circumstances are such as to show that the plaintiff had taken on himself the risk of inevitable injury (i.e. injury which is the result of neither intention nor carelessness on the part of the defendant), the plaintiff must today in this crowded world be considered as taking on himself the risk of inevitable injury from any acts of his neighbour which, in the absence of damage to the plaintiff, would not in themselves be unlawful – of which discharging a gun at a shooting party in 1957 ... [is an] obvious [example]. For Blackburn J in ... *Fletcher v Rylands* ((1866) LR 1 Exch at p. 286) was in truth doing no more than stating the converse of the principle referred to by Lord Macmillan in *Read v J Lyons & Co Ltd* ([1946] 2 All ER at p. 476), that a man's freedom of action is subject only to the obligation not to infringe any duty of care which he owes to others.

(4) The onus of proving negligence, where the trespass is not intentional, lies on the plaintiff, whether the action be framed in trespass or in negligence. This has been unquestioned law in highway cases ever since *Holmes v Mather* ((1875) LR 10 Exch 261), and there is no reason in principle, nor any suggestion in the decided authorities, why it should be any different in other cases. It is, indeed, but an illustration of the rule that he who affirms must prove, which lies at the root of our law of evidence. ...

If, as I have held, the onus of proof of intention or negligence on the part of the defendant lies on the plaintiff, then, under the modern rules of pleading, he must allege either intention on the part of the defendant, or, if he relies on negligence, he must state the facts which he alleges constitute negligence. Without either of such allegations the bald statement that the defendant shot the plaintiff in unspecified circumstances with an unspecified weapon in my view discloses no cause of action. ...

[In relation to] negligent trespass to the person, there is here the bare allegation that on a particular day at a particular place 'the defendant shot the plaintiff'. In what circumstances, indeed with what weapon, from bow and arrow to atomic warhead, is not stated. So bare an allegation is consistent with the defendant's having exercised reasonable care. It may be – I know not – that, had the circumstances been set out with greater particularity, there would have been disclosed facts which themselves shouted negligence, so that the doctrine of res ipsa loquitur would have applied. In such a form the statement of claim might have disclosed a cause of action even although the word 'negligence' itself had not been used, and the plaintiff in that event would have been limited to relying for proof of negligence on the facts which he had alleged. But I have today to deal with the pleading as it stands. As it stands, it neither alleges negligence in terms nor alleges facts which, if true, would of themselves constitute negligence; nor, if counsel for the plaintiff is right, would he be bound at any time before the trial to disclose to the defendant what facts he relies on as constituting negligence.

I do not see how the plaintiff will be harmed by alleging now the facts on which

---

1. [See now RSC, Ord. 18, r. 7(3).]
2. See *Fletcher v Rylands* (1866) LR 1 Exch 265.

he ultimately intends to rely. On the contrary, for him to do so, will serve to secure justice between the parties. It offends the underlying purpose of the modern system of pleading that a plaintiff, by calling his grievance 'trespass to the person' instead of 'negligence', should force a defendant to come to trial blindfold; and I am glad to find nothing in the authorities which compels the court in this case to refrain from stripping the bandage from his eyes.

I hold that the statement of claim in its present form discloses no cause of action.

Order accordingly. Leave to make immediate amendments to statement of claim granted; consequential amendments to defence to be made within fourteen days.

Note

At the ultimate trial of the action, the plaintiff failed because he was unable to prove whose shot had caused the injury; see *The Times*, 21st and 22nd May, 1959; G. Dworkin (1959) 22 MLR 538. For general comment, see G. Williams [1959] CLJ 33.

Letang *v* Cooper Court of Appeal [1964] 2 All ER 929

LORD DENNING MR: On 10 July 1957, Mrs Letang, the plaintiff, was on holiday in Cornwall. She was staying at a hotel and thought she would sunbathe on a piece of grass where cars were parked. While she was lying there, Mr Cooper, the defendant, came into the car park driving his Jaguar motor car. He did not see her. The car went over her legs and she was injured. On 2 February 1961, more than three years after the accident, the plaintiff brought this action against the defendant for damages for loss and injury caused by (i) the negligence of the defendant in driving a motor car and (ii) the commission by the defendant of a trespass to the person. The sole question is whether the action is statute barred. The plaintiff admits that the action for negligence is barred after three years, but she claims that the action for trespass to the person is not barred until six years have elapsed. The judge has so held and awarded her £575 damages for trespass to the person.

Under the Limitation Act 1939, the period of limitation was six years in all actions founded 'on tort'; but in 1954 Parliament reduced it to three years in actions for damages for personal injuries, provided that the actions come within these words of s. 2(1) of the Law Reform (Limitation of Actions, &c.) Act 1954:

'... in the case of actions for damages for negligence, nuisance or breach of duty (whether the duty exists by virtue of a contract or of a provision made by or under a statute or independently of any contract or any such provision) where the damages claimed by the plaintiff for the negligence, nuisance or breach of duty consist of or include damages in respect of personal injuries to any person ...'[1]

The plaintiff says that these words do not cover an action for trespass to the person, and that, therefore, the time bar is not the new period of three years, but the old period of six years.

The argument, as it was developed before us, became a direct invitation to this court to go back to the old forms of action and to decide this case by reference to them. The statute bars *an action on the case*, it is said, after three years, whereas *trespass to the person* is not barred for six years. The argument was supported by reference to text-writers, such as *Salmond on Torts* (13th edn) p. 790. I must say that if we are, at this distance of time, to revive the distinction between trespass and case, we should get into the most utter confusion. The old common lawyers tied themselves

---

1. [See now s. 11 of the Limitation Act 1980.]

in knots over it, and we should find ourselves doing the same. Let me tell you some of their contortions. Under the old law, whenever one man injured another by the *direct* and immediate application of force, the plaintiff could sue the defendant in *trespass* to the person, without alleging negligence (see *Leame v Bray*),[1] whereas if the injury was only *consequential*, he had to sue in *case*. You will remember the illustration given by Fortescue J in *Reynolds v Clarke*, in 1752:[2]

'If a man throws a log into the highway and in that act it hits me, I may maintain trespass because it is an immediate wrong; but if, as it lies there, I tumble over it and receive an injury, I must bring an action upon the case because it is only prejudicial in consequence.'

Nowadays, if a man carelessly throws a piece of wood from a house into a roadway, then whether it hits the plaintiff or he tumbles over it the next moment, the action would not be *trespass* or *case*, but simply negligence. Another distinction which the old lawyers drew was this: If the driver of a horse and gig negligently ran down a passer-by, the plaintiff could sue the driver either in *trespass* or in *case* (see *Williams v Holland*, in 1833);[3] but if the driver was a servant, the plaintiff could not sue the master in trespass, but only in case (see *Sharrod v London and North Western Rly Co* in 1849).[4] In either case today, the action would not be *trespass* or *case*, but only negligence.

If we were to bring back these subtleties into the law of limitation, we should produce the most absurd anomalies; and all the more so when you bear in mind that under the Fatal Accidents Acts the period of limitation is three years from the death.[5] The decision of Elwes J, if correct, would produce these results. It would mean that if a motorist ran down two people, killing one and injuring another, the widow would have to bring her action within three years, but the injured person would have six years. It would mean also that if a lorry driver was in collision at a cross-roads with an owner-driver, an injured passenger would have to bring his action against the employer of the lorry driver within three years, but he would have six years in which to sue the owner-driver. Not least of all the absurdities is a case like the present. It would mean that the plaintiff could get out of the three-year limitation by suing in trespass instead of in negligence.

I must decline, therefore, to go back to the old forms of action in order to construe this statute. I know that in the last century Maitland said 'the forms of action we have buried but they still rule us from their graves'. But we have in this century shaken off their trammels. These forms of action have served their day. They did at one time form a guide to substantive rights; but they do so no longer. Lord Atkin told us what to do about them:

'When these ghosts of the past stand in the path of justice, clanking their mediaeval chains, the proper course for the judge is to pass through them undeterred',

see *United Australia Ltd v Barclays Bank Ltd.*[6]

The truth is that the distinction between trespass and case is obsolete. We have a different sub-division altogether. Instead of dividing actions for personal injuries into *trespass* (direct damage) or *case* (consequential damage), we divide the causes

---

1. (1803) 3 East 593.
2. (1725) 1 Stra 634 at 636.
3. (1833) 10 Bing 112.
4. (1849) 4 Exch 580.
5. [See now ss. 12–14 and 33 of the Limitation Act 1980.]
6. [1941] AC 1 at 29, [1940] 4 All ER 20 at 37.

of action now according as the defendant did the injury intentionally or unintentionally. If one man intentionally applies force directly to another, the plaintiff has
a cause of action in assault and battery, or, if you so please to describe it, in trespass
to the person. 'The least touching of another in anger is a battery.' If he does not
inflict injury intentionally, but only unintentionally, the plaintiff has no cause of
action today in trespass. His only cause of action is in negligence, and then only on
proof of want of reasonable care. If the plaintiff cannot prove want of reasonable
care, he may have no cause of action at all. Thus, it is not enough nowadays for the
plaintiff to plead that 'the defendant shot the plaintiff'.[1] He must also allege that he
did it intentionally or negligently. If intentional, it is the tort of assault and battery.
If negligent and causing damage, it is the tort of negligence.

The modern law on this subject was well expounded by my brother Diplock J in
Fowler v Lanning[2] with which I fully agree. But I would go this one step further:
when the injury is not inflicted intentionally, but negligently, I would say that the
only cause of action is negligence and not trespass. If it were trespass, it would be
actionable without proof of damage; and that is not the law today.

In my judgment, therefore, the only cause of action in the present case (where the
injury was unintentional) is negligence and is barred by reason of the express provision of the statute.

[LORD DENNING then went on to deal with the position if, contrary to his view,
the plaintiff had a cause of action in trespass, and decided that the phrase 'breach
of duty' in the relevant legislation covered a cause of action in trespass. He
continued:]

I come, therefore, to the clear conclusion that the plaintiff's cause of action here
is barred by the statute of limitation. Her only cause of action here, in my judgment
(where the damage was unintentional), was negligence and not trespass to the person.
It is therefore barred by the word 'negligence' in the statute; but even if it was trespass
to the person, it was an action for 'breach of duty' and is barred on that ground also.

I would allow the appeal accordingly.

DIPLOCK LJ: A cause of action is simply a factual situation the existence of which
entitles one person to obtain from the court a remedy against another person.
Historically the means by which the remedy was obtained varied with the nature of
the factual situation and causes of action were divided into categories according to
the 'form of action' by which the remedy was obtained in the particular kind of
factual situation which constituted the cause of action; but that is legal history, not
current law. If A, by failing to exercise reasonable care, inflicts direct personal injury
on B, those facts constitute a cause of action on the part of B against A for damages
in respect of such personal injuries. The remedy for this cause of action could, before
1873, have been obtained by alternative forms of action, namely, originally either
trespass vi et armis or trespass on the case, later either trespass to the person or
negligence. (See Bullen and Leake's *Precedents of Pleadings*, 3rd edn.) Certain
procedural consequences, the importance of which diminished considerably after the
Common Law Procedure Act 1852, flowed from the plaintiff's pleader's choice of
the form of action used. The Supreme Court of Judicature Act 1873, abolished forms
of action. It did not affect causes of action; so it was convenient for lawyers and
legislators to continue to use, to describe the various categories of factual situations
which entitled one person to obtain from the court a remedy against another, the
names of the various 'forms of action' by which formerly the remedy appropriate to
the particular category of factual situation was obtained. But it is essential to realise
that when, since 1873, the name of a form of action is used to identify a cause of
action, it is used as a convenient and succinct description of a particular category of

---

1. See *Fowler v Lanning* [1959] 1 QB 426; [1959] 1 All ER 290.
2. [1959] 1 QB 426; [1959] 1 All ER 290.

factual situation which entitles one person to obtain from the court a remedy against another person. To forget this will indeed encourage the old forms of action to rule us from their graves.

If A, by failing to exercise reasonable care, inflicts direct personal injuries on B, it is permissible today to describe this factual situation indifferently, either as a cause of action in negligence or as a cause of action in trespass, and the action brought to obtain a remedy for this factual situation as an action for negligence or an action for trespass to the person − though I agree with Lord Denning MR that today 'negligence' is the expression to be preferred. But no procedural consequences flow from the choice of description by the pleader (see *Fowler v Lanning*).[1] They are simply alternative ways of describing the same factual situation.

In the judgment under appeal, Elwes J[2] has held that the Law Reform (Limitation of Actions, &c.) Act 1954, has, by s. 2(1) created an important difference in the remedy to which B is entitled in the factual situation postulated according to whether he chooses to describe it as negligence or as trespass to the person. If he selects the former description, the limitation period is three years; if he selects the latter, the limitation period is six years. The terms of the subsection have already been cited, and I need not repeat them.

The factual situation on which the plaintiff's action was founded is set out in the statement of claim. It was that the defendant, by failing to exercise reasonable care (of which failure particulars were given), drove his motor car over the plaintiff's legs and so inflicted on her direct personal injuries in respect of which the plaintiff claimed damages. That factual situation was the plaintiff's cause of action. It was the cause of action 'for' which the plaintiff claimed damages in respect of the personal injuries which she sustained. That cause of action or factual situation falls within the description of the tort of 'negligence' and an action founded on it, that is, brought to obtain the remedy to which the existence of that factual situation entitles the plaintiff, falls within the description of an 'action for negligence'. The description 'negligence' was in fact used by the plaintiff's pleader; but this cannot be decisive, for we are concerned not with the description applied by the pleader to the factual situation and the action founded on it, but with the description applied to it by Parliament in the enactment to be construed. It is true that that factual situation also falls within the description of the tort of 'trespass to the person'. But that, as I have endeavoured to show, does not mean that there are two causes of action. It merely means that there are two apt descriptions of the same cause of action. It does not cease to be the tort of 'negligence', because it can also be called by another name. An action founded on it is none the less an 'action for negligence' because it can also be called an 'action for trespass to the person'.

It is not, I think, necessary to consider whether there is today any respect in which a cause of action for unintentional as distinct from intentional 'trespass to the person' is not equally aptly described as a cause of action for 'negligence'. The difference stressed by Elwes J[2] that actual damage caused by failure to exercise reasonable care forms an essential element in the cause of action for 'negligence', but does not in the cause of action in 'trespass to the person', is, I think, more apparent than real when the trespass is unintentional; for, since the duty of care, whether in negligence or in unintentional trespass to the person, is to take reasonable care to avoid causing actual damage to one's neighbour, there is no breach of the duty unless actual damage is caused. Actual damage is thus a necessary ingredient in unintentional as distinct from intentional trespass to the person. Whether this be so or not, the subsection which falls to be construed is concerned only with actions in which actual damage in the form of personal injuries has in fact been sustained by the plaintiff. Where this factor is present, every factual situation which falls within the description 'trespass

1. [1959] 1 QB 426; [1959] 1 All ER 290.
2. [1964] 1 All ER 669 at 673.

to the person' is, where the trespass is unintentional, equally aptly described as negligence.

I am, therefore, of opinion that the facts pleaded in the present action make it an 'action for negligence . . . where the damages claimed by the plaintiff for the negligence . . . consist of or include damages in respect of personal injuries to' the plaintiff, within the meaning of the subsection,[1] and that the limitation period was three years.

In this respect I agree with the judgment of Adam J in the only direct authority on this point, the Victorian case of *Kruber v Grzesiak*.[2] To his lucid reasoning I am much indebted. This is yet another illustration of the assistance to be obtained from the citation of relevant decisions of courts in other parts of the Commonwealth, and I am particularly grateful to counsel for the defendant and those instructing him for drawing our attention to this case. I agree, however, with my brethren and with Adam J that this action also falls within the words 'action . . . for breach of duty (whether the duty exists by virtue of a contract or of a provision made by or under a statute or independently of any contract or any such provision)'. I say 'also falls', for in the absence of the word 'other' before 'breach of duty' that expression as explained by the words in parenthesis is itself wide enough to include 'negligence' and 'nuisance'. . . .

[DANCKWERTS LJ agreed with LORD DENNING MR.]

Appeal allowed

Questions

1. What do you understand by the 'forms of action'?

2. Shepherd threw a lighted squib into a crowded market house where it landed on the stall of Yates, a gingerbread seller. Willis, to prevent injury to himself and Yates' wares, instantly took up the squib and threw it across the market house, where it fell upon the stall of Ryal, who, to save his own goods, in turn picked it up and threw it away. It struck the plaintiff in the face and burst, putting out one of his eyes. In *Scott v Shepherd* (1773) 2 Wm Bl 892, the majority of the Court of King's Bench held that an action of trespass was properly brought against Shepherd. Blackstone J (dissenting) was of the opinion that Willis and Ryal, being free agents, were not 'instruments' in the hands of Shepherd, and so the damage was not sufficiently 'direct' for trespass to be maintainable. How would this case be pleaded today?

3. Does an action for trespass lie if the injury, though direct, was caused neither intentionally nor by negligence?

4. D accidentally parked his car on P's foot but refused to remove it when asked several times to do so. He then relented and moved the car. How would you plead this as a civil case, assuming alternatively that (a) P's foot was injured; (b) P suffered only momentary distress but no physical injury? (Cf. *Fagan v Metropolitan Police Comr* [1969] 1 QB 439; [1968] 3 All ER 442.)

---

1. Law Reform (Limitation of Actions, &c.) Act 1954, s. 2(1).
2. [1963] VLR 621.

Notes

1. Those interested in exploring the history of trespass and case will derive pleasure from the research of S. F. C. Milsom, *Historical Foundations of the Common Law* 2nd edn (London, 1981), chap. 11, and his earlier articles (1958) 74 LQR 195, 407 and 561; (1965) 81 LQR 496; [1954] CLJ 105. M. J. Prichard [1964] CLJ 234 provides an illuminating account of the line of cases which decided that the action upon the case for negligence overlapped trespass; more generally see also the same author's Selden Society Lecture (published in 1976) entitled '*Scott v Shepherd* (1773) and the Emergence of the Tort of Negligence'.

2. A number of technical distinctions between negligent trespass to the person and the tort of negligence are suggested by F. A. Trindade (1971) 20 ICLQ 706, but these would probably require the English courts to depart from *Fowler v Lanning* and *Letang v Cooper*; and see further A. J. Harding and K. F. Tan (1980) 22 Mal LR 29 at 32–33.

In *Miller v Jackson* [1977] QB 966; [1977] 3 All ER 338 Lord Denning MR reiterated his view (described as 'judicial legislation' by Bray CJ in *Venning v Chin* (1974–75) 10 SASR 299 at 307) that where injury is inflicted unintentionally, an action would not lie in trespass but only in negligence; and in *Wilson v Pringle* [1987] QB 237; [1986] 2 All ER 440 the idea that an action in trespass cannot be brought if the defendant has acted negligently met with support in the Court of Appeal. One question that was discussed in *Wilson v Pringle*, however, was whether the necessary intention for a trespass action to be available had to relate to the contact with the plaintiff or to the infliction of the injury. Counsel for the defendant argued that it was both, citing passages from *Fowler v Lanning* (Diplock J's first proposition, p. 571, ante) and *Letang v Cooper*. It will have been seen that in *Letang v Cooper* Lord Denning does distinguish between trespass and negligence in terms of the injury being inflicted intentionally or unintentionally (see p. 574, ante). However, in the Court of Appeal's view in *Wilson v Pringle* it was only the defendant's act which had to be intentional in a trespass action and neither Lord Denning's judgment nor Diplock J's first proposition in *Fowler v Lanning* were intended to support a requirement of intention to injure in such a case (see [1987] QB at p. 249). For support for this view, see F. A. Trindade (1982) 2 Oxf JLS 211 at 219–220 (and note ibid pp. 220–225 for discussion of the nature of intention in this context) and consider *Weldon v Home Office* [1990] 3 WLR 465 at 470 in the context of false imprisonment.

3. In *Williams v Humphrey* (1975) Times, 20th February the defendant pushed the plaintiff into a swimming pool with the result that the latter was injured when his foot struck the side of the pool. The defendant did not intend to cause any harm, but Talbot J found that the reasonable man would have foreseen the likelihood of harm to the plaintiff and the plaintiff succeeded in negligence. However, Talbot J went on to say that he could also succeed in trespass on proof that the defendant acted intentionally. Is this duality of action consistent with Lord Denning's judgment in *Letang v Cooper*? See further Trindade (1982) 2 Oxf JLS at 212–213; cf. *Paterson Zochonis & Co Ltd v Merfarken Packaging Ltd* [1986] 3 All ER 522 at 541. Note also that in *Wilson v Pringle* the reasoning in *Williams v Humphrey*

was said not to have gone far enough in that it did not require an element of 'hostility', but on this requirement see p. 580 and p. 602, post. Trindade's article should also be consulted more generally in relation to the next section.

4. Writers have asserted that negligence would be a sufficient state of mind for the tort of false imprisonment. The issue was raised recently in Ralph Gibson LJ's judgment in *Weldon v Home Office* [1990] 3 WLR 465 at 470, but his Lordship found it unnecessary to consider the point. If *Letang v Cooper* is followed, what is the position today of someone who is negligently falsely imprisoned? See Harding and Tan, op cit. If no actual damage is suffered, then there is no action in negligence. Cf. *Winfield & Jolowicz*, p. 59, note 52 who suggest that 'being deprived of one's liberty for a substantial period is surely damage'; and see further P. G. Heffey (1983) 14 Melb ULR 53 at 57-64.

2 Assault and battery

Stephens *v* Myers Nisi Prius (1830) 4 C & P 349

Assault. The declaration stated, that the defendant threatened and attempted to assault the plaintiff. Plea—Not guilty.

It appeared, that the plaintiff was acting as chairman, at a parish meeting, and sat at the head of a table, at which table the defendant also sat, there being about six or seven persons between him and the plaintiff. The defendant having, in the course of some angry discussion, which took place, been very vociferous, and interrupted the proceedings of the meeting, a motion was made, that he should be turned out, which was carried by a very large majority. Upon this, the defendant said, he would rather pull the chairman out of the chair, than be turned out of the room; and immediately advanced with his fist clenched towards the chairman, but was stopt by the churchwarden, who sat next but one to the chairman, at a time when he was not near enough for any blow he might have meditated to have reached the chairman; but the witnesses said, that it seemed to them that he was advancing with an intention to strike the chairman.

Spankie, Serjt., for the defendant, upon this evidence, contended, that no assault had been committed, as there was no power in the defendant, from the situation of the parties, to execute his threat—there was not a present ability—he had not the means of executing his intention at the time he was stopt.

TINDAL CJ in his summing up, said—It is not every threat, when there is no actual personal violence, that constitutes an assault, there must, in all cases, be the means of carrying the threat into effect. The question I shall leave to you will be, whether the defendant was advancing at the time, in a threatening attitude, to strike the chairman, so that his blow would almost immediately have reached the chairman, if he had not been stopt; then, though he was not near enough at the time to have struck him, yet if he was advancing with that intent, I think it amounts to an assault in law. If he was so advancing, that, within a second or two of time, he would have reached the plaintiff, it seems to me it is an assault in law. If you think he was not advancing to strike the plaintiff, then only can you find your verdict for the defendant; otherwise you must find it for the plaintiff, and give him such damages, as you think the nature of the case requires.

Verdict for the plaintiff—Damages, 1s.

Questions

1. Would there have been an assault in this case if the defendant 'was not advancing to strike the plaintiff', but the plaintiff reasonably believed that he was?

2. Would there be sufficient immediacy for an assault if the defendant, having entered an enclosed garden in the evening, intentionally frightened the plaintiff by looking through a closed window at her? (Consider *Smith v Chief Superintendent, Woking Police Station* (1983) 76 Cr App Rep 234.) What if the window had bars on it?

Note

It was said recently in *Thomas v National Union of Mineworkers (South Wales Area)* [1986] Ch 20; [1985] 2 All ER 1 that there had to be the ability to carry out the immediate intention to commit the battery at the time the act (accompanied by the intention) occurred. But note that this comment was made in the context of a situation in which the inability so to act would have been apparent. A particular problem which has arisen in this area is whether it is an assault to point a gun at a person when that gun is unloaded. In *R v St George* (1840) 9 C & P 483, a criminal case, Parke B stated in the course of argument (at p. 490), that 'it is an assault to point a weapon at a person, though not loaded, but so near, that if loaded, it might do injury' (see also p. 493). Whether the ratio decidendi of the case covers this point is a matter on which the textbooks differ — *Winfield & Jolowicz*, 12th edn, p. 56; *Street*, p. 26. The view of Lord Abinger CB in *Blake v Barnard* (1840) 9 C & P 626 is in conflict with that of Parke B but the ratio of this case is also disputed — see *Winfield & Jolowicz*, 12th edn, p. 56, note 28, and *Street*, p. 25, note 14. The case of *Logdon v DPP* [1976] Crim LR 121, however, seems to support the view stated by Parke B.

Tuberville *v* Savage Court of King's Bench (1669) 1 Mod Rep 3

Action of *assault*, *battery* and *wounding*. The evidence to prove a provocation was, that the plaintiff put his hand upon his sword and said, '*If it were not assize-time, I would not take such language from you.*' — The question was, If that were an assault? — The Court agreed that it was not; for the declaration of the plaintiff was, that he would not assault him, the Judges being in town; and *the intention* as well as *the act* makes an assault. Therefore if one strike another upon the hand, or arm, or breast in discourse, it is no assault, there being no *intention* to assault; but if one, intending to assault, strike *at* another and miss him, this is an assault: so if he hold up his hand against another in a threatening manner and say nothing, it is an assault. — In the principal case the plaintiff had judgment.

Question

Would there have been an assault if, as both parties knew, the assizes were ending that day?

Note

As *Tuberville v Savage* shows, words accompanying an act may lead the court to deny that there has been any assault, but there is a conflict of authority on the question whether words alone can amount to an assault. Compare *Meade and Belt's* case (1823) 1 Lewin 184, where Holroyd J denied that words were 'equivalent to an assault', with *R v Wilson* [1955] 1 All ER 744 at 745: 'He called out "Get out knives", which itself would be an assault . . .' (per Lord Goddard CJ). Both were criminal cases. See further *Ansell v Thomas* [1974] Crim LR 31 (a civil case) and see generally G. Williams [1957] Crim LR 219; P. R. Handford (1976) 54 Can Bar Rev 563 at 568–573; Trindade (1982) 2 Oxf JLS at pp. 231–233.

Cole *v* Turner Nisi Prius (1704) 6 Mod Rep 149

HOLT CJ: Upon evidence in trespass for assault and battery, declared,
   First, that the least touching of another in anger is a battery.
   Secondly, if two or more meet in a narrow passage, and without any violence or design of harm, the one touches the other gently, it will be no battery.
   Thirdly, if any of them use violence against the other, to force his way in a rude inordinate manner, it will be a battery; or any struggle about the passage to that degree as may do hurt, will be a battery. . . .

Note

It will have been seen that Holt CJ refers to the touching of another 'in anger' as being a battery. More recently, in *Wilson v Pringle* [1987] QB 237; [1986] 2 All ER 440 the Court of Appeal, relying, amongst other authorities, on *Cole v Turner*, asserted that for the touching of another to be a battery it has to be 'hostile'; they did not think it 'practicable to define a battery as "physical contact which is not generally acceptable in the ordinary conduct of daily life"'. This latter view had been expressed by Robert Goff LJ when discussing the defences in this area of the law in the Divisional Court in *Collins v Wilcock* [1984] 3 All ER 374; [1984] 1 WLR 1172, part of which is set out p. 599, post.
   Having asserted the 'hostility' requirement, the Court of Appeal in *Wilson v Pringle* continued (at pp. 447–448):

'Hostility cannot be equated with ill-will or malevolence. It cannot be governed by the obvious intention shown in acts like punching, stabbing or shooting. It cannot be solely governed by an expressed intention, although that may be strong evidence. But the element of hostility, in the sense in which it is now to be considered, must be a question of fact for the tribunal of fact. It may be imported from the circumstances. Take the example of the police officer in *Collins v Wilcock*. She touched the woman deliberately, but without an intention to do more than restrain her temporarily. Nevertheless, she was acting unlawfully and in that way was acting with hostility. She was acting contrary to the woman's legal right not to be physically restrained.'

This example shows that in this context 'hostility' can take on a meaning rather wider than its everyday sense. Is the penultimate sentence of this passage from *Wilson v Pringle* an example of circular reasoning? (See Clayton and Tomlinson, op cit, p. 106, who also argue that the 'hostility' requirement is not supported by the authorities.)

What is the relationship between the 'hostility' requirement and Robert Goff LJ's 'generally acceptable conduct' exception to battery in *Collins v Wilcock*? *Wilson v Pringle* seems to be requiring the element of hostility without necessarily rejecting the idea of cases failing on the 'generally acceptable conduct' category, although some cases would fail on either ground. See further p. 599, post.

The two cases were discussed in *T v T* [1988] Fam 52, [1988] 1 All ER 613 (where Robert Goff LJ's analysis was found by Wood J to be of greater assistance than the analysis in *Wilson v Pringle*) and in *Re F* [1990] 2 AC 1, sub nom *F v West Berkshire Health Authority (Mental Health Act Commission intervening)* [1989] 2 All ER 545 (p. 599, post). Particular attention should be paid to the latter decision in this context for it will be seen that Lord Goff reiterated his approach in *Collins v Wilcock* and expressed doubt about the 'hostility' requirement. Generally see further p. 599, post.

Innes *v* Wylie Nisi Prius (1844) 1 Car & Kir 257

The plaintiff belonged to a Society which purported to expel him, and a policeman, acting under the defendants' orders, stopped the plaintiff from entering a room to attend a dinner of the Society. For reasons which need not be mentioned here, Lord Denman CJ took the view that the expulsion was invalid, but his summing up to the jury also dealt with the question of assault.

LORD DENMAN CJ: . . . You will say, whether, on the evidence, you think that the policeman committed an assault on the plaintiff, or was merely passive. If the policeman was entirely passive like a door or a wall put to prevent the plaintiff from entering the room, and simply obstructing the entrance of the plaintiff, no assault has been committed on the plaintiff, and your verdict will be for the defendant. The question is, did the policeman take any active measures to prevent the plaintiff from entering the room, or did he stand in the door-way passive, and not move at all.

Verdict for the plaintiff, damages 40*s*.

[A motion for a new trial was later made, but without success.]

The Offences Against the Person Act 1861

44[1]. If the magistrates shall dismiss any complaint of assault or battery, they shall make out a certificate to that effect. — If the justices, upon the hearing of any case of assault or battery upon the merits, where the complaint[2] was preferred by or on behalf of the party aggrieved, shall deem the offence not to be proved, or shall find the assault or battery to have been justified, or so trifling as not to merit any punishment, and shall accordingly dismiss the complaint,[2] they shall forthwith make out a certificate under their hands stating the fact of such dismissal, and shall deliver such certificate to the party against whom the complaint[2] was preferred.

45. Certificate or conviction shall be a bar to any other proceedings. — If any person against whom any such complaint[2] as [is mentioned in section 44 of this Act][3] shall have been preferred by or on the behalf of the party aggrieved shall have obtained

---

1. [As amended by the Criminal Justice Act 1988, s. 170, Sch. 15 and Sch. 16.]
2. [The word should now be read as 'information' — Magistrates' Courts Act 1980, s 50.]
3. [Added by the Criminal Justice Act 1988, s. 170 and Sch. 15].

such certificate, or, having been convicted, shall have paid the whole amount adjudged to be paid, or shall have suffered the imprisonment or imprisonment with hard labour[1] awarded, in every such case he shall be released from all further or other proceedings, civil or criminal, for the same cause.

Notes

1. The problems of interpretation of these provisions are considered by P. M. North (1966) 29 MLR 16 who points out incidentally that the rule which bars later civil proceedings 'can easily be evaded by the simple expedient of suing first and making a complaint later'. He concludes (at p. 31): 'The moral is: sue first. This does not detract from the conclusion that section 45 does appear to be based upon the fallacious assumption that the rules of civil and criminal liability for assault and battery are identical.'

2. In 1980 the Criminal Law Revision Committee's Fourteenth Report (*Offences Against the Person*, Cmnd. 7844) recommended repeal (without replacement) of ss. 44 and 45 of the 1861 Act (paras. 163–164); but no such legislative activity has occurred. Consider further the proposals of the Law Commission in *A Criminal Code for England and Wales* (Law Com. No. 177), H. C. 299 Session 1988–89.

3. Under s. 35 of the Powers of Criminal Courts Act 1973 (as amended by s. 67 of the Criminal Justice Act 1982 and s. 104 of the Criminal Justice Act 1988), where a person is convicted of an offence, the court may 'make an order . . . requiring him to pay compensation for any personal injury, loss or damage resulting from that offence or any other offence which is taken into consideration by the court in determining sentence or to make payments for funeral expenses or bereavement in respect of a death resulting from any such offence, other than a death due to an accident arising out of the presence of a motor vehicle on a road'. Furthermore, a court is obliged to give reasons if it does not make an order when it could do so under this section. Subsection 3 contains provisions limiting the situations in which compensation orders can be made in relation to injury, loss or damage resulting from road accidents involving a motor vehicle. Subsections 3C and 3D also limit compensation orders in relation to bereavement: such an order can only be made for the benefit of anyone entitled to claim such damages under the Fatal Accidents Act 1976 (p. 241, ante) and the amount awarded may not exceed the amount fixed under that legislation. The means of the offender must be considered by the court (s. 35(4) but see s. 35(4A)). Where later civil proceedings are brought, no attention should be paid to an earlier compensation order in *assessing* the damages 'but the plaintiff may only recover an amount equal to the aggregate of the following — (*a*) any amount by which they exceed the compensation; and (*b*) a sum equal to any portion of the compensation which he fails to recover' (s. 38, as substituted by s. 105 of the Criminal Justice Act 1988). (Enforcement of the judgment, so far as it relates to this latter sum, requires the leave of the court.) See further s. 37 (also as substituted by s. 105 of the Criminal Justice Act 1988) dealing with the review of an order. Note also that there is a limit imposed on the amount

---

1. [The courts may no longer sentence to imprisonment with hard labour: Criminal Justice Act 1948, s. 1(2).]

magistrates' courts can award under a compensation order (s. 40 of the Magistrates' Courts Act 1980). At the time of writing it stood at £2,000 (S.I. 1984 No. 447). P. S. Atiyah [1979] Crim LR 504 pointed to the uncertainty surrounding the question whether a compensation order could be made in a case in which there could be no civil liability but it was later held in *R v Chappell* (1985) 80 Cr App Rep 31 that civil liability is not a precondition to the making of a compensation order. Guidelines on compensation orders, including the level of awards (the latter having been prepared by the Criminal Injuries Compensation Board), have been issued by the Home Office: for the main provision, see H. O. Circular No. 85/1988.

For discussion of compensation orders prior to the amendments made by the Criminal Justice Act 1988 (on which see D. Miers [1989] Crim LR 32 at 32–38), see the Report of the Hodgson Committee on the Profits of Crime and their Recovery (published under the auspices of the Howard League for Penal Reform, 1984), pp. 46–62 and 65–66, the First Report from the House of Commons Home Affairs Select Committee, *Compensation and Support for Victims of Crime*, H.C. 43, Session 1984/85, pp. xiv–xxi and the Government's reply, Cmnd. 9457, 1985. For comment of the Hodgson Committee's Report, see M. Wasik [1984] Crim LR 708 at 713–717.

4. A person who has been intentionally injured may recover compensation from the Criminal Injuries Compensation Board, but note para. 21 of the scheme, p. 924, post.

3   False imprisonment

Murray *v* Ministry of Defence House of Lords [1988] 2 All ER 521

For the purposes of this extract it is sufficient to say that one issue raised in the case concerned an unsuccessful claim for damages for false imprisonment for a period from 7 a.m. to 7.30 a.m., that the House of Lords held that the plaintiff had been under arrest (under s. 14 of the Northern Ireland (Emergency Provisions) Act 1978) during this period, and that the House rejected the challenge to the legality of the arrest.

LORD GRIFFITHS: ... Although on the facts of this case I am sure that the plaintiff was aware of the restraint on her liberty from 7.00 am, I cannot agree with the [Northern Ireland] Court of Appeal that it is an essential element of the tort of false imprisonment that the victim should be aware of the fact of denial of liberty. The Court of Appeal relied on *Herring v Boyle* (1834) 1 Cr M & R 377, 149 ER 1126 for this proposition which they preferred to the view of Atkin LJ to the opposite effect in *Meering v Grahame-White Aviation Co Ltd* (1919) 122 LT 44. *Herring v Boyle* is an extraordinary decision of the Court of Exchequer: a mother went to fetch her 10-year-old son from school on 24 December 1833 to take him home for the Christmas holidays. The headmaster refused to allow her to take her son home because she had not paid the last term's fees, and he kept the boy at school over the holidays. An action for false imprisonment brought on behalf of the boy failed. In giving judgement Bolland B said (1 Cr M & R 377 at 381, 149 ER 1126 at 1127):

'. . . as far as we know, the boy may have been willing to stay; he does not appear to have been cognizant of any restraint, and there was no evidence of any act whatsoever done by the defendant in his presence. I think that we cannot construe the refusal to the mother in the boy's absence, and without his being cognizant of any restraint, to be an imprisonment of him against his will . . .'

I suppose it is possible that there are schoolboys who prefer to stay at school rather than go home for the holidays but it is not an inference that I would draw, and I cannot believe that on the same facts the case would be similarly decided today. In *Meering v Grahame-White Aviation Co Ltd* the plaintiff's employers, who suspected him of theft, sent two of the works police to bring him in for questioning at the company's offices. He was taken to a waiting-room where he said that if he was not told why he was there he would leave. He was told he was wanted for the purpose of making inquiries about things that had been stolen and he was wanted to give evidence; he then agreed to stay. Unknown to the plaintiff, the works police had been instructed not to let him leave the waiting-room until the Metropolitan Police arrived. The works police therefore remained outside the waiting-room and would not have allowed the plaintiff to leave until he was handed over to the Metropolitan Police, who subsequently arrested him. The question for the Court of Appeal was whether on this evidence the plaintiff was falsely imprisoned during the hour he was in the waiting-room, or whether there could be no 'imprisonment' sufficient to found a civil action unless the plaintiff was aware of the restraint on his liberty. Atkin LJ said (122 LT 44 at 53–54):

'It appears to me that a person could be imprisoned without his knowing it. I think a person can be imprisoned while he is asleep, while he is in a state of drunkenness, while he is unconscious, and while he is a lunatic. Those are cases where it seems to me that the person might properly complain if he were imprisoned, though the imprisonment began and ceased while he was in that state. Of course, the damages might be diminished and would be affected by the question whether he was conscious of it or not. So a man might in fact, to my mind, be imprisoned by having the key of a door turned against him so that he is imprisoned in a room in fact although he does not know that the key has been turned. It may be that he is being detained in that room by persons who are anxious to make him believe that he is not in fact being imprisoned, and at the same time his captors outside that room may be boasting to persons that he is imprisoned, and it seems to me that if we were to take this case as an instance supposing it could be proved that Prudence had said while the plaintiff was waiting: "I have got him detained there waiting for the detective to come in and take him to prison" – it appears to me that that would be evidence of imprisonment. It is quite unnecessary to go on to show that in fact the man knew that he was imprisoned. If a man can be imprisoned by having the key turned upon him without his knowledge, so he can be imprisoned if, instead of a lock and key or bolts and bars, he is prevented from, in fact, exercising his liberty by guards and warders or policemen. They serve the same purpose. Therefore it appears to me to be a question of fact. It is true that in all cases of imprisonment so far as the law of civil liberty is concerned that "stone walls do not a prison make," in the sense that they are not the only form of imprisonment, but any restraint within defined bounds which is a restraint in fact may be an imprisonment.'

I agree with this passage. In the first place it is not difficult to envisage cases in which harm may result from unlawful imprisonment even though the victim is unaware of it. Dean William L Prosser gave two examples in 'False Imprisonment: Consciousness of Confinement' (1955) 55 Col LR 847, in which he attacked § 42 of the American Law Institute's Restatement of the Law of Torts, which at that time stated the rule that 'there is no liability for intentionally confining another unless the person physically restrained knows of the confinement'. Dean Prosser wrote (at 849):

'Let us consider several illustrations. A locks B, a child two days old, in the vault of a bank. B is, of course, unconscious of the confinement, but the bank vault cannot be opened for two days. In the meantime, B suffers from hunger and thirst, and his health is seriously impaired; or it may be that he even dies. Is this no tort? Or suppose that A abducts B, a wealthy lunatic, and holds him for ransom for a week. B is unaware of his confinement, but vaguely understands that he is in unfamiliar surroundings, and that something is wrong. He undergoes mental suffering affecting his health. At the end of the week, he is discovered by the police and released without ever having known that he has been imprisoned. Has he no action against B? ... If a child of two is kidnapped, confined, and deprived of the care of its mother for a month, is the kidnapping and the confinement in itself so minor a matter as to call for no redress in tort at all?'

The Restatement of the Law of Torts has now been changed and requires that the person confined 'is conscious of the confinement or is harmed by it' (see Restatement of the Law, Second, Torts 2nd (1965) § 35, p. 52).

   If a person is unaware that he has been falsely imprisoned and has suffered no harm, he can normally expect to recover no more than nominal damages, and it is tempting to redefine the tort in the terms of the present rule in the American Law Institute's Restatement of the Law of Torts. On reflection, however, I would not do so. The law attaches supreme importance to the liberty of the individual and if he suffers a wrongful interference with that liberty it should remain actionable even without proof of special damage. . . .

[LORD KEITH OF KINKEL, LORD TEMPLEMAN, LORD OLIVER OF AYLMERTON and LORD JAUNCEY OF TULLICHETTLE agreed with LORD GRIFFITHS' speech.]

Notes

1. In *Murray v Ministry of Defence* Lord Griffiths mentioned that, in the absence of knowledge of the imprisonment and of any harm, the plaintiff can normally only expect to be awarded nominal damages. It should be noted that in appropriate circumstances—see p. 407, ante—exemplary damages would be available to such a person.

2 Writing before the House of Lords' decision in *Murray*, *Street*, p. 31 states:

'Whether *Herring v Boyle* is to be preferred to the *Meering* case raises fundamental issues of the function of the law of torts. Is it solely a means of adjusting losses between individuals in which case the former decision must be preferred as the plaintiff unaware of his imprisonment may suffer no injury? Or does tort properly have a deterrent function to prevent wrongful behaviour and reinforce civil liberties?'

Note further Question 3, p. 594, post. Consider also A. L. Goodhart's criticism ((1934–5) 83 U Pa LR 411 at 418) that Atkin LJ in the *Meering* case 'seems to confuse in his argument the question of false imprisonment with that of slander'.

3. The point that the plaintiff in a false imprisonment action does not have to be aware of the restraint was reiterated by Ralph Gibson LJ (whose judgment met with agreement from Parker and Fox LJJ) in *Weldon v Home Office* [1990] 3 WLR 465 at 469–470. His Lordship then quoted the latter part of the passage from Atkin LJ's judgment in the *Meering* case which has been set out p. 584, ante, and continued:

'It is clear that the policy of the law is jealously to protect personal liberty. Thus, it appears that, if a man is without justification confined in a room, it would be no defence to show that, if he had not been locked in, he would not in fact have had occasion to leave the room during the period of time over which he was so confined, although . . . that would be relevant to damages. The wrong done is the infringement of the right to the ability to leave and go elsewhere. Further, it would appear to follow that, if a man should be under some restraint not to leave a particular place for a period of time, for example, because he does not have the means to leave, or because he has contracted to stay there to guard the place, or because, as a soldier or policeman, he has been ordered to remain there, he could, nevertheless, claim damages for false imprisonment if, without justification, he should be imprisoned within that place. The immediate and wholly unrestricted freedom and ability to go somewhere else are not, therefore, a precondition for asserting a claim in false imprisonment.'

The Court of Appeal in *Weldon* then proceeded to decide that, even though a prisoner was serving a sentence which justified his detention in prison (see s. 12 of the Prison Act 1952), it was possible for him to be falsely imprisoned within the confines of that prison: an example given was if a prison officer intentionally and unjustifiably sent a prisoner to his cell at a time when, under the rules in the prison, he was entitled to associate with other inmates. Prisoners enjoyed a 'residual liberty' within the prison. Ralph Gibson LJ was disposed to think, however, that bad faith on the part of the prison officer would have to be proved. See, however, *R v Deputy Governor of Parkhurst Prison, ex p Hague* [1990] 3 All ER 687; [1990] 3 WLR 1210, a later Court of Appeal decision which asserted that, apart from a case where a prisoner was kept in intolerable conditions, an action for false imprisonment would not lie against the prison authorities because of the general power justifying imprisonment under s. 12 of the Prison Act 1952.

The view that the conditions of imprisonment could be so intolerable as to render an otherwise lawful imprisonment unlawful, which was accepted in *Weldon* and *Hague*, had previously been approved in the Court of Appeal in 1985 in *Middleweek v Chief Constable of the Merseyside Police* [1990] 3 All ER 662; [1990] 3 WLR 481. An example given in *Middleweek* was where a cell became and remained badly flooded thereby seriously prejudicing the health of the prisoner. In *Weldon* Ralph Gibson LJ thought that the 'better view' was that the plaintiff would also have to show bad faith, but in *Hague* this view was rejected, Taylor LJ pointing out that Ralph Gibson LJ had not come to a final conclusion on the issue.

Middleweek involved the detention of an arrested person and in *Weldon* and *Hague* the detention of convicted prisoners was in issue, but the doctrine propounded in these cases would presumably apply outside these two contexts. It would appear that the imprisonment becomes unlawful because the statutory authority justifying it is interpreted as not covering this situation. A similar process of construction could apply in a case where the justification for imprisonment was contract or some other form of consent. The issue is, therefore, connected with the defences to false imprisonment.

Bird *v* Jones Court of Queen's Bench (1845) 7 QB 742

The following statement of facts is taken from the judgment of Patteson J: 'A part of Hammersmith Bridge which is ordinarily used as a public footway was appropriated for seats to view a regatta on the river, and separated for that purpose from the carriage way by a temporary fence. The plaintiff insisted on passing along the part so appropriated, and attempted to climb over the fence. The defendant, being clerk of the Bridge Company, seized his coat, and tried to pull him back: the plaintiff, however, succeeded in climbing over the fence. The defendant then stationed two policemen to prevent, and they did prevent, the plaintiff from proceeding forwards along the footway; but he was told that he might go back into the carriage way, and proceed to the other side of the bridge, if he pleased. The plaintiff would not do so, but remained where he was above half an hour: and then, on the defendant still refusing to suffer him to go forwards along the footway, he endeavoured to force his way, and, in so doing, assaulted the defendant: whereupon he was taken into custody.' By virtue of the pleadings in the case, the question arose whether there had been an imprisonment of the plaintiff before he committed the assault. At the trial the Lord Chief Justice told the jury that there had, and a rule nisi for a new trial was obtained on the ground of misdirection:

COLERIDGE J: . . . And I am of opinion that there was no imprisonment. To call it so appears to me to confound partial obstruction and disturbance with total obstruction and detention. A prison may have its boundary large or narrow, visible and tangible, or, though real, still in the conception only; it may itself be moveable or fixed: but a boundary it must have; and that boundary the party imprisoned must be prevented from passing; he must be prevented from leaving that place, within the ambit of which the party imprisoning would confine him, except by prison-breach. Some confusion seems to me to arise from confounding imprisonment of the body with mere loss of freedom: it is one part of the definition of freedom to be able to go whithersoever one pleases; but imprisonment is something more than the mere loss of this power; it includes the notion of restraint within some limits defined by a will or power exterior to our own.

   . . . If, in the course of a night, both ends of a street were walled up, and there was no egress from the house but into the street, I should have no difficulty in saying that the inhabitants were thereby imprisoned; but, if only one end were walled up, and an armed force stationed outside to prevent any scaling of the wall or passage that way, I should feel equally clear that there was no imprisonment. If there were, the street would obviously be the prison; and yet, as obviously, none would be confined to it.

   Knowing that my Lord has entertained strongly an opinion directly contrary to this, I am under serious apprehension that I overlook some difficulty in forming my own: but, if it exists, I have not been able to discover it, and am therefore bound to state that, according to my view of the case, the rule should be absolute for a new trial.

PATTESON J: . . . But imprisonment is, as I apprehend, a total restraint of the liberty of the person, for however short a time, and not a partial obstruction of his will, whatever inconvenience it may bring on him. . . .

LORD DENMAN CJ [dissenting]: . . . I had no idea that any person in these times supposed any particular boundary to be necessary to constitute imprisonment, or that the restraint of a man's person from doing what he desires ceases to be an imprisonment because he may find some means of escape.

   It is said that the party here was at liberty to go in another direction. I am not sure that in fact he was, because the same unlawful power which prevented him from taking one course might, in case of acquiescence, have refused him any other. But this liberty to do something else does not appear to me to affect the question of imprisonment. As long as I am prevented from doing what I have a right to do, of what importance is it that I am permitted to do something else? How does the imposition of an unlawful condition shew that I am not restrained? If I am locked in a room, am I not imprisoned because I might effect my escape through a window, or because I might find an exit dangerous or inconvenient to myself, as by wading through water or by taking a route so circuitous that my necessary affairs would suffer by delay?

It appears to me that this is a total deprivation of liberty with reference to the purpose for which he lawfully wished to employ his liberty: and, being effected by force, it is not the mere obstruction of a way, but a restraint of the person. . . .

[WILLIAMS J also delivered a judgment to the effect that there was no imprisonment on these facts.]

Rule made absolute

Robinson *v* Balmain New Ferry Co Ltd Judicial Committee of the Privy Council [1910] AC 295

The plaintiff, who intended to cross a harbour on the defendant company's ferry, paid one penny to enter the company's wharf. Between the wharf and the street there was a barrier with two turnstiles, and a notice board (above the turnstiles and on each side of the barrier) stated that a penny must be paid on entering or leaving the wharf, whether or not the passenger had used the ferry. The practice of the company was to collect fares on one side of the harbour only. The plaintiff, who had gone through the entry turnstile, discovered that there would be a twenty minute wait before the next steamer left, and, wishing to leave the wharf, he approached the exit turnstile. He refused to pay a penny, however, and was prevented from forcing his way out for some time by two of the company's officers. On appeal from a decision of the High Court of Australia by the plaintiff who claimed damages for assault and false imprisonment:

LORD LOREBURN LC [delivering the judgment of their Lordships]: . . . There was no complaint, at all events there was no question left to the jury by the plaintiff's request, of any excessive violence, and in the circumstances admitted it is clear to their Lordships that there was no false imprisonment at all. The plaintiff was merely called upon to leave the wharf in the way in which he contracted to leave it. There is no law requiring the defendants to make the exit from their premises gratuitous to people who come there upon a definite contract which involves their leaving the wharf by another way; and the defendants were entitled to resist a forcible passage through their turnstile.

The question whether the notice which was affixed to these premises was brought home to the knowledge of the plaintiff is immaterial, because the notice itself is immaterial.

When the plaintiff entered the defendants' premises there was nothing agreed as to the terms on which he might go back, because neither party contemplated his going back. When he desired to do so the defendants were entitled to impose a reasonable condition before allowing him to pass through their turnstile from a place to which he had gone of his own free will. The payment of a penny was a quite fair condition, and if he did not choose to comply with it the defendants were not bound to let him through. He could proceed on the journey he had contracted for. . . .

Their Lordships will humbly advise His Majesty that this appeal should be dismissed with costs.

Question

Why was the notice immaterial?

Herd v Weardale Steel, Coal and Coke Co Ltd House of Lords [1915] AC 67

The appellant (and his fellow workers) descended the respondent company's mine at 9.30 am and he would have been entitled to be raised to the surface at the end of his shift (about 4 pm) by a cage which was used at other times to carry coal. The cage was, in fact, the only way out of the mine. The appellant, whose verbal contract of service provided for fourteen days' notice on either side, refused to do certain work which he had been told to do on the grounds that it was unsafe, and also that the instruction was in breach of an oral agreement between the men's representative and the colliery manager. At about 11 am he asked to be allowed to use the cage, but this request was refused. The appellant was not allowed to use the cage until approximately 1.30 pm, although it had been standing at the bottom of the mine shaft since 1.10 pm and could have been used to carry him to the surface. He was employed subject to the provisions of the Coal Mines Regulation Acts 1887–1908, certain rules established under the 1887 Act and an agreement between the Durham Coal Owners' Association and the Durham Miners' Association. One of the terms of his contract was that he should be raised from the mine at the end of his shift, and a notice containing the times of raising and lowering, which had been fixed under the 1887 Act and the agreement, was posted at the pit head. In an earlier action the company were awarded 5s. damages for the appellant's breach of contract. The appellant sued for damages for false imprisonment, but Pickford J's judgment in his favour was reversed by the Court of Appeal, [1913] 3 KB 771. An appeal to the House of Lords was dismissed.

VISCOUNT HALDANE LC: My Lords, by the law of this country no man can be restrained of his liberty without authority in law. That is a proposition the maintenance of which is of great importance; but at the same time it is a proposition which must be read in relation to other propositions which are equally important. If a man chooses to go into a dangerous place at the bottom of a quarry or the bottom of a mine, from which by the nature of physical circumstances he cannot escape, it does not follow from the proposition I have enunciated about liberty that he can compel the owner to bring him up out of it. The owner may or may not be under a duty arising from circumstances, on broad grounds the neglect of which may possibly involve him in a criminal charge or a civil liability. It is unnecessary to discuss the conditions and circumstances which might bring about such a result, because they have, in the view I take, nothing to do with false imprisonment.

My Lords, there is another proposition which has to be borne in mind and that is the application of the maxim volenti non fit injuria. If a man gets into an express train and the doors are locked pending its arrival at its destination, he is not entitled, merely because the train has been stopped by signal, to call for the doors to be opened to let him out. He has entered the train on the terms that he is to be conveyed to a certain station without the opportunity of getting out before that, and he must abide by the terms on which he has entered the train. So when a man goes down a mine, from which access to the surface does not exist in the absence of special facilities given on the part of the owner of the mine, he is only entitled to the use of these facilities (subject possibly to the exceptional circumstances to which I have alluded) on the terms on which he has entered. I think it results from what was laid down by the Judicial Committee of the Privy Council in *Robinson v Balmain New Ferry Co.*[1] that that is so. There there was a pier, and by the regulations a penny was to be paid by those who entered and a penny on getting out. The manager of the exit gate refused to allow a man who had gone in, having paid his penny, but having changed

---

1. [1910] AC 295.

his mind about embarking on a steamer, and wishing to return, to come out without paying his penny. It was held that that was not false imprisonment; volenti non fit injuria. The man had gone in upon the pier knowing that those were the terms and conditions as to exit, and it was not false imprisonment to hold him to conditions which he had accepted. So, my Lords, it is not false imprisonment to hold a man to the conditions he has accepted when he goes down a mine.

My Lords, I do not wish to be understood as saying that no other question than that of contract comes into this case, for the Coal Mines Regulation Act 1887 lays down a statutory obligation on the owner of mines to provide access to the surface, and it lays down conditions as regards the availability of that access. But the material point is this: that on considering the provisions of that statute I find nothing which entitles a miner to claim to use the winding-up cage at any moment he pleases. It may be that the cage is full of coal; it may be that it is employed in drawing other people up; it may be that it is very inconvenient for other reasons to use it at the moment. It is enough that no right is given by statute which enables the workman to claim to use the cage at any moment he pleases.

Now, my Lords, in the present case what happened was this. The usage of the mine – a usage which I think must be taken to have been notified – was that the workman was to be brought up at the end of his shift. In this case the workman refused to work; it may have been for good reasons or it may have been for bad, – I do not think that question concerns us. He said that the work he had been ordered to do was of a kind that was dangerous, and he threw down his tools and claimed to come up to the surface. The manager, or at any rate the person responsible for the control of the cage, said: 'No, you have chosen to come at a time which is not your proper time, and although there is the cage standing empty we will not bring you up in it,' and the workman was in consequence under the necessity of remaining at the bottom of the shaft for about twenty minutes. There was no refusal to bring him up at the ordinary time which was in his bargain; but there was a refusal, – and I am quite ready to assume that the motive of it was to punish him, I will assume it for the sake of argument, for having refused to go on with his work – by refusing to bring him up at the moment when he claimed to come. Did that amount to false imprisonment? In my opinion it did not. No statutory right under the Coal Mines Regulation Act 1887 avails him, for the reason which I have already spoken of. Nor had he any right in contract. His right in contract was to come up at the end of his shift. Was he then falsely imprisoned? There were facilities, but they were facilities which, in accordance with the conditions that he had accepted by going down, were not available to him until the end of his shift, at any rate as of right.

My Lords, under these circumstances I find it wholly impossible to come to the conclusion that the principle to which I have alluded, and on which the doctrine of false imprisonment is based, has any application to the case. Volenti non fit injuria. The man chose to go to the bottom of the mine under these conditions, – conditions which he accepted. He had no right to call upon the employers to make use of special machinery put there at their cost, and involving cost in its working, to bring him to the surface just when he pleased. . . .

[LORD SHAW OF DUNFERMLINE and LORD MOULTON delivered speeches in favour of dismissing the appeal.]

Questions

1. Does Viscount Haldane's explanation of *Robinson*'s case accord with what is stated in that case? (See M. S. Amos (1928) 44 LQR 464 at 465–466.)

2. Once the miners got to the surface would it have been false imprisonment for the respondent to have stopped them leaving the colliery before the end

of their shift by (a) refusing to unlock the gates of the pit yard or (b) locking those gates? (See *Burns v Johnston* [1916] 2 IR 444; affd [1917] 2 IR 137 cited by G. Williams, *Law, Justice and Equity*, chap. 5, an essay which discusses both *Herd*'s case and *Robinson*'s case.)

Note

In his essay entitled 'Two Cases on False Imprisonment' (loc cit), G. Williams concludes that '*Robinson*'s case is of small general interest because it is confined to a situation that is not likely to occur frequently. A condition may be attached to exit, but only when the plaintiff has a choice of two exits, A and B, the condition being attached to A. Further, no condition may be attached when exit B is extremely onerous. . . . Nor does the decision apply when the condition attached to exit A is unreasonable, unless exit B gives practically immediate freedom. If exit B is in an intermediate position, neither being extremely onerous nor giving practically immediate freedom, the reasonableness of the condition attached to exit A becomes relevant; and this is the only case where it is relevant.' For further discussion of *Herd*'s case and *Robinson*'s case, see K. F. Tan (1981) 44 MLR 166.

4 Wrongful interference

Wilkinson *v* Downton Queen's Bench Division [1895-99] All ER Rep 267

WRIGHT J read a judgment in which he referred to the plaintiff's allegations, in the statement of claim, and continued: The defendant, in the execution of what he seems to have regarded as a practical joke, represented to the female plaintiff that he was charged by her husband with a message to her to the effect that the husband had been smashed up in an accident, and was lying at the Elms public-house at Leytonstone with both legs broken, and that she was to go at once in a cab to fetch him home. All this was false. The effect of this statement on the female plaintiff was a violent shock to the nervous system producing vomiting and other more serious and permanent physical consequences, at one time threatening her reason and entailing weeks of suffering and incapacity to her as well as expense to her husband for medical treatment of her. These consequences were not in any way the result of previous ill-health or weakness of constitution, nor was there any evidence of predisposition to nervous shock or of any other idiosyncrasy. In addition to these matters of substance there is a small claim for 1s 10½d for the cost of railway fares of persons sent by the female plaintiff to Leytonstone in obedience to the pretended message. As to this 1s 10½d expended in railway fares on the faith of the defendant's statement, it is clearly within the scope of the decision in *Pasley v Freeman*.[1] It was a misrepresentation intended to be acted on to the damage of the plaintiff.

The real question is as to the £100, the greatest part of which is given as compensation for the female plaintiff's illness and suffering. It was argued for her that she is entitled to recover this as being damage caused by fraud, and, therefore, within the doctrine established by *Pasley v Freeman*[1] and *Langridge v Levy*.[2] I am not sure that this would not be an extension of that doctrine, the real ground of which appears

---

1. (1789) 3 Term Rep 51.
2. (1837) 2 M & W 519; affd (1838) 4 M & W 337.

to be that a person who makes a false statement, intending it to be acted on, must make good the damage naturally resulting from its being acted on. Here is no injuria of that kind. I think, however, that the verdict may be supported on another ground. The defendant has, as I assume for the moment, wilfully done an act calculated to cause physical harm to the female plaintiff, i.e., to infringe her legal right to personal safety, and has thereby in fact caused physical harm to her. That proposition, without more, appears to me to state a good cause of action, there being no justification alleged for the act. This wilful injuria is in law malicious, although no malicious purpose to cause the harm which was caused, nor any motive of spite, is imputed to the defendant.

It remains to consider whether the assumptions involved in the proposition are made out. One question is whether the defendant's act was so plainly calculated to produce some effect of the kind which was produced, that an intention to produce it ought to be imputed to the defendant regard being had to the fact that the effect was produced on a person proved to be in an ordinary state of health and mind. I think that it was. It is difficult to imagine that such a statement, made suddenly and with apparent seriousness, could fail to produce grave effects under the circumstances upon any but an exceptionally indifferent person, and therefore an intention to produce such an effect must be imputed, and it is no answer in law to say that more harm was done than was anticipated, for that is commonly the case with all wrongs. The other question is whether the effect was, to use the ordinary phrase, too remote to be in law regarded as a consequence for which the defendant is answerable. Apart from authority I should give the same answer, and on the same grounds, as to the last question, and say that it was not too remote. Whether, as the majority of the Lords thought in *Lynch v Knight*,[1] the criterion is in asking what would be the natural effect on reasonable persons, or whether, as Lord Wensleydale thought, the possible infirmities of human nature ought to be recognised, it seems to me that the connection between the cause and the effect is sufficiently close and complete.

It is, however, necessary to consider two authorities which are supposed to have laid down that illness through mental shock is a too remote or unnatural consequence of an injuria to entitle the plaintiffs to recover in a case where damage is a necessary part of the cause of action. One is *Victorian Railways Comrs v Coultas*,[2] where it was held in the Privy Council that illness which was the effect of shock caused by fright was too remote a consequence of a negligent act which caused the fright, there being no physical harm immediately caused. That decision was treated in the Court of Appeal in *Pugh v London, Brighton, and South Coast Rly Co*[3] as open to question. It is inconsistent with an earlier decision of the Court of Appeal in Ireland (*Bell v Great Northern Rly Co of Ireland*[4]) where the Irish Exchequer Division declined to follow *Victorian Railways Comrs v Coultas*,[2] and it has been disapproved in the Supreme Court of New York (see *Pollock on Torts* (4th edn) p. 47 (n.)). Nor is it altogether in point, for there was not in that case any element of wilful wrong, nor was perhaps the illness so direct and natural a consequence of the defendant's conduct, as in this case.

On these grounds it seems to me that *Victorian Railways Comrs v Coultas*[2] is not an authority on which this case ought to be decided.

A more serious difficulty is the decision in *Allsop v Allsop*,[5] which was approved in the House of Lords in *Lynch v Knight*.[1] In that case it was held by Pollock CB, Martin, Bramwell and Wilde BB, that illness caused by a slanderous imputation of unchastity in the case of a married woman did not constitute such special damage as

---

1. (1861) 9 HL Cas 577.
2. (1888) 13 App Cas 222.
3. [1896] 2 QB 248.
4. (1890) 26 LR IR 428.
5. (1860) 5 H & N 534.

would sustain an action for such a slander. That case, however, appears to have been decided on the grounds that, in all the innumerable actions for slander which had occurred, there were no precedents for alleging illness to be sufficient special damage; and that it would be an evil consequence to treat it as sufficient, because such a rule might lead to an infinity of trumpery or groundless actions. Neither of these reasons is applicable to the present case, nor could such a rule be adopted as of general application without results which it would be difficult or impossible to defend. Suppose that a person is in a precarious and dangerous condition, and another person falsely tells him that his physician has said that he has but a day to live. In such a case, if death ensued from the shock caused by the false statement, I cannot doubt that the case might be one of criminal homicide; or that, if a serious aggravation of illness ensued, damages might be recovered. I think, however, that it must be admitted that the present case is without precedent. . . .

Judgment for plaintiffs

Note

For the present position where nervous shock is *negligently* inflicted, see p. 118, ante.

Janvier *v* Sweeney Court of Appeal [1918–19] All ER Rep 1056

This was an appeal by Sweeney, a private detective and Barker, his assistant from a judgment for the plaintiff for £250 entered by Avory J sitting with a jury.

BANKES LJ: . . . The case for the plaintiff was that she was employed by a lady in whose house she resided, and that, on 16 July 1917, a man called at the house and told her that he was a detective inspector from Scotland Yard representing the military authorities and that she was the woman they wanted as she had been corresponding with a German spy. The plaintiff said that she was extremely frightened, with the result that she suffered from a severe nervous shock, and she attributed a long period of nervous illness to the shock she received from the language used to her on that occasion. If she could establish the truth of that story and satisfy the jury that her illness was the direct result of the shock, she was entitled to maintain this action. At the trial the defendants disputed the plaintiff's story altogether. They said that Barker had never spoken the words alleged, and that, so far from suffering any shock, the plaintiff was a very self-possessed woman with her wits about her all the time during which the defendants were in communication with her, and that she was mainly occupied in attempting to trick these two men whom she suspected of being private inquiry agents. These matters were entirely for the jury. The court cannot interfere with their findings merely because it might think the opposite inference preferable. It is clear that the learned judge would not have arrived at the same conclusion as the jury. The defendants cannot complain of the summing-up. But in spite of that summing-up in favour of the defendants, the jury accepted the plaintiff's story, and their findings as to the words used by Barker is not challenged in this court. We must take it then that Barker went to this house and deliberately threatened the plaintiff in order to induce or compel her to commit a gross breach of the duty[1] she owed to her employer.

It is no longer contended that this was not a wrongful act which would amount to an actionable wrong if damage which the law recognises can be shown to have flowed directly from that act. But counsel for the defendant, Barker, contended that no

---

1. [I.e. to allow him to see some letters in the possession of a resident in the house.]

action would lie for words followed by such damage as the plaintiff alleges here. In order to sustain that contention it would be necessary to overrule *Wilkinson v Downton*.[1] In my opinion, that judgment was right. It has been approved in subsequent cases. It did not create any new rule of law, though it may be said to have extended existing principles over an area wider than that which they had been recognised as covering, because the court there accepted the view that the damage there relied on was not in the circumstances too remote in the eye of the law. . . .

. . . In my view of the present state of the authorities, it is impossible to suggest that *Wilkinson v Downton*[1] is not good law or that it ought to be reversed. So much for the main point. . . .

DUKE LJ: I am anxious not to overlay or weaken the force of the judgment which has just been delivered, with every word of which I agree. My observations will, therefore, be brief. This is a much stronger case than *Wilkinson v Downton*.[1] In that case there was no intention to commit a wrongful act; the defendant merely intended to play a joke upon the plaintiff. In the present case there was an intention to terrify the plaintiff for the purpose of attaining an unlawful object in which both the defendants were jointly concerned. . . .

[A. T. LAWRENCE J delivered a judgment in favour of dismissing the appeal.]

Appeal dismissed

Questions

1. A shopkeeper, as a joke, sends out a grossly inflated bill to a customer. Would there be any liability to the customer if he commits suicide as this large bill is the 'last straw' (and on this last point consider p. 322, ante and p. 342, ante)?

2. Could and should the principle in these cases cover the intentional infliction of purely mental *distress*? (See F. A. Trindade (1986) 6 Oxf JLS 219; cf. *Burnett v George*, cited by Clayton and Tomlinson, op cit, p. 119.)

3. Could the principle in these cases be used to meet Prosser's point (set out in *Murray v Ministry of Defence* [1988] 2 All ER 521 at 529, p. 585, ante) concerning liability for false imprisonment even when the plaintiff is unaware of the imprisonment? (See *Street*, p. 31, note 16.)

5 Defences

(a) Contributory negligence: consent: necessity

Murphy v Culhane Court of Appeal [1976] 3 All ER 533

LORD DENNING MR: . . . Timothy Murphy's widow . . . brings an action against John Culhane for damages under the Fatal Accidents Acts, claiming damages on behalf of herself and her baby daughter. . . . The question is whether or not Mrs Murphy is entitled to judgment on the pleadings without any trial. The statement of claim says:

---

1. [1897] 2 QB 57.

'On or about the nineteenth day of September 1974, near Grove Place, in the area of Greater London, the Defendant assaulted and beat the Deceased by striking him on the head with a plank. The said assault was unlawful. The Plaintiff intends to adduce evidence pursuant to section 11 of the Civil Evidence Act 1968, that the Defendant was on the 25th day of April 1975, convicted on his own plea of guilty before the Central Criminal Court of manslaughter of the Deceased.'

The defence admits those allegations and further admits that, by reason of the assault, Mr Murphy was killed. It then says:

'The said assault occurred during and as part of a criminal affray which was initiated by the Deceased and others who had together come to 20 Grove Place on the occasion in question with the joint criminal intent of assaulting and beating the Defendant.'

That is followed by legal contentions of ex turpi causa non oritur actio, volenti non fit injuria, and that the deceased's said death was caused in part by his own aforesaid fault.

. . . There are two cases which seem to show that, in a civil action for damages for assault, damages are not to be reduced because the plaintiff was himself guilty of provocation. Provocation, it was said, can be used to wipe out the element of exemplary damages but not to reduce the actual figure of pecuniary damages. It was so said by the High Court of Australia in 1962 in *Fontin v Katapodis*[1] and followed by this court in 1967 in *Lane v Holloway*.[2] But those were cases where the conduct of the injured man was trivial — and the conduct of the defendant was savage — entirely out of proportion to the occasion. So much so that the defendant could fairly be regarded as solely responsible for the damage done. I do not think they can or should be applied where the injured man, by his own conduct, can fairly be regarded as partly responsible for the damage he suffered. So far as general principle is concerned, I would like to repeat what I said in the later case of *Gray v Barr*[3]:

'In an action for assault, in awarding damages, the judge or jury can take into account, not only circumstances which go to aggravate damages, but also those which go to mitigate them.'

That is the principle I prefer rather than the earlier cases. Apart altogether from damages, however, I think there may well be a defence on liability. If Murphy was one of a gang which set out to beat up Culhane, it may well be that he could not sue for damages if he got more than he bargained for. A man who takes part in a criminal affray may well be said to have been guilty of such a wicked act as to deprive himself of a cause of action or, alternatively, to have taken on himself the risk. . . .

There is another point, too, even if Mrs Murphy were entitled to damages under the Fatal Accidents Acts, they fall to be reduced under the Law Reform (Contributory Negligence) Act 1945 because the death of her husband might be the result partly of his own fault and partly of the default of the defendant: see s. 1(1) and (4) of the 1945 Act. On this point I must explain a sentence in *Gray v Barr*[3] where the widow of the dead man was held to be entitled to full compensation without any reduction. Her husband had not been guilty of any 'fault' within s. 4 of the 1945 Act because his conduct had not been such as to make him liable in an action of tort or, alternatively, was not such that he should be regarded as responsible in any degree for the damage. So also in *Lane v Holloway*[4], as Winn LJ pointed out. But in the

---

1. (1962) 108 CLR 177.
2. [1968] 1 QB 379, [1967] 3 All ER 129.
3. [1971] 2 QB 554 at 569, [1971] 2 All ER 949 at 957.
4. [1968] 1 QB 379 at 393, [1967] 3 All ER 129 at 135.

present case the conduct of Mr Murphy may well have been such as to make him liable in tort.

It seems to me that this is clearly a case where the facts should be investigated before any judgment is given. It should be open to Mr Culhane to be able to put forward his defences so as to see whether or not and to what extent he is liable in damages.

I would therefore allow the appeal. The judgment[1] should be set aside and the case go for trial accordingly.

[ORR and WALLER LJJ agreed.]

Appeal allowed

Notes

1. There is a conflict of authority in relation to the question whether any provocation on the plaintiff's part can mitigate compensatory, as opposed to exemplary, damages. *Murphy v Culhane* represents one side of the argument, but in *Barnes v Nayer* (1986) Times, 19th December it was said in the Court of Appeal that the better view is that it does not have this effect.

2. On the Law Reform (Contributory Negligence) Act 1945 see p. 357, ante and see also *Glanville Williams*, pp. 197–202 and p. 318, note 3; and for an article which involves discussion of later case law, see Hudson, (1984) 4 LS 332. See esp. Hudson, op cit, pp. 337–338 for criticism of Lord Denning MR's approach to this issue in *Murphy v Culhane*. More recently, the Court of Appeal in *Barnes v Nayer* accepted that the 1945 Act can apply to assault cases (although in that case the view was taken that it — and indeed defences of volenti and ex turpi — would not succeed on the ground of the disparity on the alleged facts between the deceased's acts and the defendant's response). On the contributory negligence defence, see further *Wasson v Chief Constable of the Royal Ulster Constabulary* [1987] 8 NIJB 34.

3. On the defence of ex turpi causa non oritur actio to which Lord Denning MR referred, see p. 392, ante.

4. Consent — here a form of implied consent — was raised in *Murphy v Culhane* under the guise of volenti non fit injuria or assumption of risk. On the extent to which consent affects a criminal prosecution for assault, see *Smith & Hogan*, pp. 383–386 and especially *A-G's Reference (No 6 of 1980)* [1981] QB 715; [1981] 2 All ER 1057. Compare *Murphy v Culhane*; *Barnes v Nayer*. Why might the civil law take a different line? Consider *Fleming*, p. 75; *Winfield & Jolowicz*, pp. 700–701. Note, however, Hudson, op cit, p. 333 who argues that volenti might not provide a defence in circumstances similar to those in *Murphy v Culhane* and consider now *Re F* [1990] 2 AC 1, sub nom *F v West Berkshire Health Authority (Mental Health Commission intervening)* [1989] 2 All ER 545 (p. 599, post). When that case was in the Court of Appeal, support can be found (see [1989] 2 WLR at pp. 1038, 1049 and 1058) for the view that public policy can invalidate consent in both criminal *and* civil law, something which was indeed expressly stated by

---

1. [In Mrs Murphy's favour.]

Neill LJ. One example given was a prize fight and Neill LJ referred to the case of an assault occasioning actual bodily harm. When *F v West Berkshire Health Authority* reached the House of Lords, Lord Goff (p. 602, post) acknowledged that the public interest might negate the effect of consent 'in certain limited circumstances' and Lord Griffiths ([1989] 2 All ER at p. 562) referred to consent not being available in the case of a bare knuckle prize fight or fighting which might result in actual bodily harm. (Although this was in a part of Lord Griffiths' speech where he was dissenting, his dissent was not on this precise issue.) Both their Lordships appear to have had civil liability in mind as covered by these statements.

Herd *v* Weardale Steel Coal and Coke Co Ltd, p. 589, ante

Chatterton *v* Gerson Queen's Bench Division [1981] 1 All ER 257

This case was concerned with the extent to which a doctor must inform a patient of the nature of, and risks involved in, a particular course of treatment. A claim in negligence failed and on this aspect of the law see p. 278, ante. At this point the relevant issue is the unsuccessful claim in trespass to the person and the question of consent.

BRISTOW J: . . . *Trespass to the person and consent*
It is clear law that in any context in which consent of the injured party is a defence to what would otherwise be a crime or a civil wrong, the consent must be real. Where, for example, a woman's consent to sexual intercourse is obtained by fraud, her apparent consent is no defence to a charge of rape. It is not difficult to state the principle or to appreciate its good sense. As so often, the problem lies in its application.

No English authority was cited before me of the application of the principle in the context of consent to the interference with bodily integrity by medical or surgical treatment. . . .

In my judgment what the court has to do in each case is to look at all the circumstances and say, 'Was there a real consent?' I think justice requires that in order to vitiate the reality of consent there must be a greater failure of communication between doctor and patient than that involved in a breach of duty if the claim is based on negligence. When the claim is based on negligence the plaintiff must prove not only the breach of duty to inform but that had the duty not been broken she would not have chosen to have the operation. Where the claim is based on trespass to the person, once it is shown that the consent is unreal, then what the plaintiff would have decided if she had been given the information which would have prevented vitiation of the reality of her consent is irrelevant.

In my judgment once the patient is informed in broad terms of the nature of the procedure which is intended, and gives her consent, that consent is real, and the cause of the action on which to base a claim for failure to go into risks and implications is negligence, not trespass. Of course, if information is withheld in bad faith, the consent will be vitiated by fraud. Of course, if by some accident, as in a case in the 1940s in the Salford Hundred Court, where a boy was admitted to hospital for tonsillectomy and due to administrative error was circumcised instead, trespass would be the appropriate cause of action against the doctor, though he was as much the victim of the error as the boy. But in my judgment it would be very much against the interests of justice if actions which are really based on a failure by the doctor to perform his duty adequately to inform were pleaded in trespass. . . . I should add that getting the patient to sign a pro forma expressing consent to undergo the operation 'the effect and nature of which have been explained to me' . . . should be a valuable reminder to everyone of the need for explanation and consent. But it would be no defence to an action based on trespass to the person if no explanation had in fact been given. The consent would have been expressed in form only, not in reality. . . .

Notes

1. Bristow J's view in the final sentence of the penultimate paragraph of the extract ante was approved in *Hills v Potter* [1983] 3 All ER 716; [1984] 1 WLR 641 and see *Sidaway v Board of Governors of the Bethlem Royal Hospital and the Maudsley Hospital* [1985] AC 871 at 883 and 894. See further *Freeman v Home Office (No. 2)* [1984] QB 524; [1983] 3 All ER 589 (per McCowan J). For support for the view that 'real consent' defeats a trespass action, see *Sidaway v Board of Governors of the Bethlem Royal Hospital and the Maudsley Hospital* [1984] QB 493; [1984] 1 All ER 1018 and *Freeman v Home Office (No 2)* [1984] QB 524; [1984] 1 All ER 1036 where it is pointed out that, in addition to consent obtained by fraud being inoperative, consent induced by misrepresentation (as to the nature of the treatment) is also not 'real consent'. (This last point was not specifically mentioned in *Chatterton v Gerson*.) Note also that in *Freeman v Home Office (No 2)* the contention that a prisoner could not *as a matter of law* consent to medical treatment because of the pressures of prison life and discipline was rejected.

2. For comment on the use of the distinction between failure of advice relating to the nature of the treatment and that relating to the risks involved in it as a basis for deciding whether the action is trespass or negligence, see K. F. Tan (1987) 7 LS 149, and see M. Brazier ibid. 169 at 179–182 (though in relation to the reference to *Wilson v Pringle* [1987] QB 237; [1986] 2 All ER 440, see now p. 580, ante and p. 599, post).

3. In *Freeman v Home Office (No 2)* when dealing with the unsuccessful claim for damages for trespass to the person (based on the administration of drugs to the plaintiff prisoner), Sir John Donaldson MR stated ([1984] 1 All ER at pp. 1044–1045):

'The maxim volenti non fit injuria can be roughly translated as "You cannot claim damages if you have asked for it", and "it" is something which is and remains a tort. The maxim, where it applies, provides a bar to enforcing a cause of action. It does not negative the cause of action itself. This is a wholly different concept from consent which, in this context, deprives the act of its tortious character. Volenti would be a defence in the unlikely scenario of a patient being held not to have in fact consented to treatment, but having by his conduct caused the doctor to believe that he had consented.'

In relation to the volenti maxim, compare *Salmond & Heuston*'s view, noted p. 353, ante.

4. On the question of consent by children to medical treatment and the role of parents, see P. M. Bromley and N. V. Lowe, *Bromley's Family Law* 7th edn (London, 1987), pp. 274–277 discussing, amongst other authorities, *Gillick v West Norfolk and Wisbech Area Health Authority* [1986] AC 112; [1985] 3 All ER 402. See further note 2, p. 606, post.

5. For discussion of where the burden of proof lies in relation to the issue

of consent, see Trindade op cit, pp. 228–229 who submits that the onus of establishing consent should rest upon the defendant; but see *Street*, p. 22. Trindade finds support for his view in Bristow J's reference in the judgment in *Chatterton v Gerson* to consent being a defence, and on such a matter the onus would lie on the defendant to establish his defence. (See further note 6, post.) However, in the later case of *Freeman v Home Office (No 2)* McCowan J construed Bristow J's judgment in *Chatterton v Gerson* as favouring the view that the burden of proof lay on the plaintiff to show absence of consent, and he went on to rule to that effect. Do you agree with his interpretation of *Chatterton v Gerson*? A passage from Sir John Donaldson MR's judgment (when *Freeman v Home Office (No 2)* went on appeal) has been set out ante (and note that Fox LJ agreed with his reasons for dismissing the appeal). Does this passage support the view that the burden of proof is on the plaintiff? Does it suggest that consent in this area should not properly be regarded as a 'defence'? Whatever the answer to this question, consent has been treated by writers as a matter of defence (though see *Street*, p. 22) and, as *Street*, p. 75, acknowledges, it is convenient to do so.

6. As was stated p. 596, ante, consent can be implied. Such consent was discussed in *Collins v Wilcock* [1984] 3 All ER 374; [1984] 1 WLR 1172 in which the Divisional Court stated (at p. 378):

'Generally speaking, consent is a defence to battery; and most of the physical contacts of ordinary life are not actionable because they are impliedly consented to by all who move in society and so expose themselves to the risk of bodily contact. So nobody can complain of the jostling which is inevitable from his presence in, for example, a supermarket, an underground station or a busy street; nor can a person who attends a party complain if his hand is seized in friendship, or even if his back is (within reason) slapped. . . . Although such cases are regarded as examples of implied consent, it is more common nowadays to treat them as falling within a general exception [to the rule that touching another is a battery] embracing all physical contact which is generally acceptable in the ordinary conduct of daily life.'

For comment (in *Wilson v Pringle* [1987] QB 237; [1986] 2 All ER 440) on Robert Goff LJ's judgment in *Collins v Wilcock*, see p. 580, ante, but note that in *F v West Berkshire Health Authority*, post Lord Goff reiterated his approach in *Collins v Wilcock* and expressed doubt about the 'hostility' requirement which was referred to in *Wilson v Pringle*.

In some situations a patient cannot consent to physical contact, e.g. because of unconsciousness. In *Wilson v Pringle* an urgent operation in such a situation was thought to come within the exception referred to in the passage from *Collins v Wilcock* ante, but this view has not met with approval in later cases (*T v T* [1988] Fam 52; [1988] 1 All ER 613; *F v West Berkshire Health Authority* post and also when that case was in the Court of Appeal [1990] 2 AC 1). As will be seen from the next extract, this question takes the discussion beyond the issue of consent and onto the defence of necessity (although on the question of consent, see also notes 1 and 2, p. 606, post).

F *v* West Berkshire Health Authority (Mental Health Act Commission intervening) House of Lords [1989] 2 All ER 545

The House of Lords in this case had to consider the legality of a sterilisation operation which it was proposed to carry out on F, an adult woman whose mental capacity was such that she was unable to consent to the operation. The view of the trial judge (Scott Baker J) and of the Court of Appeal, [1990] 2 AC 1, that such an operation was in F's best interests was not challenged in this appeal to the House of Lords. Scott Baker J had granted a declaration that the sterilisation of F would not be an unlawful act by reason only of the absence of F's consent. An appeal to the Court of Appeal was unsuccessful and a further appeal to the House of Lords was dismissed. The House of Lords did, however, amend the declaration so that it read 'the operation of sterilisation proposed to be performed on the plaintiff being in the existing circumstances in her best interests can lawfully be performed on her despite her inability to consent to it'. (It was also ordered that if there was a material change in the existing circumstances before the operation took place, any party could apply to the court for such further or other declaration or order as might be just.) The House of Lords (with Lord Griffiths dissenting on this point) did not think that it was legally mandatory in the case of such a sterilisation operation to obtain a declaration from the court that the operation was lawful, but nevertheless thought that as a matter of practice such a declaration should be sought.

LORD BRANDON OF OAKBROOK: . . . At common law a doctor cannot lawfully operate on adult patients of sound mind, or give them any other treatment involving the application of physical force however small (which I shall refer to as 'other treatment'), without their consent. If a doctor were to operate on such patients, or give them other treatment, without their consent, he would commit the actionable tort of trespass to the person. There are, however, cases where adult patients cannot give or refuse their consent to an operation or other treatment. One case is where, as a result of an accident or otherwise, an adult patient is unconscious and an operation or other treatment cannot be safely delayed until he or she recovers consciousness. Another case is where a patient, though adult, cannot by reason of mental disability understand the nature or purpose of an operation or other treatment. The common law would be seriously defective if it failed to provide a solution to the problem created by such inability to consent. In my opinion, however, the common law does not fail. In my opinion, the solution to the problem which the common law provides is that a doctor can lawfully operate on, or give other treatment to, adult patients who are incapable, for one reason or another, of consenting to his doing so, provided that the operation or other treatment concerned is in the best interests of such patients. The operation or other treatment will be in their best interests if, but only if, it is carried out in order either to save their lives or to ensure improvement or prevent deterioration in their physical or mental health.

Different views have been put forward with regard to the principle which makes it lawful for a doctor to operate on or give other treatment to adult patients without their consent in the two cases to which I have referred above. The Court of Appeal in the present case regarded the matter as depending on the public interest. I would not disagree with that as a broad proposition, but I think that it is helpful to consider the principle in accordance with which the public interest leads to this result. In my opinion, the principle is that, when persons lack the capacity, for whatever reason, to take decisions about the performance of operations on them, or the giving of other medical treatment to them, it is necessary that some other person or persons, with the appropriate qualifications, should take such decisions for them. Otherwise they would be deprived of medical care which they need and to which they are entitled.

In many cases, however, it will not only be lawful for doctors, on the ground of necessity, to operate on or give other medical treatment to adult patients disabled from giving their consent: it will also be their common law duty to do so. . . .

LORD GRIFFITHS: . . . I have had the advantage of reading the speeches of my noble and learned friends Lord Brandon and Lord Goff and there is much therein with which I agree. I agree that those charged with the care of the mentally incompetent are protected from any criminal or tortious action based on lack of consent. Whether one arrives at this conclusion by applying a principle of 'necessity' as do Lord Brandon and Lord Goff or by saying that it is in the public interest as did Neill LJ in the Court of Appeal, appear to me to be inextricably interrelated conceptual justifications for the humane development of the common law. Why is it necessary that the mentally incompetent should be given treatment to which they lack the capacity to consent? The answer must surely be because it is in the public interest that it should be so.

In a civilised society the mentally incompetent must be provided with medical and nursing care and those who look after them must do their best for them. Stated in legal terms the doctor who undertakes responsibility for the treatment of a mental patient who is incapable of giving consent to treatment must give the treatment that he considers to be in the best interests of his patient, and the standard of care required of the doctor will be that laid down in *Bolam v Friern Hospital Management Committee* [1957] 2 All ER 118, [1957] 1 WLR 582. The doctor will however be subject to the specific statutory constraints on treatment for mental disorder provided by Pt IV of the Mental Health Act 1983. . . .

LORD GOFF OF CHIEVELEY: My Lords, the question in this case is concerned with the lawfulness of a proposed operation of sterilisation on the plaintiff, F, a woman of 36 years of age, who by reason of her mental incapacity is disabled from giving her consent to the operation. It is well established that, as a general rule, the performance of a medical operation on a person without his or her consent is unlawful, as constituting both the crime of battery and the tort of trespass to the person. Furthermore, before Scott Baker J and the Court of Appeal, it was common ground between the parties that there was no power in the court to give consent on behalf of F to the proposed operation of sterilisation, or to dispense with the need for such consent. This was because it was common ground that the parens patriae jurisdiction in respect of persons suffering from mental incapacity, formerly vested in the courts by royal warrant under the sign manual, had ceased to be so vested by revocation of the last warrant on 1 November 1960, and further that there was no statutory provision which could be invoked in its place. Before your Lordships, having regard to the importance of the matter, both those propositions were nevertheless subjected to close scrutiny, and counsel for the Official Solicitor deployed, with great ability, such arguments as can be advanced that the parens patriae jurisdiction is still vested in the courts as a matter of common law, and that the necessary statutory jurisdiction is to be found in Pt VII of the Mental Health Act 1983, and in particular in ss 93, 95 and 96 of that Act. However, with the assistance of counsel, I for my part have become satisfied that the concessions made below on these points were rightly made. On both points I find myself to be respectfully in agreement with the opinion expressed by my noble and learned friend Lord Brandon, and I do not think it necessary for me to add anything.

It follows that, as was recognised in the courts below, if the operation on F is to be justified, it can only be justified on the applicable principles of common law. The argument of counsel revealed the startling fact that there is no English authority on the question whether as a matter of common law (and if so in what circumstances) medical treatment can lawfully be given to a person who is disabled by mental incapacity from consenting to it. Indeed, the matter goes further, for a comparable problem can arise in relation to persons of sound mind who are, for example, rendered unconscious in an accident or rendered speechless by a catastrophic stroke. All such persons may require medical treatment and, in some cases, surgical operations. All may require nursing care. In the case of mentally disordered persons, they may require care of a more basic kind, dressing, feeding and so on, to assist them in their daily life, as well as routine treatment by doctors and dentists. It follows that, in my opinion, it is not possible to consider in isolation the lawfulness of the proposed operation of sterilisation in the present case. It is necessary first to ascertain the applicable common law principles and then to consider the question of sterilisation against the background of those principles.

Counsel for the Official Solicitor advanced the extreme argument that, in the absence of a parens patriae or statutory jurisdiction, no such treatment or care of the kind I have described can lawfully be given to a mentally disordered person who is unable to consent to it. This is indeed a startling proposition, which must also exclude treatment or care to persons rendered unconscious or unable to speak by accident or illness. For centuries, treatment and care must have been given to such persons, without any suggestion that it was unlawful to do so. I find it very difficult to believe that the common law is so deficient as to be incapable of providing for so obvious a need. Even so, it is necessary to examine the point as a matter of principle.

I start with the fundamental principle, now long established, that every person's body is inviolate. As to this, I do not wish to depart from what I myself said in the judgment of the Divisional Court in Collins v Wilcock [1984] 3 All ER 374, [1984] 1 WLR 1172, and in particular from the statement that the effect of this principle is that everybody is protected not only against physical injury but against any form of physical molestation (see [1984] 3 All ER 374 at 378, [1984] 1 WLR 1172 at 1177).

Of course, as a general rule physical interference with another person's body is lawful if he consents to it; though in certain limited circumstances the public interest may require that his consent is not capable of rendering the act lawful. There are also specific cases where physical interference without consent may not be unlawful: chastisement of children, lawful arrest, self-defence, the prevention of crime and so on. As I pointed out in Collins v Wilcock [1984] 3 All ER 374 at 378, [1984] 1 WLR 1172 at 1177, a broader exception has been created to allow for the exigencies of everyday life: jostling in a street or some other crowded place, social contact at parties and such like. This exception has been said to be founded on implied consent, since those who go about in public places, or go to parties, may be taken to have impliedly consented to bodily contact of this kind. Today this rationalisation can be regarded as artificial: and, in particular, it is difficult to impute consent to those who, by reason of their youth or mental disorder, are unable to give their consent. For this reason, I consider it more appropriate to regard such cases as falling within a general exception embracing all physical contact which is generally acceptable in the ordinary conduct of everyday life.

In the old days it used to be said that, for a touching of another's person to amount to a battery, it had to be a touching 'in anger' (see Cole v Turner (1704) Holt KB 108, 90 ER 958 per Holt CJ); and it has recently been said that the touching must be 'hostile' to have that effect (see Wilson v Pringle [1986] 2 All ER 440 at 447, [1987] QB 237 at 253). I respectfully doubt whether that is correct. A prank that gets out of hand, an over-friendly slap on the back, surgical treatment by a surgeon who mistakenly thinks that the patient has consented to it, all these things may transcend the bounds of lawfulness, without being characterised as hostile. Indeed, the suggested qualification is difficult to reconcile with the principle that any touching of another's body is, in the absence of lawful excuse, capable of amounting to a battery and a trespass. Furthermore, in the case of medical treatment, we have to bear well in mind the libertarian principle of self-determination which, to adopt the words of Cardozo J (in Schloendorff v Society of New York Hospital (1914) 211 NY 125 at 126), recognises that—

'Every human being of adult years and sound mind has a right to determine what shall be done with his own body; and a surgeon who performs an operation without his patient's consent, commits an assault . . .'

This principle has been reiterated in more recent years by Lord Reid in S v S, W v Official Solicitor [1970] 3 All ER 107 at 111, [1972] AC 24 at 43.

It is against this background that I turn to consider the question whether, and if so when, medical treatment or care of a mentally disordered person who is, by reason of his incapacity, incapable of giving his consent can be regarded as lawful. As is recognised in Cardozo J's statement of principle, and elsewhere (see eg Sidaway v

Bethlem Royal Hospital Governors [1985] 1 All ER 643 at 649, [1985] AC 871 at 882 per Lord Scarman), some relaxation of the law is required to accommodate persons of unsound mind. In *Wilson v Pringle* the Court of Appeal considered that treatment or care of such persons may be regarded as lawful, as falling within the exception relating to physical contact which is generally acceptable in the ordinary conduct of everyday life. Again, I am with respect unable to agree. That exception is concerned with the ordinary events of everyday life, jostling in public places and such like, and affects all persons, whether or not they are capable of giving their consent. Medical treatment, even treatment for minor ailments, does not fall within that category of events. The general rule is that consent is necessary to render such treatment lawful. If such treatment administered without consent is not to be unlawful, it has to be justified on some other principle.

On what principle can medical treatment be justified when given without consent? We are searching for a principle on which, in limited circumstances, recognition may be given to a need, in the interests of the patient, that treatment should be given to him in circumstances where he is (temporarily or permanently) disabled from consenting to it. It is this criterion of a need which points to the principle of necessity as providing justification.

That there exists in the common law a principle of necessity which may justify action which would otherwise be unlawful is not in doubt. But historically the principle has been seen to be restricted to two groups of cases, which have been called cases of public necessity and cases of private necessity. The former occurred when a man interfered with another man's property in the public interest, for example (in the days before we could dial 999 for the fire brigade) the destruction of another man's house to prevent the spread of a catastrophic fire, as indeed occurred in the Great Fire of London in 1666. The latter cases occurred when a man interfered with another's property to save his own person or property from imminent danger, for example when he entered on his neighbour's land without his consent in order to prevent the spread of fire onto his own land.

There is, however, a third group of cases, which is also properly described as founded on the principle of necessity and which is more pertinent to the resolution of the problem in the present case. These cases are concerned with action taken as a matter of necessity to assist another person with his consent. To give a simple example, a man who seizes another and forcibly drags him from the path of an oncoming vehicle, thereby saving him from injury or even death, commits no wrong. But there are many emanations of this principle, to be found scattered through the books. These are concerned not only with the preservation of the life or health of the assisted person, but also with the preservation of his property (sometimes an animal, sometimes an ordinary chattel) and even to certain conduct on his behalf in the administration of his affairs. Where there is a pre-existing relationship between the parties, the intervener is usually said to act as an agent of necessity on behalf of the principal in whose interests he acts, and his action can often, with not too much artificiality, be referred to the pre-existing relationship between them. Whether the intervener may be entitled either to reimbursement or to remuneration raises separate questions which are not relevant to the present case.

We are concerned here with action taken to preserve the life, health or well-being of another who is unable to consent to it. Such action is sometimes to be justified as arising from an emergency; . . .

In truth, the relevance of an emergency is that it may give rise to a necessity to act in the interests of the assisted person without first obtaining his consent. Emergency is however not the criterion or even a prerequisite; it is simply a frequent origin of the necessity which impels intervention. The principle is one of necessity, not of emergency.

We can derive some guidance as to the nature of the principle of necessity from the cases on agency of necessity in mercantile law. When reading those cases, however, we have to bear in mind that it was there considered that (since there was a pre-existing relationship between the parties) there was a duty on the part of the agent to act on his principal's behalf in an emergency. [His Lordship then referred to statements in *Prager v Blatspiel, Stamp and Heacock Ltd* [1924] 1 KB 566 at 572 and in *Australasian Steam Navigation Co v Morse* (1872) LR 4 PC 222 at 230 and continued:] ... [From these statements] can be derived the basic requirements, applicable in these cases of necessity, that, to fall within the principle, not only (1) must there be a necessity to act when it is not practicable to communicate with the assisted person, but also (2) the action taken must be such as a reasonable person would in all the circumstances take, acting in the best interests of the assisted person.

On this statement of principle, I wish to observe that officious intervention cannot be justified by the principle of necessity. So intervention cannot be justified when another more appropriate person is available and willing to act; nor can it be justified when it is contrary to the known wishes of the assisted person, to the extent that he is capable of rationally forming such a wish. On the second limb of the principle, the introduction of the standard of a reasonable man should not in the present context be regarded as materially different from that of Sir Montague Smith's 'wise and prudent man'[1], because a reasonable man would, in the time available to him, proceed with wisdom and prudence before taking action in relation to another man's person or property without his consent. I shall have more to say on this point later. Subject to that, I hesitate at present to indulge in any greater refinement of the principle, being well aware of many problems which may arise in its application, problems which it is not necessary, for present purposes, to examine. But as a general rule, if the above criteria are fulfilled, interference with the assisted person's person or property (as the case may be) will not be unlawful. Take the example of a railway accident, in which injured passengers are trapped in the wreckage. It is this principle which may render lawful the actions of other citizens, railway staff, passengers or outsiders, who rush to give aid and comfort to the victims: the surgeon who amputates the limb of an unconscious passenger to free him from the wreckage; the ambulance man who conveys him to hospital; the doctors and nurses who treat him and care for him while he is still unconscious. Take the example of an elderly person who suffers a stroke which renders him incapable of speech or movement. It is by virtue of this principle that the doctor who treats him, the nurse who cares for him, even the relative or friend or neighbour who comes in to look after him will commit no wrong when he or she touches his body.

The two examples I have given illustrate, in the one case, an emergency and, in the other, a permanent or semi-permanent state of affairs. Another example of the latter kind is that of a mentally disordered person who is disabled from giving consent. I can see no good reason why the principle of necessity should not be applicable in his case as it is in the case of the victim of a stroke. Furthermore, in the case of a mentally disordered person, as in the case of a stroke victim, the permanent state of affairs calls for a wider range of care than may be requisite in an emergency which arises from accidental injury. When the state of affairs is permanent, or semi-permanent, action properly taken to preserve the life, health or well-being of the assisted person may well transcend such measures as surgical operation or substantial medical treatment and may extend to include such humdrum matters as routine medical or dental treatment, even simple care such as dressing and undressing and putting to bed.

The distinction I have drawn between cases of emergency and cases where the state of affairs is (more or less) permanent is relevant in another respect. We are here concerned with medical treatment, and I limit myself to cases of that kind. Where, for example, a surgeon performs an operation without his consent on a patient temporarily rendered unconscious in an accident, he should do no more than is reasonably required, in the best interests of the patient, before he recovers consciousness. I can see no practical difficulty arising from this requirement, which derives

---

1. [In *Australasian Steam Navigation Co v Morse* (1872) LR 4 PC 222 at 230.]

from the fact that the patient is expected before long to regain consciousness and can then be consulted about longer term measures. The point has however arisen in a more acute form where a surgeon, in the course of an operation, discovers some other condition which, in his opinion, requires operative treatment for which he has not received the patient's consent. In what circumstances he should operate forthwith, and in what circumstances he should postpone the further treatment until he has received the patient's consent, is a difficult matter which has troubled the Canadian courts (see *Marshall v Curry* [1933] 3 DLR 260 and *Murray v McMurchy* [1949] 2 DLR 442), but which it is not necessary for your Lordships to consider in the present case.

But where the state of affairs is permanent or semi-permanent, as may be so in the case of a mentally disordered person, there is no point in waiting to obtain the patient's consent. The need to care for him is obvious; and the doctor must then act in the best interests of his patient, just as if he had received his patient's consent so to do. Were this not so, much useful treatment and care could, in theory at least, be denied to the unfortunate. It follows that, on this point, I am unable to accept the view expressed by Neill LJ in the Court of Appeal, that the treatment must be shown to have been necessary. Moreover, in such a case, as my noble and learned friend Lord Brandon has pointed out, a doctor who has assumed responsibility for the care of a patient may not only be treated as having the patient's consent to act, but also be under a duty so to act. I find myself to be respectfully in agreement with Lord Donaldson MR when he said:

'I see nothing incongruous in doctors and others who have a caring responsibility being required, when acting in relation to an adult who is incompetent, to exercise a right of choice in exactly the same way as would the court or reasonable parents in relation to a child, making due allowance, of course, for the fact that the patient is not a child, and I am satisfied that that is what the law does in fact require.'

In these circumstances, it is natural to treat the deemed authority and the duty as interrelated. But I feel bound to express my opinion that, in principle, the lawfulness of the doctor's action is, at least in its origin, to be found in the principle of necessity. This can perhaps be seen most clearly in cases where there is no continuing relationship between doctor and patient. The 'doctor in the house' who volunteers to assist a lady in the audience who, overcome by the drama or by the heat in the theatre, has fainted away is impelled to act by no greater duty than that imposed by his own Hippocratic oath. Furthermore, intervention can be justified in the case of a non-professional, as well as a professional, man or woman who has no pre-existing relationship with the assisted person, as in the case of a stranger who rushes to assist an injured man after an accident. In my opinion, it is the necessity itself which provides the justification for the intervention.

I have said that the doctor has to act in the best interests of the assisted person. In the case of routine treatment of mentally disordered persons, there should be little difficulty in applying this principle. In the case of more serious treatment, I recognise that its application may create problems for the medical profession; however, in making decisions about treatment, the doctor must act in accordance with a responsible and competent body of relevant professional opinion, on the principles set down in *Bolam v Friern Hospital Management Committee* [1957] 2 All ER 118, [1957] 1 WLR 582. No doubt, in practice, a decision may involve others besides the doctor. It must surely be good practice to consult relatives and others who are concerned with the care of the patient. Sometimes, of course, consultation with a specialist or specialists will be required; and in others, especially where the decision involves more than a purely medical opinion, an inter-disciplinary team will in practice participate in the decision. It is very difficult, and would be unwise, for a court to do more than to stress that, for those who are involved in these important and sometimes difficult decisions, the overriding consideration is that they should act in the best interests of the person who suffers from the misfortune of being prevented by incapacity from deciding for himself what should be done to his own body in his own best interests.

In the present case, your Lordships have to consider whether the foregoing principles apply in the case of a proposed operation of sterilisation on an adult woman of unsound mind, or whether sterilisation is (perhaps with one or two other cases) to be placed in a separate category to which special principles apply.

[LORD GOFF went on to decide that the 'foregoing principles' did apply to the case he had outlined.]

[LORD BRIDGE OF HARWICH and LORD JAUNCEY OF TULLICHETTLE delivered speeches in which they concurred with the reasons given for dismissing the appeal by LORD BRANDON and LORD GOFF.]

Questions

1. How would you answer the issue posed by Lord Goff (p. 605 ante)?

2. If an unconscious person who needed urgent medical treatment had to the knowledge of the defendant previously expressed the view that he did not wish to have the type of treatment in question (e.g. a Jehovah's Witness carrying a card stating that they did not wish to have a blood transfusion), would the necessity principle justify the use of this treatment? (See S. Y. S. Lam (1989) 5 PN 118, discussing the Canadian case of *Malette v Shulman* (1988) 47 DLR (4th) 18.)

Notes

1. In relation to the question of consent and the provision of medical treatment concerned with *mental disorder* where Part IV of the Mental Health Act 1983 needs to be considered, see *Clerk & Lindsell*, para. 17–49.

2. A court can grant consent for an operation if a minor who is a ward of court is involved (see *Re B (a minor)* [1988] AC 199; [1987] 2 All ER 206). See further note 4, p. 598, ante.

3. On necessity see further p. 622, post and on the *Bolam* case which was held to be applicable (e.g. pp. 601 and 605, ante, see p. 278, ante. Does *F v West Berkshire Area Health Authority* give too much latitude to the medical profession? Consider M. A. Jones (1989) 5 PN 178; J. Shaw (1990) 53 MLR 91 at 102–106. (The Court of Appeal would have been more restrictive.)

(b) Defence of the person or property

Cockcroft v Smith Court of Queen's Bench (1705) 11 Mod 43

Cockcroft in a scuffle ran his finger towards Smith's eyes, who bit a joint off from the plaintiff's finger.

The question was, whether this was a proper defence for the defendant to justify in an action of *mayhem*?

HOLT CJ, said, if a man strike another, who does not immediately after resent it, but takes his opportunity, and then some time after falls upon him and beats him, in this case, *son assault* is no good plea; neither ought a man, in case of a small assault, give a violent or an unsuitable return; but in such case plead what is necessary for a man's defence, and not who struck first; though this, he said, has been the common practice, but this he wished was altered; for hitting a man a little blow with a little stick on the shoulder, is not a reason for him to draw a sword and cut and hew the other, &c.

Note

The conduct of the *plaintiff* which is involved in this section may be a crime and in this situation the student should note s. 3 of the Criminal Law Act 1967 (replacing the common law) which provides that a 'person may use such force as is reasonable in the circumstances in the prevention of crime. . . .'. See further *Farrell v Secretary of State for Defence* [1980] 1 All ER 166; [1980] 1 WLR 172.

Green *v* Goddard Court of Queen's Bench (1702) 2 Salk 641

. . . *Et per Cur*. There is a force *in law*, as in every trespass *quare clausum fregit*: as if one enters into my ground, in that case the owner must request him to depart before he can lay hands on him to turn him out; for every *impositio manuum* is an assault and battery, which cannot be justified upon the account of breaking the close in law, without a request. The other is an *actual force*, as in burglary, as breaking open a door or gate; and in that case it is lawful to oppose force to force; and if one breaks down the gate, or comes into my close *vi & armis*, I need not request him to be gone, but may lay hands on him immediately, for it is but returning violence with violence: so if one comes forcibly and takes away my goods, I may oppose him without any more ado, for there is no time to make a request. . . .

(c) Lawful authority

Leigh *v* Gladstone King's Bench Division (1909) 26 TLR 139

The plaintiff, a suffragette, claimed damages for assault for the forcible feeding of her in prison and an injunction to restrain its repetition, the defence being that the acts were necessary to save her life and that the force used was the minimum necessary.

LORD ALVERSTONE CJ (in summing up): . . . It was the duty, both under the rules and apart from the rules, of the officials to preserve the health and lives of the prisoners, who were in the custody of the Crown. If they forcibly fed the plaintiff when it was not necessary, the defendants ought to pay damages. The plaintiff did not complain – and it did her credit – of any undue violence being used towards her. The medical evidence was that at the time she was first fed it had become dangerous to allow her to abstain from food any longer. . . . If Dr Helby had allowed the plaintiff to fast for a few days longer, and she had died in consequence, what answer could he have made? It was said that the treatment had failed. That had nothing to do with the case, for there was evidence that it had been successfully continued in some cases for 2½ years, and they had heard that two other ladies who were also guilty of this wicked folly – for it was wicked folly to attempt to starve themselves to death – had completed their full sentences although fed by force. If they thought this poor woman had been improperly treated, in the interests of justice they must not hesitate to say so.

The jury, after considering two minutes, returned a verdict for the defendants, and judgment was entered accordingly.

Questions

1. Is this case an example of the defence of necessity?

2. Is it at all relevant that suicide was then (but is not now) a crime? (In relation to this and the following question, consider p. 399, ante and p. 400, ante.)

3. If a political extremist set fire to himself in the street, would there be any defence for (a) a private person who threw water over him or (b) a fireman who did likewise?

Notes

1. See also the consideration of necessity, p. 599, ante and p. 622, post.

2. For comment on *Leigh v Gladstone*, see G. Zellick [1976] PL 153. The author refers to the Home Secretary's announcement in 1974 (877 H. C. Debs (5th Series) cols. 451–452) which in Zellick's words 'made it plain that [the then Home Secretary] did not approve of forced feeding and would like to see it abandoned unless the prisoner's capacity for rational judgment was impaired by illness'.

3. An obvious case of lawful authority justifying trespass to the person is the power of arrest, but treatment of that topic will be left to courses on constitutional law.

4. Moving away from the question of defences, the student should note, alongside the tort of false imprisonment, the possible existence of tortious liability for some abuse of the legal process, a topic which is not dealt with in this book. See *Winfield & Jolowicz*, chap. 19. For example, if the defendant has maliciously and without reasonable and probable cause instituted or continued criminal proceedings against the plaintiff and those proceedings have ended in the plaintiff's favour, the latter has a cause of action in the tort of malicious prosecution if he has suffered damage. Another point to note is the existence of s. 133 of, and Sch. 12 to, the Criminal Justice Act 1988 dealing with the question of compensation for miscarriages of justice.

14 Interference with land

It was pointed out in the Introduction (p. 1, ante) that to a lawyer from a civil law system the arrangement of English law seems faulty because the possession of land is protected in English law through trespass, an action in tort. The law regulating some aspects of the conduct of neighbouring land-owners is also dealt with in tort, through the action in respect of nuisance, rather than as a part of the law of property.

It has been seen (p. 570, ante) that fault is now an essential ingredient in trespass to the person, and this is also the position in the case of trespass to goods (*National Coal Board v Evans* [1951] 2 KB 861; [1951] 2 All ER 310): whether fault (in the sense of intention or negligence) in respect of the entry is essential in all cases of actions for trespass to land is less clear; but in an action for trespass by hounds (*League Against Cruel Sports Ltd v Scott* [1986] QB 240; [1986] 2 All ER 489) it was decided that the master of hounds was only liable if he had intended their entry or was negligent in failing to stop it. Whatever the position on that point, one common characteristic of all these trespass actions is that they are actionable without proof of damage. Nevertheless, it should be noted that a plaintiff, who has not suffered any damage, risks having a 'frivolous action' disapproved of by the awarding of 'contemptuous damages', and is likely to have to pay his own costs. (See F. H. Lawson, *The Rational Strength of English Law*, p. 132.) A further point to note about actions for trespass to land is that they can be used not simply to settle questions of title to land, but again in common with other trespass actions (in particular false imprisonment), they can be important in the constitutional sphere, protecting the Englishman's castle/home against unlawful intrusions: *Entick v Carrington* (1765) 19 State Tr 1029.

The tort of nuisance takes two forms, the one called public nuisance, the other private nuisance, but the same conduct may amount to both. Public nuisance has been said to 'cover a multitude of sins, great and small' (per Denning LJ in *Southport Corpn v Esso Petroleum Co Ltd* [1954] 2 QB 182 at 196), and a definition will be found in the judgment of Lawton J in *British Celanese Ltd v A H Hunt* (*Capacitors*) *Ltd* [1969] 2 All ER 1252; [1969] 1 WLR 959 (p. 629, post). A public nuisance is also a crime, but can give rise to a civil action by an individual where he suffers some particular damage greater than that suffered by the public. Public nuisances share with private nuisances the element of annoyance or inconvenience; more broadly, private nuisance is described (by *Winfield & Jolowicz*, p. 378) as 'unlawful inter-ference with a person's use or enjoyment of land, or some right over, or in connection with it.'

Nuisance differs from trespass in that an action will lie for nuisance, but not trespass, if the damage is merely consequential upon the defendant's act and not 'direct'; moreover, nuisance is in general actionable only on proof of actual damage. On the other hand, nuisance may overlap with liability under the rule in *Rylands v Fletcher* (1868) LR 3 HL 330 (p. 650, post) which is concerned with the escape of dangerous things from land. It too may have to be distinguished from trespass, since in *Rigby v Chief Constable of Northamptonshire* [1985] 2 All ER 985; [1985] 1 WLR 1242 Taylor J was inclined to agree with the argument that *Rylands v Fletcher* is only concerned with indirect damage, and that it does not apply in cases of intentional or voluntary release of dangerous things (which would have to be remedied in trespass). Nevertheless, whatever the historical relationship between nuisance and the rule in *Rylands v Fletcher*, on the authorities as they stand at present it does appear that the two forms of liability are somewhat divorced. For example, the plaintiff in private nuisance, as opposed to public nuisance, must have an interest in land (*Malone v Laskey* [1907] 2 KB 141), but, although the case law does not speak with one voice, it does suggest that this may not be necessary under *Rylands v Fletcher* (see e.g. the Law Commission's Report, *Civil Liability for Dangerous Things and Activities*, Law Com. No. 32, Appendix 1, pp. 17–18; cf. *Salmond & Heuston*, pp. 362–364). To this extent, therefore, it must be confessed that the materials in the *Rylands v Fletcher* section go beyond the title of this chapter; yet the close connection with the factual circumstances which may give rise to an action in nuisance suggests that it is convenient to consider the rule in *Rylands v Fletcher* immediately after the tort of nuisance has been explored. For other differences between nuisance and *Rylands v Fletcher*, see *Street*, pp. 357–358; W. A. West (1966) 30 Conv (NS) 95.

The sphere of operation of the rule in *Rylands v Fletcher* is at present rather limited. Amongst the difficulties facing the plaintiff—in addition to the doubt just mentioned concerning the status to sue of someone without an interest in land—is the uncertainty as to whether damages can be recovered for personal injuries. Furthermore, although liability under *Rylands v Fletcher* is apparently strict, it can become similar to liability in negligence: see *Perry v Kendricks Transport Ltd* [1956] 1 All ER 154; [1956] 1 WLR 85 (p. 661, post) dealing with the defence of 'act of stranger'. It will also be seen that one requirement of liability under *Rylands v Fletcher* is that there must have been a 'non-natural user' of land, and *Winfield & Jolowicz*, p. 429, suggest that this concept 'is now understood by the courts as being similar to the idea of unreasonable risk in negligence' (see also pp. 442–443; D. W. Williams [1973] CLJ 310, esp. 314–317). The relationship of negligence and the tort of nuisance has also provoked debate (p. 632, post), not least because of the decision in *The Wagon Mound* (*No 2*) [1967] 1 AC 617; [1966] 2 All ER 709 (p. 632, post) which decides that the kind of damage must be foreseeable if it is to be recoverable in nuisance (both public and private), just as in negligence. It should, however, be remembered that, in laying down the position for negligence, the Privy Council in *The Wagon Mound* [1961] AC 388; [1961] 1 All ER 404 (p. 333, ante) asserted that their judgment was not intended to 'reflect on' the rule in *Rylands v Fletcher* which they had not considered. See generally R. W. M. Dias [1962] CLJ 178 at 193–195.

In 1970 the rule in *Rylands v Fletcher* was considered by the Law Commission (op cit), but, because of the scope of the inquiry which the Law Commission was invited to undertake, that body refrained from making any recommendations to change the law. (See paras. 2, 11 and 18 of the Report.) The views of the Pearson Commission relating to this area of the law are mentioned at p. 664, post.

The final section of this chapter deals with liability for fire, which has often been considered to be within the rule in *Rylands v Fletcher*, although liability for fire at common law has its own separate history. Indeed, in a relatively recent cases *H & N Emanuel Ltd v Greater London Council* [1971] 2 All ER 835 (p. 666, post) the old common law action for damage by fire received judicial attention. A more modern hazard, nuclear installations, has been subject to special legislation, and liability for such installations should be studied in the light of that legislation, p. 533, ante. For further legislative activity relevant to 'dangerous things', see the Environmental Protection Act 1990 which can in certain circumstances entail civil liability.

1 Trespass to land

Salmond and Heuston on the Law of Torts (19th edn, p. 46)

The tort of trespass to land (trespass *quare clausum fregit*) consists in the act of (1) entering upon land in the possession of the plaintiff, or (2) remaining upon such land, or (3) placing or projecting any object upon it – in each case without lawful justification.

(a) Special situations

(i) The highway

Hickman *v* Maisey Court of Appeal [1900] 1 QB 752

A. L. SMITH LJ: This is an application for judgment or a new trial by the defendant in an action for trespass brought by the occupier of certain down land, part of which was used for the purpose of training race-horses. The application is made under the following circumstances. It appears that there is a highway across the plaintiff's land, and the defendant, who was what has been called a 'racing tout', had for a considerable period of time been using this highway for the purpose of watching therefrom the trials of race-horses upon the plaintiff's land, and availing himself of the information so obtained by him for the purposes of his business, the effect of which was to depreciate the value of the plaintiff's land as a place for the training and trial of race-horses. The defendant insisting on his right so to use the highway, the plaintiff brought his action for trespass in respect of such use of the highway by the defendant. The defendant justifies the acts complained of on the ground that the locus in quo was a highway, and that he was lawfully using it as such. The question is, therefore, whether the use of the highway in the manner in which the defendant used it was in truth a use of it for the purpose for which a highway is dedicated to the public. The evidence shews that what the defendant did was to walk up and down a short portion of the highway about fifteen yards in length for a period of about an hour and a half with a note-book, watching the horses, and taking notes of their performances. It is contended for the defendant that such a use of the highway is lawful as being a use of it in the ordinary way in which a highway is used, namely, for the purpose of passing and repassing, and therefore not a trespass. Unless what the defendant did comes within the ordinary and reasonable use of a highway as such and is therefore lawful, it is clear that it would be a trespass. Therefore the question is, What is the lawful use of a highway? Many authorities, of which the well-known case of *Dovaston v Payne*[1] is one, shew that prima facie the right of the public is merely to pass and repass along the highway; but I quite agree with what Lord Esher MR said in *Harrison v Duke of Rutland*,[2] though I think it is a slight extension of the rule as previously stated, namely, that, though highways are dedicated prima facie for the purpose of passage, 'things are done upon them by everybody which are recognised as being rightly done and as constituting a reasonable and usual mode of using a highway as such'; and, 'if a person on a highway does not transgress such reasonable and usual mode of using it,' he will not be a trespasser; but, if he does 'acts other than the reasonable and ordinary user of a highway as such' he will be a trespasser. For instance, if a man, while using a highway for passage, sat down for a time to rest himself by the side of the road, to call that a trespass would be unreasonable. Similarly, to take a case suggested during the argument, if a man took a sketch from the highway, I should say that no reasonable person would treat that as an act of trespass. But I cannot agree with the contention of the defendant's counsel that the acts which this defendant did, not really for the purpose of using the highway as such, but for the purpose of carrying on his business as a racing tout to the detriment of the plaintiff by watching the trials of race-horses on the plaintiff's land, were within such an ordinary and reasonable user of the highway as I have mentioned. It appears to me that in the case of *Harrison v Duke of Rutland*[2] the point which arises in this case was substantially determined, though the user of the highway by the plaintiff in that case was not precisely similar to that in the present case. In that case the plaintiff went upon a highway, the soil of which was vested in the defendant, while a grouse drive was taking place on adjoining land of the defendant, for the purpose of interfering with the drive, which the defendant's keepers prevented him from doing by force. The plaintiff thereupon brought an action for assault against the defendant, and the defendant counter-claimed in trespass. The plaintiff in answer to the counter-claim set up the defence that the locus in quo was a highway. It was clear upon the facts that he was not using the highway for the purpose of passing or repassing along it, but solely for the purpose of interfering with the defendant's enjoyment of his right of shooting over his land, and it was held therefore that the plaintiff's user of the highway was a trespass. I cannot see any real distinction between that case and the present. It is contended that Day J directed the jury improperly, but I do not think that is so. He told them in effect that the defendant was entitled to use the highway as a wayfarer, and that it was a question for them whether in what the defendant did he was so using it. I think that his direction was in substance a sufficient direction under the circumstances of the case. I do not agree with the argument of the defendant's counsel to the effect that the intention and object of the defendant in going upon the highway cannot be taken into account in determining whether he was using it in a lawful manner. I think that his intention and object were all-important in determining that question. The application must be dismissed.

[COLLINS and ROMER LJJ delivered judgments in favour of dismissing the application.]

Application dismissed

---

1. (1795) 2 Hy Bl 527.
2. [1893] 1 QB 142.

Question

Are any of the following trespasses on the highway?
  (a) parking a car overnight
  (b) participating in a procession along the highway, or
  (c) participating in a meeting on the highway.

Notes

1. The soil of the highway is presumed to belong (up to the middle of the highway) to the owner of the land on either side. However, it should be mentioned that by s. 263 of the Highways Act 1980 'every highway maintainable at the public expense, together with the materials and scrapings of it vests in the authority who are for the time being the highway authority for the highway'. For discussion of the interest of the highway authority, see C. A. Cross, *Encyclopedia of Highway Law and Practice*, paras. 1-002-1-004. It would seem that the highway authority could sue in trespass: see S. J. Sauvain, *Highway Law* (London, 1988), para. 1-07, deriving support from *Wiltshire County Council v Frazer* (1983) 82 LGR 313. Note, however, *Hubbard v Pitt* [1976] QB 142; [1975] 3 All ER 1, in which there was an orderly and peaceful picket outside the plaintiffs' offices. In this case Lord Denning MR stated that the plaintiffs could not maintain an action for trespass to the highway because the surface of the highway was vested in the local authority, and he continued by saying that the highway authority could not complain because 'no wrong has been done to them or their interest'. Assuming that Lord Denning thought that there had been such a use of the highway in this case as could constitute a trespass to the highway, do you agree with this view that the highway authority could not sue? See further the discussion of trespass to the highway by P. Wallington [1976] CLJ 82 at 93-97 and see s. 15 of the Trade Union and Labour Relations Act 1974 as substituted by the Employment Acts 1980 and 1982.

2. If a defendant obstructs the highway, he may commit not only a trespass but also a public nuisance. Furthermore, he may involve himself in criminal liability under statute: see s. 137 of the Highways Act 1980.

(ii) Air space

The Civil Aviation Act 1982

76. Liability of aircraft in respect of trespass, nuisance and surface damage. — (1) No action shall lie in respect of trespass or in respect of nuisance, by reason only of the flight of an aircraft over any property at a height above the ground which, having regard to wind, weather and all the circumstances of the case is reasonable, or the ordinary incidents of such flight, so long as the provisions of any Air Navigation Order and of any orders under section 62[1] above have been duly complied with and there has been no breach of section 81[2] below.

---

1. [Section 62 relates to the control of aviation in time of war or great national emergency.]
2. [This concerns aircraft being flown in a manner unnecessarily dangerous to person or property.]

(2) Subject to subsection (3) below, where material loss or damage is caused to any person or property on land or water by, or by a person in, or an article, animal or person falling from, an aircraft while in flight, taking off or landing, then unless the loss or damage was caused or contributed to by the negligence of the person by whom it was suffered, damages in respect of the loss or damage shall be recoverable without proof of negligence or intention or other cause of action, as if the loss or damage had been caused by the wilful act, neglect, or default of the owner of the aircraft.

(3) Where material loss or damage is caused as aforesaid in circumstances in which —

> (a) damages are recoverable in respect of the said loss or damage by virtue only of subsection (2) above, and
>
> (b) a legal liability is created in some person other than the owner to pay damages in respect of the said loss or damage,

the owner shall be entitled to be indemnified by that other person against any claim in respect of the said loss or damage.

Note

For a consideration of s. 76 see Shawcross and Beaumont, *Air Law*, 4th edn (London, 1990), paras. V (136)–(150) and see further the ensuing case. The section applies to 'aircraft belonging to or exclusively employed in the service of Her Majesty, not being military aircraft' (see The Civil Aviation (Crown Aircraft) Order 1970, S.I. 1970 No. 289 which by virtue of s. 101 of the Civil Aviation Act 1982 and s. 17(2)(b) of the Interpretation Act 1978 applies to the 1982 Act).

Lord Bernstein of Leigh *v* Skyviews and General Ltd Queen's Bench Division [1977] 2 All ER 902

The defendants, whose business involved the taking of aerial photographs of premises and the sale of those photographs to the owners of the premises, took an aerial photograph of the plaintiff's house. The plaintiff claimed that the defendants had trespassed and committed an actionable invasion of his privacy. The trial judge (Griffiths J) found that the defendants had without permission flown over the plaintiff's land to take the photograph.

GRIFFITHS J: . . . The plaintiff claims that as owner of the land he is also owner of the air space above the land, or at least has the right to exclude any entry into the air space above his land. He relies on the old Latin maxim, *cujus est solum ejus est usque ad coelum et ad inferos*, a colourful phrase often on the lips of lawyers since it was first coined by Accursius in Bologna in the 13th century. There are a number of cases in which the maxim has been used by English judges but an examination of those cases shows that they have all been concerned with structures attached to the adjoining land, such as overhanging buildings, signs or telegraph wires, and for their solution it has not been necessary for the judge to cast his eyes towards the heavens; he has been concerned with the rights of the owner in the air space immediately adjacent to the surface of the land.

That an owner has certain rights in the air space above his land is well established by authority. He has the right to lop the branches of trees that may overhang his boundary, although this right seems to be founded in nuisance rather than trespass: see *Lemmon v Webb*[1]. In *Wandsworth Board of Works v United Telephone Co*[2]

---

1. [1894] 3 Ch 1; [1891–4] All ER Rep 749.
2. (1884) 13 QBD 904.

the Court of Appeal did not doubt that the owner of land would have the right to cut a wire placed over his land. Fry LJ said[1]:

'As at present advised, I entertain no doubt that an ordinary proprietor of land can cut and remove a wire placed at any height above his freehold.'

Fry [LJ] added that the point was not necessary for his decision (it is therefore obiter) and I hasten to add that it would be subject to any statutory rights given to the Post Office and other undertakers to erect telegraph lines or other installations.

In *Gifford v Dent*[2] Romer J held that it was a trespass to erect a sign that projected four feet eight inches over the plaintiff's forecourt and ordered it to be removed. He invoked the old maxim in his judgment. The report reads[2]:

' . . . the Plaintiffs were tenants of the forecourt and were accordingly tenants to the space above the forecourt usque ad coelum, it seemed to him that the projection was clearly a trespass upon the property of the plaintiff.'

That decision was followed by McNair J in *Kelsen v Imperial Tobacco Co Ltd*[3], in which he granted a mandatory injunction ordering the defendants to remove a sign which projected only eight inches over the plaintiff's property. The plaintiff relies strongly on this case, and in particular on the following passage when, after citing the judgment of Romer J to which I have already referred, McNair J continued[3]:

'That decision, I think, has been recognised by the text-book writers, and, in particular, by the late Professor Winfield[5], as stating the true law. It is not without significance that in the Air Navigation Act 1920, s. 9(1), which was replaced by s. 40(1) of the Civil Aviation Act 1949,[6] the legislature found it necessary expressly to negative the action of trespass or nuisance arising from the mere fact of an aeroplane passing through the air above the land. It seems to me clearly to indicate that the legislature were not taking the same view of the matter as Lord Ellenborough in *Pickering v Rudd*,[7] but were taking the view accepted in the later cases, such as *Wandsworth Board of Works v United Telephone Co*,[8] subsequently followed by Romer J in *Gifford v Dent*[9]. Accordingly, I reach the conclusion that a trespass, and not a mere nuisance, was created by the invasion of the plaintiff's air space by this sign.'

I very much doubt if in that passage McNair J was intending to hold that the plaintiff's rights in the air space continued to an unlimited height or 'ad coelum' as counsel for the plaintiff submits. The point that the judge was considering was whether the sign was a trespass or a nuisance at the very low level at which it projected. This to my mind is clearly indicated by his reference to Winfield on Tort[10] in which the text reads: . . . it is submitted that trespass will be committed by [aircraft] to the air-space if they fly so low as to come within the area of ordinary user.' The author in that passage is careful to limit the trespass to the height at which it is contemplated an

---

1. (1884) 13 QBD 904 at 927.
2. [1926] 1 WN 336.
3. [1957] 2 QB 334; [1957] 2 All ER 343.
4. [1957] 2 QB 334 at 345; [1957] 2 All ER 343 at 351.
5. Winfield on Tort (6th edn, 1954), p. 379.
6. [See now s. 76(1) of the Civil Aviation Act 1982 (p. 613, ante).]
7. (1815) 4 Camp 219.
8. (1884) 13 QBD 904.
9. [1926] 1 WN 336.
10. 6th edn, (1954), p. 380.

owner might be expected to make use of the air space as a natural incident of the user of his land. If, however, the learned judge was by his reference to the Civil Aviation Act 1949[1], and his disapproval of the views of Lord Ellenborough in *Pickering v Rudd*[2], indicating the opinion that the flight of an aircraft at whatever height constituted a trespass at common law, I must respectfully disagree.

I do not wish to cast any doubts on the correctness of the decision on its own particular facts. It may be a sound and practical rule to regard any incursion into the air space at a height which may interfere with the ordinary user of the land as a trespass rather than a nuisance. Adjoining owners then know where they stand: they have no right to erect structures overhanging or passing over their neighbours' land and there is no room for argument whether they are thereby causing damage or annoyance to their neighbours about which there may be much room for argument and uncertainty. But wholly different considerations arise when considering the passage of aircraft at a height which in no way affects the user of the land. . . .

I can find no support in authority for the view that a landowner's rights in the air space above his property extend to an unlimited height. In *Wandsworth Board of Works v United Telephone Co*[3] Bowen LJ described the maxim, usque ad coelum, as a fanciful phrase, to which I would add that if applied literally it is a fanciful notion leading to the absurdity of a trespass at common law being committed by a satellite every time it passes over a suburban garden. The academic writers speak with one voice in rejecting the uncritical and literal application of the maxim. . . . I accept their collective approach as correct. The problem is to balance the rights of an owner to enjoy the use of his land against the rights of the general public to take advantage of all that science now offers in the use of air space. This balance is in my judgment best struck in our present society by restricting the rights of an owner in the air space above his land to such height as is necessary for the ordinary use and enjoyment of his land and the structures on it, and declaring that above that height he has no greater rights in the air space than any other member of the public.

Applying this test to the facts of this case, I find that the defendants' aircraft did not infringe any rights in the plaintiff's air space, and thus no trespass was committed. It was on any view of the evidence flying many hundreds of feet above the ground and it is not suggested that by its mere presence in the air space it caused any interference with any use to which the plaintiff put or might wish to put his land. The plaintiff's complaint is not that the aircraft interfered with the use of his land but that a photograph was taken from it. There is, however, no law against taking a photograph, and the mere taking of a photograph cannot turn an act which is not a trespass into the plaintiff's air space into one that is a trespass.

. . . Counsel for the plaintiff . . . conceded that he was unable to cite any principle of law or authority that would entitle the plaintiff to prevent someone taking a photograph of his property for an innocent purpose, provided they did not commit some other tort such as trespass or nuisance in doing so. It is therefore interesting to reflect what a sterile remedy the plaintiff would obtain if he was able to establish that mere infringement of the air space over his land was a trespass. He could prevent the defendants flying over his land to take another photograph, but he could not prevent the defendants taking the virtually identical photograph from the adjoining land provided they took care not to cross his boundary, and were taking it for an innocent as opposed to a criminal purpose.

My finding that no trespass at common law has been established is sufficient to determine this case in the defendants' favour. I should, however, deal with a further defence under the Civil Aviation Act 1949, s. 40(1)[1]. . . .

---

1. [See now s. 76(1) of the Civil Aviation Act 1982 (p. 613, ante).]
2. (1815) 4 Camp 219.
3. (1884) 13 QBD 904.

It is agreed that all the statutory provisions have been complied with by the defendants, nor is there any suggestion that the aircraft was not flying at a reasonable height; but it is submitted by the plaintiff that the protection given by the subsection is limited to a bare right of passage over land analogous to the limited right of a member of the public to pass over the surface of a highway, and my attention has been drawn to a passage in Shawcross and Beaumont on Air Law[1] in which the editors express this view. I see nothing in the language of the section to invite such a restricted reading which would withdraw from its protection many very beneficial activities carried on from aircraft. . . . As I read the section its protection extends to all flights provided they are at a reasonable height and comply with the statutory requirements. And I adopt this construction the more readily because s. 40(2)[2] imposes on the owner of the aircraft a strict liability to pay damages for any material loss or damage that may be caused by his aircraft.

It is, however, to be observed that the protection given is limited by the words 'by reason only of the flight', so although an owner can found no action in trespass or nuisance if he relies solely on the flight of the aircraft above his property as founding his cause of action, the section will not preclude him from bringing an action if he can point to some activity carried on by or from the aircraft that can properly be considered a trespass or nuisance, or some other tort. For example, the section would give no protection against the deliberate emission of vast quantities of smoke that polluted the atmosphere and seriously interfered with the plaintiff's use and enjoyment of his property; such behaviour remains an actionable nuisance. Nor would I wish this judgment to be understood as deciding that in no circumstances could a successful action be brought against an aerial photographer to restrain his activities. The present action is not founded in nuisance for no court would regard the taking of a single photograph as an actionable nuisance. But if the cir[c]umstances were such that a plaintiff was subjected to the harassment of constant surveillance of his house from the air, accompanied by the photographing of his every activity, I am far from saying that the court would not regard such a monstrous invasion of his privacy as an actionable nuisance for which they would give relief. However, that question does not fall for decision in this case and will be decided if and when it arises.

On the facts of this case even if contrary to my view the defendants' aircraft committed a trespass at common law in flying over the plaintiff's land, the plaintiff is prevented from bringing any action in respect of that trespass by the terms of s. 40(1)[3] of the Civil Aviation Act 1949.

For these reasons the plaintiff's action fails and there will be judgment for the defendants.

Judgment for the defendants

Notes

1. In *Anchor Brewhouse Developments Ltd v Berkely House Docklands Developments Ltd* [1987] 2 EGLR 173 the question arose whether there could be a trespass action in respect of tower cranes which stood on the defendant's property, but of which part would swing into the air space over another's property. Reference was made by counsel for the defendant to the passage in Griffiths J's judgment in the *Bernstein* case (p. 616, ante) concerning the need to balance the owner's rights against those of the public. However, Scott J in *Anchor Brewhouse* thought it would be wrong to apply that

---

1. 3rd edn (1966), vol 1, p. 561.
2. [See now s. 76(2) of the Civil Aviation Act 1982 (p.614, ante).]
3. [See now s. 76(1) of the Civil Aviation Act 1982 (p. 613, ante).]

approach, which in his view related to the question of aircraft, to the general
problem of invasion of the air space. In his opinion 'if somebody erects on
his own land a structure, part of which invades the air space above the land
of another, the invasion is trespass', and he pointed to an earlier passage in
Griffiths J's judgment (p. 616, ante) in which he had accepted that landowners could not erect structures passing over their neighbours' land. (Note,
however, the reference in this passage to 'ordinary user'; cf. Scott J in
Anchor Brewhouse who rejected an argument that the test should be one of
interference with the ordinary use and enjoyment.) On cranes see further
Woollerton and Wilson Ltd v Richard Costain Ltd [1970] 1 All ER 483;
[1970] 1 WLR 411 (trespass conceded); *London and Manchester Assurance
Co Ltd v O and H Construction Ltd* [1989] 2 EGLR 185.

2. The extent to which a plaintiff can obtain an injunction to prevent a
trespass where he has suffered no actual harm has been discussed in the cases
dealing with the air space (*Woollerton and Wilson Ltd*; *John Trenberth Ltd
v National Westminster Bank Ltd* (1980) 39 P & CR 104; *Anchor Brewhouse*).
In *Woollerton and Wilson Ltd* the lack of any actual harm was seen as a
reason for, rather than against, the grant of an injunction since in Stamp J's
view only nominal damages could be awarded (and see also the *Trenberth*
case); but note that in *Anchor Brewhouse* it was stated by Scott J (at p. 176)
that in these cases 'it would have been open to a court in assessment of
damages to charge the defendant with, in effect, a reasonable licence fee'.
Consequently on this view more than merely nominal damages could have
been awarded, but this did not lead Scott J to regard the grant of injunctive
relief in *Woollerton and Wilson Ltd* as unsound. The problem does, of
course, arise in cases other than those concerned with the air space, and in
Patel v W H Smith (Eziot) Ltd [1987] 2 All ER 569 at 573 Balcombe LJ stated
that it seemed to him' that . . . prima facie a landowner whose title is not in
issue is entitled to an injunction to restrain trespass on his land whether or
not the trespass harms him'. He did, however, go on to accept that there
might be exceptional circumstances where an injunction might not be
thought to be appropriate. See further *Anchor Brewhouse* where various
authorities are discussed, and for a case where there was a refusal to grant
a mandatory injunction in relation to trespass in the air space, see
Tollemache and Cobbold Breweries Ltd v Reynolds (1983) 268 Estates
Gazette 52.

The operation of the injunction that was granted in *Woollerton and
Wilson Ltd* was postponed until a particular date by which time it apperaed
that the trespass would have ceased. In *Charrington v Simons & Co Ltd*
[1971] 2 All ER 588; [1971] 1 WLR 598 the Court of Appeal reserved its opinion on the correctness of this decision and in the *Trenberth* case Walton J
stated that *Woollerton and Wilson Ltd* could not be relied on in relation to
the suspension of the injunction.

On the topics raised by this note (and note 1, ante), see E. McKendrick
(1988) 138 NLJ 23; A. J. Wait (1989) 5 Const LJ 117.

3. On privacy, in respect of which trespass to land is one tort that may provide protection in appropriate circumstances, see also p. 795, post and the
references to further reading at p. 801, post. See also the note on *Lord
Bernstein of Leigh v Skyviews and General Ltd* by R. Wacks (1977) 93 LQR
491, and consider *Patel v Patel* [1988] 2 FLR 179.

(b)   The plaintiff

Graham v Peat Court of King's Bench (1801) 1 East 244

Trespass *quare clausum fregit*. Plea the general issue (and certain special pleas not material to the question). At the trial before Graham B at the last assizes at Carlisle, the trespass was proved in fact; but it also appeared that the locus in quo was part of the glebe of the rector of the parish of Workington in Cumberland, which had been demised by the rector to the plaintiff, and that the rector had not been resident within the parish for five years last past, and no sufficient excuse was shewn for his absence. Whereupon it was objected that the action could not be maintained, the lease being absolutely void by the Act of the 13 Eliz c. 20, which enacts, 'That no lease of any benefice or ecclesiastical promotion with cure or any part thereof shall endure any longer than while the lessor shall be ordinarily resident and serving the cure of such benefice without absence above fourscore days in any one year; but that every such lease immediately upon such absence shall cease and be void.' And thereupon the plaintiff was nonsuited.

A rule was obtained in Michaelmas term last to shew cause why the nonsuit should not be set aside, upon the ground that the action was maintainable against a wrongdoer upon the plaintiff's possession alone, without shewing any title. . . .

LORD KENYON CJ: There is no doubt but that the plaintiff's possession in this case was sufficient to maintain trespass against a wrongdoer; and if he could not have maintained an ejectment upon such a demise, it is because that is a fictitious remedy founded upon title. Any possession is a legal possession against a wrongdoer. Suppose a burglary committed in the dwelling-house of such an one, must it not be laid to be his dwelling-house notwithstanding the defect of his title under that statute.

Per Curiam. Rule absolute

Notes

1. This case shows that the saying that possession is nine tenths of the law is not without truth. (On the concept of possession, see further F. Pollock and R. S. Wright, *An Essay on Possession in the Common Law* (Oxford, 1888).) Compare the action of ejectment (or action for recovery of land), on which see *Clerk & Lindsell*, paras. 23-48-23-52.

2. A person with possession of property will not always succeed in a trespass action. In *Delaney v T P Smith Ltd* [1946] KB 393; [1946] 2 All ER 23 the plaintiff made an oral agreement with an agent of the defendants for the tenancy of a house which was being repaired. Before the house was ready, the defendants decided that they would sell the house (along with several others), and wrote to the plaintiff to that effect. Some time later the plaintiff obtained a key and took possession of the premises, but nine days later was forcibly ejected by the defendants, from whom he claimed damages for trespass. He alleged that he was the tenant of the house and protected by the provisions of the Rent and Mortgage Interest (Restrictions) Acts 1920-1939, but was faced by an argument from the defendants based on s. 40 of the Law of Property Act 1925 – that no note or memorandum existed relating to the alleged tenancy. It was pointed out in the Court of Appeal that in an action for trespass to land, an allegation of possession by a plaintiff would suffice against a wrongdoer, but not against the lawful owner. Against the freeholder

here, the plaintiff had to rely on the oral agreement, to which s. 40 provided an answer. (Cf. *Lane v Dixon* (1847) 3 CB 776.) *Delaney v T P Smith Ltd* was cited in *Portland Managements Ltd v Harte* [1977] QB 306; [1976] 1 All ER 225 where the position of an owner bringing a trespass action against someone alleged to be in possession of his property was considered. In this situation it was accepted that once the court is satisfied that the plaintiff in a trespass action is the owner of the property in question and intending to regain possession, then the burden is on the defendant to establish some right to possession which is consistent with the plaintiff being the owner. On the question of who may sue in trespass, see further *Winfield & Jolowicz*, pp. 394–396; *Street*, pp. 69–72; *Clerk & Lindsell*, paras. 23-08-23-18.

3. The student should also note the doctrine of trespass by relation, which operates where a person had a right to immediate possession but did not enter until a later date. He may sue for trespasses committed between the time when the right arose and the actual entry; he is deemed to have been in possession of the land during that period.

(c)   The nature of the defendant's act

Smith *v* Stone Court of King's Bench (1647) Sty 65

Smith brought an action of trespasse against Stone pedibus ambulando, the defendant pleads this special plea in justification, viz. that he was carried upon the land of the plaintiff by force, and violence of others, and was not there voluntarily, which is the same trespasse, for which the plaintiff brings his action. The plaintiff demurs to this plea: in this case Roll Iustice said, that it is the trespasse of the party that carried the defendant upon the land, and not the trespasse of the defendant: as he that drives my cattel into another mans land is the trespassor against him, and not I who am owner of the cattell.

Gilbert *v* Stone Court of King's Bench (1647) Sty 72

Gilbert brought an action of trespasse quare clausum fregit, and taking of a gelding, against Stone. The defendant pleads that he for fear of his life, and wounding of twelve armed men, who threatened to kill him if he did not the fact, went into the house of the plaintiff, and took the gelding. The plaintiff demurred to this plea; Roll Iustice. This is no plea to justifie the defendant; for I may not do a trespasse to one for fear of threatnings of another, for by this means the party injured shall have no satisfaction, for he cannot have it of the party that threatned. Therefore let the plaintiff have his judgment.

Question

What duty does an occupier of land owe to someone who has involuntarily gone on to his property? (Cf. *Public Transport Commission of New South Wales v Perry* (1977) 14 ALR 273.)

Note

Although these two cases occur in this section on trespass to land, they illustrate a general principle. (See *Clerk & Lindsell*, para. 1-62 and see further p. 264, ante.) Cf. p. 622, post. On the question whether there is any requirement of fault, see p. 609, ante.

(d) Trespass ab initio

The Six Carpenters' Case (1610) 8 Co Rep 146a

In trespass brought by John Vaux against Thomas Newman, carpenter, and five other carpenters, for breaking his house, and for an assault and battery, 1 Sept. 7 Jac. in London, in the parish of St. Giles extra Cripplegate, in the ward of Cripplegate, &c. and upon the new assignment, the plaintiff assigned the trespass in a house called the Queen's Head. The defendants to all the trespass *praeter fractionem domus* pleaded not guilty; and as to the breaking of the house, said, that the said house *praed' tempore quo, &c. et diu antea et postea*, was a common wine tavern, of the said John Vaux, with a common sign at the door of the said house fixed, &c. by force whereof the defendants, *praed' tempore quo, &c. viz. hora quarta post meridiem* into the said house, the door thereof being open, did enter, and did there buy and drink a quart of wine, and there paid for the same, &c. The plaintiff, by way of replication, did confess, that the said house was a common tavern, and that they entered into it, and bought and drank a quart of wine, and paid for it: but further said, that one John Ridding, servant of the said John Vaux, at the request of the said defendants, did there then deliver them another quart of wine, and a pennyworth of bread, amounting to 8d. and then they there did drink the said wine, and eat the bread, and upon request did refuse to pay for the same: upon which the defendants did demur in law and the only point in this case was, if the denying to pay for the wine, or non-payment, which is all one (for every non-payment upon request, is a denying in law) makes the entry into the tavern tortious.

And first, it was resolved when an entry, authority, or licence, is given to any one by the law, and he doth abuse it, he shall be a trespasser ab initio; but where an entry, authority, or licence is given by the party, and he abuses it, there he must be punished for his abuse, but shall not be a trespasser ab initio. And the reason of this difference is, that in the case of a general authority or licence of law, the law adjudges by the subsequent act, *quo animo*, or to what intent, he entered; for *acta exteriora indicant interiora secreta.* . . . But when the party gives an authority or licence himself to do any thing, he cannot, for any subsequent cause, punish that which is done by his own authority or licence, and therefore the law gives authority to enter into a common inn, or tavern, so to the lord to distrain; to the owner of the ground to distrain damage-feasant; to him in reversion to see if waste be done; to the commoner to enter upon the land to see his cattle, and such like. . . .

But if he who enters into the inn or tavern doth a trespass, as if he carries away any thing; or if the lord who distrains for rent, or the owner for damage-feasant, works or kills the distress; or if he who enters to see waste breaks the house, or stays there all night; or if the commoner cuts down a tree, in these and the like cases, the law adjudges that he entered for that purpose; and because the Act which demonstrates it is a trespass, he shall be a trespasser ab initio, as it appears in all the said books. . . .

It was resolved *per totam Curiam*, that not doing, cannot make the party who has authority or licence by the law a trespasser ab initio, because not doing is no trespass; and, therefore, if the lessor distrains for his rent, and thereupon the lessee tenders him the rent and arrears, &c. and requires his beasts again, and he will not deliver them, this not doing cannot make him a trespasser ab initio. . . .

So in the case at Bar, for not paying for the wine, the defendants shall not be trespassers, for the denying to pay for it is no trespass, and therefore they cannot be trespassers ab initio.

Notes

1. This case has been subject to criticism in recent times. In *Chic Fashions (West Wales) Ltd v Jones* [1968] 2 QB 299; [1968] 1 All ER 229 Lord Denning MR stated emphatically (at p. 236) that the case above 'was a by-product of the old forms of action. Now that they are buried, it can be interred with their bones.' See too the judgment of Diplock LJ who expressed the following reservation (at p. 239): 'What application, if any, the rule applied in the *Six Carpenters' Case* has in the modern law of tort, may some day call for re-examination . . . '. The doctrine does seem at odds with the idea, which Lord Denning MR in particular has favoured, that the lawfulness of conduct should be judged at the time when it takes place, and not by what happens later. Nevertheless, in *Cinnamond v British Airports Authority* [1980] 2 All ER 368; [1980] 1 WLR 582 Lord Denning referred to the *Six Carpenters' Case* without any criticism in the course of applying the trespass ab initio doctrine.

2. The *Six Carpenters' Case* refers to entry on to land under a licence. This is a topic which is more fully dealt with in books on the law of property, though see *White v Blackmore* [1972] 2 QB 651; [1972] 3 All ER 158 (p. 456, ante).

(e) Necessity

Notes

1. This defence, which has been mentioned in the context of intentional interference with the person (see p. 599, ante), might also be raised as a defence to trespass to land. However, in *London Borough of Southwark v Williams* [1971] Ch 734; [1971] 2 All ER 175, a case concerning squatters, the Court of Appeal seemed determined to keep the defence within fairly limited bounds. Lord Denning MR stated (at p. 179):

'If homelessness were once admitted as a defence to trespass, no one's house could be safe. Necessity would open a door which no man could shut. It would not only be those in extreme need who would enter. There would be others who would imagine that they were in need, or would invent a need, so as to gain entry. Each man would say his need was greater than the next man's. The plea would be an excuse for all sorts of wrongdoing. So the courts must, for the sake of law and order, take a firm stand. They must refuse to admit the plea of necessity to the hungry and the homeless; and trust that their distress will be relieved by the charitable and the good.'

Edmund Davies LJ took the view that 'all the cases where a plea of necessity has succeeded are cases which deal with an urgent situation of imminent peril', citing *Leigh v Gladstone* (1909) 26 TLR 139 (p. 607, ante) as an example. Though on the need for an 'emergency' in relation to this defence in general, see now *F v West Berkshire Health Authority (Mental Health Act Commission intervening)* [1989] 2 All ER 545 at 565 (p. 603, ante). On the defence of necessity consider further the position in cases such as *Cope v Sharpe (No. 2)* [1912] 1 KB 496.

2. The necessity defence did succeed in *Rigby v Chief Constable of*

Northamptonshire [1985] 2 All ER 985; [1985] 1 WLR 1242, but it was emphasised that for the plea to be successful the necessity for taking measures must not have been caused or contributed to by any negligence on the defendant's part. Negligence is used here in the sense of the standard required by the tort of negligence, rather than any stricter standard (see [1985] 2 All ER at pp. 944–945), and once the issue of negligence is raised, the burden is on the defendant to disprove it.

2 Nuisance

(a) In general

St Helen's Smelting Co *v* Tipping House of Lords (1865) 11 HL Cas 642

The Lord Chancellor (Lord Westbury) stated the following facts: 'Now, in the present case, it appears that the Plaintiff purchased a very valuable estate, which lies within a mile and a half from certain large smelting works. What the occupation of these copper smelting premises was anterior to the year 1860 does not clearly appear. The Plaintiff became the proprietor of an estate of great value in the month of June 1860. In the month of September 1860 very extensive smelting operations began on the property of the present Appellants [defendants] in their works at St Helen's. Of the effect of the vapours exhaling from those works upon the Plaintiff's property, and the injury done to his trees and shrubs, there is abundance of evidence in the case.' The report sets out the direction which was given to the jury by Mellor J:

The learned Judge told the jury that an actionable injury was one producing sensible discomfort; that every man, unless enjoying rights obtained by prescription or agreement, was bound to use his own property in such a manner as not to injure the property of his neighbours; that there was no prescriptive right in this case; that the law did not regard trifling inconveniences; that everything must be looked at from a reasonable point of view; and therefore, in an action for nuisance to property, arising from noxious vapours, the injury to be actionable must be such as visibly to diminish the value of the property and the comfort and enjoyment of it. That when the jurors came to consider the facts, all the circumstances, including those of time and locality, ought to be taken into consideration; and that with respect to the latter it was clear that in counties where great works had been erected and carried on, persons must not stand on their extreme rights and bring actions in respect of every matter of annoyance, for if so, the business of the whole country would be seriously interfered with.

The Defendants' counsel submitted that the three questions which ought to be left to the jury were, 'whether it was a necessary trade, whether the place was a suitable place for such a trade, and whether it was carried on in a reasonable manner.' The learned judge did not put the questions in this form, but did ask the jury whether the enjoyment of the Plaintiff's property was sensibly diminished, and the answer was in the affirmative. Whether the business there carried on was an ordinary business for smelting copper, and the answer was, 'We consider it an ordinary business, and conducted in a proper manner, in as good a manner as possible.' But to the question whether the jurors thought that it was carried on in a proper place, the answer was, 'We do not.' The verdict was therefore entered for the Plaintiff, and the damages were assessed at £361 18*s* 4½*d*. A motion was made for a new trial, on the ground of misdirection, but the rule was refused (4 Best and Sm 608). Leave was however given to appeal, and the case was carried to the Exchequer Chamber, where the judgment was affirmed, Lord Chief Baron Pollock there observing, 'My opinion has not always been that which it is now. Acting upon what has been decided *in this Court*, my brother Mellor's direction is not open to a bill of exception' (4 Best and Sm 616). This appeal was then brought.

[The direction to the jury was approved by the House of Lords, and by the judges who were summoned. LORD WESTBURY LC continued:] . . . My Lords, in matters of this description it appears to me that it is a very desirable thing to mark the difference between an action brought for a nuisance upon the ground that the alleged nuisance produces material injury to the property, and an action brought for a nuisance on the ground that the thing alleged to be a nuisance is productive of sensible personal discomfort. With regard to the latter, namely, the personal inconvenience and interference with one's enjoyment, one's quiet, one's personal freedom, anything that discomposes or injuriously affects the senses or the nerves, whether that may or may not be denominated a nuisance, must undoubtedly depend greatly on the circumstances of the place where the thing complained of actually occurs. If a man lives in a town, it is necessary that he should subject himself to the consequences of those operations of trade which may be carried on in his immediate locality, which are actually necessary for trade and commerce, and also for the enjoyment of property, and for the benefit of the inhabitants of the town and of the public at large. If a man lives in a street where there are numerous shops, and a shop is opened next door to him, which is carried on in a fair and reasonable way, he has no ground for complaint, because to himself individually there may arise much discomfort from the trade carried on in that shop. But when an occupation is carried on by one person in the neighbourhood of another, and the result of that trade, or occupation, or business, is a material injury to property, then there unquestionably arises a very different consideration. I think, my Lords, that in a case of that description, the submission which is required from persons living in society to that amount of discomfort which may be necessary for the legitimate and free exercise of the trade of their neighbours, would not apply to circumstances the immediate result of which is sensible injury to the value of the property. . . .

[Having stated the facts as above, he continued:] My lords, the action has been brought upon that, and the jurors have found the existence of the injury; and the only ground upon which your Lordships are asked to set aside that verdict, and to direct a new trial, is this, that the whole neighbourhood where these copper smelting works were carried on, is a neighbourhood more or less devoted to manufacturing purposes of a similar kind, and therefore it is said, that inasmuch as this copper smelting is carried on in what the Appellant contends is a fit place, it may be carried on with impunity, although the result may be the utter destruction, or the very considerable diminution, of the value of the Plaintiff's property. My Lords, I apprehend that that is not the meaning of the word 'suitable', or the meaning of the word 'convenient', which has been used as applicable to the subject. The word 'suitable' unquestionably cannot carry with it this consequence, that a trade may be carried on in a particular locality, the consequence of which trade may be injury and destruction to the neighbouring property. Of course, my Lords, I except cases where any prescriptive right has been acquired by a lengthened user of the place.

On these grounds, therefore, shortly, without dilating farther upon them . . . I advise your Lordships to affirm the decision of the Court below, and to refuse the new trial, and to dismiss the appeal with costs.

[LORD CRANWORTH delivered a brief speech in which he concurred with the LORD CHANCELLOR. LORD WENSLEYDALE agreed with both their Lordships.]

Judgment of the Exchequer Chamber affirming the judgment of the Court of Queen's Bench affirmed. Appeal dismissed.

Notes

1. For criticism of the 'locality' principle in the *St Helen's* case, see R. A. Buckley, *The Law of Nuisance* (London, 1981), pp. 8–9; A. I. Ogus and G. M. Richardson [1977] CLJ 284 at 299.

2. As the *St. Helen*'s case shows, the nuisance action may play some part in the protection of the environment. Attention might also be paid to *Halsey v Esso Petroleum Co Ltd* [1961] 2 All ER 145; [1961] 1 WLR 683 where the defendants, who operated an oil-distributing depot near to the plaintiff's house, were held liable for: (a) damage caused by acidy smuts escaping from the depot on to laundry hung out to dry (liability in nuisance and under *Rylands v Fletcher*); (b) damage similarly caused to the plaintiff's motor car on the highway (whether or not there could be a claim in private nuisance, there was liability under *Rylands v Fletcher* and in public nuisance); (c) nuisance caused by a 'nauseating smell' escaping from the depot; (d) nuisance at night caused by noise from the plant at the depot; (e) nuisance during the night shift caused by noise from tankers arriving at and leaving the depot (liability here was based either on private nuisance or in the alternative on public nuisance by virtue of their use of the highway). The character of the neighbourhood was relevant to the question of nuisance by smell and by noise. On the question of the character of the neighbourhood, see further p. 650, post.

3. For other aspects of environmental protection, see *Winfield & Jolowicz*, pp. 375–376, though see now the Environmental Protection Act 1990.

4. For an application of economic analysis to the action in private nuisance, see Ogus and Richardson op cit. This article also discusses the position in relation to remedies on which see, in addition, Harris, *Remedies*, pp. 335–343.

5. Many circumstances may be taken into account in deciding whether there has been a nuisance. It is in this context that malice is relevant, although this statement must be read in the light of *Bradford Corpn v Pickles* [1895] AC 587. In that case, the defendant's excavations on his land interfered with percolating water under his land, and resulted in the plaintiffs' water supply being diminished and occasionally discoloured. The plaintiffs sought an injunction but were unsuccessful. The defendant had a right to act in this way (see *Chasemore v Richards* (1859) 7 HL Cas 349), and to the allegation that the defendant was acting maliciously, Lord Halsbury LC answered (at p. 594) that 'if it was a lawful act, however ill the motive might be, he had a right to do it'. In fact, Lord Macnaghten stated that it could be taken that Pickles' objective was to compel the Corporation to purchase his property at a price which suited him, but his Lordship drew attention to the lack of spite and ill-will on Pickles' part. *Salmond & Heuston* (at p. 23) suggest that the common law did not regard his motive as improper.

This decision on the irrelevance of motive must be compared with *Hollywood Silver Fox Farm Ltd v Emmett* [1936] 2 KB 468; [1936] 1 All ER 825. The plaintiff company was engaged in breeding silver foxes. There had been a disagreement between the defendant (an adjoining landowner) and the managing director of the plaintiff company about a notice on the plaintiff's land, and some months later the defendant sent his son out to the boundary of his land which was closest to the vixens' pens to fire a gun: the shooting was repeated for the next three evenings. The noise affected the vixens and caused the plaintiff loss, for there was evidence that the number of cubs reared was less than could have been expected. Some vixens did not mate and one ate her cubs. On the defendant's side, there was evidence that his son was shooting there to cut down the number of rabbits, but in fact the learned judge found that the son was sent to shoot there to frighten the vixens. Taking the view that *Bradford Corpn v Pickles* did not govern the case, and that the defendant's intention was relevant, Macnaghten J gave judgment for the plaintiff in his action for nuisance. (See also *Christie v Davey* [1893] 1 Ch 316.) The explanation of *Emmett*'s case would appear to lie in the following reasoning. Noise can be an interference with a person's use and enjoyment of land. However, the law of nuisance is concerned with balancing the interests of neighbouring landowners, and to be actionable as nuisance, it appears that there has to be an 'unreasonable' use of land by the defendant. Therefore the purpose behind the creation of the 'nuisance' becomes a relevant factor, and the presence of malice may mean that a given amount of noise constitutes an actionable nuisance, where, in the absence of malice, it would not do so. As was pointed out in a note on *Emmett*'s case, the presence of malice destroys the 'qualified privilege to act in a reasonable manner' (1936) 52 LQR 460 at 461, but see (1937) 53 LQR 1–4.

Can *Pickles*' case and *Emmett*'s case be reconciled? (See *Winfield & Jolowicz*, pp. 392–393; *Street*, pp. 322–323; *Clerk & Lindsell*, para. 1–68; G. H. L. Fridman (1958) 21 MLR 484 at 493–494.) On the position in negligence concerning percolating water, see *Stephens v Anglian Water Authority* [1987] 3 All ER 379; [1987] 1 WLR 1381, noted p. 50, ante. Malice is relevant in the tort of conspiracy but is not in itself a cause of action — see *Allen v Flood* [1898] AC 1 (p. 674, post).

6. Consider further the position of a person onto whose land water will, unless prevented, percolate. In *Home Brewery Co Ltd v William Davis & Co (Leicester) Ltd* [1987] QB 339; [1987] 1 All ER 637, noted by J. R. Spencer [1987] CLJ 205, it was accepted that, while an occupier of land had a right to allow water naturally on his land to percolate through to another's land, the latter was not obliged to receive it. Such a rejection was, however, subject to the law of nuisance, but if it was part of a reasonable user of the land, then it was not actionable. *Pickles* was distinguished on the ground that there the defendant was extracting something to which he had an entitlement, rather than repelling something coming from the plaintiff's land. See further *Ryeford Homes Ltd and Mewburn Property Co Ltd v Sevenoaks District Council* (1989) 46 BLR 34 at 47–49 where the approach in the *Home Brewery* case was followed.

Bridlington Relay Ltd v Yorkshire Electricity Board Chancery Division [1965] 1 All ER 264

The plaintiffs, who provided a sound and television broadcast relay system in Bridlington, had installed aerials on top of a tower they had built: at a later date, an electricity power line was erected by the defendants in the area. On the evening of 1 June 1964, during a test period when the line was energised, there was some interference on the plaintiffs' television set (apparently only in the case of the BBC transmission from Holme Moss — see [1965] Ch 436 at 442) and they sought an injunction to stop the defendants so operating the line as to interfere with their reception of radio and television broadcasts. Buckley J found that the interference which had been experienced could be remedied. The defendants had given an assurance to the plaintiffs that they would do their utmost to suppress interference and Buckley J decided that 'it would be wrong for this court in quia timet proceedings to grant relief by way of injunction to compel the defendants to do something which they appear to be willing to do without the imposition of an order of the court'. Nevertheless, he went on to consider whether the plaintiffs could claim in nuisance if the power line's tendency to cause interference could not be remedied, or if his view that it may be remediable was irrelevant:

BUCKLEY J: . . . If interference of the kind experienced by the plaintiffs on 1 June were to recur at all frequently, it is very probable that the plaintiffs' business would be damaged. If such damage were established, and it were shown that it would be likely to continue or recur, would the plaintiffs have a cause of action in nuisance? . . .

I was invited, and am prepared, to take judicial notice of the fact that the reception of television has become a very common feature of domestic life. The evidence has shown that the quality of reception enjoyed in different parts of the country varies widely, mainly for geographical reasons. Where the quality of reception is poor the effect of interference is more serious, for the greater the strength of the wanted signal the less the effect on the screen of interference of any given strength. Where the strength of the wanted signal is low, interference of even quite moderate intensity will degrade the picture. In taking judicial notice of the widespread reception of television in domestic circles, I do so on the footing that in those circles television is enjoyed almost entirely for what I think must be regarded as recreational purposes, notwithstanding that the broadcast programmes include material which may have some educational content, some political content and, it may be, some other content not strictly or exclusively recreational in character. Those programmes, the purposes of which are strictly educational, are not, I presume, intended for domestic consumption or very much looked at in private homes. I mention these matters because, in my judgment, the plaintiffs could not succeed in a claim for damages for nuisance if what I may call an ordinary receiver of television by means of an aerial mounted on his own house could not do so. It is, I think, established by authority that an act which does not, or would not, interfere with the ordinary enjoyment of their property by neighbours in the ordinary modes of using such property cannot constitute a legal nuisance. I quote:

'A man cannot increase the liabilities of his neighbour by applying his own property to special uses, whether for business or pleasure'.
(*Eastern and South African Telegraph Co Ltd v Cape Town Tramways Co's Ltd*[1]).

In *Robinson v Kilvert* Cotton LJ stated the principle thus:[2]

'If a person does what in itself is noxious, or which interferes with the ordinary use and enjoyment of a neighbour's property, it is a nuisance. But no case has been cited where the doing something not in itself noxious has been held a nuisance, unless it interferes with the ordinary enjoyment of life, or the ordinary use of property for the purposes of residence or business.'

The dissemination of electrical interference is not, in my judgment, 'noxious' in the

---

1. [1902] AC 381 at 393.
2. (1889) 41 Ch D 88 at 94.

sense in which, I think, the learned lord justice is there using the term. Could such interference as is here in question be held to cause an interference with the ordinary enjoyment of life or the ordinary use of the plaintiffs' property for the purposes of residence or business of such a kind as to amount to an actionable nuisance?

There are, of course, many reported cases in which something adversely affecting the beneficial enjoyment of property has been held to constitute a legal nuisance; but I have been referred to no case in which interference with a purely recreational facility has been held to do so. Considerations of health and physical comfort and well being appear to me to be on a somewhat different level from recreational considerations. I do not wish to be taken as laying down that in no circumstances can something which interferes merely with recreational facilities or activities amount to an actionable nuisance. It may be that in some other case the court may be satisfied that some such interference should be regarded, according to such 'plain and sober and simple notions' as Sir J. L. Knight Bruce V-C referred to in a well-known passage in his judgment in *Walter v Selfe*,[1] as detracting from the beneficial use and enjoyment by neighbouring owners of their properties to such an extent as to warrant their protection by the law. For myself, however, I do not think that it can at present be said that the ability to receive television free from occasional, even if recurrent and severe, electrical interference is so important a part of an ordinary householder's enjoyment of his property that such interference should be regarded as a legal nuisance, particularly, perhaps, if such interference affects only one of the available alternative programmes.

Accordingly, I do not think that even if the conditions which existed on the evening of 1 June would have produced the same effect on the screen of a householder using an aerial mounted on his own house at the site of the plaintiffs' mast, this would have constituted an actionable nuisance. . . .

The plaintiffs' complaint is concerned not with interference with domestic amenities; their complaint is that their business will be damaged. But their business is such that to prosper it requires an exceptional degree of immunity from interference. To prosper it must be able to offer its subscribers a better service than they could obtain through aerials of their own. It was not established to my satisfaction that the aerial used by the plaintiffs for receiving BBC transmissions from Holme Moss was proportionately more sensitive to interference than domestic aerials are in the same area, but it was established that the business of the plaintiffs was exceptionally sensitive in the sense which I have just indicated. The use of their aerial for this particular kind of business was, in my judgment, use of a special kind unusually vulnerable to interference, just as the business carried on by the plaintiff in *Robinson v Kilvert*[2] was exceptionally vulnerable to the effects of heat.

For these reasons as well as the other reasons given earlier in this judgment I am of opinion that the plaintiffs cannot succeed in this action. . . .

Action dismissed

Question

Do you think that this judgment, which was delivered in 1964, gives sufficient weight to the importance of television reception today? (Cf. *Nor-Video Services Ltd v Ontario Hydro* (1978) 84 DLR (3d) 221 and for further consideration of the application of nuisance to television reception, see R. Kidner [1989] Conv 279.)

---

1. (1851) 4 De G & Sm 315 at 322.
2. (1889) 41 Ch D 88.

Note

Robinson v Kilvert (1889) 41 Ch D 88, to which reference is made in the extract above, is worthy of further consideration. In that case, the defendants, who had let the ground floor of a warehouse to the plaintiff, started making paper boxes, for which heat and dry air were necessary. The heat passed into the plaintiff's room and dried his stocks of brown paper. Far from gaining any weight (which would happen if this paper was kept at a 'proper temperature' in an atmosphere with a normal moisture content) the paper lost weight and became brittle. In fact the paper was sold by weight, and the plaintiff suffered a loss of profit. Ordinary paper would not have been affected by the heat, nor was the heat such as to 'incommode' the plaintiff's workers and the action failed. Doing something which was non-noxious was not a nuisance merely because it affected a particularly sensitive trade. What sort of loss did the plaintiff sustain in this case – was it economic or physical loss? On recovery for economic loss in nuisance, see Buckley, op cit, pp. 63–65 (public nuisance) and pp. 108–109 (private nuisance) and see also the more recent case of Ryeford Homes Ltd and Mewburn Property Co Ltd v Sevenoaks District Council (1989) 46 BLR 34 at 46–47 (economic loss resulting from physical injury to land or substantial interference with its beneficial use said to be 'probably recoverable' in private nuisance).

British Celanese Ltd v A H Hunt (Capacitors) Ltd Queen's Bench Division [1969] 2 All ER 1252

This was the trial of a preliminary issue whether the defendants were liable in law for the damage claimed on the alleged facts which were as follows: The defendants, who made electrical components, occupied a site on the trading estate where the plaintiffs carried on their business. For their business purposes the defendants had collected on their site strips of metal foil, which could be blown about in the wind. An electricity supply sub-station, owned by the local Electricity Board, provided power to both the plaintiffs' and the defendants' factories. The sub-station was 120 yards away from the defendants' premises, and if the foil made contact with more than one of the 'bus-bars' which stood in the open air at the sub-station, there could be a 'flash-over', which could in turn lead to a power failure. The defendants knew this was likely to happen, and that damage would be caused to those with premises in the area through interruption of the light and power supply, because, on an earlier occasion, foil had blown into the overhead conductors causing an interruption of supply, and the district engineer of the Electricity Board had written to the defendants and told them what had happened and of the danger of interruption of supplies. Three and a half years after this incident, some foil which was lying about in the open air on or near the defendants' premises, blew away and came into contact with the bus-bars. This led to interruption in the light and power supply at the plaintiffs' factory, and their machinery came to a halt. Certain machines, in which materials had solidified, had to be cleaned: materials and time were wasted and production and profit were lost. The plaintiffs claimed that if they proved these allegations the defendants would be liable under Rylands v Fletcher (1868) LR 3 HL 330 (p. 650, post), and in negligence, nuisance and public nuisance. Only the last two heads are dealt with in the extract below, but it should be noted that, in considering the claim under Rylands v Fletcher, Lawton J took the view that the averments 'amount to an allegation of damage, including injury to property, flowing directly from the escape of the metal foil from the defendants' premises'. When considering remoteness of damage (in the context of the negligence claim), he took the view that there was an 'averment that the defendants at the very least ought reasonably to have foreseen that their conduct was likely to cause injury to the plaintiffs' property and that it in fact did so.'

LAWTON J: . . . I turn now to the plaintiffs' contention that the re-amended statement of claim discloses a cause of action both in private and public nuisance. As to private nuisance they say that the defendants' alleged method of storing metal foil resulted, as the defendants knew it would, in an interference with the beneficial enjoyment of their own premises whereby they suffered damage; and as to public nuisance their case is that the nuisance was one which affected a class of persons, namely, those members of the public supplied with electricity from the sub-station, and that as members of that class they suffered special damage.

The defendants made three answers to these contentions: first, that an isolated happening such as the plaintiffs relied on was not enough to found an action in nuisance since this tort can only arise out of a continuing condition: secondly, that if there was a nuisance on the defendants' premises, it did not affect the plaintiffs' premises directly; and thirdly that the re-amended statement of claim did not disclose enough facts to justify a ruling that a class of the public had been injuriously affected by the alleged nuisance.

In my judgment, all three answers are misconceived. Most nuisances do arise from a long continuing condition; and many isolated happenings do not constitute a nuisance. It is, however, clear from the authorities that an isolated happening by itself can create an actionable nuisance. Such an authority is *Midwood & Co Ltd v Manchester Corpn*,[1] where an electric main installed by the defendants fused. This caused an explosion and a fire whereby the plaintiffs' goods were damaged. The Court of Appeal held that the defendants were liable, all the Lord Justices being of the opinion that they had caused a nuisance. The explosion in that case arose out of the condition of the electric main: the 'flash-over' in this case was caused by the way in which the defendants stored their metal foil whereby those in the neighbourhood were exposed to the risk of having their electric power cut off. I am satisfied that the law is correctly stated in *Winfield on Tort* (8th edn) at p. 364:

'Where the nuisance is the escape of tangible things which damage the plaintiff in the enjoyment of his property, there is no rule that he cannot sue for the first escape.'

Anyway, in this case, the alleged happening of 7 December 1964 was not the first escape; there is said to have been one in 1961.

The second of the defendants' answers is a repetition of the argument which was addressed to me on remoteness of damage. I accept that those who are only indirectly affected by a nuisance cannot sue for any damage which they may suffer: but . . . I adjudge that the plaintiffs were directly and foreseeably affected.

Finally, I come to the last of the defendants' answers. Paragraph 6 of the re-amended statement of claim alleges that the defendants knew and foresaw that a 'flash-over' caused by pieces of metal foil blowing about was likely to cause an interruption of power —

'. . . to the premises of members of the public in the said area supplied [with electricity] from the said sub-station including the plaintiffs' said premises . . .'

This averment identifies the class of persons said to have been affected by the nuisance and alleges that the plaintiffs were members of that class. Whether this class was big enough to attract the description 'public' to the nuisance must await the evidence at the trial. In *A-G v PYA Quarries Ltd*[2] Romer LJ, after a learned

---

1. [1905] 2 KB 597.
2. [1957] 2 QB 169 at 184; [1957] 1 All ER 894 at 902.

examination of the authorities, summarised the law as follows:

'. . . any nuisance is "public" which materially affects the reasonable comfort and convenience of life of a class of Her Majesty's subjects. The sphere of the nuisance may be described generally as "the neighbourhood"; but the question whether the local community within that sphere comprises a sufficient number of persons to constitute a class of the public is a question of fact in every case.'

For the reasons given and to the extent specified, I adjudge that on the facts set out in the re-amended statement of claim the defendants are liable in law for the damage claimed.

Order accordingly

Notes

1. Apart from the claim in nuisance, Lawton J held that the *Rylands v Fletcher* claim failed, and this point is noted, p. 660, post, but he did not rule out the negligence claim if the allegations could be proved: cf. *Spartan Steel and Alloys Ltd v Martin & Co (Contractors) Ltd* [1973] QB 27; [1972] 3 All ER 557 (p. 230, ante).

2. For discussion of the question whether an isolated escaped is actionable, see *Winfield & Jolowicz*, pp. 390–391. The quotation from Winfield on *Tort* (8th edn) in the extract above is not to be found in those terms in the current edition of *Winfield & Jolowicz*. They do quote (at p. 391) the following statement of Thesiger J in *SCM (United Kingdom) Ltd v W J Whittall & Son Ltd* [1970] 2 All ER 417 at 430 that 'while there is no doubt that a single isolated escape may cause the damage that entitles a plaintiff to sue for nuisance, yet it must be proved that the nuisance arose from the condition of the defendant's land or premises or property or activities thereon that constituted a nuisance.' He denied that one negligent act causing damage to an electric cable was *thereby* a nuisance. An isolated escape is, of course, actionable under the *Rylands v Fletcher* principle, on which see F. H. Newark (1949) 65 LQR 480 at 488.

3. The plaintiffs in the *British Celanese* case argued that they had a cause of action in both public and private nuisance. A common example of public nuisance, which is also a crime, is causing an obstruction on the highway. Public nuisance is only actionable as a tort by a private individual where he suffers some particular damage greater than that suffered by the public. See G. Kodilyne (1986) 6 LS 182 and esp. 189–191 on the question whether the damage suffered must be greater in kind or merely greater in degree than that suffered by the public in general. On public nuisance generally (both as a crime and as a tort), see J. R. Spencer [1989] CLJ 55. It should be noted that the similarities between the two nuisance actions only go so far — see *Street*, pp. 313–314 and 341–343; Lord Wright in *Sedleigh-Denfield v O'Callaghan* [1940] AC 880 at 905; cf. the observations of Lord Romer in that case at p. 913, and see Lord Porter at p. 918.

4. In relation to nuisance and the highway, consider *Thomas v National Union of Mineworkers (South Wales Area)* [1986] Ch 20; [1985] 2 All ER 1. In this case, which was concerned with picketing during the miners' strike,

Scott J stated at one point that unreasonable interference with the rights of others was actionable in tort and, more specifically, was prepared to recognise a case as actionable in tort if there had been unreasonable interference with a person's right to use the highway. This could, in his opinion, be described 'as a species of private nuisance', though his Lordship did not think that the label mattered. The case has attracted a good deal of comment: see H. Carty [1985] PL 542; K. D. Ewing [1985] CLJ 374; S. Lee and S. Whittaker (1986) 102 LQR 35; B. A. Hepple All ER Ann Rev 1982, p. 305; R. Benedictus (1985) 14 ILJ 176 at 181–185. The two last-named authors make the point, inter alia, that Scott J's view circumvents the requirements of an interest in land in the case of private nuisance and of special damage in the case of public nuisance. Note further *News Group Newspapers Ltd v SOGAT '82 (No 2)* [1987] ICR 181 at 206 where Stuart-Smith J saw force in the defendants' criticism of Scott J's judgment, but did not need to express a final view.

(b) Foreseeability, fault and nuisance

Sedleigh-Denfield v O'Callagan (Trustees for St. Joseph's Society for Foreign Missions), p. 637, post

The Wagon Mound (No 2), Overseas Tankship (UK) Ltd v The Miller Steamship Co Pty Ltd Judicial Committee of the Privy Council [1966] 2 All ER 709

The facts are set out, p. 253, ante.

LORD REID: . . . Having made these findings Walsh J[1] went on to consider the case in nuisance. There is no doubt that the carelessness of the appellant's servants in letting this oil overflow did create a public nuisance by polluting the waters of Sydney Harbour. Also there can be no doubt that anyone who suffered special damage from that pollution would have had an action against the appellants; but the special damage sustained by the respondents was caused not by pollution but by fire. So, having held in finding (v) that risk of fire was not reasonably foreseeable, Walsh J had to consider whether foreseeability has any place in the determination of liability for damage caused by nuisance. He made an extensive survey of the case law and said that the principles which he found there[1]

'suggest that a plaintiff may set up a case depending on the following steps. The defendant has committed a "wrongful" act in that it has created a public nuisance by polluting the harbour waters with oil. As a result of the presence of that "nuisance" (i.e., of the oil) the plaintiff has suffered damage over and above that suffered by others. This gives the plaintiff an action, subject only to proof that there is the requisite relationship between the presence of that nuisance and the injury, so that it can be said that the injury suffered was direct. It matters not that the injury was different in kind from a fouling of the ship by the polluted waters.'

Then, coming to the words used by the judges in numerous cases of nuisance, he said that[2]

---

1. [1963] 1 Lloyd's Rep 402 at 426.
2. [1963] 1 Lloyd's Rep at p. 432.

'. . . by and large, the judgments are not expressed in terms of the concept of foreseeability. The term used again and again is "direct". It is true that other expressions are also used, but one does not find in express terms any testing of the matter by what the defendant might have contemplated or might have foreseen.'

And later he added[1]

'I do not find in the case law on nuisance until the time of the [*Wagon Mound*] decision,[2] any authority for the view that liability depends on foreseeability.'

Their lordships must now make their own examination of the case law. They find the most striking feature to be the variety of words used: and that is not very surprising because in the great majority of cases the facts were such that it made no difference whether the damage was said to be the direct or the natural or probable or foreseeable result of the nuisance. The word 'natural' is found very often, and it is peculiarly ambiguous. It can and often does mean a result which one would naturally expect, i.e., which would not be surprising: or it can mean the result at the end of a chain of causation unbroken by any conscious act, the result produced by so-called natural laws however surprising or even unforeseeable in the particular case. Another word frequently used is 'probable'. It is used with various shades of meaning. Sometimes it appears to mean more probable than not, sometimes it appears to include events likely but not very likely to occur, sometimes it has a still wider meaning and refers to events the chance of which is anything more than a bare possibility, and sometimes, when used in conjunction with other adjectives, it appears to serve no purpose beyond rounding off a phrase.

Their lordships must first refer to a number of cases on which Walsh J relied because they require that the damage suffered by the plaintiff must be the direct or immediate result of the nuisance (generally obstruction of a highway), and they make no reference to foreseeability or probability. But that is because they were dealing with quite a different matter from measure of damages.

'. . . by the common law of England, a person guilty of a public nuisance might be indicted; but, if injury resulted to a private individual, other and greater than that which was common to all the Queen's subjects, the person injured has his remedy by action'

(per Brett J in *Benjamin v Storr*[3]). So the first step is to decide whether the plaintiff has suffered what may for brevity be called special damage. The authorities on this matter are numerous and exceedingly difficult to reconcile; but one thing is clear. There have been excluded from the category of special damage many cases where the damage suffered by the plaintiff was clearly caused by the nuisance; it was not only foreseeable but probable, and was indeed the inevitable result of the nuisance – the obstruction by the defendant of a highway giving access to the plaintiffs' premises. The words direct and immediate have often been used in determining whether the damage caused by the nuisance is special damage. . . .

Such cases have nothing to do with measure of damages: they are dealing with the entirely different question whether the damage caused to the plaintiff by the nuisance was other and different from the damage caused by the nuisance to the rest of the public. When the word direct is used in determining that question, its meaning or connotation appears to be narrower than when it is used in determining whether damage is too remote, so their lordships do not propose to deal further with cases determining

---

1. [1963] 1 Lloyd's Rep at p. 433.
2. [1961] AC 388; [1961] 1 All ER 404.
3. (1874) LR 9 CP 400 at 406.

what is and what is not special damage. No one denies that the respondents have suffered special damage in this case within the meaning of these authorities. The question is whether they can recover notwithstanding the finding that it was not foreseeable.

Of the large number of cases cited in argument there were few in which there was separate consideration of the proper measure of damages for nuisance. Many of the cases cited deal with the measure of damages for breach of contract, and their lordships will later explain why they do not propose to examine these cases. Moreover a larger number were cases based purely on negligence in which there was no element of nuisance. Their lordships do not intend to examine these cases in detail. . . . The respondents can only succeed on this branch of the case by distinguishing nuisance from negligence, either because the authorities indicate that foreseeability is irrelevant in nuisance or because on principle it ought to be held to be irrelevant. . . .

[Having discussed several authorities he continued:] The only case cited where there is an express statement that liability does not depend on foreseeability is *Farrell v John Mowlem & Co Ltd*[1] where the defendant had without justification laid a pipe across a pavement and the plaintiff tripped over it and was injured. Devlin J held this to be a nuisance. He said:[2]

'I think the law still is that any person who actually creates a nuisance is liable for it and for the consequences which flow from it, whether he is negligent or not.'

That is quite true, but then he added[3]

'It is no answer to say "I laid the pipe across the pavement but I did it quite carefully and I did not foresee and perhaps a reasonable man would not have foreseen that anybody would be likely to trip over it".'

That case was before the *Wagon Mound*[4] and it may be that Devlin J thought that the rule was the same in negligence: or it may be that he thought that there was a different rule for nuisance. He cites no authority.

In their lordships' judgment the cases point strongly to there being no difference as to the measure of damages between nuisance and negligence, but they are not conclusive. So it is desirable to consider the question of principle.

The appellant's first argument was that damages depend on the same principles throughout the law of tort and contract. This was stated emphatically by Sir Baliol Brett MR in *The Notting Hill*[5] and by Lord Esher MR in *The Argentino*,[6] and it has often been repeated. But the matter has not been fully investigated recently.[7] There has in recent times been much development of the law of torts, and developments in the law of contract may not have proceeded on parallel lines. To give but one example, it is not obvious that the grounds of decision of the House of Lords in *Hughes v Lord Advocate*[8] are consistent with the first rule in *Hadley v Baxendale*[9] as that rule is commonly interpreted. It is unnecessary, however, to pursue this question in this case, and therefore their lordships do not intend to examine cases arising out of breach of contract.

---

1. [1954] 1 Lloyd's Rep 437.
2. [1954] 1 Lloyd's Rep at p. 440.
3. [1954] 1 Lloyd's Rep at p. 440.
4. [1961] AC 388; [1961] 1 All ER 404.
5. (1884) 9 PD 105 at 113.
6. (1888) 13 PD 191 at 197.
7. [See now *H. Parsons (Livestock) Ltd v Uttley Ingham & Co Ltd* [1978] QB 791; [1978] 1 All ER 525.]
8. [1963] AC 837; [1963] 1 All ER 705.
9. (1854) 9 Exch 341; [1843–60] All ER Rep 461.

The next argument was that at all events the measure of damages is the same throughout the law of tort; but there are many special features in various kinds of tort, and again their lordships do not find it necessary to make the extensive investigations which would be required before reaching a conclusion on this matter.

Comparing nuisance with negligence the main argument for the respondent was that in negligence foreseeability is an essential element in determining liability, and therefore it is logical that foreseeability should also be an essential element in determining the amount of damages; but negligence is not an essential element in determining liability for nuisance, and therefore it is illogical to bring in foreseeability when determining the amount of damages. It is quite true that negligence is not an essential element in nuisance. Nuisance is a term used to cover a wide variety of tortious acts or omissions, and in many negligence in the narrow sense is not essential. An occupier may incur liability for the emission of noxious fumes or noise, although he has used the utmost care in building and using his premises. The amount of fumes or noise which he can lawfully emit is a question of degree, and he or his advisers may have miscalculated what can be justified. Or he may deliberately obstruct the highway adjoining his premises to a greater degree than is permissible hoping that no one will object. On the other hand the emission of fumes or noise or the obstruction of the adjoining highway may often be the result of pure negligence on his part: there are many cases (e.g., *Dollman v Hillman*)[1] where precisely the same facts will establish liability both in nuisance and in negligence. And although negligence may not be necessary, fault of some kind is almost always necessary and fault generally involves foreseeability, e.g., in cases like *Sedleigh-Denfield v O'Callaghan*[2] the fault is in failing to abate a nuisance of the existence of which the defender is or ought to be aware as likely to cause damage to his neighbour. (Their lordships express no opinion about cases like *Wringe v Cohen*[3] on which neither counsel relied.) The present case is one of creating a danger to persons or property in navigable waters (equivalent to a highway) and there it is admitted that fault is essential — in this case the negligent discharge of the oil.

'But how are we to determine whether a state of affairs in or near a highway is [a] danger? This depends, I think, on whether injury may reasonably be foreseen. If you take all the cases in the books you will find that if the state of affairs is such that injury may reasonably be anticipated to persons using the highway it is a public nuisance'

(per Denning LJ in *Morton v Wheeler*).[4] So in the class of nuisance which includes this case foreseeability is an essential element in determining liability.

It could not be right to discriminate between different cases of nuisance so as to make foreseeability a necessary element in determining damages in those cases where it is a necessary element in determining liability, but not in others. So the choice is between it being a necessary element in all cases of nuisance or in none. In their lordships' judgment the similarities between nuisance and other forms of tort to which the *Wagon Mound*[5] applies far outweigh any differences, and they must therefore hold that the judgment appealed from is wrong on this branch of the case. It is not sufficient that the injury suffered by the respondents' vessels was the direct result of the nuisance, if that injury was in the relevant sense unforeseeable. . . .

---

1. [1941] 1 All ER 355.
2. [1940] AC 880; [1940] 3 All ER 349.
3. [1940] 1 KB 229; [1939] 4 All ER 241.
4. (1956) unreported.
5. [1961] AC 388; [1961] 1 All ER 404.

Appeal against the verdict for the respondents on the nuisance claim allowed, but the judgment for the respondents was affirmed, because their cross-appeal against the verdict for the appellants on the negligence claim was allowed.

Questions

1. In discussing the relationship of negligence and nuisance, Lord Reid used the term 'negligence in the narrow sense'. What do you think he meant by this?

2. If one applies the Privy Council's view on the foreseeability of damage (pp. 253–257, ante) and the law they laid down relating to nuisance, to the actual nuisance claim in the case, why was the appeal from the verdict in favour of the respondents on the nuisance claim allowed? (See R. J. Buxton (1966) 29 MLR 676 at 681 and the answer by L. H. Hoffmann (1967) 83 LQR 13.)

Notes

1. The use of the term 'measure of damages' by Lord Reid in this case should, it is submitted, be read as remoteness of damage, or at least so read for analytical purposes.

2. For a recent affirmation by the Privy Council of a 'fault' requirement in a nuisance claim where the defendant neither knew of nor created the nuisance, see *Montana Hotels Pty Ltd v Fasson Pty Ltd* (1986) 69 ALR 258 relying on the sentence in the extract ante concerning *Sedleigh-Denfield v O'Callaghan* [1940] AC 880; [1940] 3 All ER 349 (p. 637, post) and a passage in Lord Wright's speech in that case at p. 904. It will be seen that *Sedleigh-Denfield* concerned the act of a trespasser, but, as *Montana* indicates, its relevance extends beyond that precise situation.

3. The Privy Council expressed no opinion on cases such as *Wringe v Cohen* [1940] 1 KB 229; [1939] 4 All ER 241. This was understandable for they relate to an area where liability need not be based on fault. In *Wringe v Cohen* the plaintiff's shop stood next to the defendant's premises which he let to a tenant. There was evidence that the wall which formed the gable end of the house above this shop had been in a defective state for three years, and one day it fell, damaging the roof of the shop. In the Court of Appeal it was admitted that there was evidence on which the judge in the court below could find an agreement by the defendant with the tenant that the former would keep the premises in repair, and on which he could hold that the gable end wall had become a nuisance because of the lack of repair. Nevertheless, it was argued that the defendant could only be held liable if he knew or should have known of the want of repair. Atkinson J's reply for the Court of Appeal (at p. 243) was that:

'. . . [I]f, owing to want of repair, premises upon a highway become dangerous, and, therefore, a nuisance, and a passer-by or adjoining owner suffers damage by their collapse, the occupier, or the owner, if he has undertaken the duty of repair, is answerable, whether or not he knew, or ought to have known, of the danger. The undertaking to repair gives the owner control of the premises, and a right of access thereto for the purpose of maintaining them in a safe condition. On the other hand, if the nuisance is created, not by want of repair, but, for example, by the act of a trespasser, or by a secret and unobservable operation of nature, such as a subsidence under or near the foundations of the premises, neither an occupier nor an owner responsible for repair is answerable, unless with knowledge or means of knowledge he allows the danger to continue. In such a case, he has in no sense caused the nuisance by any act or breach of duty. I think that every case decided in the English courts is consistent with this view.'

It should be noted that today an owner can be liable if he has an express or implied right to enter to do repairs rather than an obligation to repair (*Mint v Good* [1951] 1 KB 517; [1950] 2 All ER 1159). The collapse in *Wringe v Cohen*, of course, was not onto the highway, but onto a neighbour's property. If the strict duty can be justified on the grounds of danger to the public on the highway, should it also apply for the benefit of the neighbour? Would the neighbour's action be in public or private nuisance? What, in any case, are premises upon a highway? Does this phrase include a case where the grounds stretch to the highway, and the house is 100 yards away at the end of a private drive but close to the neighbour's house? For comment on *Wringe v Cohen*, see W. Friedmann (1943) 59 LQR 63 at 67–69. Consider further Buckley, op cit, pp. 68–70 and p. 78, note 12 who argues that the judgment in *Wringe v Cohen* does not represent the law on the question of the standard of liability imposed.

4. In some situations a defendant may be liable in the torts of negligence and nuisance. However, the operation of the concept of negligence in the tort of nuisance, which is discussed by Lord Reid in *The Wagon Mound* (*No 2*), is difficult, and is not made any easier by the existence of the test of unreasonable user of land in nuisance, which has been mentioned, p. 626, ante. In addition to the standard textbooks on tort, reference should be made to R. W. M. Dias' valuable article, [1967] CLJ 62; J. M. Eekelaar (1973) 8 Ir Jur (NS) 191; Buckley, op cit, pp. 3–4, 17–21, 65–68, 87–88 and 99–101. On the interrelationship of the torts of private nuisance and negligence, see C. Gearty [1989] CLJ 214.

(c)   Act of trespasser

Sedleigh-Denfield *v* O'Callagan (Trustees for St. Joseph's Society for Foreign Missions) House of Lords [1940] 3 All ER 349

The appellant (plaintiff) owned land on the north side of which there was a ditch which, it was held, belonged to the respondents (defendants), the owners of adjoining property. A pipe (or culvert) was laid in the ditch by a trespasser, and the workmen involved did not place a grid near the mouth of the pipe so as to intercept any refuse: in fact, they laid it on top of the pipe where it served no useful purpose. When the pipe was being laid, Brother Dekker, who was then responsible for cleaning the ditch, saw the work being carried out. Further, the ditch was cleaned out twice a year on behalf of the respondents by the person in charge of it. After a heavy rainstorm the pipe became blocked with refuse and the appellant's land was flooded. In the House of Lords, Viscount Maugham expressed the view, with which in his opinion all their Lordships agreed, that before the flooding 'the respondents must be taken to have had knowledge of the existence of the unguarded culvert which for nearly 3 years had been the means by which the water coming down the ditch on the respondents' land had flowed away to the sewer in Lawrence Street.' Branson J, [1938] 3 All ER 321, had dismissed the appellant's action, and that decision had been affirmed by the Court of Appeal, [1939] 1 All ER 725. On further appeal to the House of Lords:

VISCOUNT MAUGHAM: . . . The statement that an occupier of land is liable for the continuance of a nuisance created by others, e.g., by trespassers, if he continues or adopts it — which seems to be agreed — throws little light on the matter, unless the words 'continues or adopts' are defined. In my opinion, an occupier of land 'continues' a nuisance if, with knowledge or presumed knowledge of its existence, he fails to take any reasonable means to bring it to an end, though with ample time to do so. He 'adopts' it if he makes any use of the erection, building, bank or artificial contrivance which constitutes the nuisance. In these sentences, I am not attempting exclusive definitions. . . .

My Lords, in the present case, I am of opinion that the respondents both continued and adopted the nuisance. After the lapse of nearly 3 years, they must be taken to have suffered the nuisance to continue, for they neglected to take the very simple step of placing a grid in the proper place, which would have removed the danger to their neighbour's land. They adopted the nuisance, for they continued during all that time to use the artificial contrivance of the conduit for the purpose of getting rid of water from their property without taking the proper means for rendering it safe. For these reasons, I am of opinion that this appeal should be allowed for damages to be assessed. . . .

LORD ATKIN: . . . I treat it as established that the entrance to the offending pipe, when it was laid, was on the defendants' land, abutting on the premises occupied by the plaintiff. I agree with the finding of the judge, accepted by the Court of Appeal, that the laying of a 15-ins. pipe with an unprotected orifice was, in the circumstances, the creation of a nuisance, or of that which would be likely to result in a nuisance. It created a state of things from which, when the ditch was flowing in full stream, an obstruction might reasonably be expected in the pipe, from which obstruction flooding of the plaintiff's ground might reasonably be expected to result, though I am not satisfied that, granted this reasonable expectation of obstruction, it would be necessary for the plaintiff to prove that the particular injury was such as reasonably to be expected to result from the obstruction. If the defendants had themselves laid the pipe in the manner described, I have no hesitation in saying that, once the plaintiff had suffered damage from flooding so caused, he would have had a good cause of action against them for nuisance. It is probably strictly correct to say that, as long as the offending condition is confined to the defendants' own land without causing damage, it is not a nuisance, though it may threaten to become a nuisance. Where damage has accrued, however, the nuisance has been caused. I should regard the case on this hypothesis as having the same legal consequences as if the defendants, instead of laying a pipe, had placed an obvious obstruction in the course of the ditch. The question here is what the legal position is if such an obstruction is placed by a trespasser. In the present case, I consider it established that the defendants by their responsible agents had knowledge of the erection of the pipe, of the reasonable expectation that it might be obstructed, of the result of such obstruction, and of its continued existence in the condition complained of since it was first placed in position. Brother Dekker, a member of the community, was in charge of the defendants' farming operations, and obviously represented the defendants in this matter, so far as is relevant. He had doubtless no authority to consent to a trespass, and probably no authority to incur any appreciable expense in remedying it, but the defendants obviously had to rely upon him to report to them what was found on the farm likely to be injurious to them or their neighbours.

In this state of the facts, the legal position is not, I think, difficult to discover. For the purpose of ascertaining whether, as here, the plaintiff can establish a private nuisance, I think that nuisance is sufficiently defined as a wrongful interference with another's enjoyment of his land or premises by the use of land or premises either occupied – or, in some cases, owned – by oneself. The occupier or owner is not an insurer. There must be something more than the mere harm done to the neighbour's property to make the party responsible. Deliberate act or negligence is not an essential ingredient, but some degree of personal responsibility is required, which is connoted in my definition by the word 'use'. This conception is implicit in all the decisions which impose liability only where the defendant has 'caused or continued' the nuisance. We may eliminate, in this case, 'caused.' What is the meaning of 'continued'? In the context in which it is used, 'continued' must indicate mere passive continuance. If a man uses on premises something which he finds there, and which itself causes a nuisance by noise, vibration, smell or fumes, he is himself, in continuing to bring into existence the noise, vibration, smell or fumes, causing a nuisance. Continuing in this sense, and causing are the same thing. It seems to me clear that, if a man permits an offensive thing on his premises to continue to offend – that is, if he knows that it is operating offensively, is able to prevent it, and omits to prevent it – he is permitting the nuisance to continue. In other words, he is continuing it. . . .

In the present case . . . there is, as I have said, sufficient proof of the knowledge of the defendants both of the cause and of its probable effect. What is the legal result of the original cause being due to the act of a trespasser? In my opinion, the defendants clearly continued the nuisance, for they come clearly within the terms I have mentioned above. They knew the danger, they were able to prevent it, and they omitted to prevent it. In this respect, at least, there seems to me to be no difference between the case of a public nuisance and that of a private nuisance, and *A-G v Tod Heatley*[1] is conclusive to show that, where the occupier has knowledge of a public nuisance, has the means of remedying it, and fails to do so, he may be enjoined from allowing it to continue. I cannot think that the obligation not to 'continue' can have a different meaning in 'public' and in 'private' nuisance. . . . I think, therefore, that, in the present case, the plaintiff established the liability of the defendants to him, and that the appeal should be allowed. The orders of the judge and the Court of Appeal should be set aside and judgment entered for the plaintiff for damages to be assessed. . . .

LORD PORTER: . . . [T]he true view is that the occupier of land is liable for a nuisance existing on his property to the extent that he can reasonably abate it, even though he neither created it nor received any benefit from it. It is enough if he permitted it to continue after he knew, or ought to have known, of its existence. To this extent, but to no greater extent, he must be proved to have adopted the act of the creator of the nuisance. . . .

[LORD WRIGHT and LORD ROMER delivered speeches in favour of allowing the appeal.]

Appeal allowed

Notes

1. The case above is an example where an occupier was held liable in nuisance. (Note also that one co-occupier of land on which the act complained of is done can sue the other co-occupier in respect of a nuisance affecting land occupied by the former but not the latter: *Hooper v Rogers* [1975] Ch 43; [1974] 3 All ER 417 esp. Scarman LJ.) Several textbooks take the view that the person who by some positive act creates the nuisance may be liable even though he is not an occupier of the land – but see *Street*, p. 329,

---

1. [1897] 1 Ch 560.

note 13. For the position where an independent contractor creates the nuisance, see p. 854, post, and for the potential liability of a defendant for continuation of a public nuisance committed by others, see *News Group Newspapers Ltd v SOGAT '82 (No 2)* [1987] ICR 181 relying on *Sedleigh-Denfield*: for criticism see S. Auerbach (1987) 16 ILJ 277 at 237–238. On the liabilities of landlord and tenant, see *Salmond & Heuston*, pp. 76–78; *Winfield & Jolowicz*, pp. 401–406. See also the standard textbooks on tort on the question of who can sue in nuisance, and see G. Kodilyne (1989) 9 LS 284.

2. Compare the *Sedleigh-Denfield* case with *Wringe v Cohen* [1940] 1 KB 229; [1939] 4 All ER 241, noted p. 636, ante. (See *Salmond & Heuston*, pp. 74–75; cf. *Street*, p. 334.)

3. A trespasser can alter the state of the premises and cause a nuisance (as in *Sedleigh-Denfield* itself), but the activities of trespassers can also cause a nuisance without the state of the land necessarily being altered. In *Page Motors Ltd v Epsom and Ewell Borough Council* (1982) 80 LGR 337 no distinction between these two situations was accepted for the purposes of the applicability of *Sedleigh-Denfield*.

(d) Natural hazards

Leakey v National Trust for Places of Historic Interest or Natural Beauty Court of Appeal [1980] 1 All ER 17

The plaintiffs owned houses lying at the base of Burrow Mump, a steep conical hill, which at the point where it met the plaintiffs' property took the form of a bank. The defendants admitted in their pleadings that Burrow Mump was owned and occupied by them. As a result of the operation of natural agencies, from time to time there had been slides of soil, rocks, tree roots and the like from this bank on to the plaintiffs' land, and, since 1968 at least, the defendants appreciated that the bank was a part of their property and that it was a threat to the houses below because of the real possibility of falls of material from it. In 1976 there was a large fall of the bank and shortly thereafter the plaintiffs brought an action in nuisance against the defendants. At the trial of the action O'Connor J, [1978] 3 All ER 234, held that a nuisance had been established and the defendants appealed to the Court of Appeal. The extract from the judgment contains several references to *Rylands v Fletcher* (1868) LR 3 HL 330 which can be found set out p. 650, post.

MEGAW LJ: ... O'Connor J ... based his decision on the judgment of the Judicial Committee of the Privy Council in *Goldman v Hargrave*[1]. The main issue in this appeal is whether *Goldman v Hargrave*[1] accurately states the law of England. If it does, the appeal fails, and the defendants are liable. ...

For the defendants in this appeal, the fundamental proposition was formulated by counsel as follows: in English law, neither the owner nor the occupier of land from which, solely as the result of natural causes, natural mineral material encroaches onto, or threatens to encroach onto, adjoining land, causing damage, is under any liability to the adjoining land owner.

... [T]he opening words, 'In English law', are properly and deliberately included so as to emphasise that, even if the proposition has to be treated as being inconsistent

---

1. [1967] 1 AC 645; [1966] 2 All ER 989.

with the ratio decidendi of *Goldman v Hargrave*[1], that case, however persuasive, does not have the status of a binding authority as to English law. . . .

The defendants' second proposition, which I propose to consider in the course of considering the first proposition, is that, if the first proposition be wrong, so that *Goldman v Hargrave*[1] does represent the law of England, nevertheless the liability which is imposed under the *Goldman v Hargrave*[1] principle is a liability in negligence and not in nuisance. The present claim was pleaded, and pleaded only, in nuisance. Hence, it is said, it must fail. . . .

The relevant facts of *Goldman v Hargrave*[1] were simple. A redgum tree, 100 feet high, on the defendant's land was struck by lightning and caught fire. The defendant caused the land around the burning tree to be cleared and the tree was then cut down and sawn into sections. So far there could be no complaint that the defendant had done anything which he ought not to have done or left undone anything which he ought to have done, so as in any way to increase the risk which had been caused by this act of natural forces setting fire to the tree. Thereafter the defendant (this was the state of the facts on which the Judicial Committee based their decision) did not do anything which he ought not to have done. He took no positive action which increased the risk of the fire spreading. But he failed to do something which he could have done without any substantial trouble or expense, which would, if done, have eliminated or rendered unlikely the spreading of the fire, that is, to have doused with water the burning or smouldering sections of the tree as they lay on the ground. Instead, the defendant chose to allow or encourage the fire to burn itself out. Foreseeably (again it was the forces of nature and not human action), the weather became even hotter and a strong wind sprang up. The flames from the tree spread rapidly through the defendant's land to the land of neighbours where it did extensive damage to their properties.

The judgment of the Board was delivered by Lord Wilberforce. It was held that the risk of the consequence which in fact happened was foreseeable. This, it is said, 'was not really disputed'. The legal issue was then defined[2]:

'. . . the case is not one where a person has brought a source of danger on to his land, nor one where an occupier has so used his property as to cause a danger to his neighbour. It is one where an occupier, faced with a hazard accidentally arising on his land, fails to act with reasonable prudence so as to remove the hazard. The issue is therefore whether in such a case the occupier is guilty of legal negligence, which involves the issue whether he is under a duty of care, and, if so, what is the scope of that duty.'

It is to my mind clear, from this passage and other passages in the judgment, that the duty which is being considered, and which later in the judgment is held to exist, does not involve any distinction of principle between what, in another sphere of the law, used to be known as misfeasance and non-feasance. A failure to act may involve a breach of the duty, though, since the duty which emerges is a duty of reasonable care, the question of misfeasance or non-feasance may have a bearing on the question whether the duty has been broken. It is to my mind clear, also, that no distinction is suggested in, or can properly be inferred from, the judgment as between a hazard accidentally arising on the defendant's land which, on the one hand, gives rise to a risk of damage to a neighbour's property by the encroachment of fire and, on the other hand, gives rise to such a risk by the encroachment of the soil itself, falling from the bank onto the neighbour's land. There is no valid distinction, to my mind, between an encroachment which consists, on the one hand, of the spread of fire from a tree on fire on the land, and, on the other hand, of a slip of soil or rock resulting

---

1. [1967] 1 AC 645; [1966] 2 All ER 989.
2. [1967] 1 AC 645 at 656; [1966] 2 All ER 989 at 991.

from the instability of the land itself, in each case, the danger of encroachment, and the actual encroachment, being brought about by the forces of nature.

If any such distinctions as I have referred to in the previous paragraph were sought to be made, I should have thought that their acceptance as being material, as leading to different conclusions of principle in law, would make the law on this topic incoherent, artificial, uncertain and unpredictable. In other words, they would lead to bad law.

At the point in the Board's judgment immediately following the passage which I have quoted above, the judgment goes on to deal briefly with the question of the appropriate description of the cause of action. Their Lordships in that case found it unnecessary to decide[1] –

'whether if responsibility is established it should be brought under the heading of nuisance or placed in a separate category . . . The present case is one where liability, if it exists, rests on negligence and nothing else; whether it falls within or overlaps the boundaries of nuisance is a question of classification which need not here be resolved.'

It is convenient at this stage to deal with the second proposition put forward by the defendants in the present appeal. The plaintiffs' claim is expressed in the pleadings to be founded in nuisance. There is no express reference to negligence in the statement of claim. But there is an allegation of a breach of duty, and the duty asserted is, in effect, a duty to take reasonable care to prevent part of the defendants' land from falling onto the plaintiffs' property. I should, for myself, regard that as being properly described as a claim in nuisance. But even if that were, technically, wrong, I do not think that the point could or should avail the defendants in this case. If it were to do so, it would be a regrettable modern instance of the forms of action successfully clanking their spectral chains; for there would be no conceivable pre- judice to the defendants in this case that the word 'negligence' had not been expressly set out in the statement of claim. The suggestion that if it had been so pleaded the defendants could have raised a defence of volenti non fit injuria, which they could not raise as against a claim pleaded in nuisance, is, in my judgment, misconceived. As counsel for the plaintiffs submitted, while it is no defence to a claim in nuisance that the plaintiff has 'come to the nuisance', it would have been a properly pleadable defence to this statement of claim that the plaintiffs, knowing of the danger to their property, by word or deed, had shown their willingness to accept that danger. Moreover, I find it hard to imagine circumstances in which the facts which would provide a defence of volenti non fit injuria would not also provide a defence in a case such as the present in the light of the scope of the duty which falls to be considered hereafter.

If the defendants' first and main proposition is wrong, I do not see that they can succeed on their second proposition.

I return to the judgment in *Goldman v Hargrave*[2]. The law of England as it used to be is set out in the following passage:

'. . . it is only in comparatively recent times that the law has recognised an occupier's duty as one of a more positive character than merely to abstain from creating, or adding to, a source of danger or annoyance. It was for long satisfied with the conception of separate or autonomous proprietors, each of which was entitled to exploit his territory in a "natural" manner and none of whom was obliged to restrain or direct the operations of nature in the interest of avoiding harm to his neighbours.'

---

1. [1967] 1 AC 645 at 656; [1966] 2 All ER 989 at 992.
2. [1967] 1 AC 645 at 657; [1966] 2 All ER 989 at 992.

The judgment of the Board then goes on to review the development of the law which, as the Board held[1], had changed the law so that there now exists 'a general duty on occupiers in relation to hazards occurring on their land, whether natural or man-made'.

That change in the law, in its essence and in its timing, corresponds with, and may be viewed as being a part of, the change in the law of tort which achieved its decisive victory in *Donoghue v Stevenson*[2], though it was not until eight years later, in the House of Lords' decision in *Sedleigh-Denfield v O'Callagan*[3], that the change as affecting the area with which we are concerned was expressed or recognised in a decision binding on all English courts, and, even then, the full, logical effect of the decision in altering what had hitherto been thought to be the law was not immediately recognised. But *Goldman v Hargrave*[4] has now demonstrated what that effect was in English law.

The *Sedleigh-Denfield* case[3] approved the dissenting judgment of Scrutton LJ in *Job Edwards Ltd v Birmingham Navigations*[5]. . . .

The approval by the House of Lords in the *Sedleigh-Denfield* case[3] of Scrutton LJ's judgment in the *Job Edwards* case[5] meant, at any rate unless it could properly be said that it was a decision inconsistent with an earlier decision of the House of Lords, that it was thereafter the law of England that a duty existed under which the occupier of land might be liable to his neighbour for damage to his neighbour's property as a result of a nuisance spreading from his land to his neighbour's land, even though the existence and the operative effect of the nuisance were not caused by any 'non-natural' use by the defendant of his own land. But the liability was not a strict liability such as that which was postulated by the House of Lords in *Rylands v Fletcher*[6] as arising where damage was caused to another by an 'unnatural' user of land. The obligation postulated in the *Sedleigh-Denfield* case[3], in conformity with the development of the law in *Donoghue v Stevenson*[2], was an obligation to use reasonable care. A defendant was not to be liable as a result of a risk of which he neither was aware nor ought, as a reasonable careful landowner, to have been aware.

The decision in the *Sedleigh-Denfield* case[3] was in a case where, on the facts, something which might be described as 'not natural' had been introduced onto the defendant's land in the building of the culvert, but not by the defendant. It had been done by a trespasser without the defendant's knowledge or consent. It was not a case in which the potential damage to the neighbour's land had been brought about by natural causes. Therefore it may be said that the *Sedleigh-Denfield* case[3] did not decide, so as to bind lower courts in England, that an owner or occupier of land was under a duty to exercise reasonable care where natural causes, as distinct from the act of a trespasser, brought about the dangerous condition of the land, of which he, the owner or occupier, knew or which he should have realised. If I had taken the view that the *Sedleigh-Denfield* case[3] does not bear on the question raised by the present appeal (and therefore also ought not to have influenced the decision in *Goldman v Hargrave*[4]), I should have reached a different conclusion on this appeal. I do not, however, accept the suggested distinction.

My first comment is that the whole tenor of the speeches in the *Sedleigh-Denfield* case[3] suggests that the view of their Lordships, if not their decision, was that the same duty arose. . . .

My second comment on the suggested distinction is that it involves a fallacy. I cite

---

1. [1967] 1 AC 645 at 661–662; [1966] 2 All ER 989 at 995.
2. [1932] AC 562; [1932] All ER Rep 1.
3. [1940] AC 880; [1940] 3 All ER 349.
4. [1967] 1 AC 645; [1966] 2 All ER 989.
5. [1924] 1 KB 341.
6. (1868) LR 3 HL 330; [1861–73] All ER Rep 1.

a passage from the judgment in *Goldman v Hargrave*[1] which, I respectfully suggest, makes this clear beyond dispute:

'It was suggested as a logical basis for the distinction that in the case of a hazard originating in an act of man, an occupier who fails to deal with it can be said to be using his land in a manner detrimental to his neighbour and so to be within the classical field of responsibility in nuisance, whereas this cannot be said when the hazard originates without human action so long at least as the occupier merely abstains. The fallacy of this argument is that, as already explained, the basis of the occupier's liability lies not in the use of his land: in the absence of "adoption" there is no such use; but in the neglect of action in the face of something which may damage his neighbour. To this, the suggested distinction is irrelevant.'

. . . Is there, then, anything in the ratio decidendi of *Rylands v Fletcher*[2], or in any subsequent authority binding on this court, which requires or entitles us to disregard the decision in the *Sedleigh-Denfield* case[3] or to prevent us from accepting the logical extension of it (so far as it is an extension) which was regarded as proper in *Goldman v Hargrave*[4]?

. . . It was no part of the decision, as distinct from dicta, in *Rylands v Fletcher*[2] that one who has not himself brought something of an unusual nature on his land, or used his land in an unnatural way (whatever that may mean or include), is in no circumstances liable if something from his land encroaches on his neighbour's land. . . .

Rylands v Fletcher[2] does not impose strict liability except where there has been some non-natural use of the land. But it does not hold, by way of binding authority, that there can be no duty where there has not been a 'non-natural' use of the land. . . .

So I find nothing in *Rylands v Fletcher*[2], or at least in its ratio decidendi, which could properly be used to justify the suggestion that the House of Lords in 1940 in the *Sedleigh-Denfield* case[3] departed, consciously or unconsciously, from the law as laid down in *Rylands v Fletcher*[2], or which was inconsistent with the extension, if it be an extension, of the *Sedleigh-Denfield*[3] decision to defects naturally arising on land which constitute nuisances and give rise to damage to the land of neighbours. The House of Lords was not in 1940 precluded by earlier decisions of the House from following the *Donoghue v Stevenson*[5] approach or from holding that the neighbour in Lord Atkin's speech in *Donoghue v Stevenson*[6] included one who was a neighbour in the literal sense as being the owner of adjoining land.

Is there, then, any subsequent authority binding on this court which prevents it, by the doctrine of precedent, from holding that the law of England, as laid down in the *Sedleigh- Denfield* case[3], is extended by what the Judicial Committee of the Privy Council regarded as inevitable logic?

[MEGAW LJ found no such authority. In particular, he thought that the Divisional Court's decision in *Giles v Walker*[7] should be overruled, and disapproved of Eve J's reasoning in *Pontardawe RDC v Moore-Gwyn*[8]: both were cases on which the defendants had placed 'much reliance'. He continued:] . . . Suppose that we are not bound by *Rylands v Fletcher*[2] or any other authority to hold in favour of the

---

1. [1967] 1 AC 645 at 661; [1966] 2 All ER 989 at 995.
2. (1868) LR 3 HL 330; [1861–73] All ER Rep 1.
3. [1940] AC 880; [1940] 3 All ER 349
4. [1967] 1 AC 645; [1966] 2 All ER 989.
5. [1932] AC 562; [1932] All ER Rep 1.
6. [1932] AC 562 at 580; [1932] All ER Rep 1 at 11.
7. (1890) 24 QBD 656; [1886–90] All ER Rep 501.
8. [1929] 1 Ch 656.

defendants where the nuisance arises solely from natural forces; but suppose also that we are not bound by the decision in *Sedleigh-Denfield*[1] or other binding authority to hold that there is a duty on the defendants in a case such as the present. Ought we as a matter of policy to develop the law by holding that there is a duty in a case such as the present?

If, as a result of the working of the forces of nature, there is, poised above my land, or above my house, a boulder or a rotten tree, which is liable to fall at any moment of the day or night, perhaps destroying my house, and perhaps killing or injuring me or members of my family, am I without remedy? (Of course the standard of care required may be much higher where there is risk to life or limb as contrasted with mere risk to property, but can it be said that the duty exists in the one case and not in the other?) Must I, in such a case, if my protests to my neighbour go unheeded, sit and wait and hope that the worst will not befall?. . . .

In the example which I have given above, I believe that few people would regard it as anything other than a grievous blot on the law if the law recognises the existence of no duty on the part of the owner or occupier. But take another example, at the other end of the scale, where it might be thought that there is, potentially, an equally serious injustice the other way. If a stream flows through A's land, A being a small farmer, and there is a known danger that in times of heavy rainfall, because of the configuration of A's land and the nature of the stream's course and flow, there may be an overflow, which will pass beyond A's land and damage the property of A's neighbours: perhaps much wealthier neighbours. It may require expensive works, far beyond A's means, to prevent or even diminish the risk of such flooding. Is A to be liable for all the loss that occurs when the flood comes, if he has not done the impossible and carried out these works at his own expense?

In my judgment, there is, in the scope of the duty as explained in *Goldman v Hargrave*[2], a removal, or at least a powerful amelioration, of the injustice which might otherwise be caused in such a case by the recognition of the duty of care. Because of that limitation on the scope of the duty, I would say that, as a matter of policy, the law ought to recognise such a duty of care.

This leads on to the question of the scope of the duty. This is discussed, and the nature and extent of the duty is explained, in the judgment in *Goldman v Hargrave*[3]. The duty is a duty to do that which is reasonable in all the circumstances, and no more than what, if anything, is reasonable, to prevent or minimise the known risk of damage or injury to one's neighbour or to his property. The considerations with which the law is familiar are all to be taken into account in deciding whether there has been a breach of duty, and, if so, what that breach is, and whether it is causative of the damage in respect of which the claim is made. Thus, there will fall to be considered the extent of the risk. What, so far as reasonably can be foreseen, are the chances that anything untoward will happen or that any damage will be caused? What is to be foreseen as to the possible extent of the damage if the risk becomes a reality? Is it practicable to prevent, or to minimise, the happening of any damage? If it is practicable, how simple or how difficult are the measures which could be taken, how much and how lengthy work do they involve, and what is the probable cost of such works? Was there sufficient time for preventive action to have been taken, by persons acting reasonably in relation to the known risk, between the time when it became known to, or should have been realised by, the defendant, and the time when the damage occurred? Factors such as these, so far as they apply in a particular case, fall to be weighed in deciding whether the defendant's duty of care requires, or required, him to do anything, and, if so, what.

---

1. [1940] AC 880; [1940] 3 All ER 349.
2. [1967] 1 AC 645; [1966] 2 All ER 989.
3. [1967] 1 AC 645 at 663, 664; [1966] 2 All ER 989 at 996.

There is a passage in this part of the judgment in *Goldman v Hargrave*[1] defining the scope of the duty, which, on the one hand, is said to be likely, if accepted, to give rise to insuperable difficulties in its practical working, and, on the other hand, is said to provide a sensible and just limitation on the scope of the duty, avoiding the danger of substantial injustice being caused, even in exceptional cases, by the existence of the duty. The passage in question reads as follows:

'. . . the owner of a small property where a hazard arises which threatens a neighbour with substantial interests should not have to do so much as one with larger interests of his own at stake and greater resources to protect them: if the small owner does what he can and promptly calls on his neighbour to provide additional resources, he may be held to have done his duty: he should not be liable unless it is clearly proved that he could, and reasonably in his individual circumstances should, have done more.'

. . . The difficulties which are foreseen, arising out of the passage which I have quoted, include unpredictability of the outcome of litigation, delay in reaching decisions (which in everyone's interests ought to be made promptly) as to protective measures to prevent damage, and the increased complexity, length and expense of litigation, if litigation is necessary. All this, and other disadvantages, would arise, it is suggested, because the parties and their advisers, before they could form a fair and confident view of their respective rights and liabilities, and before they could safely ask the court to decide these matters, whether finally or at an interlocutory hearing, would find it necessary, or at least desirable, to put themselves in a position to ascertain and compare the respective financial resources of the parties. This might involve detailed, embarrassing and prolonged investigation, even before the stage of discovery in an action.

If I thought that that sort of result would be likely to follow, or to follow in a substantial number or proportion of cases where this duty comes in question, I should, at least, hesitate long before accepting that this factor could be regarded as a proper factor in deciding whether the duty had or had not been broken in a particular case. But I do not think that anything of that sort is contemplated by *Goldman v Hargrave*[2]. . . .

. . . The defendant's duty is to do that which it is reasonable for him to do. The criteria of reasonableness include, in respect of a duty of this nature, the factor of what the particular man, not the average man, can be expected to do, having regard, amongst other things, where a serious expenditure of money is required to eliminate or reduce the danger, to his means. Just as, where physical effort is required to avert an immediate danger, the defendant's age and physical condition may be relevant in deciding what is reasonable, so also logic and good sense require that, where the expenditure of money is required, the defendant's capacity to find the money is relevant. But this can only be in the way of a broad, and not a detailed, assessment; and, in arriving at a judgment on reasonableness, a similar broad assessment may be relevant in some cases as to the neighbour's capacity to protect himself from damage, whether by way of some form of barrier on his own land or by way of providing funds for expenditure on agreed works on the land of the defendant.

. . . It may be that in some cases the introduction of this factor may give rise to difficulties to litigants and to their advisers and to the courts. But I believe that the difficulties are likely to turn out to be more theoretical than practical. . . . If and when problems do arise, they will have to be solved. I do not think that the existence of such potential difficulties justifies a refusal to accept as a part of the law of

1. [1967] 1 AC 645 at 663; [1966] 2 All ER 989 at 996.
2. [1967] 1 AC 645; [1966] 2 All ER 989.

England the duty as laid down in *Goldman v Hargrave*[1], including the whole of the exposition as to the scope of the duty. As I have said, no difficulty now[2] arises in this present appeal as regards the application of the *Goldman v Hargrave*[1] scope of the duty, once it is held that the duty exists.

I would dismiss the appeal.

[SHAW LJ delivered a judgment in favour of dismissing the appeal. CUMMING-BRUCE LJ agreed with MEGAW LJ.]

Appeal dismissed

Questions

1. Is the standard of care adopted in this case the same as that adopted in the materials to be found in the chapter on breach of duty (p. 247, ante)?

2. If the damage had been held to be reasonably foreseeable in *Smith v Littlewoods Organisation Ltd* [1987] AC 241; [1987] 1 All ER 710 (p. 86, ante) could there have been liability in nuisance? (Consider the comments of A. Tettenborn [1984] CLJ 19 at 20–21 and M. A. Jones (1984) 47 MLR 223 at 226–227 on *P. Perl (Exporters) Ltd v Camden London Borough Council* [1984] QB 342; [1983] 3 All ER 161, noted p. 98, ante.)

Notes

1. For discussion of the judgment of the trial judge (O'Connor J) in *Leakey*, see R. A. Buckley (1978) 94 LQR 338 and Lord Wedderburn (1978) 41 MLR 589. The latter refers to 'the authorities which at common law relieve the occupier from liability for a natural accumulation on his land of wild animals, not encouraged by any act on his part', authorities which were not expressly mentioned by O'Connor J or by the Court of Appeal in *Leakey*. Wedderburn cites as an example *Seligman v Docker* [1949] Ch 53; [1948] 2 All ER 887 in which the plaintiff complained of the presence on the defendant's land of a large number of wild pheasants which damaged his (the plaintiff's) crops. Romer J, adopting the view of Scrutton LJ in *Peech v Best* [1931] 1 KB 1 at 14, held that the plaintiff could succeed if the damage was the result of 'extraordinary, non-natural or unreasonable action' on the defendant's part, but denied that this had occurred: the large number of pheasants at the relevant time was a result of exceptionally favourable weather conditions. Furthermore, referring for support at one point to *Giles v Walker* (1890) 24 QBD 656 (which was overruled in *Leakey*), Romer J also held there was no duty on the defendant to reduce the number of pheasants. (See generally North, *Animals*, pp. 172–174 on the question of nuisance by animals.) Is the approach of the Court of Appeal in *Leakey* inconsistent with the decision in *Seligman v Docker* (and see Buckley, op cit, pp. 44–45)?

---

1. [1967] 1 AC 645; [1966] 2 All ER 989.
2. [During the proceedings in the Court of Appeal it transpired that the defendants did not challenge the judgment against them if there was a duty laid on them and its scope was that set out in *Goldman v Hargrave* [1967] 1 AC 645; [1966] 2 All ER 989.]

2. It was argued after *Leakey* that the subjective approach in that case also applied to cases where it was sought to hold the defendant liable for a nuisance brought about by the act of a third party (e.g. *Sedleigh-Denfield*), and this view is now supported by *Page Motors Ltd v Epsom and Ewell Borough Council* (1982) 80 LGR 337. Note also that *Leakey* was relied on in *Bradburn v Lindsay* [1983] 2 All ER 408 where it was held that a duty was owed by the owner of a semi-detached house (No. 53) to the owner of the other part (No. 55) to take reasonable steps to stop dry rot spreading from No. 53 to No. 55; secondly, a duty was owed to take reasonable steps to prevent damage to No. 55 through lack of repair to No. 53, there being a right of support for No. 55 from No. 53. If this view is followed, *Leakey* will have brought about a change in the law on this second point, on which see P. Jackson [1984] Conv 54. See further A. J. Waite [1987] Conv 47 at 47–49.

3. The actual circumstances of the defendant which are to be taken into account are not restricted to his physical or financial resources. Thus in the *Page Motors* case, which concerned nuisance arising from the activities of gypsies who were camped on the defendant's land, the defendant's position as a local authority had to be considered which involved factors such as the need to satisfy the 'democratic process of consultation'. There can be situations, therefore, in which a public authority might not be liable for a nuisance when a private citizen could be so liable. Contrast, however, the rejection in *Page Motors* of the 'intra vires' protection for public authorities enshrined in *Anns v Merton London Borough Council* [1978] AC 728; [1977] 2 All ER 492 (p. 99, ante): the defendant was sued in its capacity as landowner and was not exercising a statutory power. On this point, see P. Cane [1983] PL 202 at 204–205. See further S. H. Bailey and M. Bowman [1986] CLJ 430 at 453–4 and on nuisance and the question of intra vires protection, see P. Cane, *An Introduction to Administrative Law* (Oxford, 1986), p. 212.

4. For comment on Megaw LJ's view in *Leakey* (p. 642, ante) on the defence of volenti, see Buckley, op cit, pp. 99–101. In this passage Megaw LJ also mentioned that it is no defence for a plaintiff to come to a nuisance. *Sturges v Bridgman* (1879) 11 Ch D 852 provides support for this proposition and that decision was followed relatively recently, albeit with some reluctance, by a majority of the Court of Appeal in *Miller v Jackson* [1977] QB 966; [1977] 3 All ER 338.

The facts of *Miller v Jackson* were given at p. 253, ante, when the question of the plaintiffs' action in negligence was under consideration; however, the plaintiffs also sought damages and an injunction on the basis of nuisance. The majority of the Court of Appeal thought that an actionable nuisance had been established, but one of the majority (Cumming-Bruce LJ) then sided with Lord Denning MR in refusing to grant an injunction. In Lord Denning's opinion, the injunction should be refused as the private interest in the privacy of home and garden should be subordinated to the public interest in preserving playing fields, but in any event the Master of the Rolls did not think that a nuisance had been committed. Cumming-Bruce LJ felt that on the facts of the case the interest of the inhabitants of the village in question in not losing their facilities for enjoying the game of cricket should be given priority. In exercising this discretion to refuse an injunction, he made the point that the plaintiffs must or ought to have realised before completing the purchase of the house that cricket balls would be hit into their property: thus, in Cumming-Bruce LJ's judgment, the idea of coming to the nuisance was relevant at this stage and militated against the grant of an injunction, though not the initial establishment of the nuisance. The plaintiffs had to be content with damages.

Damages in lieu of an injunction can be awarded under jurisdiction originally conferred by Lord Cairns' Act (s. 2 of the Chancery Amendment Act 1858), on which see generally J. A. Jolowicz [1975] CLJ 224 and see now s. 50 of the Supreme Court Act 1981. Unless the damage to the plaintiff's interests was trivial, the general line adopted by the courts has been that the public interest in the continuation of the activity causing the nuisance should not be allowed to override the plaintiff's claim for injunctive relief, once the nuisance has been established: see e.g. *Shelfer v City of London Electric Lighting Co* [1895] 1 Ch 287; Buckley, op cit pp. 121–123; *Clerk & Lindsell*, para. 7–05. *Shelfer's* case, which also contains other guidelines on the granting of damages in lieu of an injunction, was mentioned by Cumming-Bruce LJ in *Miller v Jackson*, though not by Lord Denning.

Three years later the question of the relevance of the public interest in this area arose before a differently composed Court of Appeal in *Kennaway v Thompson* [1981] QB 88; [1980] 3 All ER 329: the nuisance in this case was constituted by noise from the activities of a motor boat racing club and the effect of an injunction on those watching or participating in the racing was put forward as an argument against the grant of such a remedy. The court was not prepared to give priority to the public interest; in particular, Lawton LJ, delivering the judgment of the Court of Appeal, expressed the view that Lord Denning's statement in *Miller v Jackson* 'that the public interest should prevail over the private interest runs counter to the principles enunciated in *Shelfer's* case and does not accord with Cumming-Bruce LJ's reason for refusing an injunction' ([1981] QB at p. 93). With respect it does seem that Cumming-Bruce LJ did take account of the public interest in retaining the cricket ground as *one* reason for refusing an injunction and thus he did lend a measure of support to Lord Denning's judgment (and see *Sevenoaks District Council v Pattullo & Vinson Ltd* [1984] Ch 211 at 222); for a criticism of the approach in *Kennaway v Thompson* to *Shelfer's* case, (though not of the result in the former case), see Buckley, op cit, p. 131. Note further Harris, *Remedies*, p. 329 who writes that the court in *Kennaway v Thompson* 'formulated the injunction in terms which did amount to a compromise which was obviously influenced by the public interest: motor-boat racing was permitted to continue on a lake, subject to restrictions as to the number and duration of the club, national and international events to be held there each season, and as to the noise level of boats using the lake at any other time.' However, it might be argued that the terms of the injunction were merely fixing what would or would not be a nuisance and were not specifically taking account of the public interest: consider R. A. Buckley (1981) 44 MLR 212 at 215: *Rosling v Pinnegar* (1986) 54 P & CR 124. The public interest can be brought into account to a certain extent on the question of *liability* (see e.g. *Winfield & Jolowicz*, p. 388), although in *Kennaway v Thompson* it was not expressly mentioned on this issue.

The precise state of the law concerning the relevance of the public interest in refusing an injunction and granting damages in lieu seems somewhat uncertain at present. Note also *Tetley v Chitty* [1986] 1 All ER 663 where McNeill J (at pp. 674–675) thought that the public interest in the provision of recreational facilities could be balanced against the plaintiffs' interests, but then referred to *Kennaway v Thompson* without making any express mention of the view in that case concerning the relevance of the public interest on the issue under consideration.

To grant damages in lieu of an injunction once a nuisance has been established could be seen as a form of expropriation of the plaintiff's rights, albeit with compensation (see Lindley LJ in *Shelfer*'s case [1895] 1 Ch at p. 316). In what situations, if any, do you think *courts* should bring about this result? Consider further Lord Denning's 'new principle' (in the context of statutory authority) in *Allen v Gulf Oil Refining Ltd* [1980] QB 156 at 168–169, but note that it was not adopted when that case reached the House of Lords, [1981] AC 1001; [1981] 1 All ER 353. On damages in lieu of an injunction, see further S. Tromans [1982] CLJ 87 and on nuisance and remedies generally, see Harris, *Remedies*, chap. 25.

More broadly on the facts of *Miller v Jackson*, note P. S. Atiyah's comment that the economic arguments 'point both ways' (*Lord Denning: the Judge and the Law*, edited by J. L. Jowell and J. P. W. B. MacAuslan, (London, 1984), p. 73), and consider further Harris, *Remedies*, p. 328.

5. For defences to nuisance, see the standard textbooks on tort; statutory authority, for example, may provide a defence. This defence will not be discussed here, but it might be noted that Cumming-Bruce LJ highlighted (in *Allen v Gulf Oil Refining Ltd* [1980] QB 156; [1979] 3 All ER 1008) one particular way in which the existence of a statute may affect certain actions in nuisance. He stated (at p. 1018):

'. . . [I]n the instant case, if as a matter of interpretation of the Act it is clear that the intention of Parliament was to change the immediate environment of the village of Waterston by the construction on the specified site immediately beside the village of a great oil refinery with jetties appropriate to the berthing of large tankers bringing in vast quantities of crude oil, and a railway to carry the products of the refinery away overland, it would follow that Parliament has authorised a dramatic change in the neighbourhood of the village. Thereafter a complaint of nuisance by interference with the enjoyment of life in the village would on any view have to show such a degree of interference with enjoyment as exceeded such levels of noise and impurity of air as are inevitable in a neighbourhood in which oil refinery business is to be regarded as the norm.'

This point met with approval when the case reached the House of Lords, [1981] AC 1001; [1981] 1 All ER 353; see Lord Wilberforce [1981] AC at pp. 1013–1014, with whose speech Lord Diplock and Lord Roskill expressly agreed.

3   Escape of dangerous things from land

Rylands *v* Fletcher Court of Exchequer Chamber and House of Lords [1861–73] All ER Rep 1

Appeal from a decision of the Court of Exchequer . . . by the defendants in an action brought against them by the plaintiff for damage done to his mines through the escape of water from a reservoir on the defendants' land.

The plaintiff was a tenant of Lord Wilton. The defendants, who were proprietors of a mill, made upon land of Lord Wilton's, in pursuance of an arrangement made with him for that purpose, a reservoir, employing competent persons to construct the same. It turned out that beneath the site of the reservoir were old shafts running down into coal workings long disused which communicated with other old workings situate under the land of one Whitehead. The plaintiff's colliery, called the Red House Colliery, adjoined Whitehead's land, and the plaintiff, soon after he had commenced working the Red House Colliery, made arrangements with Whitehead to get, by means of the Red House pit, the coal lying under Whitehead's land. In pursuance of those arrangements the plaintiff had worked through from the Red House Colliery into the coal lying under Whitehead's land, and so into the old workings situated under Whitehead's land. As a result the workings of the plaintiff's colliery were made to communicate with the old workings under the reservoir. These underground works were effected several years before the defendants commenced making their reservoir, but the fact of their existence was not known to the defendants or any agent of theirs, or any person employed by them, until the reservoir burst, as is hereinafter mentioned. In the course of constructing the reservoir the shafts were perceived, but it was not known or suspected that they had been made for the purpose of getting coal beneath the site of the reservoir. The Special Case stated in the action contained a finding that there was no personal negligence or default on the part of the defendants themselves in relation to the selection of the site or the construction of the reservoir, but reasonable and proper care was not used by the persons employed with reference to the shafts so met with to provide for the sufficiency of the reservoir to bear the pressure which, when filled, it would have to bear. The reservoir in consequence burst downwards into the shafts, and the water found its way into the plaintiff's mine. The majority of the Court of Exchequer held that the non-exercise of sufficient care upon the part of the persons employed to construct the reservoir did not, in the absence of any notice to the defendants of the underground communication, affect the defendants with any liability, there being in the absence of such notice no duty cast upon the defendants to use any particular amount of care in the construction of a reservoir upon their own land. Bramwell B was of opinion that the question of knowledge was immaterial, and that the defendants were, therefore, liable. The plaintiff appealed to the Court of Exchequer Chamber.

BLACKBURN J (reading the judgment of the Court): . . . The plaintiff, though free from all blame on his part, must bear the loss, unless he can establish that it was the consequence of some default for which the defendants are responsible.

The question of law, therefore, arises: What is the liability which the law casts upon a person who, like the defendants, lawfully brings on his land something which, though harmless while it remains there, will naturally do mischief if it escape out of his land? It is agreed on all hands that he must take care to keep in that which he has brought on the land, and keep it there in order that it may not escape and damage his neighbour's, but the question arises whether the duty which the law casts upon him under such circumstances is an absolute duty to keep it in at his peril, or is, as the majority of the Court of Exchequer have thought, merely a duty to take all reasonable and prudent precautions in order to keep it in, but no more. If the first be the law, the person who has brought on his land and kept there something dangerous, and failed to keep it in, is responsible for all the natural consequences of its escape. If the second be the limit of his duty, he would not be answerable except on proof of negligence, and consequently would not be answerable for escape arising from any latent defect which ordinary prudence and skill could not detect. Supposing the second to be the correct view of the law, a further question arises subsidiary to the first, namely, whether the defendants are not so far identified with the contractors whom they employed as to be responsible for the consequences of their want of skill in making the reservoir in fact insufficient with reference to the old shafts, of the existence of which they were aware, though they had not ascertained where the shafts went to.

We think that the true rule of law is that the person who, for his own purposes, brings on his land, and collects and keeps there anything likely to do mischief if it escapes, must keep it in at his peril, and, if he does not do so, he is prima facie answerable for all the damage which is the natural consequence of its escape. He can excuse himself by showing that the escape was owing to the plaintiff's default, or, perhaps, that the escape was the consequence of vis major, or the act of God; but, as nothing of this sort exists here, it is unnecessary to inquire what excuse would be sufficient. The general rule, as above stated, seems on principle just. The person whose grass or corn is eaten down by the escaped cattle of his neighbour, or whose mine is flooded by the water from his neighbour's reservoir, or whose cellar is invaded by the filth of his neighbour's privy, or whose habitation is made unhealthy by the fumes and noisome vapours of his neighbour's alkali works, is damnified without any fault of his own; and it seems but reasonable and just that the neighbour who has brought something on his own property which was not naturally there, harmless to others so long as it is confined to his own property, but which he knows will be mischievous if it gets on his neighbour's, should be obliged to make good the damage which ensues if he does not succeed in confining it to his own property. But for his act in bringing it there no mischief could have accrued, and it seems but just that he should at his peril keep it there, so that no mischief may accrue, or answer for the natural and anticipated consequences. On authority this, we think, is established to be the law, whether the thing so brought be beasts or water, or filth or stenches. . . .

The view which we take of the first point renders it unnecessary to consider whether the defendants would or would not be responsible for the want of care and skill in the persons employed by them. We are of opinion that the plaintiff is entitled to recover. . . .

[On appeal by the defendants to the House of Lords:]

LORD CAIRNS LC: . . . The principles on which this case must be determined appear to me to be extremely simple. The defendants, treating them as the owners or occupiers of the close on which the reservoir was constructed, might lawfully have used that close for any purpose for which it might, in the ordinary course of the enjoyment of land, be used, and if, in what I may term the natural user of that land, there had been any accumulation of water, either on the surface or underground, and if by the operation of the laws of nature that accumulation of water had passed off into the close occupied by the plaintiff, the plaintiff could not have complained that that result had taken place. If he had desired to guard himself against it, it would have lain on him to have done so by leaving or by interposing some barrier between his close and the close of the defendants in order to have prevented that operation of the laws of nature.

As an illustration of that principle, I may refer to a case which was cited in the argument before your Lordships, *Smith v Kenrick*[1] in the Court of Common Pleas. On the other hand, if the defendants, not stopping at the natural use of their close, had desired to use it for any purpose which I may term a non-natural use, for the purpose of introducing into the close that which, in its natural condition, was not in or upon it — for the purpose of introducing water, either above or below ground, in quantities and in a manner not the result of any work or operation on or under the land, and if in consequence of their doing so, or in consequence of any imperfection in the mode of their doing so, the water came to escape and to pass off into the close of the plaintiff, then it appears to me that that which the defendants were doing they were doing at their own peril; and if in the course of their doing it the evil arose to which I have referred — the evil, namely, of the escape of the water, and its passing away to the close of the plaintiff and injuring the plaintiff — then for the consequence of that, in my opinion, the defendants would be liable. . . .

---

1. (1849) 7 CB 515.

These simple principles, if they are well founded, as it appears to me they are, really dispose of this case. The same result is arrived at on the principles referred to by Blackburn J in his judgment in the Court of Exchequer Chamber. . . .

In that opinion, I must say, I entirely concur. Therefore, I have to move your Lordships that the judgment of the Court of Exchequer Chamber be affirmed, and that the present appeal be dismissed with costs.

LORD CRANWORTH: I concur with my noble and learned friend in thinking that the rule of law was correctly stated by Blackburn J in delivering the opinion of the Exchequer Chamber. . . .

Appeal dismissed

Notes

1. For an account of the background to this decision concerning the problem of legal liability for damage caused by burst reservoirs and argument as to the influence of such an historical context, see A. B. Simpson (1984) 13 J Leg Stud 208.

2. One particular mystery which surrounds this decision is neatly stated in the title of a note by R. F. V. Heuston – 'Who was the Third Lord in *Rylands v Fletcher*?' (1970) 86 LQR 160. See also a note by D. E. C. Yale (1970) 86 LQR 311 for a further contribution on this question.

3. The decision in *Rylands v Fletcher* has 'no place in Scots law': *R H M Bakeries (Scotland) Ltd v Strathclyde Regional Council* 1985 SLT 214, noted by K. Miller (1985) 101 LQR 472.

4. Blackburn J spoke of 'anything likely to do mischief if it escapes', but it should be noted that this may not necessarily be confined to 'things'. In *A-G v Corke* [1933] Ch 89, the defendant was held responsible under the *Rylands v Fletcher* principle for the nuisance created by the activities off his land of some of the caravan-dwellers who were licensees on his land. This case should be compared with *Smith v Scott* [1973] Ch 314; [1972] 3 All ER 645, the facts of which are given at p. 85, ante. In that case, Pennycuick V-C took the view that the rule could not be invoked against a landlord who let premises to undesirable tenants. He continued (at p. 649):

'The person liable under the rule in *Rylands v Fletcher* (1868) LR 3 HL 330 is the owner or controller of the dangerous "thing", and this is normally the occupier and not the owner of the land. . . . A landlord parts with possession of the demised property in favour of his tenant and could not in any sense known to the law be regarded as controlling the tenant on property still occupied by himself. I should respectfully have thought that *A-G v Corke* [1933] Ch 89 could at least equally well have been decided on the basis that the landowner there was in possession of the property and was himself liable in nuisance for the acts of his licensees; see *White v Jameson* (1874) LR 18 Eq 303.'

Both the general idea that the rule in *Rylands v Fletcher* could apply to the escape of human beings and the particular decision in *A-G v Corke* received an unsympathetic reception in *Matheson v Northcote College Board of Governors* [1975] 2 NZLR 106. For an early discussion both of 'things' within the rule and of the non-natural user of land, see W. T. S. Stallybrass (1929) 3 CLJ 376.

5. As the passage from *Smith v Scott* ante states, the defendant under *Rylands v Fletcher* is the owner or controller of the dangerous thing. In relation to this point note *Rigby v Chief Constable of Northamptonshire* [1985] 2 All ER 985; [1985] 1 WLR 1242 where it was accepted by Taylor J that someone who brings such a thing onto the highway from where it escapes to another's land can be liable under the rule in that case.

6. On the question of non-natural user of land, which is specifically mentioned in Lord Cairns' speech ante, see the following case and notes 1 and 2, p. 660, post.

Read *v* J Lyons & Co Ltd House of Lords [1946] 2 All ER 471

VISCOUNT SIMON LC: My Lords, in fulfilment of an agreement dated 26 January 1942, and made between the Ministry of Supply and the respondents, the latter undertook the operation, management and control of the Elstow Ordnance Factory as agents for the Ministry. The respondents carried on in the factory the business of filling shell cases with high explosives. The appellant was an employee of the Ministry, with the duty of inspecting this filling of shell cases, and her work required her (although she would have preferred and had applied for other employment) to be present in the shell filling shop. On 31 August 1942, while the appellant was lawfully in the shell filling shop in discharge of her duty, an explosion occurred which killed a man and injured the appellant and others. No negligence was averred or proved against the respondents. The plea of volenti non fit injuria, for whatever it might be worth, has been expressly withdrawn before this House by the Attorney-General on behalf of the respondents, and thus the simple question for decision is whether in these circumstances the respondents are liable, without any proof or inference that they were negligent, to the appellant in damages, which have been assessed at £575 2*s* 8*d*, for her injuries.

Cassels J, who tried the case, considered that it was governed by *Rylands v Fletcher*,[1] and held that the respondents were liable, on the ground that they were carrying on an ultra-hazardous activity and so were under what is called a 'strict liability' to take successful care to avoid causing harm to persons whether on or off the premises. The Court of Appeal (Scott, MacKinnon and du Parcq LJJ) reversed this decision, Scott LJ, in an elaborately reasoned judgment, holding that a person on the premises had, in the absence of any proof of negligence, no cause of action, and that there must be an escape of the damage-causing thing from the premises and damage caused outside before the doctrine customarily associated with the case of *Rylands v Fletcher*[1] can apply.

I agree that the action fails. . . .

Blackburn J, in delivering the judgment of the Court of Exchequer Chamber in *Fletcher v Rylands*[2] (LR 1 Exch 265 at 279), laid down the proposition that:

'. . . the person who, for his own purposes brings on his lands and collects and keeps there, anything likely to do mischief if it escapes, must keep it in at his peril, and, if he does not do so, is prima facie answerable for all the damage which is the natural consequence of its escape.'

It has not always been sufficiently observed that in the House of Lords, when the appeal from *Fletcher v Rylands*[2] was dismissed and Blackburn J's pronouncement was expressly approved, Lord Cairns LC emphasized another condition which must

---

1. (1868) LR 3 HL 330.
2. (1866) LR 1 Exch 265.

be satisfied before liability attaches without proof of negligence. This is that the use to which the defendant is putting his land is a 'non-natural' use (LR 3 HL 330 at 338–339). Blackburn J had made a parenthetic reference to this sort of test when he said (LR 1 Exch 265 at 280):

'. . . it seems but reasonable and just that the neighbour, who has brought something on his own property, *which was not naturally there*, harmless to others so long as it is confined to his own property, but which he knows to be mischievous if it gets on his neighbour's, should be obliged to make good the damage which ensues if he does not succeed in confining it to his own property.'

I confess to finding this test of 'non-natural' user (or of bringing on the land what was not 'naturally there,' which is not the same test) difficult to apply. . . .

The classic judgment of Blackburn J besides deciding the issue before the court and laying down the principle of duty between neighbouring occupiers of land on which the decision was based, sought to group under a single and wider proposition other instances in which liability is independent of negligence. . . . There are instances, no doubt, in our law in which liability for damage may be established apart from proof of negligence, but it appears to me logically unnecessary and historically incorrect to refer to all these instances as deduced from one common principle. The conditions under which such a liability arises are not necessarily the same in each class of case. Lindley LJ issued a valuable warning in *Green v Chelsea Waterworks Co*[1] (70 LT 547 at 549), when he said of *Rylands v Fletcher*[2] that that decision:

'. . . is not to be extended beyond the legitimate principle on which the House of Lords decided it. If it were extended as far as strict logic might require, it would be a very oppressive decision.'

It seems better, therefore, when a plaintiff relies on *Rylands v Fletcher*[2] to take the conditions declared by this House to be essential for liability in that case and to ascertain whether these conditions exist in the actual case.

Now, the strict liability recognised by this House to exist in *Rylands v Fletcher*[2] is conditioned by two elements which I may call the condition of 'escape' from the land of something likely to do mischief if it escapes, and the condition of 'non-natural use' of the land. This second condition has in some later cases, which did not reach this House, been otherwise expressed, e.g. as 'exceptional' user, when such user is not regarded as 'natural' and at the same time is likely to produce mischief if there is an 'escape'. . . . It it not necessary to analyse this second condition on the present occasion, for in the case now before us the first essential condition of 'escape' does not seem to me to be present at all. 'Escape', for the purpose of applying the proposition in *Rylands v Fletcher*[2] means escape from a place which the defendant has occupation of, or control over, to a place which is outside his occupation or control. Blackburn J several times refers to the defendant's duty as being the duty of 'keeping a thing in' at the defendant's peril and by 'keeping in' he means, not preventing an explosive substance from exploding, but preventing a thing which may inflict mischief from escaping from the area which the defendant occupies or controls. In two well-known cases the same principle of strict liability for escape was applied to defendants who held a franchise to lay pipes under a highway and to conduct water (or gas) under pressure through them: *Charing Cross West End and City Electric Supply Co v London Hydraulic Power Co*[3]; *Northwestern Utilities Ltd v London Guarantee and Accident Co Ltd*[4]. . . .

---

1. (1894) 70 LT 547.
2. (1868) LR 3 HL 330.
3. [1913] 3 KB 442.
4. [1936] AC 108.

In these circumstances it becomes unnecessary to consider other objections that have been raised, such as the question whether the doctrine of *Rylands v Fletcher*[1] applies where the claim is for damages for personal injury as distinguished from damages to property. It may be noted, in passing, that Blackburn J himself when referring to the doctrine of *Rylands v Fletcher*[1] in the later case of *Cattle v Stockton Waterworks*[2] leaves this undealt with. He treats damages under the *Rylands v Fletcher*[1] principle as covering damages to property, such as workmen's clothes or tools, but says nothing about liability for personal injuries.

On the much litigated question of what amounts to 'non-natural' use of land, the discussion of which is also unnecessary in the present appeal, I content myself with two further observations. The first is that when it becomes essential for the House to examine this question it will, I think, be found that Lord Moulton's analysis in delivering the judgment of the Privy Council in *Rickards v Lothian*[3] is of the first importance. The other observation is as to the decision of this House in *Rainham Chemical Works Ltd v Belvedere Fish Guano Co*[4] to which the appellant's counsel in the present case made considerable reference in support of the proposition that manufacturing explosives was a 'non-natural' use of land. This was a case of damage to adjoining property. I find in Scrutton LJ's judgment (in the court of first instance (123 LT 211 at 212)) that he understood it to be admitted before him that the person in possession of and responsible for the DNP was liable under the doctrine of *Rylands v Fletcher*[1] for the consequences of its explosions. The point, therefore, was not really open for argument to the contrary before the House of Lords. . . . I think it not improper to put on record, with all due regard to the admission and dicta in that case, that if the question had hereafter to be decided whether the making of munitions in a factory at the government's request in time of war for the purpose of helping to defeat the enemy is a 'non-natural' use of land, adopted by the occupier 'for his own purposes', it would not seem to me that the House would be bound by this authority to say that it was. In this appeal the question is immaterial, as I hold that the appellant fails for the reason that there was no 'escape' from the respondents' factory. I move that the appeal be dismissed with costs.

LORD MACMILLAN: . . . The action is one of damages for personal injuries. Whatever may have been the law of England in early times I am of opinion that, as the law now stands an allegation of negligence is in general essential to the relevancy of an action of reparation for personal injuries. The gradual development of the law in the matter of civil liability is discussed and traced with ample learning and lucidity in *Holdsworth's History of English Law*, Vol. 8, pp. 446 et seq., and need not here be rehearsed. Suffice it to say that the process of evolution has been from the principle that every man acts at his peril and is liable for all the consequences of his acts to the principle that a man's freedom of action is subject only to the obligation not to infringe any duty of care which he owes to others. The emphasis formerly was on the injury sustained and the question was whether the case fell within one of the accepted classes of common law actions; the emphasis now is on the conduct of the person whose act has occasioned the injury and the question is whether it can be characterised as negligent. I do not overlook the fact that there is at least one instance in the present law in which the primitive rule survives, namely, in the case of animals *ferae naturae* or animals *mansuetae naturae* which have shown dangerous proclivities.[5] . . . But such an exceptional case as this affords no justification for its extension by anology.

---

1. (1868) LR 3 HL 330.
2. (1875) LR 10 QB 453.
3. [1913] AC 263.
4. [1921] 2 AC 465.
5. [See now the Animals Act 1971, p. 521, ante.]

The appellant in her printed case in this House thus poses the question to be determined:

'Whether the manufacturer of high explosive shells is under strict liability to prevent such shells from exploding and causing harm to persons on the premises where such manufacture is carried on as well as to persons outside such premises.'

Two points arise on this statement of the question. In the first place, the expression 'strict liability', though borrowed from authority, is ambiguous. If it means the absolute liability of an insurer irrespective of negligence, then the answer, in my opinion, must be in the negative. If it means that an exacting standard of care is incumbent on manufacturers of explosive shells to prevent the occurrence of accidents causing personal injuries I should answer the question in the affirmative, but this will not avail the plaintiff. In the next place, the question as stated would seem to assume that liability would exist in the present case to persons injured outside the defendants' premises without any proof of negligence on the part of the defendants. Indeed, Cassels J in his judgment ([1944] 2 All ER 98 at 101) records that:

'It was not denied that if a person outside the premises had been injured in the explosion the defendants would have been liable without proof of negligence.'

I do not agree with this view. In my opinion, persons injured by the explosion inside or outside the defendant's premises would alike require to aver and prove negligence to render the defendants liable. . . .

The doctrine of *Rylands v Fletcher*,[1] as I understand it, derives from a conception of the mutual duties of adjoining or neighbouring landowners and its congeners are trespass and nuisance. If its foundation is to be found in the injunction *sic utere tuo ut alienum non laedas*, then it is manifest that it has nothing to do with personal injuries. The duty is to refrain from injuring not *alium* but *alienum*. The two prerequisites of the doctrine are that there must be the escape of something from one man's close to another man's close and that that which escapes must have been brought on the land from which it escapes in consequences of some non-natural use of that land whatever precisely that may mean. Neither of these features exists in the present case . . . [N]othing escaped from the defendants' premises, and, were it necessary to decide the point, I should hesitate to hold that in these days and in an industrial community it was a non-natural use of land to build a factory on it and conduct there the manufacture of explosives. I could conceive it being said that to carry on the manufacture of explosives in a crowded urban area was evidence of negligence, but there is no such case here and I offer no opinion on the point.

It is noteworthy in *Rylands v Fletcher*[1] that all the counts in the declaration alleged negligence and that on the same page of the report on which his famous dictum is recorded (LR 1 Exch 265 at 279), Blackburn J states that:

'the plaintiff . . . must bear the loss, unless he can establish that it was the consequence of some default for which the defendants are responsible.'

His decision for the plaintiff would thus logically seem to imply that he found some default on the part of the defendants in bringing on their land and failing to confine there an exceptional quantity of water. Notwithstanding the width of some of the pronouncements . . . I think that the doctrine of *Rylands v Fletcher*,[1] when studied in its setting, is truly a case on the mutual obligations of the owners or occupiers of neighbouring closes and is entirely inapplicable to the present case, which is quite outside its ambit.

It remains to say a word about the *Rainham Chemical Works* case.[2] There are

---

1. (1868) LR 3 HL 330.
2. [1921] 2 AC 465.

several features to be noted. Perhaps most important is the fact that the application of the doctrine of *Rylands v Fletcher*[1] was not contested except on the ground that it was not non-natural to use land in war-time for the manufacture of explosives. Lord Carson says ([1921] 2 AC 465 at 491) that the liability of the defendant company 'was not seriously argued.' In the next place it was a case of damage to adjoining property. The explosion caused loss of life, but we find nothing in the case about any claim for personal injuries. It is true that Lord Buckmaster states (ibid, at p. 471) (what was not contested, except to the limited extent I have indicated), that the use of the land for the purpose of making munitions was 'certainly not the common and ordinary use of the land' and thus brought the case within the doctrine of *Rylands v Fletcher,*[1] but that was a finding of fact rather than of law. In his enunciation of the doctrine he clearly confines it to the case of neighbouring lands. And the case is open to the further observation that the real contest was, not whether there was liability, but who was liable, in particular, whether two directors of the company which was carrying on the manufacture of munitions were in the circumstances liable as well as the company itself. The case clearly affords no precedent for the present plaintiff's claim. . . .

LORD PORTER: . . . Normally at the present time in an action of tort for personal injuries if there is no negligence there is no liability. To this rule, however, the appellant contends that there are certain exceptions, one of the best known of which is to be found under the principle laid down in *Rylands v Fletcher.*[1] The appellant's counsel relied on that case and naturally put it in the forefront of his argument. To make the rule applicable, it is at least necessary for the person whom it is sought to hold liable to have brought on to his premises, or, at any rate, to some place over which he has a measure of control, something which is dangerous in the sense that, if it escapes, it will do damage. Possibly a further requisite is that to bring the thing to the position in which it is found is to make a non-natural use of that place. Such, at any rate, appears to have been the opinion of Lord Cairns, and this limitation has more than once been repeated and approved: see *Rickards v Lothian*[2] ([1913] AC 263 at 280, per Lord Moulton). Manifestly, these requirements must give rise to difficulty in applying the rule in individual cases and necessitate at least a decision as to what can be dangerous and what is a non-natural use. Indeed, there is a considerable body of case law dealing with these questions and a series of findings or assumptions as to what is sufficient to establish their existence. Among dangerous objects have been held to be included gas, explosive substances, electricity, oil, fumes, rusty wire, poisonous vegetation, vibrations, a flag-pole, and even dwellers in caravans. Furthermore, in *Musgrove v Pandelis*[3] it was held that a motor-car brought into a garage with full tanks was a dangerous object, a conclusion, which, as Romer LJ pointed out in *Collingwood v Home and Colonial Stores Ltd*[4] ([1936] 3 All ER 200 at 209) involves the propositions that a motor-car is a dangerous thing to bring into a garage and that the use of one's land for the purpose of erecting a garage and keeping a motor car there is not an ordinary or proper use of the land.

My Lords, if these questions ever come directly before this House it may become necessary to lay down principles for their determination. For the present I need only say that each seems to be a question of fact subject to a ruling of the judge whether the particular object can be dangerous or the particular use can be non-natural, and in deciding this question I think that all the circumstances of the time and place and practice of mankind must be taken into consideration so that what might be regarded as dangerous or non-natural may vary according to those circumstances.

---

1. (1868) LR 3 HL 330.
2. [1913] AC 263.
3. [1919] 2 KB 43.
4. [1936] 3 All ER 200.

I do not, however, think that it is necessary for Your Lordships to decide these matters now, inasmuch as the defence admits that high explosive shells are dangerous things, and, whatever view may be formed whether the filling of them is or is not a non-natural use of land, the present case can, in my opinion, be determined upon a narrower ground. In all cases which have been decided, it has been held necessary, to establish liability, that there should have been some form of escape from the place in which the dangerous object has been retained by the defendant to some other place not subject to his control. . . .

It was urged on Your Lordships that it would be a strange result to hold the respondents liable if the injured person was just outside their premises but not liable if she was just within them. There is force in the objection, but the liability is itself an extension of the general rule, and, in my view, it is undesirable to extend it further. . . .

I would add that, in considering the matter now in issue before Your Lordships, it is not, in my view, necessary to determine whether injury to the person is one of those matters in respect of which damages can be recovered under the rule. Atkinson J thought it was: see *Shiffman v Venerable Order of the Hospital of St John of Jerusalem*[1] and the language of Fletcher Moulton LJ in *Wing v London General Omnibus Co*[2] where he says ([1909] 2 KB 652 at 665):

'This cause of action is of the type usually described by reference to the well-known case of *Rylands v Fletcher*.[3] For the purpose of to-day it is sufficient to describe this class of actions as arising out of cases where by excessive use of some private right a person has exposed his neighbour's property or person to danger.'

is to the same effect, and, although the jury found negligence on the part of the defendants in *Miles v Forest Rock Granite Co (Leicestershire) Ltd*,[4] the Court of Appeal applied the rule in *Rylands v Fletcher*[3] in support of a judgment in favour of the plaintiff for £850 in respect of personal injuries. Undoubtedly, the opinions expressed in these cases extend the application of the rule and may some day require examination. For the moment it is sufficient to say that there must be escape from a place over which a defendant has some measure of control to a place where he has not. In the present case there was no such escape and I would dismiss the appeal.

LORD SIMONDS: . . . It was urged by counsel for the appellant that a decision against her when the plaintiff in *Rainham*'s case[5] succeeded would show a strange lack of symmetry in the law. There is some force in the observation, but your Lordships will not fail to observe that such a decision is in harmony with the development of a strictly analogous branch of the law, the law of nuisance, in which also negligence is not a necessary ingredient in the case. For, if a man commits a legal nuisance, it is no answer to his injured neighbour that he took the utmost care not to commit it. There the liability is strict, and there only he has a lawful claim who has suffered an invasion of some proprietary or other interest in land. To confine the rule in *Rylands v Fletcher*,[3] to cases in which there has been an escape from the defendant's land appears to me consistent and logical. . . .

[LORD UTHWATT delivered a speech in favour of dismissing the appeal.]

Appeal dismissed

---

1. [1936] 1 All ER 557.
2. [1909] 2 KB 652.
3. (1868) LR 3 HL 330.
4. (1918) 34 TLR 500.
5. [1921] 2 AC 465.

Notes

1. The need for there to be a non-natural user of land for liability under *Rylands v Fletcher* was apparently introduced in the House of Lords, but, as Viscount Simon pointed out in *Read v J Lyons & Co Ltd* (p. 655, ante), Blackburn J did at one point refer to a neighbour bringing something onto his land 'which was not naturally there'. How does this differ from the test of non-natural user? (On non-natural user, see generally F. H. Newark (1961) 24 MLR 557; D. W. Williams [1973] CLJ 310.)

2. Although he found it unnecessary to decide whether there was a non-natural user of land in *Read v J Lyons & Co Ltd*, Viscount Simon did make some observations on the problem, and paid tribute to Lord Moulton's analysis in *Rickards v Lothian* [1913] AC 263; [1911–13] All ER Rep 71, saying it was 'of the first importance'. Lord Moulton, referring to the *Rylands v Fletcher* principle, stated (at p. 80): 'It is not every use to which land is put that brings into play that principle. It must be some special use bringing with it increased danger to others and must not merely be the ordinary use of the land or such a use as is proper for the general benefit of the community.'

This passage was quoted by Lawton J in *British Celanese Ltd v A H Hunt (Capacitors) Ltd* [1969] 2 All ER 1252; [1969] 1 WLR 959. The facts were given on p. 629, ante in detail. The statement of claim alleged, inter alia, that the defendants had collected strips of metal foil (the 'things' which had escaped) on their land for the purposes of their business (the manufacture of electrical and electronic parts) and that the premises they occupied were on a trading estate. It was held that to use these premises for manufacturing purposes was an ordinary use, that neither the manufacturing of these components nor the storing of the foil was a special use, that no special risks were created by the mere use of premises to store foil and that the manufacture of the products, in the course of which the foil was used, was beneficial to the community. Thus the plaintiffs did not bring their case within the *Rylands v Fletcher* principle. This non-natural user point is a difficult one, and the following words of warning of Windeyer J in *Benning v Wong* [1970] ALR 585 should be borne in mind. He said (at pp. 618–619) that some of the cases on non-natural user of land 'seem to me to make a natural or non-natural use of land depend not on any certain objective criteria, but on whether it is a use of such a character that the defendant ought, in the opinion of the court determining the particular case, to take the risk of having a dangerous thing where it was.'

3. A point which the speeches in *Read v J Lyons & Co Ltd* touch on, but which was not decided in that case, is whether a plaintiff, relying on the *Rylands v Fletcher* principle, can recover damages for personal injuries. Several authorities, the references to which can be found in the textbooks on tort, would give an affirmative answer to that question, but any consideration of these authorities is further complicated by the question whether the plaintiff under *Rylands v Fletcher* must be an occupier of land. Despite the recent observations by Lawton J in the *British Celanese* case that the plaintiff under *Rylands v Fletcher* need not be the occupier of adjoining land, or of any land, it cannot be said that the answer to either question is free from doubt. Although each question can arise independently of the other, both

will arise where the court is faced with a claim by a non-occupier for damages for personal injuries. Might economic loss be recoverable under *Rylands v Fletcher*? (Consider *Ryeford Homes Ltd and Mewburn Property Co Ltd v Sevenoaks District Council* (1989) 46 BLR 34 at 44.)

4. For comment on the position if the 'escape' is an intentional or voluntary release, see p. 610, ante.

Perry *v* Kendricks Transport Ltd Court of Appeal [1956] 1 All ER 154

There was a vehicle park at the south end of the defendants' premises. The defendants objected to people crossing this park, and boys who played there were chased away. In the south-west corner of the park, the defendants kept a motor coach. The petrol tank had been drained and its cap replaced by the defendants who carried out regular inspections of the vehicles in the park. The infant plaintiff gave evidence to the effect that two boys were standing near to the coach. As he approached, they jumped away and there followed an explosion in which the infant plaintiff, who had not reached the defendants' land, was badly burnt. The petrol cap had been removed from the tank, but there was no evidence as to who had done this, and the explosion was found to have been caused by the throwing of a lighted match into the petrol tank by one of the two boys. There was an appeal from the judgment of Lynskey J who had dismissed the plaintiff's claim for damages.

JENKINS LJ: . . . So far as the plaintiff's claim is founded on negligence it seems to me that he has wholly failed to make out his case. . . .

As to the alternative contentions that the defendants are liable, even if they were not negligent, on the principle of *Rylands v Fletcher*,[1] I am prepared to accept the view that this motor coach in the condition in which it was on the defendant's land was an object of the class to which the rule in *Rylands v Fletcher*[1] applies, that is to say, that it was, for this purpose, a dangerous thing, because the tank contained inflammable petrol vapour and the defendants were under an obligation under the rule to prevent it, or the dangerous element in it, escaping on to a neighbour's land and doing damage there. It was a dangerous thing for this purpose in that its tank contained inflammable petrol vapour. The fact that it was a thing to which the rule in *Rylands v Fletcher*[1] applied, and the fact that the vapour escaped, was ignited and did damage, cannot, however, conclude the matter against the defendants. It is well settled that an occupant of land cannot be held liable under the rule if the act bringing about the escape was the act of a stranger and not any act or omission of the occupier himself or his servant or agent, or any defect, latent or patent, in the arrangements made for keeping the dangerous thing under control. In this case, it seems to me plain that the escape was caused by the act of a stranger or strangers in the shape of one or both of the two small boys Whittaker and Rawlinson. Counsel for the plaintiff submitted that a child cannot for this purpose be a stranger because ability should not be imputed to a child of doing a conscious and deliberate act when he does such a thing as setting fire to petrol vapour in the tank of a vehicle. Speaking for myself, I see no necessity to confine the exception from the rule in *Rylands v Fletcher*[1] of acts of strangers to acts which proceed from the conscious volition or the deliberate act of the stranger. It seems to me that the relevance of the exception is that the stranger is regarded as a person over whose acts the occupier of the land has no control. Then the real cause of the escape is not the occupier's action in having the dangerous thing on his land, nor is it any failure on his part or on the part of his

1. (1868) LR 3 HL 330.

agents in keeping the dangerous thing on the land, nor is it due to any latent or patent defect in his protective measures. The real cause is none of these things, but the act of the stranger, for whose acts the occupier of the land is in no sense responsible, because he cannot control them. It is interesting in this connection to observe that in *Rickards v Lothian*,[1] Lord Moulton, after referring to the judgment of the Exchequer Chamber in *Nichols v Marsland*,[2] continued ([1913] AC at p. 278):

'To follow the language of the judgment just recited – a defendant cannot in their Lordships' opinion be properly said to have caused or allowed the water to escape if the malicious act of a third person was the real cause of its escaping without any fault on the part of the defendant. It is remarkable that the very point involved in the present case was expressly dealt with by Bramwell B in delivering the judgment of the Court of Exchequer[3] in the same case. He says: "What has the defendant done wrong? What right of the plaintiff has she infringed? She has done nothing wrong. She has infringed no right. It is not the defendant who let loose the water and sent it to destroy the bridges. She did indeed store it, and store it in such quantities that if it was let loose it would do as it did, mischief. But suppose a stranger let it loose, would the defendant be liable? If so, then if a mischievous boy bored a hole in a cistern in any London house, and the water did mischief to a neighbour, the occupier of the house would be liable. That cannot be. Then why is the defendant liable if some agent over which she has no control lets the water out? . . . I admit that it is not a question of negligence. A man may use all care to keep the water in . . . but would be liable if through any defect, though latent, the water escaped. . . . But here the act is that of an agent he cannot control".'

There Bramwell B gives, by way of reductio ad absurdum, the example of a mischievous boy boring a hole in a cistern. He says that if the defendant in *Nichols v Marsland*[2] was liable, then the occupier of a house in which there was a cistern, if a mischievous boy bored a hole in it, would be liable, and adds: 'That cannot be'. If we are to accept counsel's argument in its full form on this point, then if any mischievous boy chose to come on the defendants' land and chose to set fire to the petrol or the petrol vapour in the tank of a vehicle there, the defendants would be liable. I repeat, with Bramwell B, 'that cannot be'. It seems to me that this argument must be limited to saying that in the circumstances of a particular case, it may be that children doing some mischievous act whereby the dangerous thing escapes are not strangers. I cannot, however, regard that as aiding a plaintiff in an action such as this, unless it can be shown that in the circumstances of the case the dangerous thing was left by the defendants in such a condition that it was a reasonable and probable consequence of their action, which they ought to have foreseen, that children might meddle with the dangerous thing and cause it to escape. If facts such as those were made out in any particular case, then in my view, the defendants could not claim to rely on the act of the mischievous child as constituting the act of a stranger. It would be an act brought about by the defendants' own negligence in dealing with the dangerous thing, and the foreseeable consequence of a negligent act. If that were made out, however, one reaches the point where the claim based on *Rylands v Fletcher*,[4] merges into the claim in negligence: for if such a state of affairs could be made out, then it would no longer be necessary for the plaintiff to rely on *Rylands v Fletcher*[4] at all. He could rely simply on the defendants' negligence. Counsel for the plaintiff is precluded from taking that course here by the circumstance that the learned judge, in my view perfectly rightly, held that there was no negligence on the part of the defendants.

---

1. [1913] AC 263.
2. (1876) 2 Ex D 1.
3. [The judgment of the Court of Exchequer is to be found at (1875) LR 10 Ex 255.]
4. (1868) LR 3 HL 330.

Accordingly, while I feel great sympathy for this unfortunate infant plaintiff, who has sustained very serious injuries through no fault of his own, I have come to the conclusion that no ground has been shown on which this court could properly hold the defendants liable to compensate him for his hurts. . . . [T]his appeal must be dismissed.

PARKER LJ: I agree and I would only add a word in deference to the argument of counsel for the plaintiff in regard to the rule in *Rylands v Fletcher*.[1] Although the decision in *Musgrove v Pandelis*[2] has been the subject of some criticism (see the speech of Lord Porter in *Read v Lyons & Co Ltd*[3]), it is still binding on this court. Accordingly, I feel bound to approach the matter on the basis that the facts here bring the case within the rule in *Rylands v Fletcher*[1]: nor do I think it is open to this court to hold that the rule applies only to damage to adjoining land or to a proprietary interest in land and not to personal injury. It is true that in *Read v Lyons & Co Ltd*[3] Lord Macmillan, Lord Porter and Lord Simonds all doubted whether the rule extended to cover personal injuries, but the final decision in the matter was expressly left over and, as the matter stands at present, I think we are bound to hold that the defendants are liable in this case, quite apart from negligence, unless they can bring themselves within one of the well-known exceptions to the rule.

For a long time there has been an exception to the rule where the defendants can show that the act which brought about the escape was the act of a stranger, meaning thereby someone over whom they had no control. The acts in question here, first, of removing the petrol cap, and, secondly, of inserting a lighted match, are, as it seems to me, prima facie undoubtedly the acts of strangers in that sense. Counsel, however, contends that nevertheless, since at any rate the last of those acts, the insertion of the lighted match, was almost certainly the act of a young child, the exception does not apply, and for this reason, so he says, that in law the act of a young child is not a novus actus interveniens. Speaking for myself, I do not think the matter can be approached in quite that way. In a *Rylands v Fletcher*[1] case the plaintiff need only prove the escape. The onus is then on the defendants to bring themselves within one of the exceptions. Once they prove that the escape was caused by the act of a stranger, whether an adult or a child, they avoid liability, unless the plaintiff can go on to show that the act which caused the escape was an act of the kind which the occupier could reasonably have anticipated and guarded against. In that connection it seems to me that it is not sufficient for the plaintiff to show that the defendants knew that children played in the vehicle park, played on the roof of a motor car or inside a coach. They must show that the defendants reasonably should have anticipated an act of a kind which would cause the escape.

Sorry as one is for the infant plaintiff in this case, it seems to me that he has utterly failed to show that the defendants should have anticipated any such thing. I agree that this appeal should be dismissed.

[SINGLETON LJ delivered a judgment in favour of dismissing the appeal.]

Appeal dismissed

Question

If the defence of act of stranger had not been successful in this case and if it is accepted that a non-occupier can recover damages for personal injuries

---

1. (1868) LR 3 HL 330.
2. [1919] 2 KB 43.
3. [1947] AC 156.

under *Rylands v Fletcher*, could the boy have recovered damages if he had been trespassing on the land where he was standing when he was injured?

Notes

1. Contrast with the fact situation in *Perry*'s case the case where a motor car is used on the road: this does not come within the rule in *Rylands v Fletcher* (see J. R. Spencer [1983] CLJ 65).

2. Although Jenkins LJ would not confine the defence of act of stranger to 'acts which proceed from the conscious volition or the deliberate act of the stranger,' it might be noted that Singleton LJ stated that the occupier of land was excused from *Rylands v Fletcher* liability where 'the damage is caused by the mischievous, deliberate and conscious act of a stranger.' See *Clerk & Lindsell*, para. 25–16; cf. *Winfield & Jolowicz*, p. 434.

3. On the burden of proof, the following statement should be compared with those in *Perry v Kendricks Transport Ltd*. In *Hanson v Wearmouth Coal Co Ltd and Sunderland Gas Co* [1939] 3 All ER 47, Goddard LJ stated (at p. 53):

'A person who brings a dangerous thing on to his land and allows it to escape, thereby causing damage to another, is liable to that other unless he can show that the escape was due to the conscious act of a third party, and without negligence on his own part. Obviously the burden of showing that there was no negligence is on the defendants, and it is not for the plaintiff to prove negligence affirmatively.'

See also *A Prosser & Son Ltd v Levy* [1955] 3 All ER 577 at 587 per Singleton LJ; *Northwestern Utilities Ltd v London Guarantee and Accident Co Ltd* [1936] AC 108; cf. *Street*, p. 356, note 11.

4. Before leaving this section on the rule in *Rylands v Fletcher*, mention should be made of the question of reform of the law relating to dangerous things and activities. The position of the Law Commission (in 1970) was noted at the beginning of this chapter (p. 610, ante). More recently the Pearson Commission, in vol. 1, chap. 31 of its Report where the question of liability for exceptional risks was being considered, recommended that:

'strict liability should be imposed on the controllers of things or operations in each of two categories—first, those which by their unusually hazardous nature require close, careful and skilled supervision, the failure of which may cause death or personal injury; and, secondly, those which, although normally by their nature perfectly safe, are likely, if they do go wrong, to cause serious and extensive casualties' (para. 1643).

This second category includes things such as major stores and stadiums.

The favoured method for implementing this strict liability was for a statute to be passed containing general provisions which should be applied by statutory instruments (along with any other special provisions thought necessary) to certain listed dangerous things and activities (para. 1651). The Commission thought that contributory negligence and voluntary assumption of risk should be permitted as defences, although with a qualification in the case of the latter where an employee is injured (para. 1654). Statutory authority was not to provide a defence (para. 1653), nor in general was the fact that the plaintiff was a trespasser, though here it was proposed that the maker of a statutory instrument should have the power to permit it as a defence (para. 1656). Any other defences (a majority thought) should be set out in the statute and stated to be applicable to all listed things and activities (para. 1659); however, by a majority the Commission wished to exclude the defence of act of a third party (para. 1660).

For comment see J. G. Fleming, (1979) 42 MLR 249 at 265–267; *Accident Compensation After Pearson*, edited by Allen, Bourn and Holyoak, pp. 46–49 and 55–61 (J. A. Jolowicz) and pp. 234–238 (P. S. Atiyah). See further *Winfield & Jolowicz*, p. 445, who point out that 'power already exists [under the Health and Safety at Work etc. Act 1974] to utilise delegated legislation to go a good deal of the way along the road proposed by the [Pearson] Commission'.

4 Fire

The Fires Prevention (Metropolis) Act 1774

86. No action to lie against a person where the fire accidentally begins. – And . . . no action, suit or process whatever shall be had, maintained or prosecuted against any person in whose house, chamber, stable, barn or other building, or on whose estate any fire shall . . . accidentally begin, nor shall any recompence be made by such person for any damage suffered thereby, any law, usage or custom to the contrary notwithstanding: . . . provided that no contract or agreement made between landlord and tenant shall be hereby defeated or made void.

Notes

1. Despite the title of this statute, this section is not restricted to the 'Metropolis' but applies generally: *Filliter v Phippard* (1847) 11 QB 347. That case also decided that the section does not give any protection where the fire has been caused by the defendant's negligence, nor where the defendant intentionally lit the fire.

2. Further consideration was given to the 1774 Act in *Musgrove v Pandelis* [1919] 2 KB 43. In that case, a fire occurred in a garage at the back of a house of which the plaintiff was the lessee. The garage had living rooms above. Part of the garage had been let to the defendant who kept his car there, and on one occasion when his servant started the car, the petrol in the carburettor caught fire. If the servant had turned off the petrol tap straightaway the fire would have been rendered harmless, but when he did attempt to do this, the fire, which by then was burning more fiercely, thwarted his efforts. The fire spread and burnt the car, the garage, the plaintiff's rooms above and some of his furniture. The defendant relied on s. 86 of the 1774 Act, and the Court of Appeal resolved two questions relating to its construction. The word 'fire' in the Act, was interpreted to mean 'the fire which causes the damage'. This was held to be the fire, fed by petrol from the tank, which spread and burnt the car, and was to be distinguished from the original fire in the carburettor, which would have burnt itself out if the petrol tap had been turned off. Thus the Act would not protect the defendant since the later fire did not 'accidentally begin', but was a result of the servant's negligence. Is this a sensible distinction? (Note, however, that this approach was accepted by the Privy

Council in *Goldman v Hargrave* [1967] 1 AC 645; [1966] 2 All ER 989.) It was also held in *Musgrove v Pandelis* that the Act did not provide a defence where liability for fire could be based on the principle of *Rylands v Fletcher*, a principle which Bankes LJ thought had existed in the law 'long before' that decision. For criticism, see A. I. Ogus [1969] CLJ 104 at 113-116.

3. The view that the 1774 Act is inapplicable where the *Rylands v Fletcher* principle is invoked was doubted, but followed, by MacKenna J in *Mason v Levy Auto Parts of England Ltd* [1967] 2 QB 530; [1967] 2 All ER 62. Having discussed *Musgrove v Pandelis*, he went on to say (at pp. 69-70):

'What then is the principle? As Romer LJ pointed out in *Collingwood v Home and Colonial Stores Ltd* [1936] 3 All ER 200 at 208-209, it cannot be exactly that of *Rylands v Fletcher* (1868) LR 3 HL 330. A defendant is not held liable under *Rylands v Fletcher* unless two conditions are satisfied: (i) that he has brought something on to his land likely to do mischief if it escapes, which has in fact escaped, and (ii) that these things happened in the course of some non-natural user of the land. However, in *Musgrove*'s case, [1919] 2 KB 43, the car had not escaped from the land, neither had the petrol in its tank. The principle must be, Romer LJ said, [1936] 3 All ER at p. 209, the wider one on which *Rylands v Fletcher* itself was based, *Sic utere tuo ut alienum non laedas*. If, for the rule in *Musgrove*'s case to apply, there need be no escape of anything brought on to the defendant's land, what must be proved against him? There is, it seems to me, a choice of two alternatives. The first would require the plaintiff to prove (a) that the defendant had brought something on to his land likely to do mischief if it escaped, (b) that he had done so in the course of a non-natural user of the land, and (c) that the thing had ignited and that the fire had spread. The alternative would be to hold the defendant liable if (a) he brought on to his land things likely to catch fire, and kept them there in such conditions that, if they did ignite, the fire would be likely to spread to the plaintiff's land, (b) he did so in the course of some non-natural use, and (c) the thing ignited and the fire spread.
    The second test is, I think, the more reasonable one, since to make the likelihood of damage if the thing escapes a criterion of liability, when the thing has not in fact escaped but has caught fire, would not be very sensible. I propose, therefore, to apply the second test. . . .'

Honeywill and Stein Ltd *v* Larkin Bros (London's Commercial Photographers) Ltd, p. 856, post

Balfour *v* Barty-King, p. 855, post

H and N Emanuel Ltd *v* Greater London Council Court of Appeal [1971] 2 All ER 835

The London County Council (LCC — the predecessor of the Greater London Council (GLC)) managed two prefabricated bungalows for the government, who had put them up on land owned by the Council. In 1962 there was a request by the LCC to the Ministry of Housing for the bungalows to be removed, and their removal was approved by that Ministry: in the meantime, the LCC kept control and their district foreman held the keys. The Ministry of Housing asked the Ministry of Works to remove the bungalows, and the method adopted by the latter Ministry was to sell the bungalows to Mr King, a contractor. The contract specified that no rubbish was to be burnt on the site, that work was not to be started until the contractor had received written notice of the bungalows' release (which the Ministry of Works issued) and that the local authority, from whom the keys were to be obtained, must be told of the date of the commencement of the dismantling work. After the contractor obtained the written notice of release from the foreman, his men went to the site. However, they lit a bonfire, and sparks set fire to property on the plaintiff's adjoining premises. There was evidence that the burning of rubbish by the contractor was a regular practice, which was known to the Ministry of Works, and it was 'reasonable to assume' (per Lord Denning MR) that the practice and the term in the contract against it were also known by the LCC's foreman. James J held both the Council and Mr King liable and the Council appealed.

LORD DENNING MR: . . . After considering the cases, it is my opinion that the occupier of a house or land is liable for the escape of fire which is due to the negligence not only of his servants, but also of his independent contractors and of his guests, and of anyone who is there with his leave or licence. The only circumstances when the occupier is not liable for the negligence is when it is the negligence of a stranger. It was so held in a case in the Year Books 570 years ago, *Beaulieu v Finglam*,[1] which is well translated by Mr Fifoot in his book on the History and Sources of the Common Law.[2] The occupier is, therefore, liable for the negligence of an independent contractor, such as the man who comes in to repair the pipes and uses a blowlamp: see *Balfour v Barty-King*[3]; and of a guest who negligently drops a lighted match: see *Boulcott Golf Club Inc v Engelbrecht*.[4] The occupier is liable because he is the occupier and responsible in that capacity for those who come by his leave and licence: see *Sturges v Hackett*.[5]

But the occupier is not liable for the escape of fire which is not due to the negligence of anyone. Sir John Holt himself said in *Tuberville v Stampe*[6] that if a man is properly burning up weeds or stubble and, owing to an unforeseen windstorm, without negligence, the fire is carried into his neighbour's ground, he is not liable. Again, if a haystack is properly built at a safe distance, and yet bursts into flames by spontaneous combustion, without negligence, the occupier is not liable. That is to be inferred from *Vaughan v Menlove*.[7] So also if a fire starts without negligence owing to an unknown defect in the electric wiring: *Collingwood v Home and Colonial Stores Ltd*[8]; or a spark leaps out of the fireplace without negligence: *Sochacki v Sas*.[9] All those cases are covered, if not by the common law, at any rate by the Fires Prevention (Metropolis) Act 1774, which covers all cases where a fire begins or spreads by accident without negligence. But that Act does not cover a fire which begins or is spread by negligence: see *Filliter v Phippard*,[10] *Musgrove v Pandelis*[11] and *Goldman v Hargrave*.[12]

Nevertheless, as I have said earlier, the occupier is not liable if the outbreak of fire is due to the negligence of a 'stranger'. But who is a 'stranger' for this purpose? . . . I think a 'stranger' is anyone who in lighting a fire or allowing it to escape acts contrary to anything which the occupier could anticipate that he would do: such as the person in *Rickards v Lothian*.[13] Even if it is a man whom you have allowed or

---

1. (1401) YB 2 Hen 4, fo. 18, pl. 6.
2. 1949 p. 166.
3. [1957] 1 QB 496; [1957] 1 All ER 156.
4. [1945] NZLR 556.
5. [1963] 3 All ER 166; [1962] 1 WLR 1257.
6. (1697) 1 Ld Raym 264.
7. (1837) 3 Bing NC 468.
8. [1936] 3 All ER 200.
9. [1947] 1 All ER 344.
10. (1847) 11 QB 347.
11. [1919] 2 KB 43.
12. [1966] 2 All ER 989.
13. [1913] AC 263.

invited into your house, nevertheless, if his conduct in lighting a fire is so alien to your invitation that he should qua the fire be regarded as a trespasser, he is a 'stranger'. Such as the man in Scrutton LJ's well-known illustration[1]:

'When you invite a person into your house to use the staircase you do not invite him to slide down the bannisters . . .'

which was quoted by Lord Atkin in *Hillen and Pettigrew v ICI (Alkali) Ltd*[2]. . .

There has been much discussion about the exact legal basis of liability for fire. The liability of the occupier can be said to be a strict liability in this sense that he is liable for the negligence not only of his servants but also of independent contractors and, indeed, of anyone except a 'stranger'. By the same token it can be said to be a 'vicarious liability', because he is liable for the defaults of others as well as his own. It can also be said to be a liability under the principle of *Rylands v Fletcher*,[3] because fire is undoubtedly a dangerous thing which is likely to do damage if it escapes. But I do not think it necessary to put it into any one of these three categories. It goes back to the time when no such categories were thought of. Suffice it to say that the extent of the liability is now well defined as I have stated it. The occupier is liable for the escape of fire which is due to the negligence of anyone other than a stranger.

Seeing that in this case the contractors were negligent both in lighting the fire in that place and in allowing it to spread, the only question is whether the LCC were 'occupiers' of the land and whether the contractors were 'strangers' to them. The question of what is an 'occupier' was much discussed in *Fisher v CHT Ltd*[4] and *Wheat v E Lacon & Co Ltd*.[5] Those cases show that the word 'occupier' has a different meaning according to the subject-matter in which it is employed. There it was the Occupiers' Liability Act 1957. Here it is liability for the escape of fire. Adapting what I said in *Wheat v E Lacon & Co Ltd*,[5] I would say that, for purposes of fire, whenever a person has a sufficient degree of control over premises that he can say, with authority, to anyone who comes there: 'Do' or 'Do not light a fire', or 'Do' or 'Do not put that fire out', he as 'occupier' must answer for any fire which escapes by negligence from the premises. Applying this test, I am clear that the LCC were occupiers of this site. They were the owners of it. Their foreman had the keys of the prefabs. Anyone who wanted to do anything with them had to get permission from him. On behalf of the LCC he could clearly say to anyone: 'You are not to light a fire on the site'; or: 'If you do light a fire, it must be well away from the road', or as the case may be. It may be that the Ministry of Housing and the Ministry of Works were also 'occupiers' because, as I pointed out in *Wheat v Lacon*,[6] there are often many 'occupiers' who have a sufficient degree of control to be responsible. But the position of the Ministry does not arise here.

The question: who is a 'stranger'? is more difficult. But I am quite clear that the contractors' men were not strangers. They were present on the site with the leave and with the knowledge of the LCC; true it is that they were prohibited from burning rubbish, but, nevertheless, it was their regular practice to burn it. The LCC ought to have taken better steps to prevent them. Not having done so, they cannot disclaim responsibility for the fire. The LCC could reasonably have anticipated that these men might

---

1. *The Carlgarth* [1927] P 93 at 110.
2. [1936] AC 65 at 69; [1935] All ER Rep 555 at 558.
3. (1868) LR 3 HL 330; [1861–73] All ER Rep 1.
4. [1966] 2 QB 475; [1966] 1 All ER 88.
5. [1966] AC 552; [1966] 1 All ER 582.
6. [1966] AC at p. 578; [1966] 1 All ER at p. 594.

start a fire; and that is enough, just as in the case in 1401[1] the householder might-reasonably have anticipated that his guest might light a candle.

I think the judge was quite right. I would dismiss this appeal.

EDMUND DAVIES LJ: I agree. There are two main questions involved in this case. First of all, were the LCC in occupation of the site from which the fire spread? And, secondly, how was that fire caused? In other words, was it caused by some one who vis-à-vis the LCC is to be treated as a stranger, as our law understands that term in this context? Counsel for the plaintiffs, Emanuels, has sought to uphold the learned judge's decision in their favour on three grounds. First, that at common law, which he said in this respect still obtains, there was and there is strict liability for the spread of this fire on to Emanuels' land. Secondly, he says that the learned judge was perfectly right in awarding Emanuels judgment on the basis of the principle enunciated in *Rylands v Fletcher*.[2] Thirdly, he says that in any event the LCC ought to be held responsible, contrary to the learned judge's finding, on *two* grounds: (a) that they were guilty of personal negligence in all the circumstances of the case, and (b) that they were also vicariously responsible for the negligence of the second defendant, who is not, so he submitted, to be regarded as a stranger.

[C]ounsel for the GLC conceded that [the LCC] were in occupation. He contended that so also were the Ministry of Works, but in my judgment that matters not for present purposes.

The second question is, was the contractor, Mr King, a stranger? Well, he was somebody who was, first of all, there with the knowledge of the LCC. Further, he was there in order to discharge a function which the LCC desired to have performed, namely, the clearing of the site; and it is beyond belief that the LCC had no means of controlling his activities. In *Perry v Kendricks Transport Ltd*[3] Jenkins LJ said: '. . . the stranger is regarded as a person over whose acts the occupier of the land has no control.' Well, of course, the LCC had control over the activities of the contractor. It is untenable that, assuming knowledge on their part of what he was doing, they could not put a stop to it. So . . . the question of . . . whether the contractor was a stranger must in my judgment be answered contrary to the defendants.

Counsel for Emanuels, as I have already related, sought to uphold the judgment on three grounds. I do not find it necessary for the purposes of this appeal to consider the question of the strict liability at common law, nor do I propose to go into the validity—for such I believe it to be—of the decision of the learned trial judge that the LCC were in truth and in law liable under *Rylands v Fletcher*.[2] The question which remains is whether they are also liable in negligence. Were they, first of all, personally negligent? . . .

[Having found personal negligence on the part of the LCC, 'the personal negligence consisting in failure to exercise any degree of supervision at all', he continued:] I am not really concerned as to the exact role which Mr King, the contractor, occupied. I suspect it was that of a licensee. If it was that of an independent contractor, there is the abundance of authority to which Lord Denning MR has referred indicating that there can be in circumstances such as here present vicarious liability in the occupier for his acts. *Balfour v Barty-King*[4] is one illustration of the law applicable to this case; and so also is the Australian decision in *McInnes v Wardle*.[5] In *Eriksen v Clifton*[6] McGregor J said:

---

1. *Beaulieu v Fingham* (1401) YB 2 Hen 4, fo. 18, pl. 6.
2. (1868) LR 3 HL 330; [1861–73] All ER Rep 1.
3. [1956] 1 All ER 154 at 159; [1956] 1 WLR 85 at 90.
4. [1957] 1 QB 496; [1957] 1 All ER 156.
5. (1932) 45 CLR 548.
6. [1963] NZLR 705 at 709.

'If the employer delegates to an independent contractor work involving the use of fire, a duty arises to exercise control in regard to such action. If the employer fails to exercise such control he is responsible for the negligence of the independent contractor, but this is in truth personal negligence on the part of the employer in failure to exercise control.'

There was in my judgment in the present case personal negligence by the LCC in failing to exercise control in the circumstances.

Was the contractor a mere licensee, as has been submitted by counsel for the GLC? Well, that may be the role he occupied. But even so the LCC cannot be absolved from responsibility for his undoutbed negligence. Lord Denning MR has already referred in this context to the decision in New Zealand in *Boulcott Golf Club Inc v Engelbreacht*,[1] where the golf club were held liable as occupiers for the consequence of a fire negligently caused by one of the members of the golf club dropping a cigarette. For these reasons, I hold that the LCC were guilty, first of personal negligence, and secondly of vicarious responsibility for the negligence of the second defendant. On that dual ground, as well as on the principle enunciated in *Rylands v Fletcher*,[2] I concur in holding that this appeal should be dismissed.

PHILLIMORE LJ: The LCC were undoubtedly occupiers of this land. They were sued in that capacity and they did not call any evidence to suggest otherwise. As such they owed a duty to their neighbours which is best described in the old latin maxim: sic utere tuo ut alienum non laedas. As Markham J put it in *Beaulieu v Finglam*[3]:

'I shall answer to my neighbour for him who enters my house by my leave or knowledge whether he is guest to me or my servant, if either of them acts in such a way with a candle or other things that my neighbour's house is burned.'

Since the Fires Prevention (Metropolis) Act 1774 it is I think necessary to insert the word 'negligently' after the word 'acts'.

. . . Now, it seems to me that if an occupier owes a duty, he cannot, by handing over the performance of the work on his land to somebody else refrain from any sort or kind of supervision, say: 'Well, I have delegated my responsibilities to the Ministry.' I think the LCC and consequently the GLC are liable for what was in effect the negligence of the Ministry of Works in failing to supervise the activities of the contractor. The Ministry of Works was on the site with leave and licence and indeed at the request of the LCC, and the LCC cannot escape liability for their act or omission any more than could the owner of the house in *Beaulieu v Finglam*.[3] Accordingly I would agree that this appeal must be dismissed.

Appeal dismissed

Notes

1. In *H and N Emanuel Ltd v Greater London Council*, Lord Denning MR referred to *Sochacki v Sas* [1947] 1 All ER 344, where a lodger was held not liable for damage caused by a fire which spread from his room, and which was probably caused by a spark from the fire in the fireplace setting light to the floorboards. It would appear that the lodger had lit the original fire, but

---

1. [1945] NZLR 556.
2. (1868) LR 3 HL 330; [1861-73] All ER Rep 1.
3. (1401) YB 2 Hen 4, fo. 18, pl. 6.

he had not been negligent. Liablity under *Rylands v Fletcher* was denied in particular on the ground that this was an ordinary user of the room. Lord Denning MR thought that, whatever the common law position, the case would be covered by the 1774 Act. Although *Filliter v Phippard* (1847) 11 QB 347 appears to exclude from the Act's protection the intentional fire (on which see F. H. Newark (1944) 6 NILQ 134 at 137–140), Lord Denning's view can be supported on the type of analysis adopted in *Musgrove v Pandelis* [1919] 2 KB 43 – that the fire with which the Act is concerned started when the floorboards were set alight, and this fire did 'accidentally begin'. (See, however, *Musgrove v Pandelis* [1919] 2 KB at p. 51; cf. *Job Edwards Ltd v Birmingham Navigations* [1924] 1 KB 341 at 361.) *Salmond & Heuston*, pp. 375–376 take the view that the Act almost certainly applies to fires intentionally lit which spread accidentally but see the contrary view expressed in *New Zealand Forest Products Ltd v O'Sullivan* [1974] 2 NZLR 80 at 84.

2. Compare with Lord Denning's judgment in *H and N Emanuel Ltd v Greater London Council* the view of Mahon J in the case just mentioned (*N Z Forest Products Ltd v O'Sullivan*) and also in *Holderness v Goslin* [1975] 2 NZLR 46. In the former case Mahon J referred to the rule in *Rylands v Fletcher* as an accepted basis for strict liability for the escape of fire; this, he thought, was inconsistent with Lord Denning's opinion in *H and N Emanuel Ltd v Greater London Council* in so far as that opinion 'may be thought to have substituted negligence as the only basis of liability for escape of fire' ([1974] 2 NZLR at p. 88). Mahon J's dislike of the importation of negligence into liability for the escape of fire was also expressed in *Holderness v Goslin*; it was the reason why, in considering who was a stranger for whose fire a defendant would not be liable, he rejected the test (to be found in Lord Denning's judgment in *H and N Emanuel Ltd v Greater London Council*) of what the occupier could anticipate. In Mahon J's view, when the occupier has a power to control the activities of the visitor, then that person is not a stranger (and see the judgment of Edmund Davies LJ in *H and N Emanuel Ltd v Greater London Council*).

3. The New Zealand Court of Appeal in *Mayfair Ltd v Pears* [1987] 1 NZLR 459 refused to extend the strict liability at common law to a fire not resulting from any negligence of the defendant but which spread from his car parked on another's land, a situation not within the wording of the 1774 Act.

15 Deliberate interference with interests in trade or business

We have seen that the courts are reluctant to protect relational economic interests from *negligent* interference (p. 230, ante). The pragmatic objections, based on the fear of crushing liability, do not, however, apply to conduct which is specifically *aimed* at the plaintiff. Indeed, it was at one time suggested that intentionally inflicted harm is always tortious, unless justified. But this is not the rule of modern English law. Broadly speaking, liability in these so-called 'economic torts' is limited to the following circumstances, in all of which there must be proof of damage.

(1) The combination of two or more persons whose predominant purpose is to inflict damage on the plaintiff rather than to serve their own bona fide and legitimate interests (p. 680, post).
(2) The intentional interference by A with a contract between B and C with knowledge of or recklessness as to its terms, (a) by directly inducing B to break or not to perform his contract with C, or (b) by unlawful means the necessary consequence of which is to cause B to break his contract with C or to prevent him from performing that contract (p. 693, post).
(3) The threat by A to B that he will use means which are unlawful as against B with the intention of causing B to do or refrain from doing something he is at liberty to do, so causing damage either to himself or to C (p. 718, post).
(4) The intentional use by A of unlawful means with the purpose and effect of causing damage to B in his trade or business (p. 724, post). This category of interference by unlawful means is a 'genus' tort wide enough to cover species (2) and (3) above; because of its wider but uncertain scope it is convenient to discuss it separately.
(5) Representations by a trader that the plaintiff is in some way associated with his business, goods or services, where the representation is calculated to deceive (p. 733, post).

All these torts have to be considered against the background of the still authoritative decision of the House of Lords in *Allen v Flood* [1898] AC 1 (p. 674, post) that conduct which is not otherwise tortious does not become so simply because it was carried out with the deliberate purpose of harming the economic interests of another. That principle is subject to the anomalous exception of conspiracy but that tort is itself now strictly limited even where unlawful means are used, to conduct deliberately aimed at the plaintiff (p. 689, post).

There has been no Lord Atkin ready to formulate a general principle, parallel to the duty of care, which would unify these ramshackle torts.

Concepts such as 'contract', 'right', 'property' and 'trade' have been used to delimit the scope of the torts (although there seems to be no reason why some of them should not protect other intangible interests, such as the alienation of affection). Ambiguous words such as 'malice', 'inducement', 'interference' and 'unlawful means' have been used, with little consistency, to describe the conduct outlawed in the various torts. The difficulties presented to the student by these torts are compounded by the fact that many of the reported cases arise from applications for interlocutory injunctions to prevent the commission of *alleged* torts or their continuance pending the trial of the action, and so are concerned only with the question whether or not there is a serious issue to be tried, without full investigation of the facts or of the legal principles.

These torts play a residual role in the regulation of competition between traders, which may include the 'Eurotort' of breach of EEC law where this has direct effect (see H. Carty (1988) 104 LQR 250 at 255). The economic torts are increasingly important in the sphere of industrial conflict. The fundamental problem has been the incompatibility of collective action with the individualistic notions of the common law. When parliamentary policy favoured collective bargaining without legal restraint (broadly speaking, 1906–1971 and 1974–1979) legislation limited the operation of specific economic torts committed by persons acting 'in contemplation or furtherance of a trade dispute'. At times (e.g. *Rookes v Barnard* [1964] AC 1129; [1964] 1 All ER 367, p. 718, post) the courts bypassed the statutory immunities by developing new heads of tortious liability, leading Parliament to restore and even to extend the immunities. By contrast, the policy of the Employment Acts 1980, and 1982, 1988 and 1990 and the Trade Union Act 1984 is to place severe restrictions on industrial action by withdrawing the immunities in a number of circumstances which are defined with great complexity. The study of these changing policies and the immunities belongs to labour law: see in particular Lord Wedderburn, *The Worker and the Law*, 3rd edn (London, 1986), chaps. 7 and 8; *Clerk & Lindsell*, paras. 15–27 *et seq*; *Encyclopedia of Labour Relations Law* (London, 1990), Part 1B–31; Carty, op cit.

1   Conspiracy

Allen *v* Flood House of Lords [1895–9] All ER Rep 52

The plaintiffs, Flood and Taylor, were shipwrights. They were employed to repair the woodwork on the *Sam Weller*. Members of the Boilermakers' Society, who worked with iron, discovered that the plaintiffs had previously repaired ironwork on another ship. Allen, the district secretary of the Boilermakers' Society, told the employers that the boilermakers would not work if the plaintiffs were allowed to do so. As a result the plaintiffs were dismissed that same day. All the men were free to leave their employment at the end of each day and they had no right to re-engagement on the following day.

Kennedy J ruled that there was no evidence of conspiracy or of intimidation or of coercion or of breach of contract. The jury found that Allen maliciously induced the employers to discharge the plaintiffs from their employment and not to re-engage them. He gave judgment for the plaintiffs for £20 each: [1895] 2 QB 21.

The Court of Appeal affirmed that decision (Lord Esher MR, Lopes and Rigby

LJJ): [1895] 2 QB 21. Allen appealed to the House of Lords. The case was argued for four days before Lord Halsbury LC, Lords Watson, Herschell, Morris, Macnaghten, Davey and Shand. Eight judges were then summoned to attend (Hawkins, Mathew, Cave, North, Wills, Grantham, Lawrance and Wright JJ) and the case was re-argued before all of them and, in addition, Lord Ashbourne and Lord James. The judges were asked the question: 'Assuming the evidence given by the [respondent's] witnesses to be correct, was there any evidence of a cause of action fit to be left to the jury?' By a majority of 6–2 the judges answered this in the affirmative. However, the House of Lords allowed the appeal by a majority of 6–3.

LORD WATSON: . . . Although the rule may be otherwise with regard to crimes, the law of England does not, according to my apprehension, take into account motive as constituting an element of civil wrong. Any invasion of the civil rights of another person is in itself a legal wrong, carrying with it liability to repair its necessary and natural consequences, in so far as these are injurious to the person whose right is infringed, whether the motive which prompted it be good, bad, or indifferent. But the existence of a bad motive, in the case of an act which is not in itself illegal, will not convert that act into a civil wrong, for which reparation is due. A wrongful act, done knowingly, and with a view to its injurious consequences, may, in the sense of law, be malicious; but such malice derives its essential character from the circumstance that the act done constitutes a violation of the law. . . . The root of the principle is that, in any legal question, malice depends not upon evil motive which influenced the mind of the actor, but upon the illegal character of the act which he contemplated and committed. In my opinion, it is alike consistent with reason and common sense that when the act done is, apart from the feelings which prompted it, legal, the civil law ought to take no cognisance of its motive. . . .

There are, in my opinion, two grounds only upon which a person who procures the act of another can be made legally responsible for its consequences. In the first place, he will incur liability if he knowingly, and for his own ends, induces that other person to commit an actionable wrong. In the second place, when the act induced is within the right of the immediate actor, and is, therefore, not wrongful in so far as he is concerned, it may yet be to the detriment of a third party, and, in that case, according to the law laid down by the majority in *Lumley v Gye*,[1] the inducer may be held liable if he can be shown to have procured his object by the use of illegal means directed against that third party. . . .

The doctrine laid down by the Court of Appeal in this case and in *Temperton v Russell*,[2] with regard to the efficacy of evil motives in making — to use the words of Lord Esher — 'that unlawful which would otherwise be lawful,' is stated in wide and comprehensive terms; but the majority of the consulted judges who approve of the doctrine have only dealt with it as applying to cases of interference with a man's trade or employment. Even in that more limited application, it would lead, in some cases, to singular results. One who committed an act not in itself illegal, but attended with consequences detrimental to several other persons, would incur liability to those of them whom it was proved that he intended to injure, and the rest of them would have no remedy. A master who dismissed a servant engaged from day to day, or whose contract of service had expired, and declined to give him further employment because he disliked the man, and desired to punish him, would be liable in an action for tort. And ex pari ratione, a servant would be liable in damages to a master whom he disliked, if he left his situation at the expiry of his engagement and declined to be re-engaged, in the knowledge and with the intent that the master would be put to considerable inconvenience, expense, and loss before he could provide a substitute. . . .

---

1. (1853) 2 E & B 216; [1843–60] All ER Rep 208.
2. [1893] 1 QB 715; [1891–4] All ER Rep 724.

LORD HERSCHELL: . . . It is to be observed, in the first place, that the company in declining to employ the plaintiffs were violating no contract; they were doing nothing wrongful in the eye of the law. The course which they took was dictated by self-interest; they were anxious to avoid the inconvenience to their business which would ensue from a cessation of work on the part of the ironworkers. It was not contended at the Bar that merely to induce them to take this course would constitute a legal wrong, but it was said to do so because the person inducing them acted maliciously. Lord Esher MR declined in the present case to define what was meant by 'maliciously'; he considered this a question to be determined by a jury. But if acts are, or are not, unlawful and actionable, according as this element of malice be present or absent, I think it essential to determine what is meant by it. I can imagine no greater danger to the community than that a jury should be at liberty to impose the penalty of paying damages for acts which are otherwise lawful because they choose, without any legal definition of the term, to say that they are malicious. No one would know what his rights were. The result would be to put all our actions at the mercy of a particular tribunal whose view of their propriety might differ from our own.

However malice may be defined, if motive be an ingredient of it, my sense of the danger would not be diminished. The danger is, I think, emphasised by the opinions of some of the learned judges. In a case to which I shall refer immediately, Lord Esher MR included within his definition of malicious acts persuasion used for the purpose 'of benefiting the defendant at the expense of the plaintiff'. Wills J thinks this 'going a great deal too far,' and that whether the act complained of was malicious depends upon whether the defendant has, in pursuing his own interests, 'done so by such means and with such a disregard to his neighbour as no honest and fair-minded man ought to resort to'. Here it will be seen that malice is not made dependent on motive. The assumed motive is a legitimate one, the pursuit of one's own interests. The malice depends on the means used and the disregard of one's neighbour, and the test of its existence is whether these are such as no honest and fair-minded man ought to resort to. There is here room for infinite differences of opinion. Some, I dare say, applying this test, would consider that a strike by workmen at a time damaging to the employer or a 'lock-out' by an employer at a time of special hardship to the workmen were such means and exhibited such a disregard of his neighbour as an honest and fair-minded man ought not to resort to. Others would be of the contrary opinion. The truth is that this suggested test makes men's responsibility for their actions depend on the fluctuating opinions of the tribunal before whom the case may chance to come as to what a right-minded man ought or ought not to do in pursuing his own interests. Again, Cave J expressed the view that the action of the appellant might have been justified on the principles of trade competition if it had been confined to the time when the men were doing iron work, but that it 'was without just cause or excuse, and consequently malicious', inasmuch as the respondents were not at the time engaged upon iron work. On the other hand, it is evident, from the reasoning of some of the learned judges who think the respondents entitled to succeed, that they would not be prepared to adopt this distinction, and would regard the act as 'malicious' in either case. . . .

In *Temperton v Russell*,[1] the further step was taken by the majority of the court — A. L. Smith LJ reserving his opinion on the point — of asserting that it was immaterial that the act induced was not the breach of a contract, but only the not entering into a contract, provided that the motive of desiring to injure the plaintiff, or to benefit the defendant at the expense of the plaintiff, was present. It seems to have been regarded as only a small step from the one decision to the other, and it was said that there seemed to be no good reason why, if an action lay for maliciously inducing a breach of contract, it should not equally lie for maliciously inducing a person not to enter into a contract. So far from thinking it a small step from the one decision to the other, I think there is a chasm between them. The reason for a distinction between

---

1. [1893] 1 QB 715; [1891–4] All ER Rep 724.

the two cases appears to me to be this: that in the one case the act procured was the violation of a legal right, for which the person doing the act which injured the plaintiff could be sued, as well as the person who procured it, while in the other case, as no legal right was violated by the person who did the act from which the plaintiff suffered, he would not be liable to be sued in respect of the act done, while the person who induced him to do the act would be liable to an action. I think this was an entirely new departure. . . .

It has recently been held in this House in *Bradford Corpn v Pickles*[1] that acts done by the defendant upon his own land were not actionable when they were within his legal rights, even though his motive were to prejudice his neighbour. The language of the noble and learned Lords was distinct. Lord Halsbury said ([1895] AC at 594):

'This is not a case where the state of mind of the person doing the act can affect the right. If it was a lawful act, however ill the motive be, he had a right to do it. If it was an unlawful act, however good the motive might be, he would have no right to do it.'

The statement was confined to the class of case then before the House, but I apprehend that what was said is not applicable only to rights of property, but is equally applicable to the exercise by an individual of his other rights. . . .

I think these considerations (subject to a point which I will presently discuss) sufficient to show that the present action cannot be maintained. It is said that the statement that the defendant would call men out, if made, was a threat. It is this aspect of the case which has obviously greatly influenced some of the learned judges. Hawkins J says that the defendant without excuse or justification

'wilfully, unlawfully, unjustly, and tyrannically invaded the plaintiffs' right by intimidating and coercing their employers to deprive them of their present and future employment,'

and that the plaintiffs are, therefore, entitled to maintain this action. But 'excuse or justification' is only needed where an act is prima facie wrongful. Whether the defendant's act was so is the matter to be determined. To say that the defendant acted 'unlawfully', is, with all respect, to beg the question which is whether he did so or not? To describe his acts as unjust and tyrannical proves nothing, for these epithets may be, and are, in popular language constantly applied to acts which are within a man's rights, and unquestionably lawful. In my opinion, these epithets do not advance us a step towards the answer to the question which has to be solved.

The proposition is, therefore, reduced to this, that the appellant invaded the plaintiffs' right by intimidating and coercing their employers. In another passage, in his opinion, the learned judge says that there is no authority for the proposition that to render threats, menaces, intimidation, or coercion available as elements in a cause of action, they must be of such a character as to create fear of personal violence. I quite agree with this. The threat of violence to property is equally a threat in the eye of the law. And many other instances might be given. On the other hand, it is undeniable that the terms 'threat', 'coercion', and even 'intimidation' are often applied in popular language to utterances which are quite lawful and give rise to no liability either civil or criminal. They mean no more than this, that the so-called threat puts pressure, perhaps extreme pressure, on the person to whom it is addressed, to take a particular course. Of this again, numberless instances might be given. Even then, if it can be said without abuse of language that the employers were 'intimidated and coerced' by the appellant, even if this be in a certain sense true, it by no means follows that he committed a wrong or is under any legal liability for his act. Everything depends on the nature of the representation or statement by which the pressure was exercised. The law cannot

---

1. [1895] AC 587.

regard the act differently because you choose to call it a threat or coercion instead of an intimation or warning. . . .

The object which the appellant and the iron workers had in view was that they should be freed from the presence of men with whom they disliked working, or to prevent what they deemed an unfair interference with their rights by men who did not belong to their craft doing the work to which they had been trained. Whether we approve or disapprove of such attempted trade restrictions, it was entirely within the right of the iron workers to take any steps, not unlawful, to prevent any of the work which they regarded as legitimately theirs being intrusted to other hands.

Some stress was laid in the court below upon the fact that the plaintiffs were not at the time in question engaged upon iron work, although immediately before that time they had been so employed elsewhere. This, it was said, showed that the motive of the defendant and the iron workers was the 'punishment' of the plaintiffs for what they had previously done. I think that the use of the word 'punishment' has proved mis-leading. That word does not necessarily imply that vengeance is being wreaked for an act already done, though no doubt it is sometimes used in that sense. When a court of justice, for example, awards punishment for a breach of the law, the object is not vengeance. The purpose is to deter the person who has broken the law from a repetition of his act, and to deter other persons also from committing similar breaches of the law. In the present case it was admitted that the defendant had no personal spite against the plaintiffs. His object was, at the utmost, to prevent them in the future from doing work which he thought was not within their province, but within that of the iron workers. If he had acted in exactly the same manner as he did at a time when the plain-tiffs were engaged upon iron work, his motive would have been precisely the same as it was in the present case, and the result to the plaintiffs would have been in nowise different. I am unable to see, then, that there is any difference either in point of ethics or law between the two cases. The iron workers were no more bound to work with those whose presence was disagreeable to them than the plaintiffs were bound to refuse to work because they found that this was the case. The object which the defendant and those whom he represented had in view throughout was what they believed to be the interest of the class to which they belonged. The step taken was a means to that end. The act which caused the damage to the plaintiffs was that of the iron company in refusing to employ them. The company would not subordinate their own interests to the plaintiffs. It is conceded that they could take this course with impunity. Why, then, should the defendant be liable because he did not subordinate the interests of those he represented to the plaintiffs? Self-interest dictated alike the act of those who caused the damage and the act which is found to have induced them to cause it. . . .

[LORD MACNAGHTEN, LORD SHAND, LORD DAVEY and LORD JAMES OF HEREFORD delivered speeches in favour of reversing the Court of Appeal's decision and dismissing the action. LORD HALSBURY LC, LORD ASHBOURNE and LORD MORRIS delivered speeches in favour of dismissing the appeal.]

Appeal allowed

Notes

1. Although this case, and *Bradford Corpn v Pickles* [1895] AC 587, noted p. 625, ante, are usually cited as authority for the proposition that the concept of abuse of rights has no place in English law (unlike civil law systems), malicious and improper motives can be a source of liability such as for abuse of governmental power or may be evidence of unreasonable conduct, as in nuisance (p. 625, ante) or may act as a limitation on certain defences such as qualified privilege and fair comment in defamation (pp. 778 and 770, post). B. Napier (1979) VII *Estratto da M Rotondi; Inchieste di Diritto Comparato*

(Padua) 267 at 282 explains that 'the absence of any coherent, unifying principle in British law means that, in general, one cannot hope to object successfully to the exercise of a legal right, simply by pointing out that the actor's motivation is morally objectionable, and of little social utility'.

2. Despite *Allen v Flood*, is there a *tort* of unjustifiable interference in restraint of trade? The point was raised but left open by Lord Denning MR in *Hadmor Productions Ltd v Hamilton* [1981] 2 All ER 724 at 734 (a point not considered in the subsequent appeal to the House of Lords, p. 724, post). This nascent tort would be relevant in situations where a body with monopoly control of a trade arbitrarily or capriciously prevents access to that trade whether by rejecting from membership or refusing a licence. In *Nagle v Feilden* [1966] 2 QB 633; [1966] 1 All ER 689 a declaration but not damages was awarded in respect of alleged sex discrimination by stewards of the Jockey Club (which controls horse-racing on the flat) in the exercise of their discretion to grant a trainer's licence. The cause of action was not contractual, and the decision has been criticised by T. Weir [1966] CLJ 165, because adhering to an unlawful restraint of trade has not previously been recognised as a legal wrong. Cf. *Weinberger v Inglis (No 2)* [1919] AC 606 where the Stock Exchange was allowed to refuse a broker readmission on grounds of his German origin. In *Board of Governors of Seneca College of Applied Arts and Technology v Bhaudaria* (1981) 124 DLR (3d) 193, the Supreme Court of Canada decided that there was no common law tort of racial discrimination (cf. I. B. McKenna (1981) 1 LS 296). The supposed absence of such a tort led the legislature in Britain to introduce the statutory civil wrongs of unlawful discrimination on racial grounds and on grounds of sex and marital status (now contained in the Race Relations Act 1976 and the Sex Discrimination Act 1975) (see A. Lester and G. Bindman, *Race and Law* (London, 1972), p. 234).

The nascent tort of unjustifiable interference in restraint of trade would be relevant in trade union closed shops if the 'right to work' were regarded (see e.g. Slade J in *Greig v Insole* [1978] 3 All ER 449 at 510, and Lord Denning MR in *Hadmor Productions Ltd v Hamilton* [1981] 2 All ER at p. 734) as a different concept from 'restraint of trade' in respect of which s. 2(5) of the Trade Union and Labour Relations Act 1974 protects trade union purposes and rules from attack on the basis that they are in restraint of trade. Parliament has legislated extensively to control the closed shop (e.g. Employment Act 1982, ss. 12 and 14, as amended; Employment Act 1980, ss. 4 and 5; Employment Protection (Consolidation) Act 1978, s. 58, as amended; Employment Act 1988, ss. 10 and 11; Employment Act 1990, ss. 1–3) rather than await the development of a common law tort (see generally on the 'right to work' B. Hepple (1981) 10 ILJ 65).

3. Do you agree with J. D. Heydon, *Economic Torts*, 2nd edn (London, 1978), p. 28, that 'a legal system which lacks [a doctrine that malevolent action by one alone is tortious] seems deficient'? Note the inroads which have been made on *Allen v Flood* by recent developments in the tort of interference with contract (p. 693, post), and interference with trade by unlawful means (p. 724, post), and consider why a *conspiracy* is tortious if the real purpose is to inflict damage on the plaintiff rather than to serve the legitimate interests of those who combine (post).

Vegelahn v Guntner Supreme Judicial Court of Massachusetts 44 NE 1077 (1896)

HOLMES J (dissenting): . . . It is plain from the slightest consideration of practical affairs, or the most superficial reading of industrial history, that free competition means combination, and that the organisation of the world, now going on so fast, means an ever-increasing might and scope of combination. It seems to me futile to set our faces against this tendency. Whether beneficial on the whole, as I think it, or detrimental, it is inevitable, unless the fundamental axioms of society, and even the fundamental conditions of life, are to be changed.

One of the eternal conflicts out of which life is made up is that between the effort of every man to get the most he can for his services, and that of society, disguised under the name of capital, to get his services for the least possible return. Combination on the one side is patent and powerful. Combination on the other is the necessary and desirable counterpart, if the battle is to be carried on in a fair and equal way. . . .

Crofter Hand Woven Harris Tweed Co Ltd v Veitch House of Lords [1942] 1 All ER 142

The pursuers marketed cloth woven by crofters on the Isle of Lewis in the Outer Hebrides, using yarn imported from the mainland. Yarn was also produced in spinning mills on the Island and this was woven by the crofters into cloth and sold under the Harris Tweed mark. Most of the spinners in the island mills belonged to the Transport & General Workers' Union. Officials of the union asked for higher wages for mill workers but this was refused on the ground that an increase in costs would prevent the mill owners from competing with the pursuers and other firms on the island, who were importing yarn. To overcome this objection the defenders, officials of the union, instructed their members, who were dockers at Stornaway, the principal port on the island, not to handle yarn consigned to the pursuers or unfinished cloth despatched by them to the mainland. The embargo on the cloth was subsequently lifted. The pursuers sought an interdict (i.e. injunction) to prevent the continuing embargo on the yarn.

The Lord Ordinary recalled the interim interdict, and the Court of Session, Second Division (Lord Mackay dissenting) affirmed the decision: 1940 SC 141. On appeal by the pursuers to the House of Lords:

LORD WRIGHT: . . . The cause of action set out in the appellants' claim is for a conspiracy to injure, which is a tort. The classical definition of conspiracy is that given by Willes J. in advising the House of Lords in *Mulcahy v R*,[1] at p. 317:

'A conspiracy consists not merely in the intention of two or more, but in the agreement of two or more to do an unlawful act, or to do a lawful act by unlawful means.'

This must be supplemented by observing that, though the crime is constituted by the agreement, the civil right of action is not complete unless the conspirators do acts in pursuance of their agreement to the damage of the plaintiffs.

The question is, then, what the unlawful acts were with which the respondents were charged, or what the unlawful means were which they employed to do acts otherwise lawful. In other words, what is the legal right of the appellants which is infringed, or what is the legal wrong committed by the respondents? The concept of a civil

---

1. (1868) LR 3 HL 306.

conspiracy to injure has been in the main developed in the course of the last half-century, particularly since *Mogul SS Co v McGregor, Gow & Co.*[1] Its essential character is described by Lord Macnaghten in *Quinn v Leathem*,[2] at p. 510, basing himself on the words of Lord Watson in *Allen v Flood*,[3] at p. 108:

'. . . a conspiracy to injure might give rise to civil liability even though the end were brought about by conduct and acts which by themselves and apart from the element of combination or concerted action could not be regarded as a legal wrong.'

In this sense, the conspiracy is the gist of the wrong, though damage is necessary to complete the cause of action. . . . The rule may seem anomalous, so far as it holds that conduct by two may be actionable if it causes damage, whereas the same conduct done by one, causing the same damage, would give no redress. In effect, the plaintiff's right is that he should not be damnified by a conspiracy to injure him, and it is in the fact of the conspiracy that the unlawfulness resides. It is a different matter if the conspiracy is to do acts in themselves wrongful, as to deceive or defraud, to commit violence, or to conduct a strike or lock-out by means of conduct prohibited by the Conspiracy and Protection of Property Act 1875, or which contravenes the Trade Disputes and Trade Unions Act 1927. A conspiracy to injure, however, is a tort which requires careful definition, in order to hold the balance between the defendant's right to exercise his lawful rights and the plaintiff's right not to be injured by an injurious conspiracy. As I read the authorities, there is a clear and definite distinction which runs through them all between what Lord Dunedin in *Sorrell v Smith*,[4] at p. 730, calls 'a conspiracy to injure' and 'a set of acts dictated by business interests'. I should qualify 'business' by adding 'or other legitimate interests', using the convenient adjective not very precisely. It may be a difficult task in some cases to apply this distinction. It depends largely on matters of fact, but also on a legal conception of what is meant by 'intention to injure'. The appellants contend that there was here an intention to injure, even though it is negatived that the respondents were actuated by malice or malevolence. In substance, what the appellants say is that the issue between the millowners and the yarn importers was one between two sets of employers, in which the men were not directly concerned, that the union's action was an unjustifiable and meddlesome interference with the appellants' right to conduct their own businesses as they pleased, and that the union were pushing into matters which did not concern them. The appellants further say, as I understand their case, that this unjustifiable intrusion was due to the union's desire to secure the assistance of the millowners towards the union's object, which was to get 100 per cent. membership in the textile workers, and thus there was no common object among the two main parties to the combination. Each set had its own selfish object. In effect, it was said, the union were bribed by the millowners to victimise the appellants in their trade by the promise of help in the matter of the union membership, which was entirely foreign to the question of the importation of yarn. These considerations, it was said, constituted 'malice' in law, even if there was no malevolence, and prevented the respondents from justifying the injury which they wilfully did to the appellants' trade, because they could not assert any legitimate interest of their union which was relevant to the action taken. Actual malevolence or spite was, it was said, not essential. There was no genuine intention to promote union interests by the stoppage of importation. The interference with the appellants' trade by stopping import of yarn was wilful and ultroneous action on the part of the union, supported by no relevant union interest. It was malicious or wrongful because it was intentionally and unjustifiably mischievous, even though not malevolent.

---

1. [1892] AC 25.
2. [1901] AC 495.
3. [1898] AC 1.
4. [1925] AC 700.

Before I refer to the authorities, there are some preliminary observations which I desire to make. I shall avoid the use of what Bowen LJ in the *Mogul* case[1] described as the 'slippery' word 'malice' except in quotations. When I want to express spite or ill will, I shall use the word 'malevolence'. When I want to express merely intentional tortious conduct, I shall use the word 'wrongful'. As the claim is for a tort, it is necessary to ascertain what constitutes the tort alleged. It cannot be merely that the appellants' right to freedom in conducting their trade has been interfered with. That right is not absolute or unconditional. It is only a particular aspect of the citizen's right to personal freedom, and, like other aspects of that right, is qualified by various legal limitations, either by statute or by common law. Such limitations are inevitable in organised societies, where the rights of individuals may clash. In commercial affairs, each trader's rights are qualified by the right of others to compete. Where the rights of labour are concerned, the rights of the employer are conditioned by the rights of the men to give or withhold their services. The right of workmen to strike is an essential element in the principle of collective bargaining. . . .

It is thus clear that employers of workmen, or those who, like the appellants, depend in part on the services of workmen, have in the conduct of their affairs to reckon with this freedom of the men, and to realise that the exercise of the men's rights may involve some limitation on their own freedom in the management of their business. Such interference with a person's business, so long as the limitations enforced by law are not contravened, involves no legal wrong against the person. In the present case, the respondents are sued for imposing the 'embargo', which corresponds to calling out the men on strike. The dockers were free to obey or not to obey the call to refuse to handle the appellants' goods. In refusing to handle the goods, they did not commit any breach of contract with anyone. They were merely exercising their own rights. However, there might be circumstances which rendered the action wrongful. The men might be called out in breach of their contracts with their employer, and that would be clearly a wrongful act as against the employer, and an interference with his contractual right, for which damages could be claimed, not only as against the contract-breaker, but also against the person who counselled or procured or advised the breach. This is the principle laid down in *Lumley v Gye*[2] which Lord Macnaghten in *Quinn v Leathem*,[3] defined to be that [p. 510]:

'. . . a violation of legal right committed knowingly is a cause of action and . . . it is a violation of legal right to interfere with contractual relations recognised by law if there be no sufficient justification for the interference.'

That is something substantially different from a mere interference with a person's qualified right to exercise his free will in conducting his trade. A legal right was violated and needed justification, if it could be justified. This distinction was drawn by the majority of the Lords in *Allen v Flood*,[4] who disapproved of the dicta in *Bowen v Hall*[5] and *Temperton v Russell*[6] that every person who persuades another not to enter into a contract with a third person may be sued by the third person, if the object is to benefit himself at the expense of such person. However, in *Allen v Flood*,[4] this House was considering a case of an individual actor, where the element of combination was absent. In that case, it was held, the motive of the defendant is immaterial. Damage done intentionally, and even malevolently, to another thus, it was held, gives no cause of action so long as no legal right of the other is infringed.

---

1. [1892] AC 25.
2. (1853) 2 E & B 216.
3. [1901] AC 495.
4. [1898] AC 1.
5. (1881) 6 QBD 333.
6. [1893] 1 QB 715.

That I take to be the English rule laid down by this House in *Bradford Corpn v Pickles*[1] and in *Allen v Flood*,[2] though in *Sorrell v Smith*,[3] at p. 713, Lord Cave LC doubts the proposition, and says that in general what is unlawful in two is not lawful in one. This, however, seems to be inconsistent with the express rulings in *Allen v Flood*.[2] Though eminent authorities have protested against the principle, it must, I think, be accepted at present as the law in England. The precise issue does not arise in this case, which is concerned with combination or conspiracy. I need not consider whether any qualification may hereafter be found admissible.

Thus, for the purposes of the present case, we reach the position that, apart from combination, no wrong would have been committed. There was no coercion of the dockers. There were no threats to them. They were legally free to choose the alternative course which they preferred. In *Quinn v Leathem*,[4] a wide meaning was given to words like 'threats', 'intimidation' or 'coercion', especially by Lord Lindley, but that was not the ratio decidendi adopted by the House. These words, as pointed out in *Wright on Criminal Conspiracy*, are not terms of art and are consistent with either legality or illegality. They are not correctly used in the circumstances of a case like this. In *Allen v Flood*,[2] *Ware and De Freville Ltd v Motor Trade Association*[5] and *Sorrell v Smith*,[3] a more accurate definition was given. I should also refer to the admirable discussion by Peterson J in *Hodges v Webb*.[6] There is nothing unlawful in giving a warning or intimation that, if the party addressed pursues a certain line of conduct, others may act in a manner which he will not like and which will be prejudicial to his interests, so long as nothing unlawful is threatened or done. In the words of Lord Buckmaster in *Sorrell v Smith*,[3] at p. 747:

'A threat to do an act which is lawful cannot, in my opinion, create a cause of action whether the act threatened is to be done by many or by one.'

No doubt the use of illegal threats or the exercise of unlawful coercion would create by itself a cause of action, but there was nothing of the sort in this case.

The only way in this case in which the appellants can establish a cause of action in tort is by establishing that there was a conspiracy to injure, which would take the case out of the general ruling in *Allen v Flood*[2] and bring it within the exception there reserved by Lord Herschell, at pp. 123, 124:

'It is certainly a general rule of our law that an act prima facie lawful is not unlawful and actionable on account of the motive which dictated it. I put aside the case of conspiracy which is anomalous in more than one respect.'

In the same case, Lord Watson made a similar reservation, at p. 108. Lord Macnaghten, at p. 153, said that the decision in *Allen v Flood*[2] could have no bearing on any case which involved the element of oppressive combination. These reservations were acted upon in *Quinn v Leathem*,[4] to which I shall refer later. That the decision in that case turned on conspiracy cannot now be doubted, especially after *Ware and De Freville Ltd v Motor Trade Association*[7] and *Sorrell v Smith*.[3]

The distinction between conduct by one man and conduct by two or more may be difficult to justify. Lord Sumner in *Sorrell v Smith*[3] puts the very artificial case of the owner of a large business who gave a small share to a partner and 'conspired' with

---

1. [1895] AC 587.
2. [1898] AC 1.
3. [1925] AC 700.
4. [1901] AC 495.
5. [1921] 3 KB 40.
6. [1920] 2 Ch 70.
7. [1921] 3 KB 40.

him. For practical purposes, the position there is the same as if he had remained a sole trader. The fact that the sole trader employed servants or agents in the conduct of his business would not, in my opinion, make these others co-conspirators with him. The special rule relating to the effect of a combination has been explained on the ground that it is easier to resist one than two. That may appear to be true if a crude illustration is taken, such as the case of two men attacking another, but even there it would not always be true — for instance, if the one man was very strong and the two were very weak — and the power of a big corporation or trader may be greater than that of a large number of smaller fry in the trade. This explanation of the rule is not very satisfactory. The rule has been explained on grounds of public policy. The common law may have taken the view that there is always the danger that any combination may be oppressive, and may have thought that a general rule against injurious combinations was desirable on broad grounds of policy. Again, any combination to injure involves an element of deliberate concert between individuals to do harm. Whatever the moral or logical or sociological justification, the rule is as well established in English Law as I here take to be the rule that motive is immaterial in regard to the lawful act of an individual, a rule which has been strongly criticised by some high legal authorities, who would solve the apparent antinomy by holding that deliberate action causing injury is actionable whether done by one or by several.

A conspiracy to injure involves *ex vi termini* an intention to injure, or, more accurately, a common intention and agreement to injure. Both 'intention' and 'injure' need definition. The word 'injure' is here used in its correct meaning of 'wrongful harm', *damnum cum injuria*, not *damnum absque injuria*. That obviously raises the question of when the harm is wrongful. 'Intention' is generally determined by reference to overt acts and to the circumstances in which they are done. . . .

. . . On principle, I am of the opinion that malevolence is no more essential to the intent to injure, the mens rea, than it is to the intent to deceive. On practical grounds, also I prefer that view. To leave to a jury to decide on the basis of an internal mental state, rather than on the facts from which intent is to be inferred, may be to leave the issue in the hands of the jury as clay to mould at their will. After all, the plaintiff has to prove actual damage, which can only result from things done. Mere malevolence does not damage anyone. I cannot see how the pursuit of a legitimate practical object can be vitiated by glee at the adversary's expected discomfiture. Such glee, however deplorable, cannot affect the practical result. I may add that a desire to injure does not necessarily involve malevolence. It may be motivated by wantonness or some object not justifiable.

As to the authorities, the balance, in my opinion, is in favour of the view that malevolence as a mental state is not the test. I accordingly agree with the appellants' contention that they are not concluded by the finding that the respondents were not malevolent. It thus becomes necessary to consider the further arguments on which the appellants base their claim to succeed. I approach the question on the assumption that the appellants have to prove that they have been damnified by tortious action. They do not prove that by showing that they have been harmed by acts done by the respondents in combination, these acts being, apart from any question of combination, otherwise within the respondents' rights. It is not, then, for the respondents to justify these acts. The appellants must establish that they have been damnified by a conspiracy to injure — that is, that there was a wilful and concerted intention to injure without just cause and consequent damage. That was the view accepted by Lord Dunedin and Lord Buckmaster in *Sorrells*' case.[1] Lord Sumner proposes the question without deciding it, but the form in which he states it seems to me to suggest the answer. It is not a question of onus of proof. It depends on the cause of action. The plaintiff has to prove the wrongfulness of the defendant's object. Of course,

---

1. [1925] AC 700.

malevolence may be evidence tending to exclude a legitimate object or to establish a wrongful object. . . .

The respondents had no quarrel with the yarn importers. Their sole object, the courts below have held, was to promote their union's interests by promoting the interest of the industry on which the men's wages depended. On these findings, with which I agree, it could not be said that their combination was without sufficient justification. Nor would this conclusion be vitiated, even though their motives may have been mixed, so long as the real or predominant object, if they had more than one object, was not wrongful. Nor is the objection tenable that the respondents' real or predominant object was to secure the employers' help to get 100 per cent. membership of the union among the textile workers. Cases of mixed motives, or, as I should prefer to say, of the presence of more than one object, are not uncommon. If so, it is for the jury or judge of fact to decide which is the predominant object, as it may be assumed the jury did in *Quinn*'s case,[1] when they decided on the basis that the object of the combiners was vindictive punishment, and not their own practical advantage. . . .

I may here note that the doctrine of civil conspiracy to injure extends beyond trade competition and labour disputes. *Thompson v British Medical Association (NSW Branch)*[2] shows that it may extend to the affairs of a profession, as was expressly stated in that case, at p. 771, in the judgment of the Privy Council. By way of contrast, *Gregory v Duke of Brunswick*[3] may be regarded as a striking illustration of what might be held to constitute a conspiracy to injure. What was alleged was a conspiracy to hiss an actor off the stage in order to ruin him. To what legitimate interests other than those mentioned the general doctrine may extend I do not here seek to define, since beyond question it extends to the present case, whether the object of the action were the prosperity of the industry or the obtaining of 100 per cent. membership. The objects or purposes for which combinations may be formed, however, are clearly of great variety. It must be left to the future to decide, on the facts of the particular case, subject to the general doctrine, whether any combination is such as to give rise to a claim for a conspiracy to injure.

If, however, the object of securing 100 per cent. union membership were operative in inducing the respondents to combine with the employers, it was relied on by the appellants on other grounds as vitiating the combination. It was objected that there could be no combination between the employers and the union, because their respective interests were necessarily opposed. I think that that is a fallacious contention. It is true that employers and workmen are often at variance because the special interest of each side conflicts in the material respect, as, for instance, in questions of wages, conditions of hours of work, exclusion of non-union labour, but, apart from these differences in interest, both employers and workmen have a common interest in the prosperity of their industry, though the interest of one side may be in profits and of the other in wages. Hence a wider and truer view is that there is a community of interest. That view was acted upon in the present case in regard to the essential matter of yarn importation. As to the separate matter of the union membership, while that was something regarded as important by the respondents, it was probably regarded by the employers as a matter of indifference to them. It was, in any case, a side issue in the combination, even from the respondents' point of view. I may add that I do not accept as a general proposition that there must be complete identity of interest between parties to a combination. There must, however, be sufficient identity of object though the advantage to be derived from that same object may not be the same.

The appellants have further contended that the 'deal' referred to in the respondent

---

1. [1901] AC 495.
2. [1924] AC 764.
3. (1844) 6 Man & G 953.

Veitch's letter was a bargain by which the union sold to the employers the dockers' aid in return for the employers' aid in regard to union membership. In other words, the contention was that the respondents or the union were bribed, and were mercenaries, and not interested in the embargo except for the reward, which was in its nature unrelated to the embargo. The facts, however, were not as the contention assumes, so I need not discuss whether a party to a combination whose interest was merely separate and mercenary could ever be held to have a legitimate interest or justification for harm done in pursuance of the combination. I need merely add a few words on the objection that the embargo was the act of the dockers for the benefit, not of themselves, but of the textile workers. It is enough to say that both sections were members of the union, and there was, in my opinion, a sufficient community of interest, even if the matter is regarded from the standpoint of the men, as individuals, and not from the standpoint of the respondents, who were the only parties sued. Their interest, however, was to promote the advantage of the union as a whole. In my opinion, the judgment appealed from should be affirmed and the appeal dismissed.

[VISCOUNT SIMON LC, VISCOUNT MAUGHAM, LORD THANKERTON and LORD PORTER delivered speeches in favour of dismissing the appeal.]

Appeal dismissed

Notes

1. 'Why should an act which causes economic loss to A but is not actionable at his suit if done by B alone become actionable because B did it pursuant to an agreement between B and C?' (per Lord Diplock in *Lonrho Ltd v Shell Petroleum Co Ltd* [1981] 2 All ER 456 at 464, p. 688, post.) The reply given in the first 'modern' case, *Mogul SS Co Ltd v McGregor, Gow & Co* (1889) 23 QBD 598 at 616; affd [1892] AC 25, by Bowen LJ was that 'a combination may make oppressive or dangerous that which if it proceeded only from a single person would be otherwise, and the very fact of the combination may shew that the object is to do harm, and not to exercise one's own just rights'. This argument lost its force once English law accepted the doctrine of separate corporate personality (*Salomon v Salomon & Co* [1897] AC 22), with the possibility of great economic power being concentrated in a single corporation, as Lord Diplock recognised in the *Lonrho* case (p. 688, post), but the 'anomalous' tort of civil conspiracy to injure is now 'too well-established to be discarded.'

2. The historical link between the crime of conspiracy and the action for damages has been severed by s. 5(1) of the Criminal Law Act 1977 which abolishes the offence of conspiracy at common law subject to certain exceptions. This follows the Report of the Law Commission (Law Com. No. 76) on *Conspiracy and Criminal Law Reform*. The Act has no direct effect on civil proceedings. Note that husband and wife cannot be charged with a criminal conspiracy with each other (and see now s. 2(2)(a) of the 1977 Act), but they can conspire together for the purposes of the law of tort: *Midland Bank Trust Co Ltd v Green (No 3)* [1982] Ch 529; [1981] 3 All ER 744. Where the act complained of is a crime, or a conspiracy to commit a crime, and not also a tort against him, then no private person can bring an action to restrain a threatened breach of the law, unless the breach would infringe his private rights or would inflict special damage on him: *Gouriet v Union of Post Office Workers* [1978] AC 435; [1977] 3 All ER 70.

3. The pursuit of economic self-interest by traders (*Mogul SS Co Ltd v McGregor, Gow & Co* [1892] AC 25) and by trade unionists in combination with employers in the *Crofter* case have been held to be 'legitimate objects'. But a combination is unlawful if the real object is to injure. For example, in *Huntley v Thornton* [1957] 1 All ER 234; [1957] 1 WLR 321, the plaintiff had been prevented from obtaining work by a district committee of the Amalgamated Engineering Union because he had failed to participate in an official union strike, and had shown an 'arrogant attitude' to the committee at a disciplinary meeting, by describing the committee as a 'shower'. The Executive Committee of the union refused to countenance his expulsion, but the local boycott continued. Harman J held that the plaintiff was entitled to damages of £500, and he was granted leave to apply for an injunction in the event of renewed victimisation, because 'the district committee had entirely lost sight of what the interests of the union demanded and thought only of their own ruffled dignity. . . . It had become a question of the committee's prestige . . .'. It was also held that they were not entitled to the benefit of the statutory immunity against tort liability in trade disputes because they had not acted in *furtherance* of such a dispute. Two officials who had helped to implement the boycott were not liable because, being ignorant of the background to the dispute between the plaintiff and the committee, they had acted in what they sincerely believed to be the best interests of the union.

4. In *Scala Ballroom (Wolverhampton) Ltd v Ratcliffe* [1958] 3 All ER 220; [1958] 1 WLR 1057 the defendants were officials of the Musicians' Union who had organised a boycott of the plaintiffs' ballroom in protest against a colour bar operated there. The plaintiffs were refused an interlocutory injunction on the ground that no cause of action had been made out. The Court of Appeal held that the objects of the combination were legitimate, particularly in the light of an affidavit by one official in which he referred to the 'insidious effects' of a colour bar imposed on the audience because 'it is impossible for musicians to insulate themselves from their audience'. Hodson LJ said that legitimate interests were not to be confused with those which can be exchanged for cash. Morris LJ said that so long as the defendants honestly believed a certain policy to be desirable, even though it could not be translated into financial terms, there was no conspiracy to injure.

O. Kahn-Freund (1959) 22 MLR 69 comments: 'The line which separates lawful from unlawful action does not run between the markets of commodities or services and the labour market, but between a "policy of interest" and a "policy of prestige".' Does the decision mean that a boycott against members of a particular religion would not be tortious? Compare *Sweeney v Coote* [1907] AC 221 (for a fuller exposition of the facts, see [1906] IR 51-126) in which an action alleging conspiracy by Protestant parents who withdrew their children from the school of a Catholic schoolmistress, with the alleged purpose of having her dismissed from her post, failed. Earl Halsbury LC (at p. 223) said: 'If the object [was] . . . to cause her to be dismissed, not upon any ground of personal objection to her, or any spite or ill-will to her, but upon the ground that in the view of the parents . . . it was an undesirable thing for a Roman Catholic to be put into that position, I am of opinion that there would be no ground of action.' But in the *Crofter* case Lord Maugham ([1942] 1 All ER at p. 152) said that if 'the object of the combination [is] a dislike of the religious views or the politics or the race or

the colour of the plaintiff, or a mere demonstration of power by busybodies
... [t]here is, I think, no authority to be found which justifies the view that
[such] a combination ... would be lawful.' (See B. Hepple, *Race, Jobs and
the Law in Britain*, 2nd edn (Harmondsworth, 1970), p. 246; Lester and
Bindman, op cit., p. 53).

Lonrho Ltd *v* Shell Petroleum Co Ltd House of Lords [1981] 2 All ER 456

For the facts and other aspects of this case see p. 545, ante.

LORD DIPLOCK [dealing with the question whether the contravention of the sanctions
order, if proved, would amount to the tort of civil conspiracy by the respondents
jointly]: ... Your Lordships are invited to answer it on the assumption that the
purpose of Shell and BP in entering into the agreement to do the various things that
it must be assumed they did in contravention of the sanctions order was to forward
their own commercial interests, *not* to injure those of Lonrho. So the question of law
to be determined is whether an intent by the defendants to injure the plaintiff is an
essential element in the civil wrong of conspiracy, even where the acts agreed to be
done by the conspirators amount to criminal offences under a penal statute. It is
conceded that there is no direct authority either way on this question to be found in
the decided cases; so if this House were to answer it in the affirmative, your Lordships
would be making new law.

My Lords, conspiracy as a criminal offence has a long history. It consists of 'the
agreement of two or more persons to effect any unlawful purpose, whether as their
ultimate aim, or only as a means to it, and the crime is complete if there is such agreement, even though nothing is done in pursuance of it'. I cite from Viscount Simon
LC's now classic speech in *Crofter Hand Woven Harris Tweed Co Ltd v Veitch* [1942]
AC 435 at 439; [1942] 1 All ER 142 at 146. Regarded as a civil tort, however,
conspiracy is a highly anomalous cause of action. The gist of the cause of action is
damage to the plaintiff; so long as it remains unexecuted, the agreement, which alone
constitutes the crime of conspiracy, causes no damage; it is only acts done in execution of the agreement that are capable of doing that. So the tort, unlike the crime,
consists not of agreement but of concerted action taken pursuant to agreement.

As I recall from my early years in the law, first as a student and then as a young
barrister, during its chequered history between Lord Coleridge CJ's judgment at first
instance in *Mogul Steamship Co v McGregor, Gow & Co* (1888) 21 QBD 544 and the
Crofter case, the civil tort of conspiracy attracted more academic controversy than
success in practical application. Why should an act which causes economic loss to A
but is not actionable at his suit if done by B alone become actionable because B did
it pursuant to an agreement between B and C? An explanation given at the close of
the nineteenth century by Bowen LJ in the *Mogul* case 23 QBD 598 at 616 when it
was before the Court of Appeal was: 'The distinction is based on sound reason, for
a combination may make oppressive or dangerous that which if it proceeded only
from a single person would be otherwise ...' But to suggest today that acts done by
one street-corner grocer in concert with a second are more oppressive and dangerous
to a competitor than the same acts done by a string of supermarkets under a single
ownership or that a multinational conglomerate such as Lonrho or oil company such
as Shell or BP does not exercise greater economic power than any combination of
small businesses is to shut one's eyes to what has been happening in the business and
industrial world since the turn of the century and, in particular, since the end of
the 1939–45 war. The civil tort of conspiracy to injure the plaintiff's commercial
interests where that is the predominant purpose of the agreement between the defendants and of the acts done in execution of it which caused damage to the plaintiff
must I think be accepted by this House as too well-established to be discarded,

however anomalous it may seem today. It was applied by this House eighty years ago in *Quinn v Leathem* [1901] AC 495; [1900–3] All ER Rep 1, and accepted as good law in the *Crofter* case in 1942, where it was made clear that injury to the plaintiff and not the self-interest of the defendants must be the predominant purpose of the agreement in execution of which the damage-causing acts were done.

My Lords, in none of the judgments in decided cases in civil actions for damages for conspiracy does it appear that the mind of the author of the judgment was directed to a case where the damage-causing acts, although neither done for the purpose of injuring the plaintiff nor actionable at his suit if they had been done by one person alone, were nevertheless a contravention of some penal law. I will not recite the statements in those judgments to which your Lordships have been referred by Lonrho as amounting to dicta in favour of the view that a civil action for conspiracy does lie in such a case. Even if the authors' minds had been directed to the point, which they were not, I should still find them indecisive. This House, in my view, has an unfettered choice whether to confine the civil action of conspiracy to the narrow field to which alone it has an established claim or whether to extend this already anomalous tort beyond those narrow limits that are all that common sense and the application of the legal logic of the decided cases require.

My Lords, my choice is unhesitatingly the same as that of Parker J and all three members of the Court of Appeal. I am against extending the scope of the civil tort of conspiracy beyond acts done in execution of an agreement entered into by two or more persons for the purpose not of protecting their own interests but of injuring the interests of the plaintiff. . . .

[LORD EDMUND-DAVIES, LORD KEITH OF KINKEL, LORD SCARMAN, and LORD BRIDGE OF HARWICH agreed with the speech of LORD DIPLOCK in favour of dismissing the appeal.]

Metall und Rohstoff AG *v* Donaldson Lufkin and Jenrette Inc
Court of Appeal [1989] 3 All ER 14

An English company (AML) and its officers, who acted as brokers for the Swiss plaintiffs (M & R) were alleged to have traded fraudulently in the London Metal Exchange. To protect their position AML and its American parent companies had seized metal warrants and closed accounts operated by M & R (the plaintiffs), who obtained a judgment against AML which remained largely unsatisfied. In an attempt to recover the outstanding damages and costs M & R issued a writ against the American parent companies (the first and second defendants) alleging a conspiracy, not with the sole or predominant purpose to injure M & R, but as a 'conspiracy in effect to steal their warrants'. The Court of Appeal held that an alleged agreement in this form did not amount to a tortious conspiracy, even if the means used were unlawful, because the defendants had acted to protect their own commercial interests rather than to injure the plaintiffs.

SLADE LJ [delivering the judgment of the Court]: . . . The correct legal principle to be applied in this . . . situation [where a conspiracy to use unlawful means is alleged] was the subject of detailed and protracted argument . . . the crucial issue being the correct understanding of the House of Lords unanimous decision, contained in the speech of Lord Diplock in *Lonrho Ltd v Shell Petroleum Co Ltd' (No 2)*[1]. . . .

Even a speech of Lord Diplock's is not to be construed like a statute. But he was a judge noted for his clear and precise use of language. This speech was adopted without qualification or addition by the other members of the Appellate Committee.

---

1. [1982] AC 173; [1981] 2 All ER 456.

The parties to this appeal differ radically in their interpretation of what he meant. Courts here and abroad have similarly differed. Resolution of the difference is fundamental to the outcome of this part of the appeal. We feel bound to analyse what Lord Diplock said in more detail than might in other circumstances be appropriate.

(1) The appeal could have been determined on very limited grounds that the oil companies had no intention to injure the claimants or had (on the assumed facts) no relevant lawful business to protect. But throughout his speech Lord Diplock referred to the tort of conspiracy in general terms: 'conspiracy as a civil tort', 'the civil wrong of conspiracy', 'regarded as a civil tort . . . conspiracy', 'the cause of action', 'the tort', 'the civil tort of conspiracy', 'the civil tort of conspiracy to injure the plaintiff's commercial interests', 'the civil action of conspiracy', 'civil tort of conspiracy'. It could be said that Lord Diplock was not expressly referring to conspiracies outside the commercial field, such as agreements to defame the plaintiff otherwise than in his professional capacity. But subject to that possible qualification he seems to have chosen very general language.

(2) Acts done in combination pursuant to agreement may be acts which, if done by one person alone, would be (a) entirely lawful (as were the acts done in the *Mogul Steamship case*,[1] *Quinn v Leathem*,[2] *Sorrell v Smith*[3] and the *Crofter Hand Woven Harris Tweed Co*[4] case) or (b) tortious or (c) tortious and also criminal or (d) simply criminal (as were assumed acts in the *Lonrho* case). M & R submitted that the rule laid down by the House in the *Lonrho* case was intended to cover acts in categories (a) and (d), but not (b) and (c). We cannot accept this. In first posing the question for determination by the House, Lord Diplock appears to have treated the commission of criminal acts pursuant to agreement as the extreme case ('even where the acts agreed to be done by the conspirators amount to criminal offences under a penal statute'). It is not conceivable, least of all in the light of the argument and the judgments below, that the House overlooked the possibility of acts in classes (b) and (c). Yet nowhere does one find any exclusion of acts in these classes or any indication that they were to be subject to any different rule. The natural inference is that the House intended to embrace acts in all four classes within the rule laid down.

(3) The House plainly regarded the tort of conspiracy as anomalous, first because its ingredients differed from those of the crime of conspiracy and second because the fact of combination had the effect of rendering actionable conduct otherwise lawful, even though a single enterprise if large and powerful enough could do more harm to the victim acting alone than a number of smaller and less powerful enterprises could do acting in combination. Plainly also the House regarded the law of civil conspiracy as unsatisfactory in practice. So the wish of the House was to restrict the scope of civil conspiracy, not to extend it. And the House cannot have intended to introduce a new anomaly. If, however, the decision had the 'comparatively narrow' effect which Gatehouse J ascribed to it 'that a plaintiff cannot rely on a damage-causing act which is merely a breach of the criminal law but gives no right of action in tort' (see [1988] 3 All ER 116 at 123, [1988] 3 WLR 548 at 556), a new anomaly would arise, because a cause of action in conspiracy would exist where it was least needed (ie where the acts done pursuant to the agreement were torts, which would in themselves provide a cause of action) but not where it was most needed (ie where the acts done pursuant to the agreement were non-tortious crimes which would not themselves provide a cause of action).

(4) The House regarded as too well established to be discarded, despite its inherent anomaly, the rule that an agreement to injure the plaintiff's commercial interests was

---

1. [1892] AC 25.
2. [1901] AC 495.
3. [1925] AC 700.
4. [1942] AC 435; [1942] 1 All ER 142

civilly actionable where the defendants' predominant purpose in making the agreement and implementing it so as to damage the plaintiff was to injure those interests. *Quinn v Leathem*[1] was said to establish, and the *Crofter Hand Woven Harris Tweed Co*[2] case to affirm, that injury to the plaintiff, not the self-interest of the defendants, must be the predominant purpose of the agreement in execution of which the damage-causing acts were done. It would not, of course, be possible to summarise nearly a hundred pages of speeches in those two cases in one short sentence, but Lord Diplock was, as we understand him, intending to state the essential thrust of the rule. M & R contended that by 'self-interest of the defendants' Lord Diplock must have been intending to refer to the defendants' legitimate or lawful self-interest but (i) he did not make that qualification either at this point or when first expressing the antithesis nor did he make it in his final summary and (ii) the House must have had this aspect in mind, both because Eveleigh LJ[3] expressly referred to it and because the case was one involving an illegitimate or unlawful interest of the oil companies. In truth *Crofter Hand Woven Harris Tweed Co Ltd v Veitch*[2] laid down no rule on the effect of lawful acts done pursuant to agreement for the purpose not of damaging the plaintiff but of advancing an unlawful interest of the defendants because the question did not arise. But the decision in *Lonrho Ltd v Shell Petroleum Co Ltd* did establish that there was no actionable conspiracy where criminal acts were done pursuant to agreement for the purpose not of damaging the plaintiff but of advancing an unlawful interest of the defendants (trade to Rhodesia).

(5) The House held itself free the choose 'whether to confine the civil action of conspiracy to the narrow field to which alone it has an established claim or whether to extend this already anomalous tort beyond those narrow limits that are all that common sense and the application of the legal logic of the decided cases require'. We understand 'the narrow field to which alone it has an established claim' as an unmistakable reference back to the rule held to be too well established to be discarded. That is the rule established in *Quinn v Leathem*[1] and *Crofter Hand Woven Harris Tweed Co Ltd v Veitch*,[2] the essential ingredient of the tort being a predominant purpose of causing injury. To hold that agreements to commit tortious acts were being deliberately excluded from consideration by Lord Diplock is to deprive the word 'alone' of meaning. In our view the House plainly intended the presence of a predominant intention to injure to be the touchstone of an actionable conspiracy. Where that was present the plaintiff won, as in *Quinn v Leathem*,[1] although the defendants' acts were in themselves lawful. Where it was absent the plaintiff lost, whether the acts were lawful, as in the *Mogul Steamship*[5] case, *Sorrell v Smith*[4] and the *Crofter Hand Woven Harris Tweed Co*[2] case, or criminal as in the *Lonrho Ltd* case. The latter decision, as we have understood it, was consistent with common sense and the legal logic of the decided cases since the assumed conduct of the oil companies, if meriting criminal penalties, could not sensibly be regarded as entitling the plaintiffs to compensation. Where the predominant intention to injure is absent but the defendants pursuant to agreement commit torts against the plaintiff, the House held, we conclude, that common sense and the legal logic of the decided cases are satisfied if the plaintiff is denied a remedy in conspiracy and left to sue on the substantive torts.

(6) It was pointed out that although Lord Diplock twice used the word 'predominant' when referring to the existing law he did not do so when first expressing the purpose antithesis nor when expressing his final conclusion (see [1981] 2 All ER 456 at 462–463, [1982] AC 173 at 188–189). But the House would of course have appreciated that human

---

1. [1901] AC 495.
2. [1942] AC 435; [1942] 1 All ER 142
3. [In the Court of Appeal in that case.]
4. [1925] AC 700.
5. [1892] AC 25.

motives are often mixed, and Lord Denning MR[1] had quoted Viscount Simon LC's colourful metaphor on the point. We think it plain that the House intended 'predominant' or 'sole or predominant' to be understood even where these expressions were not used, since the effect of the decision was to limit the tort to the established rule under which a predominant purpose of causing injury was essential. M & R submitted that the rule laid down by the House was that adopted by Lord Denning MR in the Court of Appeal, that where there was agreement to do an unlawful act an action in conspiracy would lie if the defendant had an intention to injure, even if that intention was not predominant. That was, as it seems to us, a workable approach and it would enable M & R to succeed on this issue in this appeal, since they have pleaded an intention to injure and plainly the conspiracy alleged was aimed or directed at M & R in a secondary way. It is perhaps surprising that the House did not expressly comment on Lord Denning MR's formulation. Having read and reread Lord Diplock's speech, we cannot however construe it consistently with an intention to adopt that formulation.

(7) The House of Lords has never thought it necessary further to define 'a predominant purpose to injure'. Nor do we. It is not to be equated with spite, vindictiveness or sheer malevolence, although these will sometimes be present. But we prefer to stick to the test the House of Lords had laid down.

M & R submitted, and Gatehouse J concluded, that —

'It would be most surprising if the House of Lords had intended to alter radically the nature of all those types of conspiracy which have long been recognised and are generally known as "illegal means" conspiracies, where predominant purpose has hitherto been immaterial.'

(See [1988] 3 All ER 116 at 123, [1988] 3 WLR 548 at 557.) There is, however, no decided case in the House of Lords whose ratio depends on recognition of such a conspiracy. There are, as we have indicated, numerous dicta by eminent judges of great authority, but in regarding the law as unclear and unsatisfactory the House in the *Lonrho Ltd* case was echoing Lord Dunedin, who in *Sorrell v Smith* [1925] AC 700 at 717, [1925] All ER Rep 1 at 8 thought that it would be 'an impossible task to reconcile either the decisions or the dicta', Lord Wright, who in *Crofter Hand Woven Harris Tweed Co Ltd v Veitch* held that 'reconciliation of all the observations is impossible', and Lord Porter, who in the same case regarded the law as 'somewhat obscure' (see [1942] 1 All ER 142 at 163, 167, [1942] AC 435 at 472, 480). Recognising that the authorities contained material for almost endless debate, their Lordships may well have thought it desirable to abbreviate argument in future by laying down a clear, simple and universally applicable rule, as we think they did. It is hard to accept that the House could not reasonably have intended to lay down the rule it did when the rule laid down, as we have construed it, was almost exactly that favoured (had the slate been clean) by Lord Dunedin in *Sorrell v Smith* [1925] AC 700 at 717, [1925] All ER Rep 1 at 8 and by the arbitrators in *Lonrho* itself (at para C14 of the consultative case). . . .

Notes

1. This decision attempts to resolve the conflict between first instance judges as to the scope of unlawful means conspiracy. However, in *Derby & Co v Weldon (No 3)* [1989] 3 All ER 118; [1989] 1 WLR 1244, Vinelott J refused to strike out a conspiracy claim which did not allege that the sole or predominant purpose was to injure the plaintiffs because he thought that the House of Lords might decide the issue differently. The *Metall und Rohstoff* litigation

---

1. [In the Court of Appeal in that case.]

has since been settled, but in *Lonrho plc v Fayed* [1989] 2 All ER 65; [1989] 3 WLR 631 (p. 726, post) the Court of Appeal held that the tort of unlawful interference in the trade of another does not require proof that the defendant acted with the predominant purpose to injure the plaintiff rather than for his own financial ends. Leave to appeal to the House of Lords was granted. This may enable the House of Lords to clarify the relationship between the two torts. See generally J. Eekelaar (1990) 106 LQR 223.

2. An indication of the result of requiring a 'predominant intent to injure' in respect of conspiracy to use unlawful means is to be seen in *R C A Corpn v Pollard* [1983] Ch 135; [1982] 3 All ER 771, noted p. 549, ante, where boot-leggers committed criminal offences by taking and trading in unauthorised live recordings of Elvis Presley numbers. The Court of Appeal held that there was no civil action for breach of statutory duty nor had there been a tort of unlawful interference with contractual relations (post). It seems that the 'common sense' or 'legal logic' advanced by Lord Diplock in the *Lonrho* case would exculpate the 'criminal bootleggers from civil liability in conspiracy once they prove that although they intended to harm the recording companies, their *predominant* object was to spread the rock of Elvis (at a profit)' (W[edderburn] (1983) 46 MLR at p. 228; see too A. Evans [1983] EIPR 31). Compare the approach to 'intention' in this context with that in the 'genus' tort of interference with trade by unlawful means (p. 724, post).

3. Now that the House of Lords has accepted the 'predominant purpose' to profit selfishly by a criminal act as a 'legitimate object' does it make any difference whether the plaintiff has to prove the lack of 'justification' or the defendant has to prove that his illegal act was 'justified'? (Compare *Clerk & Lindsell*, para. 15-25, note 57 with P. Elias and K. Ewing [1982] CLJ 321 at 325.)

4. There is a statutory immunity in s. 13(4) of the Trade Union and Labour Relations Act 1974 where the agreement is to commit an act which would not be actionable in tort if committed by an individual and the act is 'in contemplation or furtherance of a trade dispute'. The precise limits of this defence are debatable (see Wedderburn in *Clerk & Lindsell*, para. 15-31), but the modern judicial acceptance of most trade union objectives as 'legitimate' (*Crofter*'s case, p. 680, ante) and the requirement of a predominant intention to injure even when unlawful means are employed (*Metall und Rohstoff* case) means that the immunity is of far less importance than when it was first introduced as s. 1 of the Trade Disputes Act 1906 to counteract *Quinn v Leathem* [1901] AC 495 (on which see P. Davies and M. Freedland, *Labour Law: Text and Materials* 2nd edn (London, 1984), pp. 710–718).

2   Interference with contract

Lumley v Gye Court of Queen's Bench [1843–60] All ER Rep 208

CROMPTON J: The declaration in this case consisted of three counts. The two first stated a contract between the plaintiff, the proprietor of the Queen's Theatre, and Miss Wagner, for the performance by her for a period of three months at the plaintiff's theatre; and it then stated that the defendant, knowing the premises and with a malicious intention, while the agreement was in full force and before the expiration of the period for which Miss Wagner was engaged, wrongfully and maliciously enticed and procured Miss Wagner to refuse to sing or perform at the theatre and to depart from and abandon her contract with the plaintiff and all service thereunder, whereby Miss Wagner wrongfully, during the full period of the engagement, refused and made default in performing at the theatre. Special damage arising from the breach of Miss Wagner's engagement was then stated. The third count stated that Miss Wagner had been hired and engaged by the plaintiff, then being the owner of the Queen's Theatre, to perform at the theatre for a specified period as the dramatic artiste of the plaintiff for reward to her in that behalf, and had become and was such dramatic artiste for the plaintiff at his theatre for profit to the plaintiff in that behalf, and that the defendant, well knowing the premises and with a malicious intention, while Miss Wagner was such artiste of the plaintiff, wrongfully and maliciously enticed and procured her, so being such artiste of the plaintiff, to depart from and out of the employment of the plaintiff, whereby she wrongfully departed from and out of the service and employment of the plaintiff, and remained and continued absent from such service and employment until the expiration of her said hiring and engagement to the plaintiff by effluxion of time. Special damage arising from the breach of Miss Wagner's engagement was then stated. To this declaration the defendant demurred, and the question for our decision is whether all or any of the counts are good in substance.

The effect of the two first counts is that a person under a binding contract to perform at a theatre is induced by the malicious act of the defendant to refuse to perform and entirely abandon her contract, whereby damage arises to the plaintiff, the proprietor of the theatre. The third count differs in stating expressly that the performer had agreed to perform as the dramatic artiste of the plaintiff, and had become and was the dramatic artiste of the plaintiff for reward to her, and that the defendant maliciously procured her to depart out of the employment of the plaintiff as such dramatic artiste, whereby she did depart out of the employment and service of the plaintiff, whereby damage was suffered by the plaintiff. It was said, in support of the demurrer, that it did not appear in the declaration that the relation of master and servant ever subsisted between the plaintiff and Miss Wagner; that Miss Wagner was not averred, especially in the two first counts, to have entered upon the service of the plaintiff; and that the engagement of a theatrical performer, even if the performer has entered upon the duties, is not of such a nature as to make the performer a servant within the rule of law which gives an action to the master for the wrongful enticing away of his servant. It was laid down broadly, as a general proposition of law, that no action will lie for procuring a person to break a contract, although such procuring is with a malicious intention and causes great and immediate injury. The law as to enticing servants was said to be contrary to the general rule and principle of law, to be anomalous, and probably to have had its origin from the state of society when serfdom existed and to be founded upon, or upon the equity of, the Statute of Labourers. It was said that it would be dangerous to hold that an action was maintainable for persuading a third party to break a contract unless some boundary or limits could be pointed out; that the remedy for enticing away servants was confined to cases where the relation of master and servant, in a strict sense, subsisted between the parties; and that, in all other cases of contract, the only remedy was against the party breaking the contract.

Whatever may have been the origin or foundation of the law as to enticing of servants, and whether it be, as contended by the plaintiff, an instance and branch of a wider rule, or, as contended by the defendant, an anomaly and an exception from the general rule of law on such subjects, it must now be considered clear law that a person who wrongfully and maliciously, or, which is the same thing, with notice, interrupts the relation subsisting between master and servant by procuring the servant to depart from the master's service, or by harbouring and keeping him as servant after he has quitted it and during the time stipulated for as the period of service, whereby the master is injured, commits a wrongful act for which he is responsible at law. I think that the rule applies wherever the wrongful interruption operates to prevent the service during the time for which the parties have contracted that the service shall continue, and I think that the relation of master and servant subsists, sufficiently for the purpose of such action, during the time for which there is in existence a binding contract of hiring and service between the parties. I think that it is a fanciful and technical and unjust distinction to say that the not having actually entered into the service, or that the service is not actually continuing, can make any difference. The wrong and injury are surely the same whether the wrongdoer entices away the gardener, who has hired himself for a year, the night before he is to go to his work, or after he has planted the first cabbage on the first morning of his service. I should be sorry to support a distinction so unjust, and so repugnant to common sense, unless bound to do so by some rule or authority of law plainly showing that such distinction exists. . . .

The objection as to the actual employment not having commenced would not apply in the present case to the third count, which states that Miss Wagner had become the artiste of the plaintiff and that the defendant had induced her to depart from the employment. But it was further said that the engagement, employment, or service, in the present case was not of such a nature as to constitute the relation of master and servant, so as to warrant the application of the usual rule of law giving a remedy in case of enticing away servants. The nature of the injury and of the damage being the same, and the supposed right of action being in strict analogy to the ordinary case of master and servant, I see no reason for confining the case to services or engagements under contracts for services of any particular description; and I think that the remedy, in the absence of any legal reason to the contrary, may well apply to all cases where there is an unlawful and malicious enticing away of any person employed to give his personal labour or service for a given time under the direction of a master or employer who is injured by the wrongful act, more especially when the party is bound to give such personal services exclusively to the master or employer though I by no means say that the service need be exclusive. . . .

In deciding this case on the narrower ground, I wish by no means to be considered as deciding that the larger ground taken by counsel for the plaintiff is not tenable, or as saying that in no case except that of master and servant is an action maintainable for maliciously inducing another to break a contract to the injury of the person with whom such contract has been made. It does not appear to me to be a sound answer to say that the [actionable] act in such cases is the act of the party who breaks the contract, for that reason would apply in the acknowledged case of master and servant. Nor is it an answer to say that there is a remedy against the contractor and that the party relies on the contract, for, besides that reason also applying to the case of master and servant, the action on the contract and the action against the malicious wrongdoer may be for a different matter, and the damages payable for such malicious injury might be calculated on a very different principle from the amount of the debt which might be the only sum recoverable on the contract. Suppose a trader, with a malicious intent to ruin a rival trader, goes to a banker or other party who owes money to his rival, and begs him not to pay the money which he owes him, and by that means ruins or greatly prejudices the party. I am by no means prepared to say that an action could not be maintained, and that damages, beyond the amount of the debt if the injury were great, or much less than such amount if the injury were less serious, might not be recovered. Where two or more parties were concerned in inflicting such injury, an indictment, or a writ of conspiracy at common law, might, perhaps, have been maintainable. Where a writ of conspiracy would lie for an injury inflicted by two, an action on the case in the nature of conspiracy will generally lie, and in such an action on the case the plaintiff is entitled to recover against one defendant without proof of any conspiracy, the malicious injury and not the conspiracy being the gist of the action: see note (4) to *Skinner v Gunton* (1669) 1 Saund at p. 230. In this class of cases it must be assumed that it is the malicious act of the defendant, and that malicious act only, which causes the servant or contractor not to perform the work or contract which he would otherwise have done. The servant or contractor may be utterly unable to pay for anything like the amount of the damage sustained entirely from the wrongful act of the defendant, and it would seem unjust, and contrary to the general principles of law, if such a wrongdoer were not responsible for the damage caused by his wrongful and malicious act. . . .

ERLE J: . . . It is clear that the procurement of the violation of a right is a cause of action in all instances where the violation is an actionable wrong, as in violations of a right to property, whether real or personal, or to personal security. He who procures the wrong is a joint wrongdoer, and may be sued, either alone or jointly with the agent, in the appropriate action for the wrong complained of. Where a right to the performance of a contract has been violated by a breach thereof, the remedy is upon the contract against the contracting party. If he is made to indemnify for such breach, no further recourse is allowed, and, as in case of the procurement of a breach of contract the action is for a wrong and cannot be joined with the action on the contract, and as the act itself is not likely to be of frequent occurrence nor easy of proof, therefore, the action for this wrong, in respect of other contracts than those of hiring, are not numerous, but still they seem to me sufficient to show that the principle has been recognised. . . .

This principle is supported by good reason. He who maliciously procures a damage to another by violation of his right ought to be made to indemnify, and that whether he procures an actionable wrong or a breach of contract. He who procures the non-delivery of goods according to contract may inflict an injury, the same as he who procures the abstraction of goods after delivery, and both ought on the same ground to be made responsible. The remedy on the contract may be inadequate, as where the measure of damages is restricted; or in the case of non-payment of a debt where the damage may be bankruptcy to the creditor who is disappointed, but the measure of damages against the debtor is interest only; or, in the case of the non-delivery of the goods, the disappointment may lead to a heavy forfeiture under a contract to complete a work within a time, but the measure of damages against the vendor of the goods for non-delivery may be only the difference between the contract price and the market value of the goods in question at the time of the breach. In such cases, he who procures the damage maliciously might justly be made responsible beyond the liability of the contractor. . . .

[WIGHTMAN J delivered a judgment agreeing with CROMPTON J. COLERIDGE J dissented.]

Note

Bowen v Hall (1881) 6 QBD 333 was the next case of inducing breach of contract to reach an appellate court. An expert bricklayer had been induced to leave his employer's service by a rival firm. As in *Lumley v Gye*, the relationship of master and servant, in the strict sense, did not exist. The Court of Appeal (Lord Selborne LC and Brett LJ; Lord Coleridge CJ dissenting) allowed the plaintiff employer an action. The majority took the view that *Lumley v Gye* had been correctly decided on the wide ground stated by Erle J, i.e. the *malicious* violation of contractual rights. However, in *Quinn v Leathem* [1901] AC 495 at 510, Lord Macnaghten said: 'I think the decision [in *Lumley v Gye*] was right, not on the ground of malicious intention—that was not, I think the gist of the action, but on the ground that a violation of a legal right committed knowingly is a cause of action, and that it is a violation of a legal right to interfere with contractual relations recognised by law if there be no sufficient justification for the interference.'

South Wales Miners' Federation *v* Glamorgan Coal Co Ltd
House of Lords [1904–7] All ER Rep 211

The Miners' Federation had ordered a number of stop-days. Bigham J, [1903] 1 KB 118, held that in doing so the Federation and the members of its executive had been actuated by an honest desire to forward the interests of the men without any prospect of personal gain to themselves and without any intention, malicious or otherwise, to injure the plaintiffs, who were colliery owners. The object had been to restrict output so as to keep up coal prices because, under the sliding scale agreement between the colliery owners and the miners, wages depended upon the selling price of coal. It was not disputed that the Federation had induced and procured workmen who were employed by the plaintiffs to break their contracts of service, so inflicting loss on the plaintiffs. It was argued, however, that the wrong was justifiable in the circumstances. The Court of Appeal held that it was not, [1903] 2 KB 545. On appeal to the House of Lords:

LORD MACNAGHTEN: . . . That there may be a justification for that which in itself is an actionable wrong I do not for a moment doubt; and I do not think that it would be difficult to give instances, putting aside altogether cases complicated by the introduction of moral considerations. But what is the alleged justification in the present case? It was said that the council, the executive of the federation, had a duty cast upon them to protect the interests of the members of the union, and that they could not be made legally responsible for the consequences of their action if they acted honestly in good faith and without any sinister or indirect motive. The case was argued with equal candour and ability. But it seems to me that the argument may be disposed of by two simple questions. How was the duty created? What in fact was the alleged duty? The alleged duty was created by the members of the union themselves, who elected or appointed the officials of the union to guide and direct their action; and then it was contended that the body to whom the members of the union have thus committed their individual freedom of action are not responsible for what they do, if they act according to their honest judgment in furtherance of what they consider to be the interest of their constituents. It seems to me that if that plea were admitted there would be an end of all responsibility. It would be idle to sue the workmen, the individual wrongdoers, even if it were practicable to do so. Their counsellors and protectors, the real authors of the mischief, would be safe from legal proceedings. The only other question is, What is the alleged duty set up by the federation? I do not think that it can be better described than it was by counsel for the plaintiffs. It comes to this: it is the duty on all proper occasions, of which the federation or their officials are to be the sole judges, to counsel and procure a breach of duty. . . .

LORD JAMES OF HEREFORD: . . . It yet remains to deal with the words 'wrongfully and maliciously' as averred in the statement of claim. As to the word 'wrongfully', I think that no difficulty arises. If the breach of the contract of service by the workmen was an unlawful act, any one who induces and procures the workmen, without just cause and excuse, to break such contract also acts unlawfully, and thus the allegation that the act done was wrongfully done is established. But the word 'maliciously' has also to be dealt with. The judgment of Bigham J ([1903] 1 KB at p. 133), proceeds on the ground that

'to support an action for procuring a breach of contract it is essential to prove actual malice.'

I cannot concur in this view of the law. The word 'maliciously' is often employed in criminal and civil pleadings without proof of actual malice, apart from the commission of the act complained of, being required. If A utters a slander of B, even if he be a stranger to him, the averment that A maliciously spoke such words of B is established by simply proving the uttering of words taken to be false until the contrary be proved. In such an action the word 'maliciously' may be treated either as an unnecessary averment or as being proved by inference drawn from the proof of the act being wrongfully committed. . . .

LORD LINDLEY: . . . The constitution of the union may have rendered it the duty of the officials to advise the men what could be legally done to protect their own interests, but a legal duty to do what is illegal and known so to be is a contradiction in terms. A similar argument was urged without success in *Read v Friendly Society of Operative Stonemasons.*[1] Then your Lordships were invited to say that there was a moral or social duty on the part of the officials to do what they did, and that, as they acted bona fide in the interests of the men and without any ill-will to the employers, their conduct was justifiable; and your Lordships were asked to treat this case as if it were like a case of libel or slander on a privileged occasion. This contention was not based on authority, and its only merits are its novelty and ingenuity. The analogy is, in my opinion, misleading; and to give effect to this contention would be to legislate and introduce an entirely new law and not to expound the law as it is at present. It would be to render many acts lawful which, as the law stands, are clearly unlawful. I have purposely abstained from using the word 'malice'. Bearing in mind that malice may or may not be used to denote ill-will, and that in legal language presumptive or implied malice is distinguished from express malice, it conduces to clearness in discussing such cases as these to drop the word 'malice' altogether and to substitute for it the meaning which is really intended to be conveyed by it. Its use may be necessary in drawing indictments; but when all that is meant by malice is an intention to commit an unlawful act, and to exclude all spite or ill-feeling, it is better to drop the word and so avoid all misunderstanding. The appeal ought to be dismissed with costs.

[EARL HALSBURY LC delivered a speech in favour of dismissing the appeal.]

Appeal dismissed

Edwin Hill & Partners (a firm) *v* First National Finance Corpn plc Court of Appeal [1988] 3 All ER 801

The defendants were a finance company who had made a substantial loan to a property developer, secured by a legal charge. The developer was unable to get the development started and unable to repay the loan. Instead of exercising their powers of sale as mortgagees, the finance company agreed to make further advances to the developer, but on terms that the developer's contract with the plaintiff architects be terminated and that new architects be appointed in their place. The developer complied with this requirement. The plaintiffs thereupon sued the defendants for inducing breach of contract. Rose J held that all the elements of the tort were made out, but that the defendants had established the defence of justification because the right of the mortgagees to receive payment of their loan and interest constituted an equal or superior right to that of the plaintiffs. The question of justification was the main issue on appeal.

STUART-SMITH LJ: . . . Counsel for the defendants submitted that the judge's approach was correct. He contended that where the interferer's conduct is within the ambit

---

1. [1902] 2 KB 732.

or compass of his legal rights he is justified. By this phrase he means that if the defendants, instead of exercising their full legal rights of calling for repayment of the loan and exercising their powers of sale or appointment of a receiver, reach some accommodation with the mortgagor, which is more beneficial both to themselves and the mortgagor, they should not be held to lose the justification which they would have had if they had exercised the remedies available to them in the strict sense.

Alternatively he submits that the question of justification should be approached by what he called the 'broad brush' approach adumbrated by Romer LJ in *Glamorgan Coal Co Ltd v South Wales Miners' Federation* [1903] 2 KB 545. This is a convenient starting point for a consideration of the authorities. Romer LJ said (at 574):

'I respectfully agree with what Bowen L.J. said in [*Mogul Steamship Co Ltd v McGregor Gow & Co* (1889) 23 QBD 598 at 618, [1891-4] All ER Rep 263 at 281], when considering the difficulty that might arise whether there was sufficient justification or not: "The good sense of tribunal which had to decide would have to analyze the circumstances and to discover on which side of the line each case fell." I will only add that, in analyzing or considering the circumstances, I think that regard might be had to the nature of the contract broken; the position of the parties to the contract; the grounds for the breach; the means employed to procure the breach; the relation of the person procuring the breach to the person who breaks the contract; and I think also to the object of the person in procuring the breach. But, though I deprecate the attempt to define justification, I think it right to express my opinion on certain points in connection with breaches of contract procured where the contract is one of master and servant. In my opinion, a defendant sued for knowingly procuring such a breach is not justified of necessity merely by his shewing that he had no personal animus against the employer, or that it was to the advantage or interest of both the defendant and the workman that the contract should be broken.'

Stirling LJ's judgment is to the same effect (at 577).

When the case reached the House of Lords ([1905] AC 239, [1904-7] All ER Rep 211) nothing was said by any members of the House to suggest that this was the wrong approach. Lord Lindley expressed entire agreement with the judgments of Romer and Stirling LJJ (see [1905] AC 239 at 252, [1904-7] All ER Rep 211 at 218). The other members of the House contented themselves with saying that the alleged justification did not amount to such in law. In my judgment it matters not that some of their Lordships treated the case as both conspiracy and wrongful interference with contracts (see for example [1905] AC 239 at 244, [1904-7] All ER Rep 211 at 244 per the Earl of Halsbury LC).

Counsel for the plaintiffs submitted that in the *Glamorgan* case the supposed justification was a duty to act in what was conceived to be the interests of both parties to the contract and that accordingly Romer LJ's test or approach should be confined to such cases, and should not extend to cases where the interferer's conduct is sought to be justified by reference to some equal or superior legal right. But I cannot see that the proposition should be so limited; in my judgment the courts have over the years worked on this principle, holding that some cases fall on one side of the line, others on the other. . . .

Thus the following matters have been held not to amount to justification. (1) Absence of malice or ill-will or intention to injure the person whose contract is broken: *Smithies v National Association of Operative Plasterers* [1909] 1 KB 310, [1908-10] All ER Rep 455 and *South Wales Miners' Federation v Glamorgan Coal Co Ltd* [1905] Ac 239, [1904-7] All ER Rep 211. (2) The commercial or other best interests of the interferer or the contract breaker: *Read v Friendly Society of Operative Stonemasons of England Ireland and Wales* [1902] 2 KB 88 at 97, [1902] 2 KB 732 at 737 per Darling J and Collins MR, the *Glamorgan* case [1905] AC 239 at 252, [1904-7] All ER Rep 211 at 217–218 per Lord James, *Pratt v British Medical Association* [1919] 1 KB 244 at 266, [1918–19] All ER Rep 104 at 115 per McCardie J and *De Jetley Marks v Lord Greenwood* [1936] 1 All ER 863 at 873 per Porter J. (3) The fact that A has broken his contract with X does not of itself justify X in revenge procuring a breach of an independent contract between A and B: *Smithies v National Association of Operative Plasterers* [1909] 1 KB 310 esp at 337, [1908–10] All ER Rep 455 esp at 467 per Buckley LJ.

On the other side of the line justification has been said to exist where (1) there is a moral duty to intervene, as for example in *Brimelow v Casson* [1924] 1 Ch 302, [1923] All ER Rep 40, where it was held that the defendants were justified in their actions since they owed a duty to their calling and its members to take all necessary steps to compel the plaintiff to pay his chorus girls a living wage so that they were not driven to supplement their earnings through prostitution, (2) where the contract interfered with is inconsistent with a previous contract with the interferer: see per Buckley LJ in *Smithies's* case [1909] 1 KB 310 at 337, [1908–10] All ER Rep 455 at 467. . . .

This leads one to a consideration of the important case of *Read v Friendly Society of Operative Stonemasons of England Ireland and Wales* [1902] 2 KB 88. Darling J said (at 96–97):

'I think their sufficient justification for interference with plaintiff's right must be an equal or superior right in themselves, and that no one can legally excuse himself to a man, of whose contract he has procured the breach, on the ground that he acted on a wrong understanding of his own rights, or without understanding of his own rights, or without malice, or bona fide, or in the best interests of himself, nor even that he acted as an altruist, seeking only the good of another and careless of his own advantage.'

Rose J adopted this test, namely whether the defendants had an equal or superior right in themselves. And much of the argument before us has been directed to the question whether he was right to hold that they did. . . .

The submission of counsel for the plaintiffs to us is to the effect that the words 'sufficient justification for interference with plaintiff's right must be an equal or superior right in themselves' must be confined to the exercise of that right by the defendant. But I can find no warrant for his proposition and in my judgment it confuses right with the remedies available to protect the right. The defendants had the rights of a secured creditor, that is to say the right to be repaid their loan together with interest; in support of that right they had the remedies or rights granted by the legal charge and the law, namely to sell the land or appoint a receiver. They were not bound to exercise these remedies in defence of their rights, but they could do so. Had they done so, it is common ground, at least in so far as the power of sale and I think probably also on the appointment of a receiver, that the plaintiffs' contract would have come to an end. If instead of exercising these remedies in their full rigour, they reach an accommodation with the mortgagor in defence and protection of their rights as secured creditor, which has the same result of putting an end to the plaintiffs' contract, it would in my judgment be anomalous and illogical if they were justified in the one case but not in the other. Nor can it make any difference that the accommodation reached is one that is more beneficial to the defendants and Mr Pulver than the straightforward exercise of the right of sale or appointment of a receiver.

Why, it may be asked, should the defendants be justified in interfering with the plaintiffs' contract if they exercise their power of sale as mortgagee in possession, but not if by agreement they permit the mortgagor to conduct the sale in the hope of achieving a better deal for both? Why should they be justified if they appoint a receiver, who has power to build-out the development and appoint architects, but not if they agree to finance the mortgagor to perform this task? I cannot find any logical answer to these questions.

Moreover, I think it would be undesirable if the law were to insist that a mortgagee in such a position should exercise his strict legal rights if he is to be justified in interference with contracts between the mortgagor and third parties, and could not be justified if he reached some sensible and reasonable accommodation which may be to the benefit of both himself and the mortgagor, but which has the same effect on the third parties' contract. The accommodation is designed to protect or defend the mortgagee's equal or superior right as a secured creditor, who had in this case financed the entire purchase and development of the site so far. And the accommodation was reached against the background of the remedy of sale or the appointment of a receiver. There can be no doubt that these rights existed once a formal demand for payment was made, a demand which could not have been met. . . .

Justification for interference with the plaintiff's contractual right based on an equal or superior right in the defendant must clearly be a legal right. Such right may derive from property real or personal or from contractual rights. Property rights may simply involve the use and enjoyment of land or personal property. To give an example put in argument by Sir Nicolas Browne-Wilkinson V-C, if X carries on building operations on his land, they may to the knowledge of X interfere with a contract between A and B to carry out recording work on adjoining land occupied by A. But, unless X's activity amounts to a nuisance, he is justified in doing what he did. Alternatively, the law may grant legal remedies to the owner of property to act in defence or protection of his property; if in the exercise of these remedies he interferes with a contract between A and B of which he knows, he will be justified. If instead of exercising those remedies he reaches an accommodation with A, which has a similar effect of interfering with A's contract with B, he is still justified notwithstanding that the accommodation may be to the commercial advantage of himself or A or both. The position is the same if the defendant's right is to a contractual as opposed to a property right, provided it is equal or superior to the plaintiff's right.

In my judgment that is the position in this case; I therefore agree with the judge's conclusion and would dismiss the appeal. . . .

[NOURSE LJ delivered a judgment, in which he agreed with STUART-SMITH LJ, in favour of dismissing the appeal. SIR NICOLAS BROWNE-WILKINSON V-C agreed with both judgments.]

Appeal dismissed

Question

Would the defence of justification have succeeded had it been shown that the defendants could have secured further advances by other means? This and other issues are considered by R. O'Dair (1991) 11 Oxf JLS (forthcoming).

Notes

1. Justification must be proved as against the *plaintiff*, irrespective of the rights and wrongs between the defendant and the middleman. In *Greig v Insole* [1978] 3 All ER 449; [1978] 1 WLR 302 the international and English cricketing authorities had directly induced breaches of contract by imposing retrospective bans on playing first-class cricket against cricketers who had entered into contracts with Mr Kerry Packer's World Series Cricket Pty Ltd (WSC). Slade J held that whatever the actions of the players might have

been, the authorities had not given much thought to the possibility that they might be infringing WSC's rights, and despite their disinterested motives the defence of justification against WSC could not succeed. One may ask whether the result would have been different had the authorities gone no further than was necessary to protect their legitimate interests of ensuring that first-class cricket is properly organised and administered ([1978] 3 All ER at p. 497). It seems that they could have done this by limiting the ban to those who contracted with WSC *after* the ban was announced (cf. ibid. p. 501). One may note that in an American case (*Knapp v Penfield* 5 NYS 41 (1932)) the promoter of a play (an 'angel') who induced the dismissal of an actress to protect his investment in the play, succeeded in the defence of justification; and in *Posluns v Toronto Stock Exchange and Gardiner* (1964) 46 DLR (2d) 210, on appeal (1966) 53 DLR (2d) 193, inducing breach of the employment contract of a broker's man to promote financial probity on the stock exchange was held to be justifiable.

2. Why were the combinations of shipping companies in *Mogul SS Co Ltd v McGregor, Gow & Co* [1892] AC 25 and of employers and trade union in the *Crofter* case (p. 680, ante) allowed to justify their actions, but not the South Wales Miners' Federation? For general discussion of the defence of justification see J. D. Heydon (1970) XX Univ Tor LJ 139 at 161–171; and *Heydon*, pp. 38–47. An earlier but still useful discussion of principle is to be found in C. E. Carpenter (1928) 41 Harv LR 728 at 745 et seq; see too J. Nockleby (1980) 93 Harv LR 540.

3. The absence of any common law defence of justification in respect of trade union activities resulted in the enactment of a statutory immunity for inducing breach of contract. The Trade Union and Labour Relations Acts 1974 and 1976, s. 13, extended this to the breach or interference with the performance of any contract provided the act is done 'in contemplation or furtherance of a trade dispute' but this has now been modified by subsequent legislation. In New Zealand, in *Pete's Towing Services Ltd v Northern Industrial Union of Workers* [1970] NZLR 32, the common law defence of justification was allowed, where a trade union defendant was found to be putting forward 'fair conditions' and the inducement was 'not being used as a sword to procure financial betterment but as a shield to avoid involvement in industrial discord' (per Speight J at p. 51). C. Grunfeld (1971) 34 MLR 181 at 185 submits, in the light of this decision, that while the defence of justification is barred in economic disputes (*South Wales Miners' Federation* case, p. 697, ante) it is not in labour disputes of 'principle' (e.g. about recognition of a union, bona fide compliance with an agreed disputes procedure, or tolerating a breakaway union). See further *Morgan v Fry* [1968] 2 QB 710; [1968] 3 All ER 452 (defence of justification for tort of intimidation, p. 723, post) and B. G. Hansen (1975) 38 MLR 217.

4. The cases so far considered involved 'direct interference' with contractual rights. In *Greig v Insole* [1978] 3 All ER 449; [1978] 1 WLR 302, Slade J (at p. 486) offered the following useful definitions:

'The phrase "direct interference" covers the case where the intervener, either by himself or his agents, speaks, writes or publishes words or does other acts which communicate pressure or persuasion to the mind or person of one of the contracting parties themselves, while "indirect interference" refers to the case where, without actually doing any of these things, the intervener nevertheless procures or attempts to procure a situation which will result or may result in a breach of the contract.'

So resolutions of the cricketing authorities which contained a threat of a ban directed at players who had contracted with a private promoter, coupled with a suggestion that they could escape from its operation by terminating their contracts with that promoter were a 'direct interference'. In *JT Stratford & Son Ltd v Lindley* [1965] AC 269; [1964] 3 All ER 102, a letter to an employers' association 'informing' them of an embargo placed on the movement of goods by a trade union was said to be a direct inducement of the association's members not to deal with the person aimed at by the embargo. Lord Pearce (at p. 333) remarked that 'the fact that an inducement to break a contract is couched as an irresistible embargo rather than in terms of seduction does not make it any the less an inducement'. See further the examples given by Lord Denning MR and Winn LJ in *Torquay Hotel Co Ltd v Cousins* [1969] 2 Ch 106; [1969] 1 All ER 522 (p. 708, post). In *CBS Songs Ltd v Amstrad Consumer Electronics plc* [1988] AC 1013; [1988] 2 All ER 484, the House of Lords in another context rejected the argument that the advertising and sale of twin-track tape recording machines constituted an incitement to procure the infringement of copyright since these acts facilitated rather than 'procured' breaches of copyright. Lord Templeman stated (at pp. 496–497):

'Generally speaking, inducement, incitement or persuasion to infringe must be by a defendant to an individual infringer and must identifiably procure a particular infringement in order to make the defendant liable as a joint infringer.'

Compare the more stringent approach taken in labour law cases, e.g. in *Union Traffic Ltd v Transport and General Workers' Union* [1989] ICR 98, the Court of Appeal indicated that the mere presence of pickets may be sufficient to constitute an 'inducement' if it is clear that their presence is intended to induce, and is successful in the object of bringing about breach of contract. S. Auerbach (1989) 18 ILJ 166 at 168 points out that 'the implication is that the fact of effective action may be taken as sufficient to satisfy the test, leaving no need for more particular evidence'.

5. The gist of the action is the 'violation of a legal right' (per Lord Macnaghten, p. 696, ante). A wider tort has been developed which includes inducing a breach of statutory duty (*Meade v London Borough of Haringey* [1979] 2 All ER 1016; [1979] 1 WLR 637; *Associated British Ports v Transport and General Workers' Union* [1989] ICR 557; [1989] 3 All ER 796, p. 728, post; revsd on a different point [1989] ICR 557; [1989] 3 All ER 822) and inducing breach of an equitable obligation (*Prudential Assurance Co Ltd v Lorenz* (1971) 11 KIR 78). However, it seems that it is not a tort to procure a breach of trust (*Metall und Rohstoff AG v Donaldson Lufkin & Jenrette Inc* [1989] 3 All ER 14 at 58–59).

6. The next three cases are concerned with the principles applicable to cases of *indirect* 'interference' or 'procurement'. They raise the problem of how the law should regulate so-called 'secondary' industrial action. The typical situation is that in pursuance of a dispute with a 'primary' employer, trade union

officials persuade the employees of another, 'secondary', employer, who is a supplier or customer of the primary employer, to 'black' supplies to or from the primary employer so as to increase pressure on him. This may involve the employees of the secondary employer in breaches of their contracts of employment with him, and a consequence of the action may be either the breach or interference with the performance of the commercial contract between the primary and secondary employers. Legal policy towards this traditional method of collective action results from the changing interaction between tort liabilities and statutory immunities. In *Temperton v Russell* [1893] 1 QB 715, the Court of Appeal extended *Lumley v Gye* (1853) 2 E & B 216 (p. 693, ante) so as to hold union officials liable for *direct* inducement of breach of *commercial* contracts. Section 3 of the Trade Disputes Act 1906 afforded immunity to those who, 'in contemplation or furtherance of a trade dispute' induced 'some other person to breach a contract of employment' but made no reference to breach of commercial contracts. The cases of *DC Thomson & Co Ltd v Deakin* [1952] Ch 646; [1952] 2 All ER 361 (post) and *Torquay Hotel Co Ltd v Cousins* [1969] 2 Ch 106; [1969] 1 All ER 522 (p. 708, post) were decided while the immunity was so limited. Subsequently, s. 13(1)(a) of the Trade Union and Labour Relations Acts 1974 and 1976 gave protection in trade disputes to the breach or interference with the performance of *any* contract. But s. 17 of the Employment Act 1980 (now repealed) removed the protection of s. 13(1) of the 1974 Act from certain forms of secondary action resulting in the procurement of breaches of commercial contracts. It was in this new statutory context that *Merkur Island Shipping Corpn v Laughton* [1983] 2 AC 570; [1983] 2 All ER 189 (p. 713, post), was decided. The Employment Act 1990, s. 4 has removed the protection of s. 13(1) from all forms of secondary action, with a narrow exception in relation to picketing.

DC Thomson & Co Ltd *v* Deakin Court of Appeal [1952] 2 All ER 361

The plaintiffs, a firm of printers and publishers, maintained a non-union shop. They dismissed a man belonging to a union, whereupon a number of unions organised a boycott. Drivers and loaders employed by Bowaters, who supplied paper to the plaintiffs, expressed reluctance to load or deliver paper to the plaintiffs. Bowaters, not wishing to become involved in the dispute, refrained from ordering any of their employees to do so. The result was that no further supplies were taken to the plaintiffs' premises. Bowaters wrote to the plaintiffs informing them that they had been prevented from performing their contract to supply paper by union action. The plaintiffs issued a writ and sought an interlocutory injunction to restrain the defendant union officials from procuring any breach of Bowaters' contract with the plaintiffs. Upjohn J refused to grant an injunction on the ground that there never was any direct action by the defendants with the object of persuading Bowaters to break an existing contract with the plaintiffs. An appeal to the Court of Appeal was dismissed on other grounds. (See the diagram p. 705, post.)

JENKINS LJ: . . . The breach of contract complained of must be brought about by some act of a third party (whether alone or in concert with the contract breaker), which is in itself unlawful, but that act need not necessarily take the form of persuasion or procurement or inducement of the contract breaker, in the sense above indicated.

Direct persuasion or procurement or inducement applied by the third party to the contract breaker, with knowledge of the contract and the intention of bringing about its breach, is clearly to be regarded as a wrongful act in itself, and where this is shown a case of actionable interference in its primary form is made out: *Lumley v Gye* (1853) 2 E & B 216; 22 LJQB 463. But the contract breaker may himself be a willing party to the breach, without any persuasion by the third party, and there seems to be no doubt that if a third party, with knowledge of a contract between the contract breaker and another, has dealings with the contract breaker which the third party knows to be inconsistent with the contract, he has committed an actionable interference: see, for example, *British Industrial Plastics Ltd v Ferguson* [1940] 1 All ER 479, where the necessary

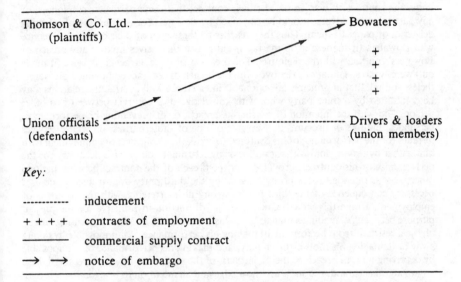

Thomson & Co. Ltd. ———————————————————→ Bowaters
    (plaintiffs)

Union officials - Drivers & loaders
    (defendants)   (union members)

Key:

- - - - - - - - - - -   inducement

+ + + +   contracts of employment

———————   commercial supply contract

→   →   notice of embargo

knowledge was held not to have been brought home to the third party; and *British Motor Trade Association v Salvadori* [1949] Ch 556; [1949] 1 All ER 208. The inconsistent dealing between the third party and the contract breaker may, indeed, be commenced without knowledge by the third party of the contract thus broken, but, if it is continued after the third party has notice of the contract, an actionable interference has been committed by him: see, for example, *De Francesco v Barnum* (1890) 45 Ch D 430; 60 LJ Ch 63. Again, so far from persuading or inducing or procuring one of the parties to the contract to break it, the third party may commit an actionable interference with the contract, against the will of both and without the knowledge of either, if, with knowledge of the contract, he does an act which, if done by one of the parties to it, would have been a breach. Of this type of interference the case of *GWK Ltd v Dunlop Rubber Co Ltd* (1926) 42 TLR 376 affords a striking example. Further, I apprehend that an actionable interference would, undoubtedly, be committed if a third party, with knowledge of a contract and intent to bring about its breach, placed physical restraint on one of the parties to the contract, so as to prevent him from carrying it out.

It is to be observed that in all these cases there is something amounting to a direct invasion by the third party of the rights of one of the parties to the contract, by prevailing on the other party to do, or doing in concert with him, or doing without reference to either party, that which is inconsistent with the contract, or by preventing, by means of actual physical restraint one of the parties from being where he should be or doing what he should do under the contract. But here the acts complained of as constituting the actionable interference do not amount to a direct invasion of the plaintiffs' contractual rights. The plaintiffs' case as regards paper is that the defendants persuaded, induced or procured employees of Bowaters (that is, drivers employed by Bowaters Sales Co Ltd, and loaders employed by Bowaters Mersey Mills Ltd) to break their contracts of employment by refusing to drive lorries loaded with, or to load lorries with, paper destined for the plaintiffs, with the object and intention of causing Bowaters Sales Co Ltd, to break, or making it impossible for them to fulfil, their contract for the supply of paper to the plaintiffs, and that the defendants did in fact by the means I have stated produce the intended result. . . .

The plaintiffs' case does seem to me to involve an extension of the range of actionable interference with contractual rights beyond any actual instance of this type of wrong to be found in the decided cases. Here there is no direct invasion of the plaintiffs' rights under the contract. It was no part of their contract that these particular employees, or any particular employees, should be employed by Bowaters for the purpose of effecting deliveries of paper to them. Thus the breaches by these men of their contract of service with Bowaters (if made out on the facts) did not in themselves involve any breach of Bowaters' contract with the plaintiffs. The breaches of the contracts of service (if made out) were, so to speak, at one remove from the breach of contract complained of. Nevertheless, I think that in principle an actionable interference with contractual relations may be committed by a third party who, with knowledge of a contract between two other persons and with the intention of causing its breach, or of preventing its performance, persuades, induces or procures the servants of one of those parties, on whose services he relies for the performance of his contract, to break their contracts of employment with him, either by leaving him without notice or by refusing to do what is necessary for the performance of his contract, provided that the breach of the contract between the two other persons intended to be brought about by the third party does in fact ensue as a necessary consequence of the third party's wrongful interference with the contracts of employment. I take this view because I see no distinction in principle for the present purpose between persuading a man to break his contract with another, preventing him by physical restraint from performing it, making his performance of it impossible by taking away or damaging his tools or machinery, and making his performance of it impossible by depriving him, in breach of their contracts, of the services of his employees. All these are wrongful acts, and, if done with knowledge and an intention to bring about a breach of a contract to which the person directly wronged is a party, and if in fact producing that result, I fail to see why they should not all alike fall within the sphere of actionable interference with contractual relations delimited by Lord Macnaghten and Lord Lindley in *Quinn v Leathem* [1901] AC 495; 70 LJPC 76. But, while admitting this form of actionable interference in principle, I would hold it strictly confined to cases where it is clearly shown, first, that the person charged with actionable interference knew of the existence of the contract and intended to procure its breach; secondly, that the person so charged did definitely and unequivocally persuade, induce or procure the employees concerned to break their contracts of employment with the intent I have mentioned; thirdly, that the employees so persuaded, induced or procured did in fact break their contracts of employment; and, fourthly, that breach of the contract forming the alleged subject of interference ensued as a necessary consequence of the breaches by the employees concerned of their contracts of employment. I should add that by the expression 'necessary consequence' used here and elsewhere in this judgment I mean that it must be shown that, by reason of the withdrawal of the services of the employees concerned, the contract breaker was unable, as a matter of practical possibility, to perform his contract. In other words, I think the continuance of the services of the particular employees concerned must be so vital to the performance of the contract alleged to have been interfered with as to make the effect of their withdrawal comparable, for practical purposes, with a direct invasion of the contractual rights of the party aggrieved under the contract alleged to have been interfered with, as, for example (in the case of a contract for personal services), the physical restraint of the person by whom such services are to be performed.

I make the above reservations in regard to the scope of this newly propounded form of actionable interference with contractual rights for these reasons. It is now well settled that, apart from conspiracy to injure, no actionable wrong is committed by a person who, by acts not in themselves unlawful prevents another person from obtaining goods or services necessary for the purposes of his business, or who induces others so to prevent that person by any lawful means. It follows, in my view, that (again apart from conspiracy to injure) there is nothing unlawful, under the law as enunciated in *Allen v Flood* [1898] AC 1 and subsequent cases, in general appeals to others to prevent a given person from obtaining goods or services, for that is a purpose capable of being lawfully carried out, and there can, therefore, be nothing unlawful in advocating it, unless unlawful means are advocated. The result of such advocacy may well be that unlawful means are adopted by some to achieve the purpose advocated, but that is not to say that a person who advocates the object without advocating the means is to be taken to have advocated recourse to unlawful means. If by reference to the form of actionable interference with contractual rights now propounded, general exhortations issued in the course of a trade dispute, such as 'Stop supplies to X', 'Refuse to handle X's goods', 'Treat X as "black"', and the like were regarded as amounting to actionable interference, because persons reached by such exhortations might respond to them by breaking their contracts of employment and thereby causing breaches of contracts between their employers and other persons, and because the person issuing such exhortations must be taken constructively to have known that the employers concerned must have contracts of some kind or other with other persons, and that his exhortations (general as they were) might lead to breaches of those contracts through breaches of contracts of employment committed by persons moved by his exhortations, then the proposition must be accepted that it is an actionable wrong to advocate objects which can be achieved by lawful means because they can also be achieved by unlawful means, and to that proposition I decline to subscribe. Furthermore, as the learned judge in effect pointed out in his judgment, almost every strike, if to any extent successful, must cause breaches of contracts between the employer against whom it is directed and the persons with whom he is doing business, the very object of the strike being to bring his business to a standstill or himself to terms. Again, many a strike embarked on in support of a strike in progress in some other concern must have had for its immediate object the cutting off of supplies to, or prevention of distribution of the products of, or the application of similar pressure on, that other concern. Yet we have been referred to no case in which the persons inciting a strike have been held liable for actionable interference with contractual relations between the strikers' employers and the persons with whom they deal, and in principle I do not think that the inciters of the strike could be held so liable in the absence of proof that they knew of the existence of a particular contract, and, with a view to bringing about its breach, counselled action by employees in itself necessarily unlawful (as for example breach of their contracts of employment) designed to achieve that end. To hold otherwise would, in my view, be to admit not only an addition to the means whereby actionable interference with contractual rights may be compassed (which addition, as I have said, I am in principle prepared to accept), but also an enlargement of the character and scope of the tort itself (which I cannot agree to).

Finally, not every breach of a contract of employment with a trading or manufacturing concern by an employee engaged in services required for the performance of a contract between his employer and some other person carries with it as a necessary consequence (in the sense above indicated) the breach of the last-mentioned contract. For instance, A induces B, C's lorry driver, to refuse, in breach of his contract of employment, to carry goods which C is under contract to deliver to D, and does so with a view to causing the breach of C's contract with D. C could, if he chose, engage some other lorry driver, or arrange alternative means of transport, but he does not do so. He fails to deliver the goods, telling D he is prevented from doing so by B's breach of contract. In such circumstances, there has been no direct invasion by A of C's rights under his contract with D, and, although A has committed an actionable wrong against C, designed to bring about the breach of C's contract with D, and a breach has occurred, it cannot be said that the breach has been caused by A's wrongful act, and, therefore, D cannot, in my view, establish as against A an actionable interference with his rights under his contract with C. . . .

SIR RAYMOND EVERSHED MR: . . . [T]here is not on this motion proved any procuring of any wrongful act by any member of any of the unions concerned. I need only add that on the evidence there was no breach of contract by any workmen, since Bowaters, for reasons which, I doubt not, were prudent, took the line that they would not order any man either to load or to deliver paper for the plaintiffs. They accepted the situation as they found it, and, again I doubt not prudently, made no attempt to contrive to get the paper to the plaintiffs by any other means. It is true, if my analysis is correct, that there was in the case of the first three defendants what might be called a direct approach to Bowaters, but, so far as I understand the evidence, I cannot see that that direct approach amounted to anything more than a statement of the facts as the members of the union understood them to be. In particular, there was a reference to picketing, which was obviously of great significance, and, whether that reference was correct or incorrect, there is no suggestion that it was not made in the bona fide belief of its truth. I appreciate that in these matters there is a difficult question of distinguishing between what might be called persuasion and what might be called advice, meaning by the latter a mere statement of, or drawing of the attention of the party addressed to the state of facts as they were. In *Camden Nominees Ltd v Forcey* [1940] Ch 352; [1940] 2 All ER 1 it was held that the advice given was of such a character that it was obviously intended to be acted on and so for all practical purposes was equivalent to persuasion. But, if the matter be advice merely (in the ordinary sense of that word), it seems to me that there can be no complaint about it, nor do I think that counsel for the plaintiffs can derive any substantial assistance by saying that Bowaters proved themselves merely chicken-hearted. The ease with which a person may be persuaded is not a relevant consideration in determining whether the persuader was wrongful in what he was doing. That may, as a general proposition, be true, but in this case it seems to me, as I have already more than once indicated, that the evidence on this motion, whatever may emerge when the matter is fully investigated, falls short of any proof of what is required to constitute a cause of action such as would entitle the plaintiffs to an injunction. Put another way, I cannot see that the evidence establishes that there was anything done by Bowaters vis-à-vis the plaintiffs which is fairly attributable to any such pressure, persuasion or procuration on the part of any of these defendants as would in any event cause them to be liable in tort. . . .

[MORRIS LJ delivered a judgment in favour of dismissing the appeal.]

Torquay Hotel Co Ltd *v* Cousins Court of Appeal [1969] 1 All ER 522

The Torbay Hotel, together with fellow members of the local Hotels Association at Torquay, had refused recognition to the Transport & General Workers' Union, whose local officials P and L called a strike and posted pickets outside the Hotel. Newspapers reported statements by C, managing director of the Imperial Hotel (owned by the plaintiff company), that the Hotels Association would 'stamp out' the TGWU. Angered by these unconfirmed reports, some of these pickets moved across and picketed the Imperial. P telephoned Esso, who supplied fuel oil to the Imperial, and warned them that fuel supplies would be stopped. Esso drivers were members of the TGWU and it was 'common knowledge' that they would not cross the picket lines. The Imperial ordered fuel from Alternative Fuels Ltd and a delivery was made while the pickets were temporarily absent. A representative of the defendant union telephoned Alternative Fuels Ltd and warned that there would be 'serious repercussions' if further supplies were made to the Imperial. The plaintiff company's solicitors asked the defendant union for an undertaking that the 'blacking' of the Imperial would be withdrawn; they also gave notice of the contract with Esso and summarized its terms. 3,000 gallons were successfully delivered to the Imperial by Esso, but the union did not give the undertaking. Stamp J granted an interlocutory injunction restraining the defendant union and certain of its officials from causing any supplier of fuel to break his contract to supply fuel oil and from picketing the Imperial to prevent the delivery of fuel oil. On appeal, the Court of Appeal held that an injunction could not be granted against the defendant union because of the provisions of s. 4 of the Trade Disputes Act 1906 (no actions in tort maintainable against trade unions) (but see now ss. 15–16 of the Employment Act 1982), but dismissed the appeals by the individual trade union officials who were also defendants.

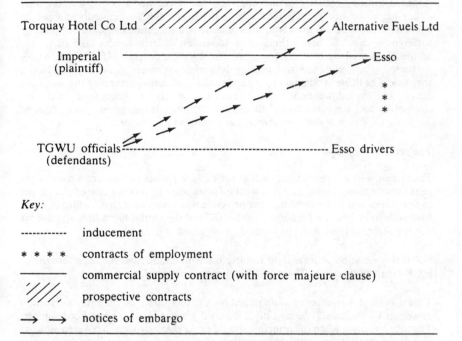

Key:

----------   inducement

* * * *   contracts of employment

————————   commercial supply contract (with force majeure clause)

///////,   prospective contracts

→ →   notices of embargo

LORD DENNING MR: . . . The Imperial Hotel had a contract with Esso under which the Imperial Hotel agreed to buy their total requirements of fuel oil from Esso for one year, the quantity being estimated at 120,000 gallons, to be delivered by road tank wagon at a minimum of 3,000 gallons a time. Under that contract there was a *course of dealing* by which the Imperial Hotel used to order 3,000 gallons every week or ten days, and Esso used to deliver it the next day. But there was a *force majeure* or *exception clause* which said that —

'Neither party shall be liable for any failure to fulfil any term of this Agreement if fulfilment is delayed, hindered or prevented by any circumstance whatever which is not within their immediate control, including . . . labour disputes . . .'

It is plain that, if delivery was hindered or prevented by labour disputes, as for instance, because their drivers would not cross the picket line, Esso could rely on that exception clause as a defence to any claim by the Imperial Hotel. They would not be liable in damages. And I am prepared to assume that Esso would not be guilty of a breach of contract. But I do not think that would exempt the defendant union officials from liability, if they unlawfully hindered or prevented Esso from making deliveries. The principle of *Lumley v Gye* extends not only to inducing breach of contract, but also to preventing the performance of it. That can be shown by a simple illustration taken from the books. In *Lumley v Gye*,[1] Miss Wagner, an actress, was engaged by Mr Lumley to sing at Her Majesty's Theatre. Mr Gye, who ran Covent Garden, procured her to break her contract with Mr Lumley by promising to pay her more, see *Lumley v Wagner*.[2] He was held liable to Mr Lumley for inducing a breach of contract. In *Poussard v Spiers and Pond*,[3] Mme Poussard was under contract with Messrs Spiers and Pond to sing in an opera at the Criterion Theatre. She fell sick and was unable to attend rehearsals. Her non-performance, being occasioned by sickness, was not a breach of contract on her part; but it was held to excuse the theatre company from continuing to employ her. Suppose now that an ill-disposed person, knowing of her contract, had given her a potion to make her sick. She would not be guilty of a breach herself. But undoubtedly the person who administered the potion would have done wrong and be liable for the damage suffered by them. So here I think the trade union officials cannot take advantage of the force majeure or exception clause in the Esso contract. If they unlawfully prevented or hindered Esso from making deliveries, as ordered by the Imperial Hotel, they would be liable in damages to the Imperial Hotel, notwithstanding the exception clause. There is another reason too. They could not rely on an excuse of which they themselves had been 'the mean' to use Lord Coke's language, see *New Zealand Shipping Co Ltd v Société des Ateliers et Chantiers de France*.[4]

The principles of law.

The principle of *Lumley v Gye*,[1] is that each of the parties to a contract has a 'right to the performance' of it; and it is wrong for another to procure one of the parties to break it or not to perform it. That principle was extended a step further by Lord Macnaghten in *Quinn v Leathem*,[5] so that each of the parties has a right to have his 'contractual relations' with the other duly observed. He said:[6]

'... it is a violation of legal right to interfere with contractual relations recognised by law if there be no sufficient justification for the interference.'

That statement was adopted and applied by a strong Board of the Privy Council in *Jasperson v Dominion Tobacco Co.*[7] It included Viscount Haldane and Lord Sumner. The time has come when the principle should be further extended to cover 'deliberate and direct interference with the execution of a contract without that causing any breach'. That was a point left open by Lord Reid in *JT Stratford & Son Ltd v Lindley*.[8] But the common law would be seriously deficient if it did not condemn

---

1. (1853) 2 E & B 216; [1843-60] All ER Rep 208.
2. (1852) 1 De GM & G 604; [1843-60] All ER Rep 368.
3. (1876) 1 QBD 410.
4. [1919] AC 1 at 7, 8.
5. [1901] AC 495; [1900-3] All ER Rep 1.
6. [1901] AC at p. 510; [1900-3] All ER Rep at p. 9.
7. [1923] AC 709.
8. [1965] AC 269 at 324; [1964] 3 All ER 102 at 107.

such interference. It is this very case. The principle can be subdivided into three elements: First, there must be *interference* in the execution of a contract. The interference is not confined to the procurement of a *breach* of contract. It extends to a case where a third person *prevents* or *hinders* one party from performing his contract, even though it be not a breach. Secondly, the interference must be deliberate. The person must know of the contract or, at any rate, turn a blind eye to it and intend to interfere with it, see *Emerald Construction Co Ltd v Lowthian*.[1] Thirdly, the interference must be *direct*. Indirect interference will not do. Thus, a man who 'corners the market' in a commodity may well know that it may prevent others from performing their contracts, but he is not liable to an action for so doing. A trade union official, who calls a strike on proper notice, may well know that it will prevent the employers from performing their contracts to deliver goods, but he is not liable in damages for calling it. *Indirect* interference is only unlawful if unlawful means are used. I went too far when I said in *Daily Mirror Newspapers Ltd v Gardner*,[2] that there was no difference between direct and indirect interference. On reading once again *DC Thomson & Co Ltd v Deakin*,[3] with more time, I find there is a difference. Morris LJ there drew the very distinction between[4] '*direct* persuasion to break a contract' which is unlawful in itself; and 'the intentional bringing about of a breach by *indirect* methods involving wrong doing'. This distinction must be maintained, else we should take away the right to strike altogether. Nearly every trade union official who calls a strike—even on due notice, as in *Morgan v Fry*[5]—knows that it may prevent the employers from performing their contracts. He may be taken even to intend it. Yet no one has supposed hitherto that it was unlawful; and we should not render it unlawful today. A trade union official is only in the wrong when he procures a contracting party *directly* to break his contract, or when he does it indirectly by *unlawful means*. On reconsideration of the *Daily Mirror* case,[6] I think that the defendants there interfered directly by getting the retailers as their agents to approach the wholesalers.

I must say a word about unlawful means, because that brings in another principle. I have always understood that if one person deliberately interferes with the trade or business of another, and does so by unlawful means, that is, by an act which he is not at liberty to commit, then he is acting unlawfully, even though he does not procure or induce any actual breach of contract. If the means are unlawful, that is enough. Thus in *Rookes v Barnard*[7] (as explained by Lord Reid in *JT Stratford & Son Ltd v Lindley*[8] and also by Lord Upjohn[9]) the respondents interfered with the employment of Rookes—and they did it by unlawful means, namely, by intimidation of his employers—and they were held to be acting unlawfully, even though the employers committed no breach of contract as they gave Rookes proper notice. And in *Stratford v Lindley*,[10] the respondents interfered with the business of Stratford—and they did it by *unlawful means*, namely, by inducing the men to *break their contracts* of employment by refusing to handle the barges—and they were held to be acting unlawfully, even in regard to *new business* which was not the subject of contract. Lord Reid said:[11]

---

1. [1966] 1 All ER 1013; [1966] 1 WLR 691.
2. [1968] 2 QB 762 at 781; [1968] 2 All ER 163 at 168.
3. [1952] Ch 646; [1952] 2 All ER 361.
4. [1952] Ch at p. 702; [1952] 2 All ER at p. 384.
5. [1968] 2 QB 710; [1968] 3 All ER 452.
6. [1968] 2 QB 762; [1968] 2 All ER 163.
7. [1964] AC 1129; [1964] 1 All ER 367.
8. [1965] AC 269 at 325; [1964] 3 All ER 102 at 107.
9. [1965] AC at p. 337; [1964] 3 All ER at p. 115.
10. [1965] AC 269; [1964] 3 All ER 102.
11. [1965] AC at p. 324; [1964] 3 All ER at p. 106.

'. . . the respondents' action made it practically impossible for the appellants to do *any new business* with the barge-hirers. It was not disputed that *such* interference . . . is tortious, if any unlawful means are employed.'

So also in the second point in *Daily Mirror Newspapers Ltd v Gardner,*[1] the defendants interfered with the business of the Daily Mirror — and they did it by a collective boycott which was held to be *unlawful* under the Restrictive Trade Practices Act 1956 — and they were held to be acting unlawfully.

This point about unlawful means is of particular importance when a place is declared 'black'. At common law it often involves the use of unlawful means. Take the Imperial Hotel. When it was declared 'black', it meant that the drivers of the tankers would not take oil to the hotel. The drivers would thus be induced to break their contracts of employment. That would be unlawful at common law.

[LORD DENNING MR then went on to deal with the relevant statutory immunity, which he decided was inapplicable in this case, and continued:]

Applying the principle in this case.

. . . [T]his case falls to be determined by the common law. It seems to me that the defendant union officials deliberately and directly interfered with the execution of the contract between the Imperial Hotel and Esso. They must have known that there was a contract between the Imperial Hotel and Esso. Why otherwise did they on that very first Saturday afternoon telephone the bulk plant at Plymouth? They may not have known with exactitude all the terms of the contract. But no more did the defendants in *Stratford v Lindley.*[2] They must also have intended to prevent the performance of the contract. That is plain from the telephone message: 'Any supplies of fuel oil will be stopped being made.' And the interference was direct. It was as direct as could be — a telephone message from the trade union official to the bulk plant.

Take next the supplies from Alternative Fuels. The first wagon got through. As it happened, there was no need for the Imperial Hotel to order any further supplies from Alternative Fuels. But suppose they had given a further order, it is quite plain that the defendant union officials would have done their best to prevent it being delivered. Their telephone messages show that they intended to prevent supplies being made by all means in their power. By threatening 'repercussions' they interfered unlawfully with the performance of any future order which Imperial Hotel might give to Alternative Fuels. And the interference was direct again. It was direct to Alternative Fuels. Such interference was sufficient to warrant the grant of an injunction *quia timet.* . . .

RUSSELL LJ: . . . The bulk supply contract between Esso Petroleum Co Ltd and the Imperial Hotel was such as might be expected for an establishment the size of the latter. It was argued that the exception clause had the effect that Esso could not be in breach of its supply contract if failure to deliver was due to labour disputes. In my view, the exception clause means what it says and no more; it *assumes* a failure to fulfil a term of the contract — i.e. a breach of contract — and excludes liability — i.e. in damages — for that breach in stated circumstances. It is an exception from liability for non-performance rather than an exception from obligation to perform. If, over a considerable period, Esso failed to deliver for one of the stated reasons, it seems to me that the hotel would be entitled to repudiate the contract on the ground of failure by Esso to carry out its terms; otherwise the hotel would be unable to enter into another bulk supply contract until the Esso contract was time expired. . . .

1. [1968] 2 QB 762; [1968] 2 All ER 163.
2. [1965] AC at p. 332; [1964] 3 All ER at p. 112.

WINN LJ: . . . The evidence does not establish that in consequence any quantity of fuel which had been ordered was not delivered; no breach of contract by Esso was induced. However, the argument of counsel for the defendants that cl. 10 of the written contract between Esso and the Imperial Hotel for a year's supply would have operated to prevent a failure or failures to deliver ordered instalments of fuel thereunder from being a breach does not seem to me to be sound. As I construe the clause it affords only an immunity against any claim for damages; it could not bar a right to treat the contract as repudiated by continuing breach; despite the clause Esso could well have been held to have committed a breach by non-delivery and Mr Pedley [P] came close to committing a tort of the *Lumley v Gye*[1] type.

It is not necessary in the instant case to consider to what extent the principle of that case may cover conduct which Lord Reid described in *JT Stratford & Son Ltd v Lindley*,[2] as 'deliberate and direct interference with the execution of a contract without that causing any breach'. For my part I think that it can at least be said, with confidence, that where a contract between two persons exists which gives one of them an optional extension of time or an optional mode for his performance of it, or of part of it, but, from the normal course of dealing between them, the other person does not anticipate such postponement, or has come to expect a particular mode of performance, a procuring of the exercise of such an option should, in principle, be held actionable if it produces material damage to the other contracting party.

It was one of counsel for the defendants' main submissions that mere advice, warning or information cannot amount to tortious procurement of breach of contract. Whilst granting arguendi causa that a communication which went no further would, in general, not, in the absence of circumstances giving a particular significance, amount to a threat or intimidation, I am unable to understand why it may not be an inducement. In the ordinary meaning of language it would surely be said that a father who told his daughter that her fiancé had been convicted of indecent exposure, had thereby induced her, with or without justification, by truth or by slander, to break her engagement. A man who writes to his mother-in-law telling her that the central heating in his house has broken down may thereby induce her to cancel an intended visit.

The court is not concerned in this case with any indirect procuring of breach, or non-performance of a contract, or with the adoption of indirect means to produce such a result; it is, therefore, not appropriate to consider whether such a mode of procuring such a result is only actionable, as counsel for the defendants submitted where unlawful means, involving, for example, breaches of contract, or actionable breaches of contract, are involved. . . .

Merkur Island Shipping Corpn *v* Laughton House of Lords [1983] 2 All ER 189

The plaintiff shipowners time-chartered the *Hoegh Apapa*, to Leif Hoegh & Co (the charterers) who subsequently sub-chartered the ship to Ned Lloyd (the sub-charterers). The sub-charterers had a contract with Rea Towing (the tugowners) to take the ship in and out of Liverpool dock at which the ship was to be loaded. The International Transport Workers' Federation (ITF) (of which the individual defendants were officials), having learnt that the shipowners were paying the crew less than the rate of wages approved by ITF, persuaded the tugmen employed by the tugowners to refuse, in breach of their contracts of employment with the tugowners, to move

---

1. (1853) 2 E & B 216; [1843–60] All ER Rep 208.
2. [1965] AC 269 at 324; [1964] 3 All ER 102 at 106.

the ship out of the dock so as to enable her to sail. Lock-keepers also refused to work the gates to allow the ship out. The shipowners were obliged under clause 8 of the charter to prosecute voyages 'with the utmost despatch'. Clauses 51 and 60 of the charter were in the following terms:

'Clause 51. Blockade/Boycott. In the event of loss of time due to boycott of the vessel in any port or place by shore labour or others, or arising from Government restrictions by reason of the vessel's flag, or arising from the terms and conditions on which the members of the crew are employed, or by reason of the trading of this vessel, payment of hire shall cease for time thereby lost.

Clause 60. Cancellation. Should the vessel be prevented from work for the reasons as outlined in Clauses 49/50/51 and 52 for more than ten days, Charterers shall have the option of cancelling this contract.'

Parker J granted an injunction requiring ITF to lift the blacking of the ship. The very same day an extraordinarily high tide enabled the ship to escape from the dock, without the use of tugs, and to proceed to sea. The shipowners' writ included claims for damages and, desirous of clarifying the law about blacking, the ITF appealed to the Court of Appeal, [1983] 1 All ER 334, which dismissed the appeal. On further appeal to the House of Lords:

```
        Merkur                                                    Leif Hoegh
(plaintiff shipowners)————————————————————————————————(charterers)
                                                                      |
                                                                 Ned Lloyd
                                                              (sub-charterers)
                                                                   / / /
                                                                 Rea Towing
                                                                 (tugowners)
                                                                      +
                                                                      +
        ITF officials ----------------------------------------------------- Tugmen
        (defendants)
```

Key:

------------	inducement
+ + + +	contracts of employment
———————	commercial contract (with off-hire clause)
/ / /	towing contract

LORD DIPLOCK: . . . The common law tort relied on by the shipowners under head (1) of the writ is the tort of interfering by unlawful means with the performance of a contract. The contract of which the performance was interfered with was the charter; the form the interference took was by immobilising the ship in Liverpool to prevent the captain from performing the contractual obligation of the shipowners under cl. 8 of the charter to 'prosecute his voyages with the utmost despatch'. The unlawful means by which the interference was effected was by procuring the tugmen and the lockmen to break their contracts of employment by refusing to carry out the operations on the part of the tugowners and the port authorities that were necessary to enable the ship to leave the dock.

The reason why the shipowners relied on interference with the performance of the charter rather than procuring a breach of it was the presence in the charter of cll. 51 and 60 [the terms of which are set out, ante]. . . .

DC Thomson & Co Ltd v Deakin [1952] Ch 646; [1952] 2 All ER 361 was a case in which the only interference with contractual rights relied on was procuring a *breach* by a third party of a contract between that third party and the plaintiff. That is why . . . Jenkins LJ restricts himself to that form of actionable interference with contractual rights which consists of procuring an actual breach of the contract that formed the subject matter of interference; but it is evident from . . . passages in his judgment . . . that Jenkins LJ, though using the expression 'breach', was not intending to confine the tort of actionable interference with contractual rights to the procuring of such non-performance of primary obligations under a contract as would necessarily give rise to secondary obligations to make monetary compensation by way of damages. All prevention of due performance of a primary obligation under a contract was intended to be included even though no secondary obligation to make monetary compensation thereupon came into existence, because the secondary obligation was excluded by some force majeure clause.

If there were any doubt about this matter, it was resolved in 1969 by the judgments of the Court of Appeal in *Torquay Hotel Co Ltd v Cousins* [1969] 2 Ch 106; [1969] 1 All ER 522. . . .

So I turn to the four elements of the tort of actionable interference with contractual rights as Jenkins LJ stated them, but substituting 'interference with performance' for 'breach', except in relation to the breaking by employees of their own contracts of employment where such breach has as its necessary consequence the interference with the performance of the contract concerned.

The first requirement is actually twofold: (1) knowledge of the existence of the contract concerned and (2) intention to interfere with its performance.

As respect knowledge, the ITF had been given an actual copy of the charter on 19 July 1980, three days after the blacking started but two days before the application to Parker J was made. Quite apart from this, however, there can hardly be anyone better informed than the ITF as to the terms of the sort of contracts under which ships are employed, particularly those flying flags of convenience. I agree with what was said by Sir John Donaldson MR on the question of the ITF's knowledge ([1983] 2 WLR 45 at 63; [1983] 1 All ER 334):

'Whatever the precise degree of knowledge of the defendants at any particular time, faced with a laden ship which, as they well knew, was about to leave port, the defendants must in my judgment be deemed to have known of the almost certain existence of contracts of carriage to which the shipowners were parties. The wholly exceptional case would be that of a ship carrying the owner's own goods. Whether that contract or those contracts consisted of a time charter, a voyage charter or one or more bill of lading contracts or some or all of such contracts would have been immaterial to the defendants. Prima facie their intention was to immobilise the ship and in so doing to interfere with the performance by the owners of their contract or contracts of carriage; immobilising a laden ship which had no contractual obligation to move would have been a pointless exercise, since it would have brought no pressure to bear on the owners.'

The last sentence of this citation deals also with intention. It was the shipowners on whom the ITF wanted to bring pressure to bear, because it was they who were employing seamen at rates of pay lower than those it was the policy of the ITF to enforce. The only way in which income could be derived by the shipowners from the ownership of their ship was by entering into contracts with third parties for the carriage of goods under which a primary obligation of the shipowners would be to prosecute the contract voyages with the utmost dispatch, and their earnings from their ship would be diminished by its immobilisation in port. Diminishing their earnings under the contract of carriage was the only way in which pressure could be brought to bear on the shipowners.

The fulfilment of the second and third requirements, that the ITF successfully procured the tugmen and lock keepers to break their contracts of employment and that the ITF's intention in doing so was to interfere with the performance by the shipowners of their primary obligations to the charterers under the charter, is beyond dispute. So is the fulfilment of the fourth requirement, that the prevention of the performance by the shipowners of their primary obligation under the charter to secure through the captain that the ship, as soon as she had completed loading should proceed from the port of Liverpool on her voyage with the utmost dispatch, was a necessary consequence of the breaches by the tugmen and the lock keepers of their contracts of employment.

On [this] point I accordingly agree with the Court of Appeal that the shipowners, on the evidence that was before Parker J, have made out a strong prima facie case that the ITF committed the common law tort of actionable interference with contractual rights.

Clauses 51 and 60 of the charterparty do not assist the ITF any more than did the force majeure clause in the *Torquay Hotels* case; but cl. 51 does show that the ITF's action did in fact succeed in causing damage to the shipowners. . . .

[His Lordship then considered whether the cause of action which was removed as against the defendants by s. 13(1)(*a*) of the Trade Union and Labour Relations Act 1974, as amended was restored by the restrictions on secondary action imposed by s. 17 of the Employment Act 1980 (now repealed), and decided this point in favour of the plaintiff shipowners.]

[LORD EDMUND-DAVIES, LORD KEITH OF KINKEL, LORD BRANDON OF OAKBROOK and LORD BRIGHTMAN agreed with the speech of LORD DIPLOCK.]

Appeal dismissed

Notes

1. Can the words of Sir John Donaldson MR, as approved by Lord Diplock on the question of ITF's knowledge and intention be reconciled with the propositions of Jenkins LJ in *DC Thomson & Co Ltd v Deakin* (p. 704, ante) that (a) it is not enough that the defendant must have known that the middleman had a contract of some kind or other with others and that his exhortations might result in breaches of them; and (b) it is not an actionable wrong to advocate objects which can be achieved by lawful means merely because they can also be achieved by unlawful means? Consider, as well, *Emerald Construction Co Ltd v Lowthian* [1966] 1 All ER 1013; [1966] 1 WLR 691 in which the defendant trade union officers sought to end a sub-contract between main building contractors and the plaintiff for the supply of labour only on a building site. They put pressure on the main contractors by industrial action. They did not know, until after the action started, of the terms of the contract, one of which gave the main contractors the option to cancel. The plaintiff's claim for an interlocutory injunction was successful. Lord Denning MR said (at p. 1017):

'Even if they did not know of the actual terms of the contract, but had the means of knowledge—which they deliberately disregarded—that would be enough. Like the man who turns a blind eye. So here, if the officers deliberately sought to get this contract terminated, heedless of its terms, regardless whether it was terminated by breach or not, they would do wrong. For it is unlawful for a third person to procure a breach of contract knowingly, or recklessly, indifferent whether it is a breach or not.'

2. Does the judgment of Jenkins LJ in *DC Thomson & Co Ltd v Deakin* (p. 704, ante) envisage liability for 'prevention of due performance of a primary obligation' short of breach of contract, without the use of unlawfulness as suggested by Lord Diplock in the *Merkur Island* case? Lord Denning's statement in *Torquay Hotel Co Ltd v Cousins* (p. 710, ante) that 'the principle of *Lumley v Gye* extends not only to inducing breach of contract, but also to preventing the performance of it' (and the similar statement, approved by Lord Diplock) has been described by P. Davies and M. Freedland as 'a major extension of the scope of the tort of inducing breach to give protection to contractual expectations as well as to contractual rights. . . . It is significant that neither of the two other judges in the *Torquay* case concurred in this view, but rather adopted the traditional English analysis of exemption clauses that they protect against liability but not against breach' (*Lord Denning: the Judge and the Law*, edited by J. L. Jowell and J. P. W. B. McAuslan (London, 1984), p. 380). The proposed extension has not been expressly supported by later authority.

In *Allen v Flood* [1898] AC 1 (p. 674, ante) a tort of malicious injury without the use of unlawful means was rejected by the House of Lords. How is this to be reconciled with the new tort, now recognised by the House of Lords (without consideration of *Allen v Flood* or *Mogul SS Co v McGregor, Gow & Co* [1892] AC 25), of deliberate (*a fortiori* malicious) interference with contractual *expectations*? Would a trader who deliberately tempts customers away from his rivals in order to drive them out of business, by offering cut prices, now commit an actionable wrong? (See the trenchant comments by W[edderburn] (1983) 46 MLR 632, and in *Clerk & Lindsell*, para. 15–05 on the threat which the new tort may pose to commercial competition.) The expansive nature of 'interference' was illustrated in *Dimbleby & Sons Ltd v National Union of Journalists* [1984] 1 All ER 117; [1984] 1 WLR 67. Journalists employed by the plaintiffs, publishers of local newspapers, who were members of the defendant union refused to supply copy to the plaintiffs for printing by TBF (Printers) Ltd in response to a call by their union. One of the torts alleged against the union was unlawful interference with the performance by the plaintiffs of their contract with TBF (Printers). The Court of Appeal rejected the argument that, because the newspapers continued to be published, there was no interference. Sir John Donaldson MR affirmed (at p. 126) that '"Interference" means hindrance as well as prevention and the loss of the services of staff journalists was quite clearly a hindrance to the performance by the plaintiffs of their contractual obligations towards TBF (Printers) Ltd. . . .'

3. In *Rickless v United Artists Corpn* [1988] QB 40; [1987] 1 All ER 679, the Court of Appeal rejected the argument that interference with contract could not be committed by interfering with a purely negative contractual obligation, the contract being otherwise fully performed.

4. What is the difference between *direct* interference short of breach by *lawful* means (what Lord Denning MR was talking about, p. 710, ante) and *indirect* interference with contract by *unlawful* means (as in *Thomson v Deakin*, or the facts in the *Merkur Island* case)? Does Lord Diplock confuse the two categories? Note the comment by Lord Denning (p. 711, ante) that 'the distinction must be maintained else we should take away the right to strike altogether'. In the *Merkur Island* case [1983] 2 All ER at pp. 196–197,

when dealing with the statutory immunities, Lord Diplock appears to suggest that indirect interference with contract by unlawful means is a species of the 'genus' tort of interference with trade by unlawful means (p. 724, post). (See the comment by H. Carty (1983) 12 ILJ 166.) The nature of the 'unlawful' means required for the 'species' tort is dealt with in that context (p. 724, post), as is the question whether a 'predominant purpose' to injure the plaintiff is necessary (p. 731, post).

3 Intimidation

Rookes v Barnard House of Lords [1964] 1 All ER 367

The plaintiff was employed by BOAC as a skilled draughtsman at London airport. He left his union, the Association of Engineering and Shipbuilding Draughtsmen, because of disagreements about its policies. The union had an informal '100 per cent union membership' agreement with BOAC. Barnard and Fistal, two fellow draughtsmen who were local unpaid union officials, and Silverthorne (a district official of the union not employed by BOAC) conveyed to BOAC the substance of a resolution passed at a members' meeting that if the plaintiff was not removed from the design office within three days, all labour would be withdrawn. As a result, BOAC at first suspended and then dismissed the plaintiff with the (long) lawful period of notice. There was a clause in another (formal) collective agreement between BOAC and the union that there would be no strike or lockout. It was *conceded* by counsel for the defendants that this clause was incorporated into each individual contract of employment with BOAC. The threat by Barnard and Fistal and other employees to withdraw their labour was, in consequence, a threat to break their contracts. The plaintiff sued Barnard, Fistal and Silverthorne for conspiracy. (See the diagram, p. 719, post.)

At the trial before Sachs J and a jury, [1961] 2 All ER 825, the plaintiff was awarded £7,500 damages, after an instruction that the jury were entitled to award exemplary damages. The Court of Appeal, [1962] 2 All ER 579, reversed this decision, unanimously taking the view that the tort of intimidation was confined to threats of violence. The House of Lords allowed the plaintiff's appeal on the question of liability (by this stage Silverthorne had died) but held that this was not a suitable case for the award of exemplary damages and sent the case for re-trial on the question of damages (on this aspect of the case see chap. 8, p. 407, ante). The case was later settled for £4,000, plus costs estimated at £30,000: [1966] 1 QB 176; [1965] 3 All ER 549.

LORD REID: . . . The question in this case is whether it was unlawful for them to use a threat to break their contracts with their employer as a weapon to make him do something which he was legally entitled to do, but which they knew would cause loss to the appellant.

The first contention of the respondents is very far reaching. They say there is no such tort as intimidation. That would mean that, short of committing a crime, an individual could with impunity virtually compel a third person to do something damaging to the plaintiff, which he does not want to do but can lawfully do: the wrongdoer could use every kind of threat to commit violence, libel or any other tort, and the plaintiff would have no remedy. And a combination of individuals could do the same, at least if they acted solely to promote their own interests. It is true that there is no decision of this House which negatives that argument. But there are many speeches in this House and judgments of eminent judges where it is assumed that that is not the law and I have found none where there is any real support for this argument. Most of the relevant authorities have been collected by Pearson LJ[1] and I see no need to add to them. It has often been stated that if people combine to do acts which they know will cause loss to the plaintiff, he can sue if either the object of their conspiracy is unlawful or they use unlawful means to achieve it. In my judgment, to cause such loss by threat to commit a tort against a third person if he does not comply with their demands is to use unlawful means to achieve their object.

. . . I can see no difference in principle between a threat to break a contract and a threat to commit a tort. If a third party could not sue for damage caused to him by the former I can see no reason why he should be entitled to sue for damage caused to him by the latter. A person is no more entitled to sue in respect of loss which he suffers by reason of a tort committed against someone else, than he is entitled to sue in respect of loss which he suffers by reason of breach of a contract to which he is not a party. What he sues for in each case is loss caused to him by the use of an unlawful weapon against him – intimidation of another person by unlawful means. So long as the defendant only threatens to do what he has a legal right to do he is on safe ground. At least if there is no conspiracy he would not be liable to anyone for doing the act, whatever his motive might be, and it would be absurd to make him liable for threatening to do it but not for doing it. But I agree with Lord Herschell

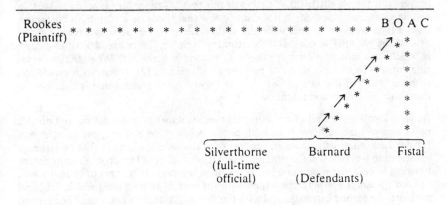

Rookes
(Plaintiff)

Silverthorne
(full-time
official)

Barnard

Fistal

(Defendants)

BOAC

Key:

* * * *   contracts of employment

→ →   threat

(*Allen v Flood*)[2] that there is a chasm between doing what you have a legal right to do and doing what you have no legal right to do, and there seems to me to be the same chasm between threatening to do what you have a legal right to do and threatening to do what you have no legal right to do. It must follow from *Allen v Flood*[3] that to intimidate by threatening to do what you have a legal right to do is to intimidate by lawful means. But I see no good reason for extending that doctrine. Threatening a breach of contract may be a much more coercive weapon than threatening a tort, particularly when the threat is directed against a company or corporation, and, if

1. [1963] 1 QB at 686–696; [1962] 2 All ER at 602–608.
2. [1898] AC 1 at 121; [1895–99] All ER Rep 52 at 79.
3. [1898] AC 1; [1895–99] All ER Rep 52.

there is no technical reason requiring a distinction between different kinds of threats, I can see no other ground for making any such distinction. . . .

LORD DEVLIN: . . . My lords, in my opinion there is a tort of intimidation of the nature described in chap. 18 of *Salmond on the Law of Torts* (13th edn) p. 697. The tort can take one of two forms which are set out in Salmond as follows:

'(1) Intimidation of the plaintiff himself.

'Although there seems to be no authority on the point, it cannot be doubted that it is an actionable wrong intentionally to compel a person, by means of a threat of an illegal act, to do some act whereby loss accrues to him: for example, an action will doubtless lie at the suit of a trader who has been compelled to discontinue his business by means of threats of personal violence made against him by the defendant with that intention.

'(2) Intimidation of other persons to the injury of the plaintiff.

'In certain cases it is an actionable wrong to intimidate other persons with the intent and effect of compelling them to act in a manner or to do acts which they themselves have a legal right to do which cause loss to the plaintiff: for example, the intimidation of the plaintiff's customers whereby they are compelled to withdraw their custom from him, or the intimidation of an employer whereby he is compelled to discharge his servant, the plaintiff. Intimidation of this sort is actionable, as we have said, in certain classes of cases; for it does not follow that, because a plaintiff's customers have a right to cease to deal with him if they please, other persons have a right as against the plaintiff to compel his customers to do so. There are at least two cases in which such intimidation may constitute a cause of action: (i) When the intimidation consists in a threat to do or procure an illegal act; (ii) When the intimidation is the act, not of a single person, but of two or more persons acting together, in pursuance of a common intention.'

As your lordships are all of opinion that there is a tort of intimidation and on this point approve the judgments in both courts below, I do not propose to offer any further authorities or reasons in support of my conclusion. I note that no issue on justification was raised at the time and there is no finding of fact on it. Your lordships have not to consider what part, if any, justification plays in the tort of intimidation.

Your lordships are here concerned with the sort of intimidation which Salmond puts into the second category, and with the first of Salmond's two cases. The second case is, so Salmond later observed, 'one form of the tort of conspiracy'.[1] That form is the *Quinn v Leathem*[2] type, so that it is no use to the appellant here. He relies on 'a threat to do or procure an illegal act', namely, a breach of contract. Doubtless it would suit him better if he could rely on the procuring of a breach of contract, for that is a tort; but immunity from that is guaranteed in terms by s. 3. So he complains only of the threat to break the service contracts, and the breach would undoubtedly be an act actionable by BOAC, though it is neither tortious nor criminal. He does not have to contend that in the tort of intimidation, as in the tort of conspiracy, there can be, if the object is injurious, an unlawful threat to use lawful means. I do not think that there can be. The line must be drawn according to the law. It cannot be said that to use a threat of any sort is per se unlawful; and I do not see how, except in relation to the nature of the act threatened, i.e. whether it is lawful or unlawful, one could satisfactorily distinguish between a lawful and an unlawful threat.

This conclusion, while not directly in point, assists me in my approach to the matter to be determined here. It is not, of course, disputed that if the act threatened is a crime, the threat is unlawful. But otherwise is it enough to say that the act

---

1. (13th edn) p. 699.
2. [1901] AC 495; [1900–3] All ER Rep 1.

threatened is actionable as a breach of contract or must it be actionable as a tort? My lords, I see no good ground for the latter limitation. I find the reasoning on this point of Professor Hamson[1] (which Sellers LJ[2] sets out in his judgment though he does not himself accept it) very persuasive. The essence of the offence is coercion. It cannot be said that every form of coercion is wrong. A dividing line must be drawn and the natural line runs between what is lawful and unlawful as against the party threatened. If the defendant threatens something that that party cannot legally resist, the plaintiff likewise cannot be allowed to resist the consequences; both must put up with the coercion and its results. But if the intermediate party is threatened with an illegal injury, the plaintiff who suffers by the aversion of the act threatened can fairly claim that he is illegally injured.

Accordingly, I reach the conclusion that the respondents' second point fails and on the facts of this case the tort of intimidation was committed. I do not share the difficulties which the lords justices felt about the idea of admitting breach of contract into the tort of intimidation. Out of respect to them I must state what those difficulties are and how in my opinion they can be satisfactorily resolved. I think that in one form or another they all stem from the error that any cause of action by the third party, that is the appellant, must in some way be supplemental to or dependent on a cause of action by BOAC. Thus, it is said to be anomalous that on the facts of this case the appellant should be able to sue the respondents when BOAC could not. The best way of answering that is to grant that BOAC would not be able to sue and to assert, as I shall seek to show, that there is nothing anomalous about it. But there was introduced into the argument a suggestion that BOAC could in fact have sued because although there was no actual breach of contract, one was threatened and therefore there was an anticipatory breach. Against that, it was said that BOAC could not have sued for an anticipatory breach unless they first elected to rescind, which they never did. I dare say that is right, but I do not think it matters at all whether BOAC could sue or not. The two causes of action — BOAC's and the appellant's — are in law quite independent; and in fact they are virtually alternative because it is difficult to visualise (except in one case) a set of facts on which both could sue.

This last statement is best examined in relation to a threat of physical violence which would unquestionably constitute intimidation. If A threatens B with physical violence unless he harms C, B can either resist or comply. If he resists, B might obtain an injunction against A (as he could also in the case of a threatened breach of contract if the contract were of a kind that permitted that remedy); or if A carries out his threat, B can sue for assault and obtain damages. In neither case can C sue because he has suffered no harm. If B complies with the threat, B cannot sue for damages because ex hypothesi there has been no assault; and he is not likely to obtain an injunction against the execution of a threat which he has already taken other means to avoid. But C will be able to sue because through B's compliance he has been injured. There is no anomaly about this; and if one substitutes 'breach of contract' for 'physical violence', the position is the same. The only case in which B and C are both likely to sue is if they both sue for the tort of intimidation in a case in which B has harmed himself by also harming C. Then it is said that to give C a cause of action offends against the rule that one man cannot sue on another's contract. I cannot understand this. In no circumstances does C sue on B's contract. The cause of action arises not because B's contract is broken but because it is not broken; it arises because of the action which B has taken to avert a breach.

Then it is asked how it can be that C can sue when there is a threat to break B's contract but cannot sue if it is broken without a threat. This means, it is argued, that if A threatens first, C has a cause of action; but if he strikes without threatening,

---

1. Cambridge Law Journal, November 1961, p. 189 at 191, 192.
2. [1963] 1 QB at p. 665; [1962] 2 All ER at p. 588.

C has no cause of action. I think that this also is fallacious. What is material to C's cause of action is the threat and B's submission to it. Whether the threat is executed or not is *in law* quite immaterial. *In fact* it is no doubt material because if it is executed (whether it be an assault or a breach of contract) it presumably means that B has not complied with it; and if B has not complied with it, C is not injured; and if C is not injured, he has no cause of action. Thus the reason why C can sue in one case and not in the other is because in one case he is injured and in the other he is not. The suggestion that it might pay A to strike without threatening negatives the hypothesis on which A is supposed to be acting. It must be proved that A's object is to injure C through the instrumentality of B. (That is why in the case of an 'innocent' breach of contract, which was remarked on by Sellers LJ[1] that is, one into which A was forced by circumstances beyond his control, there could never be the basis of an actionable threat.) If A hits B without telling him why, he can hardly hope to achieve his object. Of course A might think it more effective to hit B first and tell him why afterwards. But if then B injures C, it would not be because B had been hit but because he feared that he might be hit again. So if in the present case AESD went on strike without threatening, they would not achieve their object unless they made it plain why they were doing so. If they did that and BOAC then got rid of the appellant, his cause of action would be just the same as if BOAC had been threatened first, because the cause of the injury to the appellant would have been AESD's threat, express or implied, to continue on strike until the appellant was got rid of.

Finally, it is said that if a threat of breach of contract constitutes intimidation, one party to a contract could be sued for intimidation if he threatened reprisals. Suppose, for example, A has agreed to deliver goods to B in monthly instalments but has not made payment for the first a condition precedent to delivery of the second. If he threatens to withhold the second until payment has been made for the first, is he intimidating B? I doubt it. But the case introduces questions not in issue here — whether a threat in such circumstances would be justifiable and whether it is intimidation to try to force a man into doing what the law, if invoked, would compel him to do. I find therefore nothing to differentiate a threat of a breach of contract from a threat of physical violence or any other illegal threat. The nature of the threat is immaterial, because, as Professor Hamson points out,[2] its nature is irrelevant to the plaintiff's cause of action. All that matters to the plaintiff is that, metaphorically speaking, a club has been used. It does not matter to the plaintiff what the club is made of — whether it is a physical club or an economic club, a tortious club or an otherwise illegal club. If an intermediate party is improperly coerced, it does not matter to the plaintiff how he is coerced.

I think therefore that at common law there is a tort of intimidation and that on the facts of this case each of the respondents has committed it, both individually (since the jury has found that each took an overt and active part) and in combination with others. I must add that I have obtained no assistance from the numerous dicta cited to show what constitutes 'unlawful means' in the action of conspiracy. In some of the dicta the language suggests that the means must be criminal or tortious and in others that breach of contract would do; but in no case was the point in issue. Moreover, while a decision on that point might have been most illuminating, it is not the point that I have been considering. I have not been considering what amounts to unlawful means in the tort of conspiracy. I am not saying that a conspiracy to commit a breach of contract amounts to the tort of conspiracy; that point remains to be decided. I am saying that in the tort of intimidation a threat to break a contract would be a threat of an illegal act. It follows from that that a combination to intimidate by means of a threat of a breach of contract would be an unlawful conspiracy; but it

---

1. [1963] 1 QB at p. 671; [1962] 2 All ER at p. 592.
2. Cambridge Law Journal, November 1961, at pp. 191, 192.

does not necessarily follow that a combination to commit a breach of contract simpliciter would be an unlawful conspiracy. . . .

[LORD EVERSHED, LORD HODSON and LORD PEARCE delivered speeches in favour of allowing the appeal.]

Notes

1. The immediate repercussion of this decision was the enactment of a specific immunity for those committing the tort of intimidation in circumstances similar to *Rookes v Barnard*, by the Trade Disputes Act 1965. The immunity in extended form is now contained in s. 13 of the Trade Union and Labour Relations Act 1974 as amended.

2. Why was Silverthorne, who had no contract to threaten to break, treated as a conspirator? In *Morgan v Fry* [1968] 2 QB 710; [1968] 3 All ER 452, noted post, the only reason Lord Denning MR could find for Silverthorne not being protected from liability (by the Trade Disputes Act 1906, s. 3) for inducing breach of contract was that he was a conspirator.

3. If A breaks his contract with B, this gives no remedy to C who is not a party. Why then, if A merely threatens to break his contract, should C have a cause of action? See L. H. Hoffmann (1965) 81 LQR 116 esp. at 126; K. W. Wedderburn (1964) 27 MLR 257; J. A. Weir [1964] CLJ 225.

4. In *Morgan v Fry* [1968] 2 QB 710; [1968] 3 All ER 452 Russell LJ suggested that not every threat to break a contract of employment is sufficient to constitute intimidation. So where workers could have exerted equivalent or greater pressure on their employer by giving notice lawfully to terminate their contracts, Russell LJ said that the threat of a minor breach was not intimidatory. Arguably, this 'may depend upon absence of proof that the threat of a minor breach could cause damage', proof of damage being an essential element of the tort (see *Clerk & Lindsell*, para. 15-15). But in interlocutory proceedings the nature of the breach is unlikely to be investigated. See for example *Hadmor Productions Ltd v Hamilton* [1983] 1 AC 191; [1982] 1 All ER 1042 (p. 724, post).

5. If the deliberate contravention of a penal statute by itself gives no cause of action to the plaintiff (see *Lonrho Ltd v Shell Petroleum Ltd* [1982] AC 173; [1981] 2 All ER 456 (pp. 545 and 688, ante); cf. *Associated British Ports v Transport and General Workers' Union* [1989] ICR 557; [1989] 3 All ER 796 (p. 728, post)) would a coercive threat to commit a breach of such a statute constitute a sufficient *threat* of an illegal act for the purposes of this tort? If not, do you agree with *Winfield & Jolowicz* pp. 511–512, that 'it is perhaps surprising that a threat of a mere breach of contract should give rise to liability'? For discussion of other types of wrong which may give rise to liability, see *Clerk & Lindwell*, para. 15-15; see too p. 732, post.

6. Lord Devlin (p. 720, ante) recognised that 'an action [for intimidation] will doubtless lie at the suit of a trader who has been compelled to discontinue his business by means of threats of personal violence against him by the defendant with that intention'. Is this tort of 'two-party intimidation' appropriate in cases where the only threat is one to break a contract to which

the plaintiff is a party? Where A threatens B that he will break his contract with B so causing B damage, B may have other remedies: (a) he may be able to bring an action for anticipatory breach of contract, or await the breach and then sue for damages; or (b) he may be able to rely on the doctrine of economic duress defined by Lord Scarman in *Pao On v Lau Yiu Long* [1980] AC 614 at 635 as 'a coercion of the will so as to vitiate consent', so as to have a contract made under duress avoided or to recover money paid under duress. In *Universe Tankships Inc of Monrovia v International Transport Workers Federation* [1983] 1 AC 366 at 385, Lord Diplock said:

'The use of economic duress to induce another person to part with property or money is not a tort per se; the form that duress takes may, or may not, be tortious. The remedy to which economic duress gives rise is not an action for damages but an action for restitution of property or money exacted under any such duress and the avoidance of any contract that has been induced by it; but where the particular form taken by the economic duress used is itself a tort, the restitutional remedy for money had and received by the defendant to the plaintiff's use is one which the plaintiff is entitled to pursue as an alternative remedy to an action for damages in tort.'

(Cf. Lord Scarman at p. 400.) Duress may be wider than the tort of intimidation because it can include a threat of coercive *lawful* action; moreover, it seems that the 'threat' for the purposes of duress may amount to no more than an implied threat of non-performance of the contract: see *B & S Contracts and Design Ltd v Victor Green Publications Ltd* [1984] ICR 419 and the comments by N. E. Palmer and L. Catchpole (1985) 48 MLR 102. The development of this doctrine reduces the importance of the tort of intimidation in a contractual context. See generally E. MacDonald [1989] JBL 460; A. Phang (1990) 53 MLR 107.

7. The next case shows that the 'species' tort of intimidation may constitute 'unlawful means' for purposes of the 'genus' tort of interference with trade by unlawful means.

4 Interference with trade by unlawful means

Hadmor Productions Ltd v Hamilton Court of Appeal and House of Lords [1981] 2 All ER 724; [1982] 1 All ER 1042

The plaintiff company (Hadmor) was a facility company which made a series of fifteen filmed television programmes using freelance performers and technicians. The technicians' union had a policy of being opposed to transmission by television stations of material, produced by such companies, but the directors of Hadmor believed that they had an assurance from Hamilton, an ACTT official, that the union would not prevent the films being shown provided that they maintained a closed shop, which they did. The first two programmes were shown by Thames Television, but the local branch of the union then resolved that the programmes would be 'blacked' (i.e. that union members would refuse to handle them). Faced with the likelihood of disruption, Thames, who were under no contractual obligation to transmit them, withdrew the remaining programmes from transmission. Hadmor alleged that the acts of the union official and shop steward amounted to the tort of interference with trade by unlawful means. On an application for interlocutory injunctions, Dillon J held that there was a serious issue to be tried on this point but refused to grant the injunctions on the ground that there was a likelihood of a defence succeeding under the amended s. 13(1) of the Trade Union and Labour Relations Act 1974, as modified by s. 17 of the Employment Act 1980. The Court of Appeal reversed his decision on the latter point, but the House of Lords restored his order holding that the statutory immunity was likely to be established. The extracts relate only to the tort of interference with trade by unlawful means.

In the Court of Appeal:

LORD DENNING MR: . . . It seems to me that Hadmor have a legitimate grievance against Bob Hamilton and the shop stewards. Hadmor had cleared the position with the union. On the faith of it, they negotiated with Thames Television. They had a firm business expectation that their video films would be taken, bought and transmitted by Thames Television for the 13 weeks from 8th January 1981. That expectation was shattered by the action of Bob Hamilton and the shop stewards in 'blacking' or threatening to 'black' the series, by inducing the technicians to break their contract of employment. It was the cause of much damage to Hadmor, which is still continuing. . . .

. . . [I]t is important to recognise that we have now a separate and distinct tort of interference with the business of another by unlawful means. It was stated in *Allen v Flood* [1898] AC 1 at 138, 180; [1895-9] All ER Rep 52 at 88, 104 by Lord Herschell and Lord James; in *J T Stratford & Son Ltd v Lindley* [1965] AC 269 at 324, 328; [1964] 3 All ER 102, at 106, 109 by Lord Reid and Viscount Radcliffe; by this court in *Torquay Hotel Co Ltd v Cousins* [1969] 2 Ch 106 at 139; [1969] 1 All ER 522 at 530–531; in *Acrow (Automation) Ltd v Rex Chainbelt Inc* [1971] 3 All ER 1175 at 1181; [1971] 1 WLR 1676 at 1683; in *Ex p Island Records Ltd* [1978] Ch 122 at 136; [1978] 3 All ER 824 at 830; and in *Associated Newspapers Group Ltd v Wade* [1979] 1 WLR 697 at 708. It was accepted by Lord Wedderburn in *Clerk and Lindsell on Torts* (14th Edn, 1975, para. 808), and was admitted by counsel for the trade union officers in argument before us. . . .

In the House of Lords:

LORD DIPLOCK: . . . Since, at the time of the hearing by Dillon J, there was no evidence before him that there had been any prior agreement between Thames and ACTT that films or video tapes produced by facility companies should not be transmitted without prior consultation with ACTT, the defendants' case had to be presented to him on the basis that for a member of ACTT to disobey an order to transmit a programme produced by a facility company would be a breach of his contract of employment with Thames, and thus an 'unlawful act' of which a threat to do it or procure it is capable of constituting the common law tort of intimidation discussed by this House in *Rookes v Barnard* [1964] AC 1129; [1964] 1 All ER 367. Dillon J did not deal separately with this issue. He was content to assume that in the absence of any statutory immunity it would have raised a serious question to be tried. By the time that the matter came before the Court of Appeal Hadmor's case on this vital issue had been weakened by the uncontradicted evidence of the agreement between Thames and ACTT that Thames would not require ACTT's members to transmit programmes produced by facility companies except after prior consultation with the union. The extent to which terms relating to the performance of contracts of employment which have been agreed between an employer and a trade union of which his employees are members are to be treated as incorporated in the individual contracts of employment of those members raises interesting and difficult questions of law into which it would be inappropriate to enter on a motion for an interlocutory injunction. I would therefore hold, although not without considerable misgivings, that Hadmor does manage to scramble over the first hurdle in its path. . . .

Lonrho plc v Fayed Court of Appeal [1989] 2 All ER 65

The plaintiffs (Lonrho) and first three defendants (the Fayed brothers) were competing bidders for the share capital of House of Fraser plc which owned various department stores including Harrods. By 1979, Lonrho had acquired 19.9 per cent of the share capital and their bid was referred to the Monopolies and Mergers Commission (MMC) by the Secretary of State for Trade and Industry. At his request in 1981, Lonrho gave an undertaking to him not to purchase any more shares in the company. In 1985, the Fayeds made a bid for the company, through the medium of a company referred to as 'Holdings' (the fourth defendant), while Lonrho was still subject to their undertaking. The Secretary of State did not refer the Fayeds' bid to the Commission, and the Fayeds acquired control through Holdings. Lonrho alleged that the Secretary of State had been influenced in his decision not to refer the bid by fraudulent misrepresentations made to him by the Fayeds concerning their own commercial standing and worth. Lonrho brought an action claiming, inter alia, that the defendants had committed the tort of wrongful interference with Lonrho's trade or business. Pill J, [1988] 3 All ER 464, struck out the claim as disclosing no cause of action on the ground that the opportunity to make a take-over bid was not a legal right which this tort would protect. The plaintiffs appealed.

DILLON LJ: ... The ... cause of action alleged in the statement of claim is the common law tort of wrongful interference with trade or business. The existence of such a tort is conceded by the defendants. Reference can be made to the speech of Lord Diplock in *Merkur Island Shipping Corp v Laughton* [1983] 2 All ER 189 at 196–197, [1983] 2 AC 570 at 609–610, where he said:

'In anticipation of an argument that was addressed to your Lordships on the stage 3 point, I should mention that the evidence also establishes a prima facie case of the common law tort, referred to in s 13(2) and (3) of the [Trade Union and Labour Relations Act 1974], of interfering with the trade or business of another person by doing unlawful acts. To fall within this genus of torts the unlawful act need not involve procuring another person to break a subsisting contract or to interfere with the performance of a subsisting contract. The immunity granted by s 13(2) and (3) I will call the "genus immunity". Where, however, the procuring of another person to break a subsisting contract *is* the unlawful act involved, as it is in s 13(1), this is but one species of the wider genus of tort. This I will call the "species immunity".' (Lord Diplock's emphasis.)

There are also references to this tort in *J T Stratford & Son Ltd v Lindley* [1964] 3 All ER 102, [1965] AC 269. Lord Reid said ([1964] 3 All ER 102 at 106, [1965] AC 269 at 324):

'In addition to interfering with existing contracts the respondents' action made it practically impossible for the appellants to do any new business with the bargehirers. It was not disputed that such interference with business is tortious, if any unlawful means are employed.'

Viscount Radcliffe said ([1964] 3 All ER 102 at 109, [1965] AC 269 at 328):

'The case comes before us as one in which the respondents have inflicted injury on the appellants in the conduct of their business and have resorted to unlawful means to bring this about.'

But, although those statements indicate that the tort is a recognised tort, they cannot be taken as comprehensive definitions of what constitutes that tort.

There are several what may be called established exceptions to the generality of those definitions. In particular, although it is not relevant on the facts of the present case, the speech of Lord Diplock in *Lonrho Ltd v Shell Petroleum Co Ltd* [1981] 2 All ER 456 at 463, [1982] AC 173 at 187 establishes that the mere fact that a person has suffered injury in his business by an act of the defendant which is illegal in the sense of being in breach of a statutory prohibition does not automatically entitle the injured person to bring an action within this tort to recover damages for the injury. The complainant still has to show that on its true construction the statute which imposed the prohibition gave rise to a civil remedy. That has to be considered in the light of the principle examined in *Cutler v Wandsworth Stadium Ltd* [1949] 1 All ER 544, [1949] AC 398. Furthermore, in *RCA Corp v Pollard* [1982] 3 All ER 771 at 781, [1983] Ch 135 at 153 Oliver LJ sets out cogently that the action does not lie where the damage complained of is merely economic damage as an incidental result of the breach of a prohibition in a statute not designed to protect the interests of a class to which the plaintiff belongs.

It is submitted to us that, even with this tort, it must, as with the tort of conspiracy, have been the predominant purpose of the tortfeasor to injure the victim rather than to further the tortfeasor's own financial ends. I do not accept that. It would be inconsistent with the way Lord Diplock treated this tort and the tort of conspiracy differently in his speech in *Lonrho Ltd v Shell Petroleum Co Ltd* and in *Hadmor Productions Ltd v Hamilton* [1982] 1 All ER 1042 at 1052–1053, [1983] 1 AC 191 at 228–229. No predominant purpose to injure is required where the tortious act relied on is injury by wrongful interference with a third party's contract with the victim or by intimidation of a third party to the detriment of the victim, nor should it in my view be required where the wrongful interference has been by the practice of fraud on a third party, aimed specifically at the plaintiff, as it was put by Oliver LJ in *RCA Corp v Pollard* [1982] 3 All ER 771 at 780, [1983] Ch 135 at 151.

It is also submitted for the defendants that for this tort of wrongful interference with business to apply there must have been a complete tort as between the alleged wrongdoer and the third party against whom the wrong was practised to the detriment of the plaintiff in the action. It is said that that is not the case here, because though fraud was practised, if the allegations of Lonrho are correct, on the Secretary of State to achieve the end that the Secretary of State did not refer Holdings' bid to the MMC, the tort of deceit requires that the plaintiff should have suffered damage, and the Secretary of State suffered, it is said, no actionable damage. I, for my part, can see no valid reason why the tort should need, as against the third party, to have been complete to the extent that the third party had himself suffered damage. The distinction drawn by Lord Diplock elsewhere between primary and secondary obligations may be relevant. Apart from that, the need to show that the injured third party had suffered damage, as opposed to the plaintiff having suffered damage, was not a factor in the decision of the majority of this court in *National Phonograph Co Ltd v Edison-Bell Consolidated Phonograph Co Ltd* [1908] 1 Ch 335, [1904–7] All ER Rep 116. Causation has of course to be proved, but that is a different matter.

It also has to be proved by a plaintiff who seeks to rely on this tort, as counsel conceded for Lonrho, that the unlawful act was in some sense directed against the plaintiff or intended to harm the plaintiff. The origin of those phrases is the oft-quoted passage in the speech of Lord Watson in *Allen v Flood* [1898] AC 1 at 96, [1895–9] All ER Rep 52 at 69, which was applied by the majority of this court (Buckley and Kennedy LJJ) in *National Phonograph Co Ltd v Edison-Bell Consolidated Phonograph Co Ltd*. In that case the fraud was clearly directed against the plaintiff.

I have to bear in mind, however, as I have endeavoured to bear in mind throughout the hearing of this appeal, that this court has before it not the trial of the action or an appeal from a decision of the judge at the trial of the action on a striking out application. . . .

Here the existence of this tort is recognised, but the detailed limits of it have to be refined. I regard it as right and, indeed, essential that this should be done on the actual facts as they emerge at the trial rather than on a set of hypotheses, more or less wide, in very comprehensive pleadings. This is very far from being a case in which there is no conflict as to the facts, and the matters in conflict involve questions of intention, purpose, motive or probability. We have the general framework of the law which falls to be applied to this case laid down, and to a considerable extent refined as a result of this application. But the actual application of that law to the facts of the case should, in my judgment, be a matter for the trial of the action.

. . . It is not right to endeavour to try complicated issues of causation on a striking out application on what might or might not appear to be on paper, on the balance of probabilities, the foreseeable outcome of a trial.

There are many other issues which fall to be investigated, which are also, in my judgment, matters for investigation at the trial, such as whether the business interest which Lonrho claims to have had and which it claims has been injured by the allegedly tortious acts is a sufficient business interest to support the tort which is alleged, and whether the nature of the damage which Lonrho claims to have suffered is damage properly recoverable for that tort in the particular circumstances of this case. I have no doubt at all that these are all matters which must be investigated at the trial of the action. I underline that this tort is still in the process of judicial definition. This is not, therefore, so far as this cause of action is concerned, a proper case for striking out.

I would, accordingly, allow this appeal. . . .

RALPH GIBSON LJ: I agree that the appeal should be allowed to the extent indicated by Dillon LJ and for the reasons which he has given. . . .

. . . This is a comparatively new tort of which the precise boundaries must be established from case to case. Those points include, first, the nature of the intention which is required to satisfy the requirement that the conduct is 'directed against' the plaintiffs, in particular where the fraudulent misstatement is made by A to B about A himself in order to cause B to act in such a way that A obtains or retains a commercial advantage over C or deprives C of a commercial advantage; second, the nature of the business interest by reference to which the plaintiff must prove that he has been damaged; third, whether there is sufficient nexus or directness of impact and consequence between the unlawful means employed and the alleged loss causing effect on the plaintiffs; and, fourth, whether the damage alleged is sufficient to support the existence of a cause of action. . . .

[WOOLF LJ delivered a judgment agreeing with both judgments.]

Appeal allowed

Associated British Ports *v* Transport and General Workers' Union Court of Appeal [1989] 3 All ER 796

The Government introduced legislation in 1989 to abolish the National Dock Labour Scheme which had regulated the employment of dock workers since 1947. When negotiations with the port employers (who were registered employers under the scheme) to establish national conditions of employment no less favourable than those under the scheme broke down, the TGWU (the defendant union) representing most of the registered dock workers (RDWs) held a strike ballot which resulted in a large majority in favour of strike action. Three of the largest port employers (the plaintiffs) then sought an interlocutory injunction to restrain the union from proceeding with the threatened strike.

Millett J refused to grant the injunction. The port employers appealed contending, inter alia, that by calling a national dock strike the union would be committing the tort of intentionally causing damage to the employers' business by unlawful means. The unlawful means alleged were inducing breach of the statutory duty to 'work for such periods as are reasonable in his particular case' placed on registered dock workers by cl. 8(5)(*b*) of the scheme. On the assumption that cl. 8(5)(*b*) did impose some form of statutory duty to work, the Court of Appeal held that the port employers had an arguable case that the union would be committing the tort of interference with business by unlawful means. (This tort is outside the scope of the immunities in respect of acts in contemplation or furtherance of a trade dispute under s. 13 of the Trade Union and Labour Relations Act 1974, as amended.) The Court of Appeal granted the interlocutory injunction for the period that the scheme remained in force. The union then appealed to the House of Lords, [1989] 3 All ER 822, which considered only the issue whether cl. 8(5)(*b*) of the scheme imposed a statutory duty to work on registered dockworkers. The House held that it did not do so and consequently the strike call was only an inducement to breaches of contract within the immunity granted by s. 13 of the 1974 Act. Accordingly the union's appeal was allowed. The House of Lords did not hear argument on the issue of interference with business by unlawful means. The extracts below from the judgments in the Court of Appeal relate to this issue.

NEILL LJ: . . . The employers put their claim in tort in two ways. (1) They allege that by calling a strike the union would procure or induce a breach of statutory duty. (2) They allege that by calling a strike the union would cause intentional injury to the employers' businesses by using unlawful means; that is, by procuring or inducing a breach of statutory duty.

For its part the union contends that it would not be liable in tort because (a) the obligation imposed on RDWs by cl 8(5)(*b*) of the scheme is not a duty owed to the employer or actionable by the employers, (b) the union would only be liable in tort for procuring or inducing a breach of statutory duty if the breach by the RDWs would be actionable at the suit of the employers and (c) the breach of statutory duty which would be relied on for the purposes of the second tort could only constitute unlawful means if the breach would be actionable at the suit of the employers.

. . . First I must look further at the elements of the two torts on which the employers rely. It is important to remember, however, that at this interlocutory stage the court should not attempt finally to resolve difficult questions of law. . . .

It is common ground that the inducement of a breach of statutory duty exists as a head of tortious liability. In *Meade v Haringey London Borough* [1979] 2 All ER 1016, [1979] 1 WLR 637 it was held that a parent was entitled to bring proceedings against a local education authority who, despite a statutory duty to make schools available, had closed the schools in the borough during an industrial dispute. But Eveleigh LJ went on to say that if the union concerned had ordered or solicited a breach of the statutory duty they could not rely on the statutory immunity conferred by s 13 of the Trade Union and Labour Relations Act 1974 (see [1979] 2 All ER 1016 at 1028, [1979] 1 WLR 637 at 651).

The inducement of a breach of statutory duty is, of course, akin to the inducement of a breach of contract, which has been recognised as a tort for many years. Both species of tort can be classed as torts which involve interference with a person's legal rights.

The central issue between the parties on this aspect of the case is whether it is necessary for the employers to prove that a breach of the obligations under cl 8(5)(*b*) would give them a right of action against the RDWs in breach. It was argued on behalf of the employers that such a breach would be actionable. I shall return to this point later. In the alternative it was argued that even if a breach was not actionable, the obligation in cl 8(5)(*b*) gave the employers what is described as a correlative right to insist on its performance and that this right was sufficient to found an action for inducing a breach of a statutory duty. In this context our attention was directed to the decision of the Court of Appeal in *Torquay Hotel Co Ltd v Cousins* [1969] 1 All

ER 522, [1969] 2 Ch 106, where it was held that it was actionable to interfere with the performance of a contract for the delivery of oil even though the oil company itself was excused from liability by the inclusion in its contract of a force majeure clause. It was argued that this decision demonstrated that the existence of a right of action against the obligor was not an essential element of the tort of inducing a breach of contract, and that by analogy it was not necessary for the employers to prove that they had a right of action against the RDWs for any breach.

In my view, however, the *Torquay Hotel* case does not assist the employers' argument. Thus, in that case the primary obligation to make deliveries under the contract for the supply of oil remained even though the oil company was relieved from its secondary obligation to make monetary compensation for breach. It seems to me that in this type of tort, where the plaintiff is complaining of some interference with a right, it is necessary for him to show that the right is a legal or equitable right which is capable of forming the basis of a cause of action.

I turn, therefore, to the alternative basis of tortious liability on which the employers seek to rely. The existence of this tort seems no longer to be in doubt. Indeed, counsel for the union did not challenge its existence.

. . . [I]t was argued on behalf of the employers that it would be wholly anomalous if in this tort the breach of statutory duty had to be actionable at the suit of the plaintiff before it could constitute unlawful means when it was established by authority that a plaintiff could rely on a tort or breach of contract involving a third party other than himself and possibly, since *Lonrho plc v Fayed*, even though the third party could not sue because he had suffered no damage.

The arguments directed to this aspect of the case were sustained and clear. For my part, I see great force in counsel's argument for the union that even though it may be anomalous, a breach of statutory duty cannot be relied on as unlawful means for the purposes of this tort unless it is actionable. On careful reflection, however, I have been driven to the conclusion that it would be wrong to attempt to resolve the matter on the hearing of an interlocutory motion. The precise limits and characteristics of this tort are uncertain, and the argument, though full, has not been comprehensive. Counsel for the employers raised the possibility that some further research might be necessary. I see the force of this submission. The issue seems to me to fall fairly within Lord Diplock's category of difficult questions of law which require, as he put it, 'mature consideration'.[1] . . .

Let me pause to explain the stage which I have now reached. . . .

(a) I consider that for the purpose of the first tort it would be necessary for the employers to show that the breach of duty was actionable by them.

(b) I consider that in relation to the second tort there is an issue to be tried as to whether unlawful means can include inducement of breaches of duty which are not actionable.

(c) Without expressing a final view, I am at present of the opinion that a breach of the obligation imposed in cl 8(5)(*b*) is not actionable at the suit of the employers.

It follows, therefore, that I am expressing no final view whatever as to whether a strike would be lawful or unlawful. At this stage all that can be said is that it is *arguable* that the employers have a claim in tort which would not require them to prove that a breach of the cl 8(5)(*b*) obligation was actionable. . . .

BUTLER-SLOSS LJ [having held that there was no serious issue to be tried in respect of the tort of inducing breach of statutory duty because the breach of cl. 8(5)(*b*) of the

---

1. [In *American Cyanamid Co v Ethicon Ltd* [1975] AC 396; [1975] 1 All ER 504, on which see p. 732, post.]

Scheme was not actionable at common law between the employer and a registered dockworker, then considered the second tort of intentional interference with business by unlawful means]: . . . This tort clearly exists whether or not it is a separate tort or a limb of a wider genus, and whether or not the limits have yet been defined, which they appear not so to have been. In decisions cited to us and in the arguments placed before this court there has been a tendency to blur or even to confuse this tort of intent to injure from the 'interference with rights' tort, with which I have dealt with earlier. The intentional interference with business by unlawful means expressed in the decisions in *J T Stratford & Son Ltd v Lindley* [1964] 3 All ER 102, [1965] AC 269, in *Merkur Island Shipping Corp v Laughton* [1983] 2 All ER 189, [1983] 2 AC 570 and in *Lonrho plc v Fayed* [1989] 2 All ER 65, [1989] 3 WLR 631 has been held to cover unlawful means by breach of contract, contempt of court and breach of statutory duty. . . .

It is argued for the union that whatever may be the earlier position, since *Lonrho v Shell* [1982] AC 173; [1981] 2 All ER 456 an action under this head, where the unlawful means consists of a breach of statutory obligation, can only succeed if the breach of statutory obligation itself is capable of a right of action between the obligee and obligor. In other words, the same requirement as under the first tort of inducing a breach of statutory obligation. . . .

For my part, I see much force in the submission of counsel for [the employers] in this most difficult, not to say obscure, branch of the law of tort. If it is necessary for the unlawful means to constitute a cause of action available to the plaintiff where it is a breach of statutory obligation, it would seem to place this member of the group of these torts in an oddly anomalous position. It adds nothing and is virtually indistinguishable from the first tort which we have considered. Further, it is the only member of the group which requires a cause of action by the plaintiff in respect of the unlawful means. There is no logical distinction easily to be drawn between the various members of this group. It is strongly arguable that where the unlawful act relied on is a breach of statutory duty it is not necessary to be actionable in tort at the instance of the plaintiff. . . .

STUART-SMITH LJ: . . . Counsel for the union further submitted that the first tort was a tort of intention and there was no difference in the nature of the intention to injure required in the first tort and the second tort. I am not persuaded that this is correct. In *Clerk and Lindsell* (15th edn, 1982) p. 757 the editor, rightly in my view, distinguished the second tort from the first tort on the ground that the essence of the second tort is deliberate and intended damage. And in *Lonrho plc v Fayed* [1989] 2 All ER 65 at 69, [1989] 3 WLR 631 at 637 Dillon LJ stated that the unlawful act had to be directed against the plaintiff or intended to harm him.

Accordingly, I take the view that at the very least it is strongly arguable that where the unlawful act relied on in this tort is a breach of statute, it is not necessary that it should be one that is actionable in tort at the suit of the plaintiff. . . .

Notes

1. *Clerk & Lindsell*, para. 15–20, note 45, comment on this case as follows:

'. . . [A] distinction between the ["intent to injure" tort and the "interference with rights" tort] based upon different categories of "intent to injure", which is used to determine the meaning of unlawful means, is hard to find in previous precedents of the modern law. The tendency in these judgments is to revert to that outflanking of *Allen v Flood* [1898] AC 1 [p. 674, ante], which has from time to time characterised common law development . . . by relying on coercive intention to injure for acts otherwise lawful (as in *Quinn v Leathem* [1901] AC 495 [p. 681, ante]). The introduction of a separate category of "intent to injure" — less than predominant purpose in conspiracy [see note 1, p. 692, ante] but more than the "intention" required for procuring breach of contract or of other rights [see p. 716, ante] — injects an element of motive which may be thought irregular on orthodox principles (*Lonrho v Fayed* [1989] 2 All ER p. 73 *per* Woolf LJ; . . .). To this extent it is submitted, there are now inconsistent analyses of the nature of this tort between which the Court of Appeal is entitled to choose, even before, the House of Lords expresses its view. More generally, the case demonstrates the imperfections of the law-making process on motion in interlocutory applications, not least in trade disputes. The applicant need show only a "serious question to be tried" or an "arguable case" (*American Cyanamid Co v Ethicon Ltd* [1975] AC 396 . . .), encouraging an ingenious plaintiff to seek relief by redesigning the precedents in the knowledge that he, not the defendants, will benefit if thereby "difficult questions of law" emerge which require "mature consideration". . . .'

See further on this case B. Simpson (1989) 18 ILJ 234, and on *Lonrho v Al-Fayed* (ante) J. M. Eekelaar (1990) 106 LQR 223.

2. The tort of interference with trade by unlawful means is wide enough to embrace the specific torts of indirect procurement of breach of contract (p. 703, ante) and intimidation (p. 718, ante). How far it extends beyond those recognised heads depends upon the meaning given to 'unlawful means' for the purpose of this tort. *Clerk & Lindsell*, para. 15–20, comment that the 'reason for the requirement [of unlawful means] is clearly the same in [intimidation, indirect procurement of breach of contract, conspiracy to use unlawful means, and unlawful interference], namely, the maintenance of the right to take lawful action by way of trade competition or in pursuit of industrial objectives and the like, in defence of legitimate interests in present society.' They had earlier stated that 'it would make for brevity, logic and elegance if the principle could be stated that the definition of "illegal" or "unlawful" was the same under all four rubrics' but conclude that 'unhappily, no such clear principle emerges from the authorities'.

3. Is the tort of interference with trade by unlawful means committed where A intentionally commits a breach of his contract with B in order to damage either B or C? Weir [1964] CLJ 225 suggested that such conduct is tortious, although the logic would be to make A liable in *tort* for any deliberate breach of contract (contra: H. Carty (1988) 104 LQR 250 at 271–272; and see the analogous problem of two-party intimidation, p. 723, ante). In *Barretts & Baird (Wholesale) Ltd v Institution of Professional Civil Servants* [1987] IRLR 3 at 8–9, Henry J observed that the results of treating breach of contract as unlawful means in the law of tort were 'surprising' because they lead to 'large inroads into the doctrine of privity of contract': see S. Fredman (1987) 103 LQR 176; B. Simpson (1987) 50 MLR 506; K. Ewing [1987] CLJ 222. If non-actionable contravention of a statute is unlawful means when there is an 'intention to injure' (*Associated British Ports v TGWU*, ante), or if C can rely on A's deceit practised upon B even if B has suffered no damage (*Lonrho v Al-Fayed*, ante), does it follow that an 'intention to injure' breach of contract is tortious? *Clerk & Lindsell*, para. 15–20, comment: 'there is no way round the fact that to allow C to sue gives him a right of action on a contract to which he is a third party. That is why the courts may feel bound to introduce new, artificial barriers to the spread of breach of contract into tortious interference . . .'.

4. If A commits a common law crime, or a contempt of court, which is not itself a tort in order to harm C, can this be unlawful means? In *Chapman v*

Honig [1963] 2 QB 502; [1963] 2 All ER 513 a landlord gave a tenant notice to quit (in accordance with the lease) in order to punish him for giving evidence in an action brought by other tenants against the landlord. The majority of the Court of Appeal (Lord Denning MR dissenting) held that even if this amounted to a contempt of court, no tort had been committed. On the other hand, in *Acrow (Automation) Ltd v Rex Chainbelt Inc* [1971] 3 All ER 1175; [1971] 1 WLR 1676 (in which *Chapman v Honig* was not referred to) a refusal to continue deliveries to which the plaintiff had no contractual right was held by the Court of Appeal to be unlawful means and hence actionable in tort because the defendants were aiding and abetting the breach of an injunction, in contempt of court. (Note now that various forms of contempt of court are statutory crimes under the Contempt of Court Act 1981.)

5. Torts such as trespass and nuisance may be unlawful means: see *Messenger Newspapers Group Ltd v National Graphical Association* [1984] IRLR 397 (damages included £10,000 as aggravated damages and £25,000 exemplary damages because of intention to close down the plaintiff's business by unlawful means); *Norbrook Laboratories Ltd v King* [1984] IRLR 200; *News Group Newspapers Ltd v Society of Graphical and Allied Trades '82 (No 2)* [1987] ICR 181.

6. For general discussion, see P. Elias and K. Ewing [1982] CLJ 321; H. Carty (1983) 3 LS 193 and (1988) 104 LQR 250; N. Cohen-Grabelsky (1982) 45 MLR 241; *Clerk & Lindsell*, para. 15–20.

5 Passing-off and other forms of unlawful competition

Erven Warnink BV *v* J Townend & Sons (Hull) Ltd House of Lords [1979] 2 All ER 927

The first plaintiffs ('Warnink') manufactured an alcoholic drink known as 'advocaat' made out of a mixture of eggs and spirits. The defendants ('Keeling') produced an alcoholic drink from a mixture of dried eggs and Cyprus sherry and marketed it as 'Keeling's Old English Advocaat'. They were able to undersell Warnink because of the lower rate of excise duty appropriate to fortified wine in place of spirits. Keeling had not passed off their product as that of Warnink and it was unlikely that any purchaser would suppose Keeling's drink to be Warnink's product. Warnink applied for an injunction restraining Keeling from selling or distributing under the name 'advocaat' any product which was not made out of eggs and spirits without the addition of wine. They relied on the principle, first recognised by Danckwerts J in the Champagne case (*Bollinger v Costa Brava Wine Co Ltd* [1960] Ch 262; [1959] 3 All ER 800), and followed in the Sherry case (*Vine Products Ltd v Mackenzie & Co Ltd* [1969] RPC 1) and the Scotch Whisky case (*John Walker & Sons Ltd v Henry Ost & Co Ltd* [1970] 2 All ER 106; [1970] 1 WLR 917), that although they did not have an exclusive right to the use of the trade name 'advocaat', they were members of a class consisting of all those who had a right to use the name and as such were entitled to protect the name. The judge (Goulding J) granted the injunction. On appeal the Court of Appeal discharged the injunction and dismissed the action on the ground that the name 'advocaat' was purely descriptive and not distinctive. On appeal to the House of Lords:

LORD DIPLOCK: . . . Unfair trading as a wrong actionable at the suit of other traders who thereby suffer loss of business or goodwill may take a variety of forms, to some of which separate labels have become attached in English law. Conspiracy to injure a person in his trade or business is one, slander of goods another, but most protean is that which is generally and nowadays, perhaps misleadingly, described as 'passing off'. The forms that unfair trading takes will alter with the ways in which trade is carried on and business reputation and goodwill acquired. Emerson's maker of the better mousetrap if secluded in his house built in the woods would today be unlikely to find a path beaten to his door in the absence of a costly advertising campaign to acquaint the public with the excellence of his wares.

The action for what has become known as 'passing off' arose in the 19th century out of the use in connection with his own goods by one trader of the trade name or trade mark of a rival trader so as to induce in potential purchasers the belief that his goods were those of the rival trader. . . .

My Lords, *A G Spalding & Bros v A W Gamage Ltd*[1] and the later cases make it possible to identify five characteristics which must be present in order to create a valid cause of action for passing off: (1) a misrepresentation, (2) made by a trader in the course of trade, (3) to prospective customers of his or ultimate consumers of goods or services supplied by him, (4) which is calculated to injure the business or goodwill of another trader (in the sense that this is a reasonably foreseeable consequence) and (5) which causes actual damage to a business or goodwill of the trader by whom the action is brought or (in a quia timet action) will probably do so.

In seeking to formulate general propositions of English law, however, one must be particularly careful to beware of the logical fallacy of the undistributed middle. It does not follow that because all passing-off actions can be shown to present these characteristics, all factual situations which present these characteristics give rise to a cause of action for passing off. True it is that their presence indicates what a moral code would censure as dishonest trading, based as it is on deception of customers and consumers of a trader's wares, but in an economic system which has relied on competition to keep down prices and to improve products there may be practical reasons why it should have been the policy of the common law not to run the risk of hampering competition by providing civil remedies to everyone competing in the market who has suffered damage to his business or goodwill in consequence of inaccurate statements of whatever kind that may be made by rival traders about their own wares. The market in which the action for passing off originated was no place for the mealy mouthed: advertisements are not on affidavit; exaggerated claims by a trader about the quality of his wares, assertions that they are better than those of his rivals, even though he knows this to be untrue, have been permitted by the common law as venial 'puffing' which gives no cause of action to a competitor even though he can show that he has suffered actual damage in his business as a result.

Parliament, however, beginning in the 19th century has progressively intervened in the interests of consumers to impose on traders a higher standard of commercial candour than the legal maxim caveat emptor calls for, by prohibiting under penal sanctions misleading descriptions of the character or quality of goods; but since the class of persons for whose protection the Merchandise Marks Acts 1887 to 1953 and even more rigorous later statutes are designed are not competing traders but those consumers who are likely to be deceived, the Acts do not themselves give rise to any civil action for breach of statutory duty on the part of a competing trader even though he sustains actual damage as a result: *Cutler v Wandsworth Stadium Ltd*[2]; and see *London Armoury Co Ltd v Ever Ready Co (Great Britain) Ltd*[3]. Nevertheless the increasing recognition by Parliament of the need for more rigorous standards of

---

1. (1915) 32 RPC 273.
2. [1949] AC 398.
3. [1941] 1 KB 742; [1941] 1 All ER 364.

commercial honesty is a factor which should not be overlooked by a judge confronted by the choice whether or not to extend by analogy to circumstances in which it has not previously been applied a principle which has been applied in previous cases where the circumstances although different had some features in common with those of the case which he has to decide. Where over a period of years there can be discerned a steady trend in legislation which reflects the view of successive Parliaments as to what the public interest demands in a particular field of law, development of the common law in that part of the same field which has been left to it ought to proceed on a parallel rather than a diverging course.

The Champagne case came before Danckwerts J in two stages: the first[1] on a preliminary point of law, the second[2] on the trial of the action. The assumptions of fact on which the legal argument at the first stage was based were stated by the judge to be[3]:

'(1) The plaintiffs carry on business in a geographical area in France known as Champagne; (2) the plaintiffs' wine is produced in Champagne and from grapes grown in Champagne; (3) the plaintiffs' wine has been known in the trade for a long time as "Champagne" with a high reputation; (4) members of the public or in the trade ordering or seeing wine advertised as "Champagne" would expect to get wine produced in Champagne from grapes grown there and (5) the defendants are producing a wine not produced in that geographical area and are selling it under the name of "Spanish Champagne".'

These findings disclose a factual situation (assuming that damage was thereby caused to the plaintiff's business) which contains each of the five characteristics which I have suggested must be present in order to create a valid cause of action for passing off. The features that distinguished it from all previous cases were (a) that the element in the goodwill of each of the individual plaintiffs that was represented by his ability to use without deception (in addition to his individual house mark) the word 'champagne' to distinguish his wines from sparkling wines not made by the champenois process from grapes produced in the Champagne district of France was not exclusive to himself but was shared with every other shipper of sparkling wine to England whose wines could satisfy the same condition and (b) that the class of traders entitled to a proprietary right in 'the attractive force that brings in custom' represented by the ability without deception to call one's wines 'champagne' was capable of continuing expansion, since it might be joined by any future shipper of wine who was able to satisfy that condition. . . .

. . . [T]he familiar argument that to extend the ambit of an actionable wrong beyond that to which effect has demonstrably been given in the previous cases would open the floodgates or, more ominously, a Pandora's box of litigation leaves me unmoved when it is sought to be applied to the actionable wrong of passing off.

I would hold the Champagne case to have been rightly decided and in doing so would adopt the words of Danckwerts J where he said[4]:

'There seems to be no reason why such licence [sc. to do a deliberate act which causes damage to the property of another person] should be given to a person, competing in trade, who seeks to attach to his product a name or description with which it has no natural association so as to make use of the reputation and goodwill which has been gained by a product genuinely indicated by the name or description. In my view,

---

1. [1960] Ch 262; [1959] 3 All ER 800.
2. [1961] 1 All ER 561; [1961] 1 WLR 277.
3. [1960] Ch 262 at 273; [1959] 3 All ER 800 at 804.
4. [1960] Ch 262 at 284; [1959] 3 All ER 800 at 810-811.

it ought not to matter that the persons truly entitled to describe their goods by the name and description are a class producing goods in a certain locality, and not merely one individual. The description is part of their goodwill and a right of property. I do not believe that the law of passing off, which arose to prevent unfair trading, is so limited in scope.'

In the Champagne case the descriptive term referred to the geographical provenance of the goods, and the class entitled to the goodwill in the term was accordingly restricted to those supplying on the English market goods produced in the locality indicated by it. Something similar was true in the Sherry case where the word 'sherry' as descriptive of a type of wine unless it was accompanied by some qualifying geographical adjective was held to denote wine produced by the solera method in the province of Jerez de la Frontera in Spain and the class entitled to the goodwill in the word was restricted to suppliers on the English market of wine produced in that province. In the Scotch Whisky case the product with which the case was primarily concerned was blended whisky and the class entitled to the goodwill in the descriptive term 'Scotch whisky' was not restricted to traders who dealt in whisky that had been blended in Scotland but extended to suppliers of blended whisky wherever the blending process took place provided that the ingredients of their product consisted exclusively of whiskies that had been distilled in Scotland. But the fact that in each of these first three cases the descriptive name under which goods of a particular type or composition were marketed by the plaintiffs among others happened to have geographical connotations is in my view without significance. If a product of a particular character or composition has been marketed under a descriptive name and under that name has gained a public reputation which distinguishes it from competing products of different composition, I can see no reason in principle or logic why the goodwill in the name of those entitled to make use of it should be protected by the law against deceptive use of the name by competitors, if it denotes a product of which the ingredients come from a particular locality, but should lose that protection if the ingredients of the product, however narrowly identified, are not restricted as to their geographical provenance. . . .

. . . [O]n the findings of fact by Goulding J to which I referred at the beginning of this speech, the type of product that has gained for the name 'advocaat' on the English market the reputation and goodwill of which Keelings are seeking to take advantage by misrepresenting that their own product is of that type is defined by reference to the nature of its ingredients irrespective of their origin. The class of traders of whose respective businesses the right to describe their products as advocaat forms a valuable part of their goodwill are those who have supplied and are supplying on the English market an egg and spirit drink in broad conformity with an identifiable recipe. The members of that class are easily identified and very much fewer in number than in the Champagne, Sherry or Scotch Whisky cases. Warnink with 75 per cent of the trade have a very substantial stake in the goodwill of the name 'advocaat' and their business has been showed to have suffered serious injury as a result of Keelings putting on the English market in competition with Warnink and at a cheaper price an egg and wine based drink which they miscall advocaat instead of egg-flip which is its proper name.

My Lords, all the five characteristics that I have earlier suggested must be present to create a valid cause of action in passing off today were present in the instant case. Prima facie, as the law stands today, I think the presence of those characteristics is enough, unless there is also present in the case some exceptional feature which justifies, on grounds of public policy, withholding from a person who has suffered injury in consequence of the deception practised on prospective customers or consumers of his product a remedy in law against the deceiver. On the facts found by the judge, and I stress their importance, I can find no such exceptional feature in the instant case.

I would allow this appeal and restore the injunction granted by Goulding J.

[LORD FRASER OF TULLYBELTON delivered a speech in favour of allowing the appeal and restoring the order made by Goulding J. VISCOUNT DILHORNE, LORD SALMON and LORD SCARMAN agreed with both speeches.]

Appeal allowed

Notes

1. In *Reckitt & Colman Products Ltd v Borden Inc* [1990] 1 All ER 873 at 888, Lord Oliver said that 'the essence of the action for passing off is a deceit practised on the public and it can be no answer, in a case where it is demonstrable that the public has been or will be deceived, that they would not have been if they had been more careful, more literate or more perspicacious.'

2. In addition to the common law tort of passing-off, it is possible by registering a trade mark in respect of any specification of goods or services, under the Trade Marks Act 1938, as amended by the Trade Marks (Amendment) Act 1984, to prevent the infringement of the right to use that trade mark within the specification. The registered proprietor may prevent its use by others even in ways that involve no passing-off. The remedies are:
(a) an injunction restraining infringement;
(b) damages or alternatively an account of profits; and
(c) an order for delivery up of the infringing articles or otherwise rendering them innocuous.
For detailed discussion see *Clerk & Lindsell*, chap. 30.

3. The study of this subject and the related fields of patents and copyright belongs to specialist works on intellectual property. But a point of general interest is the relationship between this tort and the tort of negligence. Proof of an intention to deceive is not essential and, as Lord Diplock's definition (p. 734, ante) shows, the damage must be a reasonably foreseeable consequence of the misrepresentation. Is this different from a duty of care? There may even be circumstances in which a third person, such as a printer of labels, who facilitates a passing-off without actual knowledge is liable in negligence. This would be rare because 'if a person approaches a printer and asks him to carry out certain work, there must be some limit to the extent to which the printer should be expected to, so to speak, look over his shoulder and consider whether or not the material when printed might be used by the customer for passing-off his goods as another's': per Robert Goff LJ in *Paterson Zochonis & Co Ltd v Merfarken Packaging Ltd* [1986] 3 All ER 522 at 542.

4. A more generalised tort of unfair competition has not developed in England. In *Cadbury-Schweppes Pty Ltd v Pub Squash Co Pty Ltd* [1981] 1 All ER 213; [1981] 1 WLR 193, noted by G. Dworkin (1981) 44 MLR 564, a claim of unfair competition was raised but not pursued before the Privy Council where the defendant was alleged to have deliberately exploited the plaintiffs' advertising campaign so as to secure a share of a market created by the plaintiffs. In *Associated Newspapers Group plc v Insert Media Ltd* [1988] 2 All ER 420; [1988] 1 WLR 509, the defendants were inserting leaflets into the plaintiffs' newspapers without the latter's approval. An interlocutory injunction pending trial was granted on grounds that there was a

serious issue to be tried as to passing-off. However, Hoffmann J held, as a matter of law, that an allegation of unfair competition by debasing or devaluing the plaintiffs' goods was not actionable. In *Moorgate Tobacco Co Ltd v Philip Morris Ltd* (1985) 56 ALR 193 the High Court of Australia held that there was no general tort of unfair competition known to the law of Australia, but Deane J (with whose judgment Gibbs CJ, Moran, Wilson and Dawson JJ agreed) said (at p. 214) that this did 'not involve a denial of the desirability of adopting a flexible approach to traditional forms of action . . . to meet new situations and circumstances'. One example he gave was the adaptation of the doctrine of passing-off as happened in *Henderson v Radio Corpn Pty Ltd* (1960) SR NSW 576 where a well-known professional dancing partnership obtained an injunction to restrain the sale or distribution of a gramophone record cover which had as its background a photograph of them dancing, although their names did not appear on the cover. See generally W. R. Cornish (1972) 12 JSPTL (NS) 126; V. L. Knight (1978) 53 Tulane LR 164; G. Dworkin [1979] EIPR 241; T. Frazer (1983) 99 LQR 281; J. Adams [1985] JBL 26; S. Naresh [1986] CLJ 97.

16 Interests in reputation – defamation

The tort of defamation protects interests in reputation. It consists in the *publication* to a third person of matter 'containing an untrue imputation against the *reputation* of another' (*Gatley on Libel and Slander*, 8th edn (London, 1981), para. 3). Since reputation is one's estimation in the eyes of others, the element of publication is essential. Pride, self-respect and dignity may be affronted by a communication to the person defamed: but without publication to a third person there is no hurt to reputation and hence no wrong of defamation. This distinguishes defamation from the Roman law of *injuria*, which, in modified form, exists in most civil law countries, and which protects *dignitas*. It also distinguishes the tort of defamation from criminal libel, for which there may be a prosecution, in respect of a serious written defamation, without proof of publication to a third person. Another distinction is that in criminal proceedings truth is not a defence unless the defendant also proves that publication was for the public benefit. Moreover, criminal libel, unlike the civil wrong, may possibly extend to defamation of the dead, and also to incitement of public hatred against a class of people. (The Law Commission in its report on *Criminal Libel* in September 1985 (Law Com. No. 149, Cmnd. 9618) has proposed a new and more limited offence of criminal defamation to punish those who intentionally publish defamatory statements knowing or believing the statements to be untrue and seriously defamatory.)

Reputation may include a business reputation; but defamation is distinct from the tort of malicious falsehood considered p. 760, post, because the latter is committed even if reputation is not besmirched (for a comparison of the torts see *Duncan and Neill on Defamation*, 2nd edn (London, 1983), p. 3). In order to succeed in an action for defamation the plaintiff must prove: (1) that the statement was defamatory; (2) that it referred to him (p. 745, post); (3) that the defendant published it to a third person (p. 764, post); and (4) (in a few cases) that damage resulted to him. Damage is presumed to flow from the publication of defamatory matter in permanent form or by broadcast (this is called libel); but if it is in the transitory form (called slander) damage must be proved, unless it falls within certain specified categories (p. 744, post).

Since the tort of defamation limits freedom of speech, many safeguards for that freedom have been built into the legal requirements. The first of these is trial by jury. The defendant's right to this *may* be taken away only if the trial requires 'any prolonged examination of documents or accounts or any scientific or local investigation which cannot conveniently be made with a jury' (*Goldsmith v Pressdram Ltd* [1987] 3 All ER 485; [1988] 1 WLR 64n; *Viscount De L'Isle v Times Newspapers Ltd* [1987] 3 All ER 499; [1988] 1

739

WLR 49) or the probable length of the trial makes the action one which cannot conveniently be tried with a jury (Supreme Court Act 1981, s. 69). Secondly, the courts at common law might not allow the issue of a writ in an action for libel to stifle further comment on the matter in issue by treating it as contempt of court (see *Borrie & Lowe's Law of Contempt*, 2nd edn (London, 1983), pp. 135–138 and consider also the Contempt of Court Act 1981). Thirdly, the courts will not restrain the threatened publication of a defamatory statement by interlocutory injunction if there is any doubt as to whether the words are defamatory, or if the defendant swears that he intends to justify the words, or, if the occasion is a privileged one, unless it is shown that the defendant maliciously and dishonestly proposes to publish information which he knows to be untrue or that the material is being published in pursuance of a conspiracy which has the sole or predominant purpose of injuring the plaintiff (*Gulf Oil (GB) Ltd v Page* [1987] Ch 327; [1987] 3 All ER 14). Finally the defendant may, at the trial, prove any of a number of defences: (1) justification, i.e. truth (p. 767, post); (2) fair comment on a matter of public interest (p. 770, post); (3) privilege, which may be (a) absolute, or (b) qualified (p. 774, post). The plaintiff may defeat the defences of fair comment or qualified privilege by proving 'malice', a concept which here includes dishonesty, the introduction of extraneous matter, and ulterior purposes. (The word 'malicious' also appears in the plaintiff's allegation that the defendant 'maliciously' published the defamatory statement; but there it is mere verbiage.) Apology is no defence at common law, although it may reduce the damages. Section 2 of the Libel Act 1843, as amended by the Libel Act 1845 (p. 789, post), introduced a little-used and limited defence of apology and payment of money by way of amends. The conduct of the parties will affect damages: if the plaintiff has a bad reputation his damages may be reduced even down to the 'smallest coin in the realm' (p. 795, post); if the defendant's conduct has been calculated to make a profit for himself which might well exceed the compensation payable to the plaintiff as damages, then exemplary damages may be awarded (p. 790, post). An action for libel or slander must be commenced within three years from the date on which the cause of action accrued. Where the relevant facts did not become known to the plaintiff until after the expiration of this period, the action may be brought, with the leave of the High Court, at any time before the expiration of one year from the earliest date on which the plaintiff knew all the relevant facts (Administration of Justice Act 1985, s. 57).

The publication of untruths is sometimes treated as an invasion of 'privacy'; but, as the Younger Committee on Privacy (Cmnd. 5012, 1972) pointed out, the concepts of defamation and privacy need to be kept separate lest the safeguards for freedom of speech built into the defamation action be lost in a wide and vague proposed tort of invasion of privacy (p. 795, post). A right to privacy in respect of information must also be distinguished from the protection of confidence (p. 801, post); in respect of the latter the Law Commission has proposed the creation of a statutory tort of breach of confidence (p. 801, post). It is worth considering just what 'privacy' means, how far the existing law protects this interest, and what could be done in the future, although the Calcutt Committee on Privacy and Related Matters (Cm. 1102, 1990), like the majority of the Younger Committee before it, has recommended that a statutory tort of infringement of privacy should not presently be introduced (p. 797, post).

1 The distinction between libel and slander

Monson *v* Tussauds Ltd Court of Appeal [1891-4] All ER Rep 1051

The plaintiff had been tried in Scotland upon a charge of having murdered a young man named Hambrough by shooting him with a gun at a place called Ardlamont. The defence to the charge was that Hambrough was killed by the accidental discharge of his own gun. The jury returned a verdict of 'not proven'. Shortly after the trial the defendants, who were the proprietors of an exhibition in London, consisting mainly of wax figures of celebrated and notorious personages, placed in their exhibition a portrait model of the plaintiff, bearing his name, with a gun close by described as his gun. The model was displayed in a room containing figures of Napoleon I, a convicted murderer, a suicide, and another person charged in connection with the alleged Ardlamont murder. This room gave access to the Chamber of Horrors. The plaintiff applied for an interim injunction restraining the exhibition of his effigy until the trial of an action for libel. The Court of Appeal (reversing the decision of a Divisional Court) held that an interlocutory injunction ought not to be granted.

LOPES LJ: . . . Libels are generally in writing or printing, but this is not necessary; the defamatory matter may be conveyed in some other permanent form. For instance, a statue, a caricature, an effigy, chalk marks on a wall, signs, or pictures may constitute a libel. The plaintiff's case, therefore, is libel, and the application for an interlocutory injunction must be determined upon the principles which are applicable to the granting of injunctions in cases of libel. . . .

The matter of restraining libels on interlocutory motions for injunction was thought of such importance that the question was, in *Bonnard v Perryman*,[1] argued before the full Court of Appeal, and Lord Coleridge, in delivering the considered judgment of the court, said:

'We entirely approve of, and desire to adopt as our own, the language of Lord Esher in *William Coulson & Sons v James Coulson & Co*[2]:

"To justify the court in granting an interim injunction it must come to a decision upon the question of libel or not. Therefore the jurisdiction was of a delicate nature. It ought only to be exercised in the clearest cases, where any jury would say that the matter complained of was libellous, and where, if the jury did not so find, the court would set aside the verdict as unreasonable."'

I cannot help thinking that a principle was laid down in that case applicable to all libels without a limitation. . . .

[LORD HALSBURY and DAVEY LJ delivered speeches in favour of allowing the appeal.]

Youssoupoff *v* Metro-Goldwyn-Mayer Pictures Ltd Court of Appeal (1934) 50 TLR 581

The plaintiff claimed damages for an alleged libel which she said was contained in a sound film entitled *Rasputin, the Mad Monk*, alleging that the defendants had

---

1. [1891] 2 Ch 269.
2. (1887) 3 TLR 846.

published in the film pictures and words which were understood to mean that she, therein called 'Princess Natasha', had been seduced by Rasputin. The jury returned a verdict in favour of the plaintiff and awarded her £25,000 damages. The defendants unsuccessfully appealed to the Court of Appeal.

SLESSER LJ: This action is one of libel and raises at the outset an interesting and difficult problem which, I believe, to be a novel problem, whether the product of the combined photographic and talking instrument which produces these modern films does, if it throws upon the screen and impresses upon the ear defamatory matter, produce that which can be complained of as libel or as slander.

In my view, this action, as I have said, was properly framed in libel. There can be no doubt that, so far as the photographic part of the exhibition is concerned, that is a permanent matter to be seen by the eye, and is the proper subject of an action for libel, if defamatory. I regard the speech which is synchronized with the photographic reproduction and forms part of one complex, common exhibition as an ancillary circumstance, part of the surroundings explaining that which is to be seen. . . .

[SCRUTTON and GREER LJJ delivered speeches in favour of dismissing the appeal.]

Question

Does Slesser LJ's reasoning mean that the *vision* constituted the libel? If so, does this imply that a gramophone record or other sound recording would only be a slander? Is sky-writing by an aeroplane, or flag signals at sea, capable of giving rise to a libel?

Note

For the fascinating background to this case see H. Montgomery Hyde, *Sir Patrick Hastings* (London, 1960), pp. 274–283, and for the historical background of the distinction between libel and slander see the Report of the Faulks Committee, Cmnd. 5909, 1975, App. VI, and R. Helmholz (1987) 103 LQR 624; see generally J. M. Kaye (1975) 91 LQR 524.

The Defamation Act 1952

16. Interpretation. – (1) Any reference in this Act to words shall be construed as including a reference to pictures, visual images, gestures and other methods of signifying meaning.

(2) The provisions of Part III of the Schedule to this Act shall have effect for the purposes of the interpretation of that Schedule.

The Broadcasting Act 1990

166. Defamatory material. – (1) For the purposes of the law of libel and slander (including the law of criminal libel so far as it relates to the publication of defamatory matter) the publication of words in the course of any programme included in a programme service[1] shall be treated as publication in permanent form.

---

1. [Defined in s. 201.]

The Theatres Act 1968

4. Amendment of law of defamation. — (1) For the purposes of the law of libel and slander (including the law of criminal libel so far as it relates to the publication of defamatory matter) the publication of words in the course of a performance of a play shall, subject to section 7 of this Act, be treated as publication in permanent form.

(2) The foregoing subsection shall apply for the purposes of section 3[1] (slander of title, etc.) of the Defamation Act 1952 as it applies for the purposes of the law of libel and slander.

(3) In this section 'words' includes pictures, visual images, gestures and other methods of signifying meaning.

7. Exceptions for performances given in certain circumstances. — (1) Nothing in sections 2 to 4 of this Act shall apply in relation to a performance of a play given on a domestic occasion in a private dwelling.

(2) Nothing in sections 2 to 6 of this Act shall apply in relation to a performance of a play given solely or primarily for one or more of the following purposes, that is to say —

(a) rehearsal; or

(b) to enable —
   (i) a record or cinematograph film to be made from or by means of the performance; or
   (ii) the performance to be broadcast; or
   (iii) the performance to be [included in a cable programme service which is or does not require to be licensed][2];

but in any proceedings for an offence under section 2, . . .[3] or 6 of this Act alleged to have been committed in respect of a performance of a play or an offence at common law alleged to have been committed in England and Wales by the publication of defamatory matter in the course of a performance of a play, if it is proved that the performance was attended by persons other than persons directly connected with the giving of the performance or the doing in relation thereto of any of the things mentioned in paragraph (b) above, the performance shall be taken not to have been given solely or primarily for one or more of the said purposes unless the contrary is shown.

(3) In this section —

'broadcast' means broadcast by wireless telegraphy (within the meaning of the Wireless Telegraphy Act 1949), whether by way of sound broadcasting or television;

'cinematograph film' means any print, negative, tape or other article on which a performance of a play or any part of such a performance is recorded for the purposes of visual reproduction;

'record' means any record or similar contrivance for reproducing sound, including the sound-track of a cinematograph film;
. . .[4]

Gray v Jones King's Bench Division [1939] 1 All ER 798

The plaintiff brought an action for slander, alleging that the defendant had said of him: 'You are a convicted person. I will not have you here. You have a conviction.'

---

1. [See p. 761, post.]
2. [Inserted by the Cable and Broadcasting Act 1984, s. 57, Sch. 5, para. 21.]
3. [Amended by the Public Order Act 1986, s. 40(3), Sch. 3.]
4. [Amended by the Cable and Broadcasting Act 1984, s. 57, Sch. 5, para. 21, Sch. 6.]

The defendant submitted that the words were not capable of being actionable without proof of special damage. It was held that the words were actionable per se and judgment was given for the plaintiff.

ATKINSON J: ... The argument for the defendant is that the true view is that the reason why words imputing a crime are actionable is that the plaintiff is put in jeopardy of a criminal prosecution, and, therefore, if the words merely imply that the plaintiff has been guilty of a criminal offence, and has been convicted, and it is a thing of the past, then it is not actionable without proof of special damage, because the plaintiff is not put in jeopardy. That raises the question as to the real basis of the action. What is the real ground upon which a plaintiff may bring an action for such defamation without proof of special damage? Is it because the misconduct alleged is of so serious a character that the law visits it with punishment, and is therefore so likely to cause other people to shun the person defamed, and to exclude him from society, that damage is presumed? Or is the basis the fact he is put in jeopardy? In my opinion, the former view is the sound one. ...

Notes

1. In *D and L Caterers Ltd and Jackson v D'Anjou* [1945] KB 364; [1945] 1 All ER 563 the Court of Appeal left open the question whether a company can sue without proof of special damage for a slander imputing an offence punishable, had it been committed by an individual, with imprisonment.

2. *Gray v Jones* illustrates one of the four categories of slander actionable per se. The other three are:

(a) words imputing that the plaintiff is suffering from a contagious or infectious disease (e.g. *Bloodworth v Gray* (1844) 7 Man & G 334: 'He has got that damned pox [meaning the French pox otherwise known as venereal disease] from going to that woman on the Derby Road.' £50 damages awarded without proof of special damage).

(b) words imputing unchastity or adultery to any woman or girl (Slander of Women Act 1891, post); in *Youssoupoff v Metro-Goldwyn-Mayer Pictures Ltd* (p. 741, ante). Avory J, with whom Scrutton LJ agreed, said, obiter, that an allegation that a woman had been raped would fall into this category.

(c) words calculated to disparage the plaintiff in any office, profession, calling, trade or business, held or carried on by him at the time of publication (Defamation Act 1952, s. 2, post).

3. A committee of the House of Lords in 1843 and the Faulks Committee on Defamation, para. 91, in 1975, recommended the abolition of the distinction between libel and slander.

The Slander of Women Act 1891

1. Amendment of law. — Words spoken and published ... which impute unchastity or adultery to any woman or girl shall not require special damage to render them actionable.

Provided always, that in any action for words spoken and made actionable by this Act, a plaintiff shall not recover more costs than damages, unless the judge shall certify that there was reasonable ground for bringing the action.

The Defamation Act 1952

2. Slander affecting official, professional or business reputation. — In an action for slander in respect of words calculated to disparage the plaintiff in any office, profession, calling, trade or business held or carried on by him at the time of the publication, it shall not be necessary to allege or prove special damage, whether or not the words are spoken of the plaintiff in the way of his office, profession, calling, trade or business.

2   Words or matter defamatory of the plaintiff

Sim *v* Stretch House of Lords [1936] 2 All ER 1237

The defendant sent to the plaintiff a telegram concerning a housemaid who had left the plaintiff's employment and was then in the service of the defendant. The relevant part read: 'Edith resumed her service with us today. Please send her possessions and the money you borrowed also her wages to Old Barton — Sim.' The plaintiff claimed damages for libel alleging that these words were defamatory and further that by them the defendant meant and was understood to mean that the plaintiff was in pecuniary difficulties, that by reason thereof he had borrowed money from his housemaid, that he had failed to pay her wages, and that he was a person to whom no one ought to give any credit. At the trial of the action before Talbot J and a common jury judgment was given for the plaintiff who was awarded £250 damages. The defendant appealed unsuccessfully to the Court of Appeal, but his appeal to the House of Lords was upheld on the ground that the words were not reasonably capable of a defamatory meaning.

LORD ATKIN: . . . The question, then, is whether the words in their ordinary significa-   ✱ tion are capable of being defamatory. Judges and textbook writers alike have found difficulty in defining with precision the word 'defamatory'. The conventional phrase exposing the plaintiff to hatred, ridicule and contempt is probably too narrow. The question is complicated by having to consider the person or class of persons whose reaction to the publication is the test of the wrongful character of the words used. I do not intend to ask your Lordships to lay down a formal definition, but after collating the opinions of many authorities I propose in the present case the test: would the words tend to lower the plaintiff in the estimation of right-thinking members of society generally? Assuming such to be the test of whether words are defamatory or not there is no dispute as to the relative functions of judge and jury, of law and fact. It is well settled that the judge must decide whether the words are capable of a defamatory meaning. That is a question of law: is there evidence of a tort? If they are capable, then the jury is to decide whether they are in fact defamatory. Now, in the present case it is material to notice that there is no evidence that the words were published to anyone who had any knowledge at all of any of the facts that I have narrated above. There is no direct evidence that they were published to anyone who had ever heard of the plaintiff. The post office officials at Maidenhead would not be presumed to know him, and we are left without any information as to the officials at Cookham Dean. The plaintiff and his wife dealt at the shop at which was the sub-post office, but there is no evidence that the shopkeeper was the telegraph clerk; the probability is that he was not. It might, however, be inferred that the publication of the telegram at Cookham Dean was to someone who knew the plaintiff. What would he or she learn by reading the telegram? That Edith Saville had been in the plaintiff's employment; that she had that day entered the defendant's employment; and that the former employer was requested to send on to the new place of employment the servant's possessions together with the money due to her for money borrowed and for wages. How could perusal of that communication tend to lower the plaintiff in the estimation of the right-thinking peruser who knows nothing of the circumstances but what he or she derives from the telegram itself. . . .

[LORD RUSSELL OF KILLOWEN and LORD MACMILLAN concurred in allowing the appeal.]

Byrne *v* Deane Court of Appeal [1937] 2 All ER 204

Automatic gambling machines, known as 'diddler' machines, had been kept by the defendants upon golf club premises since 1932 for the use of members of the club. Someone gave information to the police as to the existence of these machines on the club premises which led the police to require the removal of the machines. The day after the machines had been removed someone put upon the wall of the club against which the automatic machines had formerly stood a typewritten paper containing the following lampoon:
    'For many years upon this spot
    You heard the sound of a merry bell
    Those who were rash and those who were not
    Lost and made a spot of cash
    But he who gave the game away
    May he byrnne in hell and rue the day'
    Diddleramus
The plaintiff brought an action for libel, alleging that by these words the defendants meant and were understood to mean that the plaintiff had reported to the police the presence of the machines upon the premises, that he was guilty of underhand disloyalty to the defendants and his fellow members of the club, that his conduct was deserving of the gravest censure, that he was a person devoid of all true sporting spirit, and further that he was a person unfit for other members of the club to associate with and should be ostracised by them. Hilbery J held that the words were defamatory of the plaintiff and awarded 40 shillings damages and costs. On appeal, all members of the Court held that it was not defamatory of a man to say that he has informed the police of a crime. Slesser and Greene LJJ held that the words in this case were not defamatory, but Greer LJ held that they were defamatory because they meant something more than that the police had been informed of a crime, namely that he had been guilty of disloyalty.

SLESSER LJ: . . . In my view, to allege of a man—and for this purpose it does not matter whether the allegation is true or is not true—that he has reported certain acts, wrongful in law, to the police, cannot possibly be said to be defamatory of him in the minds of the general public. We have to consider in this connection the *arbitrium boni*, the view which would be taken by the ordinary good and worthy subject of the King (to quote the matter which appears in the old declarations), and I have assigned to myself no other criterion than what a good and worthy subject of the King would think of some person of whom it had been said that he had put the law into motion against wrongdoers, in thinking that such a good and worthy subject would not consider such an allegation in itself to be defamatory. That is the view taken by McCardie J in *Myroft v Sleight*[1] at 884, where he quotes with approval a judgment of the Irish court in *Mawe v Piggott*[2] at 62, where Lawson J giving the judgment of the court says:

---

1. (1920) 90 LJKB 883.
2. (1869) IR 4 CL 54.

'[Counsel for the plaintiff], however, argued that amongst certain classes who were either themselves criminal, or who sympathised with crime, it would expose a person to great odium to represent him as an informer or a prosecutor, or otherwise aiding in the detection of crime; that is quite true, but we cannot be called upon to adopt that standard. The very circumstances which will make a person be regarded with disfavour by the criminal classes will raise his character in the estimation of right-thinking men. We can only regard the estimation in which a man is held by society generally . . .'

Notes

1. The views of the 'ordinary good and worthy subject of the King' are obviously subject to change. At the time of Charles II it was defamatory to call a person a Papist (*Row v Clargis* (1683) T Raym 482); during the First World War it was defamatory to describe a firm as German (*Slazengers Ltd v Gibbs & Co* (1916) 33 TLR 35); in 1964 it was thought, by Lord Denning MR, to be defamatory to call a man with an English name a Czech, if that implied communist sympathies which made him disloyal (*Linklater v Daily Telegraph Ltd* (1964) 108 Sol Jo 992); in 1981 it was defamatory to say that a person had insulted the Muslim faith (*Shaw v Akram* [1981] LS Gaz R 814). But 'would it be libellous to write of a lady of fashion that she had been seen on the top of an omnibus?' Even when Pollock CB asked this question (in *Clay v Roberts* (1863) 8 LT 397 at 398) the answer given was in the negative. An imputation of deviationism is not defamatory unless it carries with it an allegation of hypocrisy. Nor is a light-hearted comment likely to be construed as defamatory. In 1985 a High Court jury decided that it was not defamatory to compare someone, in a sketch of political life, with Sue-Ellen, a promiscuous alcoholic character of the television soap opera *Dallas*: *The Times*, 2nd February, 1985, p. 1.

2. In *Youssoupoff v Metro-Goldwyn-Mayer Pictures Ltd* (p. 741, ante), Scrutton LJ preferred the formula that defamation is a statement to a person's *discredit*. Does a statement that a woman has been raped fall within this formula, as the learned judge seemed to believe? Or does it evoke *pity*, which, so far, forms no part of the judicial definition? (See p. 748, post.)

3. The test of defamation in *Sim v Stretch* may be compared with the traditional test whether the words bring the plaintiff into 'hatred, ridicule or contempt'. The question of 'ridicule' is clearly one of degree; e.g. in *Emerson v Grimsby Times and Telegraph Co Ltd* (1926) 42 TLR 238 a newspaper published an account of the plaintiff's wedding the day before it took place and, as a result, he was subjected to ridicule. The Court of Appeal treated this as simply a feeble joke and not defamatory.

4. The Faulks Committee, para. 64, proposed that there should be a statutory definition stating: 'Defamation shall consist of the publication to a third person of matter which in all the circumstances would be likely to affect a person adversely in the estimation of reasonable people generally.' Would this lead to any different conclusion in the above cases?

Tolley *v* Fry & Sons Ltd House of Lords [1931] All ER Rep 131

In this action for libel Acton J and a common jury returned a verdict in favour of the plaintiff and awarded him £1,000 damages. The Court of Appeal by a majority held that the trial judge ought to have withdrawn the case from the jury on the ground that the document complained of as a libel was not reasonably capable of a defamatory meaning and ordered judgment to be entered for the defendants. All the Lords Justices were further of the opinion that in any event there should be a new trial on the ground that the damages were excessive. The plaintiff appealed on the first point. The House of Lords (Lord Blanesburgh dissenting) held that the document was capable of a defamatory meaning, and the new trial would be limited to the assessment of damages. The facts appear from the speech of Lord Hailsham.

LORD HAILSHAM: The plaintiff in this case is a well-known amateur golfer. The defendants are manufacturers of chocolate in various forms. In June 1928, the defendants published in the 'Daily Sketch' and 'Daily Mail', newspapers enjoying a large circulation in London and the provinces, a caricature of the plaintiff which represented him in golfing costume having just completed a drive, with a packet of the defendants' chocolate protruding from his pocket, in the company of a caddie who is holding up packets of the defendants' chocolate, and below the caricature was a limerick in the following terms:

'The caddie to Tolley said: "Oh, Sir!
Good shot, Sir! That ball, see it go, Sir.
    My word, how it flies,
    Like a Cartet of Fry's.
They're handy, they're good, and priced low, Sir."'

The caricature and the limerick were surrounded with descriptions of the merits of the defendants' chocolates, and the whole was plainly an advertisement of the defendants' goods.

The plaintiff thereupon brought this action for damages for libel. He did not complain of the caricature or the words as being defamatory in themselves; but the innuendo alleged that the

'defendants meant and were understood to mean that the plaintiff had agreed or permitted his portrait to be exhibited for the purpose of the advertisement of the defendants' chocolate, that he had done so for gain and reward, that he had prostituted his reputation as an amateur golf player for advertising purposes, that he was seeking notoriety and gain by the means aforesaid, and that he had been guilty of conduct unworthy of his status as an amateur golfer. . . .'

LORD DUNEDIN: The sole question raised by this appeal is whether the case ought to have been withdrawn from the jury by the judge, and judgment entered for the defendants. It has been stated again and again, and is not in dispute, that the question for the judge is whether the writing or publication complained of is capable of a libellous meaning. It is for the jury, if the judge so rules, to say whether it has that meaning.

The most authoritative pronouncement on actions of this sort, because it is a judgment of this House, is to be found in *Capital and Counties Bank v Henty*.[1] Both parties in this case have appealed to it as an authority in their favour. I think the ruling canon in that case is to be found in the judgment of Lord Selborne LC. That was a case where, as here, the mere words used were not libellous. But Lord Selborne then proceeded to inquire what were the circumstances in which the document was published. In that case he held the circumstances did not and could not lead to any libellous imputation. The circular was directed to Henty's customers alone, and there

---

1. (1882) 7 App Cas 741.

were quite innocent reasons which would justify the circular. But he pointedly said that if the circumstances had been otherwise, if the circular had been placarded up or published to the world at large the effect might have been quite otherwise. Now, applying this method of reasoning to the present case, I find that the caricature of the plaintiff, innocent itself as a caricature, is so to speak embedded in an advertisement. It is held out as part of an advertisement so that its presence there gives rise to speculation as to how it got there, or in other words provokes in the mind of the public an inference as to how and why the plaintiff's picture, caricatured as it was, became associated with a commercial advertisement. The inference that is suggested is that the consent was given, either gratuitously or for a consideration, to its appearance. Then it is said, and evidence on that point was given and not cross-examined to, that, if that were so, the status of the plaintiff as an amateur golfer would be called in question. It seems to me that all this is within the province of a jury to determine. The idea of the inference in the circumstances is not so extravagant as to compel a judge to say it was so beside the mark that no jury ought to be allowed to consider it.

I come to this conclusion on a consideration of the advertisement alone, explained with the evidence of the golf players and the golf secretary. There are here two separate propositions: (i) Would the caricature associated with the advertisement admit of a reasonable inference that the plaintiff had assented to be so depicted? That depends on the view taken of the picture, of its surroundings, and of its use. (ii) If that inference were drawn, would it be deleterious to the plaintiff's position as an amateur golfer, and do him harm? That depends on the evidence of the golfers. A great deal of argument was directed to the terms of [a] letter of 4 June. . . . I do not consider that to be material to the question before us. It may well have influenced the jury in coming to the verdict they did, for, to my mind, it shows clearly that the general proposition that amateur status might be called in question by association of an amateur with an advertisement was well before the eyes of the defendants and their advisers. But we are not concerned at present with the justice of the verdict, only with the question of whether there was a case for the jury to consider. I agree with the motion proposed.

[LORD BUCKMASTER and LORD TOMLIN delivered speeches in favour of allowing the appeal. LORD BLANESBURGH delivered a speech in favour of dismissing the appeal.]

Question

Would Tolley have had a cause of action in English law had he been a professional golfer? (See further *Williams v Reason* [1988] 1 All ER 262; [1988] 1 WLR 96, in which an amateur Welsh international rugby player was awarded £20,000 damages for an allegation of 'shamateurism' although a new trial was then ordered on procedural grounds.)

Note

This case has been said to be 'the nearest the law of defamation ever came to protecting "privacy" as such' (Report of the Committee on Privacy, Cmnd. 5012, 1972, App. 1, para. 5, and see p. 795, post; cf. S. Stoljar (1984) 4 LS 67 at 85). In the United States, on the contrary, a tort of putting a person in a 'false light' has been recognised. This makes it actionable to attribute to the plaintiff some opinion or utterance or to include a well-known person, without his consent, in a popularity contest or to use his photograph in a book or article with which he has no connection. However, in England, the Faulks Committee, para. 69, has endorsed the views of the Younger Committee

on Privacy (p. 795, post) that there should be no extension of the definition
of defamation to include 'placing in a false light'. Statutory protection exists,
in the Copyright, Designs and Patents Act 1988, s. 80, for the author of a
copyright literary, dramatic, musical or artistic work and for the director of
a copyright film not to have his work subjected to 'derogatory treatment'.
This is defined to cover the distortion or mutilation of the work or other
treatment which is prejudicial to the honour or reputation of the author or
director. Section 84 of the Act gives protection against false attribution of
authorship (a right which, unlike defamation, survives until 20 years after
death).

Cassidy v Daily Mirror Newspapers Ltd Court of Appeal [1929] All ER Rep 117

The plaintiff, Mrs Mildred Anna Cassidy, was and was generally known as the lawful
wife of one Kettering Edward Cassidy, who was also known as Michael Dennis
Corrigan, an owner of race horses and at one time reputed to be a general in the
Mexican Army. The plaintiff and her husband did not live together but he occasionally stayed with her at her flat. She brought an action for libel against the defendants alleging that they had printed and published in the Daily Mirror newspaper a
photograph of K. E. Cassidy and a woman whose name was not mentioned at the
trial, but who was referred to as Miss X, under a heading 'Today's gossip. News and
views about men, women, and affairs in general.' Under the photograph were the
words: 'Mr M. Corrigan, the race horse owner and Miss X, whose engagement has
been announced.' The plaintiff alleged that she had suffered damage through the
above publication inasmuch as it was intended, and by several people understood,
to mean that K. E. Cassidy was not the plaintiff's husband but was living with her
in immoral cohabitation.

McCardie J held that in the circumstances the publication was capable of conveying a meaning defamatory of the plaintiff. He directed the jury that if the publication
conveyed to reasonably minded people who knew the circumstances an aspersion on
the moral character of the plaintiff their verdict should be for the plaintiff. The jury
returned a verdict for the plaintiff of £500. The defendants appealed. The Court of
Appeal, by a majority, held that the publication was capable of conveying a meaning
defamatory of the plaintiff and dismissed the appeal.

SCRUTTON LJ: . . . In my view, the words published were capable of the meaning:
'Corrigan is a single man,' and were published to people who knew the plaintiff pro-
fessed to be married to Corrigan; it was for the jury to say whether those people could
reasonably draw the inference that the so-called Mrs Corrigan was in fact living in
immoral cohabitation with Corrigan, and I do not think their finding should be
interfered with. . . .

RUSSELL LJ: . . . Liability for libel does not depend on the intention of the defamer,
but on the fact of defamation. If you once reach the conclusion that the published
matter in the present case amounts to or involves a statement that Mr Corrigan is an
unmarried man, then, in my opinion, those persons who knew the circumstances
might reasonably consider the statement defamatory of the plaintiff. The statement
being capable of a meaning defamatory to the plaintiff, it was for the jury, upon the
evidence adduced, to decide whether the plaintiff had been libelled or not.

It was said that it would be a great hardship on the defendants if they were made
liable in consequence of a statement, innocent on its face and published by them in
good faith. The answer to this appeal for sympathy seems to be to point out that,
in stating to the world that Mr Corrigan was an unmarried man—for that construction

is the foundation of their liability—they in fact stated that which was false. From a business angle, no doubt, it may pay them not to spend time or money in making inquiries or verifying statements before publication; but if they had not made a false statement they would not now be suffering in damages. They are paying a price for their methods of business. . . .

[GREER LJ delivered a judgment in favour of allowing the appeal.]

Lewis *v* Daily Telegraph Ltd House of Lords [1963] 2 All ER 151

The Daily Telegraph newspaper published a paragraph headed 'Inquiry on firm by City Police' and the Daily Mail one headed 'Fraud Squad probe Firm', the gist of these paragraphs being that the City Fraud Squad was inquiring into the firm's affairs, and identifying the firm and its chairman, Mr Lewis. In actions for libel by Mr Lewis and the firm, the defendants admitted that the words were defamatory in their ordinary meaning, but they said that this meaning was that there was a police inquiry on foot and they sought to justify this as true. The plaintiffs, however, contended that the ordinary meaning was that they were guilty of, or suspected by the police of, fraud or dishonesty. The trial judge directed the juries in such a way as to leave it open to them to accept the plaintiffs' contention. From the amounts of damages awarded by them (£25,000 to Mr Lewis and £75,000 to the firm, in the case of the Daily Telegraph, and, the next day, by a different jury £7,000 and £100,000 respectively, against the Daily Mail) it was clear that the juries must have done this.

On appeal to the House of Lords, a majority held that the judge's failure to direct the juries whether the words were capable of imputing guilt of fraud as distinct from suspicion was a misdirection sufficient to warrant a new trial.

LORD DEVLIN: . . . If it is said of a man—'I do not believe that he is guilty of fraud but I cannot deny that he has given grounds for suspicion', it seems to me to be wrong to say that in no circumstances can they be justified except by the speaker proving the truth of that which he has expressly said that he did not believe. It must depend on whether the impression conveyed by the speaker is one of frankness or one of insinuation. Equally in my opinion it is wrong to say that, if in truth the person spoken of never gave any cause for suspicion at all, he has no remedy because he was expressly exonerated of fraud. A man's reputation can suffer if it can truly be said of him that although innocent he behaved in a suspicious way; but it will suffer much more if it is said that he is not innocent.

It is not therefore correct to say as a matter of law that a statement of suspicion imputes guilt. It can be said as a matter of practice that it very often does so, because although suspicion of guilt is something different from proof of guilt, it is the broad impression conveyed by the libel that has to be considered and not the meaning of each word under analysis. A man who wants to talk at large about smoke may have to pick his words very carefully, if he wants to exclude the suggestion that there is also a fire; but it can be done. One always gets back to the fundamental question: what is the meaning that the words convey to the ordinary man; a rule cannot be made about that. They can convey a meaning of suspicion short of guilt; but loose talk about suspicion can very easily convey the impression that it is a suspicion that is well founded.

In the libel that the House has to consider there is, however, no mention of suspicion at all. What is said is simply that the plaintiff's affairs are being inquired into. That is defamatory, as is admitted, because a man's reputation may in fact be injured by such a statement even though it is quite consistent with innocence. I daresay that it would not be injured if everybody bore in mind, as they ought to, that no man is guilty until he is proved so, but unfortunately they do not. It can be defamatory without it being necessary to suggest that the words contained a hidden allegation that there were good grounds for inquiry. A statement that a woman has been raped can affect her reputation, although logically it means that she is innocent of any impurity: *Youssoupoff v Metro-Goldwyn-Mayer Pictures Ltd.*[1] So a statement that a man has been acquitted of a crime with which in fact he was never charged might lower his reputation. Logic is not the test. But a statement that an inquiry is on foot may go further and may positively convey the impression that there are grounds for the inquiry, i.e. that there is something to suspect. Just as a bare statement of suspicion may convey the impression that there are grounds for belief in guilt, so a bare statement of the fact of an inquiry may convey the impression that there are grounds for suspicion. I do not say that in this case it does: but I think that the words in their context and in the circumstances of publication are capable of conveying that impression. But can they convey an impression of guilt? Let it be supposed, first, that a statement that there is an inquiry conveys an impression of suspicion; and, secondly, that a statement of suspicion conveys an impression of guilt. It does not follow from these two suppositions that a statement that there is an inquiry conveys an impression of guilt. For that, two fences have to be taken instead of one. While, as I have said, I am prepared to accept that the jury could take the first I do not think that in a case like the present, where there is only the bare statement that a police inquiry is being made, it could take the second in the same stride. If the ordinary sensible man was capable of thinking that wherever there was a police inquiry there was guilt, it would be almost impossible to give accurate information about anything: but in my opinion he is not. I agree with the view of the Court of Appeal.

There is on this branch of the case a final point to be considered. It is undoubtedly the law that the judge should not leave the question 'libel or no libel' to the jury unless the words are reasonably capable of a defamatory meaning. But if several defamatory meanings are pleaded or suggested, can the judge direct the jury that the words are capable of one meaning but not of another? The point is important here, because the defendants admit that the words are defamatory in one sense but dispute that they are defamatory in the senses pleaded in the statements of claim, and contend that the judge should have so directed the jury. Both counsel for the appellants appear at one time to have argued in the Court of Appeal that the function of the judge was exhausted when he ruled that the words were capable of being defamatory; and that it was not for him to inquire whether they were or were not capable of any particular defamatory meaning. But later they abandoned the point; and, therefore, did not initiate the discussion of it here. Nevertheless there was considerable discussion of it, because some of your lordships at one time felt that it was a point which ought to be considered. In the result I think that all your lordships are now clearly of the opinion that the judge must rule whether the words are capable of bearing each of the defamatory meanings, if there be more than one, put forward by the plaintiff. This supports indirectly my view on the desirability of pleading different meanings. If the plaintiff can get before the jury only those meanings which the judge rules as capable of being defamatory, there is good reason for having the meanings alleged set out precisely as part of the record.

For the reasons that I have given earlier, I agree that there must be a new trial on the ground of misdirection: but I should in any event have considered that there should be a new trial on the issue of damages as they are, in my opinion, ridiculously out of proportion to the injury suffered.

[LORD REID (with whom LORD TUCKER agreed) and LORD HODSON delivered speeches in favour of dismissing the appeal. LORD MORRIS OF BORTH-Y-GEST delivered a speech in favour of allowing the appeal.]

---

1. (1934) 50 TLR 581.

Morgan v Odhams Press Ltd House of Lords [1971] 2 All ER 1156

The plaintiff, Johnny Morgan, complained that he was libelled by an article published in the Sun newspaper, which stated: 'A girl who is likely to be a key witness in a dog doping scandal went into hiding yesterday after threats were made on her life. Margo Murray left her lodgings in Elsham Road, Shepherd's Bush, accompanied by two men . . . Miss Murray . . . was kidnapped last week by members of the gang when they heard she had made a statement to the police. She was kept at a house in Finchley but was eventually allowed to leave.' No one was named in the article except Miss Murray. The plaintiff, in whose flat Miss Murray had stayed a week before the article was published, relied on extrinsic evidence which he said would entitle an ordinary reader to understand that the article referred to him. At the trial, six witnesses who had seen the plaintiff with Miss Murray a week before the publication gave evidence that they thought the article referred to the plaintiff. In fact the plaintiff's flat was three miles from Finchley and Miss Murray had been going about freely with the plaintiff, although in a distressed condition.

In interlocutory proceedings, the Court of Appeal had refused to strike out particulars of a claim on which the plaintiff relied to show that the article referred to him. The trial judge held that in view of this refusal to strike out particulars the case was arguable and should go to the jury. The House of Lords, in this appeal, unanimously held that the trial judge was wrong in holding that he was bound by the decision of the Court of Appeal in interlocutory proceedings; the issue whether the plaintiff had a reasonable cause of action was a matter for the judge to decide at the trial in the light of the evidence. Nevertheless, by a majority (Lord Guest and Lord Donovan dissenting) the House of Lords held that the judge had been right to allow the case to go to the jury. The majority (Lord Reid, Lord Morris of Borth-y-Gest and Lord Pearson) were agreed that the judge had rightly left to the jury the question of fact whether readers having knowledge of the circumstances would reasonably have understood that the article referred to the plaintiff. Lord Reid (post), Lord Morris of Borth-y-Gest, Lord Guest and Lord Donovan expressed the view that there was no limitation to the effect that an article must contain some 'key or pointer' indicating that it referred to the plaintiff. Lord Pearson, however, thought that in order to be defamatory the article must contain something which to the mind of the reader with knowledge of the relevant circumstances contained defamatory imputations and pointed to the plaintiff. On the facts of this case, however, Lord Pearson held that the article did point to the plaintiff.

The jury had awarded £4,750 damages to the plaintiff. The Court of Appeal had allowed an appeal by the defendants. The House of Lords reversed the Court of Appeal's decision.

LORD REID: . . . It must often happen that a defamatory statement published at large does not identify any particular person and that an ordinary member of the public who reads it in its context cannot tell who is referred to. But readers with special knowledge can and do read it as referring to a particular person. A number of matters are not in dispute in this case. It does not matter whether the publisher intended to refer to the plaintiff or not. It does not even matter whether he knew of the plaintiff's existence. And it does not matter that he did not know or could not have known the facts which caused the readers with special knowledge to connect the statement with the plaintiff. Indeed the damage done to the plaintiff by the publication may be of a kind which the publisher could not have foreseen. That may be out of line with the ordinary rule limiting damage for which a tortfeasor is liable, but that point does not arise in this case.

On the other hand when people come and say that they thought that the plaintiff was referred to by a statement which does not identify anyone there must be some protection for a defendant who is thus taken unawares. It is now well settled that the plaintiff must give sufficient particulars of the special facts on which he or his witnesses rely. But that in itself may not be enough. It may be plain and obvious that no sensible person could, by reason of knowing these facts, jump to the conclusion that the defamatory words refer to the plaintiff. Then RSC Ord. 18, r. 19 can be used to stop the case from going to trial. Otherwise the case goes to trial.

The next protection for the defendant is that at the end of the plaintiff's case the judge may be called on to rule whether the words complained of are capable of referring to the plaintiff in light of the special facts or knowledge proved in evidence. The main question in this case is: how is he to make that decision? It is often said that because a question is for the judge to answer it must be a question of law. I have more than once stated my view that the meaning of words is not a question of law in the true sense, even in other departments of the law where a much stricter test of the meaning of words is adopted than in the law of libel. It is simply a question which our law reserves for the judge. . . .

. . . Let me test the matter by supposing that the statements in the defendants' article had been somewhat different. Suppose it had said that Margaret Murray had been kidnapped by the doping gang and taken to a house in Cricklewood on a date which corresponded with the date of her arrival at the plaintiff's flat in Cricklewood and suppose that instead of going about with the plaintiff she had felt unwell and had remained in that flat but that her presence there was known to a number of people. There would be no pointer to the plaintiff; there are many thousands of houses in Cricklewood and to regard a reference to a house in an area where, say, 100,000 people reside as a pointer to any one or every one of them would be to reduce this new limitation to an insubstantial formality. But I would think it impossible to say that ordinary sensible people, who knew of the arrival of Margaret Murray at the plaintiff's flat and that she had not gone out, would have been unreasonable in coming to the conclusion that the article meant that the plaintiff was one of, or was in league with, the gang.

Some people may think that the law has gone too far in holding that the publisher of a defamatory statement which identifies no one is liable if knowledge of special facts which the publisher could not know causes sensible people to think that the statement applies to someone the publisher had never heard of. That may be arguable: I express no opinion about it, farther than to say that in deciding the question one would require to have in mind not only the innocent publisher but also the person who wishes to injure the reputation of the plaintiff but tries to avoid liability by disguising his libel so that it conveys nothing to the ordinary reader but causes those with special knowledge to infer that it is aimed at the plaintiff.

If this new limitation is intended to distinguish between an innocent publisher and a publisher who has the plaintiff in mind it fails in its object. It would still leave the publishers of matter ex facie defamatory in its nature liable in at least three cases: where he uses what he thinks is a fancy name (*E Hulton & Co v Jones*[1]), where the plaintiff happens to have the same name as the person to whom he intends to refer (*Newstead v London Express Newspaper Ltd*[2]) and where he happens to put in something which could be regarded by those with special knowledge as a pointer or peg although he never intended it to point to the plaintiff. I can see no substantial distinction between that case and the case where those with special knowledge are caused to infer that there is a reference to the plaintiff by the narration of facts and circumstances which coupled with that special knowledge do indicate the plaintiff.

The principal authority cited for this novel doctrine is *Astaire v Campling*.[3] That was a very different kind of case. Defamatory statements had been made about Mr X:

---

1. [1910] AC 20; [1908–10] All ER Rep 29.
2. [1940] 1 KB 377; [1939] 4 All ER 319.
3. [1965] 3 All ER 666; [1966] 1 WLR 34.

no one knew who he was. Then the defendant published something which gave a clue to his identity but he did not in any way adopt the earlier defamatory statements. It was obviously right to hold that he incurred no liability for libels published by others. Sellers LJ said[1]:

'It may well be that in circumstances where the identity of a plaintiff is not expressly referred to in an article extrinsic evidence may be given to establish identity, but it seems to me a wholly different matter to seek to add to the alleged libel defamatory views expressed and published by somebody else.'

Diplock LJ said[2]:

'. . . the statement of fact or expression of opinion relied on as defamatory must be one which can be reasonably said to be contained in the statement in respect of which the action is brought and not merely in some other statement.'

I can find nothing in the judgments which throws any light on the question with which I am now dealing, or which indicates that this question was in the mind of any of the learned judges.

There was no peg or pointer in *Cassidy v Daily Mirror Newspapers Ltd*[3] or in *Hough v London Express Newspaper Ltd.*[4] I see nothing wrong with these decisions. They do, however, show that the court recognises that rather far-fetched inferences may be made by sensible readers. I therefore reject the argument that the plaintiff must fail because the defendants' article contained no pointer or peg for his identification. . . .

One other matter I must mention at this stage. One of the witnesses thought that the article referred to the plaintiff but completely disbelieved it; he thought it was rubbish. It was argued that he must be left out of account because no tort is committed by making a defamatory statement about X to a person who utterly disbelieves it. That is plainly wrong. It is true that X's reputation is not diminished but the person defamed suffers annoyance or worse when he learns that a defamatory statement has been published about him. There may be no clear authority that publishing a defamatory statement is a tort whether it is believed or disbelieved. But very often there is no authority for an obvious proposition: no one has had the hardihood to dispute it. . . .

Notes

1. Where a plaintiff relies on a 'true' innuendo meaning he must plead and prove that the words were published to specific persons and that they knew of specific facts which would enable them to understand the words in the innuendo meaning: *Fullam v Newcastle Chronicle and Journal Ltd* [1977] 3 All ER 32; [1977] 1 WLR 651. Moreover, since the cause of action arises as soon as the words complained of are published, any extrinsic facts relied on to support an innuendo have to be known at the time of publication by the person to whom the words were published. Inferences put on the words complained of as a result of facts coming to light after publication cannot make the words defamatory: *Grappelli v Derek Block (Holdings) Ltd* [1981] 2 All

---

1. [1965] 3 All ER at p. 667; [1966] 1 WLR at p. 39.
2. [1965] 3 All ER at p. 669; [1966] 1 WLR at p. 41.
3. [1929] 2 KB 331; [1929] All ER Rep 117.
4. [1940] 2 KB 507; [1940] 3 All ER 31.

ER 272: [1981] 1 WLR 822; cf. *Hayward v Thompson* [1982] QB 47; [1981] 3 All ER 450, explained by *Carter-Ruck on Libel and Slander*, 3rd edn (London, 1985), p. 40.

2. It was Fox's Libel Act 1792 which made the question of 'libel or no libel' essentially one for the jury. Although the Act applied to criminal proceedings only it has been regarded as declaratory of the common law. The judge must, however, be satisfied that there is sufficient evidence to go to the jury, i.e. the statement must be 'reasonably capable' of the meaning alleged. If it is not, it must be withdrawn from the jury.

E Hulton & Co *v* Jones House of Lords [1908–10] All ER Rep 29

The plaintiff, Thomas Artemus Jones Esq, barrister, brought an action for libel against the defendants, the publishers of the Sunday Chronicle newspaper. The libel was said to be contained in an article purportedly describing a motor festival at Dieppe. The material parts were as follows: 'Upon the terrace marches the world, attracted by the motor races—a world immensely pleased with itself, and minded to draw a wealth of inspiration—and, incidentally, of golden cocktails—from any scheme to speed the passing hour ... "whist! there is Artemus Jones with a woman who is not his wife, who must be, you know—the other thing!" whispers a fair neighbour of mine into her bosom friend's ear. Really, is it not surprising how certain of our fellow countrymen behave when they come abroad? Would you suppose by his goings on, that he was a churchwarden at Peckham. No one, indeed, would assume that Jones in the atmosphere of London would take on so austere a job as the duties of a churchwarden. Here, in the atmosphere of Dieppe, on the French side of the Channel, he is the life and soul of a gay little band that haunts the Casino and turns night into day, besides betraying a most unholy delight in the society of female butterflies.'

The evidence of the writer of the article and the editor of the paper which was that they knew nothing of the plaintiff, and that the article was not intended by them to refer to him, was accepted as true. At the trial, witnesses were called for the plaintiff, who said that they had read the article and thought that it referred to the plaintiff. The jury returned a verdict for the plaintiff with £1,750 damages, and Channell J gave judgment for the plaintiff. The defendants appealed unsuccessfully to the Court of Appeal. On further appeal to the House of Lords:

LORD SHAW: ... In the publication of matter of a libellous character—that is, matter which would be libellous if applying to an actual person—the responsibility is as follows. In the first place, there is responsibility for the words used being taken to signify that which readers would reasonably understand by them; in the second place, there is responsibility also for the names used being taken to signify those whom the readers would reasonably understand by those names; and, in the third place, the same principle is applicable to persons unnamed, but sufficiently indicated by designation or description. I demur to the observation so frequently made in the argument that these principles are novel. Sufficient expression is given to the same principles by Abbott CJ in *Bourke v Warren*, in which that learned judge said ((1826) 2 C & P 307 at 309, 310):

'The question for your consideration is, whether you think that the libel designates the plaintiff in such a way as to let those who knew him understand that he was the person meant? It is not necessary that all the world should understand the libel; it is sufficient if those who know the plaintiff can make out that he is the person meant.'

I think that it is out of the question to suggest that that means 'meant in the mind of the writer' or of the publisher: it must mean 'meant by the words employed'. . . .

[LORD LOREBURN LC (with whom LORD ATKINSON and LORD GORRELL concurred) delivered a speech in favour of dismissing the appeal.]

Appeal dismissed

Note

Salmond & Heuston, p. 160, note 69 comment: 'There is some evidence that the decision may have been based on the recklessness or even the spite of the defendants. . . . The plaintiff had been a contributor to the defendants' paper for twelve years and his name was well-known in their office, although not to the actual writer of the article. The managing director admitted in cross-examination that he had read the article in proof and thought at first reading that it referred to the plaintiff. . . . The point is still important, for if the actual facts of *Hulton v Jones* recurred today, the defendants might be held to have failed to establish reasonable care under s. 4 of the 1952 Act' (see post). Lord Denning, *What Next in the Law?* (London, 1982), p. 213 comments: 'I would like to see the House of Lords take *Hulton v Jones* by the scruff of the neck and throw it out of the courts and start afresh.' The Faulks Committee, para. 123, however, thought that the principle in *Hulton v Jones* should stand.

Newstead *v* London Express Newspaper Ltd Court of Appeal [1939] 4 All ER 319

The Daily Express newspaper published an account of a trial for bigamy and referred to the prisoner as 'Harold Newstead, thirty-year old Camberwell man'. The account was true as regards a Camberwell barman of that name, but was not true as regards the plaintiff, Harold Newstead, aged about thirty, who assisted his father in a hairdressing business at Camberwell Road, Camberwell. The plaintiff brought an action for damages for libel against the proprietors of the newspaper. Five questions were left to the jury who were unable to agree on the first question: 'Would reasonable persons understand the words complained of to refer to the plaintiff?' and they assessed damages at one-farthing. The defendants appealed. The Court of Appeal held that the evidence would have justified an affirmative answer to the first question by the jury; and, assuming the words were capable of a meaning defamatory of the plaintiff, the fact that they were true of another person did not afford a good defence to the defendants.

SIR WILFRED GREENE MR: . . . After giving careful consideration to the matter, I am unable to hold that the fact that defamatory words are true of A makes it as a matter of law impossible for them to be defamatory of B, which was in substance the main argument on behalf of the appellants. At first sight, this looks as though it would lead to great hardship, but the hardships are in practice not so serious as might appear, at any rate in the case of statements which are ex facie defamatory. Persons who make statements of this character may not unreasonably be expected, when describing the person of whom they are made, to identify that person so closely as to make it very unlikely that a judge would hold them to be reasonably capable of referring to someone else, or that a jury would hold that they did so refer. This is particularly so in the case of statements which purport to deal with actual facts. If there is a risk of coincidence, it ought, I think, in reason to be borne, not by the innocent party to whom the words are held to refer, but by the party who puts them into circulation. In matters of fiction, there is no doubt more room for hardship. Even in the case of matters of fact it is no doubt possible to construct imaginary facts which would lead to hardship. There may also be hardship if words, not on their faces defamatory, are true of A but are reasonably understood by some as referring to B, and, as applied to B, are defamatory. Such cases, however, must be rare. The law as I understand it is well settled, and can be altered only by legislation. The appeal must be dismissed with costs.

[DU PARCQ LJ delivered a judgment in favour of dismissing the appeal. MACKINNON LJ thought that the appeal should be allowed by reason of the smallness of the damages which would have been awarded to the plaintiff had the jury returned a verdict in his favour.]

The Defamation Act 1952

4. Unintentional defamation. — (1) A person who has published words alleged to be defamatory of another person may, if he claims that the words were published by him innocently in relation to that other person, make an offer of amends under this section; and in any such case —

(a) if the offer is accepted by the party aggrieved and is duly performed, no proceedings for libel or slander shall be taken or continued by that party against the person making the offer in respect of the publication in question (but without prejudice to any cause of action against any other person jointly responsible for that publication);

(b) if the offer is not accepted by the party aggrieved, then, except as otherwise provided by this section, it shall be a defence, in any proceedings by him for libel or slander against the person making the offer in respect of the publication in question, to prove that the words complained of were published by the defendant innocently in relation to the plaintiff and that the offer was made as soon as practicable after the defendant received notice that they were or might be defamatory of the plaintiff, and has not been withdrawn.

(2) An offer of amends under this section must be expressed to be made for the purposes of [this section and must be accompanied by an affidavit specifying] the facts relied upon by the person making it to show that the words in question were published by him innocently in relation to the party aggrieved; and for the purposes of a defence under paragraph (b) of subsection (1) of this section no evidence, other than evidence of facts specified in the affidavit, shall be admissible on behalf of that person to prove that the words were so published.

(3) An offer of amends under this section shall be understood to mean an offer —

(a) in any case, to publish or join in the publication of a suitable correction of the words complained of, and a sufficient apology to the party aggrieved in respect of those words;

(b) where copies of a document or record containing the said words have been distributed by or with the knowledge of the person making the offer, to take such steps as are reasonably practicable on his part for notifying persons to whom copies have been so distributed that the words are alleged to be defamatory of the party aggrieved.

(4) Where an offer of amends under this section is accepted by the party aggrieved —

(a) any question as to the steps to be taken in fulfilment of the offer as so accepted shall in default of agreement between the parties be referred to and determined by the High Court, whose decision thereon shall be final;

(*b*) the power of the court to make orders as to costs in proceedings by the party aggrieved against the person making the offer in respect of the publication in question, or in proceedings in respect of the offer under paragraph (*a*) of this subsection, shall include power to order the payment by the person making the offer to the party aggrieved of costs on an indemnity basis and any expenses reasonably incurred or to be incurred by that party in consequence of the publication in question;

and if no such proceedings as aforesaid are taken, the High Court may, upon application made by the party aggrieved, make any such order for the payment of such costs and expenses as aforesaid as could be made in such proceedings.

(5) For the purposes of this section words shall be treated as published by one person (in this subsection referred to as the publisher) innocently in relation to another person if and only if the following conditions are satisfied, that is to say—

(*a*) that the publisher did not intend to publish them of and concerning that other person, and did not know of circumstances by virtue of which they might be understood to refer to him; or

(*b*) that the words were not defamatory on the face of them, and the publisher did not know of circumstances by virtue of which they might be understood to be defamatory of that other person,

and in either case that the publisher exercised all reasonable care in relation to the publication; and any reference in this subsection to the publisher shall be construed as including a reference to any servant or agent of his who was concerned with the contents of the publication.

(6) Paragraph (*b*) of subsection (1) of this section shall not apply in relation to the publication by any person of words of which he is not the author unless he proves that the words were written by the author without malice.

Notes

1. 'All lawyers are thieves' (an example given in *Eastwood v Holmes* (1858) 1 F & F 347 at 349) is group defamation and not actionable. 'The reason why a libel published of a large or indeterminate number of persons described by some general name generally fails to be actionable is the difficulty of establishing that the plaintiff was in fact included in the defamatory statement. . . .' (per Lord Atkin in *Knupffer v London Express Newspaper Ltd* [1944] 1 All ER 495 at 498). Whether or not the plaintiff succeeds will depend upon 'the size of the class, the generality of the charge and the extravagance of the accusation' (per Lord Porter at p. 499).

2. Corporate bodies have been allowed to sue in respect of defamation: trading companies (*South Hetton Coal Co v North Eastern News Association* [1894] 1 QB 133), and local authorities (*Bognor Regis UDC v Campion* [1972] 2 QB 169; [1972] 2 All ER 61). There is a strong criticism of the last-mentioned decision by J. A. Weir [1972A] CLJ 238. The Faulks Committee, para. 342, has recommended that in such cases there should be proof of special damage or the likelihood of pecuniary damage, but *Duncan and Neill on Defamation* 2nd edn, p. 44, note 4, suggest that it would be better not to add this complication to the law, since it is rare for such corporations to sue. Trade unions, not being corporate bodies, lack the necessary legal personality to sue, despite the wording of s. 2(1) of the Trade Union and Labour Relations Act 1974: *Electrical, Electronic, Telecommunication and Plumbing Union v Times Newspapers Ltd* [1980] QB 585; [1980] 1 All ER 1097.

3 The distinction between defamation and malicious falsehoods

Ratcliffe v Evans Court of Appeal [1891–4] All ER Rep 699

This was an action for damages for publication in a newspaper of a statement that the plaintiff's firm had gone out of business. The plaintiff proved a general loss of business as a result of the publication, but could not prove that he had lost any particular customer or order. The jury found that the words were not libellous in the sense of reflecting on the plaintiff's character, but that they were not published bona fide. Mr Commissioner Bompas QC entered judgment for the plaintiff for £120. The defendant appealed to the Court of Appeal.

BOWEN LJ: . . . That an action will lie for written or oral falsehoods not actionable per se nor even defamatory, where they are maliciously published, where they are calculated in the ordinary course of things to produce, and where they do produce, actual damage, is established law. Such an action is not one of libel or of slander, but an action on the case for damage wilfully and intentionally done without just occasion or excuse, analogous to an action for slander of title. To support it actual damage must be shown, for it is an action which only lies in respect of such damage as has actually occurred. It was contended before us that in such an action it is not enough to allege and prove general loss of business arising from the publication, since such general loss is general, and not special, damage; and special damage — as has often been said — is the gist of such an action on the case.

Lest we should be led astray by mere words, it is desirable to recollect that the term 'special damage', which is found for centuries in the books, is not always used with reference to similar subject-matter nor in the same context. At times (both in the law of tort and of contract) it is employed to denote that damage arising out of the special circumstances of the case which, if properly pleaded, may be super-added to the general damage which the law implies in every breach of contract and every infringement of an absolute right: see *Ashby v White*.[1] In all such cases the law presumes that some damage will flow in the ordinary course of things from the mere invasion of the plaintiff's rights, and calls it general damage. Special damage in such a context means the particular damage (beyond the general damage) which results from the particular circumstances of the case and of the plaintiff's claim to be compensated, for which he ought to give warning in his pleadings, in order that there may be no surprise at the trial. But where no actual and positive right (apart from the damage done) has been disturbed, it is the damage done that is the wrong; and the expression 'special damage', when used of this damage, denotes the actual and temporal loss which has in fact occurred. Such damage is called variously in old authorities 'express loss', 'particular damage' (*Cane v Golding*),[2] 'damage in fact', 'special or particular cause of loss' (*Harwood v Lowe*,[3] *Tasburgh v Day*[4]).

. . . The rule to be laid down with regard to malicious falsehoods affecting property or trade is only an instance of the doctrines of good sense applicable to all that branch of actions on the case to which the class under discussion belongs. The nature and circumstances of the publication of the falsehood may accordingly require the admission of evidence of general loss of business, as the natural and direct result produced, and perhaps intended to be produced.

---

1. (1703) 2 Ld Raym 938.
2. (1649) Sty 169.
3. (1628) Palm 529.
4. (1618) Cro Jac 484.

An instructive illustration, and one by which the present appeal is really covered, is furnished by *Hargrave v Le Breton*,[1] decided a century and a half ago. It was an action of slander of title at an auction. The allegation in the declaration was that divers persons who would have purchased at the auction left the place; but no particular persons were named. The objection that they were not specially mentioned was, as the report tells us, 'easily' answered. The answer given was that in the nature of the transaction it was impossible to specify names; that the injury complained of was in effect that the bidding at the auction had been prevented and stopped; and that everybody had gone away. It had, therefore, become impossible to tell with certainty who would have been bidders or purchasers if the auction had not been rendered abortive. This case shows, what sound judgment itself dictates, that in an action for falsehood producing damage to a man's trade, which in its very nature is intended or reasonably likely to produce, and which in the ordinary course of things does produce, a general loss of business as distinct from the loss of this or that known customer, evidence of such general decline of business is admissible. In *Hargrave v Le Breton*[1] it was a falsehood openly promulgated at an auction. In the case before us to-day it is a falsehood openly disseminated through the press, probably read and possibly acted on by persons of whom the plaintiff never heard. To refuse with reference to such subject-matter to admit such general evidence would be to misunderstand and warp the meaning of old expressions; to depart from and not to follow old rules; and, in addition to all this, would involve an absolute denial of justice and of redress for the very mischief which was intended to be committed.
. . .

Appeal dismissed

The Defamation Act 1952

3. Slander of title, &c. – (1) In an action for slander of title, slander of goods or other malicious falsehood, it shall not be necessary to allege or prove special damage –

(a) if the words upon which the action is founded are calculated to cause pecuniary damage to the plaintiff and are published in writing or other permanent form; or

(b) if the said words are calculated to cause pecuniary damage to the plaintiff in respect of any office, profession, calling, trade or business held or carried on by him at the time of the publication.

Note

The Faulks Committee on Defamation, para. 588, has recommended that the distinction between the written and spoken word introduced in the above section be removed, and that proof of special damage be always unnecessary provided that the words are likely to cause pecuniary damage to the plaintiff. This would bring English law into line with the law in Scotland.

White *v* Mellin House of Lords [1895] AC 154

Defendant sold the plaintiff's 'Infants' Food', affixing to plaintiff's wrappers a label stating that defendant's 'food for infants and invalids' was far more nutritious and healthful than any other. It was not proved that this statement was untrue or had

---

1. (1769) 4 Burr 2422.

caused any damage to the plaintiff. Romer J dismissed an action for an injunction restraining publication and for damages. The Court of Appeal reversed this judgment. On appeal to the House of Lords:

LORD HERSCHELL LC: . . . The allegation of a tradesman that his goods are better than his neighbour's very often involves only the consideration whether they possess one or two qualities superior to the other. Of course 'better' means better as regards the purpose for which they are intended, and the question of better or worse in many cases depends simply upon one or two or three issues of fact. If an action will not lie because a man says that his goods are better than his neighbour's it seems to me impossible to say that it will lie because he says that they are better in this or that or the other respect. Just consider what a door would be opened if this were permitted. That this sort of puffing advertisement is in use is notorious; and we see rival cures advertised for particular ailments. The Court would then be bound to inquire, in an action brought, whether this ointment or this pill better cured the disease which it was alleged to cure – whether a particular article of food was in this respect or that better than another. Indeed, the courts of law would be turned into a machinery for advertising rival productions by obtaining a judicial determination which of the two was the better. . . .

LORD WATSON: . . . In the first place, I do not think the representation conveyed by the defendant's label is, in any legal sense, a representation of and concerning the infants' food of the plaintiff. It is a highly coloured laudation of Dr Vance's food and nothing else. It makes no reference to the plaintiff's goods beyond what might be implied in the case of every kind of food which is recommended and sold as being suitable for consumption by infant children. Nor, in my opinion, is the circumstance that the label was sometimes put upon the plaintiff's wrappers, however distressing it might be to him, sufficient to convert it into a disparagement of the contents of the wrapper. An advertisement in the window of a bootmaker, to the effect that he makes the best boots in the world, may be more offensive to his next neighbour in the same trade than to a bootmaker at a distance; but the disparagement in kind and degree is identical in both cases.

In the second place, assuming that the representation did refer to the plaintiff's food, I am of opinion that his evidence does not prove it to be untrue. At the best, the evidence comes to no more than this, that the plaintiff's food is the more suitable for children under six months old who cannot get their mother's milk; and that Dr Vance's food is the more suitable for children above that age who are not the victims of indigestion. In these circumstances it appears to me to be difficult to hold that it was not open to either of the parties to say that his was the best food for infants without conveying a false imputation upon the food of the other.

In the third and last place, I am of opinion that, even if the plaintiff had proved that the representation concerned his food and was wilfully false, his evidence discloses no cause of action. There is not in the whole of it an attempt to prove that the plaintiff has suffered in the past or is likely to suffer in the future any damage whatever through the representations of which he complains. . . .

[LORD ASHBOURNE concurred. LORD MACNAGHTEN and LORD SHAND delivered speeches in favour of allowing the appeal.]

Appeal allowed

Notes

1. In *De Beers Abrasive Products Ltd v International General Electric Co of New York Ltd* [1975] 2 All ER 599; [1975] 1 WLR 972, after a review of

the authorities, Walton J suggested that where a trader chooses to denigrate the goods of a rival, the test to be applied is whether a reasonable man would take the claim being made as a serious claim or not. One indication that the disparagement is intended to be taken seriously, could be a claim that the rival's goods had been subjected to a proper scientific test. The plaintiff must also prove 'malice' (see post).

2. The Code of Advertising Practice, under the supervision of the Advertising Standards Authority, says that while comparative advertising is permissible 'advertisements should not unfairly attack or discredit other products, advertisers or advertisements directly or by implication' (Code, section IIm, para. 12). A complaint to the Code of Advertising Practice Committee may often succeed where a claim for malicious falsehood would have little prospect of success.

Balden *v* Shorter Chancery Division [1933] All ER Rep 249

A servant of the defendants falsely said of the plaintiff, speaking carelessly but without any intention to injure him, that he was employed by the defendants, whereas he was in fact employed by another firm. Maugham J dismissed an action for an injunction restraining defendants from making such representations.

MAUGHAM J: . . . If I could properly conclude that the story told in the witness-box by Mr Bensted was untrue and that he knew that the plaintiff was not employed by the defendants, I should have little difficulty in determining the action in the plaintiff's favour because, if Mr Bensted said what he did say knowing it to be untrue, I should draw the inference that he did it from a dishonest motive and maliciously. But I cannot come to that conclusion.

The meaning of 'malice' in connection with injurious falsehood is dealt with in *Salmond on Torts* (7th edn, pp. 582–583) in the following passage, which I accept as correct:

'What is meant by malice in this connection? Lord Davey, in the passage already cited [from *Royal Baking Powder Co v Wright, Crossley & Co*[1] (18 RPC at p. 99)] defines it as meaning the absence of just cause or excuse. It is to be observed, however, that this is not one of the recognised meanings of the term malice in other connections. An act done without just cause or excuse is wrongful, but not necessarily malicious; for example, a trespass by mistake on another man's land or the conversion of his chattels under an erroneous claim of right. Notwithstanding Lord Davey's dictum, it is now apparently settled that malice in the law of slander of title and other forms of injurious falsehood means some dishonest or otherwise improper motive. A bona fide assertion of title, however mistaken, if made for the protection of one's own interest or for some other proper purposes, is not malicious.'

In *Greers Ltd v Pearman and Corder Ltd*[2] (1922) 39 RPC at p. 417, Bankes LJ said that 'maliciously' for the purpose which the court was considering meant 'with some indirect object', and Scrutton LJ remarked that the only question in the case was whether there was evidence on which the jury could find that the statements were made maliciously 'in the sense of being made with some indirect or dishonest motive'.

I think that in the present case the statements were, at the worst, careless statements

---

1. (1900) 18 RPC 95.
2. (1922) 39 RPC 406.

made without any indirect motive and without any intention of injuring the plaintiff, and I find that Mr Bensted believed them to be true. The allegation of malice must fail, and on that finding of fact the action must be dismissed. . . .

Question

What are the implications of cases such as *Ministry of Housing and Local Government v Sharp* [1970] 2 QB 223; [1970] 1 All ER 1009 (p. 189, ante), and *Ross v Caunters (a firm)* [1979] 3 All ER 580; [1979] 3 WLR 605 (p. 192, ante) and *Lawton v BOC Transhield* [1987] 2 All ER 608; [1987] ICR 7, noted p. 191, ante in respect of the decision in *Balden v Shorter*?

4 Publication

Huth *v* Huth Court of Appeal [1914–15] All ER Rep 242

The defendant sent a letter to his wife in an unsealed envelope suggesting that they were not married and that their children were illegitimate. The wife could not sue her husband in tort (but see now the Law Reform (Husband and Wife) Act 1962, s. 1). In order to circumvent this, his children brought this action for libel. To prove publication the family butler was called to give evidence that he had looked at the contents of the envelope before placing it on the breakfast table. The plaintiffs lost their action at first instance and appealed to the Court of Appeal.

LORD READING CJ: . . . It cannot be contended, and is not contended, as I understand, that if a person, in breach of his duty, opens an envelope and reads a letter, and there is no reason to expect that he would be likely to commit this breach of duty, the fact that he opens the envelope and reads the letter amounts to publication by the person who sends it; but it is argued in this case that, as the document was enclosed in an unsealed and ungummed envelope, it must be assumed that the defendant knew or ought to have known, or might have expected that a servant in the house would open a letter in such an envelope so addressed. It is further said that an envelope unsealed, with a halfpenny stamp on it, is liable always to be opened by the postal authorities and the document is liable to be examined and read, and consequently that it must be taken that there was some evidence of publication to the Post Office.

With regard to the first point, that is the publication to the butler, I am clearly of opinion that there is no evidence of any such publication to the butler upon the point merely whether the fact that the butler opened the letter and read it because he was curious, would make it publication by the defendant. Fortunately, it is no part of a butler's duty to open the letters that come to the house of his master or mistress addressed to the master or mistress; and in this case there is nothing exceptional in it except that his curiosity was excited by reason of the lady being addressed by her maiden name. No one can help a man's curiosity being excited, but it does not justify him in opening a letter, and it could not make the defendant liable for the publication to the butler of the contents of the envelope, because it must of course be borne in mind that, however insulting and offensive the matters may have been which the husband wrote to his wife, they were addressed to the wife and only intended for the wife, and she alone saw them, no action for libel could be brought by her. An action for libel can only be brought if there is publication to some third person. The publication to the butler in this case is not sufficient. . . .

. . . It has been laid down, and I think rightly that the court will take judicial notice of the nature of the document, which is the postcard, and will presume, in the absence of evidence to the contrary, that others besides the person to whom it is addressed will read and have read what is written thereon. In this way the presumption of law based on the authorities arises. If, of course, even in such a case as that, the defendant could establish that the postcard never was read by a single person — if it were possible to establish such a state of things, although it is very difficult to conceive — he would, notwithstanding the presumption, succeed in the action, because he would have proved that there was no publication. But of course he cannot, and does not. The fact that it is practically impossible to prove that anyone did read the postcard is the very reason why the law takes judicial notice of the nature of the document, and says the mere fact that it is written on a postcard which is posted must be taken as some evidence that a third person will read it, or has read it. Now, that is clear law, and is quite beyond dispute. . . .

. . . I cannot think that the court is entitled to presume, merely because the envelope went through the post, that it would be opened. I suppose what is said with regard to these letters is true of every package which is sent through the Post Office. It is true of every parcel which is sent through the Post Office, and in certain circumstances it may be true also of other documents, even though they may be sealed; but that does not justify the presumption to which counsel for the plaintiffs is driven in this case — that is, that such a letter in an envelope which is ungummed is to be treated just as a postcard. I think that that point fails, and that there is therefore no evidence of publication in this case. . . .

SWINFEN EADY LJ: . . . In my opinion, the question of publication can shortly be disposed of in this way. There was no publication, because there was no evidence that, to the defendant's knowledge, a letter addressed to his wife and enclosed in this envelope, but unsealed and not fastened down, would in the ordinary course be likely to be opened by the butler, or by any other person in the employ of the mistress, or at the mistress's house, before it was delivered to her.

When the cases which were referred to are looked at it will be seen that in each case the defendant, who must be taken to have intended the natural consequences of his own act in the circumstances of the case, must on that footing have intended the publication which in fact took place. . . .

[BRAY J agreed.]

Appeal dismissed

Theaker *v* Richardson Court of Appeal [1962] 1 All ER 229

The defendant wrote a defamatory letter to the plaintiff, a married woman and a fellow-member of the local district council. The letter was placed in a sealed manilla envelope similar to the kind used for distributing election addresses. The envelope was addressed to the plaintiff. The plaintiff's husband, seeing the envelope on the mat, opened it thinking it was an election address. The jury found that it was a natural and probable consequence of the defendant's writing and delivery of the letter that the plaintiff's husband would open and read it. Judgment was given for the plaintiff. The defendant appealed to the Court of Appeal.

PEARSON LJ: . . . The question arising can be put in this form. The plaintiff's husband, acting carelessly and thoughtlessly but meaning no harm, picked up and opened and began to read the letter. Was his conduct something unusual, out of the ordinary and not reasonably to be anticipated, or was it something which could quite easily and naturally happen in the ordinary course of events? In my judgment that is a fair formulation of the question, and, when so formulated, it is seen to be a question of fact which in a trial with a jury can and should be left to and decided by the jury, who have observed the witnesses giving evidence and have and are expected to use their own common sense and general knowledge of the world and perhaps some particular knowledge (if they have it) of the locality concerned and the ways of its inhabitants. In my judgment, it would not be right to substitute the opinion of this court for the opinion of the jury on such a question arising in the course of a trial with a jury. . . .

[HARMAN LJ delivered a judgment in favour of dismissing the appeal. ORMEROD LJ delivered a judgment in favour of allowing the appeal.]

Appeal dismissed

Question

A writes a defamatory statement and locks it in his desk. A thief steals it and makes its contents known. Is there publication by A? (The example is given in *Pullman v Hill* [1891] 1 QB 524 at 527.)

Notes

1. Dictation by a manager to his secretary is a publication and unless the communication is protected by some defence such as qualified privilege (as to which see p. 778, post) the manager will be liable and so will his employer on the principle of vicarious liability (*Riddick v Thames Board Mills Ltd* [1977] QB 881 per Waller LJ at pp. 906–907 and Stephenson LJ at p. 900; cf. Lord Denning MR, at pp. 893–894, who resuscitated the doctrine of common employment (p. 565, ante). Alternatively Lord Denning was prepared to utilise the 'master's tort' theory (p. 829, post) to suggest that the making of a report by one employee to another is an act of the employer so that there is no publication by the employer to anyone but himself and so the employer, in his view, cannot be sued).

2. The law relating to re-publication in defamation cases was described by Stocker LJ in *Slipper v BBC* [1991] 1 All ER 165 as 'but an example of the rules of *novus actus interveniens*' (on which see p. 319, ante). In that case the BBC made a film recounting the abortive efforts of the plaintiff, at a time when he was a chief superintendent in the Flying Squad, to bring back a bank robber from Brazil. The film was shown and published by way of a preview to press and television journalists, and it was subsequently broadcast on BBC1. The plaintiff alleged that the film was defamatory of him and, in support of his claim for general damages, he alleged that the BBC well knew and could and did foresee that the broadcast was likely to be reviewed in the national press and the contents rehearsed in such reviews; further, or alternatively, that it was the natural and probable consequence that the film and its contents were likely to be so reviewed. The Court of Appeal dismissed an appeal from an order of Michael Davies J refusing to strike out these allegations. Stocker LJ said that the questions whether the reviews reproduced the sting of the libel, and whether the BBC invited such reviews or anticipated that such reviews would repeat the sting of the libel, were matters for the jury to decide. This included the question whether or not it was a foreseeable or a natural and probable consequence of the invitation to review that such reviews would include the sting of the libel.

3. Although everyone who takes part in publishing a libel is prima facie

liable (e.g. the editor, printer, publisher and seller of a newspaper) a person who is not the author, printer or the first or main publisher of a work which contains a libel, e.g. a salesman, librarian or distributor, may raise the defence of innocent dissemination. He must prove – (a) that he did not know that the offending material contained the libel; (b) that he did not know it was of a character likely to contain a libel; and (c) that his absence of knowledge was not due to negligence on his part. In *Vizetelly v Mudie's Select Library Ltd* [1900] 2 QB 170 the defence failed because the defendant circulating library had overlooked a publisher's circular requesting them to return the offending book. The Royal Commission on the Press (Cmnd. 6810, para. 19.46) has recommended the removal of condition (b). Compare the views of Lord Denning MR on the burden of proof in *Goldsmith v Sperrings Ltd* [1977] 2 All ER 566 at 572–573. The Faulks Committee, para. 315, has proposed that the defence of innocent dissemination should be extended to printers, subject to the same conditions as apply to other distributors.

4. Publishers and printers usually protect themselves by an indemnity clause in the contract with the author. The following is a specimen clause:

'The author warrants to the Publishers that the Work will in no way whatever be a violation of any existing copyright and that it will contain nothing of a libellous or scandalous character.'

Section 11 of the Defamation Act 1952 provides:

'An agreement for indemnifying any person against civil liability for libel in respect of the publication of any matter shall not be unlawful unless at the time of the publication that person knows that the matter is defamatory, and does not reasonably believe there is a good defence to any action brought upon it.'

This section means that an insurance policy against libel damages is valid only in cases of unintentional defamation. A specimen insurance policy provides:

'The insured shall at all times exercise diligence, care and restraint in an endeavour to avoid the printed publication of matter which would reasonably be expected to cause offence such as to incur a complaint or legal proceedings which would give rise to a claim under this Policy.'

It is usual for the insured to bear some portion of the loss (e.g. the first ten per cent). A usual condition is that the insurer is to have full control of the defence of any claim for indemnity or damages and full discretion in the conduct of any negotiations or settlement proceedings. (These clauses are quoted with kind permission of the Guardian Royal Exchange Assurance Group from their specimen policy.)

5   Defences

(a) Justification

The Defamation Act 1952

5. Justification. – In an action for libel or slander in respect of words containing two or more distinct charges against the plaintiff, a defence of justification shall not fail by reason only that the truth of every charge is not proved if the words not proved to be true do not materially injure the plaintiff's reputation having regard to the truth of the remaining charges.

The Civil Evidence Act 1968

13. Conclusiveness of convictions for purposes of defamation actions. – (1) In an action for libel or slander in which the question whether a person did or did not commit a criminal offence is relevant to an issue arising in the action, proof that, at the time when that issue falls to be determined, that person stands convicted of that offence shall be conclusive evidence that he committed that offence; and his conviction thereof shall be admissible in evidence accordingly.

(2) In any such action as aforesaid in which by virtue of this section a person is proved to have been convicted of an offence, the contents of any document which is admissible as evidence of the conviction, and the contents of the information, complaint, indictment or charge-sheet on which that person was convicted, shall, without prejudice to the reception of any other admissible evidence for the purpose of identifying the facts on which the conviction was based, be admissible in evidence for the purpose of identifying those facts.

(3) For the purposes of this section a person shall be taken to stand convicted of an offence if but only if there subsists against him a conviction of that offence by or before a court in the United Kingdom or by a court-martial there or elsewhere.

Question

A writes of B: 'B has stolen bicycles from X, Y and Z.' B has in fact stolen bicycles from X and Y, but not from Z. In his statement of claim he relies only on A's allegation that he has stolen Z's bicycle. May A plead and prove the thefts from X and Y by way of justification?

Notes

1. The defendant must justify 'the sting of the libel': e.g. in *Alexander v North Eastern Rly Co* (1865) 6 B & S 340, the plaintiff brought an action for libel based on the following notice which the defendants had published: 'N. E. Railway Company. Caution. J. Alexander was charged before the magistrates at Darlington for riding in a train from Leeds, for which his ticket was not available, and refusing to pay the proper fare. He was convicted in the penalty of £9 1s 10d, including costs, or three weeks' imprisonment.' In fact the plaintiff had been sentenced to fourteen days' imprisonment in default of payment of the fine and costs. The Court of Queen's Bench held that the defence of justification succeeded. It has been said: 'It is sufficient if the substance of the libellous statement is justified . . . As much must be justified as meets the sting of the charge, and if anything be contained in a charge which does not add to the sting of it, that need not be justified' (*Edwards v Bell* (1824) 1 Bing 403 at 409, per Burrough J). The defendant cannot protect himself with a statement like: 'There is a rumour that . . .'. He must prove that the rumour is true: *Truth (NZ) Ltd v Holloway* [1960] 1 WLR 997 at 1002.

2. 'Suppose a publication stated truthfully that the plaintiff was a murderer, but falsely that he had a conviction for speeding. It would be open to the plaintiff under the present law to ignore the very grave true allegation and

to bring a libel action only on the trivial and false one. Although it is likely that a tribunal of fact would award no more than contemptuous damages for the latter allegation in such circumstances, the plaintiff would be entitled technically to succeed' (Faulks Committee, para. 132).

However, recent case law has shown that the plaintiff is not entirely free to pick and choose those matters which he believes the defendant will be unable to justify. He can do so only when the two libels are severable and distinct. In *Polly Peck (Holdings) plc v Trelford* [1986] QB 1000; [1986] 2 All ER 84, the Court of Appeal held that when several defamatory statements have a 'common sting', then the defendant is entitled to justify that sting and it is fortuitous if some or all of the facts so pleaded are culled from parts of the publication of which the plaintiff has chosen not to complain. This does not mean that the defendant can plead as justification various suspicious matters without making it clear what meaning of the defamatory words he is seeking to justify. In *Lucas-Box v News Group Newspapers Ltd* [1986] 1 All ER 177; [1986] 1 WLR 147, the Court of Appeal held that the defendant must make clear in his pleadings the fact situation which he says justifies his words. (The best practice is for the defendant to set out the meaning or meanings he intends to justify at the start of the plea: *Morrell v International Thomson Publishing Ltd* [1989] 3 All ER 733 at 378.) The jury is not fettered by the pleadings, but can determine a meaning of the defamatory words as it sees fit; it then applies the facts of justification, as confined by the particulars given by the defendant, to that meaning in order to decide whether the defence is made out (see further *Prager v Times Newspapers Ltd* [1988] 1 All ER 300; [1988] 1 WLR 77). The defendant may, however, only justify a meaning which the words are reasonably capable of bearing. So for example in *Bookbinder v Tebbit* [1989] 1 All ER 1169; [1989] 1 WLR 640, the plaintiff, leader of a Labour-controlled council, complained only of a specific charge by the defendant, chairman of the Conservative Party, that the council under the plaintiff's leadership had squandered public funds by overprinting school stationery with the caption 'Support Nuclear Free zones'. A defence of justification based on the alleged general squandering of public funds on other occasions by the council under the plaintiff's leadership was struck out by the Court of Appeal. The defendant is, however, entitled to rely in mitigation of damages on evidence of specific acts of misconduct adduced in support of an unsuccessful plea of partial justification (*Pamplin v Express Newspapers Ltd (No 2)* [1988] 1 All ER 282; [1988] 1 WLR 116n, in which the plaintiff, described as a 'slippery, unscrupulous spiv', was awarded one halfpenny damages).

3. Section 13 of the Civil Evidence Act 1968 was enacted in order to avoid a repetition of cases like *Hinds v Sparks* [1964] Crim LR 717 and *Goody v Odhams Press Ltd* [1967] 1 QB 333; [1966] 3 All ER 369, in which defendants seeking to justify their statements were prevented from relying on the criminal convictions in the subsequent actions for libel.

4. There is nothing to prevent a defendant in an action for libel or slander, founded upon the publication of the fact of a conviction which is 'spent', from relying on the defence of justification or fair comment (s. 8 of the Rehabilitation of Offenders Act 1974). A 'spent' conviction is one which s. 5 of the Act so classifies and this generally excludes sentences of imprisonment exceeding thirty months. However, s. 8(5) of the Act provides, in effect, that

if the plaintiff proves that the defendant *maliciously* published details of a 'spent' conviction, the defence of justification is defeated (cf. qualified privilege, p. 778, post). An interlocutory injunction to restrain publication of a 'spent' conviction will be granted only if the evidence of an irrelevant, spiteful or improper motive is overwhelming: *Herbage v Pressdram Ltd* [1984] 2 All ER 769; [1984] 1 WLR 1160.

(b)   Fair comment

London Artists Ltd *v* Littler Court of Appeal [1969] 2 All ER 193

The four top performers in *The Right Honourable Gentleman* terminated their contracts, through their agents, the plaintiffs. The defendant (Mr Emile Littler, the impresario) was convinced that there was a plot to stop the play. He wrote a letter to each artiste and distributed the letter to the press. In it he suggested that the plaintiffs, all of them connected with the entertainments industry, had taken part in a plot to end a successful play. In an action for libel, the defendant pleaded justification (this defence was later withdrawn), fair comment on a matter of public interest, namely the fate of the play, and publication on an occasion of qualified privilege. The trial judge, [1968] 1 All ER 1075, held that the plea of privilege failed, as did the plea of fair comment because this was not a matter of public interest. The defendant appealed on the ground that the judge had erred on a question of law when he ruled that the defence of fair comment could not be left to the jury. On appeal to the Court of Appeal:

LORD DENNING MR: . . . Three points arise on the defence of fair comment. First, was the comment made on a matter of public interest? The judge ruled that it was not.[1] I cannot agree with him. There is no definition in the books as to what is a matter of public interest. All we are given is a list of examples, coupled with the statement that it is for the judge and not for the jury. I would not myself confine it within narrow limits. Whenever a matter is such as to affect people at large, so that they may be legitimately interested in, or concerned at, what is going on; or what may happen to them or to others; then it is a matter of public interest on which everyone is entitled to make fair comment. A good example is *South Hetton Coal Co Ltd v North-Eastern News Association Ltd*.[2] A colliery company owned most of the cottages in the village. It was held that the sanitary conditions of those cottages – or rather their insanitary condition – was a matter of public interest. Lord Esher MR said[3] that it was 'a matter of public interest that the conduct of the employers should be criticised'. There the public were legitimately *concerned*. Here the public are legitimately *interested*. Many people are interested in what happens in the theatre. The stars welcome publicity. They want to be put at the top of the bill. Producers wish it too. They like the house to be full. The comings and goings of the performers are noticed everywhere. When three top stars and a satellite all give notice to leave at the same time – thus putting a successful play in peril – it is to my mind a matter of public interest on which everyone, press and all, are entitled to comment freely.

The second point is whether the allegation of a 'plot' was a fact which the defendant had to prove to be true, or was it only comment? In order to be fair, the commentator

---

1. [1968] 1 All ER at p. 1088; [1968] 1 WLR at p. 623.
2. [1894] 1 QB 133.
3. [1894] 1 QB at p. 140.

must get his basic facts right. The basic facts are those which go to the pith and substance of the matter, see *Cunningham-Howie v F W Dimbleby & Sons Ltd.*[1] They are the facts on which the comments are based or from which the inferences are drawn—as distinct from the comments or inferences themselves. The commentator need not set out in his original article all the basic facts, see *Kemsley v Foot*;[2] but he must get them right and be ready to prove them to be true. He must indeed afterwards in legal proceedings, when asked, give particulars of the basic facts, see *Burton v Board*;[3] but he need not give particulars of the comments or the inferences to be drawn from those facts. If in his original article he sets out basic facts which are themselves defamatory of the plaintiff, then he must prove them to be true: and this is the case just as much after s. 6 of the Defamation Act 1952, as it was before. It was so held by the New Zealand Court of Appeal in *Truth (NZ) Ltd v Avery*,[4] which was accepted by this court in *Broadway Approvals Ltd v Odhams Press Ltd.*[5] It is indeed the whole difference between a plea of fair comment and a plea of justification. In fair comment, he need only prove the basic facts to be true. In justification he must prove also that the comments and inferences are true also.

So I turn to ask what were the basic facts in this case? In the particulars (as amended by including para. 20A) the defendant set out very many facts which conveyed no clear picture. But, putting them together, it appears that he was relying on three basic facts. First, that the owners wanted to get *The Right Honourable Gentleman* out of Her Majesty's Theatre. Second, that the stars and satellite all gave notice by the same agents at the same time in the same form. Third, that there was a plot between the owners and the stars (through the second plaintiffs, the Grade Organisation Ltd) to bring to an end the run of *The Right Honourable Gentleman*. The defendant proved the first two basic facts, but did not prove the third. He failed to prove a plot and had to withdraw the allegation. That put him in a quandary on fair comment. He could not prove one of the basic facts. So he turned right about. He then submitted that the allegation of a 'plot' was not a fact at all but only a comment. In my view that submission cannot be sustained, and for these reasons: In the first place, the defendant in his pleadings, treated the 'plot' as a statement of fact, and I do not think we should look with favour on such a complete turnabout in the middle of the case. In the second place, the defendant in his evidence said it was a statement of fact. He was asked:

'What was said in the letters was deliberately intended by you to be said. That is right, is it not? A.—It was a statement of fact. Q.—What you believed to be a fact? A.—Yes.'

In the third place, on a fair reading of the whole letter, I think the allegation of a plot was a statement of fact. The first paragraph runs in guarded language, 'it appears'; and the fourth paragraph says 'In other words'; but the last paragraph speaks of 'the combined effort'. Reading the letter as a whole, I have no doubt that it stated *as a fact* that there was a plot between the plaintiffs to bring down a chopper on the head of *The Right Honourable Gentleman*.

Counsel for the defendant submitted, however, that the question whether the statement was a statement of fact or comment should have been left to the jury. He would be right if it was reasonably capable of being considered as comment. That is clear from many of the cases, finishing with the judgment of the Privy Council in *Jones*

---

1. [1951] 1 KB at p. 364; [1950] 2 All ER at p. 883.
2. [1952] AC 345; [1952] 1 All ER 501.
3. [1929] 1 KB 301; [1928] All ER Rep 659.
4. [1959] NZLR 274.
5. [1965] 2 All ER 523; [1965] 1 WLR 805.

v Skelton.[1] But for the three reasons which I have given, I do not think the statement of a 'plot' was reasonably capable of being considered as comment. It was a statement of fact which was itself defamatory of the plaintiffs. The defendant, in order to succeed, had to prove it to be true. He failed to do so, and along with it went the defence of fair comment.

In case, however, I am wrong about this and it could be regarded as comment, then I turn to the third point, which is this: Were there any facts on which a fair-minded man might honestly make such a comment? I take it to be settled law that, in order for the defence of fair comment to be left to the jury, there must at least be a sufficient basis of fact to warrant the comment, in this sense, that a fair-minded man might on those facts honestly hold that opinion. There is no need for the defendant to prove that his opinion was correct or one with which the jury agree. He is entitled to the defence of fair comment unless it can be said: 'No fair-minded man could honestly hold that opinion.' See what Buckley LJ said in *Peter Walker & Son Ltd v Hodgson*.[2]

In this case I am sure that the defendant acted honestly and in good faith. He honestly thought that there was a plot to bring to a stop the run of *The Right Honourable Gentleman*. He was himself so convinced of it that he took the extreme step of telling it to the world. But I fear that he went beyond the bounds of a fair-minded man. He jumped too hastily to his conclusion. He ought not to have been so precipitate. He ought to have made enquiries of the artistes. He ought to have made enquiries of his brother, or wait till he had a letter from him. We know that the brother had on 23 June, that very day, written saying 'We shall have to continue on the same basis as now'. By jumping so quickly to a conclusion the defendant came at odds with the law. He made a public condemnation not only of the artistes themselves but of the plaintiffs, Associated Television, and the agents, London Artists, Mr Lew Grade and the Grade Organisation. The judge held[3] that in alleging that all those were parties to a plot he was making an imputation without any basis of fact to support it. I think the judge was quite right in so holding and in not leaving it to the jury.

In the upshot it comes to this: the fate of *The Right Honourable Gentleman* was a matter of public interest. The defendant was fully entitled to comment on it as long as his comment was fair and honest. He was entitled to give his views to the public through the press. But I think he went beyond the bounds of fair comment. He was carried away by his feelings at the moment. He did not wait long enough to check the facts and to get them right. He had no defence except as to damages; and on that he did well. I would dismiss this appeal.

[EDMUND DAVIES and WIDGERY LJJ delivered judgments in favour of dismissing the appeal.]

Appeal dismissed

Notes

1. In *Slim v Daily Telegraph* [1968] 2 QB 157 at 170, Lord Denning MR said of fair comment: 'We must ever maintain this right intact. It must not be whittled down by legal refinements.' Yet, as Diplock LJ pointed out, in that very case two letters to the *Daily Telegraph* by Mr John Herbert, neither of which could have taken a literate reader more than 60 seconds to read,

---

1. [1963] 3 All ER 952; [1963] 1 WLR 1362.
2. [1909] 1 KB 239 at 253.
3. [1968] 1 All ER at p. 1088; [1968] 1 WLR at p. 624.

became submerged in a legal case in which the pleadings covered 83 pages, the correspondence 300 pages, the evidence 6 days followed by 2 or 3 days' argument, and a judgment of 35 pages, followed by a further 3 days of minute linguistic analysis in the Court of Appeal. The case of *London Artists Ltd v Littler* (ante) took 17 days to try, and was followed by 5 days in the Court of Appeal.

2. In *Sutherland v Stopes* [1925] AC 47 (in which Marie Stopes PhD, who worked for birth control, failed in her action for libel against a Roman Catholic doctor who had commented 'Charles Bradlaugh was condemned to jail for a less serious crime') there are some dicta which suggest that a comment which is expressed in very violent language may be regarded as unfair, although the opinion is honestly held. But dicta in *Slim v Daily Telegraph* and *Littler v London Artists Ltd* suggest that violence of expression is simply evidence that an opinion is not honestly held.

3. A defence of fair comment can be rebutted by proof of malice: *Thomas v Bradbury, Agnew & Co Ltd* [1906] 2 KB 627.

4. A statement may be a comment although no facts, on which that opinion is based, are included, provided the subject-matter is indicated with clarity (see *Control Risks Ltd v New English Library* [1989] 3 All ER 577; [1990] 1 WLR 183). In *Kemsley v Foot* [1952] AC 345; [1952] 1 All ER 501 an article in *Tribune* by Michael Foot was headed 'Lower than Kemsley', and went on to accuse another journalist and the *Evening Standard* of 'the foulest piece of journalism perpetrated in this country for many a year'. The *Evening Standard* had no connection with Kemsley, the well-known newspaper owner. Kemsley alleged that the article's heading imputed that his name was a byword for false and foul journalism. The House of Lords held that the defendant could plead fair comment because there was sufficient subject-matter on which the comment could be based. Had it been a bare inference it would have been treated as a statement of fact, and the only available defence would have been justification. Here the words implied that Kemsley was dishonest and low, but not as low as the Beaverbrook press. This was enough for the defence of fair comment because the words implied certain conduct and commented on that conduct. Moreover, where the defence is fair comment, not coupled as it often is with justification, the defendant is not asserting the truth, but simply that the comment could at the date of publication have been honestly made by a fair-minded person: *Cornwell v Myskow* [1987] 2 All ER 504; [1987] 1 WLR 630.

5. A defendant pleading fair comment has the choice of saying either that 'the said words are fair comment on a matter of public interest', in which case he must give particulars of the facts on which the comment is based, or he can adopt the 'rolled-up plea', namely 'in so far as the said words consist of statements of fact they are true in substance and in fact, and in so far as they consist of expressions of opinion they are fair comment upon the said facts which are matters of public interest', in which case he must state which of the words are statements of fact and he must particularise the facts and matters he relies on to support the allegation that the words are true. The Faulks Committee, para. 176, has recommended the abolition of the 'rolled-up' plea, and, paras. 171–174, that the defence (to be renamed 'comment') should not fail by reason only that the defendant has failed to prove the truth of every relevant assertion of fact.

The Defamation Act 1952

6. Fair comment. – In an action for libel or slander in respect of words consisting partly of allegations of fact and partly of expression of opinion, a defence of fair comment shall not fail by reason only that the truth of every allegation of fact is not proved if the expression of opinion is fair comment having regard to such of the facts alleged or referred to in the words complained of as are proved.

Question

D writes and publishes the following statement: 'P is an undischarged bankrupt and a drug addict. He is not fit to be a councillor.' D proves the truth of the allegation that P is a drug addict, but was mistaken about him being an undischarged bankrupt. Does P have any remedy? What difference would it make if D had omitted the comment?

(c) Privilege

(i) Absolute privilege

The Parliamentary Papers Act 1840

1. Proceedings, criminal or civil, against persons for publication of papers printed by order of Parliament, to be stayed upon delivery of a certificate and affidavit to the effect that such publication is by order of either House of Parliament. – ... It shall and may be lawful for any person or persons who now is or are, or hereafter shall be, a defendant or defendants in any civil or criminal proceeding commenced or prosecuted in any manner soever, for or on account or in respect of the publication of any such report, paper, votes, or proceedings by such person or persons, or by his, her, or their servant or servants, by or under the authority of either House of Parliament, to bring before the court in which such proceeding shall have been or shall be so commenced or prosecuted, or before any judge of the same (if one of the superior courts at Westminster), first giving twenty-four hours notice of his intention so to do to the prosecutor or plaintiff in such proceeding, a certificate under the hand of the lord high chancellor of Great Britain, or the lord keeper of the great seal, or of the speaker of the House of Lords, for the time being, or of the clerk of the Parliaments, or of the speaker of the House of Commons, or of the clerk of the same house, stating that the report, paper, votes, or proceedings, as the case may be, in respect whereof such civil or criminal proceeding shall have been commenced or prosecuted, was published by such person or persons, or by his, her, or their servant or servants, by order or under the authority of the House of Lords or of the House of Commons, as the case may be, together with an affidavit verifying such certificate; and such court or judge shall thereupon immediately stay such civil or criminal proceeding; and the same, and every writ or process issued therein, shall be and shall be deemed and taken to be finally put an end to, determined, and superseded by virtue of this Act.

2. Proceedings to be stayed when commenced in respect of a copy of an authenticated report, etc. – ... In case of any civil or criminal proceeding hereafter to be commenced or prosecuted for or on account or in respect of the publication of any copy of such report, paper, votes, or proceedings, it shall be lawful for the defendant or defendants at any stage of the proceedings to lay before the court or judge such report, paper, votes, or proceedings, and such copy, with an affidavit verifying such report, paper, votes, or proceedings, and the correctness of such copy, and the court or judge shall immediately stay such civil or criminal proceeding; and the same, and every writ or process issued therein, shall be and shall be deemed and taken to be finally put an end to, determined, and superseded by virtue of this Act.

Note

Compare *Church of Scientology of California v Johnson-Smith* [1972] 1 QB 522; [1972] 1 All ER 378 where the plaintiffs alleged that the defendant, a member of Parliament, had made defamatory remarks concerning them during a television interview. The defendant pleaded fair comment and privilege. In order to defeat these pleas the plaintiffs alleged malice, and, in order to establish this, sought to adduce evidence, including extracts from Hansard, of what the defendant had said and done in Parliament. Browne J held that, because of Parliamentary privilege, it was not open to either party to go directly or indirectly into anything said or done in Parliament. Accordingly, although this case arose out of something said outside Parliament, the proceedings in Parliament could not be used to support the allegation of malice and the extracts from Hansard had to be excluded. Although a resolution of the House of Commons on 31 October 1980 has made it unnecessary to petition Parliament before calling evidence of anything that has happened in Parliament, this has not altered the principle laid down in the *Johnson-Smith* case: *R v Secretary of State for Trade, ex p Anderson Strathclyde plc* [1983] 2 All ER 233; *Rost v Edwards* [1990] 2 All ER 641; [1990] 2 WLR 1280, noted p. 781, post.

The Law of Libel Amendment Act 1888

3. Newspaper reports of proceedings in court privileged. – A fair and accurate report in any newspaper of proceedings publicly heard before any court exercising judicial authority shall, if published contemporaneously. with such proceedings, be privileged: Provided that nothing in this section shall authorise the publication of any blasphemous or indecent matter.

The Defamation Act 1952

8. Extent of Law of Libel Amendment Act, 1888, s. 3. – Section three of the Law of Libel Amendment Act, 1888 (which relates to contemporary reports of proceedings before courts exercising judicial authority) shall apply and apply only to courts exercising judicial authority within the United Kingdom.

9. (2) Section seven of this Act and section three of the Law of Libel Amendment Act, 1888, as amended by this Act shall apply in relation to reports or matters broadcast by means of wireless telegraphy as part of any programme or service provided by means of a broadcasting station within the United Kingdom, and in relation to any broadcasting by means of wireless telegraphy of any such report or matter, as they apply in relation to reports and matters published in a newspaper and to publication in a newspaper; and subsection (2) of the said section seven shall have effect in relation to any such broadcasting, as if for the words 'in the newspaper in which' there were substituted the words 'in the manner in which'.

(3) In this section 'broadcasting station' means any station in respect of which a

licence granted by the Postmaster General under the enactments relating to wireless telegraphy is in force, being a licence which (by whatever form of words) authorises the use of the station for the purpose of providing broadcasting services for general reception.[1]

Notes

1. For s. 7 of the Defamation Act 1952, see p. 783, post.

2. It is not clear whether 'privileged' in s. 3 of the Law of Libel Amendment Act 1888 refers to 'qualified' or 'absolute' privilege, but it is generally understood as the latter: *McCarey v Associated Newspapers Ltd* [1964] 2 All ER 335; [1964] 1 WLR 855. If the conditions of s. 3 are not satisfied, then the qualified privilege which exists at common law to publish fair and accurate reports of judicial proceedings becomes relevant. In *Webb v Times Publishing Co Ltd* [1960] 2 QB 535; [1960] 2 All ER 789 Pearson J held that this privilege attaches to the publication of reports of foreign judicial proceedings only if there is a 'legitimate and proper interest as contrasted with an interest which is due to idle curiosity or the desire for gossip'. In the *Webb* case the plea of qualified privilege was upheld in respect of a report of the trial of a British subject in a Swiss court, during which he confessed to having committed a murder for which he had previously been acquitted by an English court and to other crimes for which he was wanted by the police in England.

3. A report is 'fair and accurate' even if the reporter selects parts of a trial to report, e.g. counsel's opening speech in a libel case: *Burnett and Hallam-shire Fuel Ltd v Sheffield Telegraph and Star Ltd* [1960] 2 All ER 157; [1960] 1 WLR 502.

4. A 'spent' conviction, as defined in the Rehabilitation of Offenders Act 1974, may be used as evidence to support a defence of absolute or qualified privilege (s. 8(3)), and where malice is alleged against a defendant who is relying on a defence of qualified privilege, evidence of such conviction is admissible to rebut the allegation (s. 8(4)). A defence that the matter published was a fair and accurate report of judicial proceedings may not be raised if the publication contains a reference to evidence of a 'spent' conviction which was inadmissible by virtue of s. 4(1) of the Act, unless the publication was in a bona fide series of law reports, not forming part of any other publication, or is published as a report or account of judicial proceedings for bona fide educational, scientific or professional purposes, or is given in the course of any lecture, class or discussion for these purposes (s. 8(6) and (7)).

Chatterton *v* Secretary of State for India Court of Appeal [1895-9] All ER Rep 1035

In his statement of claim the plaintiff claimed 'damages for libel from the defendant in that he conveyed or caused to be conveyed in writing to the Under-Secretary of

---

1. [As regards Northern Ireland, s. 9 was repealed by the Police and Criminal Evidence (Northern Ireland) Order 1989, S.I. 1989 No. 1341 (N.I.12), art. 90(2) (3), Sch. 7, pt. III.]

State untrue statements affecting the professional reputation of the plaintiff'. The statement complained of was made by the Secretary of State for India to the Parliamentary Under-Secretary for India in order to enable him to answer a question asked in the House of Commons. The Master made an order dismissing the action as vexatious. This was affirmed by a judge in chambers, and, subsequently by the Divisional Court. The plaintiff appealed to the Court of Appeal.

LORD ESHER MR: . . . The Queen's Bench Division has held that the action cannot be maintained, on the ground that such an act as that which is the subject of the action cannot be inquired into by a civil court of law. It is beyond the powers of a civil court to hold any inquiry upon the matter. In all the reported cases upon the subject it has been laid down that a judge should stop the case, if such an action came before him for trial, because he would have no jurisdiction even to entertain the question. As the action cannot be maintained at all, I think it would be vexatious to allow it to go on.

What is the reason for the existence of this law? It does not exist for the benefit of the official. All judges have said that the ground of its existence is the injury to the public good which would result if such an inquiry were allowed as would be necessary if the action were maintainable. An inquiry would take away from the public official his freedom of action in a matter concerning the public welfare, because he would have to appear before a jury and be cross-examined as to his conduct. That would be contrary to the interest of the public, and the privilege is, therefore, absolute in regard to the contents of such a document as that upon which this action is founded. I shall not go through the reported cases since they are all to the same effect. The result of them is summed up thus by Mr Fraser in his book on *Libel and Slander* (1st edn) p. 95:

'For reasons of public policy the same protection would no doubt be given to anything in the nature of an act of State—for example, to every communication relating to State matters made by one Minister to another, or to the Crown.'

I adopt that paragraph, which seems to me to be an exact statement of the law. . . .

[KAY and A L SMITH LJJ delivered judgments in favour of dismissing the appeal.]

Appeal dismissed

Notes

1. Apart from the defence of absolute privilege in these circumstances, the Crown may be able to claim public interest immunity from disclosure of certain classes of official documents: see J. Beatson and M. H. Matthews, *Administrative Law: Cases and Materials*, 2nd edn, pp. 640–668. In *Hasselblad (GB) Ltd v Orbinson* [1985] QB 475; [1985] 1 All ER 173 the Court of Appeal held that absolute privilege did not attach to documents disclosed to the Commission of the European Communities as evidence in proceedings for restrictive practices, under art. 85 of the EEC Treaty, because its procedure is administrative rather than judicial or quasi-judicial (see next note). However, the document in question could not be used as the basis of a libel action in England against the author of the document since the public interest in the effective conduct by the Commission of its task of investigating breaches of the Treaty would otherwise be severely impeded (May LJ dissented from the conclusion of Sir John Donaldson MR and O'Connor LJ on this latter point).

2. Statements made in the course of proceedings in a court of law or other tribunal with attributes sufficiently similar to a court of law are absolutely privileged: *Trapp v Mackie* [1979] 1 All ER 489; [1979] 1 WLR 377. This does not include conciliation proceedings: *Tadd v Eastwood* [1985] ICR 132. See generally on civil immunities for statements in the course of judicial proceedings, N. V. Lowe and H. F. Rawlings [1982] PL 418 at 431–440 and 445–447.

3. In *Fayed v Al-Tajir* [1988] QB 712; [1987] 2 All ER 396, the Court of Appeal held that an internal memorandum of a foreign embassy in London was protected by absolute privilege in libel proceedings. This privilege was derived not from cases such as *Chatterton v Secretary of State for India* (ante) but was said to rest upon the public policy of not meddling in the affairs of foreign states and on the law of diplomatic relations.

(ii)   Qualified privilege

The Parliamentary Papers Act 1840

3. In proceedings for printing any extract or abstract of a paper, it may be shewn that such extract was bona fide made. – . . . It shall be lawful in any civil or criminal proceeding to be commenced or prosecuted for printing any extract from or abstract of such report, paper, votes, or proceedings[1], to give in evidence . . . such report, paper, votes, or proceedings, and to show that such extract or abstract was published bona fide and without malice; and if such shall be the opinion of the jury, a verdict of not guilty shall be entered for the defendant or defendants.

The Defamation Act 1952

9. **Extension of certain defences to broadcasting.** – (1) Section three of the Parliamentary Papers Act, 1840 (which confers protection in respect of proceedings for printing extracts from or abstracts of parliamentary papers) shall have effect as if the reference to printing included a reference to broadcasting by means of wireless telegraphy.

Note

The Second Report from the Committee of Privileges HC 222, Session 1978–79, paras. 1–10, recommends that the qualified privilege accorded by the Act of 1840, as extended by the 1952 Act, should be further extended to some fair and accurate reports of parliamentary proceedings. Note that at common law a fair and accurate report of parliamentary proceedings is protected by qualified privilege: *Wason v Walter* (1868) LR 4 QB 73. Furthermore, in *Cook v Alexander* [1974] QB 279; [1973] 3 All ER 1037 it was held by the Court of Appeal that a reporter writing a sketch of parliamentary proceedings is entitled to select that part of the proceedings which he considers

---

1. [i.e. those referred to in s. 1 of the Act, p. 774, ante.]

to be of genuine public interest. Provided that the reporting is fair and accurate, it is protected by qualified privilege.

The Defamation Act 1952

10. Limitation on privilege at elections. — A defamatory statement published by or on behalf of a candidate in any election to a local government authority or to Parliament shall not be deemed to be published on a privileged occasion on the ground that it is material to a question in issue in the election, whether or not the person by whom it is published is qualified to vote at the election.

De Buse v McCarthy Court of Appeal [1942] 1 All ER 19

The defendant, a town clerk, sent out a notice convening a meeting of the borough council to consider, among other matters, a report of a committee of the council regarding the loss of petrol from one of the council's depots. Included in the notice was a long agenda of business, and a complete copy of the report of the committee. The notice was not only affixed on or near the door of the town hall, where the council was to meet, but under instructions from the council and in accordance with long-established practice, copies were also sent to each of the public libraries in the borough, where they were available for perusal by ratepayers and other frequenters of the libraries. In actions brought by four employees of the council, who complained that words in the report of the committee were defamatory of them, one of the defendant's pleas was that the notices sent to the public libraries were privileged. Wrottesley J ruled that the occasion of the publication was privileged and there was no evidence of malice to be put before the jury, and he directed that judgment be entered for the defendant with costs. The plaintiffs appealed, asking for judgment or a new trial.

LORD GREENE MR: ... The requirements for such a plea can be taken, of course, from many passages in judgments, but they are very conveniently stated in a passage in the opinion of Lord Atkinson in *Adam v Ward*[1] to which du Parcq LJ referred in the course of the argument. Lord Atkinson said, at p. 334:

'It was not disputed, in this case on either side, that a privileged occasion is, in reference to qualified privilege, an occasion where the person who makes a communication has an interest or a duty, legal, social, or moral, to make it to the person to whom it is made, and the person to whom it is so made has a corresponding interest or duty to receive it. This reciprocity is essential.'

I prefer myself that language which requires the interest or duty to be an interest or duty to make the particular communication in question to language which is sometimes found which refers to an interest in the subject-matter of the communication. The latter phrase appears to me to be vague and to leave uncertain what degree of relevance to a particular subject- matter the communication has to bear. However, adopting the language of Lord Atkinson, we have to consider, in the first instance, what interest or duty the council had to communicate to the ratepayers the report of a committee which the council was proposing to take into its consideration, and which contained not merely statements with regard to the administration of the petrol supply and with regard to the steps which had taken place, but also set out the names of employees who had been accused of complicity in those thefts and made the report and recommendation in relation to them to which I have already referred.

I cannot myself see that it can possibly be said that the council was under any duty

1. [1917] AC 309.

to make that communication to the ratepayers. The matter was at that stage, in a sense, sub judice, because the committee's report by itself was a thing which could have no practical value unless and until it had been taken into consideration by the council and the council had come to some decision upon it. That decision might have been that the report be adopted, or it might have been that the report be not adopted, or it might have been that the report be referred back to the committee. The appointment of committees of that kind is part of the internal management and administration of a body of this description, and, whatever the duty or the interest of the council might have been after it had dealt with the report and come to some decision upon it, I cannot myself see that at that stage in the operation of the machinery of the borough's administration there was any duty whatsoever to tell the ratepayers how the wheels were going round. There may well have been a duty of the council, or, if not a duty, at any rate an interest in the council, to inform the ratepayers of the result of its own deliberations.

If I am right in thinking that there was no duty to make the communication to the ratepayers at that stage, was there an interest in the council to do so? There, again, I cannot see how it can be said that the council had, at that stage of the inquiries, an interest to communicate to its ratepayers the circumstance that the committee had reported in those terms. It is perfectly true — and, indeed, obvious — that the committee itself had both an interest and a duty to make a report to the council, but there could be no common interest, as far as I can see, between the council and the ratepayers to have what, in the circumstances, was only a preliminary stage in the investigation communicated to the ratepayers in the form in which it was communicated. . . .

I have dealt with the question of the interest or duty of the council, and, looking at the other side of the picture, I cannot myself see what interest or duty the ratepayers had to receive the communication. That ratepayers are interested in the proper administration and safeguarding of their property is, of course, obvious. That they are interested in the way in which their council conducts its business is, of course, obvious, but what I may call the internal working of the administrative machine, and all the details of its domestic deliberations, in a case of this kind, are things in which I should have thought ratepayers are not interested unless and until they emerge in the shape of some practical action or practical resolution. The result, therefore, upon the whole case, is that, in my opinion, contrary to the view taken by the judge, the plea of privilege cannot be made good. . . .

I have dealt with the publication in the public libraries as though it were merely a publication to ratepayers, and, on the basis of its being a legitimate publication to ratepayers, the amended defence was drawn. I did not find it necessary to deal with the argument that, even if, as a communication to ratepayers, privilege had been established for it, nevertheless a communication which laid the whole matter open to those who frequent the public libraries was not justified. I mention this point only because I do not wish it to be thought that I am expressing any opinion one way or the other on that matter. . . .

[GODDARD and DU PARCQ LJJ delivered judgments in favour of allowing the appeal and ordering a new trial.]

Appeal allowed

Note

Complaints about the conduct of public authorities or of those with responsibilities to the public are generally protected by qualified privilege provided that they are made in good faith and communicated to a person with a proper interest in the subject-matter. So in *Beach v Freeson* [1972] 1 QB 14; [1971]

2 All ER 854, a letter by a Member of Parliament to the Law Society and the Lord Chancellor in which he set out complaints from one of his constituents concerning the conduct of a firm of solicitors was held to be protected by qualified privilege. The Third Report from the Committee of Privileges HC 417, Session 1976–77, para. 7, endorsing earlier recommendations by the Faulks Committee, para. 203 et seq., has proposed a definition of 'proceedings in Parliament' under new legislation which would make it clear that all things said or written between MPs or between MPs and Ministers to enable MPs to carry out their functions are accorded absolute, and not simply qualified, privilege. For the significance of the phrase 'proceedings in Parliament', see art. 9 of the Bill of Rights 1688 and de Smith and Brazier, *Constitutional and Administrative Law* 6th edn (London, 1989), pp. 315–319 and note *Rost v Edwards* [1990] 2 All ER 641; [1990] 2 WLR 1280 (where it was held that the Register of Members' Interests does not fall within the meaning of 'proceedings in Parliament').

Horrocks *v* Lowe House of Lords [1974] 1 All ER 662

The plaintiff, a Conservative Party councillor in Bolton, complained that at a council meeting he was slandered by the defendant, a councillor leading the Labour Party opposition. The trial judge awarded damages of £400 (costs being estimated at £9,000). The judge had decided that the occasion was privileged but that the defendant was guilty of express malice.

The House of Lords confirmed a decision of the Court of Appeal, which had allowed the defendant's appeal.

LORD DIPLOCK: . . . In the instant case Mr Lowe's speech at the meeting of the Bolton borough council was on matters which were undoubtedly of local concern. With one minor exception the only facts relied on as evidence from which express malice was to be inferred had reference to the contents of the speech itself, the circumstances in which the meeting of the council was held and the material relating to the subject-matter of Mr Lowe's speech which was within his actual knowledge or available to him on enquiry. The one exception was his failure to apologise to Mr Horrocks when asked to do so two days later. A refusal to apologise is at best but tenuous evidence of malice, for it is consistent with a continuing belief in the truth of what he said. Stirling J found it to be so in the case of Mr Lowe.

So the judge was left with no other material on which to found an inference of malice except the contents of the speech itself, the circumstances in which it was made and, of course, Mr Lowe's own evidence in the witness box. Where such is the case the test of malice is very simple. It was laid down by Lord Esher himself, as Brett LJ, in *Clark v Molyneux*.[1] It is: has it been proved that the defendant did not honestly believe that what he said was true, i.e. was he either aware that it was not true or indifferent to its truth or falsity? In *Royal Aquarium and Summer and Winter Garden Society v Parkinson*[2] Lord Esher MR applied the self-same test. . . . All Lord Esher MR was saying was that such indifference to the truth or falsity of what was stated constituted malice even though it resulted from prejudice with regard to the subject-matter of the statement rather than with regard to the particular person defamed. But however gross, however unreasoning the prejudice it does not destroy the privilege unless it has this result. If what it does is to cause the defendant honestly

---

1. (1877) 3 QBD 237.
2. [1892] 1 QB 431 at 444; [1891–94] All ER Rep 429 at 433.

to believe what a more rational or impractical person would reject or doubt he does not thereby lose the protection of the privilege. . . .

[LORD WILBERFORCE, LORD HODSON and LORD KILBRANDON agreed with LORD DIPLOCK. VISCOUNT DILHORNE delivered a speech in favour of dismissing the appeal.]

Egger v Viscount Chelmsford Court of Appeal [1964] 3 All ER 406

The plaintiff was a judge of Alsatian dogs and her name appeared on the list of names kept by the Kennel Club. The secretary of a dog club wrote to the Kennel Club asking that the plaintiff's name might be approved so that she could judge Alsatians at a show. A committee of the Kennel Club decided not to approve the plaintiff's appointment as a judge. On their instructions the assistant secretary wrote to the secretary of the dog club saying that the committee were unable to approve the plaintiff's appointment. The plaintiff sued the members of the committee for alleged libel contained in the letter. The letter was found to be defamatory, but the occasion privileged. The jury found that five members of the committee acted with malice, but acquitted the assistant secretary and three members of the committee of malice. Marshall J held himself bound by the decision in Smith v Streatfeild [1913] 3 KB 764, and gave judgment against all the defendants. The four defendants against whom malice was not found by the jury appealed to the Court of Appeal.

LORD DENNING MR: . . . I cannot help thinking that the root of all the trouble is the tacit assumption that if one of the persons concerned in a joint publication is a tortfeasor, then all are joint tortfeasors. They must, therefore, stand or fall together. So much so that the defence of one is the defence of all: and the malice of one is the malice of all. I think that this assumption rests on a fallacy. In point of law, no tortfeasors can truly be described solely as *joint* tortfeasors. They are always *several* tortfeasors as well. In any joint tort, the party injured has his choice whom to sue. He can sue all of them together or any one or more of them separately. This has been the law for centuries. It is well stated in Serjeant Williams' celebrated notes to *Saunders' Reports* (1845 edn) of *Cabell v Vaughan*.[1]

'If several persons jointly commit a *tort*, the plaintiff has his election to sue all or any number of the parties; because a *tort* is in its nature the separate act of each individual.'

Therein lies the gist of the matter. Even in a joint tort, the tort is the separate act of each individual. Each is severally answerable for it: and, being severally answerable, each is severally entitled to his own defence. If he is himself innocent of malice, he is entitled to be the benefit of it. He is not to be dragged down with the guilty. No one is by our English law to be pronounced a wrongdoer, or be made liable to be made to pay damages for a wrong, unless he himself has done wrong; or his agent or servant has done wrong and he is vicariously responsible for it. Save in the cases where the principle respondent superior applies, the law does not impute wrongdoing to a man who is in fact innocent.

My conclusion is that *Smith v Streatfeild*[2] was wrongly decided and should be overruled: that the obiter dicta on this point of their lordships in *Adam v Ward*[3] were erroneous: and that the general rule stated by Gatley does not exist. It is a

---

1. (1669) 1 Wms Saund 288 at 291.
2. [1913] 3 KB 764; [1911–13] All ER Rep 362.
3. [1917] AC 309; [1916–17] All ER Rep 157.

mistake to suppose that, on a joint publication, the malice of one defendant infects his co-defendant. Each defendant is answerable severally, as well as jointly, for the joint publication: and each is entitled to his several defence, whether he be sued jointly or separately from the others. If the plaintiff seeks to rely on malice to aggravate damages, or to rebut a defence of qualified privilege, or to cause a comment, otherwise fair, to become unfair, then he must prove malice against each person whom he charges with it. A defendant is only affected by express malice if he himself was actuated by it: or if his servant or agent concerned in the publication was actuated by malice in the course of his employment. We have come after several years to find that the law is as Lord Porter's Committee recommended that it should be. . . .

[HARMAN and DAVIES LJJ delivered judgments in favour of allowing the appeal.]

Appeal allowed

Notes

1. Lord Denning's dictum applies to the defence of fair comment as well as to qualified privilege (although Davies LJ disagreed on this point). The Faulks Committee, para. 260, proposed that Lord Denning's view should be approved by statute.

2. The ordinary rules of vicarious liability apply so that an employer or principal is liable if his employee or agent was actuated by malice in making a defamatory statement in the scope of his employment: *Riddick v Thames Board Mills Ltd* [1977] QB 881 at 900, and see p. 766, ante.

3. In *Bryanston Finance Ltd v De Vries* [1975] QB 703; [1975] 2 All ER 609 the members of the Court of Appeal differed as to the exact scope of any original privilege in the situation where a letter is dictated to a typist, but it was said that if the communication ultimately was the subject of qualified privilege, then the dictation, too, was protected, if done in the normal course of business practice.

The Defamation Act 1952[1]

7. Qualified privilege of newspapers. — (1) Subject to the provisions of this section, the publication in a newspaper of any such report or other matter as is mentioned in the Schedule to this Act shall be privileged unless the publication is proved to be made with malice.

(2) In an action for libel in respect of the publication of any such report or matter as is mentioned in Part II of the Schedule to this Act, the provisions of this section shall not be a defence if it is proved that the defendant has been requested by the plaintiff to publish in the newspaper in which the original publication was made a reasonable letter or statement by way of explanation or contradiction, and has refused or neglected to do so, or has done so in a manner not adequate or not reasonable having regard to all the circumstances.

(3) Nothing in this section shall be construed as protecting the publication of any matter the publication of which is prohibited by law, or of any matter which is not of public concern and the publication of which is not for the public benefit.

(4) Nothing in this section shall be construed as limiting or abridging any privilege subsisting (otherwise than by virtue of section four of the Law of Libel Amendment Act 1888) immediately before the commencement of this Act.

(5) In this section the expression 'newspaper' means any paper containing public

---

1. [This is applied to programme services by the Broadcasting Act 1990, s. 166(3).]

news or observations thereon, or consisting wholly or mainly of advertisements, which is printed for sale and is published in the United Kingdom either periodically or in parts or numbers at intervals not exceeding thirty-six days.

SCHEDULE

Newspaper statements having qualified privilege

PART I. STATEMENTS PRIVILEGED WITHOUT EXPLANATION OR CONTRADICTION

1. A fair and accurate report of any proceedings in public of the legislature of any part of Her Majesty's dominions outside Great Britain.

2. A fair and accurate report of any proceedings in public of an international organisation of which the United Kingdom or Her Majesty's Government in the United Kingdom is a member, or of any international conference to which that government sends a representative.

3. A fair and accurate report of any proceedings in public of an international court.

4. A fair and accurate report of any proceedings before a court exercising jurisdiction throughout any part of Her Majesty's dominions outside the United Kingdom, or of any proceedings before a court-martial held outside the United Kingdom under the Naval Discipline Act, [the Army Act 1955 or the Air Force Act 1955].

5. A fair and accurate report of any proceedings in public of a body or person appointed to hold a public inquiry by the government or legislature of any part of Her Majesty's dominions outside the United Kingdom.

6. A fair and accurate copy of or extract from any register kept in pursuance of any Act of Parliament which is open to inspection by the public, or of any other document which is required by the law of any part of the United Kingdom to be open to inspection by the public.

7. A notice or advertisement published by or on the authority of any court within the United Kingdom or any judge or officer of such a court.

PART II. STATEMENTS PRIVILEGED SUBJECT TO EXPLANATION OR CONTRADICTION

8. A fair and accurate report of the findings or decision of any of the following associations, or of any committee or governing body thereof, that is to say—
   (a) an association formed in the United Kingdom for the purpose of promoting or encouraging the exercise of or interest in any art, science, religion or learning, and empowered by its constitution to exercise control over or adjudicate upon matters of interest or concern to the association, or the actions or conduct of any persons subject to such control or adjudication;
   (b) an association formed in the United Kingdom for the purpose of promoting or safeguarding the interests of any trade, business, industry or profession, or of the persons carrying on or engaged in any trade, business, industry or profession, and empowered by its constitution to exercise control over or adjudicate upon matters connected with the trade, business, industry or profession, or the actions or conduct of those persons;
   (c) an association formed in the United Kingdom for the purpose of promoting or safeguarding the interests of any game, sport or pastime to the playing or exercise of which members of the public are invited or admitted, and empowered by its constitution to exercise control over or adjudicate upon persons connected with or taking part in the game, sport or pastime,
being a finding or decision relating to a person who is a member of or is subject by virtue of any contract to the control of the association.

9. A fair and accurate report of the proceedings at any public meeting held in the United Kingdom, that is to say, a meeting bona fide and lawfully held for a lawful purpose and for the furtherance or discussion of any matter of public concern, whether the admission to the meeting is general or restricted.

10. A fair and accurate report of the proceedings at any meeting or sitting in any part of the United Kingdom of —
   (a) any local authority or committee of a local authority or local authorities;
   (b) any justice or justices of the peace acting otherwise than as a court exercising judicial authority;
   (c) any commission, tribunal, committee or person appointed for the purposes of any inquiry by Act of Parliament, by Her Majesty or by a Minister of the Crown;
   (d) any person appointed by a local authority to hold a local inquiry in pursuance of any Act of Parliament;
   (e) any other tribunal, board, committee or body constituted by or under, and exercising functions under, an Act of Parliament,
not being a meeting or sitting admission to which is denied to representatives of newspapers and other members of the public.

11. A fair and accurate report of the proceedings at a general meeting of any company or association constituted, registered or certified by or under any Act of Parliament or incorporated by Royal Charter, not being a private company within the meaning of the Companies Act 1948.

12. A copy or fair and accurate report or summary of any notice or other matter issued for the information of the public by or on behalf of any government department, officer of state, local authority or chief officer of police.

PART III. INTERPRETATION

13. In this Schedule the following expressions have the meanings hereby respectively assigned to them, that is to say: —

   'Act of Parliament' includes an Act of the Parliament of Northern Ireland, and the reference to the Companies Act 1948, includes a reference to any corresponding enactment of the Parliament of Northern Ireland;
   'government department' includes a department of the Government of Northern Ireland;
   'international court' means the International Court of Justice and any other judicial or arbitral tribunal deciding matters in dispute between States;
   'legislature', in relation to any territory comprised in Her Majesty's dominions which is subject to a central and a local legislature, means either of those legislatures;
   ['local authority' means —

   (a) any principal council, within the meaning of the Local Government Act 1972, any body falling within any paragraph of section 100J(1) of that Act and any local authority, within the meaning of the Local Government (Scotland) Act 1973;
   (b) any authority or body to which the Public Bodies (Admission to Meetings) Act 1960 applies; and
   (c) any authority or body to which sections 23 to 27 of the Local Government Act (Northern Ireland) 1972 apply;

   and any reference to a committee of a local authority shall be construed in accordance with sub-paragraph (2) below;][1]
   'part of Her Majesty's dominions' means the whole of any territory within those dominions which is subject to a separate legislature.

[(2) Any reference in this Schedule to a committee of a local authority includes a reference —

  (a) to any committee or sub-committee in relation to which sections 100A to 100D of the Local Government Act 1972 apply by virtue of section 100E of that Act (whether or not also by virtue of section 100J of that Act); . . .]¹

14. In relation to the following countries and territories, that is to say, India, the Republic of Ireland, any protectorate, protected state or trust territory within the meaning of the British Nationality Act 1948, any territory administered under the authority of a country mentioned in [Schedule 3 to the British Nationality Act 1981]² the Sudan and the New Hebrides, the provisions of this Schedule shall have effect as they have effect in relation to Her Majesty's dominions, and references therein to Her Majesty's dominions shall be construed accordingly.

Note

In relation to s. 7, note s. 9(2) and (3) of the Defamation Act 1952 (p. 775, ante). The question under the first limb of s. 7(3), whether a publication is 'prohibited by law' is a pure question of law for the judge; but the questions under the second limb of s. 7(3) of 'public concern' and 'public benefit', are matters for the jury, according to the Court of Appeal in *Kingshott v Associated Kent Newspapers* [1990] 3 WLR 675.

Blackshaw *v* Lord Court of Appeal [1983] 2 All ER 311

The plaintiff complained of a libel in an article written by the first defendant and published by the second defendant in the *Daily Telegraph*. The article was headed '"Incompetence" at Ministry' and stated that a government department had paid £52m to North Sea oil companies which they should not have received, that the investigations of a House of Commons committee had led to a number of civil servants being reprimanded, that the plaintiff was the official in charge of the department's scheme when the overpayments were made, that the plaintiff had resigned from the Civil Service the previous month and that the Chairman of the House of Commons committee had described the events as 'a story of inefficiency, incompetence, inadequate staff and inadequate supervision'. The first defendant had obtained this information from Mr Smith, a press officer in the department, but the article did not state the information also given to him by the press officer that the plaintiff had resigned from the Civil Service for personal reasons, namely to pursue a writing career. In later editions of the newspaper the plaintiff's own explanation of his resignation was published, but the defendants refused to publish an apology and did not publish the vindications of the plaintiff issued by the government department, by the Minister and by the House of Commons committee.

The jury found that the article was defamatory of the plaintiff and that it was not a fair and accurate report of the information given to the first defendant by the press officer, and awarded the plaintiff damages of £45,000 for the libel. The defendants appealed. The Court of Appeal dismissed the appeal, deciding that there was material on which the trial judge had been entitled to leave to the jury the issue whether the article was a fair and accurate report of the information given, and furthermore that the jury had been entitled to find that the article was not a fair and accurate report of that information. The Court of Appeal also considered whether, even if (contrary

---

1. [Amended by the Local Government (Access to Information) Act 1985, s. 3(1), Sch. 2, para. 2.]
2. [Amended by the British Nationality Act 1981, s. 52(6) and Sch. 7.]

to the jury's verdict) the article was to be regarded as a fair and accurate report, it was protected by qualified privilege under s. 7(1) and para. 12 of the Schedule to the Defamation Act 1952 (p. 783, ante), and whether it was protected by qualified privilege at common law, as preserved by s. 7(4) of the 1952 Act.

STEPHENSON LJ [having set out the words of s. 7 and para. 12 of the Schedule to the Defamation Act 1952 (p. 783, ante) continued]: . . . To come therefore within the statutory protection of the privilege provided by para. 12, the defendants had to prove first that what Mr Smith said to Mr Lord was matter, other than a notice, issued for the information of the public by or on behalf of the Department of Energy. The judge ruled that it was. I am of the opinion that it was not.

The judge approached the words of the paragraph 'in not a strictly literal sense but in a fairly liberal way', to include information painfully extracted by journalists, like a tooth, from an official of a government department acting in the course of his employment, as well as formal statements released to the press by the government department. That seems to me to pay too little attention to the word 'issued' and to the language's indication that the matter issued must be of the same kind as a notice. It would unduly restrict the words to confine them to written 'hand-outs', including photographs, sketches or other pictorial representations, which are given as examples in the revised version of para. 12 suggested in the Report of the Committee on Defamation of 1975, presided over by Faulks J (still unimplemented) ((Cmnd 5909) App. XI, p. 273, para. 17); but it is right to confine them to official notices and the like, such as, for example, the police message broadcast on television in *Boston v W S Bagshaw & Sons* [1966] 2 All ER 906; [1966] 1 WLR 1126, the only reported case on the paragraph, statements 'of a genuinely official nature' formally 'issued for the information of the public', in the words accepted by Jordan CJ considering a statutory provision in similar terms in *Campbell v Associated Newspapers Ltd* (1948) 48 SRNSW 301 at 303. It may be right to include in the paragraph's ambit the kind of answers to telephoned interrogatories which Mr Lord, quite properly in the discharge of his duty to his newspaper, administered to Mr Smith. To exclude them in every case might unduly restrict the freedom of the press and I did not understand counsel for the plaintiff to submit the contrary. But information which is put out on the initiative of a government department falls more easily within the paragraph than information pulled out of the mouth of an unwilling officer of the department, and I accept the argument of counsel for the plaintiff that not every statement of fact made to a journalist by a press officer of a government department is privileged, and what is certainly outside the privilege is assumption, inference, speculation on the part of the journalist. That is not authorised; that is not official. If the assumption, inference, speculation were the press officer's, it would not be within the paragraph; Mr Smith was not speaking on behalf of his department if he told Mr Lord the reprimanded official was or must have been the plaintiff. And the defendants' case both as pleaded and as put in evidence alleged no more than that Mr Smith stated assumptions and/or it was inevitably to be inferred from what he said that the plaintiff was the man. A fortiori the reporter's own assumption, inference, speculation could not be attributed to the press officer's department. That would be to accord to investigative journalism the protection provided for reporting of official information. The question whether what Mr Smith said was matter within the paragraph is closely connected with the question whether Mr Lord's article was a report of it or a fair and accurate report of it. But in my judgment Mr Lord's version of what Mr Smith told him, put at its highest, did not bring it or his report of it in his article within the paragraph.

Was the judge also wrong in ruling that the article might be a privileged publication at common law? This point the judge found more difficult, and I have not found it easy. . . .

There is no doubt that 'the general law of qualified privilege is available to newspapers . . . as much as to any other person' (see the Report of the Faulks Committee on Defamation, p. 55, para. 215(f); cf. Duncan and Neill *Defamation* (1978) p. 109, para. 14.29; *Gatley on Libel and Slander* (8th edn, 1981) pp. 251, 277, paras. 591, 649). The common law privilege subsists and is not limited or abridged by the statute: see s. 7(4) of the 1952 Act. . . . But I approach with caution the application of common law privilege to an occasion, or more correctly a publication, which tries and fails to come within statutory privilege, and find no very clear guidance in such authorities as there are on the circumstances in which a newspaper report has the necessary qualifications for the protection of the common law. . . .

The question here is, assuming Mr Lord recorded Mr Smith's conversation with him fairly and accurately, did Mr Lord (and his newspaper) publish his report of that conversation in pursuance of a duty, legal, social or moral, to persons who had a corresponding duty or interest to receive it? That, in my respectful opinion, correct summary of the relevant authorities is taken from the Report of the Faulks Committee, p. 47, para. 184(a), repeated in *Duncan and Neill* p. 98, para. 14.01. I cannot extract from any of those authorities any relaxation of the requirements incorporated in that question. No privilege attaches yet to a statement on a matter of public interest believed by the publisher to be true in relation to which he has exercised reasonable care. That needed statutory enactment which the Faulks Committee refused to recommend (see pp. 53–55 paras. 211–215). 'Fair information on a matter of public interest' is not enough without a duty to publish it and I do not understand Pearson J's ruling in *Webb v Times Publishing Co Ltd* [1960] 2 All ER 789; [1960] 2 QB 535, that a plea of a fair and accurate report of foreign judicial proceedings was not demurrable, was intended to convey that it was enough. Public interest and public benefit are necessary (cf. s. 7(3) of the 1952 Act), but not enough without more. There must be a duty to publish to the public at large and an interest in the public at large to receive the publication; and a section of the public is not enough.

The subject-matter must be of public interest; its publication must be in the public interest. That nature of the matter published and its source and the position or status of the publisher distributing the information must be such as to create the duty to publish the information to the intended recipients, in this case the readers of the Daily Telegraph. Where damaging facts have been ascertained to be true, or been made the subject of a report, there may be a duty to report them (see e.g. *Cox v Feeney* (1863) 4 F & F 13, 176 ER 445, *Perera v Peiris* [1949] AC 1 and *Dunford Publicity Studios Ltd v News Media Ownership Ltd* [1971] NZLR 961), provided the public interest is wide enough (*Chapman v Lord Ellesmere* [1932] 2 KB 431; [1932] All ER Rep 221). But where damaging allegations or charges have been made and are still under investigation (*Purcell v Solwer* (1877) 2 CPD 215), or have been authoritatively refuted (*Adam v Ward* (1915) 31 TLR 299; *affd* [1917] AC 308; [1916–17] All ER Rep 157), there can be no duty to report them to the public. . . .

There may be extreme cases where the urgency of communicating a warning is so great, or the source of the information so reliable, that publication of suspicion or speculation is justified; for example, where there is danger to the public from a suspected terrorist or the distribution of contaminated food or drugs; but there is nothing of that sort here. So Mr Lord took the risk of the defamatory matter, which he derived from what he said were Mr Smith's statements and assumptions, turning out untrue. . . .

[DUNN and FOX LJJ delivered judgments in favour of dismissing the appeal.]

Appeal dismissed

Note

The Faulks Committee, paras. 211–215, in refusing to recommend a defence of 'fair information on a matter of public interest' cited with strong approval the remarks of Lord Goodman, when Chairman of the Newspaper Publishers Association (*New Statesman*, 31 March 1972, p. 426):

'The absorbing question is the one whether the present law prevents editors and publishers from printing material which ought to be printed in order to expose villainy and protect the public from villainy. I have heard this contention over many years and remain unrepentantly sceptical of its truth. A great newspaper – if it believes that some villainy ought to be exposed – should expose it without hesitation and without regard to the law of libel. If the editor, his reporters and his advisers are men of judgment and sense, they are unlikely to go wrong; but if they do go wrong the principle of publish and be damned is a valiant and sensible one for the newspaper and it should bear the responsibility. Publish – and let someone else be damned – is a discreditable principle for a free press. Moreover, the frequent assertion that newspapers have in their archives hundreds of files which would reveal dreadful goings-on has never been established to the satisfaction of any conscientious witness.'

On the other hand, Lord Denning in *What Next in the Law?*, pp. 213–214, advocates a defence of 'fair information on a matter of public interest'. Do the present restrictions imposed by the law of libel prevent journalists in Britain from publishing the kind of information which led to the exposure of the Watergate scandal in the United States?

6 Apology

The Libel Act 1843

[1.] Offer of an apology admissible in evidence in mitigation of damages in action for defamation. – . . . In any action for defamation it shall be lawful for the defendant (after notice in writing of his intention so to do, duly given to the plaintiff at the time of filing or delivering the plea in such action), to give in evidence, in mitigation of damages, that he made or offered an apology to the plaintiff for such defamation before the commencement of the action, or as soon afterwards as he had an opportunity of doing so, in case the action shall have been commenced before there was an opportunity of making or offering such apology.

2. In an action against a newspaper for libel, the defendant may plead that it was inserted without malice and without negligence, and that he has published or offered to publish an apology. – . . . In an action for libel contained in any public newspaper or other periodical publication it shall be competent to the defendant to plead that such libel was inserted in such newspaper or other periodical publication without actual malice, and without gross negligence, and that before the commencement of the action, or at the earliest opportunity afterwards, he inserted in such newspaper or other periodical publication a full apology for the said libel, or, if the newspaper or periodical publication in which the said libel appeared should be ordinarily published at intervals exceeding one week, had offered to publish the said apology in any newspaper or periodical publication to be selected by the plaintiff in such action; . . . and . . . to such plea to such action it shall be competent to the plaintiff to reply generally, denying the whole of such plea.

The Libel Act 1845

2. Defendant not to plead matters allowed by 6 & 7 Vict. c. 96, without payment into court. – . . . It shall not be competent to any defendant in such action, whether in

England or in Ireland, to file any such plea, without at the same time making a payment of money into court by way of amends . . ., but every such plea so filed without payment of money into court shall be deemed a nullity, and may be treated as such by the plaintiff in the action.

Note

See *Duncan and Neill on Defamation* 2nd edn, para. 16.09 as to why this defence is 'seldom if ever used in practice at the present day'.

7 Damages

Cassell & Co Ltd *v* Broome House of Lords [1972] 1 All ER 801

The plaintiff, a retired sea captain of unblemished reputation, won an action for libel arising out of the publication of the book 'The Destruction of Convoy PQ17' by David Irving. The book contained grave imputations on the conduct of the plaintiff who had been the officer commanding the naval ships escorting the ill-fated convoy PQ17. The jury awarded against the publishers and the author (1) the sum of £1,000 in respect of the publication of 60 proof copies of the book; (2) £14,000 described as 'compensatory damages' in respect of the principal or hardback edition of the book, and (3) in respect of the hardback edition a further sum of £25,000 described as 'by way of exemplary damages'. The defendants appealed against the award of £25,000 exemplary damages, but this was dismissed by the Court of Appeal, [1971] 2 All ER 187, which held that (a) the judge's direction on the subject of exemplary damages complied with *Rookes v Barnard* [1964] AC 1129; [1964] 1 All ER 367 and (b) in any event, the decision in *Rookes v Barnard* on the question of damages was arrived at per incuriam and without argument on the point by counsel. The publishers (but not the author) then appealed against the Court of Appeal's decision, to the House of Lords, which dismissed the appeal. The House of Lords held by a majority (Lord Hailsham, Lord Reid, Lord Morris, Lord Diplock and Lord Kilbrandon; Viscount Dilhorne and Lord Wilberforce dissenting) that *Rookes v Barnard* had correctly formulated the rules governing the award of exemplary damages, and that the principles enunciated in that case were applicable to defamation cases. (On this aspect of the case, see the extracts at p. 403, ante.) The House held, further (Viscount Dilhorne, Lord Wilberforce and Lord Diplock dissenting) that on the basis of those principles, the jury's award of £25,000 exemplary damages should be upheld.

The material before the jury was that the author knew fully what he was doing and persisted despite repeated warnings that the relevant passages were defamatory of the plaintiff. His original publishers refused to publish the book on the ground that it was a 'continuous witch hunt of [the plaintiff]'. The defendants then published it despite a warning that it had been rejected by the author's first publishers on the ground that it was libellous. The plaintiff himself warned the publishers that if the book was not modified they must expect an action for libel. Nevertheless the defendants went ahead and published it with a dustjacket which indicated that they were fully aware of the full implications of the passages complained of and were prepared to sell it on the basis of this sensational interpretation of the naval disaster.

LORD HAILSHAM: . . . The final point taken for the appellants was that the award of £25,000 exemplary damages or, as it was equally properly and possibly better put, the total award of £40,000 (which included the exemplary element) was so far excessive of what 12 reasonable men could have awarded that it ought to be set aside and a new trial ordered. I cannot disguise from myself that I found this an extremely difficult point in the case, and have only decided that the verdict should not be disturbed with great hesitation because I am very conscious of the fact that I would certainly have awarded far less myself, and possibly, to use a yardstick which some judges have adopted as a rule of thumb, less than half the £25,000.

A number of factors lead me, however, to the belief that the verdict should not be disturbed. The first, and paramount, consideration in my mind is that the jury is, where either party desires it, the only legal and constitutional tribunal for deciding libel cases, including the award of damages. I do not think the judiciary at any level should substitute itself for a jury, unless the award is so manifestly too large, as were the verdicts in *Lewis v Daily Telegraph Ltd*[1] or manifestly too small, as in *English and Scottish Co-operative Properties Mortgage and Investment Society Ltd v Odhams Press Ltd*[2] that no sensible jury properly directed could have reached the conclusion. . . .

The second reason which leads me to decline to interfere with the jury's verdict in this case is the peculiar gravity of the facts of this case. I share with Phillimore LJ the view that the jury must have found that[3]—

'these were grave libels perpetrated quite deliberately and without regard to their truth by a young man and a firm of publishers interested solely in whether they would gain by the publication of this book. They did not care what distress they caused.'

It is true, and I have been constrained to say, that I would have treated this heinous offence against public decency with far less severity than did the jury in this case. But, at the end of the hearing, I found myself as unable to say as were the three eminent judges in the Court of Appeal[4] that no 12 reasonable jurors could have come to a different conclusion from myself. These matters are very highly subjective, and I do not feel myself entitled to substitute my own subjective sense of proportion or properties for that of the constitutional tribunal appointed by law to determine such matters. . . .

Sutcliffe *v* Pressdram Ltd Court of Appeal [1990] 1 All ER 269

The plaintiff was the wife of a multiple murderer known as the 'Yorkshire Ripper'. The satirical magazine *Private Eye* published an article in 1983 which she alleged meant that she had agreed to sell her story to a national newspaper for £250,000. Three months before the trial of the action in 1989 the magazine published two further articles which the plaintiff alleged meant that she knew before his arrest that her husband was a murderer and had lied to the police to provide him with a false alibi and was defrauding the Department of Social Security. The plaintiff claimed aggravated damages on the basis of the two articles. At the trial the magazine put forward no evidence in support of its plea of justification but relied entirely on cross-examination to prove its case. The jury found that the magazine had libelled the plaintiff and awarded her £600,000 damages. The magazine appealed, contending that the jury's award should be set aside as being out of all proportion to the injury suffered by the plaintiff.

NOURSE LJ: . . . The conduct of a defendant which may often be regarded as aggravating the injury to the plaintiff's feelings, so as to support a claim for aggravated damages, includes: a failure to make any or any sufficient apology and

---

1. [1964] AC 234; [1963] 2 All ER 151.
2. [1940] 1 KB 440; [1940] 1 All ER 1.
3. [1971] 2 All ER at p. 215; [1971] 2 WLR at p. 887.
4. [1971] 2 All ER 187; [1971] 2 WLR 853.

withdrawal; a repetition of the libel; conduct calculated to deter the plaintiff from proceeding; persistence, by way of a prolonged or hostile cross-examination of the plaintiff or in turgid speeches to the jury, in a plea of justification which is bound to fail; the general conduct either of the preliminaries or of the trial itself in a manner calculated to attract further wide publicity; and persecution of the plaintiff by other means. I think it likely that many of these misconducts were featured in many of the recent cases in which . . . large awards have been made. Nobody could say that the jury were not entitled to view them with abhorrence. Nobody could really blame the jury if, as representatives of the public and not as lawyers, they included an exemplary element in their award.

With these general considerations in mind, I come to the particular question which we have to decide. There having been no claim for exemplary damages, is the jury's award of £600,000 by way of compensatory damages one with which this court can and ought to interfere? The various tests which have been stated in the past can be summarised by saying that a jury's award will only be interfered with on appeal if it is so large or so small as to be irrational, that is to say incapable of having been arrived at by a process of reason and necessarily arrived at through emotion, pre-judice, caprice or stupidity, or simply on a wrong basis. Among juries trying civil actions in the late 1980s, we ought to be confident that prejudice, caprice and stupidity are possibilities which exist only in theory. But we must recognise that out of the human attributes for which we prize them they may sometimes make an award on a wrong basis, seasoned perhaps with some seasonable emotion.

The basis on which it was open to the jury to make an award of damages to Mrs Sutcliffe was compensation for the injury to her reputation (in such an amount as was appropriate to vindicate her) and for the injury to her feelings, including the aggravation caused by Private Eye's misconduct. The misconduct relied on by Mrs Sutcliffe and, we must assume, found proved by a jury who regarded it as having been as injurious to the plaintiff's feelings as it was possible for it to be, included the repetition of the libel in the 1983 article, the publication of further libels in the two 1989 articles, being articles calculated to frighten the plaintiff from going on with her action, persistence in a late plea of justification, in part bogus and in its entirety bound to fail, by means of a three-day cross-examination which, although courteous, went 'up hill and down dale', as counsel for Mrs Sutcliffe described it to the jury, and was not in the end supported by any evidence led for Private Eye, and a failure, even after a final invitation made in counsel's closing speech, to make any apology. Counsel for Mrs Sutcliffe also relied on other acts of misconduct and, with further regard to Mrs Sutcliffe's feelings, he emphasised that in 1981, when the first article was published, she was in a uniquely fragile and vulnerable condition.

I have dwelt on the injury, original and aggravated, to Mrs Sutcliffe's feelings, because it is on that injury that she must principally rely in order to sustain the award of £600,000 as one exclusively of compensatory damages. But I bear in mind also that Mrs Sutcliffe was entitled to proper and vindicative compensation for the injury to her reputation. Taking account of all material considerations and with a disposition to resolve and assume everything in her favour, I nevertheless conclude that the amount of the award was very substantially in excess of any sum which could reasonably have been thought appropriate to compensate Mrs Sutcliffe. It must have been made on a wrong basis. I think that the jury, without realising that they were exceeding their function, have included a very large exemplary element in their award.

How do I arrive at that conclusion? We must look into the minds of the jury. We must look, as best we can, into the minds of ordinary sensible men and women, peo-ple with ordinary incomes and mortgages and a proper respect for the reputations and feelings of others, who have watched and listened attentively throughout the trial. Knowing the values of houses, motor cars, foreign holidays and life insurance policies, they could not regard £600,000 as anything other than an enormous sum of money, a sum which would transform the life of any of them who received it.

However grave the injury to Mrs Sutcliffe's reputation, however pressing the need for its vindication, however profound the injury to her feelings and however disgraceful Private Eye's conduct, they could not, these ordinary men and women, think that that enormous sum was appropriate, far less necessary, as compensation for one who in other circumstances might have been numbered among them. And if, with Lord Donaldson MR, they were to look at the £600,000 not simply as a capital sum but as one whose investment would both preserve it and provide Mrs Sutcliffe with a gross income of over £1,000 per week, they would think their view of it to be the more obvious still.

I therefore agree with Lord Donaldson MR that the approach of Pearson LJ in *McCarey v Associated Newspapers Ltd* [1964] 3 All ER 947 at 958, [1965] 2 QB 86 at 106 is sounder than that of Diplock LJ, who thought that, in considering whether a jury's award of damages in a defamation case ought to be interfered with, it was legitimate and valuable for the appellate court to bear in mind the sort of awards which are currently held to be proper in cases of serious physical injury ([1964] 3 All ER 947 at 960, [1965] 2 QB 86 at 109). That approach would not only, as Diplock LJ recognised, involve a comparison of like with unlike. It would require us to look into the minds of judges, who are not, at any rate for this purpose, ordinary sensible men and women.

For these reasons I agree that the jury's verdict, so far as it relates to damages, must be set aside. Had it not been for the rule established by *Cassell & Co Ltd v Broome* [1972] 1 All ER 801, [1972] AC 1027, there must have been a greater doubt whether we could properly take that course. Counsel for Mrs Sutcliffe would have relied even more strongly on the award of £25,000 which was upheld by this court in *Youssoupoff v Metro-Goldwyn-Mayer Pictures Ltd* (1934) 50 TLR 581, a sum which he has calculated might be worth about £900,000 in today's money and which was later described by the successful advocate Sir Patrick Hastings KC as enormous: see *Cases in Court* (1949) p. 39. On the other side, it could have been said with very great force that, even by today's rule, the defendants' conduct in that case merited a very large exemplary award and, moreover, that there the plaintiff's tragedy was on an altogether grander scale. It is not very helpful to attempt comparisons between cases which can never be truly comparable. It is enough to say that we cannot, in a case where there is no claim for exemplary damages, uphold an award which, if it could have been upheld at all, could only have been upheld if there had been such a claim. . . .

It has often been said that our law develops more by accident than by design. Certain it is that we are always learning by experience. Now that this jury, and perhaps others, have made an award on a wrong basis, we must do our best to see that it does not happen again. Lord Donaldson MR has pointed to the most valuable respect in which juries can be further assisted, and in the wisdom of that I wholly concur. I add two further suggestions. In a case where the plaintiff relies on the defendant's alleged misconduct, but where there is no claim for exemplary damages, the judge should emphasise that the jury may only take account of any such misconduct in order to assess the injury, original or aggravated, which it has caused to the plaintiff's feelings. He should tell them that, however great their indignation, they are not allowed to take account of it so as to include an exemplary element in their award. Further, in a case where he deems it appropriate, the judge should warn the jury of the possible consequences of awarding an excessive sum. It may be a real disservice to make an award which is at risk of being set aside by this court, an event which will expose the plaintiff, as regrettably she will now be exposed in this case, to the expense, delay and anxieties of a retrial. No sympathetic jury could want to put the plaintiff through another such ordeal.

There is nothing in an experience of this case which suggests that damages in defamation cases ought to be assessed not by the jury but by the judge. The application of the law as it stands having been clarified by this court, there is no reason to fear that juries, having the benefit of the improved guidance which judges will give them, will not keep to the ways of orthodoxy. Even if there was such a fear, it would need a far greater experience of error before a mode of trial so deeply embedded among our constitutional rights and freedoms could safely be overthrown. . . .

LORD DONALDSON OF LYMINGTON MR: . . . What is, I think, required, is some guidance to juries in terms which will assist them to appreciate the real value of large sums. It is, and must remain, a jury's duty to award lump sums by way of damages, but there is no reason why they should not be invited notionally to 'weigh' any sum which they have in mind to award.

Whether the jury did so, and how it did so, would be a matter for them, but the judge could, I think, properly invite them to consider what the result would be in terms of weekly, monthly or annual income if the money were invested in a building society deposit account without touching the capital sum awarded or, if they have in mind smaller sums, to consider what they could buy with it. Had that been done by the judge in the present case, and I stress that it would have represented a total departure from the existing practice, which he could not be expected to undertake, I think that the result would have been a very large award, but not as high as £600,000, and one with which this court would not have wished to interfere. . . .

[RUSSELL LJ delivered a judgment agreeing that the appeal should be allowed and a new trial ordered on the issue of damages.]

Appeal allowed; new trial ordered on issue of damages

Notes

1. At the time of this case, the Court of Appeal had no power, in place of ordering a new trial, to substitute for the sum awarded by the jury such sum as appeared to the court to be proper. The Courts and Legal Services Act 1990, s. 8(2) will reform the law to give the Court of Appeal this power in future. (By agreement between the parties the award of £600,000 damages in this case was subsequently reduced to £60,000.) The Faulks Committee suggested that the assessment of damages in defamation cases should be left to the judge, after selection of the appropriate category (exemplary, aggravated etc.) by the jury. Justice (the law reform body), in its 1990 report, *Freedom of Expression and the Law*, argued that, failing this, the judge should at least be able to direct the jury on the appropriate level of damages. In Scotland in the few cases where there is a jury the judge can comment on the size of damages and counsel for the parties can suggest appropriate figures; in consequence damages tend to be fairly modest. The Calcutt Committee on Privacy and Related Matters (Cm. 1102, (1990), para. 7.26, noted that since the Court of Appeal's decision in *Sutcliffe v Pressdram Ltd* damages in jury cases have tended to be awarded on a more modest level. *Sutcliffe* had been preceded by a series of very high awards (£500,000 to Mr Jeffrey Archer in 1987, £300,000 to Miss Koo Stark in 1988) and was followed by an award of £1.5m to Lord Aldington in November 1989. See further P. R. Ghandhi (1990) 10 LS 182 at 198–199.

2. The profit-calculation basis for exemplary damages upheld in *Cassell & Co Ltd v Broome* (p. 790, ante) is available where the defendants knew that the article was defamatory or were reckless in that regard and had decided that the economic benefits of publishing outweighed the risk of having to pay compensation to the injured party. Where there are multiple plaintiffs the

appropriate award of exemplary damages, if any, is a single award divided amongst the plaintiffs rather than separate awards for each plaintiff, and the total amount by way of exemplary damages should not exceed the total which the defendant ought to pay by way of punishment (*Riches v News Group Newspapers Ltd* [1985] QB 256; [1986] 2 All ER 845). See generally on the distinction between aggravated and exemplary damages, p. 409, ante.

3. At the other end of the scale from exemplary damages are 'contemptuous' damages – the smallest coin in the realm – used to express the fact that although the plaintiff has technically been libelled, he has such a bad character that the libel was very nearly justified. It is always at the discretion of the judge whether to order that either party shall pay the other's costs and where the plaintiff has only gained the pyrrhic victory of contemptuous damages the judge will be very likely to exercise his discretion to refuse to make an order for costs in the plaintiff's favour (e.g. *Dering v Uris* [1964] 2 QB 669; [1964] 2 All ER 660n).

8   Excursus: the protection of privacy

Report of the Committee on Privacy. Cmnd. 5012 (1972) [Chairman: The Rt. Hon. Kenneth Younger]

62. We consider first the broadest interpretation of privacy; the state of being let alone. We take this to mean freedom from human interference by any means. Privacy would be an element in it, but there are other elements of equal importance: protection from physical harm and restraint, freedom from direction, and peaceful enjoyment of one's surroundings. The threats to these could take the form of injurious acts by other private persons, of public impositions or of man-made disasters or nuisances, and any one of these might threaten several of the elements which constitute the state of being let alone. A badly maintained factory chimney which falls on your family in your private house causes physical harm and interferes with the peaceful enjoyment of your surroundings; it also invades your privacy, but most people would not spontaneously make that the reason for being angry about it. Arbitrary arrest at home interferes with peaceful enjoyment and involves direction; it is also an invasion of privacy, but is unlikely to be condemned primarily on that score.

63. If there were to be a right of privacy under the law it should not, in our opinion, be synonymous with a right to be let alone. An unqualified right of this kind would in any event be an unrealistic concept, incompatible with the concept of society, implying a willingness not to be let entirely alone and a recognition that other people may be interested and consequently concerned about us. If the concept were to be embodied into a right, its adaptation to the dominant pressures of life in society would require so many exceptions that it would lose all coherence and hence any valid meaning. We have concluded therefore that the type of conduct against which legal protection might be afforded on the ground of intrusion on privacy should be confined to injurious or annoying conduct deliberately aimed at a particular person or persons where the invasion of privacy is the principal wrong complained of.

69. It has been suggested to us that there are two other constituents of privacy [apart from those discussed elsewhere in the Report and not relevant in this context] – freedom from interference with moral and intellectual integrity and freedom from

being placed in a false light. These are both constituents of the Nordic Conference concept of the right to be let alone,[1] a concept we have already rejected as a whole in paragraph 63. But they occur elsewhere. As to the first, we received no serious evidence that subliminal influencing, sleep teaching, manipulative selection, group conditioning and other uses of the behavioural sciences to influence people's subconscious minds are a problem in this country or that special legal protection is needed against them.

70. Placing someone in a false light is one of the four torts into which Dean Prosser has analysed the United States law of privacy,[2] which seem to have influenced the Nordic Conference[3] and they in turn the 'Justice' Bill.[4] We consider that placing someone in a false light is an aspect of defamation rather than of privacy.[5]

71. We do not support the view of those who argue that the publication of an untruth about a person should be treated by the law as an invasion of privacy rather than under the heading of defamation. In this connection we commend the warning by Professor Harry Kalven about the way in which the 'false light' aspect of privacy has been used in the United States to extend the scope for actions of a defamation nature.[6] He says that any extensions of the law of defamation should be made openly as such, but he suggests also that the restrictions on the application of the law of defamation may reflect a wise caution about permitting its extension to the mollification of outraged dignity. We were interested in this connection to learn of the development of case law on defamation and 'false light' in the decisions of the Federal Court of the Federal Republic of Germany: defamation has lost its identity there as a separate tort and become fused into the broader tort of infringement of the right of personality (Persönlichkeitsrecht).[7] To our mind there could be a real threat to freedom of speech if the safeguards for it that have been built into the law of defamation were to be put in jeopardy by the process of subsuming defamation into a wider tort which is implied by the doctrine of 'false light'.[8] We believe that the

---

1. Conclusions of the Nordic Conference of International Jurists on the Right of Privacy, Stockholm 1967; . . .
2. 'Privacy', Dean William L. Prosser, *California Law Review*, August 1960.
3. Conclusions of the Nordic Conference of International Jurists on the Right of Privacy, Stockholm 1967.
4. 'Privacy and the Law', Appendix J, clause 9(e) and (f).
5. The law on defamation is under consideration by the Committee set up in May 1971 under the Chairmanship of Mr Justice Faulks 'to consider whether, in the light of the Defamation Act 1952, any changes are desirable in the law, practice and procedure relating to actions for defamation'.
6. 'Privacy in Tort Law—Were Warren and Brandeis Wrong?' *Law and Contemporary Problems*, Chicago University 1966:
   '. . . if the colonization of defamation by privacy does take place, it will only be because by the use of a fiction the courts have turned at last to reform of the law of defamation. It will not be because they have perceived that logically defamation is subsumed in privacy. They will simply be calling false statements by a new name . . . one may wonder if this trend represents even good judicial statesmanship. The technical complexity of the law of defamation, which has shown remarkable stamina in the teeth of centuries of acid criticism, may reflect one useful strategy for a legal system forced against its ultimate better judgment to deal with dignitary harms. . . . In any event, it would be a notable thing if the right of privacy, having, as it were, failed in three-quarters of a century to amount to anything at home, went forth to take over the traditional torts of libel and slander.'
7. Oral evidence of Professor Dr Hein Kötz, 6 January 1972.
8. See also the Report of the Porter Committee on the Law of Defamation, 1948, Cmnd. 7536, paras. 24–26.

concepts of defamation and of intrusion into privacy should be kept distinct from one another. . . .

Report of the Committee on Privacy and Related Matters. Cm 1102 (1990) [Chairman: David Calcutt QC]

Possible definition

12.17   We are satisfied that it would be possible to define a statutory tort of infringement of privacy. This could specifically relate to the publication of personal information (including photographs). . . . Personal information could be defined in terms of an individual's personal life, that is to say, those aspects of life which reasonable members of society would respect as being such that an individual is ordinarily entitled to keep them to himself, whether or not they relate to his mind or body, to his home, to his family, to other personal relationships, or to his correspondence or documents.

12.18   We would not see any advantage in laying down a more detailed definition of personal information on the face of any statute. The courts could develop their interpretation on a case by case basis. We would, however, see merit in specifically excluding any material:

a) concerning any company or other corporate entity, or any firm or partnership: or

b) concerning an individual in relation to his conduct in the way of any trade, business, calling or profession, or in relation to his carrying out of any functions or duties attaching to, or to his suitability for, any office or employment (including any elective office); or

c) required by law to be registered, recorded or otherwise available for public inspection.

Defences

12.19   All proposals for a tort of infringement of privacy have included a number of defences. These have been of two kinds: the specific and the general. Specific defences have included consent, legal privilege, lawful authority and absence of intent. Defences of this kind would clearly be necessary if a tort were ever to be introduced, perhaps that the act of publication was done:

a) with the consent, general or specific, of the individual whose privacy was infringed; or

b) in circumstances which would give rise to a defence of absolute or qualified privilege if the proceedings had been founded on the tort of defamation; or

c) in circumstances in which the defendant, having exercised all reasonable care, did not know that his act would or might constitute an infringement of the plaintiff's privacy; or

d) at a time when the personal information in question had already come into the public domain through no act or default of the defandant; or

e) under lawful authority.

Public interest

. . .

12.22   . . . [W]e have serious reservations about a general defence merely labelled 'public interest'. We should not consider it appropriate for any tort of infringement of privacy. A defence to cover the justified disclosure of personal information would, however, clearly be necessary, but it would need to be tightly drawn and specific. . . .

12.23   We consider, therefore, that the additional defence would have to be limited to any infringement where the defendant had reasonable grounds for believing that:

a) publication of the personal information would contribute to the prevention, detection or exposure of any crime or other seriously anti-social conduct; or
b) it would be necessary for the protection of public health or safety; or
c) there would, but for the publication, be a real risk that the public, or some section of the public, would be materially misled by a statement previously made public by or on behalf of any individual whose privacy would otherwise be infringed (whether the plaintiff or otherwise).

Freedom of speech

12.24   A number of arguments of principle, many of them relating to freedom of speech, have been advanced against the creation of a statutory tort of infringement of privacy. We do not accept that such a tort would be the thin end of a wedge leading towards censorship. A law designed solely for the protection of individual citizens and their personal lives should offer no scope for Government interference. Furthermore, there is no necessary inter-relationship between protection of individual privacy (in the terms in which we discuss it in this report) and censorship by Government. We cannot, therefore, accept the argument that no tort of infringement of privacy should be introduced unless balanced by some provision for the entrenchment of freedom of speech or a Freedom of Information Act.

12.25   Nor do we agree that a narrowly-drawn tort would inhibit serious investigative journalism or that responsible newspapers would suffer for the misdeeds of others. Serious investigative journalism would be outside the scope of such a law, especially when exposing serious wrong-doing. There is a clear distinction between infringements of privacy deriving from prurient curiosity and those associated with legitimate journalism. . . . Most people have little difficulty in recognising where the boundary lies. . . .

12.26   On the other hand, we are conscious that a tort of infringement of privacy would mark a new departure in the law. It might extend restrictions on the press even to situations where the information was not only true but also where it:

a) would not necessarily cause any significant or lasting harm;
b) had been obtained by reputable means; and
c) was already known within the complainant's own circle of acquaintances.

12.27   In addition a tort might have the effect of stifling reports about the failings of people in the public eye who use the media to promote themselves. We have the impression that many people would agree with the sentiments expressed by Lord Denning, the Master of the Rolls, in *Woodward v Hutchins* [1977] 1 WLR 760, at page 763, where he said:

'There is no doubt whatever that this pop group sought publicity. They wanted to have themselves presented to the public in a favourable light so that audiences would come to hear them and support them. Mr Hutchins was engaged so as to produce, or help to produce, this favourable image, not only of their public lives but of their private lives also. If a group of this kind seek publicity which is to their advantage, it seems to me that they cannot complain if a servant or employee of theirs afterwards discloses the truth about them. If the image which they fostered was not a true image, it is in the public interest that it should be corrected.'

Physical intrusion

12.33   . . . [W]e do not consider that physical intrusion as such is best tackled by means of a civil remedy. That is why we propose the creation of new criminal offences and why we would exclude such intrusion from the definition of infringement of privacy in any tort. . . . A civil remedy would, however, be valuable against the imminent or actual publication of material obtained by means of physical intrusion. Accordingly, . . . we recommend that anyone having a sufficient interest should be able to seek an injunction and damages in respect of the publication of private material or photographs obtained by committing any of certain proposed offences[1]. . . . We consider that such a tightly-drawn civil remedy, closely linked to acts that most people would regard as clearly wrong, would tackle many of the worst forms of infringement of individual privacy.

Notes

1. In *Kaye v Robertson* (1990) Times, 21st March the Court of Appeal ruled out the development of a tort of privacy in English law, and urged Parliament to consider legislation on the subject. The unauthorised intrusion of reporters and photographers into the hospital room of a seriously ill actor was described by Bingham LJ as 'a monstrous invasion of privacy'. An interlocutory injunction was granted to restrain publication of anything which could convey that the actor had consented to be photographed or interviewed, on the ground that this would constitute a malicious falsehood (see p. 760, ante). It is to be noted that s. 85 of the Copyright, Designs and Patents Act 1988 gives a right of privacy to prevent private or domestic photographs and films from being issued or shown to the public.

2. The Calcutt Committee considered arguments for and against a statutory tort of privacy and (like a majority of the Younger Committee, paras. 634–650) concluded that the case for legislation was not 'overwhelming'. The Committee said that the press should be given 'one final chance to prove that self-regulation can work' (para. 14.38) and added that, were further consideration at any time to be given to the introduction of such a tort, this should not be limited to the press. The Committee proposed that the Press Council should be disbanded and that a new Press Complaints Commission should provide redress against, inter alia, unwarranted invasions of privacy (paras. 14.38 and 15.34). If this mechanism did not work, the Committee recommended that a statutory Press Complaints Tribunal for handling complaints should be established (para. 16.9). In privacy cases, the Tribunal should be able to restrain publication in breach of a proposed code of practice by injunctions (para. 16.17).

3. The Data Protection Act 1984, implementing the European Convention on Data Protection, confers rights of access, rectification, erasure and compensation upon individuals who are the subject of data consisting of information which relates to a living individual. Data users are obliged to register on a public register. Upon payment of a prescribed fee a data subject is

---

1. [The proposed offences are: (a) entering private property, without the consent of the lawful occupant, with intent to obtain personal information with a view to its publication; (b) placing a surveillance device on private property, without the consent of the lawful occupant, with intent to obtain personal information with a view to its publication; (c) taking a photograph, or recording the voice, of an individual who is on private property, without his consent, with a view to its publication with intent that the individual shall be identifiable.]

entitled to know whether a data user holds information concerning him in a form in which it can be processed by equipment operating automatically in response to instructions (the Act does not cover manual records). If so, he is entitled to have a copy within forty days of his request. This is enforceable by court order, or by the issue of an enforcement notice by the Data Protection Registrar (s. 21). The data subject may recover compensation for damage and distress caused by inaccuracy in personal data held by a data user (s. 22(1)). Data is inaccurate for this purpose only as to any matter of fact (s. 22(4)), thus excluding expressions of opinion. It is a defence for the data user to prove that he has taken such care in all the circumstances as was reasonably required to ensure the accuracy of the data at the material time (s. 22(3)). The data subject also has a right to claim compensation from a data user or a computer bureau for damage by reason of loss of the data, or unauthorised destruction or disclosure or access to the data (s. 23(1)). There is a defence that the user or bureau has taken such care as in all the circumstances was reasonably required to prevent the loss, destruction or disclosure in question. Rectification and erasure of inaccurate data (including opinion based on inaccurate data) may be ordered by a court on application by the data subject (s. 24(1)). Even where the information is accurate, the court may order erasure of the data on the grounds of unauthorised access to or disclosure causing damage to the data subject where there is a substantial risk of further disclosure or access to the data (s. 24(3)). These obligations are subject to wide-ranging exemptions (Part IV). For a critique of the Act see R. C. Austin [1984] PL 618; and for the background see the Younger Committee Report, Cmnd. 5012 and the White Papers, *Computers and Privacy*, Cmnd. 6353, 1975, and *Computers: Safeguards for Privacy*, Cmnd. 6354, 1975, and the Report of the Lindop Committee, Cmnd. 7341, 1978 which sets out a scheme for the legislation. J. Michael, *The Politics of Secrecy* (London, 1982), chap. 9, gives a description of data protection systems in other countries.

4. In *Malone v Metropolitan Police Comr* [1979] Ch 344; [1979] 2 All ER 620, Megarry V-C held that there is no common law right in England to 'telephonic privacy' and refused to grant a declaration to the plaintiff that the tapping of his telephone on the authority of the Secretary of State was unlawful. The Crown could profit from the maxim that what is not specified to be illegal is legal; one might compare the more robust attitude of judges to civil liberties in *Entick v Carrington* (1765) 19 State Tr 1029, and *Ashby v White* (1703) 2 Ld Raym 938 (see C. Harlow, *Compensation and Government Torts* (London, 1983), pp. 43–44; *Williams & Hepple*, pp. 61–66). The European Court of Human Rights subsequently ruled that the telephone tapping in the *Malone* case was contrary to arts. 8 and 13 of the European Convention on Human Rights and Fundamental Freedoms. The Interception of Communications Act 1985 now makes unauthorised interception a criminal offence, and a special tribunal is empowered to order the payment of compensation where there were insufficient grounds for authorising interception.

5. As regards the privacy of the home see *Lord Bernstein of Leigh v Skyviews and General Ltd* [1978] QB 479; [1977] 2 All ER 902 (p. 614, ante) and *Patel v Patel* [1988] 2 FLR 179.

6. There is an enormous literature on the subject of privacy. A few useful

works are: R. Wacks, *The Protection of Privacy* (London, 1980), and *Personal Information: Privacy and the Law* (Oxford, 1989); A. F. Westin, *Privacy and Freedom* (London, 1970); W. F. Pratt, *Privacy in Britain* (Lewisburg and London, 1979); S. I. Benn (1978) 52 ALJ 601, 686; S. Stoljar (1984) 4 LS 67; Z. Segal [1982] PL 240 (a comparison of English law with the Israel Protection of Privacy Law 1981). The classic starting point of modern legal conceptions of privacy is the article by S. D. Warren and L. Brandeis (1890) 4 Harv LR 193; cf. H. Kalven Jr (1966) 31 Law and Contemporary Problems 326; P. H. Winfield (1931) 47 LQR 23; G. D. S. Taylor (1971) 34 MLR 288.

7. There is a distinction between a right of privacy in respect of information and a right of action for breach of confidence. Under the existing law, in the absence of an express or implied contract, confidentiality depends upon (a) the information having the necessary quality of confidence about it; (b) the information having been imparted in circumstances involving an obligation of confidence; and (c) unauthorised use or disclosure of the information to the detriment of the person using it (*Coco v A N Clark (Engineers) Ltd* [1969] RPC 41 at 47). It is difficult to say how far, if at all, the present action for breach of confidence rests upon tort, or rather upon a broad equitable obligation of conscience (see *A-G v Guardian Newspapers Ltd (No 2)* [1990] 1 AC 109; [1988] 3 All ER 545, and compare the views of P. M. North (1972) 12 JSPTL 149 with those of G. H. Jones (1970) 86 LQR 463). The Law Commission (*Breach of Confidence* Law Com. No 110) has proposed the abolition of the present action in order to create a statutory tort for breach of confidence replacing the courts' jurisdiction in equity and property, but leaving largely unimpaired the jurisdiction in contract. For comments see F. Gurry *Breach of Confidence* (Oxford, 1984), pp. 474–479; Y. Cripps (1984) 4 Oxf JLS 361, and [1983] PL 600; G. H. Jones [1982] CLJ 40.

Loss distribution

17 Vicarious liability

The individual defendant in a tort action is not infrequently a man of straw. The typical modern way of ensuring that the plaintiff actually receives the compensation to which he is entitled is through the device of compulsory insurance (p. 885, post). But there is also an older legal mechanism which enables the plaintiff to fix responsibility upon someone other than the impecunious actor. This is the principle of vicarious liability. The actor and the person to whom responsibility is imputed are jointly liable to the plaintiff. The person who actually pays may be able to recover that payment from the actor (p. 871, post); but so far as his liability to the plaintiff is concerned this appears as a form of strict liability, imposed regardless of personal fault. The justification for this principle is controversial (e.g. p. 821, post). The most widely accepted theory is that the person with the power of control and direction over the actor is usually the best fitted to absorb the loss: this is likely to be an enterprise which can pass on the costs of insurance or self-insurance to consumers of its products in the form of higher prices, to shareholders in the form of reduced dividends, and to employees in the form of smaller wage increases. If all those who committed torts were adequately insured there would be no need for a doctrine of vicarious liability. So goes the theory. But in reading the cases which follow the student will be unable to test its validity because the courts refuse to investigate the facts of insurance or the economics of loss distribution. *Morgans v Launchbury* [1973] AC 127; [1972] 2 All ER 606 (p. 819, post) is the clearest example of conscious judicial avoidance of policy-making in this area.

The most important factor delimiting the scope of vicarious liability is not any theoretical principle, but simply judicial precedent. As a matter of law, the defendant (D) will be made vicariously liable to the plaintiff (P) in respect of the acts of another person (X) only if P shows that —

(1) X has committed a *wrongful act* which has caused P damage;

(2) some *special relationship recognised by law* exists between D and X, for example a contract of employment, or the delegation of the task of driving a motor vehicle for the owner's purposes;

(3) some *connection* exists between the act of X and his special relationship with D — in the traditional formula the act must be in 'the course of X's employment' or, what amounts to much the same thing, in 'the scope of X's authority'.

Each of these points raises its own difficulties. In regard to the first, must X's act constitute a *tort*? Or is the real basis of this form of liability the attribution of X's *act* to D so as to make it D's tort? This point is usually only raised when it is sought to attribute X's knowledge to D (as in *Armstrong v Strain* [1952] 1 KB 232; [1952] 1 All ER 139, noted p. 829, post) or to allow

D to limit his liability by an express prohibition on certain conduct by X (like giving unauthorised lifts in *Rose v Plenty* [1976] 1 All ER 97; [1976] 1 WLR 141, p. 839, post). One notes an increasing tendency for the courts to impose primary or direct liability on the employer, rather than to resort to the device of vicarious liability (see pp. 810 and 814, post).

The second point raises problems of definition. There is only one special relationship which, as a general rule, gives rise to vicarious liability. This is the one between employer and employee ('master' and 'servant' in the older terminology). It is therefore necessary to consider the various tests by which the existence of a contract of employment (i.e. of service) as distinct from a contract with an independent contractor (i.e. for services) is to be determined, (p. 807, post). The many borderline cases which arise, particularly in the context of the growing practice of employment under Forms other than the 'contract of service', indicate the artificiality of the general rule. Another special relationship which may sometimes, but does not always, give rise to vicarious liability is that between 'principal' and 'agent'. These terms have a special connotation in the law of contract; in the law of tort they are simply a form of shorthand descriptive of circumstances in which vicarious liability has been imposed. The materials in the second section of this chapter relate to four such circumstances (p. 819, post).

The third point is a question of mixed law and fact. Factual issues such as 'Did D authorise X to drive his car?' are sometimes closely connected with legal issues such as whether particular acts should be regarded as a custom or should be implied as terms in a contract. In dealing with this question precedent must be treated with extreme caution, because the cases are so often simply concerned with applying a general test to particular facts. (It should be noted that the old Workmen's Compensation Act cases and those under social security legislation use the phrase 'arising out of and in the scope of employment'. This phrase is narrower than the common law 'course of employment', e.g. in regard to express prohibitions; moreover, those cases are concerned with the question whether the injured workman can recover compensation, not with the employer's liability to strangers *outside* the enterprise in respect of the acts of workmen.)

Consideration of the question of liability for independent contractors has been left to sections 4 and 5 (pp. 851, 858, post) since this raises the most controversial conceptual problems. The instances of such liability are rare. Do they rest upon the breach of some personal 'non-delegable' duty by the employer? Or is the notion of 'non-delegable' duties simply a 'logical fraud' (in the words of G. L. Williams [1956] CLJ 180) disguising vicarious liability? Historically, the adoption of the concept of 'non-delegable' duties enabled the courts to avoid the hardships to employees caused by the doctrine of common employment: see *Wilsons and Clyde Coal Co Ltd v English* [1938] AC 57; [1937] 3 All ER 628 (p. 566, ante). But the continued use of this terminology, despite the statutory abolition of the doctrine of common employment has led to curious results in regard to the employer's liability to his own employees in respect of the acts of an independent contractor (p. 859, post) which have only partially been remedied by the Employer's Liability (Defective Equipment) Act 1969 (p. 858, post).

The chapter concludes with a brief view of some of the problems of distinguishing 'personal' and 'vicarious' liability in the context of corporations, trade unions and associations. The plaintiff may have been injured through a failure of team-work in which case the corporation is sometimes treated as 'personally' liable; in reality this may simply be another way of saying that one or more employees of the corporation has been negligent (p. 864, post).

1 Liability for employees

Mersey Docks and Harbour Board v Coggins and Griffiths Ltd
House of Lords [1946] 2 All ER 345

The Board (the appellants) hired out to the respondents, who were master stevedores, the use of a mobile crane together with its driver, Newall, for the purpose of loading a ship. Through his negligent handling of the crane, Newall injured a stevedore called MacFarlane. The question in issue was whether Newall was to be regarded as the employee of the Board or of the respondents, when he set the crane in motion. An agreement between the Board and the respondents said that he was to be the respondents' employee, but the Board continued to pay his wages and had the power to dismiss him. The respondents had the power to tell him *what* to do, i.e. where to station the crane, whether to lift or lower the load etc., but had no power to direct *how* he should work the crane. The manipulation of the controls was a matter for Newall himself.

The Court of Appeal, [1945] 1 All ER 605, held that he was acting as employee of the Board, who were, accordingly, vicariously liable for his tortious act. On appeal:

VISCOUNT SIMON: . . . It is not disputed that the burden of proof rests upon the general or permanent employer – in this case the board – to shift the prima facie responsibility for the negligence of servants engaged and paid by such employer so that this burden in a particular case may come to rest on the hirer who for the time being has the advantage of the service rendered. And, in my opinion, this burden is a heavy one and can only be discharged in quite exceptional circumstances.

It is not easy to find a precise formula by which to determine what these circumstances must be. . . .

The Court of Appeal in this case, following its own decision in *Nicholas v F J Sparkes & Son*[1] applied a test it had formulated, where a vehicle is lent with its driver to a hirer, by propounding the question ([1945] 1 All ER 605 at 608):

'In the doing of the negligent act was the workman exercising the discretion given him by his general employer, or was he obeying or discharging a specific order of the party for whom upon his employer's direction, he was using the vehicle . . .?'

I would prefer to make the test turn on where the authority lies to direct, or to delegate to, the workman, the manner in which the vehicle is driven. It is this authority which determines who is the workman's *superior*. In the ordinary case, the general employers exercise this authority by delegating to their workman discretion in the method of driving, and so the Court of Appeal correctly points out ([1945] 1 All ER 605 at 608), that in this case the driver Newall:

'. . . in the doing of the negligent act, was exercising his own discretion as driver – a discretion which had been vested in him by his regular employers when he was sent out with the vehicle – and he made a mistake with which the hirers had nothing to do.'

---

1. [1945] KB 309n.

If, however, the hirers intervene to give directions as to how to drive which they have no authority to give, and the driver *pro hac vice* complies with them, with the result that a third party is negligently damaged, the hirers may be liable as joint tort-feasors.

I move that the appeal be dismissed with costs.

LORD PORTER: . . . Many factors have a bearing on the result. Who is paymaster, who can dismiss, how long the alternative service lasts, what machinery is employed — all these questions have to be kept in mind. The expressions used in any individual case must always be considered in regard to the subject matter under discussion, but among the many tests suggested I think that the most satisfactory by which to ascertain who is the employer at any particular time is to ask who is entitled to tell the employee the way in which he is to do the work upon which he is engaged. If someone other than his general employer is authorised to do this, he will, as a rule, be the person liable for the employee's negligence. But it is not enough that the task to be performed should be under his control, he must also control the method of performing it. It is true that in most cases no orders as to how a job should be done are given or required. The man is left to do his own work in his own way, but the ultimate question is not what specific orders, or whether any specific orders, were given, but who is entitled to give the orders as to how the work should be done. Where a man driving a mechanical device, such as a crane, is sent to perform a task, it is easier to infer that the general employer continues to control the method of performance since it is his crane and the driver remains responsible to him for its safe keeping. In the present case, if the appellants' contention were to prevail, the crane driver would change his employer each time he embarked on the discharge of a fresh ship. Indeed, he might change it from day to day, without any say as to who his master should be and with all the concomitant disadvantages of uncertainty as to who should be responsible for his insurance in respect of health, unemployment and accident.

I cannot think that such a conclusion is to be drawn from the facts established. I should dismiss the appeal.

LORD SIMONDS [read by LORD UTHWATT]: . . . It is not disputed that at the time when the respondents entered into a contract with the appellants under which the latter were to supply the former with the service of a crane and craneman, Newall was the servant of the appellants. He was engaged and paid and liable to be dismissed by them. So also, when the contract had been performed, he was their servant. If, then, in the performance of that contract he committed a tortious act, injuring McFarlane by his negligence, they can only escape from liability if they can show that *pro hac vice* the relation of master and servant had been temporarily constituted between the respondents and Newall and temporarily abrogated between themselves and him. This they can do only by proving, in the words of Lord Esher MR, in *Donovan's* case[1] that entire and absolute control over the workman had passed to the respondents. In the cited case the court held upon the facts that the burden of proof had been discharged and I do not question the decision. But it appears to me that the test can only be satisfied if the temporary employer (if to use the word 'employer' is not to beg the question) can direct not only what the workman is to do but also how he is to do it.

In the case before your Lordships, the negligence of the workman lay, not in the performance of any act which the respondents could and did direct and for which, because they procured it, they would be responsible, but in the manner in which that act was performed, a matter in which they could give no direction and for which they can have no responsibility.

The doctrine of the vicarious responsibility of the *superior*, whatever its origin, is

---

1. [1893] 1 QB 629.

to-day justified by social necessity, but, if the question is where that responsibility should lie, the answer should surely point to that master in whose act some degree of fault, though remote, may be found. Here the fault, if any, lay with the appellants who, though they were not present to dictate how directions given by another should be carried out, yet had vested in their servant a discretion in the manner of carrying out such directions. If an accident then occurred through his negligence, that was because they had chosen him for the task, and they cannot escape liability by saying that they were careful in their choice. Suppose that the negligence of the craneman had resulted in direct damage to the respondents, I do not see how the appellants could escape liability. For the obligation to supply a crane and a man to work it is an obligation to supply a crane which is not defective and a man who is competent to work it. It would be a strange twist of the law if, the negligence resulting in damage not to the respondents but to a third party, the liability shifted from the appellants to the respondents. . . .

LORD UTHWATT: . . . It may be an express term of the bargain between the general employer and the hirer that the workman is to be the servant of the hirer or is to be subject in all respects to his authority. That, in my opinion, does not of itself determine the workman's position. The workman's assent, express or implied, to such a term would, I think, conclude the point one way, and his dissent conclude it the other way. In cases where the point cannot be disposed of in this fashion, the nature of the activities proper to be demanded of the workman by the hirer and the relation of those activities to the activities of the hirer's own workmen are of outstanding importance in determining whether the hirer has in any reasonable sense authority to control the manner of execution of the workman's task. For instance, the position under the hirer of a craftsman entrusted for the hirer's purposes with the management of a machine belonging to his general employer, that machine demanding for its proper operation the exercise of technical skill and judgment, differs essentially from the position under the hirer of an agricultural labourer hired out for a period of weeks for general work. In the case of the craftsman the inference of fact may be drawn that he was not the servant of the hirer even though the bargain provided that he should be; and in the case of the agricultural labourer the inference of fact may be that he became the servant of the hirer, though the bargain provided that he should not be. The realities of the matter have to be determined. The terms of the bargain may colour the transaction; they do not necessarily determine its real character. . . .

Applying the general principles which I have stated to this case, the particular question to be determined is whether or not Coggins & Griffiths (Liverpool) Ltd had authority to give directions as to the manner in which the crane was to be operated. To my mind it is clear they were not intended to have, and did not have, any such authority. The manner in which the crane was to be operated was and remained exclusively the workman's affair as the servant of the dock board. The workman, in saying in his evidence: 'I take no orders from anybody,' pithily asserted what was involved in the hiring out of the crane committed to his charge by the dock board and, so far as the company was concerned, gave an accurate legal picture of his relations to the company. The company's part was to supply him with work: he would do that work but he was going to do it for the dock board as their servant in his own way.

. . . The proper test is whether or not the hirer had authority to control the manner of execution of the act in question. Given the existence of that authority, its exercise or non-exercise on the occasion of the doing of the act is irrelevant. The hirer is liable for the wrongful act of the workman, whether he gave any specific order or not. Where there is no such authority vested in the hirer, he may, by reason of the giving of a specific order, be responsible for harm resulting from the negligent execution of that order. But it is not every order given by the hirer that will result in liability attaching to him. The nature and terms of the order have to be considered. For instance, an order given to unload cargo from a particular hold in the ship would not — assuming that to be a proper operation — subject the hirer to liability for damage resulting from any negligent driving of the crane in carrying out the order. And lastly, where liability does attach to the hirer by reason of a specific order, that liability arises by the reason that in the particular matter he was a joint tortfeasor with the workman. The general relation arising out of the contract of hiring is in no way involved.

I would dismiss the appeal.

[LORD MACMILLAN delivered a speech in favour of dismissing the appeal.]

Appeal dismissed

Question

If the driver (Newall) had been lifting a fragile load too jerkily would the respondents (the hirers) have been entitled to control *how* he wielded the crane? Does Lord Simonds' verbal antithesis between *what* the driver was to do and *how* he was to do it afford any help? (See C. Grunfeld (1947) 10 MLR 203 at 207.)

Note

In the case ante the issue was dealt with as one of the vicarious liability of an employer for the acts of an employee which cause injury to a fellow employee. An alternative approach in the context of work injuries is to consider the employer's *personal non-delegable* duty to exercise reasonable care to provide and operate a safe system of work (see p. 566 ante). The latter approach was favoured by the House of Lords in *McDermid v Nash Dredging and Reclamation Co Ltd* [1987] AC 906; [1987] 2 All ER 878. The plaintiff was instructed by his employer, the defendant company, to work as a deckhand on a tug, owned by the defendants' parent company. As a result of the negligence of the master of the tug, the plaintiff suffered injuries involving the amputation of his leg. Staughton J held that the tug master was to be regarded as the defendants' employee, because the plaintiff had been instructed to work under his control, and so the defendants were vicariously responsible. However, both the Court of Appeal and the House of Lords held that the defendant company was under a personal duty to provide a safe system of work and to operate it. It was no defence to show that they had delegated this duty to the tug master, whether or not an employee, who was reasonably believed to be competent to perform it. Despite the delegation the employer was liable for the non-performance of the duty. D. Fleming [1988] CLJ 11 comments: 'now we have unequivocal authority for a duty owed by employers to employees, the content of which is such that resort to claims based on vicarious liability look a poor second best. Why hunt for a tortfeasor for whom the defendant *may* be responsible, when you can make him liable even when he has carefully delegated?' See E. McKendrick, (1990) 53 MLR 770.

Servants and Independent Contractors O. Kahn-Freund (1951) 14 MLR 504 at 505–506

The traditional test was that a person working for another was regarded as a servant if he was 'subject to the command of the master as to the manner in which he shall do his work',[1] but if the so-called 'master' was only in a position to determine the 'what' and not the 'how' of the services, the substance of the obligation but not the manner of its performance, then the person doing the work was said to be not a servant but an independent contractor, and his contract one for work and labour and not of employment. This distinction was based upon the social conditions of an earlier age: it assumed that the employer of labour was able to direct and instruct the labourer as to the technical methods he should use in performing his work. In a mainly agricultural society and even in the earlier stages of the Industrial Revolution the master could be expected to be superior to the servant in the knowledge, skill and experience which had to be brought to bear upon the choice and handling of the tools. The control test was well suited to govern relationships like those between a farmer and an agricultural labourer (prior to agricultural mechanisation), a craftsman and a journeyman, a householder and a domestic servant, and even a factory owner and an unskilled 'hand'. It reflects a state of society in which the ownership of the means of production coincided with the possession of technical knowledge and skill and in which that knowledge and skill was largely acquired by being handed down from one generation to the next by oral tradition and not by being systematically imparted in institutions of learning from universities down to technical schools. The control test postulates a combination of managerial and technical functions in the person of the employer, i.e. what to modern eyes appears as an imperfect division of labour. The technical and economic developments of all industrial societies have nullified these assumptions. The rule respondeat superior (and, one may add, the whole body of principles governing the contract of employment) 'applies even though the work which the servant is employed to do is of a skilful or technical character, as to the method of performing which the employer himself is ignorant'.[2] To say of the captain of a ship, the pilot of an aeroplane, the driver of a railway engine, of a motor vehicle, or of a crane,[3] that the employer 'controls' the performance of his work is unrealistic and almost grotesque. But one need not think of situations in which the employee is physically removed from his employer's premises: a skilled engineer or toolmaker, draftsman or accountant may as often as not have been engaged just because he possesses that technical knowledge which the employer lacks. If in such a case the employee relied on the employer's instructions 'how to do his work' he would be breaking his contract and possibly be liable to summary dismissal for having misrepresented his skill. No wonder that the Courts found it increasingly difficult to cope with the cases before them by using a legal rule which, as legal rules so often do, had survived the social conditions from which it had been an abstraction. The judgments in *Mersey Docks and Harbour Board v Coggins and Griffiths*,[4] show plainly enough that the control test had to be transformed if it was to remain a working rule and to be more than a mere verbal incantation.

---

1. Per Bramwell LJ in *Yewens v Noakes* (1880) 6 QBD 530.
2. Per MacKinnon LJ in *Gold v Essex County Council* [1942] 2 All ER at 244.
3. See *Mersey Docks and Harbour Board v Coggins and Griffiths Liverpool Ltd* [1947] AC 1; [1946] 2 All ER 345. In this case the House of Lords was compelled to give a new meaning to the 'control' test, see per Lord Simon, [1946] 2 All ER at 348; per Lord Porter, at 351; per Lord Simonds at 352; per Lord Uthwatt at 353. See C. Grunfeld's Note in (1947) 10 MLR 203.
4. Lord Simon's formula (at p. 348) comes very near to what one may call the 'subordination' or 'organisation' test . Where does the authority lie to direct, or to delegate to the workman the manner in which he should do the work? Who delegates the discretion the workman exercises? Here subordination to the employer's managerial power is made the criterion, and this, it is submitted, is the only possible way of dealing with the matter in the conditions of modern industry.

Cassidy v Ministry of Health Court of Appeal [1951] 1 All ER 574

The plaintiff lost the use of his left hand and had severe pain and suffering as a result of negligent treatment following an operation on his hand. The evidence showed a prima facie case of negligence on the part of persons in whose care the plaintiff was, although it was not clear whether this was to be imputed to Dr Fahrni, the full time assistant medical officer, or to the house surgeon, or to one of the nurses. The Court of Appeal held that the hospital authority was liable.

SOMERVELL LJ: . . . The question whether the defendants are so responsible depends in the first instance on examination of the decision of this court in *Gold v Essex County Council*.[1] To appreciate the problem it is necessary to go back to *Hillyer v St Bartholomew's Hospital (Governors)*.[2] That case is fully analysed and considered in *Gold*'s case,[1] and it is unnecessary to repeat in any detail all that is there set out. In his judgment in *Hillyer*'s case[2] Kennedy LJ expressed the view ([1909] 2 KB 829) that a hospital, though responsible for the exercise of due care in selecting its professional staff, whether surgeons, doctors or nurses, was not responsible if they or any of them acted negligently in matters of professional care or skill. The other reasoned judgment, that of Farwell LJ was based on narrower grounds. The Court of Appeal in *Gold v Essex County Council*,[1] after considering that case and other authorities, and certain dicta in the House of Lords, decided that the statement of Kennedy LJ so far as it related to nurses or those in the position of nurses, should not be followed. The question of doctors on the staff did not directly arise in *Gold*'s case.[1]

The evidence as to Dr Fahrni's position in the present case is that he was an assistant medical officer, that he received a sum in lieu of residential emoluments, which indicates that, if there had been accommodation, or, perhaps, if he had been a bachelor, he would have lived in, and that he was employed whole time. His engagement was subject to the standing orders of the council, but these are not before us. Dr Ronaldson was a house surgeon working under Dr Fahrni. The first question is whether the principles as laid down in *Gold*'s case[1] cover them. In considering this, it is important to bear in mind that nurses are qualified professional persons. It is also important to remember, and MacKinnnon LJ emphasised this (ibid., 244), that the principle of respondeat superior is not ousted by the fact that a 'servant' has to do work of a skilful or technical character, for which the servant has special qualifications. He instanced the certified captain who navigates a ship. On the facts as I have stated them, I would have said that both Dr Fahrni and Dr Ronaldson had contracts of service. They were employed like the nurses as part of the permanent staff of the hospital. Lord Greene MR in *Gold*'s case,[1] in considering (ibid., 242) what a patient is entitled to expect when he knocks at the door of the hospital, comes to the conclusion that he is entitled to expect nursing, and, therefore, the hospital is liable if a nurse is negligent. It seems to me the same must apply in the case of the permanent medical staff. A familiar example is an out-patient's ward. One may suppose a doctor and a sister dealing with the patients. It seems to me the patient is as much entitled to expect medical treatment as nursing from those who are the servants of the hospital. I agree that, if he is treated by someone who is a visiting or consulting surgeon or physician, he is being treated by someone who is not a a servant of the hospital. He is in much the same position as a private patient who has arranged to be operated on by 'X'. . . .

---

1. [1942] 2 KB 293, [1942] 2 All ER 237.
2. [1909] 2 KB 820.

SINGLETON LJ: . . . In *Hillyer v St Bartholomew's Hospital Governors*[1] the plaintiff's arm was burned when he was on an operating table. The examination was conducted by a consulting surgeon attached to the hospital, and it was admitted that the relationship of master and servant did not exist between the defendants and the consulting surgeon. Farwell LJ assumed that the nurses and carriers were servants of the defendants for general purposes, but added ([1909] 2 KB 826):

'. . . as soon as the door of the theatre or operating room has closed on them for the purposes of an operation . . . they cease to be under the orders of the defendants, and are at the disposal and under the sole orders of the operating surgeon until the whole operation has been completely finished; the surgeon is for the time being supreme, and the defendants cannot interfere with or gainsay his orders.'

I do not think that the words of Farwell LJ to which I have referred, can be applied to the facts of this case. The plaintiff was in the care of the hospital authorities. Those responsible for the post-operational treatment were all full-time employees of the corporation and it seems to me that it is not necessary for the plaintiff to establish precisely which individual employee was negligent. . . .

DENNING LJ: If a man goes to a doctor because he is ill, no one doubts that the doctor must exercise reasonable care and skill in his treatment of him, and that is so whether the doctor is paid for his services or not. If, however, the doctor is unable to treat the man himself and sends him to hospital, are not the hospital authorities then under a duty of care in their treatment of him? I think they are. Clearly, if he is a paying patient, paying them directly for their treatment of him, they must take reasonable care of him, and why should it make any difference if he does not pay them directly, but only indirectly through the rates which he pays to the local authority or through insurance contributions which he makes in order to get the treatment? I see no difference at all. Even if he so poor that he can pay nothing, and the hospital treats him out of charity, still the hospital authorities are under a duty to take reasonable care of him just as the doctor is who treats him without asking a fee. In my opinion, authorities who run a hospital, be they local authorities, government boards, or any other corporation, are in law under the self-same duty as the humblest doctor. Whenever they accept a patient for treatment, they must use reasonable care and skill to cure him of his ailment. The hospital authorities cannot, of course, do it by themselves. They have no ears to listen through the stethoscope, and no hands to hold the knife. They must do it by the staff which they employ, and, if their staff are negligent in giving the treatment, they are just as liable for that negligence as is anyone else who employs others to do his duties for him. What possible difference in law, I ask, can there be between hospital authorities who accept a patient for treatment and railway or shipping authorities who accept a passenger for carriage? None whatever. Once they undertake the task, they come under a duty to use care in the doing of it, and that is so whether they do it for reward or not. It is no answer for them to say that their staff are professional men and women who do not tolerate any interference by their lay masters in the way they do their work. . . . The reason why the employers are liable in such cases is not because they can control the way in which the work is done — they often have not sufficient knowledge to do so — but because they employ the staff and have chosen them for the task and have in their hands the ultimate sanction for good conduct — the power of dismissal. . . .

. . . I decline to enter into the question whether any of the surgeons were employed only under a contract for services, as distinct from a contract of service. The evidence is meagre enough in all conscience on that point, but the liability of the hospital authorities should not, and does not, depend on nice considerations of that sort. The

1. [1909] 2 KB 820.

plaintiff knew nothing of the terms on which they employed their staff. All he knew was that he was treated in the hospital by people whom the hospital authorities appointed, and the hospital authorities must be answerable for the way in which he was treated. . . .

Notes

1. In *Roe v Ministry of Health* [1954] 2 QB 66; [1954] 2 All ER 131, if negligence had been established a hospital authority would have been held liable for the acts of an anaesthetist who provided a regular service for the hospital but was also engaged in private practice. Somervell LJ (at p. 79) regarded him as part of the permanent staff; Morris LJ (at p. 91) said that he was part of the 'organisation' of the hospital, and left open the question whether the hospital was under a personal non-delegable duty; Denning LJ (at p. 82) adhered to what he had said in *Cassidy*'s case.

2. In *Wilsher v Essex Area Health Authority* [1987] QB 730; [1986] 3 All ER 801 (overruled on other grounds, [1988] AC 1034; [1988] 1 All ER 871) both Sir Nicolas Browne-Wilkinson V-C and Glidewell LJ accepted (obiter) that there might be primary or direct liability on the part of a health authority for failure to provide doctors of sufficient skill and experience to give the treatment offered at the hospital. Browne-Wilkinson V-C recognised that this duty could cause 'awkward problems'; for example, 'should the hospital be liable if it demonstrates that due to the financial stringency under which it operates, it cannot afford to fill the posts with those possessing the necessary experience?' (at p. 778). The plaintiff has the burden of proving negligence, and although the National Health Service Act 1977 lays a duty on the Secretary of State to provide medical services (which he may direct area health authorities to carry out), the court may regard the authority's exercise of discretion as a 'policy' rather than an 'operational' decision: cf. *R v Central Birmingham AHA, ex p Walker* (1987) Independent, 26th November, and p. 99, ante. A more extensive duty was suggested by Mason J in the Australian case of *Kondis v State Transport Authority* (1984) 55 ALR 225, namely a personal non-delegable duty on the part of the hospital authority to exercise reasonable care in the treatment of its patients. If this approach were to be fully accepted in English law, vicarious liability would rarely be needed and a relatively high duty of care would be placed on hospitals: see J. Bettle (1987) 137 NLJ 573; J. Montgomery (1987) 137 NLJ 703. Compare the employer's personal non–delegable duty to employees, noted p. 566, ante.

Ready-Mixed Concrete (South-East) Ltd *v* Minister of Pensions and National Insurance Queen's Bench Division [1968] 1 All ER 433

These were three appeals, by way of cases stated, from determinations by the Minister whether each of three owner-drivers were employed under a contract of service for purposes of s. 1(2) of the National Insurance Act 1965. Only those who are so employed pay 'Class One' contributions and, in turn, are entitled to certain types of social security benefit. Although not concerned with the imposition of vicarious liability, the case highlights the problems involved in applying traditional tests for identifying a contract of service in a modern 'self-employment' situation.

A company in the Ready-Mixed Group organised a scheme for the delivery of ready-mixed concrete to its customers through so-called 'owner-drivers' whom it hoped to give 'an incentive to work for a higher return without abusing the vehicle in a way which often happens if an employee is given a bonus scheme related to the use of his employer's vehicle'. The contract with each owner-driver contained many provisions suggestive of a high degree of control by the company: he was to buy the vehicle on hire-purchase from a finance company within the Group, but he was not to make alterations to, change or sell the vehicle without the employing company's permission; on termination of his engagement the company had the option to purchase the vehicle from him; he was to make the vehicle available to the company at all times of the day and night, was to comply with all rules and regulations of the company, and was 'to carry out all reasonable orders from any competent servant of the company as if he were an employee of the company', and he was not to engage in any other haulage business.

MACKENNA J: . . . I must now consider what is meant by a contract of service. A contract of service exists if the following three conditions are fulfilled: (i) The servant agrees that in consideration of a wage or other remuneration he will provide his own work and skill in the performance of some service for his master. (ii) He agrees, expressly or impliedly, that in the performance of that service he will be subject to the other's control in a sufficient degree to make that other master. (iii) The other provisions of the contract are consistent with its being a contract of service. . . .

The third and negative condition is for my purpose the important one, and I shall try with the help of five examples to explain what I mean by provisions inconsistent with the nature of a contract of service.

(i) A contract obliges one party to build for the other, providing at his own expense the necessary plant and materials. This is not a contract of service, even though the builder may be obliged to use his own labour only and to accept a high degree of control: it is a building contract. It is not a contract to serve another for a wage, but a contract to produce a thing (or a result) for a price.

(ii) A contract obliges one party to carry another's goods, providing at his own expense everything needed for performance. This is not a contract of service, even though the carrier may be obliged to drive the vehicle himself and to accept the other's control over his performance: it is a contract of carriage.

(iii) A contract obliges a labourer to work for a builder, providing some simple tools, and to accept the builder's control. Notwithstanding the obligation to provide the tools, the contract is one of service. That obligation is not inconsistent with the nature of a contract of service. It is not a sufficiently important matter to affect the substance of the contract.

(iv) A contract obliges one party to work for the other, accepting his control, and to provide his own transport. This is still a contract of service. The obligation to provide his own transport does not affect the substance. Transport in this example is incidental to the main purpose of the contract. Transport in the second example was the essential part of the performance.

(v) The same instrument provides that one party shall work for the other subject to the other's control, and also that he shall sell him his land. The first part of the instrument is no less a contract of service because the second part imposes obligations of a different kind (*Amalgamated Engineering Union v Minister of Pensions and National Insurance*).[1]

I can put the point which I am making in other words. An obligation to do work subject to the other party's control is a necessary, though not always a sufficient, condition of a contract of service. If the provisions of the contract as a whole are inconsistent with its being a contract of service, it will be some other kind of contract, and

---

1. [1963] 1 All ER 864 at 869, 870.

the person doing the work will not be a servant. The judge's task is to classify the contract (a task like that of distinguishing a contract of sale from one of work and labour). He may, in performing it, take into account other matters besides control. . . .

. . . The opinion of Lord Wright in *Montreal Locomotive Works Ltd v Montreal and A-G for Canada*,[1] forgotten by at least one of the counsel who argued the case, and discovered by Mr Atiyah, must be mentioned here. . . .

. . . Mr Atiyah cites . . . the following passage from Lord Wright's opinion:[2]

'In earlier cases a single test, such as the presence or absence of control, was often relied on to determine whether the case was one of master and servant, mostly in order to decide issues of tortious liability on the part of the master or superior. In the more complex conditions of modern industry, more complicated tests have often to be applied. It has been suggested that a fourfold test would in some cases be more appropriate, a complex involving (1) control; (2) ownership of the tools; (3) chance of profit; (4) risk of loss. Control in itself is not always conclusive. Thus the master of a chartered vessel is generally the employee of the shipowner though the charterer can direct the employment of the vessel. Again the law often limits the employer's right to interfere with the employee's conduct, as also do trade union regulations. In many cases the question can only be settled by examining the whole of the various elements which constitute the relationship between the parties. In this way it is in some cases possible to decide the issue by raising as the crucial question whose business is it, or in other words by asking whether the party is carrying on the business, in the sense of carrying it on for himself or on his own behalf and not merely for a superior.'

. . . If a man's activities have the character of a business, and if the question is whether he is carrying on that business or for another, it must be relevant to consider which of the two owns the assets ('the ownership of the tools') and which bears the financial risk ('the chance of profit', 'the risk of loss'). He who owns the assets and bears the risk is unlikely to be acting as an agent or a servant. If the man performing the service must provide the means of performance at his own expense and accept payment by results, he will own the assets, bear the risk, and be to that extent unlike a servant. I should add that there is nothing in the Canadian case to support the view that the ownership of the assets is relevant only to the question of control. Lord Wright treats his three other tests as having a value independent of control in determining the nature of the contract. . . .

There is, . . . the dictum of Denning LJ in *Bank voor Handel en Scheepvaart NV v Slatford*,[3] repeated in his Hamlyn Lectures:

'In this connexion I would observe the test of being a servant does not rest nowadays on submission to orders. It depends on whether the person is part and parcel of the organisation.'

This raises more questions than I know how to answer. What is meant by being 'part and parcel of an organisation'? Are all persons who answer this description servants? If only some are servants, what distinguishes them from the others if it is not their submission to orders? Though I cannot answer these questions I can at least invoke the dictum to support my opinion that control is not everything. . . .

It is now time to state my conclusion, which is that the rights conferred and the duties imposed by the contract between Mr Latimer and the company are not such as to make it one of service. It is a contract of carriage.

---

1. [1947] 1 DLR 161
2. [1947] 1 DLR at p. 169.
3. [1953] 1 QB 248 at 290, [1952] 2 All ER 956 at 971.

I have shown earlier that Mr Latimer must make the vehicle available throughout the contract period. He must maintain it (and also the mixing unit) in working order, repairing and replacing worn parts when necessary. He must hire a competent driver to take his place if he should be for any reason unable to drive at any time when the company requires the services of the vehicle. He must do whatever is needed to make the vehicle (with a driver) available throughout the contract period. He must do all this, at his own expense, being paid a rate per mile for the quantity which he delivers. These are obligations more consistent, I think, with a contract of carriage than with one of service. The ownership of the assets, the chance of profit and the risk of loss in the business of carriage are his and not the company's.

If (as I assume) it must be shown that he has freedom enough in the performance of those obligations to qualify as an independent contractor, I would say that he has enough. He is free to decide whether he will maintain the vehicle by his own labour or that of another, and, if he decides to use another's, he is free to choose whom he will employ and on what terms. He is free to use another's services to drive the vehicle when he is away because of sickness or holidays, or indeed at any other time when he has not been directed to drive himself. He is free again in his choice of a competent driver to take his place at these times, and whoever he appoints will be his servant and not the company's. He is free to choose where he will buy his fuel or any other of his requirements, subject to the company's control in the case of major repairs. This is enough. It is true that the company are given special powers to ensure that he runs his business efficiently, keeps proper accounts and pays his bills. I find nothing in these or any other provisions of the contract inconsistent with the company's contention that he is running a business of his own. A man does not cease to run a business on his own account because he agrees to run it efficiently or to accept another's superintendence'. . . .

Judgments accordingly

Questions

1. What would the result have been in the *Ready-Mixed* case had the judge asked 'Is this contract inconsistent with its being a contract for services'?

2. It has been suggested that the arrangement between the company and the 'owner-drivers' was no more than 'an elaborate incentive scheme' (by G. de N. Clark (1968) 31 MLR 450). Does this alter the character of the relationship into one of service?

3. Under the contract with each owner-driver the company had to insure each vehicle in the owner-driver's name and charge the premiums to him, but monies received by the owner-driver under the insurance policy had to be used to repair and replace vehicles. Assume that due to the negligent driving of an owner-driver the vehicle was damaged and a third party was injured. How would the accident costs be absorbed? What difference would it make if the owner-driver was classified as an employee of the company? (For compulsory road traffic and employer's liability insurance provisions, see p. 885, post.)

4. The *Ready-Mixed* case, like most of the decisions dealing with the criteria by which to identify a contract of service, was not concerned with the problem of vicarious liability. In employment law generally, the recent tendency has been to leave the question of definition to industrial tribunals to 'consider in the light of their industrial experience and qualifications' from a 'commonsense' point of view. In the context of vicarious liability (usually

dealt with by a High Court or county court judge) would it not be more satisfactory to base liability on economically critical factors, such as the solvency of the employee, the relative risk-bearing capacity of the parties or the extent to which the employer could be expected to avoid accidents by 'control' over the employee? (See A. O. Sykes (1984) 117 Yale LJ 1231.)

Note

The *Ready-Mixed* case indicates somes of the contractual provisions which may be inconsistent with the requirement of 'service' (for others see *Encyclopedia of Labour Relations Law*, para. IB–207). The other critical element is the existence of a 'contract'. Recent case law has emphasised the need for 'mutuality' of obligation. This may exist at two levels. In the simple 'wage-work' bargain there is an exchange of work for remuneration which may create a series of separate contracts each time a worker is engaged. At the second level, there may be a series of separate contracts which give rise to an inference that there is a 'global' or 'umbrella' contract under which the employee must be available to render service and the employer must enable the employee to earn remuneration. The Court of Appeal has been reluctant to find the existence of a 'global' contract, so excluding casual and temporary workers from employee benefits (e.g. *O'Kelly v Trusthouse Forte plc* [1984] QB 90; [1983] 3 All ER 456; *Wickens v Champion Employment* [1984] ICR 365) and also denying employee status to trawlermen who sailed exclusively for one employer for many years on voyages lasting about 21 days with short periods ashore in between (*Hellyer Bros Ltd v McLeod* [1987] ICR 526). However, the decision of the Judicial Committee of the Privy Council (in an appeal from the Court of Appeal of Hong Kong) in *Lee Ting Seng v Chung* [1990] 2 AC 374, indicates a more flexible approach to casual workers in relation to entitlement to compensation under workmen's compensation legislation. A skilled mason was one of a large pool of casual workers in the construction industry who earned his living by working for more than one employer. The Privy Council held that the courts below had made an error of law in regarding him as an independent contractor in business on his own account. Lord Bridge was critical of the use of the test whether a person 'is part and parcel of the organisation' in the context of a statute which expressly contemplated that casual workers and those working concurrently for more than one employer could be employees, and warned against relying on dicta from cases of a 'wholly dissimilar character'.

The Police Act 1964

48. Liability for wrongful acts of constables. — (1) The chief officer of police for any police area shall be liable in respect of torts committed by constables under his direction and control in the performance or purported performance of their functions in like manner as a master is liable in respect of torts committed by his servants in the course of their employment, and accordingly shall in respect of any such tort be treated for all purposes as a joint tortfeasor.

(2) There shall be paid out of the police fund—

    (a) any damages or costs awarded against the chief officer of police in any proceedings brought against him by virtue of this section and any costs incurred by him in any such proceedings so far as not recovered by him in the proceedings; and

    (b) any sum required in connection with the settlement of any claim made against the chief officer of police by virtue of this section, if the settlement is approved by the police authority.

(3) Any proceedings in respect of a claim made by virtue of this section shall be brought against the chief officer of police for the time being or, in the case of a vacancy in that office, against the person for the time being performing the functions of the chief officer of police; and references in the foregoing provisions of this section to the chief officer of police shall be construed accordingly.

(4) A police authority may, in such cases and to such extent as they think fit, pay any damages or costs awarded against a member of the police force maintained by them, or any constable for the time being required to serve with that force by virtue of section 14 of this Act, or any special constable appointed for their area, in proceedings for a tort committed by him, any costs incurred and not recovered by him in any such proceedings, and any sum required in connection with the settlement of any claim that has or might have given rise to such proceedings; and any sum required for making a payment under this subsection shall be paid out of the police fund.

Notes

1. At common law a police officer is not a servant of the police authority: *Fisher v Oldham Corpn* [1930] 2 KB 364; *Lewis v Cattle* [1938] 2 KB 454; [1938] 2 All ER 368; G. Marshall, *Police and Government* (London, 1965) comments on s. 48 of the 1964 Act: 'the individual constable's responsibility to the law for the exercise of his common law powers presumably remains compatible with this arrangement and means as much or as little as it did before the Act.' The chief officer is not liable for 'independent action by a rogue police officer' which is not in the 'performance or purported performance' of his functions or in the course of his employment: see *Makanjuola v Metropolitan Police Com* [1989] NLJR 468 (Commissioner not liable for serious sexual assault by officer). The police authority, not the chief constable, is vicariously liable for police cadets (Police Act 1964, s. 17(3); *Wiltshire Police Authority v Wynn* [1981] QB 95).

2. A servant of the Crown is not responsible for the torts of those in the same employment as himself: e.g. the First Lord of the Admiralty is not responsible for false imprisonment by his subordinates (*Fraser v Balfour* (1918) 87 LJKB 1116). At common law the Crown itself enjoyed immunity from proceedings in tort, but the Crown Proceedings Act 1947 subjects the Crown to civil liability as if it were a private person of full age and capacity in respect of torts committed by its servants or agents. The Post Office cannot be made liable in tort: Post Office Act 1969, s. 29(1). A public officer may, of course, be liable for his own torts, and exemplary damages may be available against such an officer for arbitrary and unconstitutional action (p. 407, ante).

2 Liability for delegated tasks

(a) Driving a motor vehicle

Morgans v Launchbury House of Lords [1972] 2 All ER 606

LORD WILBERFORCE: My Lords, this appeal arises out of a motor car accident in which the three respondents were injured. They were passengers in a Jaguar saloon which was registered in the name of the appellant; she was not using the car at the time. The other persons in it were the appellant's husband and a friend of his, Mr D. J. Cawfield, who was driving: both were killed. It is not disputed that the accident was caused by the negligence of Mr Cawfield. At first instance, the appellant was sued both in her personal capacity and as administratrix for her deceased husband; judgment was given against her in both capacities on the ground that both she personally and her husband, were vicariously liable for Mr Cawfield's negligence. It is only in her personal capacity that she brings the present appeal and the question involved is therefore whether as owner of the car, and in the circumstances in which it came to be used and driven, she can be held vicariously liable for the negligence of the driver.

Some further facts require to be stated. Before their marriage the appellant and her husband each had their own car, but after they had been married about a year they decided to sell one, and the one sold was the husband's. The Jaguar was, in the appellant's words, regarded as 'our car'. It was freely used by either husband and wife; the husband normally used it every day to drive to and from his place of work seven miles from his home.

On the day of the accident, the husband had driven in the car to work. In the evening he telephoned to the appellant to say that he would not be returning home for his evening meal and that he was going out with friends. He visited a number of public houses and had drinks. At some stage he realised that he was unable to drive safely and he asked Mr Cawfield to drive and gave Mr Cawfield the keys. Mr Cawfield drove the husband to other public houses. After the last one had been visited Mr Cawfield offered the three respondents, one of whom was a friend of his, a lift in the car; and, soon after, the husband got into the back of the car and fell asleep: he was certainly and heavily intoxicated. Mr Cawfield then drove off, not in the direction of the husband's home, but in the opposite direction, suggesting a meal before he finally drove the passengers home. Soon after, with Mr Cawfield driving at 90 mph, the car collided with an omnibus.

There was some important evidence as to the circumstances in which the appellant's husband may have asked Mr Cawfield to drive. According to the appellant's evidence, her husband often liked to stay out and visit public houses. In her words, 'We had an understanding, he had always told me he would never drive if he thought there was any reason he should not drive' and 'it was an understanding, he told me, "You need not worry, I would not drive unless I was fit to drive".' Some further questions were put to her and the judge felt entitled to find —

'that he promised her he never would drive himself if he had taken more drink than he felt he should have, but would do one of two things, either get a friend to drive him, or ring her up and she would come and fetch him.'

We must accept the tenor of this finding but it was to be understood in the context of discussion between husband and wife. It is unlikely that it was so crystal clear as it appears from the finding to have been. One other fact: there was no question of the appellant knowing that Mr Cawfield drove or might drive the car that evening, and he was to her merely an acquaintance.

It is on these facts that liability for the injuries sustained by the respondents must be considered. Who could they sue? In the first place, there was the estate of Mr Cawfield as the negligent driver; in the second, the estate of the husband who requested Mr Cawfield to drive, this resting on the normal principle of the law of agency. But the respondents seek to go further and to place vicarious liability on the appellant. As to this, apart from the special circumstances of the 'understanding' there would seem, on accepted principle, to be insuperable difficulties in their way. The car cannot by any fair process of analysis be considered to have been used for the appellant's purposes at the time of the accident. During the whole of the evening's progress it was as clearly used for the husband's purposes as any car should be; and if there was any doubt about this the separation from any possible purpose of the appellant's at the time of the accident can only be intensified by the fact that Mr Cawfield, the husband's agent, was taking the car away from the appellant's (and the husband's) home for some fresh purpose. It seems clear enough that this was the purpose of Mr Cawfield but even if one attributes this to her husband, I am unable to formulate an argument for attributing it to the wife.

It is said, against this, that there are authorities which warrant a wider and vaguer test of vicarious liability for the negligence of another; a test of 'interest or concern'. Skilled counsel for the respondents at the trial was indeed able to put the word 'concerned' and 'interest' into the wife's mouth and it was on these words that he mainly rested his case.

On the general law, no authority was cited to us which would test vicarious liability on so vague a test, but it was said that special principles applied to motor cars. I should be surprised if this were so, and I should wish to be convinced of the reason for a special rule. But in fact there is no authority for it. The decisions will be examined by others of your Lordships and I do not find it necessary to make my own review. For I regard it as clear that in order to fix vicarious liability on the owner of a car in such a case as the present, it must be shown that the driver was using it for the owner's purposes, under delegation of a task or duty. The substitution for this clear conception of a vague test based on 'interest' or 'concern' has nothing in reason or authority to commend it. Every man who gives permission for the use of his chattel may be said to have an interest or concern in its being carefully used, and, in most cases if it is a car, to have an interest or concern in the safety of the driver, but it has never been held that mere permission is enough to establish vicarious liability. And the appearance of the words in certain judgments (*Ormrod v Crosville Motor Services Ltd*[1] per Devlin J and per Denning LJ[2]) in a negative context (no interest or concern, therefore no agency) is no warrant whatever for transferring them into a positive test. I accept entirely that 'agency' in contexts such as these is merely a concept, the meaning and purpose of which is to say 'is vicariously liable' and that either expression reflects a judgment of value — respondeat superior is the law saying that the owner ought to pay. It is this imperative which the common law has endeavoured to work out through the cases. The owner ought to pay, it says, because he has authorised the act, or requested it, or because the actor is carrying out a task or duty delegated, or because he is in control of the actor's conduct. He ought not to pay (on accepted rules) if he has no control over the actor, has not authorised or requested the act, or if the actor is acting wholly for his own purposes. These rules have stood the test of time remarkably well. They provide, if there is nothing more, a complete answer to the respondents' claim against the appellant.

I must now consider the special circumstances on which the judge relied — the understanding between the appellant and her husband. What does it amount to? In my opinion, it is nothing more than the kind of assurance that any responsible citizen would give to his friends, any child would give to his parent, any responsible husband would give to his wife: that he intends to do what is his legal and moral duty, not to drive if in doubt as to his sobriety. The evidence is that this assurance originated from the husband and no doubt it was welcomed by the wife. But it falls far short of any authority by the wife to drive on her behalf or of any delegation by her of the task of driving. If the husband was, as he clearly was, using the car for his own purposes, I am unable to understand how his undertaking to delegate his right to drive to another can turn the driver into the wife's agent in any sense of the word. The husband remains the user, the purposes remain his. So if one applies accepted principles of the law, the case is clear; I only wish to add that I agree with the judgment of Megaw LJ in the Court of Appeal[3] both on the law and the facts.

---

1. [1953] 1 All ER 711; [1953] 1 WLR 409.
2. [1953] 2 All ER 753; [1953] 1 WLR 1120.
3. *Morgans v Launchbury* [1971] 2 QB 245 at 261; [1971] 1 All ER 642 at 652.

This is not the end of the case. The respondents submitted that we should depart from accepted principle and introduce a new rule, or set of rules, applicable to the use of motor vehicles, which would make the appellant liable as owner. Lord Denning MR in the Court of Appeal[1] formulated one such rule, based on the conception of a matrimonial car, a car used in common by husband and wife for the daily purposes of both. All purposes, or at least the great majority of purposes, he would say are matrimonial purposes: shopping, going to work, transporting children, all are purposes of the owner, the car was bought and owned for them to be carried out. And, consequently (this is the critical step) the owner is ipso jure liable whatever the other spouse is using the car for, unless, it seems, although the scope of the exception is not defined, the latter is 'on a frolic of his own'. Indeed Lord Denning MR[2] seems to be willing to go even further and to hold the owner liable on the basis merely of permission to drive, actual or assumed.

My Lords, I have no doubt that the multiplication of motor cars on our roads, their increasing speed, the severity of the injuries they may cause, the rise in accidents involving innocent persons, give rise to problems of increasing social difficulty with which the law finds it difficult to keep abreast. And I am willing to assume (although I think that more evidence is needed than this one case) that traditional concepts of vicarious liability, founded on agency as developed in relation to less dangerous vehicles, may be proving inadequate. I think, too, although counsel for the appellant argued eloquently to the contrary, that some adaptation of the common law rules to meet these new problems of degree is capable of being made by judges. I do not have to depend on my own judgment for this for it can be seen that in the United States, so long ago as 1913, the judges in the state of Washington developed, without legislative aid, a new doctrine of the family car (*Birch v Abercrombie*)[3] and some other states have, with variations, followed the same road (see *Prosser on Torts*).[4] Other states have resorted to statute. To be similarly creative, even 70 years later, has its attraction. But I have come to the clear conclusion that we cannot in this House embark on the suggested innovation. I endeavour to state some reasons.

1. Assuming that the desideratum is to fix liability in cases of negligent driving on the owner of the car (an assumption which may be disputable), there are at least three different systems which may be adopted: (a) that apparently advocated by Lord Denning MR[2] of a 'matrimonial' car, the theory being that all purposes for which it is used by either spouse are presumed to be matrimonial purposes; (b) that adopted in some American states of a 'family' car, the theory being that any user by any member of the family is the owner's 'business' (see *Prosser*);[4] (c) that any owner (including hire-purchaser) who permits another to use his motor vehicle on the highway should be liable by the fact of permission. This principle has been adopted *by statute* in certain Australian states (e.g. the Motor Vehicles Insurance Acts 1936–45 (Queensland), s. 3(2)). Yet another possibility would be to impose liability on the owner in all cases regardless of whether he had given permission or not. My Lords, I do not know on what principle your Lordships acting judicially can prefer one of these systems to the others or on what basis any one can be formulated with sufficient precision or its exceptions defined. The choice is one of social policy; there are arguments for and against each of them. If any one is preferable on purely logical grounds, to me it is the third, for I am unable to state with any precision a rational (as opposed to a policy) preference for drawing a line at either of the alternative points, the spouses or the family. But apart from the unsupported statement by Lord Denning MR in the present case I know of no judicial pronouncement in favour of

---

1. [1971] 2 QB at p. 256; [1971] 1 All ER at p. 648.
2. [1971] 2 QB at p. 256; [1971] 1 All ER at p. 648.
3. 74 Wash 486, 133 P 1020 (1913).
4. (3rd edn, 1964) pp. 494 et seq.

the third; indeed the cases, amongst them the judgments of Edmund-Davies and Megaw LJJ below,[1] contain statements to the contrary, i.e. that mere permission is not in law a sufficient basis of liability. I do not doubt that this is the existing law nor the validity of the Australian position that to base liability on permission would be a matter for legislation.

2. Whatever may have been the situation in 1913 in the youth of the motor car, it is very difficult now, when millions of people of all ages drive for a vast variety of purposes and when there is in existence a complicated legislative structure as to insurance—who must take it out, what risks it must cover, who has the right to sue for the sum assured. Liability and insurance are so intermixed that judicially to alter the basis of liability without adequate knowledge (which we have not the means to obtain) as to the impact this might make on the insurance system would be dangerous, and, in my opinion, irresponsible.

3. To declare as from the date of the decision in this House that a new and greatly more extensive principle of liability was to be applied in substitution for well-known and certain rules might inflict great hardships on a number of people, and at least would greatly affect their assumed legal rights. We cannot, without yet further innovation, change the law prospectively only; and in any event this accident occurred in 1964, so any change if it were to be relevant to this case would have to date back until then. Such is the number of accidents now occurring, and the time which elapses before the damages are settled, that any decision in this case would affect, at the least, cases over the last eight years, the parties to which could justly expect to look to the established law to guide them, and whose insurances were arranged on the basis of established law.

My Lords, we may be grateful to Lord Denning MR for turning our thoughts in a new direction, a direction perceived, if not with unity of vision, by courts beyond the seas so long ago; but I must invite your Lordships to state that his judgment does not state the law. Any new direction, and it may be one of many alternatives, must be set by Parliament.

I would allow the appeal and dismiss the action.

LORD PEARSON: . . . It seems to me that these innovations, whether or not they may be desirable, are not suitable to be introduced by judicial decision. They raise difficult questions of policy, as well as involving the introduction of new legal principles rather than extension of some principle already recognised and operating. The questions of policy need consideration by the government and Parliament, using the resources at their command for making wide enquiries and gathering evidence and opinions as to the practical effects of the proposed innovations. Apart from the transitional difficulty of current policies of insurance being rendered insufficient by judicial changes in the law, there is the danger of injustice to owners who for one reason or another are not adequately covered by insurance or perhaps not effectively insured at all (e.g. if they have forgotten to renew their policies or have taken out policies which are believed by them to be valid but are in fact invalid, or have taken their policies from an insolvent insurance company). Moreover, lack of insurance cover would in some cases defeat the object of the proposed innovation, because uninsured or insufficiently insured owners would often be unable to pay damages, awarded against them in favour of injured plaintiffs. Any extension of car owners' liability ought to be accompanied by an extension of effective insurance cover. How would that be brought about? And how would it be paid for? Would the owner of the car be required to take out a policy for the benefit of any person who may drive a car? Would there be an exception for some kinds of unlawful driving? A substantial

---

1. [1971] 2 QB 245; [1971] 1 All ER 642.

increase in premiums for motor insurance would be likely to result and to have an inflationary effect on costs and prices. It seems to me that if the proposed innovations are desirable, they should be introduced not by judicial decision but by legislation after suitable investigation and full consideration of the questions of policy involved.

I would allow the appeal.

[VISCOUNT DILHORNE, LORD CROSS OF CHELSEA and LORD SALMON delivered speeches in favour of allowing the appeal.]

Appeal allowed

Questions

1. Megaw LJ in his dissenting judgment in the Court of Appeal in this case ([1971] 1 All ER 642 at 655–656), approved by Lord Wilberforce, said: 'We do not have to decide what the position might have been if the accident had happened in the course of a normal journey to or from work.' What would the position have been?

2. Would Mrs Morgans have been liable if Mr Morgans had taken the car to do the family shopping? (Note *Norwood v Navan* [1981] RTR 457, in which Ormrod LJ said (at p. 461): 'if we were to hold that the mere fact that some part of this trip which the wife was doing was for what was called "general shopping" made her the agent of her husband, we should be getting into the position where, in any of these cases, it would be necessary to examine the contents of the shopping basket to see what had been purchased that day. We would be pushed into the absurd position of saying that, if all the purchases had been for the wife personally, there was no agency, whereas if she bought some minor household article, she would be an agent for the husband — a distinction which is really absurd'.)

3. A, a car owner, asks B, a passenger, to close the door of the car. B does so negligently, slamming the door on C's fingers. Is A liable in damages to C?

4. Mr Morgans was not the registered owner of the car. Why was he vicariously liable for Cawfield's negligence? (See *Nottingham v Aldridge* [1971] 2 QB 739; [1971] 2 All ER 751.)

5. Lord Denning MR in the Court of Appeal in this case ([1971] 1 All ER 642 at 647) said: 'The words "principal" and "agent" are not used here in the connotation which they have in the law of contract (which is one thing), or the connotation which they have in the business community (which is another thing). They are used as a shorthand to denote the circumstances in which vicarious liability is imposed.' Why is there no general principle in the law of tort that a 'principal' is liable for the acts of his 'agent'? (See Atiyah, *Vicarious Liability*, chap. 9.)

6. The Road Traffic Act 1988, ss. 143, 145 (p. 885, post) makes it a criminal offence for the owner to permit any other person to use a motor vehicle on the road unless there is in force a policy of insurance against risks of bodily injury or death to third parties. J. A. Jolowicz [1972A] CLJ 209 at 210 asks: 'Does it not follow that the owner, and thus his insurer, ought to be made civilly liable for the negligence of all permitted drivers?' How would such a change in the law affect (a) the insured owner and (b) the uninsured owner?

Was Mrs Morgans liable to be sued for breach of the statutory duty to insure? (See p. 892, post.)

7. Would the same result be reached today in each of the following cases decided before the decision of the House of Lords in *Morgans v Launchbury*?

(a) A was negotiating the sale of his car to Mrs C. He took her for a trial run allowing B, her son, to drive. A sat next to B. As a result of B's negligent driving, P was injured. A was liable because he had not abandoned his 'right of control': *Samsom v Aitchison* [1912] AC 844.

(b) D drove E's car with E's consent. After setting down E, D took the car home and negligently parked it on a steep gradient without properly applying the handbrake. P was injured as a result. E was liable because he had the 'right of control' even though he was not present: *Parker v Miller* (1926) 42 TLR 408.

(c) G borrowed his father's (F) car to take home two girl-friends. F was not liable for G's negligent driving. Two reasons were suggested: (a) such liability depends not on ownership but on the delegation of a task or duty; (b) the father had no 'social or moral duty' to convey the girls home: *Hewitt v Bonvin* [1940] 1 KB 188.

(d) H took his car to J's garage for repairs. One of J's mechanics took H to the station in H's car. H was not responsible for the mechanic's negligent driving because H had lost the 'right of control' by bailing the car to J: *Chowdhary v Gillot* [1947] 2 All ER 541.

(e) M asked O to drive M's Austin Healey from Liverpool to Monte Carlo. O collided with a bus due in part to his own negligence and, in part, to the negligence of the bus driver. O's wife was injured and she sued the bus driver's employer, who, in turn, brought the owner of the car, M, into the proceedings. At this time (which was prior to the enactment of the Law Reform (Husband and Wife) Act 1962) they could not bring in O's husband because spouses could not sue one another in tort. But if M were held responsible for O's driving, his insurance policy would cover his liability. M was held to be vicariously liable because the car was being used on M's business and for M's purposes: *Ormrod v Crossville Motor Services Co Ltd* [1953] 2 All ER 753, [1953] 1 WLR 1120.

(f) Q let R (his son) use the family car at night provided that Q's chauffeur drove. Q was liable for the chauffeur's negligent driving while on R's business, since he had asked the chauffeur to drive: *Carberry v Davies* [1968] 2 All ER 817; [1968] 1 WLR 1103; cf. *Rambarran v Gurrucharran* [1970] 1 All ER 749; [1970] 1 WLR 556.

Note

Sometimes there may be a personal non-delegable duty to provide a vehicle which is reasonably safe. In *Rogers v Night Riders (a firm)* [1983] RTR 324 a firm running a minicab service hired radios to drivers who owned, maintained and controlled their own vehicles. On receiving a telephone call from a customer they contacted a driver by radio and directed him to the customer. The plaintiff, who obtained a minicab in this way, was injured by a defective door because the driver had failed properly to maintain the vehicle. The Court of Appeal held that the minicab firm were under a personal non-delegable duty to provide a vehicle which was reasonably maintained and reasonably fit for the purpose.

(b) Transactions with third parties

Armagas Ltd v Mundogas SA, The Ocean Frost House of Lords [1986] 2 All ER 385

Mr Magelssen, vice-president of the defendant company (Mundogas), without actual or ostensible authority, contracted for the sale of the defendant's ship to the plaintiff (Armagas) and its charter back to the defendant company. The plaintiff claimed damages from the defendant, alleging, inter alia, that the defendant company was vicariously responsible for Magelssen's deceit.

The trial judge held the defendant company liable. The Court of Appeal [1985] 3 All ER 795, allowed an appeal on the ground that since Magelssen's deceit consisted of a misrepresentation, made outside his ostensible authority, the defendant company was not vicariously liable.

The plaintiff appealed to the House of Lords.

LORD KEITH OF KINKEL: . . . The broad proposition of law founded on is that an employer is vicariously liable for the torts of his employee committed in the course of his employment. 'Course of employment' is a concept which has engendered much disputation and spawned a plethora of reported decisions. The starting point should be to consider the fundamental principles which govern vicarious liability in the field of intentional wrongdoing by the servant, particularly by way of dishonest conduct. It is unnecessary to consider the development of the basis of vicarious liability in relation to torts such as negligence or trespass, which has followed a somewhat different line. Dishonest conduct is of a different character from blundering attempts to promote the employer's business interests, involving negligent ways of carrying out the employee's work or excessive zeal and errors of judgment in the performance of it. Dishonest conduct perpetrated with no intention of benefiting the employer but solely with that of procuring a personal gain or advantage to the employee is governed, in the field of vicarious liability, by a set of principles and a line of authority of peculiar application. . . .

The leading case in this field is *Lloyd v Grace Smith & Co* [1912] AC 716, [1911–13] All ER Rep 51, the facts of which are too well known to require recapitulation. The proposition established by that case is epitomised in the speech of Earl Loreburn ([1912] AC 716 at 725, [1911–13] All ER Rep 51 at 54):

'If the agent commits the fraud purporting to act in the course of business such as he was authorized, or held out as authorized, to transact on account of his principal, then the latter may be held liable for it.'

Lord Shaw said ([1912] AC 716 at 739–740, [1911–13] All ER Rep 51 at 61):

'The case is in one respect the not infrequent one of a situation in which each of two parties has been betrayed or injured by the fraudulent conduct of a third. I look upon it as a familiar doctrine as well as a safe general rule, and one making for security instead of uncertainty and insecurity in mercantile dealings, that the loss occasioned by the fault of a third person in such circumstances ought to fall upon the one of the two parties who clothed that third person as agent with the authority by which he was enabled to commit the fraud.'

Later he equiparates ostensible authority with actual authority. The principal importance of the case lies in its having dispelled misunderstanding of certain observations by Willes J in *Barwick v English Joint Stock Bank* (1867) LR 2 Exch 259, [1861–73] All ER Rep 194, and having established that it is not necessary to a master's liability for the fraud of his servant that the fraud should have been committed for the master's benefit. It was argued for Armagas that in *Lloyd v Grace Smith & Co* the fraudulent clerk was not acting within the scope of his actual or ostensible authority but was acting in the course of his employment, and that it was the latter which made the employer liable. In the present case, so it was maintained, Mr Magelssen was acting in the course of his employment though not within the scope of his actual or ostensible authority, so Mundogas was liable. In my opinion the attempted distinction has no validity in this category of case. Lord Macnaghten in *Lloyd v Grace Smith & Co* [1912] AC 716 at 736, [1911–13] All ER Rep 51 at 59 regarded the two expressions as meaning one and the same thing. The essential feature for creating liability in the employer is that the party contracting with the fraudulent servant should have altered his position to his detriment in reliance on the belief that the servant's activities were within his authority, or, to put it another way, were part of his job, this belief having been induced by the master's representations by way of words or conduct. In *Uxbridge Permanent Benefit Building Society v Pickard* [1939] 2 All ER 344 at 348, [1939] 2 KB 248 at 254–255, Sir Wilfrid Greene MR, rejecting the argument that the actions of the fraudulent solicitors' clerk who had induced the building society to advance money to a non-existent client, were analogous to a 'frolic of his own' said:

'With all respect to that argument, I cannot accept it. It appears to me to be drawing an analogy where no analogy exists, because, in the case of the servant who goes off on a frolic of his own, no question arises of any actual or ostensible authority upon the faith of which some third person is going to change his position. The very essence of the present case is that the actual authority and the ostensible authority to Conway were of a kind which, in the ordinary course of an everyday transaction, was going to lead to third persons, on the faith of it, changing their position, just as a purchaser from an apparent client or a mortgagee lending money to a client is going to change his position by being brought into contact with that client. That is within the actual and ostensible authority of the clerk.'

In further pursuance of the argument, reliance was placed on a dictum of Denning LJ in *Navarro v Moregrand Ltd* [1951] 2 TLR 674 at 680, a case where a house agent had obtained an illegal premium from a tenant and the landlord was found liable for its repayment, who after referring to *Lloyd v Grace Smith & Co* and the *Uxbridge* case, as authority for the view that a servant acting within his actual or ostensible authority was acting in the course of his employment, continued:

'But the judge inferred from those cases the converse proposition—namely, that if a servant or agent is not acting within his actual or ostensible authority, then he is not acting in the course of his employment. I do not think that that is correct: it is a confusion between the responsibility of a principal in contract and his responsibility in tort. He is only responsible in contract for things done within the actual or ostensible authority of the agent; but he is responsible in tort for all wrongs done by the servant or agent in the course of his employment, whether within his actual or ostensible authority or not. The presence of actual or ostensible authority is decisive to show that his conduct is within the course of his employment, but the absence of it is not decisive the other way.'

This dictum, which was not concurred in by the other two members of the Court of Appeal, may have some validity in relation to torts other than those concerned with fraudulent misrepresentation, but in my opinion it has no application to torts of the latter kind, where the essence of the employer's liability is reliance by the injured party on actual or ostensible authority.

... In the end of the day the question is whether the circumstances under which a servant has made the fraudulent misrepresentation which has caused loss to an innocent party contracting with him are such as to make it just for the employer to bear the loss. Such circumstances exist where the employer by words or conduct has induced the injured party to believe that the servant was acting in the lawful course of the employer's business. They do not exist where such belief, although it is present, has been brought about through misguided reliance on the servant himself, when the servant is not authorised to do what he is purporting to do, when what he is purporting to do is not within the class of acts that an employee in his position is usually authorised to do and when the employer has done nothing to represent that he is authorised to do it. In the present case Mr Magelssen was not authorised to enter into the three-year charterparty, to do so was not within the usual authority of an employee holding his position, and Armagas knew it, and Mundogas had done nothing to represent that he was authorised to do so. It was contended for Armagas that concluding the contract for the sale of the vessel was within Mr Magelssen's actual authority, and that inducing the sale by falsely representing that he had authority to enter into the charterparty amounted to no more than an improper method of performing what he was employed to do, such as in other contexts was sufficient to attract vicarious liability. But the sale of a ship backed by a three-year charterparty is a transaction of a wholly different character from a straightforward sale, even if the charterparty is not to be regarded as a transaction separate and distinct from the sale, and Mr Jensen and Mr Dannesboe knew that Mr Magelssen had no authority to enter into a transaction of the character on his own responsibility.

I conclude that the Court of Appeal rightly held that Mundogas was not vicariously liable in English law for Mr Magelssen's deceit. ...

My Lords, for these reasons I would dismiss the appeal with costs.

[LORD BRANDON OF OAKBROOK, LORD TEMPLEMAN, LORD GRIFFITHS and LORD OLIVER OF AYLMERTON agreed with the speech of LORD KEITH.]

Appeal dismissed

Notes

1. In the Court of Appeal in this case [1985] 3 All ER 795, Robert Goff LJ suggested (at p. 810) that 'torts which involve reliance by the plaintiff on a representation by the servant should be distinguished from other wrongs, for example those which involve intentional or negligent physical acts by the servant. In the latter class of case, the ostensible authority of the servant does not provide the criterion for the master's vicarious liability.' The latter class is discussed p. 832, post. In the former class 'the plaintiff is placing his reliance exclusively on the servant; and it is understandable that it should be the policy of the law in those circumstances, not merely that the unauthorised act should not be imputed to the master, but also that the master should not be vicariously liable for the servant's wrong, (ibid.). See too *Kooragang Investments Pty Ltd v Richardson and Wrench Ltd* [1982] AC 462; [1981] 3 All ER 65, where Lord Wilberforce, delivering the opinion of the Privy Council (in an appeal from the Supreme Court of New South Wales) suggested that an employer cannot be vicariously liable for negligent misstatements which his employee was neither actually nor ostensibly authorised to make.

2. In *Lloyd v Grace Smith & Co* [1912] AC 716 (referred to by Lord Keith, p. 826, ante) a solicitor was held liable for the fraud of his managing clerk

who induced a client to transfer property to him and then disposed of the property for his own benefit. The basis of the decision was that the managing clerk had been authorised to transact business on behalf of the firm. Lord Loreburn LC said (at p. 725): 'If the agent commits the fraud purporting to act in the course of business such as he was authorised, or held out as authorised, to transact on account of his principal, then the latter may be held liable for it.'

3. In *Armstrong v Strain* [1952] 1 KB 232; [1952] 1 All ER 139 the issue arose whether a principal can be held responsible for the misrepresentation of an agent where the agent making the statement honestly believed it to be true, but the principal knew it to be false but had not authorised the making of the statement. The Court of Appeal held that in the absence of actual fraud on the part of the principal, he was not liable for fraudulent misrepresentation. The traditional justification for this (see too *Cornfoote v Fowke* (1840) 6 M & W 358) is that one cannot add two innocent states of mind to make a fraudulent state of mind. This, in turn, rests on the theory that vicarious liability is imposed on one person for the tort of another (e.g. *Salmond & Heuston*, p. 509). Another view, that propounded by G. L. Williams (1956) 72 LQR 522, is that the law attributes the *act* of the employee to his employer. It is the employer's duty which is broken. If this, the 'master's tort' theory, were applied to the facts of *Armstrong v Strain* the principal would be liable for the composite fraud. Does the decision in *The Ocean Frost* rest implicitly upon the 'master's tort' theory or upon the theory of vicarious liability?

(c)   Joint enterprises

Brooke *v* Bool King's Bench Division [1928] All ER Rep 155

The plaintiff was the tenant of certain premises and she requested her landlord, the defendant, to search for a suspected gas leak in her basement. The defendant procured the help of a third party, Morris, who applied a naked light to the pipe they were examining, with the result that there was an explosion damaging the plaintiff's property. The county court judge gave judgment for the defendant. On appeal:

SALTER J: . . . In my opinion there are three grounds on which it was competent in law for the learned judge to find that the defendant was responsible for what was obviously a grossly reckless act on the part of Morris — namely, holding a naked light near to a place where he suspected an escape of gas. First, I think that there was evidence of agency. The defendant desired to examine this pipe, and examined it himself so far as he could in a most reckless and dangerous way with a naked light. He then desired to examine the upper part of it. Now the defendant was an old man of nearly eighty years of age, and he had in his company a much younger man. I think that there was ample evidence that the defendant impliedly invited and instructed Morris to get up on to the counter and complete the examination, when it was not convenient for him to continue it himself, and that Morris did what he did on the instructions of the defendant. The maxim *Qui facit per alium facit per se* applies, and on that first ground I think that there was evidence on which the judge could have found the defendant responsible.

Secondly, he could have been held responsible on the score of the control which he exercised over the proceedings. It is necessary to bear in mind the difference between the position of the defendant and that of Morris. The defendant was on the premises lawfully, at the request of the plaintiff, whereas Morris was a trespasser, unless the defendant had a right to invite him there to help. There was ample evidence on which the judge could find that the invitation by the plaintiff to the defendant to keep a watch over the premises extended to the right to bring in someone to help him on an occasion of that kind. In my opinion, Morris was there by the permission and invitation of the defendant, since otherwise he would have been a trespasser, and the defendant was in control of the enterprise. . . .

Thirdly, I think there was here a joint enterprise on the part of the defendant and Morris, and that the act which was the immediate cause of the explosion was their joint act done in pursuance of a concerted enterprise. . . .

. . . Here the defendant and Morris went into the room, obviously proceeding by tacit agreement to examine this pipe and both employing the same negligent means. I think that what Morris did negligently was done by him in concert with the defendant and in pursuance of their common enterprise. In [a] passage to which I wish to refer, Scrutton LJ says:[1]

'I am of opinion that the definition in *Clerk and Lindsell on Torts* (7th edn) 59, is much nearer the correct view: "Persons are said to be joint tortfeasors when their respective shares in the commission of the tort are done in furtherance of a common design . . . but mere similarity of design on the part of independent actors, causing independent damage, is not enough: there must be concerted action to a common end."'

That appears to me precisely to describe this case, and on that third ground also I think that the county court judge was fully entitled in law to find for the plaintiff. . . .

TALBOT J: I am of the same opinion, and I do not differ from the judgment just delivered or from any part of it. There is, I think, another principle on which the liability of the defendant can be satisfactorily based. . . .

In my opinion, the defendant having undertaken this examination was under a duty to take reasonable care to avoid damage resulting from it to the shop and its contents; and, if so, he could not escape liability for the consequences of failure to discharge this duty by getting (as he did) someone to make the examination, or part of it, for him, whether that person was an agent or a servant or a contractor or a mere voluntary helper. . . . The principle is that if a man does work on or near another's property which involves danger to that property unless proper care is taken, he is liable to the owner of the property for damage resulting to it from the failure to take proper care, and is equally liable, if, instead of doing the work himself, he procures another, whether agent, servant or otherwise, to do it for him. . . .

It appears to me, therefore, that the defendant is liable to the plaintiff for damage caused to her property by the negligence of Morris, who, by the defendant's authority, continued the examination of the premises which the defendant had undertaken and begun. It is, I think, a reasonable inference from the evidence that the defendant thought that Morris would use lighted matches just as he himself had been doing, but it is quite immaterial. It was the defendant's duty to take care that the dangerous operation which he had undertaken was done safely; and he is as much liable for the carelessness of Morris in doing part of the work as he would have been if he had done it himself in the same way.

Appeal allowed

---

1. *The Koursk* [1924] P 140 at 156.

Notes

1. The only other English case in which liability was imposed on the ground of joint enterprise is *Scarsbrook v Mason* [1961] 3 All ER 767, in which Glyn-Jones J held that a passenger who had agreed to contribute 4s towards the cost of petrol for a pleasure trip by car to Southend, was liable for the driver's negligence. He said: 'They knew they were joining a party, all equally concerned in the trip to Southend, and that one member of the party was going to drive on behalf of the others, so that the party could get to Southend. The members of that party are jointly and severally liable for the manner in which that motor car was driven.' Atiyah, *Vicarious Liability*, p. 124, suggests that 'being a road traffic case [*Scarsbrook v Mason*] may well have been influenced by special policy considerations.' What are these policy considerations? How have they been affected by *Morgans v Launchbury* (p. 819, ante)? Atiyah, loc. cit., discusses the American cases in which the tendency is to require something more than a mere common purpose in the journey. Note further that in *S v Walsall Metropolitan Borough Council* [1985] 3 All ER 294; [1985] 1 WLR 1150, considerable reservations were expressed about *Scarsbrook v Mason*.

2. What do you understand by Salter J's use of the word 'agency'? Cf. p. 824, ante.

3. As regard Talbot J's alternative reason for holding the defendant liable, see p. 851, post.

4. In *R v Salmon* (1880) 6 QBD 79, a criminal case, several persons shot at a target in a negligent manner so that a stranger was killed. It was held that there was no need to show who fired the fatal shot. They were all principals in manslaughter. Do you agree with G. L. Williams (1953) 31 Can BR 315 at 316 that 'had the marksmen been sued in tort they could well have been held joint tortfeasors'? Cf. *Cook v Lewis* [1951] SCR 830, criticised by T. B. Hogan (1961) 24 MLR 331.

(d)   Partners

The Partnership Act 1890

10. Liability of the firm for wrongs. — Where, by any wrongful act or omission of any partner acting in the ordinary course of the business of the firm, or with the authority of his co-partners, loss or injury is caused to any person not being a partner in the firm, or any penalty is incurred, the firm is liable therefor to the same extent as the partner so acting or omitting to act.

11. Misapplication of money or property received for or in custody of the firm. — In the following cases; namely —
  (a) Where one partner acting within the scope of his apparent authority receives the money or property of a third person and misapplies it; and
  (b) Where a firm in the course of its business receives money or property of a third person, and the money or property so received is misapplied by one or more of the partners while it is in the custody of the firm;
the firm is liable to make good the loss.

12. Liability for wrongs joint and several. — Every partner is liable jointly with his co-partners and also severally for everything for which the firm while he is a partner therein becomes liable under either of the two last preceding sections.

3 The course of employment

Salmond & Heuston on Torts (19th edn, p. 521)

It is clear that the master is responsible for acts actually authorised by him: for liability would exist in this case, even if the relation between the parties was merely one of agency, and not one of service at all. But a master, as opposed to an employer of an independent contractor, is liable even for acts which he has not authorised, provided that they are so connected with acts which he has authorised that they may rightly be regarded as modes — although improper modes — of doing them . . . On the other hand if the unauthorised and wrongful act of the servant is not so connected with the authorised act as to be a mode of doing it, but is an independent act, the master is not responsible; for in such a case the servant is not acting in the course of his employment, but has gone outside of it.

Whatman v Pearson Court of Common Pleas (1868) LR 3 CP 422

A contractor's men were allowed an hour for dinner but were not permitted to go home to dine or to leave their horses and carts unattended. One of the men went home about a quarter of a mile out of the direct line of his work to his dinner and left his horse unattended in the street before his door. The horse ran away and damaged the plaintiff's railings.

Byles J reserved leave to the defendant to move to enter a non-suit on the ground that there was no evidence that the driver was acting in the scope of his employment. The Court of Common Pleas held that it was properly left to the jury to decide this question and that they were justified in finding that he was within the scope of his employment.

BYLES J: . . . When the defendant's servant left the horse at his own door without any person in charge of it, he was clearly acting within the general scope of his authority to conduct the horse and cart during the day. . . .

[BOVILL CJ, KEATING and MONTAGU SMITH JJ delivered judgments in favour of refusing the rule.]

Rule refused

Storey v Ashton Court of Queen's Bench (1869) LR 4 QB 476

The defendant, a wine merchant, sent his carman and clerk with horse and cart to deliver wine. On their return, about a quarter of a mile from the defendant's offices, the carman was induced by the clerk, it being after business hours, to drive in another direction to visit the clerk's brother-in-law. While driving in that direction the plaintiff was run down due to the carman's negligent driving.

A verdict was directed for the defendant with leave to move to enter judgment for the plaintiff if the Court should be of opinion, on the evidence, that the defendant was responsible for the negligence of his servant. A rule having been obtained accordingly, the defendant showed cause. *Whatman v Pearson* (ante) was referred to in argument in support of the rule, but is not discussed in the judgments.

COCKBURN CJ: I am of opinion that the rule must be discharged. I think the judgments of Maule and Cresswell JJ in *Mitchell v Crassweller*[1] express the true view of the law, and the view which we ought to abide by; and that we cannot adopt the view of Erskine J in *Sleath v Wilson*,[2] that it is because the master has intrusted the servant with the control of the horse and cart that the master is responsible. The true rule is that the master is only responsible so long as the servant can be said to be doing the act, in the doing of which he is guilty of negligence, in the course of his employment as servant. I am very far from saying, if the servant when going on his master's business took a somewhat longer road, that owing to this deviation he would cease to be in the employment of the master, so as to divest the latter of all liability; in such cases, it is a question of degree as to how far the deviation could be considered a separate journey. Such a consideration is not applicable to the present case, because here the carman started on an entirely new and independent journey which had nothing at all to do with his employment. It is true that in *Mitchell v Crassweller*[1] the servant had got nearly if not quite home, while, in the present case, the carman was a quarter of a mile from home; but still he started on what may be considered a new journey entirely for his own business, as distinct from that of his master; and it would be going a great deal too far to say that under such circumstances the master was liable.

[MELLOR and LUSH JJ delivered judgments in favour of discharging the rule.]

Rule discharged

Notes

1. Compare the definition of the 'act' found to be authorised in each of the above cases: in *Whatman v Pearson* (1868) LR 3 CP 422 it was the 'care and management of the vehicle'; in *Storey v Ashton* (1869) LR 4 QB 476 it was to drive the vehicle on a specific journey. In *Feldman (Pty) Ltd v Mall* 1945 AD 733, the Appellate Division of the Supreme Court of South Africa, rejecting *Storey v Ashton*, said (per Tindall JA at p. 757) that a servant entrusted with the driving of a vehicle has a twofold duty: 'to drive it for the [purposes authorised] and to keep control of it for his employer and return it to his employer's garage'.

2. In *Ruddiman & Co v Smith* (1889) 60 LT 708, the defendants were lessees of premises, occupying the upper floors themselves and sub-letting the ground floor and basement to the plaintiffs. An employee of the defendants left off work at seven o'clock in the evening and a few minutes afterwards went to the lavatory on the second floor to wash his hands before leaving. He went home without turning off the tap. The overflow of water broke through the floor on to the plaintiffs' premises and damaged their goods. It was held by the Divisional Court that the employee's negligent act was an incident to the ordinary duties of his employment, and it was not less an incident that it was done when the day's work was over. Would the defendants have been liable had their employee negligently collided with another employee while going up the stairs after knocking-off? Was it material that the employee's negligence related to the employers' premises which, as an employee, he was under an implied obligation to his employers to protect?

---

1. (1853) 13 CB 237.
2. (1839) 9 C & P 607 at 612.

3. In *Harvey v R G O'Dell Ltd* [1958] 2 QB 78; [1958] 1 All ER 657, McNair J held that it was 'fairly incidental' to their work for employees to get a meal during working hours, so a journey for this purpose was held to be impliedly authorised. In *Hilton v Burton (Rhodes) Ltd* [1961] 1 All ER 74; [1961] 1 WLR 705, however, Diplock J held that it was not within the course of their employment for a group of workmen to travel seven or eight miles from their work site for tea, immediately after finishing their lunch in a public-house. Does this mean (a) that a tea break immediately after lunch is not impliedly authorised, or (b) that, in the second case, the workmen had, in effect, finished off their work for the day? On 'skylarking' see, for example, *Harrison v Michelin Tyre Co Ltd* [1985] 1 All ER 918; [1985] ICR 696, cf. *Aldred v Nacanco* [1987] IRLR 292.

4. In *Kay v ITW Ltd* [1968] 1 QB 140; [1967] 3 All ER 22, the issue was whether an employee instructed to drive a fork-lift truck had implied authority to remove obstacles in his path and, if so, what kind of obstacle. The Court of Appeal held that the removal of a five-ton diesel lorry was within the course of his employment. Although agreeing with this result, Danckwerts LJ was led to say (at p. 27): '[i]t would be a good deal safer to keep lions or other wild animals in a park than to engage in business involving the employment of labour. In fact the position comes close to that in *Rylands v Fletcher* (1868) LR 3 HL 330.'

Smith *v* Stages House of Lords [1989] 1 All ER 833

Mr Machin was employed by the Darlington Insulation Co Ltd (the second defendants) as a peripatetic lagger to install insulation at power stations. In August 1977 he and Mr Stages (the first defendant), a fellow lagger employed by the second defendants, were taken off work on Drakelow power station in Staffordshire and instructed by their employers to go to do urgent work at Pembroke power station in Wales, starting at 8 a.m. on Tuesday, 23 August and to report back for work in Staffordshire at 8 a.m. on Wednesday, 31 August. They were paid for an 8-hour day for the journey to Pembroke and for an 8-hour day for the journey back to Staffordshire, and were given the equivalent of rail fare as travelling expenses, but no stipulation was made as to their mode of travel. The two employees travelled to Wales in Stages' car, did the work, and by dint of working for 24 hours in order to finish the job they finished by 8.30 a.m. on Monday, 29 August. They then decided to drive straight back to Staffordshire without any sleep and on the way the car, driven by Stages, left the road and crashed into a brick wall. Both men were seriously injured. Machin brought proceedings against Stages for damages and later joined the second defendants alleging that they were vicariously liable for Stages' negligence. In 1979, Machin died from unrelated causes and the action was continued by his widow and administratrix, Mrs Smith. Stages was uninsured. The trial judge held that the accident had been caused by Stages' negligence but that the second defendants were not liable because Stages had not been acting in the course of his employment. On appeal, the Court of Appeal, [1988] ICR 201, reversed the decision and held that the second defendants were vicariously liable.

The second defendants appealed to the House of Lords.

LORD GOFF OF CHIEVELEY: . . . The present case can be seen as one of those cases, which have troubled the courts in the past, in which the question has arisen whether an employee, travelling to or from a place of work, is acting in the course of his employment. . . .

. . . The fundamental principle is that an employee is acting in the course of his employment when he is doing what he is employed to do, to which it is sufficient for present purposes to add, or anything which is reasonably incidental to his employment. . . .

. . . We can begin with the simple proposition that, in ordinary circumstances, when a man is travelling to or from his place of work, he is not acting in the course of his employment. So a bank clerk who commutes to the City of London every day from Sevenoaks is not acting in the course of his employment when he walks across London Bridge from the station to his bank in the City. This is because he is not employed to travel from his home to the bank: he is employed to work at the bank, his place of work, and so his duty is to arrive there in time for his working day. Nice points can arise about the precise time, or place, at which he may be held to have arrived at work; but these do not trouble us in the present case. Likewise, of course, he is not acting in the course of his employment when he is travelling home after his day's work is over. If, however, a man is obliged by his employer to travel to work by means of transport provided by his employer, he may be held to be acting in the course of his employment when so doing.

These are the normal cases. There are, however, circumstances in which, when a man is travelling to (or from) a place where he is doing a job for his employer, he will be held to be acting in the course of his employment. Some of these are listed by Lord Atkin in *Blee v London and North Eastern Rly Co* [1937] 4 All ER 270 at 273, [1938] AC 126 at 131–132. So, if a man is employed to do jobs for his employer at various places during the day, such as a man who goes from door to door canvassing for business, or who distributes goods to customers, or who services equipment like washing machines or dishwashers, he will ordinarily be held to be acting in the course of his employment when travelling from one destination to another, and may also be held to do so when travelling from his home to his first destination and home again after his last. Again, it has been held that, in certain circumstances, a man who is called out from his home at night to deal with an emergency may be acting in the course of his employment when travelling from his home to his place of work to deal with the emergency: see *Blee v London and North Eastern Rly Co*. There are many other cases.

But how do we distinguish the cases in this category in which a man is acting in the course of his employment from those in which he is not? The answer is, I fear, that everything depends on the circumstances. As Sir John Donaldson MR said in *Nancollas v Insurance Officer* [1985] 1 All ER 833 at 836, the authorities —

'approve an approach which requires the court to have regard to and to weigh in the balance every factor which can be said in any way to point towards or away from a finding that the claimant was in the course of his employment. In the context of the present appeals, there are a number of such factors to which we must have regard, but none is of itself decisive.'

For example, the fact that a man is being paid by his employer in respect of the relevant period of time is often important, but cannot of itself be decisive. . . .

. . . [T]o me, the question is this. Was Mr Stages employed to travel to and from Pembroke? Or was the pay given to him simply in recognition of the fact that he had lost two days' work at Drakelow because, in order to work at the power station at Pembroke, he would have to make his own way to Pembroke and back again to the Midlands? If we can solve that problem, we can answer the question whether Mr Stages was acting in the course of his employment when, worn out, he crashed his car on the A40 near Llandeilo. . . .

I approach the matter as follows. I do not regard this case as an ordinary case of travelling to work. It would be more accurate to describe it as a case where an employee, who has for a short time to work for his employers at a different place of work some distance away from his usual place of work, has to move from his ordinary base to a temporary base (here lodgings in Pembroke) from which he will travel to work at the temporary place of work each day. For the purpose of moving base, a normal working day was set aside for Mr Stages' journey, for which he was paid as for an eight-hour day. In addition to his day's pay he was given a travel allowance for his journey, and an allowance for his lodgings at his temporary base in Pembroke. In my opinion, in all the circumstances of the case, Mr Stages was required by the employers to make this journey, so as to make himself available to do his work at the Pembroke power station, and it would be proper to describe him as having been employed to do so. The fact that he was not required by his employer to make the journey by any particular means, nor even required to make it on the particular working day made available to him, does not detract from the proposition that he was employed to make the journey. Had Mr Stages wished, he could have driven down on the afternoon of Sunday, 21 August, and have devoted the Monday to (for example) visiting friends near Pembroke. In such circumstances it could, I suppose, be said that Stages was not travelling 'in his employers' time'. But this would not matter; for the fact remains that the Monday, a normal working day, was made available for the journey, with full pay for that day to perform a task which he was required by the employers to perform.

I have it very much in mind that Mr Machin and Mr Stages were described by counsel for the employers as peripatetic laggers working at such sites as were available. This may well be an accurate description of their work. If so, their contracts of service may have provided at least an indication as to how far they would be acting in the course of their employment when changing from one power station to another. Indeed, accepting the description as correct, it is difficult to know how much weight to give to it in the absence of their contracts of service. However, the present case can in any event be differentiated on the basis that it was a departure from the norm in that it was concerned with a move to a temporary base to deal with an emergency, on the terms I have described.

I turn to Mr Stages' journey back. Another ordinary working day, Tuesday, 30 August, was made available for the journey, with the same pay, to enable him to return to his base in the Midlands to be ready to travel to work on the Wednesday morning. In my opinion, he was employed to make the journey back, just as he was employed to make the journey out to Pembroke. If he had chosen to go to sleep on the Monday morning and afternoon for eight hours or so, and then to drive home on the Monday evening so that he could have Tuesday free (as indeed Mr Pye[1] expected him to do), that would not have detracted from the proposition that his journey was in the course of his employment. For this purpose, it was irrelevant that Monday was a bank holiday. Of course, it was wrong for him to succumb to the temptation of driving home on the Monday morning, just after he had completed so long a spell of work; but once again that cannot alter the fact that his journey was made in the course of his employment.

For these reasons, I would dismiss the appeal.

LORD LOWRY: . . . The paramount rule is that an employee travelling on the highway will be acting in the course of his employment if, and only if, he is at the material time going about his employer's business. One must not confuse the duty to turn up for one's work with the concept of already being 'on duty' while travelling to it.

It is impossible to provide for every eventuality and foolish, without the benefit of argument, to make the attempt, but some prima facie propositions may be stated with reasonable confidence. (1) An employee travelling from his ordinary residence to his regular place of work, whatever the means of transport and even if it is provided by the employer, is not on duty and is not acting in the course of his employment, but, if he is obliged by his contract of service to use the employer's transport, he will normally, in the absence of an express condition to the contrary, be regarded as acting

---

1. [The employers' contract manager.]

in the course of his employment while doing so. (2) Travelling in the employer's time between workplaces (one of which may be the regular workplace) or in the course of a peripatetic occupation, whether accompanied by goods or tools or simply in order to reach a succession of workplaces (as an inpector of gas meters might do), will be in the course of the employment. (3) Receipt of wages (though not receipt of a travelling allowance) will indicate that the employee is travelling in the employer's time and for his benefit and is acting in the course of his employment, and in such a case the fact that the employee may have discretion as to the mode and time of travelling will not take the journey out of the course of his employment. (4) An employee travelling *in the employer's time* from his ordinary residence to a workplace other than this regular workplace or in the course of a peripatetic occupation or to the scene of an emergency (such as a fire, an accident or a mechanical breakdown of plant) will be acting in the course of his employment. (5) A deviation from or interruption of a journey undertaken in the course of employment (unless the deviation or interruption is merely incidental to the journey) will for the time being (which may include an overnight interruption) take the employee out of the course of his employment. (6) Return journeys are to be treated on the same footing as outward journeys.

All the foregoing propositions are subject to any express arrangements between the employer and the employee or those representing his interests. They are not, I would add, intended to define the position of salaried employees, with regard to whom the touchstone of payment made in the employer's time is not generally significant. . . .

[LORD KEITH OF KINKEL and LORD GRIFFITHS agreed with LORD LOWRY's speech. LORD BRANDON OF OAKBROOK agreed with the speeches of LORD GOFF and LORD LOWRY.]

Appeal dismissed

Century Insurance Co Ltd *v* Northern Ireland Road Transport Board House of Lords [1942] 1 All ER 491

The respondents' employee, Davison, was delivering petrol from a tanker into the storage tank of a Belfast garage proprietor. While the petrol was flowing into the tank, Davison lighted a cigarette and threw away the lighted match causing a conflagration in which the tanker, a motor vehicle belonging to the garage proprietor, and several houses in the street were damaged. The appellants had insured the respondents against liability to third parties and, in answer to the claims based on this policy, one of their contentions was that the tanker driver's negligence was not done in the course of his employment so as to make the respondents liable.

The Court of Appeal of Northern Ireland held that the respondents were liable for the driver's negligence and were entitled to claim under the policy. The appellants appealed to the House of Lords. The appeal was dismissed.

LORD WRIGHT: . . . The act of a workman in lighting his pipe or cigarette is an act done for his own comfort and convenience and at least, generally speaking, not for his employer's benefit. That last condition, however, is no longer essential to fix liability on the employer. (*Lloyd v Grace, Smith & Co*).[1] Nor is such an act prima facie negligent. It is in itself both innocent and harmless. The negligence is to be found by considering the time when and the circumstances in which the match is struck and thrown down. The duty of the workman to his employer is so to conduct himself in doing his work as not negligently to cause damage either to the employer himself or his property or to third persons or their property, and thus to impose the same liability on the employer as if he had been doing the work himself and committed

---

1. [1912] AC 716.

the negligent act. This may seem too obvious as a matter of common sense to require either argument or authority. I think that what plausibility the contrary argument might seem to possess results from treating the act of lighting the cigarette in abstraction from the circumstances as a separate act. This was the line taken by the majority judgment in *Williams v Jones*[1] from which Mellor and Blackburn JJ as I think, rightly dissented. . . .

[VISCOUNT SIMON LC, with whom LORD ROMER concurred, delivered a speech in favour of dismissing the appeal. LORD PORTER concurred.]

Williams *v* Jones Court of Exchequer Chamber (1865) 3 H & C 602

The defendant's employee negligently dropped a wood shaving, with which he had been lighting his pipe, causing a fire in the plaintiff's shed. A majority of the Court of Exchequer Chamber (Keating J, Erle CJ and Smith J) held that the defendant was not liable. Blackburn and Mellor JJ dissented. Their judgments were approved by the House of Lords in *Century Insurance Co Ltd v Northern Ireland Road Transport Board* (ante).

BLACKBURN J (dissenting): . . . Now the general rule of law is clear, that where the relation of master and servant exists between one directing a thing to be done and those employed to do it, the master is considered in law to do it himself, and as a consequence that the master is responsible, not only for the consequences of the thing which he directed to be done, but also for the consequences of any negligence of his servants in the course of the employment, though the master was no party to such negligence and even did his best to prevent it; as in the ordinary case where a master, selecting a coachman believed to be sober, sends him out with orders to drive quietly, and the coachman gets drunk and drives furiously. In such a case it may seem hard that the master should be responsible, yet he no doubt is if he be his master within the definition stated by Parke B in *Quarman v Burnett* (1840) 6 M & W 499 at 509, that the person is liable 'who stood in the relation of master to the wrongdoer – he who had selected him as his servant, from the knowledge of or belief in his skill and care, and who could remove him for misconduct, and whose orders he was bound to receive and obey.' But the master is not liable for any negligence or tort of the servant which is not in the course of the employment, for such negligence or tort cannot be considered as in any way the act of the master.

In the present case the difficulty is to apply these rules to the facts. It is said that Davies, the servant, was not employed by his master to smoke or to light his pipe, and that is no doubt true; but the act of lighting a pipe was in itself a harmless act; it only became negligent and a breach of duty towards the plaintiff because it was done when using his shed and working there amongst inflammable materials. Had the action been brought against Davies himself, it could not have been maintained for merely lighting his pipe, but that under the circumstances would have been evidence that he failed to take reasonable care when using the plaintiff's shed and working there, which would have been the true ground of action. The action would have lain against Davies personally for negligence in doing that very thing which he was employed by the defendant to do as his servant and not otherwise. It seems to me, therefore, that it was negligence in the course of his employment, such as to be in law the negligence of his master, the defendant. The point is not one admitting of being elucidated by argument or by decided cases: in truth the whole case depends upon whether this is a correct statement of the effect of the facts. . . .

---

1. (1865) 3 H & C 602.

Rose v Plenty Court of Appeal [1976] 1 All ER 97

Mr Plenty, the first defendant, was a milk roundsman, employed by the second defendants, Co-operative Retail Services Ltd. His duties were to drive his float on his round delivering milk and collecting payment. There were notices up at the depot making it clear that roundsmen were not allowed in any circumstances to employ children in the performance of their duties or to give lifts on the milk float. Contrary to these prohibitions, Plenty invited Leslie Rose, then aged 13, to help him with his milk round in return for payment. On 21 June 1970, whilst riding on the float in the course of helping Plenty, Rose was injured when Plenty drove negligently. By his father and next friend, he brought an action for damages against Plenty and the Co-op. The judge found that Rose was 25 per cent to blame for the accident and gave judgment against Plenty for 75 per cent of the assessed damages of £800. He held that Plenty was acting outside the scope of his employment and that Rose was a trespasser on the float. On appeal, it was contended for Rose that the Co-op were liable for the acts of Plenty.

LORD DENNING MR: . . . This raises a nice point on the liability of a master for his servant. I will first take the notices to the roundsmen saying they must not take the boys on. Those do not necessarily exempt the employers from liability. The leading case is *Limpus v London General Omnibus Co*[1]. The drivers of omnibuses were furnished with a card saying they 'must not on any account race with or obstruct another omnibus . . .' Nevertheless the driver of one of the defendants' omnibuses did obstruct a rival omnibus and caused an accident in which the plaintiff's horses were injured. Martin B[2] directed the jury that, if the defendants' driver did it for the purposes of his employer, the defendants were liable; but if it was an act of his own, and in order to effect a purpose of his own, the defendants were not responsible. The jury found for the plaintiff. The Court of Exchequer Chamber[3] held that the direction was correct. It was a very strong court which included Willes and Blackburn JJ. Despite the prohibition, the employer was held liable because the injury resulted from an act done by the driver in the course of his service and for his master's purposes. The decisive point was that it was *not* done by the servant for his own purposes, but for his master's purposes.

I will next take the point about a trespasser. The boy was a trespasser on the milk float so far as Co-operative Services were concerned. They had not given him any permission to be on the float and had expressly prohibited the milk roundsman from taking him on. There are two early cases where it was suggested that the employer of a driver is not liable to a person who is a trespasser on the vehicle. They are *Twine v Bean's Express Ltd*[4] and *Conway v George Wimpey & Co Ltd*[5]. But these cases are to be explained on other grounds; and the statements about a trespasser are no longer correct. Those statements were made at a time when it was commonly supposed that occupiers of premises were under no duty to use care in regard to a trespasser. But that stern rule has now been abandoned, especially when the trespasser is a child: see *British Railways Board v Herrington*[6]; *Southern Portland Cement Ltd v Cooper*[7] and *Harris v Birkenhead Corp*[8,9]. So far as vehicles are concerned, I venture to go

---

1. (1862) 1 H & C 526.
2. 1 H & C at 529, 530.
3. (1863) 9 Jur NS 333; [1861–73] All ER Rep 556.
4. (1946) 175 LT 131.
5. [1951] 2 KB 266; [1951] 1 All ER 363.
6. [1972] AC 877; [1972] 1 All ER 749.
7. [1974] AC 623; [1974] 1 All ER 87.
8. [1975] 1 All ER 1001; [1975] 1 WLR 379.
9. [See now s. 1 of the Occupiers' Liability Act 1984 (p. 442, ante).]

back to my own judgment in *Young v Edward Box & Co Ltd*[1], when I said:

'In every case where it is sought to make the master liable for the conduct of his servant the first question is to see whether the servant was liable. If the answer is Yes, the second question is to see whether the employer must shoulder the servant's liability.'

That way of putting it is, I think, to be preferred to the way I put it later in *Staveley Iron and Chemical Co Ltd v Jones*[2].

Applying the first question in *Young v Box*[3], it is quite clear that the driver, Mr Plenty, was liable to the boy, Leslie Rose, for his negligent driving of the milk float. He actually invited the boy to ride on it. So the second question arises, whether his employers, Co-operative Services, are liable for the driver's negligence. That does not depend on whether the boy was a trespasser. It depends, as I said in *Young v Box*[3], on whether the driver, in taking the boy on the milk float, was acting in the course of his employment.

In considering whether a prohibited act was within the course of the employment, it depends very much on the purpose for which it is done. If it is done for his employers' business, it is usually done in the course of his employment, even though it is a prohibited act. That is clear from *Limpus v London General Omnibus Co*[4]; *Young v Box*[3] and *Ilkiw v Samuels*[5]. But if it is done for some purpose other than his master's business, as, for instance, giving a lift to a hitchhiker, such an act, if prohibited, may not be within the course of his employment. Both *Twine v Bean's Express Ltd*[6] and *Conway v George Wimpey & Co Ltd*[7] are to be explained on their own facts as cases where a driver had given a lift to someone else contrary to a prohibition and not for the purposes of the employers. *Iqbal v London Transport Executive*[8] seems to be out of line and should be regarded as decided on its own special circumstances. In the present case it seems to me that the course of Mr Plenty's employment was to distribute the milk, collect the money and to bring back the bottles to the van. He got or allowed this young boy, Leslie Rose, to do part of that business which was the employers' business. It seems to me that although prohibited, it was conduct which was within the course of the employment; and on this ground I think the judge was in error. I agree it is a nice point in these cases on which side of the line the case falls; but, as I understand the authorities, this case falls within those in which the prohibition affects only the conduct within the sphere of the employment and did not take the conduct outside the sphere altogether. I would hold this conduct of Christopher Plenty to be within the course of his employment and the master is liable accordingly, and I would allow the appeal.

In parting with the case, it may be interesting to notice that this type of case is unlikely to arise so much in the future, since a vehicle is not to be used on a road unless there is in force an insurance policy covering, inter alia, injury to passengers.

LAWTON LJ (dissenting): Ever since 1946 employers of drivers have been entitled to arrange their affairs on the assumption that if they gave clear and express instructions to their drivers that they were not to carry passengers on the employers' vehicles, the employers would not be liable in law for any injury sustained by such passengers. They were entitled to make that assumption because of the decision of this court in

---

1. [1951] 1 TLR 789 at 793.
2. [1955] 1 QB 474 at 480; [1955] 1 All ER 6 at 8.
3. [1951] 1 TLR 789.
4. (1862) 1 H & C 526.
5. [1963] 2 All ER 879; [1963] 1 WLR 991.
6. (1946) 175 LT 131.
7. [1951] 2 KB 266; [1951] 1 All ER 363.
8. (1973) Times, 6th June.

Twine v Bean's Express Ltd[1]. No doubt since 1946 employers when negotiating with their insurers have sought to get reductions in premiums and have done so because of the assumption which, so it seems to me, they were entitled to make about freedom from liability to unauthorised passengers. . . .

. . . The first defendant had been employed to drive the milk float and deliver the milk. He had not been authorised to sub-contract his work. What he was doing was setting the plaintiff to do the job for which he had been employed and for which he was getting paid. In my judgment in so doing he was acting outside the scope of his employment — just as in the same way as was the driver in *Conway v George Wimpey & Co Ltd*[2].

If a general principle should be needed to support my opinion in this case, I would adopt the same approach as Lord Greene MR in *Twine's* case[1]. What duty did the second defendants owe to the plaintiff? Counsel for the plaintiff says: 'Oh well, they put the driver with the milk float on the road; they put him into a position to take passengers if he were minded to disobey his instructions and therefore it is socially just that they should be responsible.' I do not agree. When they put the first defendant with his float on the road they put him into a position where he had to take care not to injure those with whom he was reasonably likely to have dealings or to meet, that is all other road users and his customers. They expressly excluded anyone travelling as a passenger on his milk float. He was instructed expressly that he was not to carry passengers. Had he obeyed his instructions, he would not have had a passenger to whom he owed a duty of care. It was his disobedience which brought the injured plaintiff into the class of persons to whom the second defendants vicariously owed a duty of care. He had not been employed to do anything of the kind. In my judgment, the plaintiff has failed to establish that the second defendants owed him any duty of care. . . .

SCARMAN LJ: . . . I think it important to realise that the principle of vicarious liability is one of public policy. It is not a principle which derives from a critical or refined consideration of other concepts in the common law, e.g. the concept of trespass or indeed the concept of agency. No doubt in particular cases it may be relevant to consider whether a particular plaintiff was or was not a trespasser. Similarly, when, as I shall indicate, it is important that one should determine the course of employment of the servant, the law of agency may have some marginal relevance. But basically, as I understand it, the employer is made vicariously liable for the tort of his employee not because the plaintiff is an invitee, nor because of·the authority possessed by the servant, but because it is a case in which the employer, having put matters into motion, should be liable if the motion that he has originated leads to damage to another. What is the approach which the cases identify as the correct approach in order to determine this question of public policy? First, as Lord Denning MR has already said, one looks to see whether the servant has committed a tort on the plaintiff. In the present case it is clear that the first defendant, the servant of the dairy company, who are the second defendants, by the negligent driving of the milk float, caused injury to the plaintiff, a boy 13½ years old, who was on the float at his invitation. There was therefore a tort committed by the servant. The next question, as Lord Denning MR has said, is whether the employer should shoulder the liability for compensating the person injured by the tort. With all respect to the points developed by Lawton LJ, it does appear to me to be clear, since the decision of *Limpus v London General Omnibus Co*[3], that that question has to be answered by directing attention to what the first defendant was employed to do when he committed the tort that has caused damage to the plaintiff. The first defendant was, of course, employed at the time of the accident

---

1. (1946) 175 LT 131.
2. [1951] 2 KB 266; [1951] 1 All ER 363.
3. (1862) 1 H & C 526.

to do a whole number of operations. He was certainly not employed to give the plaintiff a lift, and if one confines one's analysis of the facts to the incident of injury to the plaintiff, then no doubt one would say that carrying the plaintiff on the float — giving him a lift — was not in the course of the first defendant's employment. But in *Ilkiw v Samuels*[1] Diplock LJ indicated that the proper approach to the nature of the servant's employment is a broad one. He said:

'As each of these nouns implies [he is referring to the nouns used to describe course of employment, sphere, scope and so forth] the matter must be looked at broadly, not dissecting the servant's task into its component activities — such as driving, loading, sheeting and the like — by asking: What was the job on which he was engaged for his employer? and answering that question as a jury would.'

Applying those words to the employment of the first defendant, I think it is clear from the evidence that he was employed as a roundsman to drive his float round his round and to deliver milk, to collect empties and to obtain payment. That was his job. He was under an express prohibition — a matter to which I shall refer later — not to enlist the help of anyone doing that work. And he was also under an express prohibition not to give lifts on the float to anyone. How did he choose to carry out the task which I have analysed? He chose to disregard the prohibition and to enlist the assistance of the plaintiff. As a matter of common sense, that does seem to me to be a mode, albeit a prohibited mode, of doing the job with which he was entrusted. Why was the plaintiff being carried on the float when the accident occurred? Because it was necessary to take him from point to point so that he could assist in delivering milk, collecting empties and, on occasions, obtaining payment. The plaintiff was there because it was necessary that he should be there in order that he could assist, albeit in a way prohibited by the employers, in the job entrusted to the first defendant by his employers.

. . . In *Twine*'s case[2], at the very end of the judgment, Lord Greene MR said: 'The other thing that he [i.e. the servant] was doing simultaneously was something totally outside the scope of his employment, namely, giving a lift to a person who had no right whatsoever to be there.' In that case the conclusion of fact was that the express prohibition on giving lifts was not only a prohibition but was also a limiting factor on the scope of the employment; and, of course, once a prohibition is properly to be treated as a defining or limiting factor on the scope of employment certain results follow. In *Twine*'s case[3] the driver was engaged to drive his employers' van, his employers having a contract with the Post Office. When so doing, he gave Mr Twine a lift from A to B. True A and B happened to be, both of them, offices of the Post Office. Yet I can well understand why the court reached the conclusion that in the circumstances of that case it was not possible to say that the driver in giving Mr Twine a lift was acting within the scope of his employment or doing improperly that which he was employed to do. Similarly when one looks at *Conway*'s case[4], one again sees that on the facts of that case the court considered it right so to define the scope of employment that what was done, namely giving somebody a lift, was outside it and was not a mode of doing that which the servant was employed to do. That also was a case of a lift: the person lifted was not in any way engaged, in the course of the lift or indeed otherwise, in doing the master's business or in assisting the servant to do the master's business; and no doubt it was for that reason that Asquith LJ was able to say[5] that what was done — that is giving somebody else's employee a lift from

---

1. [1963] 2 All ER at p. 889; [1963] 1 WLR at p. 1004.
2. (1946) 175 LT at p. 132.
3. (1946) 175 LT 131.
4. [1951] 2 KB 266; [1951] 1 All ER 363.
5. [1951] 2 KB at p. 276; [1951] 1 All ER at p. 367.

the airport home—was not a mode of performing an act which the driver was employed to do, but was the performance of an act which he was not employed to perform. In the present case the first defendant, the servant, was employed to deliver milk, to collect empties, to obtain payment from customers. The plaintiff was there on the float in order to assist the first defendant to do those jobs. I would have thought therefore that whereas *Conway v George Wimpey & Co Ltd*[1] was absolutely correctly decided on its facts, the facts of the present case lead to a very different conclusion. The dividing factor between, for instance, the present case and the decisions in *Twine v Bean's Express Ltd*[2] and *Conway v George Wimpey & Co Ltd*[1] is the category into which the court, on the study of the facts of the case, puts the express prohibition issued by the employers to their servant. In *Ilkiw v Samuels*[3] Diplock LJ, in a judgment to which I have already referred, dealt with this problem of the prohibition, and quoted a dictum of Lord Dunedin in *Plumb v Cobden Flour Mills Co Ltd*[4], which itself has been approved in the Privy Council case of *Canadian Pacific Rly Co v Lockhart*[5]. Lord Dunedin said[6]: '. . . there are prohibitions which limit the sphere of employment, and prohibitions which only deal with conduct within the sphere of employment.' . . . [In *Iqbal v London Transport Executive*[7]] the Court of Appeal had to consider whether London Transport Executive was liable for the action of a bus conductor in driving, contrary to his express instructions, a motor bus a short distance in a garage. Of course, the court had no difficulty at all in distinguishing between the spheres of employment of a driver and a conductor in London Transport. Accordingly, it treated the prohibition on conductors acting as drivers of motor buses as a prohibition which defined his sphere of employment. Now there was nothing of that sort in the prohibition in this case. The prohibition is twofold: (1) that the first defendant was not to give lifts on his float; and (2) that he was not to employ others to help him in delivering the milk and so forth. There was nothing in those prohibitions which defined or limited the sphere of his employment. The sphere of his employment remained precisely the same after as before the prohibitions were brought to his notice. The sphere was as a roundsman to go round the rounds delivering milk, collecting empties and obtaining payment. Contrary to instructions, this roundsman chose to do what he was employed to do in an improper way. But the sphere of his employment was in no way affected by his express instructions.

Finally, I think one can see how careful one must be not to introduce into a study of this sort of problem ideas of trespass and agency. It is perfectly possible, on the principle that I am now considering, that an employer may authorise his servant, if the servant chooses to do it—'permit' is perhaps a better word—to give lifts. But the effect of that permission does not make the employer liable if in the course of recreational or off duty but permitted activity the servant drives the vehicle negligently and injures the passenger. *Hilton v Thomas Burton (Rhodes) Ltd*[8] is a case in which the plaintiff failed although the journey was a permitted journey, because he was not able to show that the journey on which he was being carried was a journey which occurred in the course of the servant's employment. Conversely one has the classic case of *Limpus v London General Omnibus Co*[9] when what the servant was doing was a defiance and disregarded of the bus company's instructions.

---

1. [1951] 2 KB 266; [1951] 1 All ER 363.
2. (1946) 175 LT 131.
3. [1963] 2 All ER at p. 889; [1963] 1 WLR at p. 1004.
4. [1914] AC 62 at 67.
5. [1942] AC 591; [1942] 2 All ER 464.
6. [1914] AC at 67.
7. (1973) 16 KIR 329.
8. [1961] 1 All ER 74; [1961] 1 WLR 705.
9. (1862) 1 H & C 526.

Nevertheless the plaintiff who was injured by the defiant and disobedient acts was entitled to recover against the employer. . . .

Appeal allowed; judgment for the plaintiff against the second defendants for £620 damages plus £63.90 interest.

Notes

1. As Lord Denning MR pointed out, since 1 December 1972 it has been compulsory to insure against liability to passengers, and under s. 149 of the Road Traffic Act 1988 the user cannot restrict his liability by agreement or by the operation of the defence volenti non fit injuria (p. 888, post).

2. Is Lawton LJ's dissenting judgment, in which he states that the employers did not owe a duty of care to the plaintiff, consistent with the essential nature of vicarious liability? For a critique of Lord Greene MR's judgment in *Twine v Bean's Express Ltd* (1946) 175 LT 131, upon which Lawton LJ relied, see F. H. Newark (1954) 17 MLR 102. Cf. Atiyah, *Vicarious Liability*, p. 250.

3. Is it relevant whether the person injured as a result of the employee's negligence is aware of the prohibition? In *Stone v Taffe* [1974] 3 All ER 1016 [1974] 1 WLR 1575, Stephenson LJ suggested, obiter (at p. 1022), that a plaintiff who knew of the prohibition and who had the chance to avoid the danger of injury from the prohibited act cannot hold the employer liable; furthermore he thought it would be sufficient for the employer to prove that the prohibition was likely to be known to the injured person. Where the injured person is a fellow employee of the wrongdoer he is more likely to know of the prohibition (as in *Iqbal v London Transport Executive* (1973) 16 KIR 329). For comment see I. M. Yeats (1976) 39 MLR 94 at 95–96.

4. It appears to be easier to limit the scope of a delegated task than the scope of authority of an employee. In *Watkins v Birmingham City Council* (1975) Times, 1st August; (1976) 126 NLJ 442, the deputy headmistress of a school was injured when she fell over a tricycle which had been negligently placed near a classroom door by a ten-year-old boy in the course of carrying out his assigned task of distributing milk in classrooms. There was a strict rule, which the boy had disobeyed, that tricycles were not to be moved from their safe position in the middle of the assembly hall. The Court of Appeal held that the boy was not an employee of the authority, since it was part of his education to render the services. Buckley LJ is reported to have said that 'the boy might well have been acting as an agent of the school authority, but it has been conceded that if the relationship was that of principal and agent but not master and servant, the strict school rule . . . was effective to protect the school from vicarious liability for any breach of the rule . . .'. The court indicated that had the boy been an employee, the rule against moving the tricycle would not have restricted the scope of the employment. Cf. *Armagas Ltd v Mundogas SA* [1986] AC 717; [1986] 2 All ER 385 (p. 826, ante).

Poland v John Parr and Sons Court of Appeal [1926] All ER
Rep 177

Mr Hall, a carter employed by the defendants, honestly and reasonably believed that
the plaintiff, a boy aged twelve years, was pilfering or about to pilfer sugar from a
bag on the defendants' wagon. He hit him on the back of the neck, causing him to
fall under one of the wheels of the wagon, which injured his foot. In an action for
damages judgment was entered for the defendants in the Liverpool Court of Passage.
The plaintiff appealed.

SCRUTTON LJ: . . . In order to make a master liable for the act of a person alleged to
be his servant, the act must be one of a class of acts which the person was authorised
or employed to do. If the act complained of is one of that class, the master is liable,
although the act is done negligently, or, in some cases, even if it is done with excessive
violence. But the excess may be so great as to take the act in question out of the class
of acts which the person is employed or authorised to do. Whether it is so or not is
a question of degree. It has been argued that a master cannot be liable if the act of
his servant is illegal or excessive. In my opinion, *Dyer v Munday*[1] negatives the proposition that a master cannot be liable if the act of his servant is illegal. In that case,
Lord Esher MR put the question whether the act complained of was or was not for
the master's benefit. That may be one test, but where excessive violence is charged,
another question must be considered—namely, whether the excess is such as to take
the act complained of out of the class of authorised acts. It was also argued that a
master could not authorise an act which he could not lawfully do himself. But in
many cases masters have been held responsible for acts of their servants which, if
done by themselves, would have been illegal. . . .

ATKIN LJ: . . . Any servant is, as a general rule, authorised to do acts which are for the
protection of his master's property. I say 'authorised', for although there are acts which
the servant is bound to do, and for which, therefore, his master is responsible, it does not
follow that the servant must be bound to do an act in order to make his master responsible for it. For example, a servant may be authorised to stop a runaway horse, but it
would be hard to say that every servant was bound to do this, or that a servant commits a
breach of his duty if he refrains from doing so, or if he refrains from extinguishing a fire.
Some men may have the necessary courage to encounter such dangers, others may shrink
from facing them. It cannot be said that all are bound to face such dangers. Thus there is
a class of acts which, in an emergency, a servant, though not bound, is authorised to do.
And then the question is not whether the act of the servant was for the master's benefit,
but whether it is an act of this class. I agree that, where the servant does more than the
emergency requires, the excess may be so great as to take the act out of the class. For
example, if Mr Hall had fired a shot at the boy, the act might have been in the interests of
his masters, but that is not the test. The question is whether the act is one of the class of
acts which the servant is authorised to do in an emergency.
  In the present case, Mr Hall was doing an act of this class—namely, protecting his
masters' property, which was or which he reasonably and honestly thought was being
pillaged. His mode of doing the act is not, in my opinion, such as to take the act out
of the class. He was, therefore, doing an authorised act for which the defendants are
responsible. The appeal must be allowed and judgment must be entered for the plaintiff.

[BANKES LJ delivered a judgment in favour of dismissing the appeal.]

Appeal allowed

---

1. [1895] 1 QB 742.

Warren v Henley's Ltd King's Bench Division [1948] 2 All ER 935

Beaumont, employed by the defendants as a petrol pump attendant, erroneously accused the plaintiff, in violent language, of having tried to drive away without paying for petrol which had been put into the tank of his car. The plaintiff paid his bill, called the police and told the pump attendant that he would be reported to his employers. The attendant then assaulted and injured the plaintiff, who brought this action for damages against the defendants who were held not liable.

HILBERY J: . . . Is there any evidence here on which a jury could find that this assault, committed in the circumstances which I have just given, was so connected with the acts which the servant was expressly or impliedly authorised to do as to be a mode of doing those acts? It seems to me the answer must be 'No'. Of course, as in *Dyer v Munday*,[1] if a manager, who, in the course of the very duties in the business goes to recover furniture, so conducts himself in recovering the furniture that he commits an assault, that is a tortious mode of doing the class of act which he is authorised to do. . . . Clearly, there is no evidence here that this act belonged to the class of acts that Beaumont was authorised to do. In extension of what Scrutton LJ[2], has said, I have also examined the matter in the light of that statement of the law which I have already read from Salmond on Torts, so as to ask whether, although it was not of the class of acts which Beaumont was authorised to do, it was so connected with that class of acts as to be a mode of doing some act within that class. It seems to me that it was an act entirely of personal vengeance. He was personally inflicting punishment, and intentionally inflicting punishment, on the plaintiff because the plaintiff proposed to take a step which might affect Beaumont in his own personal affairs. It had no connection whatever with the discharge of any duty for the defendants. The act of assault by Beaumont was done by him in relation to a personal matter affecting his personal interests, and there is no evidence that it was otherwise. . . .

Notes

1. In *Keppel Bus Co Ltd v Sa'ad bin Ahmad* [1974] 2 All ER 700; [1974] 1 WLR 1082 employers were held not liable for an assault by one of their bus conductors on a passenger after the passenger had objected to the conductor's use of abusive language to himself and an elderly lady. It was held that insults to passengers were not part of a conductor's duty and there was no evidence of disorder among passengers calling for forcible action. Could a different result have been achieved by examining whether the bus company were in breach of their duty of care to passengers to safeguard them against the risk of assaults by conductors? Compare *Home Office v Dorset Yacht Co Ltd* [1970] AC 1004; [1970] 2 All ER 294 (p. 72, ante). Generally, see F. D. Rose (1977) 40 MLR 420.

2. In *General Engineering Services Ltd v Kingston and St Andrew Corpn* [1988] 3 All ER 867, [1989] ICR 88 as part of industrial action against their employers, firemen operated a 'go-slow' policy. As a result it took them 17 minutes to cover the distance to the plaintiff's premises instead of the normal

---

1. [1895] 1 QB 742.
2. [In *Poland v John Parr & Sons* [1927] 1 KB 236 at 243.]

three-and-a-half minutes. The delay caused the plaintiff's premises to be completely destroyed. The Privy Council (on appeal from the Court of Appeal of Jamaica) decided that the employers of the firemen were not vicariously liable. Lord Ackner, delivering the judgement of the Board, regarded the mode and manner in which the firemen went to the fire in order to put pressure on their employers in an industrial dispute as a wrongful repudiation by the firemen of their contracts of employment and not in furtherance of their employers' business. This conduct was 'the very negation of carrying out some act authorised by the employer, albeit in a wrongful and unauthorised mode' (at p. 91).

Morris v C W Martin & Sons Ltd Court of Appeal [1965] 2 All ER 725

The plaintiff sent her mink stole to Mr Beder, a furrier, for cleaning. With her consent, he sent it to the defendants, one of the biggest cleaners in the country, who knew that it belonged to an unspecified customer of Mr Beder. The current trade conditions were that 'goods belonging to customers' on the defendants' premises were held at the customer's risk and the defendants would 'not be responsible for loss or damage however caused'. Whilst the fur was with the defendants, it was stolen by one of their employees, named Morrissey.

The plaintiff brought an action for damages for loss of the fur against the defendants. The trial judge found that the defendants were not negligent in employing Morrissey, that they had taken all proper steps to safeguard the fur while on their premises and that the act of Morrissey was not done in the scope of his employment. He gave judgment for the defendants. The plaintiff appealed to the Court of Appeal.

LORD DENNING MR: . . . The law on this subject has developed greatly over the years. During the nineteenth century it was accepted law that a master was liable for the dishonesty or fraud of his servant if it was done in the course of his employment *and* for his master's benefit. Dishonesty or fraud by the servant for his *own* benefit took the case out of the course of his employment. The judges took this simple view: No servant who turns thief and steals is acting in the course of his employment. He is acting outside it altogether. But in 1912 the law was revolutionised by the case of *Lloyd v Grace, Smith & Co*,[1] where it was held that a master was liable for the dishonesty or fraud of his servant if it was done within the course of his employment, no matter whether it was done for the benefit of the master or for the benefit of the servant. Nevertheless there still remains the question: What is meant by the phrase 'in the course of his employment'? When can it be said that the dishonesty or fraud of a servant, done for his *own* benefit, is in the course of his employment?

On this question the cases are baffling. In particular those cases, much discussed before us, where a bailee's servant dishonestly drives a vehicle for his own benefit. These stretch from *Coupé Co v Maddick*[2] to the present day. Let me take an illustration well fitted for a moot. Suppose the owner of a car takes it to a garage to be repaired. It is repaired by a garage hand who is then told to drive it back to the owner. But instead, he takes it out on a 'frolic of his own' (to use the nineteenth century phrase) or on a 'joy-ride' (to come into the twentieth century). He takes it out, let us say, on a drunken escapade or on a thieving expedition. Nay more, for it is all the same, let us suppose the garage-hand steals the car himself and drives off at speed. He runs into a motor-cyclist. Both the car and the motor-cycle are damaged. Both

1. [1912] AC 716; [1911–13] All ER Rep 51.
2. [1891] 2 QB 413; [1891–94] All ER Rep 914.

owners sue the garage proprietor for the negligence of his servant. The motor-cyclist clearly cannot recover against the garage proprietor for the simple reason that at the time of the accident the servant was not acting in the course of his employment; see *Storey v Ashton*.[1] You might think also that the owner of the car could not recover, and for the self-same reason, namely, that the servant was *not* acting in the course of his employment. Before 1912 the courts would undoubtedly have so held; see *Sanderson v Collins*;[2] *Cheshire v Bailey*,[3] as explained by Lord Shaw of Dunfermline in *Lloyd v Grace, Smith & Co*[4] itself. But since 1912 it seems fairly clear that the owner of the damaged car could recover from the garage proprietor; see *Central Motors (Glasgow) Ltd v Cessnock Garage and Motor Co*,[5] on the ground that, although the garage-hand was using the car for his own private purposes, 'he should be regarded as still acting in the course of his employment' (see *Aitchison v Page Motors Ltd*):[6] and even if he stole the car on the journey, it was a conversion 'in the course of the employment' (see *United Africa Co Ltd v* Saka Owoade (1954)).[7] I ask myself, how can this be? How can the servant on one and the same journey, be acting both within and without the course of his employment? Within qua the car owner. Without qua the motor-cyclist. It is time we got rid of this confusion. And the only way to do it, so far as I can see, is by reference to the duty laid by the law on the master. The duty of the garage proprietor to the owner of the car is very different from his duty to the motor-cyclist. He owes to the owner of the car the duty of a bailee for reward, whereas he owes no such duty to the motor-cyclist on the road. He does not even owe him a duty to use care not to injure him.

If you go through the cases on this difficult subject, you will find that in the ultimate analysis, they depend on the nature of the duty owed by the master towards the person whose goods have been lost or damaged. If the master is under a duty to use due care to keep goods safely and protect them from theft and depredation, he cannot get rid of his responsibility by delegating his duty to another. If he entrusts that duty to his servant, he is answerable for the way in which the servant conducts himself therein. No matter whether the servant be negligent, fraudulent, or dishonest, the master is liable. But not when he is under no such duty. The cases show this:. . . .

[His Lordship then considered a number of decided cases and continued:]

From all these instances we may deduce the general proposition that when a principal has in his charge the goods or belongings of another in such circumstances that he is under a duty to take all reasonable precautions to protect them from theft or depredation, then if he entrusts that duty to a servant or agent, he is answerable for the manner in which that servant or agent carries out his duty. If the servant or agent is careless so that they are stolen by a stranger, the master is liable. So also if the servant or agent himself steals them or makes away with them. . . .

So far I have been dealing with the cases where the owner himself has entrusted the goods to the defendant. But here it was not the owner, the plaintiff, who entrusted the fur to the cleaners. She handed it to Mr Beder, who was a bailee for reward. He in turn, with her authority, handed it to the cleaners who were sub-bailees for reward. Mr Beder could clearly himself sue the cleaners for loss of the fur and recover the whole value (see *The Winkfield*),[8] unless the cleaners were protected by some exempting conditions. But can the plaintiff sue the cleaners direct for the

---

1. (1869) LR 4 QB 476.
2. [1904] 1 KB 628; [1904–7] All ER Rep 561.
3. [1905] 1 KB 237; [1904–7] All ER Rep 882.
4. [1912] AC at p. 741; [1911–13] All ER Rep at p. 62.
5. 1925 SC 796.
6. [1935] All ER Rep 594 at 596–598.
7. [1955] AC 130 at 144; [1957] 3 All ER 216 at 247.
8. [1902] P 42; [1900–03] All ER Rep 346.

misappropriation by their servant? And if she does, can she ignore the exempting conditions? . . .

. . . See the history of the matter fully discussed in *Holmes on the Common Law*, pp. 164–180. But now an action does lie by the owner direct against the wrongdoer if he has the right to immediate possession; see *Kahler v Midland Bank Ltd*.[1] Even if he has no right to immediate possession, he can sue for any permanent injury to, or loss of, the goods by a wrongful act of the defendant; see *Mears v London and South Western Rly Co*.[2] But what is a wrongful act as between the owner and the sub-bailee? What is the duty of the sub-bailee to the owner? Is the sub-bailee liable for misappropriation by his servant? There is very little authority on this point. *Pollock and Wright on Possession* say this (at p. 169):

'If the bailee of a thing sub-bails it by authority . . . and there is no direct privity of contract between the third person and the owner *it would seem that both the owner and the first bailee have concurrently the rights of a bailor against the third person according to the nature of the sub-bailment.*'

By which I take it that if the sub-bailment is for reward, the sub-bailee owes to the owner all the duties of a bailee for reward: and the owner can sue the sub-bailee direct for loss of or damage to the goods; and the sub-bailee (unless he is protected by any exempting conditions) is liable unless he can prove that the loss or damage occurred without his fault or that of his servants. So the plaintiff can sue the defendants direct for the loss of the goods by the misappropriation by their servant, and the cleaners are liable unless they are protected by the exempting conditions. . . .

[His Lordship went on to find that the exempting conditions did not protect the defendants since, as a matter of construction, the word 'customer' meant the furrier and not the plaintiff.]

DIPLOCK LJ: . . . If the bailee in the present case had been a natural person and had converted the plaintiff's fur by stealing it himself, no one would have argued that he was not liable to her for its loss; but the defendant bailees are a corporate person. They could not perform their duties to the plaintiff to take reasonable care of the fur and not to convert it otherwise than vicariously by natural persons acting as their servants or agents. It was one of their servants, to whom they had entrusted the care and custody of the fur for the purpose of doing work on it, who converted it by stealing it. Why should they not be vicariously liable for this breach of their duty by the vicar whom they had chosen to perform it? Sir John Holt, I think, would have answered that they were liable 'for seeing that [if] someone must be the loser by this deceit it is more reason that he who employs and puts a trust and confidence in the deceiver should be the loser than a stranger' (*Hern v Nichols*).[3] . . .

If the principle laid down in *Lloyd v Grace, Smith & Co*[4] is applied to the facts of the present case, the defendants cannot in my view escape liability for the conversion of the plaintiff's fur by their servant Morrissey. They accepted the fur as bailees for reward in order to clean it. They put Morrissey as their agent in their place to clean the fur and to take charge of it while doing so. The manner in which he conducted himself in doing that work was to convert it. What he was doing, albeit dishonestly, he was doing in the scope or course of his employment in the technical sense of that infelicitous but time-honoured phrase. The defendants as his masters are responsible for his tortious act.

I should add that we are not concerned here with gratuitous bailment. That is a

---

1. [1950] AC 24 at 33, 56; [1949] 2 All ER 621 at 627, 628, 641.
2. (1862) 11 CBNS 850.
3. (1701) 1 Salk 289.
4. [1912] AC 716; [1911–13] All ER Rep 51.

relationship in which the bailee's duties of care in his custody of the goods are different from those of a bailee for reward. It may be that his duties being passive rather than active, the concept of vicarious performance of them is less apposite. However this may be, I express no views as to the circumstances in which he would be liable for convertion of the goods by his servant. Nor are we concerned with what would have been the liability of the defendants if the fur had been stolen by another servant of theirs who was not employed by them to clean the fur or to have the care or custody of it. The mere fact that his employment by the defendants gave him the opportunity to steal it would not suffice. . . .

I base my decision in this case on the ground that the fur was stolen by the very servant whom the defendants as bailees for reward had employed to take care of it and to clean it.

I agree that the appeal should be allowed.

SALMON LJ: . . . I accordingly agree with my lords that the appeal should be allowed. I am anxious, however, to make it plain that the conclusion which I have reached depends on Morrissey being the servant through whom the defendants chose to discharge their duty to take reasonable care of the plaintiff's fur. The words of Willes J, in *Barwick*'s case[1] are entirely applicable to these facts. The defendants

'put [their] agent [Morrissey] in [the defendants'] place as to such a class of acts, and . . . must be answerable for the manner in which the agent conducts himself in doing the business which is the business of the master.'

A bailee for reward is not answerable for a theft by any of his servants, but only for a theft by such of them as are deputed by him to discharge some part of his duty of taking reasonable care. A theft by any servant who is not employed to do anything in relation to the goods bailed is entirely outside the scope of his employment and cannot make the master liable. So in this case, if someone employed by the defendants in another depot had broken in and stolen the fur, the defendants would not have been liable. Similarly in my view if a clerk employed in the same depot had seized the opportunity of entering the room where the fur was kept and had stolen it, the defendants would not have been liable. The mere fact that the master, by employing a rogue, gives him the opportunity to steal or defraud does not make the master liable for his depredations. *Ruben and Ladenburg v Great Fingall Consolidated*.[2] It might be otherwise if the master knew or ought to have known that his servant was dishonest, because then the master could be liable in negligence for employing him. . . .

Appeal allowed

Question

Do you agree with Lord Denning MR that the solution to cases like this is to abandon the notion of vicarious liability in favour of that of a primary non-delegable duty of the bailee? (See *Winfield & Jolowicz*, pp. 574–576).

Note

The dishonest employee could be personally liable for the tort of conversion: see the remarks of Kerr J in *Fairline Shipping Corpn v Adamson* [1975] QB 180, [1974] 2 All ER 967, noted by A. Diamond (1975) 38 MLR 198.

---

1. (1867) LR 2 Exch at p. 266; [1861–73] All ER at p. 198.
2. [1906] AC 439; [1904–07] All ER Rep 460.

4 Liability for independent contractors

Salsbury *v* Woodland Court of Appeal [1969] 3 All ER 863

The first defendant, an occupier of property adjoining a highway, engaged the second defendant, an experienced and apparently competent tree-feller, as an independent contractor, to fell a large tree in his front garden. If competently felled, there was no risk of injury, but the second defendant did the work so negligently that the tree fouled telephone wires which ran from a telegraph pole on the far side of the highway, bringing them down so that they lay across the highway. The plaintiff, a bystander, attempted to remove the wires from the roadway and while attempting to do so was injured when he took action to avoid an oncoming car as it struck the wires. Judgment for damages was obtained against the second defendant in default of defence. At the trial, judgment was also given against the first defendant, who appealed to the Court of Appeal.

WIDGERY LJ: . . . So far as the first defendant is concerned, he personally committed no negligent act, and it is not challenged that in selecting the second defendant as the means of having this tree felled he selected a person who was apparently competent and fit to do it. The whole basis of the case against the first defendant is that the second defendant was negligent and that the first defendant is responsible for that negligence. Counsel for the first defendant was prepared to challenge the judge's finding of negligence on the part of the second defendant, and was prepared to challenge the difficult questions of causation which arose in the course of that issue, but, the court having concluded that the first defendant's appeal succeeded on a different ground, I need not go into those matters now. The basis of the decision of this court (which has already been indicated to the parties) on the liability of the first defendant is simply that the first defendant was not responsible for the negligence of the second defendant even if the second defendant was negligent; and it is to that matter only that I need now direct myself.

It is, of course, trite law that an employer who employs an independent contractor is not vicariously responsible for the negligence of that contractor. He is not able to control the way in which the independent contractor does the work and the vicarious obligation of a master for the negligence of his servant does not arise under the relationship of employer and independent contractor. I think it is entirely accepted that those cases — and there are some — in which an employer has been held liable for injury done by the negligence of an independent contractor are in truth cases where the employer owes a direct duty to the person injured, a duty which he cannot delegate to the contractor on his behalf. The whole question in this case is whether, in the circumstances which I have briefly outlined, the first defendant is to be judged by the general rule, which would result in no liability, or whether he comes within one of the somewhat special exceptions — cases in which a direct duty to see that care is taken rests on the employer throughout the operation.

This is clear from authority . . .

. . . In truth, according to the authorities there are a number of well-determined classes of case in which this direct and primary duty on an employer to see that care is taken exists. Two such classes are directly relevant for consideration in this case. The first class concerns what have sometimes been described as 'extra hazardous acts' — acts commissioned by an employer which are so hazardous in their character that the law has thought it proper to impose this direct obligation on the employer to see that care is taken. An example of such a case is *Honeywill and Stein Ltd v Larkin Bros (London's Commercial Photographers) Ltd*.[1] Other cases which one finds in the

---

1. [1934] 1 KB 191; [1933] All ER Rep 77.

books are cases where the activity commissioned by the employer is the keeping of dangerous things, within the rule in *Rylands v Fletcher*,[1] and where liability is not dependent on negligence at all.

I do not propose to add to the wealth of authority on this topic by attempting further to define the meaning of 'extra hazardous acts'; but I am confident that the act commissioned in the present case cannot come within that category. The act commissioned in the present case, if done with ordinary caution by skilled men, presented no hazard to anyone at all.

The second class of case which is relevant for consideration of the present dispute concerns dangers created in a highway. There are a number of cases on this branch of the law, a good example of which is *Holliday v National Telephone Co*.[2] These, on analysis, will all be found to be cases where work was being done in a highway and was work of a character which would have been a nuisance unless authorised by statute. It will be found in all these cases that the statutory powers under which the employer commissioned the work were statutory powers which left on the employer a duty to see that due care was taken in the carrying out of the work, for the protection of those who passed on the highway. In accordance with principle, an employer subject to such a direct and personal duty cannot excuse himself if things go wrong merely because the direct cause of the injury was the act of the independent contractor.

This again is not a case in that class. It is not a case in that class because in the instant case no question of doing work in the highway, which might amount to a nuisance if due care was not taken, arises. In my judgment, the present case is clearly outside the well-defined limit of the second class to which I have referred. Counsel for the plaintiff accordingly invited us to say that there is a third class into which the instant case precisely falls and he suggested that the third class comprised those cases where an employer commissions work to be done *near* a highway in circumstances in which, if due care is not taken, injury to passers-by on the highway may be caused. If that be a third class of case to which the principle of liability of the employer applies, no doubt the present facts would come within the description. The question is, is there such a third class?

Reliance is placed primarily on three authorities. The first is *Holliday*'s case,[2] to which I have already referred. *Holliday*'s case[2] was a case of work being done in a highway by undertakers laying telephone wires. The injury was caused by the negligent act of a servant of the independent contractor who was soldering joints in the telephone wires. The cause of the injury was the immersion of a defective blow-lamp in a pot of solder, and the pot of solder was physically on the highway—according to the report, on the footpath. The Earl of Halsbury LC holding the employers responsible for that negligence, in my view, on a simple application of the cases applicable to highway nuisance to which I have already referred, put his opinion in these words:[3]

'Therefore, works were being executed in proximity to a highway, in which in the ordinary course of things an explosion might take place.'

Counsel for the plaintiff draws our attention to the phrase 'in proximity to a highway' and submits that that supports his contention on this point. I am not impressed by this argument, because the source of danger in *Holliday*'s case[2] was itself on the highway and also because I do not think it follows (although one need not decide the point today) that in the true highway cases to which I have referred the actual source of injury must arise on the highway itself. Counsel for the plaintiff said that in *Holliday*'s case[2] it would have been ridiculous if there had been liability because the pot of solder was on the highway but no liability if it was two feet off the highway. That is an observation

---

1. (1868) LR 3 HL 330; [1861–73] All ER Rep 1.
2. [1899] 2 QB 392; [1895–99] All ER Rep 359.
3. [1899] 2 QB at p. 399; [1895–99] All ER Rep at p. 361.

with which I entirely sympathise; but I can find nothing in Lord Halsbury's use of the word 'proximity' to justify the view that there is therefore a special class of case on the lines submitted by counsel.

The second case relied on is *Tarry v Ashton*,[1] where a building adjoining the highway had attached to it a heavy lamp which was suspended over the footway and which was liable to be a source of injury to passers-by if allowed to fall into disrepair. It fell into disrepair, and injury was caused. The defendant sought to excuse himself by saying that he had employed a competent independent contractor to put the lamp into good repair and that the cause of the injury was the fault of the independent contractor. Counsel for the plaintiff argues that that case illustrates the special sympathy with which the law regards passers-by on the highway. He says this demonstrates that the law has always been inclined to give special protection to persons in that category and so supports his argument that any action adjacent to the highway may be subject to special rights. But in my judgment that is not so. *Tarry v Ashton*[1] seems to me to be a perfectly ordinary and straightforward example of a case where the employer was under a positive and continuing duty to see that the lamp was kept in repair. The duty was imposed on him before the contractor came and after the contractor had gone; and on the principle that such a duty cannot be delegated the responsibility of the employer in that case seems to me to be fully demonstrated. I cannot find that it produces on a side-wind, as it were, anything in support of counsel for the plaintiff's contention.

The last case to which I will refer on this point is *Walsh v Holst & Co Ltd*,[2] a decision of this court. In that case the occupier of premises adjoining the highway was carrying out works of reconstruction which involved knocking out large areas of the front wall. He employed for this purpose a contractor, and the contractor employed a sub-contractor. It was obvious to all, no doubt, that such an operation was liable to cause injury to passers-by by falling bricks unless special precautions against that eventuality were taken. Indeed very considerable precautions were so taken. However, on a day when the only workman employed was an employee of the sub-contractor one brick escaped the protective net, fell in the street and injured a passer-by. The passer-by-plaintiff brought his action against the occupier, the contractor, and the sub-contractor, relying on the doctrine of res ipsa loquitur. In my judgment, the only thing that was really decided by that case was that on those facts the precautions which had been taken against such an injury rebutted the presumption of negligence which might otherwise have arisen under the doctrine of res ipsa loquitur. No attempt appears to have been made in argument to distinguish the liability of the occupier as compared with that of the contractor or sub-contractor, and it certainly was not material to the decision; . . .

. . . Accordingly, in my judgment, there is no third class of cases of the kind put forward by counsel for the plaintiff; and it was for those reasons that I concurred in the court's decision, already announced, that the appeal of the first defendant should be allowed, and the judgment against him set aside.

SACHS LJ: . . . I would add an observation that . . . I derived no assistance at all from any distinction between 'collateral and casual' negligence and other negligence. Such a distinction provides too many difficulties for me to accept without question, unless it simply means that one must ascertain exactly what was the occupier's duty and then treat any act that is not part of that duty as giving rise to no liability on his part. How, in *Walsh v Holst & Co Ltd*[2] could one distinguish between a falling half-brick and a falling cold chisel?

Again, I would observe that counsel for the plaintiff, in his attempt to bring the instant case into what might be called a special and new category, was constrained to

---

1. (1876) 1 QBD 314; [1874–80] All ER Rep 738.
2. [1958] 3 All ER 33; [1958] 1 WLR 800.

urge that an occupier would be liable if an independent contractor, engaged to fell a tree 100 yards or so away from a highway and remove it from the occupier's property, chose, out of a large number of different routes to an exit gate, the only one that lay close to a highway and then allowed the tree to roll into the road. That seems to me to indicate what unnecessarily absurd results would follow from assenting to the proposition urged on behalf of the plaintiff. . . .

[HARMAN LJ delivered a judgment in favour of allowing the first defendant's appeal.]

Appeal allowed

Note

As regards an occupier's liability for the acts of independent contractors see s. 2(4)(b) of the Occupiers' Liability Act 1957 (p. 443, ante); and for the liability of highway authorities see s. 58 of the Highways Act 1980.

Matania *v* National Provincial Bank Ltd Court of Appeal [1936] 2 All ER 633

The defendant Bank demised the second and third floors of certain premises to the plaintiff with a covenant for quiet enjoyment. Without the plaintiff's consent the second defendants, who proposed to occupy the first floor of the building, instructed contractors to carry out extensive alterations. No proper precautions being taken, the plaintiff suffered damage by reason of the dust and noise from the operations. The Court of Appeal, allowing an appeal, held the second defendants liable for damages for nuisance although they had employed an independent contractor to do the work.

SLESSER LJ: . . . Now there remains one other matter, and an important one, which Mr Morris has argued before us with great force and with which I have to deal. There is no doubt in this case that Messrs Adamson are independent contractors, and being independent contractors, save for exceptional circumstances, in the ordinary way those employing them would not be liable for their wrongful acts in negligence or in nuisance. . . . Here, of course, we are not concerned with danger such as might found an action for negligence. We are here concerned with annoyance such as may found an action for nuisance, but the principles in my opinion are the same as regards the liability of a person who employs an independent contractor, that is to say, that if the act done is one which in its very nature involves a special danger of nuisance being complained of, then it is one which falls within the exception for which the employer of the contractor will be responsible if there is a failure to take the necessary precautions that the nuisance shall not arise. Now, what are the facts of the present case? They are these. It is really not in dispute that as regards the place where this work was to be done this noise and this dust were inevitable. That is the evidence of both the plaintiff and the defendants, and it is the conclusion of the learned judge. The only question which I see is whether in that state where the production of noise and dust is inevitable, sufficient precautions were taken to prevent that noise and dust affecting Mr Matania. In every case, whether it be a case of ordinary employment of a contractor or whether it be a case of a hazardous operation, the problem must arise whether a precaution would or would not prevent the result of an operation. To say that a precaution will prevent the result of an operation does not by itself take the case outside the rule that a person may be responsible, where the act is a hazardous one, for the acts of his contractor. Where the act is hazardous, to presume that every hazardous act would result in the danger or the nuisance would be to say that the act was inevitable in its consequences, regardless of any question of precaution or not, but that is not the right way of looking at it. In the case to which I referred, the case of *Honeywill and Stein Ltd v Larkin Bros Ltd*[1] it was not inevitable that the fire, which was brought into the theatre, would necessarily under proper precautions set the theatre on fire, but it was a hazardous operation to bring the fire into the theatre. So it was hazardous as regards the possible nuisance to Mr Matania to bring the noise and dust immediately below his apartment. Wh·t is said is with sufficient and proper precaution the result of that hazardous operation could have been avoided without detriment to him. I am of opinion that this was a hazardous operation within the meaning of the exceptions stated in *Honeywill and Stein v Larkin Bros Ltd* that the principle which is there dealing with a case of negligence applies equally to the tort of nuisance, and that, therefore, this being a case of this kind, I think that the Elevenist Syndicate are responsible for the fact that neither they nor the contractors, Messrs Adamson, took those reasonable precautions which could have been taken to prevent this injury to the plaintiff.

I say nothing about the action in so far as it is framed in trespass. There are difficulties in stating an action in trespass and in nuisance except alternatively. The textbook writers seem to differ in their opinions on this point. Sir John Salmond in his book seems to think that the actions are alternative. Sir Frederick Pollock is of the contrary opinion. I think there would be difficulties apart from those, in succeeding in trespass in this case. I think the dust and the noise which were allowed to come upon the premises of Mr Matania were the result probably of an act indirect and not direct on the part of the contractor, and so probably would found an action in case rather than an action in trespass, but in so far as I have come to the conclusion that the Elevenist Syndicate are liable in nuisance to Mr Matania, I do not think it necessary to deal with the question of trespass at all. . . .

[ROMER LJ and FINLAY J delivered judgments in favour of allowing the appeal.]

Balfour *v* Barty-King Court of Appeal [1957] 1 All ER 156

The defendants' water-pipes were frozen. Mrs Barty-King asked two men at work on a nearby site to help unfreeze the pipes. Instead of using a heated brick to do this, they applied a blow-lamp to a pipe in the loft of the Barty-Kings' house. This was highly dangerous because the pipes were lagged with felt and it was draughty. The lagging caught fire and the fire spread to the plaintiff's adjoining premises causing extensive damage. Havers J gave judgment against the defendants, who appealed.

LORD GODDARD CJ read the judgment of the Court (which included MORRIS LJ and VAISEY J): . . . The question which this court has to consider is whether Havers J was right in holding that for the spread of the fire from their premises to those of the plaintiff the defendants are responsible, although the fire was caused by the negligence of independent contractors brought on to the defendants' premises to do the work which I have described. On this matter there seems to be no direct authority. . . .

. . . Although there is a difference of opinion among eminent text writers whether at common law the liability was absolute or depended on negligence, at the present day it can safely be said that a person in whose house a fire is caused by negligence is liable if it spreads to that of his neighbour, and this is true whether the negligence is his own or that of his servant or his guest, but he is not liable if the fire is caused by a stranger.

Who then is a stranger? Clearly a trespasser would be in that category, but, if a man is liable for the negligent act of his guest, it is, indeed, difficult to see why he is not liable for the act of a contractor whom he has invited to his house to do work on it, and who does the work in a negligent manner. We do not get much assistance from

1. [1934] 1 KB 191; [1933] All ER Rep 77.

Black v Christchurch Finance Co ([1894] AC 48), although Sir William Holdsworth cites that case in support of his opinion that there is liability for the acts of a contractor in this respect. In that case the fire was certainly the fire of the defendants, for the contractor had been employed by them to make a fire to burn the scrub and saplings on the land, and in carrying out the work the contractor did a negligent act and one which was in breach of a stipulation in the contract. He started the fire in unfavourable weather. The lighting of the fire was not a casual, or, as it is sometimes put, a collateral act of negligence; it was the very thing that he was employed to do, and Lord Shand's judgment is really mainly concerned with whether, as the contractor had diregarded a special term in the contract, the employers were liable.

The argument of counsel for the defendants was that in the present case it was not the defendants' fire, as the contractor was not employed to light a fire or to use a blow-lamp or any other form of fire. That, however, is answered by the fact that the use of a blow-lamp is an ordinary way of freeing frozen pipes. The negligence was in using the lamp in proximity to inflammable material. Counsel also relied on the dictum of Lord Watson in *Dalton v Angus* ((1881) 6 App Cas 740 at 831), where he said:

'When an employer contracts for the performance of work, which properly conducted can occasion no risk to his neighbour's house which he is under obligation to support, he is not liable for damage arising from the negligence of the contractor.'

This observation, no doubt, states the general rule with regard to liability, or the lack of it, for the negligence of an independent contractor; but the noble and learned Lord was not dealing with the case of the escape of a dangerous thing from land to which it has been brought or on which it has been created. We do not think that it is necessary to consider the doctrine of *Rylands v Fletcher* ((1868) LR 3 HL 330) as a separate head of liability. No doubt the doctrine of that case applies to fire, and is subject to the exception of the damage being caused by a stranger.

In *Perry v Kendricks Transport Ltd* ([1956] 1 All ER 154 at 161), Parker LJ referred to a stranger as a person over whom the defendant had no control. From one point of view it may be said that the test of an independent contractor is that he is left to carry out the work in his own way, but that is not the sense, I think, in which the lord justice was using the word 'control'. The defendants here had control over the contractor in that they chose him, they invited him to their premises to work, and he could have been ordered to leave at any moment. It was left to the men who were sent how to do the work, and in our opinion the defendants are liable to the plaintiff for this lamentable occurrence, the more lamentable in that the persons ultimately responsible are insolvent. The appeal must be dismissed with costs.

Appeal dismissed

Honeywill and Stein Ltd *v* Larkin Bros (London's Commercial Photographers) Ltd Court of Appeal [1933] All ER Rep 77

A cinema company engaged the plaintiffs to do acoustics work in their cinema. The plaintiffs, with the cinema company's permission, employed the defendants, an independent firm of photographers to take photographs of the interior of the cinema. At the time, the taking of flashlight photographs was 'inevitably attended with danger' because it involved the ignition in a metal tray or holder, held above the lens, of an ounce or more of magnesium powder, which on being ignited flared up and caused intense heat. As a result of the negligence of the operator in lighting the magnesium at a distance of less than four feet from the curtains, the curtains caught fire and were damaged to the extent of £261 4s 3d. The plaintiffs paid these damages to the cinema company and now sought an indemnity from the photographers (the defendants in this action) who contended that since they were independent contractors the plaintiffs were not responsible for their actions and so should not have reimbursed the cinema company. The trial judge found for the defendants. The plaintiffs appealed to the Court of Appeal.

SLESSER LJ read the following judgment of the court— . . . It is well established as a general rule of English law that an employer is not liable for the acts of his independent contractor in the same way as he is for the acts of his servants or agents, even though these acts are done in carrying out work for his benefit under the contract. The determination whether the actual wrongdoer is a servant or agent, on the one hand, or an independent contractor, on the other, depends on whether or not the employer not only determines what is to be done, but retains the control of the actual performance, in which case the doer is a servant or agent, but, if the employer, while prescribing the work to be done, leaves the manner of doing it to the control of the doer, the latter is an independent contractor. . . .

It is clear that the ultimate employer is not responsible for the acts of an independent contractor merely because what is to be done will involve danger to others if negligently done. The incidence of this liability is limited to certain defined classes, and for the purpose of this case it is only necessary to consider that part of this rule of liability which has reference to extra hazardous acts, that is, acts which, in their very nature involve in the eyes of the law special danger to others. . . .

. . . To take a photograph in the cinema with a flashlight was, on the evidence stated above, a dangerous operation in its intrinsic nature, involving the creation of fire and explosion on another person's premises, that is, in the cinema, the property of the cinema company. The plaintiffs, in procuring this work to be performed by their contractors, the defendants, assumed an obligation to the cinema company which was, as we think, absolute, but which was at least an obligation to use reasonable precautions to see that no damage resulted to the cinema company from those dangerous operations. That obligation they could not delegate by employing the defendants as independent contractors, but they were liable in this regard for the defendants' acts. For the damage actually caused the plaintiffs were, accordingly, liable in law to the cinema company, and are entitled to claim and recover from the defendants damages for their breach of contract or negligence in performing their contract to take photographs.

The learned judge has found for the defendants because he has held (founding himself on the words of Lord Watson in *Dalton v Angus*)[1] that the work to be done by the defendants for the plaintiffs,

'was not necessarily attended with risk. It was work which, as a general rule, would seem to be of quite a harmless nature.'

But, with respect, he is ignoring the special rules which apply to extra hazardous or dangerous operations. Even of these it may be predicated that, if carefully and skilfully performed, no harm will follow. As instances of such operations may be given those of removing support from adjoining houses, doing dangerous work on the highway, or creating fire or explosion. Hence it may be said in one sense that such operations are not necessarily attended with risk. But the rule of liability for independent contractors attaches to those operations, because they are inherently dangerous, and hence are done at the principal employer's peril.

For these reasons, we are of opinion that the appeal must be allowed, the judgment set aside and judgment entered for the appellants for the amount of the damage.

Appeal allowed

---

1. (1881) 6 App Cas 740.

Notes

1. 'Even if one goes so far as to say that the use of flashlight powder is "dangerous" it is hyperbolical to describe it as "extra-hazardous". If this is "extra-hazardous" we are left with no language to describe really dangerous conduct': G. L. Williams [1956] CLJ at 186. What do you understand by 'extra-hazardous'?

2. The cinema company was probably insured in this case, and the photographers may not have been insured. Which of these two potential defendants was best equipped to absorb the loss? G. L. Williams, op cit, pp. 193–198 argues that 'it may be questioned whether the social evil of the occasional insolvent tortfeasant contractor is of sufficient gravity to justify the imposition of vicarious liability'.

3. How would this case have been argued if the plaintiffs' *contract* with the cinema company had permitted them to take photographs (or have photographs taken), i.e. if they had not simply been *licensees* for the purpose of taking photographs?

4. In *Read v J Lyons & Co Ltd* [1947] AC 156, [1946] 2 All ER 471 (p. 654, ante), the House of Lords refused to establish a general tort of liability for 'extra-hazardous' activities. Atiyah, *Vicarious Liability*, p. 373, argues that *Honeywill's* case is the 'first cousin' of the rejected doctrine and should suffer the same fate.

5. Consider the liability of the following:
   (a) a solicitor for the negligence of counsel in non-litigious work (cf. *Saif Ali v Sydney Mitchell & Co (a firm)* [1980] AC 198; [1978] 3 All ER 1033, noted p. 173, ante);
   (b) a carrier for the negligence of an independent contractor (see *Riverstone Meat Pty Ltd v Lancashire Shipping Co Ltd* [1961] AC 807; [1961] 1 All ER 495);
   (c) a bailee for reward who entrusts the care of goods to an independent contractor (*Morris v C W Martin & Sons*, p. 847, ante; on gratuitous bailees, see Atiyah, *Vicarious Liability*, p. 367);
   (d) a main contractor on the construction of a building for an independent sub-contractor with whom he has contracted for some of the work to be done (*D & F Estates Ltd v Church Comrs for England* [1989] AC 177; [1988] 2 All ER 992).

Consider also *Rogers v Night Riders (a firm)* [1983] RTR 324, noted p. 825, ante, *Luxmoore-May v Messenger May Baverstock* [1990] 1 All ER 1067, [1990] 1 WLR 1009 and section 5, post.

5 Employer's liability to employees

The Employer's Liability (Defective Equipment) Act 1969

1. Extension of employer's liability for defective equipment. – (1) Where after the commencement of this Act –
   (*a*) an employee suffers personal injury in the course of his employment in

consequence of a defect in equipment provided by his employer for the purposes of the employer's business; and

(b) the defect is attributable wholly or partly to the fault of a third party (whether identified or not),

the injury shall be deemed to be also attributable to negligence on the part of the employer (whether or not he is liable in respect of the injury apart from this sub-section), but without prejudice to the law relating to contributory negligence and to any remedy by way of contribution or in contract or otherwise which is available to the employer in respect of the injury.

(2) In so far as any agreement purports to exclude or limit any liability of an employer arising under subsection (1) of this section, the agreement shall be void.

(3) In this section—

'business' includes the activities carried on by any public body;

'employee' means a person who is employed by another person under a contract of service or apprenticeship and is so employed for the purposes of a business carried on by that other person, and 'employer' shall be construed accordingly;

'equipment' includes any plant and machinery, vehicle, aircraft and clothing;

'fault' means negligence, breach of statutory duty or other act or omission which gives rise to liability in tort in England and Wales or which is wrongful and gives rise to liability in damages in Scotland;

'personal injury' includes loss of life, any impairment of a person's physical or mental condition and any disease.

(4) This section binds the Crown, and persons in the service of the Crown shall accordingly be treated for the purposes of this section as employees of the Crown if they would not be so treated apart from this subsection.

Notes

1. The purpose of this statute was to overcome the effects of the decision in *Davie v New Merton Board Mills Ltd* [1959] AC 604; [1959] 1 All ER 346. In that case the plaintiff employee was blinded when a particle of metal chipped off the tool with which he was working. The employer had purchased the tool from reputable suppliers who, in turn, had bought it from reputable manufacturers. There had been negligence in the course of manufacture which had caused the tool to become excessively hard, but outwardly the tool was in good condition. The manufacturers were liable under the *M'Alister* (or *Donoghue*) *v Stevenson* rule (p. 40, ante). Most people believed that in such circumstances the employer would be liable too, because in *Wilsons and Clyde Coal Co Ltd v English* [1938] AC 57; [1937] 3 All ER 628 (p. 566, ante) the House of Lords had held that the employer's three-fold duty (to provide (a) competent staff, (b) proper plant, premises and material, and (c) a safe system of work) was *personal* and *non-delegable*. It was thought to follow from this that an employer cannot delegate to an 'independent contractor' his duty to provide proper tools. However, in *Davie*'s case the House of Lords held that an employer who buys a tool from a reputable supplier or manufacturer does not 'delegate' his duty: he 'discharges' it. This restriction on the 'non-delegation' doctrine was criticised on legal and social grounds. C. J. Hamson [1959] CLJ 157 showed that the result was due to the way in which the House of Lords classified the duty as *tortious* rather than *contractual*. Lord Wright had favoured the contractual approach in *Wilsons and Clyde Coal Co Ltd v English* (p. 566, ante) and had this been followed

in *Davie* the standard of care would have amounted to a warranty that the tool was safe (as it would have been had the employer *hired* or *sold* the tool to the employee). The practical effect of the decision was to leave the injured employee without compensation where the negligent manufacturer or supplier could not be identified or was bankrupt. The Employer's Liability (Defective Equipment) Act does not, however, entirely remedy the situation: see B. A. Hepple [1970] CLJ 25; and *Clarkson v William Jackson & Sons Ltd* (1984) Times, 21st November.

(Another Act passed around the same time to ensure that employees actually receive their compensation is the Employers' Liability (Compulsory Insurance) Act 1969: see p. 894, post.)

2. In *Coltman v Bibby Tankers Ltd* [1988] AC 276; [1987] 3 All ER 1068, the House of Lords held that the word 'equipment' in s 1(1) of the Act includes a ship provided by the employer for the purposes of his business. The case arose out of the sinking of *The Derbyshire* with all hands off the coast of Japan in 1980. It was alleged that due to the manufacturer's negligence the ship was defectively constructed and designed rendering her unseaworthy and that these were defects in 'equipment' deemed under the Act to be attributable to the negligence of the employers. On a preliminary question of law, the House of Lords rejected the view of a majority in the Court of Appeal [1987] 1 All ER 932; [1987] 2 WLR 1098 that 'equipment' denoted something ancillary to something else and could not apply to the workplace provided by the employer. Although their Lordships could not find any rational basis for the failure to mention ships, alongside vehicles and transport, in the statutory definition, the width of that definition as well as the purpose of the Act led them to conclude that the Act covers defective plant of every sort with which the employee is compelled to work.

Questions

1. Would it be correct to say that the Act of 1969 simply restores the law as laid down in *Wilsons and Clyde Coal Co Ltd v English* (p. 566, ante)?

2. A self-employed window cleaner is supplied with a defective ladder by a householder as a result of which the window cleaner is injured. (a) Whom should he sue? (b) Who is likely to be insured against such risks?

3. A refuse removal worker is injured by an object placed in a dustbin by a householder and which unexpectedly explodes. Does he have any claim against (a) his employer, (b) the householder? (See *Pattendon v Beney* (1934) 50 TLR 204.)

4. A travelling salesman (who cannot later be traced) sells a weed exterminator to X, but fails to pass on the information that the substance must not be used unless gloves are worn to protect the skin. X gives the weed exterminator to his gardener who suffers severe skin burns. Advise the gardener.

Sumner *v* William Henderson & Sons Ltd Queen's Bench Division [1963] 1 All ER 408

In an action begun by writ issued on 27 July 1960, the plaintiff Isaac Sumner claimed damages under the Fatal Accidents Acts 1846 to 1959, in respect of the death of his wife, Louise Sumner, which was alleged to have been caused by the negligence or breach of duty of the defendants, their servants or agents. The defendants denied negligence and breach of duty. The parties stated certain questions of law in a special case for the opinion of the court, as follows. On 22 June 1960, the defendants were owners and occupiers of a department store in which a fire broke out. On that day the plaintiff's wife was employed by the defendants and died as a result of asphyxiation by smoke from the fire when she was in the course of her employment by the defendants as a restaurant supervisor, on the fourth floor of the store. In the amended statement of claim the plaintiff alleged (a) that the fire originated in a fault in an electrical cable running between the third and fourth floors of the defendants' store and (b) that a cause of his wife's death was the fact that parts of the store were so constructed or installed as to cause a fire to spread with great rapidity. The defendants by their amended defence alleged, (i) that the cable was manufactured by another company, manufacturers of such equipment, and was installed by electrical contractors in accordance with a specification prepared by consultant electrical engineers and under their supervision, and that all these companies or firms were reputable, competent and skilled contractors, who were fully capable of carrying out the work that they did, which was work calling for the exercise of specialised knowledge, skill and experience not possessed by the defendants or their servants. The defendants further alleged, (ii) that the relevant parts of the defendants' store were constructed or installed by building and engineering contractors, their servants or agents; that the parts of the store were constructed or installed in accordance with plans and specifications prepared by architects and under their supervision; that the building contractors, their servants, or agents, and the architects, were competent and properly skilled contractors and architects, who were fully capable of carrying out the work which they did, and of advising the defendants thereon, and that the work called for the exercise of specialised knowledge, skill and experience not possessed by the defendants or their servants. The court was asked for the purposes of the special case to assume the truth of each of the allegations of the plaintiff and the defendants set out as (a), (b) and (i) and (ii) previously in this report.

By para. 10 of the special case the questions for the opinion of the court were stated as being whether, on the facts and assumptions hereinbefore set out, the defendants were liable to the plaintiff in any of the following events, which are here briefly summarised — if the death of the plaintiff's wife was caused or contributed to either (a) by negligence of the manufacturers of the cable; or (b) by negligence of the electrical contractors in installing, inspecting or testing the electrical cable; or (c) by negligence on the part of the consultant electrical engineers in preparing the specification for the installation of the cable or supervising its installation or in inspecting or testing the cable; or (d) by negligence of the building contractors, their servants or agents, in constructing or installing the parts of the store which were assumed to have been so constructed as to have caused the fire to spread with great rapidity; or (e) by negligence of the architects, either in preparing plans and specifications for the construction and installation of the relevant parts of the store or in supervising the construction or installation thereof.

PHILLIMORE J: . . . The short point which I have to determine is whether the defendants, in the circumstances which I have to assume, remain liable to their servant, the deceased, for the negligence of the manufacturers of the cable or for the negligence of one or other of the firms or companies employed to do the work, such negligence having either caused or promoted a fire which resulted in the deceased's death. I was told by learned counsel that, although the claim had been laid in tort, an amendment was under consideration, and I was asked to deal with the matter on the footing that liability, if any, arises either in contract or in tort.

Counsel for the plaintiff contends that, with the possible exception of the manufacturers of the cable, the defendants as employers are liable for the negligence, if any, of the other firms and companies which did or supervised the doing of the work. He contends that the defendants owed their employee, the deceased, a duty to take reasonable care to provide safe premises; that this was a personal or inalienable duty so that, if they chose to delegate its performance to someone else, whether a servant, agent, or independent contractor, they remained liable to their employee for any negligence in its performance.

Counsel on behalf of the defendants does not seek to deny that an employer owes a certain duty to his employee, the nature of which is personal and inalienable, or that, if he delegates the performance of that duty to an independent contractor, he remains liable to his employee for any negligence in its performance. He contends that the duty is more limited than that contended for by the plaintiff. He put it as follows. First, in regard to anything necessary to the carrying on or establishing of his operations, the master owes a personal duty of care for the safety of a servant so that, if he delegates performance to an independent contractor, he remains personally liable for negligence by that contractor. Secondly, in regard to anything which is not necessary for the carrying on or establishing of his operations, any duty that he may owe is not a personal duty, so that, if it is something which he is not qualified to do, he can delegate the work to a competent independent contractor, for whose negligence the employer will not be liable to his employee.

The phrase 'the carrying on or establishing of his operations' was explained by counsel for the defendants, as referring to the essential nature of the employer's business. Thus, a butcher would have a personal and inalienable duty to take reasonable care to provide a safe system of butchery, proper appliances such as choppers and a chopping block, and safe premises to the extent of a floor for his shop which was both sound and not unduly slippery. In regard to the structure of the premises, however, as not being sufficiently connected with his trade and a matter outside his personal competence, he could appoint a competent contractor, and would thereafter be free of liability if, for example, negligence on the part of the contractor resulted in the collapse of the roof, with consequent injury to the butcher's employees. As I understand it, counsel for the defendants agreed that, if the employer was a company owning many shops and having its own repairs department, the company might remain liable for injury to those engaged in butchery as a result of negligence by the employees of the repairs department when engaged in repairing the structure of the premises, since repairs in that event would form part of the employer's operations. I confess that I find the argument of counsel for the defendants quite unacceptable. The anomalies to which it would give rise are obvious, and I cannot think that the liability of the employer depends on so artificial a basis. . . .

In *Davie v New Merton Board Mills Ltd*,[1] the House of Lords held that the employers, being under a duty to take reasonable care to provide a reasonably safe tool – in that case a chisel – had discharged that duty by buying one from a reputable supplier, who, in turn, had procured it from a reputable manufacturer. The employers had no means of discovering the latent defect which in fact existed in the chisel. The ratio of this decision is, I think that on the facts the employers could not be said to have delegated their duty to the manufacturers, to whose negligence the latent defect was presumably due. Delegation must always be a question dependent on the facts of the individual case, and it would seem impossible to say of an employer who merely went into a shop to buy a standard tool that he was delegating his responsibility for his employee's safety either to the supplier, who had merely bought it as a standard tool from the manufacturer, or, still less, that he was delegating it to the manufacturer, with whom he entered into no contract and who had manufactured it months, or even years, before. There were observations in the opinions both of Viscount Simonds and of Lord Reid which, taken in isolation, might be thought to impair the principle that the employer remains responsible when he delegates his duty to an independent contractor. On the other hand, there are passages, notably in

---

1. [1959] AC 604; [1959] 1 All ER 346.

Lord Simon's opinion[1] and in Lord Reid's opinion[2] which show that this was not intended. Indeed, if any doubt remained, it is disposed of by the opinions expressed by their Lordships in *Riverstone Meat Co Pty Ltd v Lancashire Shipping Co Ltd*[3]. . . .

It is not clear from the Case as drafted what were the circumstances in which the cable was obtained from the manufacturers, and I accordingly invited counsel to agree a further statement to cover this point. Counsel accordingly agreed the following addendum to the special case:

'Messrs Sloan and Lloyd Barnes [the electrical engineers] ordered from [the manufacturers] a cable capable of carrying a given load of electric current and in giving such order they contemplated that the cable would be delivered from stock or, perhaps though unusually, it would be manufactured against the order.'

On this somewhat meagre statement of the facts, I find it impossible to hold that the defendants, acting through their agents, the electrical engineers, were delegating their duty to the manufacturers. They were simply ordering a length of a certain type of cable, just as in *Davie*'s case,[4] they ordered a certain tool. . . .

In contrast, it seems to me that, in employing the electrical contractors to install the cable and the electrical engineers to order it and to supervise its testing and installation, the defendants were delegating any duty they owed. Likewise, in regard to the reconstruction of the premises, if the defendants were under any duty to their employees, they were clearly delegating it to the architects and to the contractors. . . .

I would accordingly answer the specific questions raised in the case as follows: para. 10(a), 'No'; para. 10(b), (c), (d) and (e), 'Yes'. In regard to para. 11, I direct as I am invited to do, that the plaintiff may not adduce at the trial evidence which is solely directed to showing that negligence on the part of the manufacturers of the electrical cable caused or contributed to the death of the plaintiff's wife.

Questions

1. What difference would it have made if the plaintiff's wife had not been an 'employee', but a self-employed labour-only sub-contractor? (See *Sole v W J Hallt Ltd* [1973] QB 574; [1973] 1 All ER 1032.)

2. Is an employer liable to his employee for an injury caused by the negligent driving of a lorry by a driver employed by a trade supplier to deliver goods to the employer?

3. What difference (if any) does it make if the employer's liability is classified as contractual rather than tortious? (See *Sole v W J Hallt Ltd*; *Davie v New Merton Board Mills Ltd* [1959] AC 604; [1959] 1 All ER 346; J. A. Jolowicz [1973] CLJ 209.)

4. Would the Employer's Liability (Defective Equipment) Act 1969 (p. 858, ante) make the manufacturer liable to the plaintiff, had these facts been stated after that Act came into operation?

---

1. [1959] AC at pp. 621, 623; [1959] 1 All ER at pp. 351, 354.
2. [1959] AC at pp. 642, 646, [1959] 1 All ER at pp. 365, 367, 368.
3. [1961] AC 807; [1961] 1 All ER 495.
4. [1959] AC 604; [1959] 1 All ER 346.

Note

On an employer's liability to an employee see further p. 810, ante where *McDermid v Nash Dredging and Reclamation Co Ltd* [1987] AC 906, [1987] 2 All ER 878 is noted and generally McKendrick, (1990) 53 MLR 770.

6 Corporations, trade unions and associations

Lennard's Carrying Co Ltd *v* Asiatic Petroleum Co Ltd House of Lords [1914–15] All ER Rep 280

Section 502 of the Merchant Shipping Act 1894 provides that the owner of a British sea-going ship is not liable to make good to any extent whatever 'any loss or damage happening without his actual fault or privity' where any goods are lost or damaged by reason of fire on board the ship.

Mr Lennard was the active director of a ship-owning company. One of the company's ships was in an unseaworthy state and as a result the ship became stranded in a gale and the cargo belonging to the respondents was destroyed by fire.

VISCOUNT HALDANE LC: . . . Did what happened take place without the actual fault or privity of the owners of the ship who were the appellants? A corporation is an abstraction. It has no mind of its own any more than it has a body of its own; its active and directing will must consequently be sought in the person of somebody who for some purposes may be called an agent, but who is really the directing mind and will of the corporation, the very ego and centre of the personality of the corporation. That person may be under the direction of the shareholders in general meeting; that person may be the board of directors itself, or it may be, and in some companies it is so, that that person has an authority co-ordinate with the board of directors given to him under the articles of association, and is appointed by the general meeting of the company, and can only be removed by the general meeting of the company. Whatever is not known about Mr Lennard's position, this is known for certain, Mr Lennard took the active part in the management of this ship on behalf of the owners, and Mr Lennard as I have said, was registered as the person designated for this purpose in the ship's register. Mr Lennard, therefore, was the natural person to come on behalf of the owners and give full evidence not only about the events of which I have spoken, and which related to the seaworthiness of the ship, but about his own position and as to whether or not he was the life and soul of the company. For if Mr Lennard was the directing mind of the company, then his action must, unless a corporation is not to be liable at all, have been an action which was the action of the company itself within the meaning of s. 502. It has not been contended at the Bar, and it could not have been successfully contended, that s. 502 is so worded as to exempt a corporation altogether which happened to be the owner of a ship, merely because it happened to be a corporation. It must be upon the true construction of that section in such a case as the present one that the fault or privity is the fault of somebody who is not merely a servant or agent for whom the company is liable upon the footing respondeat superior, but somebody for whom the company is liable because his action is the very action of the company itself. . . .

[LORD DUNEDIN, LORD ATKINSON, LORD PARKER OF WADDINGTON and LORD PARMOOR concurred.]

Questions

1. If some officers of a company are 'the directing mind and will of the corporation' is there any need for a doctrine of vicarious responsibility for the acts of corporations? (See Atiyah, *Vicarious Liability*, pp. 381–383; Gower, *Modern Company Law* 4th edn, pp. 205 et seq.) Note that directors who order an act which amounts to a tort may be liable as joint tortfeasors, and it is not necessary that the directors should know that the act is tortious: *C Evans & Sons Ltd v Spritebrand Ltd* [1985] 2 All ER 415, [1985] 1 WLR 317.

2. Consider *Carmarthenshire County Council v Lewis* [1955] AC 549, [1955] 1 All ER 565 (p. 67, ante). The Court of Appeal treated the Council as vicariously liable for the teacher's negligence in allowing the boy to escape on to the highway, while the House of Lords treated the Council as 'personally' negligent in allowing such an easy method of escape. Which approach is preferable? Note, as well, the cases on hospital authorities (p. 812, ante).

Notes

1. In the case of unincorporated members' clubs there is liability for acts expressly or impliedly authorised in accordance with the rules of the club: *Flemyng v Hector* (1836) 2 M & W 172; *Re St James Club* (1852) 2 De G M & G 383.

2. A trade union is not, and is not to be treated as if it were, a corporate body (Trade Union and Labour Relations Act 1974, s. 2(1)). However, it can sue or be sued in its own name (s. 2(1)(c)) and judgments are enforceable against any property held in trust for the union (s. 2(1)(e)). Section 15(1) of the Employment Act 1982 removed the immunity from certain actions in tort previously enjoyed by trade unions, although some restrictions were placed by s. 16 on the amount of damages recoverable in certain proceedings. These limits, ranging from £10,000 if the union has less than 5,000 members to £250,000 if it has 100,000 or more members, do not apply to any proceedings for negligence and nuisance or breach of duty resulting in personal injury or to breach of duty in connection with the ownership, occupation, posssession, control or use of property. Moreover, the limit applies separately to *each* set of proceedings, so if a large number of plaintiffs sue in separate proceedings the amounts awarded in total could be substantial. Section 17 of the Employment Act 1982 does, however, protect certain funds of the union (especially the provident benefit funds) from awards of damages and costs, but not from fines for contempt of court. Since a trade union can act only through natural persons the question of vicarious liability arises. In the case of proceedings in tort against a union on a ground specified in s. 13(1)(a) or (b) of the Trade Union and Labour Relations Act 1974, as amended (broadly speaking, interference with contract or a threat to interfere with contract or for conspiracy, special rules are prescribed by s. 15(2)–(9) of the Employment Act 1982, as amended or by the Employment Act 1990, s. 6. The union is responsible if the act in question was done, authorised or endorsed by (a) any person empowered by the rules of the union to do so; (b) the principal executive committee, or the president or general secretary; (c) any other

committee of the union or any other official of the union (whether employed by it or not). The union is responsible for such officials (including shop stewards), and for committees whose purposes include the calling of industrial action, unless the union repudiates the action in accordance with the Act's detailed requirements for notice to the official or committee in question and to 'do its best' to give individual written notice of repudiation to every member whom the union has reason to believe is taking part or might otherwise take part, and to the employer of every such member. Sections 10 and 11 of the Trade Union Act 1984, as amended, render the union liable for acts authorised or endorsed without a secret ballot in accordance with the provisions of that Act.

3. In the case of all torts other than those specified by s. 15 of the Employment Act 1982 the question of vicarious liability has to be determined according to common law principles. The guidance given in *Heatons' Transport (St Helens) Ltd v Transport and General Workers' Union* [1973] AC 15; [1972] 3 All ER 101 by the House of Lords (at p. 109) in respect of union responsibility for shop stewards committing statutory unfair industrial practices under the Industrial Relations Act 1971 (repealed in 1974) was that the test to be applied is 'was the servant or agent acting on behalf of, and within the scope of the authority conferred by, the master or principal?'. On the facts of the case it was held that the stewards had *implied* authority from the membership as a whole *by custom* to authorise industrial action. It is not clear whether, in the *Heatons* case, the House of Lords was espousing a general principle of liability for acts of agents (unlikely in view of *Morgans v Launchbury* [1973] AC 127; [1972] 2 All ER 606, p. 819, ante), or was really concerned with the *personal* liability of a quasi-corporation (see B. Hepple (1972) 1 ILJ 197; K. W. Wedderburn (1973) 36 MLR 226; O. Kahn-Freund (1974) 3 ILJ 186). In a later case under the 1971 Act (*General Aviation Services (UK) Ltd v TGWU* [1985] ICR 615), the House of Lords emphasised that each case of liability for stewards turns on its own facts, and in the *Heatons* case itself ([1972] 3 All ER at p. 110) Lord Wilberforce was careful to state that what was said in that case 'does not necessarily apply' to liability for tortious acts. However, in *Thomas v National Union of Mineworkers (South Wales Area)* [1985] ICR 886 at 916–918, Scott J applied the principle of the *Heatons* case to common law torts committed in the course of picketing outside colliery gates. This may be compared with *News Group Newspapers Ltd v SOGAT '82* [1987] ICR 181, in which Stuart-Smith J avoided the vicarious liability issue by holding that a union could be liable for 'continuing or adopting' a nuisance by organising pickets and marches in the knowledge or presumed knowledge that nuisance and other torts are being committed by those whom the union organises. For the development of these 'organisational' torts against unions in the context of picketing, see S. Auerbach (1987) 16 ILJ 227 at 237–239; (1988) 17 ILJ 227; (1989) 18 ILJ 166.

18 Joint liability

The problems with which the materials in this chapter are concerned arise where the *same* damage is attributable to the conduct of two or more tortfeasors. If they have all participated in the same act leading to that damage they are called *joint* tortfeasors. The main examples of joint tortfeasors are (a) the person who authorises or instigates the commission of a tort and the person who carries out his instructions; (b) those who participate in a joint enterprise (p. 829, ante); and (c) employer and employee where the employer is vicariously liable for the torts of his employee (p. 807, ante). If, on the other hand, there are several *independent* acts all leading to the same damage, then they are called *several concurrent* tortfeasors. An example would be an accident in which two cars collide due to the negligent driving of each driver, causing injury to a pedestrian. The drivers are *severally* liable, and they cannot be described as *joint* tortfeasors. (For an illustration from maritime law see *The Koursk* [1924] P 140.)

The distinction between joint tortfeasors and several concurrent tortfeasors is of little practical significance, except in one situation. This is that the release of one joint tortfeasor from his liability discharges all others liable with him, while the release of one of two or more several concurrent tortfeasors will not have this effect (*Cutler v McPhail* [1962] 2 QB 292; [1962] 2 All ER 474, p. 868, post). This is an anachronism and the courts have mitigated the strict rules in two ways: (a) by deciding that a mere promise not to sue does not amount to a release; and (b) by allowing the plaintiff, when releasing one joint tortfeasor, to make an express reservation of rights against the other joint tortfeasors. Indeed, this reservation may even be implied: *Gardiner v Moore* [1969] 1 QB 55; [1966] 1 All ER 365.

In all other respects joint tortfeasors and several concurrent tortfeasors are alike. Each tortfeasor is liable in full for the whole of the damage caused to the plaintiff. Satisfaction by any one tortfeasor usually discharges the liability of the others to the plaintiff. Although two or more tortfeasors may be joined as co-defendants in the action, only one sum can be awarded as damages and that sum must, accordingly, be the *lowest* sum for which any of the individual defendants can be held liable (*Cassell & Co Ltd v Broome* [1972] AC 1027; [1972] 1 All ER 801, p. 870, post). If a judgment is obtained against one tortfeasor this is not a bar to later proceedings against the others (Civil Liability (Contribution) Act 1978, s. 3) but the plaintiff is not entitled to his costs in the second action (ibid., s. 4).

There is a right of contribution between tortfeasors and it is with this right that the chapter is principally concerned. The Law Reform (Married Women and Tortfeasors) Act 1935 abolished the common law rule (*Merryweather v Nixan* (1799) 8 Term Rep 186) which denied this right. The relevant parts of this Act have been repealed and replaced (with effect from 1 January 1979) by the Civil Liability (Contribution) Act 1978 (p. 871, post), which clarifies and reforms the earlier legislation and extends the principle of the 1935 Act to all wrongdoers, whether the basis of liability is tort, breach of contract, breach of trust or otherwise (s. 6(1)). The Act is based, with some important modifications, on the Law Commission's *Report on Contribution* (Law Com. No. 79).

The right to recover contribution under the 1978 Act supersedes any other right except (a) an express or implied contractual or other (e.g. statutory) right to an indemnity; or (b) an express contractual provision regulating or excluding contribution (s. 7(3)). An example of an implied contractual right will be found in *Lister v Romford Ice and Cold Storage Co Ltd* [1957] AC 555; [1957] 1 All ER 125 (p. 875, post). It was held that there is an implied term which allows an employer to recover an indemnity from the employee for whose torts he is vicariously liable. The exact scope of this implied term, particularly where insurance by the employer is compulsory (either as vehicle owner or as employer), is a matter for debate (p. 878, post). In practice this right of indemnity is of importance only where the employer's insurers choose to exercise their rights of subrogation and sue the employee in the employer's name, a rare occurrence because of a self-denying ordinance (p. 881, post).

1   Effect of release of joint tortfeasor

Cutler *v* McPhail Queen's Bench Division [1962] 2 All ER 474

SALMON J: The points raised on release are extremely interesting and by no means easy. The principle is quite plain, that, if there is a release of one joint tortfeasor, the cause of action against all the tortfeasors is extinguished; on the other hand, if there is merely an agreement not to sue one of several joint tortfeasors, the cause of action does not die and the other tortfeasors can properly be sued. What I have to decide here in respect of the publication in 'The Villager', is whether there has been a release of the plaintiffs' cause of action against the defendant. In the *Price v Barker*[1] line of cases, the court has had to consider a release by deed, where, in the body of the document, there is an express release followed by words purporting to retain the right to sue other joint tortfeasors — an express reservation of right. In such cases, it is clear from the authorities that, there is no magic in the use of the word 'release' in the deed. The deed has to be looked at as a whole, and, if it appears from the deed, looked at as a whole, that, although the parties have used the word 'release', the deed is not intended to operate as a release but is merely an agreement or a promise not to sue, then it is merely a promise not to sue and not a release. But in the class of case to which I have referred, the decision, when it has been in favour of the view that the deed did not operate as a release, has always proceeded on the basis that the express reservation of rights in the document showed that it was not intended to operate as a release.

Here, one has to consider a release by accord and satisfaction, and the release with which I am particularly concerned is the release of the Pinner Association officers. They are the persons responsible for the publication in 'The Villager', and they settled their case with the plaintiffs on the basis that they paid £250 damages and costs,

---

1. (1855) 4 E & B 760.

and published an apology. As far as they are concerned, the matter starts with the letter written by the plaintiffs' solicitor to Messrs Wyld, Collins and Crosse, appearing for the Pinner Association and its officers. I need not read the whole of the letter, but the vital paragraph reads:

'Upon the apologies being published and the sum mentioned paid over, then my client will, of course, release from any further liability in respect of the publication complained of, all officers and members of the committee including, of course, the editor of "The Villager".'

Presumably that letter means what it says. One can guess what the probability is; no doubt, when the letter was written the plaintiffs hoped to go on with their action against the present defendant. But I cannot see that stated anywhere in the letter, and, when I look at the rest of the correspondence following that letter, between the plaintiffs' solicitor and the solicitors for the Pinner Association officers, I still cannot find anything to indicate that, when the plaintiffs' solicitor used the word 'release' in his letter of 19 February 1959, he did not mean precisely what he said; nor is there any evidence before me from which I can come to the conclusion that a contrary intention was ever expressed by the plaintiffs to the Pinner Association officers.

Counsel for the plaintiffs has sought to rely on a letter which was written by the plaintiffs' solicitor to the solicitors for the printers and publishers, the Pinner Press, Ltd; that letter also uses these words:

'Upon the publication of the apologies by your clients and payment by them of my costs, they will of course be released from all further liability in the matter',

and adds:

'As a matter of interest, it has not proved possible to effect a settlement of the matter with [the defendant] and I have instructed counsel to settle writ and statement of claim.'

It is suggested that those last words amount to an express reservation of rights and an intimation that this letter was intended only as an agreement not to sue. In my judgment, the letter does not contain an express reservation of rights; it is at least as consistent with the view that the solicitor writing the letter intended to release without fully appreciating the legal consequences of a release, as it is with any other suggested interpretation. But, as far as the release to the Pinner Association officers is concerned, there are no such additional words in the relevant letter and, as I have already indicated, I have looked, and looked in vain, to find anything which expresses an intention, or from which an intention could properly be deduced, negativing what the letter of February 19 says in the plainest terms.

It may be that the law relating to release might be reconsidered with advantage; the difference between a release and an agreement not to sue is highly technical but very real in its effect, but, whilst the law remains as it is, I feel bound to hold in this case that there has been a release of the Pinner Association officers, and that that release in law extinguishes the claim in respect of the separate tort alleged to have been committed by the defendant in causing his letter to be published in 'The Villager'. . . .

Notes

1. In *Gardiner v Moore* [1969] 1 QB 55; [1966] 1 All ER 365 Thesiger J held that there was no material difference between an express and an implied covenant not to sue. Being satisfied, on the facts, that there had been no

intention to release the author of a libel when a claim against the newspaper proprietors and printers was settled, he held that the author had not been discharged from liability.

2. The common law rule of release by accord and satisfaction has been abolished in several jurisdictions and Lord Denning MR has stated, obiter, (in *Bryanston Finance Ltd v De Vries* [1975] QB 703 at 723) that it should be disregarded. However, the Civil Liability (Contribution) Act 1978 (p. 871, post) appears to leave the rule unaffected.

2   A single award

Cassell & Co Ltd *v* Broome House of Lords [1972] 1 All ER 801

For the facts and other material aspects of the case see p. 403, ante, and p. 790. ante.

LORD HAILSHAM: . . . Less meritorious, in my view, was the second criticism of the direction put before us. This was in effect that the judge did not correctly direct the jury as to the principles on which a joint award of exemplary damages can be made against two or more defendants guilty of the joint publication of a libel in respect of which their relevant guilt may be different, and their means of different amplitude. . . . I think the effect of the law is . . . that awards of punitive damages in respect of joint publications should reflect only the lowest figure for which any of them can be held liable. This seems to me to flow inexorably both from the principle that only one sum may be awarded in a single proceeding for a joint tort, and from the authorities which were cited to us by counsel for the appellants in detail in the course of his argument. . . . I think that the inescapable conclusion to be drawn from these authorities is that only one sum can be awarded by way of exemplary damages where the plaintiff elects to sue more than one defendant in the same action in respect of the same publication, and that this sum must represent the highest *common* factor, that is the *lowest* sum for which any of the defendants can be held liable on this score. Although we were concerned with exemplary damages, I would think that the same principle applies generally and in particular to aggravated damages, and that dicta or apparent dicta to the contrary can be disregarded. As counsel conceded, however, plaintiffs who wish to differentiate between the defendants can do so in various ways, for example, by electing to sue the more guilty only, by commencing separate proceedings against each and then consolidating, or, in the case of a book or newspaper article, by suing separately in the same proceedings for the publication of the manuscript to the publisher by the author. Defendants, of course, have their ordinary contractual or statutory remedies for contribution or indemnity so far as they may be applicable to the facts of a particular case. But these may be inapplicable to exemplary damages. . . .

LORD REID: . . . Unless we are to abandon all pretence of justice, means must be found to prevent more being recovered by way of punitive damages from the least guilty th[a]n he ought to pay. We cannot rely on his being able to recover some contribution from the other. Suppose printer, author and publisher of a libel are all sued. The printer will probably be guiltless of any outrageous conduct but the others may deserve punishment beyond compensatory damages. If there has to be one judgment against all three then it would be very wrong to allow any element of punitive damages at all to be included because very likely the printer would have to pay the whole and the others might not be worth suing for a contribution. The only logical way to deal with the matter would be first to have a judgment against all the defendants for the compensatory damages and then to have a separate judgment against each of the defendants for such additional sum as he should pay as punitive damages. I would agree that that is impracticable. The fact that it is impracticable to do full justice appears to me to afford another illustration of how anomalous and indefensible is the whole doctrine of punitive damages. But as I have said before we must accept it and make the best we can of it.

So, in my opinion, the jury should be directed that, when they come to consider what if any addition is to be made to the compensatory damages by way of punitive damages, they must consider each defendant separately. If any one of the defendants does not deserve punishment or if the compensatory damages are in themselves sufficient punishment for any one of the defendants, then they must not make any addition to the compensatory damages. If each of the defendants deserves more punishment than is involved in payment of the compensatory damages then they must determine which deserves the least punishment and only add to the compensatory damages such additional sum as that defendant ought to pay by way of punishment. I do not pretend that that achieves full justice but it is the best we can do without separate awards against each defendant. . . .

3   Contribution between tortfeasors

(a)   By statute

The Civil Liability (Contribution) Act 1978

Proceedings for contribution

1. Entitlement to contribution. — (1) Subject to the following provisions of this section, any person liable in respect of any damage suffered by another person may recover contribution from any other person liable in respect of the same damage (whether jointly with him or otherwise).

(2) A person shall be entitled to recover contribution by virtue of subsection (1) above notwithstanding that he has ceased to be liable in respect of the damage in question since the time when the damage occurred, provided that he was so liable immediately before he made or was ordered or agreed to make the payment in respect of which the contribution is sought.

(3) A person shall be liable to make contribution by virtue of subsection (1) above notwithstanding that he has ceased to be liable in respect of the damage in question since the time when the damage occurred, unless he ceased to be liable by virtue of the expiry of a period of limitation or prescription which extinguished the right on which the claim against him in respect of the damage was based.

(4) A person who has made or agreed to make any payment in bona fide settlement or compromise of any claim made against him in respect of any damage (including a payment into court which has been accepted) shall be entitled to recover contribution in accordance with this section without regard to whether or not he himself is or ever was liable in respect of the damage, provided however, that he would have been liable assuming that the factual basis of the claim against him could be established.

(5) A judgment given in any action brought in any part of the United Kingdom by or on behalf of the person who suffered the damage in question against any person from whom contribution is sought under this section shall be conclusive in the proceedings for contribution as to any issue determined by that judgment in favour of the person from whom the contribution is sought.

(6) References in this section to a person's liability in respect of any damage are references to any such liability which has been or could be established in an action brought against him in England and Wales by or on behalf of the person who suffered

the damage; but it is immaterial whether any issue arising in any such action was or would be determined (in accordance with the rules of private international law) by reference to the law of a country outside England and Wales.

2. Assessment of contribution. — (1) Subject to subsection (3) below, in any proceedings for contribution under section 1 above the amount of the contribution recoverable from any person shall be such as may be found by the court to be just and equitable having regard to the extent of that person's responsibility for the damage in question.

(2) Subject to subsection (3) below, the court shall have power in any such proceedings to exempt any person from liability to make contribution, or to direct that the contribution to be recovered from any person shall amount to a complete indemnity.

(3) Where the amount of the damages which have or might have been awarded in respect of the damage in question in any action brought in England and Wales by or on behalf of the person who suffered it against the person from whom the contribution is sought was or would have been subject to —

(a) any limit imposed by or under any enactment or by any agreement made before the damage occurred;

(b) any reduction by virtue of section 1 of the Law Reform (Contributory Negligence) Act 1945 or section 5 of the Fatal Accidents Act 1976; or

(c) any corresponding limit or reduction under the law of a country outside England and Wales;

the person from whom the contribution is sought shall not by virtue of any contribution awarded under section 1 above be required to pay in respect of the damage a greater amount than the amount of those damages as so limited or reduced.

Proceedings for the same debt or damage

3. Proceedings against persons jointly liable for the same debt or damage. — Judgment recovered against any person liable in respect of any debt or damage shall not be a bar to an action, or to the continuance of an action, against any other person who is (apart from any such bar) jointly liable with him in respect of the same debt or damage.

4. Successive actions against persons liable (jointly or otherwise) for the same damage. — If more than one action is brought in respect of any damage by or on behalf of the person by whom it was suffered against persons liable in respect of the damage (whether jointly or otherwise) the plaintiff shall not be entitled to costs in any of those actions, other than that in which judgment is first given, unless the court is of the opinion that there was reasonable ground for bringing the action.

6. Interpretation. — (1) A person is liable in respect of any damage for the purposes of this Act if the person who suffered it (or anyone representing his estate or dependants) is entitled to recover compensation from him in respect of that damage (whatever the legal basis of his liability, whether tort, breach of contract, breach of trust or otherwise).

(2) References in this Act to an action brought by or on behalf of the person who suffered any damage include references to an action brought for the benefit of his estate or dependants.

(3) In this Act 'dependants' has the same meaning as in the Fatal Accidents Act 1976.

(4) In this Act, except in section 1(5) above, 'action' means an action brought in England and Wales.

7. Savings. — (1) Nothing in this Act shall affect any case where the debt in question became due or (as the case may be) the damage in question occurred before the date on which it comes into force.

(2) A person shall not be entitled to recover contribution or liable to make contribution in accordance with section 1 above by reference to any liability based on breach of any obligation assumed by him before the date on which this Act comes into force.

(3) The right to recover contribution in accordance with section 1 above supersedes any right, other than an express contractual right, to recover contribution (as distinct from indemnity) otherwise than under this Act in corresponding circumstances; but nothing in this Act shall affect —

(*a*) any express or implied contractual or other right to indemnity; or

(*b*) any express contractual provision regulating or excluding contribution;

which would be enforceable apart from this Act (or render enforceable any agreement for indemnity or contribution which would not be enforceable apart from this Act).

Notes

1. *Scope of the right to contribution.* Section 1(1) is much wider in scope than s. 6(1)(*c*) of the Law Reform (Married Women and Tortfeasors) Act 1935 which merely provided that a tortfeasor liable in respect of damage suffered by any person as a result of tort could recover contribution from any other tortfeasor who was, or would if sued have been liable, in respect of the same damage. There were situations in which there was no right of contribution, for example between a person liable in contract and a tortfeasor, although both were liable in respect of the same damage, or between persons liable under separate contracts for breaches of different kinds causing the same damage. This has now been remedied.

2. *Persons entitled to claim.* Sections 1(2) and 1(4) deal with the problem which arose under the 1935 Act, where one tortfeasor (D1) had settled with the plaintiff. In order to recover a contribution from the other tortfeasor (D2) D1 had to show that he was 'liable' (*Stott v West Yorkshire Road Car Co Ltd* [1971] 2 QB 651; [1971] 3 All ER 534). This could deter settlements where there were doubts about D1's liability because D1 would not wish to put his right to contribution at risk. Section 1(4) removes this obstacle. The proviso, that the person claiming a contribution 'would have been liable assuming the factual basis of the claim against him could be established', was added during the Committee stage in the belief that it would prevent settlements based solely on the requirements of foreign law. However, as A. M. Dugdale (1979) 42 MLR 182 at 184 points out, the proviso has the effect of excluding all settlements based on legal rather than factual doubts.

3. *Persons liable to contribute.* Section 1(3) clarifies a point on which there was much difference of opinion in the House of Lords in *George Wimpey & Co Ltd v BOAC* [1955] AC 169; [1954] 3 All ER 661. D1 can bring a contribution claim against D2 within two years of his own liability to P being determined, but by then the limitation period between P and D2 may have expired. *Wimpey*'s case was generally regarded as authority for the proposition that D2 was to be regarded as 'liable' unless he had actually been sued by P and found not liable because of the expiration of the limitation period. In other words, D2's obligation to make a contribution depended upon whether P had attempted to sue after the limitation period had expired.

Following the Law Commission's proposals, s. 1(3) means that a wrongdoer who has been held not liable to P because of the expiry of the limitation period or the dismissal of the claim by P for want of prosecution can still be regarded as liable to make a contribution. However, if the expiry of a limitation or prescription period extinguished not merely the remedy but also the right on which the claim against him was based, then he is not liable to make a contribution.

4. *Effect of contributory negligence.* Where P and D1 and D2 are all to blame, both the Law Reform (Contributory Negligence) Act 1945 (p. 357, ante) and the 1978 Act are relevant. In *Fitzgerald v Lane* [1989] AC 328; [1988] 2 All ER 961, noted p. 310, ante, the House of Lords held that the essential principles in this situation are that (a) where P successfully sues D1 and D2 and there is a claim between D1 and D2 for contribution, the apportionment between D1 and D2 is a separate issue which should be considered only after the issues of contributory negligence and apportionment between P on the one hand and D1 and D2 on the other hand have been decided; and (b) in determining the issue of contributory negligence between P and D1 and D2, P's conduct should be compared with the totality of D1 and D2's conduct rather than the extent to which the conduct of D1 and D2 each contributed to the damage (per Lord Ackner, at pp. 338–339).

5. *Assessment.* Sections 2(1) and 2(2) reproduce s. 6(2) of the 1935 Act. Section 2(3), which is new, limits the court's discretion. For example, if P suffers a £1,200 loss due equally to a tort by D1 and a breach of contract by D2 but D2's contract limits the damages for which he can be liable to P to £400, the court should first apportion the loss between D1 and D2 at £600 each and then reduce D2's share to £400 leaving D1 to pay £800 (Dugdale, op cit).

6. *Successive actions.* Section 3, replacing s. 6(1)(a) of the 1935 Act, refers not only to tortfeasors but to 'any person liable in respect of any debt or damage' (see s. 6(1) of the 1978 Act). It also makes it clear that this provision applies not only to successive actions but also to a single action against two or more persons, thus adopting the view of Lord Denning MR on the old s. 6(1)(a) in *Bryanston Finance Co Ltd v De Vries* [1975] QB 703 at 722. See *Cutler v McPhail* (p. 868, ante) regarding release. Section 4 is intended to replace s. 6(1)(b) of the 1935 Act, but differs from that section, first in covering not only tortfeasors but also 'persons liable in respect of the damage' (s. 6(1) of the 1978 Act), and secondly, in setting no limit on sums recoverable under judgments other than the judgment first given.

7. *Limitation.* Section 10 of the Limitation Act 1980 provides that the right to claim contribution becomes statute-barred after the end of the period of two years from the date when the right accrued. The relevant date is the date of judgment against the first tortfeasor, or, where he makes or agrees to make any payment to one or more persons in compensation for the damage, the earliest date on which the amount to be paid is agreed between him and the person to whom the payment is to be made. (As regards the situation where the breach of duty occurred before the 1978 Act came into force, but the damage occurred after that date, see *Lampitt v Poole Borough Council* [1990] 2 All ER 887; [1990] 3 WLR 179.)

(b)   Under the contract of employment

Lister v Romford Ice & Cold Storage Co Ltd House of Lords [1957] 1 All ER 125

The appellant, Lister, was employed as a lorry driver by the respondents. He negligently ran down his mate (his father) while backing his lorry in a yard. The father recovered damages against the respondents on grounds of their vicarious liability. The respondents' insurers, acting in their name by virtue of a term in the contract of insurance, brought an action against the appellant for damages for breach of an implied term in his contract of employment that he would exercise reasonable care and skill in his driving. The appellant pleaded that it was an implied term that he was entitled to the benefit of any insurance which his employer either had effected or as a reasonable and prudent person should have effected and consequently the respondents could not claim an indemnity or contribution from him.

The Court of Appeal, Denning LJ dissenting, held that the respondents' action succeeded both under the Act of 1935 and because of the appellant's breach of the implied term. In the House of Lords this judgment was affirmed on the point of the implied term by 3:2 (the dissentients being Lord Radcliffe and Lord Somervell). Although all five of their Lordships held that there was an implied term to use reasonable care, the dissentients took the view that the employee was protected by an implied term that the employer will not seek an indemnity where it is understood that the employer will take out a third-party liability policy. The majority (Viscount Simonds, Lord Morton and Lord Tucker) said that such a term could not be implied.

VISCOUNT SIMONDS: . . . It is, in my opinion, clear that it was an implied term of the contract that the appellant would perform his duties with proper care. The proposition of law stated by Willes J in *Harmer v Cornelius* ((1858) 5 CBNS 236 at 246) has never been questioned:

'When a skilled labourer, artisan, or artist is employed, there is on his part an implied warranty that he is of skill reasonably competent to the task he undertakes, — Spondes peritiam artis. Thus, if an apothecary, a watchmaker, or an attorney be employed for reward, they each impliedly undertake to possess and exercise reasonable skill in their several arts . . . An express promise or express representation in the particular case is not necessary.'

I see no ground for excluding from, and every ground for including in, this category a servant who is employed to drive a lorry which, driven without care, may become an engine of destruction and involve his master in very grave liability. Nor can I see any valid reason for saying that a distinction is to be made between possessing skill and exercising it. No such distinction is made in the cited case; on the contrary, 'possess' and 'exercise' are there conjoined. Of what advantage to the employer is his servant's undertaking that he possesses skill unless he undertakes also to use it? I have spoken of using skill rather than using care, for 'skill' is the word used in the cited case, but this embraces care. For even in so-called unskilled operations an exercise of care is necessary to the proper performance of duty.

I have already said that it does not appear to me to make any difference to the determination of any substantive issue in this case whether the respondents' cause of action lay in tort or breach of contract. But, in deference to Denning LJ I think it right to say that I concur in what I understand to be the unanimous opinion of your Lordships that the servant owes a contractual duty of care to his master, and that the breach of that duty founds an action for damages for breach of contract, and that this (apart from any defence) is such a case. It is trite law that a single act of negligence may give rise to a claim either in tort or for breach of a term express or implied in a contract. Of this, the negligence of a servant in performance of his duty is a clear example.

I conclude, then, the first stage of the argument by saying that the appellant was under a contractual obligation of care in the performance of his duty, that he committed a breach of it, that the respondents thereby suffered damage and they are entitled to recover that damage from him, unless it is shown either that the damage is too remote or that there is some other intervening factor which precludes the recovery. . . .

My Lords, undoubtedly there are formidable obstacles in the path of the appellant, and they were formidably presented by counsel for the respondents. First, it is urged that it must be irrelevant to the right of the master to sue his servant for breach of duty that the master is insured against its consequences. As a general proposition it has not, I think, been questioned for nearly two hundred years that, in determining the rights inter se of A and B, the fact that one or other of them is insured is to be disregarded: see, e.g. *Mason v Sainsbury* ((1782) 3 Doug KB 61). This general proposition, no doubt, applies if A is a master and B his man; but its application to a case or class of case must yield to an express or implied term to the contrary, and, as the question is whether that term should be implied, I am not constrained by an assertion of the general proposition to deny the possible exception. Yet I cannot wholly ignore a principle so widely applicable as that a man insures at his own expense for his own benefit and does not thereby suffer any derogation of his rights against another man.

Next — and here I recur to a difficulty already indicated — if it has become part of the common law of England that, as between the employer and driver of a motor vehicle, it is the duty of the former to look after the whole matter of insurance (an expression which I have used compendiously to describe the plea as finally submitted), must not that duty be more precisely defined? It may be answered that in other relationships duties are imposed by law which can only be stated in general terms. Partners owe a duty of faithfulness to each other; what that duty involves in any particular case can only be determined in the light of all its circumstances. Other examples in other branches of the law may occur to your Lordships where a general duty is presented and its scope falls to be determined partly by the general custom of the country which is the basis of the law and partly, perhaps, by equitable considerations; but even so, the determination must rest on evidence of the custom or on such broad equitable considerations as have from early times guided a court of equity.

In the area in which this appeal is brought, there is no evidence to guide your Lordships. The single fact that, since the Road Traffic Act 1930 came into force, a measure of insurance against third-party risk is compulsory affords no ground for an assumption that an employer will take out a policy which covers more than the Act requires, for instance, a risk of injury to third parties not on the road but in private premises. There is, in fact, no assumption that can legitimately be made what policy will be taken out and what its terms and qualifications may be. I am unable to satisfy myself that, with such a background, there can be implied in the relationship of employer and driver any such terms as I have indicated. And though, as I have said, I feel the force of the argument as presented by Denning LJ, I must point out that, at least in his view, the indemnity of the driver was conditional on a policy which covered the risk having in fact been taken out. It may be that this was because his mind was directed to a case where such a policy was taken out, and that he would have gone on to say that there was a further implication that the employer would take out a policy whether required by law to do so or not. But here we are in the realm of speculation. Is it certain that, if the imaginary driver had said to his employer: 'Of course you will indemnify me against any damage that I may do however gross my negligence may be', the employer would have said: 'Yes, of course!' For myself, I cannot answer confidently that he would have said so or ought to have said so. It may well be that, if such a discussion had taken place, it might have ended in some agreement between them or in the driver not entering the service of that employer. That I do not know. But I do not know that I am ever driven further from an assured certainty what is the term which the law imports into the contract of service between the employer and the driver of a motor vehicle.

Another argument was, at this stage, adduced which appeared to me to have some weight. For just as it was urged that a term could not be implied unless it could be defined with precision, so its existence was denied if it could not be shown when it came to birth. Here, it was said, was a duty alleged to arise out of the relation of master and servant in this special sphere of employment which was imposed by the common law. When, then, did it first arise? Not, surely, when the first country squire exchanged his carriage and horses for a motor car or the first haulage contractor bought a motor lorry. Was it when the practice of insurance against third-party risk became so common that it was to be expected of the reasonable man, or was it only when the Act of 1930 made compulsory and, therefore, universal what had previously been reasonable and usual?

Then, again, the familiar argument was heard asking where the line is to be drawn. The driver of a motor car is not the only man in charge of an engine which, if carelessly used, may endanger and injure third parties. The man in charge of a crane was given as an example. If he, by his negligence, injures a third party who then makes his employer vicariously liable, is he entitled to assume that his employer has covered himself by insurance and will indemnify him, however gross and reprehensible his negligence? And does this depend on the extent to which insurance against third-party risks prevails and is known to prevail in any particular form of employment? Does it depend on the fact that there are fewer cranes than cars and that the master is less likely to drive a crane than a car? . . .

LORD MORTON OF HENRYTON: . . . If any such term is to be implied in this case, it must surely be implied in all cases where an employee is employed to drive any kind of vehicle which might cause damage to third parties. And the implied term cannot be limited to cases where the vehicle is being driven on a public highway, for the accident in the present case occurred in a yard. Surely it must logically extend to cases such as a crane driver in factory premises, and many other cases come to mind which cannot logically be distinguished from the present case. Such an obligation might have been imposed on the employer by statute, and it is, perhaps, of some significance that the legislature did not take this course when the law was so strikingly altered by the Road Traffic Act 1930. It cannot be said, in my view, that the implication of either of these terms is necessary in order to give 'to the transaction such efficacy as both parties must have intended that . . . it should have'. (*The Moorcock* (1889) 14 PD 64 at 68, per Bowen LJ)

Turning now to another branch of the argument for the appellant, I cannot see that any events which have occurred in modern times, such as the passing of the Road Traffic Act 1930, could justify your Lordships in holding it to be the law today that one or other of the implied terms now under discussion forms part of every contract whereby a man is employed to drive a vehicle. No provision of the Act of 1930 suggests to me that the terms to be implied in such a contract immediately after the Act became law should differ in any respect from the terms to be implied immediately before the Act became law. This matter is fully dealt with in the opinion about to be delivered by my noble and learned friend, Lord Tucker, which I have read, and I need only say that I entirely agree with his views on it.

Counsel for the appellant finally suggested that some such term ought to be implied because, in its absence, the employee was placed in a most unfortunate position. It is, however, your Lordships' task to decide what the law is, not what it ought to be. In saying this, I am far from suggesting that either of the terms now under discussion ought to be implied. . . .

LORD TUCKER: . . . It is said that the passing of the Road Traffic Act 1930, has created the new situation which gives rise to the necessity for these implied terms. It is common knowledge that, for many years before 1930, the great majority of prudent motor car owners protected themselves by insurance. Section 35 and s. 36 of the Act were passed not for the protection of the bank balances of car owners, or the life savings of their employees, but simply and solely to ensure that persons injured by the negligent driving of motor cars who established their claims in court might not be deprived of compensation by reason of the defendant's inability to satisfy their judgments. Again, it is said that the passing of the Act has admittedly resulted in the introduction of one implied term, viz. that the servant shall not be required to drive a motor vehicle the user of which has not been covered by insurance as required by the Act. This is merely the application of an existing term to the situation created by the Act. It has always been an implied term that the master will indemnify the servant from liability arising out of an unlawful enterprise on which he has been required to embark without knowing that it was unlawful. When the Road Traffic Act 1930 required the user to be covered by insurance, a journey which would previously have been lawful became unlawful in the absence of the required cover. My Lords, I cannot accept the view that the impact of this Act on the previously existing obligation of the master is in any way comparable to the implied terms which it is now sought to introduce into the contract of service. . . .

[LORD RADCLIFFE and LORD SOMERVELL OF HARROW delivered speeches in favour of allowing the appeal.]

Notes

1. In *Gregory v Ford* [1951] 1 All ER 121 Byrne J held that it was an implied term of the contract of employment that the employer would not require the employee to do an unlawful act and, consequently, the employer had a contractual duty to the employee to comply with the compulsory insurance provisions of the Road Traffic Act in respect of vehicles the employee was required to drive. The validity of this decision was accepted by both sides in *Lister's* case (note, however, Lord Morton's remarks, ante). G. L. Williams (1957) 20 MLR 220 at 226 argues that *Gregory v Ford* cannot demonstrably be founded on the wording of the Road Traffic Act. The present Road Traffic Act 1988 (p. 885, post) requires the person who uses or causes or permits a motor vehicle to be used on a road to be covered against third party risks. The Act, like its predecessors, does not require the employer to take out a policy which covers the personal liability of his employee. If this is so, how can the Act be said to create an implied contractual duty to insure the employee?

2. In one exceptional case the employee does have a right to indemnity. This is where a road traffic policy is taken out under the provisions of the Road Traffic Act 1988 (p. 885, post). In *Lister's* case the insurance was not compulsory (the accident did not occur on a 'road') and, in any event, the insurance company which claimed by subrogation was not the company which issued the road traffic policy, but another company which had issued an employer's liability policy. Since 1 January 1972, employers' liability insurance has been compulsory (p. 894, post) but the Employers' Liability (Compulsory Insurance) Act 1969 contains no statutory right of indemnity for an employee analogous to that contained in the Road Traffic Act. Since the Employers' Liability (Compulsory Insurance) Act requires the employer to cover *his* liability to employees and not the personal liability of employees

to fellow employees or others, it does not seem that the Act creates an implied contractual duty to insure the employee (cf. *Gregory v Ford*, ante).

3. Section 4 of the Unfair Contract Terms Act 1977 subjects indemnity clauses in certain cases to a reasonableness test. The section might now catch the implied term in *Lister*'s case that the employee would use reasonable care, but see Rogers and Clarke, *The Unfair Contract Terms Act 1977*, who argue that 'since the right to indemnity arises from a term implied by law, the courts could hardly say the term was unreasonable'.

4. In a case concerning a hire of plant with a worker (*Thompson v T Lohan (Plant Hire) Ltd* [1987] 2 All ER 631; [1987] 1 WLR 649, noted p. 392, ante), a clause providing that the hirer was to be liable for the negligence of the owner's employee while operating hired plant was held not to be an exclusion of liability clause and hence not invalidated by s. 2(1) of the 1977 Act (p. 872, ante); cf. *Phillips Products Ltd v Hyland* [1987] 2 All ER 620; [1987] 1 WLR 659n.

Jones *v* Manchester Corporation Court of Appeal
[1952] 2 All ER 125

In an action for damages by the widow of a patient who died under negligent hospital treatment, the hospital board claimed an indemnity from Dr Wilkes, an inexperienced physician who had administered the fatal anaesthetic under the instructions of Dr Sejrup, a house surgeon.

SINGLETON LJ: . . . The employer cannot have a right of indemnity if he himself has contributed to the damage or if he bears some part of the responsibility therefor, and the same reasoning applies if some other and senior employee's negligence has contributed to the damage. On the facts of this case I feel bound to reject the claim of the hospital board to an indemnity against Dr Wilkes. I mentioned in the course of the argument the desirability of pleadings and of discovery if a question such as this was to be raised. Without this it is not easy to determine the true terms of the contract between the parties. All that we know is that Dr Wilkes was appointed a house surgeon at the hospital a short time after she had been qualified, and after an interview. There is no evidence to show that she was ever instructed, or advised, at the hospital as to the use of drugs. . . .

DENNING LJ: . . . The hospital authorities cannot come down on every negligent member of the staff for a full indemnity. Such a course could only be justified if the hospital authorities could be regarded as innocent parties who have been made vicariously liable without any fault in them. But the law does not regard them as innocent. It says that they are themselves under a duty of care and skill, and, if that duty is not fulfilled, it regards them as tortfeasors and makes them liable as such, no matter whether the negligence be their personal negligence or the negligence of their staff.

In all these cases the important thing to remember is that when a master employs a servant to do something for him, he is responsible for the servant's conduct as if it were his own. If the servant commits a tort in the course of his employment, then the master is a tortfeasor as well as the servant. The master is never treated as an innocent party. This is well seen by taking a simple case where two cars are damaged in a collision by the fault of both drivers. One is driven by a servant, the other by an owner-driver. The owner-driver can obviously only recover a proportion of the damage to his own car from the owner of the other one, and likewise the owner of the chauffeur-driven car can only recover a proportion of the damage to his car. He cannot recover the whole damage from the owner-driver. He cannot claim as if he was an innocent person damaged by the negligence of the two drivers. He can only claim upon the footing that he himself is a tortfeasor and that the damage is partly the result of his own fault within the Law Reform (Contributory Negligence) Act 1945. Now suppose that a third person was injured in the collision, so that the owners of both cars are liable in tort to the injured person for his full damages. The owner of the chauffeur-driven car obviously cannot recover a full indemnity from his servant or from the owner-driver. He cannot claim as if he were an innocent person who has suffered damage as the result of the negligence of the two drivers. He can only claim as a tortfeasor for contribution under the Act of 1935[1].

My conclusion, therefore, is that the hospital authorities in this case were themselves tortfeasors who have no right to indemnity or contribution from any member of their staff except in so far as the court thinks it just and equitable having regard to the extent of that person's responsibility for the damage. In considering what is just and equitable, I think the court can have regard to extenuating circumstances which would not be available as against the injured person. Errors due to inexperience or lack of supervision are no defence as against the injured person, but they are available to reduce the amount of contribution which the hospital authorities can demand. It would be in the highest degree unjust that hospital authorities, by getting inexperienced doctors to perform their duties for them, without adequate supervision, should be able to throw all the responsibility on to those doctors as if they were fully experienced practitioners. Applying this principle to the present case, I find it very difficult to place much blame on Dr Wilkes. . . .

[HODSON LJ delivered a dissenting judgment.]

Harvey v R G O'Dell Ltd (Galway, Third Party) Queen's Bench Division [1958] 1 All ER 657

Galway was employed by the first defendants as a storekeeper. On their instructions he went from London to Hurley to do some repair work, taking the plaintiff, a fellow employee with him as a passenger in his motor cycle combination. While on a journey from fetching some tools and materials, there was an accident partly due to Galway's negligence in which he was killed and the plaintiff was injured. In an action by the plaintiff against the defendants as Galway's employers, the defendants served a third party notice on Galway's administratrix claiming a contribution against his estate under s. 6(1)(c) of the Act of 1935[1] or alternatively for breach of an implied term in Galway's contract of service that he would indemnify them for any liability arising out of his negligence. McNair J held that, as joint tortfeasors, the defendant employers were entitled to a 100 per cent contribution from Galway's estate. He also considered the alleged implied term.

MCNAIR J: . . . Mr Galway was engaged and employed by the first defendants as a storekeeper; as a concession to the first defendants he from time to time used his own motor cycle on their business and was so using it at the time of the accident. I find it difficult to see on what grounds of justice and reason I should hold that, by making his motor cycle combination available for his employers' business on a particular occasion, he should be held in law to have impliedly agreed to indemnify them if he committed a casual act of negligence. Suppose in a time of labour disturbance in the docks master stevedores, as sometimes happens, induce their office staff to man the cranes or to do stevedoring; if a third party is injured through the negligence of such staff, no doubt the master stevedores would be vicariously liable, as, indeed, they

---

1. [Now replaced by the Civil Liability (Contribution) Act 1978, p. 871, ante.]

might be primarily liable, on the basis that they had employed unskilled persons. But it would surely be contrary to all reason and justice to hold that the willing office staff, by abandoning their ledgers and undertaking manual tasks, had impliedly agreed to indemnify their employers against liability arising from their negligence in performing work which they were not employed to do.

I should, therefore, dismiss the claim of the first defendants against the third party, in so far as it rests on an allegation of breach of the contract of employment. . . .

Question

Did McNair J pose the right question? Should it have been 'Did Galway agree to exercise reasonable care about his employer's business?' (See J. A. Jolowicz (1959) 22 MLR 71, 189.)

Notes

1. The student who relied simply on the law reports for an understanding of the contribution arrangements between employers and their employees would be seriously misled. *Lister*'s case produced an uproar if for no other reason than that 'the friendliest relation between the employer and his staff can now be disrupted, and the employee impoverished, by the action of an insurance company, which finds itself in the happy position of having received premiums for a risk that it does not have to bear.' (G. L. Williams (1957) 20 MLR 220 at 221.) An inter-departmental committee was set up to investigate the position and suggested that trade unions might, by collective bargaining, seek insurance cover for their members. This does not seem to have happened on any significant scale and, in any event, has now been over-taken by the Employers' Liability (Compulsory Insurance) Act 1969 (p. 894, post). Moreover, a so-called 'gentlemen's agreement' among the majority of insurers not to enforce their subrogation rights against employees except in cases of collusion or wilful misconduct, had, according to the inter-departmental committee, prevented any 'practical problem' arising out of *Lister*'s case. Mr (later Lord) Gardiner commented: 'It is not clear that the Committee realised that the "gentlemen's agreement" leaves it open to the insurers to say to a trade union, "If you go on with this action on behalf of your insured member, and we choose with the consent of the assured to claim over against the foreman whose negligence is alleged to have caused the injury, the foreman who is also one of your members, may have to sell up his home."' ((1959) 22 MLR 652 at 654). The 'agreement' was later extended to cover all members of the British Insurance Association, all Lloyd's under-writers concerned with this class of business and nearly all other insurance companies. See generally R. Lewis (1985) 4 SMLR 270.

2. In *Morris v Ford Motor Co Ltd* [1973] QB 792; [1973] 2 All ER 1084, the Court of Appeal sought to limit the application of *Lister*'s case. C was engaged by F to perform cleaning services at F's factory. M, an employee of C, was injured due to the negligent driving of a fork-lift truck by R, one of F's employees. F's insurers paid M's damages and then, in F's name, recovered the full amount from C, in terms of a clause in the contract for cleaning services which obliged C to indemnify F against all losses. C then claimed an indemnity from R, the negligent employee of F. The Court of Appeal acknowledged that C, as indemnitor, was entitled to every right of

action of the person indemnified. However, Lord Denning MR and James LJ (Stamp LJ dissenting) held that, in an industrial setting, subrogation was unacceptable and unrealistic and so there was an implied term that this right was excluded. Lord Denning MR also held that subrogation was an equitable right, and it was not just or equitable to compel F to lend its name to proceedings against R, because this might lead to a strike and, anyway, C had been imprudent in failing to heed advice to insure.

19 Insurance and compensation

'As a general proposition it has not, I think, been questioned for nearly two hundred years that in determining the rights inter se of A and B, the fact that one of them is insured is to be disregarded': per Viscount Simonds in *Lister v Romford Ice and Cold Storage Co Ltd* [1957] 1 All ER 125 at 133 (p. 875, ante).

'Liability and insurance are so intermixed that judicially to alter the basis of liability without adequate knowledge (which we do not have the means to obtain) as to the impact this might make upon the insurance system would be dangerous and, in my opinion, irresponsible': per Lord Wilberforce in *Morgans v Launchbury* [1972] 2 All ER 606 at 611 (p. 823, ante).

These observations reveal a fundamental judicial dilemma implicit in many of the cases collected together in this sourcebook. The common law method of determining liability rests upon the notion of *loss shifting*: either the plaintiff or the defendant, or sometimes both, must individually bear the loss. The predominant mechanism is fault. At the same time, the fact of insurance makes it possible for losses to be *distributed*. Some large enterprises are able to operate as self-insurers and absorb the cost of paying compensation from their own resources. Most organisations and individuals, however, have recourse to insurance. This spreads the risk among those engaged in the same kind of activity—such as manufacturers, motorists or employers—and paying premiums against similar risks. Once this loss distributing function of the law of tort is acknowledged many of the old arguments in favour of the fault principle have to be modified: in particular the imposition of liability on the defendant will not be a crushing economic burden. Occasionally (e.g. the views of Lord Denning MR in cases of economic loss) the courts have denied the existence of a duty of care on the ground that the defendant is not a suitable loss distributor; or (as in *Ackworth v Kempe* (1778) 1 Doug KB 40 and *Lloyd v Grace, Smith & Co* [1912] AC 716) have allowed recovery against an employer for his employee's wrongdoing on the ground that he could protect himself by fidelity insurance. However, these are exceptional cases. The observations in *Morgans v Launchbury* [1973] AC 127, [1972] 2 All ER 606 (p. 819, ante) indicate that English judges are not willing to innovate any general principle of risk distribution, i.e. the imposition of liability upon those parties best placed to act as a conduit of distribution. Any major change in the basis of liability from fault to risk must be sought from Parliament, not the courts.

This does not mean that the student can afford to ignore the facts of insurance. The materials gathered together in this chapter have been relevant in other chapters. It has been suggested that the legal rules have been 'invisibly' affected by the existence of insurance: examples are the development of the manufacturer's duty in negligence (p. 492, ante), the raising of the standard of care required from learner drivers (p. 260, ante), the conversion from 'fault' to 'negligence without fault' through the res ipsa loquitur doctrine (p. 287, ante), the imposition of strict liability for dangerous escapes (p. 650, ante). There is also the power of the insurance companies, having obtained a decision in their favour, to 'buy off' an appeal by paying ample compensation to the appellant so that they will have a legal precedent on their side for use in settling later cases (per Lord Denning MR in *Davis v Johnson* [1979] AC 264 at 278). Legislative policy has also been affected by the insurance situation: examples are the abolition of the rule against actions between husband and wife (Law Reform (Husband and Wife) Act 1962), the removal of the protection afforded to highway authorities Highways (Miscellaneous Provisions) Act 1961, s. 1(1) and see now the Highways Act 1980, s. 58), and the imposition of strict liability for nuclear incidents upon site licensees (Nuclear Installations Act 1965, p. 533, ante).

By far the most important reason for understanding the insurance background is that it enables one to examine how far tort law is coping with the social and economic problem of allocating accident losses. Those who criticise the legal rules often do so because they are seen to be deficient in the performance of this function. The materials in this chapter begin, in s. 1, with the attempts made by Parliament to remedy one obvious injustice, that created by the defendant who is unable to pay. The Road Traffic Act 1988 re-enacts, with later amendments, provisions first enacted in 1930 to compel insurance in respect of death or bodily injury arising from the use of a motor vehicle on a road. The Employers' Liability (Compulsory Insurance) Act 1969, which has been in operation since 1 January 1972, adopts a similar policy in regard to an employer's liability to his employees. Parliament has also assisted the victims of bankrupt tortfeasors by means of the Third Parties (Rights Against Insurers) Act 1930 (p. 896, post) and the Road Traffic Act 1988, s. 153 (p. 890, post).

The courts attempted to create a remedy against the uninsured motorist in *Monk v Warbey* [1935] 1 KB 75 (p. 892, post). But this obviously unsatisfactory device has now almost been supplanted by a fascinating instance of 'private legislation': the agreements between the insurance industry and the government which, ignoring the formal legal rules, promise compensation to the victims of uninsured and untraced motorists. Like the 'gentlemen's agreement' not to rely on *Lister v Romford Ice and Cold Storage Co Ltd* [1957] AC 555, [1957] 1 All ER 125 (p. 881, ante), these agreements remind the student of law that 'black letter' legal rules sometimes bear little relation to social reality. The agreements are printed in the second section of this chapter. There are no corresponding institutions to protect the victims of uninsured or 'fly-by-night' employers.

The third section contains examples of policies offered by a particular insurance company. Insurance is a matter of contract between insurer and insured. The policy may be one of *liability* insurance (e.g. products, employers' or 'public' liability) by which the insurer agrees, in consideration of a premium, to cover specified types of legal liability which the insured may incur. Or it may be one of *loss* (sometimes called 'first-party' or 'personal accident') insurance (e.g. on the life of the insured, or his home or business) by which the insurer agrees, in consideration of a premium, to indemnify the insured in respect of particular losses. Or it may be a combination of liability and loss insurance (e.g. a comprehensive motor insurance policy). A particular risk may be covered by both types of insurance (e.g. the owner of a damaged motor vehicle may claim under his own *loss* insurance policy or make a tort claim against the negligent motorist whose insurer will pay under the latter's *liability* policy). The student of tort is not concerned with the many problems of contract interpretation which may arise under policies such as these. His or her questions ought primarily to be functional ones such as: (1) what limits are there on the various types of liability insurance? (2) what is the effect of the law of contributory negligence on liability insurance? (3) what risks are covered by loss insurance that are not covered by liability insurance? (4) what is the nature and likely effect of no-claims discount clauses? (5) what are the advantages of loss (first-play) insurance in comparison with liability insurance? These and related questions can best be answered by reading the policies in conjunction with *Atiyah*, chaps. 10 and 12; *Williams & Hepple*, chap. 5.

The institution of insurance has an important effect on the conduct of litigation, in particular because of the insurer's right of subrogation (p. 916, post) and his right to full control over the conduct of legal proceedings in the insured's name (the latter being a contractual condition, e.g. p. 913, post). This gives the insured the advantage of expert assistance; but by the same token it means that the uninsured party may find himself without similar assistance. The factors which influence the nature and amount of settlements of tort claims are considered in the fourth section of this chapter.

Tort provides only about one-quarter of all the compensation for personal injury in Britain. The main burden falls on the highly developed and complicated social security system. A brief guide to the main benefits under that system is provided in the fifth section (p. 917, post). One of the state benefits is criminal injuries compensation and the text of the current scheme is printed (p. 920, post).

These other sources of compensation are important to the student of tort in respect of the assessment of tort damages (p. 403, ante). They also have to be understood if there is to be any intelligent discussion of the likely future of tort as a method of compensation for incapacity. The comprehensive social security approach, as in New Zealand, and the alternative strategy of a 'mixed' system avoiding duplication, advocated by the Pearson Commission, are indicated in extracts in the last section of this chapter.

1   Compulsory insurance provisions

The Road Traffic Act 1988

PART VI. THIRD-PARTY LIABILITIES

Compulsory insurance or security against third-party risks

143. Users of motor vehicles to be insured or secured against third-party risks —
(1) Subject to the provisions of this Part of this Act —
   (*a*) a person must not use a motor vehicle on a road unless there is in force in relation to the use of the vehicle by that person such a policy of insurance or such a security in respect of third party risks as complies with the requirements of this Part of this Act, and

(b) a person must not cause or permit any other person to use a motor vehicle on a road unless there is in force in relation to the use of the vehicle by that other person such a policy of insurance or such a security in respect of third party risks as complies with the requirements of this Part of this Act.

(2) If a person acts in contravention of subsection (1) above he is guilty of an offence.

(3) A person charged with using a motor vehicle in contravention of this section shall not be convicted if he proves —

(a) that the vehicle did not belong to him and was not in his possession under a contract of hiring or of loan,

(b) that he was using the vehicle in the course of his employment, and

(c) that he neither knew nor had reason to believe that there was not in force in relation to the vehicle such a policy of insurance or security as is mentioned in subsection (1) above.

(4) This Part of this Act does not apply to invalid carriages.

144. Exceptions from requirement of third-party insurance or security — (1) Section 143 of this Act does not apply to a vehicle owned by a person who has deposited and keeps deposited with the Accountant General of the Supreme Court the sum of £15,000, at a time when the vehicle is being driven under the owner's control.

[Sub-s. (2) provides that s. 143 shall not apply to specified local and police and certain other authorities.]

145. Requirements in respect of policies of insurance — (1) In order to comply with the requirements of this Part of this Act, a policy of insurance must satisfy the following conditions.

(2) The policy must be issued by an authorised insurer.

(3) Subject to subsection (4) below, the policy —

(a) must insure such person, persons or classes of persons as may be specified in the policy in respect of any liability which may be incurred by him or them in respect of the death of or bodily injury to any person or damage to property caused by, or arising out of, the use of the vehicle on a road in Great Britain, and

(b) must insure him or them in respect of any liability which may be incurred by him or them in respect of the use of the vehicle and of any trailer, whether or not coupled, in the territory other than Great Britain and Gibraltar of each of the member States of the Communities according to the law on compulsory insurance against civil liability in respect of the use of vehicles of the State where the liability may be incurred, and

(c) must also insure him or them in respect of any liability which may be incurred by him or them under the provisions of this Part of this Act relating to payment for emergency treatment.

(4) The policy shall not, by virtue of subsection (3)(a) above, be required —

(a) to cover liability in respect of the death, arising out of and in the course of his employment, of a person in the employment of a person insured by the policy or of bodily injury sustained by such a person arising out of and in the course of his employment, or

(b) to provide insurance of more than £250,000 in respect of all such liabilities as may be incurred in respect of damage to property caused by, or arising out of, any one accident involving the vehicle, or

(c) to cover liability in respect of damage to the vehicle, or

(d) to cover liability in respect of damage to goods carried for hire or reward in or on the vehicle or in or on any trailer (whether or not coupled) drawn by the vehicle, or

(e) to cover any liability of a person in respect of damage to property in his custody or under his control, or

(f) to cover any contractual liability.

(5) In this Part of this Act 'authorised insurer' means a person or body of persons carrying on insurance business within Group 2 in Part II of Schedule 2 to the Insurance Companies Act 1982 and being a member of the Motor Insurers' Bureau (a company limited by guarantee and incorporated under the Companies Act 1929 on 14th June 1946).

(6) If any person or body of persons ceases to be a member of the Motor Insurers' Bureau, that person or body shall not by virtue of that cease to be treated as an authorised insurer for the purposes of this Part of this Act—

    (a) in relation to any policy issued by the insurer before ceasing to be such a member, or

    (b) in relation to any obligation (whether arising before or after the insurer ceased to be such a member) which the insurer may be called upon to meet under or in consequence of any such policy or under section 157[1] of this Act by virtue of making a payment in pursuance of such an obligation.

148. Avoidance of certain exceptions to policies or securities—(1) Where a certificate of insurance or certificate of security has been delivered under section 147 of this Act to the person by whom a policy has been effected or to whom a security has been given, so much of the policy or security as purports to restrict—

    (a) the insurance of the persons insured by the policy, or

    (b) the operation of the security,

(as the case may be) by reference to any of the matters mentioned in subsection (2) below shall, as respects such liabilities as are required to be covered by a policy under section 145 of this Act, be of no effect.

(2) Those matters are—

    (a) the age or physical or mental condition of persons driving the vehicle,

    (b) the condition of the vehicle,

    (c) the number of persons that the vehicle carries,

    (d) the weight or physical characteristics of the goods that the vehicle carries,

    (e) the time at which or the areas within which the vehicle is used,

    (f) the horsepower or cylinder capacity or value of the vehicle,

    (g) the carrying on the vehicle of any particular apparatus, or

    (h) the carrying on the vehicle of any particular means of identification other than any means of identification required to be carried by or under the Vehicles (Excise) Act 1971.

(3) Nothing in subsection (1) above requires an insurer or the giver of a security to pay any sum in respect of the liability of any person otherwise than in or towards the discharge of that liability.

(4) Any sum paid by an insurer or the giver of a security in or towards the discharge of any liability of any person which is covered by the policy or security by virtue only of subsection (1) above is recoverable by the insurer or giver of the security from that person.

(5) A condition in a policy or security issued or given for the purposes of this Part of this Act providing—

    (a) that no liability shall arise under the policy or security, or

    (b) that any liability so arising shall cease,

in the event of some specified thing being done or omitted to be done after the happening of the event giving rise to a claim under the policy or security, shall be of no effect in connection with such liabilities as are required to be covered by a policy under section 145 of this Act.

(6) Nothing in subsection (5) above shall be taken to render void any provision in a policy or security requiring the person insured or secured to pay to the insurer or the giver of the security any sums which the latter may have become liable to pay

---

1. [Section 157 deals with payment for hospital treatment of traffic casualties.]

under the policy or security and which have been applied to the satisfaction of the claims of third parties.

(7) Notwithstanding anything in any enactment, a person issuing a policy of insurance under section 145 of this Act shall be liable to indemnify the persons or classes of persons specified in the policy in respect of any liability which the policy purports to cover in the case of those persons or classes of persons.

149. Avoidance of certain agreements as to liability towards passengers — (1) This section applies where a person uses a motor vehicle in circumstances such that under section 143 of this Act there is required to be in force in relation to his use of it such a policy of insurance or such security in respect of third-party as complies with the requirements of this Part of this Act.

(2) If any other person is carried in or upon the vehicle while the user is so using it, any antecedent agreement or understanding between them (whether intended to be legally binding or not) shall be of no effect so far as it purports or might be held —

(*a*) to negative or restrict any such liability of the user in respect of persons carried in or upon the vehicle as is required by section 145 of this Act to be covered by a policy of insurance, or

(*b*) to impose any conditions with respect to the enforcement of any such liability of the user.

(3) The fact that a person so carried has willingly accepted as his the risk of negligence on the part of the user shall not be treated as negativing any such liability of the user.

(4) For the purposes of this section —

(*a*) references to a person being carried in or upon a vehicle include references to a person entering or getting on to, or alighting from, the vehicle, and

(*b*) the reference to an antecedent agreement is to one made at any time before the liability arose.

151. Duty of insurers or persons giving security to satisfy judgment against persons insured or secured against third-party risks — (1) This section applies where, after a certificate of insurance or certificate of security has been delivered under section 147 of this Act to the person by whom a policy has been effected or to whom a security has been given, a judgment to which this subsection applies is obtained.

(2) Subsection (1) above applies to judgments relating to a liability with respect to any matter where liability with respect to that matter is required to be covered by a policy of insurance under section 145 of this Act and either —

(*a*) it is a liability covered by the terms of the policy or security to which the certificate relates, and the judgment is obtained against any person who is insured by the policy or whose liability is covered by the security, as the case may be, or

(*b*) it is a liability, other than an excluded liability, which would be so covered if the policy insured all persons or, as the case may be, the security covered the liability of all persons, and the judgment is obtained against any person other than one who is insured by the policy or, as the case may be, whose liability is covered by the security.

(3) In deciding for the purposes of subsection (2) above whether a liability is or would be covered by the terms of a policy or security, so much of the policy or security as purports to restrict, as the case may be, the insurance of the persons insured by the policy or the operation of the security by reference to the holding by the driver of the vehicle of a licence authorising him to drive it shall be treated as of no effect.

(4) In subsection (2)(*b*) above 'excluded liability' means a liability in respect of the death of, or bodily injury to, or damage to the property of any person who, at the time of the use which gave rise to the liability, was allowing himself to be carried in or upon the vehicle and knew or had reason to believe that the vehicle had been stolen or unlawfully taken, not being a person who —

(a) did not know and had no reason to believe that the vehicle had been stolen or unlawfully taken until after the commencement of his journey, and

(b) could not reasonably have been expected to have alighted from the vehicle.

In this subsection the reference to a person being carried in or upon a vehicle includes a reference to a person entering or getting on to, or alighting from, the vehicle.

(5) Notwithstanding that the insurer may be entitled to avoid or cancel, or may have avoided or cancelled, the policy or security, he must, subject to the provisions of this section, pay to the persons entitled to the benefit of the judgment—

(a) as regards liability in respect of death or bodily injury, any sum payable under the judgment in respect of the liability, together with any sum which, by virtue of any enactment relating to interest on judgments, is payable in respect of interest on that sum,

(b) as regards liability in respect of damage to property, any sum required to be paid under subsection (6) below, and

(c) any amount payable in respect of costs.

(6) This subsection requires—

(a) where the total of any amounts paid, payable or likely to be payable under the policy or security in respect of damage to property caused by, or arising out of, the accident in question does not exceed £250,000, the payment of any sum payable under the judgment in respect of the liability, together with any sum which, by virtue of any enactment relating to interest on judgments, is payable in respect of interest on that sum,

(b) where that total exceeds £250,000, the payment of either—

(i) such proportion of any sum payable under the judgment in respect of the liability as £250,000 bears to that total, together with the same proportion of any sum which, by virtue of any enactment relating to interest on judgments, is payable in respect of interest on that sum, or

(ii) the difference between the total of any amounts already paid under the policy or security in respect of such damage and £250,000, together with such proportion of any sum which, by virtue of any enactment relating to interest on judgments, is payable in respect of interest on any sum payable under the judgment in respect of the liability as the difference bears to that sum,

whichever is the less, unless not less than £250,000 has already been paid under the policy or security in respect of such damage (in which case nothing is payable).

(7) Where an insurer becomes liable under this section to pay an amount in respect of a liability of a person who is insured by a policy or whose liability is covered by a security, he is entitled to recover from that person—

(a) that amount, in a case where he became liable to pay it by virtue only of subsection (3) above, or

(b) in a case where that amount exceeds the amount for which he would, apart from the provisions of this section, be liable under the policy or security in respect of that liability, the excess.

(8) Where an insurer becomes liable under this section to pay an amount in respect of a liability of a person who is not insured by a policy or whose liability is not covered by a security, he is entitled to recover the amount from that person or from any person who—

(a) is insured by the policy, or whose liability is covered by the security, by the terms of which the liability would be covered if the policy insured all persons or, as the case may be, the security covered the liability of all persons, and

(b) caused or permitted the use of the vehicle which gave rise to the liability.

(9) In this section—

(a) 'insurer' includes a person giving a security,

(b) 'material' means of such a nature as to influence the judgment of a prudent insurer in determining whether he will take the risk and, if so, at what premium and on what conditions, and

(c) 'liability covered by the terms of the policy or security' means a liability which is covered by the policy or security or which would be so covered but for the fact that the insurer is entitled to avoid or cancel, or has avoided or cancelled, the policy or security.

[Section 152 sets out exceptions to s. 151.]

153. Bankruptcy, etc, of insured or secured persons not to affect claims by third parties — (1) Where, after a certificate of insurance or certificate of security has been delivered under section 147 of this Act to the person by whom a policy has been effected or to whom a security has been given, any of the events mentioned in subsection (2) below happens, the happening of that event shall, notwithstanding anything in the Third Parties (Rights Against Insurers) Act 1930[1], not affect any such liability of that person as is required to be covered by a policy of insurance under section 145 of this Act.

(2) In the case of the person by whom the policy was effected or to whom the security was given, the events referred to in subsection (1) above are —

(a) that he becomes bankrupt or makes a composition or arrangement with his creditors or that his estate is sequestrated or he grants a trust deed for his creditors,

(b) that he dies and —

(i) his estate falls to be administered in accordance with an order under section 421 of the Insolvency Act 1986,

(ii) an award of sequestration of his estate is made, or

(iii) a judicial factor is appointed to administer his estate under section 11A of the Judicial Factors (Scotland) Act 1889,

(c) that if that person is a company —

(i) a winding-up order or an administration order is made with respect to the company,

(ii) a resolution for a voluntary winding-up is passed with respect to the company,

(iii) a receiver or manager of the company's business or undertaking is duly appointed, or

(iv) possession is taken, by or on behalf of the holders of any debentures secured by a floating charge, of any property comprised in or subject to the charge.

(3) Nothing in subsection (1) above affects any rights conferred by the Third Parties (Rights Against Insurers) Act 1930 on the person to whom the liability was incurred, being rights so conferred against the person by whom the policy was issued or the security was given.

[Section 154 provides for a duty to give information as to insurance or security where a claim is made.]

Notes

1. The duty to insure rests upon the person who 'uses' or 'causes or permits any other person to use' the vehicle. Subject to s. 143(3), a person may breach this duty even though he does not know that there is no policy of insurance in force for the permitted use: *Houston v Buchanan* 1940 SC (HL) 17. In

---

1. [See p. 896, post for this Act.]

addition to a fine or imprisonment, the offender's driving licence must be endorsed and he may be disqualified from driving: Road Traffic Offenders Act 1988, Sch. 2. There may also be a civil action for breach of statutory duty: see post.

2. It is the *use* of the vehicle which must be covered by insurance and not the personal or vicarious liability of the owner. So a situation may arise in which the owner is responsible in law (limited in *Morgans v Launchbury* [1972] AC 127, [1972] 2 All ER 606, p. 819, ante, to the delegation of driving for the owner's purposes) but the use is not insured. This can happen because, by contract with the insurer, the owner may stipulate that the insurance covers the use of the vehicle only when used by himself or particular named drivers. If he nevertheless permits someone other than those named to use the vehicle he commits a criminal offence and may be liable in damages for breach of statutory duty. This is cumbersome and of little value to the person who suffers loss by virtue of the owner's failure to insure because, ex hypothesi, the owner will be uninsured in such cases and probably without funds to pay. Some other countries arrange matters more sensibly by attaching the insurance to the *vehicle* and not its *user* by particular drivers.

3. The provisions of ss. 145(1) and 145(3)(a) of the Road Traffic Act 1988 do not require insurance against the death or personal injury of the person actually driving the vehicle but are only intended to cover the user's liability to third parties: *Cooper v Motor Insurers' Bureau* [1985] QB 575, [1985] 1 All ER 449.

4. Since 1 December 1972, it has been compulsory to insure against liability to passengers (now Road Traffic Act 1988, s. 145). Under s. 149(3) the user cannot restrict his liability, either through agreement or by operation of the defence of volenti non fit injuria, by a notice on the dashboard saying 'Passengers ride at their own risk and on the condition that no claim shall be made against the driver or owner'. See further p. 389, ante.

5. Section 148(7) overcomes the inconvenient 'privity of contract' rule by enabling any person covered by the policy to sue upon the contract of insurance: *Tattersall v Drysdale* [1935] 2 KB 174 (decided under provisions of the 1930 Road Traffic Act corresponding to s. 148(7) of the 1988 Act). But the person covered must take the policy as he finds it and must comply with all conditions: *Austin v Zurich Accident and Liability Insurance Co* [1945] KB 250, [1945] 1 All ER 316.

6. Liability to employees will not be covered by a road traffic policy (s. 145(4)(a), but by an employer's liability policy (p. 894, post).

7. Section 7 of the Policyholders Protection Act 1975 requires the Policyholders Protection Board, set up by that Act and financed by levies on the insurance industry, to secure payment of the full amount that an insurance company in liquidation is liable to pay to a person entitled to the benefits of a judgment under s. 151 of the Road Traffic Act 1988. Section 6 requires the Board to secure payment to the full extent that a company in liquidation is liable to pay to a UK policyholder in respect of liability subject to compulsory insurance (including under Part VI of the Road Traffic Act 1988).

Monk *v* Warbey Court of Appeal [1934] All ER Rep 373

GREER LJ: This appeal raises one question of considerable public importance, and though I might in other respects have been content with saying that I have read Charles J's very careful judgment and that I agree with every word of it, having regard to the fact that other cases may be affected by our judgment, I think it necessary to add some few words.

The facts can be stated quite shortly. Warbey, the defendant to the action in the court below and the appellant in this court, was the owner of a motor car which he had insured under a Lloyd's policy in which the liability was described under the head of 'Liability to the public' as 'liability at law for compensation for death or bodily injury caused by the use of the car'. The question whether or not the events which happened in this case were within the terms of the policy has not been presented for argument either in the court below or in this court. It was conceded by the parties when this came before the court that the policy did not cover the events that happened, and the action which was brought by the plaintiff was an action on the ground that there had been a breach of the statutory duty imposed by s. 35 of the Road Traffic Act 1930, and the damages which he sought to recover were alleged to be the result of that breach of the statute.

In his clear-cut argument counsel for the defendant takes three points. First, he submits to this court that the learned judge was wrong in deciding that a breach of s. 35 was available for the benefit of the plaintiff, who alleged that he had been injured by the negligent driving of the motor car by the servant of an uninsured person, and his contention is — and the matter is capable of considerable argument — that, having regard to the fact that a very serious penalty is imposed by the statute for the breach of s. 35, it cannot be concluded that that section was intended to create any right on the part of a member of the public who was injured by reason of the breach. Numbers of cases have been cited. In my judgment, this is a stronger case in favour of the plaintiff than *Groves v Lord Wimborne*[1] and the cases which relate to breaches of statutory duties towards minors, such as *Britannic Merthyr Coal Co Ltd v David*.[2]

The Road Traffic Act 1930, was passed in these circumstances. It had become apparent that people who were injured by the negligence of drivers of motor cars on the roads were in a parlous situation if they happened to be injured by somebody who was unable to pay damages for the injuries which they had suffered, and, accordingly, two Acts were passed. One was for the purpose of enabling persons who were so injured to recover, in the case of the bankruptcy of the insured person, the money which would be payable to him by the insurance company — that is the Third Parties (Rights Against Insurers) Act 1930. It was thought right by Parliament that in such a case the insurers' money should not go to the general creditors of the bankrupt, but should be available for the purpose of compensating the injured person, and it was provided that in the case of bankruptcy proceedings being taken against a defendant who could not pay the amount of the damage, but was insured, then in the course of the bankruptcy the person injured could make the insurance company liable for the damage caused to him although he was not a party to the contract of insurance. But that did not meet the whole difficulty because the owners of motor cars sometimes lent their motor cars to uninsured persons, and if the person causing the injury was an uninsured person then the remedy provided by that Act to which I have just referred was unavailable for the injured person. Provision, therefore, was made in the Road Traffic Act 1930, for the protection of third persons against the risks arising out of the negligent driving of a motor vehicle by an uninsured person to whom an insured owner had lent his car and, in connection with such protection, to amend the

---

1. [1898] 2 QB 402.
2. [1910] AC 74.

Assurance Companies Act 1909. How could Parliament make provision for the protection of third parties against such risks if it did not enable an injured third person to recover for a breach of s. 35 of the Road Traffic Act 1930? That section is to be found in Part II of the Act, which is headed 'Provision against third party risks arising out of the use of motor vehicles'. It would be a very poor protection of the person injured by the negligence of an uninsured person to whom a car had been lent by an insured person if the person injured had no civil remedy for a breach of the section. . . .

The power to prosecute for a penalty is no protection whatever to the injured person except in the sense that it affords a strong incentive for people not to break the provisions of the statute. But the power to prosecute is a poor consolation to the man who has been damaged by reason of a breach of the provisions of s. 35. . . .

[MAUGHAM and ROCHE LJJ delivered judgments in favour of dismissing the appeal.]

Appeal dismissed

Notes

1. In *Martin v Dean* [1971] 2 QB 208, [1971] 3 All ER 279, John Stephenson J held that it is not necessary for the plaintiff in an action of the *Monk v Warbey* type to show that the uninsured driver will not pay at all. The plaintiff may claim damages in the same action against the driver alleging negligence and against the vehicle owner alleging breach of the statutory duty to insure. Judgment will be given against the owner if the evidence shows that the driver is a man of limited means, unable to satisfy the judgment against him promptly.

2. We have seen that breach of the Motor Vehicles (Use and Construction) Regulations, which prescribe in detail the mode of construction of motor vehicles, has been held not to give a private remedy to the person injured (p. 545, ante). Is there any justification for allowing an action in tort in the *Monk v Warbey* situation, when it is not allowed in other cases of breach of road safety legislation? Do you agree with G. L. Williams (1960) 23 MLR 233 at 259, that *Monk v Warbey* is an 'improper type of judicial invention'? Note that it imposes liability without fault upon a defendant who is, ex hypothesi, uninsured.

3. The plaintiff nowadays will give notice of the bringing of proceedings against an uninsured driver, within seven days after the commencement of the proceedings, to the Motor Insurers' Bureau. (See the agreement between the Secretary of State for the Environment and the MIB, p. 898, post.) Although the MIB may require the plaintiff to take all reasonable steps to 'obtain judgment against all the persons liable' (para. 5(1)(d)), any unsatisfied judgment will be paid by the MIB. The practical importance of *Monk v Warbey* therefore seems to be limited to those situations in which there is a relatively wealthy owner who has permitted his vehicle to be used without compulsory insurance cover. But in law the existence of the MIB agreements does not affect the action for breach of statutory duty: *Corfield v Groves* [1950] 1 All ER 488.

The Employers' Liability (Compulsory Insurance) Act 1969

An Act to require employers to insure against their liability for personal injury to their employees, and for purposes connected with the matter aforesaid

1. Insurance against liability for employees. — (1) Except as otherwise provided by this Act, every employer carrying on any business in Great Britain shall insure, and maintain insurance, under one or more approved policies with an authorised insurer or insurers against liability for bodily injury or disease sustained by his employees, and arising out of and in the course of their employment in Great Britain in that business, but except in so far as regulations otherwise provide not including injury or disease suffered or contracted outside Great Britain.

(2) Regulations may provide that the amount for which an employer is required by this Act to insure and maintain insurance shall, either generally or in such cases or classes of case as may be prescribed by the regulations, be limited in such manner as may be so prescribed.

(3) For the purposes of this Act —

(a) 'approved policy' means a policy of insurance not subject to any conditions or exceptions prohibited for those purposes by regulations;

(b) 'authorised insurer' means a person or body of persons lawfully carrying on in [the United Kingdom insurance business of a class specified in Schedule 1 or 2 to the Insurance Companies Act 1982][1] and issuing the policy or policies in the course thereof;

(c) 'business' includes a trade or profession, and includes any activity carried on by a body of persons, whether corporate or unincorporate;

(d) except as otherwise provided by regulations, an employer not having a place of business in Great Britain shall be deemed not to carry on business there.

2. Employees to be covered. — (1) For the purposes of this Act the term 'employee' means an individual who has entered into or works under a contract of service or apprenticeship with an employer whether by way of manual labour, clerical work or otherwise, whether such contract is expressed or implied, oral or in writing.

(2) This Act shall not require an employer to insure —

(a) in respect of an employee of whom the employer is the husband, wife, father, mother, grandfather, grandmother, step-father, step-mother, son, daughter, grandson, granddaughter, step-son, step-daughter, brother, sister, half-brother or half-sister; or

(b) except as otherwise provided by regulations, in respect of employees not ordinarily resident in Great Britain.

3. Employers exempted from insurance. — (1) This Act shall not require any insurance to be effected by —

(a) any such authority as is mentioned in subsection (2) below; or

(b) any body corporate established by or under any enactment for the carrying on of any industry or part of an industry, or of any undertaking, under national ownership or control; or

(c) in relation to any such cases as may be specified in the regulations, any employer exempted by regulations.

(2)[2] The authorities referred to in subsection (1)(a) above are the Common Council of the City of London [. . .] the council of a London borough, the council of a county,

---

1. [Amended by the Insurance Companies Act 1981, s. 36(1), Sch. 4, Part II, para. 19, and the Insurance Companies Act 1982, s. 99(2), Sch. 5, para. 8.]
2. [As amended by various statutes.]

[. . .] or county district in England or Wales, [the Boards Authority,] a [regional, islands] or district in Scotland, any joint board or joint committee in England and Wales or joint committee in Scotland which is so constituted as to include among its members representatives of any such council, [. . .] a joint authority established by Part IV of the Local Government Act 1985] and any police authority.

5. Penalty for failure to insure. — An employer who on any day is not insured in accordance with this Act when required to be so shall be guilty of an offence and shall be liable on summary conviction to a fine not exceeding [level 4 on the standard scale][1]; and where an offence under this section committed by a corporation has been committed with the consent or connivance of, or facilitated by any neglect on the part of, any director, manager, secretary or other officer of the corporation, he, as well as the corporation shall be deemed to be guilty of that offence and shall be liable to be proceeded against and punished accordingly.

The Employers' Liability (Compulsory Insurance) General Regulations 1971, S.I. 1971 No. 1117

The Secretary of State, in exercise of his powers under sections 1(2) and (3)(*a*), 2(2), 4(1) and (2) and 6 of the Employers' Liability (Compulsory Insurance) Act 1969 (hereinafter referred to as 'the Act') and of all other powers enabling him in that behalf, hereby makes the following Regulations . . .

Prohibition of certain conditions in policies of insurance. — **2.** — (1) Any condition in a policy of insurance issued or renewed in accordance with the requirements of the Act after the coming into operation of this Regulation which provides (in whatever terms) that no liability (either generally or in respect of a particular claim) shall arise under the policy, or that any such liability so arising shall cease —
  (*a*) in the event of some specified thing being done or omitted to be done after the happening of the event giving rise to a claim under the policy;
  (*b*) unless the policy holder takes reasonable care to protect his employees against the risk of bodily injury or disease in the course of their employment;
  (*c*) unless the policy holder complies with the requirements of any enactment for the protection of employees against the risk of bodily injury or disease in the course of their employment; and
  (*d*) unless the policy holder keeps specified records or provides the insurer with or makes available to him information therefrom,
is hereby prohibited for the purposes of the Act.
  (2) Nothing in this Regulation shall be taken as prejudicing any provision in a policy requiring the policy holder to pay to the insurer any sums which the latter may have become liable to pay under the policy and which have been applied to the satisfaction of claims in respect of employees or any costs and expenses incurred in relation to such claims.

Limit of amount of compulsory insurance. — **3.** The amount for which an employer is required by the Act to insure and maintain insurance shall be two million pounds in respect of claims relating to any one or more of his employees arising out of any one occurrence.

---

1. [Inserted by the Criminal Justice Act 1982, s. 46.]

Notes

1. It will be observed that the employee is not given a statutory right, analogous to that given to the road traffic victim by s. 148(7) of the Road Traffic Act 1988, to sue upon the contract of insurance. What is the significance of the Employers' Liability (Compulsory Insurance) General Regulations 1971, reg. 2(2), ante? (See the Employers' Liability policy, p. 906, post.)

2. There is no Employers' Liability Insurers' Bureau comparable to the Motor Insurers' Bureau (p. 898, post) but the Policyholders Protection Board is required to secure in full any payment that a company in liquidation is liable to pay to a UK policyholder in respect of liability subject to compulsory insurance under the 1969 Act (Policyholders Protection Act 1975, s. 6). For general comment on the Act, see R. C. Simpson (1972) 35 MLR 63; R. A. Hasson (1974) 3 ILJ 79.

The Third Parties (Rights Against Insurers) Act 1930

1. Rights of third parties against insurers on bankruptcy, etc, of the insured.[1] —
(1) Where under any contract of insurance a person (hereinafter referred to as the insured) is insured against liabilities to third parties which he may incur, then —
> (a) in the event of the insured becoming bankrupt or making a composition or arrangement with his creditors; or
> (b) in the case of the insured being a company, in the event of a winding-up order [or an administration order] being made, or a resolution for a voluntary winding-up being passed, with respect to the company, or of a receiver or manager of the company's business or undertaking being duly appointed, or of possession being taken, by or on behalf of the holders of any debentures secured by a floating charge, of any property comprised in or subject to the charge [or of[a voluntary arrangement proposed for the purposes of Part I of the Insolvency Act 1986 being approved under the Part]];

if, either before or after that event, any such liability as aforesaid is incurred by the insured, his rights against the insurer under the contract in respect of the liability shall, notwithstanding anything in any Act or rule of law to the contrary, be transferred to and vest in the third party to whom the liability was so incurred.

(2) Where [the estate of any person falls to be administered in accordance with an order under section [421 of the Insolvency Act 1986]], then, if any debt provable in bankruptcy [(in Scotland, any claim accepted in the sequestration)] is owing by the

---

1. [The words in the first pair of square brackets and the words in the second (outer) pair of square brackets in sub-s. (1) were inserted by the Insolvency Act 1985, s. 235(1), Sch. 8, para. 7(2), and the words in the third (inner) pair of square brackets in that subsection were substituted by the Insolvency Act 1986, s. 439(2), Sch. 14.

    The words in the first (outer) pair of square brackets in sub-s. (2) were inserted by s. 235(1) of, and Sch. 8, para. 7(2) to, the 1985 Act and the words in the second (inner) pair of square brackets in that subsection were substituted by s. 439(2) of, and Sch. 14 to, the 1986 Act. The words in the third pair of square brackets in that subsection were inserted by the Bankruptcy (Scotland) Act 1985, s. 75(1), Sch. 7, Pt. I, para. 6(1). The words in the fourth pair of square brackets in that subsection were substituted by the Insolvency Act 1985, s. 235(1), Sch. 8, para. 7(2).

    The words in the first (outer) pair of square brackets in sub-s. (3) were inserted by the Insolvency Act 1985, s. 235(1), Sch. 8, para. 7(2), and the words in the second (inner) pair of square brackets in that subsection were substituted by s. 439(2) of, and Sch. 14 to, the 1986 Act.]

deceased in respect of a liability against which he was insured under a contract of insurance as being a liability to a third party, the deceased debtor's rights against the insurer under the contract in respect of that liability shall, notwithstanding anything in [any such order], be transferred to and vest in the person to whom the debt is owing.

(3) In so far as any contract of insurance made after the commencement of this Act in respect of any liability of the insured to third parties purports, whether directly or indirectly, to avoid the contract or to alter the rights of the parties thereunder upon the happening to the insured of any of the events specified in paragraph (a) or paragraph (b) of subsection (1) of this section or upon the [estate of any person falling to be administered in accordance with an order under section [421 of the Insolvency Act 1986]], the contract shall be of no effect.

(4) Upon a transfer under subsection (1) or subsection (2) of this section, the insurer shall, subject to the provisions of section three of this Act, be under the same liability to the third party as he would have been under to the insured, but —

(a) if the liability of the insurer to the insured exceeds the liability of the insured to the third party, nothing in this Act shall affect the rights of the insured against the insurer in respect of the excess; and

(b) if the liability of the insurer to the insured is less than the liability of the insured to the third party, nothing in this Act shall affect the rights of the third party against the insured in respect of the balance.

(5) For the purposes of this Act, the expression 'liabilities to third parties', in relation to a person insured under any contract of insurance, shall not include any liability of that person in the capacity of insurer under some other contract of insurance.

(6) This Act shall not apply —

(a) where a company is wound up voluntarily merely for the purposes of reconstruction or of amalgamation with another company; or

(b) to any case to which subsections (1) and (2) of section seven of the Workmen's Compensation Act 1925 applies.

3. Settlement between insurers and insured persons.[1] — Where the insured has become bankrupt or where in the case of the insured being a company, a winding-up order [or an administration order] has been made or a resolution for a voluntary winding-up has been passed, with respect to the company, no agreement made between the insurer and the insured after liability has been incurred to a third party and after the commencement of the bankruptcy or winding-up [or the day of the making of the administration order], as the case may be, nor any waiver, assignment, or other disposition made by, or payment made to the insured after the commencement [or day] aforesaid shall be effective to defeat or affect the rights transferred to the third party under this Act, but those rights shall be the same as if no such agreement, waiver, assignment, disposition or payment had been made.

Notes

1. This Act does not prevent the insurer from avoiding the policy, e.g. on grounds of material non-disclosure by the insured: *McCormick v National Motor and Accident Insurance Union Ltd* (1934) 49 Ll L Rep 361.

2. The liability of the assured has to be established before there can be any basis for an action against the liability insurers under the Act. In *Bradley v Eagle Star Insurance Co Ltd* [1989] AC 957, [1989] 1 All ER 961 the House

---

1. [The words in square brackets were inserted by the Insolvency Act 1985, s. 235(1), Sch. 8, para. 7(4).]

of Lords, Lord Templeman dissenting, held that the dissolution of a company prevented it from being sued and thus prevented its liability to the plaintiff from being established. This decision affected a large number of pending cases involving plaintiffs who did not realise that they had claims against the company which had employed them or their relatives, until after the company had been removed from the register of companies. Under s. 651 of the Companies Act 1985, application could be made to the court for the revival of a company to allow it to be sued, but this was of no use in *Bradley* because the application had to be made within two years of dissolution. As a result of amendments to s. 651 introduced by the Companies Act 1989, the two-year limitation has been removed in cases where the applicant is seeking damages in relation to death or personal injury and these amendments are retroactive for twenty years. Consequently claims such as those in *Bradley* are now possible under the 1930 Act, provided that the claim against the company is not statute-barred and the plaintiff can prove that the company's negligence or breach of duty caused the loss.

2 Motor Insurers' Bureau

Compensation of Victims of Uninsured Drivers: Text of an Agreement Dated 21st December 1988 Between the Secretary of State For Transport and the Motor Insurers' Bureau

In accordance with the Agreement made on 31st December 1945 between the Minister of War Transport and insurers transacting compulsory motor vehicle insurance business in Great Britain (published by the Stationery Office under the title 'Motor Vehicle Insurance Fund') a corporation called the 'Motor Insurers' Bureau' entered into an agreement on 17 June 1946 with the Minister of Transport to give effect from 1 July 1946 to the principle recommended in July 1937 by the Departmental Committee under Sir Felix Cassel, (Cmnd 5528), to secure compensation to third party victims of road accidents in cases where, notwithstanding the provisions of the Road Traffic Acts relating to compulsory insurance, the victim is deprived of compensation by the absence of insurance, or of effective insurance. That Agreement was replaced by an Agreement which operated in respect of accidents occurring on or after 1 March 1971 which in turn was replaced by a new Agreement which operated in respect of accidents occurring on or after 1 December 1972. The Agreement of 1972 has now been replaced by a new Agreement which operates in respect of accidents occurring on or after 31 December 1988.

The text of the new Agreement is as follows—

MEMORANDUM OF AGREEMENT made the 21st day of December 1988 between the Secretary of State for Transport and the Motor Insurers' Bureau, whose registered office is at New Garden House, 78 Hatton Garden, London EC1N 8JQ (hereinafter referred to as 'M.I.B.') SUPPLEMENTAL to an Agreement (hereinafter called 'the Principal Agreement') made the 31st Day of December 1945 between the Minister of War Transport and the insurers transacting compulsory motor insurance business in Great Britain by or on behalf of whom the said Agreement was signed and in pursuance of paragraph 1 of which M.I.B. was incorporated.

IT IS HEREBY AGREED AS FOLLOWS—

Definitions

1. In this Agreement—

'contract of insurance' means a policy of insurance or a security;
'insurer' includes the giver of a security;
'relevant liability' means a liability in respect of which a policy of insurance must insure a person in order to comply with Part VI of the Road Traffic Act 1972[1], and references to the Road Traffic Act 1972 are references to that Act as amended by the Motor Vehicles (Compulsory Insurance) Regulations 1987 (No. 2171).

Satisfaction of Claims by M.I.B.

2. (1) If judgment in respect of any relevant liability is obtained against any person or persons in any Court in Great Britain whether or not such a person or persons be in fact covered by a contract of insurance and any such judgment is not satisfied in full within seven days from the date upon which the person or persons in whose favour the judgment was given became entitled to enforce it then M.I.B. will, subject to the provisions of paragraphs (2), (3) and (4) below and to Clauses 4, 5 and 6 hereof, pay or satisfy or cause to be paid or satisfied to or to the satisfaction of the person or persons in whose favour the judgment was given any sum payable or remaining payable thereunder in respect of the relevant liability including any sum awarded by the Court in respect of interest on that sum and any taxed costs or any costs awarded by the Court without taxation (or such proportion thereof as is attributable to the relevant liability) whatever may be the cause of the failure of the judgment debtor to satisfy the judgment.

(2) Subject to paragraphs (3) and (4) below and to Clauses 4, 5 and 6 hereof, M.I.B. shall incur liability under paragraph (1) above in respect of any sum awarded under such a judgment in respect of property damage not exceeding £250,000 or in respect of the first £250,000 of any sum so awarded exceeding that amount.

(3) Where a person in whose favour a judgment in respect of a relevant liability which includes liability in respect of damage to property has been given, has received or is entitled to receive in consequence of a claim he has made, compensation from any source in respect of that damage, M.I.B. may deduct from the sum payable or remaining payable under paragraph (1) above an amount equal to the amount of that compensation in addition to the deduction of £175 by virtue of paragraph (4) below. The reference to compensation includes compensation under insurance arrangements.

(4) M.I.B. shall not incur liability under paragraph (1) above in respect of any amount payable or remaining payable under the judgment in respect of property damage liability where the total of amounts so payable or remaining payable is £175 or less, or, where the total of such amounts is more than £175, in respect of the first £175 of such total.

Period of Agreement

3. This Agreement shall be determinable by the Secretary of State at any time or by M.I.B. on twelve months' notice without prejudice to the continued operation of the Agreement in respect of accidents occurring before the date of termination.

---

1. [See now Part VI of the Road Traffic Act 1988, part of which has been set out p. 885, ante.]

Recoveries

4. Nothing in this Agreement shall prevent insurers from providing by conditions in their contracts of insurance that all sums paid by them or by M.I.B. by virtue of the Principal Agreement or this Agreement in or towards the discharge of the liability of their insured shall be recoverable by them or by M.I.B. from the insured or from any other person.

Conditions Precedent to M.I.B.'s Liability

5. (1) M.I.B. shall not incur any liability under Clause 2 of this Agreement unless—
  (*a*) notice in writing of the bringing of the proceedings is given within seven days after the commencement of the proceedings—
    (i) to M.I.B. in the case of proceedings in respect of a relevant liability which is either not covered by a contract of insurance or covered by a contract of insurance with an insurer whose identity cannot be ascertained, or
    (ii) to the insurer in the case of proceedings in respect of a relevant liability which is covered by a contract of insurance with an insurer whose identity can be ascertained;
  Such notice shall be accompanied by a copy of the writ, summons or other document initiating the proceedings;
  (*b*) the person bringing the proceedings furnishes to M.I.B.—
    (i) such information (in such form as M.I.B. may specify) in relation thereto as M.I.B. may reasonably require; and
    (ii) such information (in such form as M.I.B. may specify) as to any insurance covering any damage to property to which the claim or proceedings relate and any claim made in respect of that damage under the insurance or otherwise and any report which may have been made or notification which may have been given to any person in respect of that damage or the use of the vehicle giving rise thereto, as M.I.B. may reasonably require;
  (*c*) the person bringing the proceedings has demanded the information and, where appropriate, the particulars specified in section 151 of the Road Traffic Act 1972[1] in accordance with that section or, if so required by M.I.B., has authorised M.I.B. to do so on his behalf;
  (*d*) if so required by M.I.B. and subject to full indemnity from M.I.B. as to costs the person bringing the proceedings has taken all reasonable steps to obtain judgment against all the persons liable in respect of the injury or death or damage to property and, in the event of any such person being a servant or agent, against his principal; and
  (*e*) the judgment referred to in Clause 2 of this Agreement and any judgment referred to in paragraph (*d*) of this Clause which has been obtained (whether or not either judgment includes an amount in respect of a liability other than a relevant liability) and any order for costs are assigned to M.I.B. or their nominee.

(2) In the event of any dispute as to the reasonableness of a requirement by M.I.B. for the supply of information or that any particular step should be taken to obtain judgment against other persons it may be referred to the Secretary of State whose decision shall be final.

(3) Where a judgment which includes an amount in respect of a liability other than a relevant liability has been assigned to M.I.B. or their nominee in pursuance of paragraph (1)(*e*) of this Clause M.I.B. shall apportion any monies received in pursuance of the judgment according to the proportion which the damages in respect of

---

1. [See now s. 154 of the Road Traffic Act 1988.]

the relevant liability bear to the damages in respect of the other liabilities and shall account to the person in whose favour the judgment was given in respect of such monies received properly apportionable to the other liabilities. Where an order for costs in respect of such a judgment has been so assigned monies received pursuant to the order shall be dealt with in the same manner.

Exceptions

6. (1) M.I.B. shall not incur any liability under Clause 2 of this Agreement in a case where —
   (a) the claim arises out of the use of a vehicle owned by or in the possession of the Crown, except where any other person has undertaken responsibility for the existence of a contract of insurance under Part VI of the Road Traffic Act 1972[1] (whether or not the person or persons liable be in fact covered by a contract of insurance) or where the liability is in fact covered by a contract of insurance;
   (b) the claim arises out of the use of a vehicle the use of which is not required to be covered by a contract of insurance by virtue of section 144 of the Road Traffic Act 1972[1], unless the use is in fact covered by such a contract;
   (c) the claim is in respect of a judgment or any part thereof which has been obtained by virtue of the exercise of a right of subrogation by any person;
   (d) the claim is in respect of damage to property which consists of damage to a motor vehicle or losses arising therefrom if at the time of the use giving rise to the damage to the motor vehicle there was not in force in relation to the use of that vehicle when the damage to it was sustained such a policy of insurance as is required by Part VI of the Road Traffic Act 1972[2] and the person or persons claiming in respect of the loss or damage either knew or ought to have known that that was the case;
   (e) at the time of the use which gave rise to the liability the person suffering death or bodily injury or damage to property was allowing himself to be carried in or upon the vehicle and either before the commencement of his journey in the vehicle or after such commencement if he could reasonably be expected to have alighted from the vehicle he —
       (i) knew or ought to have known that the vehicle had been stolen or unlawfully taken, or
       (ii) knew or ought to have known that the vehicle was being used without there being in force in relation to its use such a contract of insurance as would comply with Part VI of the Road Traffic Act 1972[2].
   (2) The exception specified in sub-paragraph (1)(e) of this Clause shall apply only in a case where the judgment in respect of which the claim against M.I.B. is made was obtained in respect of a relevant liability incurred by the owner or a person using the vehicle in which the person who suffered death or bodily injury or sustained damage to property was being carried.
   (3) For the purposes of these exceptions —
   (a) a vehicle which has been unlawfully removed from the possession of the Crown shall be taken to continue in that possession whilst it is kept so removed;
   (b) references to a person being carried in a vehicle include references to his being carried in or upon or entering or getting on to or alighting from the vehicle; and

---

1. [See now Part VI of the Road Traffic Act 1988, part of which has been set out p. 885, ante.]
2. [See now s. 144 of the Road Traffic Act 1988 (p. 886, ante).]

(c) 'owner' in relation to a vehicle which is the subject of a hiring agreement or a hire-purchase agreement, means the person in possession of the vehicle under that agreement.

Agents

7. Nothing in this Agreement shall prevent M.I.B. performing their obligations under this Agreement by Agents.

Operation

8. This Agreement shall come into operation on 31 December 1988 in relation to accidents occurring on or after that date. The Agreement made on 22 November 1972 between the Secretary of State and M.I.B. shall cease and determine except in relation to claims arising out of accidents occurring before 31 December 1988.[1]

Notes

1. There is a separate agreement, dated 22 November 1972, and a supplemental agreement dated 7 December 1977, between the Secretary of State and the MIB to secure compensation for third party victims of road accidents when the driver responsible for the accident cannot be traced. There is a right of appeal to an arbitrator against the decision of the MIB: clause 11. See generally D. B. Williams, *Claiming Against the Motor Insurers' Bureau: A Short Guide* (London, 1989).

2. These agreements are contracts between the Secretary of State for the Environment and the MIB; there is no privity of contract with third party victims of uninsured or untraced drivers. However, the MIB has said it will never take the point (see the remarks of Viscount Dilhorne in *Albert v Motor Insurers' Bureau* [1972] AC 301 at 320, and Lord Denning MR in *Hardy v Motor Insurers' Bureau* [1964] 2 QB 745 at 757, and the Court of Appeal has not been willing to take the point of its own accord: *Coward v Motor Insurers' Bureau* [1963] 1 QB 259 at 265). The Bureau is entitled to be added as a defendant in an action by a third party victim where this is necessary to ensure that all issues are dealt with. (Compare *Gurtner v Circuit* [1968] 2 QB 587, [1968] 1 All ER 328, where the MIB was joined, with *White v London Transport Executive* [1971] 2 QB 721, [1971] 3 All ER 1, where it was not joined as a defendant.) For the history and difficulties of the use of this kind of private agreement to which members of the public are not party, see R. Lewis (1985) 48 MLR 275 at 279–281.

3. The MIB is bound to pay even though the driver intentionally causes the injury: *Gardner v Moore* [1984] AC 548, [1984] 1 All ER 1100, in which the House of Lords approved *Hardy v Motor Insurers' Bureau* [1964] 2 QB 745, [1964] 2 All ER 742. Diplock LJ said in this latter case (at p. 752):

'The liability of the assured, and thus the rights of the third party against the insurers, can only arise out of some wrongful (tortious) act of the assured. I can see no reason in public policy for drawing a distinction between one kind of wrongful act, of which

---

1. [The text of the Agreement made on 22 November 1972 will be found in the 3rd edn of this book, pp. 781–783.]

a third party is the innocent victim, and another kind of wrongful act; between wrongful acts which are crimes on the part of the perpetrator and wrongful acts which are not crimes, or between wrongful acts which are crimes of carelessness and wrongful acts which are intentional crimes. It seems to me to be slightly unrealistic to suggest that a person who is not deterred by the risk of a possible sentence of life imprisonment from using a vehicle with intent to commit grievous bodily harm would be deterred by the fear that his civil liability to his victim would not be discharged by his insurers. I do not, myself, feel that, by dismissing this appeal, we shall add significantly to the statistics of crime.'

4. The MIB is bound to pay only if the vehicle is on a 'road' at the time of the accident: *Randall v Motor Insurers' Bureau* [1969] 1 All ER 21, [1968] 1 WLR 1900 (part of lorry on private ground but greater part on public road; held use on road caused injury).

3 Insurance documents

There are considerable variations in the type and form of policies available from different companies. Those below are reproduced by kind permission of the Guardian Royal Exchange Assurance Group. Since most students have access to a private motor car insurance policy and a home insurance policy, we have, for reasons of space, limited our selection to two types of policy: liability insurance and business interruption.

Liability Insurance Policy

The Insured by a proposal (including supplementary information) which shall be the basis of and incorporated in this contract having applied to the GRE (UK) Limited (the Company) for this insurance and having paid or agreed to pay the Premium.

The Company will provide insurance as described in the following pages in respect of the Sections indicated in the Schedule.

SECTION A – PUBLIC LIABILITY

The Company will subject to the terms of and endorsements to this section and the conditions of this Policy indemnify the Insured against all sums which the Insured becomes legally liable to pay as damages in respect of
  (1) bodily injury (including death or disease) to any person
  (2) loss of or damage to property
  (3) trespass nuisance or any interference with any right of way light air or water happening
    (*a*) within Great Britain Northern Ireland the Channel Islands and the Isle of Man
    (*b*) elsewhere in the world in connection with visits by Employees normally resident in and travelling from the territories mentioned in (*a*)
    during the Period of Insurance in connection with the Business
The indemnity provided shall include an indemnity against liability arising from defective work carried out by or on behalf of the Insured to any premises within the territories mentioned in (*a*) above disposed of by the Insured prior to the occurrence of the bodily injury or damage to property giving rise to liability
  The Company will also pay Legal Costs and Solicitor's Fees

LIMIT OF INDEMNITY

The liability of the Company for all damages payable arising out of one occurrence or series of occurrences consequent on one original cause shall not exceed the Limit of Indemnity

EXCEPTIONS

(1) The Company will not indemnify the Insured against liability arising from
   (a) bodily injury sustained by an Employee and arising out of and in the course of their employment or engagement by the Insured
   (b) loss of or damage to property belonging to or in the custody or control of the Insured or any Employee other than personal effects (including vehicles) of directors visitors or Employees. This exception shall not apply to premises leased or rented (but not owned) by the Insured unless liability arises solely under the terms of a lease or rental agreement. Provided that the Insured shall be responsible for the first £100 of each and every claim for damage to leased or rented premises caused otherwise than by fire and explosion
   (c) (i) libel or slander
      (ii) infringement of plans copyright patent trade name trade mark or registered design
   (d) bodily injury loss or damage trespass nuisance or any interference with any right of way light air or water
      (i) deliberately caused by or on the instructions of the Insured or an Employee whilst engaged in supervisory duties unless caused by the wilful misconduct of such Employee
      (ii) arising from any Products whether or not described in the Schedule (after they have ceased to be in the custody or under the control of the Insured) sold supplied repaired altered treated or installed other than food and drink for consumption on the Insured's premises
   (e) the non-performance non-completion or delay in completion of any contract or agreement or the payment of penalty sums fines or liquidated damages
   (f) the ownership possession or use of any aircraft hovercraft drilling platform or rig or mechanically propelled watercraft
   (g) the ownership possession or use of any mechanically propelled vehicle whilst in use in circumstances in which a Certificate of Motor Insurance or surety is required under any Road Traffic Act or similar legislation
   This exception shall not apply in respect of
      (i) liability arising out of the operation of such vehicle as a tool except in respect of liability compulsorily insurable under any Road Traffic Act or similar legislation
      (ii) the loading or unloading of any mechanically propelled vehicle unless indemnity is granted by any other insurance
      (iii) the use of Employees' own vehicles on the Insured's Business but Definition 3(b)(i) shall not be operative
(2) The Company will not indemnify the Insured in respect of
   (a) any legal liability of whatsoever nature directly or indirectly caused by or contributed to by or arising from
      (i) ionising radiations or contamination by radioactivity from any nuclear fuel or from any nuclear waste from the combustion of nuclear fuel
      (ii) the radioactive toxic explosive or other hazardous properties of any explosive nuclear assembly or nuclear component thereof
   (b) any consequence whether direct or indirect of war invasion act of foreign enemy hostilities (whether war be declared or not) civil war rebellion revolution insurrection or military or usurped power

SECTION B – PRODUCTS LIABILITY

The Company will subject to the terms of and endorsements to this section and the conditions of this Policy indemnify the Insured against all sums which the Insured becomes legally liable to pay as damages in respect of
(1) bodily injury (including death or disease) to any person
(2) loss of or damage to property
happening anywhere in the world during the Period of Insurance and caused by the Products sold supplied repaired altered treated or installed from or in Great Britain Northern Ireland the Channel Islands and the Isle of Man in connection with the Business
The Company will also pay Legal Costs and Solicitor's Fees

LIMIT OF INDEMNITY

The liability of the Company for all damages in respect of all bodily injury loss or damage happening in any one Period of Insurance shall not in the aggregate exceed the Limit of Indemnity

EXCEPTIONS

(1) The Company will not indemnify the Insured against liability arising from
    (*a*) bodily injury sustained by an Employee and arising out of and in the course of their employment or engagement by the Insured
    (*b*) loss of or damage to property belonging to or in the custody or control of the Insured
    (*c*) (i) libel or slander
        (ii) infringement of plans copyright patent trade name trade mark or registered design
    (*d*) bodily injury loss or damage arising directly or indirectly from Products sold supplied repaired altered treated or installed by the Insured on terms less favourable to the Insured than the ordinary process of law governing their sale supply repair alteration treatment or installation
        This exception shall not apply if liability would have attached in the absence of such terms
(2) The Company will not indemnify the Insured against liability
    (*a*) in respect of loss of or damage to the Products
    (*b*) for the cost of repair alteration or replacement of the Products including the cost of demolition breaking out dismantling delivery rebuilding supply and installation of the Products and any other property (unless physically damaged by the Products) essential to such repair alteration or replacement
    (*c*) to make any refund of the payment received for the Products
(3) The Company will not indemnify the Insured in respect of
    (*a*) any legal liability of whatsoever nature directly or indirectly caused by or contributed to by or arising from
        (i) ionising radiations or contamination by radioactivity from any nuclear fuel or from any nuclear waste from the combustion of nuclear fuel
        (ii) the radioactive toxic explosive or other hazardous properties of any explosive nuclear assembly or nuclear component thereof
    (*b*) any consequence whether direct or indirect of war invasion act of foreign enemy hostilities (whether war be declared or not) civil war rebellion revolution insurrection military or usurped power

SECTION C – EMPLOYERS' LIABILITY

The Company will subject to the terms of and endorsements to this section and the conditions of this Policy indemnify the Insured against all sums which the Insured becomes legally liable to pay as damages in respect of bodily injury (including death or disease) sustained by an Employee arising out of and in the course of his employment or engagement by the Insured in the Business and caused
  (*a*) within Great Britain Northern Ireland the Channel Islands and the Isle of Man
  (*b*) elsewhere in the world in respect of Employees normally resident in and travelling from the territories mentioned in (*a*) but this Policy shall not apply to liability incurred under any Workers Compensation or similar legislation during the Period of Insurance
  The Company will also pay Legal Costs and Solicitor's Fees
  The Indemnity granted by this section is deemed to be in accordance with the provisions of any law relating to the compulsory insurance of liability to employees in Great Britain (and Northern Ireland the Isle of Man and the Channel Islands in so far as this clause applies to those territories) but the Insured shall repay to the Company all sums paid by the Company which the Company would not have been liable to pay but for the provisions of such law

EXTENSION

Unsatisfied Court Judgements
In the event of a judgement for damages being obtained
by any Employee or the personal representative of any Employee in respect of bodily injury (including death or disease) sustained by any Employee arising out of and in the course of employment or engagement by the Insured in the Business and caused during the Period of Insurance against any company or individual operating within premises in Great Britain, Northern Ireland, the Channel Islands or the Isle of Man in any court situate in those territories and remaining unsatisfied in whole or in part six months after the date of such judgement the Company will at the request of the Insured pay to the Employee the amount of any such damages and any awarded costs to the extent they remain unsatisfied
  Provided always that
      (i) there is no appeal outstanding
      (ii) if any payment is made under the terms of this extension the Employee or the personal representative of the Employee shall assign any such damages and any awarded costs to the Company

DEFINITIONS

1. Business
The term 'Business' shall include
  (*a*) the provision and management of catering social sports and welfare organisations for the benefit of Employees
  (*b*) first aid fire and ambulance services
  (*c*) private work carried out by any Employee for the Insured or any director partner or senior official of the Insured

2. Employee
The term 'Employee' shall include
  (*a*) any person under a contract of service or apprenticeship with
      (i) the Insured
      (ii) any other party and who is borrowed by or hired to the Insured

(b) any labour master or person supplied by him

(c) any person supplied by a labour only subcontractor

(d) any self-employed person working for the Insured

(e) any person supplied to the Insured under a contract or agreement the terms of which deem such person to be in the employment of the Insured for the duration of such contract or agreement

(f) any student provided by a local Education Authority within the terms of a Work Experience Programme Agreement

(g) any trainee provided by the Manpower Services Commission or any other Central or Local Government body under the terms of a Work Experience Agreement

3. Insured
The term 'Insured' shall include

(a) any party for whom the Insured is carrying out a contract away from the Insured's own premises but only to the extent required by such contract and in respect of Section C—Employers' Liability—only in so far as concerns bodily injury sustained by an Employee of the Insured

(b) at the request of the Insured

   (i) any director partner or Employee of the Insured in respect of liability for which the Insured would have been entitled to claim under this insurance if the claim had been made against the Insured

   (ii) any officer or member of the Insured's catering social sports or welfare organisations first aid fire or ambulance services in his respective capacity as such

(c) in the event of the death of the Insured any personal representative of the Insured in respect of liability incurred by the Insured

4. Legal Costs
The term 'Legal Costs' shall mean legal costs and expenses recoverable by any claimant and all costs and expenses incurred with the written consent of the Company

The Company will also indemnify the Insured and at the request of the Insured any director or Employee of the Insured in respect of legal fees and expenses incurred with the written consent of the Company and any prosecution costs awarded against such person in respect of

(a) the defence of any criminal proceedings brought against the Insured director or Employee for an alleged offence occurring during the Period of Insurance under the Health and Safety at Work etc. Act 1974 (the Act) and similar safety legislation arising from the Business relating to

   (i) if section A—Public Liability is operative

   matters affecting the safety health and welfare of persons other than Employees of the Insured (but excluding legal fees and expenses arising from a breach of Section 6 of the Act unless Section B—Products Liability is operative)

   (ii) if Section C—Employers' Liability is operative

   matters affecting the safety health and welfare of Employees of the Insured

(b) an appeal against a conviction arising from such proceeding

Provided always that

(a) the Company shall not be liable for the payment of fines or penalties

(b) such director or Employee shall comply with the terms of the Policy

5. Solicitor's Fees
The term 'Solicitor's Fees' shall mean the solicitor's fees incurred with the written consent of the Company for representation of the Insured at

(a) any coroners inquest or fatal inquiry arising from any death (*b*) proceedings in any Court of Summary Jurisdiction arising out of any alleged breach of a statutory duty resulting in bodily injury or loss of or damage to property

which may be the subject of a claim under this Policy

POLICY CONDITIONS

1. Interpretation
Any word or expression to which a specific meaning has been attached in any part of this Policy or Schedule shall bear such meaning wherever it may appear

2. Precautions
The Insured shall take and cause to be taken all reasonable precautions to
  (*a*) prevent bodily injury and loss of and damage to property and the sale or supply of Products which are defective in any way
  (*b*) comply with all statutory obligations and regulations imposed by any Authority

3. Alterations
The Insured shall give notice to the Company as soon as possible of any alteration which materially affects the risk

4. Claims
  (*a*) The Insured shall give written notice to the Company of any bodily injury loss or damage or claim or proceeding as soon as possible after the same shall have come to the knowledge of the Insured or any representative of the Insured
  (*b*) The Insured shall not admit liability for or negotiate the settlement of any claim without the written consent of the Company which shall be entitled to conduct in the name of the Insured the defence or settlement of any claim or to prosecute for its own benefit any claim for indemnity or damages or otherwise and shall have full discretion in the conduct of any proceedings and in the settlement of any claim and the Insured shall give all such information and assistance as the Company may require
  (*c*) If under Section A – Public Liability – the Company is required to indemnify more than one party named in Definition 3 (Insured) the liability of the Company for all damages payable shall not exceed in all the Limit of Indemnity
  (*d*) In connection with any one claim or number of claims other than in respect of claims under Section C – Employers' Liability – occurring in any one Period of Insurance the Company may at any time pay to the Insured the amount of the Limit of Indemnity (after deduction of any sum or sums already paid as compensation) or any less amount for which such claim or claims can be settled and thereafter the Company shall be under no further liability under this Policy in connection with such claim or claims except for Legal Costs incurred prior to the date of such payment

5. Cancellation
The Company may cancel any section by sending thirty days' notice by registered letter to the Insured's last known address and shall return to the Insured the Premium less the pro rata portion thereof for the period the section has been in force subject to adjustment under Condition 6

6. Adjustment
If any part of the Premium is calculated on estimates the Insured shall within one month from the expiry of each Period of Insurance furnish such details as the Company may require and the Premium for such period shall be adjusted subject to
  (*a*) No refund of premium where the Premium for any Section is less than £1,000

(*b*) The retention by the Company of £1,000 or the Minimum Premium whichever
is the greater where the Premium for any Section is £1,000 or more

If the Insured fails to furnish such details the Company shall be entitled to estimate
those details and adjust the Premium accordingly

7. Other Insurances

If an indemnity is or would but for the existence of this insurance be granted by any
other insurance the Company shall not provide indemnity except in respect of any
excess beyond the amount which is or would but for the existence of this insurance
be payable

8. Observance

The observance and fulfilment of the terms exceptions and conditions of and
endorsements applying to this Policy in so far as they relate to anything to be undertaken or complied with by the Insured shall be a condition precedent to the right of
the Insured to claim under this Policy

Policy of Insurance – Business Interruption

Guardian Royal Exchange Assurance plc (the Insurer) agrees (subject to the conditions contained herein or endorsed or otherwise expressed hereon which conditions
shall so far as the nature of them respectively will permit be deemed to be conditions
precedent to the right of the Insured to recover hereunder) that if after payment of
the premium any building or other property or any part thereof used by the Insured
at the premises for the purpose of the business be destroyed or damaged by any of
the contingencies specified in the schedule during the period of insurance or of any
subsequent period in respect of which the Insured shall have paid and the Insurer
shall have accepted the premium required for the renewal of this policy and the
business carried on by the Insured at the premises be in consequence thereof interrupted or interfered with then the Insurer will indemnify the Insured

PROVIDED THAT –

(1) at the time of the happening of the destruction or damage there shall be in force
an insurance covering the interest of the Insured in the property at the premises
against such destruction or damage and that
  (i) payment shall have been made or liability admitted thereof
  or
  (ii) payment would have been made or liability would have been admitted
therefor but for the operation of a proviso in such insurance excluding
liability for losses below a specified amount
(2) the liability of the Insurer shall in no case exceed in respect of each item the sum
expressed in the schedule to be insured thereon or in the whole the total sum
insured hereby or such other sums as may be substituted therefor by memorandum signed by or on behalf of the Insurer

THE CONTINGENCIES

FIRE (whether resulting from explosion or otherwise) but excluding
  (*a*) explosion occasioned by fire
  (*b*) earthquake or subterranean fire
  (*c*) destruction of or damage to property as a result of
    (i) its own spontaneous fermentation or heating or
    (ii) its undergoing any process involving the application of heat

LIGHTNING

EXPLOSION
- (a) of boilers used for domestic purposes only
- (b) of any other boilers or economisers on the premises
- (c) in a building not being part of any gas works, of gas used for domestic purposes or used for lighting or heating the premises

but excluding destruction or damage caused by earthquake or subterranean fire

EXPLOSION excluding
- (a) destruction or damage occasioned by the bursting of any vessel, machine or apparatus (not being a boiler or economiser on the premises) in which internal pressure is due to steam only and belonging to or under the control of the Insured
- (b) loss sustained in consequence of the Insured being deprived of the use of any vessel, machine or apparatus (not being a boiler or economiser on the premises) or its contents as a result of the explosion thereof

Pressure waves caused by aircraft and other aerial devices travelling at sonic or supersonic speeds shall not be deemed explosion

EARTHQUAKE but limited to destruction or damage by fire only

SUBTERRANEAN FIRE

Fire only of or to any property or part thereof caused by its own SPONTANEOUS FERMENTATION, HEATING OR COMBUSTION

AIRCRAFT and other aerial devices or articles dropped therefrom excluding destruction or damage occasioned by pressure waves caused by aircraft and other aerial devices travelling at sonic or supersonic speeds

RIOT OR CIVIL COMMOTION but limited to destruction or damage by fire only and excluding loss destruction or damage
- (a) occasioned by or happening through confiscation or destruction or requisition by order of the Government or any Public Authority
- (b) to property in Northern Ireland

RIOT, CIVIL COMMOTION, STRIKERS, LOCKED-OUT WORKERS or persons taking part in labour disturbances or MALICIOUS PERSONS, excluding
- (a) destruction or damage resulting from confiscation or requisition by order of the government or any public authority
- (b) destruction or damage resulting from cessation of work
- (c) destruction or damage by fire caused by strikers, locked-out workers or persons taking part in labour disturbances or malicious persons

EARTHQUAKE but not destruction or damage caused by fire

STORM OR TEMPEST AND FLOOD excluding
- (a) destruction or damage by lightning, frost, subsidence or landslip
- (b) destruction or damage attributable solely to change in the water table level
- (c) destruction or damage to fences, gates and moveable property in the open

ESCAPE OF WATER FROM WATER TANKS, APPARATUS OR PIPES excluding
- (a) destruction or damage by water discharged or leaking from an automatic sprinkler installation
- (b) destruction or damage occurring whilst the premises are empty or disused

IMPACT by any road vehicle or animal not belonging to or under the control of the Insured or their employees

WATER ACCIDENTALLY DISCHARGED OR LEAKING FROM ANY AUTOMATIC SPRINKLER INSTALLATION(S) in the premises not occasioned by or happening through—
    (a) freezing whilst the premises in the Insured's ownership and/or tenancy are empty or disused,
    (b) explosion (including the blowing up of buildings or blasting) earthquake or subterranean fire or heat caused by fire.

POLICY EXCLUSIONS

The policy does not cover loss resulting from
    (1) destruction or damage directly or indirectly occasioned by or happening through or in consequence of
        (a) riot and civil commotion unless these contingencies are specified in the schedule and then only to the extent stated,
        (b) war, invasion, act of foreign enemy, hostilities (whether war be declared or not), civil war, rebellion, revolution, insurrection or military or usurped power;
    (2) destruction or damage occasioned by or happening through or occasioning loss or destruction of or damage to any property whatsoever or any loss or expense whatsoever resulting or arising therefrom or any consequential loss directly or indirectly caused by or contributed to by or arising from
        (a) ionising radiations or contamination by radioactivity from any nuclear fuel or from any nuclear waste from the combustion of nuclear fuel,
        (b) the radioactive, toxic, explosive or other hazardous properties of any explosive nuclear assembly or nuclear component thereof;
    (3) destruction or damage in Northern Ireland occasioned by or happening through
        (a) civil commotion,
        (b) any unlawful, wanton or malicious act committed maliciously by a person or persons acting on behalf of or in connection with any unlawful association;
    For the purpose of this exclusion
    'unlawful association' means any organisation which is engaged in terrorism and includes an organisation which at any relevant time is a proscribed organisation within the meaning of the Northern Ireland (Emergency Provisions) Act 1973
    'terrorism' means the use of violence for political ends and includes any use of violence for the purpose of putting the public or any section of the public in fear
    In any action, suit or other proceedings where the Insurer alleges that by reason of the provisions of this exclusion any loss is not covered by this policy the burden of proving that such loss is covered shall be upon the Insured;
    (4) pollution or contamination except loss resulting from destruction or damage, not otherwise excluded, caused by
        (a) pollution or contamination at the premises which itself results from an insured contingency
        (b) any insured contingency which itself results from pollution or contamination.

POLICY CONDITIONS

A) General Conditions

Identification
This policy and the schedule (which forms an integral part of this policy) shall be read

together as one contract and words and expressions to which specific meanings have been attached in any part of this policy or of the schedule shall bear such specific meanings wherever they may appear.

Policy Voidable

This policy shall be voidable in the event of misrepresentation, misdescription or non-disclosure in any material particular.

Alteration

This policy shall be avoided if at any time after the commencement of this insurance

(a) the business be wound up or carried on by a liquidator or receiver or permanently discontinued

or

(b) the Insured's interest ceases otherwise than by death

or

(c) any alteration be made either in the business or in the premises or property therein whereby the risk of destruction or damage is increased

unless its continuance be admitted by memorandum signed by or on behalf of the Insurer.

POLICY CONDITIONS

B) Claims Conditions

Action by the Insured

(a) On the happening of any destruction or damage in consequence of which a claim is or may be made under this policy the Insured shall forthwith give notice thereof in writing to the Insurer.

(b) In respect of destruction or damage caused by riot, civil commotion, strikers, locked-out workers, persons taking part in labour disturbances or malicious persons the Insured shall furnish the Insurer with full details of such destruction or damage within seven days of its happening.

(c) The Insured shall with due diligence do and concur in doing and permit to be done all things which may be reasonably practicable to minimise or check any interruption of or interference with the business or to avoid or diminish the loss and in the event of a claim being made under this policy shall, not later than thirty days after the expiry of the indemnity period or within such further time as the Insurer may in writing allow, at his own expense deliver to the Insurer in writing a statement setting forth particulars of his claim together with details of all other insurances covering the destruction or damage or any part of it or consequential loss of any kind resulting therefrom. The Insured shall at their own expense also produce and furnish to the Insurer such books of account and other business book, vouchers, invoices, balance sheets and other documents, proofs, information, explanation and other evidence as may reasonably be required by the Insurer for the purpose of investigating or verifying the claim together with (if demanded) a statutory declaration of the truth of the claim and of any matters connected therewith. No claim under this policy shall be payable unless the terms of this condition have been complied with and in the event of non-compliance therewith in any respect, any payment on account of the claim already made shall be repaid to the Insurer forthwith.

Fraud

If any claim be in any respect fraudulent or if any fraudulent means or devices be used by the Insured or anyone acting on their behalf to obtain any benefit under this policy or if any destruction or damage be occasioned by the wilful act or with the connivance of the Insured all benefit under this policy shall be forfeited.

Contribution
If at the time of any destruction or damage resulting in a loss under this policy there be any other insurance effected by or on behalf of the Insured covering such loss or any part of it the liability of the Insurer hereunder shall be limited to its rateable proportion of such loss.

Subrogation
Any claimant under this policy shall at the request and at the expense of the Insurer do and concur in doing and permit to be done all such acts and things as may be necessary or reasonably required by the Insurer for the purpose of enforcing any rights and remedies or of obtaining relief or indemnity from other parties to which the Insurer shall be or would become entitled or subrogated upon its paying for or making good any loss under this policy, whether such acts and things shall be or become necessary or required before or after indemnification by the Insurer.

Arbitration
If any difference shall arise as to the amounts to be paid under this policy (liability being otherwise admitted) such difference shall be referred to an arbitrator to be appointed by the parties in accordance with the statutory provisions in that behalf for the time being in force. Where any difference is by this condition to be referred to arbitration the making of an award shall be a condition precedent to any right of action against the Insurer.

4   The settlement process

Hard Bargaining: Out of Court Settlement in Personal Injury Actions Hazel Genn (Clarendon Press: Oxford, 1987), pp. 13–15, 163–169.

THE SIGNIFICANCE OF SETTLEMENT

Because claims are settled without any court formalities there is no official source of information about the claims settlement process. No records of settlements are publicly available, nor are there any official statistics relating to the volume of claims pursued and compromised, the level of settlements, or the costs involved in achieving settlements. The research conducted by the Pearson Commission (1978) and detailed evidence from the Oxford national survey do, however, shed some light on these questions. The Oxford study obtained information from plaintiffs and their solicitors about the administration and settlement of claims. It showed that only a small proportion of those people injured in accidents each year actually initiate claims for damages; that only 80 per cent of those claims initiated achieve any kind of settlement . . .; [that] the settlements reached are generally for relatively small amounts (Harris *et al.* (1984); and that in two-thirds of cases the settlement is concluded on the basis of the *first* offer made by the defendant's insurers (Harris *et al.* (1984), p. 94). On the other hand, the evidence from both the Pearson Commission and the Oxford study indicates that the total cost of achieving these settlements is very high. For example, the Oxford study found that average total legal expenses for damages under £1,000 were 29 per cent of damages (Harris *et al.* (1984), p. 131); for damages over £1,000, average legal expenses were 15 per cent of damages (Harris *et al.* (1984), Figures 3.5A and 3.5B). The Pearson Commission, on the basis of data collected in

1972, estimated that the total cost of operating the tort system was 87 per cent of the total damages paid out as compensation (Pearson (1978), Table 158).

Although these studies provide valuable statistical information not previously available about the volume of claims, the characteristics of personal injury plaintiffs, and the amounts of damages obtained, the effect of the data is to raise more questions than are answered about the settlement process itself. For example, the most simple-minded assumptions about bargaining strategies would anticipate rather fewer than two-thirds of plaintiffs capitulating on the basis of the first offer to be made by a defendant insurance company.

The system of out of court claims settlement is essentially 'unsupervised'. Without a court hearing, plaintiffs and defendants are largely free to reach whatever compromise they choose, except in the case of infant plaintiffs, where court approval is necessary for agreed settlements made on their behalf. A plaintiff may instruct a solicitor to press his claim for him and authorize him to reach a settlement with the defendant; or the plaintiff may negotiate personally with the defendant unrepresented. In either situation he may accept a figure in full and final settlement of his claim against the defendant with no interference from outside parties or bodies. It is essentially a private matter for the individual plaintiff.

If things go badly wrong a plaintiff may have grounds to sue his solicitor or have a contract of settlement (if negotiated personally with the defendant insurers) set aside by the courts if it was deemed to be an unconscionable bargain or if made as a result of undue influence (*Horry v Tate and Lyle* [1982] 2 Lloyd's Rep 416; *Beach v Eames* (1978) 82 DLR (3rd) 736). However, the value of these potential remedies is severely constrained. They will only be used if the plaintiff ever becomes aware, subsequent to the conclusion of the settlement, that some mistake has been made . . .

One of the distinguishing features of personal injury litigation, in contrast with other forms of litigation (e.g. actions for breach of contract between businessmen; breach of contract in sale of goods; employment law litigation), is the fact that the injured plaintiff rarely has any informed or realistic expectation of the amount of compensation to which he may be entitled. He may know that he has a cause of action and that he might get *some* money, but he will generally be guided by his legal advisers or, possibly more perilously, by the defendant insurer, as to the quantum of his potential damages.

The obvious danger for the plaintiff in this unsupervised system of claims settlement is that the damages paid by defendants are once and for all payments in respect of past and *any* possible future losses. On signing the settlement contract most defendants will ensure that the plaintiff relinquishes any future rights of action in respect of his injury and its consequences.

One is looking, then, at a system of claims settlement which is of crucial importance to injured plaintiffs. For many it represents the only opportunity to obtain restitution for financial losses suffered as a result of injury, and yet there is considerable imprecision in this area of law and there is no person or body independent of the parties or their representatives overseeing the process. . . .

CONCLUSION . . .

Within [the] general climate of uncertainty surrounding the legal principles which form the basis of claims, the parties to personal injury actions do not meet on equal terms and their objectives are diametrically opposed. It has been argued in [an earlier part of the book] that there are both structural and situational inequalities between the parties in personal injury litigation and . . . the effect of these inequalities is evident throughout negotiations and the final out of court settlement of a claim. The law requires the injured plaintiff to prove that the defendant was guilty of negligence. The plaintiff is in a disadvantaged position from the outset. He is the person who has been injured, and in the early stages after his accident is more likely to be concerned about his recovery than about collecting good, fresh evidence, which might be necessary to prove some future claim arising from his injuries. He is unlikely to have had experience of bringing a claim for damages, may delay in deciding to make a claim, has limited resources, and may have no obvious means of locating an expert in personal injury litigation.

Insurance companies, on the other hand, by virtue of their position as 'repeat players' in litigation, are themselves specialists in the field. They are experienced negotiators and litigators and have the informational and financial resources to obtain expert legal advice whenever it is needed. They also have the resources to collect or to construct, from expert witnesses, the information necessary to help them refute the plaintiff's allegations of negligence. In many cases, however, the exertion of insurance companies in this respect is rendered unnecessary because the plaintiff's solicitor fails to undertake the same degree of case preparation on behalf of his client. It has been argued that this failure is both a direct result of limited resources on the plaintiff's side, and also an indirect result of the remunerative basis of civil litigation which deters solicitors from devoting sufficient time to case investigation and preparation. . . .

A common response to the problems of uncertainty, lack of expertise in personal injury work, and concern about legal costs is to adopt an approach to claims settlement based on co-operation with the opponent rather than confrontation: reasonable negotiation, without the commencement of proceedings, rather than litigation. The co-operative approach is universally welcome and encouraged by insurance companies, who regard it as the most sensible way of dealing with the claims settlement process. . . .

. . . Co-operation in this context does not mean being pleasant or courteous in dealings with the opponent. It means that in order to avoid 'antagonizing' the defendant, or in order to establish or maintain good relations with insurance companies, solicitors will postpone, or fail even to consider, the issue of formal proceedings. This approach can be developed into an extreme form, as was displayed by the solicitor . . . who claimed that he would not use the threat of litigation as a weapon against an insurance company. The problem arising from this situation is that the nature of personal injury claims settlement is inherently adversarial. The plaintiff wants to maximize his damages, while the defendant wants to avoid or minimize payment. Despite the emphasis on co-operation, the language of the parties is couched in the terminology of warfare or competition: for example, 'Going for the big prize – no liability'. . . .

When a plaintiff relinquishes his claim for damages out of court, the defendant insurance company is spared the increase in two sets of legal costs that a trial would involve, and the risk that, in addition, a judge might have awarded the plaintiff more than he has now accepted. But what benefits accrue to the plaintiff? The plaintiff, it is said, is spared the uncertainty, the delay, and the stress of costs considerations. It is on these grounds that he accepts a discounted offer. It was argued in [an earlier part of the book], however, that there is a self-serving circularity in this contention and that much of the uncertainty, delay, and costs pressures which plague plaintiffs and weaken their resolve is deliberately manufactured or exacerbated by defendants' manipulation of legal and procedural rules. It was further argued that such tactics by defendants are capable of containment by plaintiffs' solicitors if they are able and willing to pressurize defendants into action by pushing them toward trial . . .

The understandable reluctance of insurance companies to part with their money is strengthened by the effects of the inequalities between the parties which have been stressed. Evidence from claims inspectors of the influence of legal aid on bargaining strategy . . . and their admission that they adopt a different approach when faced with trade union specialist solicitors, leads to the conclusion that, when the imbalance between the parties is somewhat redressed, plaintiffs are more likely to obtain better settlements of their claims than otherwise.

Should these findings give cause for concern? Should the pervasive practice of settling claims in the absence of formal adjudication or supervision be greeted with less enthusiasm? The settlement of some 99 per cent of claims for damages without a court hearing obviously serves the civil justice system by freeing congested courts for other business and the public interest in smoothing the administration of justice is widely acknowledged. But is there also a public interest in seeing that justice is being done when parties settle their claims out of court, or is it simply a private matter for the parties to resolve as they wish? . . .

If there is, indeed, a public interest in seeing that injured plaintiffs obtain 'fair' compensation for their injuries, then the analysis of out of court settlement processes contained in this study suggests that there is a strong argument for attempting to reduce some of the imbalance between the parties by improving the access of unknowledgeable plaintiffs to solicitors who genuinely specialize in personal injury litigation; for speeding-up personal injury litigation procedure, particularly for low-value claims; for providing incentives to defendants to settle claims quickly; and for providing a means by which out of court settlements become more visible or subject to scrutiny.

Notes

1. When an insurance company has paid a claim under a policy it is subrogated to the rights of the insured against third parties. This means that the insurer can sue third parties to the same extent as the insured could have done. The insurer, who sues in the name of the insured, has full control of the proceedings. The effect of this may be seen from cases such as *Lister v Romford Ice and Cold Storage Co Ltd* [1957] AC 555, [1957] 1 All ER 125 (p. 875, ante), *Morris v Ford Motor Co Ltd* [1973] QB 792, [1973] 2 All ER 1084 (p. 881, ante) and *Esso Petroleum Co Ltd v Hall Russell & Co Ltd* [1989] AC 643, [1989] 1 All ER 37 noted p. 235, ante). In the case of property insurance, 'knock-for-knock' agreements between insurance companies mean that the insurers' rights of subrogation are not exercised. Suppose that P and D are each comprehensively insured by different insurers and that D negligently damages P's car. Under a 'knock-for-knock' agreement, P's insurer will settle his claim and will not claim from D's insurer. Where, as is usually the case, P is not fully insured (e.g., he is subject to an excess clause or not insured against loss of use of his car while being repaired), the 'knock-for-knock' agreement does not prevent P from bringing proceedings against D in respect of damage to his vehicle. If P has already been partially indemnified by his insurers he would be obliged to reimburse them from the damages recovered from D: *Hobbs v Marlowe* [1978] AC 16, [1977] 2 All ER 241, noted by J. Birds (1978) 41 MLR 201. R. Hasson (1985) 5 Oxf JLS 416 argues that subrogation leads to overlapping insurance coverage and wasteful litigation and that subrogated claims do not deter negligent behaviour.

2. There is a growing literature on the settlement process. Among the leading works (in addition to Genn, op cit) are: H. L. Ross, *Settled Out of Court: The Social Process of Insurance Claims Adjustment* 2nd edn (Chicago, 1980); R. H. Mnookin and L. Kornhauser (1979) 88 Yale LJ 950; *Atiyah*, chap. 11. *Harris et al*, p. 319; J. Phillips and K. Hawkins (1976) 39 MLR 497.

5 Other compensation systems

Social security benefits

About half of the total amount of compensation for personal injury and death comes from social security and a quarter from the tort system (see p. 35, ante). There was a dramatic growth of state provision in the period from 1945 to 1980 (traced in vol. 1, chap. 5 of the Pearson Report, with detailed statistics in vol. 2, chap. 4). However, since then there have been profound changes. Reductions have been made in the real value of many benefits, responsibility for income maintenance during short periods of sickness and injury has been transferred from the state to the employer, benefits have been restructured, supplementary benefits have been replaced by income support, and the right to single and urgent needs payments has been replaced by a discretionary social fund subject to cash limits. New conditions have been imposed upon benefits aimed at providing incentives to work and at encouraging labour mobility. The following is a brief guide to the principal benefits relevant to compensation for personal injury and death. (The reference to 'contributory' benefits means that certain national insurance contributions must have been made by or credited to the claimant.) For details, A.I.Ogus and E. Barendt, *The Law of Social Security* 3rd edn (London, 1988), D. Bonner et al, *Non-Means Tested Benefits: the Legislation* 1990 edn (London, 1990), and C.P.A.G., *Income Support, The Social Fund and Family Credit* 1990 edn (London, 1990) should be consulted.

COMPENSATION FOR LOSS OF INCOME

Statutory sick pay (SSP). Employers are obliged to pay this to employees when off sick for four days or more. Spells of sickness with eight weeks or less between them are linked. SSP is paid at two rates, depending upon earnings, for up to 28 weeks. Then the claimant is transferred to (state) invalidity benefit. SSP is taxable. Although it is non-contributory, employees earning less than the lower earnings limit for national insurance contributions are not eligible, nor are those employed for less than three months or those over pensionable age. It is not means-tested, but it counts as income for means-tested benefits.

Sickness benefit. This is paid for incapacity for work because of sickness or disablement to those not eligible for SSP who are off sick for four or more days in a row. It is paid for up to 28 weeks; then the claimant is transferred to invalidity benefit. Sickness benefit is tax free, but is subject to national insurance contributions unless the injury was suffered at work or the claimant is suffering from a prescribed industrial disease. It is not means-tested but it counts as income for means-tested benefits.

Invalidity benefit. This consists of invalidity pension and invalidity allowance. The pension is paid for incapacity for work and replaces SSP or sickness benefit after 28 weeks. Invalidity allowance is payable on top of invalidity pension to people who were under 55 (women) or 60 (men) when they became chronically sick. These benefits are tax free (but invalidity allowance is taxable when paid with retirement pension). They are contributory (as for sickness benefit) and not means-tested, but they count as income for means-tested benefits.

Severe disablement allowance. This is a weekly benefit, at a lower rate, for those of working age who have not been able to work for at least 28 weeks but cannot get sickness or invalidity benefit because they have not paid the required national insurance contributions. Those who became incapable of work after their 20th birthday must be 80 per cent or more disabled. As from December 1990, there is an age-related addition.

Vaccine damage payments. These are available to those aged two or over who were severely disabled as a result of routine vaccination for specified common diseases. Claims must be made within six years of the vaccination, which must have been done before the claimant was 18 (except for polio and rubella). The payment is a £20,000 lump sum which is tax free, not contributory, and not means-tested. If paid to a dependant child the payment is not taken into account in assessing means-tested benefits. The same applies to a payment to an adult which is held in trust for two years (or longer, if reasonable).

Haemophilia/HIV payments. The Macfarlane Trust (1987) set up by the Government makes grants and regular payments on the basis of need to haemophiliacs with HIV infection as a result of receiving infected blood products (Factor 8). In addition, under the Special Payments Trust, all who qualify on medical grounds receive lump sums of £20,000 each.

War disablement pensions. These are payable to those disabled as a result of service in the armed forces 1914–1918, to civilians and service people disabled in 1939–1945, and to service people disabled since 1945.

Criminal injuries compensation. See p. 920, post.

Income support. This is the 'topping-up' benefit intended to keep incomes up to a statutory minimum level for persons working less than 24 hours a week. It is payable to persons over 60, those who are lone parents, those who are too sick or disabled to work including the registered blind, those staying at home to look after a severely disabled person or getting invalid care allowance, those who are unemployed and actively seeking work, and those working 24 hours a week or more but, because of physical or mental disability, earning 75 per cent or less of what would be normal for a fit person. The claimant's capital must not exceed £8,000 and between this figure and £3,000 an amount of 'notional income' will be assumed. Income support is made up of personal allowances (at a lower rate for under 25s) and premiums which depend upon age and health. These premiums include a family premium, a lone parent's premium, a disabled child's premium, a carer's premium, a disability premium and a severe disability premium.

Housing benefit. This is to help those on low incomes to pay rent and is dependent upon income, the number in the family and the age or disability of the claimant, partner or child. Those with disabilities receive more housing benefit because income is calculated as for income support, i.e. a personal allowance plus disability premium. If a non-dependant is living with the claimant a deduction is made from housing benefit, unless the claimant or partner is blind or gets attendance allowance or similar benefit.

COMPENSATION FOR NON-PECUNIARY LOSS

Disablement benefit. This is a pension payable after SSP or sickness benefit stops to employed earners who suffer disablement caused by an accident arising out of and in the course of employment or a prescribed industrial disease. The amount of benefit depends upon the degree of disablement as assessed by a medical board. There are prescribed degrees of disablement, e.g. absolute deafness, 100 per cent; amputation of both feet resulting in end-bearing stumps, 90 per cent; loss of one eye, without complications, the other being normal, 40 per cent, etc. Payment does not begin until 90 days after the start of the disability and can continue even if the employee resumes work. It is tax free, non-contributory and not means-tested. It counts as income for the assessment of means-tested benefits.

COMPENSATION FOR EXPENSES

Attendance allowance. This is a tax free allowance for the severely disabled who have needed a lot of care in connection with 'bodily functions' for at least six months. Since October 1990 there has been no six-month waiting period for terminally ill people. For others claims have to be made on the social fund during the waiting period. There are two rates of allowance, a higher rate if care is needed day and night, and a lower rate if needed by day only. It is non-contributory, not means-tested and does not count as income for means-tested benefits.

Constant attendance allowance. This is paid to those receiving disablement benefit (i.e. as the result of industrial injury or prescribed disease) who are 100 per cent disabled and need constant care and attendance for the necessities of life. There are four rates.

Exceptionally severe disablement allowance. This is an additional amount for those receiving constant attendance allowance at a higher rate, and whose need for such allowance is likely to be permanent.

Mobility allowance. This is a tax free allowance to assist with the extra costs of travel for those who are unable or virtually unable to walk outdoors, or for whom the exertion of trying to do so would cause serious harm. The inability must be due to a physical cause and likely to last for at least a year. It is non-contributory, not means-tested and does not count as income for means-tested benefits.

Invalid care allowance. This is a taxable allowance for people spending at least 35 hours a week looking after someone who gets or has claimed attendance allowance or constant attendance allowance. It is non-contributory and not means-tested but counts as income for means-tested benefits.

Independent living fund. This is a charitable trust established by the Government to help severely disabled people to pay for personal care or domestic help so that they do not have to go into residential care. The claimant must live alone and must be entitled to attendance allowance or constant attendance allowance. The claimant's income must not be higher than that fixed for income support and savings must be below £8,000. Payments are not taxable and do not affect means-tested benefits.

Social fund. This makes grants and loans, mainly to those on income support, for some exceptional expenses which cannot be paid for out of regular income. Savings must be below £500 (£1,000 for cold weather payments to those aged 60 or over). Disabled people receive priority for the discretionary community care grants which are paid to those who remain in or re-establish themselves in the community rather than being in residential care.

Family fund. This assists families of children with very severe disabilities and makes grants for items not covered by statutory schemes. It is funded by the Government but administered by the Joseph Rowntree Memorial Trust. The means of families are taken into account.

REFORMS

A number of changes in the above benefits are due to come into effect by April 1992. These include the following. (1) A new disability allowance will replace attendance allowance and mobility allowance, with a common qualifying period of three months; (2) A disability employment credit will supplement the wages of disabled people who receive disability allowance or who have been receiving invalidity benefit or the disability premium payable with income support or housing benefit before starting work and who are certified as only partially capable of work.

Criminal Injuries Compensation Scheme

The Scheme for compensating victims of crimes of violence was announced in both Houses of Parliament on 24 June 1964, and in its original form came into operation on 1 August 1964.

The Scheme has since been modified in a number of respects. The revised 1990 Scheme which applies to all applications received by the Board on and after 1 February 1990 (see para. 28) is set out below.

Administration

1. The Compensation Scheme will be administered by the Criminal Injuries Compensation Board, which will be assisted by appropriate staff. Appointments to the Board will be made by the Secretary of State, after consultation with the Lord Chancellor and, where appropriate, the Lord Advocate. A person may only be appointed to be a member of the Board if he is a barrister practising in England and Wales, an advocate practising in Scotland, a solicitor practising in England and Wales or Scotland or a person who holds or has held judicial office in England and Wales or Scotland. The Chairman and other members of the Board, will be appointed to serve for up to five years in the first instance, and their appointments will be

renewable for such periods as the Secretary of State considers appropriate. The Chairman and other members will not serve on the Board beyond the age of 72, or after ceasing to be qualified for appointment, whichever is the earlier except that, where the Secretary of State considers it to be in the interests of the Scheme to extend a particular appointment beyond the age of 72 or after retirement from legal practice, he may do so. The Secretary of State may, if he thinks fit terminate a member's appointment on the grounds of incapacity or misbehaviour.

2. The Board will be provided with money through a Grant-in-Aid out of which payments for compensation awarded in accordance with the principles set out below will be made. Their net expenditure will fall on the Votes of the Home Office and the Scottish Home and Health Department.

3. The Board, or such members of the Board's staff as the Board may designate, will be entirely responsible for deciding what compensation should be paid in individual cases and their decisions will not be subject to appeal or to Ministerial review. The general working of the Scheme will, however, be kept under review by the Government, and the Board will submit annually to the Home Secretary and the Secretary of State for Scotland a full report on the operation of the Scheme, together with their accounts. The report and accounts will be open to debate in Parliament.

Scope of the Scheme

4. The Board will entertain applications for ex gratia payments of compensation in any case where the applicant or, in the case of an application by a spouse or dependant (see paragraphs 15 and 16 below), the deceased, sustained in Great Britain, or on a British vessel, aircraft or hovercraft or on, under or above an installation in a designated area within the meaning of section 1 subsection (7) of the Continental Shelf Act 1964 or any waters within 500 metres of such an installation, or in a lighthouse off the coast of the United Kingdom, personal injury directly attributable —
   (a) to a crime of violence (including arson or poisoning); or
   (b) to the apprehension or attempted apprehension of an offender or a suspected offender or to the prevention or attempted prevention of an offence or to the giving of help to any constable who is engaged in any such activity; or
   (c) to an offence of trespass on a railway.
Applications for compensation will be entertained only if made within three years of the incident giving rise to the injury, except that the Board may in exceptional cases waive this requirement. A decision by the Chairman not to waive the time limit will be final. In considering for the purposes of this paragraph whether any act is a criminal act a person's conduct will be treated as constituting an offence notwithstanding that he may not be convicted of the offence by reason of age, insanity or diplomatic immunity.

5. Compensation will not be payable unless the Board are satisfied that the injury was one for which the total amount of compensation payable after deduction of social security benefits, but before any other deductions under the Scheme, would not be less than the minimum amount of compensation. This shall be £750. The application of the minimum level shall not, however, affect the payment of funeral expenses under paragraph 15 below or, where the victim has died otherwise than in consequence of an injury for which compensation would have been payable to him under the terms of the Scheme, any sum payable to a dependant or relative of his under paragraph 16.

6. The Board may withhold or reduce compensation if they consider that —
   (a) the applicant has not taken, without delay, all reasonable steps to inform the police, or any other authority considered by the Board to be appropriate for

the purpose, of the circumstances of the injury and to co-operate with the police or other authority in bringing the offender to justice; or

(*b*) the applicant has failed to give all reasonable assistance to the Board or other authority in connection with the application; or

(*c*) having regard to the conduct of the applicant before, during or after the events giving rise to the claim or to his character as shown by his criminal convictions or unlawful conduct – and, in applications under paragraphs 15 and 16 below, to the conduct or character as shown by the criminal convictions or unlawful conduct, of the deceased and of the applicant – it is inappropriate that a full award, or any award at all, be granted.

Further, compensation will not be payable –

(*d*) in the case of an application under paragraph 4(*b*) above where the injury was sustained accidentally, unless the Board are satisfied that the applicant was at the time taking an exceptional risk which was justified in all the circumstances.

7. Compensation will not be payable unless the Board are satisfied that there is no possibility that a person responsible for causing the injury will benefit from an award.

8. Where the victim and any person responsible for the injuries which are the subject of the application (whether that person actually inflicted them or not) were living in the same household at the time of the injuries as members of the same family, compensation will be paid only where –

(*a*) the person responsible has been prosecuted in connection with the offence, except where the Board consider that there are practical, technical or other good reasons why a prosecution has not been brought; and

(*b*) in the case of violence between adults in the family, the Board are satisfied that the person responsible and the applicant stopped living in the same household before the application was made and seem unlikely to live together again; and

(*c*) in the case of an application under this paragraph by or on behalf of a minor, i.e. a person under 18 years of age, the Board are satisfied that it would not be against the minor's interest to make a full or reduced award.

For the purposes of this paragraph, a man and a woman living together as husband and wife shall be treated as members of the same family.

9. If in the opinion of the Board it is in the interests of the applicant (whether or not a minor or a person under an incapacity) so to do, the Board may pay the amount of any award to any trustee or trustees to hold on such trusts for the benefit of all or any of the following persons, namely the applicant and any spouse, widow or widower, relatives and dependants of the applicant and with such provisions for their respective maintenance, education and benefit and with such powers and provisions for the investment and management of the fund and for the remuneration of the trustee or trustees as the Board shall think fit. Subject to this the Board will have a general discretion in any case in which they have awarded compensation to make special arrangements for its administration. In this paragraph 'relatives' means all persons claiming descent from the applicant's grandparents and 'dependants' means all persons who in the opinion of the Board are dependent on him wholly or partially for the provision of the ordinary necessities of life.

10. The Board will consider applications for compensation arising out of acts of rape and other sexual offences both in respect of pain, suffering and shock and in respect of loss of earnings due to consequent pregnancy, and, where the victim is ineligible for a maternity grant under the National Insurance Scheme, in respect of the expenses of childbirth. Compensation will not be payable for the maintenance of any child born as a result of a sexual offence, except that where a woman is awarded

compensation for rape the Board shall award the additional sum of £5,000 in respect of each child born alive having been conceived as a result of the rape which the applicant intends to keep.

11. Applications for compensation for personal injury attributable to traffic offences will be excluded from the Scheme, except where such injury is due to a deliberate attempt to run the victim down.

Basis of compensation

12. Subject to the other provisions of this Scheme, compensation will be assessed on the basis of common law damages and will normally take the form of a lump sum payment, although the Board may make alternative arrangements in accordance with paragraph 9 above. More than one payment may be made where an applicant's eligibility for compensation has been established but a final award cannot be calculated in the first instance — for example where only a provisional medical assessment can be given. In a case in which an interim award has been made, the Board may decide to make a reduced award, increase any reduction already made or refuse to make any further payment at any stage before receiving notification of acceptance of a final award.

13. Although the Board's decisions in a case will normally be final, they will have discretion to reconsider a case after a final award of compensation has been accepted where there has been such a serious change in the applicant's medical condition that injustice would occur if the original assessment of compensation were allowed to stand, or where the victim has since died as a result of his injuries. A case will not be re-opened more than three years after the date of the final award unless the Board are satisfied, on the basis of evidence presented with the application for re-opening the case, that the renewed application can be considered without a need for extensive enquiries. A decision by the Chairman that a case may not be re-opened will be final.

14. Compensation will be limited as follows —
   (a) the rate of net loss of earnings or earning capacity to be taken into account shall not exceed one and a half times the gross average industrial earnings at the date of assessment (as published in the Department of Employment Gazette and adjusted as considered appropriate by the Board);
   (b) there shall be no element comparable to exemplary or punitive damages.
Where an applicant has lost earnings or earning capacity as a result of the injury, he may be required by the Board to produce evidence thereof in such manner and form as the Board may specify.

15. Where the victim has died in consequence of the injury, no compensation other than funeral expenses will be payable for the benefit of his estate, but the Board will be able to entertain applications from any person who is a dependant of the victim within the meaning of section 1(3) of the Fatal Accidents Act 1976 or who is a relative of the victim within the meaning of Schedule 1 to the Damages (Scotland) Act 1976. Compensation will be payable in accordance with the other provisions of this Scheme to any such dependant or relative. Funeral expenses to an amount considered reasonable by the Board will be paid in appropriate cases, even where the person bearing the cost of the funeral is otherwise ineligible to claim under this Scheme. Applications may be made under this paragraph where the victim has died from his injuries even if an award has been made to the victim in his lifetime. Such cases will be subject to conditions set out in paragraph 13 for the re-opening of cases and compensation payable to the applicant will be reduced by the amount paid to the victim.

16. Where the victim has died otherwise than in consequence of the injury, the Board may make an award to such dependant or relative as is mentioned in paragraph 15 in respect of loss of wages, expenses and liabilities incurred by the victim before death as a result of the injury whether or not the application for compensation in respect of the injury has been made before the death.

17. Compensation will not be payable for the loss of or damage to clothing or any property whatsoever arising from the injury unless the Board are satisfied that the property was relied upon by the victim as a physical aid.

18. The cost of private medical treatment will be payable by the Board only if the Board consider that, in all the circumstances, both the private treatment and the cost of it are reasonable.

19. Compensation will be reduced by the full value of any present or future entitlement to —
  (a) United Kingdom social security benefits;
  (b) any criminal injury compensation awards made under or pursuant to statutory arrangements in force at the relevant time in Northern Ireland;
  (c) social security benefits, compensation awards or similar payments whatsoever from the funds of other countries; or
  (d) payments under insurance arrangements except as excluded below which may accrue, as a result of the injury or death, to the benefit of the person to whom the award is made.
In assessing this entitlement, account will be taken of any income tax liability likely to reduce the value of such benefits and, in the case of an application under paragraph 15, the value of such benefits will not be reduced to take account of prospects of remarriage. If, in the opinion of the Board, an applicant may be eligible for any such benefits the Board may refuse to make an award until the applicant has taken such steps as the Board consider reasonable to claim them. Subject to paragraph 18 above, the Board will disregard monies paid or payable to the victim or his dependants as a result of or in consequence of insurance personally effected, paid for and maintained by the personal income of the victim or, in the case of a person under the age of 18, by his parent.

20. Where the victim is alive compensation will be reduced to take account of any pension accruing as a result of the injury. Where the victim has died in consequence of the injury, and any pension is payable for the benefit of the person to whom the award is made as a result of the death of the victim, the compensation will similarly be reduced to take account of the value of that pension. Where such pensions are taxable, one-half of their value will be deducted; where they are not taxable, e.g. where a lump sum payment not subject to income tax is made, they will be deducted in full. For the purposes of this paragraph, 'pension' means any payment payable as a result of the injury or death, in pursuance of pension or other rights whatsoever connected with the victim's employment, and includes any gratuity of that kind and similar benefits payable under insurance policies paid for by employers. Pension rights accruing solely as a result of payments by the victim or a dependant will be disregarded.

21. When a civil court has given judgement providing for payment of damages or a claim for damages has been settled on terms providing for payment of money, or when payment of compensation has been ordered by a criminal court, in respect of personal injuries, compensation by the Board in respect of the same injuries will be reduced by the amount of any payment received under such an order or settlement. When a civil court has assessed damages, as opposed to giving judgement for damages agreed by the parties, but the person entitled to such damages has not yet

received the full sum awarded, he will not be precluded from applying to the Board, but the Board's assessment of compensation will not exceed the sum assessed by the court. Furthermore, a person who is compensated by the Board will be required to undertake to repay them from any damages, settlement or compensation he may subsequently obtain in respect of his injuries. In arriving at their assessment of compensation the Board will not be bound by any finding of contributory negligence by any court, but will be entirely bound by the terms of the Scheme.

Procedure for determining applications

22. Every application will be made to the Board in writing as soon as possible after the event on a form obtainable from the Board's offices. The initial decision on an application will be taken by a single member of the Board, or by any member of the Board's staff to whom the Board has given authority to determine applications on the Board's behalf. Where an award is made the applicant will be given a breakdown of the assessment of compensation except where the Board consider this inappropriate, and where an award is refused or reduced, reasons for the decision will be given. If the applicant is not satisfied with the decision he may apply for an oral hearing which, if granted, will be held before at least two members of the Board excluding any member who made the original decision. The application for a hearing must be made within three months of notification of the initial decision; however the Board may waive this time limit where an extension is requested with good reason within the three month period, or where it is otherwise in the interests of justice to do so. A decision by the Chairman not to waive the time limit will be final. It will also be open to a member of the Board, or a designated member of the Board's staff, where he considers that he cannot make a just and proper decision himself to refer the application for a hearing before at least two members of the Board, one of whom may be the member who, in such a case, decided to refer the application to a hearing. An applicant will have no title to an award offered until the Board have received notification in writing that he accepts it.

23. Applications for hearing must be made in writing on a form supplied by the Board and should be supported by reasons together with any additional evidence which may assist the Board to decide whether a hearing should be granted. If the reasons in support of the application suggest that the initial decision was based on information obtained by or submitted to the Board which was incomplete or erroneous, the application may be remitted for reconsideration by the member of the Board who made the initial decision or, where this is not practicable or where the initial decision was made by a member of the Board's staff, by any member of the Board. In such cases it will still be open for the applicant to apply in writing for a hearing if he remains dissatisfied after his case has been reconsidered and the three-month limitation period in paragraph 22 will start from the date of notification of the reconsidered decision.

24. An applicant will be entitled to an oral hearing only if —
   (a) no award was made on the ground that any award would be less than the sum specified in paragraph 5 of the Scheme and it appears that applying the principles set out in paragraph 26 below, the Board might make an award; or
   (b) an award was made and it appears that, applying the principles set out in paragraph 26 below, the Board might make a larger award; or
   (c) no award or a reduced award was made and there is a dispute as to the material facts or conclusions upon which the initial or reconsidered decision was based or it appears that the decision may have been wrong in law or principle.
An application for a hearing which appears likely to fail the foregoing criteria may be reviewed by not less than two members of the Board other than any member who made the initial or reconsidered decision. If it is considered on review that if any facts

or conclusions which are disputed were resolved in the applicant's favour it would have made no difference to the initial or reconsidered decision, or that for any other reason an oral hearing would serve no useful purpose, the application for a hearing will be refused. A decision to refuse an application for a hearing will be final.

25. It will be for the applicant to make out his case at the hearing, and where appropriate this will extend to satisfying the Board that compensation should not be withheld or reduced under the terms of paragraph 6 or paragraph 8. The applicant and a member of the Board's staff will be able to call, examine and cross-examine witnesses. The Board will be entitled to take into account any relevant hearsay, opinion or written evidence, whether or not the author gives oral evidence at the hearing. The Board will reach their decision solely in the light of evidence brought out at the hearing, and all the information and evidence made available to the Board members at the hearing will be made available to the applicant at, if not before, the hearing. The Board may adjourn a hearing for any reason, and where the only issue remaining is the assessment of compensation may remit the application to a Single Member of the Board for determination in the absence of the applicant but subject to the applicant's right to apply under paragraph 22 above for a further hearing if he is not satisfied with the final assessment of compensation. While it will be open to the applicant to bring a friend or legal adviser to assist him in putting his case, the Board will not pay the cost of legal representation. They will, however, have discretion to pay the expenses of the applicant and witnesses at a hearing. If an applicant fails to attend a hearing and has offered no reasonable excuse for his non attendance the Board at the hearing may dismiss his application. A person whose application has been dismissed by the Board for failure to attend a hearing may apply in writing to the Chairman of the Board for his application to be reinstated. A decision by the Chairman that an application should not be reinstated will be final.

26. At the hearing the amount of compensation assessed by a Single Member of the Board or a designated member of the Board's staff will not be altered except upon the same principles as the Court of Appeal in England or the Court of Session in Scotland would alter an assessment of damages made by a trial judge.

27. Procedure at hearings will be as informal as is consistent with the proper determination of applications, and hearings will in general be in private. The Board will have discretion to permit observers, such as representatives of the press, radio and television, to attend hearings provided that written undertakings are given that the anonymity of the applicant and other parties will not in any way be infringed by subsequent reporting. The Board will have power to publish information about its decision in individual cases; this power will be limited only by the need to preserve the anonymity of applicants and other parties.

Implementation

28. The provisions of this Scheme will take effect from 1 February 1990. All applications for compensation received by the Board on or after 1 February 1990 will be dealt with under the terms of this Scheme except that in relation to applications in respect of injuries incurred before that date the following provisions of the 1990 Scheme shall not apply—

  (a) Paragraph 4(c);
  (b) Paragraph 8, but only in respect of injuries incurred before 1 October 1979 where paragraph 7 of the 1969 Scheme will continue to apply;
  (c) Paragraph 10 but only insofar as it requires the Board to award an additional sum of £5,000 in the circumstances therein prescribed;
  (d) Paragraphs 15 and 16 but only insofar as they enable the Board to entertain applications from a person who is a dependant within the meaning of section

1(3)(b) of the Fatal Accidents Act 1976 or who is a relative within the meaning of paragraph 1(aa) of Schedule 1 to the Damages (Scotland) Act 1976 other than such a person who is applying only for funeral expenses.

29. Applications for compensation received by the Board before 1 February 1990 will continue to be dealt with in accordance with paragraph 25 of the Scheme which came into operation on 1 October 1979 ('the 1979 Scheme') or the Scheme which came into operation on 21 May 1969 ('the 1969 Scheme') except that the following paragraphs of this Scheme will apply in addition to or in substitution for provisions of these Schemes as specified below —
  (a) Paragraph 3 of this Scheme will apply in substitution for paragraph 4 of the 1969 Scheme and paragraph 3 of the 1979 Scheme;
  (b) Paragraph 6(c) of this Scheme will apply in substitution for paragraph 17 of the 1969 Scheme and paragraph 6(c) of the 1979 Scheme;
  (c) Paragraph 14 of this Scheme will apply additionally to applications otherwise falling to be considered under the 1969 or 1979 Schemes but only insofar as it allows the Board to require an applicant to produce evidence of loss of earnings or earning capacity;
  (d) Paragraphs 22, 23 and 25 of this Scheme will apply in substitution for paragraphs 21 and 22 of the 1969 Scheme and paragraphs 22 and 23 of the 1979 Scheme;
  (e) Paragraph 26 of this Scheme will apply additionally to applications otherwise falling to be considered under the 1969 of 1979 Schemes;
  (f) Paragraph 27 of this Scheme will apply in substitution for paragraph 23 of the 1969 Scheme and paragraph 24 of the 1979 Scheme.

30. Applications to re-open cases received before 1 February 1990 will continue to be dealt with under the terms of paragraph 25 of the 1979 Scheme. Applications to re-open cases received on or after 1 February 1990 will be considered and determined under the terms of this Scheme.

Notes

1. The Criminal Justice Act 1988, Part VII, contains provisions to put the Criminal Injuries Compensation Scheme on a statutory basis. The impetus for this was the adoption of the European Convention on the Compensation of Victims of Violent Crimes (Cmnd. 9167) and the Report of an Interdepartmental Working Party, *Criminal Injuries Compensation: a Statutory Scheme* (HMSO, 1986). However, the legislation has not yet (October 1990) been brought into operation. In its Twenty-Fifth Report (Cm. 900, 1989), para. 1.8, the Criminal Injuries Compensation Board strongly urged that the Board should be permitted for a reasonable period to continue with the existing non-statutory Scheme, on the grounds that implementation of the statutory Scheme would exacerbate the problem of delay. The backlog of cases under or awaiting consideration by the Board at 31st March 1989 was more than 82,000 as against 78,000 at the end of the previous year. The number of new applications received in 1988–1989 was 43,385, higher than ever before in the history of the Scheme. It was estimated that over 50,000 new cases would be received in the following year (para. 1.1). In 1988–1989 73.1 per cent of cases took over 12 months between registration of the application and submission to a single member of the Board for decision, a worsening of delay since 1986–1987 when 50.2 per cent took over 12 months (para. 6.1). See further *Compensating Victims Quickly: the Administration of the Criminal Injuries*

Compensation Board, House of Commons Home Affairs Committee, H.C. 92, Session 1989–90; P. Duff (1989) 52 MLR 518.

2. At present the only form of control over the decisions of the Board is by way of judicial review: see e.g. *R v Criminal Injuries Compensation Board, ex P Lain* [1967] 2 QB 864, [1967] 2 All ER 770. This power of review will be exercised only if the Board misconstrues the terms of the Scheme or reaches a decision which is 'plainly wrong' (*R v Criminal Injuries Compensation Board, ex Thompstone* [1984] 3 All ER 572, [1984] 1 WLR 1234 dealing with para. 6(c) of the Scheme on which cf. p. 399, ante.) Note further *R v Criminal Injuries Compensation Board, ex P Webb* [1986] QB 184, [1986] 2 All ER 478 where the Court of Appeal, affirming the decision of the Divisional Court, refused to interfere with the decision of the Board that suicide by jumping onto a railway line in the path of an oncoming train was not a 'crime of violence' which could be compensated under the Scheme. (The Scheme has since been amended so as to cover personal injury attributable to 'an offence of trespass on a railway'; see para. 4(c) of the Scheme, ante.) Lawton LJ, giving the judgment of the court, said that rather than construing the guidelines of the Board as if they were a statute or a technical definition, the proper approach was to consider whether a reasonable and literate man would consider he ought to be compensated under the Scheme. Looking at the nature of the crime, rather than its consequences, the Court of Appeal was not willing to disturb the Board's finding that the facts in this case did not disclose a 'crime of violence'. When the statutory Scheme comes into force there will be an appeal on any ground which involves a question of law alone to the High Court in England and Wales or the Court of Session in Scotland (Criminal Justice Act 1988, s. 113).

3. In the first 25 years of its operation the Board awarded over £431m in compensation. The Board assesses compensation on tort principles, but the awards are generally smaller than would be awarded by a court. In particular, the rate of net loss of earnings or earning capacity to be taken into account may not exceed one and a half times the gross average industrial earnings at the date of assessment, and there is no element comparable to exemplary or punitive damages (para. 14 of the Scheme). The highest award by the Board in 1988–1989 was £307,781. There is also a minimum amount (currently £750) below which compensation will not be awarded. Compensation normally takes the form of a lump sum payment (para. 12, subject to para. 9). In its Fourteenth Annual Report (Cmnd. 7396, 1978) the Board expressed 'grave doubts' about the beneficial effects of changing to a system of periodic payments as proposed by the Pearson Commission, and the Criminal Justice Act 1988, Sch. 7, para. 6(1) will continue the system of lump sum payments when the Scheme is on a statutory basis.

4. Research by Joanna Shapland on Compensation for Victims of Crimes of Violence (summarised in Appendix B of the First Report of the House of Commons Home Affairs Select Committee, H. C. 43, Session 1984–85, *Compensation and Support for Victims of Crime*, pp. 20–22) looked at the experiences of a sample of victims with various sources of compensation. Among the findings were that (a) ignorance among victims about compensation was widespread; (b) compensation orders from criminal courts for crimes of violence (on which see p. 582, ante) have always been of lower frequency and amounts than those for property crimes; (c) victims who applied

to the Criminal Injuries Compensation Board had a higher success rate than those receiving compensation orders in court. 'Victims saw compensation, whatever its source, as symbolic – a judgment about their offence [sic] and their suffering' (p.22). For a general comparative review, see P. Burns, *Criminal Injuries Compensation* (Vancouver, 1980); and generally, T. Newburn, *The Settlement of Disputes at the Criminal Injuries Compensation Board* (London, 1989).

6 The future of compensation

The tort system is the 'junior partner' of social security (in the words of the Pearson Commission) in compensating for accidental injuries and death (see p. 33, ante). The strategic question for accident compensation in Britain therefore concerns the future relationship between tort and social security. The practical alternatives are either to replace the tort system with enlarged social security benefits, or to retain a 'mixed' system in which one form of compensation complements but does not duplicate the other. The former is the model adopted in New Zealand based on the Woodhouse Report on Compensation for Personal Injury (December 1967), and this section opens with a short summary of that country's comprehensive approach. The alternative 'mixed' system was, however, the one favoured by the Pearson Commission. The 'strategy' and some of the 'concluding reflections' of the Commission are printed (p. 931, post). For reasons of space, it has been possible to include only one short extract from the literature which is critical of the Pearson Report's approach (p. 937, post) but there is a select bibliography of writings on the theory and future of tort (p. 938, post). For a general discussion, see *Williams & Hepple*, chap. 7; *Atiyah*, chaps. 22–25.

(a)   Comprehensive approaches

The Law of Torts 7th edn. John G. Fleming (Sydney, 1987), pp. 375–377

Following the famous Woodhouse Report, New Zealand launched in 1974 a comprehensive system of exclusive compensation, replacing tort recovery not only for traffic and industrial accidents but for all 'personal injury by accident', including certain industrial diseases and criminal injuries. The decision to embrace all accidents was based as much on the difficulty of justifying special treatment for road casualties as on the practical problems of demarcation and the manageable extra cost of covering the residue.

The guiding principle of the scheme is to replace financial loss rather than the social welfare philosophy of assuring a minimally adequate living standard. Accordingly benefits are not flat but earnings-related and fixed at a level which the public could fairly accept in exchange for their common law rights. The standard is 80 per cent of pre-accident earnings, payable in weekly instalments up to $817 in 1986. There are reasons for questioning the avowed fairness of this standard: past earnings are perhaps adequate enough for short-term benefits but hardly for longer lasting incapacity by persons with substantially increasing (or decreasing) earning potential. Provision for inflation adjustment has also proved inadequate.

Besides, a lump sum up to $17,000 is payable for permanent loss or impairment of bodily functions, like loss of an eye or leg, akin to the scheduled injuries under workers' compensation; also up to $10,000 for loss of 'amenities or capacity for enjoying life, including loss or disfigurement' and for 'pain and suffering, including nervous shock and neurosis'. Both evoke memories of common law damages, the one for loss of faculty, the other for pain and suffering. But there are important differences: the first is measured objectively by reference to a schedule as a specified percentage of the maximum, on the model of scheduled injuries under workers' compensation; the second calls for an individualised judgment and is conceived merely as a supplement to periodical payments for the economic loss, to be awarded moderately and only for serious suffering, with a ceiling rather than a graduated scale. Even so, the whole idea of compensating non-economic[1] (representing a political compromise) has been criticised less for the direct extra cost it involves than for its disproportionate administrative burden and disincentive to rehabilitation.

Although coverage of all 'personal injury by accident' has the virtue of being very inclusive, it does not eliminate all questions of demarcation. Since 'medical misadventure' is now specifically included in the definition, a more liberal interpretation appears to be gaining. Provided the injury is 'course by mischance or accident, unexpected and undesigned, in the nature of medical error or mishap', it can include nonfeasance (for example failure to detect a lesion), even an unsuccessful sterilisation so long as the risk of failure is not medically accepted. Also covered are intentional acts like battery and rape, which are an 'accident' to the victim; moreover, pregnancy, like all actual bodily harm, arising from a criminal act, is specifically included. On the other hand, heart attacks and strokes were excluded unless shown to be the consequences of an accident or of an effort or stress in the cause of employment, which was abnormal, excessive or unusual.

The financing of the scheme reveals a tension between the philosophies of social welfare and resource allocation. Dominated primarily by the desire to capture the same funds available to the old system and to avoid general taxation, the original proposal of raising a flat levy from employers of 1 per cent of all wages was abandoned in favour of establishing two separate funds. The Motor Vehicle Fund is fed by levies on motor vehicles and covers the whole population; the Earners' Fund derives from levies on employees (paid by their employer) and the self-employed at differential rates according to occupational risks, and covers only these segments of the population. This eliminates more 'externalities' than a flat rate, by allocating costs more discriminatingly to accident causing activities, although it remains questionable whether this will realistically exert accident preventive deterrence sufficiently to justify the resulting complexity of funding and the exclusion of the non-earning population from some of its benefits, all the more as so many other 'externalities' remain.

At the heart of the scheme is the complete elimination of tort recovery for those covered by its benefits. The substantial savings from reduction of administrative costs and channelling funds away from minor claims permit the considerable expansion of benefits for hitherto uncompensated major injuries, without noticeably increasing the total previous cost of workers' compensation and third-party insurance for motor vehicles. To the same end, the administration is taken out of the hands of private insurance companies and vested in an Accident Compensation Corporation, which uses the Post Office for collecting premiums and the State Insurance Office for processing claims. Appeals from the Corporation lie to an Appeal Authority and thence (with leave) to the High Court.

---

1. [I.e. non-pecuniary.]

Further reading

(i) New Zealand

Report of the Committee on Absolute Liability (Wellington, 1963)

Report of the Royal Commission of Inquiry, Compensation for Personal Injury in New Zealand (Wellington, December 1967) ('the Woodhouse Report')

Government of New Zealand. Personal Injury—A Commentary on the Report of the Royal Commission of Inquiry into Compensation for Personal Injury in New Zealand (presented to the House of Representatives by Leave, October 1969)

Report of the Select Committee on Compensation for Personal Injury in New Zealand (Wellington, October 1970) ('the Gair Report')

Accident Compensation Commission, Annual Reports, 1975—

Report of the Royal Commission on Civil Liability and Compensation for Personal Injury. Cmnd. 7054. Vol. III, chap. 10. ('the Pearson Report')

D. R. Harris, 'Accident Compensation in New Zealand: A Comprehensive Insurance System' (1974) 37 MLR 361

T. G. Ison, *Accident Compensation. A Commentary on the New Zealand Scheme* (London, 1980)

G. W. Palmer, *Compensation for Incapacity: A Study of Law and Social Change in New Zealand and Australia* (Wellington, 1979)

(ii) Australia

Report of the Royal Commission of Inquiry on Compensation and Rehabilitation 1974. Parliamentary Paper No. 100 (Canberra, 1974)

Parliament of the Commonwealth of Australia. Clauses of the National Compensation Bill 1974. Report from the Senate Standing Committee on Constitutional and Legal Affairs (Canberra, July, 1975)

Report of the Royal Commission on Civil Liability and Compensation for Personal Injury. Cmnd. 7054. Vol. III, chap. 9 ('the Pearson Report')

H. Luntz, *Compensation and Rehabilitation in Australia* (Melbourne, 1975)

(b) 'Mixed' approaches

Report of the Royal Commission on Civil Liability and Compensation for Personal Injury. Cmnd. 7054. Vol. 1

Our Strategy

A mixed system

273 The fundamental problem with which we were faced was the balance between no-fault and tort. The extreme options might be thought of as exclusive reliance on one or the other. A total dependence on the tort system, however, would be unrealistic

—there could be no question of sweeping away the growing structure of social security provision. On the other hand, the possibility of relying exclusively on no-fault required more careful consideration, particularly as this was a model which had gained wide support following the Woodhouse report in New Zealand, and the subsequent implementation of a comprehensive accident compensation scheme in that country. Our consideration of such a possibility involved asking two main questions—how far no-fault should be extended; and whether tort should be abolished.

274 ... [O]ur terms of reference precluded us from considering whether to recommend a no-fault scheme covering all injuries. To recommend a scheme for all injuries within our terms of reference would have been impracticable. In a no-fault scheme, such as the social security system, it would not be feasible to adjudicate on the dividing line between injuries inside and outside our remit; this would involve determining such issues as whether or not a given injury was suffered through the act or omission of another. We therefore came of necessity to ask ourselves whether there were persuasive reasons for extending no-fault provision for particular categories of injury, and whether any new no-fault schemes could be satisfactorily financed.

275 Our decision to approach the extension of no-fault in this manner had an obvious bearing on the question whether tort should be abolished. It was clear to us that social security should be regarded as the primary method of providing compensation—it is quick, certain and inexpensive to administer, and it already covers a majority of the injured. But, in the absence of a no-fault scheme covering all injuries, the abolition of tort for personal injury would deprive many injured people of a potential source of compensation, without putting anything in its place. We concluded that tort must be retained; and most of us saw good reason for keeping tort even where all injuries in a given category are covered by a no-fault scheme.

276 The retention of a mixed system, including both social security and tort, still leaves a wide variety of mixed systems to choose from. We now summarise our main strategic conclusions. . . .

No-fault

281 We reached three main conclusions on the extension and improvement of no-fault provision. These were that the structure of the industrial injuries scheme should remain basically unchanged, albeit with some improvements; that a new scheme should be introduced for road injuries; and that a new social security benefit should be introduced for severely handicapped children. [Since this Report, the benefits for the severely handicapped have been restructured; see p. 917, ante.]

282 We considered the introduction of new no-fault schemes for other categories covered by our terms of reference, but, in broad terms, we thought that the case for such schemes was less compelling; that our proposals as they stood would be enough, for the present at any rate, for the administrative system to absorb; and that the miscellaneous circumstances of accidents would make it difficult, and sometimes impracticable, to construct and finance schemes other than those covered by our main conclusions.

Work injuries
283 There was a remarkable unanimity among our witnesses that the structure of the industrial injuries scheme had stood the test of time. We could see no better alternative in overseas models, nor any way of devising one ourselves. We concluded that the scheme should remain essentially as it is, but extended and improved in some respects. [Since this Report, the industrial injuries scheme has been subject to major reform. Industrial injury benefit has been abolished, with short-term loss of earnings

being met by standard statutory sick pay or sickness benefit; industrial death benefit and some special allowances payable with disablement benefit have also been abolished. Special hardship allowance was replaced by a reduced earnings allowance for those still at work, but the latter too was removed in 1990 for new claimants.] ...

Road injuries
286 Our decision to recommend a special no-fault scheme for road injuries sprang largely from our review of the operation of the tort system in this field. We were impressed by evidence that some of the criticisms levelled against tort applied with especial force to road accident compensation. In particular, we were convinced that the fault principle operates with particular capriciousness. ...

287 There were other considerations, too. Road accidents are numerous, particularly likely to be the cause of serious injury, and an unavoidable hazard for most of the population. It was noticeable that those witnesses who pressed for more no-fault compensation tended to consider road injuries an exceptionally strong case. Similar considerations have led other countries to the same conclusion.

288 In seeking a model, the industrial injuries scheme was the obvious choice, in that it would provide inflation proofing and adequate benefits for long term incapacity. In using it, we thought it essential to make one important modification. There is necessarily no place in that scheme for benefits for non-earners, but we felt that there should be some provision for non-earners, injured in road accidents. ...

Tort

Possible exceptions to the retention of tort
299 In the light of our conclusions on the extension of no-fault, we considered the possibility of abolishing tort for certain categories of injury. In doing so, we kept in mind two considerations which could apply to any such category, although not all of us would place the same emphasis on each.

300 First, we were not convinced that the social security system could provide machinery suitable for determining the appropriate award under certain heads of damage which most of us felt should be compensated, in particular, pain and suffering and promotion prospects, in such a way as to take account of individual circumstances.

301 Secondly, the earnings relation of social security benefits is subject to limits, for the present at least. Whilst this is so, most of us thought it not unreasonable that high income earners should be free to pursue full reparation in tort. [Since this Report, earnings related supplements to short-term benefits were abolished in 1982.]

302 If tort were to be abolished for any particular categories of injury, the most obvious possibility would be where all injuries would be within a no-fault scheme, that is to say, under our proposals, for work and road injuries. In either case, however, there would be the difficulty that other categories of injury would remain covered by the tort system. This means that someone injured by the fault of another at work or on the roads might receive less compensation than if he had suffered an identical injury, also through the fault of another, in different circumstances.

303 We felt unable to defend such an anomaly for road injuries. For work injuries, however, there is a strong case for abolishing tort on accident prevention grounds. ... The Robens Report, 'Safety and Health at Work' (Cmnd. 5034), referred to a number of ways in which the tort system was said to work to the detriment of accident prevention. The main argument was that the task of framing and enforcing statutory

provisions for prevention of accidents, and the task of investigating individual accidents, were made more difficult than they should be. Employers and trade unions were inevitably concerned with safeguarding or strengthening their respective positions in the event of a tort action. If employers were no longer to be held liable in tort, it was argued, everyone could concentrate on the task of preventing accidents, and perhaps devote to it some of the money previously spent on litigation. It was also suggested that the tort system had a detrimental impact on industrial relations.

304 Our evidence showed that not everyone accepted these arguments in the Robens Report. We for our part acknowledge the force of the arguments, but most of us concluded that they were not sufficiently powerful to justify depriving the worker injured alone of the right to claim tort compensation. We recommend . . . that tort should be retained for work injuries as a means of supplementing industrial injury benefits.

305 We considered the possibility of abolishing tort for two other categories of injury, medical and ante-natal. In relation to medical injuries, it was put to us that it was particularly difficult to prove negligence and, still more important, that it was often impossible to ascertain whether or not the injury was indeed a 'medical injury'. It might not be clear whether a given deterioration in the patient's condition would have occurred but for the act or omission complained of. It was also put to us that there were widespread fears that the risk of litigation was proving an obstacle to good and economical medical practice, and that, if litigation became more common, insurance premiums might rise to prohibitive levels. But we did not find these arguments strong enough to justify making medical injuries a special case where tort liability would not apply, especially as we received much evidence from medical and other witnesses which favoured the retention of tort. . . .

306 In relation to ante-natal injuries, the main problem is one we have already mentioned in another context, namely that it is only rarely that a physical cause of a congenital deformity can be identified. There is also the risk that acts or omissions of the child's parents may be called into question, with serious consequences for relationships within the family. Again, however, we did not find these arguments strong enough to justify removing the right to a tort action, save in certain exceptional cases[1]. . . .

Liability
312 To describe the future role of tort as essentially one of supplementing no-fault compensation is not to say that that role would be insubstantial. For example, not all long term social security benefits are earnings related and it will be some time before they are[2]. Even then, the upper limit on the earnings related element would continue to leave high earners with a substantial gap to try to fill. There would continue to be cases where substantial losses or expenses were incurred over and above lost earnings. There would remain considerable scope for compensating non-earners who were injured otherwise than in a road accident and were not entitled to non-contributory social security benefits.

313 We considered whether it should be made easier for an injured or bereaved person to recover tort compensation. For most categories of injury, the basis of liability remains the proof of negligence. We reviewed each category separately and considered two main options — either a statutory reversal of the burden of proof or strict liability.

---

1. [See p. 147, ante.]
2. [Since the Report, earnings-related benefits have been phased out rather than extended.]

314 In the event, we decided not to recommend a reversal of the burden of proof for any category of injury, and we decided against strict liability for work or road injuries. But there remained a wide range of other circumstances for which we found we had to consider strict liability.

315 By definition, strict liability is not concerned with fault (except in so far as fault on the part of the injured person may be permitted to reduce or eliminate his entitlement to damages). Subject to any defences which might be allowed, its effect is to impose the cost of compensation on the person who causes an accident or is responsible for something which causes it.

316 A relevant question is the insurability of the risk. Can those who may cause an injury take out insurance more conveniently and cheaply than those who may be injured? This is a practical issue. For example, depending on market conditions, the owner of a business might be able to spread the financial burden over those who ultimately pay for his goods or services. Another question is whether the victim is likely to experience particular difficulty in proving fault.

317 Our answers to these questions have led us to conclude . . . that strict liability should be imposed on producers for injuries caused by defective products.[1]

318 We also felt that where particular things or activities involved exceptional risks of injury, the cost of compensating such injury ought to be charged to those responsible for the things or activities concerned. This principle already lies behind the imposition of strict liability on the 'keepers' of dangerous animals in England, Wales and Northern Ireland[2]. We concluded that the principle should be extended and applied systematically to things or activities which either have a high risk potential (such as highly flammable gases or liquids), or where a malfunction might cause multiple casualties (such as dams). . . . We recommend a scheme whereby strict liability would be imposed on the controllers of such things or activities.

319 In most other areas of our remit, strict liability was less clearly appropriate, for reasons which we shall explain in each of the chapters concerned. In broad terms, we concluded that liability should continue to be for negligence except where there were exceptional risks or where, as with defective products, there were other reasons for introducing a scheme of strict liability.

Compulsory insurance
320 Our terms of reference mentioned specifically the possibility of recovering compensation through compulsory insurance. At present, third party insurance cover is compulsory for employers and motorists, and also in respect of nuclear installations, dangerous wild animals, riding establishments, and oil pollution from merchant ships. The central argument in its favour is that it ensures, so far as is possible, that those entitled to tort compensation actually receive it.

321 We saw a number of practical difficulties in the way of widening the scope of compulsory insurance. A requirement to insure would have to be effectively enforced. All the present requirements are linked to a system of licensing or certification; but for many other risks the cost of effective enforcement—in money and manpower—might prove disproportionate.

---

1. [See now p. 504, ante.]
2. [For the position in Scotland, see now the Animals (Scotland) Act 1987.]

322 Furthermore, the cost of the cover required would have to be economic; it might not be reasonable to compel the insurance of small risks. The cover required would also have to be available; it would not be sensible to require unlimited cover which insurers would consider unrealistic to provide.

323 We also considered whether the basis of liability was relevant. It can be argued that insurance is essential to the effectiveness of tort as a provider of compensation; and that, if legislation were to impose strict liability with the object of improving a victim's chances of being entitled to compensation, it would be logical also to insist that such liabilities should be insured. On the other hand, it may be thought no less unfortunate for people not to receive damages when they have gone to the trouble and expense of proving negligence.

324 We concluded that the imposition of compulsory insurance was essentially a matter of weighing up the practical possibilities. We shall be recommending that consideration be given to imposing a new requirement in only two areas, namely in respect of exceptional risks for which strict liability would be imposed . . . and in respect of private aircraft. . . . We shall not be recommending the removal of the requirement in any instance where it exists at present, although we doubt whether we should ourselves have proposed introducing one or two of the provisions in minor areas had we been starting afresh. . . .

CONCLUDING REFLECTIONS

1714 Some of us would welcome an eventual extension of no-fault compensation beyond the spheres of employment and road traffic to cover the other categories of accident within our terms of reference (such as accidents arising from the use of services), and those accidents which are outside our terms of reference (such as accidents in the home). In the long run, too, they would see little justification for distinguishing between the injured and the sick. The cost of introducing a comparable no-fault scheme covering both sickness and injury would be substantial, there are those of us who believe that it is a socially desirable objective.

1715 Some of us who look forward to considerable extensions of no-fault provision are also doubtful about the permanent value of the tort system of compensation as a means of supplementing what can be obtained from social security. In their view the tort system is too costly, too cumbersome, too prone to delay and too capricious in its operation to be defensible; and they do not accept, having regard to the availability of liability insurance, that the tort action is an effective deterrent to accidents in general. They regard our present, limited recommendations as providing, if implemented, a time for testing the capacity of the social security system to cope with the new demands which those recommendations would put upon it. In the light of that experience they think it would be possible to find acceptable ways of providing an overall no-fault scheme of compensation without reliance on tort. Compensation would be related to lost income and special needs which have arisen as a result of injury. They do not think, however, that compensation should necessarily be restricted to state benefits. Greater facilities, for example, by way of tax concessions or otherwise, might be offered for additional cover by first party insurance.

1716 Others among us hope, and believe, that there would always be a role for the tort system, whatever happened to no-fault provision. They would argue that tort would remain uniquely well equipped to compensate the widest possible range of the particular losses suffered by a given individual; that, despite the role of liability insurance, tort would continue to embody the socially valuable principle that, where a person negligently or intentionally causes injuries to another, amends should be made for the consequences of his fault; and that the continued existence of tort would, of itself, be some safeguard against a system of total dependence on the state.

1717 In addition it is felt that no-fault compensation, with no recourse to tort, might involve or lead to abandoning the common law principle of *restitutio in integrum* (making up to the injured party, so far as money can serve, the loss and injury which he has sustained) and the replacement of this principle by a statutory tariff determined, not by practice and accepted custom, but by governmental regulation. There would then be no court awards independent of the tariff to give guidance as to its sufficiency; and there could be changes in the tariff for reasons other than the interests of injured persons. Adjudication by statutory tribunals, however careful and impartial, might not be accepted as an adequate substitute for the existing right of the subject to seek reparation for personal injury from the independent courts of the realm. Those who hold this view would also maintain that there is another factor which goes deeply into the structure of society. A sense of responsibility for the effect of one's actions on others, and a sense that one does have a duty of care towards one's fellow citizens, is an essential element in a civilised community, and a lapse in the discharge of that responsibility is a matter of blame—in other words fault or *culpa*. They would regard the continued existence of the law of tort or delict as a measure of deterrence against general irresponsibility and a positive encouragement to a sense of individual responsibility towards one's fellows.

1718 Then there are yet others of us who take the view that, in the light of all the uncertainties, it would be best to wait until it is possible to assess the social and practical consequences of our proposals, in particular our road scheme, before trying to judge, even in principle, in which direction it would be appropriate to move next. . . .

Compensation and Support for Illness and Injury Donald Harris et al. Oxford Socio-Legal Studies (Clarendon Press: Oxford, 1984), pp. 327–328

We believe, in the light of the data presented in this [study], that the future policy-maker should plan to phase out all existing compensation systems which favour accident victims (or any category of them) over illness victims. This proposal obviously applies to the damages system, whose deficiences as revealed by the survey [see the summary p. 31, ante] are too deep-rooted to be removed by any modification of the system. Relatively few accident victims recover any damages at all; most amounts recovered are low and therefore can do little to 'compensate'; and the cost of administering the system is very high. Delay and uncertainty are inherent in the system; the adversarial game permits defendants to adopt negotiating strategies which exploit— quite legitimately under the present rules—each uncertainty to defeat a claim, or to reduce the amount paid. The advantages claimed for the system do not, in our opinion, outweigh the disadvantages. Deterrence of carelessness operates in a random way, and accident victims themselves perceive no clear concept of fault or blame underlying the attribution of liability to pay damages. Our data establish that the roles of sick pay and social security in providing income support following illness and injury are now, in the aggregate, of much greater importance than the damages system. Yet the illness/injury demarcation is ignored by sick pay schemes and by all social security benefits introduced since 1946: within social security, only the historically anomalous industrial injuries scheme continues the preference for accident victims. We believe that the damages system for death and personal injury should be abolished as soon as improvements in sick pay and social security provision produce a rational, coherent, and integrated system of compensation for illness and injury.

Our view that we should move towards the abolition of every compensation scheme which is based on a particular category of causation means that we oppose the implementation of many of the recommendations of the Pearson Royal Commission, 1978. The Commission recommended many improvements to the tort claim; a new, no-fault scheme for injuries caused by road accidents; a special benefit for severely handicapped children; and that the criminal injuries scheme should be placed on a statutory basis. In our opinion, these proposals are difficult to justify in social policy terms, and would only increase the complexity of the present web of compensation systems, which are based, not on the relative extent of disabilities, but on the circumstances which give rise to disabilities. . . .

Our proposals . . . are designed to permit some of the advantages of the tort system to be retained in any new schemes to replace tort: the individualized assessment of damages to be replaced by better and more flexible types of social security benefits for long-term cases of disability; and deterrence of carelessness through some risk-relationship, by extension of sick pay entitlement, and by new types of risk-related social security contributions. Our proposals would also allow the policy-maker (contrary, however, to our own preference) to choose to implement risk-relationship by special, no-fault schemes as part of the overall scheme. . . .

Further reading

The literature on the theory and future of compensation is vast, expanding and international. The following is a highly select bibliography.

(i) Great Britain
D. K. Allen, C. J. Bourn, J. H. Holyoak (eds.) *Accident Compensation after Pearson* (London, 1979)

P. S. Atiyah, *Accidents, Compensation and the Law* 4th edn by P. Cane (London, 1987)

P. W. J. Bartrip and S. B. Burman, *The Wounded Soldiers of Industry: Industrial Compensation Policy 1833–1897* (Oxford, 1983)

D. W. Elliott and H. Street, *Road Accidents* (Harmondsworth, 1968)

W. L. F. Felstiner and R. Dingwall, *Asbestos Litigation in the United Kingdom: an Interim Report* (Oxford, Centre for Socio-Legal Studies, 1988)

J. G. Fleming, 'The Pearson Report: Its Strategy' (1979) 42 MLR 251

C. Ham et al, *Medical Negligence: Compensation and Accountability* (Oxford, Centre for Socio-Legal Studies, Briefing Paper 6, 1989)

D. Harris et al, *Compensation and Support for Illness and Injury* (Oxford, 1984)

R. A. Hasson, 'The Pearson Report' (1979) 6 Br J Law and Soc 119

T. G. Ison, *The Forensic Lottery* (London, 1967)

J. A. Jolowicz, 'Liability for Accidents' [1968] CLJ 50

D. Kretzmer, 'Transformation of Tort Liability in the 19th Century: the Visible Hand' (1984) 4 Oxf JLS 46

R. Lewis, *Compensation for Industrial Injury* (Abingdon, 1987)

R. Lewis, 'No-Fault Compensation for Victims of Road Accidents: Can it be Justified?' (1981) J Soc Pol 161

N. S. Marsh, 'The Pearson Report on Civil Liability and Compensation for Death and Personal Injury' (1979) 95 LQR 513

A. I. Ogus, P. Corfield and D. R. Harris, 'Pearson: Principled Reform or Political Compromise?' (1978) 7 ILJ 143

J. Stapleton, *Disease and the Compensation Debate* (Oxford, 1987)

S. D. Sugarman, 'Personal Injury Law Reform: a Proposed First Step' (1987) 16 ILJ 30

F. A. Trindade, 'A No-Fault Scheme for Road Accident Victims in the United Kingdom' (1980) 96 LQR 581

(ii) United States and Canada
R. L. Abel, 'A Critique of American Tort Law' (1981) Br J Law and Soc 199

J. G. Fleming, *The American Tort Process* (Oxford, 1988)

R. E. Keeton and J. O'Connell, *Basic Protection for the Traffic Victim* (Boston, 1965)

J. O'Connell, *The Lawsuit Lottery: Injuries, Insurance and Injustice* (Urbana, 1979)

J. O'Connell and C. B. Kelly, *The Blame Game: Injuries, Insurance and Injustice* (Lexington, Mass, 1987)

Report of the Royal Commission on Civil Liability and Compensation for Personal Injury. Cmnd. 7054, vol. III, chaps. 2 and 3 (the Pearson Report)

G. T. Schwartz, 'Tort Law and the Economy in 19th Century America: a Reinterpretation' (1981) 90 Yale LJ 1717

S. D. Sugarman, *Doing Away with Personal Injury Law* (New York, 1989)

G. E. White, *Tort Law In America: An Intellectual History* (New York and Oxford, 1980)

A. I. Widdiss et al, *No-Fault Automobile Insurance in Action: the Experiences in Massachusetts, Florida, Delaware and Michigan* (New York, 1977)

(iii) Other countries
C. Oldertz and E. Tidefelt, *Compensation For Personal Injury in Sweden and Other Countries* (Stockholm, 1988)

Report of the Royal Commission on Civil Liability and Compensation for Personal Injury, Cmnd. 7054, vol. III (the Pearson Report)

A. Tunc, 'Traffic Accident Compensation: Law and Proposals'. Chap. 14 of the *International Encyclopedia of Comparative Law* (vol. XI Tort) (Tubingen, Hague, Paris, New York, 1972)

(iv) General theory

R. L. Abel, 'A Socialist Approach to Risk' (1982) 41 Maryland LR 699

R. L. Abel, 'Torts' in *The Politics of Law*, edited by D. Kairys (New York, 1982), pp. 185–200

P. Burrows, 'Tort and Tautology: the Logic of Restricting the Scope of Liability' (1984) 13 J Leg Stud 399

P. Burrows and C. G. Veljanovski (eds.), *The Economic Approach to Law* (London, 1981), chaps. 5, 6 and 7

G. Calabresi, *The Costs of Accidents: a Legal and Economic Analysis* (New Haven and London, 1970)

G. Calabresi and J. T. Hirschoff, 'Towards a Test for Strict Liability in Torts' (1972) 81 Yale LJ 1055

P. Cane, 'Justice and Justifications for Tort Liability' (1982) 2 Oxf JLS 30

P. Danzon, *Medical Malpractice: Theory, Evidence and Public Policy* (Cambridge, Mass, 1985)

I. Englard, 'The System Builders: a Critical Appraisal of Modern American Tort Theory' (1980) 9 J Leg Stud 27

R. A. Epstein, *A Theory of Strict Liability: Toward a Reformulation of Tort Law* (San Francisco, 1980) (also in (1973) 2 J Leg Stud 151 and (1974) 3 J Leg Stud 165); see too (1975) 4 J Leg Stud 391

R. A. Epstein, 'Social Consequences of Common Law Rules' (1982) 95 Harv LR 1717

J. G. Fleming, 'Is There a Future for Tort?' (1984) 58 Aust LJ 131

G. P. Fletcher, 'Fairness and Utility in Tort Theory' (1972) 85 Harv LR 573

A. C. Hutchinson and D. Morgan, 'The Canengusian Connection: The Kaleidoscope of Tort Theory' (1984) 22 Osgoode Hall LJ 69

T. G. Ison, *Accident Compensation* (London, 1980)

W. M. Landes and R. A. Posner, *The Economic Structure of Tort Law* (Cambridge, Mass, 1987)

R. E. Litan and C. Winston (eds.), *Liability: Perspectives and Policy.* (Washington DC, 1988).

A. I. Ogus, 'Do We have a General Theory of Compensation?' (1984) 37 Current LP 29

R. L. Rabin, *Perspectives on Tort Law* 2nd edn (Boston, 1983)

S. Shavell, *Economic Analysis of Accident Law* (Cambridge, Mass, 1987)

G. Williams, 'The Aims of the Law of Tort' (1951) 4 Current LP 137

Index